WORLDMARK

ENCYCLOPEDIA
of Religious
Practices

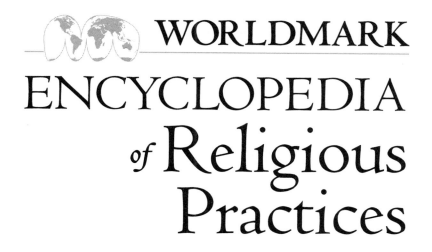

WORLDMARK

ENCYCLOPEDIA

of Religious

Practices

Volume 1

RELIGIONS AND DENOMINATIONS

Thomas Riggs, Editor

THOMSON

GALE

Detroit • New York • San Francisco • San Diego • New Haven, Conn. • Waterville, Maine • London • Munich

THOMSON
GALE

Worldmark Encyclopedia of Religious Practices, Volume 1
Thomas Riggs

Product Managers
Carol DeKane Nagel, Bonnie Hawkwood

Project Editors
Michael L. LaBlanc, Thomas Carson, Jason M. Everett, Bernard Grunow

Editorial
Mary Rose Bonk, Andrew Clapps, Sara Constantakis, Angela Doolin, Anne Marie Hacht, Gillian Leonard, Stephanie Macomber, Ellen McGeagh, Ira Mark Milne, Rebecca Parks, Mark E. Rzeszutek, Jennifer York Stock.

Rights Acqusition and Management
Peg Ashlevitz, Jacqueline Key, Susan J. Rudolph

Manufacturing
Wendy Blurton

Imaging and Multimedia
Lezlie Light, Dan Newell, Christine O'Bryan

Product Design
Kate Scheible

LIBRARY OF CONGRESS CATALOGING-IN-PUBLICATION DATA

Worldmark encyclopedia of religious practices / Thomas Riggs, editor in chief.
    p. cm.
      Includes bibliographical refrences and index.
      ISBN 0-7876-6611-4 (set hardcover : alk. paper)—
      ISBN 0-7876-6612-2 (vol 1 : alk paper)—;
      ISBN 0-7876-6613-0 (vol 2 : alk. paper)—;
      ISBN 0-7876-6614-9 (vol 3 : alk. paper)
      1. Religions. I. Riggs, Thomas, 1963-

BL80.3.W67 2006
200.9—dc22
                                              2005027456

This title is also available as an e-book.
ISBN 0-7876-9390-1

Contact your Thomson Gale representative for ordering information.

Printed in the United States of America
10 9 8 7 6 5 4 3 2 1

Contents

CONTENTS

VOLUME 3: COUNTRY ENTRIES
M–Z

CONTENTS

Editor's Preface

In 2001 Thomson Gale had a simple but ambitious goal: to produce an encyclopedia outlining the contemporary religious practices of every country in the world—from the very largest, such as China, India, Brazil, and Russia, to the smallest, such as Tuvalu, Andorra, and Antigua and Barbuda. Because this information has not been readily available in books or other sources in libraries, as well as on the Internet, the project required years of planning and hard work by a large group of people: our distinguished board of 10 advisers, the 245 scholars and other subject specialists commissioned to write essays or to review the text of their colleagues, and the editorial staff of Thomson Gale. The result was this publication, the *Worldmark Encyclopedia of Religious Practices*. It joins an already existing series of Worldmark encyclopedias, including the *Worldmark Encyclopedia of the Nations* and the *Worldmark Encyclopedia of Cultures and Daily Life*.

Organization

The *Worldmark Encyclopedia of Religious Practices* has three volumes. Volume 1 includes essays on the history, beliefs, and contemporary practices of 13 major faith groups—African Traditional Religions, Bahá'í, Buddhism, Christianity, Confucianism, Hinduism, Islam, Jainism, Judaism, Shinto, Sikhism, Taoism, and Zoroastrianism—and 28 of their subgroups, such as Anglicanism, Reform Judaism, Mahayana Buddhism, and Vaishnavism. These essay topics, selected by our advisory board, represent not only the world's largest religious groups but also smaller faiths that have had significant historical, cultural, or theological impact. Because of space limitations, we could not include essays on all groups worthy of discussion. Each essay in volume 1 is organized with the same subject headings—for example, "Moral Code of Conduct" and "Sacred Symbols"—allowing easy comparison of a topic from one religion or subgroup to another. Printed at the top

of each essay in volume 1 is a population map displaying the group's distribution throughout the world.

By discussing broadly various religions and subgroups, volume 1 provides the background or context for more fully understanding the information in volumes 2 and 3. These subsequent volumes together contain 193 essays, each focusing on the contemporary religious practices of a particular country. Organizing the topic of religious practices by country assumes that geographical and, in particular, political boundaries—because in varying degrees they mark off areas of unique history, culture, and influence—encourage distinctive ways in which a religion is practiced, despite shared beliefs held by all members of a religion.

The essays in volumes 2 and 3 follow a standard format: statistical information, an overview of the country, one or more sections on major religions, a discussion of other religions, and a bibliography. The statistical information includes the country's total population and a breakdown by percentage of the major religious groups. The "Country Overview" section contains an "Introduction," providing a geographical or historical summary of the country needed to understand religious activities in the area, and a subsection on "Religious Tolerance," discussing such topics as freedom of worship, religious discrimination, ecumenical movements, and the relationship between church and state.

Every country essay then proceeds with a major religion section on each religion whose followers make up 25 percent or more of the country's population. In some countries just one religion, such as Christianity, Islam, or Buddhism, has at least this percentage of followers, but in other countries two or three religions each have more than 25 percent, thus resulting in the essay including two or three major religion sections. Exceptions to the rule were made for a small number of essays, most notably for China, where Buddhism, at 8 percent of the population, and Christianity, at 6.5 percent, were given their own sections. China's population, however, is immense, and Buddhism's 8 percent, for example, represents 103 million people, more than the entire population of most countries. In some essays the major religion section is on a religious subgroup; this occurs when a subgroup, such as Roman Catholicism, dominates the country or when the country, such as Sweden, has had a historically important state church.

Each major religion section is broken down into the following 18 subsections, which describe the religion's distinctive qualities in that country. "Date of origin," for example, refers to the year not when the religion was founded but when it was introduced into the country. "Major Theologians and Authors" discusses significant religious writers from the country. "Mode of Dress" details any clothing or styles distinctive to adherents in the country. Because each major religion section is divided into the same 18 subject headings, religions can be easily compared from one country to another.

1. Date of Origin
2. Number of Followers
3. History
4. Early and Modern Leaders
5. Major Theologians and Authors
6. Houses of Worship and Holy Places
7. What is Sacred?
8. Holidays and Festivals
9. Mode of Dress
10. Dietary Practices
11. Rituals (outlining such practices as worship services, prayer, and pilgrimages)
12. Rites of Passage
13. Membership (discussing ways of encouraging new members)
14. Social Justice (in relation to poverty, education, and human rights)
15. Social Aspects (focusing on marriage and family)
16. Political Impact
17. Controversial Issues
18. Cultural Impact (in the arts, such as literature, painting, music, dance, and architecture)

Each country essay ends with a summary of other religions—those that make up less than 25 percent of the population—and a bibliography, which recommends other books and articles for further reading.

Acknowledgments

I would like to express my appreciation to the encyclopedia's editorial staff. Among those in-house at Thomson Gale are Bonnie Whitaker, who helped identify the need for the book and develop its main outline; Bernard Grunow, who calmly guided the early in-house steps; Thomas Carson, whose wisdom and background in religious studies kept the encyclopedia on the right path; Rita Runchock, whose editorial judgment proved essential at various stages of the project; Carol Nagel, who in the final months provided editorial focus, in the process finding solutions to lingering problems; and Michael LaBlanc, whose good humor, common sense, and fine editorial skills helped bring the project to a needed and gentle ending.

I am also grateful to Stephen Meyer, the associate editor, who was involved from the very beginning of the project, helping develop the book's editorial plan, contacting scholars to write essays and working with them on their revisions, and involving himself in other tasks too numerous to list; Mariko Fujinaka, an assistant editor, whose day-to-day organizational skills made all our lives easier; Erin Brown, our other assistant editor, who was involved in photo selection, contacting and corresponding with peer reviewers, and many other areas; Joyce Meyer, who translated a number of essays from French into English; Robert Rauch, the senior line editor, who helped create the editing guidelines and oversee the other line editors; and the line editors themselves—Lee Esbenshade, Laura Gabler, Natalie Goldstein, Anne Healey, Elizabeth Henry, and Janet Moredock—who were asked to ensure that the text, even when containing challenging or esoteric information, be accessible to a wide range of readers.

Finally, I would like to thank the advisers and contributors. Much of the information in the essays cannot be readily found in any other source, and without the involvement of our advisers and contributors, this encyclopedia, of course, could not have been produced.

Thomas J. Riggs

Comments

Although great effort has gone into this work, we would appreciate any suggestions for future editions of the *Worldmark Encyclopedia of Religious Practices*. Please send comments to the following address:

Editor
Worldmark Encyclopedia of Religious Practices
Thomson Gale
27500 Drake Road
Farmington Hills, Michigan 48331

Introduction

While religion is universal throughout human culture, its variations are so extensive that authorities do not always agree on a definition. Scholars have identified more than 50 characteristics of religion, from belief in gods or God to sophisticated ideas about a philosophical worldview. Some authorities regard religion as a particular kind of human experience, as a special way of living together, or as offering answers to certain vexing questions, such as why there is something rather than nothing or whether there is a larger purpose for evil. Religion is sometimes held to be bound up with what a particular group chooses as sacred, whether that be an object (totem), a being (God), a text (scripture), or a fundamental law of nature. Some believers hold that religion is beyond comprehension by the human mind, with study of it reserved for specially gifted people, a view that makes religion an esoteric, or secret, activity. On the other hand, many languages have no specific word to identify the human sensibility we call "religion." In these cases, acts of piety are simply considered natural or ordinary, so that there is no need to identify a distinctive experience.

In addition, how are innovations in religion under the pressures of modern life to be understood? For example, is the cooking and eating of a wild boar by a contemporary urban Melanesian a religious rite, even if it is not accompanied by the ceremony and ideology that traditionally attended such an act? Is a pious attitude sufficient for the act to be called religious? Further, if ideas are modern, are they less religious than views established long ago? What, for example, is to be made of the belief held by some Muslims that the best community existed at the time of the Prophet Muhammad, that the Islamic community today is somehow "less Muslim" than it was then? Or how is one to understand ancient gods? Osiris, for example, was once widely worshipped in Egypt but has few, if any, followers today. Does this mean that the most powerful beings humans once identified with and worshipped can "die"? And is a rule dating from biblical times still applicable today, or can "timeless" revelations be modified in the light of new discoveries? Despite the fact that there seem to be thousands of new religions, is it possible to say that a new religion is "better" than an old one? These and other issues surrounding contemporary religion are staggering in their complexity.

In spite of the difficulties in defining religion, it is essential to understand the phenomenon, for it touches almost every facet of life, from themes in popular culture, to perceptions of well-being, to motivations for global terrorism. Even those who reject religion, who blame it for human problems, or who regard it as a relic of the past should understand contemporary religion. It is also important that people understand the history of religion, including its power and its spread. Consider Christianity, for example, which began as an obscure movement in a tiny place outside Jerusalem some 2,000 years ago but which spread to Byzantium and Rome, centers of the then-known world, where it was adopted as the state religion. It later spread throughout Europe and followed European movement into the New World, and it has since spread to virtually every part of the earth. In the late twentieth century, reform movements from countries outside its traditional home, as with the doctrines of the Korean evangelist Sun Myung Moon, began to return to the heartland of Christianity with a revitalized vision. Thus, there are Christians from the so-called Third World who are now challenging Western nations to become "religious" once again. Such dynamism cannot be ignored by those who wish to understand the forces that motivate societies today.

The *Worldmark Encyclopedia of Religious Practices* focuses on contemporary expressions of world religion. It accepts the fact that there are international communities of faith, along with numerous branches within them, and that these define the world of religion today.

Volume I contains articles on the following I3 major religious groups: African indigenous beliefs, the Bahá'í faith, Buddhism, Christianity, Confucianism, Hinduism, Islam, Jainism, Judaism, Shinto, Sikhism, Taoism, and Zoroastrianism. In addition, there are separate articles on a number of major branches within these groups—for example, in Buddhism, on the Mahayana, Theravada, and Tibetan traditions.

This organization may seem misleading, for it does not indicate that religious ideas interact with one another or that similar perceptions are found in several religions. In addition, there is far more variety within each of these religions and subgroups than this approach suggests. Such matters are dealt with in Volumes 2 and 3 of the encyclopedia, where the diversity of religious practices in the various countries of the world is discussed. Still, the organization of Volume I is useful in showing that the subject is not limitless. It is possible to sketch the main dimensions of religious practice according to the traditions with which believers identify, an approach that scholarship has come to accept.

Common Elements in Religious Practice

Given the religious diversity found throughout the world, how can one hope to gain adequate knowledge of the subject? Are there basic ways of approaching the study of religion? It is often said that religion insists on a certain kind of reality, something that is larger than the individual or the immediate community. Such a reality is usually defined as a force or person of greater "power," something beyond human creation. What results from human interaction with this power may be called "religious." It may not be possible to prove such a reality, or to "know" it, conclusively. Nonbelievers, for example, do not accept its existence or share in the relationship. What is possible, however, is to document how people act when they are acting religiously. Thus, what appears to be crucial in understanding religion is practice—that is, activity related to the experience of a greater power.

Consider prayer, for example. Although there are considerable variations in how people pray, normally it is possible to tell the difference between believers at prayer and believers acting in an "ordinary" way. In prayer there are certain ways of moving, stances adopted, demeanors assumed, and words uttered—all of which appear to indicate a direct relationship between the believer and the greater power. Prayer brings believers into communication with the transforming agent, or higher power, that is the basis of their religion and their world.

Every religion has a system that establishes how that religion is experienced (as, for example, in prayer), giving a structure to its activities and providing an intellectual basis for the believer's perception of reality. Students of religion have an number of terms for such systems, including "philosophy," "theology," "beliefs," "values," and "doctrines." In some religions these systems are spelled out in an elaborate manner, as, for example, in the doctrine of the Trinity (Father, Son, and Holy Spirit) in Christianity. They may be part of a larger system of teaching and learning, as with Dianetics in the Church of Scientology. In some religions, however, there is less emphasis on theory than on acts, with reference made to basic beliefs only when queries are raised or when disagreements arise. This can be seen, for example, among Japanese shamans who perform healing rituals but who seldom talk about the spirit world they are encountering.

It is important to note that many religious practices arose from ancient rituals related to major life passages—for example, rites for girls and boys when they reach puberty. Some practices, such as those surrounding birth, marriage, and death, are as old as humankind. For many believers there is something reassuring about religion's connection with the stages and cycles of life, and people may actively participate in such rites even when they are not sure about the meaning of what they are doing.

Although every religion has distinctive practices, several common features are discussed here.

RITUALS Throughout life, rituals are used to express meaning. There are formal words used when greeting someone of an official rank, for example; gifts for people on special occasions; and the shaking of a hand when it is offered. It is possible for a person to ignore these practices, but there may be repercussions in doing so. By providing a grounding for life, rituals, rites, and ceremonies take on critical importance.

One of the most important ways of expressing religious feeling is through rituals. Believers, for example, use rituals to interact with their conception of the source of life. The indigenous people of the Plains tradition in North America smoke a pipe as a means of sending their prayers to the Spirit World, and Tibetan Buddhists chant in meditation to encounter the

Thunderbolt reality that lies beyond ordinary perception. In conveying their concerns and feelings to their sacred entities, believers do not see themselves as "using" rituals to manipulate the situation. Rather, they believe that such acts are a way of communicating with the object of their religious sensibilities.

For those who hold that communication with the gods or God is the purpose of religion, worship is a basic ritual, and in most religions worship is demanded of the faithful. Even in Buddhism, where the basis of religion is not worship, loving adoration of the Buddha is ordinarily a crucial part of the believer's rituals. In addition, most religions have developed rites that chart the growth of a person from birth to death and beyond, thus providing activities called rites of passage. These rites move a person through various levels of privilege and responsibilities. In some religions the performance of rites and ceremonies is considered so critical that they can be carried out only by specially endowed people, usually called priests, who operate as mediators between divine power and the individual believer.

The practices and rituals of any religion are directly affected by its conception of the spiritual world, that is, by its system of beliefs. When theism (belief in God) is a central tenant, the resulting religious practices in one way or another invoke the deity in its rituals. Further, how people conceive of the gods or God directly shapes practices. Christians speak of God's love as revealed through Jesus Christ and hold that God offers spiritual fulfillment and personal redemption through the doctrines reflected in the Trinity. As a result, Christians have developed rituals that embrace this belief, such as the commemorations and celebrations of Easter or the rituals of baptism. Jews, on the other hand, stress the worship of "the God of our Fathers, the God of Abraham, Isaac and Jacob," emphasizing the importance of a spiritual lineage with God. For Jews this lineage is demonstrated through the reading of the laws of God as set forth in the Hebrew Scriptures. By contrast, Hinduism has embraced many names for the diversity of spiritual reality, and Hindus observe a great number of rituals to express this exuberance of deities. On the other hand, those religions that do not involve belief in gods, including those of certain indigenous peoples, have quite different rituals. For example, in the past, Inuit shamans and medicine people maintained a vigorous religious life that involved spirits of the "other" world. They performed ceremonies honoring and submitting to these spirits, although they did not "worship" them in the sense commonly understood in Western religious rituals.

CELEBRATIONS AND OBSERVANCES Festive occasions bring people together and foster a sense of belonging, reflecting the deep-seated need within humans to move beyond the everyday. People celebrate birthdays, couples toast each other on a wedding anniversary, and victories on battlefields give rise to ceremonies of remembrance and introspection. Likewise, religions pause throughout the year to celebrate those events that make them unique, the result being an array of religious holidays and festivities. From the wandering Hindu sannyasi (mendicant), whose presence is regarded as beneficial, to the reaction of an infant upon first seeing Santa Claus, celebrations bond people to their religious families.

Many religions also celebrate their founding. Such celebrations look to a defining time in the past and rejoice at its continuing influence. For believers such a celebration brings with it a sense of liberation and freedom. Sometimes such observances, along with their accompanying feasts and festivals, are criticized for the waywardness they encourage or for their expense on the public purse. Critics, for example, often single out Christmas decorations and gift giving as reflections of such extravagance. Despite this, they are treasured by people for the benefits they bestow.

SCRIPTURE Authoritative religious teachings are those sources of inspiration that embody a tradition's wisdom. They take on a hallowed character that puts them beyond normal human creativity. For believers such teachings are not exhausted through reading, for they can become the source of theology, meditation, or even healing, to say nothing of their use to provoke division and militancy. The teachings also reveal the standards by which the believer is to live. In most religions there is a written document, or scripture, that conveys this material. The oldest is thought to be the Rig Veda, which includes materials that may date from before the beginning of writing—that is, to around 4000 B.C.E. Scripture is sometimes held to be timeless, as, for example, with the Koran—thewords were delivered by the Prophet Muhammad but the message is believed to date to the very establishment of humans upon the earth.

Because writing is relatively recent in human history, religion has not always relied on a written text. Even some literate peoples have never assigned true authority to written forms, preferring instead the immediacy of the oral version. Devout Muslims, for example, pointing to the oral origins of the Koran, regard the oral version of "pure Arabic" as the only authoritative version. Others, like the Quakers, hoping to ward off dogma and worrying that a text might become frozen into literalism, have refused to accept anything but a flexible interpretation. Further, in certain religious contexts, such as ritual activity, there remains a preference for oral versions among some groups—for example, Buddhists—even though they have written texts. In place of a written canon some religions have sacred stories that are passed on orally from one authoritative speaker to another. The stories may take on the character of scripture, with people referring to them as the basis for their actions. In such traditions the authorities have the freedom of recasting the stories according to the audience and the spiritual need of the moment.

One of the most important uses of scripture is to provide the language of religious rites, with believers using its passages as a means of communicating with the living object of their faith. In this case the text becomes a vehicle of communication at another, perhaps deeper spiritual level than when it is simply used to affirm a specific doctrine. At this level scripture fosters a state of spiritual being and unites those focused upon it in ways that few other writings can. This is why it is difficult to disassociate scripture from the ritual life and personal piety of the group. The use of a scriptural text in scholarship outside the religious tradition is sometimes said to distort its original purpose, provoking criticism from believers that outsiders are trying to interpret what are essentially sacred sources.

Not all scriptures are conceived of as written by God. The Analects of Confucius, for example, are regarded as inspired writings that give details on a properly ordered life, but they are held up not as the word of God but rather as spiritually superior insights from a master. In addition, many practitioners of New Age beliefs argue that true religion is syncretic or eclectic, that people may pick and choose which scriptures or parts thereof are most meaningful and then make up their own authoritative text. Such individualism seems to violate the traditional sense of a sacred text as the focus of group loyalty. Thus, not only can scripture undergo transformation within the life of a tradition itself but its traditional meaning has been challenged in the contemporary world.

THEOLOGY In many religions it is particularly important to describe the intellectual basis of the faith. Throughout history great minds have wrestled with the problems of explaining the reality behind one or another religion, their efforts producing an interpretation of God and related terminology that is called "theology." As with activities like prayer or sacrifice, the theologies of the various religions show considerable diversity, and despite the attempt to use words and phrases that can be understood by ordinary people, the subject is sometimes difficult. Further, in some religions certain ideas are not discussed in a systematic way, even though they involve important doctrines of the tradition. Ideas surrounding death and life after death are examples.

Theology has been of particular importance in Western religions, especially in Christianity. In the Christian tradition theology is a highly organized profession, with the various churches exercising vigorous control over the ideas perpetrated in their names. At least in Western culture, theology has a long history separate from both philosophy and science, and it often involves intellectual activity at a sophisticated level. When theology addresses doctrine, it attempts to explain the principal ideas of a religion in a way that both adherents and interested observers can understand. It also develops ways of dealing with puzzles that are created by its own system of thought. For example, in Judaism, Christianity, and Islam, which as monotheistic religions embrace the doctrine of God as all-powerful and all-good, the existence of evil in the world is a problem. For the ordinary believer some of these complications may be beyond solution, and believers sometimes simply embrace such difficulties as part of the weakness of the human mind in trying to comprehend what is beyond the everyday.

ETHICS Every religion serves as the foundation for a system of ethics, or standards of moral behavior. For some religions adherence to such standards is regarded as the very basis of the believer's relationship with God, as, for example, with the Torah, or teachings, in Judaism. For others ethics promotes well-being and a healthy society. In the Confucian tradition, for example, devotees believe that the successful person is one who is neighborly and giving. In effect, that person's key moral goal in life is to express *ren* (or *jen*). Such a person is held to be dedicated to human relationships and consequently subjects all personal acts to the rule of moral conduct. Acting out that value in life is religion. Confucius thus summed up the standard for human relationships in the

Analects as "Never do to others what you would not like them to do to you," which is strikingly similar to the biblical adage "Do unto others as you would have others do into you" (Matt. 7:12). Islam also asserts that God has established the true way and that living according to the Shariʻah, or religious law, is the most basic responsibility of the Muslim.

Most religions share the concern that their moral values be expressed concretely in people's lives. There is, for example, an almost universal interest among religions in helping the poor and in providing education for children. Religion affirms that there are certain principles that should be enshrined in society, since the values they represent are the foundation of a beneficial community life. It is for this reason that religions advocate such qualities as honesty and truthfulness and oppose greed and materialism. Likewise, everywhere religion thrives there is concern for the uniqueness and sanctity of human life. Agreements on matters such as these suggest deeper patterns that transcend religious boundaries.

Ethical questions also arise in the relationship between religion and science. There was a time when science, seen as objective and free of "beliefs," was held to be a type of knowledge unfettered by religious convictions. Few people would agree with this view now, however, for modern science itself has come to be seen as the result of particular cultural assumptions. Science has developed in certain ways because of complex influences from the culture in which it has grown, with one of these influences being religion. The freedom to pursue research regardless of the consequences, for example, reflects an aggressive individualism that could not have developed without belief in the individual's responsibility for knowledge, a view derived from religion.

Scientists are themselves human, of course, and they respond to various religious sensibilities. Because science is a human activity, scientists are not "outside" culture or totally "objective," especially when they deal with human problems. Thus, science sometimes comes into conflict with a deeper sense of what is right. Issues like human cloning, for example, are debated by all people, and scientists must sometimes arbitrate between their religious feelings and values and what is scientifically possible. Further, questions have been raised about the legitimacy of any science that operates without social and cultural oversight—that is, outside a solidly-based ethics.

It has been argued that, since different religions promote different standards of moral behavior, ethics should not be grounded in religious belief. Further, some people have pointed to new problems, such as the international scourge of HIV/AIDS, faced by humans today as evidence that religion cannot handle modern ethical problems. Others have claimed that some of the problems of the modern world are legacies of religion itself.

Such critics usually advocate a system of secular ethics. Religious believers, however, argue that in a secular system people are not schooled in and do not internalize the age-old patterns that have undergirded human civilization. Believers maintain, for example, that secular ethics seems not to provide an educational grounding in matters of respect and dutifulness, which have traditionally been provided by religion as the foundation for relationships among people. Moreover, believers point out that charges of inadequacy against religious ethics are unfair, since the world is littered with failed attempts to shape a secular moral sensibility. The rise and fall of Marxism is a notable example. The history of such attempts gives little comfort to those making the secular argument, and the result has been a renewed attempt to reaffirm religious value as a foundation of modern life.

Thus, although the modern world poses many difficulties for believers in every culture, religious groups maintain that their perspective is essential for civilization. Most believers argue that religious tradition addresses issues in a more positive way than does any other approach. Using the tools of promotion and advertising, religions have entered into competition with other forces as they challenge individuals and societies to live according to a better plan. Seen from this perspective, religion has taken on a business hue, with the various traditions competing for followers in the marketplace of contemporary life.

OBSERVANCE AND EXPLANATION OF DEATH Most religions deal with death by providing rituals of condolence and assurances that life goes on, even if in a different way and on another level. Some religions claim to hold keys to eternal life as part of their mandate, while others claim to provide the means by which a person can face the next phase of life. Even those religions that do not maintain a belief in life after death provide means for a sense of closure and acceptance at the ending of life.

Most cultures accept the idea that death falls within the compass of religion. As in other matters, there is a wide variety of approaches. Indigenous peoples anticipate living on in an ancestral world, sometimes characterized by festivities that provide endless moments of delight before some part of a person once again takes on bodily form in this world. Hindus believe in a form of transmigration: with the death of the body in this world a movement into a transitory state from which a person, depending on his or her karma, ultimately exits in another form. Buddhists hope to achieve nirvana, a state that is not material. Western religions, on the other hand, are based on a strong sense of linear time, and although they hold that death is the end of earthly life, they believe that at least a spiritual element lives on. Such religions hold that following death there occur various events, including judgment, purification, and, ultimately for believers, a glorious life in a paradise, or heaven.

Geographic Variations in Religious Practice

In the contemporary world there is great diversity within religious groups, and religious practices often vary by country or region. Consider meditation, for example. As practiced across India in early Hinduism, meditation seems to have been associated with mendicants, those who left their families and homes, took vows, and became wandering holy men. When the practice was adopted by Buddhism, which spread from India to China, it seems initially to have been restricted to monks. In Zen Buddhism, which took root in Japan, meditation eventually took on much broader forms, for the possibility of instant awareness had the effect of weakening the commitment to a monastic life and made the benefits of meditation available to the lay population.

Volumes 2 and 3 of this encyclopedia, containing essays on the contemporary religious practices of individual countries, reveal that religions have frequently been influenced by and vary according to political and geographical boundaries. For example, people do not celebrate Christmas in the same way in Sweden, Uganda, and China. This "mixture" of forms is, however, a contentious issue, for postcolonial critics argue that contemporary political boundaries sometimes reflect the historical presence of imperialism, not the "natural" configuration of an ethnic or religious group. It is also true that religion seldom is restrained by national borders, as is seen by the spread of fundamentalism. Nonetheless, whatever its limitations, the view that political bound-

aries play a critical role in shaping religious life is commonly accepted, even as it makes analysis more difficult.

Trends in Contemporary Religion

One important trend in the contemporary world is the growth of local religious groups made up of small but highly engaged memberships. These groups, whose practices are especially diverse, claim to redefine traditional views, and they sometimes challenge tradition over the "proper" way to practice religion. The numbers of such groups are staggering, with perhaps thousands having sprung up throughout the world in the past quarter century alone.

Contemporary religion is also characterized by its close relation to politics. As religion has come to play an increasing role in political life, nearly every major government in the world now faces pressure from groups that form political movements clothed in religious mantles and that raise ethical questions over public policy. Further, the rise of radical religious groups like al-Qaeda or the Tamil Tigers of Sri Lanka has sometimes made religion a prime force in political events. All of this demonstrates that religion has not retreated, even in the face of the widespread embrace of secularism by governments. Even in countries that might be conceived as firmly advanced in secularism, such as France, the official banning of a religious symbol like the *hijab* can raise a storm of protest, signaling that religious sensitivities are far from quiescent. Indeed, many governments in Muslim countries have quietly abandoned their secular stance, with one eye toward the rising tide of religious revivalism.

Obviously not even Western democratic governments are free from religious influence. This is a striking change compared with, say, Europe during the sixteenth-century Protestant Reformation, when whole countries and peoples became Protestant or Roman Catholic at the conversion of a ruler and stroke of a pen. Today it tends to be the other way around, with the religious values of the people having a direct impact on the government. Religious issues, moreover, are receiving more and more attention in the media. Whereas newspapers, for example, once were restrained in their reporting of religious issues, such matters are now front-page news. At the same time powerful religious organizations like the Roman Catholic Church are no longer free from scrutiny by the public press.

Another feature of contemporary religion is the changing role of women. Holding everything from volunteer to executive positions, women are more important than ever before in religious organizations. While some organizations have been slow to revise their official policies on the role of women, women themselves often have developed their own ways of circumventing the system. Their influence in religion has also changed many people's views about the relationship between the sexes, despite the view of women in traditional theology.

Along with this challenge from women, religious groups have also faced greater demands from the laity. Many laypeople have come to insist that their understanding of tradition is just as valid as that of the professional religionist, something that has consequences for everything from ritual activity to doctrine and organization. Prominent in this movement is the use of the Internet and other modern technology to promote alternative religious views. Whereas a traditional religious organization tends to adopt this technology only to serve its existing structures and approaches, lay leaders often use it as a means for developing new ideas and ways of interacting, which further alienates them from the traditional centers of authority.

The practice of religion without the trappings of wealth and privilege, what is called "antiformalism," is another contemporary idea of global significance. Although it is difficult to see the outlines of the movement clearly, one noticeable feature is the rejection of elaborate settings for worship. In Christianity, for example, architecture has historically played a major role, with basilicas, monasteries, and other religious and educational edifices being central to the life of the Church. The trend in Christianity away from embodying tradition in ornate, expensive buildings may have important ramifications for all religions, as this movement can be seen as part of a broader challenge to established religious understanding and practice.

Hand in hand with these movements are those associated with fundamentalism. A complex phenomenon that arose in American Christianity in the early twentieth century, variations of this movement have spread to most major religions and countries around the world. Fundamentalism involves a militant return to first principles, even as its very existence requires the presence of modernity, with which it clashes. It is not a return to traditional views, for most fundamentalists see such views as hopelessly entwined with political and secular issues. Instead, for fundamentalists religion is primary. Resisting the concept of compromise, fundamentalism affirms a direct and literal interpretation of what is seen as essential in religion. While it is claimed that the roots of fundamentalism connect it to ancient religious founders, there is no mistaking the modern tone and strident individualism of the movement, regardless of the religion in which it occurs.

An Invitation to Explore

These, then, are some of the ways in which people have fashioned responses to their religious sensibilities. It is this material that is summarized, or, perhaps better, sketched in the *Worldmark Encyclopedia of Religious Practices*. The essays in the encyclopedia attempt to describe the rich detail of religious activity in an accessible way. Given the wealth to be found in contemporary religion, however, it is not possible in the essays to do more than provide a sampling, supplemented by suggestions for further reading in the bibliographies. In fact, given limitations of time and space and of human understanding, it is impossible ever to fully describe contemporary religious practices. While acknowledging these limitations, we invite you to engage in studying this cultural wealth with us.

Earle H. Waugh

Advisory Board

EARLE H. WAUGH, CHAIR
Professor of Religious Studies
University of Alberta
Edmonton, Canada

STEPHEN D. CROCCO
James Lennox Librarian
Princeton Theological Seminary
Princeton, New Jersey

JAY DOLAN
Professor Emeritus of History
University of Notre Dame
Notre Dame, Indiana

GARY EBERSOLE
Professor of History and Religious
  Studies
Director, Center for Religious
  Studies
University of Missouri
Kansas City, Missouri

NORMAN GIRARDOT
University Distinguished Professor of
  Religion
Lehigh University
Bethlehem, Pennsylvania

GERRIE TER HAAR
Professor of Religion, Human
  Rights, and Social Change
Institute of Social Studies
The Hague, The Netherlands

VALERIE J. HOFFMAN
Associate Professor of Religion
University of Illinois
Urbana, Illinois

VASUDHA NARAYANAN
Former President, American
  Academy of Religion
Professor of Religion
University of Florida
Gainesville, Florida

GRANT WACKER
Professor of Church History
The Divinity School
Duke University
Durham, North Carolina

BERNARD WASSERSTEIN
Harriet and Ulrich E. Meyer
  Professor of Modern European
  Jewish History
University of Chicago
Chicago, Illinois

Notes on Contributors

ABELA, ANTHONY M. Contributor and peer reviewer. Associate professor of sociology and social policy, University of Malta; principal investigator, European Values Study, Malta; and member, European Values Steering Committee, Tilburg, The Netherlands. Author of *Transmitting Values in European Malta*, 1991, *Changing Youth Culture*, 1992, *Shifting Family Values*, 1994, *Secularized Sexuality: Youth Values in a City-Island*, 1998, *Women and Men in the Maltese Islands: A Comparative European Perspective*, 2000, *Youth Participation in Voluntary Organizations*, 2001, and *Women's Welfare in Society*, 2002. Essay: Malta.

AGUILAR, MARIO I. Contributor and peer reviewer. Dean, Faculty of Divinity, Saint Mary's College, University of Saint Andrews, Scotland. Author of *Being Oromo in Kenya*, 1998, *The Rwanda Genocide and the Call to Deepen Christianity in Africa*, 1998, and *Current Issues on Theology and Religion in Latin America and Africa*, 2002. Editor of *The Politics of Age and Gerontocracy in Africa: Ethnographies of the Past and Memories of the Present*, 1998. Essays: Rwanda, Uganda.

AKERS, DEBORAH S. Contributor. Assistant professor of anthropology, Miami University, Oxford, Ohio. Author, with Abubaker Bagader, of *They Die Strangers: Selected Works by Abdel-Wali*, 2001, *Whispers from the Heart: Short Stories from Saudi Arabia*, 2003, and *Oranges in the Sun: Short Stories from the Persian Gulf*, 2004. Essays: Qatar, Saudi Arabia.

AKINADE, AKINTUNDE E. Contributor. Associate professor of world religions, High Point University, North Carolina. Coeditor of *The Agitated Mind of God: The Theology of Kosuke Koyama*, 1996. Essay: Gambia.

AMAYA, BENJAMÍN. Contributor. Assistant professor of anthropology and sociology, University College of Cape Breton, Nova Scotia, Canada. Author of *Violencia y culturas juveniles en El Salvador*, 2002. Author of book reviews for the scholarly journals *Anthropologie et Société* and *Culture*. Essay: El Salvador.

ANDERSON, LEONA. Contributor and peer reviewer. Professor of religious studies, University of Regina, Saskatchewan, Canada. Author of *The Vasantotsava: The Spring Festivals of India: Texts and Contexts*, 1993. Producer of the video documentaries *The Kumbh Mela*, 1991, and *The Ganesh Festival: Ten Days in the Presence of God*, 1999. Essay: India.

ANDERSON, PAUL N. Contributor. Professor of biblical and Quaker studies and chair, Department of Religious Studies, George Fox University, Newberg, Oregon. Author of *The Christology of the Fourth Gospel: Its Unity and Disunity in the Light of John 6*, 1997, and *Navigating the Living Waters of the Gospel of John: On Wading with Children and Swimming with Elephants*, 2000. Editor of *Evangelical Friend*, 1990–94, and *Quaker Religious Thought*, since 2000. Contributor to such journals as *Semeia*, *Horizons in Biblical Theology*, *Review of Biblical Literature*, *Journal of Biblical Literature*, *Critical Review of Books in Religion*, *Princeton Seminary Bulletin*, and *Pastoral Theology*, as well as to various Friends journals and collections. Author of the *Meet the Friends* series, 2003. Essay: Religious Society of Friends (Quakers).

ANDREEVA, LARISSA A. Contributor. Senior research fellow, Department of Cultural Anthropology, Center for Civilizational and Regional Studies, Russian Academy of Sciences, Moscow. Author of the monographs, in Russian, *Religion and Power in Russia*, 2001, and *Vicarius Christi on the Royal Throne: The Christian Civilization Model of Power Sacralization*, 2002. Essays: Belarus, Russia.

APRAHAMIAN, SIMA. Contributor. Research associate and lecturer, Simone de Beauvoir Institute, Concordia University, Quebec, Canada. Author of articles on Armenia and Lebanon in numerous scholarly journals and edited volumes. Essay: Armenia.

ARENS, WILLIAM. Contributor and peer reviewer. Professor of anthropology and dean of International Academic Programs, State University of New York, Stony Brook. Author of *On the Frontier of Change*, 1979, *The Man-Eating Myth*, 1979, and *The Original Sin*, 1986. Editor of *A Century of Change in Eastern Africa*, 1976. Coeditor of *Creativity of Power*,

1989. Author of numerous articles and essays in scholarly journals and other publications. Essay: Tanzania.

ARMSTRONG, CHARLES. Peer reviewer. Associate professor of history, Columbia University, New York, New York. Author of *Korean Society: Civil Society, Democracy, and the State,* 2002, and *The North Korean Revolution, 1945–1950,* 2003. Contributor to journals, including *Journal of Asian Studies, Critical Asian Studies,* and *Acta Koreana.*

AZEVEDO, MARIO J. Contributor and peer reviewer. Chair and Frank Porter Graham Professor, Department of African-American and African Studies, University of North Carolina, Charlotte. Author of *The Returning Hunter,* 1978, *Roots of Violence: A History of War in Chad,* 1998, and *Tragedy and Triumph: Mozambique Refugees in Southern Africa,* 2002. Coauthor of *Chad: A Nation in Search of Its Future,* 1998, and *A Historical Dictionary of Mozambique,* 2003. Editor of *Cameroon and Chad in Historical and Contemporary Perspectives,* 1988, *Africana Studies: A Survey of Africa and the African Diaspora,* 1998, and *Kenya: The Land, the People, and the Nation,* 1993. Author of articles in numerous scholarly journals, including *African Studies Review, African Affairs, Current History, Journal of Negro History,* and *Science and Medicine.* Essays: Central African Republic, Chad, Kenya, Lesotho, Mozambique, Nigeria.

BAKER, DONALD L. Contributor and peer reviewer. Professor of Asian studies, as well as director, Centre for Korean Research, University of British Columbia, Vancouver, Canada. Coeditor of *Sourcebook of Korean Civilization,* 1996. Author of numerous journal articles and book chapters on the history of Korean religion and traditional science. Essay: North Korea.

BALISKY, E. PAUL. Contributor. Lecturer, Ethiopian Graduate School of Theology, Addis Ababa. Director, Serving in Mission (SIM) Ethiopia, 1999–2003. Author of articles for the 14th International Conference of Ethiopian Studies, 2000, and the online *Dictionary of African Christian Biography.* Essay: Ethiopia.

BARBOSA DA SILVA, ANTÓNIO. Peer reviewer. Professor of systematic theology, philosophy of religion, ethics, and health care ethics, Misjonshøgskolen, Stavanger, Norway. Author of *The Phenomenology of Religion as a Philosophical Problem with Particular Reference to Mircea Eliade's Phenomenological Approach,* 1982, and *Is There a New Imbalance in Jewish-Christian Relations?* Author, in Norwegian, of *Hva er religionsfenomenologi?* Author of numerous articles.

BARCLAY, HAROLD B. Contributor and peer reviewer. Professor emeritus of anthropology, University of Alberta, Edmonton, Canada. Author of *Buurri al Lamaab, a Suburban Village in the Sudan,* 1964, *The Role of the Horse in Man's Culture,*

1980, *Culture, the Human Way,* 1986, and *People without Government: An Anthropology of Anarchy,* 1990. Author of the chapters "Egypt: Struggling with Secularization" and "Sudan: On the Frontier of Islam" in *Religions and Societies, Asia and the Middle East,* edited by Carlo Caldarola, 1982. Essays: The Sudan, Tunisia.

BAREJA-STARZYNSKA, AGATA. Contributor. Assistant professor, Department of Inner Asia, Institute of Oriental Studies, University of Warsaw, Poland. Author of "The History of Ancient Tibet according to the 17th Century Mongolian Chronicle 'Erdeni-yin tobci' by Sagang Secen," in *Proceedings of the 5th International Seminar on Tibetan Studies in Narita, Japan, 1989,* edited by S. Ihara and Z. Yamaguchi, 1992, and "The Essentials of Buddhism in the 'Ciqula kereglegci,' the 16th Century Mongolian Buddhist Treatise," in *Proceedings of the International Seminar on Buddhism 'Aspects of Buddhism' in Liw, Poland, 1994,* edited by A. Bareja-Starzynska and M. Mejor, 1997. Essay: Mongolia.

BARLOW, PHILIP L. Peer reviewer. Professor of theological studies, Hanover College, Indiana. Author of *Mormons and the Bible: The Place of the Latter-Day Saints in American Religion,* 1991. Coauthor of *New Historical Atlas of Religion in America,* 2000. Editor of *A Thoughtful Faith: Essays on Belief by Mormon Scholars,* 1986, and *Religion and Public Life in the Midwest: Microcosm and Mosaic,* 2004.

BEBBINGTON, DAVID. Peer reviewer. Professor of history, University of Stirling, Scotland. Author of *Evangelicalism in Modern Britain: A History from the 1730s to the 1980s,* 1989, and *Holiness in Nineteenth-Century England,* 1998. Editor of *The Baptists in Scotland: A History,* 1988, and *The Gospel in the World: International Baptist Studies,* 2002. Coeditor of *Evangelicalism: Comparative Studies of Popular Protestantism in North America, the British Isles and Beyond, 1700–1990,* 1994, and *Modern Christianity and Cultural Aspirations,* 2003.

BERNAL, VICTORIA. Contributor. Associate professor of anthropology, University of California, Irvine. Author of *Cultivating Workers: Peasants and Capitalism in a Sudanese Village,* 1991. Author of articles in such scholarly journals as *American Ethnologist, American Anthropologist, Comparative Studies in Society and History, Cultural Anthropology, African Studies Review,* and *Political and Legal Anthropology Review.* Essay: Eritrea.

BERRY, MOULOUK. Contributor. Assistant professor of Arabic, as well as director of the Arab and Chaldean American Writers Series and the Quranic Forum, University of Michigan-Dearborn. Essay: Lebanon.

BESNIER, NIKO. Peer reviewer. Visiting professor, Department of Anthropology, University of California, Los Angeles. Author of *Literacy, Emotion, and Authority: Reading and*

Writing on a Polynesian Atoll, 1995, and *Tuvaluan: A Polynesian Language of the Central Pacific*, 2000. Contributor to numerous journals in anthropology and linguistics, including *American Ethnologist, American Anthropologist, Anthropological Quarterly, Ethnos, Social Anthropology, Journal of Anthropological Research, Annual Review of Anthropology, Language,* and *Language in Society*, as well as many edited volumes.

BLUMHOFER, EDITH. Contributor. Professor of history, as well as director, Institute for the Study of American Evangelicals, Wheaton College, Illinois. Author of *The Assemblies of God: A Chapter in the Story of American Pentecostalism,* 1989, *Aimee Semple McPherson: Everybody's Sister,* 1993, and *Restoring the Faith: The Assemblies of God, Pentecostalism, and American Culture,* 1993. Coeditor of *Modern Christian Revivals,* 1993, and *Pentecostal Currents in American Protestantism,* 1999. Essay: Pentecostalism.

BOELDERL, ARTUR R. Contributor. Assistant professor of philosophy, Private Catholic University of Linz, Austria. Author of *Alchimie, Postmoderne und der arme Hölderlin: Drei Studien zur Philosophischen Hermetik,* 1995, and *Literarische Hermetik: Die Ethik zwischen Hermeneutik, Psychoanalyse und Dekonstruktion,* 1997. Coeditor of several volumes, including *Rituale: Zugänge zu einem Phänomen,* 1999, and *Die Sprachen der Religion,* 2003. Essay: Austria.

BONK, JONATHAN J. Peer reviewer. Executive director, Overseas Ministries Study Center, New Haven, Connecticut, as well as editor, *International Bulletin of Missionary Research,* and project director, *Dictionary of African Christian Biography.* Author of *An Annotated and Classified Bibliography of English Literature Pertaining to the Ethiopian Orthodox Church,* 1984, *The World at War, the Church at Peace: A Biblical Perspective,* 1988, *The Theory and Practice of Missionary Identification, 1860–1920,* 1989, *Missions and Money: Affluence as a Western Missionary Problem,* 1991, and *Between Past and Future: Evangelical Mission Entering the Twenty-First Century,* 2003.

BOOLELL, SHAKUNTALA. Contributor. Senior lecturer in French, Department of Humanities and Social Sciences, University of Mauritius. Author of *La femme enveloppée et autres nouvelles de Maurice,* 1996, and *De l'ombre à la lumière: Sur les traces de l'Indo-Mauricienne,* 1998. Coauthor of *Fonction et représentation de la Mauricienne dans le discours littéraire,* 2000. Essay: Mauritius.

BOROWIK, IRENA. Peer reviewer. Professor of religion and post-Communist transformation, Institute of Religious Studies, Jagiellonian University, Kraków, Poland. Author, in Polish, of *Charyzma a codziennosc: Studium wplywu religii na zycie codzienne,* 1990, *Procesy instytucjonalizacji i prywatyzacji religii w powojennej Polsce,* 1997, and *Odbudowywanie pamieci: Przemiany religijne w Srodkowo-wschodniej Europie po upadku komunizm',* 2000. Coauthor, with Tadeusz Doktór, in Polish, of *Religijny i*

moralny pluralizm w Polsce, 2001. Editor of *State Relations in Central and Eastern Europe after the Collapse of Communism,* 1999, and *Religions, Churches and the Scientific Studies of Religion: Poland and Ukraine,* 2003. Coeditor, with Miklos Tomka, of *Religion and Social Change in Post-Communist Europe,* 2001. Coeditor and contributor to *The Future of Religion,* 1995, and *New Religious Phenomena in Central and Eastern Europe,* 1997.

BOYARIN, DANIEL. Peer reviewer. Hermann P. and Sophia Taubman Professor of Talmudic Culture, Department of Near Eastern Studies and Rhetoric, University of California, Berkeley. Author of *Carnal Israel: Reading Sex in Talmudic Culture,* 1995, *A Radical Jew: Paul and the Politics of Identity,* 1997, *Unheroic Conduct: The Rise of Heterosexuality and the Invention of the Jewish Man,* 1997, *Dying for God: Martyrdom and the Making of Christianity and Judaism,* 1999, and *Border Lines: The Partition of Judaeo-Christianity,* 2004. Coauthor, with Jonathan Boyarin, of *Powers of Diaspora: Two Essays on the Relevance of Jewish Culture,* 2002. Coeditor, with Jonathan Boyarin, of *Jews and Other Differences: The New Jewish Cultural Studies,* 1997, and, with Daniel Itzkovitz and Ann Pellegrini, of *Queer Theory and the Jewish Question,* 2003.

BRATT, JAMES D. Peer reviewer. Professor of history, as well as director of the Calvin Center for Christian Scholarship, Calvin College, Grand Rapids, Michigan. Author of *Dutch Calvinism in Modern America: A History of a Conservative Subculture,* 1984. Coauthor of *Gathered at the River: Grand Rapids, Michigan, and Its People of Faith,* 1993. Editor of *Viewpoints: Exploring the Reformed Vision,* 1992, and *Abraham Kuyper: A Centennial Reader,* 1998.

BRINKMAN, INGE. Contributor. Research fellow, Ghent University, Belgium. Author of *Kikuyu Gender Norms and Narratives,* 1996, as well as various articles in such scholarly journals as *Journal of African History, Africa, Journal of South African Studies,* and *Historische Anthropoligie.* Editor of *Singing in the Bush: MPLA Songs during the War for Independence in South-East Angola (1966–1975),* 2001. Coeditor of *Grandmother's Footsteps: Oral Tradition and South-East Angolan Narratives on the Colonial Encounter,* 1999. Essay: Angola.

BROWERS, MICHAELLE. Contributor. Assistant professor of political science, Wake Forest University, Winston-Salem, North Carolina. Coeditor of *An Islamic Reformation?,* 2003. Essay: Syria.

BUCHENAU, KLAUS. Contributor. Research assistant, Eastern European Institute, Free University of Berlin. Author of two monographs, as well as various articles on religion in the former Yugoslavia. Essay: Bosnia and Herzegovina.

BUCKSER, ANDREW. Contributor. Associate professor of anthropology, Purdue University, Lafayette, Indiana. Author of *Communities of Faith: Sectarianism, Identity, and Social Change on a Danish Island,* 1996, and *After the Rescue: Jewish Identity and Community in Contemporary Denmark,* 2003. Coeditor of *The Anthropology of Religious Conversion,* 2003. Essay: Denmark.

CAHN, PETER S. Contributor. Assistant professor of anthropology, University of Oklahoma, Norman. Author of *All Religions Are Good in Tzintzuntzan: Evangelicals in Catholic Mexico,* 2003, and a chapter in *Chronicling Cultures: Long-Term Field Research in Anthropology,* 2002. Essay: Brazil.

CALKOWSKI, MARCIA. Contributor and peer reviewer. Associate professor and head, Department of Anthropology, University of Regina, Saskatchewan, Canada. Author of articles in edited volumes and journals, including *Canadian Review of Sociology and Anthropology, Anthropologica, American Ethnologist, Journal of Asian Studies, Tibetan Review,* and *Culture.* Essays: Myanmar, Thailand, Tibetan Buddhism.

CAMPBELL, SIRI. Contributor. Journalist. Author of *Inside Monaco,* 2000, and contributor to numerous television organizations and travel shows, including the Discovery Channel, BBC *Travel Show,* NBC *Today Show, CBS News,* and Denmark 2. Essay: Monaco.

CAMPO, JUAN E. Peer reviewer. Associate professor, Religious Studies Department, University of California, Santa Barbara. Author of *The Other Sides of Paradise: Explorations into the Religious Meanings of Domestic Space in Islam,* 1991. Contributor to *Merriam-Webster's Encyclopedia of World Religions,* 1999, and to journals, including *Traditional Dwellings and Settlements Review, Contention, Annals of the American Academy of Political and Social Science,* and *Muslim World.*

CAREY, PATRICK. Peer reviewer. Professor of theology, Marquette University, Milwaukee, Wisconsin. Author of *An Immigrant Bishop: John England's Adaptation of Irish Catholicism to American Republicanism,* 1982, *People, Priests and Prelates: Ecclesiastical Democracy and the Tensions of Trusteeism,* 1987, *The Roman Catholics,* 1993, and *The Roman Catholics in America,* 1996. Editor of *American Catholic Religious Thought,* 1987, and *The Early Works of Orestes A. Brownson,* 2000. Coeditor of *Theological Education in the Catholic Tradition: Contemporary Challenges,* 1997, and *Biographical Dictionary of Christian Theologians,* 2002.

CASEBOLT, JAMES. Contributor. Associate professor of psychology, Ohio University Eastern Campus, Saint Clairsville. Contributor to the edited volume *Measures of Religiosity,* 1999, and to various journals, including *AURCO Journal.* Essay: Unitarianism and Universalism.

CATE, SANDRA. Contributor. Lecturer, Department of Anthropology, San Jose State University, California. Author of *Making Merit, Making Art: A Thai Temple in Wimbledon,* 2003. Coeditor of *Converging Interests: Travelers, Traders, and Tourists in South East Asia,* 1999. Essay: Laos.

CAULKINS, D. DOUGLAS. Contributor. Earl D. Strong Professor of Social Studies, Department of Anthropology, Grinnell College, Iowa. Formerly a visiting researcher at the Institute for Social Research, Oslo, Norway, and at the universities of Trondheim, Norway; Bergen, Norway; Stirling, Scotland; and Durham, England. Author of numerous articles in journals, including *Cross-Cultural Research, Journal of Anthropological Research, Field Methods,* and *Practicing Anthropology.* Essay: Norway.

CHAKANZA, J.C. Contributor. Associate professor and head, Department of Theology and Religious Studies, Chancellor College, Zomba, Malawi. Author of *Voices of Preachers in Protest: The Ministry of Two Malawian Prophets: Elliot Kamwana and Wilfrid Gudu,* 1998, *Religion in Malawi: An Annotated Bibliography,* 1998, *Islam in Malawi Week,* 1999, and *Wisdom of the People: 2000 Chinyanja Proverbs,* 2001. Author of articles in various journals, including *Lamp.* Essay: Malawi.

CHEVANNES, BARRY. Contributor. Professor of social anthropology and dean of the Faculty of Social Sciences, University of the West Indies at Mona, Kingston, Jamaica. Author of *Rastafari: Roots and Ideology,* 1994, and *Learning to Be a Man: Culture, Socialisation and Gender in Five Caribbean Communities,* 2001. Editor of *Rastafari and Other African-Caribbean Worldviews,* 1995. Essay: Jamaica.

CHEYEKA, AUSTIN. Contributor. Lecturer in religious studies, University of Zambia, Lusaka. Author of articles in various scholarly journals, including *African Ecclesial Review (AFER)* and *African Christian Studies.* Essay: Zambia.

CHILTON, TUTII. Contributor. Assistant professor of social science, Palau Community College, Republic of Palau. Essay: Palau.

CHOKSY, JAMSHEED. Peer reviewer. Professor of central Eurasian studies, professor of history, and adjunct professor of religious studies, Indiana University, Bloomington. Author of *Purity and Pollution in Zoroastrianism: Triumph over Evil,* 1989, *Conflict and Cooperation: Zoroastrian Subalterns and Muslim Elites in Medieval Iranian Society,* 1997, and *Evil, Good, and Gender: Facets of the Feminine in Zoroastrian Religious History,* 2002. Contributor to *Women in Iran from the Rise of Islam to 1800,* edited by G. Nashat and L. Beck, 2003, *Jamshid Soroush Soroushian Memorial Volume,* edited by C. Cereti and F.J. Vajifdar, 2003, and the periodicals *Indo-Iranian Journal, Iranian Studies, Iranica Antiqua, Journal of the American Oriental Society, Journal of*

Ritual Studies, Journal of the Royal Asiatic Society of Great Britain and Ireland, and *Studia Iranica,* among others.

CINNAMON, JOHN. Contributor. Assistant professor of anthropology, Miami University, Hamilton, Ohio. Author of various articles on religion and political ecology in Gabon. Essays: Comoros, Equatorial Guinea, Gabon, São Tomé and Príncipe.

CLAYER, NATHALIE. Contributor and peer reviewer. Researcher, Centre Nationale de la Recherche Scientifique (CNRS), Paris. Author of *L'Albanie: Pays des derviches,* 1990, and *Mystiques, etat et société: Les halvetis dans l'aire balkanique de la fin du XVe siècle à nos jours,* 1994. Coeditor, *Le nouvel Islam balkanique: Les musulmans, acteurs du post-communisme,* 2001. Essay: Albania.

COLE, JUAN R. Peer reviewer. Professor of modern Middle East and South Asian history, Department of History, University of Michigan, Ann Arbor. Author of *Roots of North Indian Shi'ism in Iran and Iraq: Religion and State in Awadh, 1722–1859,* 1988, *Colonialism and Revolution in the Middle East: Social and Cultural Origins of Egypt's 'Urabi' Movement,* 1993, *Modernity and the Millennium: The Genesis of the Baha'i Faith in the Nineteenth-Century Middle East,* 1998, and *Sacred Space and Holy War: The Politics, Culture and History of Shi'ite Islam,* 2002. Translator of *Miracles and Metaphors,* by Mirza Abu'l-Fadl Gulpaygani, 1982, *Letters and Essays 1886–1913,* by Mirza Abu'l-Fadl Gulpaygani, 1985, *Spirit Brides,* by Kahlil Gibran, 1993, *The Vision,* by Kahlil Gibran, 1998, and *Broken Wings: A Novel,* by Kahlil Gibran, 1998. Contributor to and coeditor of *From Iran East and West: Studies in Babi and Baha'i History,* 1984. Coeditor of *Shi'ism and Social Protest,* 1986. Editor of *Comparing Muslim Societies,* 1992, and *Religion in Iran: From Zoroaster to Baha'u'llah,* by Alessandro Bausani, 2000. Author of articles in numerous journals and books.

COLEMAN, SIMON. Contributor. Reader in anthropology, University of Durham, England. Author of *The Globalisation of Charismatic Christianity: Spreading the Gospel of Prosperity,* 2000. Coauthor of *Pilgrimage: Past and Present in the World Religions,* 1995. Coeditor of *Tourism: Between Place and Performance,* 2002, *Religion, Identity, and Change: Perspectives on Global Transformations,* 2003, *Pilgrim Voices: Narrative and Authorship in Christian Pilgrimage,* 2003, *The Cultures of Creationism: Antievolution in English-Speaking Countries,* 2003, and *Reframing Pilgrimage: Cultures in Motion,* 2004. Essay: Sweden.

COLLINGE, WILLIAM J. Contributor. Knott Professor of Theology and professor of philosophy, Mount Saint Mary's College, Emmitsburg, Maryland. Author of *A Historical Dictionary of Catholicism,* 1997, and *The A to Z of Catholicism,* 2001, as well as articles in various journals, including

Horizons, Living Light, Faith and Philosophy, and *Augustinian Studies.* Essay: Roman Catholicism.

COSENTINO, DONALD. Contributor and peer reviewer. Professor of world arts and cultures, University of California, Los Angeles, as well as editor of *African Arts,* since 1988. Author of *Defiant Maids and Stubborn Farmers: Tradition and Invention in Mende Story Performance,* 1982, and *Vodou Things: The Art of Pierrot Barra and Marie Cassaise,* 1998. Editor of *Sacred Arts of Haitian Vodou,* 1995. Author of articles in numerous journals, magazines, and catalogs, from *Aperture* to *Playboy.* Essay: Haiti.

COWE, S. PETER. Peer reviewer. Narekatsi Professor of Armenian Studies, University of California, Los Angeles. Author of *The Armenian Version of Daniel,* 1992, and *Catalogue of the Armenian Manuscripts in the Cambridge University Library,* 1994. Editor of *Mxit'ar Sasnec'i's Theological Discourses,* 1993, and *Ani: World Architectural Heritage of a Medieval Armenian Capital,* 2001. Coeditor of *Modern Armenian Drama: An Anthology,* 2001. Translator of *Commentary on the Divine Liturg,* by Xosrov Anjewac'I, 1991.

CROCCO, STEPHEN D. Adviser. James Lennox Librarian, Princeton Theological Seminary, Princeton, New Jersey. Editor, *The Essential Paul Ramsey: A Collection,* 1994.

DAIBER, KARL-FRITZ. Contributor. Professor emeritus, College of Protestant Theology, University of Marburg, Germany. Author of *Praktische Theologie als Handlungswissenschaft,* 1977, *Diakonie und Kirchliche Identitaet,* 1988, *Religion unter den Bedingungen der Moderne—Die Situation in der Bundesrepublik Deutschland,* 1995, and *Religion in Kirche und Gesellschaft: Theologische und Soziologische Studien zur Präsenz von Religion in der Gegenwärtigen Kultur,* 1997. Coeditor of *Religion in den Gegenwartsströmungen der Deutschen Soziologie,* 1983. Essay: Germany.

DAMATTA, ROBERTO. Peer reviewer. Professor emeritus, Department of Anthropology, University of Notre Dame, Indiana. Author of *Carnivals, Rogues and Heroes: An Interpretation of the Brazilian Dilemma* and *A Divided World: Apinayé Social Structure.* Contributor to *Revisão do paraíso: Os brasileiros e o estado em 500 anos de história,* edited by Mary Del Priori, 2000, and *Brazil 2001: A Revisionary History of Brazilian Literature and Culture,* 2001. Coauthor and coeditor of *The Brazilian Puzzle* and coauthor of *Aguias, burros e borboletas: Um estudo antropologico do jogo do bicho,* 1999.

DARROW, WILLIAM. Contributor. Jackson Professor of Religion, Williams College, Williamstown, Massachusetts. Author of articles in various edited volumes and journals, including *Journal of the American Academy of Religion, Harvard Theological Review,* and *History of Religions.* Essay: Zoroastrianism.

DAVIS, MARTHA ELLEN. Contributor. Affiliate associate professor of anthropology and music, University of Florida, Gainesville. Member, Dominican Academy of Sciences, and researcher, Museo del Hombre Dominicana, Santo Domingo, Dominican Republic. Author of *Afro-Dominican Religious Brotherhoods: Structure, Ritual, and Music,* 1976, *Cries from Purgatory: A Study of the Dominican "Salve,"* 1981, and *The Other Science: Dominican Vodú as Folk Religion and Medicine,* 1987. Essay: Dominican Republic.

DIAGNE, SOULEYMANE BACHIR. Contributor. Professor of philosophy, Northwestern University, Evanston, Illinois. Author of *Boole: 1815–1864: L'oiseau de nuit en plein jour,* 1989, *Reconstruire le sens: Textes et enjeux de prospectives africaines,* 2000, *Islam et société ouverte: La fidélité et le mouvement dans la philosophie de Muhammad Iqbal,* 2001, and *100 mots pour dire l'Islam,* 2002. Coauthor of *The Cultural Question in Africa,* 1996. Essay: Senegal.

DIALLO, GARBA. Contributor. Director of international programs, International People's College, Elsinore, Denmark. Author of *Mauritania, the Other Apartheid,* 1993, *Indigenous Learning Forms in West Africa: The Case of Mauritania,* 1994, *Entrance to Hell—The Concentration Camp (Goree) That Lasted for 400 Years,* 1996, and *Mauritania—Neither Arab nor African,* 2001, as well as articles in journals, including *Global Ecology* and *Kontakt.* Editor of *Educators' Contribution to the Peace Process in the Middle East,* 1998. Essay: Mauritania.

DOLAN, JAY. Adviser. Professor emeritus of history, University of Notre Dame, Indiana. Author of *The Immigrant Church: New York's Irish and German Catholics, 1815-1865,* 1975, *Catholic Revivalism: The American Experience, 1830-1900,* 1978, *The American Catholic Experience: A History from Colonial Time to the Present,* 1985, and *In Search of an American Catholicism: A History of Religion and Culture in Tension,* 2002. Coauthor of *The American Catholic Parish: A History from 1850 to the Present,* 1987, and *Transforming Parish Ministry: The Changing Roles of Catholic Clergy, Laity, and Women Religious in the United States, 1930-1980,* 1989.

DOUGLAS, IAN T. Contributor. Professor of mission and world Christianity, as well as director of Anglican, global, and ecumenical studies, Episcopal Divinity School, Cambridge, Massachusetts. Author of *Fling Out the Banner: The National Church Ideal and the Foreign Mission of the Episcopal Church,* 1993. Editor of *Waging Reconciliation: God's Mission in a Time of Globalization and Crisis,* 2002. Coeditor of *Beyond Colonial Anglicanism: The Anglican Communion in the Twenty-First Century,* 2001. Essay: Anglicanism.

EBERSOLE, GARY. Adviser, contributor, and peer reviewer. Professor of history and religious studies, as well as director of the Center for Religious Studies, University of Missouri-Kansas City. Author of *Ritual Poetry and the Politics of Death in Early Japan,* 1989, and *Captured by Texts: Puritan to Postmodern Images of Indian Captivity,* 1995. Author of articles in numerous journals, including *History of Religions, Religion, Journal of Religion, Journal of Japanese Studies,* and *Momumenta Nipponica.* Essays: Japan, Shinto.

EDGECOMBE-HOWELL, OLIVIA. Contributor. Head, University Centre, University of the West Indies, Basseterre, St. Kitts. Essay: Saint Kitts and Nevis.

EL-ASWAD, EL-SAYED. Contributor. Professor of anthropology and chair, Department of Sociology, Tanta University, Egypt, as well as adjunct professor, Wayne State University, Detroit, Michigan. Author of books in Arabic and English, including *Religion and Folk Cosmology: Scenarios of the Visible and Invisible in Rural Egypt,* 2002, and *Symbolic Anthropology,* 2002. Author of articles in journals, including *AAA Anthropology Newsletter* and *Anthropos.* Essay: United Arab Emirates.

EL-HASSAN, KHALID. Contributor. Research assistant professor and program coordinator, African Studies Resource Center, University of Kansas, Lawrence. Author of articles and book reviews in edited volumes and journals, including *Horizons, Journal of International Programs for the University of Kansas,* and *African Studies Quarterly.* Essay: Bahrain.

ELOLIA, SAMUEL K. Contributor. Associate professor of Christian doctrine and missiology, Emmanuel School of Religion, Johnson City, Tennessee. Author of articles in several edited volumes. Essays: Burundi, Djibouti.

ESPOSITO, JOHN L. Contributor. Professor, School of Foreign Service and Theology, Georgetown University, Washington, D.C. Author of *Islam and Politics,* 1998, and coauthor of *Islam and Democracy,* 1996. Editor of *Islam and Development: Religion and Sociopolitical Change,* 1980, *Voices of Resurgent Islam,* 1983, *Islam in Asia: Religion, Politics, and Society,* 1987, *The Iranian Revolution: Its Global Impact,* 1990, and *The Islamic World: Past and Present,* 2004. Coeditor of *Islam, Gender, and Social Change,* 1998, *Muslims on the Americanization Path?,* 2000, *Religion and Global Order,* 2000, *Islam and Secularism in the Middle East,* 2001, *Daughters of Abraham: Feminist Thought in Judaism, Christianity, and Islam,* 2001, *Iran at the Crossroads,* 2001, *Muslims and the West: Encounter and Dialogue,* 2001, *Religion and Immigration: Christian, Jewish, and Muslim Experiences in the United States,* 2003, and *Turkish Islam and the Secular State: The Gülen Movement,* 2003. Essay: Islam.

ESTGEN, ALOYSE. Contributor. Member, Centre Luxembourgeois de Documentation et d'études MÇdiÇvales, and former instructor of medieval history.

Author of numerous articles, as well as coeditor of *Les Actes de Jean l'Aveugle*, 1997. Essay: Luxembourg.

ESTGEN, PAUL. Contributor. Sociologist, SESOPI-Centre Intercommunautaire, Luxembourg. Contributor to *Les valeurs au Luxembourg: Portrait d'une société au tournant du 3e millénaire*, 2002. Essay: Luxembourg.

FERNEA, ELIZABETH. Peer reviewer. Professor emeritus of English and Middle Eastern studies, University of Texas, Austin. Author of *Guests of the Sheik: An Ethnography of an Iraqi Village*, 1965, *A View of the Nile*, 1970, *A Street in Marrakech*, 1975, and *In Search of Islamic Feminism*, 1998. Coauthor, with Robert A. Fernea, of *The Arab World: Personal Encounters*, 1985, *Nubian Ethnographies*, 1991, and *The Arab World: Forty Years of Change*, 1997. Editor of *Women and the Family in the Middle East: New Voices of Change*,1985, *Children of the Muslim Middle East*, 1995, and *Remembering Childhood in the Middle East: Memoirs from a Century of Change*, 2001. Coeditor of *Middle Eastern Muslim Women Speak*, 1977, and *The Struggle for Peace: Israelis and Palestinians*, 1992. Ethnographer and consultant for the film *Some Women of Marrakech*, 1976. Producer of numerous documentaries, including *A Veiled Revolution, Women and Religion in Egypt*, 1982, *The Price of Change*, 1982, *Women under Siege*, 1982, *The Struggle for Peace: Israelis and Palestinians*, 1991, *The Road to Peace: Israelis and Palestinians*, 1995, and *Living with the Past: Historic Cairo*, 2001.

FINE-DARE, KATHLEEN. Peer reviewer. Professor of anthropology and women's studies, Fort Lewis College, Durango, Colorado. Author of *Cotocollao: Ideología, historia, y acción en un barrio de Quito*, 1991, and *Grave Injustice: The American Indian Repatriation Movement and NAGPRA*, 2002. Contributor to journals, including *Radical History Review* and *Anthropological Quarterly*.

FLAKE, KATHLEEN. Contributor. Assistant professor of American religious history, Graduate Department of Religion and Divinity School, Vanderbilt University, Nashville, Tennessee. Author of *The Politics of American Religious History: The Seating of Senator Reed Smoot, Mormon Apostle*, 2004. Essay: The Church of Jesus Christ of Latter-day Saints.

FOHR, SHERRY. Contributor. Assistant professor of world religions, Wofford College, Spartanburg, South Carolina, and board member, Southeastern Commission for the Study of Religions. Essay: Jainism.

GALINIER-PALLEROLA, JEAN-FRANÇOIS. Contributor. Member, Department of Theology, Institut Catholique de Toulouse, France. Author of *La religion populaire en Andorre*, 1990, and of articles in *Bulletin de Literature Ecclésiastique*. Essay: Andorra.

GATTAMORTA, LORENZA. Contributor. Research associate of the sociology of culture, University of Bologna, Forli, Italy. Author of *La memoria delle parole: Luzi tra Eliot e Dante*, 2002. Author of articles in numerous journals, including *Strumenti Critici, Lingua e Stile, Ideazione,* and *Sociologia e Politiche Sociali.* Essay: San Marino.

GAUSSET, QUENTIN. Contributor. Associate professor, University of Copenhagen, Denmark. Author of articles in numerous journals, including *Africa, Journal of the Royal Anthropological Institute, Cahiers d'Études Africaines, Social Sciences and Medicine,* and *Anthropos.* Essay: Cameroon.

GEFFEN, RELA MINTZ. Contributor. President, Baltimore Hebrew University, and editor of the journal *Contemporary Jewry.* Coauthor of *The Conservative Movement in Judaism: Dilemmas and Opportunities*, 2000. Editor of *Celebration and Renewal: Rites of Passage in Judaism*, 1993. Coeditor of *A Double Bond: The Constitutional Documents of American Jewry*, 1992, and *Freedom and Responsibility: Exploring the Challenges of Jewish Continuity*, 1998. Essay: Conservative Judaism.

GHANNAM, FARHA. Contributor. Visiting assistant professor of anthropology, Swarthmore College, Pennsylvania. Author of *Remaking the Modern: Space, Relocation, and the Politics of Identity in a Global Cairo*, 2002. Author of articles in various journals, including *Visual Anthropology, City and Society,* and *Middle East Report.* Essay: Egypt.

GIBBS, PHILIP. Contributor and peer reviewer. Faculty member, Melanesian Institute, Soroka, Papua New Guinea. Author of *The Word in the Third World*, 1996. Author of articles in journals, including *Point 24* and *Studia Missionalia.* Essay: Papua New Guinea.

GIBSON, KEAN. Contributor. Senior lecturer in linguistics, University of the West Indies, Cave Hill, Barbados. Author of *Comfa Religion and Creole Language in a Caribbean Community*, 2001, and *The Cycle of Racial Oppression in Guyana*, 2003. Author of articles in numerous journals, including *Lingua, American Speech, International Folklore Review, Mankind Quarterly, Lore and Language,* and *Journal of Caribbean Studies.* Essay: Guyana.

GILL, ANTHONY. Contributor. Associate professor of political science, University of Washington, Seattle. Author of *Rendering unto Caesar: The Catholic Church and State in Latin America*, 1998, and of articles in numerous journals, including *American Journal of Political Science, Rationality and Society, Politics and Society,* and *Journal of Church and State.* Essays: Argentina, Chile, Uruguay.

GIRARDOT, NORMAN. Adviser and peer reviewer. University Distinguished Professor, Department of Religious Studies,

Lehigh University, Bethlehem, Pennsylvania. Author of *Myth and Meaning in Early Taoism*, 1983, and *The Victorian Translation of China*, 2002. Editor of the section on China in the *HarperCollins Dictionary of Religion*, edited by Jonathan Z. Smith and William Scott Green, 1995. Coeditor of *Imagination and Meaning: The Scholarly and Literary Worlds of Mircea Eliade*, 1982, and *Daoism and Ecology*, 2001. Cotranslator of *Taoist Meditation*, 1993. Contributor to books, including *Self-Taught Artists of the 20th Century: An American Anthology*, edited by Elsa Longhauser, 1998, and *Changing Religious Worlds, the Meaning and End of Mircea Eliade*, edited by Bryan Rennie, 2001, and to journals such as the *Journal of the American Academy of Religion*.

GOLDSMITH, MICHAEL. Contributor and peer reviewer. Senior lecturer in anthropology, University of Waikato, Hamilton, New Zealand. Coauthor of *The Accidental Missionary: Tales of Elekana*, 2002. Coeditor of *Other Sites: Social Anthropology and the Politics of Interpretation*, 1992. Author of numerous book chapters and encyclopedia entries, as well as of articles in various journals, including *Journal of Pacific History*, *Journal of Pacific Studies*, and *Ethnologies Comparées*. Essay: Tuvalu.

GOOREN, HENRI. Contributor. Researcher, IIMO Utrecht University, The Netherlands. Coeditor of *Under Pressure: Essays on Development Research*, 1997. Author of chapters in books, as well as of articles in various journals, including *Journal for the Scientific Study of Religion* and *Dialogue*. Essay: Nicaragua.

GOOSEN, GIDEON. Contributor. Associate professor of theology, Australian Catholic University, Sydney. Author of *Religion in Australian Culture: An Anthropological View*, 1997, *Australian Theologies: Themes and Methodologies into the Third Millennium*, 2000, and *Bringing Churches Together: A Popular Introduction to Ecumenism*, 2001. Author of articles in numerous journals, including *Theological Studies*, *Compass*, *Australasian Catholic Record*, *Word in Life*, *St. Mark's Review*, and *Peace and Change*. Essay: Australia.

GOTHÓNI, RENÉ. Peer reviewer. Professor of comparative religion, University of Helsinki, Finland. Author of several books, including *Paradise within Reach: Monasticism and Pilgrimage on Mt. Athos*, 1993, and *Attitudes and Interpretations in Comparative Religion*, 2000.

GRANT, BRUCE. Peer reviewer. Associate professor of anthropology, Swarthmore College, Pennsylvania. Author of *In the Soviet House of Culture: A Century of Perestroikas*, 1995, and editor of and author of the foreword and afterword to *The Social Organization of the Gilyak*, by Lev Shternberg, 1999. Contributor to *Paranoia within Reason: A Casebook on Conspiracy as Explanation*, edited by George Marcus, 1999, and to journals, including *American Ethnologist*.

GREEN, KATHRYN L. Contributor. Independent scholar. Contributor to various publications on African and Middle Eastern history. Essay: Mali.

GROELSEMA, ROBERT. Contributor. Civil society analyst, U.S. Agency for International Development. Author of articles on African politics, culture, and current events for encyclopedias and other publications, as well as regular articles on Guinea and the Seychelles in *Africa Contemporary Record*. Essays: Republic of the Congo, Ghana, Guinea, Seychelles, Sierra Leone.

HAAR, GERRIE TER. Adviser. Professor of religion, human rights, and social change, Institute of Social Studies, The Hague, The Netherlands. General Editor, Religion in Contemporary Africa (series), as well as author of *Faith of Our Fathers: Studies on Religious Education in Sub-Saharan Africa*, 1990, *Spirit of Africa: The Healing Ministry of Archbishop Milingo of Zambia*, 1992, *African Traditional Religions in Religious Education*, 1992, *Halfway to Paradise: African Christians in Europe*, 1998, and *Worlds of Power: Religious Thought and Political Practice in Africa*, 2004.

HALE, JOE. Peer reviewer. General secretary, 1976–2001, then emeritus, World Methodist Council.

HAMM, THOMAS D. Peer reviewer. Professor of history and archivist and curator of the Friends Collection and College Archives, Earlham College, Richmond, Indiana. Author of *God's Government Begun: The Society for Universal Inquiry and Reform, 1842–1846*, 1995, *The Transformation of American Quakerism: Orthodox Friends, 1800–1907*, 1998, and *The Quakers in America*, 2003.

HEITZENRATER, RICHARD P. Contributor. William Kellon Quick Professor of Church History and Wesley Studies, Duke University, Durham, North Carolina. Author of *Mirror and Memory: Reflections on Early Methodism*, 1989, and of several books about John Wesley, including *John Wesley As Seen by Contemporaries and Biographers*, 1984, *Wesley and the People Called Methodists*, 1995, and *The Elusive Mr. Wesley*, 2003. Editor of *Diary of an Oxford Methodist, Benjamin Ingham, 1733–1734*, 1985, *The Poor and the People Called Methodists, 1729–1999*, 2002, and other volumes. Essay: Methodism.

HERMANSEN, MARCIA. Peer reviewer. Professor of theology, Loyola University Chicago, Illinois. Author of *The Conclusive Argument from God*, including a translation from the Arabic of *Hujjat Allah al-Baligha*, by Shah Wali Allah, 1996. Coeditor of *Encyclopedia of Islam and the Muslim World*, 2003. Contributor to books, including *Women and Revolution in Iran*, edited by G. Nashat, 1983, *God Experience or Origin*, 1985, *Muslims of America*, edited by Yvonne Haddad, 1991, *Muslim Communities in America*, edited by Yvonne Haddad, 1994, *New*

Trends and Developments in the World of Islam, edited by Peter Clarke, 1997, and *Teaching Islam*, edited by Brannon Wheeler, 2002. Contributor to numerous journals, including *Studies in Islam*, *Journal of Near Eastern Studies*, *Arabica*, *Islamic Quarterly*, *Studies in Religion*, and *Muslim Education Quarterly*.

HEZEL, FRANCIS. Peer reviewer. Director, Micronesian Seminar, Kolonia, Pohnpei, Federated States of Micronesia. Author of *The First Taint of Civilization: A History of the Caroline and Marshall Islands in Pre-Colonial Days, 1521–1885*, 1983, *From Conquest to Colonization: Spain in the Mariana Islands, 1690 to 1740*, 1989, *The Catholic Church in Micronesia*, 1991, *Strangers in Their Own Land*, 1995, and *The New Shape of Old Island Cultures: A Half Century of Social Change in Micronesia*, 2001.

HILL, JACK A. Contributor. Assistant professor of religion, Texas Christian University, Fort Worth. Author of *I-Sight: The World of Rastafari: An Interpretive Sociological Account of Rastafarian Ethics*, 1995, and *Seeds of Transformation: Discerning the Ethics of a New Generation*, 1998. Author of numerous articles in scholarly journals, including *Annual of the Society of Christian Ethics*, *Journal of Religious Thought*, *Journal of Beliefs and Values*, *Journal for the Study of Religion*, and *Pacific Journal of Theology and Missiology*. Essays: Fiji, Federated States of Micronesia.

HILLERBRAND, HANS. Peer reviewer. Professor of religion and history, Duke University, Durham, North Carolina. Author of numerous books, including *The Reformation: A Narrative History Related by Contemporary Observers and Participants*, 1964, *Christendom Divided: The Protestant Reformation*, 1971, *The World of the Reformation*, 1973, *Anabaptist Bibliography, 1520–1630*, 1991, and *Historical Dictionary of the Reformation and Counter-Reformation*, 1999. Editor of many books, including *Protestant Reformation*, 1968, *Oxford Encyclopedia of the Reformation*, 1996, and *Encyclopedia of Protestantism*, 2003. Contributor to numerous journals.

HJELM, TITUS. Contributor. Researcher, Department of Comparative Religion, University of Helsinki, Finland. Author of Finnish high school philosophy textbooks, as well as various articles on satanism and new religious movements in Finnish and English anthologies. Essay: Finland.

HOFFMAN, VALERIE. Adviser and contributor. Associate professor of religion, University of Illinois, Urbana-Champaign. Author of *Sufism, Mystics, and Saints in Modern Egypt*, 1995. Author of numerous articles in scholarly journals, including *International Journal of Middle East Studies*, *Journal of American Academy of Religion*, *Muslim World*, *Religion*, *Religion and the Arts*, and *Mystics Quarterly*, as well as for *Encyclopedia of Modern Islam*, *The Encyclopedia of the Qur'an*, *Holy People: An Encyclopedia*, *HarperCollins Dictionary of Religion*, and *The Dictionary of Feminist Theologies*. Essay: Oman.

HOLLAND, CLIFTON L. Contributor. Director of PRO-LADES (Latin American Socio-Religious Studies Program), San José, Costa Rica, and editor of *Mesoamerica*, a monthly news journal published by the Institute of Central American Studies (ICAS), San José. Author of *Religious Dimension in Hispanic Los Angeles: A Protestant Case Study*, 1974, as well as numerous published research reports, documents, and magazine articles. Editor of *World Christianity: Central American and the Caribbean*, 1981. Essays: Belize, Costa Rica, Mexico, Paraguay, Portugal, Spain, Suriname.

HOLMBERG, DAVID H. Contributor. Professor of anthropology and Asian studies, as well as chair of the Anthropology Department, Cornell University, Ithaca, New York. Author of *Order in Paradox: Myth, Ritual, and Exchange among Nepal's Tamang*, 1989, as well as articles in numerous journals, including *Journal of Asian Studies*, *Signs*, *American Ethnologist*, *Journal of Ritual Studies*, and *Himalayan Research Bulletin*. Essay: Nepal.

HOLT, JOHN C. Contributor and peer reviewer. William R. Kenan Professor of the Humanities and Religion, as well as chair of the Religion Department, Bowdoin College, Brunswick, Maine. Author of *Discipline: The Canonical Buddhism of the Vinayapitaka*, 1981, *Buddha in the Crown: Avalokitesvara in the Buddhist Traditions of Sri Lanka*, 1991, *The Religious World of Kirti Sri: Buddhism, Art, and Politics in Late Medieval Sri Lanka*, 1996, and *The Buddhist Visnu: Religious Assimilation, Politics, and Culture*, 2004. Essay: Sri Lanka.

HUDEPOHL, KATHRYN A. Contributor. Assistant professor of modern language and intercultural studies, Western Kentucky University, Bowling Green. Essay: Saint Lucia.

HURLEY, SCOTT. Contributor. Visiting assistant professor of religion, Department of Religion and Philosophy, Luther College, Decorah, Iowa. Coauthor of "Some Thoughts on the Theory of Religious Capital in a Global Era: The Tzu Chi Movement and the Praxis of Charity," in *The Annual Bulletin of the Japan Academy for Foreign Trade*, 2003, and "The Lotus of Capital: Tzu Chi Foundation and the Praxis of Charity," in *Kokushikan Journal of Asia*, 21, 2003. Essay: Taiwan.

HUSSAINMIYA, B.A. Contributor. Senior lecturer in history, University of Brunei Darussalam. Author of *Orang Rejimen: The Malays of the Ceylon Rifle Regiment*, 1990, and *Sultan Omar Ali Saifuddin and Britain: The Making of Brunei Darussalam*, 1995. Essay: Brunei.

ISAAK, PAUL JOHN. Contributor. Head, Department of Religion, University of Namibia, Windhoek. Author of *Religion and Society: A Namibian Perspective*, 1997. Editor of *The Evangelical Lutheran Church in the Republic of Namibia in the 21st Century*, 2000. Author of articles in numerous journals, including *Black Theology: An International Journal, African Theological Journal, African Bible Commentary, Journal of Religion and Theology in Namibia, Panorama, Journal of Constructive Theology, Southern Africa,* and *Ecumenical Review.* Essay: Namibia.

ISKENDEROVA, MAYA. Contributor. Doctoral candidate, Institute of History, Azerbaijan Academy of Sciences, Baku. Essay: Azerbaijan.

JACKSON, ROGER. Peer reviewer. Professor of religion and director of Asian studies, Carleton College, Northfield, Minnesota. Author of *Is Enlightenment Possible?*, 1993, and *Tantric Treasures,* 2004. Coauthor of *The Wheel of Time: Kalachakra in Context,* 1985. Coeditor of *Tibetan Literature: Studies in Genre,* 1996, and *Buddhist Theology,* 1999. Author of numerous articles and reviews.

JACOBS, CLAUDE. Contributor. Associate professor of behavioral science, University of Michigan-Dearborn. Coauthor of *The Spiritual Churches of New Orleans: Origins, Beliefs, and Rituals of an African-American Religion,* 1991. Author of articles in numerous journals. Essay: Panama.

JAFFEE, MARTIN. Peer reviewer. Professor, Henry M. Jackson School of International Studies, University of Washington, Seattle. Author of *Mishnah's Theology of Tithing: A Study of Tractate Maaserot,* 1981, *The Talmud of the Land of Israel: A Preliminary Translation and Explanation,* Vol. 7, 1987, *The Talmud of Babylonia: An American Translation,* 1987, *Early Judaism: Religious Worlds of the First Judaic Millennium,* 1997, and *Torah in the Mouth: Writing and Oral Tradition in Palestinian Judaism,* 2001. Coauthor of *Jews, Christians, Muslims: A Comparative Introduction to Monotheistic Religions,* 1998. Coeditor of *Innovation and Religious Traditions: Essays in the Interpretation of Religious Change,* 1992, and *Readings in Judaism, Christianity, and Islam,* 1998. Contributor to numerous books and journals.

JAHANBAKHSH, FOROUGH. Contributor. Assistant professor of religious studies, Queen's University, Kingston, Ontario, Canada. Author of *Islam, Democracy and Religious Modernism in Iran (1953–2000),* 2001. Author of articles in journals, including *Brown Journal of World Affairs, ISIM Newsletter,* and *Historical Reflection.* Essays: Iran, Shiism.

JAKSIC, IVAN. Peer reviewer. Professor of history, University of Notre Dame, Indiana. Author of *Academic Rebels in Chile: The Role of Philosophy in Higher Education and Politics,* 1989, and *Andres Bello: Scholarship and Nation Building in Nineteenth-Century Latin America,* 2001. Editor of *Selected Writings of Andres Bello,*1998, and *The Political Power of the Word: Press and Oratory in Nineteenth-Century Latin America,* 2002. Coeditor of *Filosofia e identidad cultural en America Latina,* 1988, *The Struggle for Democracy in Chile, 1982–1990,* 1991, and *Sarmiento: Author of a Nation,* 1994.

JOCHIM, CHRISTIAN. Contributor. Professor of comparative religious studies, as well as director, Center for Asian Studies, and chair of the Humanities Department, San Jose State University, California. Author of *Chinese Religions: A Cultural Perspective,* 1986. Author of articles in various journals, including *Journal of Chinese Religions, Modern China,* and *Philosophy East and West.* Essay: Confucianism.

JOHNSON, MICHELLE C. Contributor. Assistant professor of anthropology, Bucknell University, Lewisburg, Pennsylvania. Author of chapters in *Female Circumcision in Africa: Culture, Controversy, and Change,* 2000, and *A World of Babies: Imagined Child-Care Guides for Seven Societies,* 2000. Essay: Guinea-Bissau.

JOHNSON, RHONDA. Contributor. Assistant professor and head of access services, Hostos Community College Library, Bronx, New York. Researcher for *Encyclopedia of the United Nations and International Agreements,* by Edmund Jan Osmanczyk, 2003. Essay: Saint Kitts and Nevis.

JONES, STEVEN. Contributor. Associate director, Center on Religion and Democracy, as well as lecturer, Department of Sociology, University of Virginia, Charlottesville. Author of various articles on religion and democracy, including essays on Alexis de Tocqueville, the Nation of Islam, and the intersection of religion and globalization. Essays: Baptist Tradition, Honduras.

KAPLAN, DANA EVAN. Contributor. Visiting research fellow, University of Miami, Coral Gables, Florida. Author of *American Reform Judaism,* 2003, and coauthor of *Platforms and Prayer Books,* 2002. Editor of *Conflicting Visions: Contemporary Debates in American Reform Judaism,* 2001, and *Cambridge Companion to American Judaism,* 2004. Essay: Reform Judaism.

KAUFMAN, PETER IVER. Peer reviewer. Professor of religious studies, University of North Carolina, Chapel Hill. Author of several books, including *Augustinian Piety and Catholic Reform: Augustine, Colet, and Erasmus,* 1982, *The "Polytyque Churche": Religion and Early Tudor Political Culture, 1485–1516,* 1986, and *Prayer, Despair, and Drama: Elizabethan Introspection,* 1996.

KERKHOFS, JAN. Contributor and peer reviewer. Professor emeritus, Kotholieke Universiteit, Leuven, Belgium, and founder, European Values Study. Author of many books in Dutch, as well as *Europe without Priests,* 1995, and *A Horizon of Kindly Light,* 1999, both in English. Essay: Belgium.

KHAN, AISHA. Contributor. Associate professor, Department of Anthropology, New York University, New York. Author of articles and essays, including "Juthaa in Trinidad: Food, Pollution, and Hierarchy in a Caribbean

Diaspora Community," in *American Ethnologist,* 1994, "'Rurality' and 'Racial' Landscapes in Trinidad," in *Knowing Your Place: Rural Identity and Cultural Hierarchy,* edited by Barbara Ching and Gerald Creed, 1997, and "Journey to the Center of the Earth: The Caribbean as Master Symbol," in *Cultural Anthropology,* 2001. Essay: Trinidad and Tobago.

KHAZANOV, ANATOLY M. Contributor. Ernest Gellner Professor of Anthropology, University of Wisconsin, Madison. Author and editor of many books, including *Nomads and the Outside World,* 1984, *Soviet Nationality Policy during Perestroika,* 1991, and *After the USSR: Ethnicity, Nationalism and Politics in the Commonwealth of Independent States,* 1995. Essay: Kazakhstan.

KHODJIBAEV, KARIM. Contributor. Voice of America radio broadcaster. Author of *U.N. Special Report of Tajikistan,* 1994, as well as a series of radio features on American democracy, 1995, and articles in journals, including *Central Asia Monitor.* Essay: Tajikistan.

KIMMERLING, BARUCH. Contributor. George S. Wise Professor of Sociology, Hebrew University of Jerusalem, Israel. Author of numerous books and articles, including *Zionism and Territory,* 1983, *The Interrupted System: Israeli Civilians in War and Routines,* 1985, *The Invention and Decline of Israeliness: State, Society and the Military,* 2001, and *Immigrants, Settlers and Natives: Israel between Multiculturalism and Kulturkampf,* 2003. Coauthor of *The Palestinians: A History,* 2003. Essay: Israel.

KINNARD, JACOB. Contributor and peer reviewer. Assistant professor of religion, College of William and Mary, Williamsburg, Virginia. Author of *Imagining Wisdom: Seeing and Knowing in the Art of Indian Buddhism,* 1999. Coeditor of *Constituting Communities: Theravada Buddhism and the Religious Cultures in South and Southeast Asia,* 2003. Essay: Buddhism.

KIRKLAND, J. RUSSELL. Contributor. Associate professor of religion, University of Georgia, Athens. Author of *Taoism: An Enduring Tradition,* 2004, as well as articles in numerous journals, including *History of Religions* and *Journal of the American Academy of Religion.* Essay: Taoism.

KIVILU, SABAKINU. Contributor. Professor and president, Institut de Recherche et d'Études Historiques du Présent, University of Kinshasa, Democratic Republic of the Congo. Contributor to *Démocratie et paix en République Démocratique du Congo,* 2000, *Élites et démocratie en République Démocratique du Congo,* 2002, *Les consequences de la guerre de la République Démocratique du Congo en Afrique Centrale,* 2003, as well as to journals, including *Journal of African Studies,* 1999, and *Laurent Monnier,* 2000. Essay: Democratic Republic of the Congo.

KNOWLTON, DAVID. Contributor. Associate professor, Behavioral Science Department, Utah Valley State College, Orem, Utah. Essays: Bolivia, Colombia, Ecuador.

KNYSH, ALEXANDER. Peer reviewer. Professor of Islamic studies, as well as chairman, Department of Near Eastern Studies, University of Michigan, Ann Arbor. Author of *Ibn al-'Arabi in the Later Islamic Tradition: The Making of a Polemical Image in Medieval Islam,* 1998, and *Islamic Mysticism: A Short History,* 2000. Author, in Russian, of *Ibn al-'Arabi: The Meccan Revelations: Selected Translations of Ibn al-'Arabi's Early Works and a Chapter from al-Futuhat al-makkiya,* 1995. Contributor to books, including *History of Islamic Philosophy,* edited by S.H. Nasr and O. Leaman, 1996, *Hadhrami Traders, Scholars, and Statesman in the Indian Ocean, 1750s–1960s,* edited by U. Freitag and W. Clarence-Smith, 1997, *Companion to Arabic Literature,* 1998, and *Cambridge History of Arabic Literature: The Literature of al-Andalus,* edited by M.R. Menocal, R. Sheindlin, and M. Sells, 2000. Contributor to numerous journals.

KOLB, ROBERT. Contributor and peer reviewer. Missions Professor of Systematic Theology, Concordia Seminary, Saint Louis, Missouri. Author of *The Christian Faith: A Lutheran Exposition,* 1993, *Speaking the Gospel Today: A Theology for Evangelism,* 1995, *Luther's Heirs Define His Legacy: Studies on Lutheran Confessionalization,* 1996, and *Martin Luther as Prophet, Teacher, Hero: Images of the Reformer, 1520–1620,* 1999. Coeditor of *The Book of Concord: The Confessions of the Evangelical Lutheran Church,* 2000, and other books. Essay: Lutheranism.

KOLLAR, NATHAN R. Contributor. Professor of religious studies, Saint John Fisher College, Rochester, New York; senior lecturer, Department of Education and Human Development, University of Rochester, New York; and chair, Center for Interfaith Studies and Dialogue, Nazareth College, Rochester, New York. Author of *Death and Other Living Things,* 1973, and *Songs of Suffering,* 1982, as well as numerous articles in edited volumes and journals. Editor of *Options in Roman Catholicism: An Introduction,* 1983. Essay: Canada.

KRINDATCH, ALEXEI. Contributor. Research associate, Center for Geopolitical Studies, Institute of Geography, Russian Academy of Sciences, Moscow, and research associate, Institute for the Study of American Religion, University of California, Santa Barbara. Author of *Geography of Religions in Russia,* 1996, as well as articles in numerous journals, including *Osteuropa, Journal for the Scientific Study of Religion,* and *Religion, State, and Society.* Essays: Lithuania, Moldova.

KRÜGGELER, MICHAEL. Contributor. Project manager, Schweizerisches Pastoralsoziologisches Institut (SPI), Saint Gall, Switzerland. Author of *Individualisierung und Freiheit: Eine Praktisch-Theologische Studie zur Religion in der Schweiz,* 1999, and coauthor of *Solidarität und Religion: Was Bewegt Menschen in Solidaritätgruppen?*, 2002. Coeditor of *Religion und Moral: Entkoppelt oder Verknüpft?*, 2001. Essay: Liechtenstein.

KUBURIĆ, ZORICA. Contributor. Professor of the sociology of religion, Faculty of Philosophy, University of Novi Sad, Serbia and Montenegro, and president, Center for Empirical Researches of Religion, Novi Sad. Author of *Religion, Family, and Youth*, 1996, *Faith, Freedom, and Religious Institutions in Yugoslavia*, 2002, *Faith and Freedom: Religious Institutions in Yugoslavia*, 2002, and *Religion and Mental Health*, 2003. Editor of *Religion, Religious Education and Tolerance*, 2002. Essay: Serbia and Montenegro.

KVASNIĆKOVÁ, ADELA. Contributor. Lecturer in sociology, Comenius University, Bratislava, Slovakia. Author of an essay in the edited volume *Slovakia in the 90s*, 2003. Essay: Slovakia.

LAMB, CONNIE. Contributor. Middle East librarian, Brigham Young University, Provo, Utah. Coeditor of *Agricultural and Animal Sciences Journals and Serials: An Analytical Guide*, 1986, and *Jewish American Fiction Writers: An Annotated Bibliography*, 1991. Essay: Jordan.

LANG, KAREN C. Peer reviewer. Associate professor of religious studies, University of Virginia, Charlottesville. Author of *Four Illusions: Candrakirti's Advice to Travelers on the Bodhisattva Path*, 2002. Contributor to *Buddhist-Christian Studies*, 1982, *Feminist Studies in Religion*, 1986, and *Off with Her Head! The Denial of Women's Identity in Myth, Religion, and Culture*, edited by Howard Eilberg-Schwartz and Wendy Doniger, 1995.

LEFFERTS, LEEDOM. Contributor. Professor of anthropology, as well as director of the Asian Studies Department, Drew University, Madison, New Jersey. Cocurator of and coauthor of the catalog for *Textiles and the Tai Experience in Southeast Asia*, an exhibition at the Textile Museum, Washington, D.C., 1992. Author of numerous articles on textiles, social organization, and women's roles in Lao and Thai Theravada Buddhism and on Lao and Thai material culture. Essay: Laos.

LEGRAND, MICHEL. Contributor. Sociologist, SESOPI-Centre Intercommunautaire, Luxembourg. Editor of *Les valeurs au Luxembourg: Portrait d'une société au tournant du 3e millénaire*, 2002. Essay: Luxembourg.

LEHTSAAR, TÕNU. Contributor. Professor of practical theology, as well as vice rector for academic affairs, University of Tartu, Estonia. Author of *Religious Experiencing: A Psychological Study of Religious Experiences in the Lifelong Perspective*, 2000. Essay: Estonia.

LEUSTEAN, LUCIAN N. Contributor. Graduate research student, Interfaculty Institute of Central and Eastern Europe, University of Fribourg, Switzerland. Author of a book chapter, as well as articles in such journals as *Romania, Journal for the Study of Religions and Ideologies,* and *Romanian Military Thinking*. Essay: Romania.

LITTLEWOOD, ROLAND. Peer reviewer. Professor of psychiatry and anthropology, Department of Anthropology, University College, London. Author of *The Butterfly and the Serpent: Essays in Psychiatry, Race and Religion*, 1988, *Pathology and Identity: The Work of Mother Earth in Trinidad*, 1993, *Religion, Agency, Restitution: The Wilde Lectures in Natural Religion*, 1999, and *Pathologies of the West: An Anthropology of Mental Illness in Europe and America*, 2002. Coauthor, with Maurice Lipsedge, of *Aliens and Alienists: Ethnic Minorities and Psychiatry*, 1982, and, with Simon Dein, of *Cultural Psychiatry and Medical Anthropology*, 2000. Coeditor, with Jafar Kareem, of *Intercultural Therapy*, 1999. Contributor to numerous books and journals.

LOBBAN, JR., RICHARD. Contributor. Professor of anthropology and African studies, as well as director of the program in African and Afro-American studies, Rhode Island College, Providence, and vice president of the Rhode Island Black Heritage Society, Providence. Author of *Cape Verde: Crioulo Colony to Independent Nation*, 1995, *Cape Verde Islands*, 2001, and *Historical Dictionary of Ancient and Medieval Nubia*, 2004. Coauthor of *Cape Verdeans in Rhode Island*, 1990, and *Historical Dictionary of the Republic of Cape Verde*, 1995. Essay: Cape Verde.

LOVELL, NADIA. Contributor. Lecturer, University of Linkoping, Sweden. Author of *Locality and Belonging*, 1998, and *Cord of Blood: Possession and the Making of Voodoo*, 2002. Contributor to various journals, including *Ethnos*. Essay: Togo.

MAKRIDES, VASILIOS. Contributor and peer reviewer. Professor and chair of religious studies, Faculty of Philosophy, University of Erfurt, Germany. Author of *Die Religiöse Kritik am Kopernikanischen Weltbild in Griechenland zwischen 1794 und 1821: Aspekte Griechisch-Orthodoxer Apologetik Angesichts Naturwissenschaftlicher Fortschritte*, 1995, as well as numerous other books and articles in German, Greek, English, French, and Italian. Essays: Cyprus, Greece.

MALIK, SAADIA. Contributor. Independent researcher. Author of "Displacement as Discourse" in **Ìrìnkèrindò: A Journal of African Migration*. Essay: Bahrain.

MANN, GURINDER SINGH. Peer reviewer. Professor of Sikh and Punjab studies, University of California, Santa Barbara. Author of *The Goindval Pothis*, 1996, *The Making of Sikh Scripture*,

2001, *Sikhism*, 2004, and all Sikhism-related entries in *Merriam-Webster's Encyclopedia of World Religions*, 1999.

MANSURNOOR, IIK A. Contributor. Associate professor of history, University of Brunei Darussalam. Author of *Islam in an Indonesian World: Ulama of Madura*, 1990, as well as chapters in books and articles in numerous journals, including *Islamic Quarterly*, *Islamic Studies*, *Journal of Al-Islam*, *Oxford Journal of Islamic Studies*, *Prajna Vihara*, and *Islamic Culture*. Essay: Kuwait.

MARINOV, MARIO. Contributor. Assistant professor of sociology, South-West University "Neofit Rilski," Blagoevgrad, Bulgaria, and adjunct assistant professor, Sofia University "Saint Kliment Ohridski," Bulgaria. Author of articles in various publications, including the journal *Sociologicheski Problemi*. Essay: Bulgaria.

MARSTON, JOHN. Contributor. Professor and researcher, Centro de Estudios de Asia y África, El Colegio de México, Mexico City. Author of *Cambodia 1991–94: Hierarchy, Neutrality, and Etiquettes of Discourse*, 1997, as well as articles in numerous edited volumes and such journals as *Estudios de Asia y África*, *Southeast Asian Affairs*, and *Crossroads: An Interdisciplinary Journal of Southeast Asia*. Essay: Cambodia.

M'BAYO, TAMBA. Contributor. Ph.D. candidate, African history, Michigan State University, East Lansing. Author of articles and book reviews for journals, including *H-West-Africa* and *Historian*. Essays: Benin, Côte d'Ivoire.

MCCLYMOND, MICHAEL J. Contributor. Clarence Louis and Helen Irene Steber Professor of Theological Studies, Saint Louis University, Missouri. Author of *Encounters with God: An Approach to the Theology of Jonathan Edwards*, 1998, and *Familiar Stranger: An Introduction to Jesus of Nazareth*, 2004. Editor of *Embodying the Spirit: New Perspectives on North American Revivalism*, 2004. Coeditor of *The Rivers of Paradise: Moses, Buddha, Confucius, Jesus, and Muhammed as Religious Founders*, 2001, and *Dimensions of North American Revivalism*, 2002. Essay: Christianity.

MCKIM, DONALD K. Contributor. Academic and reference editor, Westminster John Knox Press, Louisville, Kentucky. Author of numerous books, including *What Christians Believe about the Bible*, 1985, *Ramism in William Perkins' Theology*, 1987, *Theological Turning Points*, 1988, *The Bible in Theology and Preaching*, 1994, *Westminster Dictionary of Theological Terms*, 1996, *Introducing the Reformed Faith*, 2001, *Presbyterian Beliefs: A Brief Introduction*, 2003, and *Presbyterian Questions, Presbyterian Answers: Exploring Christian Faith*, 2003. Editor of numerous books, including *The Authoritative Word: Essays on the Nature of Scripture*, 1983, *Readings in Calvin's Theology*, 1984, *How Karl Barth Changed My Mind*, 1986, *God Never Forgets: Faith, Hope, and Alzheimer's Disease*, 1997, *Historical Handbook of Major Biblical Interpreters*, 1998, and

The Cambridge Companion to Martin Luther, 2003. Essays: Protestantism, Reformed Christianity.

MEADOW, MARY JO. Contributor. Professor emeritus, Minnesota State University, Mankato, and founder, Resources for Ecumenical Spirituality, Forest Lake, Minnesota. Author of *Other People*, 1984, *Gentling the Heart: Buddhist Loving-Kindness Practice for Christians*, 1994, and *Through a Glass Darkly: A Spiritual Psychology of Faith*, 1996. Coauthor of *Psychology of Religion: Religion in Individual Lives*, 1984, and *Purifying the Heart: Buddhist Insight Meditation for Christians*, 1994. Coeditor of *A Time to Weep, a Time to Sing: Faith Journeys of Women Scholars of Religion*, 1985. Essay: Theravada Buddhism.

MENDES-FLOHR, PAUL. Contributor. Professor of modern Jewish thought, Divinity School, University of Chicago, Illinois, and director, Franz Rosenzweig Research Center in German-Jewish Literature and Cultural History, Hebrew University of Jerusalem, Israel. Essay: Judaism.

MICALLEF, ROBERTA. Contributor. Assistant professor of language and literature, University of Utah, Salt Lake City. Coauthor of *Islam in Turkic Central Asia*, 1997, as well as articles in numerous edited volumes and journals. Essay: Uzbekistan.

MIŠOVIC, JÁN. Contributor. Researcher, Institute of Sociology of the Academy of Science of the Czech Republic, Prague. Author of articles in various edited volumes in Czech and English, including *New Religious Phenomena in Central and Eastern Europe*, 1997, and *Church-State Relations in Central and Eastern Europe*, 1999. Essay: Czech Republic.

MOFFIC, EVAN. Contributor. Rabbinic student, Jewish Institute of Religion, Hebrew Union College, Cincinnati, Ohio. Author of articles in *CCAR Journal*. Essay: Reform Judaism.

MOLNAR, ANDREA. Contributor. Associate professor of anthropology, Northern Illinois University, DeKalb. Author of *Grandchildren of the Ga'e Ancestors: Social Organization and Cosmology among the Hoga Sara of Flores*, 2000, as well as essays in various edited volumes and articles in journals, including *Anthropos* and *Antropologi Indonesia*. Essay: East Timor.

MOLNÁR, ATTILA KAROLY. Contributor. Assistant professor, Eötvös University and Pázmány Péter Catholic University, Budapest, Hungary. Author of the monographs *The "Protestant Ethic" in Hungary*, 1994, *Notes from the Chaotic Prison*, 1999, and *Edmund Burke*, 2000. Essay: Hungary.

MOSAAD, MOHAMED. Contributor. Anthropologist and director, Religion and Society Studies Center, Cairo, Egypt. Author of a biography of the Prophet Muhammad, 2000, and of *Islam and Postmodernity: The New Islamic Discourse in Egypt*, 2004. Author of articles in various publications, including the newspaper *Al Qahira* and the magazine *Ar-Risala* magazine. Essays: Algeria, Iraq.

MULLIN, ROBERT BRUCE. Peer reviewer. Subdean of academic affairs and the Society for the Promotion of Religion and Learning, professor of history and world mission, and professor of modern Anglican studies, General Theological Seminary of the Episcopal Church, New York, New York. Author of *Episcopal Vision/American Reality: High Church Theology and Social Thought in Evangelical America*, 1986, *Miracles and the Modern Religious Imagination*, 1996, and *The Puritan as Yankee: A Life of Horace Bushnell*, 2002. Coauthor of *The Scientific Theist: A Life of Francis Ellingwood Abbot*, 1987, and coeditor of *Reimagining Denominationalism: Interpretive Essays*, 1994.

MUZOREWA, GWINYAI H. Contributor. Professor and chair, Religion Department, Lincoln University, Pennsylvania. Author of *The Origin and Development of African Theology*, 1987, *An African Theology of Mission*, 1990, and *Mwari: The Great Being God: God Is God*, 2001. Essay: Zimbabwe.

NADEAU, KATHLEEN M. Contributor. Assistant professor of anthropology, California State University, San Bernardino. Author of articles in various journals, including *Philippine Quarterly of Culture and Society, East Asian Pastoral Review*, and *Journal for the Scientific Study of Religion*. Essay: Philippines.

NARAYANAN, VASUDHA. Adviser and contributor. Professor of religion, University of Florida, Gainesville, and former president, American Academy of Religion. Author of *The Way and the Goal: Expressions of Devotion in the Early Srivaisnava Tradition*, 1987, and *The Vernacular Veda: Revelation, Recitation, and Ritual*, 1994. Coauthor of *The Tamil Veda: Pillan's Interpretation of the Tiruvaymoli*, 1989. Coeditor of *Monastic Life in the Christian and Hindu Traditions: A Comparative Study*, 1990. Author of articles in various journals, including *Journal of the American Academy of Religion, Journal of Vaishnava Studies*, and *Daedalus: Journal of the American Academy of Arts and Sciences*. Essays: Hinduism, Vaishnavism.

NDLOVU, HEBRON. Contributor. Senior lecturer in theology and religious studies, as well as dean of the Faculty of Humanities, University of Swaziland, Kwaluseni. Author of *Phenomenology in Religion*, 1997, as well as articles in edited volumes and various journals, including *UNISWA Research Journal, Theologia Viatorum, ATISCA Bulletin*, and *Journal of Black Theology in South Africa*. Essay: Swaziland.

NELSON, JOHN K. Peer reviewer. Associate professor of theology and religious studies, University of San Francisco, California. Author of *A Year in the Life of a Shinto Shrine*, 1996,

and *Enduring Identities: The Guise of Shinto in Contemporary Japan*, 2000.

NEUMAIER, EVA. Contributor. Professor emeritus, University of Alberta, Edmonton, Canada. Author of several volumes, some under the name Eva Dargyay, including *The Rise of Esoteric Buddhism in Tibet*, 1979, *Tibetan Village Communities: Structure and Change*, 1982, and *The Sovereign All-Creating Mind—the Motherly Buddha: A Translation of the Kun-byed rgyal po'i mdo*, 1992. Coauthor of *Ladakh: Innenansicht eines Landes*, 1980, and coeditor of *Gender, Genre, and Religion: Feminist Reflections*, 1995. Essay: Mahayana Buddhism.

NEUSNER, JACOB. Peer reviewer. Research professor of theology and senior fellow, Institute of Advanced Theology, Bard College, Annandale-on-Hudson, New York. Author of more than 900 books and articles. Editor of the *Encyclopedia of Judaism*, 1999, editorial board chairman of *Review of Rabbinic Judaism*, and editor in chief of the Brill Reference Library of Judaism.

NKOMAZANA, FIDELIS. Contributor. Senior lecturer and head, Department of Theology and Religious Studies, University of Botswana, Gaborone. Author of *A New Approach to Religious Education in Botswana*, 1999, as well as articles in various edited volumes and journals, including *PULA: Botswana Journal of African Studies, Scriptura, Journal of Religion and Theology in Namibia*, and *Religion and Theology*. Essay: Botswana.

NORDBECK, ELIZABETH C. Contributor. Moses Brown Professor of Ecclesiastical History, Andover Newton Theological School, Wolfeboro, New Hampshire. Author of *Thunder on the Right: Understanding Conservative Christianity*, 1990, and coeditor of *Living Theological Heritage of the United Church of Christ*, 1999. Essay: United Church of Christ.

NUMBERS, RONALD. Peer reviewer. Hilldale and William Coleman Professor of the History of Science and Medicine, University of Wisconsin, Madison. Author of numerous books, including *The Creationists*, 1992, and *Darwinism Comes to America*, 1998. Coeditor of *God and Nature: Historical Essays on the Encounter between Christianity and Science*, 1986, *Caring and Curing: Health and Medicine in the Western Religious Traditions*, 1986, *Disseminating Darwinism: The Role of Place, Race, Religion, and Gender*, 1999, and *When Science and Christianity Meet*, 2003. Contributor to numerous books and journals.

OLADIPO, CALEB. Contributor and peer reviewer. Assistant professor, Baylor University, Waco, Texas, and director of the Baylor in West Africa Program. Author of *Development of the Doctrine of the Holy Spirit in the Yoruba (African) Indigenous Christian Movement*, 1996, as well as articles in numerous edited volumes and journals, including *International Christian Digest*,

Chicago Studies, Interpretation: A Journal of Bible and Theology, and *Journal of Church-State Studies.* Essays: Somalia, South Africa.

OLDSTONE-MOORE, JENNIFER. Peer reviewer. Associate professor, Department of Religion, Wittenberg University, Springfield, Ohio. Author of *Confucianism: Origins, Beliefs, Practices, Holy Texts, Sacred Places,* 2002, and *Taoism: Origins, Beliefs, Practices, Holy Texts, Sacred Places,* 2003. Contributor to *World Religions: The Illustrated Guide,* edited by Michael Coogan, 1998, *China: Empire and Civilization,* edited by Edward Shaughnessy, 2000, and to journals and encyclopedias.

OLSON, ERNEST. Contributor. Associate professor of anthropology and religion, as well as chair of the sociology/anthropology major, Wells College, Aurora, New York. Author of articles in various journals, including *Journal of Ritual Studies.* Essay: Tonga.

OLUPONA, JACOB K. Contributor. Director, African and African-American Studies, University of California, Davis. Author of *Religion, Kingship and Rituals in a Nigerian Community,* 1991, editor of *African Traditional Religions in Contemporary Society,* 1991, and coeditor of *Religious Pluralism in Africa: Essays in Honor of John Mbiti,* 1993. Essay: African Traditional Religions.

OTTENHEIMER, MARTIN. Peer reviewer. Professor of anthropology, Kansas State University, Manhattan. Author of *Marriage in Domoni: Husbands and Wives in an Indian Ocean Community,* 1985, and *Forbidden Relatives,* 1996. Coauthor of *Historical Dictionary of the Comoro Islands,* 1994. Contributor to books, including *The Encyclopedia of Vernacular Architecture of the World,* 1997, and *The Encyclopedia of Sub-Saharan Africa,* 1997. Contributor to numerous journals, including *Journal of Cognition and Culture, Choice, Czech Sociological Review,* and *American Anthropologist.*

PAPONNET-CANTAT, CHRISTIANE. Contributor. Professor and chair, Department of Anthropology, University of New Brunswick, Fredericton, Canada. Author of articles in various French-, Spanish-, and English-language journals, including *Agalter, Anthropologica, Canadian Review of Sociology and Anthropology, Ciencias Agrarias, Culture, Egalité, Extension Rural,* and *Journal of Clinical Engineering.* Essay: France.

PATTERSON, MARY. Contributor. Senior lecturer in anthropology, University of Melbourne, Australia. Author of book chapters on the arts, sorcery, and witchcraft in Oceania, as well as articles in various scholarly journals, including *Anthropological Forum, Oceania,* and *Australian Journal of Anthropology.* Essay: Vanuatu.

PENTON, M. JAMES. Contributor. Professor emeritus, University of Lethbridge, Alberta, Canada. Author of

Jehovah's Witnesses in Canada: Champions of Freedom of Speech and Worship, 1976, and *Apocalypse Delayed: The Story of Jehovah's Witnesses,* 1997, as well as articles in various edited volumes and journals, including *Journal of Church and State.* Essay: Jehovah's Witnesses.

PETERSON, WILLIAM. Contributor. Associate professor, California State University, San Bernardino. Author of *Theatre and the Politics of Culture in Contemporary Singapore,* 2001. Author of numerous articles on theater and politics in Singapore, Maori theater, Australian theater, Indonesian dance, and American performance art for journals, including *Contemporary Dramatists, Theatre Research International, Asian Theatre Journal, Australasian Drama Studies, Theatre Journal, Journal of Dramatic Theory and Criticism, High Performance,* and *Theatre Insight.* Essay: Singapore.

PÉTURSSON, PÉTUR. Contributor. Professor of theology, University of Iceland, Reykjavík. Author of numerous books and articles on modern Icelandic church history, new religious movements, and Christian themes in film, art, and literature. Essay: Iceland.

PHUNTSHO, KARMA. Contributor. Scholar of Buddhism and Bhutan studies, as well as a trained Tibetan Buddhist. Author of various articles on Buddhism, Bhutan, and Tibetan studies and of a book on Buddhist epistemology. Essay: Bhutan.

POLLAK-ELTZ, ANGELINA. Contributor. Professor, Universdad Católica A. Bello, Caracas, Venezuela. Author of numerous books, including *Umbanda en Venezuela,* 1989, *Los santos populares en Venezuela,* 1989, *La religiosidad popular en Venezuela,* 1993, *Religiones Afroamericanos,* 1994, *Trommel und Trance: Afroamerikanische Religionen,* 1995, *El pentecostalismo en Venezuela,* 2000, and *La medicina tradicional en Venezuela,* 2001. Essay: Venezuela.

POLLOCK, NANCY J. Contributor. Acting director of development studies, Victoria University, Wellington, New Zealand. Author of *These Roots Remain: Food Habits in Islands of the Central and Eastern Pacific since Western Contact,* 1992. Coeditor of *Social Aspects of Obesity,* 1995. Essays: Fiji, Marshall Islands, and Nauru.

POTOCNIK, VINKO. Contributor. Associate professor, Faculty of Theology, University of Ljubljana, Slovenia. Contributor to *Mate-Toth,* 2001, as well as to numerous journals. Essay: Slovenia.

PRANDI, CARLO. Contributor and peer reviewer. Professor of the sociology of religion, University of Parma, Italy. Author of *I dinamismi del sacro fra storia e sociologia,* 1990, *La*

tradizione religiosa, 2000, and *La religione populare fra tradizione e modernita*, 2002. Essay: Italy.

RAUSCH, MARGARET JEAN. Contributor and peer reviewer. Assistant professor of religious studies, University of Kansas, Lawrence. Author of various scholarly articles on the social and spiritual role of women in Morocco. Coauthor of *Modern Literary Arabic*, 1981. Essay: Morocco.

REINSCHMIDT, MICHAEL C. Contributor. Lecturer, Department of Anthropology, California State University, Chico, and research associate, UCLA Fowler Museum of Cultural History, Los Angeles, California. Author of articles in various edited volumes and for conferences. Coeditor of *Strengthened Abilities: Assessing the Vision of Tosan Ahn Chang-Ho*, 1998. Essay: South Korea.

ROBBINS, JOEL. Peer reviewer. Associate professor, Department of Anthropology, University of California, San Diego. Coeditor of *Money and Modernity: State and Local Currencies in Contemporary Melanesia*, 1999. Coeditor of a special issue of the journal *Anthropology and Humanism*, 1997. Author of articles in journals, including *Ethnology*, *Social Analysis*, *Anthropological Quarterly*, and *Anthropology and Humanism*.

ROBERTS, ALLEN F. Peer reviewer. Director, James S. Coleman Center for African Studies, University of California, Los Angeles. Curator and contributor to exhibition catalogs, including *The Rising of a New Moon*, 1985, *Animals in African Art*, 1995, and, with Mary Nooter Roberts, *Memory: Luba Art and the Making of History*, 1996, and *A Sense of Wonder*, 1997.

ROEBER, A. GREGG. Contributor. Professor of early modern history and religious studies and head of the History Department, Penn State University, University Park, Pennsylvania, and member of the Orthodox Theological Society of America. Author of *Faithful Magistrates and Republican Lawyers: Creators of Virginia Legal Culture, 1680–1810*, 1981, and *Palatines, Liberty, and Property: German Lutherans and Colonial British North America*, 1993, as well as articles in edited volumes and in such journals as *Lutheran Forum* and *William and Mary Quarterly*. Essay: Eastern Orthodoxy.

SALAMONE, FRANK A. Contributor. Professor of sociology and anthropology, Iona College, New Rochelle, New York. Author of *Gods and Goods in Africa: Persistence and Change in Ethnic and Religious Identity in Yauri Emirate, North-Western State, Nigeria*, 1974, *The Hausa People, a Bibliography*, 1983, *Who Speaks for Yanomami?*, 1996, *The Yanomami and Their Interpreters: Fierce People or Fierce Interpreters?*, 1997, *Italians in Rochester, New York, 1900–1940*, 2000, and *Popular Culture in the Fifties*, 2001, as well as numerous articles for journals, including *American*

Anthropologist, *African Studies Review*, *Popular Culture*, and *Eastern Anthropologist*. Essays: Liberia, Niger, Vatican City.

SAMSON, C. MATHEWS. Contributor. Visiting lecturer, Department of Anthropology, University of Oklahoma, Norman. Author of articles in various journals, including "Texts and Context: Social Context and the Content of Liturgical Texts in Nicaragua and El Salvador," in *Human Mosaic*, 1991, and "The Martyrdom of Manuel Saquic: Constructing Maya Protestantism in the Face of War in Contemporary Guatemala," in *La Fait Missionaire*, 2003. Essay: Guatemala.

SANDS, CANON KIRKLEY C. Contributor. Lecturer, School of Social Sciences, College of The Bahamas, Nassau, and associate priest, Holy Trinity Church, Nassau. Author of *The Christian Church and the Penal Code: A Christian Response to Crime in The Bahamas*, 1983, and contributor to *Bahamas: Independence and Beyond*, 2003, *Cultural Perspectives*, 2003, and *Junkanoo and Religion: Christianity and Cultural Identity in The Bahamas*, 2003. Essay: The Bahamas.

SARNA, JONATHAN. Peer reviewer. Joseph H. and Belle R. Braun Professor of American Jewish History, Department of Near Eastern and Judaic Studies, Brandeis University, Waltham, Massachusetts. Author of *Jacksonian Jew: The Two Worlds of Mordecai Noah*, 1981, *JPS: The Americanization of Jewish Culture*, 1989, and *American Judaism: A History*, 2004. Coauthor of *American Synagogue History: A Bibliography and State-of-the-Field Survey*, 1988, *The Jews of Cincinnati*, 1989, *Yahadut Amerika: American Jewry: An Annotated Bibliography of Publications in Hebrew*, 1991, *The Jews of Boston*, 1995, and *Religion and State in the American Jewish Experience*, 1997. Editor of *Jews in New Haven*, 1978, *People Walk on Their Heads: Moses Weinberger's Jews and Judaism in New York*, 1982, *Observing America's Jews*, by Marshall Sklare, 1993, *The American Jewish Experience: A Reader*, 2nd edition, 1997, and *Minority Faiths and the American Protestant Mainstream*, 1997. Coeditor of *Jews and the Founding of the Republic*, 1985, *Yehude Artsot Ha-Berit*, 1992, *Ethnic Diversity and Civic Identity: Patterns of Conflict and Cohesion in Cincinnati since 1820*, 1992, *A Double Bond: The Constitutional Documents of American Jewry*, 1992, *Abba Hillel Silver and American Zionism*, 1997, and *Woman and American Judaism: Historical Perspectives*, 2001. Contributor to numerous journals.

SAUL, MAHIR. Contributor. Associate professor of anthropology, University of Illinois, Urbana. Coauthor of *West African Challenge to Empire: Culture and History in the Volta-Bani Anticolonial War*, 2001. Author of articles in numerous journals, including *American Anthropologist*, *American Ethnologist*, *Journal of the Royal Anthropological Institute*, *Africa*, and *International Journal of African Historical Studies*. Essay: Burkina Faso.

SCHOEPFLIN, RENNIE. Peer reviewer. Professor of history, La Sierra University, Riverside, California. Author of *Christian Science on Trial: Religious Healing in America,* 2003.

SHANKLAND, DAVID. Contributor. Senior lecturer in social anthropology, University of Bristol, England. Author of *Islam and Society in Turkey,* 1999, and *The Alevis in Turkey: The Emergence of a Secular Islamic Tradition,* 2003. Editor of *The Turkish Republic at Seventy-Five Years: Progress, Development, Change,* 1999. Essay: Turkey.

SHIPPS, JAN. Peer reviewer. Professor emeritus of religious studies and history, Indiana University–Purdue University, Indianapolis. Author of *Mormonism: The Story of a New Religious Tradition,* 1985, and *Sojourner in the Promised Land: Forty Years among the Mormons,* 2000. Editor of *Religion and Public Life in the Mountain West: Sacred Landscapes in Tension,* 2004. Coeditor of *The Journals of William E. McLellin, 1831–1836,* 1994.

SIDKY, HOMAYUN. Contributor. Associate professor of anthropology, Miami University, Oxford, Ohio. Author of *Irrigation and State Formation in Hunza: The Anthropology of a Hydraulic Kingdom,* 1997, *Witchcraft, Lycanthropy, Drugs, and Disease: An Anthropological Study of the European Witch-Hunts,* 1997, *Bitan: Oracles and Healers in the Karakorams,* 2000, *The Greek Kingdom of Cactria: From Alexander to Eurcratides the Great,* 2000, *Halfway to the Mountain: The Jirels of Eastern Nepal,* 2000, *A Critique of Postmodern Anthropology—In Defense of Disciplinary Origins and Traditions,* 2003, and *Perspectives on Culture: A Critical Introduction to Theory in Cultural Anthropology, 2003.* Essays: Afghanistan, Pakistan, Turkmenistan.

SIMONTON, MICHAEL J. Contributor. Lecturer in anthropology, Northern Kentucky University, Highland Heights, and adjunct professor, Wilmington College of Ohio. Essays: Antigua and Barbuda, Ireland.

SINGH, PASHAURA. Contributor. Assistant professor of Sikh studies, University of Michigan, Ann Arbor. Author of *The Guru Granth Sahib: Canon, Meaning and Authority,* 2000, and *The Bhagats of the Guru Granth Sahib: Sikh Self-Definition and the Bhagat Bani,* 2003. Coeditor of *The Transmission of Sikh Heritage in the Diaspora,* 1996, and *Sikh Identity: Continuity and Change,* 1999. Author of articles in numerous journals, including *Journal of American Academy of Religion, Journal of American Oriental Society, Religious Studies Review,* and *Studies in Religion/Sciences Religieuses.* Essay: Sikhism.

SOTIRIU, ELENI. Contributor. Instructor in sociology and social anthropology, University of Erfurt, Germany. Author of various articles in Greek and English on women's issues and Orthodox Christianity. Essays: Cyprus, Greece.

SPINDLER, MARC. Contributor and peer reviewer. Professor emeritus of missiology and ecumenics, University of Leiden and University of Utrecht, The Netherlands, and research associate, Centre d'Étude d'Afrique Noire, Institut d'Études Politiques de Bordeaux, France. Author of *La mission, combat pour le salut du monde,* 1967, and *Pour une théologie de l'espace,* 1968. Coeditor of *Missiology: An Ecumenical Introduction: Texts and Contexts of Global Christianity,* 1995, *Cultures of Madagascar: Ebb and Flow of Influences,* 1995, *Chrétiens d'outre-mer en Europe: Un autre visage de l'immigration,* 2000, *Dictionnaire oecuménique de missiologie,* 2001, and *Les relations églises-états; en situation post-coloniale,* 2003. Essay: Madagascar.

STENHOUSE, JOHN. Contributor. Lecturer in history, University of Otago, Dunedin, New Zealand. Coeditor of *Science and Theology: Questions at the Interface,* 1994, *God and Government: The New Zealand Experience,* 1999, and *Disseminating Darwinism: The Role of Place, Race, Religion, and Gender,* 1999. Contributor to journals, including *Journal of the History of Biology, Journal of Religious History, Journal of Law and Religion, New Zealand Journal of History,* and *British Journal for the History of Science.* Essay: New Zealand.

ST JOHN, RONALD BRUCE. Contributor and peer reviewer. Author and independent scholar. Author of numerous books, including *Qaddafi's World Design: Libyan Foreign Policy, 1969–1987,* 1987, *Boundaries, Trade, and Seaports: Power Politics in the Atacama Desert,* 1992, *The Foreign Policy of Peru,* 1992, *Historical Dictionary of Libya,* 1998, *The Land Boundaries of Indochina: Cambodia, Laos, and Vietnam,* 1998, and *Libya and the United States: Two Centuries of Strife,* 2002. Author of articles in numerous journals, including *Asian Affairs: An American Review, Asian Survey, Contemporary Southeast Asia,* and *Asian Affairs: Journal of the Royal Society for Asian Affairs.* Essays: Libya, Vietnam.

STILLMAN, NORMAN. Peer reviewer. Professor and Schusterman/Josey Chair in Judaic History, Department of History, University of Oklahoma, Norman. Author of *The Jews of Arab Lands,* 1979, *The Language and Culture of the Jews of Sefrou,* 1988, *The Jews of Arab Lands in Modern Times,* 1991, and *Sephardi Religious Responses to Modernity,* 1995. Coauthor, with Yedida K. Stillman, of *Samuel Romanell's Travail in an Arab Land,* 1989, and, with Yedida K. Stillman, of *From Iberia to Diaspora: Studies in Sephardic History and Culture,* 1998. Editor of *Arab Dress: A Short History,* by Yedida K. Stillman, 2000.

STOCKMAN, ROBERT. Contributor. Director, Institute for Bahá'í Studies, Wilmette, Illinois. Author of *The Bahá'í Faith in America,* Vol. 1, *Origins, 1892–1900,* 1985, *The Bahá'í Faith in America,* Vol. 2, *Early Expansion, 1900–1912,* 1995, and *Thornton Chase: First American Bahá'í,* 2002, as well as articles in various edited volumes and journals, including *World Order, Religion, The Bahá'í Studies Review, Iranian Studies, Bahá'í News,* and *Theosophical History.* Essay: Bahá'í Faith.

STOFFELS, HIJME C. Contributor. Professor of the sociology of religion, Faculty of Theology, Vrije Universiteit, Amsterdam, The Netherlands; member of the steering committee of the International Society for the Study of Reformed Communities and of the steering committee of the Hollenweger Center for the Study of Pentecostal and Charismatic Movements, Amsterdam. Author of *Walking in the Light: Values, Beliefs, and Social Positions of Dutch Evangelicals*, 1990. Coeditor of *Reformed Vitality: Continuity and Change in the Face of Modernity*, 1998, and *Reformed Encounters with Modernity: Perspectives from Three Continents*, 2001. Essay: The Netherlands.

STOLZ, JÖRG. Contributor and peer reviewer. Professor of the sociology of religion, University of Lausanne, Switzerland, and director of the Observatoire des Religions en Suisse (ORS). Author of *Soziologie der Fremdenfeindlichkeit: Theoretische und Empirische Analysen*, 2000, and of numerous articles on the sociology of religion and on migration. Essay: Switzerland.

STRAUGHN-WILLIAMS, MARITZA. Contributor. Assistant professor of anthropology and African-American studies, Colby College, Waterville, Maine. Essays: Barbados, Dominica.

SUÁREZ, MARGARITA. Contributor. Assistant professor, Department of Religion and Philosophy, Meredith College, Raleigh, North Carolina. Author of "Across the Kitchen Table: Cuban Women Pastors and Theology," in *Gender, Ethnicity and Religion: Views from the Other Side*, edited by Rosemary Radford Ruether, 2002, and "Cubana/os," in *Handbook on Latino/a Theologies*, edited by Edwin David Aponte and Miguel A. de la Torre, 2005. Essay: Cuba.

SUSANTO, BUDI. Contributor. Director, Realino Study Institute, Sanata Dharma University, Yogyakarta, Indonesia. Author of *People (Trick) Theater: Politics of the Past in Present Day Java*, 2000. Contributor to *Indonesian Heritage*, Vol. 9, *Religion and Ritual*, 1998. Essay: Indonesia.

SYNAN, VINSON. Peer reviewer. Professor and dean, Regent University Divinity School, Virginia Beach, Virginia. Author of *The Twentieth-Century Pentecostal Explosion: The Exciting Growth of Pentecostal Churches and Charismatic Renewal Movements*, 1987, *The Spirit Said "Grow,"* 1992, *The Holiness-Pentecostal Tradition: Charismatic Movements in the Twentieth Century*, 1997, *Oldtime Power: A Centennial History of the International Pentecostal Holiness Church*, 1998, *In the Latter Days: The Outpouring of the Holy Spirit in the Twentieth Century*, 2001, *Century of the Holy Spirit: 100 Years of Pentecostal and Charismatic Renewal*, 2001, and *Voices of Pentecost: Testimonies of Lives Touched by the Holy Spirit*, 2003.

TABYSHALIEVA, ANARA. Contributor. Chair, Institute for Regional Studies, Bethesda, Maryland. Author of articles on Kyrgyzstan and Central Asia in various edited volumes and journals, including *Anthropology and Archaeology of Eurasia*, *Nordic Newsletter of Asian Studies*, and *OSCE Yearbook*. Essay: Kyrgyzstan.

TAIVANS, LEONS. Contributor. Professor of religion, University of Latvia, Riga. Author, in Russian, of *Po Latgalyi*, 1988, and *Vostochnaya misteriya: Politiya v relifioznom soznanii indoneziycev*, 2001. Author, in Latvian, of *Teologijas vesture I. Primkristigo laikmets, AD 1–313*, 1995, as well as numerous articles in edited volumes and journals, including *Religion in Eastern Europe*. Essay: Latvia.

TAYLOR, CHRIS. Peer reviewer. Associate professor of anthropology, University of Alabama, Birmingham. Author of *Milk, Honey, and Money: Changing Concepts in Rwandan Healing*, 1992, and *Sacrifice as Terror: The Rwandan Genocide of 1994*, 1999. Contributor to *Culture and AIDS: The Human Factor*, edited by D. Feldman, 1990, *Anthropological Approaches to the Study of Ethnomedicine*, edited by M. Nichter, 1992, *Encyclopedia of Cultures and Daily Life*, 1997, *Annihilating Difference: The Anthropology of Genocide*, edited by Alex Hinton and Nancy Scheper-Hughes, 2002, and *Anthropology and Chaos Theory*, edited by Mark Mosko and Fred H. Damon, 2004. Contributor to numerous journals, including *Social Science and Medicine*, *Medical Anthropology*, *Political and Legal Anthropology Review*, and *Anthropos*.

TEAIWA, KATERINA. Contributor. Assistant professor, Center for Pacific Islands Studies, School of Hawaiian, Asian and Pacific Studies, University of Hawaii at Manoa, Honolulu. Member of the editorial board of *Contemporary Pacific: A Journal of Island Affairs*. Essay: Kiribati.

TITUS, NOEL. Contributor. Principal and professor of church history, Codrington College, St. John, Barbados. Author of *The Church and Slavery in the English-Speaking Caribbean*, 1983, *The Development of Methodism in Barbados, 1823–1883*, 1994, and *Conflicts and Contradictions*, 1998, as well as articles in various journals, including *Howard Journal of Religion*, *Journal of Negro History*, *Anglican and Episcopal History*, and *Mission Studies*. Essays: Grenada, Saint Vincent and the Grenadines.

TRANQUILLE, DANIELLE. Contributor. Lecturer, University of Mauritius, Reduit. Coauthor of *Anthologie de la littérature Mauricienne d'expression française*, 2000. Coeditor of *Rencontres: Translation Studies*, 2000. Essay: Mauritius.

TROMPF, GARRY W. Contributor. Professor of the history of ideas, University of Sydney, Australia. Author or coauthor of numerous books, including *Melanesian Religion*, 1991, *Payback: The Logic of Retribution in Melanesian Religions*, 1994, and *The Religions of Oceania*, 1995. Editor of various books, including *Cargo Cults and Millenarian Movements: Transoceanic*

Comparisons of New Religious Movements, 1990. Essay: Solomon Islands.

TUITE, KEVIN. Contributor. Professor of anthropology, Université de Montréal, Québec, Canada. Author of *Kartvelian Morphosyntax: Number Agreement and Morphosyntactic Orientation in the South Caucasian Languages,* 1988, as well as articles in various journals, including *Anthropos, Historiographia Linguistica, Lingua, Anthropological Linguistics, Journal of Indo-European Studies,* and *Cosmos.* Editor of *Anthology of Georgian Folk Poetry,* 1994. Essay: Georgia.

UDDIN, SUFIA MENDEZ. Contributor. Assistant professor of religion, University of Vermont, Burlington. Author of articles in various edited volumes and journals, including *Journal for Islamic Studies.* Essay: Bangladesh.

UHL, FLORIAN. Contributor. Professor of philosophy and head of the Philosophy Department, Private Catholic University of Linz, Austria, and president, Austrian Society for the Philosophy of Religion (ÖGRph), Linz. Editor of *Roger Bacon in der Diskussion,* 2001, and *Roger Bacon in der Diskussion II,* 2002. Coeditor of *Rituale: Zugänge zu einem Phänomen,* 1999, *Zwischen Verzückung und Verzweiflung: Dimenensionen religiöser Erfahrung,* 2001, and *Die Sprachen der Religion,* 2003. Author of articles in various edited volumes and journals. Essay: Austria.

UNDERBERG, NATALIE M. Contributor. Visiting assistant professor of folklore, University of Central Florida, Orlando. Author of articles in edited volumes and journals, including *Folklore Forum,* 1997. Essay: Peru.

URBAN, HUGH B. Contributor and peer reviewer. Associate professor, Department of Comparative Studies, Ohio State University, Columbus. Author of *The Economics of Ecstasy: Tantra, Secrecy and Power in Colonial Bengal,* 2001, and *Tantra: Sex, Secrecy, Politics and Power in the Study of Religion,* 2003. Essay: Saivism.

VA'A, UNASA L.F. Contributor. Senior lecturer in Samoan language and culture and anthropology, National University of Samoa, Apia. Author of *Saili Matagi: Samoan Migrants in Australia,* 2001, as well as articles in various edited volumes and journals. Essay: Samoa.

VALK, PILLE. Contributor. Docent of religious education, Faculty of Theology, Tartu University, Estonia. Author of *Uhest heledast laigust Eesti kooli ajaloos 1918.1940,* 1997, and *Eesti kooli religiooniõpetuse kontseptsioon,* 2002. Author of articles in various journals, including *Panorama* and *International Journal of Practical Theology.* Essay: Estonia.

VAN BEMMELEN, PETER M. Contributor. Professor of theology, Andrews University, Berrien Springs, Michigan. Author of articles in various edited volumes, including *Adventist Missions Facing the 21st Century: A Reader,* 1990, *Women in Ministry: Biblical and Historical Perspectives,* 1998, and *Handbook of Seventh-day Adventist Theology,* 2000. Essay: Seventh-day Adventist Church.

VAN DOORN-HARDER, NELLY. Contributor and peer reviewer. Associate professor of world religions, Valparaiso University, Indiana. Author of *Contemporary Coptic Nuns,* 1995, and *Between Desert and City: The Coptic Orthodox Church Today,* 1997, as well as numerous articles about the Copts and Islam. Essay: Coptic Christianity.

VAN ROMPAY, LUCAS. Peer reviewer. Professor of Eastern Christianity, as well as director of the Center for Late Ancient Studies, Duke University, Durham, North Carolina. Coeditor of *After Chalcedon: Studies in Theology and Church History Offered to Professor Albert Van Roey for His Seventieth Birthday,* 1985, *Studies in Hebrew and Aramaic Syntax: Presented to Professor J. Hoftijzer on the Occasion of His Sixty-Fifth Birthday,* 1991, and *The Book of Genesis in Jewish and Oriental Christian Interpretation: A Collection of Essays,* 1997. Editor and translator of *Fragments syriaques du commentaire des psaumes,* by Théodore de Mopsueste, 1982, and *Le commentaire sur Genèse-Exode 9,32 du manuscrit (olim) Diaybakir 22,* 1986.

VICTOR, ISAAC HENRY. Contributor. Research fellow, Milan V. Dimic Institute for Comparative Literary and Cultural Studies, as well as visiting professor, University of Alberta, Edmonton, Canada. Author of articles in numerous journals, including *Sri Lanka Journal for South Asian Studies, Indian Church History Review,* and *Vidyajyoti.* Essay: Maldives.

VOAS, DAVID. Contributor. Simon Research Fellow, Centre for Census and Survey Research, University of Manchester, England, and lecturer in sociology, University of Sheffield, England. Author of *The Alternative Bible,* 1993, and *The Bad News Bible,* 1994, as well as articles in various journals, including *Transactions of the Institute of British Geographers, American Sociological Review,* and *British Journal of Sociology.* Essay: United Kingdom.

VOM BRUCK, GABRIELE. Contributor. Lecturer in the anthropology of the Middle East, University of Edinburgh, Scotland. Author of articles in various journals, including *Journal of Material Culture, Die Welt der Islams, History and Anthropology,* and *Annales, Histoire, Sciences Sociales.* Essay: Yemen.

WACKER, GRANT. Adviser. Professor of church history, The Divinity School, Duke University, Durham, North Carolina. Author of *Augustus H. Strong and the Dilemma of Historical Consciousness,* 1985, *Religion in Nineteenth Century America,* 2000 (expanded in *Religion in American life: A Short History*, 2003), and *Heaven Below: Early Pentecostals and American Culture*, 2001. Coeditor of *Pentecostal Currents in American Protestantism*, 1999, *Portraits of a Generation: Early Pentecostal Leaders*, 2002, and *The Foreign Missionary Enterprise at Home: Explorations in North American Cultural History*, 2003.

WALKER, RANDI. Peer reviewer. Associate professor of church history, Pacific School of Religion, Berkeley, California. Author of *Protestantism in the Sangre de Cristos 1850–1920*, 1991, and *Emma Newman: A Frontier Woman Minister*, 2000. Contributor to *Religion and Modern New Mexico*, edited by Ferenc M. Szasz and Richard W. Etulain, 1997, *Religion and American Culture*, 1998, and *The Evolution of a UCC Style: Essays on the History and Ecclesiology of the United Church of Christ*, 2004. Contributor to journals, including *Prism*.

WASSERSTEIN, BERNARD. Adviser. Harriet and Ulrich E. Meyer Professor of Modern European Jewish History, University of Chicago, Illinois. Author of *The British in Palestine: The Mandatory Government and the Arab-Jewish Conflict*, 1978, *Britain and the Jews of Europe, 1939-1945*, 1979, *The Secret Lives of Trebitsch Lincoln*, 1988, *Herbert Samuel: A Political Life*, 1992, *Vanishing Diaspora: The Jews in Europe since 1945*, 1996, *Secret War in Shanghai*, 1999, *Divided Jerusalem: The Struggle for the Holy City*, 2001, and *Israelis and Palestinians: Why Do They Fight? Can They Stop?*, 2003. Editor of two volumes of the letters of the Zionist leader Chaim Weizmann, as well as coeditor of *The Jews in Modern France*, 1985.

WAUGH, EARLE H. Chair of advisory board, contributor, and peer reviewer. Professor of religious studies, University of Alberta, Edmonton, Canada. Author of *Peace As Seen in the Qur'an*, 1986, and *The Munshidin of Egypt: Their World and Their Song*, 1989. Coeditor of *The Muslim Community in North America*, 1983, *Muslim Families in North America*, 1991, and *The Shaping of an American Islamic Discourse: A Memorial to Fazlur Rahman*, 1999. Essay: Sunnism.

WELLMAN, JAMES K., JR. Contributor. Assistant professor of Western Christianity and comparative religion, University of Washington, Seattle. Author of *The Gold Coast Church and the Ghetto: Christ and Culture in Mainline Protestantism*, 1999. Coeditor of *The Power of Religious Publics: Staking Claims in American Society*, 1999. Author of articles in various journals, including *Review of Religious Research* and *Journal of Presbyterian History*. Essay: World Evangelicalism.

WHITE, DAVID. Peer reviewer. Professor, Department of Religious Studies, University of California, Santa Barbara. Author of *Myths of the Dog-Man*, 1991, *The Alchemical Body: Siddha Traditions in Medieval India*, 1996, and *Kiss of the Yogini: "Tantric Sex" in Its South Asian Contexts*, 2003. Editor and

author of the introductory essay, *Tantra in Practice*, 2000. Translator of *The Making of Terrorism*, by Michel Wieviorka, 1993, and cotranslator of *Ashes of Immortality: Widow-Burning in India*, by Catherine Weinberger-Thomas, 1999. Contributor to journals, including *Numen* and *History of Religions*.

WILLEMSEN, HEINZ. Contributor. Ph.D. candidate, Ruhr Universität, Bochum, Germany. Author of articles in various edited volumes and journals, including *Osteuropa*, *Südosteuropa*, and *Jahrbücher für Geschichte und Kultur Südosteruopas*. Essay: Macedonia.

WILLIAMS, PETER. Contributor and peer reviewer. Distinguished professor of comparative religion and American studies, Miami University, Oxford, Ohio. Author of *Houses of God: Region, Religion, and Architecture in the United States*, 1997, *America's Religions: Traditions and Cultures*, 1998, and *Popular Religion in America: Symbolic Change and the Modernization Process in Historical Perspective*, 2002. Essay: United States.

WOLDEMIKAEL, TEKLE. Contributor. Associate professor and chair, Department of Sociology and Anthropology, University of Redlands, California. Author of *Becoming Black American: Haitians and American Institutions in Evanston, Illinois*, 1989, as well as articles in various journals, including *African Studies Review*. Essay: Eritrea.

WU, SILAS. Contributor. Professor emeritus of Chinese and Japanese history, Boston College, Massachusetts, and associate, Fairbank Center for East Asian Research, Harvard University, Cambridge, Massachusetts. Author of *Communication and Imperial Control in China: Evolution of the Palace Memorial System, 1693–1735*, 1970, *Passage to Power: K'ang-hsi and His Heir Apparent, 1661–1722*, 1979, and *Dora Yu and Christian Revival in 20th Century China*, 2002, as well as articles in numerous journals, including *Harvard Journal of Asiatic Studies*, *American Historical Review*, *Tong Pao*, and *Academia Sinica*. Essay: China.

YOUSIF, AHMAD. Contributor. Associate professor, Institute of Islamic Studies, University of Brunei Darussalam. Author of *Muslims in Canada: A Question of Identity*, 1993, and *Religious Freedom, Minorities and Islam: An Inquiry into the Malaysian Experience*, 1998, as well as articles in various edited volumes and journals, including *Journal of Religious Studies and Theology*, *ISIM Newsletter*, and *Studies in Contemporary Islam*. Essay: Malaysia.

YURASH, ANDRIJ. Contributor. Assistant professor, Ivan Franko L'viv National University, Ukraine. Author, in Russian, of *Religious Organizations of Contemporary Ukraine*, 1997, as well as articles in various edited volumes and journals in

Ukraine, Poland, Russia, Germany, The Netherlands, England, and the United States. Essays: Eastern Catholic Churches, Ukraine.

ZALECKI, PAWEL. Contributor. Assistant professor of sociology, Nicolaus Copernicus University, Toruń, Poland. Author, in Polish, of *Religious Community as a Primary Group*, 1997, and *Between Triumphs and the Feeling of Danger: The Roman Catholic Church in Contemporary Poland in the Eyes of Its Representatives*, 2001. Coeditor, in Polish, of *Cultural Tools of Rule*, 2002. Essay: Poland.

ZOHAR, ZION. Contributor. Associate director, Institute for Judaic and Near Eastern Studies, Florida International University, Miami. Author of *Song of My People: A High Holy Day Machzor*, 1995, as well as articles in various edited volumes and journals, including *Jewish Studies.* Essay: Orthodox Judaism.

ZRINŠČAK, SINIŠA. Contributor. Associate professor of comparative social policy, Department of Social Work, Faculty of Law, University of Zagreb, Croatia, and vice president, International Study of Religion in Central and Eastern Europe Association (ISORECEA). Author, in Croatian, of *Sociology of Religion: The Croatian Experience*, 1999, as well as numerous articles in edited volumes and journals. Essay: Croatia.

Chronology

c. 1800 B.C.E.   Zarathustra, founder of Zoroastrianism, is born in Persia (modern-day Iran).

c. 1500 B.C.E.   Vishnu, the supreme deity of Vaishnava Hinduism, appears in the Vedas, the earliest sacred compositions in India.

c. 587 B.C.E.   Babylonian armies destroy the Temple in Jerusalem. The occupation of Palestine initiates the Jewish Diaspora.

c. 565 B.C.E.   Siddhartha Gautama, founder of Buddhism, is born in a small village on the border of modern-day Nepal and India.

c. 551 B.C.E.   Master Kong, or Confucius, is born in China.

c. 550 B.C.E.   Lord Mahavira, an ascetic living in Bihar, India, first sets forth the doctrines and practices of Jainism.

c. 550 B.C.E.   Rudra-Shiva is described as the lord and creator of the universe in the Upanishads, the final portion of the Hindu Vedas, laying the foundation of Shaivism.

c. 550 B.C.E.   The Achaemenian dynasty, the first empire to adopt Zoroastrianism as a state religion, originates in Persia.

c. 525 B.C.E.   In Varanasi, India, the Buddha introduces the Four Noble Truths to the public. These fundamental beliefs soon came to form the core of Theravada Buddhist teachings.

500 B.C.E.   Vishnu is featured in two popular Indian epics, the *Mahabharata* and the *Ramayana.* By portraying Vishnu as the supreme being who alone can grant salvation, the epics help establish Vaishnavism as a distinct system of faith and practices within Hinduism.

c. 285 B.C.E.   Scholars in China complete the *Tao-te Ching,* or *Lao-tzu,* a written record of the oral tradition of the southern land of Ch'u and the earliest foundation of Taoism.

c. 250 B.C.E.   The emperor Ashoka, of the Mauryan dynasty, converts to Buddhism and soon begins propagating Buddhist precepts throughout India.

c. 247 B.C.E.   Venerable Mahinda, son of the Indian emperor Ashoka, carries Theravada Buddhism to Sri Lanka.

c. 30 C.E.   Roman authorities in Palestine execute Jesus of Nazareth.

c. 48 C.E.   The evangelist Saint Mark introduces Christianity to Egypt, laying the foundation of the Coptic Orthodox Church.

95 C.E.   A letter of Clement asserts the authority of the Christian church in Rome over the church in Corinth, laying the foundation of the Roman Catholic papacy.

c. 135 C.E.   Simeon Bar Kokhba, the leader of a Jewish revolt against occupying Roman forces, is killed in battle. Jews are subsequently banished from Jerusalem, while the Land of Israel becomes a non-Jewish state.

175 C.E.   The emperor Han Xiaoling orders that stelae inscribed with sacred texts of Confucianism be erected at the Chinese national university.

c. 200 C.E.   The Indian monk Nagarjuna sets forth the fundamental precepts of Mahayana Buddhism.

c. 200 c.e. The Pashupata tradition, the earliest known Shaivite branch of Hinduism, originates in India.

c. 313 c.e. Emperor Constantine revokes the ban on Christianity in the Roman Empire.

325 c.e. Constantine calls the first ecumenical council of Christian bishops at Nicaea, leading to the formation of the Eastern Orthodox Church.

c. 400 c.e. The Shvetambara branch of Jainism establishes its principal doctrines at the Council of Valabhi, creating a permanent rift with the Digambara branch.

406 c.e. Lu Hsiu-ching, a scholar and sage who collected diverse Chinese scriptures and religious teachings to create a coherent Taoist tradition, is born.

431 c.e. The Council of Chalcedon accepts Pope Leo I's solution to the question of Jesus' divinity and humanity, solidifying the authority of the papacy over Christian churches.

c. 525 c.e. Bodhidharma, a disciple of Mahayana Buddhism, founds Ch'an, or Zen, Buddhism in China.

c. 610 c.e. On what is known in Muslim tradition as the Night of Power, Muhammad ibn Abdullah, a Meccan businessman and the founder of Islam, receives his first revelation from Allah.

617 c.e. King Songtsen Gampo, responsible for laying the foundation of Buddhism in Tibet, is born.

c. 622 c.e. Muhammad forms the first Muslim community in the northern Arabian city of Yathrib, later renamed Medinat al-Nabi (modern-day Medina), or "City of the Prophet."

632 c.e. Sunni Islam originates following the death of the Prophet Muhammad.

c. 650 c.e. Followers of Zoroastrianism flee Persia in the wake of the Muslim invasion, resettling in the Gujarat region of India.

c. 656 c.e. Ali, son-in-law of the Prophet Muhammad, becomes the fourth caliph of Islam. He is recognized as the first imam of Shiism.

680 c.e. Hussein, son of Ali and the third imam of Shiism, is martyred at the hands of the Umayyads in the Battle of Karbala.

c. 712 c.e. The *Kojiki* ("Record of Ancient Matters"), a narrative that contains the earliest known written record of Shinto mythology, practices, and beliefs, appears in Japan.

859 c.e. The Yoshida Shrine, one of the oldest and most revered holy structures in the Shinto tradition, is established in Kyoto, Japan.

1054 c.e. Cardinal Humbert of Rome excommunicates the patriarch of Constantinople, precipitating what is known as the Great Schism between Roman Catholicism and Eastern Orthodoxy.

1182 c.e. The Maronite Church declares unity with the Roman Catholic Church, establishing the Uniate, or Eastern Catholic, tradition.

c. 1200 c.e. Jagachandrasuri founds Tapa Gaccha (austere practices) branch of Jainism.

c. 1209 c.e. Saint Francis of Assisi forms the order of Franciscan friars, founded on principles of "holy poverty."

1435 c.e. Yoshida Kanetomo, a Japanese scholar and the founder of Yoshida Shinto, is born. His vigorous defense of purist principles helped define Shinto culture in Japan for centuries.

1463 c.e. Guru Nanak, the founder of Sikhism, is born to an upper-caste Hindu family in the village of Talwandi, India (modern-day Nankana Sahib, Pakistan).

1517 c.e. Martin Luther nails his "Ninety-five Theses," an attack on Roman Catholic practices, to a church door, thus planting the seeds of the Protestant Reformation.

1523 c.e. After public debate the canton of Zurich, Switzerland, moves to adopt the theological doctrines of Ulrich Zwingli, one of the founders of the Reformed movement in Christianity.

c. 1530 c.e. King Henry VIII of England severs ties with the Roman Catholic Church, laying the foundation for the creation of the national Church of England, or Anglican Church.

1536 C.E. John Calvin publishes *Institutes of the Christian Religion*, outlining the theology that would prove pivotal to the development of Reformed Christianity.

1565 C.E. The Minor Reformed Church, the first organized body founded on Unitarian theology, is established in Poland.

c. 1580 C.E. The Congregationalist Church, one of four groups making up the modern-day United Church of Christ, is formed in England in reaction to the liberal doctrines of the Anglican Church.

1596 C.E. The Brest Union Council leads to the formation of national Uniate churches in Ukraine and Belarus.

1606 C.E. Guru Arjan becomes the first Sikh martyr after his execution by the Mughal emperor Jahangir.

1609 C.E. John Smyth, a dissenting pastor and the founder of the Baptist tradition, rebaptizes himself in an act of protest against the Church of England.

1652 C.E. George Fox, an English preacher, founds the Religious Society of Friends (Quakers).

1656 C.E. "Dragon Gate" Taoism, widely regarded as the foundation of modern-day "Northern Taoism," is established at the White Cloud Abbey in Beijing by disciples of the Taoist sage Wu Shou-yang.

1666 C.E. Philipp Jakob Spener becomes the pastor of the Lutheran Church in Frankfurt. The founder of the movement known as Pietism, Spener preached a Christian faith based on the individual's personal devotion to Jesus Christ, a belief that lies at the core of modern-day evangelicalism.

1699 C.E. Guru Gobind Singh creates the Khalsa Panth, or "pure path," based on strict Sikh principles.

1729 C.E. John Wesley forms a religious society with fellow students in Lincoln College, Oxford, thus laying the foundation of the Methodist Church.

1741 C.E. George de Benneville, the founder of Universalism in England, emigrates to the United States, where he soon begins preaching Universalist theology.

1746 C.E. The American pastor Jonathan Edwards writes *A Treatise concerning Religious Affections*, which describes the principal characteristics of the evangelical experience.

1775 C.E. Anglicans in the United States break from the Church of England to form the Protestant Episcopal Church.

1776 C.E. At the Philadelphia Yearly Meeting members of the Religious Society of Friends move to prohibit American Quakers from owning slaves.

1795 C.E. The term "orthodox" is first used by Jewish reformers to disparage those who refuse to adapt their faith to modern society. Almost immediately the term comes to represent Jewish groups who adhere to traditional beliefs and practices.

1801 C.E. Israel Jacobson, a seminal figure in Reform Judaism, forms the first Reform prayer chapel in Westphalia, Germany.

1824 C.E. American Reform Judaism originates in Charleston, South Carolina.

1830 C.E. Joseph Smith founds the Church of Jesus Christ of Latter-day Saints, or Mormon Church.

1831 C.E. William Miller, a farmer in upstate New York, publishes the pamphlet *Evidences from Scripture and History of the Second Coming of Christ about the Year 1843, And of His Personal Reign of One Thousand Years.* Some of Miller's disciples would later found the Seventh-day Adventist movement.

1836 C.E. The rabbi Samson Raphael Hirsch publishes *Nineteen Letters,* in which he elucidates the central tenets of modern Orthodox, or Neo-Orthodox, Judaism.

1844 C.E. 'Alí-Muhammad of Shiraz, an Iranian merchant and the founder of the Bábíacute; movement, declares himself to be the "hidden Imam" of the Shiites, laying the foundation for the Bahá'í faith.

1845 C.E.   American Baptists split into Northern and Southern conventions, with the Southern Baptist Convention eventually becoming the largest Protestant group in North America.

1850 C.E.   Brigham Young becomes the governor of the Utah Territory, and the headquarters of the Church of Jesus Christ of Latter-day Saints is relocated in Salt Lake City.

1863 C.E.   The Bábí leader Mírzá Husayn-'Alí of Núr, or Bahá'u'lláh, launches his public ministry, declaring himself the divine messenger of the Bahá'í faith.

1870 C.E.   The doctrine of papal infallibility is established at the First Vatican Council.

1879 C.E.   Charles Taze Russell, founder of the Bible Students (renamed Jehovah's Witnesses in 1931), establishes the journal *Zion's Watch Tower and Herald of Christ's Presence* in order to propagate his beliefs.

1881 C.E.   The World Methodist Council is formed.

1886 C.E.   With the establishment of the Jewish Theological Seminary in New York City, Conservative Judaism is founded in the United States.

1901 C.E.   Charles Fox Parham, an evangelist living in eastern Kansas, preaches that speaking in tongues is evidence of baptism with the Holy Spirit, launching the Pentecostal revival in Christianity.

1913 C.E.   Solomon Schechter founds the United Synagogue of America, a confederation of Conservative congregations in the United States and Canada.

1917 C.E.   The Bolsheviks come to power in Russia, establishing a Communist government and pursuing a policy of forced atheism.

1918 C.E.   The Sunday School Movement helps launch a major revival of Coptic Christianity in Egypt.

1921 C.E.   The Chinese scholar Liang Shuming publishes *Eastern and Western Cultures and Their Philosophies,* a modern defense of traditional Confucian principles.

1928 C.E.   Hasan al-Banna, an Egyptian schoolteacher, founds the Ikhwan al-Muslimin, or Muslim Brotherhood, in reaction to European colonial domination in the Middle East.

1947 C.E.   British territory in the Indian subcontinent is partitioned along religious lines into two independent nations—India, with a majority of Hindus, and Pakistan, becoming the first modern state founded on Sunni Muslim principles.

1947 C.E.   Shoghi Effendi authorizes representation of the Bahá'í faith, under the name Bahá'í International Community, at the United Nations.

1948 C.E.   The modern Jewish state of Israel is founded.

1957 C.E.   Four American groups—the Congregational Church, Christian Churches, German Reformed Church, and German Evangelical Church—join to form the United Church of Christ.

1959 C.E.   In the wake of China's occupation of Tibet, the 14th Dalai Lama, Tibet's head of state and the spiritual leader of Tibetan Buddhism, is forced into exile.

1962 C.E.   Pope John XXIII convenes the Second Vatican Council to reform and modernize the Roman Catholic Church.

1966 C.E.   The Chinese Communist Party under Chairman Mao begins the Cultural Revolution, suppressing all religious activity in the world's most populous country and lasting until 1976.

1977 C.E.   The Universal Church of the Kingdom of God is founded in Brazil, reflecting the growth of evangelical churches in Latin America.

1979 C.E.   The Islamic Revolution, lead by Ayatollah Ruhollah Khomeini, overthrows the Shah of Iran and establishes an Islamic republic.

1991 C.E.   The Union of Soviet Socialist Republics, composed of Russia and other Eastern European and Asian countries, dissolves, resulting in greater religious freedom in the area.

1994 C.E.   In Memphis, Tennessee, white and black Pentecostal churches of the United States, long divided along racial lines, formally unify to create the Pentecostal/Charismatic Churches of North America.

2003 C.E.   The Right Reverend V. Gene Robinson is consecrated in the United States as bishop of the Episcopal Diocese of New Hampshire, becoming the first openly gay, noncelibate bishop in the Anglican Communion.

List of Holy Days

2005

DECEMBER 2005

1 THURSDAY

New Moon

4 SUNDAY

Advent begins (Christian)

15 THURSDAY

Full Moon

21 WEDNESDAY

Winter Solstice

25 SUNDAY

Christmas (Christian)

26 MONDAY

Chanukah begins (Jewish)

31 SATURDAY

New Moon

Oharae, or Great
Purification (Shinto)

Begin Maidhyaiya, mid-
year/winter feast
(Zoroastrian)

2006

JANUARY 2006

1 SUNDAY

Oshogatsu, or New Year
(Shinto)

2 MONDAY

Chanukah ends (Jewish)

4 WEDNESDAY

End Maidhyaiya, mid-
year/winter feast
(Zoroastrian)

5 THURSDAY

Parkash (Birthday) Guru
Gobind Singh (Sikh)

6 FRIDAY

Epiphany (Christian)

10 TUESDAY

Id-al-Adha begins
(Muslim)

12 THURSDAY

Id-al-Adha ends (Muslim)

14 SATURDAY

Full Moon

New Year (Mahayanan)

15 SUNDAY

Seijin no hi, or *Coming of Age
Day* (Shinto)

20 FRIDAY

Id al-Ghadir (Shi'a)

27 FRIDAY

Tse Gutor (Tibetan
Buddhist)

29 SUNDAY

New Moon

New Year (Tibetan
Buddhist, Confucian)

31 TUESDAY

Muharram, New Year
(Muslim)

FEBRUARY 2006

1 WEDNESDAY

Begin Mönlam Chenmo,
the great prayer ceremo-
ny (Tibetan Buddhist)

2 THURSDAY

Setsubun no hi, Change
of Seasons, (Shinto)

9 THURSDAY

Ashura (Shi'a Muslim)

13 MONDAY

Full Moon

Tu Bi-Shevat (Jewish)

20 MONDAY

End Mönlam Chenmo,
the great prayer ceremo-
ny (Tibetan Buddhist)

26 SUNDAY

Maha Shivaratri (Saivism)

28 TUESDAY

New Moon

MARCH 2006

1 WEDNESDAY

Ash Wednesday, begin-
ning of Lent (Christian)

2 THURSDAY

Annual Fast begins
(Bahá'í)

3 FRIDAY

Hina matsuri Doll
Festival, or Girls' Day
(Shinto)

14 TUESDAY

Full Moon

Holi (Hindu, Vaishnava)

15 WEDNESDAY

Holi (Hindu, Vaishnava)

16 THURSDAY

Begin
Hamaspathmaêdaya,
feast of All Souls
(Zoroastrian)

20 MONDAY

Annual Fast ends (Bahá'í)

End Hamaspathmaêdaya,
feast of All Souls
(Zoroastrian)

21 TUESDAY

Spring Equinox

Naw-Rúz, or New Year
(Bahá'í, Zoroastrian)

29 WEDNESDAY

New Moon

APRIL 2006

5 WEDNESDAY

Qing Ming festival
(Confucian)

6 THURSDAY

Ram Navami (Hindu,
Vaishnava)

9 SUNDAY

Palm Sunday
(Christianity)

11 TUESDAY

Mawlid-al-Nabi
(Muslim)

13 THURSDAY

Full Moon

New Year (Theravadan)

Passover begins (Jewish)

14 FRIDAY

Good Friday (Christian)

Vaisakhi, Birth
Anniversary of Khalsa,
(Sikh)

16 SUNDAY

Easter (Christianity)

20 THURSDAY

Passover ends (Jewish)

21 FRIDAY

Ridván festival holy day
(Bahá'í)

25 TUESDAY

Yom Hashoah, or
Holocaust Memorial
Day (Jewish)

27 THURSDAY

New Moon

29 SATURDAY

Ridván festival holy day (Bahá'í)

30 SUNDAY

Begin Maidhyõizarêmaya, mid-spring feast (Zoroastrian)

MAY 2006

2 TUESDAY

Ridván festival holy day (Bahá'í)

3 WEDNESDAY

Yom Ha'atzmaut, or Israel Independence Day: (Jewish)

4 THURSDAY

End Maidhyõizarêmaya, mid-spring feast (Zoroastrian)

5 FRIDAY

Tango no sekku, Boys' Day (Shinto)

13 SATURDAY

Full Moon

Vesak, Buddha's Birthday (Buddhist)

23 TUESDAY

Declaration of the Báb (Bahá'í)

27 SATURDAY

New Moon

29 MONDAY

Ascension of Bahá'u'lláh (Bahá'í)

JUNE 2006

2 FRIDAY

Shavuot (Jewish)

3 SATURDAY

Shavuot (Jewish)

4 SUNDAY

Pentecost, or Whitsunday (Christian)

11 SUNDAY

Full Moon

16 FRIDAY

Guru Arjan, martyrdom day (Sikh)

25 SUNDAY

New Moon

29 THURSDAY

Begin Maidhyõishêma, mid-summer feast (Zoroastrian)

30 FRIDAY

Oharae, or Great Purification (Shinto)

JULY 2006

3 MONDAY

End Maidhyõishêma, mid-summer feast (Zoroastrian)

9 SUNDAY

Martyrdom of the Báb (Bahá'í)

11 TUESDAY

Full Moon

Asalha Puja (Buddhist)

21 FRIDAY

Summer Solstice

25 TUESDAY

New Moon

AUGUST 2006

3 THURSDAY

Tishah be-Av (Jewish)

9 WEDNESDAY

Full Moon

13 SUNDAY

Obon, Festival of the Dead begins (Shinto)

16 WEDNESDAY

Obon, Festival of the Dead ends (Shinto)

Krishna Janmashthami (Hindu, Vaishnava)

23 WEDNESDAY

New Moon

27 SUNDAY

Ganesh Chaturthi (Hindu)

SEPTEMBER 2006

7 THURSDAY

Full Moon

12 TUESDAY

Begin Paitishaya, feast of bringing in the harvest (Zoroastrian)

16 SATURDAY

End Paitishaya, feast of bringing in the harvest (Zoroastrian)

21 THURSDAY

Autumn Equinox

22 FRIDAY

New Moon

Begin Ulambana, or Ancestor Day, (Mahayana)

23 SATURDAY

Rosh Hashana, New Year (Jewish)

Begin Navaratri (Hindu, Vaishnava)

24 SUNDAY

Rosh Hashana, New Year (Jewish)

Begin Ramadan (Muslim)

28 THURSDAY

Master Kong Birthday (Confucian)

OCTOBER 2006

1 SUNDAY

End Navaratri (Hindu, Vaishnava)

2 MONDAY

Yom Kippur (Jewish)

6 FRIDAY

End Ulambana, or Ancestor Day, (Mahayana)

7 SATURDAY

Full Moon

Begin Sukkot (Jewish)

12 THURSDAY

Begin Ayathrima, bringing home the herds (Zoroastrian)

13 FRIDAY

End Sukkot (Jewish)

14 SATURDAY

Shemini Atzeret (Jewish)

15 SUNDAY

Simchat Torah (Jewish)

16 MONDAY

End Ayathrima, bringing home the herds (Zoroastrian)

20 FRIDAY

Birth of the Báb (Bahá'í)

21 SATURDAY

Dipavali, Festival of Lights (Hindu, Vaishnava, Jain, Sikh)

22 SUNDAY

New Moon

24 TUESDAY

End Ramadan Id al-Fitr (Muslim)

NOVEMBER 2006

5 SUNDAY

Full Moon

Parkash (Birthday) of Guru Nanak (Sikh)

12 SUNDAY

Birth of Bahá'u'lláh (Bahá'í)

15 WEDNESDAY

Shichi-go-san, children's rite of passage, (Shinto)

20 MONDAY

New Moon

23 THURSDAY

Niiname-sai, harvest festival (Shinto)

24 FRIDAY

Niiname-sai, harvest festival (Shinto)

Guru Tegh Bahadur, martyrdom day (Sikh)

26 SUNDAY

'Abdu'l-Bahá, Day of the Covenant (Bahá'í)

28 TUESDAY

Ascension of 'Abdu'l-Bahá (Bahá'í)

DECEMBER 2006

3 SUNDAY

Advent begins (Christian)

5 TUESDAY

Full Moon

16 SATURDAY

Chanukah begins (Jewish)

20 WEDNESDAY

New Moon

21 THURSDAY

Winter Solstice

23 SATURDAY

Chanukah ends (Jewish)

25 MONDAY

Christmas (Christian)

31 SUNDAY

Id-al-Adha begins (Muslim)

Oharae, or Great Purification (Shinto)

Begin Maidhyaiya, mid-year/winter feast (Zoroastrian)

2007

JANUARY 2007

1 MONDAY

Oshogatsu, or New Year (Shinto)

2 TUESDAY

Id-al-Adha ends (Muslim)

3 WEDNESDAY

Full Moon

New Year (Mahayanan)

4 THURSDAY

End Maidhyaiya, mid-year/winter feast (Zoroastrian)

5 FRIDAY

Parkash (Birthday) Guru Gobind Singh (Sikh)

6 SATURDAY

Epiphany (Christian)

10 WEDNESDAY

Id al-Ghadir (Shi'a)

15 MONDAY

Seijin no hi, or Coming of Age Day (Shinto)

19 FRIDAY

New Moon

20 SATURDAY

Muharram, New Year (Muslim)

29 MONDAY

Ashura (Shi'a Muslim)

FEBRUARY 2007

2 FRIDAY

Full Moon

Setsubun no hi, Change of Seasons, (Shinto)

3 SATURDAY

Tu Bi-Shevat (Jewish)

16 FRIDAY

Maha Shivaratri (Saivism)

Tse Gutor (Tibetan Buddhist)

17 SATURDAY

New Moon

18 SUNDAY

New Year (Tibetan Buddhist, Confucian)

21 WEDNESDAY

Ash Wednesday, beginning of Lent (Christian)

Begin Mönlam Chenmo, the great prayer ceremony (Tibetan Buddhist)

MARCH 2007

2 FRIDAY

Annual Fast begins (Bahá'í)

3 SATURDAY

Full Moon

Hina matsuri, Doll Festival, or Girls' Day (Shinto)

Holi (Hindu, Vaishnava)

4 SUNDAY

Holi (Hindu, Vaishnava)

12 MONDAY

End Mönlam Chenmo, the great prayer ceremony (Tibetan Buddhist)

16 FRIDAY

Begin Hamaspathmaêdaya, feast of All Souls (Zoroastrian)

19 MONDAY

New Moon

20 TUESDAY

Annual Fast ends (Bahá'í)

End Hamaspathmaêdaya, feast of All Souls (Zoroastrian)

21 WEDNESDAY

Spring Equinox

Naw-Rúz, or New Year (Bahá'í, Zoroastrian)

27 TUESDAY

Ram Navami (Hindu, Vaishnava)

31 SATURDAY

Mawlid-al-Nabi (Muslim)

APRIL 2007

1 SUNDAY

Palm Sunday (Christian)

2 MONDAY

Full Moon

3 TUESDAY

New Year (Theravadan)

Passover begins (Jewish)

5 THURSDAY

Qing Ming festival (Confucian)

6 FRIDAY

Good Friday (Christian)

8 SUNDAY

Easter (Christian)

10 TUESDAY

Passover ends (Jewish)

14 SATURDAY

Vaisakhi, Birth Anniversary of Khalsa, (Sikh)

15 SUNDAY

Yom Hashoah, or Holocaust Memorial Day (Jewish)

17 TUESDAY

New Moon

21 SATURDAY

Ridván festival holy day (Bahá'í)

23 MONDAY

Yom Ha'atzmaut, or Israel Independence Day: (Jewish)

29 SUNDAY

Ridván festival holy day (Bahá'í)

30 MONDAY

Begin Maidhyõizarêmaya, mid-spring feast (Zoroastrian)

MAY 2007

2 WEDNESDAY

Full Moon

Vesak, Buddha's Birthday (Buddhist)

Ridván festival holy day (Bahá'í)

4 FRIDAY

End Maidhyõizarêmaya, mid-spring feast (Zoroastrian)

5 SATURDAY

Tango no sekku, Boys' Day (Shinto)

16 WEDNESDAY

New Moon

23 WEDNESDAY

Declaration of the Báb (Bahá'í)

Shavuot (Jewish)

24 THURSDAY

Shavuot (Jewish)

27 SUNDAY

Pentecost, or Whitsunday (Christian)

29 TUESDAY

Ascension of Bahá'u'lláh (Bahá'í)

JUNE 2007

1 FRIDAY

Full Moon

15 FRIDAY

New Moon

16 SATURDAY

Guru Arjan, martyrdom day (Sikh)

29 FRIDAY

Begin Maidhyõishêma, mid-summer feast (Zoroastrian)

30 SATURDAY

Full Moon

Oharae, or Great Purification (Shinto)

JULY 2007

3 TUESDAY

End Maidhyõishêma, mid-summer feast (Zoroastrian)

9 MONDAY

Martyrdom of the Báb (Bahá'í)

14 SATURDAY

New Moon

21 SATURDAY

Summer Solstice

24 TUESDAY

Tishah be-Av (Jewish)

30 MONDAY

Full Moon

Asalha Puja (Buddhist)

AUGUST 2007

5 SUNDAY

Ganesh Chaturthi (Hindu)

12 SUNDAY

New Moon

13 MONDAY

Obon, Festival of the Dead begins (Shinto)

16 THURSDAY

Obon, Festival of the Dead ends (Shinto)

28 TUESDAY

Full Moon

SEPTEMBER 2007

4 TUESDAY

Krishna Janmashthami (Hindu, Vaishnava)

11 TUESDAY

New Moon

Begin Ulambana, or Ancestor Day, (Mahayana)

12 WEDNESDAY

Begin Paitishaya, feast of bringing in the harvest (Zoroastrian)

13 THURSDAY

Begin Ramadan (Muslim)

Rosh Hashana, New Year (Jewish)

14 FRIDAY

Rosh Hashana, New Year (Jewish)

16 SUNDAY

End Paitishaya, feast of bringing in the harvest (Zoroastrian)

21 FRIDAY

Autumn Equinox

22 SATURDAY

Yom Kippur (Jewish)

25 TUESDAY

End Ulambana, or Ancestor Day, (Mahayana)

26 WEDNESDAY

Full Moon

27 THURSDAY

Begin Sukkot (Jewish)

28 FRIDAY

Master Kong Birthday (Confucian)

OCTOBER 2007

3 WEDNESDAY

End Sukkot (Jewish)

4 THURSDAY

Shemini Atzeret (Jewish)

5 FRIDAY

Simchat Torah (Jewish)

11 THURSDAY

New Moon

12 FRIDAY

Begin Ayathrima, bringing home the herds (Zoroastrian)

Navaratri (Hindu, Vaishnava)

13 SATURDAY

End Ramadan, Id-al-Fitr (Muslim)

16 TUESDAY

End Ayathrima, bringing home the herds (Zoroastrian)

20 SATURDAY

Birth of the Báb (Bahá'í)

Navaratri (Hindu, Vaishnava)

26 FRIDAY

Full Moon

NOVEMBER 2007

9 FRIDAY

New Moon

Dipavali, Festival of Lights (Hindu, Vaishnava, Jain, Sikh)

12 MONDAY

Birth of Bahá'u'lláh (Bahá'í)

15 THURSDAY

Shichi-go-san, children's rite of passage, (Shinto)

23 FRIDAY

Niiname-sai, harvest festival (Shinto)

24 SATURDAY

Full Moon

Niiname-sai, harvest festival (Shinto)

Parkash (Birthday) of Guru Nanak (Sikh)

Guru Tegh Bahadur, martyrdom day (Sikh)

26 MONDAY

'Abdu'l-Bahá, Day of the Covenant (Bahá'í)

28 WEDNESDAY

Ascension of 'Abdu'l-Bahá (Bahá'í)

DECEMBER 2007

2 SUNDAY

Advent begins (Christian)

5 WEDNESDAY

Chanukah begins (Jewish)

9 SUNDAY

New Moon

12 WEDNESDAY

Chanukah ends (Jewish)

20 THURSDAY

Id-al-Adha begins (Muslim)

21 FRIDAY

Winter Solstice

22 SATURDAY

Id-al-Adha ends (Muslim)

24 MONDAY

Full Moon

25 TUESDAY

Christmas (Christian)

30 SUNDAY

Id al-Ghadir (Shi'a)

31 MONDAY

Oharae, or Great Purification (Shinto)

Begin Maidhyaiya, mid-year/winter feast (Zoroastrian)

2008

JANUARY 2008

1 TUESDAY

Oshogatsu, or New Year (Shinto)

4 FRIDAY

End Maidhyaiya, mid-year/winter feast (Zoroastrian)

5 SATURDAY

Parkash (Birthday) Guru Gobind Singh (Sikh)

6 SUNDAY

Epiphany (Christian)

8 TUESDAY

New Moon

10 THURSDAY

Muharram, New Year (Muslim)

15 TUESDAY

Seijin no hi, or *Coming of Age Day* (Shinto)

19 SATURDAY

Ashura (Shi'a Muslim)

22 TUESDAY

Full Moon

New Year (Mahayanan)

Tu Bi-Shevat (Jewish)

FEBRUARY 2008

2 SATURDAY

Setsubun no hi, Change of Seasons, (Shinto)

5 TUESDAY

Tse Gutor (Tibetan Buddhist)

6 WEDNESDAY

Ash Wednesday, beginning of Lent (Christian)

7 THURSDAY

New Moon

New Year (Tibetan Buddhist, Confucian)

10 SUNDAY

Begin Mönlam Chenmo, the great prayer ceremony (Tibetan Buddhist)

21 THURSDAY

Full Moon

29 FRIDAY

End Mönlam Chenmo, the great prayer ceremony (Tibetan Buddhist)

MARCH 2008

2 SUNDAY

Annual Fast begins (Bahá'í)

3 MONDAY

Hina matsuri, Doll Festival, or Girls' Day (Shinto)

6 THURSDAY

Maha Shivaratri (Saivism)

7 FRIDAY

New Moon

16 SUNDAY

Palm Sunday (Christian)

Begin amaspathmaêdaya, feast of All Souls (Zoroastrian)

20 THURSDAY

Mawlid-al-Nabi (Muslim)

Annual Fast ends (Bahá'í)

End Hamaspathmaêdaya, feast of All Souls (Zoroastrian)

21 FRIDAY

Full Moon

Spring Equinox

Naw-Rúz, or New Year (Bahá'í, Zoroastrian)

Good Friday (Christian)

Holi (Hindu, Vaishnava)

22 SATURDAY

Holi (Hindu, Vaishnava)

23 SUNDAY

Easter (Christian)

APRIL 2008

5 SATURDAY

Qing Ming festival (Confucian)

6 SUNDAY

New Moon

14 MONDAY

Ram Navami (Hindu, Vaishnava)

Vaisakhi, Birth Anniversary of Khalsa, (Sikh)

20 SUNDAY

Full Moon

New Year (Theravadan)

Passover begins (Jewish)

21 MONDAY

Ridván festival holy day (Bahá'í)

27 SUNDAY

Passover ends (Jewish)

29 TUESDAY

Ridván festival holy day (Bahá'í)

30 WEDNESDAY

Begin Maidhyôizarêmaya, mid-spring feast (Zoroastrian)

MAY 2008

1 THURSDAY

Yom Hashoah, or Holocaust Memorial Day (Jewish)

2 FRIDAY

Ridván festival holy day (Bahá'í)

4 SUNDAY

End Maidhyôizarêmaya, mid-spring feast (Zoroastrian)

5 MONDAY

New Moon

Tango no sekku, Boys' Day (Shinto)

10 SATURDAY

Yom Ha'atzmaut, or Israel Independence Day: (Jewish)

11 SUNDAY

Pentecost, or Whitsunday (Christian)

20 TUESDAY

Full Moon

Vesak, Buddha's Birthday (Buddhist)

23 FRIDAY

Declaration of the Báb (Bahá'í)

29 THURSDAY

Ascension of Bahá'u'lláh (Bahá'í)

JUNE 2008

3 TUESDAY

New Moon

9 MONDAY

Shavuot (Jewish)

10 TUESDAY

Shavuot (Jewish)

16 MONDAY

Guru Arjan, martyrdom day (Sikh)

18 WEDNESDAY

Full Moon

29 SUNDAY

Begin Maidhyôishêma, mid-summer feast (Zoroastrian)

30 MONDAY

Oharae, or Great Purification (Shinto)

JULY 2008

3 THURSDAY

New Moon

End Maidhyôishêma, mid-summer feast (Zoroastrian)

9 WEDNESDAY

Martyrdom of the Báb (Bahá'í)

18 FRIDAY

Full Moon

Asalha Puja (Buddhist)

21 MONDAY

Summer Solstice

AUGUST 2008

1 FRIDAY

New Moon

10 SUNDAY

Tishah be-Av (Jewish)

13 WEDNESDAY

Obon, Festival of the Dead begins (Shinto)

16 SATURDAY

Full Moon

Obon, Festival of the Dead ends (Shinto)

24 SUNDAY

Krishna Janmashthami (Hindu, Vaishnava)

30 SATURDAY

New Moon

31 SUNDAY

Begin Ulambana, or Ancestor Day, (Mahayana)

SEPTEMBER 2008

2 TUESDAY

Begin Ramadan (Muslim)

3 WEDNESDAY

Ganesh Chaturthi (Hindu)

12 FRIDAY

Begin Paitishaya, feast of bringing in the harvest (Zoroastrian)

14 SUNDAY

End Ulambana, or Ancestor Day, (Mahayana)

15 MONDAY

Full Moon

16 TUESDAY

End Paitishaya, feast of bringing in the harvest (Zoroastrian)

21 SUNDAY

Autumn Equinox

28 SUNDAY

Master Kong Birthday (Confucian)

29 MONDAY

New Moon

30 TUESDAY

Rosh Hashana, New Year (Jewish)

Navaratri (Hindu, Vaishnava)

OCTOBER 2008

1 WEDNESDAY

Rosh Hashana, New Year (Jewish)

2 THURSDAY

End Ramadan, Id-al-Fitr (Muslim)

8 WEDNESDAY

Navaratri (Hindu, Vaishnava)

9 THURSDAY

Yom Kippur (Jewish)

12 SUNDAY

Begin Ayathrima, bringing home the herds (Zoroastrian)

14 TUESDAY

Full Moon

Begin Sukkot (Jewish)

16 THURSDAY

End Ayathrima, bringing home the herds (Zoroastrian)

20 MONDAY

Birth of the Báb (Bahá'í)

End Sukkot (Jewish)

21 TUESDAY

Shemini Atzeret (Jewish)

22 WEDNESDAY

Simchat Torah (Jewish)

28 TUESDAY

New Moon

Dipavali, Festival of Lights (Hindu, Vaishnava, Jain, Sikh)

NOVEMBER 2008

12 WEDNESDAY

Birth of Bahá'u'lláh (Bahá'í)

13 THURSDAY

Full Moon

Parkash (Birthday) of Guru Nanak (Sikh)

15 SATURDAY

Shichi-go-san, children's rite of passage, (Shinto)

23 SUNDAY

Niiname-sai, harvest festival (Shinto)

24 MONDAY

Niiname-sai, harvest festival (Shinto)

Guru Tegh Bahadur, martyrdom day (Sikh)

26 WEDNESDAY

'Abdu'l-Bahá, Day of the Covenant (Bahá'í)

27 THURSDAY

New Moon

28 FRIDAY

Ascension of 'Abdu'l-Bahá (Bahá'í)

30 SUNDAY

Advent begins (Christian)

DECEMBER 2008

9 TUESDAY

Id-al-Adha begins (Muslim)

11 THURSDAY

Id-al-Adha ends (Muslim)

12 FRIDAY

Full Moon

19 FRIDAY

Id al-Ghadir (Shi'a)

21 SUNDAY

Winter Solstice

22 MONDAY

Chanukah begins (Jewish)

25 THURSDAY

Christmas (Christian)

27 SATURDAY

New Moon

29 MONDAY

Muharram, New Year (Muslim)

Chanukah ends (Jewish)

31 WEDNESDAY

Oharae, or Great Purification (Shinto)

Begin Maidhyaiya, mid-year/winter feast (Zoroastrian)

2009

JANUARY 2009

1 THURSDAY

Oshogatsu, or New Year (Shinto)

4 SUNDAY

End Maidhyaiya, mid-year/winter feast (Zoroastrian)

5 MONDAY

Parkash (Birthday) Guru Gobind Singh (Sikh)

6 TUESDAY

Epiphany (Christian)

7 WEDNESDAY

Ashura (Shi'a Muslim)

11 SUNDAY

Full Moon

New Year (Mahayanan)

15 THURSDAY

Seijin no hi, or *Coming of Age Day (Shinto)*

24 SATURDAY

Tse Gutor (Tibetan Buddhist)

26 MONDAY

New Moon

New Year (Tibetan Buddhist, Confucian)

29 THURSDAY

Begin Mönlam Chenmo, the great prayer ceremony (Tibetan Buddhist)

FEBRUARY 2009

2 MONDAY

Setsubun no hi, Change of Seasons, (Shinto)

9 MONDAY

Full Moon

Tu Bi-Shevat (Jewish)

17 TUESDAY

End Mönlam Chenmo, the great prayer ceremony (Tibetan Buddhist)

23 MONDAY

Maha Shivaratri (Saivism)

25 WEDNESDAY

New Moon

Ash Wednesday, beginning of Lent (Christian)

MARCH 2009

2 MONDAY

Annual Fast begins (Bahá'í)

3 TUESDAY

Hina matsuri Doll Festival, or Girls' Day (Shinto)

9 MONDAY

Mawlid-al-Nabi (Muslim)

11 WEDNESDAY

Full Moon

Holi (Hindu, Vaishnava)

16 MONDAY

Begin Hamaspathmaêdaya, feast of All Souls (Zoroastrian)

20 FRIDAY

Annual Fast ends (Bahá'í)

End Hamaspathmaêdaya, feast of All Souls (Zoroastrian)

21 SATURDAY

Spring Equinox

Naw-Rúz, or New Year (Bahá'í, Zoroastrian)

26 THURSDAY

New Moon

APRIL 2009

3 FRIDAY

Ram Navami (Hindu, Vaishnava)

5 SUNDAY

Palm Sunday (Christian)

Qing Ming festival (Confucian)

9 THURSDAY

Full Moon

New Year (Theravadan)

Passover begins (Jewish)

10 FRIDAY

Good Friday (Christian)

12 SUNDAY

Easter (Christian)

14 TUESDAY

Vaisakhi, Birth Anniversary of Khalsa, (Sikh)

16 THURSDAY

Passover ends (Jewish)

21 TUESDAY

Ridván festival holy day (Bahá'í)

Yom Hashoah, or Holocaust Memorial Day (Jewish)

25 SATURDAY

New Moon

29 WEDNESDAY

Ridván festival holy day (Bahá'í)

Yom Ha'atzmaut, or Israel Independence Day: (Jewish)

30 THURSDAY

Begin Maidhyōizarêmaya, mid-spring feast (Zoroastrian)

MAY 2009

2 SATURDAY

Ridván festival holy day (Bahá'í)

4 MONDAY

End Maidhyōizarêmaya, mid-spring feast (Zoroastrian)

5 TUESDAY

Tango no sekku, Boys' Day (Shinto)

9 SATURDAY

Full Moon

Vesak, Buddha's Birthday (Buddhist)

23 SATURDAY

Declaration of the Báb (Bahá'í)

24 SUNDAY

New Moon

29 FRIDAY

Ascension of Bahá'u'lláh (Bahá'í)

Shavuot (Jewish)

30 SATURDAY

Shavuot (Jewish)

31 SUNDAY

Pentecost, or Whitsunday (Christian)

JUNE 2009

7 SUNDAY

Full Moon

16 TUESDAY

Guru Arjan, martyrdom day (Sikh)

22 MONDAY

New Moon

29 MONDAY

Begin Maidhyōishêma, mid-summer' feast (Zoroastrian)

30 TUESDAY

Oharae, or Great Purification (Shinto)

JULY 2009

3 FRIDAY

End Maidhyōishêma, mid-summer feast (Zoroastrian)

7 TUESDAY

Full Moon

Asalha Puja (Buddhist)

9 THURSDAY

Martyrdom of the Báb (Bahá'í)

21 TUESDAY

Summer Solstice

22 WEDNESDAY

New Moon

30 THURSDAY

Tishah be-Av (Jewish)

AUGUST 2009

6 THURSDAY

Full Moon

13 THURSDAY

Obon, Festival of the Dead begins (Shinto)

14 FRIDAY

Krishna Janmashthami (Hindu, Vaishnava)

16 SUNDAY

Obon, Festival of the Dead begins (Shinto)

20 THURSDAY

New Moon

22 SATURDAY

Begin Ramadan (Muslim)

23 SUNDAY

Ganesh Chaturthi (Hindu)

SEPTEMBER 2009

4 FRIDAY

Full Moon

12 SATURDAY

Begin Paitishaya, feast of bringing in the harvest (Zoroastrian)

16 WEDNESDAY

End Paitishaya, feast of bringing in the harvest (Zoroastrian)

19 SATURDAY

New Moon

Rosh Hashana, New Year (Jewish)

Begin Ulambana, or Ancestor Day, (Mahayana)

Navaratri (Hindu, Vaishnava)

20 SUNDAY

Rosh Hashana, New Year (Jewish)

21 MONDAY

Autumn Equinox

End Ramadan, Id-al-Fitr (Muslim)

27 SUNDAY

Navaratri (Hindu, Vaishnava)

28 MONDAY

Master Kong Birthday (Confucian)

Yom Kippur (Jewish)

OCTOBER 2009

3 SATURDAY

Begin Sukkot (Jewish)

Ulambana, or Ancestor Day, (Mahayana)

4 SUNDAY

Full Moon

9 FRIDAY

End Sukkot (Jewish)

10 SATURDAY

Shemini Atzeret (Jewish)

11 SUNDAY

Simchat Torah (Jewish)

12 MONDAY

Begin Ayathrima, bringing home the herds (Zoroastrian)

16 FRIDAY

End Ayathrima, bringing home the herds (Zoroastrian)

17 SATURDAY

Dipavali, Festival of Lights (Hindu, Vaishnava, Jain, Sikh)

18 SUNDAY

New Moon

20 TUESDAY

Birth of the Báb (Bahá'í)

NOVEMBER 2009

2 MONDAY

Full Moon

Parkash (Birthday) of Guru Nanak (Sikh)

12 THURSDAY

Birth of Bahá'u'lláh
(Bahá'í)

15 SUNDAY

Shichi-go-san, children's
rite of passage, (Shinto)

16 MONDAY

New Moon

23 MONDAY

Niiname-sai, harvest festival (Shinto)

24 TUESDAY

Niiname-sai, harvest festival (Shinto)

Guru Tegh Bahadur, mar-
tyrdom day (Sikh)

26 THURSDAY

'Abdu'l-Bahá, Day of the
Covenant (Bahá'í)

28 SATURDAY

Ascension of 'Abdu'l-
Bahá (Bahá'í)

Id-al-Adha begins
(Muslim)

30 MONDAY

Id-al-Adha ends (Muslim)

DECEMBER 2009

2 WEDNESDAY

Full Moon

8 TUESDAY

Id al-Ghadir (Shi'a)

12 SATURDAY

Chanukah begins (Jewish)

16 WEDNESDAY

New Moon

18 FRIDAY

Muharram, New Year
(Muslim)

19 SATURDAY

Chanukah ends (Jewish)

21 MONDAY

Winter Solstice

25 FRIDAY

Christmas (Christian)

27 SUNDAY

Ashura (Shi'a Muslim)

31 THURSDAY

Full Moon

Oharae, or Great
Purification (Shinto)

Begin Maidhyaiya, mid-
year/winter feast
(Zoroastrian)

Practices and Beliefs

Worldmark Encyclopedia of Religious Practices

Religion	Year founded	Prominent leaders	Place of origin	Primary texts	Number of followers
African Traditional Religions	200,000–100,000 B.C.E.	priests and priestesses, sacred kings and queens, prophets and prophetesses, and seers	Africa	• myths and oral narratives	84.5 million
Anglicanism	sixteenth century C.E.	King Henry VIII (1491–1547) Thomas Cranmer (1489–1556) William Tyndale (c. 1492–1536)	England	• Bible • Book of Common Prayer	84.5 million
Bahá'í Faith	1863 C.E.	'Alí-Muhammad, or the Báb (1819–50) Bahá'u'lláh (1817–92) 'Abdu'l-Bahá (1844–1921) Shoghi Effendi Rabbani (1897–1957)	Iran	• writings of Bahá'u'lláh, the Báb, and of 'Abdu'l-Bahá	6.5 million
Baptist Tradition	1690 C.E.	John Smyth (died in 1612) William Carey (1761–1834) Martin Luther King, Jr. (1929–68)	England	• Bible	117 million
Buddhism	fifth century B.C.E.	Siddhartha Gautama, or the Buddha (sixth century B.C.E.) Bodhidharma (sixth century C.E.) Padmasambhava (eighth century C.E.	northern India	• Tipitaka ("three baskets") • Additional books, such as the Lotus Sutra and the Prajnaparamita (Perfection of Wisdom) texts	390 million
Christianity	first century C.E.	Peter (died c. 64) Paul (died c. 64) Ignatius of Antioch (c. 35–c. 107) Constantine I (died 337) Saint Augustine (354–430) Saint Patrick (c. 390–c. 460) Pope Gregory I (reigned 590–604) Francis of Assisi (c. 1181–1226) Pope Innocent III (reigned 1198–1216) Martin Luther (1483–1546) Ulrich Zwingli (1484–1531) John Calvin (1509–64)	Palestine	• Bible	2.21 billion
Confucianism	c. 1050–256 B.C.E.	Confucius, or Master Kong (551–479 B.C.E.) Mencius, or Master Meng (c. 391–308 B.C.E.) Dong Zhongshu (c. 176–104 B.C.E.) Zhu Xi (1130–1200 C.E.) Wang Yangming (1472–1529 C.E.) Ngo Thi Nham (1746–1803 C.E.) Motoda Nagazane (1818–91 C.E.)	China	• Yijing (Book of Changes) • Shujing (Book of Documents) • Shijing (Book of Odes) • Liji (Book of Rites) • Zhouli (Rites of Zhou) • Yili (Book of Etiquette and Ritual) • Lun yu (Analects) • Xiaojing (Scripture of Filiality) • the Chinese dictionary Erya • Mengzi (Master Meng) • Chunqiu (Spring and Autumn Annals)	6.5 million
Conservative Judaism	1886 C.E.	Solomon Schechter (1847–1915) Cyrus Adler (1863–1940) Louis Ginzberg (1872–1953) Mordecai Kaplan (1881–1983)	United States	• Tanakh (Hebrew Bible) • Talmud (Oral Torah)	1.56 million

[continued]

Worldmark Encyclopedia of Religious Practices [CONTINUED]

Religion	Year founded	Prominent leaders	Place of origin	Primary texts	Number of followers
Coptic Christianity	48 C.E.	Saint Mark the Evangelist (first century) Athanasius (c. 293–373) Patriarch Cyril I (reigned 412–44)	Egypt	• Bible • Liturgy of Saint Basil, the Liturgy of Saint Gregory of Nazianzus, and the ancient liturgy of Saint Mark, also known as the Liturgy of Saint Cyril • *Katamaros,* a study of the stages of Christ's life • *Agbiya,* the book of the hours, contains the Psalms, prayers, and Gospels for the seven daily prayers • in addition, Copts use a psalmody, a book of doxologies (praise), and the *Synaxarium,* a book that commemorates Coptic saints	7.8 million
Eastern Catholic Churches	twelfth century C.E.	Patriarch Jeremias II al-Amshitti (early thirteenth century) Saint Josaphat Kuntsevych (died in 1623) Patriarch Abraham Pierre I (eighteenth century)	Lebanon and Armenia	• Bible • Euchologions, the Books of Needs, the Anthologions, the Festal Anthologies, the Floral and the Lenten Triodions, Oktoechos, Horologions, Typikons, Menologions, Menaions, the Books of Akathistos, and the Books of Commemoration	13 million
Eastern Orthodox Christianity	325 C.E.	Constantine I (died in 337) Saint Basil the Great (329–79) Saint John Chrysostom (347–407)	eastern half of the Roman Empire (now Turkey, Greece, Bulgaria, Romania, and Serbia)	• Septuagint Greek version of the Old Testament • Greek New Testament	227.5 million
Hinduism	before 3000 B.C.E.	Shankara (eighth century C.E.) Ramanuja (c. 1017–1137 C.E.) Madhva (c. 1199–1278 C.E.) Ram Mohan Roy (1772–1833 C.E.) Dayananda Sarasvati (1824–83 C.E.) Ramakrishna (1836–86 C.E.)	India	• Vedas • *Ramayana* ("Story of Rama") • *Mahabharata* ("Great Sons of Bharata") • *Puranas* ("Ancient Lore") • *Dharma Sastras*	910 million
Islam	622 C.E.	Prophet Muhammad (570–632) **Four Rightly Guide Caliphs:** Abu Bakr (reigned 632–34) Umar (reigned 634–44) Uthman (reigned 644–56) Ali (reigned 656–61)	Mecca and Medina (now in Saudi Arabia)	• Koran	1.3 billion
Jainism	c. 550 B.C.E.	Lord Mahavira (sixth century B.C.E.)	India	• **Shvetambara tradition:** • 45 texts organized into five groups: • Angas ("Limbs") • Upanga ("Supplementary Limbs") • Chedasutras ("Delineating Scriptures") • Mulasutras ("Root Scriptures") • Prakirnaka ("Miscellaneous")	6.5 million

[continued]

Worldmark Encyclopedia of Religious Practices [CONTINUED]

Religion	Year founded	Prominent leaders	Place of origin	Primary texts	Number of followers
				• **Digambara tradition:** • it is believed that the original canon has been lost • Shatakanda Agama Kashayaprabhrita • others	
Jehovah's Witnesses	1879 C.E.	Charles Taze Russell (1852–1916) Joseph Franklin Rutherford (1869–1942)	United States	• Bible	15.6 million
Judaism	c. eighteenth century B.C.E.	Abraham (eighteenth century B.C.E.) Isaac Jacob Moses (fourteenth–thirteenth centuries B.C.E.) Joshua (twelfth century B.C.E.) Samuel (eleventh century B.C.E.) David (eleventh–tenth centuries B.C.E.) Solomon (tenth century B.C.E.) Elijah (ninth century B.C.E.) Isaiah (eighth century B.C.E.) Rabbi Johanan ben Zakkai (died c. 80 C.E.)	Mesopotamia	• Tanakh (Hebrew Bible), divided into three parts: the Torah (also called the Pentateuch), the Prophets (Nevi'im), and the Writings (Ketuvim or Hagiographa) • Talmud (Oral Torah)	16.25 million
Lutheranism	1517 C.E.	Martin Luther (1483–1546) Philipp Melanchthon (1497–1560) Johannes Bugenhagen (1485–1558)	Germany	• Bible	65 million
Mahayana Buddhism	c. 200 C.E.	Nagarjuna (born in 150) Tenzin Gyatso, the 14th Dalai Lama (born in 1935)	India	• Perfection of Wisdom Sutras	208 million
Methodism	1729 C.E.	John Wesley (1703–91)	England	• Bible • Bible	76 million 12.35 million
The Church of Jesus Christ of Latter-day Saints	1830 C.E.	Joseph Smith (1805–44) Brigham Young (1801–77)	Fayette, New York, U.S.A.	• Book of Mormon • Pearl of Great Price • Doctrine and Covenants	
Orthodox Judaism	nineteenth century C.E.	**Hasidic community:** Rabbi Israel ben Eliezer, also called the Baal Shem Tov (c. 1700–60), **non-Hasidic Haredi community:** Rabbi Elijah ben Shlomo Zalman, known as the Vilna Gaon (1720–97) **Modern Orthodox community:** Rabbi Samson Raphael Hirsch (1808–88)	Europe	• Tanakh (Hebrew Bible) • Talmud (Oral Torah)	2.6 million
Pentecostalism	1901 C.E.	Charles Fox Parham (1873–1929) William J. Seymour (1870–1922)	Kansas, U.S.A.	• Bible	552.5 million

[continued]

Worldmark Encyclopedia of Religious Practices [CONTINUED]

Religion	Year founded	Prominent leaders	Place of origin	Primary texts	Number of followers
Protestantism	1517 C.E.	Martin Luther (1483–1546) John Calvin (1509–64) Ulrich Zwingli (1484–1531) Menno Simons (1496–1561)	Germany	• Bible	377 million
Reformed Christianity	sixteenth century C.E.	John Calvin (1509–64) Ulrich Zwingli (1484–1531)	Switzerland	• Bible	77.35 million
Reform Judaism	early nineteenth century C.E.	Israel Jacobson (1768–1828) Rabbi Isaac Mayer Wise (1819–1900)	western and central Europe	• Tanakh (Hebrew Bible) • Talmud (Oral Torah)	3.9 million
Religious Society of Friends (Quakers)	1652 C.E.	George Fox (1624–91) William Penn (1644–1718)	England	• Bible	390,000
Roman Catholicism	first century C.E.	Peter (died c. 64) Saint Ignatius of Loyola (1491–1556) Pope Pius IX (reigned 1846–78) Pope John XXIII (reigned 1958–63) Pope John Paul II (reigned 1978–2005)	Rome	• Bible, with 46 books in the Old Testament—the 39 from the Hebrew canon as well as 7 deutercanonical books	1.105 billion
Seventh-day Adventist Church	1863 C.E.	Ellen Gould White (1827–1915) James Springer White (1821–81) Joseph Bates (1792–1872)	United States	• Bible	13 million
Shaivism	second century C.E.	Lakulisha (c. second century) Basava (died in 1167) Sathya Sai Baba (born in 1926)	South Asia	• Upanishads • Shaivite Puranas • individual Shaivite groups have various other texts	208 million
Shiism	632 C.E.	Prophet Muhammad (570–632) Ali (c. 600–661) Husayn (626–80) Ja'far al-Sadiq (702–65)	Medina (now in Saudi Arabia)	• Koran	143 million
Shinto	c. 500 C.E.	Yamazaki Ansai (1618–82) Keichū (1640–1701) Motoori Norinaga (1730–1801)	Japan	• none sacred to all Shinto worshippers	117 million
Sikhism	c. 1499 C.E.	Guru Nanak (1469–1539) Guru Gobind Singh (1666–1708)	the Punjab (now in India and Pakistan)	• Adi Granth (Original Book) • Dasam Granth (Book of the 10th Guru) • Works of Bhai Gurdas and Bhai Nand Lal Goya • janam-sakhis (birth narratives) • rahit-namas (manuals of code of conduct) • gur-bilas (pleasure of the Guru) literature	19.5 million
Sunnism	632 C.E.	Prophet Muhammad (570–632) **Four Rightly Guided Caliphs:** Abu Bakr (reigned 632–34) Umar (reigned 634–44) Uthman (reigned 644–56) Ali (reigned 656–61)	Medina (now in Saudi Arabia)	• Koran	975 million

[continued]

Worldmark Encyclopedia of Religious Practices [CONTINUED]

Religion	Year founded	Prominent leaders	Place of origin	Primary texts	Number of followers
Taoism	c. 450–500 C.E.	Lu Hsiu-ching (406–77) T'ao Hung-ching (456–536) Ssu-ma Ch'eng-chen (646–735)	China	• *Tao-tsang*	65 million
Theravada Buddhism	fifth century B.C.E.	Mahasi Sayadaw (1904–82 C.E.) Ajahn Chah (1918–92 C.E.)	India	• *Tipitika*	123.5 million
Tibetan Buddhism	seventh and eighth centuries C.E.	Santaraksita (eighth century) Padmasambhava (eighth century) Tenzin Gyatso, the 14th Dalai Lama (born in 1935)	Tibet	• *Kanjur* • *Tenjur*	195,000
Unitarianism and Universalism	1565 C.E. (Unitarianism) and 1723 C.E. (Universalism)	Ferenc Dávid (1510–79) Faustus Socinus (1539–1604)	Poland and Transylvania (now in Romania) (Unitarianism) England (Universalism)	• Bible • many congregations include the sacred writings of all religions in worship	325,000
United Church of Christ	1957 C.E.	**Congregational:** John Winthrop (1588–1649) Jonathan Edwards (1703–58) **Reformed:** John Williamson Nevin (1803–86) **German Evangelical:** Reinhold Niebuhr (1892–1971)	United States	• Bible	1.3 million
Vaishnavism	c. 500 B.C.E.	Ramanuja (c. 1017–1137 C.E.) Madhvacarya (1296–1386 C.E.) Chaitanya (1485–1533 C.E.) Ghanshyam, or Swaminarayan (born in 1781 C.E.)	India	• Vedas • *Ramayana* • *Mahabharata* • Vaishnava Puranas	617.5 million
World Evangelicalism	seventeenth century C.E.	Philipp Jakob Spener (1635–1705) Charles Grandison Finney (1792–1875) Aimee Semple McPherson (1890–1944) Billy Graham (born in 1918)	Germany	• Bible	780 million
Zoroastrianism	second millennium B.C.E.	Tansar, or Tosar (died in 240 C.E.) Kirdīr, or Kartir (third century C.E.) K.R. Cama (1831–1909 C.E.)	Central Asia or eastern Iran	• Avesta, containing the *Yasna, Yasht*s, and *Vendidad*	149,500

Quotations on Beliefs

I. God or gods

"Acts of God are like riddles."

African Traditional Religions
African proverb

"To every discerning and illuminated heart it is evident that God, the unknowable Essence, the Divine Being, is immensely exalted beyond every human attribute, such as corporeal existence, ascent and descent, egress and regress. Far be it from His glory that human tongue should adequately recount His praise, or that human heart comprehend His fathomless mystery."

Bahá'í Faith
Bahá'u'lláh

"God then is infinite and incomprehensible and all that is comprehensible about Him is His infinity and incomprehensibility. . . . For when you speak of Him as good, and just, and wise, and so forth, you do not tell God's nature but only the qualities of His nature."

Christianity
John of Damascus

"Heaven/God [Tian] bestows one's inner nature; the Way [Tao] consists in following one's inner nature; the Teaching [Jiao] derives from cultivating the Way."

Confucianism
Doctrine of the Mean 1

"You are the supreme being, the supreme abode, the supreme purifier, the eternal one, the divine being. You are the Primordial deity without birth."

Hinduism
Bhagavad Gita 10:22

"Say: He is Allah, the One and Only; Allah, the Eternal, Absolute. He begetteth not, nor is He begotten; And there is none like unto Him."

Islam
Koran 112

"Hear, O Israel! The Lord our God, the Lord is one. You shall love the Lord your God with all your heart and with all your soul and with all your might."

Judaism
Deuteronomy 6:4-6

"Generally speaking, 'kami' denotes . . . all kinds of beings—including not only human beings but also such objects as birds, beasts, trees, grass, seas, mountains, and so forth—any being whatsoever which possesses some eminent quality out of the ordinary and awe-inspiring."

Shinto
Motoori Norinaga

"My Master is the One. He is the One, brother, and He alone exists."

Sikhism
Guru Nanak, Adi Granth, p. 150

"Then as holy I have recognized Thee, Ahura Mazda, when I saw Thee at first at the birth of life, when Thou didst appoint rewards for acts and words, bad for the bad, a good recompense for the good, by Thy innate virtue, at the final turning point of creation."

Zoroastrianism
Yasna 43:5

II. Prayer

"The prayer of the chicken hawk does not get him the chicken."

African Traditional Religions
Swahili proverb

"The state of prayer is the best of conditions, for man is then associating with God. Prayer verily bestoweth life, particularly when offered in private and at times, such as midnight, when freed from daily cares."

Bahá'í Faith
'Abdu'l-Bahá

"Sitting cross-legged,
They should wish that all beings
Have firm and strong roots of goodness
And attain the state of immovability.
Cultivating concentration,
They should wish that all beings
Conquer their minds by concentration
Ultimately, with no reminder.
When practicing contemplation,
They should wish that all beings
See truth as it is
And be forever free of oppression and contention."

Buddhism
Garland Sutra (Gandavyuha) 11

"When you are praying, do not use meaningless repetition, as the Gentiles do, for they suppose that they will be heard for their many words. Therefore do not be like them; for your Father knows what you need, before you ask Him."

Christianity
Matthew 6:7

"Knowing in what to abide, one can settle the mind; with settled mind, one can achieve quiet; in quietude, one can reach a state of calm; in calmness, one can contemplate; in contemplation, one can attain the goal."

Confucianism
Great Learning 1

"Lead me from unreality to reality; lead me from darkness to light; lead me from death to immortality. Om Peace, Peace, Peace."

Hinduism
Brihadaranyaka Upanishad 1:3:28

"Recite what is sent of the Book by inspiration to thee, and establish regular Prayer: for Prayer restrains from shameful and unjust deeds; and remembrance of Allah is the greatest [thing in life] without doubt. And Allah knows the [deeds] that ye do."

Islam
Koran 29:45

"Homage to the Jinas.
Homage to the perfected souls.
Homage to the renouncer-leaders.
Homage to the renouncer-teachers.
Homage to all renouncers."

Jainism
Namaskar Mantra

"What then is left for us to do except to pray for the ability to pray, to bewail our ignorance of living in His presence? And even if such prayer is tainted with vanity, His mercy accepts and redeems our feeble efforts. It is the continuity of trying to pray, the unspoken loyalty to our duty to pray, that lends strength to our fragile worship; and it is the holiness of the community that bestows meaning upon our individual acts of worship. These are three pillars on which our prayer rises to God: our own loyalty, the holiness of Israel, and the mercy of God."

Judaism
Abraham Joshu Heschel

"When [the Shinto priest] pronounces the ritual prayers,
the heavenly deities will push open the heavenly rock door,
and pushing with an awesome pushing,
through the myriad layers of heavenly clouds,
will hear and receive [these prayers]."

Shinto
From ninth-century norito (prayer)

"Nanak prays: the divine Name may be magnified;
May peace and prosperity come to one and all by your grace, O Lord!"

> *Sikhism*
> *Ardas prayer*

"Those Beings, male and female, whom Ahura Mazda knows the best for worship according to truth, we worship them all."

> *Zoroastrianism*
> *Yenghe Hatam prayer*

III. Duty toward other people

"A lone traveler is swept away by a stream."

> *African Traditional Religions*
> *Tonga proverb*

"Be generous in prosperity, and thankful in adversity. Be worthy of the trust of thy neighbor, and look upon him with a bright and friendly face. Be a treasure to the poor, an admonisher to the rich, an answerer of the cry of the needy. . . . Be unjust to no man, and show all meekness to all men. Be as a lamp unto them that walk in darkness, a joy to the sorrowful, a sea for the thirsty, a haven for the distressed, an upholder and defender of the victim of oppression. Let integrity and uprightness distinguish all thine acts. Be a home for the stranger, a balm to the suffering, a tower of strength for the fugitive. Be eyes to the blind, and a guiding light unto the feet of the erring. Be an ornament to the countenance of truth, a crown to the brow of fidelity, a pillar of the temple of righteousness, a breath of life to the body of mankind, an ensign of the hosts of justice, a luminary above the horizon of virtue, a dew to the soil of the human heart, an ark on the ocean of knowledge, a sun in the heaven of bounty, a gem on the diadem of wisdom, a shining light in the firmament of thy generation, a fruit upon the tree of humility."

> *Bah·á·í Faith*
> *Bahá'u'lláh*

"Hatred is never quelled by hatred in this world. It is quelled by love. This is an eternal truth."

> *Buddhism*
> *Dhammapada 1:5*

"You shall love your neighbor as yourself."

> *Christianity*
> *Mark 12:31*

"The duties of universal obligation are five . . . those between ruler and subject, father and child, husband and wife, older and younger siblings, and two friends."

> *Confucianism*
> *Doctrine of the Mean 20*

"Lack of enmity to all beings in thought, word, and deed; compassion and generous giving—these are the marks of the eternal faith; this is the eternal duty."

> *Hinduism*
> *Mahabharata*

"It is not righteousness that ye turn your faces towards east or west; but it is righteousness to believe in Allah and the Last Day, and the Angels, and the Book, and the Messengers; to spend of your substance, out of love for Him, for your kin, for orphans, for the needy, for the wayfarer, for those who ask, and for the ransom of slaves; to be steadfast in prayer, and practice regular charity; to fulfill the contracts which ye have made; and to be firm and patient, in pain (or suffering) and adversity, and throughout all periods of panic. Such are the people of truth, the Allah-fearing."

> *Islam*
> *Koran 2:177*

"The observer of vows should cultivate friendliness towards all living beings, delight in the distinction and honor of others, [show] compassion for miserable, lowly creatures and equanimity towards the vainglorious."

> *Jainism*
> *Tattvartha Sutra*

"Love your fellow as yourself: I am the Lord."

> *Judaism*
> *Leviticus 19:18*

"The hearts of all you encounter shall be as a mirror to you, reflecting the face you have presented to them."

> *Shinto*
> *Kurozumi Munetada*

"One should live on what one has earned through hard work and share with others the fruit of one's exertion." Guru Nanak

> *Sikhism*
> *Adi Granth, p. 1,245*

"The sage does not accumulate [for himself].
The more that he expends for others, the more does he possess of his own;
the more that he gives to others, the more does he have himself."

> *Taoism*
> *Tao te ching 81*

"I pledge myself to the well-thought thought, I pledge myself to the well-spoken word, I pledge myself to the well-acted act."

> *Zoroastrianism*
> *Yasna 12:8*

Worldmark Encyclopedia of Religious Practices

IV. Poverty and wealth

"The lack of money does not necessarily mean that one is poor."

African Traditional Religions
African proverb

"O CHILDREN OF DUST!
Tell the rich of the midnight sighing of the poor, lest heedlessness lead them into the path of destruction, and deprive them of the Tree of Wealth. To give and to be generous are attributes of Mine; well is it with him that adorneth himself with My virtues."

Bahá'í Faith
Bahá'u'lláh

"Goodwill, and wisdom, a mind trained by method
The highest conduct based on good morals
This makes humans pure, not rank or wealth."

Buddhism
Samyutta Nikaya

"For I was hungry, and you gave me something to eat; I was thirsty, and you gave me drink; I was a stranger, and you invited me in; naked, and you clothed me; I was sick, and you visited me; I was in prison, and you came to me."

Christianity
Matthew 25:35-36

"Facilitate their cultivation of fields, lighten their tax burden, and the common people can be made wealthy."

Confucianism
Master Meng [Mencius] VII:2:23

"This body—it is for the service of others."

Hinduism
Anonymous

"Alms are for the poor and the needy, and those employed to administer the [funds]; for those whose hearts have been [recently] reconciled [to Truth]; for those in bondage and in debt; in the cause of Allah and for the wayfarer: [thus is it] ordained by Allah, and Allah is full of knowledge and wisdom."

Islam
Koran 9:60

"Speak up for the dumb,
For the rights of all the unfortunate.
Speak up, judge righteously,
Champion the poor and the needy."

Judaism
Proverbs 31:8

"True service is the service of poor people; I am not inclined to serve others of higher social status; charity will bear fruit, in this and the next world if given to such worthy and poor people."

Sikhism
Guru Gobind Singh, Adi Granth, p. 1,223

"There is no guilt greater than to sanction ambition;
no calamity greater than to be discontented with one's lot;
no fault greater than the wish to be getting.
Therefore the sufficiency of contentment is an enduring and unchanging sufficiency."

Taoism
Tao te ching 46

"As the Master, so is the Judge to be chosen in accord with truth. Establish the power of acts arising from a life lived with good purpose, for Mazda and for the lord whom they made pastor for the poor."

Zoroastrianism
Ahuna Vairya prayer

V. Women

"And among the teachings of Bahá'u'lláh is the equality of women and men. The world of humanity has two wings—one is women and the other men. Not until both wings are equally developed can the bird fly."

Bahá'í Faith
'Abdu'l-Bahá

"Whoever has such a vehicle, whether it is a woman or a man, by means of that vehicle shall come to nirvana."

Buddhism
Samyutta Nikaya

"The knot of Eve's disobedience was loosed by the obedience of Mary. For what the virgin Eve had bound fast through unbelief, this did the virgin Mary set free through faith."

Christianity
Saint Irenaeus

"To be a woman, one must develop as a person; to do this, strive to establish one's purity and chastity. With purity, one remains undefiled; with chastity, one keeps one's virtue."

Confucianism
Analects for Women 2:1a

"If any do deeds of righteousness—be they male or female—and have faith, they will enter Heaven, and not the least injustice will be done to them."

Islam
Koran 4:124

"Jewish feminism focuses on three issues: attaining complete religious involvement for Jewish women; giving Jewish expression to women's experiences and self-understanding; and highlighting the imagery, language, rituals already present within the tradition that center around the feminine and the women. These efforts involve changing or eliminating aspects of Jewish law, customs, and teachings that prevent or discourage women from developing positions of equality to men within Judaism as well as bringing new interpretations to bear on the tradition."

Judaism
Susannah Heschel

"Woman is the foundation of the faith."

Shinto
Nakayama Miki

"Blessed are they, both men and women, who endlessly praise their Lord. Blessed are they in the True One's court; there shall their faces shine."

Sikhism
Guru Nanak, Adi Granth, p. 473

"The valley spirit dies not, aye the same;
The female mystery thus do we name.
Its gate, from which at first they issued forth,
Is called the root from which grew heaven and earth.
Long and unbroken does its power remain,
Used gently, and without the touch of pain."

Taoism
Tao te ching 6

"We call upon you the Waters, and you the milk cows, and you the mothers, giving milk, nourishing the poor, possessed of all kinds of sustenance; who are the best, the most beautiful. Down we call you, O good ones, to be grateful for and pleased by shares of the long-armed offering, you living mothers."

Zoroastrianism
Yasna 38:5

VI. Death

"The elephant has fallen."

African Traditional Religions
Yoruba metaphor for the death of an elderly person

"O SON OF THE SUPREME!
I have made death a messenger of joy to thee. Wherefore dost thou grieve?"

Bahá'í Faith
Bahá'u'lláh

"[D]eath, which we want nothing to do with, is unavoidable. This is why it is important that during our lifetime we become familiar with the idea of death, so that it will not be a real shock to us at the moment it comes. We do not meditate regularly on death in order to die more quickly; on the contrary, like everyone, we wish to live a long time. However, since death is inevitable, we believe that if we begin to prepare for it at an earlier point in time, on the day of our death it will be easier to accept it."

Buddhism
Dalai Lama

"Death has been swallowed up in victory. Where, O death, is your victory? Where, O death, is your sting? . . . Thanks be to God! He gives us the victory through our Lord Jesus Christ."

Christianity
1 Corinthians 15:54-55

"If one is not yet able to serve living persons, how can one serve spirits of the dead? If one does not yet understand life, how can one understand death?"

Confucianism
Analects of Confucius 11:12

"Just as one casts away old clothes and gets new ones, so too, after casting away worn-out bodies, the soul gets new ones."

Hinduism
Bhagavad Gita 2:22

"Every soul shall have a taste of death: And only on the Day of Judgment shall you be paid your full recompense. Only he who is saved far from the Fire and admitted to the Garden will have attained the object [of Life]: For the life of this world is but goods and chattels of deception."

Islam
Koran 3:185

"The physical body with all its sense organs, its health and youth, strength, radiance, good fortune and beauty—all resemble the rainbow which vanishes within seconds. They are impermanent."

Jainism
Acharya Kundakunda

"By the sweat of your brow
Shall you get bread to eat,
Until you return to the ground—
For from it you were taken.
For dust you are,
And to dust you shall return."

Judaism
Genesis 3:19

"Death proceeds from life, and life is the beginning of death. The [Ise] Shrine official informed me that this was handed down as the reason for the taboos surrounding both birth and death."

Shinto
Muju Ichien

"To whom should one complain, O Nanak, when death carries the mortal away without one's consent?"

Sikhism
Guru Nanak, Adi Granth, p. 1,412

"Death and life are not within our power, so we must be content with death. In this world we are like a foreign traveler and our body is just like a hired shell which we are in. From it man goes to his original abode. There should be no deep mourning for that. Everybody dies; others go before us, and we have to follow. Thus to be mournful is a sinful act."

Zoroastrianism
Dastur Erachji Sohrabji Meherjirana

Populations

African Traditional Religions 79,913,910

Anglicanism 79,913,910

Baha'I 6,147,224

Baptist Tradition .110,650,029

Buddhism 368,833,430

Christianity .2,090,056,103

Church of Jesus Christ of Latter-day Saints . .11,679,725

Confucianism 6,147,224

Conservative Judaism 1,475,334

Coptic Christianity 7,376,669

Eastern Catholicism 12,294,448

Eastern Orthodox Christianity 215,152,834

Evangelicalism 737,666,860

Hinduism 860,611,337

Islam 1,229,444,767

Jainism 6,147,224

Jehovah'S Witnesses 14,753,337

Judaism 15,368,060

Lutheranism 61,472,238

Mahayana Buddhism 196,711,163

Methodism 71,922,519

Orthodox Judaism 2,458,890

Pentecostalism .522,514,026

Protestantism 356,538,982

Reform Judaism .3,688,334

Reformed Christianity 73,151,964

Religious Society of Friends 368,833

Roman Catholicism 1,045,028,052

Seventh-day Adventist 12,294,448

Shaivism 196,711,163

Shiism 135,238,924

Shinto 110,650,029

Sikhism 18,441,671

Sunnism 922,083,575

Taoism 61,472,238

Theravada Buddhism 116,797,253

Tibetan Buddhism .184,417

Unitarianism 307,361

United Church of Christ 1,229,445

Vaishnavism 583,986,264

Zoroastrianism 141,386

Combined populations exceed total world population since some people qualify as members more than one religious group. A Buddhist, for example, may also practice Confucianism. Likewise, a Methodist might also be counted as a Christian, a Protestant, an Evangelical, and a Pentecostal, depending on their beliefs.

Glossary

10 paramitas (Buddhism) 10 perfections of the bod-hisattva: (1) *dana* (generosity), (2) *sila* (morality), (3) *ksanti* (patience and forbearance), (4) *virya* (vigor, the endless and boundless energy that bodhisattvas employ when helping others), (5) *dhyana* (meditation), (6) *prajna* (wisdom), (7) *upaya* (skillful means), (8) conviction, (9) strength, and (10) knowledge

Abaluhya (African Traditional Religions) an ethnic group in Kenya

Achaemenian dynasty (Zoroastrianism) dynasty that ruled Iran from 550 to 330 B.C.E.

acharya (Hinduism) a formal head of a monastery, sect, or subcommunity

acharya (Jainism) head of a subsect or smaller group of renouncers

Adi Granth (Sikhism) Original Book; the primary Sikh scripture

Advent (Christianity) period of four weeks, beginning four Sundays before Christmas, sometimes observed with fasting and prayer

afrinagan (Zoroastrianism) Zoroastrian ceremony involving the distribution of blessings

Aggadah (Judaism) nonlegal, narrative portions of the Talmud and Mishna, which include history, folklore, and other subjects

ahimsa (Jainism) nonviolence

Ahura Mazda (Zoroastrianism) supreme deity of Zoroastrianism; likely an honorific title meaning "Wise Lord" rather than a proper name

Akal Purakh (Sikhism) Timeless One; God

al-hajj / al-hajji (Islam) pilgrim; prefix added to a name to indicate that the person has made the hajj

Allah (Islam) God

Amaterasu (Shinto) the sun goddess

Amesha Spentas (Zoroastrianism) the six entities that aid Ahura Mazda, sometimes with an additional figure, Spenta Mainyu, to compose the divine heptad (group of seven)

amrit (Sikhism) divine nectar; sweetened water used in the initiation ceremony of the Khalsa

anagarika (Buddhism) ascetic layperson

anekant (Jainism) doctrine of the multiplicity of truth

Anglicanism (Christianity) Church of England, which originated in King Henry VIII's break with Rome in 1534, and those churches that developed from it, including the Episcopal Church in the United States; with a wide spectrum of doctrines and practices, it is sometimes called Episcopalianism

Angra Mainyu (Zoroastrianism) primordial evil spirit, twin of Spenta Mainyu

Apocrypha (Christianity) books of the Old Testament included in the Septuagint (Greek translation used by early Christians) and Catholic (including the Latin Vulgate) versions of the Bible but not in Protestant or modern Jewish editions

arahitogami (Shinto) a *kami* in human form

arhat (Buddhism) worthy one

aryika (Jainism) a Digambara nun who wears white clothing

asha (Zoroastrianism) truth; righteousness

Ashkenazim (Judaism) Jews whose ancestors in the Middle Ages lived in Germany (Ashkenaz in Hebrew) and the surrounding countries

ashrama (Hinduism) one of the four stages of life

atashkadeh (Zoroastrianism) "place of fire"; fire temple; more narrowly, the enclosed chamber in a fire temple that contains a fire continuously fed by the priests

atman (Hinduism) the human soul

Atonement (Christianity) doctrine that the death of Jesus is the basis for human salvation

Avestan (Zoroastrianism) ancient East Iranian language

Ayurveda (Hinduism) "knowledge of a long life"; a Hindu healing system

Ba Kongo (African Traditional Religions) a group of Bantu-speaking peoples who largely reside in Congo (Brazzaville), Democratic Republic of the Congo (Kinshasa), and Angola

Ba Thonga (African Traditional Religions) a group of Bantu-speaking peoples who live in the southern African countries of Mozambique, Zimbabwe, Swaziland, and South Africa

babalawo (African Traditional Religions) a divination specialist in Yoruba culture

Babi (Bahá'í) a follower of Ali-Muhammad of Shiraz (1819–50), who took the title of the Bab (Arabic: "gate")

Baganda (African Traditional Religions) the largest ethnic group in Uganda

Baha (Bahá'í) glory, splendor, or light; the greatest name of God; the root word in Bahaullah, the title of the founder of the Bahá'í faith, and in Bahá'í

Bambara (African Traditional Religions) an ethnic group in Mali

Bantu (African Traditional Religions) a large group of languages spoken in central, eastern, and southern Africa

baptism (Christianity) sacrament practiced by Christians in which the sprinkling, pouring of, or immersion in water is a sign of admission into the faith community

bar mitzvah (son of commandment) (Judaism) initiation ceremony for boys at age 13, when they are held to be responsible for their actions and hence are obliged to observe all of the commandments of the Torah; bat mitzah, a similar ceremony for girls at age 12, is observed by some Jews

barashnum (Zoroastrianism) Zoroastrian purification ceremony used primarily by priests to prepare for their ordination

Bhagavad Gita (Hinduism) one of the most sacred texts of the Hindus; a book of 18 chapters from the epic the *Mahabharata*

bhakti (Hinduism) devotion; the practice of devotion to God

bhikkhu (Buddhism) monk

bhikkhuni (Buddhism) female monk

bodhi (Buddhism) enlightenment; awakening

bodhisattva (Buddhism) an enlightened being who works for the welfare of all those still caught in samsara

Brahma (Hinduism) a minor deity; the creator god

brahmacharya (Jainism) chastity in marriage or celibacy

Brahman (Hinduism) the upper, or priestly, caste

Brahman (Hinduism) the term used in the Upanishads to refer to the supreme being

Brit Milah (Judaism) circumcision of a male infant or adult convert as a sign of acceptance of the covenant

caliph (Islam) successor; deputy to the Prophet Muhammad

caste (Hinduism) a social group (frequently one that a person is born into) in Hindu society

casuistry (Christianity) type of moral reasoning based on the examination of specific cases

catechesis (Christianity) formal instruction in the faith

"Celestial Masters" tradition (T'ien-shih) (Taoism) Taoist tradition of late Han times, with which several later traditions, especially Cheng-i, claimed affiliation

Ch'an (Zen in Japan) (Buddhism) a school of Mahayana Buddhism

ch'i (Taoism) life-energy

ch'i-kung (qigong) (Taoism) the skill of attracting vital energy

Ch'ing dynasty (Taoism) dynasty that ruled China from 1644 to 1911; also called the Manchu dynasty

Ch'ing-wei (Taoism) "Clarified Tenuity"; a Taoism sub-tradition the emerged in the tenth century; it involves a system of therapeutic rituals

ch'uan-ch'i (Taoism) type of traditional Chinese literary tale

Ch'üan-chen (Taoism) "Integrating the Perfections"; practice that originated in the eleventh century and continued in modern "Dragon Gate" Taoism; sometimes called "Northern Taoism"

chai (Taoism) type of Taoist liturgy that originated in the Ling-pao tradition in the fifth century

charismatics (Christianity) major expression of Christianity that includes those who affirm the gifts of the Holy Spirit but who are not affiliated with Pentecostal denominations

chen (Taoism) perfection or realization; ultimate spiritual integration

Cheng-i (Taoism) "Orthodox Unity"; Taoist tradition that emerged during the conquest period (approximately the twelfth through fourteenth centuries) and became a part of "Southern Taoism"

chen-jen (Taoism) perfected ones; a term used both for angelic beings and for the human ideal of fully perfected or realized persons

chiao (Taoism) extended Taoist liturgy; a sequence of events over several days that renews the local community by reintegrating it with the heavenly order

Chin dynasty (Taoism) dynasty that ruled China from 266 to 420 C.E.

ching (Taoism) vital essence

Ching-ming (Taoism) "Pure Illumination"; a Taoism subtradition that emerged during the Ming dynasty; it was absorbed into the "Dragon Gate" tradition

chin-tan (Taoism) "Golden Elixir"; a set of ideas about spiritual refinement through meditation

chrismation (Christianity) anointing with oil

Chuang-tzu (Taoism) classical text compiled c. 430 to 130 B.C.E.

classical China (Taoism) the period before 221 B.C.E.

conciliar (Christianity) governance through councils of bishops

confirmation (Christianity) sacrament marking membership in a church

congregationalism (Christianity) self-governance by a local congregation

Conservative Judaism (Judaism) largest denomination of American Judaism, with affiliated congregations in South America and Israel; advocating moderate

modifications of Halakhah, it occupies a middle ground between Reform and Orthodox Judaism

cosmogony (African Traditional Religions) a theory about the creation of the universe

cosmology (African Traditional Religions) an explanation of the nature of the universe

daeva (Zoroastrianism) demon

Dagara (African Traditional Religions) an ethnic group of the Niger region of western Africa

dakhma (Zoroastrianism) "tower of silence"; a tower in which a corpse is traditionally exposed

dan (Sikhism) charity; a person's relation with society

dana (Buddhism) proper giving; generosity

dar-i Mihr (Zoroastrianism) "the court of Mithra"; the room in a fire temple where the *yasna* is performed

Dashalakshanaparvan (Jainism) yearly Digambara festival during which the Tattvartha Sutra is read and that ends in atonement

dastur (Zoroastrianism) "master"; honorific title for a Zoroastrian priest

dawa (Islam) call to Islam; propagation of the faith

de (Confucianism) virtue; potential goodness conferred on a person by *Tian* (Heaven)

deva (Buddhism) deity; divine being; divine

deva (Hinduism) a divine being

Devi (Hinduism) in the Sanskrit literary tradition, the name for the Goddess

dharma (Hinduism) duty, or acting with a sense of what is righteous; sometimes used to mean "religion" and "ethics"

dharma (Pali, dhamma) (Buddhism) the teachings of the Buddha

Dharma Sastra (Hinduism) any of a set of treatises on the nature of righteousness, moral duty, and law

dhimmi (Islam) protected person, specifically a Jew or Christian

Diaspora (Judaism) communities of Jews dispersed outside the Land of Israel, traditionally referred to as the Exile

Digambara (Jainism) wearing the sky; sect of Jainism, largely based in southern India, in which full monks do not wear any clothing

diksha (Jainism) rite of initiation for a monk or a nun

divination (African Traditional Religions) any of various methods of accessing sacred knowledge of the deities; it often involves interpreting signs

"Dragon Gate" tradition (Lung-men) (Taoism) Taoist tradition that originated in the seventeenth century, incorporating Ch'üan-chen and Ching-ming; the dominant form of Taoism in mainland China today

dua (Islam) personal prayer

duhkha (Pali, dukkha) (Buddhism) suffering; unsatisfactoriness

Durga (Hinduism) a manifestation of the Goddess (represented as a warrior)

Edo (African Traditional Religions) an ethnic group of southern Nigeria

Eightfold Path (marga; Pali, magga) (Buddhism) a systematic and practical way to realize the truth and eliminate suffering, traditionally divided into three distinct phases that should be progressively mastered

Epiphany (Christianity) January 6, a celebration of the coming of the Magi and, in Orthodoxy, of the baptism of Jesus

eschatology (Christianity) doctrine concerning the end of the world, including the Second Coming of Christ, God's judgment, heaven, and hell

Eucharist (Communion; Lord's Supper) (Christianity) sacrament practiced by Christians in which bread and wine become (in Roman Catholicism and Orthodoxy) or stand for (in Protestantism) the body and blood of Christ

evangelicalism (Christianity) movement that emphasizes the authority of the Scriptures, salvation by faith, and individual experience over ritual

extreme unction (Christianity) sacrament; blessing of the sick

Fang (African Traditional Religions) an ethnic group of west-central Africa

fasli (Zoroastrianism) seasonal calendar that places New Year's Day in March; compare with *qadimi*

fast of Ramadan (Islam) fast during ninth month; fourth pillar

fatwa (Islam) legal opinion or judgment of a mufti, a specialist in Islamic law

Five Pillars of Islam (Islam) fundamental observances

Five Scriptures (Confucianism) *Wujing;* Confucianism's most sacred texts

Fon (African Traditional Religions) an ethnic group of Benin

Four Books (Confucianism) *Sishu;* central texts of Confucian philosophy and education

frashkard (Zoroastrianism) the renewal of the world at the end of history

Fukko Shintō (Shinto) the "pure Shinto" of the scholar Motoori Norinaga

Gāthā (Zoroastrianism) one of the 17 hymns traditionally ascribed to Zoroaster

gūji (Shinto) Shinto head priest

Gahambar (Zoroastrianism) one of six five-day Zoroastrian festivals

Ganesha (Hinduism) a popular Hindu god; a son of the goddess Parvati, he is depicted with an elephant head

Gathic (Zoroastrianism) older Avestan dialect

getig (Zoroastrianism) form; physical world

ghusl (Islam) ritual cleansing before worship

Goddess (Hinduism) a powerful, usually gracious, deity in female form sometimes seen as a manifestation of Parvati, the wife of Shiva; she is called any number of names, including Shakti, Durga, Kali, or Devi

gon-gūji (Shinto) Shinto assistant head priest

goryō (Shinto) haunting spirit of a wronged individual

gotra (Hinduism) a clan group

grace (Christianity) unmerited gift from God for human salvation

granthi (Sikhism) reader of scripture and leader of rituals in the *gurdwara*

gurdwara (Sikhism) door of the Guru; house of worship

Gurmukh (Sikhism) a person oriented toward the Guru

guru (Hinduism) a charismatic teacher

Guru (Sikhism) spiritual preceptor, either a person or the mystical "voice" of Akal Purakh

Guru Granth, or Guru Granth Sahib (Sikhism) the Adi Granth, or scripture, functioning as Guru

Guru Panth (Sikhism) the Sikh Panth, or community, functioning as Guru

Hachiman (Shinto) a Shinto-Buddhist deity popular with samurai

hadith (Islam) tradition; reports of Muhammad's sayings and deeds

Haggadah (Judaism) book used at the Passover seder, containing the liturgical recitation of the Passover story and instructions on conducting the ceremonial meal

hajj (Islam) pilgrimage to Mecca; fifth pillar

Halakhah (Judaism) legal portions of the Talmud as later elaborated in rabbinic literature; in an extended sense it denotes the ritual and legal prescriptions governing the traditional Jewish way of life

halal (Islam) meat slaughtered in a religious manner

Han dynasty (Taoism) dynasty that ruled China from 206 B.C.E. to 221 C.E.

Hand of the Cause of God (Bahá'í) one of 50 individuals appointed by Bahaullah, Abdul-Baha, or Shoghi Effendi whose duties included encouraging Bahá'ís and their institutions, advising them about the development of the Bahá'í community worldwide, and informing the head of the faith about conditions and developments in local Bahá'í communities

haoma (Zoroastrianism) sacred drink, now pressed from ephedra and pomegranate twigs

haoxue (Confucianism) love of (moral) learning

harae (Shinto) purification rites

Hasidism (Judaism) revivalist mystical movement that originated in Poland in the eighteenth century

hijab (Islam) Muslim dress for women, today often referring to a headscarf

hijra (hegira) (Islam) migration of early Muslims from Mecca to Medina

himorogi (Shinto) sacred space demarcated by a rope (*shimenawa*) or other marker

hitogami (Shinto) a living *kami* in human form

honji-suijaku (Shinto) Buddhist philosophy of the assimilation of Buddhas and *kami*

Hsiang-erh (Taoism) "Just Thinking"; text that is couched as a commentary on the *Lao-tzu*

hsin (Taoism) heart/mind

hsing (Taoism) inner nature; internal spiritual realities

hsiu chen (Taoism) cultivating reality; term by which Taoists frequently refer to religious practice

hsiu tao (Taoism) cultivating Tao; nearly synonymous with *hsiu chen*

hsiu-lien (Taoism) cultivation and refinement; an enduring Taoist term for self cultivation

hukam (Sikhism) divine order

huququllah (Bahá'í) "right of God"; a 19-percent tithe that Bahá'ís pay on their income after essential expenses

Ifa (African Traditional Religions) a form of divination that originated in West Africa

Igbo (African Traditional Religions) an ethnic group of Nigeria

imam (Islam) Shiite prayer leader; also used as the title for Muhammad's successors as leader of the Muslim community, consisting of male descendants through his cousin and son-in-law Ali

Inner Alchemy (Taoism) *nei-tan*; a generic term used for various related models of meditative self-cultivation

ishnan (Sikhism) purity

Islam (Islam) submission to the will of God; peace

iwasaka (Shinto) sacred stone circles

janam-sakhi (Sikhism) birth narrative; a hagiographical biography

jashan (Zoroastrianism) festival

jati (Hinduism) birth group

jihad (Islam) strive, struggle; a holy war

Jina (Jainism) victor or conqueror; periodic founder or reviver of the Jain religion; also called a Tirthankara (ford or bridge builder)

jingzuo (Confucianism) "quiet sitting"; meditation

jiva (Jainism) soul; every soul is endowed with perfect energy, perfect bliss, perfect perception, and perfect knowledge

jizya (Islam) poll, or head, tax paid by Jews and Christians

juma (Islam) Friday congregational prayer

Jurchen (Taoism) Manchurian tribe; founders of the Chin dynasty (1115–1234)

Kaaba (Islam) sacred structure in Mecca; according to tradition, built by Abraham and Ismail

Kabbalah (Judaism) mystical reading of the Scriptures that arose in France and Spain during the twelfth century, culminating with the composition in the late thirteenth century of the *Zohar* ("Book of Splendor"), which, especially as interpreted by Isaac Luria (1534–72), exercised a decisive influence on late medieval and early modern Jewish spiritual life

kagura (Shinto) Shinto ritual dances

Kaguru (African Traditional Religions) an ethnic group in Tanzania

kami (Shinto) Shinto deity or deities

kannushi (Shinto) lower-ranking Shinto priest

karah prashad (Sikhism) sanctified food, prepared in a large iron dish, or *karahi*

karma (Buddhism) law of cause and effect; act; deed

karma (Hinduism) literally "action"; the system of rewards and punishments attached to various actions

karma (Jainism) microscopic particles that float in the universe, stick to souls according the quality of their actions, and manifest a like result before becoming detached from them

karma (Sikhism) influence of a person's past actions on his future lives

kasruth (Judaism) rules and regulations for food and its preparation, often known by the Yiddish "kosher"

katha (Sikhism) a discourse on scripture in a *gurdwara;* homily

Kaur (Sikhism) female surname meaning Princess

kegare (Shinto) bodily or spiritual pollution

Khalsa (Sikhism) order of "pure" Sikhs, established by Guru Gobind Singh in 1699

ki (Shinto) vital spirit or energy

kirpan (Sikhism) sword

kirtan (Sikhism) devotional singing

Kojiki (Shinto) eighth-century Japanese mythological text

kokoro (Shinto) heart-mind

kokugaku (Shinto) Japanese nativist school of scholarship

Koran (Quran) (Islam) revelation; Muslim scripture

Krishna (Hinduism) a manifestation of the supreme being; one of the most popular Hindu deities, he is considered by many Hindus to be an incarnation of the god Vishnu

kuan (Taoism) Taoist abbeys or temples

kundalini (Hinduism) the power that is said to lie dormant at the base of a person's spine and that can be awakened in the search for enlightenment

kusti (Zoroastrianism) sacred cord worn around the torso by Zoroastrians and tied and untied during prayer

Lakshmi (Hinduism) a goddess; wife of the god Vishnu

langar (Sikhism) community dining

Lao-tzu (Taoism) the supposed author of the *Tao te ching;* also another name for the *Tao te ching*

Legalism (Taoism) Chinese school of philosophy that advocated a system of government based on a strict code of laws; prominent in the fifth through third centuries B.C.E.

Lent (Christianity) period of 40 days from Ash Wednesday to Easter, often marked by fasting and prayer

li (Confucianism) cosmic ordering principle

li (Confucianism) norms for the interaction of humans with each other and with higher forces (a different Chinese character from the other *li,* meaning "principle," above)

liangzhi (Confucianism) innate moral knowledge

libationers (Taoism) *chi-chiu;* men and women officiants in the early "Celestial Masters" organization

lien-shih (Taoism) refined master or mistress; an honorific term that was the highest Taoist title in T'ang times

Ling-pao (Taoism) "Numinous Treasure"; a set of Taoist revelations produced in the fourth century C.E.

Lixue (Confucianism) "study of principle"; Neo-Confucian philosophical movement

Lupupa (African Traditional Religions) a subgroup of the Basongye, an ethnic group of Democratic Republic of the Congo (Kinshasa)

madrasah (Islam) Islamic religious school

Magi (Zoroastrianism) priestly group that was initially active in western Iran under the Medes

Mahabharata (Hinduism) "Great Epic of India" or the "Great Sons of Bharata"; one of the two Hindu epics

Mahavira Jayanti (Jainism) celebration of the birth of Lord Mahavira, the 24th and last Jina of the current period, by Shvetambaras and Digambaras in March–April

Mahayana (sometimes called Northern Buddhism) (Buddhism) one of two major schools of Buddhism practiced mainly in China, Japan, Korea, and Tibet; evolved from the Mahasanghika (Great Assembly)

Man'yōshū (Shinto) eighth-century Japanese poetry anthology

mandala (Hinduism) a geometric design that represents sacredness, divine beings, or sacred knowledge or experience in an abstract form

manifestation of God (Bahá'í) an individual recognized in Bahá'í authoritative writings as a source of divine revelation and usually as the founder of a religion

mantra (Hinduism) a phrase or string of words, with or without meaning, recited repeatedly during meditation

Manyika (African Traditional Religions) an ethnic group of the southern African countries of Zimbabwe and Mozambique

marebito (Shinto) wandering spirits of the dead

Masai (African Traditional Religions) a nomadic people who inhabit Tanzania and Kenya

masjid (Islam) place for ritual prostration; mosque

matrimony (Christianity) sacrament; the joining of a man and woman in marriage

matsuri (Shinto) Shinto festivals

meng-wei (Taoism) covenant

Messiah (Christianity) the "anointed one," Jesus

Midrash (Judaism) commentary on the Scriptures, both Halakhic (legal) and Aggadic (narrative), originally in the form of sermons or lectures

mihrab (Islam) niche in mosque indicating the direction of Mecca

miko (Shinto) female medium or shaman

millet (Islam) protected religious community

minbar (Islam) raised platform in mosque; pulpit

ming (Taoism) destiny; the realities of a person's external life

Ming dynasty (Taoism) dynasty that ruled China from 1368 to 1644

Mishnah (Judaism) collection of the Oral Torah, or commentary on the Torah, first compiled in the second and third centuries C.E.

moksha (Hinduism) liberation from the cycle of birth and death

moksha (Jainism) nirvana; enlightenment achieved when practitioners purify themselves of all karma so that they will not be reborn

Mongols (Taoism) originally nomadic people who established the Yüan dynasty in China in the thirteenth century

muhapatti (Jainism) mouth guard worn by some renouncers to avoid harming insects and air beings

muni (Jainism) a Digambara monk who wears no clothing

Murtipujak (Jainism) a Shvetambara subsect that worships by means of images

Mwari (African Traditional Religions) a creator god worshiped in the southern African countries of Zimbabwe and Botswana

nam (Sikhism) the divine name

Namaskar Mantra (Jainism) the preeminent mantra that all Jains know and recite

negi (Shinto) senior Shinto priest

neisheng waiwang (Confucianism) "sage within and king without"; phrase used to describe one who is both a spiritual seeker and a social leader

nei-tan (Taoism) "Inner Alchemy"; the practice of spiritual refinement through meditation

Nei-yeh (Taoism) "Inner Cultivation"; an early Taoist text, likely a prototype for the well-known text *Tao te ching*

Neo-Confucianism (Taoism) Confucian teachings that were turned into a sociopolitical orthodoxy in China in the twelfth century

nigoda (Jainism) microscopic being

Nihon shoki (Shinto) eighth-century chronicle of Japanese history

Nineteen Day Feast (Bahá'í) a special meeting of the Bahá'í community held once every Bahá'í month, with devotional, business, and social portions

nirvana (Buddhism) the absolute elimination of karma; the absence of all states (the Sanskrit word literally means "to blow out, to extinguish")

norito (Shinto) Shinto liturgical prayers

Northern Sung dynasty (Taoism) dynasty that ruled China until 1126; part of the Sung dynasty

"Northern Taoism" (Taoism) modern term for Taoist traditions (Ch'üan-chen and Lung-men) that stress self-cultivation

odu (African Traditional Religions) poetic oral narratives memorized by *Ifa* diviners and recited during divination

Olódùmarè (African Traditional Religions) the Supreme Being in the religion of the Yoruba people

oni (Shinto) demon

opele (African Traditional Religions) a divining chain used in *Ifa* divination

ordination (Christianity) sacrament, in which a person is invested with religious authority or takes holy orders

orisa (African Traditional Religions) in the Yoruba religious tradition, the pantheon of deities

Orthodox Judaism (Judaism) traditional Judaism, characterized by strict observance of laws and rituals (the Halakhah)

Orthodoxy (Christianity) one of the main branches of Christianity, with a lineage that derives from the first-century apostolic churches; historically centered in Constantinople (Istanbul), it includes a number of autonomous national churches

Pahlavi (Zoroastrianism) middle Persian language of the Sasanian period; also the name of an Iranian dynasty (twentieth century)

pancha sila (Buddhism) five ethical precepts; the basic ethical guidelines for the layperson

panth (Sikhism) path

parahom (Zoroastrianism) sacred drink prepared during the *yasna*; a mixture of *haoma* and milk

Parsi (Zoroastrianism) member of a Zoroastrian group living mainly in western India and centered around Mumbai (Bombay)

Parvati (Hinduism) a goddess; the wife of the god Shiva

Paryushan (Jainism) yearly Shvetambara festival during which the Kalpa Sutra is read and that ends in atonement

Passover (Pesach) (Judaism) festival marking the deliverance of the Israelites from Egyptian bondage

pati (Sikhism) the core of a person, including self-respect

Pentecost (Christianity) seventh Sunday after Easter, commemorating the descent of the Holy Spirit on the apostles

Pentecostalism (Christianity) movement that emphasizes grace, expressive worship, evangelism, and spiritual gifts such as speaking in tongues and healing

People of the Book (Islam) Jews and Christians, who Muslims believe received divine revelations in the Torah and Gospels, respectively

Petrine primacy (Christianity) view that, as the successor to Peter, the bishop of Rome (pope) is supreme

prajna (Buddhism) wisdom

presbyterianism (Christianity) governance by a presbytery, an assembly of local clergy and lay representatives

Prophets (Nevi'im) (Judaism) second of the three parts of the Tanakh, made up of the books of 7 major and 12 minor prophets

Protestantism (Christianity) one of the main branches of Christianity, originating in the sixteenth-century

Reformation; rejecting the authority of the pope, it emphasized the role of grace and the authority of the Scriptures

puja (Jainism) rite of worship

puja (Buddhism) honor; worship

puja (Hinduism) religious rituals performed in the home

Purana (Hinduism) "Ancient Lore"; any of a set of sacred texts known as the old narratives

Purvas (Jainism) oldest scriptures of Jainism, now lost

qadimi (Zoroastrianism) "old" Zoroastrian calendar, which has New Year's Day in late July; compare with *fasli*

qi (Confucianism) matter-energy; life force pervading the cosmos

qiblih (Bahá'í) "point of adoration"; the location toward which Bahá'ís face when saying their obligatory prayer

rahit (Sikhism) code

Ramayana (Hinduism) "Story of Rama"; one of the two Hindu epics

raspi (Zoroastrianism) assistant priest, who feeds the fire during the *yasna*

reconciliation (Christianity) sacrament; the confession of and absolution from sin

Reconstructionist Judaism (Judaism) movement founded in the United States in the early twentieth century by Mordecai M. Kaplan (1881–1983) that holds Judaism to be not only a religion but also a dynamic "civilization" embracing art, music, literature, culture, and folkways

Reform Judaism (Judaism) movement originating in early nineteenth-century Germany that adapted the rituals and liturgy of Judaism to accommodate modern social, political, and cultural developments; sometimes called Liberal Judaism

ren (Confucianism) humaneness; benevolence

renyu (Confucianism) human desires

renzheng (Confucianism) humane government

riba (Islam) usury

Roman Catholicism (Christianity) one of the main branches of Christianity, tracing its origins to the apostle Peter; centered in Rome, it tends to be uniform in organization, doctrines, and rituals

Rosh Hashanah (Judaism) Jewish New Year; also known as the Day of Judgment, it is a time of penitence

sacrament (Christianity) any rite thought to have originated with or to have been sanctioned by Jesus as a sign of grace

sacramental (Christianity) devotional action or object

sadaqah (Islam) almsgiving for the poor, for thanksgiving, or to ward off danger

sadre (Zoroastrianism) sacred shirt; a thin, white, cotton garment worn that is worn under clothes and should never be removed

salat (Islam) prayer or worship; second pillar

sallekhana (Jainism) ritual fasting until death

salvation (Christianity) deliverance from sin and its consequences

samadhi (Hinduism) the final state of absorption into, and union with, the divine

samsara (Buddhism) the cyclical nature of the cosmos; rebirth

samsara (Hinduism) continuing rebirths; the cycle of life and death

samsara (Jainism) the cycle of reincarnation

samudaya (Buddhism) arising (of suffering); the second noble Truth

sanatana dharma (Hinduism) "eternal dharma"; in the *Dharma Sastra*s, virtues common to all human beings; also, a word used to denote Hinduism in general after the nineteenth century

sangat (Sikhism) holy fellowship; a congregation

sangha (Buddhism) community of monks

Sanhedrin (Judaism) supreme religious body of ancient Judaism, disbanded by the Romans early in the fifth century C.E.

sansar (Sikhism) rebirth; transmigration

Sanskrit (Hinduism) a classical language and part of the Indo-European language family; the language of ancient India

Sasanian dynasty (Zoroastrianism) dynasty that ruled Iran from 224 to 651 C.E.

sati (Jainism) virtuous woman; a chaste wife or a nun

Sephardim (Judaism) Jews of Spain and Portugal and their descendants, most of whom, in the wake of expulsion in 1492, settled in the Ottoman Empire and in North Africa; in the early seventeenth century small groups of descendants of Jews who had remained on the Iberian Penin

shabad (Sikhism) the divine word

Shabuoth (Feast of Weeks) (Judaism) originally a harvest festival, now observed in commemoration of the giving of the Torah to the Israelites

shahadah (Islam) declaration of faith; first pillar

shakti (Hinduism) energy or power, frequently used for the power of the Goddess; also a name for a manifestation of the Goddess

shan (Taoism) goodness

Shang-ch'ing (Taoism) "Supreme Clarity"; a tradition involving visualization meditation

Shariah (Islam) Islamic law

shen (Taoism) spirit; spiritual consciousness

shen-hsien (Taoism) spiritual transcendence

Shiite (Islam) member of second-largest Muslim sect, believing in the hereditary succession of Ali, the cousin and son-in-law of Muhammad, to lead the community

shinjin goitsu (Shinto) the essential identity of *kami* and humans

shintai (Shinto) the "body" of a *kami*, the object into which it descends following a ritual summons

Shiva (Hinduism) "the auspicious one"; a term for the supreme being; one of the most important deities in the Hindu tradition

shramana (Buddhism) wanderer

Shvetambara (Jainism) wearing white; sect of Jainism, largely based in northwestern India, in which monks and nuns wear white clothing

sikh (Sikhism) learner

Sikh Panth (Sikhism) the Sikh community

Sikh Rahit Maryada (Sikhism) Sikh Code of Conduct

sila (Buddhism) ethics; morality

Singh (Sikhism) male surname meaning Lion

smriti (Hinduism) "remembered"; a set of sacred compositions that includes the two epics, the *Puranas*, and the *Dharma Sastra*s

"Southern Taoism" (Taoism) modern term for the Chengi Taoist tradition that survives mainly in Taiwan and along China's southeast coast; it stresses public liturgies such as *chiao* rather than self-cultivation

Spenta Mainyu (Zoroastrianism) primordial good spirit, twin of Angra Mainyu

sruti (Hinduism) "that which is heard"; a set of sacred compositions more popularly known as the Vedas

Sthanakwasi (Jainism) Shvetambara aniconic subsect

Sufi (Islam) mystic

Sung dynasty (Taoism) dynasty that ruled China from 960 to 1279

sunnah (Islam) example of Muhammad

Sunni (Islam) member of largest Muslim sect, holding that the successor (caliph) to Muhammad as leader of the community should be elected

surah (Islam) chapter of the Koran

svastika (Jainism) well-being; symbol representing the four realms into which souls are reincarnated, the three jewels, the abode of enlightened beings, and the enlightened beings themselves

swami (Hinduism) "master"; a charismatic teacher

T'ai-ch'ing (Taoism) "Great Clarity"; a tradition involving ritual alchemy

t'ai-p'ing (Taoism) grand tranquillity; a classical Chinese term for peace and harmony throughout the world; the most common Taoist political ideal

T'ai-p'ing ching (Taoism) "Scripture of Grand Tranquillity," an important early Taoist text

T'ang dynasty (Taoism) dynasty that ruled China from 618 to 907 C.E.

t'ien-shih (Taoism) celestial master; historical title for certain eminent Taoists, especially figures related to Chang Tao-ling

Talmud (Judaism) also known as the Gemara, a running commentary on the Mishnah written by rabbis (called *amoraim*, or "explainers") from the third to the fifth centuries C.E. in Palestine and Babylonia; the

Tamil (Hinduism) a classical language of southern India that is still spoken

Tanakh (Judaism) anagram for Jewish Scriptures, comprising the Torah, Prophets, and Writings

Tantra (Hinduism) literally "loom" or "to stretch"; generic name given to varied philosophies and rituals that frequently involve mantras, meditation on mandalas, or forms of yoga, leading to a liberating knowledge and experience

Tao (Taoism) classical Chinese term for any school's ideals and practices; among Taoists a term generally used to suggest the highest dimensions of reality, which can be attained by practitioners of traditional spiritual practices

tao (also dao) (Confucianism) "the way"; the Confucian life path

Tao te ching (Taoism) classical Taoist text; also known as the *Lao-tzu*

Tao-chiao (Taoism) the teachings of the Tao; the Taoist's name for their religion

Taoism (Taoism) *Tao-chiao;* a Chinese religious tradition that emphasizes personal transformation and integration with the unseen forces of the universe

tao-shih (Taoism) Taoist priest or priestess; a person recognized by the Taoist community as having mastered a specific body of sacred knowledge and the proper skills and dedication necessary to put that knowledge into effect for the sake of the community

Tao-tsang (Taoism) today's library of Taoist literature

tap (tapas, tapasya) (Jainism) austerities performed to purify the soul of karma

tattva (Jainism) any of the nine realities that characterize the universe and that include souls (*jivas*), matter (*ajiva*), matter coming in contact with souls (*ashrava*), the binding of karma and the soul (*bandha*), beneficial karma (*punya*), harmful karma (*papa*), inhibiting the influx of karma (*samvara*), purifying the soul of karma (*nirjara*), and liberation (*moksha,* or *nirvana*)

Tattvartha Sutra (Jainism) the only Jain scripture shared by both Shvetambaras and Digambaras, composed by Umasvati in c. 300 C.E.

tawhid (Islam) oneness, or unity, of God; monotheism

Terapanthi (Jainism) Shvetambara aniconic subsect that has only one *acharya*

Theravada (sometimes called Southern Buddhism) (Buddhism) one of two major schools of Buddhism practiced mainly in Cambodia, Laos, Myanmar [Burma], Sri Lanka, and Thailand; evolved from the Sthavira (Elders)

Three Bonds (Confucianism) obedience of subject to ruler, child to parent, and wife to husband

three jewels (Jainism) right faith, right understanding, and right conduct

Three Refuges, or Triple Gem (Buddhism) the Buddha, the dharma, and the sangha; the taking of the Three Refuges is a basic rite of passage in Buddhism

Tian (Confucianism) "Heaven"; entity believed to represent cosmic and moral order

tianli (Confucianism) ultimate, Heaven-rooted cosmic ordering principle permeating all phenomena

tianming (Confucianism) Mandate of Heaven

Torah (Pentatuch or Law) (Judaism) first division of the Tanakh, constituting the five books of Moses

torii (Shinto) gate marking the entrance to the grounds of a Shinto shrine

Trinity (Christianity) God as consisting of three persons—the Father, Son, and Holy Spirit

tripitaka (Pali, tipitaka) (Buddhism) three baskets, or three sets; the Tripitaka (Pali, Tipitaka), a collection of the Buddha's teachings—the Vinaya (Discipline), the Dharma (Doctrine), and the Abhidharma (Pali, Abhidhamma; Advanced Doctrine—forms the basis of the Buddhist canon

ubasoku, or hijiri (Shinto) mountain ascetics and holy men

ulama (Islam) religious leader or scholar

ummah (Islam) the transnational community of followers of Islam

Uniate (Christianity) any group observing Eastern rites but recognizing the authority of the pope

Universal House of Justice (Bahá'í) the supreme governing body of the worldwide Bahá'í community

upadesa (Hinduism) the sacred teaching

Upanishad (Hinduism) any of the Hindu sacred texts composed in about the sixth century B.C.E.; generally considered to be the "last" and philosophically the most important part of the Vedas

upaya (Buddhism) the concept of skillful means

Vaishnava (Hinduism) a member of a group of people devoted to Vishnu; also used to describe an object or an institution devoted to Vishnu

Vajrayana, or Tantra (Buddhism) a school of Mahayana Buddhism

vak (Sikhism) divine command

varna (Hinduism) literally "color"; the social class into which a person is born

varna-ashrama dharma (Hinduism) the behavior recommended for each class and each stage of life

Veda (Hinduism) literally "knowledge"; any of a set of compositions dating from the second millennium B.C.E. that is the highest scriptural authority for many educated Hindus

Vedanta (Hinduism) a philosophical school within Hinduism

Vishnu (Hinduism) literally "all-pervasive"; a term for the supreme being; one of the most important deities in the Hindu tradition; his incarnations include Rama and Krishna

wai-tan (Taoism) alchemy; a process of self-perfection involving the preparation of spiritualized substances called *tan* (elixirs)

wali (Islam) friend of God; Sufi saint

Wheel of the Dharma (Buddhism) visual symbol representing the Buddha's preaching his first sermon and also, with its eight spokes, Buddhism's Eightfold Path Yogacara, or Consciousness-Only school of Buddhism

Writings (Ketuvim or Hagiographa) (Judaism) third division of the Tanakh, including the Psalms and other works said to have be written under holy guidance

wu-wei (Taoism) nonaction; in the *Tao te ching*, a behavioral ideal of trusting the world's natural processes instead of one's own activity

wudu (Islam) ablution before worship

xin (Confucianism) heart-mind; human organ of moral evaluation

xing (Confucianism) inner human nature

Xinxue (Confucianism) "study of mind"; Neo-Confucian philosophical movement

ya Baha ul-abha (Bahá'í) "O Glory of the Most Glorious"; a form of the greatest name of God

Yasht (Zoroastrianism) one of a group of hymns to Iranian deities

yasna (Zoroastrianism) main Zoroastrian ritual; also the name of the main liturgical text, which is recited during the ritual

yazata (Zoroastrianism) any of a number of Zoroastrian divinities, the two most important of which are Mithra and the river goddess Anahita

yi (Confucianism) rightness; to act justly

yoga (Hinduism) physical and mental discipline by which one "yokes" one's spirit to a god; more generally, any path that leads to final emancipation

Yom Kippur (Day of Atonement) (Judaism) end of 10 days of penitence that begin with Rosh Hashana; the most holy of Jewish days

Yoruba (African Traditional Religions) an ethnic group residing in Nigeria and parts of Benin and Togo

yuga (Hinduism) in Hindu cosmology, any of four ages into which each cycle of time is divided

yuitsu genpon sōgen shintō (Shinto) "unique original essence Shinto"

zakat (Islam) purification; tithe or almsgiving; third pillar

zaotar (Zoroastrianism) priest

Zardushti (Zoroastrianism) name for the Zoroastrian tradition in Iran

Zoroaster (Zoroastrianism) founder of the Zoroastrian tradition; his Iranian name is Zarathustra

Zoroastrianism (Zoroastrianism) religion of pre-Islamic Iran; now represented by two communities, Parsi (Indian) and Zardushti (Iranian)

zot (Zoroastrianism) chief priest who performs the *yasna*

Zulu (African Traditional Religions) a large ethnic group in South Africa

African Traditional Religions

FOUNDED: 200,000–100,000 B.C.E.

RELIGION AS A PERCENTAGE OF WORLD POPULATION: 1.3 percent

OVERVIEW Africa, the place of origin of all humankind, is divided into numerous political and cultural regions, reflecting its diverse range of histories, ethnicities, languages, beliefs, attitudes, and behaviors. Its various indigenous spiritual systems, usually called African traditional religions, are many. Every ethnic group in Africa has developed a complex and distinctive set of religious beliefs and practices. Despite their seemingly unrelated aspects, there are common features to these systems, suggesting that African traditional faiths form a cohesive religious tradition.

Africans are a deeply spiritual people. Their traditional religions, however, are perhaps the least understood facet of African life. Although historically non-Africans have emphasized the multiple deities and ancestral spirits in African traditional religions, there are other notable features. For example, African cosmogony posits the existence of a Supreme Being who created the universe and everything in it. African myths frequently describe numerous lesser deities who assist the Supreme Being while performing diverse functions in the created world. Spirits may be divided into human spirits and nature spirits. Each has a life force devoid of physical form. Individuals who have died, usually ancestors in particular lineages, are the human spirits. These spirits play a role in community affairs and ensure a link between each clan and the spirit world. Natural objects, such as rivers, mountains, trees, and the Sun (as well as forces such as wind and rain), represent the nature spirits. Africans integrate this religious worldview into every aspect of life.

Although a large proportion of Africans have converted to Islam and Christianity, these two world religions have been assimilated into African culture, and many African Christians and Muslims maintain traditional spiritual beliefs. Furthermore, African cultural practices contain elements of indigenous religion. Thus, traditional African cosmologies and beliefs continue to exert significant influence on Africans today.

HISTORY African indigenous religions are timeless, beginning with the origin of human civilization on the continent, perhaps as early as 200,000 B.C.E., when the species *Homo sapiens* is believed to have emerged. Because they date back to prehistoric times, little has been written about their history. These religions have evolved and spread slowly for millennia; stories about gods, spirits, and ancestors have passed from one generation to another in oral mythology. Practitioners of traditional religions understand the founders of their religions to be God or the gods themselves, the same beings who created the universe and everything in it. Thus, religious founders are described in creation stories.

For indigenous African peoples "history" often refers to accounts of events as narrated in stories, myths, legends, and songs. Myth and oral history are integral elements of their culture. Such history, however, can be difficult to cross-reference with historical world events. Nevertheless, the truths and myths conveyed through an

GYE NYAME. This Ghanaian Adinkra symbol means "except for God" and symbolizes the supremacy of God. The symbol can be found throughout Ghana. It is the most popular for decoration and can often be seen printed on cloth or stamped on pottery. (THOMSON GALE)

oral culture may be as authentic as those communicated through the written word. Evidence such as archaeological finds, carbon dating, and DNA has corroborated certain elements contained in African myths, legends, and narratives.

Over the years African traditional religions have increased and diminished in regional importance according to social and political changes. One of the biggest influences on African traditional religions has been outside cultures. In particular, both Islam and Christianity have affected the practice of African traditional religions. Christianity, the first world religion to appear on the continent, was taken there in about the first century C.E., spreading across North Africa. It was overtaken in the region by Islam in the seventh century—frequently by military incursion, commercial trading, and the nonviolent missionary efforts of merchants. Persian and Arab merchants introduced Islam in East Africa by trading in coastal towns up and down the eastern seaboard. Islam was readily adapted in many instances because of its compatibility, or at least tolerance of, traditional African religions. By the 1700s Islam had diversified and grown popular.

In the fifteenth century Christian missionaries became the first wave of Europeans to invade and occupy African lands. They relied on the backing of European medicinal remedies and colonial military power. By using local languages and converting Africans from their ancestral religions to Christianity, missionaries paved the way for early modernization and Western colonialism. Western colonialists negotiated and drafted treaties with African leaders, stripping Africans of their lands, depopulating the countryside, destabilizing their economies, overturning political rule, and uprooting cultural and lineage continuity. By the 1900s Christianity was firmly entrenched in most of Africa.

Today Muslims worship throughout much of Africa. The success of Islam is partially a result of its continued toleration of traditional beliefs and practices—or at least its allowance of indigenous beliefs to adapt to a form compatible with Islam. At the end of the twentieth century, Islam spread into areas such as Rwanda, where the trauma of civil war, ethnic violence, and genocide implicated Christianity and left Islam with a reputation for being on a higher moral level. On the other hand, in predominantly Muslim states such as the Sudan, Islamic fundamentalists and pro-Arab Sudanese have been implicated in the oppression and slavery of millions of Sudanese Christians and ethnic minorities.

The rapid spread of Pentecostal Christianity and fundamentalist Islam has greatly affected the role of indigenous religion in African society. African traditional religions have creatively responded to this religious onslaught by formulating new ways of survival, such as developing literature, institutionalizing the traditions, establishing associations of priests, and creating schools for the training of its priests. Moreover, they have also extended outward and influenced global culture, especially in African diaspora communities. From the 1500s to the 1900s the transatlantic slave trade took African religions to the Americas and the Caribbean. Contact with Catholicism in Brazil, Cuba, and Haiti produced new forms of religious syncretism called Candomblé, Santeria, and Vodun. Since the 1980s the religions of African immigrants have influenced American culture. A new wave of conversion to indigenous African traditions has been noticeable in the United States, especially among African Americans. New forms of Yoruba religion have been emerging that are quite different from the Yoruba *orisa* traditions in Nigeria. These forms have introduced African healing practices among the black population of the United States. There are a number of West African *babalawo*s (diviners) of African origin practicing in major American urban centers, such as Atlanta, Miami, and New York City.

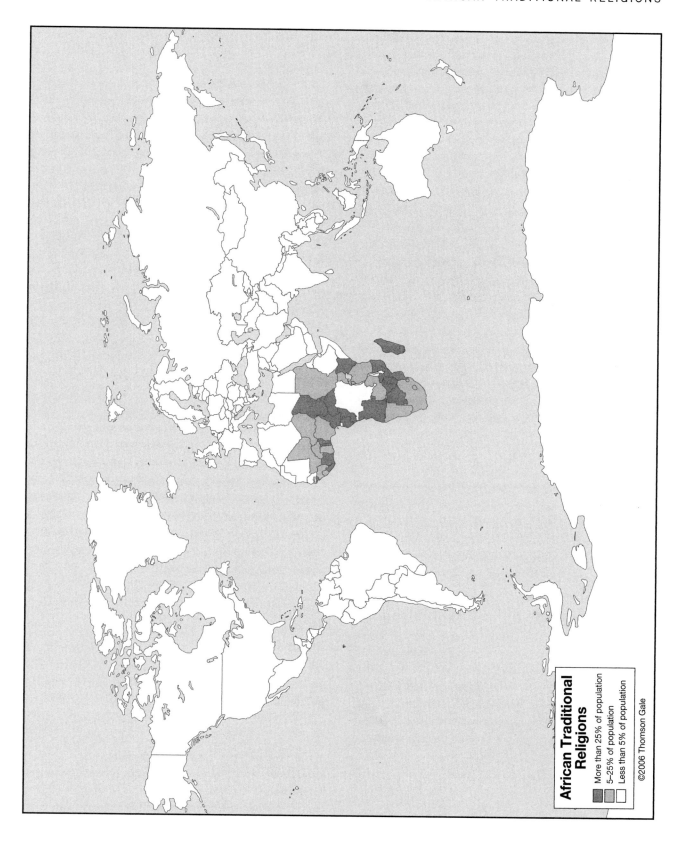

African Traditional Religions

More than 25% of population

5–25% of population

Less than 5% of population

©2006 Thomson Gale

A male fetishist carrying gear on his back at a Vodun ritual in Benin in western Africa. © DANIEL LAINÉ/CORBIS.

The interaction between Western and traditional African religious traditions has influenced religious innovations in Africa, such as African Initiated Churches and Islamic mystical traditions (Sufism). As a result, Islam and Christianity have become Africanized on the continent, significantly changing the practice of the two traditions and leading to a distinct African expression of them.

CENTRAL DOCTRINES Unlike other world faiths, African traditional religions have no predominant doctrinal teachings. Rather, they have certain vital elements that function as core beliefs. Among these beliefs are origin myths, the presence of deities, ancestor veneration, and divination. African cosmology (explanation of the nature of the universe) tends to assert that there is a Supreme God who is helped by a number of lesser deities. Spirits are the connection between the living and the invisible worlds. Anyone can communicate with the spirits, but priests, priestesses, prophets, and diviners have more direct access to invisible arenas of the world.

In African traditional religions the sense of time is often described in cyclical rather than linear imagery. In

the cosmology of the Dagara (an ethnic group in the Niger region of West Africa), for instance, the wheel or circle represents the cyclical nature of life as well as of the Earth. The wheel contains everything found on Earth. According to the Yoruba (an ethnic group from Nigeria), the life force that pervades all phenomena exists in an eternal cycle of complex interactions between cosmic domains; these interactions should always remain in balance. In African traditional religions the cosmogony (theory of the origin of the universe) usually describes humans appearing near the end of creation. In many creation stories God is likened to a potter who creates humans out of clay and then pours the breath of life into them.

African religions rely on the memory of oral stories. Thus, doctrine tends to be more flexible than it is in text-based religions, and it changes according to the immediate needs of religious followers. African traditional religions are a communal endeavor, and it is not required that an individual believe in every element. As in any democratic system, individuals may participate in ways that benefit their interests, their community roles, or their status as religious leaders. Because religion per-

A group of Vodun initiates perform a ceremony with a doll inside a kapame, *a secret ritual enclosure, near Lome, Togo.* © CAROLINE PENN/CORBIS.

meates all aspects of a traditional African culture, if an individual rejects the culture's religion, he or she may become isolated from family, friends, and the community.

Narratives about the creation of the universe (cosmogony) and the nature and structure of the world (cosmology) form the core philosophy of African religions. These narratives are conveyed in a linguistic form that scholars often refer to as myth. The term "myth" in African religions means sacred stories that are believed to be true by those who hold to them. To the African people who espouse them, myths reveal significant events and episodes of the most profound and transcendent meaning. They are not fixed, because accounts may vary from generation to generation or even among individuals who tell these stories. Myths do, however, retain similar structures and purposes: to describe the way things were at the beginning of time and to explain the cosmic order. They generally involve superhuman entities, gods, demigods, spirits, and ancestors.

The notion that myth is nonrational and unscientific, while history is critical and rational, is not always accurate, nor does it represent the outlook of practitioners of traditional religions. Many African myths deal with events that devotees consider as authentic and "real" or as symbolic expressions of historical events. Furthermore, scholars today assert that the supposedly accurate records of missionaries, colonial administrators, and the indigenous elite were susceptible to distortion. The fact that myths have endured for generations gives them their authority. Each generation expresses and reinterprets the myths, making the events revealed in them relevant to contemporary conditions.

African cosmogonic narratives explain how the world was put into place by a divine personality, usually the Supreme God in collaboration with lesser supernatural beings who act on his behalf or aid in the creative process. In several cultures a supreme deity performs creation through mere thought processes. In other cases the Supreme Being instructs lesser deities on how to create by providing them with materials to undertake

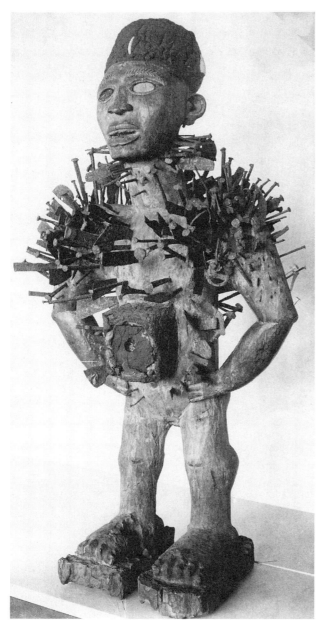

A fetish that the tribespeople of the Belgian Congo believe wards off illness.
© BETTMANN/CORBIS.

inhabited by animate beings. In African cosmological narratives creation is always portrayed as a complex process, whether the universe is said to have evolved from preexisting matter or from divine thought.

The Fon of Benin, in western Africa, and their neighbors, the Yoruba of Nigeria, share many elements of a highly intricate cosmology. They worship a number of the same deities—including Sango, god of thunder and lightning; Ògún, god of war and iron; Èsù, messenger of the gods; and Ifa, the god of divination. The names given to the specific deities in Benin may vary slightly from those of the Yoruba. There are similar motifs in the cosmological narratives of both cultures, though the Fon narratives are more complex than the Yoruba's.

In the Fon creation myth the Supreme Being, Mawu, is of indeterminate gender. Mawu is sometimes female and sometimes male. Mawu is often associated with a partner, Lisa. In one version of Fon cosmogony Nana Buluku, a creator god, gives birth to Mawu and Lisa. As a female, Mawu is associated with the Moon and has power over the nighttime and the western universe. Lisa, as the male, commands the Sun and occupies the eastern universe. These twin creators give birth to another set of twin deities, who in turn beget seven pairs of twin offspring. Therefore, twins are esteemed in Fon culture. Mawu-Lisa once gathered their children together to distribute what they owned among them. To the most senior set of twins Mawu-Lisa bestowed authority to rule the Earth. Another set, "Twins of Storm," retained authority to govern thunder and lightening. Representing iron and metal, the most powerful pair maintained jurisdiction over the manufacture of iron implements such as knives, hoes, arrows, and, beginning in the twentieth century, guns and automobiles. According the mythology, these twin gods took command of vital functions in developing the Fon economy: cultivating land for agriculture, building roads and paths, manufacturing tools, and improving weapons of war, farming, and hunting.

Mawu-Lisa positioned human beings in the region between the sky and the underworld, commanding humans to dwell there and to return to his own abode after a specified number of years. Mawu-Lisa also created spirits and deities, bestowing upon each a special "esoteric" ritual language through which they communicate among themselves. By ministering to deities and humans in liturgical worship, the clergy learn these rituals and languages. In this narrative Legba (messenger of the Su-

the process. For instance, the Yoruba believe that the Supreme Being, Olódùmarè, designated the *orisa* (deities) responsible for creating the universe. In the creation story of the Abaluhya of Kenya, the Supreme Being, called Wele Xakaba, created the universe in a manner that resembles the seven-day creation of the world by God in the Bible, with the seventh day being a time of rest. There are myths that say the world was created out of an existing abyss or a watery universe un-

Glossary

Abaluhya an ethnic group in Kenya

babalawo a divination specialist in Yoruba culture

Baganda the largest ethnic group in Uganda

Bambara an ethnic group in Mali

Bantu a large group of languages spoken in central, eastern, and southern Africa

Ba Kongo a group of Bantu-speaking peoples who largely reside in Congo (Brazzaville), Congo (Kinshasa), and Angola

Ba Thonga a group of Bantu-speaking peoples who live in the southern African countries of Mozambique, Zimbabwe, Swaziland, and South Africa

cosmogony a theory about the creation of the universe

cosmology an explanation of the nature of the universe

Dagara an ethnic group of the Niger region of western Africa

divination any of various methods of accessing sacred knowledge of the deities; it often involves interpreting signs

Edo an ethnic group of southern Nigeria

Fang an ethnic group of west-central Africa

Fon an ethnic group of Benin

Ifa a form of divination that originated in West Africa

Igbo an ethnic group of Nigeria

Kaguru an ethnic group in Tanzania

Lupupa a subgroup of the Basongye, an ethnic group of Congo (Kinshasa)

Manyika an ethnic group of the southern African countries of Zimbabwe and Mozambique

Masai a nomadic people who inhabit Tanzania and Kenya

Mwari a creator god worshiped in the southern African countries of Zimbabwe and Botswana

odu poetic oral narratives memorized by *Ifa* diviners and recited during divination

Olódùmarè the Supreme Being in the religion of the Yoruba people

opele a divining chain used in *Ifa* divination

orisa in the Yoruba religious tradition, the pantheon of deities

Yoruba an ethnic group residing in Nigeria and parts of Benin and Togo

Zulu a large ethnic group in South Africa

preme Being and other gods) gained knowledge of all sacred languages of the divinities, enabling himself to initiate communication among other deities.

That other West African cultures have similar creation myths and ensuing social traditions is evidence of influence between cultures. The Winye of Burkina Faso center their creation myth on female and male twins, whom the Supreme God sent as primordial parents to establish human life in the created world. Their rebellious behavior, however, caused dismay; they resorted to acts of sorcery and refused to submit to the natural succession of generations. The female twin held back her own offspring for a year; after she finally gave birth, the children—twins themselves—rebelled against their parents by establishing themselves as an autonomous pair.

Recognizing the superiority of their own children, the parents pledged to obey them, and they sacrificed a goat in acknowledgment. The story conveys the division and crisis between two generations; through sacrifice, order is restored. This myth acknowledges the importance of primordial beings and their innate procreative powers, which ultimately benefit civilization. Several other African cosmologies are also characterized by an emphasis on primordial disorder, conflict, or chaos. Though such disorder at first comprises "negative" forces, ultimately it becomes the source of a workable social universe.

In some traditional African cosmologies primordial divinities have a dispute in which subordinate gods must take sides. While the Supreme God serves as the adjudicator in such conflicts, one demigod eventually takes command over the others. Such myths of conflict often provide humanity with unwritten guidelines for establishing institutions of morality, ethics, and behavior.

Some African societies have creation myths that correlate with their social and political organization. An example is the northern Yatenga society (of western Africa). The Nioniosse "rose up" from the underworld, and the Foulse descended from the sky. The Nioniosse command the "cult of the earth" and other rites relating to fertility, and the Foulse command the reigning monarchy, personnel, chiefs, and kings. The two complementary realms represent the world's governance and agricultural life. This myth gives credence to the importance of the underworld as the sphere that nourishes human life. Unlike Western myth, which seems partial to the reign of sky beings and portrays heaven as the abode of the Supreme Being, many African cosmologies consider the sky and the earth as equally significant spheres through which the divine create an enchanted universe.

African cosmogonic myths, which explain the origins of the universe, contain a people's conception of superhuman beings—the Supreme Being, the divinities, the demigods, and the spirits that operate in the created world. The African pantheon of gods, goddesses, spirits, and other superhuman beings is difficult for outside observers to comprehend. Deities are varied in number and complex in character. In most places in the African world it is believed that the supernatural and the natural realms interact. The lives of gods and humans become entangled through daily experiences. The gods and goddesses often populate the expression of core community beliefs, and people make frequent and daily references to them. Deities inhabit a world primarily created for humans, and they exercise tremendous influence over day-to-day human affairs. Because the spirits inhabit the natural world, no practical distinction exists between the natural and the supernatural world.

The pantheon of deities is often given a collective name; for the Yoruba of Nigeria it is *orisa,* and for the Baganda of Uganda it is *balubaale.* The intricate myths and legends describing African deities provide ample evidence of their habits, functions, powers, activities, status, and influence. In several traditions myth portrays the divinities as anthropomorphic beings who share many characteristics with humans. They can speak, they are visible, and they endure punishments and rewards. Yet they are unlike humans in that they are immortal, superhuman, and transcendent.

The most significant superhuman being is the Supreme God, who represents universality and greatness. The myths of many African cultures describe the Supreme God's global significance and place him or her high above the other deities in the pantheon. At times supreme gods are understood to be females and males who complement each other as husband and wife or brother and sister, similar to Mawu-Lisa in the religion of the Fon of Benin. In some cultures the pair's kinship bond may signify the unity of divine energy.

Although the Supreme God is a creator god, the work of creating the universe, especially when such acts entail physical labor, is often delegated to subordinates who act according to the Supreme God's instructions. The Supreme God may also be seen as a divine principle embodying the idea of life abundance and the blessings of human procreation and agricultural fertility. In many myths the Supreme God, after creating the universe, withdraws to a comfortable distance and delegates the affairs of the universe to lesser divinities. Some African groups have cults dedicated to the Supreme Being, but in general the creator does not have a special cult of devotees. This is because he occupies the realm beyond the physical abode of humans and thus remains outside their immediate influence. In some southern African religious groups, however, the Supreme God is not considered to be remote. A classic example is the regional cult of Mwari (a creator god) in western Zimbabwe and eastern Botswana. Members of the Mwari cult engage primarily in rituals that are intended to influence the economy and maintain environmental balances.

Many Africans practice ancestor veneration. Ancestors are generally the deceased elders (of either gender) who have passed from the realm of the living to that of the superhuman. They retain membership in their family, community, clan, and kin groups. Beliefs and practices of ancestor worship vary according to the local culture and religious traditions. For example, for the Komo of Congo (Kinshasa) the ancestors play a role equally prominent to that of deities. They serve as guardians of the living, and they pass down the various Komo rituals. In some other groups notions of ancestors are more expansive and may include various categories of human spirits; in others ancestors include spirits of deceased children. For the Ba Thonga people of southern Africa, among whom the ancestral system is well developed, ideas and ritual practices relating to the cult of the dead are central aspects of community life.

Communities in the Congo, like many other African cultures, often view kinship, lineage, chieftaincy, and elderhood as factors that unite the ancestors with the living. For example, in the Ba Kongo (a group of peoples who live in the Congo and Angola) and Kaguru (an ethnic group of Tanzania) societies, the elders are closest to the ancestors, and they wield much influence on how to consult and propitiate them. The elders determine what displeases the ancestors, whom to blame for the ancestors' displeasure with the living, and who will interpret the ancestors' will. Ancestors maintain a strong moral authority over the living; the elders speak for the ancestors when they intervene in and resolve conflicts. Ancestral propitiation takes many forms in Kaguru society, including cleaning the graves of the deceased, pouring libations of beer, and making offerings of flour or tobacco. Crises call for more elaborate sacrifices, such as the slaughter of chickens, goats, and sheep. In many instances the Kaguru ancestors are approached communally.

Traditional African cultures have various standards and restrictions for attaining ancestral status and spirituality, and at times even a child may become an ancestor. There is no standard or widespread characteristic of ancestorhood, but the criteria used throughout Africa share similarities. For instance, ancestors often attain their status after they have received proper burial rituals. Gender is a major factor in many traditional ancestral cultures; males rather than females have tended to benefit from ancestral ideology. The Manyika of Zimbabwe bestow ancestor status only on males, and the status is not necessarily associated with fatherhood; a childless Manyika adult male who dies may become an ancestor if a nephew includes him in his own ancestor cult. The matrilineal agricultural people of central Zambia require that males offer sacrifices to the ancestors on the right side of a doorway, while females offer sacrifices on the left. Certain sacred children may also become ancestors. The Sukuma and Nyamwezi people of Tanzania believe that twins are ancestors because multiple births indicate an excess of fertility. Women retain exclusive rights to direct any rituals related to twin ancestors, perhaps because they are responsible for their physical birth.

In the African cosmological vision death does not cease or annihilate human life—it is merely the inevitable transition to the next stage of life. It initiates the process of attaining ancestorhood. Proper burial rites and ceremonies ensure a peaceful passage. For the Bambara of Mali a death causes great anxiety, confusion, and unpredictability. It is thought that the fortune of the deceased and that of their descendants become equally volatile and that the community is thus temporarily endangered. The Bambara fear that the death of a lineage head may disturb the entire lineage. The Yoruba believe that the death of an elder who has worked diligently to provide unity and strength in the lineage causes the entire household to become empty and devoid of cohesion.

In most African communities a deceased person must be properly buried to become an ancestor. Proper burial entails a performance of elaborate funeral ceremonies by all members of the deceased's descendants. In addition, the deceased must have died a good death; Africans regard premature death that results from an accident or a "shameful disease" (such as smallpox, leprosy, and AIDS) to be a dreadful death. Most significantly, the deceased must have lived to an old age, meaning that they will have possessed wisdom and experience. When an elderly person dies, Africans traditionally avoid using the word "death." The Yoruba, for example, refer to a traumatic event or death circuitously by using metaphors such as "the elephant has fallen" (erin wo) or "the tiger is gone" (ekun lo). In avoiding the word "death," people uphold the belief that an individual is greater than death itself.

The African understanding of immortality is tied to remembrance after death. Thus, to have many children who can preserve one's memory is to secure one's immortality. Among some peoples of East Africa it is thought that a person dies only if he or she has no one to remember him or her.

In African traditional religions it is believed that ancestors sometimes experience what is generally referred to as reincarnation. The ancestors are responsible for perpetuating their lineage, not only by making possible the procreation of the living members of the lineage but also through rebirth. The Yoruba hold that children born soon after the death of grandparents or parents are reincarnated (if they are of the same sex as the deceased). For instance, a girl born after the death of a grandmother or mother is called Yetunde or Iyabo ("mother has returned"), and a boy born after the death of a grandfather or father is called Babatunde ("father has returned"). The Yoruba purport that such children normally show the traits and characteristics of the deceased. While the Kaguru have no such generic naming system, their naming patterns are closely associated with ancestral veneration. Newborns are said to come from the place of the ancestors, not necessarily in actual physical rebirth but in terms of the particular qualities of the deceased. Through divination every Kaguru infant is given the name of the closest ancestor in time.

There is an apparent contradiction in the simultaneous belief in ancestor veneration and reincarnation. How can the ancestors live in the underworld and at the same time return to their lineage to live again? The religion of the Lupupan people of Congo (Kinshasa) illustrates how this belief is sustained in most African communities. The Lupupans believe that the body (*mbidi*) houses the spirit (*kikudi*) and that when death occurs, the spirit leaves for *elungu*, a special land that the ancestors inhabit. Wild pigs protect and guide *elungu* and run errands for the ancestors. If the living maintain a cordial relationship with the ancestors, one of the spirits returns to be reborn into the lineage. In principle, an individual's spirit can reside on Earth in another body three times, after which the cycle is complete; that individual may appear a fourth time as a fierce totemic animal, perhaps a leopard. Rebirth of the deceased spirit occurs through a grandchild (not a child, because the spirit must skip a generation). Thus, newborn grandsons take the name of their deceased grandfathers. Western notions of the afterlife came to the Lupupans in the nineteenth century with the arrival of Christianity. The Lupupans incorporated Christian ideas into their systems. While other traditional African societies may possess fewer elaborate details of reincarnation, several of them hold the view that ancestors are born into their lineage.

Another essential aspect of African traditional religion is divination, which devotees use to access the sacred knowledge of the deities and the cosmos. The process of divination allows the deities' feelings and messages to be revealed to humans. Individuals or groups of people practice divination in order to discern the meanings and consequences of past, present, and future events. Various forms of divination exist in African societies. Perhaps the most common is the appearance of signs that the elders consider to have significant meanings—for themselves, the people around them, the family, the clan, or the village. For instance, howling dogs signify the impending death of a relative. An injured toe means that a visit will be dreadful. A nightmare indicates the coming of an unpleasant event.

Evan Zuesse, a scholar of religious studies, suggests that the Fon people of Benin practice three basic types of divination: possession divination, wisdom (also called instrumental or interpretive) divination, and intuitive

divination. In possession divination a spirit possesses the diviner or sacred objects. By contacting the supernatural realm of spirits, gods, ancestors, or other divine beings, the diviner attains a state of possession or shamanic trance, usually through dancing and other ritual performance. The spirit takes hold of the diviner and speaks in spirit voices, which are interpreted by the diviner's assistants. In wisdom divination the client seeks help from a diviner, who uses certain divination instruments to diagnose the cause of illness and prescribes appropriate ritual sacrifices and medicine. Intuitive divination uses the deep spiritual insight of the diviner, who has great power to reveal issues and concerns of the client.

The Yoruba, a people of southwestern Nigeria, practice perhaps the most complex African divinatory process, a classic form of wisdom divination called *Ifa*, discussed below under SACRED BOOKS. *Ifa* divination spread in West Africa between the Edo of the Benin kingdom (now in southern Nigeria) and the Fon of the Republic of Benin, as well as among the people of African descent in the Caribbean, Brazil, and the United States. In *Ifa* divination a client consults a diviner (*babalawo*), who throws a divining chain (*opele*) made of nuts on a mat and then recites the message of the *Ifa* deity who appears. Clients listen to the poetic recital and identify aspects of it that relate to their problem. A precise response emerges through additional inquiry, and the diviner prescribes appropriate sacrifices.

MORAL CODE OF CONDUCT Various African cultures have developed intricate sets of ethical customs, rules, and taboos. Many societies believe that their morals originated with God and the ancestors and were imparted to humans as elements of God's creation of the world. These moral values are thus embedded in the religious ethos and cosmology. Because the gods and ancestors created the society's ideals, people are highly reluctant to stray from them. The Igbo people of Nigeria's Owerri region traditionally believe that Alà, goddess of Earth, together with Amadióhà, god of thunder and lightning, oversee the essential aspects of village life. As goddess of peace and mother of her people, Alà provides and protects them, deriving her great strength from the land. If offended, however, she can exhibit extremely violent reactions. Any crime is considered to defile the land and thus to offend Alà; violations include incest, adultery, larceny, birthing abnormal children, hostility, kidnaping, and murder.

In most traditional African cultures morals are of two classes—those that govern individual conduct and those that govern social and community relations. Morals that govern social conduct and community relations, and thus protect the group, tend to be rigorous, because the welfare of the group is highly valued. Fundamental human rights are often seen as important not for the sake of individuals but for the collective survival of the group. Community morals govern the family unit, from maternal and paternal relatives to extended families, clans, and lineages. Family members must adhere to specific roles, privileges, and rights. Because they regulate an infinitely larger number of relationships and personal interactions, morals governing the community are complex. To promote the welfare of communities, societies have established taboos and consequences for breaking them. Marriage to a close relative, incest, and disrespect of property and life are taboo. It is forbidden in most places for the young to disobey the elders. This is because Africans assume that respecting elders is a way of acknowledging the wealth of their experiences, their contributions to community growth, and that they are close to the world of the ancestors.

Many African societies anchor their moral values on belief in the ancestors, who are regarded as the ultimate custodians of family mores. Breaking the laws of the community offends the ancestors, who may wreak disaster upon the offender and community as well. The ancestors often reward devotion to ancestral traditions by bestow blessings upon members of their lineages.

Specific deities are ordained by the Supreme God as custodians of rectitude. Ògún, for example, is the Yoruba god of justice. The gods are concerned with many issues in the day-to-day life of the people, including their fertility, agricultural production, governance, and health and well-being. The gods watch over a person's values, morals, and sense of justice.

Although African religions have not embarked on a systematic theology, the myths, rituals, and stories of the gods and ancestors point to a profound statement on moral justice. The gods and ancestors are guardians of morality. They profess habits of truth, justice, honesty, good character, and diligence. They reward good deeds and punish bad deeds. A number of the traditions talk about judgment, through which evil deeds are punished and good deeds are rewarded. Africans believe that punishment may be communal or may pass from one generation to another. Lineage or familial misfortune signifies punishment for the past sins of members of the

Sacred Kingship

African religious leaders include the sacred kings and chiefs who often serve as both spiritual and community leaders. Kingship is integral to African belief systems for at least two reasons. First, in the origin myths of several peoples, such as the Baganda of Uganda and the Edo of Nigeria, the first king or chief of the community was endowed with the sacred power of the Supreme Deity. At times rulers have been described as gods or as endowed with God's divinity. Second, the physical well-being of a king reflects the well-being of his people, including their agricultural and hunting life. Indeed, in ancient African kingdoms, whenever the power of the king waned, he committed suicide to save the community.

In modern African societies, such as that of the Zulu of South Africa, the king's roles as ruler, judge, and ritual specialist are often critical in maintaining a functioning society. Even with the advance of literacy and the impact of Islam and Christianity in Africa, the king continues to function as a sacred canopy under which foreign traditions are subsumed and celebrated.

lineage. Certain antisocial behaviors, such as theft, witchcraft, and sorcery, are taboo, and offenders may suffer punishment of death. Because African religions focus on contemporary worldly salvation, Africans believe that bad character is punished in this world.

SACRED BOOKS Africans who follow a traditional religion rely on no scriptures, canonical texts, or holy books to guide them. In African traditional religions guidance is provided through myths, which are handed down orally. Elders, priests, and priestesses have served as guardians of the sacred traditions. Throughout Africa innumerable myths explain the creation of the universe, how man and woman appeared, the origin of the culture, and how people arrived in their current location. Oral narratives define morals and values for traditional religions, just as written texts do for religions that have sacred books. Because of the oral nature of African sacred texts, the faithful who transmit this knowledge are considered sacred.

Among many African ethnic groups, however, some sets of oral narratives exist that serve as sacred texts. A classic example is *Ifa* divination, which is popular among the Yoruba of southwestern Nigeria. The *Ifa* corpus is a large body of poetic oral narratives that are memorized by diviners and recited during divination performances. There is hardly a topic or issue that *Ifa* fails to address.

To learn about divine will and directives, an *Ifa* diviner (*babalawo*) uses 16 specially selected palm nuts or a divining chain (*opele*) made of 8 half palm nuts tied into a chain. The diviner holds the chain by the middle and throws it on a mat, making a *U* shape, so that four nuts fall on each side of the mat. The nuts expose either convex or concave sides, thus displaying 16 possible forms of *Ifa* signature. Each signature stands for a symbol called an *odu*, each of which corresponds to a chapter (also called an *odu*) containing several verses of oral poems. The diviner then recites the *odu* that appear in the divination castings. After the recitation the client tells the diviner if any of the verses is relevant to the crisis. At this stage the client may reveal to the diviner the nature of his or her inquiry. The diviner recalls and interprets an appropriate text and, through further questioning, arrives at a definitive cause of the client's quest. The diviner prescribes a remedy, which is usually a sacrificial ritual, but in a case of grave illness medicinal herbs may offer a cure.

During their long periods of apprenticeship diviners memorize *Ifa* verses, which may be as long as 256 *odu*. The message and sacrifices contained in *Ifa* verses are a genre of oral tradition; they preserve the Yoruba religious worldview through myths, proverbs, songs, and poetry.

Highly trained diviners have largely been responsible for memorizing and transmitting important historical and cultural events to the living generation. Because there are no sacred books, however, it is impossible to know what traditional religions were like 500 or 1,000 years ago. Oral myths elude permanent display on paper, stone, or other media; African traditional religions remain changeable according to the needs of their followers. Accordingly, if religious believers no longer find a belief or ritual useful for daily spiritual life, it may easily be set aside forever.

SACRED SYMBOLS African art is a central part of traditional religious expression. It is known worldwide for its powerful ability to represent abstract ideas and spiritual forces. African artists produce sacred icons and symbols of traditional religions in an enormous array of forms, both abstract and representational. Traditional artists typically carve images that express the powers of God, demigods, ancestors, and spirits as intermediaries between deities and humans. A royal stool may depict powerful animals such as leopards and tigers. Practitioners of African traditional religions are generally familiar with the symbols and icons, but often only a few trained individuals can interpret the significance of such symbolic and iconic forms, which are used to imply religious meaning in initiation, divination, and secret societies.

In addition to abstract forms, many religious artists borrow from forms found in nature—such as insects, trees, leafs, and animals—to produce intricate design motifs. Common animal motifs are the chameleon, centipede, butterfly, lizard, snake, tortoise, and fish. Many species of birds, including the ostrich, vulture, dove, and heron, inspire artists. Cultural objects and status symbols—such as an amulet, royal crown, staff, divination sign, or dance wand—often inspire designs. Such designs are incorporated into everyday objects; these may be a writing board, comb, game board, or scissors. In certain regions of Africa traditional hairstyles have their own religious significance. A male priest or a traditional ruler may wear a long hairstyle signifying a female deity, thereby assuming the persona of the deity and establishing a special connection with her. Shrines, religious objects, and sacred places are decorated with many forms, shapes, and colors to express religious concepts.

EARLY AND MODERN LEADERS While there have been great male and female religious leaders throughout Africa's history, none can be elevated above others in their importance to religious history. In indigenous traditions the leaders are the mythic beings and culture heroes who were responsible for founding empires, civilizations, clans, and lineages that later formed the core of the religioethnic traditions of their peoples. Such mythic figures and culture heroes include Oduduwa in Nigeria, Shaka the Zulu in South Africa, and Osei Tutu in Ghana.

Many people are involved in religious leadership, and a single religion can have priests, priestesses, sacred kings and queens, prophets, prophetesses, and seers, all of whom have been important religious leaders throughout the ages. This "democratization" of religious responsibility is in line with a general tendency of avoiding the concentration of spiritual powers in the hands of a single individual. Leaders in African traditional religions are the people who impart religious wisdom and guidance to believers. African societies do not clearly delineate an individual's religious title. A priest can be a diviner, a king can be a seer, and a prophet can be a priest and a diviner. Even if a person has a number of spiritual skills, however, he or she may concentrate efforts in a single area. Various roles carry distinct names in West African languages. A priest connected with a god is referred to as an *obosōmfo, vodunō, olorisa,* and *atama* in Twi, Fon, Yoruba, and Igbo, respectively. A seer in these respective languages is an *okōmfo, bokonō babalawo,* and *amoma.* Similarly, the name for a medicine healer is *sumānkwafo, amawato, onisegun,* and *dibia.*

Religious leaders play numerous roles in a traditional African society. Many offer sacrifices or make verbal demands on the behalf of believers. The most powerful religious leaders are spirit mediums, members of a family or clan who are responsible for communication between an ancestor and his or her descendants. Diviners are vital for communicating with the spirit world. People consult diviners for any number of issues, but the most common reasons are for a misfortune, such as sickness, death, or calamity; spirits are likely to have knowledge about the causes of a misfortune. Diviners have vast accumulations of secret knowledge and are highly intuitive about human nature.

Priests and priestesses are natural leaders because they are in direct service to God and dedicate themselves to the deities for life. The oldest man of the family or community is often a priest, because he is the closest to the dead and has lived the longest life. In a village one priest usually leads all other priests. A head priest is chosen by his predecessor; otherwise, village elders or a chief's council make this decision.

According to traditional belief, there are powerful spirits who, acting through spirit mediums, have been involved in historical events in Africa. For instance, Mbuya (grandmother) Nehanda, a spirit medium in Zimbabwe, played an important role in mobilizing people in the fight against for political independence beginning in the late nineteenth century. Nehanda, considered an incarnation of an oracle spirit, was eventually hanged by colonial authorities in 1898. Nevertheless, throughout the twentieth century her spirit, speaking through other spirit mediums, continued to work closely with the freedom fighters in the struggle for independence.

Contemporary African religious leaders include those who have been interested in reviving traditional religion. One of the foremost of these is Wande Abimbola (born in 1936), who in 1987 was selected by the elder *babalawo*s in Nigeria to be the *awise awo agbaye* (chief spokesperson of Ifa and Yoruba religion and culture). In 2003 Abimbola was appointed the adviser to the president of Nigeria on culture and tradition.

MAJOR THEOLOGIANS AND AUTHORS Numerous scholars in diverse fields of interest carry out studies of African religions. Major scholarly research about African traditional religions had a late start. In the fourteenth century "outsiders" began to inquire into the nature of African cultures and religions. Muslim and European colonial traders, travelers, slavers, missionaries, military personnel, mercenaries, and administrators frequently recorded naive accounts of African cultural customs, traditions, and religions. Although their inquiries were fraught with bias, some outsiders were more reliable than others.

Much of the early authorship was conducted by anthropologists working for colonial governments or by Christian missionaries. By the 1930s colonial governments in Africa had opened several colleges (as offshoots of European institutions) across the continent. Although the standards for these colleges were high, the curriculum did not include the study of European or African religions. During the 1940s and 1950s departments of religious studies were created in universities in Nigeria, Kenya, Uganda, Ghana, and Sierra Leone. Colonial offices continued to govern universities and colleges. Departments of religious studies did not appear in East Africa until the 1960s. In West Africa colleges gained autonomy during the struggle for independence in the 1960s. With autonomy came a revitalized study of religions, which recognized the religious pluralism of independent countries. The emphasis on Christian studies that had long dominated the religious studies field was replaced by an emphasis Islamic studies and African traditional religions.

The early African scholarship of J.B. Danquah (1895–1965) from Ghana and J. Olumide Lucas (from Nigeria) in the first part of the twentieth century produced interesting studies of African indigenous religion. In the 1940s Africans entered into the scholarly discourse on African indigenous religions. For example, John Mbiti from Kenya, the most prolific of the African scholars, challenged the Eurocentric notion that Africans had no notion of a Supreme God. Mbiti's work inspired numerous studies on God in African religions.

Among the scholars responding to accusations that Africans lack a notion of God was E. Bolaji Idowu, who did research on the Yoruba Supreme God, publishing *Olodumare: God in Yoruba Belief* in 1962. Idowu, with J.O. Awolalu and Geoffrey Parrinder (an English Methodist minister who taught religion in Nigeria), put in place a structure for the study of African religions that later scholars adapted for their own studies. These three scholars established the idea of the centrality of a Supreme God surrounded by myriad lesser gods. Some of the academic priests, including Parrinder, Father Placid Temple, and Zaireois V. Mulago, were influenced by the inclusive views of liberal theology developed by Protestant and Catholic academic theologians in North American and European universities. They began to abandon their doctrinal, orthodox, and christocentric views of African religion.

From the postcolonial years in the 1960s to the early 1990s, the study of African religions entered a mature phase. During this period many scholars of African religious studies were passionately nationalistic. In the forefront was E. Bolaji Idowu. Perhaps the finest critic of African religious scholarship was Ugandan writer and anthropologist O. p'Bitek. In *African Religions in Western Scholarship* (1971) p'Bitek wrote that the viewing of African religions through Euro-Christian spectacles should cease.

The study of African religions today is a global phenomenon, with methodologies and theoretical approaches that range from collecting ethnographic data to addressing the works of missionaries who try to convert the indigenous people to Christianity. During the 1980s and 1990s many African scholars began to study abroad. The overwhelming majority of scholars in religious studies departments are now Africans.

ORGANIZATIONAL STRUCTURE In contrast to structured Western religions, traditional African religions are organized with relatively little concern for formal structure. African religions rely on no single individual as a religious leader but instead depend upon an entire community to do religious work. Priests, priestesses, diviners, elders, chiefs, kings, and other authority figures may perform sacred and ceremonial rituals. Depending on the kind of religious activity, various religious authorities may preside over specific rituals.

Africans do, however, precisely define the structure of their cosmos. From greatest to least significance, African traditional religions begin the hierarchy with a being or god who remains supreme. Next are divinities and ancestors, who represent the invisible world. Then there are priests and holy persons, who are intermediaries between the seen (the living) and the unseen worlds. Finally, living humans remain for a time in the visible world. Members of an African religious tradition are often divided into the initiated and the uninitiated. The initiated are priests and priestesses and may hold titles within the cult. They carry out specialized duties. The uninitiated are the rest of the members of the religious group, who have not performed any major initiation rituals that qualify them to serve in the group's inner circles.

HOUSES OF WORSHIP AND HOLY PLACES Every African community and ethnic group has its own religious places, which can take several forms. Some are fabricated, some are found in nature, and others are natural but altered in some fashion. Some structures are built for specific religious purposes, to protect the faithful from inclement weather, or to protect religious objects from the elements. Larger buildings, such as temples, function exclusively for religious purposes; there are numerous temples for the worship of various deities. Temples are located all over the continent, especially among the ethnic groups in southern Africa, Ghana, Nigeria, and Uganda. In some cases kings, queens, and other nobility are buried in temples. Some harbor shrines and ancestor graves.

Shrines, the most common religious structure, exist throughout Africa. Shrines may be exclusively for family members or for public use. They usually contain revered religious objects and are used for religious activities such as pouring libations, performing rituals, saying prayers, and making offerings. Shrines are usually the center of a family's religious life and are the connection between the visible and invisible world. Priests or priestesses watch over both community shrines and family shrines.

Altars are small structures where offerings can be placed and sacrifices performed. They may be in shrines or temples, or they may stand on their own. Shrines and altars are most often found in natural spaces or in locations that are considered powerful places for connecting with the invisible. A taboo frequently restricts the kinds of materials used for building shrines and altars. Often only local materials found in the environment may be used to build these structures.

Shrines are often established above familial and ancestral gravesites; the grave itself may also serve as a shrine. Families memorialize deceased relatives and lineages at their gravesites. At such shrines the living may communicate with the departed person; the family may also convey messages to God through the deceased. Graves play a more important religious role for farming communities than for pastoralists, who are constantly moving from one place to another. The location of graves varies from group to group. In most West African communities burials take place on pieces of land within the family's compound; these are regarded as secured places where the dead will be at peace. Graves may also be located in a sacred forest where the spirits of the ancestors concentrate. A bad death (suicide or murder) may cause the victim to be buried in the "waste bush" to discourage the spirit from reincarnating or disturbing the peace of the living.

Natural religious sites are vast in number, and every traditional African culture has many. These sites include forests (or parts of forests), rivers, lakes, trees, mountains, waterfalls, and rocks. They are thought to be the meeting places between heaven and earth and between visible and invisible worlds. Thus, they are important places to communicate with spirits of the dead, with God, and with the heavenly world. The faithful usually designate natural places as sacred sites based on historical or special events. Such natural spaces are usually set aside from everyday uses such as grazing cattle, washing clothes, and growing crops. They are used only for ceremonies, rituals, prayers, and sacrifices. Òsun Grove in Òsogbo, Nigeria, is a good example of an environmental landmark that has been moved into the realm of the sacred.

WHAT IS SACRED The African worldview is based on a belief that every living and inanimate object is sacred on some level. Some are deemed more sacred than others. Devotees of traditional religions recognize domestic and wild animals as sacred and full of great power. Domestic animals such as dogs, goats, and roosters are often used for sacrificial purposes, and certain of their body parts—such as feathers, nails, entrails, horns, beaks, and blood—are used as offerings and for divining.

Many wild animals are sacred because they have wisdom and powers, because they are believed to be in-

habited by spirits, and because it is said that in some cases they were sent to earth by God to communicate with humans. An example is a story among Zulus in which a chameleon and then a lizard are sent to Earth by God to tell men that he has arranged death to be a part of the cycle of human life. There is a continuing belief about the sacredness of lizards and chameleons in Zulu culture. Devotees attach great importance to animals because, at any moment, an animal may be preparing to deliver a message to humans from anywhere in the spirit world.

Various herbs and plants contain special powers that are useful for religious purposes. Certain herbs are sacred, and those priest specialists who have deep knowledge of how to use them are called herbalists. In addition to having medicinal uses, the herbs carry symbolic properties and qualities that make them appropriate for religious uses.

HOLIDAYS/FESTIVALS In traditional African cultures festivals are scheduled to occur during major rites of passage, including birth, circumcision, coming-of-age initiation, marriage, and death. Many communities maintain elaborate calendars of festivals that run throughout the year. Seasonal festivals commemorate annual events such as field preparation, planting, harvesting, hunting and fishing periods, and the New Year. Other festivals celebrate victory at war, the coronation of kings or chiefs, and changes in leadership. Community festivals are designed to purify villages or larger communities (ridding them of evil and bad fortune), to carry on life-sustaining activities successfully, and to bring harmony to the village. Festivals are often accompanied by sacrifices and offerings to ancestors and deities, who, it is believed, then transmit information to God.

It is common for the various African gods and deities to have their own yearly festivals. Deities who usually do not garner much attention during daily and weekly worship schedules often draw massive crowds during their annual festivals. These are usually colorful affairs with dancing, music, eating, drinking, praying (and other religious activities), wearing masks and costumes, and general merrymaking.

In African traditional religions certain days are declared by community leaders to honor the gods. During such days ordinary community activities—fishing, farming, and buying or selling at the market—are prohibited to honor the deities. In festivals commemorating the deeds of the gods, ancestors, and sacred kings, devo-

Racism in the Early Study of African Religions

The first academic studies of African traditional religions were written in the eighteenth, nineteenth, and early twentieth centuries by Muslim and European scholars. Trained in the new method of "fieldwork"—which entailed observing participants and speaking the language of the community—these anthropologists worked for their governments. Their studies avoided describing African cultures in indigenous terms. They were expected to assess colonial projects, predict the behavior of the natives, distinguish between rumor and fact, and develop mechanisms for colonial command and control.

Early scholars viewed African indigenous religions as "primitive," comparing them adversely with European Christian beliefs. At this time two main schools of thought prevailed. The first questioned the origin of African civilizations and religions. Scholars attempted to link African cultures with external sources—for instance, suggesting that sub-Saharan black Africans had come from the Middle East or Egypt. This notion built upon evolutionary theories that posited that cultures gradually evolve, becoming "less primitive" over time. The second school put forward a diffusionist, or "contact," theory of development to explain sophisticated African belief systems and artifacts (such as exquisite bronzes and terracotta sculptures). Westerners deemed Africans incapable of producing such ideas and objects. The diffusionist theory held that religious ideas of the Mediterranean region had proliferated, eventually reaching the peoples of sub-Saharan Africa. A concept that gained wide currency under the theory of diffusion was the erroneous idea that Africans lacked a Supreme God and instead were polytheists. These two schools reflect an insidious racist ideology that influenced the initial study of African religions.

tees take time off from farming, hunting, and fishing to dedicate themselves completely to celebrating with the community or region. They observe certain taboos, such as abstinence from sex, or they make pilgrimages to sacred forests, rivers, and mountains in honor of the deities.

MODE OF DRESS Modes of dress in African traditional religions vary depending upon the kind of devotee, geographical location, and a person's age. Despite this, certain kinds of clothes, accessories, and permanent or temporary bodily accoutrements distinguish devotees from others. Priests and followers often wear white clothes as a sign of purity. Deities are usually represented by signs or symbols on clothing or the skin.

Colors adorning the body identify devotees and carry meaning. For instance, Yoruba devotees of an *orisa* (deity) wear red and white marks on their foreheads. Painting the body with white chalk or another substance for ceremonial purposes is also a common way to identify a devotee's beliefs or stage of life. Priests usually carry signs of their social status, including horsehair whisks, brass figures, embellished staffs, jewelry, diamonds, gold, feathers, or priestly stools or chairs; they may also wear white chalk on the body.

Scarification or tattoo is a permanent mode of cultural adornment signifying identification with beliefs; motifs are often based on abstract designs, leaf forms, and totemic flora and fauna. Although most body art carries little association with Ògún (the Yoruba god of iron), raised-scarification design has been associated with Ògún because Yoruba body artists traditionally use iron implements to create intricate patterns and shapes on the skin. The palm tree design on a person's body signifies identification with Ògún. This is because traditional weavers manufacture textiles from palm fronds and also because Ògún's preferred food and drink come from the oil palm tree.

DIETARY PRACTICES In traditional African cultures family members habitually offer food and drink to their ancestors. Such offerings are often placed in or on family shrines, which are usually located behind the family house or compound. All kinds of seeds and the most delicious parts of domesticated crops are appropriate for ritual offerings. Materials may be ground into powders and mixed with other substances. Offerings may be done for purification, for protection from adverse forces, and for divination.

According to African traditional beliefs, deities normally prefer certain foods and drinks and abstain from others. In Yoruba religion, for example, each deity has likes and dislikes, and care is taken to respect the deities' preferences. Òrìsà-Nlá loves snails cooked in shea butter, Òrúnmílá prefers rat and fish, and Èsù loves rooster. These deities consume no other foods, except perhaps kola nuts, a standard ritual ingredient in many African cultures. Òrìsà-Nlá disdains palm wine, and Èsù dislikes *adin* (palm-kernel oil). It is taboo to bring unfavorable foods near the shrines, and devotees of these deities refrain from partaking of these foods. Because of their personal associations with a divinity, priests and certain religious specialists honor food taboos; it is also thought that, by doing so, they can perform rituals effectively for observers of these restrictions.

Accordingly, dietary prohibitions and peculiarities are associated with the deceased and the diets of those who inhabit the heavenly world. Eating habits and diet differ vastly among regions of Africa. They are based on seasonal availability and environmental, social, cultural, and religious differences. Dietary restrictions take place for various reasons, including a person's stage of life, gender, or social class. A twin in Yoruba culture is forbidden to eat the meat of the colobus monkey, because the Yoruba believe that twins have kinship relationships with them.

RITUALS Ritual and ceremony are the most important entry points to understanding the religious life of African communities. To the observer of religious practices, rituals are more visible than mythic narratives, but rituals often relate to myths by conveying and reinforcing the meanings and values that communities hold sacred. Ritual can have an extremely broad meaning that refers to many aspects of human life.

All traditional religious practices incorporate ritual, although the forms vary greatly from region to region, ethnic group to ethnic group, and even from individual to individual within the same religious tradition. Not every member of society performs all rituals; instead, a particular ritual may be prescribed for certain members of a community. In hierarchical African societies a few skilled elites who possess status, knowledge, authority, and power are chosen to use sacred ritual icons. In nonhierarchical societies individuals share authority and power equally.

In spite of their differences, African religions share certain common features, especially in their rituals and ceremonies. They always involve larger groups of people or entire communities. For example, agricultural rituals function communally to benefit the group. Great numbers of Africans continue to work in subsistence, cash crop, and other agricultural economies, and they have preserved spiritual practices and sacred rituals to induce the gods to ensure rains, successful harvests, and abundant agricultural production. Rituals related to rain are considered communal, because the availability of water affects the lives of so many. Devotees of African traditional religions often perform rituals to induce rain; such rituals feature dancing, singing, and chanting.

Some religious rituals involve the devotees offering the gods and ancestors sacrificial animals, libations of water or alcohol, or small amounts of favored food. Sacrificial rituals and festivals in which food is shared reinforce the communal bond between the participants, the ancestors, God, and the lesser deities. Much social ritual takes place at shrines, temples, and altars. These are rituals performed to cement the bond of unity among a community or to celebrate the achievements of individual members of the group. On important occasions (such as hunting expeditions, healing ceremonies, and rites of passage), the faithful honor their gods, ancestors, and spirits with ritual festivals, ceremonies, divination, and animal sacrifice. In the case of drought, flooding, volcanoes, famine, illness, and other disasters, devotees offer a sacrificial animal to appease the spirit deity thought to be responsible for the calamity.

African religious traditions and ritual practices have been passed down from generation to generation for centuries; thus, practitioners experience history in every religious ritual that is performed. Although ritual has changed over time according to the social, political, environmental, and spiritual needs of individuals, it continues to be a real connection with the past—a connection that Africans take seriously as they pass their culture from one generation to the next.

RITES OF PASSAGE The primary rites of passage in African religious life are birth and naming, puberty, marriage, achieving elder status, and death. Such rites provide a transition from one age to the next. Puberty rituals signify the coming of age, when elders reveal to the younger generation the ancestral secrets of deep knowledge. Marriage rituals signify the betrothal of individuals to each other, to the lineage, and to the community. Although the rituals marking elderhood are more rare today, certain cultures, such as the Owo Yoruba (a subgroup of the Yoruba people of Nigeria) and the Masai (of Tanzania and Kenya), celebrate transition to the honored elder status.

Personal or individual rituals often surround events that happen in everyday life. Birth, transition to adulthood, marriage, and death are four of the most prominent kinds of life events celebrated with religious ritual. The rites for these stages often contain aspects of both communal and personal ritual. The Fang of Central Africa retain a personal ritual associated with birth, the *biang ndu*, or *biang nzí* (sometimes called the "roof medicine" ritual). If delivery becomes difficult, the father of the child climbs onto the roof of the house to a spot above the mother's belly. After piercing the thatched roof with a hollow banana stem, he pours medicinal water through the stem directly onto her pregnant belly. Only the father can perform the *biang ndu*, which is witnessed by family members and neighbors.

In African cultures celebrating the transition from childhood to adulthood takes many forms. Initiation ceremonies occur most commonly during puberty. There is much ritual involved with initiation, which is a time for the younger generation to learn how to be contributing members of society. A youth undergoes the rituals in seclusion with children of the same age. Participants are taught about their people's beliefs, history, and traditions as well as about raising a family, the secrets of marriage, and other practical information. Initiation is a deeply religious affair and a sign of unity with the larger community and the ancestors. Before, during, and after initiation ceremonies, the community offers many prayers and sacrifices to God; they ask for blessings and good luck for the youths undergoing the arduous process. Female and male circumcisions are often a part, but not the focus, of initiation rites. The ceremonies are usually performed apart from the community to preserve an aura of mystery for initiates. Initiation often takes place for several days or months in auspicious natural locations, such as forests or grasslands, where the initiates are afforded closer contact with the invisible realm, the spirits, and God.

Outside observers and anthropologists have written many descriptions of traditional African initiation rites. One of the best, however, is the account by Malidoma Patrice Somé (born in 1956) of his own initiation as a member of the Dagara of Burkina Faso. As a young boy he had been kidnaped by a French Jesuit missionary; he was initiated when he returned to his village at age 20. The initiation Somé describes is full of associations with nature. Male initiates leave the village, and while they are still in the presence of family and friends, they remove their clothing. Nakedness is common in tradi-

tional African cultures. There is no shame associated with it, because it is perceived as an expression of a relationship with the spirits of nature.

Death is one of the most important events of an African community, and often there are extended and complex rituals associated with it. With death comes a permanent physical separation between the deceased and the living, and ritual helps to accentuate this transition. There is great variation in the traditions and rituals surrounding death. Attendants use natural objects to wash, clothe, and bury the body, which is often covered in animal skins, leather, cotton, bark cloth, or leaves. These objects emphasize that the body, conceived in the earth, returns to the earth. The deceased person's soul remains a presence in the lives of individuals and must be respected by the living. In traditional African culture the world of the ancestors and the abode of the dead is understood as a sphere beyond the realm of the living. In some societies this realm, called *il`*, is considered to exist within the earth itself.

MEMBERSHIP Requirements for membership in an African indigenous religion have varied according to local traditions. Typically, traditional cults limited membership solely to birthright. Members of Igbo, Masai, or Edo groups, for example, belonged to and practiced the religion of their lineage, clan, and family. With the advent of Islam and Christianity in Africa—and the widespread conversion to these two monotheistic traditions—the numbers of adherents to African religions dwindled. Devotees of traditional religions awakened to the possibility of losing their faith, and to compensate they extended the criteria for membership. Most traditional African religious cultures have thus become more inclusive.

Throughout the centuries of transatlantic slave trading, Africans took their religious practices to the Americas and the Caribbean. The large numbers of Africans living in North, Central, and South America introduced enduring forms of African religious culture through music, dance, festivals, and martial arts. This occurred especially in Brazil, Peru, Cuba, Trinidad, Haiti, Puerto Rico, and other locations where African populations were extensive. Traditional devotees in the New World realized that, to preserve their religious heritage, they had to accept converts.

As African religious cultures spread from Cuba, Brazil, Trinidad, and other places of the diaspora to the United States, new forms emerged that catered to the spiritual needs of many peoples. Perhaps the most fascinating of these pioneer movements are the Yoruba-inspired African American traditions. Beginning in the late twentieth century hundreds of African Americans embraced Yoruba traditions by founding the Kingdom of Oyotunji African Village near the city of Sheldon, South Carolina. It was named after its namesake Yoruba kingdom in West Africa.

RELIGIOUS TOLERANCE African traditional religions do not proselytize because traditional religious expression is accepted as unique to an ethnic group. Religion is so intimately tied to place that African religions do not give themselves easily to the influence of exogenous groups. African cultures are, however, often flexible enough to absorb values and traditions from other religious belief systems. Competing indigenous religions may incorporate useful or similar aspects of each other. The most common religions that have been incorporated into traditional belief systems are Christianity and Islam. Even if followers of indigenous African religions convert to Christianity of Islam, they often continue to practice their traditional rituals. This is because, for them, Christianity lacks the breadth to signify all their religious feelings, values, and beliefs. Islam has, overall, been more compatible with and tolerant of African traditional religions and cultural practices. Ancestor veneration, polygamy, circumcision, magic, and beliefs in spirits and other divinities are common in both popular Islam and African traditional religions.

Practitioners of African traditional religions have been victims of conversion and intolerance. Adherents to Western religions have sometimes viewed African religions as "inferior." In his novel *Things Fall Apart* (1958), Chinua Achebe (born in 1930) discusses the ethnic slurs used in his native Igbo language; Christians refer to followers of traditional religions as "nonbelievers, heathens, and lowly people (*ndi nkiti*)." In Yoruba and Hausa-Fulani (Nigeria and Niger) societies, Muslims call traditional believers *keferi* (unbelievers) and people of *jahiliyya* (local and inferior tradition).

SOCIAL JUSTICE Major social concerns for followers of African traditional religions include poverty and the environment. A contemporary response to the crisis of poverty in African villages is the linking of development with ethnoreligious identity. In Nigeria, Ghana, and other parts of West Africa, for instance, village and town associations meet for purposes of economic unity

and social development. Although these groups are no longer connected to the worship of traditional gods (most of them have converted to Islam and Christianity), they have established a platform that involves the reinvention of traditional value systems such as sacred kingship, totemic concepts, and old tribal gods reimagined in modern secular idioms. By invoking tribal myth and historic symbols, they galvanize members of their communities at home and abroad to contribute to the economic growth of villages, towns, and communities. In this way Africans have been responding to a crisis using their own metaphysical and epistemological worldview.

In many African societies deceased souls live in forests, rivers, riverbanks, hills, or other natural places. The living must avoid and respect the resting places of the dead. Communities often preserve these sacred natural places from exploitation and mining by establishing certain land-use restrictions. Thus, traditional funerary ritual in many cases has been effective in inspiring wise use of natural resources. Without a natural landscape and the reverence for the spirituality and mystery to be found in nature, much of the power of African culture would be greatly diminished.

SOCIAL ASPECTS In traditional African cultures marriage, raising children, and fulfilling familial obligations are religious duties. Marriage agreements usually involve both sets of parents of the couple to be married. Binding the couple is accompanied by exchanging gifts, which is largely a way of thanking the parents of the bride or groom for bringing up their child in a good manner. The gifts do, however, hold some local legal weight, because if a marriage does not last, it is expected that the value of gifts be returned to the family who gave them.

Religious traditions reinforce the idea that family members must adhere to specific roles. Younger generations must care for their elders, children must obey their parents and elders, and parents must teach, provide, and care for their children. At times parents must care for their sibling's offspring.

CONTROVERSIAL ISSUES In contemporary Africa the persistence of sacred practices is a source of conflict between devotees of African religions and outsiders. When outsiders evaluate indigenous cultures and religions, they often judge practices and beliefs as controversial. Western religious cultures regard many aspects of African religions—such as witchcraft, ritual killing of animals, female circumcision, polygamy, and approaches to gender relations—as peculiar compared with Western cultural practices. Among the adherents of an African religious tradition, however, these practices generally do not cause controversy.

Traditional religion in any culture affirms the identity of that culture, provides a source of knowledge, and defines a people's existence. Religion provides an education for individuals and is a rich source of cultural knowledge about many different subjects. A crisis of identity has been created in Africa as Africans' own indigenous sources of knowledge are steadily replaced by global values dictated by Western capitalism. Another issue is conversion to Christianity and Islam in Africa, which has not only created conflicts between indigenous religions and these two traditions but also set Christianity and Islam against each other.

CULTURAL IMPACT African traditional religions and African arts dovetail. Religion gives meaning and value to all forms of African artistic expression, including literature, music, visual art, and dance. Because indigenous societies are mainly nonliterate, oral traditions expressed in poetry, proverbs, and mythic narratives are sources of African literary traditions. Examples are *Ifa* divination verses, which amount to 256 chapters of text.

Similar to the oral traditions, the arts of architecture, design, sculpture, textiles, dance, drumming, and music function as sacred "texts," transmitting and reinforcing traditional religions for new generations. The arts are used to convey feelings, illustrate proverbs, express the wisdom of the people, and give spiritual meaning and function to inanimate objects. Shrines and temples are adorned with elaborate carved images of the deities that convey the power of the gods and ancestors. Rites of passage are particularly important in the religious use of arts. Carved totemic and ritual objects may serve as important sources of knowledge for the newly initiated. Masks, costumes, and body design accompany religious ceremonies.

Like all elements of African traditional religion, artistic expressions are integrated with everyday life. African arts and religious meaning overlap in visual symbols, music, dance, proverbs, riddles, names of people and places, myths, legends, beliefs, and customs. In this sense, every member of society contributes to the religion's living oral "texts."

Jacob K. Olupona

Bibliography

Abimbola, Wande. *Ifá: An Exposition of Ifá Literary Corpus.* Ibadan: Oxford University Press Nigeria; New York: Oxford University Press, 1976.

Awolalu, J. Omosade. *Yoruba Beliefs and Sacrificial Rites.* London: Longman, 1979.

Bascom, William Russell. *Ifa Divination: Communication between Gods and Men in West Africa.* Bloomington: Indiana University Press, 1991.

Beidelman, T.O. *Moral Imagination in Kaguru Modes of Thought.* Washington, D.C.: Smithsonian Institution Press, 1986.

Berber, Karin. "How Man Makes God in West Africa: Yoruba Attitudes toward the Orisa." *Africa* 51, no. 3 (1981): 724–45.

Cole, H.M. (1982). *Mbari Art and Life among the Owerri Igbo.* Bloomington: Indiana University Press, 1982.

Evans-Pritchard, E. *Witchcraft, Oracles, and Magic among the Azande.* Oxford: Clarendon Press, 1937.

Idowu, E. Bolaji. *African Traditional Religion: A Definition.* London: S.C.M. Press, 1973.

———. *Olódùmarè: God in Yoruba Belief.* New York: Praeger, 1963.

Jacobson-Widding, Anita, and Walter van Beek, eds. *The Creative Communion: African Folk Models of Fertility and the Regeneration of Life.* Uppsala, Sweden: Uppsala University, 1990.

Khapoya, V.B. *The African Experience: An Introduction.* Englewood Cliffs, N.J.: Prentice Hall, 1994.

MacGaffey, Wyatt. *Religion and Society in Central Congo: The Bakongo of Lower Zaire.* Chicago: University of Chicago Press, 1986.

Mbiti, John S. *African Religions and Philosophy.* Portsmouth, N.H.: Heinemann, 1990.

———. *Introduction to African Religion.* Portsmouth, N.H.: Heinemann Educational Books, 1991.

Meek, Charles K. *Law and Authority in a Nigerian Tribe.* New York: Oxford University Press, 1937.

Merriam, Alan P. *An African World: The Basongye Village of Lupupa Ngye.* Bloomington: Indiana University Press, 1974.

Moyo, A. "Religion in Africa." In *Understanding Contemporary Africa,* edited by A.A. Gordon and D.L. Gordon. Boulder, Colo.: Lynne Rienner Publishers, 2001.

Mudimbe, V.Y. *The Invention of Africa.* Bloomington: Indiana University Press, 1988.

Olupona, Jacob K., ed. *African Spirituality: Forms, Meanings, and Expressions.* New York: Crossroad, 2000.

———. *Kingship, Religion, and Rituals in a Nigerian Community: A Phenomenological Study of Ondo Yoruba Festivals.* Stockholm, Sweden: Almqvist and Wiksell International, 1991.

Parrinder, Edward Geoffrey. *African Mythology.* London: Paul Hamlyn, 1967.

———. *West African Religion: A Study of the Beliefs and Practices of Akan, Ewe, Yoruba, Ibo, and Kindred Peoples.* London: Epworth Press, 1961.

p'Bitek, Okot. *Religion of the Central Luo.* Nairobi: East African Literature Bureau, 1971.

Platvoet, J., J. Cox, and J. Olupona. *The Study of Religions in Africa: Past, Present, and Prospects.* Cambridge, England: Roots and Branches, 1996.

Rasmussen, Susan. "Myth and Cosmology." In *Encyclopedia of Africa South of the Sahara,* edited by John Middleton. Vol. 3. New York: Charles Scribner's Sons, 1997.

Smith, Edwin W., ed. *African Ideas of God.* London: Edinburgh House, 1966.

Somé, Malidoma P. *The Healing Wisdom of Africa.* New York: J.P. Tarcher/Putnam, 1999.

Turner, Victor W. *The Ritual Process: Structure and Anti-Structure.* Ithaca, N.Y.: Cornell University Press, 1977.

Van Binsbergen, Wim, and Matthew Schoffeleers. *Theoretical Explorations in African Religion.* Berkeley: University of California Press, 1985.

The Religion, Spirituality, and Thought of Traditional Africa. Chicago: University of Chicago Press, 1979.

Zuesse, Evan M. *Ritual Cosmos: The Sanctification of Life in African Religions.* Athens, Ohio: Ohio University Press, 1979.

Bahá'í Faith

FOUNDED: 1863 C.E.

RELIGION AS A PERCENTAGE OF WORLD POPULATION: 0.1 percent

OVERVIEW The Bahá'í faith, which developed in nineteenth-century Iran, is relatively new, compared with other major world religions. It has only five million members, but it is, after Christianity, the second most widespread religion in the world, with adherents in 218 countries and dependent territories. The term Bahá'í derives from the Arabic word *Baha*, meaning glory, splendor, or light.

The Bahá'í faith was founded by Bahaullah (1817–92), an Iranian noble, who claimed to be the latest of God's messengers. Over a 40-year period Bahaullah penned the core texts of the Bahá'í scriptures and defined such basic Bahá'í beliefs as the oneness of God, the need for divine messengers or manifestations of God to guide humanity, and the unity of the world's major religions. He taught the unity of humankind; the equality of all humans; the centrality of the principle of unity for reforming society and constructing a just global civilization; the essential role of consultation in creating love, agreement, and justice; and the need for the basic education of all people. He delineated a path for individual spiritual transformation, which included the daily recitation of an obligatory prayer, the study of scripture, and holding oneself accountable before God; service to humanity; marriage and the raising of children; and working, not only to earn a living but also to serve others. He established a Bahá'í community that had no clergy but elected coordinating bodies; worshiped together in ways that minimized ritual; focused on the education and transformation of its members; served humanity; and sought to attract new members by word and deed.

Bahaullah was succeeded by his son, Abdul-Baha (1844–1921), whom he appointed head of the faith, exemplar of the teachings, and interpreter of his revelation. Abdul-Baha oversaw the expansion of the Bahá'í faith from the Middle East to Europe and the Americas. He clarified many of Bahaullah's teachings, and he proclaimed Bahá'í social teachings during his travels in the West.

Abdul-Baha appointed Shoghi Effendi Rabbani (1897–1957) as his successor and Guardian of the Cause of God. He bestowed on Shoghi Effendi authority to interpret the Bahá'í teachings. Shoghi Effendi built the Bahá'í organizational system of elected consultative councils defined by Bahaullah and Abdul-Baha and then used it as an instrument to spread the Bahá'í faith systematically around the globe. He clarified many basic Bahá'í beliefs and translated many of the most important works of Bahaullah from Arabic and Persian into English. The foundation he built allowed for the establishment of the Universal House of Justice, the supreme coordinating council of the Bahá'í faith, in 1963.

Since its establishment the Universal House of Justice has coordinated the rapid growth of the Bahá'í faith around the world and has made strenuous efforts to protect the Bahá'í community from persecution. Bahá'ís live in 127,000 localities, have 12,000 elected local coordinating councils, and 180 national coordinating councils. The United States has 150,000 members re-

NINE-POINTED STAR. A nine-pointed star is generally used by Bahá'ís as the unofficial symbol of their faith. The numerical value of the Arabic word ìbahaî is nine, which, as the highest single-digit number, symbolizes completeness. It is for this reason that all Baháíí houses of worship have nine sides. (THOMSON GALE)

siding in 7,000 localities, with 1,200 local coordinating councils.

HISTORY The Bahá'í faith traces its beginnings to the Babi movement. The Babi faith was founded by Ali-Muhammad of Shiraz (1819–50), a merchant who declared himself a divine messenger in 1844. He took the title of the Bab (Arabic: "gate"), which implied that he was the gate to the "hidden imam," a messianic figure expected by Iran's Shiite population. In his extensive writings, however, the Bab claimed to be the hidden imam himself. He attracted followers from across Iran, particularly among seminary students, the clergy, the merchant class, and some villagers. The Bab emphasized the coming of another divine messenger even greater than himself. He was imprisoned for his teachings, eventually condemned for blasphemy and heresy, and executed by firing squad in Tabriz, Iran, in 1850. Before his death, the Bab appointed Mirza Yahya Azal (1831–1912) to serve as his successor and the leader of the community. Beginning in 1848 persecution of the Babi communities resulted in the deaths of most Babi leaders and decimated the community.

A prominent early leader of the Babi movement was Mirza Husayn-Ali of Nur (1817–92), a member of an aristocratic family from north of Tehran. He soon became active in spreading Babi teachings in northern Iran,

and he protected Babi leaders from persecution when his prominence and court connections allowed him to do so. He took the title of Bahaullah (glory of God). In 1851 he left Iran for a year at request by the prime minister. When he returned, an attempt by two young Babis to assassinate the king triggered a massive persecution of Babis and resulted in Bahaullah's imprisonment from August through December 1852. While in prison he received a revelation that marked the symbolic beginning of his ministry as the Bab's messianic successor.

On his release from prison Bahaullah, exiled permanently from Iran, settled in Baghdad. There he reinvigorated the local Babi community. He began to produce works on mystical and theological subjects, including *The Hidden Words* (1858), *The Seven Valleys* (c. 1858–62), *The Four Valleys* (c. 1858–62), *Gems of Mysteries* (c. 1858–62), and *The Book of Certitude* (1862). Babis who visited Baghdad brought his advice back to Iran, gradually consolidating and strengthening the scattered and dispirited communities there. As a result, the Iranian government formally requested the Ottoman Turkish government ruling Baghdad and the surrounding territories to remove Bahaullah farther from Iran. On the eve of his departure for Istanbul, in late April 1863, Bahaullah announced to his assembled followers that he was the promised one foretold by the Bab and a divine messenger. Bahaullah's announcement is considered the beginning of his public ministry and the end of the Babi dispensation and is the most important event in the Bahá'í calendar.

Bahaullah remained in Istanbul until December 1863, when the Ottoman government exiled him to Edirne, a small city in Turkey near the present-day borders with Bulgaria and Greece. The Istanbul and Edirne periods of Bahaullah's life saw several key developments. He composed many additional mystical works and prayers. He sent epistles to some of the world's political and ecclesiastical leaders, formally announcing his claim to be a divine messenger or manifestation of God and specifically stating that he was the return of Christ. His divine claim spread widely in Iran, with the result that the vast majority of the Babis became Bahá'ís. But relations with his half brother Mirza Yahya Azal, the symbolic head of the Babi religion, progressively broke down. Yahya attempted to poison Bahaullah and came out in opposition to him in 1867–68. As a result, the Ottoman government exiled both brothers from Edirne: Mirza Yahya to Cyprus and Bahaullah to Acre, a prison city in what is today northern Israel.

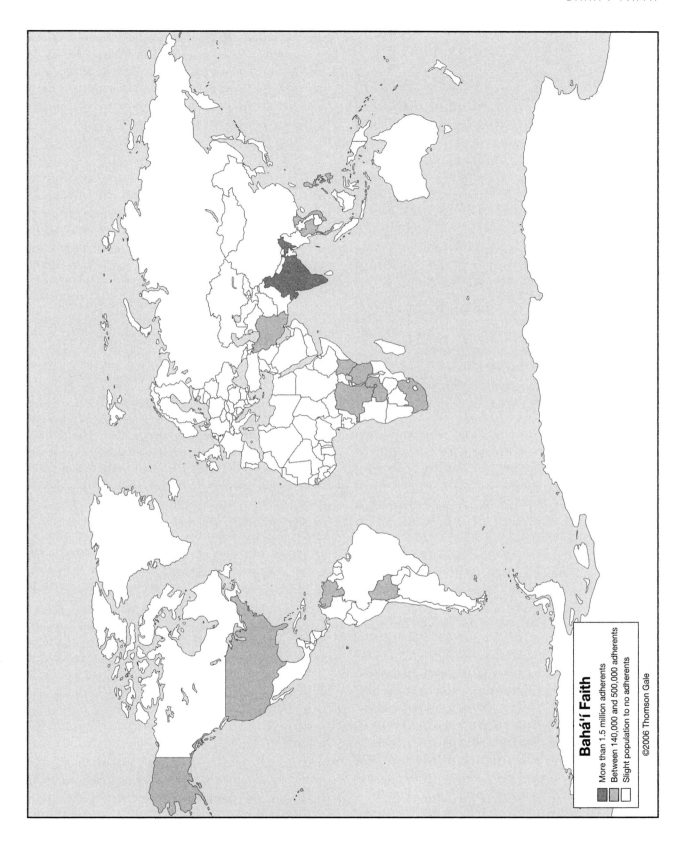

Bahá'í Faith

More than 1.5 million adherents

Between 140,000 and 500,000 adherents

Slight population to no adherents

©2006 Thomson Gale

The Bahá'í World Center and its terraced gardens on Mount Carmel in Haifa, Israel. The gardens are designed in nine concentric circles around the Shrine of the Bab, the resting place of the prophet. © AFP/CORBIS.

Bahaullah spent the next two years—from August 1868 to October 1870—in a prison barracks in Acre and then passed the remaining 22 years of his life in rented houses in Acre or just outside the city. The conditions of confinement gradually ameliorated, and Bahaullah was allowed to receive visitors, among them the British Orientalist Edward G. Browne, who interviewed Bahaullah in 1890 and published the account. Bahaullah was also able to write extensively. He continued to write epistles to kings and ecclesiastics, announcing his claims. In 1873 he composed the *Kitab-i-Aqdas* (Most Holy Book), a work containing laws of personal conduct, mystic guidance, numerous exhortations, and principles of social reconstruction. A series of short works amplified themes in the Most Holy Book, explored philosophical and theological matters, and commented on social matters, such as the importance of democracy and modernization of the Islamic world. *Epistle to the Son of the Wolf* was composed around 1891 as a response to a persecutor of Bahá'ís in Isfahan whose father, "the wolf," had been a major instigator of pogroms against Bahá'ís; it quoted some of Bahaullah's most celebrated

passages. In his Book of the Covenant (exact date unknown, though probably 1891) Bahaullah appointed his eldest son, Abbas, later titled Abdul-Baha; (Arabic: "servant of glory"), as his successor and the interpreter of his teachings. More than 15,000 works from Bahaullah's pen are extant, most of them letters, many of which include advice and prayers. He wrote in Arabic and Persian, sometimes interweaving both languages.

Through his correspondence with and guidance of visiting Bahá'ís, Bahaullah coordinated efforts to spread the Bahá'í faith beyond Iran and the Ottoman lands of Iraq, Turkey, Lebanon, Syria, and Palestine to Russian Central Asia, Egypt, The Sudan, India, Burma, and Indonesia. He also encouraged Bahá'ís to attract Sunni Muslims, Jews, Zoroastrians, Christians, and possibly Buddhists to the fold. He appointed several individuals as Hands of the Cause of God, a special position of responsibility to assist in teaching the Bahá'í faith and in protecting it from opposition. While they were termed "learned" (in Arabic, ulama), they did not have a clerical rank because Bahaullah had abolished the clergy.

Bahaullah's passing on 29 May 1892 was a shock to the Bahá'í community, which numbered perhaps 100,000 people. His written instructions guaranteed a reasonably smooth transition to the leadership of his son Abbas (1844–1921), who took the title of Abdul-Baha. Abdul-Baha's half brother Muhammad-Ali opposed Abdul-Baha's leadership but attracted few followers himself, partly because Abdul-Baha told his followers to break off contact with Muhammad-Ali and his followers. No lasting schism of the Bahá'í community resulted. Abdul-Baha's ministry as head of the Bahá'í faith lasted almost 30 years, until his passing in 1921. An early development during his tenure was the arrival of Bahá'ís of Lebanese Christian background in the United States in 1892 and the conversion of Americans, mostly blue- and white-collar Protestants of English, German, and Scandinavian backgrounds. The Americans in turn took the Bahá'í faith to Europe (1898), Hawaii (1901), Mexico (1909), Japan (1914), Brazil (1919), and Australia (1920). When the Americans heard that construction had begun on a Bahá'í house of worship in Ashgabat (modern Turkmenistan) in late 1902, they requested permission to build one in the Chicago area.

After the Young Turk Revolution freed Abdul-Baha from his confinement in Acre in 1908, he was able to travel, visiting Egypt (1910–11), Europe (1911–13), and the United States and Canada (1912). His North

Worshipers gather near a Bahá'í temple in New Delhi, India. The Bahá'í community possesses a house of worship in each geographical region of the world.
© GEORGE W. WRIGHT/CORBIS.

American tour resulted in hundreds of newspaper articles about the Bahá'í faith, greater public knowledge of the religion, the dedication of the site of the future Bahá'í house of worship outside Chicago (in Wilmette), and consolidation of the Bahá'í community. While Abdul-Baha was never able to visit Iran again, he strengthened its Bahá'í community through his letters, guided it in the establishment of the first Bahá'í administrative institutions, encouraged the creation of elementary schools for boys and girls, and fostered the gradual emancipation of Iranian Bahá'í women.

Like Bahaullah, Abdul-Baha maintained an extensive correspondence; some 16,000 letters are extant in Arabic, Persian, and Turkish. In these epistles he clarified his authority as interpreter and his position as exemplar of the Bahá'í teachings; emphasized the importance of the Bahá'í principles for social reform and international organization; answered numerous questions about theology, philosophy, and the spiritual path of the individual; offered extensive practical advice about how to live one's life, raise children, and pursue

a career; laid down the details of the Bahá'í administrative structure, especially in his Will and Testament (1935), which he wrote between 1901 and 1908; and, in 1916 and 1917, outlined the expansion of the faith worldwide in his *Tablets of the Divine Plan* (1936).

After Abdul-Baha's passing in November 1921, his will and testament was read in public and, as specified in it, authority passed to Shoghi Effendi Rabbani (1897–1957), his grandson, a student at Oxford University at the time. Shoghi Effendi was appointed the Guardian of the Bahá'í Faith. He made it a priority to establish annually elected, nine-member local and national Bahá'í governing councils (Spiritual Assemblies), as specified in Abdul-Baha's will. As that document stated, the national Spiritual Assemblies eventually would constitute the electors of the Universal House of Justice, an international governing council to which Bahaullah and Abdul-Baha had given the authority to legislate on matters about which Bahaullah was silent.

The shift from an informal to a formal organization of the Bahá'í community was not without controversy,

Located in the Chicago suburb of Wilmette, Illinois, this Bahá'í house of worship is the only temple of its kind in the United States. The building and lacelike dome of concrete and glass are nine sided. © HULTON-DEUTSCH COLLECTION/CORBIS.

but it consolidated the religion and initiated a period of sustained growth. In the United States, Bahá'í membership doubled from about 1,500 to almost 3,000. By the late 1930s the administrative bodies were sufficiently established in a few countries to allow systematic pursuit of the goals of spreading the religion laid out in Abdul-Baha's *Tablets of the Divine Plan.* Shoghi Effendi gave the North American Bahá'ís a seven-year plan, covering the period from 1937 to 1944, that called for the establishment of a Bahá'í community in every state in the United States and every province in Canada, the establishment of the nuclei of Bahá'í communities in every country in Latin America, and the completion of the exterior of the Bahá'í house of worship in Wilmette. Thus, as war raged across much of the planet, the least-disturbed portion was systematically exposed to the Bahá'í teachings. All the goals were achieved. The number of American Bahá'ís exceeded 5,000, and the number in Latin America was in the hundreds. After a two-year respite, a second seven-year plan (1946–53) gave as goals the completion of the interior of the Bahá'í house of worship in Wilmette; the election of a national

Spiritual Assembly for Canada, as well as one Spiritual Assembly each for Central America and South America; and the reestablishment of the Bahá'í faith in western Europe, where every community except the United Kingdom's had been destroyed by World War II. The German Bahá'í community had suffered severely at the hands of the Nazi government, who banned the religion and threw some members into prisons and death camps. This plan was also a complete success. The number of American Bahá'ís grew to 7,000, membership in Latin America may have reached 1,000, and Europe's Bahá'í communities counted hundreds of members. Shoghi Effendi gave the next plan, the Ten Year Crusade (1953–63), to the 12 national Spiritual Assemblies, the goals being to more than double the number of countries where Bahá'ís resided and to raise the number of national Spiritual Assemblies to 57. Except where persecution intervened, the crusade was successful. By the end of the crusade U.S. membership exceeded 10,000.

Shoghi Effendi expanded the institution of the Hands of the Cause of God, established by Bahaullah, by appointing additional individuals to the position and defining their individual and collective responsibilities as "chief stewards" of the faith. He established the Auxiliary Board, consisting of individuals appointed by the Hands of the Cause, who served under the Hands of the Cause and were responsible for encouraging and educating Bahá'ís in states or regions. Defining the nature, purpose, and chief characteristics of the Bahá'í organizational system—which was established in the same basic form in all Bahá'í communities—may be Shoghi Effendi's greatest accomplishment.

In spite of warfare and instability Shoghi Effendi developed the Bahá'í World Center in Haifa, Israel (then British-administered Palestine). The world center is both the spiritual center of the faith—Bahaullah, the Bab, and Abdul-Baha are all interred there, and it includes many holy places associated with the life of Bahaullah—and its administrative headquarters. Shoghi Effendi's efforts included the purchase of Bahá'í holy places and their restoration and beautification; completion of the Shrine of the Bab, which is also the resting place of Abdul-Baha; construction of several of the 19 monumental terraced gardens that Abdul-Baha said should extend from the top of Mount Carmel to its base in the city of Haifa; and erection of the International Archives building, the first edifice on the Arc, a semi-circle of monumental buildings that stand uphill from the Shrine of the Bab and east of the terraces. He estab-

Glossary

Babi a follower of Ali-Muhammad of Shiraz (1819–50), who took the title of the Bab (Arabic: "gate")

Baha glory, splendor, or light; the greatest name of God; the root word in Bahaullah, the title of the founder of the Bahá'í faith.

Hand of the Cause of God one of 50 individuals appointed by Bahaullah, Abdul-Baha, or Shoghi Effendi whose duties included encouraging Bahá'ís and their institutions, advising them about the development of the Bahá'í community worldwide, and informing the head of the faith about conditions and developments in local Bahá'í communities

huququllah "right of God"; a 19-percent tithe that Bahá'ís pay on their income after essential expenses

manifestation of God an individual recognized in Bahá'í authoritative writings as a source of divine revelation and usually as the founder of a religion

Nineteen Day Feast a special meeting of the Bahá'í community held once every Bahá'í month, with devotional, business, and social portions

qiblih "point of adoration"; the location toward which Bahá'ís face when saying their obligatory prayer

Universal House of Justice the supreme governing body of the worldwide Bahá'í community

ya Baha ul-abha "O Glory of the Most Glorious"; a form of the greatest name of God

lished a formal secretariat to assist him with correspondence and appointed an International Bahá'í Council to handle relations with the local governments. In 1947 Shoghi Effendi authorized representation of the Bahá'í faith, under the title Bahá'í International Community, at the United Nations.

Shoghi Effendi composed some 36,000 letters to individuals and Bahá'í institutions, and dozens of compilations of his writings have been published. He wrote *God Passes By* (1944), a history and interpretation of the Bahá'í faith's development during the period from 1844 to 1944. He also answered some theological questions, applied the spiritual path to life in the modern world, and wrote at length on such vital matters as living a life free of racism and prejudice. He translated most of Bahaullah's chief works into English, setting the pattern and defining the principles for later translations, not only into English but into all the languages of the world.

Shoghi Effendi died suddenly on 4 November 1957. He did not write an official will and testament and was unable to appoint a successor because Abdul-Baha's will and testament specified that future Guardians had to be male descendants of Bahaullah, and in 1957 no male descendants were Bahá'ís. Based on Shoghi Effendi's designation of the Hands of the Cause of God as "chief stewards" of the faith, they served as interim international coordinators of the faith until the

Universal House of Justice could be elected. The Hands took the extraordinary step of disqualifying themselves from the election, so that they could continue their service to the institution of the Hands of the Cause.

While the Bahá'í global community was shocked by Shoghi Effendi's passing, its members accepted the Hands almost unanimously, as did legal authorities concerned with the disposition of Bahá'í properties. The chief exception was one elderly Hand of the Cause, Charles Mason Remey, who declared himself the second Guardian in 1960. His claim was ignored by all but a few hundred Bahá'ís (Bahá'í membership worldwide was about 400,000 at the time).

In April 1963 Shoghi Effendi's Ten Year Crusade ended, and delegates representing 56 national Spiritual Assemblies elected the nine-member Universal House of Justice. It has since been elected every five years. It guided the steady growth of the Bahá'í faith worldwide through a series of plans (1964–73, 1974–79, 1979–86, 1986–92, 1993–2000, and 2001–06) generally known by their period of duration (Nine Year Plan, for example). It also managed several developmental milestones in the growth of the Bahá'í community.

During the turbulent 1960s and early 1970s the Bahá'í faith experienced explosive growth in every region of the globe except the countries behind the Iron Curtain and most Islamic countries, where it was prohibited or severely restricted. Developed countries saw the enrollment of tens of thousands of youth in the Bahá'í community. Even more dramatic was the attraction of a few million members of minorities—such as blacks and American Indians in the United States and Rom (gypsies) in Europe—and traditional rural peoples in Africa, Latin America, Asia, and Oceania. Demand for Bahá'í literature dramatically increased. The rapid expansion of Bahá'í membership created significant consolidation challenges for a religion that had no clergy and that was organized by elected governing bodies. The dramatic expansion among minorities continued in some places into the 1990s.

The expansion of the Bahá'í faith among populations in lesser-developed areas of the globe stimulated projects for social and economic betterment. Some projects had begun before 1921, especially in Iran, but for the next 60 years the focus was on firmly establishing Bahá'í administrative bodies. Starting in 1979 radio stations geared to the needs of rural populations were established in Ecuador, Bolivia, Peru, Chile, Liberia, and South Carolina, where about 10,000 rural African Americans had become Bahá'ís. Bahá'ís instituted village schools in hundreds of localities; a number of larger regional schools had significant budgets. Other projects focused on health, agriculture, tree planting, and the empowerment of women. Reinforcing these efforts was the Universal House of Justice's decision in 1983 to establish an Office of Social and Economic Development at the Bahá'í World Center.

Persecution of members of the Bahá'í faith in Iran dramatically increased after a revolution swept away Iran's secular monarchy and established an Islamic republic in 1978 and 1979. All Bahá'í institutions were banned, thousands of Bahá'ís were imprisoned, some 200 were executed for their beliefs, and Bahá'í community property and the community's development bank—worth several billion dollars—were confiscated. Iran's 300,000 Bahá'ís were banned from the universities. Many Bahá'ís were fired from government jobs, and Bahá'ís experienced various forms of discrimination because of their religion, such as having their insurance policies declared invalid, denial of hospital treatment, harassment by mobs, denial of justice in the courts, and burglary. Some 30,000 Bahá'ís fled the country. To mobilize public opinion Bahá'í communities throughout the world expanded their offices of public information to bring the plight of Iran's Bahá'ís to the attention of the media. Offices of external affairs were established

or expanded to present the Iranian Bahá'í's situation to governments, which resulted in a number of legislative resolutions condemning the persecution of the Iranian Bahá'ís, including resolutions by the United States Congress and the European Parliament. The Bahá'í International Community's office at the United Nations was expanded, and it became a leading nongovernmental organization affiliated with the UN system.

The expansion in membership resulted in a corresponding increase in Bahá'í literature and art. The number of books published about the Bahá'í faith every year increased about tenfold in the 1980s. The number of Bahá'í musical recordings expanded similarly; in 1992 Bahá'í gospel music became popular. The number of languages in which at least a few Bahá'í prayers and scriptural passages could be found increased to more than 800. The Bahá'í scriptures in English were enriched with the translation of four volumes of works by Bahaullah and one each by the Bab and Abdul-Baha. The first Association for Bahá'í Studies was founded in Canada in 1974; a dozen more were subsequently established around the world. A great increase in the number of Bahá'ís with graduate degrees in religious studies, Middle Eastern studies, and other subjects in the humanities—coupled with a wave of expatriated Iranian Bahá'ís deeply knowledgeable about the Bahá'í scriptures in the original Persian and Arabic languages—produced important scholarly works in Bahá'í history, theology, and scriptural studies. The expansion of Bahá'í scholarship created some tensions among intellectuals over interpretations by Shoghi Effendi and the Universal House of Justice, the need of National Spiritual Assemblies to continue conducting prepublication reviews of books and articles about the faith, and the role of discourse in the Bahá'í community.

The development of Bahá'í institutions continued during this period. Since Hands of the Cause could only be appointed by a Guardian, and because the Universal House of Justice had ruled that no additional Guardians could be appointed, in 1968 the Universal House of Justice created the institution of the Counselors to carry the responsibilities of the Hands into the future. Continental Boards of Counselors are appointed to a renewable term every five years. In 1973 the Universal House of Justice established the International Teaching Center at the Bahá'í World Center to advise it about the expansion and protection of the Bahá'í faith and coordinate the Continental Boards of Counselors. The Universal House of Justice appointed all the Hands and a group of international Counselors to its membership, transferred the Auxiliary Boards to the jurisdiction of the Counselors, and called for the appointment of assistants to the Auxiliary Board members, who are to be appointed by individual Auxiliary Board members with the approval of the Counselors.

The growth of the Bahá'í community also necessitated creation of a new level of elected coordinating councils between the local and national Spiritual Assemblies. The Universal House of Justice approved the request of a number of national Spiritual Assemblies—the first was India—to establish Bahá'í councils in states or regions. In 1997 it established regional Bahá'í councils more widely throughout the world. In some nations councils are elected annually by the members of the local Spiritual Assemblies in the council's region; in other nations the national Spiritual Assembly appoints the council directly or appoints the council from among the people who received the highest number of votes from local Spiritual Assembly members. Starting in 2001 national Bahá'í communities were divided into small planning units called "clusters." Since local Bahá'í communities are defined according to civic jurisdictional lines and because some cities, such as Los Angeles, have very large Bahá'í communities, local communities were in many cases allowed to divide themselves into "sectors."

The continued expansion of the Bahá'í faith required the creation of additional institutions and departments at the Bahá'í World Center, such as the International Teaching Center, the Office of Public Information, the Research Department, and the Office for Social and Economic Development. The support staff in Haifa expanded from a dozen persons in 1963 to some 700 in 2000. The need to explain the Bahá'í faith and its principles prompted the Universal House of Justice to release a peace statement in 1985, a statement in 1988 about individual rights and responsibilities in the world order of Bahaullah, and a letter to the world's religious leaders in 2002.

The increase in staff required a considerable expansion in facilities, and the growing Bahá'í community was in the position to support a building program. Shoghi Effendi's plans to build a series of buildings of great beauty and majesty on the Arc in Haifa were advanced when the Seat of the Universal House of Justice, the Seat of the International Teaching Center, and the Center for the Study of the Sacred Texts—each clad in Pendelikon marble and built in a modified classical style—were completed by 2000. The 19 terraces climbing the

side of Mount Carmel from base to summit were also completed and opened to the hundreds of thousands of tourists who visit each year. Bahá'í holy places in or near Haifa were purchased, restored, beautified, and opened to visiting Bahá'í pilgrims.

CENTRAL DOCTRINES The basic teachings of the Bahá'í religion are found in the writings of Bahaullah and Abdul-Baha and in the authoritative interpretations of Shoghi Effendi. The central teachings are often summarized as the oneness of God, the oneness of religion, and the oneness of humanity.

Bahaullah describes God's essence as qualitatively different from that of human beings and thus ultimately beyond their understanding. The essence of God can be understood as having such attributes as omniscience, omnipotence, and omnipresence and as having a relationship with human beings based on such qualities as love, justice, majesty, mercy, compassion, patience, generosity, kindness, beneficence, and self-subsistence. Thus, in spite of God's ultimate unknowability and otherness, Bahá'ís maintain a personal, prayer-filled relationship with their Creator.

The Bahá'í scriptures say that God created the spiritual and physical worlds but that there was never a time when creation did not exist; the relationship is causal, not temporal. All things are said to reflect attributes or qualities of God, and thus one can learn about God through contemplation and the study of creation. Human beings have a unique station in creation because they can know and love God and because they potentially can reflect all the attributes of God.

The Bahá'í concept of the oneness of religion stems from the Bahá'í concept of the manifestation of God, one of the special souls sent by God to educate humanity. Unlike human beings, manifestations are preexistent (whereas humans come into existence at the moment of conception) and have a special relationship with the divine that includes direct access to revelation. Manifestations are born in this world with ordinary human bodies, and they mature and acquire language and a culture, but they always have access to innate knowledge. They often begin their missions by withdrawing into the wilderness. They preach or write down their teachings, which eventually become expressed in scriptural form. They speak about how humans should live their lives in a loving and moral relationship with others and how they should prepare for what comes after death. They often criticize existing social and cultural institutions and are strongly opposed by their generation, often suffering death or exile as a result. But their revelation becomes the basis of a movement that endures and grows into a religious tradition, with its own doctrines, structures, and rituals. Sometimes a manifestation's particularly prominent followers or successors also have a lesser form of prophethood conferred on them (the Old Testament prophets or the Shiite Muslim imams, for example). Finally, manifestations prophesy, in symbolic language, the coming of a future manifestation, thereby inspiring messianic expectations among some of their followers.

The Bahá'í scriptures identify as many as 14 individuals as manifestations of God. Adam and Noah are mythic figures whose status as manifestations may be symbolic. Salih and Hud are prophetic figures who came to Arab tribes before the advent of Islam (they are also mentioned in the Koran) and may be manifestations. The Sabean religion, mentioned in the Koran and the Bahá'í scriptures, was founded by a manifestation whose name is lost. Abraham, Moses, Jesus, Muhammad, the Bab, Bahaullah, and Zoroaster are described by Bahaullah as manifestations. Abdul-Baha spoke of the Buddha as a manifestation, and Shoghi Effendi added Krishna. Bahaullah noted that the names of countless manifestations have been lost to history. Bahaullah, Abdul-Baha, and Shoghi Effendi state that information about manifestations and their teachings is often limited, especially manifestations that arose in preliterate societies. While all the above figures are male, there is nothing in the Bahá'í scriptures that precludes female manifestations, and many preliterate cultures have had female cultural heroes. Revelation must be relevant to culture and the needs of contemporary society; consequently, all revelations are partially time-bound and eventually are superceded. This includes Bahaullah's revelation, which Bahaullah said would endure at least a thousand years and then be followed by the teachings of another manifestation.

Because the Bahá'í scriptures view all religions as founded by manifestations, they are seen as progressively unfolding stages in the same religion of God. Bahá'ís are encouraged to "consort" with the followers of all religions in friendliness and fellowship because they all are heirs to divine guidance. The Bahá'í faith, however, does not maintain that all the past religions interpreted their founding revelations infallibly or that the traditions developed in a perfect way. Differences of doctrine among the traditions are attributed to differing social conditions shaping the expression of the revelation and to human-inspired interpretations. As a result, the major religions share some common ethical and spiritual principles but differ vastly in the details of their doctrines and rituals.

The oneness of humanity is the principle of the Bahá'í faith that shapes its ethical and social teachings. One aspect of the teaching is that humanity has its origin in a common stock, and all peoples have been equally endowed with intelligence, creativity, morality, and divine guidance. Thus, the principle implies the fundamental equality of all human beings.

The Bahá'í scriptures understand the oneness of humanity to include the equality of men and women. An important metaphor likens humanity to a bird with two wings, the male and female; unless both wings are equally developed, the bird of humanity cannot fly. To promote the equality of men and women, Bahá'í communities make efforts to improve the condition of women inside the Bahá'í community, especially in developing countries, and often engage in projects to assist women in general, such as vocational and literacy training or cooperative business projects. Bahá'í communities are particularly aware of the insight, reported in the professional development literature, that in many countries the emancipation of women is crucial to lowering the birthrate, improving infant health, and raising family income.

The Bahá'í scriptures explicitly condemn racism, especially in the context of the relations between whites and blacks in the United States. While traveling in the United States, Abdul-Baha spoke about strengthening the love between whites and blacks. He addressed the 1912 annual convention of the National Association for the Advancement of Colored People (NAACP), and he advocated interracial marriage as a way to overcome racial prejudice. Shoghi Effendi offered many specific suggestions for improving race relations (see sidebar). The American Bahá'í community has a long history of building racially integrated communities, even when the local laws made it extremely difficult, and has achieved a degree of success in attracting African Americans and other minorities to its membership. Worldwide the Bahá'í faith has often spread among members of minority groups before gaining a significant following from the majority group. Because they are defined by existing civic boundaries rather than neighborhoods, Bahá'í communities typically are racially and ethnically diverse.

The abolition of prejudices of all kinds is a principle clearly related to equality of the sexes and races. It is also associated with the Bahá'í principle of independent investigation of truth (that is, that each individual must develop the capacity to make independent judgments about the world) and is essential to the Bahá'í practice of consultation, which is considered vital to the achievement of social justice.

The manifestations devote much of their attention to guiding individuals in how to live their lives. Bahaullah states that human beings have the "twin duties" of recognizing the manifestation of God in their age—Bahaullah, for example, in this age—and obeying the manifestation's laws and teachings. Neither duty, he notes, is acceptable to God without the other, a position that, in Christian terms, could be said to call for both faith and good works, though Bahaullah does not use the Christian term "salvation" extensively. In order to accept the manifestation, individuals must search for the truth, freeing themselves from prejudices and the opinions of others, in compliance with the principle of independent investigation. (In abolishing the clergy, Bahaullah eliminated its role in guiding or mediating the search.) Bahaullah's mystic writings are replete with metaphors and stories of the mystic journey and the quest for the divine. In passages that fuse mystical and ethical qualities, he also describes in great, often poetic, detail the virtues and divine attributes a person must strive to obtain throughout life (see sidebar).

Bahaullah revealed specific laws and principles of spiritual conduct. Echoing the Five Pillars of Islam, he required Bahá'ís to repeat an obligatory prayer daily, to fast, to go on pilgrimage, and to pay a tithe. He emphasized that the true spiritual path lies not in celibacy, monasticism, and asceticism but in creating loving marriages, raising spiritually attuned children, and pursuing a vocation that serves humanity. Service to others is one of the most important virtues one can exercise.

According to the Bahá'í scriptures, human social evolution has been guided by the manifestations and has been characterized by ever-larger social units: family, tribe, city-state, and nation. Bahaullah says that humanity has now reached a stage of maturity comparable to adolescence and is capable of creating social and governing systems on a global scale. He claims that his religion brings the principles for such a social reorganization.

Central to the Bahá'í approach to implementing all of its principles is the concept of unity. Unity can be understood as existing at various levels. The simplest involves collaboration between persons in areas of common concern. Unity deepens, however, as trust grows

stronger and as prayer creates spiritual ties and fosters mutual love, until those involved achieve the ideal of being "one soul in many bodies." Building unity is a constant concern of Bahá'ís, both among themselves and in the world around them. When Bahá'ís meet to discuss matters together, they often begin with prayer, partly to create a spirit of unity. The relationship of Bahá'ís to non-Bahá'ís is similarly to be characterized by openness and a desire to work cooperatively in areas of mutual concern.

The Bahá'í practice of consultation provides the practical means to strengthen and deepen unity. Consultation involves a series of principles expressed as behaviors in a decision-making context: that all participants in consultation must be respected and feel free to contribute; that all ideas deserve consideration free from prejudice; that ideas belong to the group once they have been voiced, not to the person who voiced them; that no one should feel insulted or intimidated in the consultation process; and that advocacy of ideas must be replaced by an effort to seek the truth together.

Antithetical to the ultimate goal of spiritual unity is partisanship, which creates a lesser loyalty to a smaller group, fosters distrust and superstition between groups, and can even prevent collaboration. Bahá'í governing councils have no organized factions or caucuses. Terms like "liberal Bahá'í," "conservative Bahá'í," or "fundamentalist Bahá'í" have no clear meaning to Bahá'ís. Bahá'í elections are held without nominations, slates of candidates, or campaigns because such activities are seen as partisan and divisive. Bahá'í elections are a sacred act. Voting always begins with prayer and often includes the reading of authoritative Bahá'í texts that describe the spiritual prerequisites for those who hold elected office. Each individual votes silently and privately according to his or her consideration of the needs of the office or body being filled by election and to the dictates of personal conscience.

The Bahá'í rejection of partisanship means that Bahá'ís are forbidden from joining political parties. When Bahá'ís petition governments for assistance—as in the case of the persecuted Iranian Bahá'ís—they seek multiparty support for their concerns. Since the rule of law is essential for the functioning of any society, Bahá'ís obey laws and do not involve themselves in nonviolent civil disobedience to bring about social change. Rather, they demonstrate their principles through personal example and in ways that strengthen unity.

Racism and Racial Prejudice: A Passage from the Bahá'í Authoritative Texts

As to racial prejudice, the corrosion of which, for well-nigh a century, has bitten into the fiber, and attacked the whole social structure of American society, it should be regarded as constituting the most vital and challenging issue confronting the Bahá'í community at the present stage of its evolution. The ceaseless exertions which this issue of paramount importance calls for, the sacrifices it must impose, the care and vigilance it demands, the moral courage and fortitude it requires, the tact and sympathy it necessitates, invest this problem, which the American believers are still far from having satisfactorily resolved, with an urgency and importance that cannot be overestimated. White and Negro, high and low, young and old, whether newly converted to the Faith or not, all who stand identified with it must participate in, and lend their assistance, each according to his or her capacity, experience, and opportunities, to the common task of fulfilling the instructions, realizing the hopes, and following the example, of Abdul-Baha. Whether colored or noncolored, neither race has the right, or can conscientiously claim, to be regarded as absolved from such an obligation, as having realized such hopes, or having faithfully followed such an example. A long and thorny road, beset with pitfalls, still remains untraveled, both by the white and the Negro exponents of the redeeming Faith of Bahaullah. On the distance they cover, and the manner in which they travel that road, must depend, to an extent which few among them can imagine, the operation of those intangible influences which are indispensable to the spiritual triumph of the American believers and the material success of their newly launched enterprise. SHOGHI EFFENDI, *THE ADVENT OF DIVINE JUSTICE* (1939)

MORAL CODE OF CONDUCT Bahá'í ethical and moral teachings may be classified into three categories: duties to God, duties to oneself, and duties to others. Much of the following discussion has been summarized from Udo Schaefer's "Towards a Bahá'í Ethics," which appeared in *The Bahá'í Studies Review* (1995).

The first category encompasses loving and worshiping God, accepting God's manifestation, obeying the laws that God reveals, trusting in God, fearing God, and maintaining steadfastness of faith, servitude, and piety. Bahaullah assigned the highest rank to these duties.

The second category comprises the duties of personal spiritual development and transformation, including detachment, self-renunciation, selflessness, self-denial, purity, and chastity. These assist the individual in establishing the correct relationship to the physical world. While the Bahá'í scriptures do forbid certain behaviors—such as backbiting, lying, consuming alcohol, taking mind-altering drugs, and sexual relationships outside marriage—moderation is generally emphasized. The physical world is not seen as evil or as a source of temptation as much as it is seen to provide opportunities to do either good or bad. It should be enjoyed in moderation and with an attitude of detachment.

The third category encompasses virtues guiding our relationships with others. Unity may be seen as its key principle, for the ultimate goal of the Bahá'í faith is spiritual and social unity among human beings. Crucial to the achievement of this unity are love and justice; the former binds humans together and motivates individuals to live virtuously with others, while the latter requires corrective action, even punishment, to regulate behaviors when they go beyond their bounds. The two also balance each other, with love preventing justice from degenerating into cruelty and with justice preventing love from slipping into sentimentality and laxity. Other essentials for creating unity include truthfulness, trustworthiness, moderation, wisdom, prudence, compassion, mercy, devotion to others, kindliness, courtesy, and respect.

It is noteworthy that the supreme Bahá'í governing body is termed the Universal House of Justice and that the local and national Spiritual Assemblies are eventually to be named local and national Houses of Justice. Their names underline the role of these bodies in establishing justice in the world in order to foster unity. It is also notable that the virtues enumerated in the second and third categories are essential for the Bahá'í practice of consultation to be successful, for it calls individuals to rise to as high a level of maturity as possible, relating to each other with respect and courtesy, treating ideas with detachment, examining issues with wisdom, and always viewing everything from the point of view of unity, love, and justice.

The Bahá'í scriptures not only describe positive qualities necessary for living an ethical life. They also call on individuals to eschew wickedness, the making of mischief, envy, covetousness, malice, naughtiness, pride, sloth, idleness, cruelty to animals, bigotry, hate, strife, dissension, rancor, unseemly talk, backbiting, cursing, hypocrisy, and fanaticism.

SACRED BOOKS The sacred texts of the Bahá'í faith consist of the writings of Bahaullah, the Bab, and Abdul-Baha. Bahaullah, the founder, composed at least 15,000 letters and a hundred or so essays and books. A few hundred writings of the Bab are extant. Abdul-Baha wrote some 16,000 letters, and he wrote or approved the compilation of a half dozen authoritative books, which have been translated into English. The writings of Shoghi Effendi are authoritative and binding, but not sacred; he also wrote about 36,000 letters. About 20 volumes of his writings (mostly compilations of letters) have been published in English. Finally, the Universal House of Justice writes letters itself and oversees a department that writes letters on its behalf in response to questions from individuals and organizations. The letters receive institutional review and approval and thus are considered authoritative.

Because of their uplifting inspirational quality and status as scripture, the Bible, the Koran, and sacred texts of other religions are used by Bahá'ís in their worship alongside the writings of Bahaullah, the Bab, and Abdul-Baha. But because some of their guidance on how to conduct life has been superceded by the Bahá'í scriptures, Bahá'ís do not use the scriptures of other religions to determine how to live their lives. Accounts about Bahaullah, Abdul-Baha, and Shoghi Effendi by individuals often contain recollections of statements they made, but such accounts, termed pilgrim's notes, are not considered scriptural or authoritative unless a head of the faith has reviewed the text and approved it.

SACRED SYMBOLS The Bahá'í faith has two sacred symbols that are variants of the Arabic word *Baha* (glory). The Greatest Name (*ya Baha ul-abha*, "O Glory of the Most Glorious"), written in calligraphic Arabic script, is often displayed on walls in a place of honor. The ringstone symbol, derived from the Arabic letters in *Baha*, is incorporated in jewelry and is sometimes placed on walls. Bahá'ís commonly use the nine-pointed star as the principal Bahá'í symbol, but it is not an official symbol of the faith.

Bahaullah was painted and photographed, but pictures of him are regarded as too sacred to publish. Only a few copies exist. They are displayed only in the archives at the Bahá'í World Center, and only on special occasions, and are treated with great reverence. The same practices are followed with a painted portrait of the Bab. Many photographs and painted portraits of Abdul-Baha exist, as well as a short motion picture. The pictures are widely displayed but are treated with great respect.

EARLY AND MODERN LEADERS Because the Bahá'í faith has no clergy and emphasizes organization through governing councils, leadership is defined as exemplifying the qualities of the servant, such as humility, patience, active listening, and putting the needs of others first. Charismatic personalities are not favored, though they were more common before the Bahá'í organizational system was established. Many of the early prominent figures in the Bahá'í faith were teachers who spread it widely. A few are described below.

Jamal Effendi (died in 1898), born a Shiite Muslim in Iran, became a Babi in the 1850s or 1860s, and then he became a Bahá'í. In about 1874 or 1875 Bahaullah asked him to travel to India to teach the Bahá'í faith there. He crisscrossed the country repeatedly and spoke to large crowds—mostly Muslim—about the Bahá'í teachings, attracting some people to the religion. In 1878 he traveled to Burma (Myanmar), where he settled for several years, initiating Bahá'í communities in Mandalay and Rangoon (now Yangon). From 1884 to 1886 Effendi traveled to Thailand, Singapore, Malaysia, Java, and Sulawesi to teach the Bahá'í faith. His was the earliest effort to spread the religion in those regions. After Effendi visited Bahaullah in Acre to make a report of his travels in 1888, Bahaullah sent him on a trip to Aden and India that also included a journey through Tibet to Central Asia and Afghanistan. He returned to Acre in 1896, at which time Abdul-Baha sent him to Iran to teach the faith. He spent his last days in Acre, passing away there in 1898.

Thornton Chase (1847–1912) is generally recognized as the first American member of the Bahá'í faith. Born in Springfield, Massachusetts, and raised a northern Baptist, Chase served in the Union army during the American Civil War as a white officer of a black infantry unit, attended Brown University, started a series of unsuccessful businesses, and went on to become an actor, chorus director, silver prospector, poet, and inventor. He began a spiritual search that led him to Swedenborgianism for five years and then to the Bahá'í faith in 1894. He gradually emerged as perhaps the central member of the governing council of the Chicago Bahá'ís. He was one of the first Americans to grasp the importance of organization as it later emerged under Shoghi Effendi and to stress the Bahá'í principles of consultation. He spread knowledge of the Bahá'í Fast and holy days widely in the United States. He published two of the earliest important books on the faith: *In Galilee* (1908), an account of his visit to Abdul-Baha in Acre, and *The Bahá'í Revelation* (1909), an introductory text.

Martha Root (1872–1939) was the most important American Bahá'í itinerant teacher. An 1895 graduate of the University of Chicago, she was a journalist with some experience of international travel when she became a Bahá'í in 1909. In 1915 she began her first trip to teach the Bahá'í faith, visiting Bahá'í communities in Europe, Egypt, India, Burma, Japan, and Hawaii. In 1919 Abdul-Baha's *Tablets of the Divine Plan,* a series of epistles to the North American Bahá'ís calling on them to spread the Bahá'í faith across the world, were read at the national Bahá'í convention in New York City, and Root immediately left for South America, where there were as yet no Bahá'ís. For the next 20 years—until she died of cancer in Honolulu on her way back to the mainland United States—Root traveled almost continually, visiting every inhabited continent. She earned her living by selling travel stories to American newspapers. She usually visited a local newspaper when entering a city for the first time and used reprints of the resulting newspaper articles about her visit as a Bahá'í pamphlet. She contacted Theosophists, Esperantists, and other groups open to new ideas to tell them about the Bahá'í faith. Other Bahá'ís corresponded with and visited her contacts if Root was unable to follow up. Upon her passing, Shoghi Effendi declared her a Hand of the Cause of God.

Ruhiyyih Rabbani (Amatul-Baha Ruhiyyih Khanum, née Mary Maxwell) (1910–2000) was the daughter of May Bolles Maxwell and William Sutherland Maxwell, a prominent Canadian architect. Her parents hosted Abdul-Baha when he visited Montreal in 1912. In 1937 Mary Maxwell married Shoghi Effendi, who gave her the titles Amatul-Baha (Handmaiden of Baha) and Ruhiyyih Khanum (Lady Ruhiyyih, a name that means "spiritual"). She served as one of Shoghi Ef-

fendi's chief secretaries and assistants, and he named her a Hand of the Cause of God in 1952. Upon Shoghi Effendi's unexpected death in 1957, she played a central role in holding the Bahá'í community together through the organizational crisis that followed. Once the Universal House of Justice was established she began a series of extensive journeys, and in the next 30 years she visited virtually every country in the world, focusing in particular on encouraging Bahá'ís of tribal backgrounds and rural Bahá'ís in developing countries. She often served as the official representative of the Bahá'í faith at important ceremonial and diplomatic events. She wrote several noteworthy Bahá'í books, as well as a volume of poetry. She is buried in Haifa, Israel.

MAJOR THEOLOGIANS AND AUTHORS Mirza Abul-Fadl (1844–1914) was a Shiite clergyman who became a Bahá'í in 1876. He was instrumental in taking the Bahá'í faith to Iranian Jews and Zoroastrians and was imprisoned in Tehran for his beliefs. Subsequently he moved to Ashgabat, Turkmenistan, and played an active role in the Bahá'í community there. In 1894 Abdul-Baha urged him to move to Egypt, the intellectual capital of the Arab world. There he became a faculty member at Al-Azhar University, where he introduced the Bahá'í faith to dozens of Egyptians until he was fired for his beliefs. In 1900 Abdul-Baha asked him to move to the United States, where he was instrumental in deepening the new faith of American Bahá'ís. In 1904 he returned to Egypt, where he spent the last decade of his life. He authored three important studies of the Bahá'í faith, one of which, *Bahá'í Proofs* (1902), was an early textbook on the Bahá'í faith. His writing demonstrates a vast knowledge of the Jewish, Christian, and Muslim scriptures and sensitivity to such matters as scientific history and higher biblical criticism, even though he could not read any Western languages. He wrote several responses to written attacks against the Bahá'í faith. Two of his works are still in print in English.

Horace Holley (1877–1960) was a Connecticut Yankee and Williams College graduate who became a part of the American expatriate community in Paris, where he joined the Bahá'í community during Abdul-Baha's visit in 1911. Returning to the United States, he settled in New York and became a writer and editor. He published several books and articles on the Bahá'í faith, including *Bahá'ism: The Modern Social Religion* (1913) and *The Social Principle* (1915). Because of his organizational skills, he was elected to the Spiritual Assembly

Bahaullah, the founder of the Bahá'í faith, on How to Live One's Life

Be generous in prosperity, and thankful in adversity. Be worthy of the trust of thy neighbor, and look upon him with a bright and friendly face. Be a treasure to the poor, an admonisher to the rich, an answerer to the cry of the needy, a preserver of the sanctity of thy pledge. Be fair in thy judgment, and guarded in thy speech. Be unjust to no man, and show all meekness to all men. Be as a lamp unto them that walk in darkness, a joy to the sorrowful, a sea for the thirsty, a haven for the distressed, an upholder and defender of the victim of oppression. Let integrity and uprightness distinguish all thine acts. Be a home for the stranger, a balm to the suffering, a tower of strength for the fugitive. Be eyes to the blind, and a guiding light unto the feet of the erring. Be an ornament to the countenance of truth, a crown to the brow of fidelity, a pillar of the temple of righteousness, a breath of life to the body of mankind, an ensign of the hosts of justice, a luminary above the horizon of virtue, a dew to the soil of the human heart, an ark on the ocean of knowledge, a sun in the heaven of bounty, a gem on the diadem of wisdom, a shining light in the firmament of thy generation, a fruit upon the tree of humility. BAHAULLAH, *EPISTLE TO THE SON OF THE WOLF*, C. 1891

of the Bahá'ís of New York City. In 1923 he was elected to the National Spiritual Assembly of the Bahá'ís of the United States and Canada, and he served as executive secretary for that body for most of the next 35 years. In that position he was able to serve Shoghi Effendi closely while the latter used the American Bahá'í governing body to develop and test the practical implementation of Bahá'í administrative principles. The resulting practices were then applied elsewhere in the Bahá'í world. Holley was also chief editor of various Bahá'í quarterly magazines and a yearbook called *The Bahá'í World*. Holley drafted many statements made by the National Spiritual Assembly. In 1951 Shoghi Effendi named him a Hand of the Cause of God. On Shoghi

Effendi's passing in 1957, Holley moved to Haifa, Israel, to serve on the nine-member temporary coordinating body of the Bahá'í faith. He died in Haifa in 1960.

Alain Leroy Locke (1885–1954) was the first African-American Rhodes scholar and one of the first African-Americans to complete a Ph.D. in philosophy at Harvard University. He was a longtime member and chair of Howard University's philosophy department and is generally considered the dean of the Harlem Renaissance. In 1918 Locke became a Bahá'í. He played an important role in proclaiming Bahá'í principles directly in public gatherings throughout the American South and indirectly through scores of books and articles about race relations, adult education, multiculturalism, democracy, and black art and culture. He remains the most important Bahá'í contributor to American thought and culture.

ORGANIZATIONAL STRUCTURE To exemplify and spread the Bahá'í principles, Bahaullah established the Bahá'í community. (Bahá'ís do not use the term church to describe themselves collectively). If the Bahá'í community were described in terms of the human body, the organizational system, termed the administrative order, would be its skeleton and nervous system. It has two branches: elected councils and their agencies (at the local, regional, national, and international levels) and appointed individual consultants (at the local, regional, continental, and international levels). At the local level the elected branch is represented in the local Spiritual Assembly, the nine-member governing council chosen annually by all the adult members according to the Bahá'í principles of election. Local Spiritual Assemblies are responsible for such functions as assisting Bahá'ís, counseling them when they are in need, renting or purchasing a Bahá'í center for community meetings, handling community funds and property, demonstrating the Bahá'í principles through projects of social betterment, proclaiming the Bahá'í faith in the local media, teaching the Bahá'í faith to others, coordinating Bahá'í marriages and funerals, overseeing Bahá'í classes for children and adults, holding devotional meetings, and sponsoring Nineteen Day Feasts and holy day observances. In many nations the members of the local Spiritual Assemblies vote for the nine-member Regional Council every 26 November, all adult Bahá'ís in the region being eligible for election. The Regional Council coordinates Bahá'í activities in its geographic area, encouraging in particular the teaching of the Bahá'í faith to others.

Above the local Spiritual Assembly and the Regional Council is the nine-member national Spiritual Assembly. Each nation is divided into electoral units, each of which elects one or more delegates to the annual national convention. The delegates can elect to the national Spiritual Assembly any adult Bahá'í (except a Counselor) who resides in the nation and who has full membership privileges. The national Spiritual Assembly elects officers from among its own members (a chair, vice chair, secretary, and treasurer, at minimum) and hires staff as needed. National Spiritual Assemblies oversee relations with national governments, interact with the national media, own office buildings and other property (such as schools, radio stations, and houses of worship), often publish and distribute Bahá'í literature, set the jurisdictional boundaries of local Spiritual Assemblies (usually following legally recognized civil boundaries), discipline Bahá'ís for violations of Bahá'í law, coordinate efforts to emancipate women or empower minorities, sponsor social and economic projects, and organize national campaigns to proclaim Bahá'í teachings and to teach the Bahá'í religion to others.

At the international level the Universal House of Justice is the nine-member governing body. It is elected every five years in late April by members of all national Spiritual Assemblies. All male Bahá'ís with full membership privileges are eligible for election.

Abdul-Baha and Shoghi Effendi emphasized the importance of the Universal House of Justice in their writings. They stressed that the Universal House of Justice was infallible in matters essential to the Bahá'í faith and had to be obeyed by Bahá'ís. The Universal House of Justice devotes much of its time to guiding national Spiritual Assemblies and the Bahá'í world in general, setting international priorities, defending the Bahá'ís from persecution, fostering study of the Bahá'í scriptures, overseeing the translation and publication of Bahá'í texts, and answering thousands of questions from Bahá'ís and Bahá'í institutions. It issues statements about aspects of the Bahá'í faith. It maintains representation at the United Nations in New York and Geneva under the name of the Bahá'í International Community. It sets the boundaries of national Bahá'í communities and can disband a national Spiritual Assembly and call for a new election if it determines that Bahá'í electoral principles were violated.

The Universal House of Justice also appoints Counselors, the members of the principal institution of the appointed branch of the Bahá'í administrative order.

In 2003 there were 81 Counselors divided among five "continental" boards, plus nine serving at the International Teaching Center in Haifa. The Continental Boards of Counselors, in turn, appoint the 990 Auxiliary Board members who work in specific regions within the continents. They, in turn, appoint assistants, numbering in the thousands, who serve at the local level. Counselors and Auxiliary Board members are appointed to five-year terms; assistants are usually reappointed annually. The Counselors, Auxiliary Board members, and assistants encourage Bahá'ís, advise the Bahá'í elected bodies within their spheres of responsibility, inform Bahá'ís and institutions about national and international priorities, and generate reports to the International Teaching Center about developments at the local, regional, and national levels. The Counselors and their auxiliary institutions have no judicial or decision-making authority over the community, but by virtue of the Bahá'í principle of consultation they play a central role in strengthening the Bahá'í faith and fostering communication.

HOUSES OF WORSHIP AND HOLY PLACES Bahá'í holy places are associated with the founders of the faith and prominent early followers. The house of the Bab in Shiraz, Iran, where he announced his mission as a manifestation of God in 1844, is considered a holy place and an official place of Bahá'í pilgrimage. Confiscated from the Bahá'í faith by the Islamic revolutionary government in 1979, the building was destroyed. The house of Bahaullah in Baghdad, also an official place of pilgrimage, was confiscated from the Bahá'í community in 1922. Finally, the tombs of the Bab and Bahaullah in Haifa and Acre, Israel, respectively, are holy places and places of pilgrimage. Other holy places at the Bahá'í World Center include the tombs of Bahaullah's son Mirza Mihdi, his daughter Bahiyyih Khanum, his wife Navvab, and Abdul-Baha's wife, Munirih Khanum, as well as houses where Bahaullah and Abdul-Baha lived. Houses where Bahaullah resided in Iran and Turkey are also holy places.

The heads of the faith have designated various other sites as holy places, such as the tombs of individuals martyred for their belief in Iran and those of prominent early believers who sacrificed their time and efforts to spread the religion. In North America the Maxwell home in Montreal, where Abdul-Baha stayed, is a holy place.

The Bahá'í community possesses a house of worship in each geographical region of the world: New Delhi, India; Frankfurt, Germany; Wilmette, Illinois (United States); Panama City, Panama; Sydney, Australia; Kampala, Uganda; and Apia, Western Samoa. A house of worship was built in Ashgabat, Turkmenistan, but was confiscated and later torn down by the Soviet authorities. A house of worship is planned for Santiago, Chile. After this last "continental" house of worship is completed, the focus will turn to building national Houses of Worship around the world and, eventually, local Houses of Worship.

A Bahá'í house of worship has few architectural requirements. All houses of worship must have nine sides and nine doors. All have a dome, though this is not required, and most are surrounded by gardens. Houses of Worship are places where Bahá'ís gather for dawn prayers, teach their children to chant prayers, and frequently hold devotional services. In the prayer hall sermons are not allowed, and instrumental music is forbidden; programs consist of the recitation of sacred scripture by individual readers, the singing of a cappella music based on scripture, and silent prayer.

Each house of worship is intended to be at the center of a larger institution, the Mashriqul-Adhkar ("Dawning Place of the Mention of God"), which is to include educational, social, and charitable facilities, such as a library, university, hospital, hostel for visitors, and home for the elderly and disabled. The existing Houses of Worship do not yet have such facilities. At present local Bahá'í communities purchase or rent centers for devotional gatherings, classes, administrative activities, and social gatherings, or they meet in homes.

WHAT IS SACRED? The Bahá'í faith recognizes some places as sacred but holds few objects sacred. Most such objects are associated with the Bab, Bahaullah, and, to a lesser extent, Abdul-Baha. The Bahá'í International Archives in Haifa houses such relics as Bahaullah's writings, clothing, and personal effects; tufts of Bahaullah's hair; painted portraits and photographs of Bahaullah; and a portrait of the Bab. A Bahá'í pilgrimage includes a visit to the International Archives. The visit is carried out in an atmosphere of solemnity and dignity. Images of Bahaullah are regarded as sacred; the few copies that exist are brought out for viewing only on rare occasions. In a more general sense the Bahá'í faith considers all of creation to reflect the names and attributes of God and thus to be imbued with sacredness.

HOLIDAYS AND FESTIVALS The Bahá'í faith has nine holy days annually on which work is to be suspended. They are Naw-Ruz (New Year), which falls on the equinox in March; three days during the 12-day festival of Ridvan, which celebrates Bahaullah's public announcement of his mission as a divine messenger in 1863, of which the 1st, 9th, and 12th days (21 and 29 April and 2 May) are holy days; the Declaration of the Bab (23 May), which commemorates the day he announced his mission as a divine messenger in 1844; the Ascension of Bahaullah (29 May); the Martyrdom of the Bab (9 July); the Birth of the Bab (20 October); and the Birth of Bahaullah (12 November). Bahá'í communities often sponsor public commemorations of these events.

Two holy days are associated with the ministry of Abdul-Baha: the Day of the Covenant (26 November), which commemorates his role as the center of the covenant of Bahaullah; and the Ascension of Abdul-Baha (28 November). Work is not suspended on these days.

The Bahá'í faith has a calendar of 19 months of 19 days each. Each month is named for an attribute of God, such as Baha (splendor), Jalal (glory), Jamal (beauty), Nur (light), and Rahmat (mercy). Each month—usually on the first day—local Bahá'í communities host a gathering termed a Nineteen Day Feast, which includes a devotional program, a consultative portion in which community business is discussed, and a social portion, during which the community shares fellowship. Only Bahá'ís can attend Feast. The Bahá'í community does not have a required weekly service, mass, or other devotional program, though weekly devotional programs are often held, especially in connection with children's classes ("Bahá'í Sunday school").

Since the Bahá'í calendar is solar, and 19 months of 19 days each totals 361 days, 4 days are added to the calendar each year (or 5 in a leap year) to keep it synchronized with the seasons. This period—the intercalary days—is a time of fellowship, family gatherings, service to those in need, and gift giving.

The last month of the year—2 through 20 March, the 19 days between the intercalary days and the New Year—is a fast, when Bahá'ís refrain from eating and drinking from sunrise to sunset. The purpose of the fast is to detach the individual from the material world and focus attention on the spiritual life. Exemptions from physical fasting are granted to children under 15, senior citizens over 70, and adults who are pregnant, nursing, menstruating, traveling, ill, or performing heavy labor.

Even those who are unable to keep the physical fast, however, are able to keep the fast spiritually by focusing on prayer and detachment.

MODE OF DRESS Beyond the requirement that Bahá'ís dress modestly (a requirement that is itself defined according to local cultural norms) and cleanly, the Bahá'í faith does not prescribe a mode of dress for members. But Bahaullah specified that Bahá'ís should not allow themselves to be "playthings of the ignorant," suggesting that they should avoid fads and frivolous dress.

DIETARY PRACTICES The Bahá'í faith does not ban any types of food—its scriptures declare all things should be "clean"—nor does it require anything to be eaten or drunk. The only dietary restrictions on Bahá'ís involve a ban on alcohol and other substances that are significantly mind-altering, such as hashish, unless the substance has been prescribed by a physician as part of a medical treatment.

Bahaullah and Abdul-Baha urged a simple diet and discussed the importance of a healthy diet in preventing and overcoming disease. Abdul-Baha stated that eventually a vegetarian diet would be adopted widely. The Bahá'í writings on diet and health stress the importance of being guided by scientific research.

RITUALS The Bahá'í faith possesses no clergy (in the sense of full-time ordained religious professionals with specialized religious training) and virtually no communal ritual. Worship generally consists of celebration of the word of God through recitation of scriptural passages and prayers, which can be selected and read by anyone. In some cultures—notably the Iranian culture—it is customary to chant Bahá'í scripture. Worship also includes music, especially singing. (Instrumental music is forbidden in Houses of Worship but is often used in other contexts.) Bahá'í worship often includes songs from other religious traditions that are theologically appropriate; in the United States, for example, "Amazing Grace" is sometimes sung. A devotional program may include brief addresses, except in the prayer hall in a house of worship, where addresses are not permitted. Since only Bahá'ís can make financial contributions to the Bahá'í faith, and their contributions are strictly voluntary and private, Bahá'í worship never includes a public donation of money.

The form of worship described above may be found in various contexts: the devotional portion of the Nineteen Day Feast, the monthly gathering of the local Bahá'í community, daily worship programs at a Bahá'í house of worship, or weekly devotional programs held by local Bahá'í communities. Bahá'í weddings and funerals usually involve devotions in this form as well.

Bahá'ís are directed by scripture to perform an obligatory prayer daily. They may choose one of three obligatory prayers: the Short Obligatory Prayer, to be said once a day between noon and sunset; the Medium Obligatory Prayer, to be said three times a day (in the morning, the afternoon, and the evening); and the Long Obligatory Prayer, to be said any time within a 24-hour period. Both the medium and long prayers include ritual movements. All three are to be recited while facing the *qiblih* (Bahaullah's tomb). Unlike the Muslim obligatory prayer (*salat*), Bahá'í obligatory prayers are said privately, not congregationally. Bahá'í personal worship also includes repetition of the phrase Allah-u-Abha ("God is most glorious") 95 times each day. The obligatory prayer and repetition of Allah-u-Abha are preceded by the performance of ablutions.

The Bab, Bahaullah, and Abdul-Baha revealed numerous prayers for believers to use, usually in response to a specific need in relation to such matters as marriage, children, spouses, health, the passing of loved ones, life tests, and the acquisition of virtues and divine qualities like compassion and patience. Collections of prayers, which have been published in prayer books in many languages, are often recited by Bahá'ís in their private devotionals. Bahaullah exhorted Bahá'ís to hold themselves accountable each day before God, an effort that constitutes a form of prayer in the individual's own words; Bahá'ís otherwise seldom pray in their own words. Bahaullah urged Bahá'ís to recite the word of God every morning and evening. Finally, work performed in service to humanity is considered worship.

A Bahá'í marriage ceremony consists of the recitation of a vow ("We will, all, verily, abide by the Will of God") by the bride and groom in the presence of at least two witnesses. Bahá'ís are free to choose the location and program for the wedding ceremony. In many countries the Bahá'í community is empowered to conduct marriages, making a civil ceremony unnecessary.

A Bahá'í funeral, like a Bahá'í wedding, has no fixed program. Before interment of an adult Bahá'í, it is obligatory to recite the congregational prayer for the dead. The prayer, which includes six verses to be repeated 19 times each, is recited by one person on behalf of everyone present. Bahá'í prayers are often recited and songs sung during the funeral or at the grave site. Funeral and memorial services might include biblical texts or passages from other scriptures, especially if the family of the deceased is not Bahá'í.

Bahá'í law specifies that Bahá'ís should not be cremated. The body of the deceased is to be washed and wrapped in cotton or silk and placed in a coffin of wood, stone, or crystal, and a burial ring is to be placed on the finger. The body should not be transported more than an hour's distance from the place of death and should be buried facing the *qiblih,* the holiest place to Bahá'ís.

Bahá'ís are encouraged to go on pilgrimage once in their lifetime if they are able. Pilgrimage to the Bahá'í World Center is a nine-day event that includes visits to various holy places, such as the tombs of the Bab and Bahaullah. Unlike the Muslim pilgrimage to Mecca, it can be performed any time of the year, but it requires submitting an application to the Universal House of Justice.

RITES OF PASSAGE The Bahá'í faith does not have a prescribed baptism, a rite of passage for youth, or a required ceremony for converts. When someone wishes to become a Bahá'í, he or she first declares his or her faith in some manner, often by signing an enrollment card. Sometimes one or more persons appointed by the local Spiritual Assembly meet with the declarant to make sure the person understands the Bahá'í faith, at least at a minimal level. Then the person is enrolled as a member of the Bahá'í community. Membership is clearly defined because it has privileges: Only members can attend Feast, vote or be voted for in Bahá'í elections, and contribute money to the Bahá'í faith.

MEMBERSHIP Bahá'ís have a spiritual obligation to teach the Bahá'í faith to others, and the scriptures give ethical guidelines as to how the faith is to be taught. Three principles stand out: that people are taught the Bahá'í faith in ways that involve no coercion, bribery, or deceit; that, in their personal relations with people who inquire about the faith, Bahá'ís follow the principles of consultation, such as active listening and seeking the truth together; and that Bahá'ís teach their religion to others through personal moral and spiritual example, establishing warm and reciprocal friendships, offering a wise and appropriate explanation of their beliefs, quoting appropriate passages from the Bahá'í scriptures, and actualizing the teachings in their daily activities. Bahá'í

institutions organize events to present Bahá'í teachings to the public, orchestrate media campaigns to proclaim Bahá'í principles, and sponsor social and economic development projects that express Bahá'í principles in action. Bahá'í institutions also encourage Bahá'ís to move to cities and villages to establish new Bahá'í communities, an effort known as pioneering. Most major Bahá'í institutions maintain informational websites. Some run informational radio stations.

RELIGIOUS TOLERANCE Bahaullah exhorted the Bahá'ís to "consort with the followers of all religions in friendliness and fellowship." The Bahá'ís have a long history of lively and positive interchange with members of other religions and, since the rise of the modern interfaith movement, of involvement in efforts to work with other faiths. Because the Bahá'í scriptures recognize the validity of all major religions and see them all as derived from revelation or inspired by the same divine source, the Bahá'í religion has no problem with accepting, praying with, and working with other religions. Bahá'ís may attend services of other faiths, and most Bahá'í events are open to all. The Bahá'í principle of consultation means that Bahá'ís should approach other religionists positively and openly. Bahá'ís have been active in planning the Parliaments of the World Religions held in 1993, 1999, and 2004. Bahá'í communities are members of many international, national, and local interfaith organizations.

The Bahá'í faith forbids the use of physical coercion in matters of religion and supports the principle of freedom of worship and religious assembly. Bahá'ís are subject to severe oppression in many Islamic countries and, in the past, were persecuted by fascist and some communist regimes and by a few dictators, such as Idi Amin of Uganda. In Iran as many as 20,000 Babis and Bahá'ís were killed for their beliefs between 1844 and 1900. Since the Islamic Revolution of 1978–79, some 200 Bahá'ís have been executed for their beliefs, and thousands more have been fired from their jobs, harassed, imprisoned, tortured, denied hospital treatment or insurance coverage, refused equal rights in courts, expelled from universities, and in many cases expelled from public elementary and high schools.

SOCIAL JUSTICE The Bahá'í scriptures exhort Bahá'ís to be "anxiously concerned" about the world around them. They also stress that the social problems of the world are caused by the lack of recognition of such principles as the oneness of humanity and the ethic of unity that are fundamental to Bahá'í belief.

Bahaullah called on the nations of the world to renounce armaments, reduce their militaries to a size sufficient to meet internal security threats only, and enter into collective agreements to defend one another in case of outside attack. He called for a summit of world leaders to meet and deliberate on the common problems of humanity. He also called on humanity to establish a universal currency and universal weights and measures and to adopt a universal auxiliary language to supplement existing languages in the international arena.

Bahaullah singled out the British system of government as praiseworthy and "good" because it embraced both the principle of monarchy and of consultation of the people through Parliament. He stressed the importance of consultation in all matters, raising it to a principle of central importance to society and culture. He exhorted monarchs and presidents to be concerned about the poor and to uphold justice.

Bahaullah and his son Abdul-Baha showed a deep interest in economic development and modernization. Bahaullah abolished the Islamic ban on interest, thereby allowing the creation of modern banking systems. He and Abdul-Baha supported the creation of modern schools, including the first Bahá'í school in Iran. Bahaullah described work as a form of worship, a way to express one's creativity, serve humanity, carry forward the advance of civilization, and earn a living for one's family. He thus abolished notions that secular work was unspiritual or inferior to a lifestyle of contemplation and prayer. Abdul-Baha rejected the idea, prevalent in much of the Middle East at the time, that European or foreign ideas are automatically suspect. He called on nations to accept or reject ideas based on consultation and experimentation rather than prejudice.

The Bahá'í scriptures call for universal compulsory education to assure that everyone acquires literacy and a basic knowledge of the world. The scriptures offer at least two reasons for universal literacy: so that everyone can read and study the word of God on their own, without the need of intermediaries to interpret or explain it; and so that everyone can make a contribution to humanity's "ever-advancing civilization." Village literacy schools are among the most common projects for social improvement sponsored by Bahá'í communities in underdeveloped regions. In the United States after-school tutoring is sponsored by some local Bahá'í communities. Worldwide both individual Bahá'ís and Bahá'í commu-

nities sponsor or collaborate with others in thousands of projects for the social and economic betterment of human beings.

The Bahá'í scriptures delineate a few basic economic principles for adjusting the economy of the world. The acquisition of wealth is not condemned; rather, it is seen as essential in order to provide for one's family and assist the poor. Wealth confers a responsibility on its possessor. The Bahá'í scriptures enjoin everyone to acquire a vocation in order to earn a living in the world; neither the rich nor the poor are to be idle, and begging is forbidden. Abdul-Baha advocated a graduated income tax by which those unable to support their families are assisted by the surplus income of the wealthier members of the community.

Bahaullah's law of *huququllah* ("right of God") is relevant here. The law states that Bahá'ís must examine their expenditures, divide them into two categories (necessary and surplus), and periodically pay to the Bahá'í faith a 19 percent "tithe" on the surplus. While there are guidelines about how to determine one's necessary expenses, the individual has considerable leeway in applying the guidelines. For example, housing expenses can be regarded as necessary expenses, but an individual can decide that because he or she has a larger house that is necessary, it would be appropriate to regard the difference between a smaller and a larger house as a surplus on which the right of God must be paid. The law requires that Bahá'ís examine the material dimension of their lives and consider whether they are living in too much luxury.

The principles mentioned above foster among Bahá'ís a sense of financial responsibility and develop recognition of the importance of generosity and material sacrifice for others. They also intended to result in feelings of solidarity with all peoples, regardless of skin color, religion, class, or temperament.

While Bahá'ís are often involved in projects for social betterment, they are careful to avoid partisanship and partisan politics. The Bahá'í emphasis on unity means that Bahá'ís reject approaches to social improvement that are based on divisiveness and the solidarity of one group at the expense of others. When Bahá'ís support specific legislation—such as ratification of United Nations treaties against genocide and violence toward women—they seek to contribute to efforts that have broad support.

SOCIAL ASPECTS The Bahá'í scriptures regard marriage as the foundational institution in human society. Bahaullah referred to marriage as a "fortress for well-being and salvation." He recommended it highly and discouraged celibacy.

The Bahá'í scriptures forbid arranged marriages but require the permission of all living parents before a marriage can take place, unless the parents are unable to give permission because of mental incapacity. The wedding vow ("We will, all, verily, abide by the Will of God") establishes a Bahá'í marriage as a kind of love triangle, with God at its apex. Sexuality is regarded as only one aspect of marriage, albeit an important one. The only proper expression of sexuality, from the point of view of the Bahá'í scriptures, is a heterosexual relationship inside a marriage. Bahaullah stated that, in the future, Bahá'ís who commit adultery should pay a fine to the House of Justice; the sum starts small but doubles each time the offense is repeated.

Divorce is strongly discouraged but allowed. A couple having marital difficulties should seek counseling and, if that fails, should initiate a year of waiting while they reside separately and continue to attempt to reconcile. Any resumption of sexual relations or cohabitation requires a new start to the year of waiting. During the year of waiting the husband has an obligation to support the wife and children. After the year is over, if reconciliation has proved impossible, the couple may divorce.

Bahaullah in a verse exhorted married couples to bring forth one who will "remember" God, which has been interpreted to mean that a couple should strive to have at least one child. The mother is understood to be the first educator of the child, but the father has important educational responsibilities as well. The father is seen as the principal breadwinner of the family. But families are free to arrange their lives so that the mother works and the father stays at home with the children if that is best for them.

The Bahá'í scriptures use the metaphor of a growing tree to describe the raising of children. Just as a tree must be pruned and directed to grow straight, children must be guided and sometimes disciplined, but without resort to harsh punishment, beating, or tongue-lashing. The spiritual education of children—that is, to raise them as generous, loving, caring human beings who serve others and worship their Creator—is of paramount importance, though literacy and other basic education are also compulsory.

CONTROVERSIAL ISSUES The Bahá'í community seldom takes public stands on controversial issues that are matters of individual conscience. It does not expect those who are not Bahá'ís to adhere to Bahá'í standards of behavior.

The Bahá'í authoritative texts state that an individual's soul comes into existence at the time of conception. Birth control techniques that prevent the implantation of a fertilized egg and thus kill it, such as intrauterine devices, are not to be used by Bahá'ís. Bahá'ís may use birth control methods that prevent conception (such as birth control pills and condoms) in order to plan the timing and spacing of their children. Bahá'í couples are exhorted not to use birth control in order to remain childless, as the raising of at least one child is regarded as an important part of marriage. A couple's birth control decisions are considered private, and Bahá'í communities or institutions do not concern themselves with such matters.

Since the Bahá'í authoritative texts regard life as beginning at the moment of conception, abortion is seen as taking a life. Accordingly, Bahá'ís should not regard it as a birth control option. If the life of the mother is endangered, however, or if other medical problems arise, it is left to individuals to make their decisions regarding abortion in consultation with their doctors. The Universal House of Justice has chosen not to legislate about such matters. Bahá'ís are not asked whether they have had abortions, nor are they penalized for having them. Because the abortion issue has become immensely politicized, the Bahá'í community does not take any position on such matters as legalizing or banning abortions.

The Bahá'í faith permits divorce, though it discourages the practice. The Bahá'í community does not take positions on the legalization or legal restriction of divorce.

Since the Bahá'í faith has no clergy, it has none of the problems that many religious communities have with women serving as clergy. Women have been members of local and national Spiritual Assemblies since the formation of the first such bodies in the United States in the first decade of the twentieth century. Women also have served as Hands of the Cause of God, which is considered the highest-ranking position a Bahá'í can occupy. The Bahá'í scriptures said in the mid-nineteenth century that women had the right to marry whom they wished, divorce, own property, and practice a vocation—rights that did not exist in most societies of that day. In the early twentieth century Abdul-Baha said that women should enter all the fields occupied by men, becoming great scientists and physicians, and that women should be elected as presidents and prime ministers of nations. It may therefore seem surprising that women cannot serve in the Universal House of Justice, the Bahá'í faith's highest coordinating council. The Bahá'í scriptures give no reason for this exception but state that the reason will be clear in the future. The Universal House of Justice has added that the exemption has nothing to do with the issue of equality of the sexes.

Like other religious communities, the Bahá'í faith has had to deal with dissidence and schism. Abdul-Baha strongly emphasized the covenant, which among other things is a teaching that God will protect and guide the Bahá'í community through the individual or institution at its head and that the community will obey the head's decisions. Individuals who disagree with a position of the head of the faith—currently the Universal House of Justice—are free to hold their views privately and to enter into dialogue with the Universal House of Justice on the subject in dispute.

In rare circumstances individuals have come out in active opposition to the head of the Bahá'í faith and have sought to create their own alternative version of the faith. In those cases, after an effort to bring about reconciliation, the head of the faith has declared the person a covenant breaker. Bahá'ís are not to associate with covenant breakers in social and religious contexts and are discouraged, though not forbidden, from reading the person's writings or maintaining economic contact with the person—through business transactions, for example. Historically this policy has been remarkably effective in preventing the creation of Bahá'í sects. When Bahaullah, Abdul-Baha, and Shoghi Effendi died, a few individuals disputed the succession and claimed leadership for themselves, but the resulting movements rarely acquired more than a few hundred followers and usually lost their momentum in two or three decades. Currently there exist two or three small groups who disputed the succession after Shoghi Effendi's passing, earlier such groups having all faded away. For example, the Orthodox Bahá'ís, with 100 or so members concentrated in New Mexico, claim that Charles Mason Remey was the rightful successor to Shoghi Effendi. Another group, the Bahá'ís Under the Provision of the Covenant (BUPC), who separated from the Orthodox Bahá'ís, also has about 100 members.

Dissidence within the mainstream Bahá'í community has been relatively rare, in spite of the religion's diversity of ethnic and religious backgrounds. Although it has supported scholarly collaboration and the creation of international distance-learning courses, since the 1990s the Internet has fostered controversy over such issues as the role of women in the Bahá'í community, especially their ineligibility for membership in the Universal House of Justice, as well as the practice of institutional review before publication of all works written by Bahá'ís about the faith; the rejection of nominations and campaigns in Bahá'í elections; the rejection of homosexuality as a legitimate lifestyle for Bahá'ís; the relationship between Bahá'í institutions and academic scholarship; and the nature and purpose of discourse in the Bahá'í community, especially in changing teachings and policies. Although only a few hundred persons may have taken part in this lively discussion, they have included individuals of some intellectual influence. Perhaps a dozen of the latter have separated from the mainstream Bahá'í community because of their differences over beliefs and practices, and several have published works critical of the Bahá'í community.

CULTURAL IMPACT Because the Bahá'í faith is only a little more than 150 years old and has a relatively small number of widely scattered adherents, its cultural and artistic impact remains nascent. While Bahá'í-inspired art forms may emerge in the future, the emphasis remains on the expression of Bahá'í principles through the existing diverse cultures of the world.

Bahá'í Houses of Worship, also called Bahá'í temples, are perhaps the best example of this effort. All temples must have nine sides and nine doors, with an auditorium facing toward Bahaullah's tomb in northern Israel. All have domes and gardens. But beyond these characteristics, the temples are architectural expressions of culture. The first Bahá'í temple, in Ashgabat, Turkmenistan, had a principal entrance resembling the grand entrances of mosques typical of Iran and central Asia, and it had structures resembling minarets. The Bahá'í temple in Wilmette, Illinois, was an attempt to express Bahá'í principles in a wholly new architectural form, one with some features of cathedral domes and mosque minarets and with geometric interior and exterior ornamentation that included both European Christian and Islamic motifs. The temple in Kampala, Uganda, was designed to resemble a traditional African hut and used native art forms in its decoration. The temples in Panama and Western Samoa also extensively utilized native art forms in their ornamentation. The temple outside

Frankfurt, Germany, featured an ultramodern glass and steel design expressing the rebirth of postwar German society. The temple in New Delhi, India, represents a gigantic opening lotus flower in marble. The lotus is an ancient symbol in various Indian religions.

The Bahá'í World Center in Haifa, Israel, has also expressed Bahá'í principles in its structures. The exteriors of the buildings generally have used classical Greek and Roman architectural forms, such as marble pillars and marble cladding to convey a sense of timelessness and majesty. The building interiors have been filled with furniture and objets d'art that express the richness and diversity of culture around the world, such as Persian carpets, Chinese vases, classical European furniture, African sculpture, and modern abstract paintings. The administrative buildings have been laid out on an arc that crosses the slope of Mount Carmel, pivoting around several sacred tombs. The buildings and tombs are set in magnificent and extensive gardens. Another set of 19 garden terraces stretches from the foot to the summit of Mount Carmel. The tenth and centermost terrace is occupied by the Shrine of the Bab, the resting place of both the Bab and Abdul-Baha, the holiest Bahá'í place in Haifa. The effect of the proximity of sacred tombs and administrative buildings is to fuse the timeless sacred and the administrative, underlining the essential nature of the latter to the Bahá'í faith's development and progress. Set in immense gardens, both the sacred and the administrative structures are infused with an Edenic, utopian quality.

Individual Bahá'ís have made numerous contributions to the arts, though it is not necessarily clear to what extent their contributions reflected their identities as Bahá'ís. The best known Western examples are Dizzy Gillespie (1917–93), in jazz music; Jim Seals (born in 1941) and Dash Crofts (born in 1940), in popular music; Mark Tobey (1890–1976), in abstract painting; Bernard Leach, in pottery (1887–1979); Alain Locke (1886–1954), in philosophy; and Robert Hayden (1913–80), in poetry. Bahá'í principles that most often are used as themes in art by Bahá'ís are the unity of religion, the oneness of humanity, unity in diversity, and appreciation for forms and motifs drawn from many cultural contexts.

Robert Stockman

Bibliography

Abdul-Baha Abbas. *Writings of Abdul-Baha: A Compilation.* New Delhi: Bahá'í Publishing Trust, 1994.

Bab, Ali Muhammad Shirazi. *Selections from the Writings of the Bab.* Compiled by the Research Department of the Universal House of Justice and translated by Habib Taherzadeh. Haifa: Bahá'í World Centre, 1976.

Bahaullah. *Writings of Bahaullah: A Compilation.* New Delhi: Bahá'í Publishing Trust, 1986.

———. *Bahá'í Prayers: A Selection of Prayers.* Wilmette, Ill.: Bahá'í Publishing Trust, 1982.

Browne, Edward Granville. *Selections from the Writings of E.G. Browne on the Babi and Bahá'í Religions.* Edited by Moojan Momen. Oxford: George Ronald, 1987.

Cole, Juan R.I. *Modernity and the Millennium: The Genesis of the Bahá'í Faith in the Nineteenth-Century Middle East.* New York: Columbia University Press, 1998.

Hatcher, John S. *The Purpose of Physical Reality: The Kingdom of Names.* Wilmette, Ill.: Bahá'í Publishing Trust, 1987.

Hatcher, William S., and J. Douglas Martin. *The Bahá'í Faith: The Emerging Global Religion.* San Francisco: Harper and Row, 1984.

Buddhism

FOUNDED: Fifth century B.C.E.

RELIGION AS A PERCENTAGE OF WORLD POPULATION: 6 Percent

OVERVIEW Buddhism is the world's oldest missionary religion. Since its beginnings some 2,500 years ago in northern India, it has spread to nearly every region of the world. There are now more than 350 million Buddhists in the world, most of whom belong to one or the other of the two major schools: the Mahayana and the Theravada. About 98 percent of the world's Buddhists can be found in Asia, but there are significant Buddhist communities throughout Europe, North America, and Australia. There are Buddhists who are poor rice farmers in Malaysia and who are wealthy business owners in Chicago.

As it has spread, Buddhism has by necessity also changed, expanding to adapt to many different cultural, linguistic, and geographical settings, incorporating local beliefs and practices, and shifting to accommodate often fluid social and political contexts. The Buddhist tradition thus displays an incredible variety of beliefs and practices. There is no central Buddhist organization, single authoritative text, or simple set of defining practices. Buddhism is, to its core, a pluralistic religion.

Despite its incredible diversity, though, there are elements that cut across the many contexts in which Buddhism and Buddhists flourish. These elements include beliefs and traditions that, although perhaps slightly different depending on their specific settings, could be recognized and practiced by all Buddhists. For instance, all

Buddhists recite the simple formula known as the Three Refuges (also known as the Triple Gem): "I go for refuge to the Buddha, I go for refuge to the dharma, I go for refuge to the sangha." Buddhists can be heard chanting these lines in Colombo, Bangkok, Beijing, Sidney, Rome, or Los Angeles. Certain core philosophical tenets and beliefs that cut across the Buddhist world include karma, nirvana, and renunciation. While attention must be paid to the diverse contexts, beliefs, and practices of Buddhism, the Buddhist tradition as a whole can also be fruitfully examined.

Perhaps the single most significant unifying factor for the world's diverse Buddhist populations is the figure of the Buddha himself, Siddhartha Gautama. Although the various schools of Buddhism have different specific understandings of and attitudes toward the Buddha, each of them, without exception, recognizes, respects, and reveres him. What makes the Buddha so significant in Buddhism is not simply that he is the founder of the religion but also that he serves as the template for every Buddhist, the model for the life of the individual. It is not enough to receive and understand his teachings or to worship him; rather, one must strive to be like the Buddha—to replicate his life.

HISTORY The founder of Buddhism, Siddhartha Gautama, who would later be known simply as the Buddha, was by birth what we would now call a Hindu. Although Buddhism breaks with the Hindu tradition in significant ways, it was at the start very much a reform movement from within Hinduism. It is thus essential to understand something of the religious worldview of

WHEEL OF THE DHARMA. The Wheel of the Dharma symbolizes aspects of the Buddha's teachings. It represents the preaching ("turning") of his first sermon and also, with its eight spokes, Buddhism's Eightfold Path. The path is a guide to living life compassionately and nonviolently. (THOMSON GALE)

India in the sixth century B.C.E. in order to understand the Buddha's own religious worldview and why Buddhism took the particular shape that it did.

The Buddha was born into a world in flux, of shifting religious ideals and changing social structures. The dominant religion in northern India up until this point was Brahmanism, based on a body of texts called the Vedas, which had developed orally beginning about 1500 B.C.E. This religious system was also beginning to be challenged from a number of fronts.

The Vedic religious world was one of numerous deities, or *devas*, many of whom were personified forces of nature. Humans could interact with and influence these *devas* via sacrifice; offerings such as grain, milk, and animals were placed in a sacrificial fire by a priest, or Brahman, and "consumed" by the gods. In return, according to the Vedas, humans would receive boons from the gods: abundant crops, healthy sons, protection, and so on.

This was, furthermore, a hierarchical religious world, formally defined by the division of society into four classes, or *varnas*, membership in which was determined solely by birth. At the top were the sacrificial priests, the Brahmans. It was their role and duty to perform the religious rituals and to preserve and recite the Vedas—to memorize the thousands of verses, to chant them at the sacrificial rituals, and to orally pass these texts on to successive generations of Brahmans. In so doing, the Brahmans maintained the order, or dharma (Pali, *dhamma*), of the world, assuring that the gods would be appeased. Directly below the Brahmans in the hierarchy were the Kshatriyas, the warriors and sociopolitical rulers. Just as it was the duty of the Brahmans to maintain the order of the divine world, so was it the dharma of the Kshatriyas to preserve order in the human realm. Below the Kshatriyas were the Vaishyas, the cultivators and keepers of domestic animals. It was their dharma, accordingly, to provide food and material goods. Below them were the Shudras, the laborers and servants, whose dharma it was to ensure the cleanliness of the other three classes of humans. Outside this system was a group called untouchables, or outcasts, who had no defined role in the social system and who were viewed as disorderly, as adharmic in character and nature.

This was a system of mutual dependence but also of restriction. There was no upward mobility in this system. One Vedic text (the "Purusha Shukta" of the Rig Veda) that describes the creation of the universe envisions this social system as a human being who is sacrificed to create the world: the Brahmans are the mouth of the human (because of their oral preservation and performance of the sacred verses of the Veda); the Kshatriyas are the arms (because they are the "strong arms" of the social world); the Vaishyas are the thighs (the support of the body); and, significantly, the Shudras are the feet (the lowest but in many ways the most fundamental). Thus, social and cosmic order (dharma) can be maintained only if each part of the body is present and "healthy." Certainly the feet are lower than the head, but without the feet the body cannot stand.

A new genre of religious discourse, a body of texts known as the Upanishads, began to emerge out of the Vedic ritual religious world sometime between the seventh and the fifth century B.C.E. Although they would eventually become part of Hinduism, these texts—orally transmitted, like the Vedas—began to question the efficacy of the formal sacrifice and introduced essential new religious ideas that would be adopted, in part, by the Buddha: the idea of rebirth (samsara), the law of cause and effect (karma), the concept of liberation (moksha) from samsara, and the practice of asceticism and meditation (yoga).

As the ideas of the Upanishads began to spread, some individuals took them to heart and set out to experience the liberation that they described. These individ-

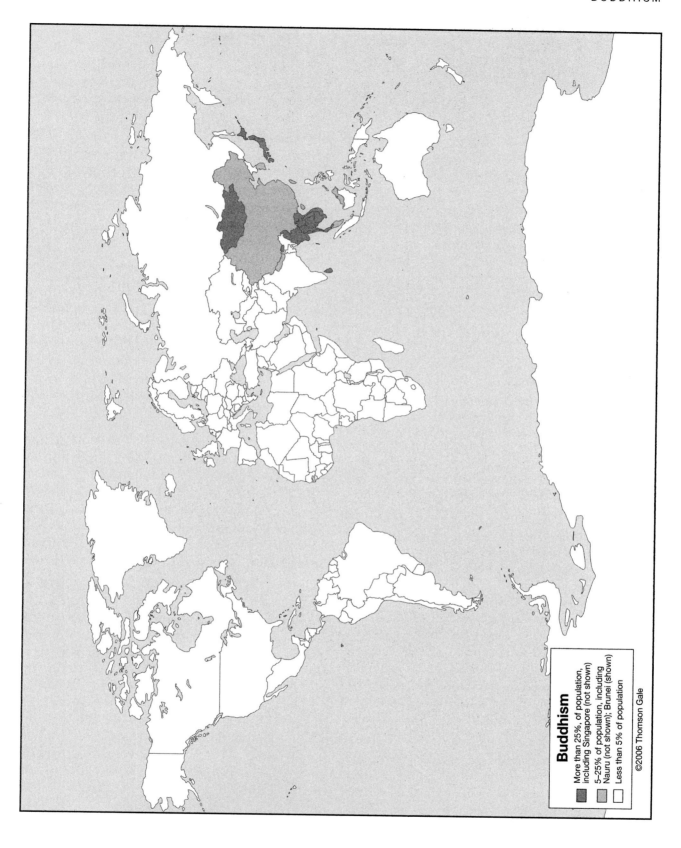

Buddhism

More than 25%, of population, including Singapore (not shown)

5–25% of population, including Nauru (not shown); Brunei (shown)

Less than 5% of population

©2006 Thomson Gale

A Buddhist devotee prays at a temple in Bodh Gaya. Bodh Gaya is the site of Buddha's enlightenment and continues to be a major place of pilgrimage for monks and laypeople throughout the Buddhist world. © DAVID CUMMING; EYE UBIQUITOUS/CORBIS.

uals renounced their ties to the material world and set out as wanderers, spreading these new ideas even farther and debating philosophical and meditational points. These various wanderers were called *shramana*s, and the earliest Buddhists saw themselves as a subset of this group of itinerant religious seekers. Also among these individuals was Mahavira, the founder of another new religious tradition, Jainism.

At about the same time, important social changes were in process along the Gangetic Plain in northern India. Kingdoms began to emerge out of the smaller kinship structures, and with these kingdoms came cities and highly structured systems of government. Furthermore, trade routes began to develop between these cities, and with trade came both economic growth and the emergence of a monied merchant class. This latter group is particularly important in the emergence of Buddhism, for although they had economic status, they, as members of the Vaishya caste, did not have religious status; the Buddha would offer a new religious path that allowed them to develop that status.

Buddhist tradition holds that the man who would become the Buddha was born in a small village near what is now the border between Nepal and India in the middle of the sixth century B.C.E. He was born into a Kshatriya family, part of the Shakka clan, and was given the name Siddhartha (he whose goal will be accomplished) Gautama.

According to legend, his birth was asexual. In a dream that his mother had, the fetus was implanted in her womb by a white elephant. His father, upon learning of his wife's unusual impregnation, had the dream interpreted by a group of Brahman priests, who stated that the boy was destined to greatness, either as a great king (*cakravartin*) or a religious leader. From the start it was clear that he would be an extraordinary human being. Siddhartha emerged from the womb—some versions have him diving out of his mother's side—and immediately took seven steps in each of the four directions, proclaiming that he was the foremost creature in each of them.

Because of the prediction of the priests, Siddhartha's father kept him confined to the palace grounds, making sure that the young boy could see and experience only sweetness and light. In an early sermon, the Buddha describes his childhood this way: "Bhikkhus [monks], I was delicately nurtured, exceedingly delicately nurtured, delicately nurtured beyond measure. In my father's residence lotus-ponds were made: one of blue lotuses, one of red and another of white lotuses, just for my sake. . . . My turban was made of Kashi cloth [silk from modern Varanasi], as was my jacket, my tunic, and my cloak. . . . I had three palaces: one for winter, one for summer and one for the rainy season. . . . In the rainy season palace, during the four months of the rains, I was entertained only by female musicians, and I did not

Pilgrims place flower petals on a set of large footprints cast in a circular stone. The footprints symbolize both the Buddha's former physical presence on earth and his temporal absence. © LINDSAY HEBBERD/CORBIS.

come down from the palace" (from the Anguttara Nikaya). Within the confines of the palace, Siddhartha lived, essentially, a normal Brahmanical life, passing from the student stage to the beginnings of the house-holder stage, but all the while being groomed to eventually become king. He married and had a child, a son named Rahula.

One day Siddhartha persuaded his chariot driver to take him outside the gates of the palace, and there he saw the first of four things that would transform his life. Upon seeing an old man, Siddhartha asked his driver, "Good charioteer, who is this man with white hair, supporting himself on the staff in his hand, with his eyes veiled by the brows, and limbs relaxed and bent? Is this some transformation in him, or his original state, or mere chance?" The driver answered that it was old age, and the prince asked, "Will this evil come upon me also?" The answer was, of course, "Yes."

On two subsequent trips outside the palace grounds, Siddhartha saw a diseased man and then a dead

man, and on each occasion he had much the same discussion with the driver. These first encounters with suffering (*duhkha*; Pali, *dukkha*) transformed the happy prince into a brooding young man. As one text puts it, "He was perturbed in his lofty soul at hearing of old age, like a bull on hearing the crash of a thunderbolt nearby." Siddhartha wondered if perhaps this luxurious palace life was not reality but instead was an illusion of some sort, and he thenceforth wandered around in a profound existential crisis.

The fourth thing he saw was a wandering ascetic, and having encountered not only the *duhkha* that characterizes the world but also, in the ascetic, a potential way out of this realm of suffering, Siddhartha resolved to leave the palace and go out into the world and wander in search of the truth. He sneaked out in the middle of the night after first going to his sleeping father to explain that he was not leaving out of lack of respect nor out of selfishness but because he had a profound desire to liberate the world from old age and death, from the

The Wheel of the Dharma stands between statues of deer in Deer Park in Sarnath, Tibet. Early Buddhism employed a variety of visual symbols to communicate aspects of the Buddha's teachings. © CHRISTINE KOLISCH/CORBIS.

fear of suffering that comes with old age and death. In short, Siddhartha wanted to rid the world of suffering.

He went off and quickly mastered meditation with a variety of teachers, but he was frustrated and thought that there must be something more than what he experienced as only temporary meditational trances. He thus set out on his own and was soon joined by five other *shramanas*. Together they began a course of rigorous asceticism. Siddhartha applied himself with great rigor to this radical lifestyle for several years, getting to the point that he could sit in meditation for days, barely eating. The narratives of his life story say that at this point he could exist on a daily diet consisting of one sesame seed, one grain of rice, or one jujube. Eventually he reached a state in which he was barely breathing, barely alive: "Because of so little nourishment, all my limbs became like some withered creepers with knotted joints; my buttocks like a buffalo's hoof; my back-bone protruding like a string of balls; my ribs like rafters of a dilapidated shed; the pupils of my eyes appeared sunk deep in their sockets as water appears shining at the bottom of a deep well; my scalp became shriveled and shrunk as a bitter

gourd cut unripe becomes shriveled and shrunk by sun and wind . . . the skin of my belly came to be cleaving to my back-bone; when I wanted to obey the calls of nature, I fell down on my face then and there; when I stroked my limbs with my hand, hairs rotted at the roots fell away from my body" (from the Majjhima Nikaya).

While meditating one day Siddhartha remembered a passing moment in his childhood when he had slipped into a state of utter calm and equilibrium as he watched a plough turn the earth. He realized with this simple vision that he must somehow return to that humble moment and forge a middle path between the extreme asceticism he had been practicing (and which only leads to more suffering) and the sensual indulgence of his former life in the palace. His fellow *shramanas* abandoned him, cursing and denouncing him as weak willed. At this point a passing woman named Sujata saw the emaciated renouncer that he had become and offered him a simple gift, a bowl of rice gruel. With this modest nourishment Siddhartha sat down beneath a ficus tree near the town of Gaya (known as Bodh Gaya after the Buddha attained enlightenment here) and made rapid progress. In the middle of his meditations he was challenged by an evil superhuman being named Mara, the embodiment of temptations of all kinds, as well as of fear, delusion, and death. In defeating Mara, Siddhartha metaphorically overcame all such hindrances and quickly attained enlightenment, or *bodhi* (awakening).

After his awakening, at the age of 35, the Buddha spent several weeks meditating on the various aspects of the truth, which he called dharma, that he had realized. He was initially hesitant to share his teachings, however, for he felt that the complexity of his meditational vision would be too difficult for humans to grasp and would lead to further confusion and suffering. At this point, according to the tradition, the gods went to the Buddha to convince him to accept his vocation of teacher, appealing to his compassion and assuring him that in fact there were people capable of understanding the dharma. One god used the image of a lotus pond: In a lotus pond there are some lotuses still under water or even under the mud; there are others that have risen only up to the water level; and there are still others that stand above water and are untouched by it. In a similar way, in this world there are people of different levels of development. Thus challenged, the Buddha determined to proclaim the insight he had gained and set out for nearby Sarnath, where he would offer his first discourse on the dharma.

The Buddha's first "sermon" was given to the very ascetics who had earlier joined him during his meditations but had lost faith in him. They gathered around him as he spoke of what is known as the first turning of the Wheel of the Dharma. He laid out the basic outline of his knowledge and experience of enlightenment to these five *shramana*s. This first discourse represents, in many ways, the beginning of Buddhism, since it is with the sharing of his personal religious experience that the Buddha created the organized religion that is Buddhism.

The content of that first sermon was so powerful, the tradition maintains, that the Buddha's first five disciples quickly—after one week—attained enlightenment, becoming *arhat*s (worthy ones). These first five followers, in turn, went forth and began to teach the dharma that the Buddha had shared with them; this is the beginning of the Buddhist sangha, the community and institution of monks that is at the heart of the religion. For the next 40 years the Buddha traveled almost without stop throughout India, sharing the dharma and gathering followers. He did, however, stay in one place for three months out of every year during the monsoon season. This period, known later as the rain season retreat, became an essential element in the formation not only of Buddhist monasticism but also of a Buddhist lay community. Monks settled in small communities throughout India, debating amongst themselves, establishing a formal religious canon and an accepted body of religious practices, and sharing the Buddha's teachings with the laypeople. The laity, in turn, supported the monks materially by providing them with shelter, food, robes, and alms bowls.

Toward the end of his life, the Buddha instructed his followers that no single person or group of people could hold authority over the community of monks and laypeople. Rather, the authority was to be shared by all. As much as this created an egalitarian religious community, it also, after the Buddha's death, opened the way both for productive debate about the meaning and significance of the teachings that the Buddha had left behind and for disagreement and schism. Initially the Buddha's teachings were only preserved orally by followers who had actually heard his discourses. These teachings were gathered in three collections, or "baskets." These three sets of what the tradition regards as the Buddha's actual words are known as the *Tripitaka* (Pali, Tipitaka): the *Vinaya* (Discipline), the *Dharma* (Doctrine), and the *Abhidharma* (Pali, Abhidhamma; Advanced Doctrine). As these collections were being formed, debates arose among the different groups of monks about the content of these discourses as well as their significance. Furthermore, new situations that had not been explicitly addressed by the Buddha arose, leading to the need for new rules and resulting in further disagreements.

These debates often led to schisms within the Buddhist community. The tradition records that shortly after the Buddha's death a council was held in the town of Rajagriha (present-day Rajgir, in Bihar) to discuss issues of doctrine and practice; another council was held about a century later. As a result of the disagreements—over proper practice and doctrine—voiced at these councils, the sangha eventually divided into two different lines of monastic ordination, the *Sthavira* (Elders) and the *Mahasanghika* (Great Assembly), whose differences initially mostly revolved around issues of monastic discipline, or Vinaya. These two groups would evolve into the Theravada and Mahayana, respectively, developing different doctrinal and ritual standards and becoming established in different parts of Asia.

Glossary

anagarika ascetic layperson

arhat worthy one

bhikkhu monk

bhikkhuni female monk

bodhi enlightenment; awakening

bodhisattva an enlightened being who works for the welfare of all those still caught in samsara

Ch'an (Zen in Japan) a school of Mahayana Buddhism

dana proper giving; generosity

deva deity; divine being; divine

dharma (Pali, dhamma) the teachings of the Buddha; order (in Hinduism)

duhkha (Pali, dukkha) suffering; unsatisfactoriness

Eightfold Path (marga; Pali, magga) a systematic and practical way to realize the truth and eliminate suffering, traditionally divided into three distinct phases that should be progressively mastered

Four Noble Truths the doctrinal foundation of Buddhism: (1) the existence of suffering, (2) the arising of suffering, (3) the cessation of suffering, and (4) the Eightfold Path

karma law of cause and effect; act; deed

Mahayana (sometimes called Northern Buddhism) one of two major schools of Buddhism practiced mainly in China, Japan, Korea, and Tibet; evolved from the Mahasanghika (Great Assembly)

nirvana the absolute elimination of karma; the absence of all states (the Sanskrit word literally means "to blow out, to extinguish")

pancha sila five ethical precepts; the basic ethical guidelines for the layperson

prajna wisdom

puja honor; worship

samsara the cyclical nature of the cosmos; rebirth

samudaya arising (of suffering); the second noble Truth

sangha community of monks

shramana wanderer

sila ethics; morality

10 paramitas 10 perfections of the bodhisattva: (1) *dana* (generosity), (2) *sila* (morality), (3) *ksanti* (patience and forbearance), (4) *virya* (vigor, the endless and boundless energy that bodhisattvas employ when helping others), (5) *dhyana* (meditation), (6) *prajna* (wisdom), (7) *upaya* (skillful means), (8) conviction, (9) strength, and (10) knowledge

Theravada (sometimes called Southern Buddhism) one of two major schools of Buddhism practiced mainly in Cambodia, Laos, Myanmar [Burma], Sri Lanka, and Thailand; evolved from the Sthavira (Elders)

Three Refuges, or Triple Gem the Buddha, the dharma, and the sangha; the taking of the Three Refuges is a basic rite of passage in Buddhism

tripitaka (Pali, tipitaka) three baskets, or three sets; the Tripitaka (Pali, Tipitaka), a collection of the Buddha's teachings—the Vinaya (Discipline), the Dharma (Doctrine), and the Abhidharma (Pali, Abhidhamma; Advanced Doctrine—forms the basis of the Buddhist canon

upaya the concept of skillful means

Vajrayana, or Tantra a school of Mahayana Buddhism

Wheel of the Dharma visual symbol representing the Buddha's preaching his first sermon and also, with its eight spokes, of Buddhism's Eightfold Path Yogacara, or Consciousness-Only school of Buddhism

---

One of the most important figures in the history of Buddhism was Ashoka, the ruler (230–207 B.C.E.) of a large empire in India who not only became a Buddhist himself but established a model of dharmic kinship that would remain the standard template for all Buddhist rulers to follow. Ashoka erected numerous large stone pillars throughout India with edicts inscribed on them. These edicts laid out many of the basic aspects of the Buddha's teachings as well as guidelines for how to live a good Buddhist life. Furthermore, Ashoka established the standard of royal support for the monks by building monastic shelters, planting shade trees and digging wells to aid travelers, and spreading the physical remains of the Buddha throughout India. The physical remains were particularly important in the spread and growth of Buddhism. Enshrined in *chaitya*s and *stupa*s—burial mounds of varying size—they became objects of devotion and important gathering places, often associated with significant events in the Buddha's life, allowing the monks to spread the dharma to larger and larger groups. Ashoka also sent out a number of missionaries, including his own son, Mahinda, to introduce Buddhism and establish monastic orders in other parts of the world, such as Sri Lanka, Southwest and Southeast Asia, and even Greece.

Ashoka had set an important precedent in his support for Buddhism; the support of rulers was an essential element in the expansion and vitality of the religion. For their part, kings were attracted to Buddhism because of its emphasis on individual morality, the lack of caste hierarchy, and the symbiosis between the sangha and the state. The monks needed the king to provide land, food, and protection, while the king found in the sangha a moral legitimization of his righteous rule. The ideal king was a *dharmaraja* (king of dharma)—just, generous, and moral, upholding and promoting the teachings of the Buddha. This basic model is one that continues to be replicated in Buddhist countries today.

As Buddhism spread, the Theravada school (sometimes called Southern Buddhism) became particularly well established in Southern Asia, in Sri Lanka, Thailand, Myanmar (Burma), Laos, and Cambodia. The Mahayana school (sometimes called Northern Buddhism) spread north, first to China and then to the rest of East Asia. These two major divisions in turn divided into many different subgroups and schools, adapting to their particular settings. In Tibet, for instance, the form of Mahayana that became established was Tantra (or Vajrayana), an extrapolation from the core Mahayana beliefs that puts particular emphasis on the transformative effects of ritual. In China and then later Japan, the Ch'an (Zen in Japan) school developed a form of the Mahayana that places particular emphasis on the meditation experience. Thus, although Buddhism essentially died out in India by the thirteenth century, its fundamentally missionary character, and its ability to adapt and adopt, enabled it to flourish elsewhere in Asia.

Buddhism first entered the Western consciousness with colonialism. In the nineteenth century intellectual interest in Buddhism developed in Europe and North America, creating a distinct scholarly field focused on the translation of Buddhist texts from their original languages, as well as their philosophical analysis, an offshoot of which was the gradual availability of accessible books on Buddhist belief and practice. Although there have never been huge numbers of Buddhists in the West—estimates vary, but probably no more than 5 million of the world's 500 million Buddhists live in the West—they have been an important religious presence. In the nineteenth and twentieth centuries the West also saw an influx of Asian immigrants who brought with them Buddhism, establishing small temples and communities throughout Europe and North America.

CENTRAL DOCTRINES As Buddhism gained followers and monks began to form distinct groups, often united on the basis of doctrinal commonalities and matters of monastic discipline, Buddhism was marked by a doctrinal explosion. By the first millennium of the common era, substantial new texts began to appear: commentaries on the Buddha's sermons, new Vinaya texts, and entirely new texts that were claimed to have been hidden by the Buddha himself. This doctrinal profusion is truly one of the hallmarks of Buddhism. That said, however, certain key doctrines also are shared by all Buddhists.

Underlying virtually all of Buddhism is the basic doctrine of samsara, which Buddhism shares with Hinduism. Samsara is really a fundamental worldview or ethos, an understanding of the world that holds that all beings, including animals, are part of an endless (and beginningless) cycle of birth, life, death, and rebirth. Furthermore, Buddhism holds that the physical universe is itself made up of infinite world systems, spread out infinitely in space, and that these world systems, like the individual person, are also subject to the cycle of birth and rebirth. It was, in many ways, the realization of the horror of samsara that led to the Upanishads and the *shramana* movements. These movements attempted to devise a religious mode of action and thought that would provide a way out of this endless cycle of rebirth.

The Buddhist view of the cosmos is predicated on samsara and holds that there are both different world systems and different realms that are arranged in a tripartite structure: the "sense-desire" realm at the bottom, the "pure form" realm above that, and the "formless" realm at the top. Within these three divisions are further subrealms into which a being can be reborn: the human realm, the animal realm, the hungry ghost (*preta*) realm, various hells, and, higher up, *deva* (divine) realms. Although it is not the highest realm, the human realm is considered the most promising because in this realm are both suffering, which acts as a motivation to advance, and free will, which enables humans to act on this impulse. It is important to note that Buddhism holds that even the divine beings, despite their power, are subject to the laws of samsara.

Karma (which means "act" or "deed"), another concept shared with Hinduism, is the linchpin of the whole religious system of Buddhism, in that karma is what determines the quality of each rebirth and keeps the individual in the samsara. On its most basic level, karma is the natural law of cause and effect, inherent in the very structure of the world, a cumulative system in which good acts produce good results, bad acts bad results. Beings are then reborn in good or bad realms, depending on their cumulative karma in each birth. Karma is frequently described in Buddhist texts as being a seed (*phalam*) that will eventually grow fruit, which is, naturally, dependent on what sort of seed was sown.

The Buddhist understanding of karma, though, further stipulates that it is not just the act that determines the karmic result but also the motivation behind the act. Thus, good acts done for the wrong reason can produce negative karmic results, and likewise bad acts that might have been done for good reasons (or accidentally) do not necessarily produce negative karmic results. Indeed, Buddhism holds that bad thoughts are every bit as detrimental as intentional bad actions.

Negative karma is most typically created through intentionally harming other beings and through greed. Positive karma is most easily created through compassionate acts and thoughts and through giving selflessly (which is, ultimately, motivated by compassion).

The doctrine of impermanence (*anitya*) is rooted in the four visions that prompted Siddhartha to abandon his life in the palace. What he realized, when he saw old age, disease, and death, was that all beings are in a fundamental state of flux and, ultimately, decay. This is, in an important sense, a fundamental corollary to the reality of samsara—the human being, just as the world, is constantly evolving, decaying, and reforming. Furthermore, it is the failure to recognize this flux that causes beings to suffer, since they grasp on to that which is impermanent—life, love, material objects, and so on—wishing it will last. The Buddha condenses this basic idea in a simple pronouncement (in Pali): *yad aniccam tam dukkham* (whatever is impermanent is suffering). Since everything is necessarily impermanent, then everything ultimately involves suffering, which he succinctly expresses in the phrase *sabbam dukkham* (everything is suffering).

The doctrine of no self (*anatman*; Pali, *anatta*) is frequently misunderstood in the West. The Buddha does not mean that human beings have no personality but, rather, that because everything in the world is impermanent, there can be no permanent self. In this way Buddhism significantly breaks from Hindu doctrine, which holds that there does exist a permanent self that is reborn time and time again in samsara. But if there is no permanent self, what is it that is reborn? It is karmic residue alone. In his second sermon, the Buddha explains that what we think of as the self is only a collection of personality traits (*skandas*). They create the impression that there are both objects to be perceived and a person to perceive the objects, when in fact all of these objects are impermanent, constantly changing.

One of the clearest expressions of this basic Buddhist idea is demonstrated in a conversation between the monk Nagasena and King Milinda, contained in the *Milindapanha*. Nagasena uses the example of a chariot to illustrate no self, explaining to Milinda that although one can point to, ride, or see a chariot, it only exists insofar as it is a collection of parts—axles, wheels, reins, and so on—and that since no single part can be called the chariot, there is no essential, independent thing called a chariot, just as there is no essential, independent self.

Often called "the chain of conditioned arising" or "the chain of becoming," *pratitya-samutpada* (Pali, *paticca-samuppada*) is broken into 12 links and is one of the most important Buddhist doctrines, one about which Buddha's disciple Sariputta says, "Whoever understands conditioned arising understands the dharma." This is a more elaborate understanding of karma and samsara, a vision of cause and effect in which everything in the world is dependent on some other thing for its existence, succinctly expressed in this simple formula, which occurs in any number of Pali texts: "When this is, that is / This arising, that arises / When this is not, that is not / This ceasing, that ceases." In other words, one thing begets another. Birth begets life, which begets decay, which begets death, which begets birth, and around and around. To get out of the circle, one must break the chain somewhere, most efficiently at its weakest link, ignorance, which is done by applying oneself to mastering the dharma.

The Four Noble Truths is really the doctrinal foundation of Buddhism, a kind of basic blueprint of the

Buddha's teachings, delivered in his first sermon at Sarnath after attaining enlightenment.

The first Noble Truth, suffering (*duhkha*; Pali, *dukkha*), posits that suffering exists in the world. This we see in the story of Siddhartha in the palace: The young prince is made aware that the world is not all wonderful, as it appears to be in the palace, but in fact that the rosy life was just an illusion. In the first sermon, the Buddha says that birth is *duhkha*, old age is *duhkha*, sickness is *duhkha*, death is *duhkha*—in fact, everything is *duhkha*, including things that seem to be pleasurable.

The first Noble Truth is intended not to engender a pessimistic worldview in Buddhists but, rather, to alert them to the reality of the world and to promote a clear, truthful view of that world. Furthermore, the response to the reality of suffering, as we see clearly in the Buddha's own desire to realize and share the dharma, is to show compassion (*karuna*) and kindness (*maitri*) to all living beings.

The second Noble Truth is the arising (*samudaya*) of suffering. Since suffering exists, the Buddha posits, it must have a cause, which is most simply expressed as *tanha* (thirst or desire). This thirst takes many forms: the desire for life, for things, for love. Although on its face this, too, may seem to engender a pessimistic worldview, in which the individual must stifle all sensual pleasure, it is important again to stress that the Buddha advocates a middle path, between sensual indulgence and extreme asceticism. Pleasurable experiences should be experienced for what they are, without grasping. Indeed, the Buddha pronounces that it is precisely because humans mindlessly grasp things and experiences, always rushing to the next, that they fail to fully experience their lives, including that which is pleasurable. The point then is not to deny the sensual but to fully experience sensations and thoughts as they are happening.

The third Noble Truth is cessation (*nirodha*) of suffering. Just as the Buddha saw that if suffering exists it must logically have an origin, so, too, must it have an end. The end of *duhkha* is, logically, related to its source; *nirodha* comes as a result of ending craving, of stopping the grasping after things that are impermanent. When one stops grasping, one stops generating karma, and it is karma and karma alone that keeps beings trapped in samsara. The absolute elimination of karma is nirvana, eternal freedom from the bondage of samsara.

Of all Buddhist concepts, nirvana has perhaps been the most misunderstood. Although it is frequently equated with heaven or described as a state of bliss, nirvana is actually the absence of all states. The Sanskrit word literally means "to blow out, to extinguish," as one would blow out a candle. Nirvana then refers to the absolute elimination of karma. Since karma is what keeps us in samsara, what constitutes our very being, the elimination of karma logically means an elimination of being. This is the end of *duhkha*, the end of the cycle of birth, life, death, and rebirth, beyond all states of existence.

Despite the fact that nirvana is the Buddhist understanding of ultimate salvation, the Buddha himself had little to say on the topic, often warning his followers of the dangers of grasping on to the end goal at the expense of living a focused, compassionate life. He describes it as the "extinction of desire, the extinction of illusion" and also as the "abandoning and destruction of desire and craving for these Five Aggregates of attachment; that is the cessation of *duhkha*." When asked once if nirvana were a state or not a state of existence, however, the Buddha responded that this was an unanswerable question and left it at that. The point again is that the focus should be on mindful progression on the path, not on the destination. The person who spends too much time obsessively focusing on nirvana—or on any aspect of existence or doctrinal complexity—is, the Buddha said, like the man who, upon being shot by a poison arrow, asks who shot it, how did he aim, what sort of wood the arrow was made of, and so on. The point is that the man must first remove the arrow before the poison kills him.

That said, however, later Buddhist schools inevitably took up the question of nirvana, frequently engaging in long philosophical analysis of the possibility of describing it in positive terms. In some Mahayana schools nirvana is, in fact, often described as a kind of state of blissful calm.

The fourth Noble Truth is the Eightfold Path (*marga*; Pali, *magga*). Often envisioned as the Wheel of the Dharma with eight spokes, this is the middle path between extreme asceticism and extreme hedonism, a systematic and practical way to realize the truth and eliminate suffering. The Eightfold Path is traditionally divided into three distinct phases that should, ideally, be progressively mastered.

The first phase is *sila* (ethics) and involves purifying one's outward behavior (and motivations for such behavior). The Buddha describes three elements in *sila* (the first three steps of the Eightfold Path): (1) right action, (2) right speech, and (3) right livelihood. Next comes *samadhi* (meditation), which is broken down, likewise, into three elements (the next three steps): (4) right effort, (5) right mindfulness, and (6) right concentration. The third phase is *prajna* (wisdom) and is broken down into two elements (the last two steps): (7) right understanding and (8) right intentions. *Prajna* is not just knowledge or things one learns. Rather, it is a profound way of understanding being in the world. *Prajna* is often described as a sword that cuts through all illusion, a mental faculty that enables one to fully experience the world as it is without grasping. A later Mahayana school uses an image of geese reflected on a perfectly still pond to describe this state: The average person looks at the pond and, upon seeing the reflection of a flock of geese, immediately looks up. But the person who has perfected *prajna* does not look up but, rather, fully experiences the thing that he or she is seeing in the moment, the reality of the reflection, without distractions. In a sense such a person does not think at all but only sees the world as it is—what the Buddha called *yathabhutam* (in a state of perpetual flux).

With the rise of Mahayana Buddhism sometime shortly after the turn of the first millennium, new and increasingly more complex doctrines emerged, extending the original teachings of the Buddha. In particular, new understandings of both the character and activity of the Buddha emerged, and new doctrines evolved that held that the Buddha had not, in fact, completely left the world when he died and attained nirvana but was still an active presence in the world.

This is first articulated in the doctrine of the various bodies (*kaya*s) of the Buddha. The first of these bodies—which are not, in fact, conceived of strictly as physical forms but rather more like the different ways in which the Buddha continues to be present in the world—is the *dharmakaya,* or "body of the teachings." This is the Buddha's form as wisdom, truth, and the real nature of reality (emptiness). This is that which characterizes the Buddha as the Buddha. Sometimes called Buddhaness, *dharmakaya* is the whole collection of wonderful qualities that are known as the Buddha. It also refers to the teachings, in their essence. The second body is called the *nirmanakaya,* or "transformation body" (also sometimes called the *rupakaya,* or "form body"). This is the earthly form, or manifestation, of the Buddha. Finally there is a more rarified form of the Buddha called the *sambhogakaya,* or "enjoyment body," the form of the Buddha that those who have attained enlightenment enjoy and interact with.

Related to this idea of the multiple bodies of the Buddha was the emergence of the concept of the bodhisattva—an enlightened being who works for the welfare of all those still caught in samsara—which is perhaps the hallmark of the Mahayana schools. Although bodhisattva was a common word in the earliest of Buddhist texts, these pre-Mahayana schools held that once the Buddha had attained enlightenment, he taught the dharma to his disciples and then, on his death, entered nirvana, or parinirvana, thus ending his existence in the realm of samsara forever. The Buddha's immediate disciples were known as arhats (worthy ones) upon attaining enlightenment, and they too entered nirvana upon death. The Mahayana, however, were critical of this position—they derisively called the arhats *pratyekabuddha*s, or "solitary Buddhas"—and posited that the Buddha and all other enlightenment beings postponed final nirvana out of their compassion for the sufferings of other beings, choosing to remain in samsara to perfect their own Buddhahood and work for the benefit of all other beings, until each one attains enlightenment.

There are a number of important elements here. For one thing, all beings were now conceived as at once having the innate potential to become a Buddha and also sharing in a kind of universal enlightenment as well. The path then was reconceived as being the path of the bodhisattva, a path that takes many, many lives but is intent on developing *bodhicitta* (the awakened mind and the very quality of enlightenment), a quality that fundamentally shifts one's attention away from the self to a selfless concern for the well-being of others. Each bodhisattva takes a vow to help other beings and to continue to do so indefinitely, a vow that involves cultivating a set of six—later expanded to 10—perfections, or *paramitas*. The 10 perfections are (1) *dana* (generosity), (2) *sila* (morality), (3) *ksanti* (patience and forbearance), (4) *virya* (vigor, the endless and boundless energy that bodhisattvas employ when helping others), (5) *dhyana* (meditation), (6) *prajna* (wisdom), (7) *upaya* (skillful means), (8) conviction, (9) strength, and (10) knowledge. Once a bodhisattva has mastered these 10 perfections, then he is fully realized as a buddha.

With the rise of the ideal of the bodhisattva came also the development of a complex pantheon of enlightened beings. Three of the most popular and most important bodhisattvas are Maitreya, Avalokiteshvara, and Manjushri.

Eventually the Buddha's teachings will lose their potency owing to the natural decay of the world. When things become unbearable, Maitreya will be reborn and will provide for the welfare of all beings and promote a new set of teachings.

The quintessential Buddhist savior figure and the embodiment of compassion, Avalokiteshvara is perhaps the most popular of all bodhisattvas. His name is significant: He is the "lord who sees all," in the sense that he sees all suffering and responds immediately. He saves us from dangers: fire, drowning in a river, being lost at sea, murder, demonic attack, fierce beasts and noxious snakes or insects, legal punishment, attack by bandits, falling from steep precipices, extremes of weather, internecine civil or military unrest, and others.

Especially associated with wisdom, Manjushri is a key figure in numerous Mahayana scriptures, and he has been the focus of significant cultic activity throughout Mahayana Buddhist countries. His name means "gentle glory," although he is called by many names and epithets, some of which refer to his relation to speech (Vagishvara, "lord of speech") or to his disarming youth (Kumarabhuta, "in the form of a youth" or "having become the crown prince"). Because he is destined soon to become a Buddha, Manjushri is often called "prince of the teachings."

A concept that first appears in the Prajnaparamita (Perfection of Wisdom) texts, the idea of emptiness (shunyata) extends the Buddha's teachings about dependent origination and posits that all phenomena are dependent for their being on some other thing. The first-century thinker Nagarjuna introduced the most radical understanding of this concept, arguing that just as the terms "long" and "short" take on meaning only in relation to each other and are themselves devoid of independent qualities (longness or shortness), so too do all phenomena (all dharmas) lack their own being (svabhava). If a thing were to have an independent and unchanging own being, Nagarjuna reasons, then it would follow that it is neither produced nor existent, because origination and existence presuppose change and transience. All things, physical as well as mental, can originate and develop only when they are empty of their own being. Nevertheless, Nagarjuna contends, elements do have what he calls a conventional reality, so that we still interact with them, think thoughts, and so on, even if ultimately they are empty of reality. Related to this is the concept of skillful means, upaya, which refers to the bodhisattva's employment of whatever means are necessary to help beings toward enlightenment. Language, for instance, is itself empty, in that it depends on external references to make sense, but language is necessary to communicate and is therefore a skillful means through which to spread the dharma.

MORAL CODE OF CONDUCT One of the things that makes the theory and practice of ethics (sila) particularly interesting in the Buddhist context is the tension that exists, right on the surface, between the individual's responsibility for his or her own salvation—as exemplified by the Buddha's advice that one must be one's own island (atta dipa), dependent on no one other than one's self for salvation—and the individual's connection with social life, as governed by the collective nature of karma. This is perhaps most dramatically illustrated by the Buddha's own life story. For instance, in Johnston's translation of The Buddhacarita, or, Acts of the Buddha, the young Siddhartha's wife, Yashodhara, when she hears that Siddhartha has abandoned her, falls upon the ground "like a Brahminy duck without its mate"—a common symbol of lifelong marital partnership, such that one duck will die of remorse upon the death of the other. Likewise, his son is described as "poor Rahula," who is fated "never to be dandled in his father's lap" (pp. viii, 58).

The ethical and moral challenge is always to strike a balance between one's concern for the suffering of others and one's own progress on the path; too much concern for other people can be a hindrance, just as not enough can generate negative karma. The key to Buddhist ethics, if not in fact to the whole of the Buddha's teachings, is the cultivation of mindfulness (sati)—to develop a mental attitude of complete and selfless awareness, a mental attitude that necessarily influences the manner in which one acts toward other living beings, a mental awareness that fundamentally informs one's every act and intention to act.

For the monk the ethical system is extremely complex and extensive, contained primarily and explicitly in the Vinaya but secondarily and implicitly in every utterance of the Buddha. To be a monk is to be necessarily ethical. For the layperson the ethical guidelines are less specific, seeming to amount to "live the proper life." This means that one must be aware that all acts and all beings are part of samsara and are thus caught up in karma and pratitya-samutpada (Pali, paticca-samuppada; the chain of conditioned arising). Whatever one does has effects, and those effects are not always obvious. The implications here are perhaps best ethically stated when the Buddha says, "Oh Bhikkhus, it is not easy to find a being who has not formerly been your mother, or your father, your brother, your sister or your son or daughter" (Samyutta Nikaya, vol. II, p. 189). In other words, any act necessarily affects not only the immediate actor but all beings, who are, logically, karmically connected.

It is also important to remember that we are still within the basic Brahmanical milieu here. What we see in Buddhism, however, is an emphasis on the individual as he or she fits into society, not an emphasis on how society molds or controls the individual, as we see in Hinduism, where the emphasis is on order and duty, on making sure that everything and everyone stays in the proper place—hence caste, life stages, and so on. This is not to say that this societal component is entirely absent in Buddhism, since one of the motivations for the individual to act ethically is to make society work. Without social order things would fall utterly apart, as is perhaps best articulated in what is sometimes called the Buddhist book of Genesis, the Aganna Sutta, which describes a social world in which chaos and decay emerge precisely because beings act greedily and selfishly. Proper, ethical action in Buddhism is not performed out of duty or some higher cosmic order, however; rather, one acts ethically out of one's own free will, because without such proper action, the individual can make no progress on the path.

The importance of proper giving (dana) is utterly central to Buddhist ethics and to the life of both the layperson and the monk; indeed, dana can be said to be the key to monk-lay relations. The first principle that must be noted here is that in Buddhism there is a marked ambiguity about material wealth. The concept of nonattachment, the absence of grasping, is of crucial importance here; from the Buddhist perspective material goods are only important as a means of cultivating nonattachment. Again, however, the middle way is emphasized: Too many possessions can lead to attachment, just as too few can lead to craving. Any material prosperity offers at once the opportunity for greater giving and the cultivation and expression of nonattachment, but such prosperity also offers a temptation toward the kind of antidharmic self-indulgence that leads to increased entrapment in the web of worldly existence.

The model donor in Buddhism is the laywoman Sujata, who gave Siddhartha the simple and selfless gift of rice gruel, which enabled him to gain the strength to make the final push to enlightenment. What makes this act of dana so important is that Sujata gave her gift modestly, with no self-interest, no expectation of gain or reward; she was responding with selfless compassion to Siddhartha's obvious need.

Equally important as a model donor is the king Vessantara, whose story is told in a popular tale from the Jataka collection that provides not only a model of ethical giving but also a cautionary tale about the karmic consequences of giving too much. In this story Vessantara eventually gives away his kingdom and prosperity, his wife and children, everything, and the result is suffering for all until everything is restored and Vessantara realizes the need to give modestly.

Monks also engage in dana, although rather than giving material goods, which they necessarily depend on the laity for, they give what the Dhammapada says is the best gift of all: "The gift of dharma excels all gifts."

Two important metaphors for proper ethical giving are bija and khsetra. Bija basically means "seed" but is nearly always used to describe the seed of an auspicious act. This act, if it is indeed done with the correct selfless motives, bears karmic fruit (phala); the act itself is called kushala, which can be defined as "good, moral, skillful, proper," or, to use the best Buddhism definition, that which is "karmically wholesome"—in other words, a gift that is given with proper intention, given out of selfless compassion. The best field in which to plant a seed is the sangha (community of monks), and the best seed to plant is an act of giving, dana. The sangha is thus consistently referred to as a fertile karmic field. This imagery is further developed in times when there are monastic schisms or crises, in which case the monks are sometimes described as a barren field in which no seeds will bear fruit. This imagery is not limited to the monks and gifts to them but refers to any auspicious action.

Buddhist acts of charity, then, are fundamentally symbiotic in nature. The laypeople provide the monks with the material support that they need—shelter, robes, food, and so on—and in the process cultivate the crucial attitudes of nonattachment and compassion, a kind of domestic asceticism that is not disruptive of the social order. The monks, in turn, depend on the laypeople and return the material gifts with the gift of the Buddha's teachings. Furthermore, the ideology of dana is such that the laypeople's gifts will only bear "fruit" (that is, positive karma) if the monks are pure (in other words, a fertile field). If a particular monastery becomes corrupt, then the laypeople will give somewhere else, providing a kind of ethical imperative for monastic purity.

A crucial element in all of this is the concept of *punya* (merit), which is positive karma. By giving selflessly, one "earns" merit, accumulating positive karma, which determines the quality of one's next rebirth. If one is too attached to this merit, though—too focused on the end products and not the selfless and compassionate act of giving (and giving up)—then one in fact earns not positive karma but negative, which will hinder one's ultimate spiritual progress.

The *pancha sila* are the basic ethical guidelines for the layperson, although they are not necessarily followed rigidly by everyone. In some ways they are rather like the Ten Commandments in Judaism and Christianity, in that they are the basis for ethical behavior, a kind of practical blueprint. A fundamental difference from the Ten Commandments, though, is that the *pancha sila* are voluntarily followed and are a matter of personal choice, not an imperative to act in a particular manner.

The first guideline is No killing. The basic idea here is that every individual is connected with all other living beings. Buddhists go to considerable lengths to qualify this precept, giving five conditions that govern it: (1) presence of a living being, (2) knowledge of this, (3) intention to kill, (4) act of killing, and (5) death.

What is most important about this first precept is not its negative form, injunction against killing, but its positive aspect, that of compassion and loving kindness. This positive aspect is one of the most common things upon which laypeople meditate, often with this verse from the Metta Sutta: "May all beings be happy and secure; / May their hearts be wholesome. / Whatever living beings there be— / Feeble or strong, tall, stout or medium, / Short, small or large, without exception— / Seen or unseen, / Those dwelling far or near, / Those who are born or who are to be born, / May all beings be happy."

The second guideline is No taking what is not given. This is particularly important for the monks. Here the concept of *dana* is crucial. Because one of the chief ethical activities of the layperson is to give unselfishly to the sangha, this giving is contingent on the monks accepting, also unselfishly, whatever is given. The monks are not to take anything that is not given to them. This holds true also for the layperson, in that he or she is not to steal.

The third guideline is No sexual misconduct. This prevents lust and envy, which are the most powerful forms of thirst (*tanha*).

The fourth guideline is No false speech. Lies create deception and illusion and lead to grasping. Also, for the monks, this is about not speaking false doctrines.

The fifth guideline is No liquor, which clouds the mind and prevents *sati* (mindfulness).

In addition to these five basic principles, monks follow additional basic rules, sometimes three, sometimes five: No untimely meals (thereby promoting group sharing of food and hindering the desire to hoard); No dancing or playing of music (thereby promoting a sober, nonfrivolous life); No adornments or jewelry (which would be against the basic ascetic attitude of the monk); No high seats (an injunction intended to promote equality in the sangha); and No handling of money (thereby preventing greed and attachments).

SACRED BOOKS The Buddha famously told his chief disciple, Ananda, that after his death, the dharma he was leaving behind would continue to be the present teacher, the "guiding light," to all future Buddhists, a scene that establishes the paramount importance of sacred texts in Buddhism. Tradition holds that during the first rainy-season retreat after the Buddha's death, thus sometime in the latter half of the sixth century B.C.E., the Buddha's disciples gathered at Rajagriha (present-day Rajgir, in Bihar) and orally collected all of the Buddha's teachings into three sets, or "three baskets" (*tripitaka*; Pali, *tipitaka*). By about the end of the first century C.E., these oral texts were written down. These three collections form the basis of the Buddhist canon.

The first collection of the Pali Tipitaka is the Sutta Pitaka, some 30 volumes of the Buddha's discourses as well as various instructional and ritual texts. The Vinaya Pitaka, or collection of monastic rules, includes the list of 227 rules for the monks (311 for nuns), called the Patimokkha, and detailed accounts as to how and why they were developed. The Vinaya also contains narratives of the Buddha's life, rules for rituals, ordination instructions, and an extensive index of topics covered. The third group of texts is the Abhidhamma Pitaka, or collection of scholastic doctrines. These are highly abstract, philosophical texts dealing with all manner of issues, particularly the minutiae that make up human experience. The last of these texts, the Patthana Abhidhamma, stretches for some 6,000 pages.

In addition to the fundamental texts of the Tipitaka, each text also is accompanied by an extensive commentary, and often several subcommentaries, that

The Practice of Deity Yoga

One of the most common meditational practices in Tibetan Buddhism is deity yoga. Tantric practitioners learn to think, speak, and act as if they were already a fully enlightened buddha through visualizing their body, speech, and mind as the body, speech, and mind of an enlightened being, in order to actualize, or make real in the present, their latent potential for enlightenment.

These practitioners meditate, often with the use of mandalas and mantras, on a particular deity—an enlightened being, such as the bodhisattva Avalokiteshvara—that represents their own potential for enlightenment, their own Buddha nature, which is, according to the Vajrayana schools, always there, albeit obscured by illusion and ignorance. In the case of deity yoga directed to Avalokiteshvara, the meditator sits before an image of the bodhisattva and mentally focuses on his compassion and wisdom, often beginning with thoughts of praise (*sadhana*s), progressing to contemplation of the deity's sublime qualities, and sometimes constructing an elaborate mental "world" inhabited by the deity; then gradually the meditator envisions everything, including his or her own mind, as being a manifestation of the deity. Accordingly, the practitioner eventually realizes through this meditation that there is no difference between the mind of the deity—or, for that matter, the Buddha himself—and his or her own mind.

clarifies the grammatical and linguistic ambiguities of the text and also extends the analysis, serving as a kind of reader's (or listener's) guide through the book's sometimes confusing philosophical and ritual points.

With the rise of the Mahayana, new books were added to this basic canonical core, most of them composed in Sanskrit; the tradition holds, however, that these were not new sacred texts but were the higher teachings of the Buddha himself that were set aside for a later revealing. Perhaps the best known of these is the Lotus Sutra, composed probably around the turn of the first millennium, and also the Prajnaparamita (Perfec-

tion of Wisdom) texts. Additional texts continued to be added as the Mahayana schools developed in India. As Buddhism branched out, these texts, and the earlier Tipitaka, were translated by Buddhist monks from both Tibet and China. These translations sometimes led to further expansion of the canon, particularly in Tibet, where the rise of the Vajrayana (Tantric) schools led to more new texts; likewise, as Ch'an (Zen in Japan) developed, new sacred texts were written and preserved.

SACRED SYMBOLS Early Buddhism employed a variety of visual symbols to communicate aspects of the Buddha's teachings: the Wheel of the Dharma, symbolic of his preaching ("turning") his first sermon and also, with its eight spokes, of Buddhism's Eightfold Path; the bodhi tree, which symbolizes not only the place of his enlightenment (under the tree) but the enlightenment experience itself; the throne, symbolizing his status as "ruler" of the religious realm and also, through its emptiness, his passage into final nirvana; the deer, symbolizing the place of his first sermon, the Deer Park at Sarnath, and also the protective qualities of the dharma; the footprint, symbolizing both his former physical presence on earth and his temporal absence; and the lotus, symbolic of the individual's journey up through the "mud" of existence, to bloom, with the aid of the dharma, into pure enlightenment. Later Buddhism added countless other symbols. Among them, in the Mahayana, for instance, the sword becomes a common symbol of the incisive nature of the Buddha's teachings; in Tibet the *vajra* (diamond or thunderbolt) is a ubiquitous symbol of the pure and unchanging nature of the dharma.

EARLY AND MODERN LEADERS The Buddha's immediate disciples not only formed the first Buddhist community but also were responsible for orally preserving his teachings. One of the most important of these early followers was Ananda, the Buddha's cousin, who accompanied the Buddha for more than 20 years and figures prominently in many early Buddhist texts. Sariputta, one of the Buddha's first converts (along with Mahamogallana), was the Buddha's most trusted disciple and was often depicted as the wisest. Sariputta also served as the Buddha's son's teacher when he joined the sangha (community of monks). Another important early figure is Mahakassapa, a Brahman who became a close disciple of the Buddha. Mahakassapa presided over the first Buddhist Council at Rajagriha (present-day Rajgir, in

Bihar) and was later celebrated in Ch'an (Zen in Japan) as the receiver of the first transmission of the Buddha's special, esoteric teachings, when the Buddha, upon being asked a question about the dharma, is said to have held up a flower and Mahakassapa smiled, silently signifying his reception of this special teaching. The Buddha's aunt, Mahapajapati, also figures prominently in several early texts. Not only did she raise him after his mother's death but she was ordained as the first woman admitted to sangha.

The Greco-Bactrian king Milinda, also called Menander or Menandros, reigned over Afghanistan and Northern India in the latter half of the second century B.C.E. and is one of the most important royal converts to Buddhism. He had a series of discussions with a Buddhist monk, Nagasena, which were compiled into a famous work entitled the *Milindapanha*. Perhaps the most famous of all historical figures in Buddhism is the Indian king Ashoka (ruled 230–207 B.C.E.). He was the founder of the Maurya Dynasty and the first king to rule over a united India, as well as being one of Buddhism's first royal patrons. Ashoka abolished war in his empire, restricted killing for food, built hospitals, erected thousands of stupas (Buddhist burial mounds), and engraved a series of edicts on rocks and pillars throughout his empire that articulated the basic moral and ethical principle of Buddhism. Ashoka was also instrumental in the spread of Buddhism outside of India. His son, Mahinda (third century B.C.E.), was the leader of a Buddhist missionary enterprise to Sri Lanka and was thus instrumental in the spread of Buddhism outside of India.

Another important early Buddhist king was Harsha-vardhana (606–47). He ruled a large empire in northern India and became an important Buddhist convert. Like his predecessor Ashoka, he is described in Buddhist texts as a model ruler—benevolent, energetic, and just, active in the administration and prosperity of his empire—and, like Ashoka, he is frequently invoked as a model for all righteous rulers.

There are many early historical figures outside of India. One of the most important records of the early Buddhist world comes to us from the Chinese pilgrim Fa-hsien (fourth to fifth century). Not only did he obtain many Sanskrit texts of the Pali Tipitaka that he translated upon his return to China in 414, but he also wrote an influential record of his travels that remains one of the most informative views of the early Buddhist world in India. He was followed by another Chinese pilgrim, Hsuan-tsang (602–64). Hsuan-tsang, like his predecessor Fa-hsien, was a Buddhist monk who traveled throughout India collecting doctrinal texts, which he then translated from Sanskrit into Chinese, and left a detailed record of his travels. Hsuan-tsang was also the founder in China of the Consciousness-Only (Yogacara) school.

The sixth-century South Indian Buddhist monk Bodhidharma is a central figure in Chinese and, later, Japanese Buddhism. He arrived at the Chinese court in 520 and is credited with founding the Ch'an (Zen) school of Buddhism. Other important East Asian historical figures are Honen (1133–1212), also called Genku, who in 1175 established the Jodo (Pure Land) school in Japan; Shinran (1173–1263), founder of the True Pure Land School of Japanese Buddhism, who is also credited with popularizing congregational worship and introducing reforms, such as salvation by faith alone, marriage of priests, and meat eating; and Nichiren (1222–82), founder of the Nichiren sect in Japan.

In Tibet the monk Padmasambhava (eighth century) is one of the best-known and important figures. He is a Tantric saint who was instrumental in introducing Buddhism to Tibet; mythologically he is credited with converting to Buddhism the local demons and gods who tormented the Tibetan people, turning them into protectors of the religion. Atisha (982–1054) was an Indian monk and scholar who went to Tibet in 1038. He is credited with entirely reforming the prevailing Buddhism in Tibet by enacting measures to enforce celibacy in the existing order and to raise the level of morality within the Tibetan sangha. He founded the Kadampa school, which later became the Geluk-pa school. Like his Chinese counterparts Fa-hsien and Hsuan-tsang, Buston (1008–64), a Tibetan Buddhist, translated much of the Buddhist sacred literature, including Tantra texts, into classic Tibetan and is sometimes credited with making the definitive arrangements of the Kanjur and Tanjur, the two basic Tibetan collections of Buddhist principles. He also produced a history of Buddhism in Tibet that is among the most important documents for Buddhism's early development in that region. Finally, two extremely important semihistorical figures are Marpa (1012–96) and Milarepa (1040–1143). Marpa was a Tibetan layman thought to have imported songs and texts from Bengal to Tibet, but he is best known and most venerated as the guru of Milarepa. Milarepa was a saint and poet of Tibetan Buddhism who continues to be extremely popular. His well-known autobiography recounts how in his youth he practiced black magic in order to take revenge on relatives who deprived his mother of the family inheritance and then later repented and sought Buddhist teaching. Milarepa stands figuratively as the model for all Tibetans.

One of the most important religious and social leaders in Tibet is the Panchen Lama, who ranks second only to the Dalai Lama among the Grand Lamas of the Geluk-pa sect of Tibetan Buddhism. His seat is in the Tashilhumpo monastery at Shigatse. The current Dalai Lama (born in 1935) is the spiritual and political leader of Tibetan Buddhists. He has lived in exile since 1959, when the Chinese invaded Tibet. The Dalai Lama has been instrumental not only in aiding the Tibetan people but also in spreading Buddhism to the West.

The Sri Lankan Buddhist Anagarika Dharmapala (1864–1933) stands as one of the most important Buddhist propagandists of the modern era. Dharmapala was intimately involved in the restoration of Bodh Gaya in India, the birthplace of Buddhism, and with spreading Buddhism to the West. He was for much of his life closely associated with Henry Steele Olcott (1832–1907), an American who, along with H.H. Blavatsky, founded the Theosophical Society. Olcott worked to establish a new lay Buddhism in Sri Lanka, where he founded schools and lay organizations, and he wrote *The Buddhist Catechism*, which was an important tool in reestablishing and preserving Buddhism among the lay population of Sri Lanka.

One of the most important early scholars of Buddhism was T.W. Rhys Davids (1843–1922). Rhys Davids was professor of Pali at London University and one of the founders of the university's School of Oriental and African Studies. Along with his wife, Caroline, he pioneered the translation, study, and transmission of Pali text in the West. Ananda Metteyya (Charles Henry Allan Bennett; 1872–1923) is another important Western Buddhist. The son of an electrical engineer, he was born in London and trained as an analytical chemist before becoming the first British *bhikkhu* (monk) and Buddhist missionary. Bhikkhu Ñanamoli (Osbert Moore; 1905–60) was a pioneer British *bhikkhu* and Pali scholar who went to Sri Lanka and was ordained as a monk. He translated *The Visuddhimagga* into English as *The Path of Purification*; he also translated *Nettippakarana* (*The Guide*) and *Patisambhidamagga* (*Path of Discrimination*), as well as most of the sections of the Majjhima Nikaya and several from the Samyutta Nikaya. Ayya Khema (Ilse Ledermann; 1923–97) was born in Berlin to Jewish parents;

in 1938 she escaped from Germany and began studying Buddhism. In 1978 she helped to establish Wat Buddha-Dhamma, a forest monastery near Sydney, Australia. She later set up the International Buddhist Women's Centre as a training center for Sri Lankan nuns and the Parappuduwa Nun's Island at Dodanduwa, Sri Lanka.

MAJOR THEOLOGIANS AND AUTHORS One of the most important biographical accounts of the Buddha's life, the *Buddhacarita*, is also the first complete biography of the Buddha; it was written by Asvaghosa (second century). Perhaps the most important theologian of early Buddhism was Nargarjuna (second to third century), sometimes called "the second Buddha." Nagarjuna is considered to be the founder of the Madhyamika (Middle Way) school and is counted as a patriarch of both Zen and Vajrayana (Tantra). He is held in the highest regard by all branches of the Mahayana. Another important early author was Kumarajiva (344–413), a Buddhist scholar and missionary who had a profound influence in China as a translator and a clarifier of Buddhist terminology and philosophy. Buddhaghosa (fifth century) was one of the greatest Buddhist scholars in the religion's history. He translated Sinhalese commentaries into Pali, wrote numerous commentaries himself, and composed the *Visuddhimagga* (later translated as *Path of Purification* by Bhikkhu Ñanamoli). Asanga (310–90) was the founder of the Yogacara (Consciousness-Only) school of Buddhism. He is closely associated with the Indian philosopher Vasubandhu (420–500). The two founded the Yogacara school of Mahayana Buddhism. Vasubandhu's *Abhidharmakosa* is one of the fullest expositions of the Abhidharma teachings of the Theravada school. Dhammapala (sixth to seventh century) was the author of numerous commentaries on the Pali canon and stands as one of the most influential figures in the Theravada. Shantideva (seventh to eighth century) is a later representative of the Madhyamika school of Mahayana Buddhism and author of two important surviving works, the *Shikshasamuccaya* (*Compendium of Doctrines*) and *Bodhisattva Avatara* (*Entering the Path of Enlightenment*), the latter of which is still used in Tibetan Buddhism as a teaching text.

ORGANIZATIONAL STRUCTURE The fundamental structure of Buddhism is that it is a self-governing body of individuals, each of whom is theoretically equal and intent on his or her own salvation while compassionately mindful of fellow beings. As soon as Buddhist monks began to form into groups, however, there was a need for rules (contained in the Vinaya Pitaka) and also for a degree of hierarchy that was needed to keep order, to enforce the rules, and to maintain religious purity within the community. This hierarchy was, and continues to be, based on seniority—the longer one has been a monk, the more seniority he or she has. There is thus no single authority in the Buddhist world. Rather, each school has a leader or group of leaders who provide guidance to the community as a whole, and the degree of internal hierarchy varies considerably from school to school and country to country.

There has always been a symbiosis between the sangha (community of monks) and the laity. The former depends on the latter for material support, while the latter depends on the former for religious instruction. In these roles they keep each other in check. The laity ensures the purity of the sangha in that unless the community of monks remains well regulated and pure, the laity's gifts will not bear fruit (positive karma); likewise, the sangha serves as a constant reminder and model to the laity of the proper, salvifically beneficial religious life.

HOUSES OF WORSHIP AND HOLY PLACES The earliest holy sites in Buddhism were probably associated with the places where the Buddha's relics were located. The tradition holds that after the Buddha's body was cremated, his remains were divided into several portions that were set up in burial mounds (stupas) at important crossroads. These places provided opportunities for laypeople and monks to contemplate the Buddha's teachings. The number of these reliquaries soon multiplied—Ashoka, the early Indian king, was said to have divided the relics into 84,000 pieces, placing them in stupas throughout India—and generally were under the care and protection of monasteries. Hence, not only were monasteries places of residence for the monks, they also became meeting places for the laity, places to hear the dharma and also to pay homage to the Buddha. Now virtually every monastic complex has a reliquary or stupa and a central meeting hall where the monks gather to recite the twice-monthly Patimokkha (the Vinaya rules) and receive donations from the laity, and also where the laity gather to hear dharma talks.

In medieval India eight special pilgrimage places developed, all associated with significant events in the Buddha's life. Bodh Gaya, for instance, is the site of his enlightenment and continues to be a major place of pilgrimage for monks and laypeople from throughout the Buddhist world, as well as being home to several important monasteries representing Buddhists from many different countries and traditions. Outside of India new holy places developed as Buddhism developed, some places having mythological significance, some having specific historical or national significance associated with famous monks.

WHAT IS SACRED? The earliest Buddhist traditions placed particular emphasis on the remains of the Buddha, which were divided into three basic categories: physical relics, such as bones and teeth; objects that the Buddha had used, such as his robe and relic bowl; and representations or images of the Buddha. The tradition holds that Ashoka divided the physical relics into 84,000 portions and distributed them throughout India. This is clearly an exaggeration, since the number of bodily relics enshrined in stupas throughout the Buddhist world vastly extends beyond the limits of a single physical body. Images of the Buddha are the most common object of devotion. Although it is typically held that images are to serve as objects of contemplation and emulation, an opportunity to cultivate the Buddha's own auspicious qualities, they are also often invested with a kind of physical power and, like the relics, said to embody something of the presence of the Buddha himself (particularly in the Mahayana and Vajrayana schools). In addition to sculptural images of the Buddha, there is in the Mahayana and Vajrayana a vast pantheon of bodhisattvas who become objects of devotion. Significant monks, likewise, frequently become objects of devotion. In Japan, for instance, the bodies of particularly famous monks are embalmed and sometimes encased in shellac and then put on display, thus displaying a kind of present master.

HOLIDAYS AND FESTIVALS There are a great many special days in the Buddhist tradition. Some of these days celebrate significant birthdays (of the Buddha or of the bodhisattvas), whereas others have to do with significant events in the monastic world. Typically on a festival day laypeople go to their local temple or monastery and offer food to the monks, vow to uphold the five ethical precepts (pancha sila), and listen to the dharma; they also distribute food to the poor and make offerings of food, robes, and money to the monks.

In countries where the Theravada prevails (Thailand, Myanmar [Burma], Sri Lanka, Cambodia, and

Laos), the Buddhist New Year is celebrated for three days from the first full-moon day in April. In predominantly Mahayana countries (China, Japan, Korea, and Tibet), the New Year typically starts on the first full-moon day in January, although this varies from country to country.

Vesak (the Buddha's birthday) is the most significant Buddhist festival of the year, as it celebrates the birth, enlightenment, and death of the Buddha, all of which tradition holds occurred on the same day. Vesak takes place on the first full-moon day in May.

On the full-moon day of the eighth lunar month (approximately July), the Asalha Puja Vesak takes place. This holiday commemorates the Buddha's first teaching, "The Turning of the Wheel of the Dharma," at the Deer Park in Sarnath.

Uposatha (or Poya) Days are four monthly holy days—when there is a new moon, a full moon, and quarter moons—that are observed in Theravada countries.

Pavarana Day marks the conclusion of the rainy-season retreat (*vassa*).

The Kathina (Robe Offering) Ceremony is held on an auspicious day within one month of the conclusion of the three-month rainy-season retreat for the monastic order. The ceremony marks not only the return of the monks into the larger community but the time when new robes and other requisites may be offered by the laity to the monks and nuns.

Specific to Myanmar (Burma), Abhidhamma Day celebrates the occasion when the Buddha is said to have gone to the Tushita heaven to teach his dead mother the Abhidharma. It is held on the full moon of the seventh month of the Burmese lunar year starting in April, which corresponds to the full-moon day in October.

In Thailand, at the end of the Kathin Festival season, the Loy Krathong (Floating Bowls) Festival takes place on the full-moon night of the 12th lunar month. People bring bowls made of leaves that they fill with flowers, candles, and incense and then float in the water. As the bowls float away, all bad luck is said to disappear. The traditional practice of Loy Krathong was meant to pay homage to the holy footprint of the Buddha on the beach of the Namada River in India.

Specific to Sri Lanka, the Festival of the Tooth takes place in Kandy, where the tooth relic of the Buddha is enshrined. The tooth itself, kept deep inside many caskets, is never actually seen. But once a year in August, on the night of the full moon, there is a special procession for it, which was traditionally said to protect the kingdom.

Ulambana (Ancestor Day) is celebrated throughout the Mahayana tradition from the first to the 15th days of the eighth lunar month. It is believed that the gates of hell are opened on the first day, and the ghosts may visit the world for 15 days. Food offerings are made during this time to relieve the sufferings of these ghosts. On the 15th day (Ulambana), people visit cemeteries to make offerings to the departed ancestors. Many Theravadins from Cambodia, Laos, and Thailand also observe this festival.

Avalokiteshvara's birthday is a festival that celebrates the bodhisattva ideal represented by Avalokiteshvara (Kuan Yin), who represents the perfection of compassion in the Mahayana traditions of Tibet and China. The festival occurs on the first full-moon day in March.

MODE OF DRESS The most distinct mode of dress in the Buddhist world is the robes worn by monks and nuns. The symbolic significance of this form of dress can be easily seen in the common phrase for becoming a monk, "taking the robes." Although the color and style of robes varies considerably from country to country, as well as from school to school, all monastics wear robes. Not only does the robe physically mark the monk as distinct from the layperson, but it also serves as a physical reminder of the monk's ascetic lifestyle. The Buddha himself fashioned his own robe out of donated scraps and recommended that his followers do the same. Buddhist robes continue to be symbolically constructed in the same manner, sewn together out of many smaller pieces of cloth (although not usually actual scraps). Robes are most often saffron in color, although the range of colors goes from yellow to red, depending on the monastery.

On auspicious days throughout the Buddhist world, particularly full-moon days (Uposatha Days), pious laypeople will often wear special clothing, usually all white, to signify their purity and taking of the *pancha sila* (five ethical vows). In Sri Lanka the reformer Anagarika Dharmapala (1864–1933) formalized this mode of dress by proposing a special kind of ascetic layperson (called *anagarika*) who always adhered to the Buddhist ethical guidelines and always wore the simple, all-white garb.

DIETARY PRACTICES Specific meals for specific occasions vary considerably throughout the Buddhist world, but virtually all traditions in all countries share two basic dietary prohibitions: alcohol is typically prohibited (always for monks), being regarded as a clouder of reason; likewise, meat is typically not eaten. One of the most basic ethical principles in Buddhism is that which prohibits the killing of any other being; this principle fundamentally informs Buddhist dietary practices. Vegetarianism is the ideal, certainly, but not always the practice, even in monasteries. Monks in particular are put in a kind of ethical double bind when it comes to eating. As much as they may wish to practice vegetarianism, in countries where monks go from home to home begging for their meals, they are also under an ethical and philosophical obligation to take (without grasping) whatever is offered; this provides the laity with the opportunity for a kind of domestic asceticism. Thus, if a layperson offers meat, the monk is obligated to accept it. The prohibition against killing or harming other beings, however, importantly involves intention, and if the monk had no say in the killing of the animal and if it was not killed specifically for him, then no karmic taint adheres to him because there was no ill intention on his part.

On particularly important holidays or festival days, Buddhists often eat special foods. For instance, in many countries laypeople eat a special milk and rice mixture, a kind of gruel intended to symbolically replicate Sujata's initial gift of rice gruel to the Buddha, which enabled him to gain the strength for enlightenment.

RITUALS *Puja*, or "honor," is a ubiquitous form of worship throughout the Buddhist world, most typically directed at images of the Buddha and the various bodhisattvas and at the Buddha's relics. Although the Buddha himself explicitly stated that he was not to be worshiped, either while he was alive or after his death—and that it was the dharma that should, instead, be learned and practiced—*puja*, in fact, often looks very much like worship, sometimes involving a great outpouring of emotion and adoration, even amounting to what seems like worship of a god. Buddhists frequently make offerings to images, typically fruit but sometimes money, as a gesture of respect, as an act of renunciation, or, in some cases, in the hopes of some favor in return, perhaps happiness or prosperity. Such acts of devotion are often performed in temples but can also be performed in small shrines in the home.

Puja typically involves not only the making of an offering but also meditation and prayer. Frequently a Buddhist layperson will approach an image, make his or her offering, and then kneel in prayer or meditation. These meditations sometimes involve a mental reconstruction of the Buddha's auspicious qualities—perhaps his compassion or his profound wisdom—with the hope of cultivating those qualities oneself. The meditation might be directed to the well-being of others, one's family members in particular, or one's ancestors. These are often individual acts of quiet and contemplative devotion, but in some settings they can also be congregational as well. Likewise, such devotion sometimes is quite physical in nature. In Tibet, for instance, Buddhist laypeople will frequently circumambulate a stupa, turning smaller prayer wheels as they do (symbolically turning the Wheel of the Dharma), a ritual act that is also sometimes performed by making a series of bodily prostrations. Increasingly, laypeople are also becoming involved in formal meditation, traditionally the province of monks only. In Thailand, Myanmar (Burma), and Sri Lanka, for instance, lay meditation classes are held at monasteries and temples.

Buddhist weddings are a relatively recent phenomenon, largely developed as a result of colonial exclusion of those who were not formally married. In some instances monks officiate at such events, although this is unusual. Funerals, though, quite often involve monks, who recite sacred texts, offer prayers for the dead intended to ensure their speedy and auspicious rebirth, and in some cases chant special "protective" verses intended to ward off potentially evil spirits associated with incomplete karmic transference from one birth to the next.

The first places of pilgrimage in Buddhism were associated with the Buddha's relics. The Buddha said his followers could go to these places and feel great joy and tranquility. Furthermore, the Buddha explicitly stated that even those who died on the journey to such a place would experience the same mental and physical benefits as those who reached their destination. As Buddhism spread throughout India and the rest of Asia, new pilgrimage places emerged, some directly associated with the Buddha's relics or with important events in his life and others more local in significance. The physical act of pilgrimage became, by extension, analogous to the inner journey that one "on the path" was to make. As such, pilgrimage is a kind of renunciation in microcosm, a departure from—and symbolic renunciation of—the mundane and domestic world in pursuit of a higher religious goal. Pilgrims, like monks, frequently dress in simple, distinctive clothes; they take vows of chastity and abstain from any karmically harmful acts; they meditate and study. Certainly the pilgrim, unlike the monk, eventually returns to normal life, but the ideal is that he or she returns changed by the experience and shares this change with those who did not make the journey.

RITES OF PASSAGE The most basic rite of passage in Buddhism is the taking of the Three Refuges (also known as the Triple Gem): "I go for refuge to the Buddha, I go for refuge to the dharma, I go for refuge to the sangha." This is a ritual recitation of the intent to live as a Buddhist, to embody the dharma, and to seek guidance from the dharma, and, as such, it is a kind of minimal condition for becoming a Buddhist. For the monk, this simple ritual is the first step in a far more elaborate rite of passage: formal ordination into the sangha. The first step in this elaborate process is severing one's ties with domestic life, a ritual renunciation that is usually called "leaving home for homelessness." It is followed by a series of vows, particularly the vow to follow the code of monastic discipline, the Vinaya. For lay Buddhists other significant rites of passage are birth; marriage, which in many Buddhist countries is frequently marked by the taking of specifically Buddhist vows; and death, which marks not only the end of this life but the transition to the next rebirth.

MEMBERSHIP The Buddha stressed several key issues with regard to membership within the Buddhist tradition, among these the following two: first, Buddhism was open to anyone, regardless of social status or gender (this would later become an issue within the sangha, however, as women were excluded in at least some Buddhist schools); and second, that becoming a Buddhist was an entirely self-motivated act. In a sense the Buddha and his early followers did engage in missionizing activities, but they did so not so much to gain converts to their new religion as to share the dharma out of compassion, out of an attempt to alleviate the suffering (*duhkha*; Pali, *dukkha*) that, according to the Buddha, characterizes life. The first formal Buddhist mission was initiated by Ashoka (third century B.C.E.), who sent his son, Mahinda, to Sri Lanka to establish a lineage of monks in that country.

Buddhists have never been particularly zealous in spreading their religion. Rather, Buddhist ideals have historically been imported and incorporated into indigenous practices, such as the integration of Buddhism with

Temporary Ordination

An important way for the sangha (community of monks) and the laity to interact in many Theravada countries—such as Thailand, Myanmar (Burma), Cambodia, and Sri Lanka—is through the practice of temporary ordination, a relatively recent innovation. Men of varying ages are ordained as monks temporarily, for anywhere from a few days to several weeks. They undergo the same initiation process that a novice monk would undergo: the departure from home life, the shaving of the head, the donning of the monk's robes, and the taking of the ritual recitation known as the Three Refuges (also known as the Triple Gem). These temporary monks live as all monks live, observing the rules of monastic discipline (the Vinaya), studying the dharma (the teachings of the Buddha), and meditating.

The benefits of temporary ordination are not only that it spreads the dharma directly, affording the temporary monk to gain a firsthand understanding of what it means to live according to the Buddha's teaching, but that it is also an effective means to involve laypeople in the workings of the monastery without compromising the monk's asceticism. The temporary monk returns to his domestic life and spreads what he has learned to his family and friends, and typically he and his family maintain a closer relationship with the monks and the monastery. In Sri Lanka, for instance, where temporary ordination is a new phenomenon, some prominent monks have gone so far as to say publicly that this practice will save the religion and stop the moral decay of the young.

Taoism and Confucianism in China or the integration of Buddhism and the indigenous Bon tradition in Tibet. This has meant, in practice, that Buddhism has typically grown and spread through would-be converts coming to the religion rather than the religion actively seeking them out. One important way Buddhism has grown in the modern era is through immigration of Asians to Europe and North America, particularly since the end of World War II. These immigrants gradually set up temples in their adopted countries, and frequently curious non-Asians were drawn in. Furthermore, because temples were often begun by lay Buddhists, new and expanded roles for the laity emerged.

In Asia, also, many popular new movements have emerged during this same period. The lay movement Soka Gakkai International, which began in Japan but has spread throughout the world, adopts the teachings of the thirteenth-century Zen teacher Nichiren and focuses on a kind of practical self-transformation through chanting. In Sri Lanka the Sarvodaya movement has expanded Buddhist membership by focusing on practical, village-oriented development projects with a decidedly Buddhist orientation. In Thailand the Dhammakaya movement, founded by a laywoman, has become enormously popular. And in India there has been a resurgence of Buddhism among the untouchable population since the public conversion of the first president of India, A.K. Ambedkar, in 1956 (there are now some 6 million Ambedkar, or Dalit, Buddhists in India).

RELIGIOUS TOLERANCE Because of its emphasis on self-effort and its recognition that people learn and progress at different rates, Buddhism has always been a profoundly tolerant religious tradition, tending to view other religions not so much as competitors but as different versions of the same basic quest for truth and salvation. Indeed, the Buddha never proposed that his was the only path but rather that it was the most efficacious; a person following some other religious tradition, an early text states, would be like a man slowly walking to his destination, whereas the Buddhist was like a man riding a cart to that same place. Certainly the walker and the rider would both, in time, reach their destinations, but the latter would arrive much sooner.

This is not to say that Buddhists have not engaged in polemical attacks against other religions. Certainly they have, such as the scholarly attacks on Hinduism that were common in Buddhism in the medieval Indian milieu. This is also not to say that Buddhists have not clashed, sometimes violently, with members of other religions. In modern Sri Lanka, for instance, Buddhists and Hindus have been fighting against each other in a civil war that has taken the lives of tens of thousands; however, this and other such clashes tend not to be wars about differing religious ideologies so much as they are about ethnic and political tensions.

SOCIAL JUSTICE On the surface it would appear that Buddhism would not be a religion that lends itself to taking an active role in social issues, given that at its core is the individual search for individual salvation. It is imperative, however, to understand that the Buddha set out for his quest for enlightenment not out of a selfish quest for spiritual fulfillment but out of compassion and the burning desire to alleviate the suffering of all beings, and it is this fundamental emphasis on compassion that informs and orients the Buddhist sense of social justice.

In the latter part of the twentieth century there emerged across the Buddhist world a phenomenon that scholars and Buddhists alike have labeled engaged Buddhism, a broad and varied movement that addresses issues such as poverty, education, and human rights.

The number of Buddhist organizations addressing economic issues throughout the world has grown tremendously since the middle of the twentieth century. These organizations participate in a staggering range of activities, from those that operate purely on the village level to those with a decidedly international scope. One of the most interesting modern Buddhist groups to deal with the issue of poverty is Sarvodaya, which began in 1958 with the purpose of addressing social, economic, and environmental issues in Sri Lanka. In 1987 Sarvodaya started Sarvodaya Economic Enterprises Development Services (SEEDS), intended explicitly to address poverty and economic issues. The goals of SEEDS are nothing short of the eradication of poverty, accomplished through developing, at the local and village level, means for sustainable livelihood. SEEDS provides vocational training, helps local groups develop projects related to agriculture and marketing, assists in technical issues, and provides low-interest loans to help start sustainable projects. Although this is a movement specific to Sri Lanka, countless other such movements have emerged in South, Southeast, and East Asia. For instance, the Metta Dana Project, based in central Myanmar (Burma), is a similar grassroots organization that focuses not only on poverty but also on health care and educational issues. Likewise, the Tzu Chi Foundation, in Taiwan, in addition to addressing a large range of social issues, provides a range of charities and economic relief, including home repair, medical aid, food distribution, and funeral assistance. In India the Karuna Trust, formed in 1980 by a group of Western Buddhists, focuses specifically on India's approximately 6 million formerly untouchable Buddhist converts, sometimes called Dalit Buddhists, providing disaster relief and support for a wide range of economic development projects.

Buddhist education has traditionally been in the monasteries—this is where monks receive their formal education and where laypeople traditionally go to hear dharma talks. One of the first people to promote a more formal educational system was Henry Steele Olcott, who, along with the Sri Lankan reformer Anagarika Dharmapala, established a network of distinctly Buddhist schools in Sri Lanka in the latter half of the nineteenth century. Since then Buddhist schools have been founded, with varying degrees of success, throughout Asia. One particularly important aspect of this has been the education of women. As new female monastic movements have emerged across Asia, such groups have focused specifically on the education of girls and young women. In Taiwan the Fo Kuang Shan movement has been active in Buddhist education, establishing a network of Buddhist schools from primary schools to college.

Buddhist groups specifically concerned with human rights began to draw widespread recognition during the Vietnam War, when Buddhist monks took an active role in protesting not only American military involvement in Vietnam and Cambodia but also the activities of the communist governments in those countries. One particularly prominent figure in this movement has been Thich Nhat Hanh, an outspoken monk who left Vietnam in 1966 and took up residence in France, where he has continued to be an important voice. He is the founder of Plum Village, a Buddhist retreat that promotes a cross-cultural, interdenominational appreciation of human life.

Buddhist human rights activists have been particularly active in Myanmar (Burma) and Tibet. The Free Burma Coalition (FBC), for instance, is an umbrella organization that was founded in 1995 by a group of Burmese and American graduate students to address human rights violations by Myanmar's military. FBC is associated with the National League for Democracy, a group that has been led by Aung San Suu Kyi, the 1991 winner of the Nobel Peace Prize. FBC is a large network, particularly active on the Internet, of activists, dissident academics in exile, labor groups, and refugees, all working to ensure the protection of human rights in Myanmar's highly volatile political climate. Tibet has been an even more consistent focus of human rights groups since the 1950s and the exile of the Dalai Lama to India. In part motivated by the Dalai Lama himself, numerous groups in the West and in Tibet have worked to monitor and protect human rights in that country by organizing pro-

tests, mounting letter-writing campaigns, appealing to foreign governments for political and economic pressure, and so on. Prominent Buddhist organizations such as Soka Gakkai and Fo Kuang Shan in East Asia are also actively engaged in human rights issues, as are countless distinctly Buddhist human rights organizations and movements throughout Asia and the West.

SOCIAL ASPECTS Buddhist texts are essentially silent on the subject of marriage. Although the Buddha did not lay out rules on married life, he did offer basic guidelines for how to live happily within marriage. Married people should be honest and faithful and avoid adultery—indeed, one of the ethical rules in the *pancha sila* is the prohibition against sexual misconduct, which is frequently taken in practice to be the endorsement of marital fidelity and monogamy. In the Parabhava Sutta, for instance, a significant cause of human error and negative karma is involvement with multiple women. As for polygamy, the Buddhist laity are advised to limit themselves to one wife.

In traditionally Buddhist countries marriage is a completely secular affair taking various forms: monogamy or polygamy. In many South and Southeast Asian countries, marriage is traditionally arranged, based on, among other elements, social standing, education, and compatibility of horoscopes. Although monks may be invited to a marriage ceremony, their role is not to conduct the marriage itself but, rather, to bless the newly married couple as they set out on a new stage of their lives. Ceremonies vary considerably from country to country and school to school. In the Theravada, for instance, the couple might recite a text such as the Sigalovada Sutta, which deals generally with marital duties, and they might also recite a devotional text such as the Mangala Sutta.

Likewise, Buddhist views about the family tend to be general in nature, based in principle on the interconnectedness of karma. Because the traditional Buddhist family is a large and extended group that includes aunts, uncles, cousins, grandparents, and so on, one has a duty to honor and respect both one's immediate family and one's extended family. In a famous statement the Buddha remarked that one should be kind and compassionate to all living beings because there can be found no being who was not once in some former life one's brother, sister, mother, or father. In many Buddhist countries, particularly those of East Asia, one of the most important familial duties is toward one's dead ancestors, who are thought to exist in a special realm and who depend on the living to continue to honor and care for them.

CONTROVERSIAL ISSUES In general, because Buddhism has no single, centralized religious authority, and because it philosophically and practically places the emphasis on individual effort, there is no single stance on any controversial issue. Buddhists, if it is possible to generalize, tend to believe that most issues are decided by the individual or by the basic ethical guidelines that were first laid out by the Buddha himself and then subsequently elaborated on in the Vinaya Pitaka. One central tenet that informs Buddhist's understanding of such controversial issues as capital punishment and abortion is the prohibition against harming any living beings. Issues such as divorce, which can frequently be governed by religious rules and authorities, are generally left up to the individuals involved.

There is no foundation in Buddhism for Buddhists to oppose birth control. Generally it is held that Buddhist laypeople may use any traditional or modern measures to prevent conception, since birth control simply prevents a potential being from coming into existence and does not harm any sentient beings.

Abortion presents a more difficult, more ambiguous issue. The precept that prohibits killing (and harming) beings stipulates that killing is governed by five conditions, the first of which is the presence of a living being, and so it very much depends on one's stance on this issue, which is as contested in Buddhism as it is in the West.

One would think that Buddhism would have been entirely open to women, because it is purely one's own effort, one's own ability to understand the nature of the dharma and to realize the truth of impermanence, that determines where one is on the path. In other words, we might expect to find inclusiveness in Buddhism, and to a certain extent we do. One's gender should not, in theory, hinder one's spiritual attainment any more than one's caste would. In practice, however, the status of women has been anything but clear in Buddhism.

In the early textual tradition the vision of women is often quite negative, and women become a kind of hindrance and a distraction, the embodiment of illusion and the objects of lustful grasping. There are, to be sure, also positive images of women—as mothers, as devoted wives, as model givers. This last role is particularly important, for among the laity it is the women of the community who are often most actively involved in supporting the sangha and, as a result, in receiving the dharma.

The issue of female monks has been a consistently contested one, since the Buddha himself reluctantly allowed his aunt Mahapajapati to join the sangha but with the stipulation that female monks (Pali, *bhikkhuni*) would be subject to additional rules. In practice, though, the lineage of female monastics died out fairly early in the Theravada, and it has only been in the modern era, often as the result of the efforts of Western female Buddhists, that the female sangha has been revived, and even in these cases women monks are sometimes viewed with suspicion and even open hostility. Nonetheless, in Southeast Asia and Sri Lanka, women monastics have been an important voice and an important symbolic presence. In the Mahayana and Vajrayana schools, as well as in Zen, female monks, although certainly not the norm, are more common than in the Theravada. China and Korea are the only East Asian countries to allow for full female ordination. Beginning in the early 1980s a move for full female ordination began in Tibetan Buddhism, with the first all-female monastery being built in Ladakh, India, home of many Tibetan Buddhists since the Dalai Lama's exile in 1959. Similarly, Thai Buddhist woman began to organize a female monastic order in the 1970s. In Sri Lanka a German woman, Ayya Khema, began a female monastic order in the 1980s, one that has continued to grow. In 2000 the International Association of Buddhist Women was founded. This umbrella organization brings together the various female sanghas and provides a vital nexus of unity and activism.

CULTURAL IMPACT Monks are prohibited from listening to music and from dancing; such things represent, from a monastic point of view, a lack of control of the senses, a kind of indulgence and distraction that is not conducive to mindfulness. Nonetheless, monks have often chanted Buddhist texts, and the effect can be almost musical. In contemporary Sri Lanka a special class of monks is trained in such chanting, and recordings of their recitations are frequently sold as popular music, although the monks themselves have been careful to stipulate that this is simply a more effective means of transmitting the dharma and not intended for aesthetic enjoyment. Elsewhere, in Tibet and East Asia, different forms of chanting, sometimes with musical accompaniment, are common and popular. From the lay perspective, music can sometimes be a significant form of offering, or *dana*, and an expression of faith in, and attention to, the Buddha's teachings. Furthermore, at many Buddhist temples drumming, flute and horn playing, and lyrical chanting all accompany devotional and ritual activity.

Some of the earliest examples of Buddhist art and architecture are the great stupas of Bharhut, Sanchi, and Amaravati; not only did these stupas contain relics of the Buddha, but they were embellished with spectacular stone reliefs. More than decoration or ornamentation, these sculptures were intended to visually convey the Buddha's teachings, to instruct laypeople and monks alike in the dharma. Key events in the Buddha's life are depicted—for example, his defeat of the evil Mara or the simple gift of sustenance offered by the laywoman Sujata that enabled Siddhartha to attain enlightenment.

The very nature of a sculptural image in Buddhism is complex. Although there has been some debate about the matter, it is clear that Buddhists began to depict the Buddha early on, perhaps even before he died. The Buddha himself said that images of him would be permissible only if they were not worshiped. Rather, such images should provide an opportunity for reflection and meditation. Virtually all Buddhist temples and monasteries throughout the world contain sculptural images of the Buddha and the bodhisattvas. These images range from simple stone sculptures of the Buddha to incredibly intricate depictions of a bodhisattva like Kanon in Japan, with his thousand heads and elaborate hand gestures and iconographic details. And although these images function in the ritual context of the temple and monastery, they also serve an artistic and aesthetic purpose.

In Tibet particularly, an important artistic form is the mandala, an aid in meditation that symbolically depicts a world populated by bodhisattvas and other beings. Mandalas, which are often painted on cloth scrolls but can also be depicted in three-dimensional media or made out of sand (to emphasize the impermanence of all things), are intended to lead the meditator visually from the outer world of appearance and illusion to the inner core of being, the very nature of the self and emptiness. In East Asia, Zen has profound influence on the arts, and there is a long, rich tradition of Buddhist painting. Painting is seen as a form of meditation, a method of attaining insight into the immediacy of the moment and the transiency of the natural world. Other important artistic Buddhist endeavors in East Asia include archery, gardening, and the tea ceremony, all of which combine ritual action, meditation, and artistic expression.

Most of the Buddhist architecture of India is long gone, although Bodh Gaya, where the Buddha attained enlightenment, continues to be a vital center of activity not only for India's Buddhists but for Buddhist pilgrims throughout the world. Some of the most spectacular examples of Buddhist architecture can be found in Southeast Asia. At Angkor Wat, in Cambodia, for instance, Buddhist kings constructed an enormous monument that re-creates the cosmic hierarchy of divine and semi-divine beings in order to symbolically convey the concept that their earthly rule paralleled a celestial one; the ruins of similar monuments can be found in Pagan, Myanmar (Burma), in the ancient cities of Anuradhapura and Polonnaruwa in Sri Lanka, and in several ancient cities in Thailand. One of the most magnificent examples of Buddhist art and architecture is the temple complex at Borobudur, on the island of Java in Indonesia, an almost unfathomably elaborate and extensive architectural marvel.

Jacob Kinnard

See Also Vol. I: *Mahayana Buddhism, Theravada Buddhism, Tibetan Buddhism*

Bibliography

Bartholomeusz, Tessa J. *Women under the Bo Tree: Buddhist Nuns in Sri Lanka*. Cambridge: Cambridge University Press, 1994.

Bechert, Heinz, and Richard Gombrich, eds. *The World of Buddhism: Monks and Nuns in Society and Culture*. London: Thames and Hudson, 1984.

Cabezon, Jose Ignacia, ed. *Buddhism, Sexuality, and Gender*. Albany: State University of New York Press, 1992.

Carrithers, Michael. *The Forest Monks of Sri Lanka*. Delhi: Oxford University Press, 1983.

Conze, Edward. *Buddhism: Its Essence and Development*. New York: Harper Torchbooks, 1965.

———, ed. *Buddhist Texts through the Ages*. New York: Harper Torchbooks, 1964.

Cowell, E.B., ed. *Jataka Stories*. 3 vols. London: Pali Text Society, 1956.

Dehejia, Vidya. *Discourse in Early Buddhist Art: Visual Narratives of India*. Delhi: Munshiram Manoharlal, 1997.

Eckel, Malcolm David. *To See the Buddha: A Philosopher's Quest for the Meaning of Emptiness*. Princeton, N.J.: Princeton University Press, 1992.

Gombrich, Richard F. *Buddhist Precept and Practice.* Delhi: Motilal Banarsidass, 1991.

———. *Theravada Buddhism: A Social History from Ancient Benares to Modern Colombo.* London: Routledge and Kegan Paul, 1988.

Gombrich, Richard F., and Gananath Obeyesekere. *Buddhism Transformed: Religious Change in Sri Lanka.* Princeton, N.J.: Princeton University Press, 1988.

Johnston, E.H., trans. *The Buddhacarita, or, Acts of the Buddha.* 3rd ed. Delhi: Motilal Banarsidass, 1984.

Kalupahana, David J. *Nagarjuna: The Philosophy of the Middle Way.* Albany: State University of New York Press, 1986.

Keown, Damien, et al., eds. *Buddhism and Human Rights.* London: Curzon, 1998.

LaFleur, William. *The Karma of Words: Buddhism and the Literary Arts in Medieval Japan.* Berkeley: University of California Press, 1983.

Lamotte, Etienne. *History of Indian Buddhism: From the Origins to the Saka Era.* Louvain-La-Neuve: Institut Orientaliste, 1988.

Lopez, Donald S., Jr., ed. *Buddhism in Practice.* Princeton, N.J.: Princeton University Press, 1995.

———. *Religions of China in Practice.* Princeton, N.J.: Princeton University Press, 1996.

Mitra, Debala. *Buddhist Monuments.* Calcutta: Sahitya Samsad, 1971.

Murcott, Susan. *The First Buddhist Women.* Berkeley: Parallax Press, 1991.

Ñanamoli, Bhikkhu. *The Life of the Buddha.* Kandy, Sri Lanka: Buddhist Publication Society, 1972.

Ñanamoli, Bhikkhu, and Bhikkhu Bodhi, trans. *The Middle Length Discourses of the Buddha: A New Translation of the Majjhima Nikaya.* Boston: Wisdom Publications, 1995.

Pal, Pratapaditya. *Light of Asia: Buddha Sakyamuni in Asian Art.* Los Angeles: County Museum of Art, 1984.

Prebish, Charles S., ed. *Buddhist Ethics: A Cross-Cultural Approach.* Dubuque, Iowa: Kendall/Hunt, 1992.

———. *Luminous Passage: The Practice and Study of Buddhism in America.* Berkeley: University of California Press, 1999.

Prebish, Charles S., and Kenneth K. Tanaka, eds. *The Faces of Buddhism in America.* Berkeley: University of California Press, 1998.

Queen, Christopher, and Sallie B. King, eds. *Engaged Buddhism: Buddhist Liberation Movements in Asia.* Albany: State University of New York Press, 1996.

Rawson, Philip. *The Art of Southeast Asia.* New York: Praeger, 1967.

Ray, Reginald A. *Buddhist Saints in India: A Study in Buddhist Values and Orientations.* Oxford: Oxford University Press, 1994.

Reynolds, Frank E., and Jason A. Carbine, eds. *The Life of Buddhism.* Berkeley: University of California Press, 2000.

Schober, Juliane, ed. *Sacred Biography in the Buddhist Traditions of South and Southeast Asia.* Honolulu: University of Hawai'i Press, 1997.

Schopen, Gregory. *Bones, Stones, and Buddhist Monks: Collected Papers on the Archaeology, Epigraphy, and Texts of Monastic Buddhism in India.* Honolulu: University of Hawai'i Press, 1996.

Snellgrove, David L. *The Image of the Buddha.* Tokyo: Kodansha International, 1978.

———. *Indo-Tibetan Buddhism: Indian Buddhists and Their Tibetan Successors.* Boston: Shambhala, 1987.

Streng, Frederick J. *Emptiness: A Study in Religious Meaning.* Nashville: Abingdon Press, 1967.

Strong, John. *The Experience of Buddhism: Sources and Interpretations.* 2nd ed. Belmont, Calif.: Wadsworth, 2001.

———. *The Legend of King Asoka.* Princeton, N.J.: Princeton University Press, 1983.

Swearer, Donald K. *The Buddhist World of Southeast Asia.* Albany: State University of New York Press, 1995.

Tambiah, S.J. *Buddhism and the Spirit Cults in Northeast Thailand.* Cambridge: Cambridge University Press, 1970.

Tharpar, Romila. *Asoka and the Decline of the Mauryas.* Delhi: Oxford University Press, 1983.

Walshe, Maurice O'Connell, trans. *The Long Discourses of the Buddha: A Translation of the Digha Nikaya.* Boston: Wisdom Publications, 1996.

Warder, A.K. *Indian Buddhism.* 2nd ed., rev. Delhi: Motilal Banarsidass, 1980.

Wijayaratna, Mohan. *Buddhist Monastic Life according to the Texts of the Theravada Tradition.* Translated by Claude Grangier and Steven Collins. Cambridge: Cambridge University Press, 1990.

Williams, Paul. *Mahayana Buddhism: The Doctrinal Foundations.* London and New York: Routledge and Kegan Paul, 1989.

Mahayana Buddhism

FOUNDED: c. 200 C.E.

RELIGION AS A PERCENTAGE OF WORLD POPULATION: 3.2 percent

OVERVIEW Mahayana (Grand Method) Buddhism began in India as a movement to address issues that had arisen in the existing traditions, which the Mahayana followers subsequently referred to derogatorily as Hinayana (Lower, or Inferior, Method). These questions concerned the status and nature of the arhat (fully enlightened being), the nature of the Buddha (that is, whether or not the Buddha should be considered a historical figure or an ahistorical and transcendental being), and the nature of reality. They began to emerge around the beginning of the Common Era among numerous sects of pre-Mahayana Buddhists. Each sect addressed only some of the questions, and each defined its own answers. By the second century C.E., however, the various ideas began to consolidate. They found their primary expression in the Perfection of Wisdom Sutras, which are traditionally attributed to the Buddha, and in the works of the Indian monk and philosopher Nagarjuna (born in 150 C.E.). During the following centuries the Mahayana set itself in opposition to the Hinayana. Over time most of the pre-Mahayana sects disappeared, with Theravada being the only one to survive in Southeast Asia.

The Mahayana, like Buddhism in general, is marked by a plurality of doctrinal positions. No attempt to unify or harmonize them has ever been made; on the contrary, Buddhists see this plurality as one of the strengths of their creed. In the words of the scholar Paul Williams, "Mahayana is not, and never was, a single unitary phenomenon. It is not a sect or school, but rather, perhaps, a spiritual movement which initially gained its identity not by a definition but by distinguishing itself from alternative spiritual movements or tendencies."

The elements that provide Mahayana Buddhism with a distinct and coherent face are the monastic institution, the behavior of monks and nuns, and the ethics adopted by the laity, as well as some of its beliefs. The latter include the belief that, besides the historical Buddha, innumerable transcendental Buddhas and bodhisattvas (enlightened beings on the way to Buddhahood) act as guides and teachers on the path to enlightenment; that the worship of these bodhisattvas and Buddhas is important to the practice of the Mahayana; that the ideal of the bodhisattva who delays the realization of nirvana until all sentient beings can join him or her replaces the ideal of the arhat; that the path to enlightenment extends over many lifetimes; and, finally, that the "word of the Buddha," as Buddhist scripture is defined, is not restricted to the utterances of the historical Buddha but flows from a numinous source called Buddhamind.

The Mahayana originated in India but spread all over Asia from the early centuries of the Common Era onward. Its main contemporary footholds are in China (including Tibet), Japan, Vietnam, Korea, and Mongolia, and its adherents in the Western world have become increasingly numerous.

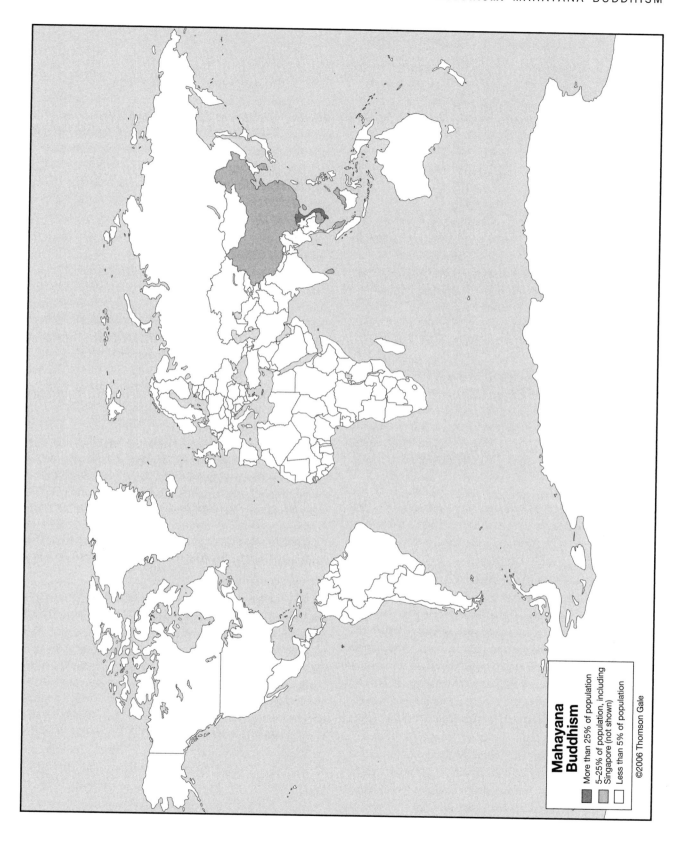

Mahayana
Buddhism

More than 25% of population

5-25% of population, including
Singapore (not shown)

Less than 5% of population

©2006 Thomson Gale

A monk sculpts a Tara figure out of yak butter. The female bodhisattva Tara is invoked to help with such problems as female infertility, the crossing of dangerous rivers, and escape from robbers. © CRAIG LOVELL/CORBIS.

HISTORY Nagarjuna is credited with formulating the main philosophical concepts of the Mahayana in the first century C.E. in his *Mulamadhyamaka-karika* (Stanzas on the Middle Way). At the same time, the Perfection of Wisdom Sutras began to appear in India. As a broad stream of Buddhist ideas and practices, the Mahayana proliferated throughout India and Southeast, East, and Central Asia, branching out into many schools. In India Madhyamaka and Yogachara flourished as the main philosophical camps from about the second to the eleventh century. During this time Mahayana Buddhism also spread into Southeast Asia, where it thrived until about the thirteenth century in such places as Sumatra and Bali. The Mahayana entered China in the second century, though it remained largely the religion of foreigners there until the fourth century, when native Chinese began to enter the monastic order. Chinese Bud-

dhist schools formed around individual scriptures. The most important of these schools were T'ien-t'ai (based on the Lotus Sutra), Hua-yen (based on the Avatamsaka, or Garland, Sutra), Fa-hsiang (based on the writings of the fifth-century philosophers Asanga and Vasubandhu), the Pure Land School (based on the Sukhavativyuha, or Pure Land, Sutra), and the Ch'an School (based on the teachings of its patriarchs).

The rulers of Tibet introduced Mahayana Buddhism to their court and to some noble families in the eighth century, but the country's general population did not embrace Buddhism until centuries later. In Tibet Mahayana Buddhism organized itself according to spiritual lineages—that is, the transmission of specific teachings from master to disciple. Four schools gained prominence: the Nyingma-pa, or Old School, founded by the eighth-century Indian mystic Padmasambhava; Kagyu-pa, founded by Marpa (1012–96); Sakya-pa, founded by Drogmi (992–1072); and Geluk-pa, which had absorbed the earlier Kadam-pa school, founded by Tsongkhapa (1357–1419).

From Korea and China, Mahayana Buddhism spread to Japan in the sixth century. In the sixteenth century it spread from Tibet to Mongolia, and from there to Siberia and parts of Russia. By the sixteenth century all of Buddhist Asia—with the exception of Sri Lanka, Myanmar (Burma), Thailand, and Laos—had accepted the Mahayana in one form or another. From India, however, the Mahayana, together with all other Buddhist traditions, disappeared by the thirteenth or fourteenth centuries because of several causes, among them persecution by hostile invaders, decreased royal patronage, and internal strife.

Philosophical reasoning became the domain of the intellectual elite in the monasteries, and contemplative practices were embraced by meditation masters and mystics, while numerous stories and rituals addressed the spiritual needs of ordinary people. Under the umbrella of the Mahayana, large monastic centers of learning evolved that were similar to the medieval universities of Europe—Nalanda and Takshashila in India, for example, and Drepung and Sera in Tibet. Rulers and the political elite embraced Mahayana rituals to enhance their glory. Monarchs of some Buddhist countries presented themselves to their subject as embodiments of specific Buddhas or bodhisattvas.

A rich literature evolved that supplied the Mahayana laity with narratives of exemplary spiritual lives. Numerous rituals came to address mundane as well as spiri-

The Yungang Caves in China are home to over 51,000 stone sculptures, examples of early Buddhist cave art. In China as well as Inner Asia, temples were often carved into cliffs and steep riverbanks, like the cave temples at Longmen, Dunhuang, and Yungang. © KEREN SU/CORBIS.

tual needs. For instance, the female bodhisattva Tara is invoked to help with such problems as female infertility, the crossing of dangerous rivers, and escapes from robbers. Mahayana traditions also gave rise to exquisite forms of art and architecture and were a major force in civilizing nomads and illiterate tribes who inhabited the steppes of Inner Asia.

Asian monarchs and aristocracies were the main financial supporters of Mahayana Buddhism until Western colonial powers overwhelmed them. A period of decline followed that lasted from roughly the sixteenth to the late nineteenth century. The Buddhist laity, less dependent on royal donations and support, provided many leaders in the effort to rejuvenate and modernize Buddhism in the late colonial and early postcolonial periods. Mahayana communities in various Asian countries have regained their vitality and established branch institutions around the world. Thus, Mahayana Buddhism is no longer a religion confined to Asia but a true world religion.

CENTRAL DOCTRINES The main doctrines of the Mahayana are contained in the *Prajnaparamita-sutra* (Perfection of Wisdom Sutras). Scholars view the *Astasahasrika prajnaparamita-sutra* (Perfection of Wisdom in Eight Thousand Lines) as the oldest version. The central doctrines of the sutras are: (1) *prajna* (wisdom), or insight into the true nature of things, will result in the understanding that all existence lacks inherent being and is for this reason empty, a doctrine that was expounded by Nagarjuna; (2) compassion as a fundamental approach toward all that exists is a necessary balance to wisdom and leads to *bodhicitta*, the Awakened Mind or Mind of Enlightenment; (3) wisdom and the Awakened Mind together provide the road map to enlightenment and constitute the path of the bodhisattva; and (4) the ideal of the bodhisattva should be pursued as the goal of Buddhist practice.

Two philosophical schools became paramount within the Mahayana: Madhyamaka and Cittamatra. Nagarjuna argued that the nature of the world as we perceive it is essentially ineffable because the basic questions of causality lead either to a logical conundrum (same begets not-same) or to the assumption that the true nature of reality is static, which contradicts the fact of apparent constant change. Thus, he concluded, reality is beyond comprehension and articulation, and the true nature of reality is empty of inherent being. (The term "emptiness" [in Sanskrit, *shunyata*] has to be understood as total potentiality and not as an expression of nihilism.) The teaching of the doctrine of emptiness became the hallmark of the Mahayana. Thinkers following in Nagarjuna's footsteps—such as Aryadeva (early third century), Buddhapalita (fifth century), Bhavaviveka (sixth century), and Candrakirti (seventh century)—developed the Mahayana philosophical school of Madhyamaka, which flourished in Tibet and, to a lesser degree, in China.

By the fourth century there had emerged several texts—variously attributed to Asanga, Vasubandhu, or Maitreya—promoting the idea that in emptiness the subject-object dichotomy collapses. These texts argued that the perceived world is colored by the mind of the perceiver; therefore, reality beyond perception remains unknown to human beings. Furthermore, these texts proposed that, separate from normal mental activity, there exists a Mind that is inherently existing and nondual. This Mind is fundamental to all existence; it is the matrix of Buddhahood (*tathagata-garbha*), or Buddhamind, which is the ineffable source of existence. These ideas flourished mainly within the Cittamatra, or Mindonly, School as well as within Zen (Chinese Ch'an) Buddhism.

MORAL CODE OF CONDUCT The moral precepts of pre-Mahayana Buddhism remain a valid code of ethics for Mahayana practitioners. Mahayana laypersons are expected to honor the *pancha sila,* or the "five precepts"—abstinence from taking life, taking what is not given, sensuous misconduct, false speech, and taking intoxicants—though the last one is often disregarded. On certain days—the new moon, for example—laypersons observe an additional three or five rules. In theory Mahayana monks and nuns are expected to observe the ten precepts along with hundreds of rules governing the monastic lifestyle. In practice, however, the precepts of eating only one meal per day and refraining from taking gold and silver (that is, handling money) are often disregarded.

For the laity as well as members of the monastic orders, the moral code of conduct inherited from pre-

Mahayana Buddhism has expanded with the ideals of the bodhisattva—wisdom and the Awakened Mind that is based on universal compassion. A serious follower of the Mahayana will strive to assist all sentient beings in their pursuit of enlightenment. Thus, to avoid harming any living thing is essential to the Mahayana practitioner. Throughout the world Mahayanists have protested against war and violence, particularly against the use of nuclear weapons in Japan and against the Vietnam War. Followers of Engaged Buddhism practice social activism in Asia as well as in the West.

SACRED BOOKS The foremost scriptures of the Mahayana are the Perfection of Wisdom Sutras, which enjoy universal recognition. The Perfection of Wisdom Sutras are often ascribed iconic status and are revered not so much for their teachings but for their protective potency. Other scriptural texts—such as the Ratnagotravibhaga, Avatamsaka-sutra (Garland Sutra), Saddharmapundarika-sutra (Lotus Sutra), or Sukhavativyuhasutra (Pure Land Sutra)—have a more circumscribed (and, one may say, more sectarian) following. All of these texts are in the form of a dialogue between an allegoric Buddha and one or more bodhisattvas, who request instruction in the typical Mahayana topics.

SACRED SYMBOLS There are two types of symbols in the Mahayana: anthropomorphic and nonanthropomorphic. Among the anthropomorphic symbols the traditional Buddha image commands a reverence equaled only by that conveyed upon the Perfection of Wisdom (*Prajnaparamita*), which is represented as a beautiful young noblewoman sitting cross-legged on a lotus throne. Many abstract concepts, such as generosity or compassion, are represented in the anthropomorphic forms of deities. The concept of wisdom, for example, is embodied by the bodhisattva Manjushri, who wields a sword as a symbol of the wisdom that cuts through ignorance. Besides these allegoric deities, who originated in Buddhist texts, many local deities have been adopted into the Buddhist pantheon, including figures from Chinese folklore as well as Tibetan gods of mountains and other geographic landmarks.

The most common nonanthropomorphic symbols in the Mahayana are the eight-spoked wheel, which symbolizes the eight-fold path to Buddhahood; the stupa or pagoda, representing the Buddha-mind as well as the eternal knot, which itself symbolizes the interdependency of reality; and the bell and *vajra* (diamond, or thunderbolt), symbols of wisdom and compassion.

EARLY AND MODERN LEADERS The leading thinkers and meditation masters of the Mahayana are mainly known through the works attributed to them. Little or no historical information about them is available. Nagarjuna was born into a Brahmanical family in southern India sometime in the second century C.E., but beyond that, not much else is known about his life. Santaraksita and Kamalashila introduced Indian Buddhism to the Tibetan nobility in the eighth century. Bodhidharma founded Ch'an (Zen) Buddhism in the sixth century. The Chinese monks Fa-hsien and Hsuan-tsang traveled to India in the fourth and seventh centuries, respectively, and left behind invaluable historical accounts of their journeys. A gifted organizer and translator, Hsuan-tsang, with the financial support of the Chinese emperor, also oversaw the translation into Chinese of numerous Buddhist texts.

In modern times Bhimrao Ramji Ambedkar (1891–1956), India's law minister from 1947 to 1951 and a leader of the untouchables, interpreted Buddhism to be mainly a social theory of revolution, which led to the conversion of many untouchables in India. Buddhadasa Bhikkhu (1906–1993) and Thich Nhat Hanh (born in 1926), as well as Tenzin Gyatso (born in 1935), the 14th Dalai Lama, have approached social and political problems from a Buddhist perspective.

MAJOR THEOLOGIANS AND AUTHORS The 14th Dalai Lama has written extensively on Mahayana topics. In his works he speaks from the vantage point of Buddhist philosophy as taught in the Tibetan monasteries, expounding the Madhyamaka view in particular. The Vietnamese Zen master Thich Nhat Hanh has published more than 30 books explaining Buddhism to Western audiences, including *The Heart of the Buddha's Teaching* (1998), as well as books that focus on how to live a Buddhist life in the modern world, such as *Present Moment, Wonderful Moment* (1990). The Chinese Ch'an master Sheng-yen (born in 1930) has expounded key Ch'an texts (*Complete Enlightenment* [1997]) and addressed the concerns of Western practitioners (*Zen Wisdom* [1993]). Chogyam Trungpa (1939–87) reinterpreted Tibetan Buddhism for a Western audience and authored many books, among them *Cutting through Spiritual Materialism* (1973).

ORGANIZATIONAL STRUCTURE Mahayana Buddhism has no unified organizational structure. Individual masters have created movements or schools that adhere to

The Bodhisattva

In all Buddhist traditions a sentient being (*sattva*) striving for enlightenment (*bodhi*) is called a bodhisattva, but with the Mahayana the bodhisattva became the supreme ideal. Mahayana followers believe that the pre-Mahayana ideal of the arhat, or enlightened individual, does not represent full enlightenment. Thus, the arhat does not deserve the title *mahasattva* (great being), which is reserved for those striving after Buddhahood—that is, the Mahayana bodhisattva.

According to the Mahayana, the bodhisattva, at the beginning of his or her career, vows to reach Buddhahood and, with it, consummate enlightenment for the good of all living creatures. Enlightenment, an individual affair in the pre-Mahayana traditions, thus became a universal event with the advent of the Mahayana. Throughout an arduous career spanning innumerable lifetimes, the bodhisattva cultivates *karuna* (compassion) and *prajna* (the right insight into the nature of reality) until he or she becomes a Buddha. But the bodhisattva will not enter Buddhahood until the entire universe presents itself in an enlightened state.

their teachings and disseminate them. Leadership within a movement passes from master to disciple, thereby creating something like a spiritual dynasty. Throughout history disputes have sometimes arisen as to the legitimacy of claims of succession within the movements. These disputes have resulted in divisions and the founding of new branches.

The leadership of the individual schools and traditions lies solidly in the hands of learned and influential monks. No woman has ever become master of a whole school or tradition. In recent times laypeople have often been involved in innovative Buddhist movements, but once such movements became established, the leadership was then handed over to a revered monk. The leader of a Mahayana school exercises his power by means of the monastic institution and its often significant economic resources. What unites the various traditions and schools of the Mahayana is their shared philosophical, ethical, and religious beliefs and acknowledgment of diversity.

HOUSES OF WORSHIP AND HOLY PLACES The Buddhist temple is primarily a place where monks—and, to a lesser degree, nuns—recite the scriptures or sutras and receive instruction. The Mahayana temple is a rectangular hall supported by several rows of pillars. The wall opposite the entrance is lined with statues of various Buddhas and bodhisattvas or similar saintly figures. The remaining walls either are decorated with murals depicting the lives of Buddhas and bodhisattvas or contain a library of Buddhist scriptures and commentaries. Such a temple, called an assembly hall, is always part of a monastery. Relics are often housed in shrines attached to the temple and form a major attraction for pilgrims. Besides the assembly halls, smaller shrines are often used for personal initiation rites or exist as places of special sanctity. In Tibet many such shrines house images of protective deities and their entourages in the form of stuffed animal hides.

Laypersons rarely visit temples, except on such occasions as a local festival or the death of a close relative. In China Buddhist temples, with their affiliated teahouses and vegetarian restaurants, often serve as focal points for community gatherings. Famous Mahayana temples in China include the so-called Lama Temple, or Yonghegong, in Beijing; Labrang Tashikyil (also known as Labuling) in Gansu; and Samye in the Tibet Autonomous Region. In China as well as Inner Asia, temples were often carved into cliffs and steep riverbanks, like the cave temples at Longmen, Dunhuang, and Yungang.

The stupa, initially used as a burial mound in India, underwent significant changes during its spread throughout Mahayana countries. In China the stupa is a multitiered tower, like the Big Goose Pagoda in Xi'an, while in Tibet it is often a solid, domelike building that rests on a square platform and is crowned with a pyramid of discs and emblems of the sun and moon. These monuments symbolize the Buddha-mind.

WHAT IS SACRED? To the Mahayana Buddhist all that exists—humans, animals, and inanimate objects—is surrounded with an aura of sanctity, though none of these things is sacred per se. The worship of relics, however, has played an important role in all Buddhist traditions, with the Mahayana being no exception. Many of the relics stored in prominent Mahayana temples and shrines are the remains of Buddhist masters or—in some rare cases, such as the Baoguang-si near Chengdu, China—of the Buddha himself. These remains may be ashes from cremation or mummified bodies, which are common in Tibetan shrines.

HOLIDAYS AND FESTIVALS Mahayana Buddhists do not have a unified calendar of religious festivals, but they do celebrate the Buddha's birthday, day of enlightenment, and passage into nirvana—all on one day, which usually falls on the first full moon after the spring equinox. Because of their use of different lunar calendars, Mahayana communities in different countries do not necessarily celebrate this occasion on the same day. Festivals in general have strong local and cultural connotations. Commemoration of the dead occurs in most East Asian and Central Asian Mahayana communities in the midst of summer. People visit graveyards or cremation sites and offer a meal, flowers, and alcohol to deceased family members.

MODE OF DRESS The robes of fully ordained monks and nuns consist of three garments that represent the simple dress of ascetics in ancient India. The Mahayana has maintained these robes to a certain degree; however, local adjustments and adaptations to climate and social habits have occurred. In general the robes consist of yellow or reddish-brown loose garments. Chinese monks and nuns wear grey robes outside the temple. There are no prescriptions for laypeople's dress.

DIETARY PRACTICES According to the monastic rules monks and nuns are supposed to eat only one meal per day, which they ought to collect as alms from laypeople, but this restriction is often disregarded. Abstention from eating meat or animal products is not required, but a Mahayana practitioner should not participate in the killing of an animal or order it. Many Chinese, Korean, Vietnamese, and Western Mahayana Buddhists have become vegetarians, though Tibetan, Mongolian, and Nepalese followers of the Mahayana usually eat meat.

RITUALS The oldest written evidence, from the second century B.C.E., indicates that the worship of stupas (as the resting places of the remains of saintly Buddhists) was part of the earliest ritual practices, and it continues to be performed in Mahayana communities. The recitation of sutras is a daily practice for monks and nuns. Meditation, carried out either individually or communally, is a standard of Mahayana practice. Laypeople occasionally join in these practices of their own will. As local folk beliefs were adopted by Mahayana Buddhism, rich systems of rituals evolved in each country. Mahayana monks from East and Central Asia often went on pilgrimages to the sacred sites of India. Members of the laity occasionally undertake pilgrimages to Bodh Gaya, India, the village where the Buddha attained enlightenment.

Mahayana Buddhists, like Buddhists in general, consider weddings secular events, for they affirm the desires for economic security, progeny, and sexual pleasure; thus, no rituals "bless" such an event. In the West, however, Mahayana monks are often asked to create a wedding ceremony ad hoc in order to meet laypeople's expectations.

Mahayana Buddhists cremate their dead in most cases but refrain from elaborate funeral rites, except in China. After a person dies, a monk addresses the mind of the deceased, which is assumed to linger around the body, and gives instructions as to how to achieve enlightenment or at least a good rebirth. Cremation or, in Tibet, sky burial, in which the body is left for vultures to devour, follows on an astrologically determined day but never before three days have passed. The ashes are often deposited in a stupa. In Tibet the bodies of important personages are often either mummified or cremated, while ordinary people's bodies are given sky burials, after which nothing is preserved of the remains.

RITES OF PASSAGE As a religion that, in its core, is contemplative and that focuses on mystical transmutation of the self, Buddhism has no interest in addressing any of the life events often marked by rites of passage. This is also true with regard to Mahayana Buddhism. The sole exception is death. For instance, the Tibetan Book of the Dead provides specific guidance intended to lead the mind of a dying person into an enlightened state.

MEMBERSHIP Mahayana Buddhism is not a proselytizing religion, nor is it a closed community. Conversions occur when a person has informed himself or herself about the religion and when he or she feels a need to convert. Thus, monks and nuns respond to questions and give advice but never seek to convert people. On the contrary, Mahayana Buddhists see such attempts to convert as acts of violence.

As there are no specific requirements for being a Mahayana Buddhist and no identifiable markers separating the Mahayana Buddhist from other Buddhist traditions, no statistics describing the worldwide Mahayana population are available. Furthermore, in many East Asian countries people see themselves as followers of several religious practices at the same time. A Chinese may say that he or she follows Confucian ethics and ancestor worship, applies Taoist ideas to matters of diet and health, but adopts Buddhist philosophy and opts for a Buddhist cremation. Based on general population statistics, however, the number of followers of Mahayana Buddhism worldwide may be roughly estimated to be between 200 and 250 million.

RELIGIOUS TOLERANCE In general Mahayana Buddhism is tolerant vis-à-vis other Buddhist and non-Buddhist traditions and agnosticism, but insists on its own spiritual and philosophical superiority. In more recent times interest in Christian-Buddhist dialogue has increased, and some Benedictine and Buddhist monks—mainly Tibetan and Ch'an—have celebrated services of both faiths together. Some Catholic monks, like Thomas Merton, have lived in Zen or other Mahayana monasteries. Meditation and contemplative practices have formed additional bridges between certain strands of Christianity and the Mahayana. In most cases only Mahayana monks (no nuns) participate in these activities.

SOCIAL JUSTICE The Indian emperor Asoka has always been lauded for his civilizing actions—such as building a road system, water wells, and homes for old people and retired farm animals—and later Mahayana rulers followed in his footsteps. In modern times many lay and monastic Buddhists have fought for equal rights on behalf of India's outcastes and have founded a social work movement, Engaged Buddhism, based on Buddhist concepts. While some of these activities have taken place in non-Mahayana communities, such leading figures of Mahayana Buddhism as the Dalai Lama, the Ch'an master Sheng-yen, and Thich Nhat Hanh have emphasized Buddhist concerns regarding poverty, education, and human rights. Increasingly, socially engaged Buddhists of all traditions, including Mahayana followers, have promoted social justice. For example, Fo kuan shan, a Mahayana movement that originated in Taiwan, not only maintains schools, mobile health centers, and orphanages but also provides homes for seniors and home care for the sick and frail in many countries. Samye Ling, a Tibetan Mahayana Buddhist center based in Scotland, operates soup kitchens and cares for street children in Great Britain, Tibet, and several African countries.

SOCIAL ASPECTS Like Buddhism in general, Mahayana Buddhism views marriage and family as secular issues that, in most cases, impede spiritual progress, because they entail too many duties and distractions. The ideal Buddhist way of life is to live as a celibate monk or nun.

CONTROVERSIAL ISSUES Because of the lack of a central authority in Mahayana Buddhism, no general binding opinions are offered with regard to such issues as birth control, divorce, abortion, women and religion, and sexual orientation. Birth control, as well as divorce, is seen as a secular issue to be dealt with according to society's standards. Most Mahayanists assume that the mind of a dead person enters a new being at the moment of conception; therefore, abortion is seen as harming or killing a living creature. But in Japan, where abortion is widespread, Mahayana Buddhism has developed rituals to guide the mind of the aborted fetus into a better rebirth and to heal the trauma experienced by the parents.

In Asian countries Mahayana Buddhist women have been secondary to men and have played no significant role in the hierarchy of the religion or in its decision-making process. Modernity has changed this situation; nevertheless, recent studies have shown that Tibetan Buddhist nuns in India could not imagine that the next Dalai Lama could be born as a woman. While Buddhists are quite tolerant of a variety of sexual behaviors, homosexual acts, according to the Dalai Lama, are inappropriate sexual conduct. Nevertheless, it is well known that male homosexuality was widespread in some Mahayana monasteries in Tibet and was even seen as a way to enlightenment by the Shingon sect in Japan.

CULTURAL IMPACT Mahayana Buddhism shaped the great civilizations of Asia and gave them a distinct flavor and unique aesthetics. A rich literature narrating the lives of ancient holy men and women and their exploits stimulated dance theaters, literature, and paintings, particularly in the form of murals on temple walls. Buddhists, including Mahayanists, love grand architecture, whether it is that of the recently destroyed Buddha relief that was cut into rock faces in Afghanistan, a gigantic Buddha statue in Hong Kong, or magnificent temples. In recent times the Mahayana has exercised an increasing influence on Western culture, including music, Beat poetry and other literature, and environmentalism.

Eva Neumaier

See Also Vol. I: *Buddhism*

Bibliography

Bechert, Heinz, and Richard Gombrich, eds. *The World of Buddhism: Buddhist Monks and Nuns in Society and Culture.* London: Thames and Hudson, 1991.

Conze, Edward. *Buddhist Scriptures.* Harmondsworth, England, and Baltimore: Penguin Books, 1959.

Guenther, Herbert V. *Buddhist Philosophy in Theory and Practice.* Baltimore: Penguin Books, 1972.

Gyatso, Tenzin, 14th Dalai Lama. *The Buddhism of Tibet and the Key to the Middle Way.* Translated by Jeffrey Hopkins and Lati Rimpoche. London: Allen and Unwin, 1975.

Kawamura, Leslie, ed. *The Bodhisattva Doctrine in Buddhism.* Waterloo, Ontario, Canada: Wilfred Laurier University Press, 1981.

Nhat Hanh, Thich. *The Heart of the Buddha's Teaching: Transforming Suffering into Peace, Joy and Liberation.* New York: Broadway Books, 1999.

Queen, Christopher S., and Sallie B. King. *Engaged Buddhism: Buddhist Liberation Movements in Asia.* Albany, N.Y.: State University of New York Press, 1996.

Strong, John S., comp. *The Experience of Buddhism: Sources and Interpretations.* Belmont, Calif.: Wadsworth Publishing, 1995.

Trungpa, Chogyam. *Cutting through Spiritual Materialism.* Edited by John Baker and Marvin Casper. Berkeley, Calif.: Shambhala, 1973.

Williams, Paul. *Mahayana Buddhism: The Doctrinal Foundations.* London and New York: Routledge, 1996.

Buddhism

Theravada Buddhism

FOUNDED: Fifth century B.C.E.

RELIGION AS A PERCENTAGE OF WORLD POPULATION: 1.9 percent

OVERVIEW Theravada Buddhism comes from the teachings of the Buddha, who lived in the fifth century B.C.E. The Theravada (School of the Elders, in the Pali language) is the sole surviving branch of the earliest Buddhism. Its primary emphasis was on monastic life, with the single goal of individual liberation through enlightenment, until the early twentieth century, when it became more widely available. Laypeople are encouraged to practice generosity (*dana*) and morality (*sila*) in hopes of a better rebirth with the opportunity for more meditation practice.

The number of Theravadins within the worldwide Buddhist community is difficult to assess since many contemporary Western Buddhists freely incorporate elements of various Buddhist groups in their practice. The Theravada are sometimes pejoratively called the Hinayana (Lesser, or Smaller, Vehicle) by other branches of Buddhism. Its disparagers see it as a teaching for only an elite few.

HISTORY The Buddha taught in what is modern-day India and Nepal. A sangha (community) of monks and nuns was well established by the time of his death. He apparently did not intend to found a religion. He said he taught one thing only: suffering and how to end suffering.

The growth of Buddhism in India was greatly enhanced in the third century B.C.E. by the emperor Ashoka, a warrior who became disenchanted with battle after a particularly bloody victory. He found the teachings of the Buddha on nonviolence appealing and established the Buddha's teachings as the moral background of his realm. His reign constituted a high point of early Buddhist culture. Trade and the growth of cities enhanced the growth of Buddhism. Buddhism in India later declined, in part due to the rise of Islam there in the thirteenth century. By that time, however, it had pervaded most of Southeast Asia.

Within several hundred years of the Buddha's birth, at the second major assembly of fully enlightened monks, schisms within the sangha led to new schools that wrote additional scriptures. The groups that formed Mahayana (Greater, or Large, Vehicle) Buddhism migrated north into China, Korea, Japan, and Tibet. This branch produced a more popularized form of the Buddha's teachings that incorporated strains of folk religion and other philosophies indigenous to the regions into which it traveled.

Although practiced worldwide, the Theravada has remained mainly Southeast Asian in its culture. It has major strongholds in Thailand, Myanmar (Burma), Sri Lanka, Cambodia, Nepal, Laos, and other Southeast Asian countries, but only remnants of it are now found in India. Since the middle of the twentieth century, it has held a strong presence in the West, where it tends to attract more educated people.

Theravadin teachings arrived in Great Britain in the late nineteenth century. They reached the United States

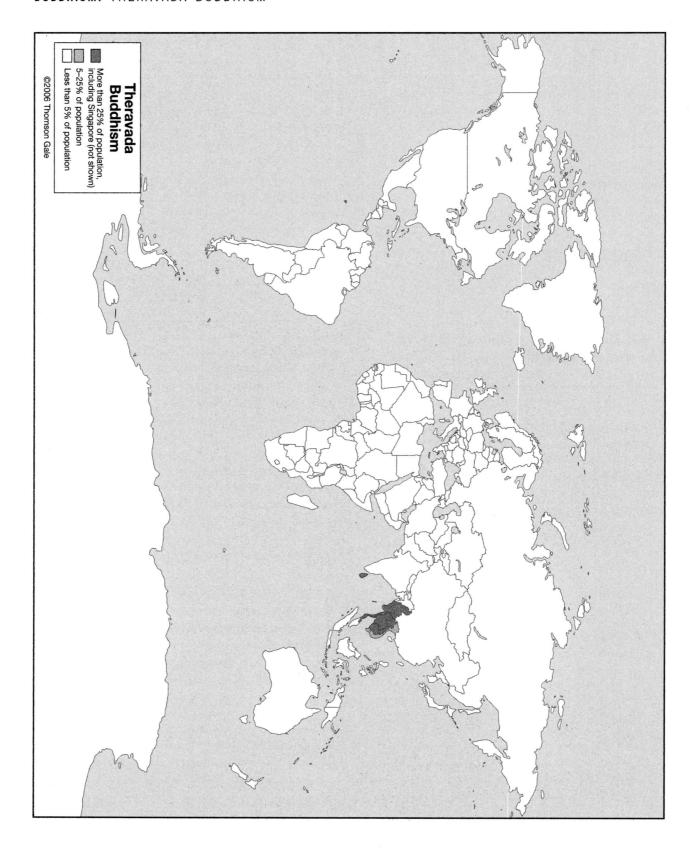

Theravada Buddhism

More than 25% of population, including Singapore (not shown)

5–25% of population

Less than 5% of population

A Buddhist Monk meditates at the Shwe Dagon Pagoda in Myanmar. Among Buddhists, the Theravadin have the fewest rituals, and meditation remains the chief practice. © SERGIO PITAMITZ/CORBIS.

later than the Mahayana, becoming established in the mid-1970s. They were brought mainly by young people returning from Peace Corps duty in Asia and by wayfarers searching Asia for spiritual riches. Although traditionally the Theravada emphasized monasticism, few observant monasteries exist in the West. England, Australia, and the United States have a few. The Theravadin presence in the West is sustained mainly by meditating laypeople.

CENTRAL DOCTRINES Theravadins share belief in the core teachings of the Buddha with all schools of Buddhism. The core teaching that the Theravada emphasizes is summarized in the Four Noble Truths, which the Buddha taught in his first sermon. These truths are that human existence is ultimately unsatisfactory and made up of suffering; that this suffering is caused by craving; that suffering ceases when craving ends; and that a path of practice leading to liberation from suffering exists.

Theravadins commonly divide the fourth noble truth, which outlines the path to liberation from suffering, into three main parts: morality (*sila*), stability of mind (*samadhi*), and wisdom (*panna*). The wisdom steps are right understanding and right intention. The morality steps are right livelihood, right conduct, and right speech. The steps involved in meditation, which lead to stability of mind and, ultimately, wisdom are right effort, right mindfulness, and right concentration. Such distinctions are important to Theravadins since their tradition has a strong base in monastic discipline and meditation.

Theravadins often speak of *kamma* (karma) in terms of their cosmology's realms of existence. This law of moral cause and effect states that chosen actions create states of mind, and that this has consequences. At death the quality of a mind creates its next experience. Having a mind dominated by an unwholesome state of mind brings about rebirth in a lower realm of suffering. For example, minds dominated by hatred create hell realms for themselves, and those dominated by greed, a hungry

Nuns carry the Buddha's remains during Vesak (Wesak) Day celebrations. Vesak, which honors the Buddha's birth, enlightenment, and death (parinibbana), is celebrated on the first full-moon day of May. © REUTERS NEWMEDIA INC./CORBIS.

ghost existence. Those in voluntary ignorance or delusion, such as that caused by polluting the mind with intoxicants, will be reborn in an animal realm. Excessive egotism and self-concern produce the demon realms.

Rebirth in the human realm can be gained through possession of some minimum of morality and generosity. This realm is considered the most propitious for spiritual practice since it has enough suffering to be motivating and enough happiness to prevent becoming overwhelmed. Those with highly developed morality and generosity can inhabit the realms of *devas*, or lesser gods. The *brahma* realms are attained through mental purity, such as being highly concentrated on beautiful states of mind. All of these realms are temporary and fall short of the fruition of *nibbana* (nirvana), which is explained below.

Theravadins teach that not all *kamma* necessarily ripens, or has a determining influence on future realms of existence. Although actions plant seeds, other factors determine whether or not the seed will ripen. Weighty *kamma*, however, will override all other factors. Some ex-

amples of negative weighty kamma are killing a parent or harming a very holy person. These inevitably earn a long sojourn in the deepest hell. Attaining the first degree of enlightenment is positive weighty *kamma*. Those who attain this will never again be born in a realm lower than the human one.

The Theravada and Mahayana schools share a fundamental belief in the *paramis* (perfections of the Buddha). Theravadins describe 10 *paramis* in a list that differs somewhat, however, from the usual Mahayana *paramitas*, but there is considerable overlap. Theravadins hold that, from the moment when he vowed to become a Buddha for the good of all beings, Gautama set about developing these 10 attributes to a high degree of perfection. When they appear in any being's life, they signal that some spiritual progress has been made, though their attainment remains a continuing spiritual task throughout life.

The foremost *parami* is *dana* (generosity). Generosity reflects the openhandedness needed for spiritual development; it is the opposite of the grasping that causes suffering. Asian laypeople commonly sign up months in advance to supply a day's food to a monastery, for example. *Sila* (morality), which is right conduct, is explained below in MORAL CODE OF CONDUCT. Renunciation is surrendering whatever stands in the way of coming to *nibbana*. Wisdom, or correct understanding and intention, is a fruit of spiritual practice and the final liberator of beings. Diligence, often called effort, energy, or courage, is persistent application to right living and spiritual practice. This quality appears in more Theravadin lists than any other as a necessary attribute to develop.

Patience involves acceptance of the rate of growth and of what happens in the process of growth. Truthfulness goes beyond the morality of not lying. It requires that a being become truth. When truthful beings give their word, they will follow though. They see themselves clearly and without sham. Resolution or resolve is staying with the task of spiritual work; sometimes this involves taking special vows to further the work. *Metta* is loving-kindness or gentle friendliness practiced toward all beings without discrimination. Finally, equanimity is having a balanced mind that is not altered by changes in fortune.

Theravadins teach four basic realities: *nibbana*, consciousness, matter, and mental formations. The latter are "colorations" of or contents in the mind through which all else is experienced. For example, when a person is angry, all is perceived through that filter or "dye" of anger. Each of the four realities exists in its own right, and all but *nibbana* are conditioned—that is, subject to laws of cause and effect. Theravadin thought defines laws governing matter, life, mind, volition (the law of *kamma*), and the dispensation of the Buddhas.

Like other Buddhists, Theravadins emphasize three characteristics of conditioned reality: impermanence (*anicca*), unsatisfactoriness (*dukkha*), and "no-self" (*anatta*), the condition of there being no permanent essences. The latter is considered the most difficult of the Buddha's teachings. Contemporary teachers commonly approach it in terms of the interconnectedness and the mutual interdependence of all things. The Pali canon offers unique details for understanding these characteristics.

Dukkha is classified according to several types. First are things easily seen as *dukkha*. They include the discomforts of many bodily processes (*dukkha dukkha*), including hunger, tensions, aches, accidents, illness, aging, and death. There are also the torments of the mind—unwelcome emotions, obsessive patterns of thought, unpleasant moods, the inability to control the mind, mental illness. All entail a loss of happiness (*viparinama dukkha*).

Incessant change that cannot be altered or controlled is also a form of *dukkha* (*anicca dukkha*); since nothing lasts, nothing can be relied on as a dependable support. *Samsara dukkha* is the ceaseless battering of the senses with harassing experiences. Finally, there is the deep *dukkha* of being an apparently individual being, of attachment to the processes making up that being, and of clinging to the sense of being a separate self. The mind creates this prison.

Theravadins also speak of conventional realities created and sustained by human thought. Such realities do not have the basic status of matter, mind states, consciousness, and *nibbana*. They continue to exist only so long as human minds hold them in existence. All of culture, religions, political systems, philosophies, and other human creations have the same reality status as dreams and trains of thought; their survival depends upon human minds continuing to support them.

Theravadins see the nature of *nibbana* somewhat differently from other Buddhist schools, and differences exist even within the Theravada. *Nibbana* is most commonly considered the sole unconditioned reality—the unborn, undying, unchanging, and completely satisfying. In contrast to some other groups, Burmese Theravadins tend to see it as beyond consciousness, which contrasts with a Mahayana notion of nirvana as a state of consciousness. Some Thai Theravadins consider *nibbana* to be the pure released mind resting in objectless, pure consciousness.

The Pali scriptures also describe *nibbana* as haven, rest, and perfect satisfaction. It is the ultimate goal of spiritual practice, a point on which other Buddhists have taken the Theravada to task as lacking a social dimension. Theravadins note, however, that spiritual practice, which requires getting deeply in touch with suffering, necessarily brings compassion in its wake.

Theravadins commonly refer to *nibbana* as a cessation experience. It involves the "blowing out" of the fires of desire. Sometimes it is called the "coolness" that follows the extinguishing of desire. Others speak of it as the cessation of "thingness" or separateness. The Pali canon portrays the Buddha as emphasizing that *nibbana* is neither nonexistence nor a state of existence as we commonly think of such states. It is also not annihilation or extinction, nor is it a realm of existence. Theravadins tend to see enlightenment as the result of considerable personal effort sustained over a long period of practice. This contrasts with some Mahayana schools, which speak of sudden, seemingly unbidden, breakthroughs.

While other schools have different maps of the journey, the Theravadin Vissuddhimagga (Path of Purification) says that *nibbana* is "touched" at four levels on the path to full enlightenment. The first touch is called "stream entry" and makes the practitioner a noble being. It soundly establishes faith in spiritual practice, rules out the possibility of faults serious enough to merit a disastrous rebirth, removes all notions of "magical" religion, and grounds the practitioner in recognizing *anatta*, or "no-self." The second enlightenment greatly reduces greed and hatred, and the third eliminates them. The fourth removes all remaining hindrances, including conceit and restlessness, and is the culmination of the path.

For Theravadins, the final level of enlightenment means that, upon death, the enlightened will "die into" *nibbana* and never again be reborn into the rounds of existence, or *samsara*. This represents the ultimate goal of practice. With their understanding of the *bodhisattwa* (bodhisattva), the Mahayana developed the ideal of the fully developed being who returns to assist all others. This teaching is one basis for the dismissal of the Theravada by some Mahayana schools as lacking social consciousness.

MORAL CODE OF CONDUCT Buddhists all tend to accept the same basic moral code, though even within schools some differences of opinion exist. Morality is extremely important in the Theravadin tradition, which sometimes refers to itself as an ethical psychology. Morality offers guidelines about what causes suffering so one can avoid harmful action. It is never seen as commandments or injunctions handed down by authority.

Theravadins have deeply analyzed the three morality steps of the Noble Eightfold Path. Regarding right livelihood, professions that necessarily involve infliction of suffering are to be avoided. Theravadins are not to be butchers or soldiers. They are not to deal in weapons, intoxicants, or living beings. For laypeople the moral code for right speech and right action is most commonly expressed in five precepts or guidelines for conduct. Detailed lists in the Pali canon describe the conditions that must apply for a violation of right action to have occurred.

The first precept, of not striking at any being's life force, has produced differences of opinion regarding vegetarianism. The Buddha allowed his monks, who were itinerant beggars, to eat what was given them so long as no one killed an animal especially for them and the food was clearly leftovers. Some Theravadins, including some monks, continue to accept this guideline. Other contemporary people, invoking knowledge of the law of supply and demand, argue for vegetarianism. All agree that directly taking life, even that of insects, is forbidden.

The second precept is not to take what is not given. It covers various forms of stealing and fraud, which the Pali scriptures carefully detail. Many contemporary Buddhists add that the right to use something should not be assumed and that borrowing without permission is not acceptable.

The third precept is to avoid sexual misconduct; it is often expanded to include control regarding all sensory appetites. The underlying principle is not to use sensuality in a way that harms anyone. Two major guidelines require honoring the sexual commitments of all parties and avoiding sexual contact with inappropriate partners, which include children and criminals. Contemporary Buddhists have added to this list relationships in which there is an imbalance of power, such as those with clients or students. Most rule out casual sexual contact because it cannot be known what harm it might cause. Homosexual contact is a debated issue.

The fourth precept of avoiding wrong speech has four major parts. Lying is always seriously wrong, as is speech that foments discord among people, such as malicious gossip, slander, and tale bearing. This latter is seen as an especially serious offense that can lead to expulsion from a monastic community. The third guideline is to avoid unnecessarily harsh speech; one should not speak in anger or other uncontrolled states. Finally, frivolous speech without a purpose should be avoided. What is spoken is to be said at appropriate times and in appropriate situations.

The fifth precept is to avoid the use of intoxicants that cloud consciousness and dull awareness. Most in the monastic communities hold that this prohibits all mind-altering substances, including alcohol. Some contemporary Buddhists argue that it means that such substances should not be used to the point of intoxication.

Some laypeople take additional precepts, especially at the time of an important feast, the new moon, or the full moon. The most common are to avoid eating after noon, to refrain from adorning the body, to avoid certain forms of entertainment, to eschew high and luxurious beds and chairs, and to avoid handling money, gold, or silver.

Contemporary nuns commonly follow 8 or 10 precepts, based on these additional precepts, although initially their code of conduct was more extensive than that of monks. The monks have an elaborately detailed monastic code with precepts governing minute details of life.

SACRED BOOKS At an uncertain date, believed to be within 100 years of the Buddha's death, an organizational assembly of 500 fully enlightened monks met to discuss teachings and writings. They formed three major divisions of the scriptures (*Tipitika*): the *Vinaya*, which deals with monastic discipline; the *Dhamma*, the sermons of the Buddha; and the *Abhidhamma*, which presents a philosophy and psychology. They are all written in Pali, a dialect of Sanskrit, and are thus known as the Pali canon. The Theravada recognizes only this canon and does not use the later Mahayana texts.

Legend says that the Buddha's beloved disciple Ananda was present at every discourse of the Buddha and committed to perfect memory each word said. His recollection formed the basis of the *sutta*s (sutras [sermons]) of the Buddha, the major component of the *Dhamma*. These sermons begin with "Thus have I heard," citing Ananda's recall of the Buddha's words. The *Vinaya* was said to come from another monk's perfect recall of the precepts of the monastic discipline.

SACRED SYMBOLS The Theravada uses few symbols in contrast to many other Buddhist schools, some of which make great use of icons and other sacred objects. Theravadin altars often bear flowers. A symbol for the Triple Gem of the Buddha, *dhamma* (teachings), and sangha (community) is sometimes present. Stupas, sacred mounds originally designed to hold relics of the Buddha, dot the landscape in many Theravadin countries. Various icons and statues are found all over Cambodia, Sri Lanka, Thailand, Myanmar (Burma), and other Buddhist locations. In Afghanistan the Taliban destroyed many stone Buddhas.

Theravadins generally do not consider the Buddha divine, although some of the laity have divinized and worshiped him. Officially the Theravada reveres the Buddha as a great man who found a solution to a common human problem. A statue of the Shakyamuni Buddha commonly sits on the altar in monasteries. It shows the Buddha reaching down to touch the ground, responding to the challenge of Mara (evil personified) by calling upon the earth to bear witness to his years of spiritual practice and his right to seek enlightenment.

EARLY AND MODERN LEADERS Until fairly recently Theravada Buddhism remained relatively hidden in its monasteries in Southeast Asia. In the early twentieth century the Burmese master Mahasi Sayadaw (1904–82) made the Theravada more universally available by opening meditation practice to the laity with his mental noting method for *vipassana*, or insight meditation. Somewhat later U Ba Khin (1889–1971) developed the body scanning method and began teaching the laity. The chief contemporary leaders of the schools of Mahasi Sayadaw and U Ba Khin are U Pandita Bivamsa (born in 1921) and S.N. Goenka (born in 1924), respectively.

Joseph Goldstein (born in 1944) and Sharon Salzberg (born in 1952), who were taught primarily in India by the late Anagarika Sri Munindra (1913 [1914]–2003), a disciple of Mahasi Sayadaw, have remained guiding teachers of the Insight Meditation Society, the first major center in the United States, which has a Burmese flavor. Jack Kornfield (born in 1945), who was also instrumental in founding this group, later established a West coast center. Two U.S. monasteries have a Burmese flavor. Bhante Gunaratana (born in 1927)

guides one in West Virginia, and Bhante Silananda (born in 1927) guides another in California.

The late Thai master Ajahn Chah (1918–92) had many disciples. Some of them have founded major centers in Australia and England with the flavor of the Thai Theravada. Ajahn Sumedho (born in 1934), a major disciple of Ajahn Chah, guides an English center, Amaravati.

MAJOR THEOLOGIANS AND AUTHORS Although not considered scripture, Buddhaghosa's *Visuddhimagga*, composed around 500 C.E., is the major classic Theravadin Buddhist work. Some important contemporary Theravadin writers include Bhikkhu Bodhi (born in 1944), Bhikkhu Nyanamoli (died in 1960), Nyanaponika Thera (born in 1901), Matara Sri Nanarama (1901–92), Narada Maha Thera (1898–1993), Nyanatiloka Thera (1878–1957), Piyadassi Thera (born in 1914), Sayadaw U Pandita Bivamsa, Mahasi Sayadaw, Ajahn Chah, Ajahn Sumedho, Joseph Goldstein, Sharon Salzberg, and Jack Kornfield.

ORGANIZATIONAL STRUCTURE The Theravada has no central authority. Monastic houses are relatively autonomous and are overseen by a head monk. A hierarchy within the monastery is based on length of time served as a monk, and monks usually eat in the order of the date of their ordination. In Asia men commonly precede women in all matters; this is usually not true in the West. Laypeople look to monks for teaching and to receive their vows.

HOUSES OF WORSHIP AND HOLY PLACES The holiest place for the Theravada is Bodh Gaya, in central India, which is considered the site of the Buddha's enlightenment. A temple marks the reputed spot of enlightenment and a *bodhi* tree, said to be a descendent of the original tree under which the Buddha sat, is adjacent to the temple. Nearly as important is Sarnath, north of Benares, where the Buddha preached his first sermon. The original deer park where the sermon was given no longer exists, but the site is adorned with statues of figures involved in that first sermon. Near both sites various groups have built monasteries.

Many lay Theravada Buddhists travel to practice at monasteries for full-moon days or more extended periods of time. Stupas, reliquaries of the Buddha, are also holy sites where people often choose to meditate. Although sacred space has been established in other locations worldwide, India contains the holiest sites.

WHAT IS SACRED? Although a lay devotional life exists, most Theravadin Buddhists acknowledge no high gods. They consider heaven realms to be temporary abodes on the path to *nibbana*. They revere enlightened beings. They tend not to celebrate other holy beings, such as *bodhisattwas*, who defer full and final enlightenment to help other beings. Some practice devotion to *devas*, lesser gods in the realms just superior to the human one, who are believed to help moral and generous humans.

Theravadins hold sensate life forms sacred and do not choose to take life. Contemporary Theravadins also tend to be highly environmentally conscious.

HOLIDAYS AND FESTIVALS There is one major feast day for the Theravada. Vesak (Wesak), which honors the Buddha's birth, enlightenment, and death (*parinibbana*), is celebrated on the first full-moon day of May. Uposatha days, whose dates are determined by the phases of the moon, are times throughout the year for extra meditation practice and the taking of vows.

MODE OF DRESS As in most other Buddhist groups, Theravadin monks and nuns wear monastic robes. The color varies from country to country. Most common for monks are russet, saffron, or brown and, for nuns, pink, peach, or gray. Laypeople who bind themselves to the eight-vow system of precepts sometimes wear white and refer to themselves as *anagarika* (homeless). The laity has no common mode of dress, though many wear white on special days, such as full-moon days.

DIETARY PRACTICES Theravadin monastics do not eat until day has broken and commonly refrain from eating solid foods after the noon meal. Monasteries differ on whether they allow caffeine after midday. Laypeople often adopt these practices on full-moon days or on extended meditation retreats. Some Theravadins practice vegetarianism. Rice gruel is sometimes served on special practice days.

RITUALS While some Buddhist traditions have elaborate rituals, others are starker. The Theravadin has the fewest rituals, and meditation remains the chief practice. There are vow ceremonies to become a monk or nun. Often "taking refuge" in the Buddha, the *dhamma*, and the sangha is chanted along with the moral precepts. Buddhist monastics frequently confess their faults. Some monasteries chant a loving-kindness practice in the evening, and some Theravadins practice sharing merit. *Suttas* are sometimes chanted, and occasionally other chants are sung. At Mother Teresa's funeral a Buddhist monk chanted "anicca vata sankara"; this chant proclaims the peace that results from accepting impermanence. Some laypeople meditate, and some practice devotions (*puja*) to the Buddha and heavenly beings. In some cases civic ceremonies are imbued with a Buddhist flavor.

Meditation develops the three meditation steps of the noble Eightfold Path: effort or diligence in practice, concentration or steadiness of mind, and mindful awareness of the ongoing flow of experience. It leads to the wisdom steps of the path of right intention (mostly compassionate care and non-harming) and right wisdom (clearly seeing and understanding reality).

As Theravadins describe the process, seven important qualities of mind develop through meditation practice. In addition to diligence, concentration, and mindfulness, these are raptness or captivated attention, investigation or having insights into reality, calm or stillness or mind, and equanimity or balanced acceptance of all experience. The path develops through alternating periods of ease and difficulty during which the wisdom knowledges unfold. These include understanding body and mind, *kamma* and cause-effect relationships, the characteristics of conditioned reality, right practice, and, ultimately, *nibbana*.

RITES OF PASSAGE Theravadins do not sacralize most life transitions. Taking refuge in the Buddha, *dhamma*, and sangha, by which one becomes a Buddhist, is the major one. Entry into monastic life is also celebrated. Often a dying person is reminded of his or her good deeds, and scripture is read to him or her. Theravadin marriage ceremonies are also available.

MEMBERSHIP Although historically some Theravadins proselytized, contemporary ones usually do not do so actively. Compassion leads them to make teaching available to anyone who is interested enough to inquire. Western groups maintain websites and publish newsletters and schedules of retreats, which are sent to parties that have expressed interest. There has been outreach to some particular groups, such as prison inmates, minority populations, and the gay and lesbian community.

RELIGIOUS TOLERANCE As with many Buddhists, tolerance is probably the cardinal virtue for Theravadins. They do not attempt to impose their beliefs or practices on anyone. Some Theravadins, like some in the Zen community, have entered into dialogue with other monastics—most commonly Christians. Many support the Society for Buddhist-Christian Studies, and Resources for Ecumenical Spirituality offers retreats combining Theravadin and Christian teachings.

SOCIAL JUSTICE Historically the Theravadin tradition has not been a prime mover regarding social justice issues, and some other Buddhist groups have faulted them for this. Many contemporary Theravadins, however, especially in the West, are part of the movement called "engaged Buddhism." They are involved with many social justice issues—most notably, peace issues, environmental concerns, criminal justice issues and prison ministry, and the treatment of minorities. The Buddhist Peace Fellowship has many Theravadin members. In recent times Myanmar and Sri Lanka have seen considerable active work for social justice among Buddhists.

SOCIAL ASPECTS In contrast to some other Buddhist schools, monastic life is the most highly valued Theravadin lifestyle. In Asia monks are almost a caste apart from other men and all women, including nuns. For the laity Theravadin positions are similar to those of all Buddhist groups. Honesty and fidelity are considered extremely important for those engaged in relationships. Parents are to be responsible for their children without forcing their own views upon them, and children are to respect their parents. The Buddha reportedly said that carrying a parent on your back for your entire life would not be adequate repayment for the gift of life.

CONTROVERSIAL ISSUES Although the Theravadin tradition is strongly sexist in Asia, Western Theravadins have achieved relative gender equality. In the West positions of leadership are fairly evenly divided between the genders.

With regard to abortion, debates occur about when a fetus becomes a sensate being, since the taking of sensate life is forbidden. Vegetarianism and the moderate use of alcohol are also debated issues. Beyond the guidelines of non-harming, little is said of personal sexual morality and issues like birth control or sexual orientation. While some monastics frown on homosexuality, some Western Theravadin centers invite those with alternative lifestyles to participate.

CULTURAL IMPACT Traditionally Theravadins have considered investment in artistic production a worldly distraction. Nevertheless, some religious art is associated with the Theravada. It began with the stupas and progressed to the building of other temples and shrines. Early carvings of groups of the laity and monks assembled to hear the Buddha speak did not depict the Buddha. At some uncertain date representations of the Buddha began to appear, and some areas, especially Sri Lanka, boast magnificent stone statues of the Buddha. The Shakyamuni Buddha statue, discussed above in SACRED SYMBOLS, derives from the Theravada, as do some symbolic depictions of the Triple Gem of the Buddha, *dhamma,* and sangha.

Mary Jo Meadow

See Also Vol. I: *Buddhism*

Bibliography

Anuruddha. *A Manual of Abhidhamma: Being Abhidhammattha Sangaha of Bhadanta Anuruddhacariya.* 5th rev. ed. Edited in the original Pali text with English translation and explanatory notes by Narada Maha Thera. Kandy, Sri Lanka: Buddhist Publication Society, 1979.

Bivamsa, U Pandita. *In This Very Life: The Liberation Teachings of the Buddha.* Translated by U. Aggacitta. Boston: Wisdom Publications, 1992.

———. *On the Path to Freedom: A Mind of Wise Discernment and Openness.* Selangor, Malaysia: Buddhist Wisdom Centre, 1995.

Bodhi, Bhikkhu. *The Noble Eightfold Path.* Kandy, Sri Lanka: Buddhist Publication Society, 1984.

Buddhaghosa. *The Path of Purification: Visuddhimagga.* 4th ed. Translated from the Pali by Bhikkhu Nyanamoli. Kandy, Sri Lanka: Buddhist Publication Society, 1979.

Goldstein, Joseph. *The Experience of Insight: A Simple and Direct Guide to Buddhist Meditation.* Boulder, Colo.: Shambhala, 1983.

———. *Insight Meditation: The Practice of Freedom.* Boston and London: Shambhala, 1993.

———. *One Dharma: The Emerging Western Buddhism.* San Francisco: HarperSanFrancisco, 2002.

Inquiring Mind official website. 14 Sept. 2004. http://www.inquiringmind.com.

Insight Meditation Society and the Barre Center for Buddhist Studies official website. 14 Sept. 2004. http://www.dharma.org.

Jayasuriya, W.F. *The Psychology and Philosophy of Buddhism: Being an Introduction to the Abhidhamma.* Colombo, Sri Lanka: Y.M.B.A. Press, 1963.

Nanarama, Sri Matara. *The Seven Stages of Purification and the Insight Knowledges.* Kandy, Sri Lanka: Buddhist Publication Society, 1983.

Narada, Maha Thera. *The Buddha and His Teachings.* 3rd ed. Colombo, Sri Lanka: The Buddhist Missionary Society, 1977.

Nhat Hanh, Thich. *The Miracle of Mindfulness: A Manual on Meditation.* Translated by Mobi Ho. Rev. ed. Boston: Beacon Press, 1987.

Nyanatiloka. *Path To Deliverance.* Kandy: Sri Lanka: Buddhist Publication Society, 1952.

————. *The Word of the Buddha.* Kandy, Sri Lanka: Buddhist Publication Society, 1981.

Piyadassi, Thera. *The Buddha's Ancient Path.* Kandy, Sri Lanka: Buddhist Publication Society, 1979.

Resources for Ecumenical Spirituality official website. 14 Sept. 2004. http://www.laycontemplative.org/res.html.

Sayadaw, Mahasi. *Practical Insight Meditation: Basic and Progressive Stages.* Kandy, Sri Lanka: Buddhist Publication Society, 1971.

————. *Progress of Insight: A Treatise on Buddhist Satipatthana Meditation.* Kandy, Sri Lanka: Buddhist Publication Society, 1985.

Salzberg, Sharon, ed. *Voices of Insight.* Boston: Shambhala, 1999.

Society for Buddhist-Christian Studies official website. 14 Sept. 2004. http://www.cssr.org/soc_scbs.htm.

Tibetan Buddhism

FOUNDED: Seventh–Eighth century
C.E.

**RELIGION AS A PERCENTAGE OF
WORLD POPULATION:** 0.003
percent

OVERVIEW Tibetan Buddhism, which originated during the seventh and eighth centuries in Tibet, has approximately 20 million followers. Founded by the Indian masters Santaraksita and Padmasambhava, it is the major religion in Tibet; Bhutan; Mongolia; regions of China; the Russian republics of Tuva, Buryatia, and Kalmykia; and the Ladakh region of India. It is well represented in Nepal, the Indian states of Himachal Pradesh and Sikkim, India's northeastern border regions, and the Tibetan refugee settlements in northern India. Following the flight of the 14th Dalai Lama and thousands of his followers into exile in 1959, Tibetan Buddhism spread to many Western countries.

Drawing many of its ritual practices from Indian Tantric Buddhism, Tibetan Buddhism stresses that the body, speech, and mind must be engaged in order for the individual to gain enlightenment and that the guidance of the lama, or spiritual teacher, is essential to the individual's mastery of esoteric knowledge. The religion's four major sects are the Nyingma-pa, Sakya-pa, Kagyu-pa, and Geluk-pa.

HISTORY The Tibetan king Songtsen Gampo (617–50) laid the foundation for Tibetan Buddhism by building temples for the Buddhist images brought to Tibet by his Nepalese and Chinese wives and by having a script developed for translating Buddhist texts into Tibetan. Trisong Detsen, who reigned from 754 to 797, invited to Tibet the great Indian Buddhist masters Santaraksita, who promoted the construction of the first Tibetan monastery, and Padmasambhava, a Tantric practitioner whose magical feats and charismatic presence drew many converts to Buddhism. During his reign from 815 to 836 the last Buddhist king, Ralpachen, sponsored the translation of the entire Buddhist canon into Tibetan. In the mid-ninth century the Tibetan kingdom disintegrated and Buddhism in central Tibet declined

A major Buddhist revival in Tibet began in the mid-eleventh century. The arrival of the Indian master Atisa (982–1054) inspired the emergence of a new Tibetan Buddhist sect, the Kadam-pa, whose members vowed strict adherence to an ascetic lifestyle. Atisa's contemporary Marpa (1012–96), a great transmitter of Indian Tantric doctrines who had learned in India how to transfer consciousness into another body or realm, ultimately inspired the development of the Kagyu-pa sect. Konchok Gyalpo (1034–1102) founded a monastery in Sakya in 1073 and established the Sakya-pa order. Those who continued the Tantric householder life introduced by Padmasambhava came to be called Nyingma-pa (followers of the old order).

During the late fourteenth century the reformist scholar Tsongkhapa (1357–1419) and his followers founded the fourth major Tibetan Buddhist sect, the Geluk-pa, which stressed monastic discipline. In the

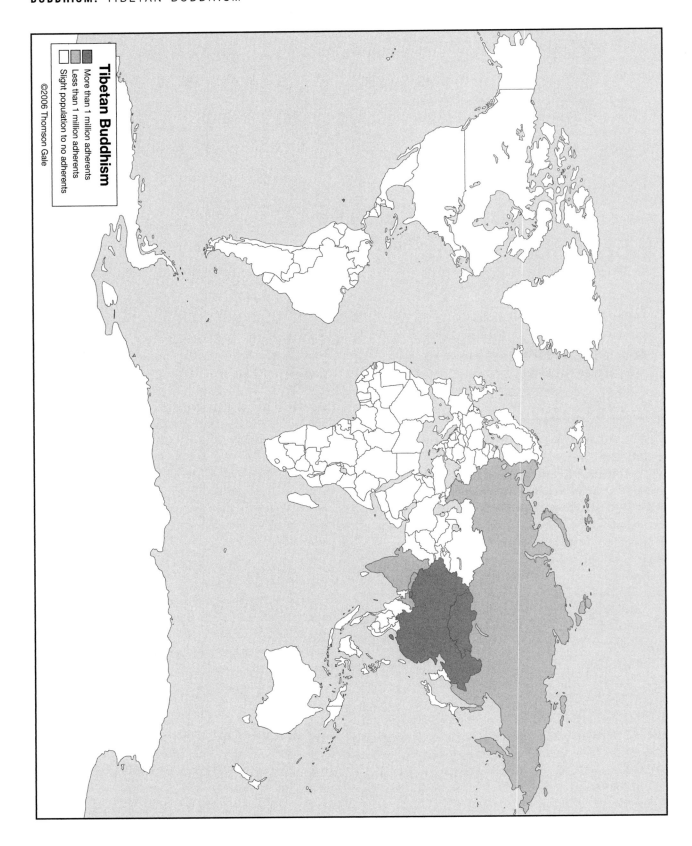

Tibetan Buddhism

More than 1 million adherents
Less than 1 million adherents
Slight population to no adherents

©2006 Thomson Gale

Pilgrims prostrate themselves at a festival at Mount Kailash. Among the most important sacred sites in Tibet is Mount Kailash, which Tibetan Buddhists regard as the center of the world. © DAVID SAMUEL ROBBINS/CORBIS.

sixteenth century the Mongol prince Altan Khan bestowed the title Dalai Lama on Sonam Gyatso, the third reincarnation of one of Tsongkhapa's chief disciples. In 1642 Mongol troops succeeded in establishing the fifth Dalai Lama (1617–82) as the spiritual and temporal leader of Tibet, effectively creating a theocracy dominated by the Geluk-pa sect with the Dalai Lama at its apex. By the mid-nineteenth century the Rimey movement, which adopted a nonsectarian approach to Tibetan Buddhist teachings, emerged in eastern Tibet, revitalizing the Sakya-pa, Nyingma-pa, and Kagyu-pa schools.

In 1950 troops of the People's Republic of China occupied Tibet, and in 1959 the 14th Dalai Lama and 100,000 of his followers fled the war-torn country for refuge in Dharmsala, India. Although the Chinese have substantively repressed Tibetan Buddhism in the Tibet Autonomous Region and the Tibetan areas that have been incorporated into Chinese provinces, numerous monasteries have been rebuilt by Tibetans in exile.

CENTRAL DOCTRINES Unlike other forms of Buddhism, Tibetan Buddhism stresses Tantric practice as a means of attaining enlightenment in the practitioner's current lifetime. Tantric practitioners incorporate rituals, symbols, and visualization techniques in their efforts to control or identify with beings in other realms of existence. Identification with these deities ultimately enables the practitioner to transform his or her consciousness into a higher state of being.

A key factor distinguishing Tibetan Buddhism from other forms of Mahayana Buddhism is the profound importance of the lama in the disciple's spiritual progress. (Because of this, Tibetan Buddhism has often been referred to—erroneously—as Lamaism by Westerners.) The lama selects the disciple's tutelary, or guiding, deity and determines when a disciple is ready for initiation into successively higher levels of secret teachings. The initiate is granted permission to read esoteric texts by the lama, who also provides instruction pertaining to the texts and empowers the meditations associat-

A Tibetan Buddhist lama wears a traditional headdress of yak fur. Hats of different colors and shapes distinguish the four sects of Tibetan Buddhism, as well as the monastic or spiritual rank of the wearer. © GALEN ROWELL/CORBIS.

ed with them. Ideally, the disciple progresses until he or she can merge with the tutelary deity and the lama and thereby attain enlightenment. Spiritually advanced, reincarnated lamas are regarded as bodhisattvas, enlightened beings who have chosen to remain on earth. These lamas, known as *tulku*, embody the authority and power attributed to their previous incarnations and can thus perpetuate the transmission of a particular line of teachings.

MORAL CODE OF CONDUCT Different rules of conduct apply to monks, who must observe the Vinaya code of discipline (attributed to the Buddha), and to Tantrists, who do not generally reside in monasteries and who may drink alcoholic beverages. Although celibacy is expected of all monks, reincarnated lamas of the Nyingma-pa, Sakya-pa, and Kagyu-pa sects are viewed as *nag-pa* (also

sngags pa; a kind of Tantric practitioner) and typically have female consorts or wives. Essential to the Tibetan Buddhist moral code is the practitioner's absolute devotion to his or her lama.

SACRED BOOKS In addition to two great canons translated from Indic languages, the *Kanjur* (consisting of works attributed to the Buddha himself) and the *Tenjur* (a collection of commentaries on the *Kanjur*), Tibetan Buddhism has inspired a vast collection of sacred texts written by scholars from each sect. A number of important texts known as *terma* were believed to have been written and buried by Padmasambhava and later discovered by his disciples.

SACRED SYMBOLS Sacred symbols in Tibetan Buddhism include the *vajra* (Tibetan *dorje;* "thunderbolt"), which represents the union of method and wisdom that constitutes enlightened consciousness; a bell, typically combined with the *vajra* and symbolizing ultimate wisdom; and the mandala, a diagram or three-dimensional rendering of concentric circles that maps a sacred realm.

EARLY AND MODERN LEADERS Throughout the history of Tibetan Buddhism, hierarchs of the various sects have been key political figures. Sakya Pandita (1182–1251) and his nephew Phakpa (1235–80) were granted rulership over central Tibet by, respectively, the Mongol prince Godan and Kublai Khan. The fifth Dalai Lama (1617–82), as the first theocratic ruler, engaged in nation building and instituted the office of the Panchen Lama, the second highest-ranking Geluk-pa hierarch. The 13th Dalai Lama (1875–1933) proclaimed Tibet's independence from China, and the 14th Dalai Lama (born in 1935) received the 1989 Nobel Peace Prize for his nonviolent efforts to free Tibet from Chinese control.

The most prominent modern leaders of Tibetan Buddhism, apart from the 14th Dalai Lama, have included Rangjung Rigpe Dorje (1924–81), the 16th Karma-pa (head of the Karma Kagyu sect), and Ogyen Trinley Dorje (born in 1985), the17th Karma-pa; the Karma Kagyu lamas Tai Situ Rinpoche (born in 1954) and Shamar Rinpoche (born in 1952); the Nyingma-pa lamas Mindroling Trichen (born in 1931), head of the Nyingma-pa sect, and Dudjom Rinpoche (1904–1987); and Sakya Trizin (born in 1945), head of the Sakya-pa sect. Chogyam Trungpa (1939–87), a Karma Kagyu *tulku*, and Geshe Rabten (1920–86), a Geluk-pa

Exorcisms

Tibetan Buddhist rituals are concerned not only with attaining enlightenment but also with potential obstacles to enlightenment. The evil spirits or cosmic entities that cause sickness, death, crop failure, bad fortune, and other troubles can be exorcised using one of four general strategies: *zhi* (appeasement), *gye* (enticement through the false promise of wealth, power, and high status), *wang* (entrapment of the spirit), and *trak* (destruction and transformation of the spirit).

A Tantric exorcist may first try to distract an attacking spirit with an effigy of its victim (*gye* ritual). If this fails, the exorcist may employ a *wang* ritual to trap the spirit in an image of itself. The most wrathful ritual, *trak*, involves annihilating the spirit and sending it on to a better rebirth. Certain Tantric specialists are renowned for their abilities to stop hailstorms or to bring rain through their appeasement or enticement of the entities that control the weather.

monk who attained a *geshe* degree, the Tibetan Buddhist equivalent of a doctor of divinity degree, were important Tibetan Buddhist missionaries.

MAJOR THEOLOGIANS AND AUTHORS A key Nyingma-pa theologian was Longchen Rabjam (1308–63). Jamyang Khentse Wangpo (1820–92), a cofounder of the nonsectarian Rimey movement, exerted a major influence on such modern theologians as Dilgo Khyentse Rinpoche (1910–91), and Dudjom Rinpoche (1904–87). Prominent contributors to the other sects include Sakya Pandita (1182–1251) of the Sakya-pa; Gampopa (1079–1153) and Milarepa (1040–1123) of the Kagyu-pa; and Tsongkhapa and the 14th Dalai Lama of the Geluk-pa.

ORGANIZATIONAL STRUCTURE Tibetan Buddhist monasteries are headed by a *khenpo* (abbot). Monks assume a variety of official roles within the monastery. Large Geluk-pa monasteries may be divided into two branches and subdivided into houses that represent the regional affiliations of their respective members. Each house has a guardian deity. Monasteries are typically associated with at least one reincarnated lama, who has his own *labrang* (personal estate) and attendants.

HOUSES OF WORSHIP AND HOLY PLACES Tibetan Buddhist temples consist of a central hall containing a statue of the Buddha and an altar. The entrance itself is topped by renderings of the dharma wheel and two deer. Temples may have a second floor and smaller chapels dedicated to specific deities flanking the main hall. Among the most important sacred sites in Tibet are Lhamo Lhatso, a lake whose waters are believed to reveal prophetic visions; Mount Kailash, which is regarded as the center of the world; Lake Manasarovar, where the Buddha's mother is believed to have bathed; the Potala palace of the Dalai Lama in Lhasa; and the Jokhang, a temple near the Potala that houses the most sacred Buddha statue in Tibet.

WHAT IS SACRED? Consecrated statues, masks, and paintings of the Buddha and Buddhist deities; consecrated amulets; Buddhist texts; relics of spiritual masters; food offerings that have been ritually blessed; prayer flags; stupas; and reincarnated lamas are considered sacred by Tibetan Buddhists.

HOLIDAYS AND FESTIVALS Monlam Chenmo, the annual great prayer ceremony, commencing on the fourth day of the New Year and lasting 20 days, commemorates the Buddha's expounding of the dharma at Sravasti. Two days prior to the New Year, the Tse Gutor, a monastic dance exorcising the accumulated evil of the past year, is performed. Drugpa Tsechu, which celebrates the birthday of Padmasambhava, features a series of monastic dances. Dzamling Chisang is an incense offering that marks Padmasambhava's transformation of Tibet's local deities into protectors of Buddhism. Lhabap Duchen is the anniversary of the Buddha's descent from the Tushita heaven, which is devoid of suffering.

MODE OF DRESS A monk's basic dress consists of a red wrapped skirt with a yellow or red sleeveless shirt and a red shawl. Nuns may wear similar attire or a sleeveless red *chupa*, a long wrapped dress, over a yellow shirt. Tantric masters of the Nyingma-pa and Kagyu-pa sects wear off-white raw silk shawls with pink to red stripes over a red *chupa* and secure their long hair in topknots. Hats of different colors and shapes distinguish the four sects as well as the monastic or spiritual rank of the wearer.

DIETARY PRACTICES Most Tibetan Buddhists eat meat, but many avoid fish. Ritual foods include *dre-see,* a dish made from rice, brown sugar, raisins, and a root called *droma,* and dough cakes made from barley flour, butter, and brown sugar. Besides its ritual uses, butter may adorn gifts of black tea and is dabbed on the rims of cups or glasses containing beverages served during New Year festivities.

RITUALS Tibetan Buddhism has a rich variety of rituals. The most widely practiced include prostration, which expresses one's desire to take refuge in the Buddha, dharma, and *sangha* (monastic order); the turning of prayer wheels; and the recitation of mantras. Pilgrims may journey to holy places by prostrating themselves repeatedly over distances of hundreds of miles. Prayer wheels, which range in size from those that can be held in the hand to huge mounted cylinders inscribed with the mantra *om mani padme hum,* are rotated clockwise to generate merit. Tibetan Buddhists attempt to gain the blessings of certain deities by raising prayer flags and burning juniper branches. Prayer flags are made from cloths in the five elemental colors of white, red, yellow, blue, and green and are stamped with woodblocks carved with mantras and auspicious animal images.

Many rituals entail constructing an altar and making offerings to the deities. These offerings include dough cakes, which are intended to serve as temporary abodes for the deities. At the completion of a ritual consecrated food offerings are distributed to all in attendance. Tantric practice requires the officiating lama to merge with a deity during the ritual.

RITES OF PASSAGE Following the death of a *tulku* a variety of divinatory techniques are employed to identify the child who is his—or (rarely) her—reincarnation. The child officially so recognized then undergoes an enthronement ceremony, during which offerings are made to persuade him not to leave this life.

Corpses may be conveyed to a funeral ground, where they are ritually dismembered and offered to vultures in a process known as sky burial, though Tibetan Buddhists commonly cremate their dead. Lamas are either cremated or, in exceptional cases, mummified. The soul, or, more precisely, consciousness, is believed to undertake a 49-day journey through an intermediary state known as *bardo* before it is reborn. Monks read the *Bardo Thosgrol,* the Tibetan book of the dead, every seven days for seven weeks to guide the consciousness to an auspicious rebirth.

MEMBERSHIP The success of Tibetan Buddhist missionaries in converting Mongol princes in the thirteenth century had a major impact on Tibet's political history as well as on the propagation of Tibetan Buddhism in Siberia and parts of China. Today Tibetan Buddhist dharma centers may be found in many Western countries, and many have their own Internet sites.

RELIGIOUS TOLERANCE Tibetan Buddhism embraces tolerance of other religions. There have been occasions in Tibet's history, however, when political rivals who supported different Tibetan Buddhist sects encouraged sectarian intolerance. In the early twentieth century several Geluk-pa lamas, against the wishes of the 13th Dalai Lama, forcibly converted some followers of other sects to the Geluk-pa order.

SOCIAL JUSTICE Tibetan Buddhist monks and nuns have engaged in numerous peaceful demonstrations in Tibet, India, and Western countries advocating freedom for Tibet. Several monks and nuns who were imprisoned and tortured by the Chinese were finally released to the West following international diplomatic efforts, and they have become prominent campaigners for human rights. Among these are the monk Palden Gyatso (born in 1931), who was imprisoned in Tibet from 1959 to 1992, and the nun Pasang Lhamo, imprisoned from 1994 to 1999. The 14th Dalai Lama, in addition to his endeavors to negotiate Tibet's future with China, has also participated in world conferences to preserve the environment.

SOCIAL ASPECTS In Tibetan Buddhism weddings are not perceived as religious rituals, although monks may be invited to read prayers to bless a marriage. Tibetan Buddhist parents petition a lama to name a new child since they believe that the lama can identify the most auspicious name for the child. It is customary for families with several sons to send one to a monastery.

CONTROVERSIAL ISSUES Despite the important roles played by women in the development of Tibetan Buddhism, nuns generally have had less access than monks to higher religious education, and they have not enjoyed equal status with monks. Birth control is acceptable to Tibetan Buddhists, but abortion and euthanasia are, according to the 14th Dalai Lama, permissible only in exceptional cases. In contravention of their vows many Tibetan monks took up arms against the Chinese in the

1950s in response to attacks on Tibetan monasteries and to safeguard the escape of the Dalai Lama from Tibet.

CULTURAL IMPACT Tibetan Buddhism is expressed and represented through a rich variety of performing and material art forms. Tibetan operas (Ache Lhamo) recount Jataka stories, tales about the Buddha's previous lives, through glottal-stop vocalizing, dancing, and clowning to the accompaniment of a drum and cymbals. Monastic dances (*cham*) portray various Buddhist deities. Tibetan Buddhist material art includes statues of the Buddha, Buddhist deities, and lamas; scroll paintings (*tangkas*); butter sculptures; masks; and mandalas made of colored grains of sand.

Marcia Calkowski

See Also Vol. 1: *Buddhism*

Bibliography

Powers, John. *Introduction to Tibetan Buddhism.* Ithaca, N.Y.: Snow Lion Publications, 1995.

Samuel, Geoffrey. *Civilized Shamans: Buddhism in Tibetan Societies.* Washington, D.C.: Smithsonian Institution Press, 1993.

Snellgrove, David. *Indo-Tibetan Buddhism: Indian Buddhists and Their Tibetan Successors.* 2 vols. Boston: Shambhala, 1987.

Snellgrove, David, and Hugh Richardson. *A Cultural History of Tibet.* New York: F.A. Praeger, 1968.

Stein, R.A. *Tibetan Civilization.* Translated by J.E. Stapleton Driver. Stanford, Calif.: Stanford University Press, 1972.

Thurman, Robert A.F. *Essential Tibetan Buddhism.* Edison, N.J.: Castle Books, 1997.

Tucci, Giuseppe. *The Religions of Tibet.* Translated by Geoffrey Samuel. Berkeley and Los Angeles: University of California Press, 1980.

Christianity

FOUNDED: First century c.e.

RELIGION AS A PERCENTAGE OF WORLD POPULATION: 34 percent

OVERVIEW Christianity is the religion of those who believe in Jesus Christ as Lord and Savior and follow the way of life inaugurated by him. More than other major religions, Christianity centers on a person. Muslims do not claim the sort of relationship to Muhammad that Christians claim with Jesus, and the same holds true for Judaism, Confucianism, Taoism, and most forms of Buddhism with regard to their respective founders. The New Testament refers to the community of believers as "the body of Christ," which signifies an intimate bond between Jesus and the church.

Christianity inherited from its parent religion, Judaism, a monotheistic belief that there is only one true God, who is personal, the creator of all things, all-powerful, holy, loving, forgiving, and yet opposed to sin and evil. Christian monotheism, however, is fundamentally shaped by belief in Jesus. Christianity can be understood as a doctrine concerning Jesus, an experience of communion with Jesus, an ethic taught by Jesus, a community in relationship to Jesus, and a social institution emerging from the life and ministry of Jesus. Alongside the stress on Jesus is an experience of life in the Holy Spirit. From the earliest period Christians have worshiped God as Father, Son, and Spirit, and the doctrine of the Trinity encapsulates a distinctively Christian conception of God.

Christianity exists in a great variety of forms, and different Christian groups highlight different aspects. Roman Catholic, Eastern Orthodox, and Protestant Christians all stress in varying fashion the need for correct doctrine, while mystics, saints, Pietists, evangelicals, and Pentecostals speak in divergent ways of an immediate experience of God. Other Christians underscore the ethical imperatives of the faith, and still others are primarily concerned with the life of the community, its institutional forms, traditions, and self-government. Because of its 2,000-year history and global extension, Christianity has become astonishingly complex, and a predominant characteristic throughout history, especially evident today, is its cultural diversity.

During the 1900s, the two world wars in Europe, the spread of communism, and the growth of secularism in Europe brought an effective end to the perceived link between Christianity and Western culture. Following World War II, there has been an astonishing expansion of Christianity in Africa, Asia, and Latin America. China, with only a million Christians in 1949, today has somewhere between 50 and 100 million Christians, and about 10,000 new converts every day. In Africa during the 1900s, the Christian population mushroomed from 9 to 335 million Christians. In Latin America, Pentecostalism has overtaken Roman Catholicism as the dominant faith in many regions. During the last decade, millions of Dalits in India (formerly known as "untouchables") have converted to Christianity. While the churches of Europe are losing members, and those of North America are statistically stagnant, the situation in the developing world is different. The intense prayer, evangelistic fervor, and openness to the miraculous that

CROSS. One of the most widely known symbols of the Christian faith is the cross. It is a figure formed by two intersecting lines. In this version (the Latin, or Roman Catholic cross) the vertical line is longer than the horizontal line. For some it symbolizes Christ's death on the cross for the sins of humans and also the life of self-denial to which he calls his followers. It also represents Christ's victory over death and sin. (THOMSON GALE)

characterize the Pentecostal movement—now numbering 524 million adherents—could set the future direction for world Christianity. Today Korean, Brazilian, and Chinese missionaries are being sent out to evangelize Muslims, and some are going as missionaries to secular Europeans, a trend that Philip Jenkins has dubbed "the empire strikes back."

HISTORY Christianity arose out of a close and yet conflicted relationship with Judaism. In about 30 C.E. Roman authorities in Palestine, with the cooperation of Jewish leaders, executed Jesus on a charge of treason. Soon after, followers of Jesus reported having seen him alive. The earliest Christians had a deep sense of Jesus' living presence among them; a confidence that he was "Lord," in the sense of having triumphed over sin and death; and an expectation that he would soon return to reign on earth. They believed that Jesus was the Messiah, the "anointed one" sent to save Israel, and they found prophecies in the Hebrew Bible, renamed the Old Testament, pointing to Jesus.

Initially all of the central leaders of the Christian community, and probably the overriding number of followers as well, were Jews. Most regarded Christianity as a sect within Judaism rather than a separate religion.

The New Testament highlights the leadership role of Simon, called Peter (the Rock) by Jesus, who seems to have been the acknowledged head of the original 12 apostles. James, called the "brother" of Jesus, guided the earliest Christian community in Jerusalem and adhered to Jewish traditions while maintaining faith in Jesus as the Messiah. Saul of Tarsus, renamed Paul, followed a different path, and he was so influential that some historians regard him as a second founder. Paul received an excellent Greek education as well as training in Jewish law, which, together with his burning sense of mission, made him a bridge between the Jewish and Gentile worlds. Paul claimed to have had a vision of the resurrected Jesus while he was engaged in persecuting Christians. In time Paul became known as the "apostle to the Gentiles," and he undertook a monumental effort to establish new congregations of believers throughout the eastern part of the Mediterranean.

Paul's general method was to go "to the Jew first, and also to the Greek [Gentile]" (Romans 1:16). Jews were scattered throughout the Roman Empire, and Paul went from synagogue to synagogue to preach about Jesus, causing consternation wherever he appeared. Paul was controversial not only because he proclaimed that Jesus was Savior but also because he taught that Gentiles could be saved without first becoming Jews. The New Testament shows that at first Paul's opinion was not shared by most fellow Jews who believed in Jesus. The early church's decision to admit Gentiles into the community without first making them Jews (Acts 15) set the future direction for Christianity as a multicultural, multiethnic, and multilinguistic religion. If Paul's position had not won out, Christianity might have kept its Hebrew and Jewish character.

In the first centuries of its existence, Christianity was a despised movement. Not only Jewish leaders but also Roman emperors and governors opposed it. When the emperor Nero wanted to blame someone for a fire in Rome in 64, he unjustly charged the Christians. Soon Christians were exposed to wild beasts in the Roman arenas, a punishment normally reserved for heinous criminals. Many of the earliest Christians were slaves, a status that did not win them favor with authorities. Christians were accused of immorality and cannibalism, the latter probably explained by the reference to the bread and wine of the Lord's Supper as "the body and blood of Christ." Moreover, Christians seemed to be political subversives when they confessed that "Jesus is

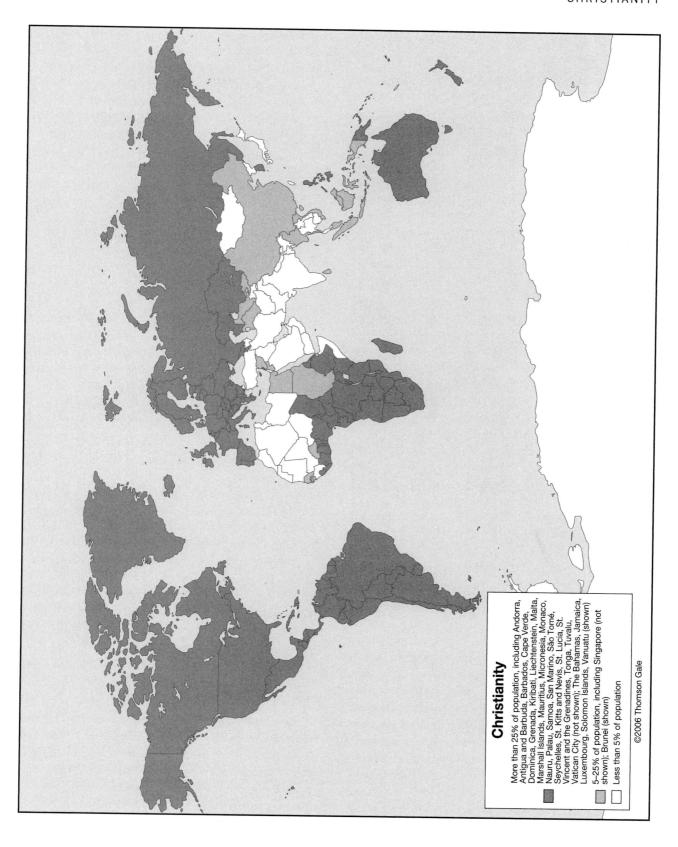

Christianity

More than 25% of population, including Andorra, Antigua and Barbuda, Barbados, Cape Verde, Dominica, Grenada, Kiribati, Liechtenstein, Malta, Marshall Islands, Mauritius, Micronesia, Monaco, Nauru, Palau, Samoa, San Marino, São Tomé, Seychelles, St. Kitts and Nevis, St. Lucia, St. Vincent and the Grenadines, Tonga, Tuvalu, Vatican City (not shown); The Bahamas, Jamaica, Luxembourg, Solomon Islands, Vanuatu (shown)

5–25% of population, including Singapore (not shown); Brunei (shown)

Less than 5% of population

©2006 Thomson Gale

A young Sudanese boy wears a picture of Jesus Christ around his neck during a Christian religious service. More than any other major religion, Christianity centers on a single person: Jesus Christ. © ADRIAN ARBIB/CORBIS.

Lord" and refused to acknowledge the divinity of the Roman rulers.

Despite persecution, the Christian movement spread. Congregations of believers, meeting in private homes, gathered for services that included the reading of scripture, a sermon, a prayer of thanksgiving, and a shared meal, with bread and wine representing the body and blood of Jesus (the Eucharist). A bishop carried responsibility for all congregations in a region. Those who departed from the essential beliefs and moral standards of the Christian communities were known as "heretics," with their members, pastors, and bishops not recognized by the majority of Christians, known as "Catholics." Controversial issues were debated and decided at local councils of bishops, while the first truly universal, or "ecumenical," council occurred in 325.

The foundations of the medieval church were laid by the Roman emperor Constantine (reigned 307–37), who first made the Christian faith legal and then made it his own. In 392 Christianity became the official religion of the empire. The Roman Empire took the church under its protection, and the church in turn provided spiritual sanction and support for the rule of the Roman Caesars (as the emperors following Augustus Caesar were called). While some have seen the empire's endorsement of the church as an immense blessing, others regard it as the cause of spiritual decline, the clergy's domination over laypeople, and forcible means for propagating the faith. Nonetheless, when the emperor Constantine converted to the Christian faith, it was the beginning of an effort to create a Christian civilization that blended together the best of pagan Rome with the church's traditions. In *City of God,* Augustine (354–430) distinguished between a "city of man," based on material desires and needs, and a "city of God," oriented toward eternal life. The book laid the foundation for the medieval idea of the church and state as two realms that are distinct and yet work in harmony.

During the Middle Ages the ideal of the Christian empire took two distinct forms: one in the eastern, Greek-speaking portion of the Mediterranean and the other in the western, Latin-speaking region. In 330 Constantine established a new capital in the city of Constantinople. Until its conquest by the Muslim Turks in 1453, Constantinople was the political and religious focus of the Eastern Christian, or Byzantine, civilization. Constantine and his successors saw themselves as the heirs of the pagan Caesars and yet also as spiritual leaders who had the right to involve themselves in the affairs of the church. While the Eastern emperors were not exactly popes, they had a degree of authority in the church that was unparalleled in the West. After the Islamic conquest of Constantinople (renamed Istanbul), the Russian rulers, or tsars, viewed themselves as the legitimate successors of the Byzantine rulers and helped to shape the Russian Orthodox Church.

Along with its differing conception of the Christian empire, Eastern Orthodoxy stressed the mystical or contemplative dimensions of the faith. The ideal life was given to *theoria,* or unceasing meditation on God, and was exemplified by holy men and women who went to the desert to purify themselves of worldly desires. Images of Christ, Mary, and the saints, known as icons, came to play a central role in devotional life. Orthodoxy held firmly to the decisions of the early Christian councils that convened in the empire's eastern portion and was generally reluctant to add to or modify what had been decided. Indeed, Orthodoxy is known for its relative constancy during the past 1,500 years. Some Eastern Christians—including the Coptic Church in Egypt; the Nestorians, or Assyrians, in Iraq; and other "separated" groups—are not a part of Orthodoxy. Though they differ on certain doctrinal points, their practice of the Christian life has more in common with Orthodoxy than with the Latin West.

Orthodoxy resisted the claim that the bishop of Rome, or pope, was leader over the whole of Christianity and held instead that decisions should be made by a consensus of bishops. In the first three centuries, three important centers of Christianity, known as "apostolic sees," emerged: Alexandria, in Egypt; Antioch, in Syria; and Rome. Constantinople and Jerusalem were later added, and some spoke of a "pentarchy" of five leading cities in the Christian world. Yet Rome followed an increasingly independent course. When Pope Leo III crowned Charlemagne as emperor in Rome in 800, an emperor already reigned in Constantinople, and the stage was set for estrangement between Eastern and Western Christians. After a period of theological debate, the pope in 1054 issued a writ of excommunication declaring all Orthodox believers to be separated from the one true and catholic faith. Orthodoxy responded with its own excommunication against the Roman church. (The mutual excommunications were abolished only in 1965.) For Orthodox Christians the most appalling act by the Latin Christians occurred in 1204, when the armies of the Crusaders, at war with the Muslims, sacked and looted the Christian city of Constantinople.

In the Western, Latin-speaking empire, it was not the Christian emperor but rather the Roman bishop, or pope, who set the tone for the historical development of Christianity. Within a century after Constantine, the bishops of Rome referred to themselves as the *pontifex maximus* (supreme pontiff), a title that had belonged to the pagan Caesars. Because of the relative weakness of political authority in the Western empire, the popes could not avoid playing a political role. When Huns and Vandals threatened Italy in 452 and 455, for example, it was Pope Leo I who represented the city of Rome in negotiations. Rome's prestige also grew from its association with the apostles Peter and Paul, who were both said to have died there.

A fresco by Fra Angelico depicts the nativity of Christ. In the early fourth century, Roman Christians began celebrating Jesus' birth on December 25. © MASSIMO LISTRI/CORBIS.

As early as the second century, some Christian writers suggested that Rome might serve as a kind of supreme court for church disputes. There gradually emerged the idea of "Petrine primacy," asserting that Peter and his successors in Rome, the popes, had authority over the whole of the church. In 1302 Pope Boniface VIII issued the statement *Unam Sanctam* ("One Holy"), declaring that it was necessary for salvation to submit to the pope. The process of defining the authority of the popes did not reach its culmination until 1870, however, when Pope Pius IX led the First Vatican Council, though with dissent among bishops, to state that the pope possesses infallibility when he makes an official declaration (ex cathedra) concerning the Catholic faith. The claims of Petrine primacy in the early church and of papal authority in the medieval and modern periods have played a role in the estrangement between Orthodoxy and Roman Catholicism, and they were decisive in the emergence of the Protestant Reformation during the 1500s. Certain Eastern churches known as Eastern Rite (also called Eastern Catholic or Uniate) recognized the primacy of Rome and yet retained their non-Latin liturgies. These include the Mar-

Legionnaires of Brigade King Alfonso XIII carry the Christ of Buena Muerta (Good Dead) statue during a Holy Week procession in Malaga, Spain. In the Christian tradition, the period from Palm Sunday through Easter Sunday is known as Holy Week. © REUTERS NEWMEDIA INC./CORBIS.

onites of Lebanon and the Eastern Rite Catholics of Ukraine.

During the medieval period Christianity grew and flourished through the efforts of monks, nuns, and members of newly established religious orders. The original Christian monks, led by Anthony (251–356), went into the Egyptian desert to pray and lead simple and largely solitary lives. The colder climate of Europe forced monks there to erect buildings and engage in farming and craftwork to support themselves. In European monasticism, led by Benedict (c. 480–c. 545), male monks and female nuns served the needs of the communities around them. In their work of copying manuscripts, monks preserved both pagan and Christian traditions and so insured that civilization would continue through the Dark Ages of the 800s and 900s. Patrick (c. 390–c. 460), a missionary from Britain to Ireland, was influential in the westward spread of Christianity.

Nestorian Christians sent missionaries into Persia, India, and western China during the sixth and seventh centuries. The Chinese churches lasted for about two centuries, while the Nestorian churches of India have continued to the present time. In Europe missionary monks took the Christian gospel into new regions. Boniface (680–754) preached in Germany, Cyril and Methodius (mid-800s) went from Constantinople to the Slavs of eastern Europe, and Bede (c. 673–735) laid the

foundation for scholarship in England. In the 800s Bulgarian leaders considered affiliation with Rome but were repelled by the insistence on papal authority, priestly celibacy, and Latin in worship, and Bulgaria thus turned toward Constantinople. Russian Orthodoxy, which began with the baptism of Prince Vladimir in 988, flourished in the region of Kiev until the invasion of the Mongols in 1240. It was almost three centuries before Russian Christians fully regained their political and religious independence and Moscow displaced Kiev as the Russian religious and cultural capital.

Many reformers of the Middle Ages, who called the church back to its ancient faith and fervor, arose from the ranks of the monks. They included Bernard of Clairvaux (1090–1153) and Francis of Assisi (1181/2–1226). The greatest of the medieval theologians were all associated with monastic or religious orders. Anselm of Canterbury (1033–1109) was head of a Benedictine community, Thomas Aquinas (1225–74) was a Dominican, and both Bonaventure (1217–74) and Duns Scotus (1266–1308) were Franciscans. Beginning in the eleventh and twelfth centuries, universities were founded throughout Europe as centers for training in theology, medicine, law, and the liberal arts. In its Scholastic form theology played a unifying role as the "the queen of the sciences." Though women's roles were limited, the church's literature was enriched by the writings of great women mystics, including Hildegard of Bingen (1098–1179) and Julian of Norwich (mid-1300s–early 1400s).

With Martin Luther (1483–1546) and Protestantism, the call for reform turned against monasticism and the papacy, even though Luther himself had been a monk. Prior to Luther, both John Wycliffe (c. 1330–84) in England and Jan Hus (1372/3–1415) in Bohemia had questioned the pope's supreme authority, criticized the church for its wealth, and cast doubt on the doctrine of transubstantiation (that the bread and the wine of the Lord's Supper literally become the body and blood of Jesus). Yet in Luther's time these criticisms fell on fertile ground, and the invention of the printing press in the mid-1400s allowed Luther to reach a larger reading public than would otherwise have been possible. Beginning with a dispute in 1517 over the sale of indulgences (written statements from the church declaring that "temporal penalties" for sin were removed), the controversy surrounding Luther came to focus on the issue of authority. The question was whether the word of the pope or the word of God contained in the Bible was final. Luther's opponents asserted that the popes were the authorized interpreters of the Bible, while Luther asserted that he could not accept anything that seemed to contradict the Bible. Within the next generation Luther and his followers rejected the supreme authority of the pope, belief in purgatory, mandatory celibacy for priests, and prayer to Mary and the saints, and they asserted that salvation occurs purely through God's grace, not human merit.

While Protestants agreed in rejecting the leadership of the popes, they differed over how much of Roman Catholicism to retain. Luther wanted to preserve much of Catholic tradition. He held to the written prayers, or liturgy, of the church (with a few changes), the baptism of infants, the real presence of Jesus in the bread and wine of the Eucharist (Communion, or Lord's Supper), and the government of the church by bishops. The most radical of the new Protestants rejected all of these. The Anabaptists, so termed because of their practice of re-baptizing as adults those who had been baptized as infants, were opposed by Luther and suffered persecution from Catholics and Protestants alike. In Zurich, during the 1520s, some were drowned to death in a cruel parody of their practice of baptism by immersion. The Anabaptists, or Radical Reformers, wanted to return to the days before Constantine, when there was no state-supported church and when Christians gathered in private homes to listen to the Bible read aloud and to break bread together. They wanted a "voluntary church," in which standards of membership would be high, with those who did not follow the Bible excluded. Although certain small groups of Radical Reformers used force against their opponents, many were pacifists. They were ready to die rather than take up arms against their persecutors. The Radical Reformers were early advocates for the separation of church and state.

The Protestant leader John Calvin (1509–64) was more radical than Luther but more traditional than the Anabaptists. Like the Anabaptists, Calvin held that the church must maintain high standards and exclude those who fell short. Unlike the Anabaptists, however, Calvin believed that the state had a role to play in promoting religion, and Geneva became his laboratory for creating an ideal Christian society. Protestant leaders went to Geneva from England and Scotland, carried Calvin's ideas back to their homelands in the mid-1500s, and, because of their desire to purify the Church of England from its Roman Catholic elements, became known as "Puritans." English Puritans were the earliest European settlers in New England, beginning with the landing of the *Mayflower* at Plymouth Rock in 1620. The Massachusetts Bay Colony, along with Geneva, became one of two major attempts to create a model society according to Calvin's principles.

Calvin held that the leaders of the New Testament churches were roughly on a par with one another, and thus he opposed the idea of a church hierarchy. Consequently, Calvinists played a role in the rise of modern political democracy. By 1700 Calvinism had taken root in Switzerland, France, the Netherlands, South Africa, Scotland, England, and colonial North America. Lutheranism became dominant in Germany and in the Scandinavian countries of Denmark, Norway, Sweden, and Finland. Southern Europe—France, Italy, Spain, and Portugal—remained largely Roman Catholic.

The overall situation in the English Reformation was more complex than in any other European nation. In 1534 King Henry VIII declared the Church of England separate from the pope and made himself the titular head of a new "Anglican" Church. Until 1688, when it was established that the monarch must be Protestant, there remained a distinct possibility that the Church of England might return to the Roman fold. Perhaps for this reason, the Anglican Church embraced a larger spectrum of theological viewpoints than did the churches on the continent of Europe. Though all Anglicans used the same prayer book in Sunday worship, some continued to hold to Catholic opinions, while others were moderately Protestant, and still others had Puritan sympathies. Some have called Anglicanism a "middle way" between Roman Catholicism and Protestantism.

The Roman Catholic Church was not passive in the face of the Protestant challenge. The Council of Trent (1545–63) set the basic direction for the church until the Second Vatican Council in the 1960s. It defined Catholic doctrine in opposition to Protestantism, unified the approach to worship and practice, and concentrated authority in the papacy and the Curia (Vatican bureaucracy). Following the Council of Trent, the Catholic Church made up for what it had lost in Europe through a major expansion into Latin America. The church expanded there through the efforts of priests, often members of such religious orders as the Jesuits, Dominicans, and Franciscans. Although voices of protest—including that of Bartolomé de la Casas (1514–c. 1566)—arose against the mistreatment of the indigenous, or Indian, peoples, the general attitude of colonists and missionaries was paternalistic if not exploitative. The colonist's *encomienda* system and the Jesuit's reductions (settlements) tied the Indians to the land and made them like indentured servants. For much of Latin America the process of Christianization proceeded slowly. Because of the paucity of priests and the lack of adequate instruction in the faith, many were baptized without much understanding of the Catholic religion. The blending of Catholicism with indigenous traditions (syncretism) is obvious in Brazilian Umbanda and Haitian voodoo.

Scholastic theology experienced a golden age during this time. Both Catholics and Protestants produced massive volumes of Latin prose. It was an era of great saints, such as Ignatius Loyola (1491–1556), founder in 1540 of the Society of Jesus, or Jesuits; Teresa of Avila (1515–82); John of the Cross (1542–91); Blaise Pascal (1623–62); and Philipp Jakob Spener (1635–1705), each of whom called Christians to spiritual renewal. Yet the century from 1550 to 1650 was also characterized by immense conflict throughout Europe along the fracture lines between Catholics and Protestants. A third of the population of Germany perished during the Thirty Year's War (1618–48). The seeds of the Enlightenment were sown during the 1600s, when theological disputes seemed to be at the root of violence and hatred. People of goodwill sought social harmony, not in a vision of Christian empire but in universal principles of human rationality.

The philosopher Immanuel Kant (1724–1804) defined the Enlightenment as "man's release from his self-incurred tutelage" and urged his readers to "have courage to use your own reason." The appeal to individual reason was a challenge to Catholics and Protestants alike, since it equally called into question the authority of church traditions and the text of the Bible. Since the eighteenth century the church's intellectual leaders have grappled with the ideas of the Enlightenment and modernist thought, though in varying ways. Among Roman Catholics the "modernist crisis" came at the beginning of the twentieth century, when Pope Pius X, in his encyclical *Pascendi Dominici Gregis* (1907; "Feeding the Lord's Flock"), attacked what he saw as an emerging rationalistic assault upon Christianity. Although the anti-modernist movement supported by the church suppressed some dubious tendencies in the academy, for a time it probably also stifled legitimate theological inquiry. Protestants were more directly affected by Enlightenment ideas at an earlier stage. Friedrich Schleiermacher (1768–1834) sought a middle way between traditional Christian faith and the Enlightenment's "cultured despisers of religion." Protestant thinkers have been concerned with establishing the "reasonableness" of Christianity. Karl Barth (1886–1968), the twentieth century's most influential Protestant theologian, rejected Schleiermacher's mediating style and insisted that Protestant theology needed to become again a "theology of the Word of God."

The Enlightenment had political as well as intellectual repercussions. In Roman Catholic countries it led to calls for the secularization of the governmental and educational systems. In the Catholic nations of southern Europe—Spain, Portugal, France, and Italy—and in Latin America, secular forms of government gradually took hold in the 1800s and 1900s, while Catholic leaders resisted these changes and favored a state-authorized and state-subsidized church. Although some national constitutions in Latin America specify that Catholicism is the official religion, freedom of religion is now widely accepted, and state support for the Catholic Church has diminished. European countries with state-supported Protestantism—for example, England, Germany, The Netherlands, and Scandinavian nations—have moved in the same general direction.

While academic theologians debated the merits of Enlightenment ideas, popular Christianity from 1700 to 2000 experienced growth and resurgence on many levels. Beginning with the spiritual revivals in English-speaking Protestantism during the mid-1700s, the evangelical movement brought the church a new vitality and sense of mission. Evangelicals stressed the need for individual conversion, a personal relationship with God, Bible reading, evangelistic activity, and social reform. The world missionary movement among Protestants in the 1800s and early 1900s emerged from the evangelical awakening, whose leaders included the Anglican preacher George Whitefield (1714–70), the Congregationalist theologian Jonathan Edwards (1703–58), and the founder of Methodism, John Wesley (1703–88). During the 1800s evangelicals were leaders in the campaign against African slavery, in the reform of labor laws, and in the temperance movement. Though evangelicalism originated in England and North America, it has spread throughout the world and is strong today in South Korea, in China and the Chinese diaspora, and in parts of Africa and Latin America.

In the Orthodox world regions originally under the jurisdiction of the patriarch, or bishop, of Constantinople broke away to become autocephalous (self-governing) national churches. Moscow became an independent patriarchate in 1589. In 1833 the patriarch of Constantinople acknowledged the independence of the Greek Orthodox Church, followed by churches in Bulgaria (1870), Serbia (1879), and Romania (1885). Peter the Great removed the patriarch as head of the Russian Church in 1721 and established the Holy Synod, which included laypersons. This situation, an anomaly in Orthodoxy, remained until the Revolution of 1917, when the Moscow Patriarchate was reestablished. During the twentieth century Communist governments in the Soviet Union and eastern Europe persecuted Orthodox churches, and the documented cases of martyrdom run into the tens of millions. Because of opposition from Islam and Communism, Orthodoxy has a historical experience of persecution and martyrdom that sets it apart from the churches of western Europe and North America. Yet Orthodoxy has experienced a resurgence in its historic heartland during the post-Communist generation.

Roman Catholicism entered a time of trials during and following the French Revolution, when revolutionary leaders called for the overthrow of the church in France and throughout Europe. The suppression of the Jesuits in 1773—reinstated in 1814—for a time removed one of the most important religious orders in the church. The papacy began to recover strength as the nineteenth century progressed, however, and Pope Pius IX symbolized the church's new confidence when he declared Mary's Immaculate Conception in 1854 and the doctrine of papal infallibility in 1870. Yet the *Syllabus of Errors* (1864), which condemned freedom of religion, freedom of speech, and the separation of church and state, proved irksome to Catholics living under governments where these principles were established. Pope Leo XIII's *Rerum Novarum* (1891; "Of New Things") called for the church to become engaged in promoting justice for workers and a decent standard of living for all. The emphasis on social justice has been a feature of Catholic philosophy ever since, and it emerged in a challenging way during the second conference of Latin-American bishops, held in Medellín, Colombia, in 1968, and in the "liberation theology" of Gustavo Gutiérrez (born in 1928) and others.

The twentieth century brought massive changes in world Christianity. In 1900 nearly 80 percent of all Christians were white, and the demographic center of Christianity lay in Europe and North America. By 2000 only 45 percent of the world's Christians were white,

and the most dynamic and rapidly growing Christian communities were located in Latin America, Africa, and Asia. In Africa the Christian population mushroomed from 9 million to 335 million during the twentieth century. Until the 1960s African Christianity was tied to colonialism, yet the expansion of Christianity occurred through Bible translations, village schools, and traveling African catechists (religious instructors) as much as through the activities of missionaries. The cultural impact of Bible translations, the first written texts in most African languages, is hard to overestimate. The translations helped to preserve indigenous languages and, with them, many oral traditions. Today African Christianity is phenomenally diverse, with thousands of groups and movements. Some African Initiated Churches (AICs) hold to customs, such as polygamy and ancestor veneration, that were forbidden by European colonists and missionaries.

Christianity entered China through the Nestorians in the sixth century, the Franciscans in the fourteenth, and the Jesuits in the sixteenth. Yet it was only with the arrival of Protestant missionaries in the mid-1800s that an enduring Chinese church was established. Communist persecution since 1949 seems only to have enhanced the growth of Christianity, and today the number of Chinese Christians may be between 70 million and 100 million. Many belong to unregistered "house churches" rather than official denominations. Following Francis Xavier's visit to Japan in 1549, large numbers converted to Christianity, and by 1600 there may have been 300,000 Christians. In the early 1600s Japanese Christians experienced severe persecution, and Japan cut off contact with foreigners until the mid-1800s. During the twentieth century there has been a numerically small but influential Christian community in Japan. Korean Christianity, especially in its Presbyterian and Pentecostal forms, expanded rapidly during the twentieth century to become one of the world's most dynamic movements. The largest Christian congregation in the world is located in Seoul, and Korean churches send missionaries throughout the world.

The Philippines have long been the only predominantly Christian nation in Asia. The Spanish arrived in 1538, remained in power for three and a half centuries, and established a form of Roman Catholicism that is much like that of Latin America. Vietnam is predominantly Buddhist but has a strong Catholic minority. In Burma, Baptist missionaries in the 1800s spread Christianity among the non-Burmese minority. Indonesia is the nation with the largest number of Muslims converting to Christianity. In part this arose as a reaction to the violence committed by Muslims against real or suspected Communists in the failed coup of 1965. Since that time millions have converted to Christianity, including the Bataks of Sumatra. In India, Christian origins go back to the fourth, second, or perhaps first century. According to early tradition, the apostle Thomas took Christianity to India. Since the 1800s outcaste groups with little stake in Hindu society and non-Hindu tribal peoples, such as the Naga, have entered the Christian church in growing numbers.

Anglicanism spread to Australia and New Zealand in the late 1700s, followed by other Protestant groups and Roman Catholicism. Christianity is now the religion of almost all of the original inhabitants of the Pacific Islands. Typically the dominant form of Christianity is that of the first missionaries to arrive—for example, Congregationalism in Hawaii and Methodism in Fiji. The Pacific Islanders converted in "people movements" (also found in Africa and Asia and among Latin-American Indians), in which the tribal leaders and entire society entered the church at the same time. New Guinea received missionaries in the late 1800s and early 1900s from Samoa, Fiji, and Tonga and today is overwhelmingly Christian.

A major part of the modern expansion of Christianity lies in the Pentecostal, or charismatic, movements that emerged after 1900 and spread rapidly and widely. Pentecostal Christianity has come to dominate large portions of Africa and Latin America, where more people may attend weekly Pentecostal services than the Roman Catholic Mass. The movement began with the Azusa Street Revival in Los Angeles in 1906, led by the African-American preacher William Seymour (1870–1922). After several days of fasting and praying, a number of people began to speak in unknown languages, taken to be an outward sign of the experience known as "baptism in the Holy Spirit," which soon became the hallmark of Pentecostalism. Within a generation small groups of Spirit-baptized Christians were found throughout the world. Pentecostals emphasize supernatural elements in Christianity, such as divine healing, prophecy and visions, the casting out of demons, and "speaking in tongues," or glossolalia.

The ecumenical movement arose out of a conference on world evangelization in Edinburgh in 1910. Delegates became aware that divisions in the Christian world were a major hindrance for missionaries, and the discussions begun at Edinburgh gave rise to a number of organizations concerned with Christian reunion. In 1948 they merged into the World Council of Churches (WCC). The WCC has promoted dialogue and joint action among Protestant, Anglican, and Orthodox churches, with some Roman Catholic participation as well. The statement "Baptism, Eucharist, and Ministry" (1982) reflected broad agreements on these points. In 1999 the Catholic Church and the Lutheran World Federation offered the "Joint Declaration on the Doctrine of Justification," another sign of a gradually emerging theological consensus.

In North America the early twentieth century brought controversy and ultimately division between liberal and conservative Protestants, termed "fundamentalists" but later described as "evangelicals." The liberals inherited the church's denominational and theological institutions, while the conservatives left the mainline denominations and started over. Conservative churches in the United States, however, have been growing at the expense of more liberal groups. One region of the world that shows less Christian vitality is western Europe, where services in massive cathedrals may attract a mere handful of worshipers. In England, for example, less than a million Anglicans attend Sunday services, while in Nigeria the Anglican Church has 17 million members and the attendance rate is 89 percent. Thus, the future of the Church of England may lie not in England but in Africa and other regions that were the object of earlier missionary efforts.

The great Christian event of the twentieth century was almost certainly the Second Vatican Council (1962–65), which in a single generation transformed the lives of Roman Catholics throughout the world. Vatican II allowed worship in vernacular languages rather than Latin, taught that Protestants were "separated brethren" rather than heretics or schismatics, opened a door for dialogue with non-Christians, and called for the church to become engaged in the struggle for justice and dignity for all human beings. Following the council, however, the declining number of new vocations to the priesthood and religious orders has threatened the viability of Catholicism. Debates over women's ordination and artificial birth control, as well as sexual abuse scandals in the United States, also are challenges for Catholics.

CENTRAL DOCTRINES Christian theology seeks to understand God and his relation to the world in light of the salvation brought by Jesus Christ. It is based on the Bible—both the Old and New Testaments—as interpreted in the light of tradition, reason, and experience. Anselm of Canterbury described theology as *fides quaerens intellectum*, or "faith seeking understanding." Faith does not exclude intellectual inquiry but rather invites it. Christians have generally been more concerned with orthodoxy (correct doctrinal expression) than have the adherents of other religions. Judaism and Islam have been more preoccupied with orthopraxy (right practice). Buddhists and Hindus have tended to be flexible about doctrines, seeing them as guidelines rather than fixed standards of belief. Thus, in many ways Christianity is the most theological of the major religions.

Roman Catholic and Orthodox Christians make individual opinion and private interpretation in understanding Scripture subordinate to the inherited traditions of the church. By contrast, Protestants make the text of the Bible the final authority. During the past three centuries many Christian thinkers have emphasized human reason as much as Scripture or tradition. The Enlightenment taught that human beings must use their own reason to evaluate all truth claims, including the texts of the Bible and the traditions of the church. Pietistic and Pentecostal Christians claim that theology emerges from personal experience, which can be a source and test of theological truth. Thus, today Christian theology involves a complex interplay of Scripture, tradition, reason, and experience.

Christian theology rests on an understanding of God as Holy Trinity. The first universal, or ecumenical, council of the Christian church, held at Nicea in Asia Minor in 325, affirmed that Jesus is "of one nature [Greek, *homoousios*] with the Father" and thus that both Father and Son are divine. In 381 a council at Constantinople affirmed that the Holy Spirit is also fully divine. Thus, the existence of three persons in one God was established as a formal principle at an early stage. The Apostle's Creed and the Nicene Creed summarize Christian beliefs, including the doctrine of the Trinity, and almost all Christian groups affirm them. The Trinity provides the basic framework for understanding salvation, which comes from the Father, through the Son, and in the Spirit. Prayer, worship, and service to God reverse this movement and are offered in the Spirit, through the Son, and toward the Father.

The classical concept of God taught in Christianity was carried over from Judaism and is summarized in the Westminster Confession of Faith (1646): "There is but one only, living, and true God, who is infinite in being and perfection, a most pure spirit, invisible, without body, parts, or passions; immutable, immense, eternal, incomprehensible, almighty, most wise, most holy . . . working all things . . . for his own glory; most loving, gracious, merciful, long-suffering, abundant in goodness and truth, forgiving iniquity . . . and withal, most just . . . hating all sin." These basic assertions regarding God's infinity, mercy, and justice continue to be affirmed, although many contemporary theologians stress God's intimate relationship with creatures rather than his power over them.

Both the Bible itself and the Apostle's Creed begin with the assertion that God created all things. There is nothing that exists apart from God's will, and God has unlimited dominion over all things. God not only created the world but also directs natural and historical events in accordance with a purpose. The story of Jesus, whose crucifixion preceded his resurrection from the dead and ascension into heaven, encourages Christians to believe that God is working out a plan that turns evil toward good: "We know that all things work together for good for those who love God" (Romans 8:28). Christian faith interprets evil in the light of a gracious God who will one day remove it altogether: "He will wipe every tear from their eyes. Death will be no more; mourning and crying and pain will be no more . . . And the one who was seated on the throne said, 'See, I am making all things new'" (Revelation 21:4–5).

Divine providence somehow concurs with genuine human choice and thus is not a negation of human freedom. Yet Christian theologians have never arrived at a consensus regarding the relation of God's will to human wills. Augustine argued that God could cause certain events to take place necessarily but without abolishing human choice. He claimed that from the beginning God had decided the exact number of those who would be saved (predestination). By contrast, in the early 400s Pelagius taught that humans could serve God through their own volition and apart from grace, but his viewpoint has found little favor in mainstream Christianity. Many theologians in Western Christianity, including Anselm, Martin Luther, John Calvin, the Jansenists, Jonathan Edwards, and Karl Barth, have followed Augustine's position. An intermediate position, known as semi-Pelagianism or Arminianism and associated with John Cassian (c. 360–435), the Jesuits, and John Wesley and Methodism, asserts that salvation begins with a human choice that is then aided and strengthened by God and divine grace. Orthodoxy generally has not shared the West's concern for probing the intricacies of divine grace and human volition but has been more concerned with Christology (the doctrine concerning Christ) and the Trinity.

For Christian theology human beings are made in "the image of God" (Genesis 1:27) and thus are distinct from other creatures. The "image" is variously identified with reason, conscience, the soul, self-awareness, or the power of dominion over other created things. Genesis states that all things made by God were "very good" (1:31), which means that human beings commit sin and yet never become evil per se. As traditionally interpreted, the story of the "fall" of humanity in Genesis 3 indicates that sin and death entered the world through the transgression of the first human pair, Adam and Eve. The doctrine of original sin asserts that all human beings are born with an inclination toward evildoing: "All have sinned and fall short of the glory of God" (Romans 3:23). The exception is Jesus Christ, who was born without the taint of original sin. Roman Catholicism, in its doctrine of Immaculate Conception—first defined in 1854—asserts that Mary, like Jesus, was also conceived without original sin.

The center of Christian theology lies in its affirmations regarding Jesus as Messiah, Lord, Savior, Redeemer, Priest, Prophet, and Returning King. While each generation of Christians has tended to re-create Jesus in its own image, certain doctrines have remained relatively constant. Chief among these is the doctrine of Jesus' divinity, humanity, and unity as a single, undivided person. The term "incarnation" refers to the affirmation that God took on human nature in Jesus: "The Word became flesh and lived among us" (John 1:14). The early Christian councils were largely devoted to elaborating basic doctrines concerning Jesus, with all departures from them defined as heresies. The heresy of Ebionitism presented a Jesus who was human but not divine, while Docetism portrayed Jesus as divine but not human. The Jesus of Arianism was neither fully human nor fully divine. Nestorianism depicted Jesus as divine and human and yet divided into two distinct persons.

Because they believe that salvation is at stake, Christian thinkers of all eras have been preoccupied with describing Jesus' character. In 451 the Council of Chalcedon sought to define the exact relationship between his divine and human natures. Jesus' role as Savior requires that he function as the mediator between God and humanity. Salvation depends on a full and true incarnation of God in human life. As God, Jesus can save fallen humanity; as human, he represents other humans and offers to God the perfect obedience that all owe to God. As a single, undivided person, he brings divinity and humanity into connection. The Incarnation affirms that God enters into human experience, understands humans from the inside out, and validates the material world and physical body through his union with it: "For we do not have a high priest [Jesus] who is unable to sympathize with our weaknesses, but we have one who in every respect has been tested as we are, yet without sin" (Hebrews 4:15). Because of the Incarnation, human beings find God to be approachable and empathetic.

Not only who Jesus is but also what he does matters for Christian theology. When he wished to summarize the gospel he preached, Paul spoke of two things—the crucifixion of Jesus and his resurrection from the dead (1 Corinthians 15:3–4). Paul writes that through the cross of Jesus God mysteriously identifies himself with the guilt, weakness, and suffering of humanity in order to remove them (1 Corinthians 1:18–31). The doctrine of Atonement states that the death of Jesus is the basis for salvation. Various theories of the Atonement seek to explain this. Jesus' death frees believers from Satan's dominion (classical theory), awakens a love for God by showing the depth of God's love for humans (exemplary theory), presents an offering of perfect obedience to God (Anselmian theory), or serves as vicarious punishment inflicted on Jesus in place of all other humans (substitutionary theory). Each theory offers a partial glimpse into the significance of Jesu's cross. The resurrection of Jesus is his public vindication, whereby he is "declared to be the Son of God with power" (Romans 1:4), and it is the ultimate basis for the Christian hope in life beyond life. Because he rose from the dead, those who believe in him have hope for their own resurrection (1 Corinthians 15:12–22).

The Christian doctrine of salvation follows from the doctrine of sin. Because human beings are estranged, God undertakes to bring them back into a closer relationship with him: "In Christ God was reconciling the world to himself, not counting their trespasses against them" (2 Corinthians 5:19). The process starts with God's eternal will to bring salvation (election, or predestination); unfolds as human beings exercise faith and repentance; ushers sinners into a new relationship of gracious acceptance by God; finds expression in the daily struggle to grow in faith, obedience, and holiness before God; and reaches its culmination when believers are raised from the dead and transformed into a glorious and immortal state. Orthodox theology speaks of salvation as "divinization" or "deification" (Greek, *theosis*), a process whereby human beings are brought to share in God's own life and so participate in his holiness and glory.

Roman Catholic, Orthodox, and many Anglican Christians view salvation as something mediated through the Christian community. In this view salvation comes through participation in the church, with baptism as the sign of that participation. Traditional Catholic theology states that unbaptized persons cannot be saved. Following baptism, a believer's strengthening in the faith comes from participation in the Eucharist and the other sacraments—confirmation, penance (reconciliation), holy orders (ordination), matrimony, and extreme unction (anointing of the sick). Some Catholic theologians emphasize the correct performance of the rituals, though others stress the importance of approaching the sacraments in faith. Like Catholics, Orthodox and Anglican Christians understand the church to be a sacramental community. In these traditions the church exhibits an unbroken line of leaders, or "apostolic succession," extending from the first century to the present time. Catholics emphasize the succession of Roman bishops, or popes, beginning with Peter (Matthew 16:17–19), as the leaders of Christendom, while Orthodox and Anglican Christians hold that the bishops collectively share in decision making and responsibility.

Protestants show a less communal interpretation of salvation, Christian life, and church leadership. Luther had been a faithful monk and yet lacked "assurance of salvation," which he found through Bible reading and a conversion experience in which God's mercy suddenly became real to him. Since that time Protestants have stressed the Bible and personal experience of God. Neither the outward forms of the church nor baptism and the sacraments are as important as the individual's experience of Christ. Most Protestants hold to two basic church rituals—baptism and the Eucharist. Lutherans and Calvinists hold that the outward actions are genuine sacraments with spiritual power attached to them. Baptists, Pentecostals, and nondenominational Protestants believe that the outward actions are merely signs attesting to and confirming the faith of those who share in them. Thus, this latter group of Protestants baptize only adults and older children on a profession of faith (believer's baptism). Though all Protestants deny the su-

preme spiritual authority of the papacy, they differ as to what they put in its place. Anglicans, Methodists, and Lutherans preserve the ancient system of church government by bishops, while Baptists, Pentecostals, and Congregationalists allow each local gathering to govern itself, with Presbyterians placing local gatherings under the direction of a representative assembly.

Christian theology includes eschatology, or a doctrine of "last things"—Jesus' return (or Second Coming), judgment by God, heaven, and hell. In the Gospels, Jesus' teaching focused on the kingdom of God, and the Lord's Prayer includes a petition for God to bring an earthly realization of his purposes: "Your kingdom come, Your will be done, on earth as it is in heaven" (Matthew 6:10). Although the kingdom of God is already present in a limited way, it will attain perfection only when Jesus returns, "coming on the clouds of heaven with power and great glory" (Matthew 24:30). Christian eschatology offers confidence that God will ultimately transform individuals, society, and the world at large into "a new heaven and a new earth" (Revelation 21:1). Jesus' resurrection shows God's purpose to overcome all that threatens humanity, including death itself. Though some versions of eschatology have encouraged Christians to retreat from the world, many have driven believers to struggle for mercy, peace, and justice. Eschatology has been an engine of social change and even revolution. The Book of Revelation offers an elaborate picture of the Christian hope, and yet the text is notoriously hard to interpret. Some theologians view it as a more or less literal account of what is to happen before Jesus returns, while others see it as symbolic in character or as referring to events that have already transpired.

MORAL CODE OF CONDUCT Christianity offers a revelation concerning God's love and human salvation. Similarly, it offers instruction in moral and spiritual life, also based on revelation. At the same time, most Christian thinkers maintain that Christians and non-Christians alike are accountable to conscience or natural law. Thus, when the Bible gives the commands "you shall not steal" and "you shall not bear false witness" (Exodus 20:15–16), these imperatives agree with human nature and can be discerned as ethically binding apart from divine revelation. Discussions of Christian ethics thus shift back and forth between natural law and biblical revelation, with Roman Catholic thinkers characteristically emphasizing the former and Protestants the latter.

If there is something distinctive about Christian ethics, it lies in the commandments to "love the Lord your God" and "love your neighbor as yourself," with the added assertion that "all the law" depends on these two commandments (Matthew 22:37–40). By linking love for God with love for neighbor, Jesus' teaching connects spirituality and ethics. Furthermore, Christian love as commanded in the New Testament goes beyond the bounds of natural law or everyday ethics. Ordinary morality tells a person that he ought not steal from his neighbor, but "love your neighbor as yourself" means that a person must meet his neighbor's needs, even if this requires personal sacrifice. Jesus himself presents the ultimate model of sacrifice on behalf of others: "No one has greater love than this, to lay down one's life for one's friends" (John 15:13).

As Christian ethics evolved through time, it developed divergent emphases. One way of summarizing the Christian way of life is "imitation" of Christ. Paul wrote, "Be imitators of me, as I am of Christ Jesus" (I Corinthians 11:1). Various branches of Christianity have all held that the goal of the Christian life is to embody Jesus' character. This theme underlies the most popular book of Christian devotion ever written, *The Imitation of Christ* by Thomas à Kempis (c. 1379–1471). The imitation of Christ was so strong a theme in early Christianity that the notion of imitating anyone else, such as saints, did not become prevalent until the fourth and fifth century.

Early Christian literature included exhortations to patience and perseverance in the face of difficulty, persecution, and martyrdom. It also stressed the need for prayer, almsgiving, and fasting and the avoidance of idolatry, violence, and sexual immorality. When Christianity became the religion of the Roman Empire and believers were no longer persecuted, monks went into the desert to pursue God in prayer and self-denial and to undergo a voluntary martyrdom for Christ. Monastic literature is concerned with eliminating wrongful desires and growing in spiritual joy and contemplation of God. Beginning in the fourth century, Christian authors began to look for harmony between pagan wisdom and biblical ethics. Ambrose modeled his *De Officiis* on a comparable work by Cicero and carried over Greco-Roman teachings on the virtues. Augustine followed along these lines but also used the Ten Commandments and love commandments as a framework. For Augustine love involved spontaneity and not rigidity: "Love, and do what you will." Only God was to be loved for his own sake,

claimed Augustine, while all creatures were to be loved "in God," or for the sake of God. Different kinds of love engendered different sorts of human communities. Augustine distinguished a "city of man," centering on material things, from a "city of God," directed toward eternal bliss.

As the centuries passed, Eastern and Western Christianity diverged in their emphases. In the East monks served as confessors and spiritual directors for laypersons, and so the monastic experience permeated the entire notion of the Christian life. Asceticism, prayer, and contemplation led to *theosis*, or "divinization" (a process of growth into Godlikeness). The spiritual standards were high, if not perfectionistic. Humans were made in the "image" of God but had to restore the "likeness" through lengthy self-discipline. Orthodox ethics are generally simpler and less formal than Roman Catholic ethics.

Western theology reached a climax in the work of Thomas Aquinas, who synthesized many strands of ethical thought. Following Aristotle, Aquinas held that humans are teleological, or goal oriented. Human fulfillment consists of knowing and choosing good ends. The natural virtues of wisdom, justice, prudence, and temperance contribute to this fulfillment. The supernatural virtues of faith, hope, and love complement the natural virtues in such a way that "grace does not destroy nature but perfects it." Perfect fulfillment comes only in the "beatific vision" of the saints who see God in heaven. Aquinas and his Dominican order emphasized reason, while Bonaventure and the Franciscans highlighted the will and the exercise of love as the chief features in human fulfillment.

A more down-to-earth form of ethical reflection developed in connection with the sacrament of confession. Beginning in the ninth century, guidebooks for confessors ("Irish penitentials") specified what penance was appropriate for a given transgression. Over time an emerging tradition of moral theology took into account not only the acts themselves but also circumstances and intentions. Mortal sins concerned grave matters, occurred when the act was done deliberately and with full consent, and blocked a person from receiving grace. Venial sins were less serious, though they still required "satisfaction," or outward actions, to show contrition and to compensate for the wrong committed. Beginning in the Middle Ages, the church taught that purgatory provided a place where those who died without mortal sin but without having made satisfaction for their venial sins could make reparation through cleansing fire. In the period from the 1600s to the 1960s, Roman Catholic moral theology took the form of multivolume works of casuistry, or moral reasoning, that considered every conceivable sort of transgression. Since the Second Vatican Council, Catholic moral theology has moved away from this formal and legal style to a more personal and humanistic approach.

Protestants laid emphasis on Scripture as the basis for ethics and generally rejected casuistry. Since they had no centralized teaching authority, Protestants developed a diversity of approaches. Both Martin Luther and John Calvin used the Ten Commandments as a broad framework for ethical teaching, and both invoked Jesus' love commandments. They rejected medieval notions of merit, or "works-righteousness," and asserted that the Christian life was fundamentally a response to the salvation already given by God. Salvation was a matter of grace, and ethics of gratitude. Luther was reluctant to describe the Christian life as a journey in which the person gradually approached a goal. Instead, every day was a new beginning. Holy living required spontaneity and not calculation. Freedom was fundamental, and "faith is a living, active, busy thing." Given Luther's assumptions, there was little place for honoring the saints as models of the Christian life.

Calvin's teaching was closer to that of Roman Catholics. He held that growth in holiness, or sanctification, could be tracked through time, and the English Calvinists, or Puritans, used personal journals as a way of "reading the evidence" of God's grace in their lives. Some Puritans wrote works of casuistry akin to Roman Catholic manuals. Many early Calvinists adopted an abstemious, self-denying, and even monklike attitude in all spheres of life, which led the sociologist Max Weber to conclude that Calvinist attitudes lay at the root of the strenuous work ethic and growth of capitalism in northern Europe during the 1500s and 1600s.

The Radical Reformers turned not to the Ten Commandments but to Jesus' Sermon on the Mount. They focused on the radical imperatives to "love your enemies," "turn the other [cheek]," and "give to everyone who begs from you" (Matthew 5:44, 39, 42). Luther and Calvin, they said, had preached only on the "sweet Christ" who offered forgiveness of sins, not on the "bitter Christ" who called his followers to forsake all worldly comforts and undergo persecution. The Christian ideal was martyrdom. While Roman Catholics and mainstream reformers sought to find harmony between church and state, or the Bible and culture, the Radical Reformers perceived a disjunction. They formed themselves into countercultural communities, and within these groups they exercised discipline, admitting or removing members based on whether or not they followed Jesus' strict demands.

The basic concepts for the Christian life vary markedly. The major saints and founders of new religious traditions all had different emphases. Anthony recounted his battles with demons through prayer. John Climacus described a "ladder of ascent," in which each rung led on to the next. Benedict summarized his monastic movement in the words *ora et labora* (work and prayer). Francis spoke of "holy poverty" and stressed total abandonment to God. Gregory Palamas and the Hesychasts (Greek, *hesychia,* or "quietness") practiced contemplation until they experienced a divine illumination akin to that exhibited by Jesus on the Mount of Transfiguration. Some medieval mystics referred to God as their heavenly spouse. Johann von Staupitz spoke of "nakedly following the naked Christ."

Luther wrote of "the freedom of a Christian," in which a believer was perfectly free and yet yielded that freedom to serve others. Ignatius Loyola viewed the church as the *militia Christi* (army of Christ) and called his followers to disciplined service. Calvin was concerned with the proper "use" of the present life and an attitude of detachment from material things. Teresa of Avila described stages in prayer, leading from strenuous effort (watering a garden), to growing ease (an irrigation system), and pure receptivity (receiving a drenching rain). John of the Cross described a "dark night of the soul" that brought detachment from earthly things and attachment to God. Quietists, such as Miguel de Molina and Madame Guyon, taught that holiness followed not from effort but from the renunciation of effort.

The Puritans were activists who continually sought to organize their lives so as to bring the greatest glory to God. Jonathan Edwards wrote that religion "consists most essentially in holy affections." John Wesley taught that "total sanctification," or freedom from all conscious sin, was possible in the present life and should be sought after. During the nineteenth century the Holiness movement followed in Wesley's tradition and gave rise to twentieth-century Pentecostalism. Liberation theologians have highlighted the "preferential option for the poor" and encouraged the creation of "base communities" that address both spiritual and economic concerns. Thus, although a few basic themes run through Christian ethics—the love commandments, the Ten Commandments, and the imitation of Christ—the overall picture is one of kaleidoscopic diversity.

SACRED BOOKS The Christian Bible includes the Old Testament and the New Testament. Christians accept the books of the Jewish, or Hebrew, Bible as sacred Scripture and designate them collectively as the Old Testament. An addendum, or New Testament, contains the accounts of the life and ministry of Jesus in the four Gospels (Matthew, Mark, Luke, and John), along with the Acts of the Apostles, the letters of Paul, other letters (Catholic Epistles), and the Book of Revelation. Much of the New Testament consists of reinterpretations of Old Testament writings in relation to the life, teaching, ministry, and person of Jesus.

When Christianity emerged, the Jewish people had synagogue services in which the Hebrew Bible was read aloud, sometimes in a Greek translation known as the Septuagint, and yet there was variation in the books that were used. A larger canon that was prevalent among Greek-speaking Jews included various books and added portions of books (Tobit, Judith, Ecclesiasticus, Additions to Esther, and others), while a smaller canon was common among non-Greek-speaking Jews. The books included in the larger canon became known as the Apocrypha, or deuterocanonical books. Jewish Bibles published in modern times do not include the Apocrypha, and Protestant Bibles typically follow the Jewish custom of excluding them. The situation in early and medieval Christianity, however, was fluid. Some groups used the Apocrypha in their worship services, while others did not. In 1548 the Council of Trent decreed that the Apocrypha was a part of the Old Testament, and since then Catholic Bibles have consistently included it.

The debate regarding the Apocrypha pertains only to the Old Testament, and all major Christian groups agree about which books belong in the New Testament. The so-called New Testament Apocrypha (Gospel of Thomas, Gospel of Peter, and others) consists of books that claim to come from the time of the apostles but probably originated many decades later. These books have not played a part in Christian worship in any of the historic churches.

SACRED SYMBOLS One of the earliest Christian symbols was the fish, associated with the fishermen who followed Jesus. The Greek word for fish (*ichthus*) is an acronym for the words "Jesus Christ, God's Son, Savior."

Today the symbol is especially popular among evangelical Christians. A dove, with wings outstretched, symbolizes the Holy Spirit and is widely used by Pentecostal and charismatic Christians.

During the era of Roman persecution, Christians produced their first enduring artistic images on the walls of underground tombs, or catacombs. One of the earliest images was of a shepherd carrying a sheep on his shoulders, a representation of God's love in seeking out sinners. Other images portrayed dramatic scenes from Israel's history.

After Constantine made Christianity legal in the fourth century, Christians erected basilicas, and the Christian artistic tradition then began to unfold in rich variety. Every episode in Jesus' life was treated in loving detail. His birth, baptism, crucifixion, resurrection, and ascension were especially common images. Not only biblical events but also the saints were commemorated in pictures and statues. Images of Mary and Jesus, the Madonna and Child, were among the most widespread. Pope Gregory I argued that images in church buildings were "books for the illiterate" and so had educational value. During much of the seventh and eighth centuries, however, controversy concerning the use of images raged in the eastern Mediterranean. The Iconoclasts argued that icons, or Christian images, were a violation of the second of the Ten Commandments—"you shall not make for yourself an idol" (Exodus 20:4)—and so had to be removed from churches. Those who insisted that reverence shown to an icon was reverence shown to God ultimately triumphed. Veneration for icons, such as kissing images and lighting candles, continues to play a major role in Orthodox Christianity. While the Western church tends to think of images as educational aids, the Eastern church has adopted a more explicitly devotional attitude toward them.

The cross is a fundamental Christian symbol, although Eastern Christians portray the cross differently than do Western Christians. The Greek cross has four arms of equal length, while the Latin cross has three arms of roughly equal length, with one longer arm. Eastern crosses sometimes have small crossbars near the ends of the arms. In honor of Andrew, who is said to have died on a cross in the form of an *X*, the Russian cross has three arms across the vertical shaft, two parallel to the ground and one at a 45-degree angle. The crucifix, a three-dimensional representation of Jesus on the cross, appeared in about 1000 in the Rhineland. It subsequently became one of the most distinctive Christian symbols and is especially associated with Roman Catholicism. Orthodox Christians have not generally favored the crucifix, since they view the cross as Jesus' moment of triumph.

Some Protestants did away with all images, while others abolished three-dimensional images, thought to be idolatrous, and yet allowed two-dimensional images in books or in stained glass. A simple cross, without Jesus' body, is one of the few symbols widely shared among Protestant groups. Protestants sometimes use images of books or open pages, a testimony to the importance of the Bible in their tradition.

EARLY AND MODERN LEADERS The earliest church seems to have regarded Peter as the leader of the 12 apostles chosen by Jesus. Numerous passages in the New Testament suggest a unique role for him (Matthew 16), and Roman Catholicism asserts that Peter was the first pope, or universal leader, of Christendom. Paul (or Saul of Tarsus) did more than any other person in the early church to spread the Christian message and establish new congregations throughout the eastern Mediterranean. Early traditions assert that both Peter and Paul died as martyrs in Rome under Emperor Nero around 64 C.E. James, known as the "brother" of Jesus—variously understood as a kinsman (Roman Catholicism), stepbrother (Orthodoxy), or half brother (Protestantism) of Jesus—was a leader among Jewish Christians in Jerusalem.

Ignatius of Antioch (c. 35–c. 107) was a bishop who wrote letters that reveal much regarding the early church. After being condemned to die, he welcomed his impending martyrdom in the Roman arena and underscored the authority of the bishop with the words *ubi episcopus, ibi ecclesia* (where the bishop is, there is the church). Anthony (c. 251–356) initiated and promoted the monastic tradition in Egypt. Athanasius (c. 296–373), the patriarch of Alexandria, was repeatedly deposed and reinstated during a decades-long struggle with the Arians, who denied the full divinity of Jesus. While Anthony promoted a solitary (anchoritic, or eremitic) life, Pachomius (c. 290–346) encouraged a communal (cenobitic) approach to monasticism. In Europe, Benedict (c. 480–c. 545) carried on this communal tradition with his *Rule*. Constantine (died in 337), who first made Christianity legal in the Roman Empire, presided over the Nicene Council and may have played a role in its theological outcome.

Augustine (354–430) was not baptized until his early thirties, after a dramatic conversion experience that is immortalized in his *Confessions*. Perhaps no one after the time of the apostles had a greater impact on Christian theology. His teachings on the church and sacraments laid the foundation for medieval and modern Catholicism, and his emphasis on grace and personal experience of God laid the foundation for the Protestant movement. Patrick (c. 390–c. 460) was taken from Britain to Ireland as a slave, escaped some years later, and eventually returned to evangelize the Irish. Arguably the most important Christian missionary since apostolic times, he was the founder of a culturally Irish and non-Roman form of Christianity. Pope Gregory I (c. 540–604) described himself as a "servant of the servants of God," wrote major works on the Christian life (*Moralia, Pastoral Rule*), and sent missionaries to strengthen the church in England. Francis of Assisi (1181/2–1226), perhaps the most popular saint of all time, called the church back to simplicity through his embrace of "holy poverty." The order of Franciscans, which he founded, is among the most influential in the history of Christianity. Innocent III (1160–1216), who reigned as pope during the time of the papacy's greatest power, initiated the Fourth Crusade in 1204 and the Fourth Lateran Council in 1215.

Martin Luther (1483–1546) may have done more than anyone else to shape the development of modern Christianity. Luther began as a faithful monk and loyal member of the church, but his emphasis on the priority of grace and the authority of the Bible provoked a series of revolutionary changes that transformed the map of Europe and forever altered theology, politics, economics, art, literature, and family life. Ulrich Zwingli (1484–1531) and John Calvin (1509–64) were second-generation reformers in the Swiss cities of Zurich and Geneva, respectively, and their Reformed version of Protestantism had influence in England, Scotland, France, Germany, Hungary, the Netherlands, North America, and South Africa. Menno Simons (1496–1561) was among the best-known and most irenic figures in the Radical Reformation, and his followers are known to this day as Mennonites.

Ignatius Loyola (1491–1556) was originally a soldier, and while recovering from battle wounds, he read the lives of the saints and decided to offer himself as a soldier for Christ. The order he founded in 1540, the Society of Jesus, has long been a leader in Catholic theology and educational work. Teresa of Avila (1515–82) led in the founding of the order of discalced (barefoot) Carmelites, and her spiritual writings, including *Autobiography* and *The Interior Castle,* were so well received that she became the first woman ever to be named a "doctor" of the Catholic Church. (Catherine of Siena [1347–80] and Teresa of Lisieux [1873–97], "the Little Flower," were subsequently given this title.) John of the Cross (1542–91), Teresa of Avila's disciple, was also a major spiritual teacher and stressed even more than Teresa the need for detachment from earthly things. Robert Bellarmine (1542–1621) was a cardinal and outstanding Catholic theologian, though he is also known as the clergyman who sought to silence Galileo. Philipp Jakob Spener (1635–1705), who began the Pietist movement in German Lutheranism, called on Christians to have not only doctrinal knowledge but also a deep and affective experience of God's grace.

There were three major figures in the evangelical movement of the 1700s. George Whitefield (1714–70), while still in his twenties, was so powerful a preacher that thousands gathered to hear him in England and America. John Wesley (1703–88) worked alongside Whitefield, but his abilities were more organizational than oratorical. After Wesley's death, and against his wishes, his renewal movement separated from the Church of England to become the Methodist Church. The writings of Jonathan Edwards (1703–58), America's greatest and most original theologian, have had tremendous influence on evangelical Christianity throughout the world.

During the nineteenth century William Wilberforce (1759–1833) entered the English Parliament to agitate for the elimination of the slave trade, and he achieved his goal in 1807. Samuel Ajayi Crowther (c. 1807–91), an Anglican, became the first African appointed a bishop under missionary auspices, and though snubbed by European missionaries during his later years, he has inspired generations of African Christians. Seraphim of Sarov (1759–1833) entered a cave in Russia, where he remained in solitary prayer for 15 years. When he opened his door for visitors, many were astonished by his wisdom, and he became a spiritual director for many. Pope Pius IX (1792–1878) promulgated the doctrines of Mary's Immaculate Conception in 1854 and the infallibility of the pope in 1870. Charles Spurgeon (1834–92), a Baptist preacher, drew thousands to his Metropolitan Tabernacle on the outskirts of London and presided over the largest congregation in England.

According to statistician David B. Barrett, 45 million Christians died as martyrs during the twentieth century. Among the best known were Dietrich Bonhoeffer (1906–45), a Lutheran minister who resisted Nazi totalitarianism and was executed; Martin Luther King, Jr. (1929–68), a Baptist minister who led in the civil rights struggle in the United States and who was assassinated; Janani Luwun (1922–77), an Anglican archbishop in Uganda who was executed under dictator Idi Amin; and Oscar Romero (1917–80), a Catholic bishop in El Salvador who sided with the poor and who was murdered while celebrating Mass. The influential Russian priest Alexander Men (1935–90), described as a "one-man antidote" to Marxist propaganda, was murdered with an ax as he left his automobile.

When Russia restored the Moscow Patriarchate in 1917, Tikhon (1866–1925) was the first to enter the office, and he led Russian Orthodoxy during the period of Stalinist repression. Aleksandr Solzhenitsyn (born in 1918), an Orthodox Christian who documented the Soviet Union's prison camps in *The Gulag Archipelago,* received the Nobel Prize in Literature in 1970. Pope John Paul II (born Karol Wojtyła in 1920; served as pope, 1978–2005), who helped to abolish Communism in his native Poland and who upheld conservative doctrinal and moral positions in the church, was a towering figure of twentieth-century Catholicism. Mother Teresa (born Agnes Gonxha Bojaxhiu; 1910–97), leader of the Sisters of Charity in Calcutta, drew international attention for her work serving the poor and was canonized in 2003. The Anglican bishop Desmond Tutu (born in 1931) was a leader of the South African movement against apartheid. Through the Catholic Worker movement Dorothy Day (1897–1980) was part of the struggle for social justice in American cities. Billy Graham (born in 1918), an American evangelist, preached to more people than anyone in history. New church-related organizations emerged in North America in the twentieth century. Cameron Townsend (1896–1982) founded Wycliffe Bible Translators; Bill Bright (1921–2003), Campus Crusade for Christ; and Demos Shakarian (1913–93), the Full Gospel Businessmen's Association. Prominent in the developing nations were Watchman Nee (1903–72) in China and Bakht Singh (1903–2000) in India, both responsible for establishing several hundred new congregations.

MAJOR THEOLOGIANS AND AUTHORS Beginning in the mid-second century, Christian apologists presented a defense of their faith, often in terms drawn from Greek philosophy, to a pagan Greco-Roman society. Among the best known were Justin Martyr (c. 100–c. 165), Athenagoras (second century), and Origen (c. 185–c. 254). Irenaeus (c. 130–c. 200) sought to refute the heresies of his day. Tertullian (c. 160–c. 225), who was the first major Christian author in Latin, contributed to the establishment of the doctrine of the Trinity. He wrote brilliant and often stinging prose and held rigorous and uncompromising standards for the Christian life.

In addition to being an apologist, Origen was among the finest biblical scholars of all time. He suggested that all beings, including the Devil, might ultimately find salvation, and he is reputed to have committed self-castration to avoid fleshly temptation. Although his works were widely read, Origen was judged heretical by some early Christian councils. In the fourth century several brilliant thinkers—Athanasius (c. 296–373), who, against the Arians, insisted on Jesu's divinity; Gregory of Nyssa (c. 330–c. 395); Gregory Nazianzen (329–89); and Basil (c. 330–79)—upheld the doctrines that emerged as orthodoxy. With his *Ecclesiastical History,* Eusebius of Caesarea (c. 260–c. 340) laid the foundation for all later histories of Christianity. Jerome (c. 342–424) wrote on the Christian life and produced the Latin translation of the Bible, or Vulgate, that was practically the only version used in Western Christianity for more than a thousand years. John Chrysostom (c. 347–407), meaning "golden mouthed," was a gifted preacher and theologian who served as bishop of Constantinople until his challenging sermons aroused opposition and his enemies deposed him. John of Damascus (c. 675–c. 749), who summarized the Orthodox faith in his writings, is still consulted as an authority.

Augustine (354–430) was the greatest and most influential of the early theologians in the Latin-speaking empire. Peter Lombard (c. 1100–60) wrote the *Sentences,* which served for centuries as the basic text for theological education in Europe. Anselm (1033–1109) was influenced by Augustine but was an innovator who introduced a more formal method in theology. Thomas Aquinas (1225–74) was probably the greatest of the medieval theologians, and some regard his *Summa Theologica* as the finest theological work ever written. In the later Middle Ages, Duns Scotus (1266–1308) and William Ockham (c. 1285–1347) stressed God's freedom and omnipotence. Gregory Palamas (c. 1296–1359), who defended the Hesychasts and their claim of divine illumination during prayer, was among the most original thinkers in Orthodoxy after the eighth century.

Martin Luther (1483–1546) was a prodigious writer and theologian, and the complete edition of his works in German and Latin fills 125 large volumes. Huldrich Zwingli (1484–1531) and John Calvin (1509–64) defined the Reformed movement, as distinct from Lutheranism. Calvin's *Institutes* may be the finest summary of sixteenth-century Protestant theology. In England, Thomas More (1478–1535) defended Roman Catholic positions against Lutheranism and was executed for opposing the divorce of King Henry VIII. Richard Hooker (c. 1554–1600) synthesized Protestant ideas with an appeal to episcopacy (church government by bishops) and natural law and so set a direction for Anglicanism. During the 1600s and 1700s theologians wrote massive Latin tomes that are little read today. Robert Bellarmine (1542–1621) is a representative Catholic writer of the period, while Johann Gerhard (1582–1637) is typical of Lutherans and Francis Turrentin (1623–87) of Calvinists. Teresa of Avila (1515–82) and John of the Cross (1542–91), who embodied a Spanish Carmelite school of spirituality, continue to exert influence.

The Enlightenment brought enormous changes in the style and content of Christian theology. The New Englander Jonathan Edwards (1703–58), who offered a brilliant synthesis of experiential religion and empirical philosophy, developed his theology as a reflection on the spiritual revival that occurred in America in 1740–41. Friedrich Schleiermacher (1768–1834) founded modern theology when he sought to steer a middle course between traditional Christian belief and Enlightenment skepticism. G.W.F. Hegel (1770–1831) was more a philosopher than a theologian, but his all-embracing intellectual synthesis provoked the religious existentialism of Søren Kierkegaard (1813–55) as well as the atheism of Ludwig Feuerbach (1804–72) and Karl Marx (1818–83). John Henry Newman (1801–90) began his life in the Church of England, shared in its Tractarian, or High Church, movement of the 1830s, and later became a Roman Catholic and rose to the rank of cardinal. His many books shaped the development of twentieth-century Catholic thought.

The most influential Protestant thinker of the twentieth century was the Swiss pastor Karl Barth (1886–1968), who led a revolt against the German liberal tradition that had begun with Schleiermacher. Barth sought to return theology to what he called "the strange

Worldmark Encyclopedia of Religious Practices

119

new world of the Bible." Emil Brunner (1889–1966) shared credit for establishing Barth's neo-orthodox, or dialectical, theology. Paul Tillich (1886–1965), with his "theology of culture," was closer in style to Schleiermacher. Dietrich Bonhoeffer (1906–45) had much in common with Barth but was an original and independent thinker. The brothers Reinhold Niebuhr (1892–1971) and H. Richard Niebuhr (1894–1962) were influential American theologians. Modern Orthodox thinkers have included Georges Florovsky (1893–1979), a neopatristic, or traditionalist, scholar, and Sergei Bulgakov (1871–1944), a Russian ex-Marxist who applied Orthodoxy to the intellectual and social issues of his day. The leading twentieth-century Catholic thinkers—Yves Congar (1904–95), Henri de Lubac (1896–1991), Jean Daniélou (1905–74), and Karl Rahner (1904–84)— were part of the *nouvelle théologie* (new theology) of the 1940s and 1950s. Inspired by the early church writers rather than the medieval scholastics, their ideas aroused controversy during the 1950s but found favor at the Second Vatican Council. Bernard Lonergan (1904–84), a Canadian Catholic, wrote influential works on theological method and fundamental theology.

Notable contemporary theologians have included Gustavo Gutiérrez (born in 1928), who was instrumental in the rise of liberation theology. Wolfhart Pannenberg (born in 1928) and Jürgen Moltmann (born in 1926) wrote theology from an eschatological standpoint, understanding God's kingdom as a future reality that impinges on the present.

ORGANIZATIONAL STRUCTURE Throughout history an underlying issue in Christianity has been the tension between centralized control and localized leadership and decision making. Prior to the third century there were variations in church governance, with certain areas—for example, Asia Minor—having a single bishop over all congregations in a city or region (monoepiscopacy), while others—for example, Corinth—were led by committee. By the third century a greater uniformity existed, and single bishops over cities or regions became the norm. Christians regarded bishops as the only persons with the power to ordain new clergy, and the consecration of a bishop by fellow bishops was said to establish a chain of leadership.

Cyprian (died in 258) believed that the bishops collectively held decision-making authority in the church, and in this conciliar viewpoint the highest authority belongs to an ecumenical council of bishops. In the second century Irenaeus and others suggested that the bishop of Rome might serve as a court of appeal for disputed issues, a viewpoint known as Petrine primacy, after Peter, the first bishop of Rome. Today Roman Catholicism holds to Petrine primacy, while Orthodoxy, Anglicanism, and those Protestant groups that have bishops maintain some version of the conciliar perspective. Since Orthodoxy gives no official recognition to any councils that have met since the eighth century, it has a built-in resistance to innovation. In practice the patriarchs of the national churches of Orthodoxy have considerable authority.

Beginning in the sixteenth century, various groups broke from the custom of government by bishops. In 1534 King Henry VIII declared himself the rightful head of the English church, and in some Lutheran regions princes replaced bishops as church leaders. John Calvin judged that the pastors referred to in the New Testament fell into a single order, or rank, and were not in any hierarchical relationship. He thus repudiated the whole idea of bishops, which led to two new models for church organization. Some Calvinists held to congregationalism, in which each local community of believers was in charge of its own affairs. Others favored presbyterianism, which linked together local congregations under the authority of a general assembly of ministers and lay leaders.

During the twentieth century the fastest-growing branches of Christianity were Pentecostal, charismatic, and nondenominational, and these traditions are generally congregationalist, though sometimes with a central government alongside local leaders. Today Christianity is divided between those groups that claim apostolic succession (an unbroken chain of leaders from the earliest church) and generally regard it as crucial and those that make no such claim and regard the issue as unimportant.

HOUSES OF WORSHIP AND HOLY PLACES Until Constantine's Edict of Milan, in 313 C.E., the Roman Empire did not acknowledge Christianity as a legitimate religion, and so Christian buildings generally were not erected. Services were held in homes, in underground tombs (catacombs), in fields, and even aboard ships. Thus, the traditions of Christian architecture began after the time of Constantine.

Among the major styles that evolved were the basilica (300s–1000), the Romanesque (1050–1150), and the Gothic (1150–1500). Gothic cathedrals may be the pinnacle of Christian architecture, although humbler churches often incorporate elements of the Gothic style—for example, the tall spire, or steeple, and stained glass. Protestants generally wanted a simple and unadorned architecture, although Lutherans preserved more of Catholic adornment in their church buildings than did Calvinists. The New England Calvinists erected meetinghouses with plain white walls and without statues, stained glass, or even a cross. During the twentieth century some Protestant groups used auditorium-style buildings or rented sports facilities. In the developing world church buildings are simpler and may consist only of a thatched hut or raised tin roof to block the wind and rain.

Constantine's mother, Helena (c. 225–c. 330), visited the Holy Land in 326 and founded basilicas on the Mount of Olives, outside Jerusalem, and at Bethlehem. According to later tradition, she also discovered the cross on which Jesus was crucified. Helena encouraged a kind of Christian archaeology, resulting in the establishment of holy sites that in time became places of pilgrimage. The best known are the Church of the Nativity and Church of the Holy Sepulchre, associated with Jesu's birth, death, and burial. Other sites in Galilee pertain to Jesus' ministry.

Christian holy sites are not confined to Palestine. For Orthodox Christians the Church of the Holy Wisdom (Hagia Sophia) in Constantinople is an important center, though since 1453 the building has been a mosque and museum. Mount Athos, in northern Greece, contains a vast complex of Orthodox monasteries, where at its peak, in the 1400s, 40,000 monks may have been in residence. For Anglicans the town of Canterbury was an early Christian center and the archbishop's seat. Glastonbury, in England, is the site where Joseph of Arimathea is said to have taken the Holy Grail, the cup Jesus used at the Last Supper. In Spain the shrine of Saint James in Compostela is a major pilgrimage center. Several sacred sites are connected with reported appearances of the Virgin Mary, including Lourdes in France (1858), Fátima in Portugal (1917), and Medjugorje in Croatia (1981). Lourdes has become the most famous center for healing in Christendom.

Many Protestants reject the whole idea of holy sites and insist that all places are equally sacred in God's sight. Yet Protestant tours to the Holy Land and to cities connected with the sixteenth-century Reformation—for example, Wittenberg and Geneva—indicate that the notion of holy ground may still be present.

WHAT IS SACRED? The term "martyr" originally meant "witness," and those who had died rather than renounce the Christian faith were regarded as the ultimate witnesses to the truth of the gospel. The martyrs had undergone a "baptism of blood" that was a sure mark of saintliness. By the end of the second century, the anniversary of a martyr's death was kept as a feast, with a worship service at the tomb. Churches were later built on these sites.

Early Christians believed that a dying martyr had the power to declare the forgiveness of a person's sins. Eventually the idea of a martyr's "intercession" was carried beyond death, and people prayed to deceased martyrs for their aid. Originally *ora pro nobis* (pray for us) was a collective prayer to all deceased martyrs and saints. In time individual saints emerged as intercessors for particular classes—for example, those bearing a certain name or following a given occupation—or for particular issues. Thus, Christopher became the patron saint of travelers and Jude the champion of hopeless causes.

Until about 1000 C.E. Christian martyrs and saints were known and celebrated locally. Over time, especially in Rome, a universal calendar developed that specified which deceased Christians were to be honored as saints. Canonization emerged as a process whereby the Roman Catholic Church could authenticate a deceased person as a saint. A person may be declared "blessed" or "venerable" without attaining the full status of sainthood. If the church declares sainthood, it is attested that the person is in heaven, the saint is invoked in public prayers, churches are dedicated to the saint's memory, festival days are celebrated, images are made showing the saint surrounded by light or with a halo, and the saint's physical remains, or relics, may be enclosed in vessels and publicly honored.

Mary, the mother of Jesus, also known as the Blessed Virgin Mary, holds a special place of honor for Roman Catholics, Orthodox, and many Anglicans. Thomas Aquinas argued that God alone was to receive worship in the full sense (Greek, *latreia*), while the saints generally deserved veneration (*douleia*), with Mary worthy of something more than veneration and less than worship, which he termed *hyperdouleia*. In general this describes Mary's place within Roman Catholic and Orthodox Christianity. The two most common Catholic prayers may be the Our Father and the Hail Mary.

Early church writers seldom mentioned Mary, though occasionally they contrasted her obedience with the disobedience of Eve. By the fourth century, however, Christian writers were asserting that Mary was not only a virgin at the time of Jesus' birth but also a virgin throughout her life (Greek, *aeiparthenos,* or "ever virginal"). Protestants typically deny this, asserting that those called the brothers of Jesus in the New Testament were children born to Mary after the birth of Jesus. In 421 the Council of Ephesus assigned to Mary the title Theotokos, or Mother of God. Though some Christian leaders—for example, Nestorius—objected that the term might imply that Mary gave birth to God rather than to Christ, it became universal in Roman Catholic and Orthodox contexts. In 1854 the Catholic Church promulgated the dogma of Mary's Immaculate Conception and in 1950 her Bodily Assumption. According to the former, Mary, like Jesus, was conceived without the taint of original sin, while the latter asserts that Mary was assumed directly into heaven.

In Roman Catholicism sacramentals are physical objects or rituals that hold sacred meaning but do not convey grace in the theologically defined way of the sacraments. Included among the sacramentals are holy water (for baptism and sprinkling), holy oil (for anointing the baptized and the sick), crucifixes, pictures or statues of saints, medallions and scapulars (worn on the body for a person's spiritual good), relics of the saints, and water from Lourdes. While the number of Catholic sacraments is fixed at seven, there is no limit to the possible number of sacramentals. Orthodoxy also acknowledges sacramentals, though not in a theologically defined fashion.

HOLIDAYS AND FESTIVALS The earliest Jewish believers in Jesus worshiped in synagogues on Saturdays and gathered again on Sundays for Christian worship. By the second century the number of Jews in the church had declined, and worship on Sunday, understood as the day of Jesus' resurrection, displaced Saturday worship within the mainstream of Christianity. An exception was Ethiopian Orthodoxy, which kept a number of Jewish practices, including Saturday Sabbath observance.

Beginning with the Protestant Reformation, and especially in Britain, there was discussion regarding the Old Testament commandment to "remember the Sabbath day, and keep it holy" (Exodus 20:8). Some British Protestants were Sabbatarians who held that Sunday needed to be observed, like the Jewish Sabbath, as a day of complete rest. Their spiritual descendants, the Puritans, took the Sabbatarian viewpoint to New England and helped to establish Sunday blue laws. Some of the stricter Sabbatarians held that the Old Testament law was binding in its original form and that Saturday, rather than Sunday, was the appropriate day for worship. A small group of Seventh Day (Saturday-worshiping) Baptists emerged in England, followed by Seventh-day Adventists in the United States beginning in the 1840s.

The Christian liturgical year consists of both movable and fixed celebrations. The former include those whose calendar dates vary each year with the date of Easter (the celebration of Jesus' resurrection from the dead), while the latter always fall on the same date. Essentially there are two annual cycles, one connected with Easter, Christmas, and the life of Jesus, which is known as *temporale,* or the Proper of Seasons. A second cycle includes the festivals of the saints, which is known as *sanctorale,* or the Proper of Saints.

In 325 C.E., at the Council of Nicea, the date of Easter was fixed as the Sunday following the first full moon after the vernal equinox. Despite this decision, the difference between the Gregorian and Julian calendars resulted in a celebration of Easter on different days among Western and Eastern Christians. As the tradition developed, the period from Palm Sunday, commemorating Jesus' triumphal entry into Jerusalem, to Easter Sunday was set aside as Holy Week. Thursday through Saturday of Holy Week became known as triduum, and the Saturday Easter Vigil was an extended service for biblical lessons and the lighting of candles.

In early Christianity the Easter Vigil became the most appropriate time for baptizing new members, with a part of their preparation being a period of fasting that was gradually extended to 40 days, in imitation of Jesus' fast in the wilderness. Over time the fast was extended to include all Christians, with the church defining Lent as a period for self-denial and contrition for sins. Lent did not require a total fast, and in its modern Roman Catholic form it typically involves refraining from eating meat on Fridays from Ash Wednesday until Easter. In Orthodoxy there are differing dietary restrictions, forbidding milk and eggs as well as meat, and the total period of time was extended, since neither Saturdays nor Sundays were regarded as appropriate for fasting and Orthodoxy wished to keep the number of fast days at exactly 40. Orthodox Christians also fast during Advent and before certain major festivals.

By the second century the Christian Easter celebration initiated a 50-day period of rejoicing, the season of Pentecost. By the fourth century a celebration of Jesus' ascension into heaven occurred on the 40th day following Easter, and the sending of the Holy Spirit 10 days later, on the day of Pentecost, or Whitsunday.

In addition to Easter, the major annual festivals are Christmas (commemorating Jesus' birth) and Epiphany. In the early fourth century Roman Christians celebrated December 25 as the festival of Jesus' birth and the beginning of the year. This date coincided with the pagan solstice festival of Sol Invictus, yet December 25 may have been selected by adding nine months to March 25, already celebrated as the date of Jesus' conception. Orthodoxy also celebrates Jesus' nativity on December 25. In Eastern Christianity, perhaps as early as the second century, a festival of Epiphany was set on January 6 to commemorate Jesus' baptism and his revelation as a member of the Holy Trinity. In most Latin cultures Epiphany is a time for exchanging gifts, after the example of the Magi. In northern Europe and in English-speaking countries, the exchange of gifts takes place on December 25. Just as Lent prepares for Easter, Advent, usually lasting four weeks, is a season of preparation for Christmas.

The calendar of saint's days has never been uniform throughout Christendom. Lutherans and Anglicans have tended to commemorate only those saints who were biblical characters, and many Protestants have ceased from honoring saint's days altogether. At the time of the Reformation, Protestants emphasized Sunday worship as the chief feature of the Christian calendar. Some Protestants do not celebrate any events in the liturgical year, including Christmas and Easter. Yet secular holidays, like Mother's Day and the Fourth of July in the United States, have sometimes found their way into church celebrations as quasi-sacred events.

MODE OF DRESS No specifically Christian mode of dress is attested in the earliest centuries of the church, except perhaps for the white garb of those to be baptized. Today Christian worship rarely involves any special attire for its lay participants.

Clerical vestments developed during the fourth to ninth centuries, and their style was based on ordinary secular clothes worn in antiquity. Among traditional vestments are the surplice and alb (white garments), stole, chasuble and tunicle (outer cloaks), and, for bishops, sandals, a miter, a pallium, and gloves. The crosier

is a crook-shaped staff carried by bishops and sometimes by abbots and abbesses (heads of religious communities). Another mark of the Christian minister is the clerical collar, a black band with a white rectangle in front that is worn around the neck. Roman Catholic cardinals wear distinctive red vestments, and popes formerly wore a tiara, a custom abolished in the 1960s. Orthodox priests and bishops have beards—since Jesus and the apostles are traditionally shown this way—and often wear black clothing and pectoral crosses (suspended by a chain or cord around the neck).

Lutherans and Anglicans have kept some of the Catholic clerical vestments, while many Protestant ministers dress in businessmen's suits or in everyday garb. Reformed ministers may wear a black gown and a variant of the clerical collar known as "Geneva tabs." As women have entered into the ordained ministry, they have adapted vestments for their use.

DIETARY PRACTICES The New Testament states that Jesus "declared all foods clean" (Mark 7:19). Paul's letters condemn those who "demand abstinence from foods" and add that "everything created by God is good, and nothing is to be rejected" (I Timothy 4:4–5). While some early followers of Jesus continued to follow the Jewish dietary laws (Acts 15), the practice faded as Gentile Christianity grew.

The early Christians celebrated the Eucharist in the context of a complete meal, known as an agape, or "love feast." As time passed, the Eucharist involved diminishing portions of bread and wine, and by the fifth or sixth century its connection with a full meal had faded. The church continued to provide charity meals for the poor, which had been one of the functions of the agape. In modern times church potlucks and soup kitchens show some analogy to the ancient agape, though usually without any link to the Eucharist.

Fasting may be more distinctive to Christianity than dietary customs. It can involve refraining from all food and drink (an absolute fast), forgoing all food but not fluids, or refraining from certain kinds of food or drink (for example, meat). The second-century *Didache* ("Teaching") indicates that the earliest Christians fasted on Wednesdays and Fridays. During the course of history, fasting developed in two directions. Some Christians came to fast according to a church calendar, especially during Lent, while others fasted at times and in ways they chose. Monastic communities have sometimes practiced fasting as a way of life. Some fourth-century monks, for example, prayed and fasted each day until the ninth hour (3 P.M.), at which time they ate their first meal. Others have rejected meat or rich foods such as butter, oil, wine, or spicy cuisine. Some modern groups have taught that a restricted or bland diet is conducive to holy living. The nineteenth-century American prophetess Ellen White sought simple food for her followers, and her disciple John Harvey Kellogg invented cornflakes.

Fasting is common among contemporary Pentecostal and charismatic Christians, who view the practice, combined with fervent prayer, as a means of releasing spiritual power and overcoming obstacles. Pentecostals may enter into prolonged fasts for up to 40 days, in imitation of Jesus, Moses, and Elijah. Woon Mong Ra (born in 1914) trained his Korean followers to withdraw to a "prayer mountain" and fast for weeks at a time, and he reported that dramatic conversions, healings, and exorcisms followed.

RITUALS Christianity is expressed in rituals as much as in theology or ethics. Rituals include the sacraments of the church and other simple and widespread actions. One is signing, or making the sign of the cross. The sign may have been used originally during baptism and then extended to other situations and modified to include the torso rather than the forehead alone. Orthodox Christians make the horizontal portion of the sign with a right to left movement, and Roman Catholics left to right. Signing occurs also among Anglicans and Lutherans.

Another simple ritual is closing the eyes and folding the hands for prayer. Pentecostals may stand during worship services and raise their hands into the air while singing and praying. The acts of kneeling or genuflecting (among Roman Catholics), bowing or prostrating (among Orthodox), processing and recessing in worship, pronouncing written prayers in unison, sprinkling holy water, anointing with oil, wearing a crucifix or medal that has been blessed, and dancing in worship are all Christian rituals. Evangelicals use an "altar call" for dedication or rededication to Christ, while Pentecostals may lay hands on a person during prayer and invoke God for healing, the casting out of demons, or the "baptism in the Holy Spirit." Certain Protestant groups practice foot washing. Christian rituals thus include actions that are not officially sacraments and may not have received much theological scrutiny or sanction.

A single ritual often has multiple meanings, and participants may perceive one meaning but not another. An infant baptism, for example, signifies the gift of divine grace, the child's incorporation into the church, a pledge by parents to raise the child in the faith, and a pledge by godparents and others to aid the parents. None of the major Christian rituals is limited to a single meaning.

Christians describe their leading rituals under the term "sacraments," a word used by the ancient Romans to refer to a sacred pledge of fidelity, later adapted by Tertullian to denote baptism. During the first centuries of Christianity, the term had a broad meaning and could be used for any church ritual or the symbolic elements it contained. For example, Pope Innocent I referred to both the eucharistic bread and wine and the consecrated oil as sacraments. Augustine defined a sacrament simply as "a sign of something sacred." It was not until the Middle Ages that theologians came to distinguish between sacraments and sacramentals, the former referring to rituals that were deemed to have spiritual effects by virtue of their proper performance (Latin, *ex opere operato*; "through the act performed") and the latter to rituals that transmitted grace in less specific ways. Thus, the Eucharist counted as a sacrament, while the sprinkling of holy water was a sacramental. Peter Lombard and, following him, Thomas Aquinas defined the church's sacraments as seven in number (which Orthodox Christians follow Roman Catholics in acknowledging): baptism, confirmation, penance (reconciliation), the Eucharist, holy orders (ordination), matrimony, and extreme unction (anointing of the sick).

The seven sacraments commemorate major life transitions (baptism after birth, and anointing and Eucharist before death), allow the restoration of a person who has sinned (penance), set people apart for one another (marriage), and set others apart for Christian service (ordination). The Eucharist plays an integral role by sustaining fellowship with God and the church. Taken together, the seven sacraments form a comprehensive system and make Roman Catholicism a sacramental community.

During the Middle Ages, Roman Catholicism came to assert that a "sacrifice of the Mass" takes place in the eucharistic liturgy and that this sacrifice is beneficial for both the living and the dead. Clergy began to offer masses for the dead. Catholicism also taught that the bread and wine of the Eucharist become the body and blood of Christ at the time of their consecration by the priest. This doctrine, proposed in the early Middle Ages and officially defined at the Fourth Lateran Council in 1215, is known as "transubstantiation" and is central to Catholic life and thought. Orthodox Christianity holds to Christ's real presence in the consecrated bread and wine but does not insist on the term "transubstantiation." Orthodoxy teaches that the change in the elements occurs at the epiclesis, or invocation of the Holy Spirit in the liturgy. In Catholicism the belief in transubstantiation gave rise to the customs of genuflection (bending one knee before the altar), to kneeling during the Mass as a sign of respect for Christ's body and blood, and to eucharistic adoration, wherein the consecrated bread is set aside in a tabernacle, or receptacle, before which believers engage in prayers and vigils.

Beginning with Martin Luther, Protestants have reacted against the alleged superstitions connected with the medieval sacraments. Many Protestants are suspicious of the idea that the church transmits grace through its rituals and believe that correct belief, knowledge of the Bible, and individual faith and sincerity toward God matter more. The Protestant tendency is to deny the label "sacrament" to all practices not directly supported by the Bible. On this basis Protestants generally affirm only baptism and the Eucharist, which were directly sanctioned by Jesus in the New Testament. Anglicans sometimes acknowledge the other five sacraments but see them as instituted by the church rather than by Christ. Baptists and nondenominational Protestants usually reject the term "sacrament," since it signifies a practice that transmits grace, and substitute the term "ordinance." More radical still are the Society of Friends (Quakers) and the Salvation Army, which reject baptism and the Eucharist and for whom spiritual life is an inward reality disconnected from outward actions. In some ways, though not labeled as such, the Bible itself is a central sacrament for Protestants. Following Augustine, Luther judged that the bread and wine of the Eucharist are "visible words," and he asserted that ritual actions carry their meaning only in the context of the spoken liturgy, or preached word of God.

Other Christian rituals include divine healing (through prayer); exorcism, or the casting out of demons; pilgrimages to holy sites; the practice of making vows or offerings to God, Jesus, Mary, or a saint in the hope of a blessing to be given or in response to a blessing received; and practices connected with saint's days and the Virgin Mary. These vary from region to region in the Roman Catholic and Orthodox traditions.

RITES OF PASSAGE The fundamental Christian ritual of initiation is baptism, which marks the transition from unbelief to faith, from sin to repentance, from death to life, and from the world to the church. Almost all Christian groups agree on its centrality. From an early period the ritual was performed with water and the three-fold formula "in the name of the Father and of the Son and of the Holy Spirit" (Matthew 28:19). In the Acts of the Apostles, there are references to baptism "in the name of Jesus," which has led some Pentecostals to use only Jesu's name. With this exception, baptism is universally performed in the name of the Trinity.

Many disputed issues surround baptism. One concerns the mode—that is, whether the proper procedure involves the sprinkling of water, pouring, or full immersion. The New Testament provides no detailed description of the ritual, and early church teaching seems flexible on the matter. In modern times Baptists and certain revivalistic groups have been concerned with the issue, with some regarding baptism as invalid unless performed by full immersion.

An especially divisive issue is whether infants can receive baptism. Roman Catholicism, Orthodoxy, Anglicanism, and many traditional Protestant groups practice infant baptism, while Baptists, nondenominational Christians, and Pentecostals prefer adult, or "believer's," baptism. They argue that New Testament baptism required a profession of faith, which an infant cannot supply. Catholics, the Orthodox, and some Anglicans teach that baptism confers grace ("baptismal regeneration") apart from any conscious response to God. Traditional Catholic theology asserted that baptism is necessary to remove the guilt of original sin and that unbaptized persons cannot therefore be saved. Luther defended infant baptism by appealing to an infant faith implicit in the child, and he also invoked the parent's or church's faith as standing in for the recipient's. Calvinists, including Presbyterians, think of the church as a covenant community in which baptism is an outward mark of belonging though not a guarantee of final salvation. Such Protestants link baptism to faith and yet allow for the baptism of infants.

Another issue concerns the validity of a prior baptism when a person moves from one Christian group to another. Following Augustine, Roman Catholicism holds that all baptisms done in the name of the Holy Trinity are valid if performed with genuine intent. Thus, a Protestant baptized as an infant is not rebaptized. Protestants, however, have mixed views on the matter. Some rebaptize members who come from Catholicism, Orthodoxy, or even from other Protestant groups, while others do not. Orthodoxy generally opposes such rebaptisms. Baptists and others who do not recognize the validity of infant baptisms tend to perform adult rebaptisms.

During the first several centuries Christians initiated new members, who were adults, through a process of catechesis (instruction in the faith) followed by a period of fasting, a ritual of exorcism, and baptism, together with an anointing with oil (chrismation) and the laying on of hands. In later centuries the ritual of anointing and the laying on of hands became separated from baptism, and from the 400s the Roman Catholic church began to teach that only bishops could perform the postbaptismal anointing. Thus, confirmation, originally part of the baptism ritual, became a separate sacrament. By contrast, Orthodoxy administers an anointing with oil and a first Communion to an infant at the time of baptism. Those Protestants who practice confirmation typically focus on doctrinal instruction in the faith for teenagers, while Catholics offer confirmation in late childhood.

In addition to baptism and confirmation, rituals of initiation and rites of passage in Christianity include marriage customs, in all their variety; funeral practices; ceremonies of ordination to the priesthood or ministry; the Catholic priest's first Mass or the Protestant minister's first sermon; the rituals for entering a religious order, such as the 30-day retreat practiced by the Jesuits; and the vows for the monastic life or for religious sisters.

MEMBERSHIP The Gospels say that Jesus commanded his followers to carry on his mission, most famously in the words of the "Great Commission": "All authority in heaven and on earth has been given to me. Go therefore and make disciples of all nations, baptizing them in the name of the Father and of the Son and of the Holy Spirit, and teaching them to obey everything that I have commanded you" (Matthew 28:18–20). Thus, the call to spread the gospel is central to Christianity. Some writers distinguish evangelism from missions. The former denotes any Christian sharing the good news, while the latter involves a more deliberate effort to establish new churches in cultures or regions without Christians. However the terms are defined, the Christian act of bearing witness flows from the conviction that Jesus is Savior and that salvation comes through him.

The expansion of Christianity from its homeland in Palestine to the rest of the world has been a continual process of translation. Linguists have rendered the Bible into thousands of languages, each with a different word for God and a different set of cultural and religious assumptions. Christianity is thus a religion of cultural adaptation, and the faith must be "incarnated" in each new setting. For the message about Jesus to be credible, however, there must be actions as well as words. Francis of Assisi reportedly said to "preach the gospel always and use words when necessary." In missionary work Roman Catholics stress tangible acts of service and compassion for non-Christians, while Protestants tend to emphasize preaching, conversation, and other verbal methods of evangelism. Yet exemplary missionaries throughout history have worked in both ways. Catholic and Protestant missionaries, for example, established many of the first hospitals and orphanages in Africa and Asia.

Throughout history missionaries went into new territories because they were convinced that non-Christians were doomed to hell. The early church writer Cyprian coined the phrase *extra ecclesiam nulla salus* (there is no salvation outside the church). Some modern Christians have rejected this exclusivist position, that only those who consciously turn to Christ are saved, in favor of an inclusivist position, that some are saved by Christ without knowing him by name. The twentieth-century Roman Catholic theologian Karl Rahner argued that faithful members of non-Christian religions may be "anonymous Christians," a view that has been widespread in Catholicism since the Second Vatican Council. A related idea is that evangelism should be preceded by dialogue with non-Christians, in which a Christian listens before speaking. More radical is the pluralist position that all religions lead to salvation and to the same ultimate reality, or God, and according to this view, conversion should be replaced by interreligious dialogue.

RELIGIOUS TOLERANCE The record of Christianity in allowing people to follow their religious beliefs without external constraint is mixed. The Roman Empire allowed people to continue worshiping ancestral gods, while insisting that all groups acknowledge the divinity of the Caesars. Most Christians refused to make even a token gesture on behalf of Caesar and so were harassed or killed. The lines of division were equally apparent in early Christian attitudes toward heretics. Those who broke from the main body of Christians were no longer acknowledged as fellow believers, and a chief concern in the first centuries lay in establishing the doctrines and practices that distinguished orthodoxy from heresy. While Christians lacked political power, there was no question of their persecuting non-Christians, though Christians could remove heretics from their worshiping communities.

After Constantine's conversion paganism became increasingly unpopular. In 415 the pagan philosopher Hypatia was executed by a Christian lynch mob in Alexandria. In 529 the emperor Justinian closed the philosophical academies in Athens and forced pagans to accept baptism. Augustine encouraged coercive policies when he interpreted the biblical phrase *compelle intrare* ("compel them to come in"; Luke 14:23) to mean that force was a legitimate means for bringing people into communion with the true church. According to the theory of two swords, the clergy could not coerce heretics and pagans, but since the state was charged with maintaining true religion, heretics apprehended by the church could be turned over to the state for punishment. This was the theory underlying the papal and Spanish inquisitions (authorized in 1231 and 1478, respectively), which allowed hearsay evidence, torture, and forced confessions and so resulted in the conviction of many innocent persons. Stimulated by the 1487 book *Malleus Maleficarum* ("Hammer of Witches"), the so-called witch craze of the 1500s and 1600s brought as many as 110,000 to trial, and perhaps 60,000 were executed.

Among Protestants, John Calvin consented to the execution of the anti-Trinitarian Michael Servetus in 1553, and New England clergy applied the death penalty to Quakers in the early 1600s and during the 1692 Salem witch trials. Luther justified his opposition to the papacy when he declared in 1521 that "my conscience is captive to the Word of God," yet neither he nor most Protestants were ready to allow others to follow their own consciences. When the Pilgrims went to America in 1619, they went not for freedom of religion but for freedom to practice their own religion. Roger Williams (c. 1604–83) and Anne Hutchinson were both ejected from Massachusetts in the 1630s for holding unacceptable theological views. Williams's *The Bloody Tenent of Persecution* (1644) was an eloquent plea for religious liberty.

As a result of the Reformation, Protestant countries passed laws against Catholics and Catholic nations against Protestants. In England the Test Act (1673) required all officeholders to renounce Roman Catholic beliefs, and it remained in force until 1829. In 1685 King Louis XIV of France revoked the Edict of Nantes,

which since 1598 had provided for the toleration of Protestants, and the result was a mass exodus.

Among the earliest proponents of church-state separation and freedom of conscience were the Radical Reformers of the early 1500s. Some argue that they advocated religious freedom simply so that they themselves would not be persecuted, but in fact their entire conception of a voluntary rather than state-subsidized church required that religious practice be uncoerced. The government might enforce outward obedience through the threat of punishment, they argued, yet this would hardly make anyone more devout. Today their arguments seem so self-evident that it is difficult to understand the perspective of medieval and early modern Christians, who viewed heresy as a moral and spiritual plague and thought that the death of heretics was necessary for the good of society.

In many ways, however, it was the Enlightenment rather than Roman Catholic or Protestant theology that did the most to promote the ideal of religious tolerance. Secular thinkers regarded the religious wars of the 1500s and 1600s with horror and argued that the state needed to rest on a nonreligious and nonsectarian foundation. Some founders of the United States, such as Benjamin Franklin and Thomas Jefferson, were Enlightenment deists rather than traditional Christians, and the U.S. constitution provided for freedom of religion and the nonestablishment of any church. In Europe during the early 1800s, Jews, who were the largest non-Christian minority in most regions, were gradually given citizenship rights that had formerly been limited to Christians.

The principle of church-state separation, though growing in influence throughout the 1800s, provoked a backlash in Roman Catholicism. In the *Syllabus of Errors* (1864), Pope Pius IX rejected the principles of freedom of religion and of the press and favored a state-sponsored church. The "Americanist" controversy, provoked by Pope Leo XIII's *Testem Benevolentiae* (1899; "Witness to Good Will"), involved similar ideas. Yet the Second Vatican Council, which explicitly affirmed freedom of conscience, has revised earlier Catholic teaching, and many nations in Europe and Latin America that formerly declared Roman Catholicism to be the national church have amended their constitutions.

SOCIAL JUSTICE Christian attitudes toward social issues follow from the basic themes of the Hebrew and Judaic tradition. The God of the Hebrews was not tribal but rather a universal deity. The Bible declares God to be just and compassionate toward all humanity, and the Hebrews had to exhibit the same traits. Thus, Christianity carried over from Judaism a transcendent God and social ideal. The early church brought together people from widely separated social classes, including slaves, noblemen, barbarians, highborn women, and Jews. Equally surprising to pagans was Christian's compassion. They raised abandoned infants as their own, fed the poor, and attended the sick. Christian inclusiveness and compassion derived not only from Judaism but also from the example of Jesus, who associated with disreputable people in his society and so set a pattern for ministry to outcasts. His ministry touched women as well as men, and, contrary to the rabbinical customs of the time, he allowed women to be his pupils.

In the fifth century Patrick, a former slave, became one of the first persons in history to condemn slavery in principle. Early and medieval monasticism included service to the community as practiced by Benedictines, Dominicans, Franciscans, and Jesuits. Many female religious orders, including the Poor Clares, Sisters of Mercy, and Sisters of Charity, have been almost exclusively oriented toward serving the needy. The early Protestants also demonstrated a concern for social needs. During the 1540s and 1550s, John Calvin created a social welfare system in Geneva that cared for the poor and needy. The Radical Reformers, though not institution builders, were generous toward outsiders, and to the present day the Mennonite Central Committee sends emergency workers all over the globe. Like the Mennonites, George Fox (1624–91) and his followers (Quakers) were known for their pacifism, and the Quakers have strenuously worked toward the nonviolent resolution of conflicts. The Pietist movement in Germany, led by August Francke in the early 1700s, had a strong bent toward social welfare. The Moravians, led by Count Nicholas Zinzendorf (1700–60), were radical Pietists who lived in community, prayed in shifts 24 hours a day, and, in one case, allowed themselves to be sold into slavery so that they could serve among Caribbean slaves.

The evangelical revivals of the 1700s brought a new concern for social issues. John Wesley's movement brought many working-class people into the church, and in time Methodism became an engine of social reform. Historically the British Labour Party found inspiration and support in Methodism, which emerged outside the ruling class and voiced the concerns of ordinary people.

Evangelicals like William Wilberforce led in the campaign to end the slave trade and make slavery illegal. In 1861 William Booth (1829–1912) and Catherine Booth (1829–90) founded the Salvation Army to meet the needs of the urban poor by providing "soap, soup, and salvation." In the United States the separation of church and state led in the 1800s to the formation of many voluntary societies devoted to such causes as temperance, the abolition of slavery, observance of the Sabbath, and foreign missions. The revivalist Charles Finney (1792–1875) and Harriet Beecher Stowe (1811–96), the novelist daughter of a revivalist, did much to initiate the abolitionist movement. After the Civil War a new generation of reformers lobbied for labor reforms and woman suffrage. American Protestant women, meeting in ladie's guilds or church auxiliaries, played a growing role in social reform movements. In Germany the Innere Mission sought prison reform and better provision for the homeless and mentally deficient.

In his encyclical *Rerum Novarum* (1891), Pope Leo XIII laid the foundation for more than a century of Roman Catholic social teaching. Though the Catholic Church had earlier shown ambivalence toward labor groups, this document marked a new era in which the church identified with the concerns of workers. *Rerum Novarum* sought a middle way between unregulated capitalism and state-sponsored socialism. Later encyclicals by Pope Pius XI and Pope John Paul II brought further refinements to this approach. The Catholic Worker movement of Dorothy Day (1897–1980) and Peter Maurin (1877–1949) gave concrete expression to the church's concern for the urban poor. Thomas Merton (1915–68), Philip Berrigan (1923–2002), and Daniel Berrigan (born in 1921) were critics of U.S. intervention in Vietnam, and the Berrigan brothers were imprisoned for destroying draft records and for other acts of civil disobedience.

Among Protestants the twentieth century brought division. Modernists, who were socially progressive and theologically nontraditional, felt increasingly estranged from conservatives, who after 1910 became known as "fundamentalists." Throughout the 1800s conservatives had been active in social causes, but by the early 1900s such social activism was associated with the Social Gospel movement of Walter Rauschenbusch (1861–1918) and theological modernism. Beginning in the 1970s, however, conservative Protestants in the United States began to reenter the field of social activism in greater numbers. Since the 1960s liberation theology has brought a radical rethinking of Christian theology from the standpoint of God's special concern for the poor.

SOCIAL ASPECTS The cultural impact of Christianity becomes conspicuous when it is set against the backdrop of Greco-Roman society. Slaves and women had little status, and most people regarded life as expendable. Individuals had value only to the extent that they contributed to the greater good of the family and the state. Christianity exhibited a strikingly different attitude. Because God loved all individuals, Christians opposed abortion, infanticide, child abandonment, and the gladiatorial games. They maintained a moral standard of chastity outside marriage and faithfulness within, though some early Christian councils upheld a more stringent law for women than for men. Sex belonged in married life and was not for public display.

Thus, Christian attitudes toward sex, marriage, and the family had pronounced effects in the lives of women. The exhortation for husbands to "love your wives" (Ephesians 5:25) was unknown in the Greco-Roman world. Christianity gave men ideals, even if they did not always live up to them. In disapproving of extramarital sex, spousal neglect, divorce, polygamy, and power mongering, Christianity did much to create a new ideal of domestic respect and familial harmony.

It is clear from the biblical stories concerning Jesus that he respectfully addressed women who were social outcastes and drew many female followers. Paul referred to Phoebe as a "deacon" (Romans 16:1), or officeholder in the church, and designated Euodia and Syntyche as his "co-workers" (Philippians 4:2–3). Women's legal rights changed because of Christian influence. Greek and Roman women had little personal freedom. They could not divorce their husbands and could not receive an inheritance unless they were under *manus* (a man's control). Beginning in the 400s, however, wives under Roman law were able to divorce an unfaithful husband. Polygamy slowly disappeared in Christian regions, and women also received inheritance rights.

In modern times Christians have opposed many of the egregious abuses of women around the world. Christian principles led the British authorities in 1829 to ban the Indian practice of suttee, the burning alive of widows at their husband's funerals. Foot binding, which caused pain and often led to infection or amputation, was outlawed in China in 1912, with Christian missionaries leading the opposition. Neither the giving of child brides nor female genital mutilation (clitoridecto-

my) has endured in regions with a strong Christian influence. Those who led the campaign for woman suffrage in the United States included many, like Frances Willard, who began as social activists in churches, and the civil rights struggle of the 1960s was rooted in the Christian church.

CONTROVERSIAL ISSUES Jesus condemned divorce as well as the lustful attitudes that lead husbands and wives to reject their spouses to marry someone else (Matthew 5:27–32; Mark 10:1–12). Both Jesus and Paul appealed to the statement in Genesis that "they become one flesh" (2:24), interpreting this to mean that a husband and wife enter into an indissoluble unity. Certain New Testament texts intimate, however, that divorce might be allowed in the case of adultery (Matthew 5:32) and perhaps if willful desertion has occurred, especially on the part of an unbelieving spouse (I Corinthians 7:15). Martin Luther suggested that impotence might be grounds for divorce. In modern times Christian pastors and counselors have discussed whether physical or verbal abuse, substance addiction, or simple marital unhappiness is a basis for divorce.

Today many Christian churches agree that at least some divorces are justified and allow divorced members to remarry with the church's blessing. Orthodoxy, for instance, allows remarriage but uses a more subdued ceremony than for a first marriage. Evangelical Protestants and Pentecostals tend to oppose divorce. The Roman Catholic Church does not acknowledge the legitimacy of divorce but insists that a physical separation of spouses, without the right to remarry in the church, is all that can be offered. On the other hand, it allows for annulment, which declares that an alleged marriage has no sacramental validity.

Jesus' teaching refers to a "husband" and "wife" in the singular, and references to Genesis also make it clear that monogamy rather than polygamy is understood as normative. Paul seems to have excluded polygamists from leadership in churches (Titus 1:6). As Christianity became dominant, many nations passed laws forbidding polygamy. The question reemerged during the nineteenth and twentieth centuries, especially in Africa, where before contact with Christianity there had been a strong tradition of multiple wives for one husband. Many Western missionaries excluded polygamous households from the full benefits of church membership, and if they wished to be baptized, polygamists sometimes had to separate from all but one spouse.

Glossary

Advent period of four weeks, beginning four Sundays before Christmas, sometimes observed with fasting and prayer

Anglicanism Church of England, which originated in King Henry VIII's break with Rome in 1534, and those churches that developed from it, including the Episcopal Church in the United States; with a wide spectrum of doctrines and practices, it is sometimes called a "middle way" between Roman Catholicism and Protestantism

Apocrypha books of the Old Testament included in the Septuagint (Greek translation used by early Christians) and Catholic (including the Latin Vulgate) versions of the Bible but not in Protestant or modern Jewish editions

Atonement doctrine that the death of Jesus is the basis for human salvation

baptism sacrament practiced by Christians in which the sprinkling, pouring of, or immersion in water is a sign of admission to the faith community

casuistry type of moral reasoning based on the examination of specific cases

catechesis formal instruction in the faith

charismatics major expression of Christianity that includes those who affirm the gifts of the Holy Spirit but who are not affiliated with Pentecostal denominations

chrismation anointing with oil

conciliar governance through councils of bishops

confirmation sacrament marking membership in a church

congregationalism self-governance by a local congregation

Epiphany January 6, a celebration of the coming of the Magi and, in Orthodoxy, of the baptism of Jesus

eschatology doctrine concerning the end of the world, including the Second Coming of Christ, God's judgment, heaven, and hell

Eucharist (Communion; Lord's Supper) sacrament practiced by Christians in which bread and wine become (in Roman Catholicism and Orthodoxy) or stand for (in Protestantism) the body and blood of Christ

---

Some African Initiated Churches defend polygamy on the precedents offered by such Old Testament patriarchs as Abraham.

Paul used Genesis 2:24 as the basis for sexual ethics. Because sex creates a bond of "one flesh" between the partners, it is not to be pursued outside a marriage covenant (I Corinthians 6:12–20). Many societies throughout the world have been tolerant of sexual activity between unmarried persons, but Christianity regards this as a sin almost as serious as adultery. Homosexual practice is debated in some Christian churches, but it is hard to find biblical texts or Christian writings before the late 1900s that favor it. Some argue that the church might reconsider the issue, however, just as it has its stance on slavery and women's rights.

The first imperative given in the Bible is to "be fruitful and multiply" (Genesis I:28), and some people argue that the bearing of offspring is an inherent part of God's purpose for sexuality. Roman Catholic teach-

ing, made explicit in the encyclical *Humanae Vitae* (1968; "Of Human Life"), holds that it is sinful to interfere with the process of conception by means of artificial birth control. Not only is it wrong to destroy an actual life through abortion but it is also wrong to prevent life from coming into existence through contraception. Catholic teaching allows for "natural family planning," which restricts sexual intercourse to the monthly periods when a woman is infertile and unlikely to conceive. In the decades since *Humanae Vitae,* however, many Catholics in developed nations have ignored the official church ban on contraception. Protestants generally accept the legitimacy of contraception for married couples, while the Orthodox attitude has been ambivalent.

Political attitudes vary among Christians. In *Christ and Culture* H. Richard Niebuhr concluded that Christians have sometimes pulled away from secular society ("Christ against culture"), sought to create a synthesis of church and society ("Christ of culture"), or applied

evangelicalism movement that emphasizes the authority of the Scriptures, salvation by faith, and individual experience over ritual

extreme unction sacrament; blessing of the sick

grace unmerited gift from God for human salvation

Lent period of 40 days from Ash Wednesday to Easter, often marked by fasting and prayer

matrimony sacrament; the joining of a man and woman in marriage

Messiah the "anointed one," Jesus

ordination sacrament, in which a person is invested with religious authority or takes holy orders

Orthodoxy one of the main branches of Christianity, with a lineage that derives from the first-century apostolic churches; historically centered in Constantinople (Istanbul), it includes a number of autonomous national churches

Pentecost seventh Sunday after Easter, commemorating the descent of the Holy Spirit on the apostles

Pentecostalism movement that emphasizes grace, expressive worship, evangelism, and spiritual gifts such as speaking in tongues and healing

Petrine primacy view that, as the successor to Peter, the bishop of Rome (pope) is supreme

presbyterianism governance by a presbytery, an assembly of local clergy and lay representatives

Protestantism one of the main branches of Christianity, originating in the sixteenth-century Reformation; rejecting the authority of the pope, it emphasized the role of grace and the authority of the Scriptures

reconciliation sacrament; the confession of and absolution from sin

Roman Catholicism one of the main branches of Christianity, tracing its origins to the apostle Peter; centered in Rome, it tends to be uniform in organization, doctrines, and rituals

sacrament any rite thought to have originated with or to have been sanctioned by Jesus as a sign of grace

sacramental devotional action or object

salvation deliverance from sin and its consequences

Trinity God as consisting of three persons-the Father, Son, and Holy Spirit

Uniate any group observing Eastern rites but recognizing the authority of the pope

Christian principles to reform society ("Christ transforming culture"). When the church has existed as a small countercultural group—the early Christians, the Radical Reformers of the 1500s, or modern communes—it has often ignored politics. When the church has been culturally dominant, as with Roman Catholicism or Orthodoxy, it has generally attempted to incorporate Christian principles into political life. When the church has been an expanding social force, as with Puritanism, it has sought to transform society, sometimes with the aim of achieving an ideal Christian community on earth.

Those who hold the ideal of "Christ against culture" are often pacifists, rejecting all use of violence. Quakers, Mennonites, Amish, and some Roman Catholics share this viewpoint. The Sermon on the Mount, in which Jesus commands his followers to turn the other cheek (Matthew 5:39), is cited in favor of pacifism. Yet most Christians hold that force is legitimate under spe-

cific situations, explained in terms of the just-war theory. For a war to be just, there must be a genuine effort to find peaceful means of resolving the conflict, the cause itself must be just and not for selfish ends, a distinction must be maintained between combatants and noncombatants, and the force used must be proportionate to the situation. Just-war proponents cite Paul's teaching that the political state is given a "sword" to protect the innocent (Romans 13:1–4).

In distinction to the just-war theory is the idea of a holy war, a conflict of the righteous against the wicked inaugurated by God himself. While certain Old Testament passages speak of God commanding the Israelites to destroy the Canaanites, the New Testament contains nothing of the kind. Instead, Jesus tells Peter, "Put your sword back into its place; for all who take the sword will perish by the sword" (Matthew 26:52). Although the idea of holy war is not commonplace in Christianity, it appeared in the medieval Crusades, in the sixteenth-century radical Thomas Muentzer, and among white European colonists in New England, Latin America, and South Africa who sought to justify their actions against indigenous peoples.

CULTURAL IMPACT The limited powers of government and the rights of the individual are basic principles in Judeo-Christian civilization. The Israelites considered their kings as subject to a higher law (Deuteronomy 17:14–20). They concerned themselves with offenses against people, and crimes committed against the lower classes were punished. Thus, the notion of the equality of all persons under the law had its roots in ancient Israel, and Christianity carried this tradition into the medieval and modern period. For example, the Magna Carta of 1215, which received strong endorsement from the head of the English church, laid the foundation for individual rights in England and, indirectly, for the U.S. Constitution and Bill of Rights, which itself has been a model for other nation-states.

Whereas the Greeks and Romans regarded manual labor as fit only for slaves, the early Christians, who often arose from the lower classes, had a positive attitude toward such work. Jesus, a carpenter before he began his ministry, served as a role model. Thus, Christianity has had the effect of giving dignity to ordinary work. During the Reformation, Martin Luther and John Calvin insisted that ordinary lay Christians—in distinction from priests, monks, and nuns—had a "vocation," or "calling," to serve God in their everyday activities. This teaching had a powerful effect in promoting economic development, with the sociologist Max Weber arguing in *The Protestant Ethic and the Spirit of Capitalism* (1905) that Calvinistic Protestantism laid the foundation for modern capitalism.

The Romans spoke of *liberalitas* (generosity) as something given to impress others and win favors in return. Christian *caritas* (charity), however, was given to those in need without concern for repayment. Early Christians had a fund to support widows, the disabled, orphans, the sick, and prisoners and to provide for burials for the poor and the release of slaves. When plagues broke out, Christians cared for the sick in peril to their own health. In the late 300s Christians founded the *nosocomia*, probably the first institutions to provide ongoing care for the sick in the general populace. The church also founded orphanages, houses for travelers, institutions for the blind, and the first homes for the aged (*gerontocomia*). By the end of the thirteenth century, the

Order of the Holy Ghost had opened more than 800 orphanages, and by the mid-1500s some 37,000 Benedictine monasteries cared for the sick. The Young Men's Christian Association (YMCA), founded in 1844 in London, provided aid in urban regions, as did the Salvation Army of William and Catherine Booth. Anthony Ashley Cooper, Lord Shaftesbury, a devout Christian and member of Parliament, was instrumental in the Factory Act of 1833, which protected children from economic exploitation. In the nineteenth century Christian compassion motivated Dorothea Dix, who led a movement to improve care for the mentally ill; Florence Nightingale and Clara Barton, important figures in the field of nursing; and Jean Henry Dunant, who founded the International Red Cross.

As early as the second century, Christians founded catechetical schools for new converts, which may have been the first to teach both sexes in the same setting. From the beginning Christian education was not limited to the upper classes, as was customary in Greco-Roman civilization. During the ninth and tenth centuries, monks kept alive the traditions of classical learning by recopying texts that would otherwise have vanished. The monastic leader Benedict has been called the "the godfather of libraries," and his Benedictines collected and loaned books. From the fourth to the tenth centuries, cathedral schools offered instruction in the seven liberal arts: the trivium (grammar, rhetoric, and logic) and the quadrivium (arithmetic, music, geometry, and astronomy). While these schools were primarily for the clergy, they admitted others as well. Girls were educated in monasteries and nunneries.

It can be argued that the European university emerged out of the monasteries. During the medieval period the Christian character of the universities—Paris, Bologna, Salamanca, Oxford, Cambridge, and others—was unmistakable. In the 1500s and 1600s Protestanism was a religion of the book, and the desire to prepare learned ministers led to the founding of new institutions in Europe (Tübingen, Heidelberg, and Leiden) and America (Harvard, Yale, and Princeton). Protestants believed in universal education, and Martin Luther seems to have been the first modern author to urge compulsory school attendance. In 1837 Friedrich Froebel, son of a Lutheran pastor, began the first kindergarten in Europe. A number of Christians, including Thomas Gallaudet and Louis Braille, led in the education of the deaf and the blind. With the exception of the University of Pennsylvania, every college founded in America before the

Revolutionary War began through the effort of a Christian church. Churches established more than 90 percent of all U.S. colleges founded before the Civil War.

The early Christians wrote doctrinal, moral, and apologetic works. By the fourth century they had begun to exhibit a new confidence, as shown in Jerome's *On Illustrious Men* (393), which argued that Christian orators, philosophers, and writers could rival the best that paganism had to offer. Augustine's *City of God* (426) argued that Christians could pursue the life of the mind as a form of service to God. Major works that are distinctly Christian include Alcuin's *Rhetoric and Virtue* (790s); Dante's *Divine Comedy* (c. 1321); Geoffrey Chaucer's *Canterbury Tales* (1380s); Desiderius Erasmus's *In Praise of Folly* (1511); the seventeenth-century Metaphysical poetry of John Donne and George Herbert; John Milton's *Paradise Lost* (1667), perhaps the greatest poem in the English language; Blaise Pascal's *Pensées* (1670); John Bunyan's *The Pilgrim's Progress* (1678); Charles Dicken'ss *A Christmas Carol* (1843); Harriet Beecher Stowe's *Uncle Tom's Cabin* (1852); Fyodor Dostoyevsky's *The Brothers Karamazov* (1880); *Four Quartets* (1943) and other poetry and prose by T.S. Eliot; J.R.R. Tolkien's *The Lord of the Rings* (1954–55); C.S. Lewis's *The Screwtape Letters* (1942), *Mere Christianity* (1943), and *The Chronicles of Narnia* (1950); and the works of G.K. Chesterton, Thomas Merton, Flannery O'Connor, and Shusako Endo.

Bible translations have had a major impact on literature. During the ninth century Cyril and Methodius invented the Glagolitic alphabet to render the sounds of the Slavic language and thus laid the foundation for Russian and other Slavic literatures. Through his translation of the complete Bible in 1534, Martin Luther established the modern German language. Similarly, the Authorized, or King James, Version of 1611 had an extensive influence on English usage, with hundreds of common expressions derived from it. In addition, biblical themes percolate through the entire Western literary tradition.

According to the New Testament, Jesus sang with his disciples on the night before his death (Matthew 26:30). Paul wrote to the Ephesians that they were to "speak to one another in psalms, hymns, and spiritual songs" (Ephesians 5:19), and evidence indicates that certain biblical texts were sung before the New Testament was written (I Timothy 3:16; Philippians 2:5–11). In the fourth century Ambrose had members of his congregation sing psalms, wrote hymns in metrical

forms that all could follow, and thus laid the basis for congregational singing in the Western church. By the ninth century plainsong—music sung monophonically and without accompaniment and named Gregorian chant in honor of Pope Gregory I—was in common use. As early as the ninth century, biblical stories were dramatized and performed in the altar area of French churches, and modern opera evolved out of these dramas.

Ubaldus Hucbald (840–930), a French Benedictine, combined two or more melodies in harmony, thus ushering in polyphony, and Guido of Arezzo (c. 995–1050), another Benedictine, introduced the musical staff to indicate the pitch of notes and introduced the system of naming them. From the high Middle Ages until the twentieth century, every new form in Western music emerged in the context of church sponsorship and patronage. Johann Sebastian Bach (1685–1750), one of the greatest composers of all time, was a man of such profound Christian faith that he has been called "the fifth evangelist." At the end of each manuscript he wrote *Soli Deo Gloria* (to God alone be the glory). Great religious works by classical composers include Bach's masterpiece, *Saint Matthew Passion*, George Frideric Handel's *Messiah*, Felix Mendelssohn's *Elijah*, and Franz Joseph Haydn's *The Seven Last Words of Christ* and *The Creation*, as well as numerous works by such modern composers as Igor Stravinsky and Olivier Messiaen. These composers were practicing Christians who saw their music as an expression of worship.

The rich traditions of Christian hymnody, which began in the eighteenth century with Isaac Watts and Charles Wesley, have continued to proliferate. There seems to be no musical style that has not been used for Christian purposes. Moreover, the direction of influence has often run from the sacred to the secular. Ray Charles, for example, scandalized some Christians in the mid-twentieth century when he used the emotive spiritual style of the black church in such secular songs as "Hallelujah, I Love Her So." Even earlier, blues and jazz grew out of black spirituals, which were a form of sacred song.

Before 200, Christianity developed little in terms of a tradition of visual arts, and this has been attributed to the persecution of the church, to the expectation of the speedy end of the world, and to the Jewish prohibition against the making of images that persisted among early Christians. Yet Christian ossuaries from the first and second centuries bore simple symbols—ships, plows, stars, trees, etc—that carried a Christian mean-

African Initiated Churches

African Initiated Churches (AICs; also called African Independent, Instituted, or Indigenous Churches) are denominations or congregations founded and governed by Africans. Some are much like missionary churches, while others are strikingly different. They tend to read the Bible literally and emphasize themes ignored by most Western Christians, such as revelation through dreams, divine healing, the struggle against witchcraft, and the need to destroy non-Christian religious objects. Whether directly or indirectly, AICs offer a critique of European missionary practice. Few mission churches allow polygamy, and yet many Africans regard the practice as consistent with biblical teaching. Likewise, Africans find that Westerners give insufficient attention to the spirit world, viewing technology and modern medicine as solutions for every need. AICs share the worldview of African traditional religions but forbid their members to participate in traditional ceremonies because of their alleged association with evil spirits. Members sometimes wear distinctive dress, such as white robes and headgear. AICs may observe the Sabbath (Saturday) as well as Sunday and follow Old Testament dietary laws, often expanded to include abstention from beer and tobacco.

One early African Initiated Church emerged in 1913–14 from the preaching of Prophet William Wadé Harris, who converted and baptized more than 120,000 villagers in what is now Côte d'Ivoire. Harris had been reared in the Episcopal Church but was expelled because of his ideas on polygamy. The theological foundation of Harrism lies in the biblical encounter between Jesus and Simon of Cyrene, the African who carried his cross, a moment that sealed God's promise to the African continent. Joseph Ositelu founded the Church of the Lord (Aladura) in 1925, when he served as a catechist for the Anglican mission. The Aladura Church prays over water, which is then used for healing. Women as well as men can serve as priests, though a woman, following the Israelite precedent, may not approach the altar during her menstrual period. AICs related to Roman Catholicism include the Jamaa movement, the Legion of Mary, and the Catholic Church of the Sacred Heart. The largest AIC is the Kimbanguist Church. Though Simon Kimbangu's preaching lasted less than a year (1921) and he suffered imprisonment until his death in 1951, the movement he inspired has 7 million members.

ing. Early Christians borrowed from Greco-Roman artistic traditions. Jesus appeared in the guise of the pagan gods Orpheus, Apollo, and Dionysius, and holding a magician's wand when he healed. In the late third century, Roman catacombs were decorated with images of Jesus as the Good Shepherd (a pre-Christian, Mediterranean motif), and a host of Old Testament figures—e.g., Jonah, Noah, and Daniel—in dramatic scenes of rescue and deliverance, often in the orans (lit., "praying") posture with hands upraised. When Christianity received sanction in the Roman Empire, the theme of rescue diminished and artistic works began to depict such regal and imperial scenes as Jesus' triumphal entry into Jerusalem and Jesus' enthronement as cosmic ruler (as in the Byzantine Pantokrator or "universal ruler").

The imperial sponsorship of Christianity encouraged new architectural traditions. The basilica—a place for Greco-Roman public gatherings—was adapted for Christian use beginning in the fourth century, with an altar set in the curved apse that had contained a statue of the emperor. The round tombs of rulers and heroes were used for saint's graves and sites of martyrdom. The floors often contained stone mosaics. Jesus appeared as clean-shaven youth, and only later portrayed as bearded and middle-aged. For centuries there were virtually no images of the crucifixion or a suffering Christ. Because of the destruction of Ethiopian Christian art by Muslims, most remaining monuments in Ethiopia date from the tenth or eleventh centuries, and these include the rock churches of Lalibela as well as vibrant murals and altarpieces exhibiting a distinctive Ethiopian style.

Constantine (d. 337) helped create a Byzantine artistic tradition when he moved his capital to Constantinople, and, with help from his mother, Helena, erected the Church of the Holy Sepulcher (328–36) on the supposed site of Jesu's death and burial in Jerusalem.

Christian sculpture was rare until well into the medieval period, and yet painting on wood panels offered images of Jesus, Mary, and the saints. Justinian created an enduring legacy of Christian architecture in the Church of the Holy Wisdom (Hagia Sophia, 532–37) in Constantinople, a structure melding the basilica and round church into a huge, light-filled space, with a largest dome ever created up to that time. The iconoclastic controversy in the Eastern Church (726–843) resulted in the destruction of icons, mosaics, and paintings, yet ended with an affirmation of art's devotionality. Reverence for an icon was reverence for Christ. Icon-painting reached a pinnacle with Andrei Rublev (ca. 1360–1430), whose images exude warmth and humanness.

In the west, the Celtic monks of Ireland and Scotland exhibited a unique aesthetic style in the dense ornamentation of the illustrated Book of Kells (ca. 800). On the continent, Charlemagne erected an octagonal chapel at Aachen (792–805) patterned after Byzantine models. Breaking with Byzantium, Franco-German artists began to produce images of a suffering Savior—including a dead, life-sized crucifix at Cologne—starting in the 900s. In the later eleventh and the twelfth centuries, the Romanesque style of architecture adopted the arch and vault of the ancient Romans, and merged the basilica plan with a system of aisles and ambulatories. Booty brought back from the crusades allowed Europeans artisans to produce reliquaries and liturgical objects with precious metals and gemstones. Though some criticized this lavish used of wealth, Abbot Suger (1081–1151) considered the contemplation of precious things as a path to God. The Gothic style, beginning in the twelfth century, is generally regarded as the highest Christian achievement in architecture. By shifting the weight of stone roofs and towers onto columns, piers, and external butresses, Gothic churches rose in height. Walls were no longer load-bearing, and so contained stained-glass windows that flooded the interior with light.

The 1200s and 1300s witnessed a newer, naturalistic style in painting and sculpture—a trend culminating in the artistic brilliance of the Renaissance era. The bubonic plague of 1348-50 temporarily reversed the trend, and brought a return to more somber themes and less naturalistic images. By the 1400s Flemish painters showed the Virgin Mary in the cozy surroundings of a middle-class home, with household objects as spiritual symbols (e.g., a vase of lilies representing purity). Those who commissioned paintings were sometimes represented in the works alongside of Jesus, Mary, and the saints.

Mathematical principles, such as symbolic ratios, geometry, and one-point perspective, were seen as reflections of God's own mind, and began to govern the work of artists and architects. Raphael was considered to have attained a perfect style. Yet Michelangelo—perhaps the first fully independent artist—produced the even more celebrated masterworks of the Sistine Chapel and statues of David and Moses. By the late 1500s, Benvenuto Cellini (1500–71) and others in the Mannerist style broke with earlier traditions by presenting elongated figures that strain and twist. Christian art in Germany continued to highlight suffering and compassion, as shown in Matthias Gruenwald's Isenheim altarpiece (1510–15) and its poignant image of the crucifixion.

Many early Protestants were iconoclasts like Ulrich Zwingli (1484–1531), who stripped medieval churches of all artwork and whitewashed their interiors. The iconoclastic style was also in vogue among John Calvin and his followers, including the Puritans of colonial New England, whose meetinghouses lacked representational art. Martin Luther acknowledged that religious art served a didactic function, and so Lutherans were never strict iconoclasts—though they like other Protestants often rejected religious sculpture. Anglican artistic sensibilities owed something to both Protestant and Catholic viewpoints. Protestant church buildings of the 1500s and 1600s eliminated the high altar, and raised the pulpit higher than ever—symbolizing the importance of the preached word.

Roman Catholics responded to Protestantism by highlighting the visual arts, though carefully controlling their content. (A Venetian artist, Veronese [1528–1588], who portrayed the Last Supper in 1573 was called before the Inquisition for incorporating dwarves, animals, and Germans into his painting!) Ironically, this highly controlled church art was also highly sensual, and featured saints of both sexes (sometimes nearly nude) writhing in agony or ecstasy. Bernini's "Ecstasy of St. Teresa" (1545–52) is a kind of religious theater, with erotic undertones. In the 1600s and 1700s, the Spaniard Diego Velázquez (1599–1660) offered stark scenes of saints lost in devotion, the Flemish artist Peter Paul Rubens painted allegorical scenes in bright colors, while the Dutchman Rembrandt van Rijn (1606–1669) treated religious themes with a finesse and psychological depth that has never been surpassed, as in his "Return of the Prodigal Son" (ca. 1665). In seventeenth- and eighteenth-century France, aristocratic patrons of the arts lost interest in religious themes, and

Christianity and Feminism

Christian feminists have argued that the subjection of women to men throughout history is not a reflection of God's purpose but a consequence of human sin, as shown in the biblical text concerning the fall of Adam and Eve: "Your desire shall be for your husband, and he shall rule over you" (Genesis 3:16). This subjection, they argue, has been removed: "There is no longer male and female; for all of you are one in Christ Jesus" (Galatians 3:28). Consequently the traditional role distinctions between men and women in marriage and in the church are no longer in force. During the 1900s Christian feminism led women and men to launch a campaign, especially successful in Protestantism, to allow women to enter the ordained ministry. Feminist theologians have also challenged the traditional picture of God and developed an approach stressing God's mutuality, reciprocity, and intimacy with creatures.

Christian antifeminists have argued that the role distinctions between man as leader and woman as follower are part of God's original purpose, that the husband is to be "head" of his wife (1 Corinthians 11:3) and that the ordained ministry is limited to males (1 Corinthians 14:34–35; 1 Timothy 2:12–15). Some argue that Adam sinned because Eve tempted him, which shows that women must not lead men. They regard Jesus' decision to appoint 12 male apostles as a sign that the ministry belongs to men. Roman Catholicism argues that females cannot represent Jesus' priesthood in the celebration of the sacraments.

Another question is whether the traditional masculine language and imagery for God are acceptable in contemporary worship. Proposals for inclusive language have suggested new designations for people ("children of God" for "sons of God") and new terms for God ("Parent" for "Father God"). Such proposals have provoked controversy, especially when favorite hymns, traditional liturgies, or the Bible itself have been altered.

Today Christian feminism is an international movement. Among its leading authors are María Pilar Aquino (Mexico), Chung Hyum Kyung (Korea), Mercy Amba Oduyoye (Ghana), Teresa Okure (Nigeria), Kwok Pui-lan (China), Rosemary Radford Ruether (United States), and Margaret Shanti (India).

a secularizing tendency was apparent. Jacques-Louis David (1748–1825) painted historical images with moral themes that substituted for traditional religious art.

Because of the influence of Enlightenment thought, which regards religion as a personal preference rather than an ultimate truth, the relationship between art and faith has become problematic during the modern era. Some consider "Christian art" as an antiquated category since about 1800. During the 1800s and 1900s, romantics, impressionists, cubists, expressionists, surrealists, and abstract artists offered works that touched on Christian themes, but often used religious images in ambiguous ways. Christian artists found themselves in a precarious position, since fellow artists did not share their faith commitment and fellow Christians did not welcome their aesthetic innovations. Critics of modern art have stigmatized it as formless, chaotic, and unsuitable for expressing spiritual truths. Yet earlier Roman-

tics, such as William Blake (1757-1827) and P. O. Runge (1777–1810), delved deeply into religious themes. C. D. Friedrich (1774-1840) sought a religious dimension in his landscape painting. Paul Gauguin (1848–1903) experimented with religious themes in his "Yellow Christ" (1889) and "Ave Maria" (1891), as Vincent van Gogh (1853-90)—preacher-turned-artist—dreamt of renewing Christian art, and conveyed a spiritual presence through his intense expressionism. The Eisenach regulation (1861) mandated the Gothic style for church buildings in Germany, and church architecture of the last two centuries has generally mimicked earlier Christian styles or else followed a more functional and secular approach.

Religious themes occur marginally, though impressively, in works by Emil Nolde (1867–1956) and Marc Chagall (1887–1985). A twentieth-century artist of international stature known for his Christian faith is Georges Rouault (1871–1958). The Jesuit order has established the Museum of Contemporary Religious Art (St. Louis, USA) and the Center for Contemporary Art (Cologne, Germany). Pope John Paul II has sought to reestablish the relationship of the church to artists, and of artists to the church, through his "Letter to Artists" (1999). A recent development is the Christian use of non-Western artistic media and content by Third World artists in Africa, Latin America, the Caribbean, India, Sri Lanka, Bali, China, Korea, Japan, and the Philippines. In light of this growing trend, the future development of Christian art could occur largely outside of the Western nations.

Michael J. McClymond

See Also Vol. I: *Anglicanism, Baptist Tradition, Church of Jesus Christ of Latter-day Saints (Mormons), Coptic Christianity, Eastern Catholicism, Eastern Orthodoxy, Evangelicalism, Jehovah's Witnesses, Lutheranism, Methodism, Pentecostalism, Protestantism, Reformed Christianity, Religious Scoiety of Friends (Quakers), Roman Catholicism, Seventh-day Adventists, Unitarianism, United Church of Christ*

Bibliography

Ahlstrom, Sydney. *A Religious History of the American People.* New Haven: Yale University Press, 1972.

Atiya, Aziz Suryal. *A History of Eastern Christianity.* Notre Dame, Ind.: University of Notre Dame, 1968.

Barrett, David B., George T. Kurian, and Todd M. Johnson, eds. *World Christian Encyclopedia: A Comparative Survey of Churches and Religions in the Modern World.* 2nd ed. 2 vols. New York: Oxford University Press, 2001.

Burgess, Stanley M., and Eduard M. van der Maas, eds. *The New International Dictionary of Pentecostal and Charismatic Movements.* Grand Rapids, Mich.: Zondervan, 2002.

Catechism of the Catholic Church. Mahwah, N.J.: Paulist Press, 1994.

Catholic University of America. *New Catholic Encyclopedia.* 15 vols. Detroit: Thomson Gale; Washington, D.C.: Catholic University of America, 2003.

Chidester, David. *Christianity: A Global History.* San Francisco: HarperSanFrancisco, 2000.

Childress, James F., and John Macquarrie, eds. *The Westminster Dictionary of Christian Ethics.* Philadelphia: Westminster Press, 1986.

Dussel, Enrique. *The Church in Latin America, 1492–1992.* Maryknoll, N.Y.: Orbis, 1992.

Fahlbusch, Erwin, et al., eds. *The Encyclopedia of Christianity.* 2 vols. Grand Rapids, Mich.: Eerdmans; Leiden: E.J. Brill, 1999–.

Feguson, Everett, Michael P. McHugh, and Frederick W. Norris, eds. *Encyclopedia of Early Christianity.* 2nd ed. 2 vols. New York: Garland, 1997.

Flannery, Austin, ed. *Vatican Council II: The Conciliar and Postconciliar Documents.* Wilmington, Del.: Scholarly Resources, 1975.

Florovsky, Georges. *Ways of Russian Theology.* 2 vols. Belmont, Mass.: Nordland, 1979, 1987.

Ford, David F., ed. *The Modern Theologians: An Introduction to Christian Theology in the Twentieth Century.* 2nd ed. Cambridge, Mass.: Blackwell, 1997.

Ford, David F., and Mike Higton, eds. *Jesus.* New York: Oxford University Press, 2002.

Hastings, Adrian, ed. *A World History of Christianity.* Grand Rapids, Mich.: Eerdmans, 1999.

Hillerbrand, Hans J., ed. *The Oxford Encyclopedia of the Reformation.* 4 vols. New York: Oxford University Press, 1996.

Isichei, Elizabeth Allo. *A History of Christianity in Africa: From Antiquity to the Present.* Grand Rapids, Mich.: Eerdmans, 1995.

Jenkins, Philip. *The Next Christendom: The Coming of Global Christianity.* New York: Oxford University Press, 2003.

Kazhdan, Alexander P., et al., eds. *The Oxford Dictionary of Byzantium.* 3 vols. New York: Oxford University Press, 1991.

Kinnamon, Michael, and Brian E. Cope, eds. *The Ecumenical Movement: An Anthology of Key Texts and Voices.* Geneva: WCC Publications; Grand Rapids, Mich.: Eerdmans, 1997.

LaCugna, Catherine Mowry, ed. *Freeing Theology: The Essentials of Theology in Feminist Perspective.* San Francisco: HarperSanFrancisco, 1993.

Livingston, E.A., ed. *The Oxford Dictionary of the Christian Church.* 3rd ed. New York: Oxford University Press, 1997.

Livingston, James C. *Modern Christian Thought: From the Enlightenment to Vatican II.* New York: Macmillan; London: Collier Macmillan, 1971.

McClymond, Michael J. *Familiar Stranger: An Introduction to Jesus of Nazareth.* Grand Rapids, Mich.: Eerdmans, 2004.

McDannell, Colleen. *Material Christianity: Religion and Popular Culture in America.* New Haven: Yale University Press, 1995.

McGinn, Bernard. *The Presence of God: A History of Western Christian Mysticism.* 3 vols. New York: Crossroad, 1991–2004.

McNamara, Jo Ann. *Sisters in Arms: Catholic Nuns through Two Millennia.* Cambridge, Mass.: Harvard University Press, 1996.

Meyendorff, John. *Rome, Constantinople, Moscow: Historical and Theological Studies.* Crestwood, N.Y.: Saint Vladimir's Seminary Press, 1996.

Moffett, Samuel H. *A History of Christianity in Asia.* 2 vols. Maryknoll, N.Y.: Orbis Books, 1998, 2004.

Niebuhr, H. Richard. *Christ and Culture.* New York: Harper, 1951.

Ozment, Steven. *Protestants: The Birth of a Revolution.* New York: HarperCollins, 1993.

Pelikan, Jaroslav. *The Christian Tradition: A History of the Development of Doctrine.* 5 vols. Chicago: University of Chicago Press, 1971–89.

———. *Jesus through the Centuries: His Place in the History of Culture.* New York: Perennial Library, 1987.

Pelikan, Jaroslav, and Valerie Hotchkiss, eds. *Creeds and Confessions of Faith in the Christian Tradition.* 4 vols. New Haven: Yale University Press, 2003.

Placher, William C., ed. *Readings in the History of Christian Theology.* 2 vols. Philadelphia: Westminster Press, 1988.

Remond, Rene. *Religion and Society in Modern Europe.* Malden, Mass.: Blackwell, 1999.

Roberts, Alexander, and James Donaldson, eds. *Ante-Nicene Fathers.* 10 vols. Peabody, Mass.: Hendrickson, 1994.

Sanneh, Lamin O. *Translating the Message: The Missionary Impact on Culture.* Maryknoll, N.Y.: Orbis Books, 1989.

Schaff, Philip, ed. *Nicene and Post-Nicene Fathers.* First and Second Series. 28 vols. Peabody, Mass.: Hendrickson, 1994.

Schmidt, Alvin J. *Under the Influence: How Christianity Transformed Civilization.* Grand Rapids, Mich.: Eerdmans, 2001.

Southern, R.W. *The Making of the Middle Ages.* New Haven: Yale University Press, 1959.

Stark, Rodney. *For the Glory of God: How Monotheism Led to Reformations, Science, Witch-Hunts, and the End of Slavery.* Princeton, N.J.: Princeton University Press, 2003.

Strayer, Joseph R., ed. *Dictionary of the Middle Ages.* 13 vols. New York: Scribner, 1982–89.

Wakefield, Gordon S., ed. *The Westminster Dictionary of Christian Spirituality.* Philadelphia: Westminster Press, 1983.

Walsh, Michael. *Dictionary of Christian Biography.* Collegeville, Minn.: Liturgical Press, 2001.

Ware, Kallistos. *The Orthodox Church.* Baltimore: Penguin, 1963.

World Christian Database. Center for the Study of Global Christianity, Gordon-Conwell Theological Seminary. 9 April 2004. www.worldchristiandatabase.org/wcd.

Anglicanism (Episcopalianism)

FOUNDED: Sixteenth century C.E.

RELIGION AS A PERCENTAGE OF WORLD POPULATION: 1.3 percent

OVERVIEW Anglicanism is a tradition of worldwide churches that trace their history to the Christian church in England. It sees itself as the via media ("middle way") between Roman Catholicism and Protestantism. Although the Church of England broke ties with the Catholic Church during the sixteenth-century Protestant Reformation, the English and subsequent Anglican churches have maintained customs and a liturgy similar to those in Roman Catholicism. Also like Catholics, Anglicans believe they are connected through an unbroken succession of bishops to the early church of the apostles. The Protestant Reformation, however, has informed Anglican belief and teachings.

As a result of British colonial expansion and missionary activity from the seventeenth through the twentieth century, the Church of England spread across the world, eventually resulting in a global family of interdependent churches called the Anglican Communion. At the beginning of the twenty-first century, the Anglican Communion was made up of 38 self-governing regional or national churches located in 164 countries, with an estimated 75–80 million members. The archbishop of Canterbury is recognized as the titular head of the Anglican Communion. The majority of Anglicans live in the southern hemisphere, with the greatest concentration in Africa south of the Sahara.

HISTORY Christianity was introduced to England in the late second or early third century. In the sixth century the Irish missionary Columba brought a Celtic form of Christianity to northern England, and in 597 Pope Gregory sent Saint Augustine to the island, where he established a Roman Catholic monastery in Canterbury, later to become the primary English bishopric. From the sixth to the sixteenth century there was tension in the English church between its connection with Roman Catholicism and its identification with the English monarch and people.

The English church officially broke ties with Rome in the 1530s. It is popularly understood that the cause was the pope's refusal to grant an annulment of King Henry VIII's marriage to Catherine of Aragon (who had failed to produce a male heir). In response, Henry rejected the authority of the pope, becoming Supreme Head of an independent Church of England, separate from Rome, though he changed little in the worship ritual. The church's move toward independence, however, was the result of a larger European development, the Protestant Reformation, and was influenced by such Reformation leaders as Martin Luther, John Calvin, and Ulrich Zwingli. At its heart the founding of the Church of England was based on the desire of the English monarch and people to create a national church. The competing sympathies for a church of England and a church loyal to Rome characterized the monarchies of Henry VIII (reigned 1509–47); Mary (reigned 1553–58), who sought to return the church to its Roman identity; and Elizabeth (reigned 1558–1603), who, in a series of acts known as the Elizabethan settlement, finally resolved

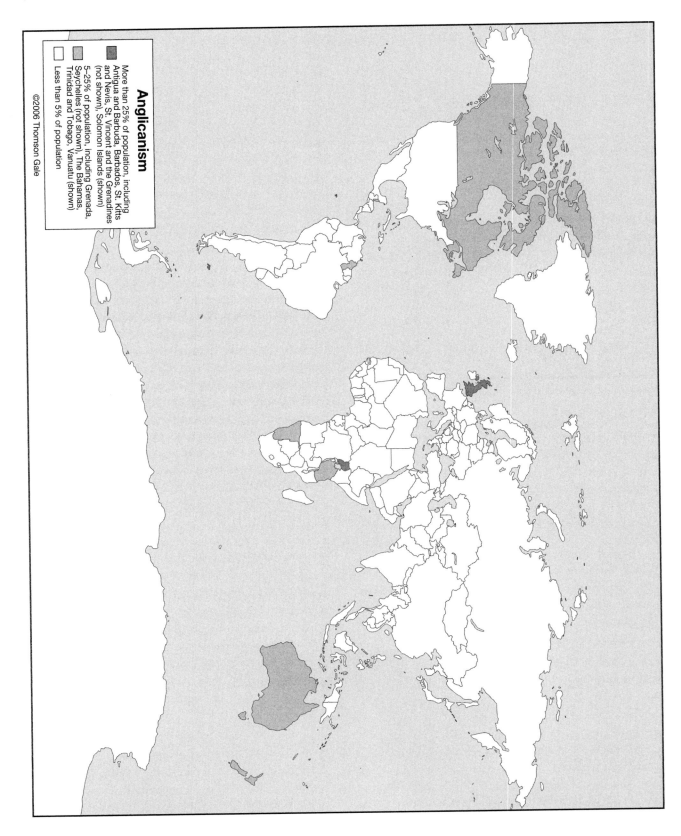

Anglicanism

More than 25% of population, including Antigua and Barbuda, Barbados, St. Kitts and Nevis, St. Vincent and the Grenadines (not shown), Solomon Islands (shown)

5–25% of population, including Grenada, Seychelles (not shown), The Bahamas, Trinidad and Tobago, Vanuatu (shown)

Less than 5% of population

©2006 Thomson Gale

the dispute by reestablishing the independent Church of England.

From the late sixteenth century to the present day, the Church of England has been the official church in the country, with the monarch as its supreme governor and the archbishop of Canterbury its ecclesial head. With the establishment of English colonies in other parts of the world from the seventeenth through the nineteenth century, the Church of England likewise expanded beyond the British Isles as both a chaplain to, and a criticizer of, English colonialism. In 1785, as a result of the American Revolution, Anglicans in the newly created United States of America separated themselves from the Church of England, becoming the Protestant Episcopal Church in the United States, the first self-governing Anglican church outside of Great Britain. Similarly, along with the decline of the British empire and Western imperialism in the mid-twentieth century, foreign missions of the Church of England and of the American-based Protestant Episcopal Church in Africa, Asia, Latin America, and the Pacific became autonomous Anglican churches in their own right. Consistent with the changing face of global Christianity, most Anglicans in the world today live in Africa, Asia, Latin America, and the Pacific and are no longer primarily identified with the English culture and language.

CENTRAL DOCTRINES As part of the ongoing, universal Christian Church, Anglicans hold that the Bible—specifically the books of the Old and New Testaments—constitutes Holy Scripture and contains all things necessary for salvation. Although influenced by the sixteenth-century Reformation, Anglicans do not, like many Protestants, subscribe to a confession of faith. Rather, they believe and affirm that the ancient creeds—in particular the Apostle's Creed and the Nicene Creed—are sufficient statements of faith. In some Anglican churches the historic articulation of the Elizabethan settlement, known as the Thirty-Nine Articles, outlines Anglican belief and practice.

Anglicans believe in and orient their lives around the two primary sacraments found in the Bible: baptism and the Eucharist. Anglicans also affirm five other "lesser" sacraments of the church: confirmation, ordination, holy matrimony, reconciliation of a penitent (confession), and unction. The authority of bishops as representative of the historic episcopate (the succession of bishops dating back to the early church) is stressed in all Anglican churches. In addition to bishops, Anglicans

A member of the Anglican clergy prepares purses of maundy money to be given to the less fortunate in a traditional ceremony. Anglicans are well known for their concern for the social welfare of their communities. © TIM GRAHAM/CORBIS.

maintain two other orders of ministry: priests (or presbyters) and deacons.

Possessing neither a confession as a point of unity nor a centralized authority structure to determine beliefs and doctrine, Anglicanism allows a certain latitude and openness in theological outlook, following the principle *lex orandi lex credendi* (the law of prayer determines the law of belief). All Anglicans, however, use for their liturgy the Book of Common Prayer, first published in 1549 and subsequently revised, translated into vernacular languages, and further adapted to various cultures. Fundamental to Anglicanism is the lived experience of the local worshiping community, or parish, where the Word of God is proclaimed and the sacraments are celebrated.

A female priest is ordained in Bristol, England. Ordination of female priests is a controversial subject within the Anglican community. © B.E.N. POLAK MATTHEW/CORBIS SYGMA.

MORAL CODE OF CONDUCT Although in Anglicanism the moral code of conduct is based on the Bible, most Anglicans believe that it needs to be interpreted within the unique circumstances and experiences of each local church. As a result, Anglicans read and interpret the Bible in various ways. For example, in some Anglican churches it is acceptable for church leaders to remarry after divorce, while others frown upon the practice. Polygamist men and their wives who are newly converted to Christianity are allowed to become members of some Anglican churches and not of others. Differing views on human sexuality—particularly homosexuality—have caused tension within the Anglican Communion.

SACRED BOOKS Anglicans hold the books of the Old and New Testaments as their sacred scripture. In addition, they place great emphasis on the Book of Common Prayer, initially written and revised by the Church of England and subsequently adapted by other Anglican churches.

SACRED SYMBOLS The cross, with or without the figure of the crucified Christ, is considered a primary sacred symbol within Anglicanism. Some Anglicans (often referred to as Anglo-Catholics, or "high-church" Anglicans) use symbols and ceremonies identified with Catholic practice, while other Anglicans (known as evangeli-

cals, or "low-church" Anglicans) are more similar to Protestants and shy away from these practices.

EARLY AND MODERN LEADERS Great leaders and thinkers of the English Reformation associated with Anglicanism include King Henry VIII (1491–1547); Thomas Cranmer (1489–1556), who created the first Book of Common Prayer; and William Tyndale (c. 1492–1536), who first translated the Bible into English. Major founding figures of the Episcopal Church in the United States include Samuel Seabury (1729–1796), the first American bishop, and William White (1747–1836) of Christ Church in Philadelphia, who was a colleague of many American patriots. The first bishop of African American origin was James Theodore Holly (1829–1911), consecrated for the Episcopal Church of Haiti in 1874. The first woman bishop in the Anglican Communion was Barbara C. Harris (born in 1930), consecrated suffragan bishop of the Diocese of Massachusetts in 1989. Globally recognized Anglicans today include Archbishop Desmond Tutu (born in 1931) of South Africa, who won the Nobel Peace Prize in 1984, and Terry Waite (born in 1939), who was an envoy of the archbishop of Canterbury and held hostage in Lebanon from 1987 to 1991.

MAJOR THEOLOGIANS AND AUTHORS In addition to foundational church leaders, such as Thomas Cranmer and William Tyndale, other Anglican theologians include Richard Hooker (1554?–1600), author of *Treatise on the Laws of Ecclesiastical Polity* (1594–97), and Frederick Denison Maurice (1805–72), a theologian of Christian socialism. The Most Reverend Rowan Williams, archbishop of Canterbury beginning in 2002, is one of the foremost Anglican theologians today.

ORGANIZATIONAL STRUCTURE Each regional or national Anglican church is divided into dioceses, and each diocese is made up of parish churches. Dioceses are headed by a diocesan bishop, sometimes assisted by suffragan or assisting bishops. While headed by bishops, each diocese and national church is governed by a synod, convention, or council that generally includes both lay and ordained leaders in the decision-making process.

Each of the 38 churches of the worldwide Anglican Communion is independent, but they relate to one another with mutual responsibility and interdependence as Christians belonging to a common fellowship. As the first bishop of the Church of England, the archbishop of Canterbury is the titular, or symbolic, head of the Anglican Communion.

HOUSES OF WORSHIP AND HOLY PLACES Anglicans worship in local communities generally known as parish churches. In some parts of the Anglican Communion—particularly in the southern hemisphere—parishes consist of multiple congregations worshiping in basic church buildings in different locations. Anglicans are particularly proud of their cathedrals. Canterbury Cathedral, York Minster, and Westminster Abbey in England and Washington National Cathedral and the Cathedral of Saint John the Divine (New York) in the United States are popular sites for both devotional visits and tourists.

WHAT IS SACRED? Anglicans view their churches and cathedrals as holy but generally do not set apart specific items for sacred worship and adoration (although individual Anglicans might do so). Anglicans hold that there is the real presence of Christ in the bread and wine of the Holy Eucharist.

HOLIDAYS AND FESTIVALS Anglicanism follows the traditional liturgical seasons of Christianity (Advent, Christmas, Epiphany, Lent, Easter, and Pentecost). Christmas (the birth of Jesus Christ) and Easter (the resurrection of Jesus Christ) are the two most significant holidays. Regional and national churches have appointed various days of remembrance for major and lesser saints throughout the liturgical year. Specific biblical passages to be read in worship each day and on Sundays are assigned from a regular lesson cycle, generally put forward in the Book of Common Prayer.

MODE OF DRESS Ordained individuals in the Anglican Communion usually wear clerical attire, most often black or gray (although occasionally other colors are worn) with a white clerical collar; bishops often wear purple. Liturgical dress includes a colored stole (a lengthy piece of cloth, of appropriate color for the liturgical season, worn around the neck) over an alb (a simple white gown). Other vestments include a cassock (a long black gown) worn with a surplice (a white overgarment). More ceremonial liturgical vestments, often in the color of the liturgical season, include a chasuble (an ornate garment worn during the Eucharist) and a cope (cape). Bishops often wear a cope and a miter (hat) and carry a crosier (staff) as a sign of their office.

DIETARY PRACTICES There are no prescribed dietary practices within Anglicanism. Some Anglicans, for reasons of personal piety, will fast from time to time or before receiving the Eucharist.

RITUALS Anglican worship is based on the monastic practice of regular community prayer throughout the day. Services for morning prayer, noonday prayer, midday prayer, evening prayer, and compline (the final prayers of the day) are found in most Anglican prayer books. Sunday worship is the primary liturgical celebration for most Anglicans and includes either a morning prayer with a sermon (in more "low-church," or low ceremony, parishes) or the Holy Eucharist (in most churches). Public services of common prayer and celebration are also provided for at significant transitions in a person's life, such as confirmation, marriage, and funerals. Depending on personal beliefs and practices, some Anglicans will go on pilgrimages or retreats for spiritual growth and development.

RITES OF PASSAGE In Anglicanism baptism with water (usually not involving immersion), both of infants and adults, marks an individual's entry into the universal fellowship of the church. Most Anglican churches also provide services for confirmation (in which adolescents or adults confirm their Christian beliefs) and reception (in which people from another Christian tradition are received into the Anglican faith). Confirmation and reception services are presided over by bishops and include the laying on of hands by the bishop as a sign of the rite of passage.

MEMBERSHIP In some countries, such as the United Kingdom, the Anglican church has been the state church, and citizens who do not profess some other religious identification have been considered part of the Anglican church. In most other countries membership in the Anglican church has been voluntary. Anglicans believe in the possibility of universal salvation through Jesus Christ and thus are involved in evangelistic outreach through various means, including missionary societies, websites, and social service.

RELIGIOUS TOLERANCE Anglicanism is generally considered a tolerant Christian tradition that is open to interreligious dialogue. Anglicans have been deeply involved in and committed to ecumenism and the ecumenical movement. The Chicago-Lambeth Quadrilateral of 1886 and 1888 was an early Anglican statement of ecumenical principles. Archbishop of Canterbury William Temple (1881–1944) and Presiding Bishop Henry Knox Sherrill (1890–1980) of the Episcopal Church in the United States were significant leaders in twentieth-century ecumenical councils.

SOCIAL JUSTICE Anglicans the world over have vigorously participated in outreach programs, expressing a concern for the social welfare of their communities. Anglican schools and hospitals have provided for the educational and health needs of all people, regardless of religious identification. Reflecting the global reach of the Anglican Communion and its presence in 164 countries, Anglicans have advocated international debt relief for poor countries and have played a significant role in efforts to combat the HIV/AIDS pandemic.

SOCIAL ASPECTS The social teachings of Anglicanism are based on the Bible but are interpreted within the specific dynamics of the local culture. For example, although Anglicans traditionally consider marriage to be a lifelong, committed, monogamous relationship between a man and a women, some Anglican churches are in countries more open to homosexuality and have considered blessing same-sex unions.

CONTROVERSIAL ISSUES Because Anglicanism is a worldwide Christian tradition that believes biblical teachings should be interpreted within a church's particular cultural and social context, there is room for different interpretations of controversial issues. Disagreements over some issues—for example, abortion, remarriage after divorce, the role of women in ordained ministry, and the place of homosexuals in the Christian community—have caused tension within the Anglican Communion.

CULTURAL IMPACT Anglicanism has contributed much to the development of Western civilization, especially in England and the territories of the former British Empire. Great thinkers, composers, authors, poets, artists, and political leaders throughout history have been motivated by their Anglican Christian faith. In many parts of the world—particularly in the West—Anglicans are identified with the cultural elite. Anglican cathedrals the world over stand as testimony to Anglican patronage of the arts and the intersection of the sacred and secular in Anglicanism.

Ian T. Douglas

The Controversy over a Gay Bishop

On 2 November 2003 the Right Reverend V. Gene Robinson was consecrated in the United States as bishop of the Episcopal Diocese of New Hampshire. A homosexual man living in a lifelong committed relationship with another man, he became the first openly gay, noncelibate bishop in the Anglican Communion. Bishop Robinson's consecration, combined with an increasing openness toward blessing same-sex relationships in some Anglican dioceses and churches (notably the Diocese of New Westminster in the Anglican Church of Canada), has exacerbated disagreements in the Anglican Communion over biblical interpretation and moral norms. Some have warned of a possible schism between the Episcopal Church in the United States and other churches in the Anglican Communion. The controversy has led to questions about what are the acceptable limits of Anglican diversity and how the Anglican Communion will continue to live together as a family of interdependent yet self-governing churches.

See Also Vol. 1: *Christianity*

Bibliography

Avis, Paul D.L. *Anglicanism and the Christian Church: Theological Resources in Historical Perspective.* 2nd ed. Edinburgh: T and T Clark, 2002.

Douglas, Ian T., and Kwok Pui Lan, eds. *Beyond Colonial Anglicanism: The Anglican Communion in the Twenty-first Century.* New York: Church Publishing, 2001.

Harris, Mark. *The Challenge of Change: The Anglican Communion in the Post-Modern Era.* New York: Church Publishing, 1998.

Howe, John. *Anglicanism and the Universal Church: Highways and Hedges.* Toronto: Anglican Book Centre, c. 1990.

Kaye, Bruce. *Reinventing Anglicanism: A Vision of Confidence, Community, and Engagement in Anglican Christianity.* New York: Church Publishing, 2004.

McGrath, Alistair E. *The Renewal of Anglicanism.* Harrisburg, Pa.: Morehouse Publishing, 1993.

Neill, Stephen. *Anglicanism.* 4th ed. New York: Oxford University Press, 1978.

Quinn, Frederick. *To Be a Pilgrim: The Anglican Ethos in History.* New York: Crossroad Publishing, 2001.

Sachs, William L. *The Transformation of Anglicanism: From State Church to Global Communion.* Cambridge: Cambridge University Press, 1993.

Sykes, Stephen. *Unashamed Anglicanism.* Nashville: Abingdon Press, 1995.

Sykes, Stephen, John Booty, and Jonathan Knight. *The Study of Anglicanism.* London: SPCK, 1998.

Wingate, Andrew, Kevin Ward, Carrie Pemberton, and Wilson Sitshebo, eds. *Anglicanism: A Global Communion.* New York: Church Publishing, 1998.

Christianity

Baptist Tradition

FOUNDED: 1609 C.E.

RELIGION AS A PERCENTAGE OF WORLD POPULATION: 1.8 percent

OVERVIEW Baptists, who effectively were founded in 1609 by John Smyth, an English dissenting pastor, have become one of the world's principal forms of Protestantism. Beginning in the seventeenth century, Baptist churches spread to the United States, where they have become the largest single Protestant denomination.

Baptists adhere to the traditional tenets of the Protestant Reformation, including the primacy of grace, the need for faith, and the authority of the Bible in all questions pertaining to religion. Most Baptists also affirm the classical statements of the Christian faith, such as the early church creeds, although they reject the use of creeds as a mandatory statement of belief. An often quoted maxim in Baptist life is "No creeds but the Bible!"

Within the larger family of Baptists, there is much diversity of opinion and practice. The emphasis Baptists have long placed on individual freedom and on the absence of ecclesiastical authority have resulted in the lack of a recognized theological authority in matters of biblical interpretation. The loose structure and voluntary association of Baptist life have contributed greatly to the denomination's numbers and success, but they have also made it notoriously difficult to define who is, and who is not, a Baptist.

HISTORY In 1609 John Smyth, a Cambridge graduate, rebaptized himself in the company of like-minded dissenters from the Church of England. Three years before his rebaptism, Smyth had helped form a small dissenting congregation in Gainsborough, England, and he served as their pastor. This small body of believers was formed around the principle that consenting adults could unite together to worship and serve God without a priestly intermediary. The threat of persecution from the Anglican Church prompted the group to move to Amsterdam, where a few years later Smyth performed his defiant self-baptism, apparently by affusion. Although he was not the first to do so, Smyth's act in 1609 is usually considered to be the inauguration of modern Baptist life.

Thomas Helwys, who was also rebaptized by Smyth, eventually led a small band of followers back to England in an attempt to witness to his countrymen. Often persecuted, those who returned are normally credited with founding the first Baptist church in England. Over the course of the seventeenth century, Baptists multiplied numerically but were divided theologically. The main division in English Baptist life was over the nature of the Atonement. All agreed that Christ's death on the cross atoned for human sin, but the question as to whom the Atonement was for proved controversial. The General Baptists held that the Atonement was for everyone, while the Particular Baptists held that Christ died only for an elect. Although passions on the matter eventually became less inflamed, in seventeenth-century Protestantism it was a volatile issue. By the end of the 1600s there were several dozen Baptist congregations in England, with additional churches in Ireland

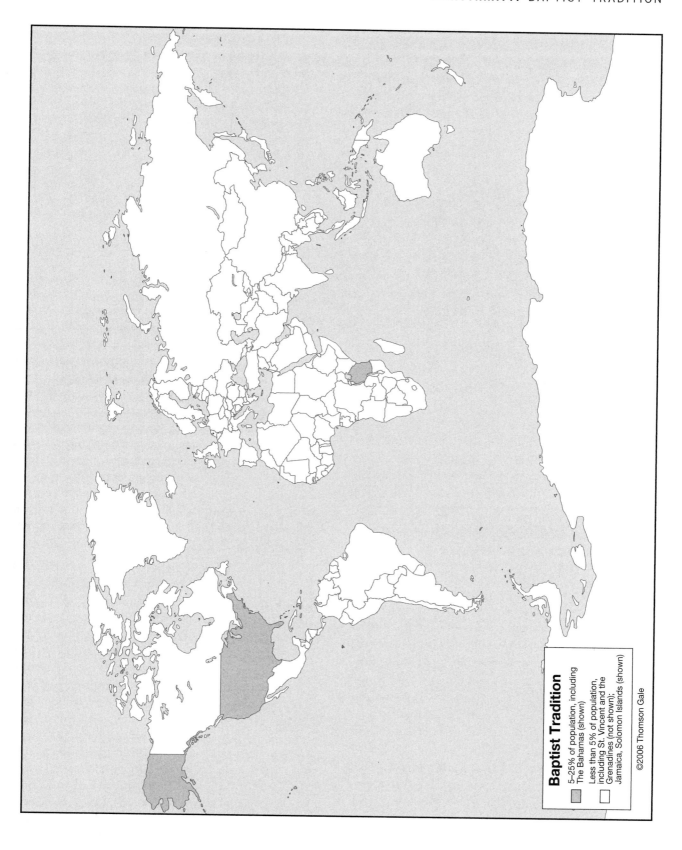

Baptist Tradition

5–25% of population, including The Bahamas (shown)

Less than 5% of population, including St. Vincent and the Grenadines (not shown); Jamaica, Solomon Islands (shown)

©2006 Thomson Gale

A Baptist pastor preaches from the pulpit. A significant architectural feature of Baptist churches is the centrality of the pulpit, which is usually, but not always, located front and center in the sanctuary, reflecting the importance of the written word in Baptist life. © ALLEN T. JULES/CORBIS.

and Wales. The great period of expansion for Baptists, however, was to come in the eighteenth and nineteenth centuries across the Atlantic in America.

The explosive growth of Baptists in America cannot be understood without reference to the revivalism and religious fervor associated with the Great Awakening of the early 1700s. Although no denomination can claim ownership of the Great Awakening, Baptists benefited more than most. Not only did they grow numerically in terms of individual conversions, but many of the new congregations formed by converts in the Great Awakening also moved into some version of Baptist life as a result of these revivals. By the end of the eighteenth century, it is estimated that there were as many as 750 Baptist churches in the new nation, representing perhaps 80,000 members. It is important to note that a geographical shift was taking place at this time as well, with more and more Baptists moving to the agrarian South.

In the nineteenth century Baptist churches continued to grow in the United States, and in those years three evolutions of Baptist life proved significant. First, the missionary movement, which had begun in the late eighteenth century, continued to expand, and Baptists became, as they have remained, a major part of the effort. Second, Baptists made significant inroads among African-Americans, with separate churches generally being formed in the wake of the Civil War (1861–65). Third, in 1845 Baptists split into Northern and Southern conventions, a split that even today is very much a part of Baptist activity in the United States. The Southern Baptist Convention has become the largest Protestant group in the country, and its tenor sets the tone for much of America's Baptist life.

The nineteenth century was significant not just for Baptists in the United States but for Baptists in other parts of the world as well. From 1815 to 1900, in less than a century, Baptist churches emerged in every corner of Europe. Baptist efforts in Germany and Sweden were particularly successful, although significant Baptist communities could also be found in Russia and other eastern European countries. By the end of the twentieth century,

Baptists could be found in virtually every land throughout the world.

CENTRAL DOCTRINES Most Baptists affirm the central tenets of the Christian faith as the Protestant Reformation presented them. It is difficult to point to a central theological doctrine that defines Baptist identity, but any list of influential ideas that have shaped Baptist life would have to include the notion of individual and collective freedom. This overarching commitment to freedom is visible in several aspects of Baptist life. For instance, while Baptists have always had great confidence in the Bible as the revealed word of God, they have held that individual freedom of interpretation is important as well. Thus, while all are agreed that the Bible is authoritative in matters of faith and practice, not all Baptists understand various biblical passages in the same way. This has led to numerous splits at both the local and national levels.

The Baptist commitment to freedom also extends to congregations. Baptist churches are free churches, meaning that each congregation is independent and autonomous. Local churches cooperate with one another on various projects, but each church is free to participate in various Baptist associations as much or as little as it pleases. These associations are formed at the local, state, national, and even international levels. Once again, however, participation on the part of a congregation, or by an individual Baptist, is entirely voluntary. There is no central theological or ecclesiastical authority in Baptist life that can compel support, financial or otherwise, from individual churches. Associations are formed on the basis of like-minded cooperation rather than through any form of coercion.

The commitment to freedom extends even to salvation. Most Baptists embrace an experiential notion of faith that trusts in a personal and individualistic encounter with the person of Christ, often called a conversion experience. There is no such thing as automatic membership in Baptist life. Only those who have accepted Christ's Atonement, symbolized by public baptism, are regarded as members of the true church, which is itself formed not at the institutional level but in the hearts and minds of individual believers.

MORAL CODE OF CONDUCT Although there is significant variance, Baptist life is normally associated with strict codes of conduct, particularly in the realm of personal piety. Many Baptists abstain from alcohol and to-

Parishioners worship in a Baptist church. While all Baptists agree that the Bible is authoritative in matters of faith and practice, not all Baptists interpret various biblical passages in the same way. © PHILIP GOULD/CORBIS.

bacco, though they do so more out of concern for setting a good witness for their neighbors than out of an obligation to a scriptural or theological command. Baptists promote chastity before marriage and complete faithfulness to one's spouse after marriage. Many Baptists have been at the forefront of the debate over the acceptance of homosexuality, with the majority opposing homosexual practice. Baptists are encouraged to tithe to their local congregations and to make additional financial gifts for specific offerings, usually associated with missions.

SACRED BOOKS There is only one source of sacred revelation for Baptists, and that is the Bible itself. Baptists have been among the staunchest defenders of both the Old and New Testaments as authoritative sources for faith and life. Although there are numerous ministerial guidebooks and explanations of Baptist belief, none is considered even remotely sacred.

SACRED SYMBOLS There are no sanctioned symbols for Baptists, although many churches have adopted traditional Christian images such as the cross, a dove, or a flame as part of their logo.

Diversity among Baptists

A remarkable diversity exists among Baptists along ethnic, racial, regional, and especially theological fault lines. There are literally dozens of Baptist groups, some barely larger than a single congregation and some representing thousands of churches and millions of members. They may be at odds with one another on virtually every issue on which it is possible to have a position. For instance, in the last quarter of the twentieth century the largest U.S. Baptist convention, the Southern Baptists, suffered years of controversy and an eventual split, ostensibly over the issue of scriptural inerrancy. Some churches left to form the Cooperative Baptist Fellowship, while others simply stopped affiliating with any national body in substantive ways. And this is just one fault line among many. Baptists, then, are a remarkably diverse group. Indeed, it is often easier to see what different groups of Baptists disagree on than to find what they agree on.

EARLY AND MODERN LEADERS In addition to John Smyth (died in 1612) and Thomas Helwys (c. 1550–c. 1616), there are several influential figures in Baptist history. The clergyman Roger Williams (1603?–83), who founded Rhode Island, was, at least temporarily, a Baptist. The Englishman William Carey (1761–1834), the founder of the Baptist Missionary Society, traveled to India in 1793 to begin a long career as a preacher and translator of the Bible. Lott Carey (1780–1828), born a slave in Virginia, was also a Baptist missionary who eventually served as vice president of the African nation of Liberia. The American Charlotte Moon (1840–1912) was a Baptist missionary in China who, in an act of solidarity with the Chinese to whom she ministered, starved herself during a famine.

More contemporary figures include the noted American civil rights leader Martin Luther King, Jr. (1929–68). The American clergyman Harry Emerson Fosdick (1878–1969) was a leading figure in liberal Protestantism for much of the twentieth century, although his relations with Baptists conventions were often strained because of his progressivism.

MAJOR THEOLOGIANS AND AUTHORS Individual Baptist theologians and pastors have been leaders in various movements that swept through Protestantism. The nineteenth-century English pastor C.H. Spurgeon (1834–92), who at one time led the largest Protestant congregation in the world, was enormously influential. He is sometimes called the "last Puritan," and annual volumes of his sermons were published. Walter Rauschenbusch (1861–1918), a German-American Baptist, was a central figure in the Social Gospel movement. For several decades the American Billy Graham (born in 1918), an important figure in modern evangelicalism, has had one of the most influential ministries in the world.

There have been several American figures of importance for their leadership in Baptist theological history. In the late eighteenth and early nineteenth centuries, John Leland (1754–1841) defended baptism by immersion and religious liberty. E.Y. Mullins (1860–1928) was a professor and the eventual president of the Southern Baptist Seminary, and he led Baptists through several controversial issues in the early part of the twentieth century. These included the battle with modernism and the Landmark controversy, which argued that a direct line could be established from the New Testament churches to modern Baptist congregations and that the New Testament sanctioned only the Baptist form of church governance. Herschel Hobbs (1907–95) was a leading figure in the production of the 1963 version of *Baptist Faith and Message*, an influential, though not uncontested, document in Baptist life.

ORGANIZATIONAL STRUCTURE Baptist churches are independent and autonomous, although they are bound together at various levels. Several local churches may form what is called an association, which can range in size from a few congregations to several hundred. There are also state and regional conventions and finally national conventions. In addition, there are international cooperatives, usually formed around particular projects or causes. Most national bodies are affiliated with the Baptist World Alliance (1905). Participation in any of these structures is entirely voluntary, with elected representatives from each church attending and voting as necessary at larger gatherings.

Churches are normally served by one or more pastors, in some countries not necessarily ordained, and by one or more deacons. The variety in Baptist organization, however, even includes bishops in the countries of Latvia and Georgia.

HOUSES OF WORSHIP AND HOLY PLACES Baptist churches range from converted houses and storefronts to enormous campuses with sanctuaries that seat several thousand. Most Baptists meet for worship, study, and fellowship on Sunday mornings, with other activities throughout the week. Many Baptists worldwide worship twice or more on Sunday. An architectural feature of Baptist churches that is often commented on is the centrality of the pulpit, usually, but not always, located front and center in the sanctuary and reflecting the importance of the written word in Baptist life. There are no shrines or places of historical importance that are especially revered by Baptists, although many claim an affinity for the land of Israel.

WHAT IS SACRED? While most Baptists believe that the body is a temple for the indwelling of the Holy Spirit, they do not attach a special significance to the physical body as such. There are no sacred objects or totems that are unique to Baptists.

HOLIDAYS AND FESTIVALS Like other Christians, Baptists celebrate Easter and Christmas, setting them aside for special worship services. Thanksgiving is also prominent in the United States, although less so for its religious than its cultural significance. There are other times of the year that are set aside for special offerings, usually for missions. Many Baptist churches also celebrate their annual homecoming, when former members of a congregation gather for worship and fellowship. Many state and national conventions are held throughout the year, although in themselves they are not considered religious events.

MODE OF DRESS Baptists have no specific mode of dress, although depending upon the congregation, ministers may wear clerical robes. Even then, however, the significance of the robe is downplayed. Generally speaking, Baptists prefer modest attire.

DIETARY PRACTICES The use of alcohol and tobacco are often frowned upon but not specifically prohibited. There are no other restrictions on diet for most Baptists.

RITUALS Baptist worship services often reflect local cultural influences more than a historically transmitted pattern. Features of the service may include songs of praise, special prayers, and preaching, as well as informal fellowship and the giving of tithes and offerings. Weddings and funerals also follow local patterns. Preaching is central to most Baptist services, with opportunities to make a public profession of faith in Christ often following the sermon.

RITES OF PASSAGE Baptists practice both baptism and Communion, the latter often called the Lord's Supper. Baptists participate in these acts out of obedience to Christ's example in the New Testament rather than from a belief that they are in any way necessary for salvation. Baptism is reserved for those who have made a profession of faith in Christ and is done not by sprinkling but by totally immersing the believer under water. Historically this has been controversial and the cause of some persecution, but Baptists have held firm to the practice, basing it on their reading of the New Testament. All Baptists observe Communion, though they differ in frequency.

MEMBERSHIP Baptists are well known for their emphasis on evangelism, both through formal church and mission projects and through personal witness. Methods of evangelism have included sending missionaries to various people and groups, summer camps for children, the use of evangelical tracts distributed in public forums, revivals, and electronic media. Baptists have attracted attention for their practice of sending volunteers to major meetings and events, such as political conventions or the Olympics, to witness to those in attendance.

The evangelizing efforts of some Baptists have been controversial. In the 1990s, for instance, the Southern Baptist Convention was criticized for encouraging members to target specifically the adherents of other religions for evangelization during their religious holidays and observances.

RELIGIOUS TOLERANCE From their origins in England through their emergence as a significant presence in the New World, Baptists have been persecuted for their lack of support for the established church. Their strict separationist views on matters of church and state, their emphasis on conversion and the believer's baptism, and their practice of immersion have all at times led them to suffer persecution. In light of their history, Baptist's consistent support for religious liberty, while at times a matter of self-preservation, is also noteworthy.

Baptists have participated in ecumenical dialogue, but the lack of hierarchy makes it impossible for any one group to claim to represent all Baptists in such settings.

SOCIAL JUSTICE Although congregations may be active in local efforts, it is through networks and associations that most individual Baptists have participated in campaigns for social justice. In the United States the Baptist Peace Fellowship, for instance, is a voluntary association promoting peace and reconciliation among individuals and nations. Similarly, Baptist groups such as the Woman's Missionary Union have been active in international relief work. Baptist missionaries have been an integral part of their denomination's eyes and ears around the world, drawing attention to and promoting human rights, education, and religious freedom.

SOCIAL ASPECTS Although Baptists do not speak with one voice on these matters, many Baptists hold fairly conservative views on matters of marriage and family. Much has been made of Baptist opposition to state-sanctioned homosexual unions, for instance. In addition, in the late 1990s the Southern Baptist Convention attracted international attention when it amended the Baptist Faith and Message to include a statement declaring that a wife should submit to her husband's authority. While there has been criticism of Baptists along these lines, it has also been noted that Baptists have consistently opposed the extension of state authority into matters concerning the home.

CONTROVERSIAL ISSUES Since no theological or church authority has the ability to speak for all Baptists, it is impossible to do more than generalize about Baptist opinion. Baptists have not taken a strict stance on birth control, although within a monogamous marriage there is little opposition to its preventative use. Although divorce continues to be decried by most Baptists, evidence suggests that the divorce rate for Baptists is not much different from that of the general population. Most Baptist groups have opposed abortion on demand, arguing that life begins at conception. The role of women in Baptist life is especially difficult to describe. Many churches do not ordain women to the ministry or to the position of deacon. Some moderate Baptist churches, however, have embraced women in the ministry.

CULTURAL IMPACT The influence of Baptists on culture has been twofold. First, Baptists comprise a major portion of the larger evangelical audience. Evangelical authors, artists, musicians, and other performers have found a willing audience for their work, fueling what is a multimillion dollar industry, and Baptists have been a large part of that audience. Customer surveys carried out by Christian retailers in the United States estimate that Baptists make up a large share of their total customer base. Second, some Baptist groups have been critical of what they perceive as a moral decline in American culture and in Western culture generally. They have been public, and in some cases influential, critics of music, dance, art, and especially movies that they consider objectionable. In the 1990s, for instance, the Southern Baptist Convention boycotted Disney theme parks and movies for promoting what the group called antifamily messages.

Steven Jones

See Also Vol. I: *Christianity, Protestantism*

Bibliography

Ammerman, Nancy Tatom. *Baptist Battles: Social Change and Religious Conflict in the Southern Baptist Convention.* New Brunswick, N.J.: Rutgers University Press, 1990.

Brackney, William H. *The Baptists.* New York: Greenwood Press, 1988.

George, Timothy, and David Dockery, eds. *Baptist Theologians.* Nashville: Broadman Press, 1990.

Goodwin, Everett C., ed. *Baptists in the Balance: The Tension between Freedom and Responsibility.* Valley Forge, Pa.: Judson Press, 1997.

Leonard, Bill J. *Baptist Ways: A History.* Valley Forge, Pa.: Judson Press, 2003.

McBeth, H. Leon. *The Baptist Heritage: Four Centuries of Baptist Witness.* Nashville: Broadman, 1987.

———. *A Sourcebook for Baptist Heritage.* Nashville: Broadman, 1990.

Shurden, William. *The Baptist Identity: Four Fragile Freedoms.* Macon, Ga.: Smyth and Helwys, 1993.

Starr, Edward Caryl. *A Baptist Bibliography.* 25 vols. Philadelphia: Judson Press, 1947–76.

Wardin, Albert W. *Baptists around the World.* Nashville: Broadman and Holman, 1995.

Christianity

Church of Jesus Christ of Latter-day Saints

FOUNDED: 1830 C.E.

RELIGION AS A PERCENTAGE OF WORLD POPULATION: 0.19 percent

OVERVIEW The Latter-day Saint movement began in the late 1820s during a time of religious ferment in the United States. It shared with other "restorationist" movements the conviction that existing churches had strayed so completely from early Christianity that they were incapable of reform from within. But unlike other groups at the time who organized new churches based on close readings of the Bible, the Latter-day Saints believed in the immediate revelation of God and in the prophetic authority of its founder, Joseph Smith. Though a variety of faith communities trace their origins to Smith, by far the largest and best known is the Church of Jesus Christ of Latter-day Saints (LDS Church), founded in 1830 and headquartered in Salt Lake City, Utah.

HISTORY According to Joseph Smith (1805–44), in 1820, at the age of 14, he had his first revelation. He was in the woods near his home in Palmyra, New York, when God and Jesus Christ appeared before him, telling him not to join any of the existing churches. A few years later the Book of Mormon, purportedly an ancient record written on golden plates, was given to Smith by an angel and translated by Smith through divine inspiration. In 1830, one month after the publication of the Book of Mormon, Smith organized the LDS Church in

Fayette, New York, restoring, he claimed, the early, primitive church of Jesus Christ. For believers the Book of Mormon was a revealed companion to the Bible. Others, however, thought that it was a blasphemous competitor to the Bible and that Smith was a false prophet.

As Smith's followers grew in numbers, so also did hostility toward them, leading to the pejorative terms "Mormonite" and, later, "the Mormons" (a term eventually embraced by the LDS Church). This antagonism also helped rationalize violence toward the new church and soon caused its removal to the Ohio frontier. A pattern of new revelation by Smith, renewed hostility toward Mormons, and migration west was repeated in the church's successive relocations to Missouri and Illinois, the latter in 1839. With each move Smith built relatively sophisticated towns, forming sites for the gathering of large numbers of proselytes from throughout North America and eventually the British Isles. The influx of a large and socially exclusive population to an already volatile American frontier threatened the political and economic status quo and created increasingly organized, even state-sponsored, attacks on the LDS Church. In 1838 Missouri's governor directed his militia to assist the ad hoc efforts of mobs to expel from the state more than 10,000 Latter-day Saints.

The Missouri refugees fled to Illinois, where they converted swampland on the banks of the Mississippi into the "City of Joseph," Smith's last and most complete effort to create a social order expressive of his theological vision. Formally named Nauvoo, the city was given unique independence by the state and became

Worldmark Encyclopedia of Religious Practices

153

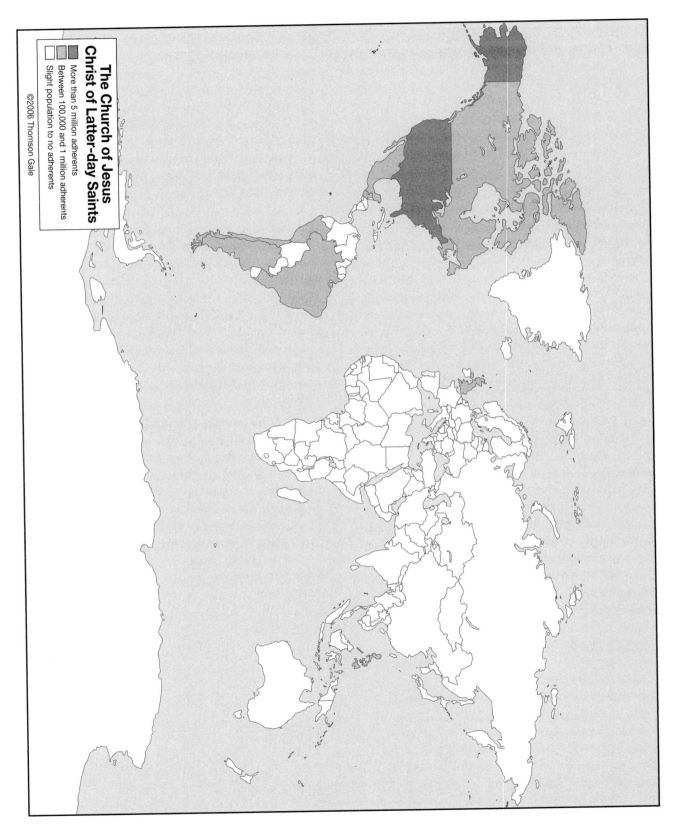

The Church of Jesus
Christ of Latter-day Saints

More than 5 million adherents
Between 100,000 and 1 million adherents
Slight population to no adherents

©2006 Thomson Gale

the site of Mormonism's first public practice of "plural marriage," or polygamy. Again, the combination of new doctrine and political power proved a catastrophic combination for the Latter-day Saints. In 1844 Joseph Smith and his brother Hyrum were killed by a mob. Upon the death of its founder, the Latter-day Saint movement splintered in several directions. Contesting claimants to his presidency led small groups to Wisconsin and Texas. Individuals, too, scattered under pressure from mobs that raided Nauvoo and its environs following Smith's murder. Many of the scattered were gathered in 1860 into what became the Reorganized Church of Jesus Christ of Latter Day Saints (later headquartered in Independence, Missouri, and in 2001 renamed the Community of Christ).

The majority of the Saints from Nauvoo followed Brigham Young (1801–77) to the West, and along with large numbers of converts from Europe, they pioneered settlements throughout the Rocky Mountain territories, establishing a theocracy. In 1850 Young became governor of the newly created territory of Utah. At the same time, however, the U.S. government attempted, both violently and nonviolently, to make Mormonism conform to nineteenth-century American moral and political norms. Because of his support for polygamy and his defiance of federal authority, Young was replaced as governor in 1857, though he continued as president of the church. It was the Mormon's subsequent separation of ecclesiastical and political office, and its late-century renunciation of polygamy, that allowed for Utah statehood in 1896 and that led to a measure of social acceptance for the Latter-day Saints. The church spent the twentieth century expanding beyond its North American borders. Today, growing at an annual rate of 3 percent per year, it is comprised of nearly 12 million members in approximately 123 nations and 21 territories.

CENTRAL DOCTRINES The Latter-day Saints worship a godhead comprised of three separate divine persons: God the Father, his Son Jesus Christ, and the Holy Ghost. Thus, the Latter-day Saints do not believe in the Trinity, the view held by traditional Christianity that the Father, Son, and Holy Ghost are united in one God. This, combined with the church's doctrine of "eternal progression," a belief that humans have divine potential, has led some to argue that the LDS Church is not Christian. Yet the church shares with traditional Christianity the doctrine of the Father's sovereignty and of Christ's

An archivist holds open Joseph Smith's diary. Joseph Smith organized the Church of Jesus Christ of Latter-day Saints in 1830. © JIM RICHARDSON/CORBIS.

divinity as God's only begotten son in the flesh, whose sacrificial atonement and resurrection is the sole means of overcoming human sin and death. Equally central to Latter-day Saint belief are the traditional Christian doctrines of repentance, faith in Christ, baptism, and the gift of the Holy Ghost.

Distinctive doctrines include a belief in modern revelation. While endorsing the traditional biblical revelation of God through Jesus Christ, the Latter-day Saints also believe that God has spoken and continues to speak to his covenant people through prophets, who are called to lead the church according to contemporary needs. The chief example of such a prophet is, of course, Joseph Smith. In addition the Latter-day Saints believe that God continues to speak through the church's president, designated as its prophet. Individual members seek divine revelation on matters of individual concern, espe-

The Mormon temple in Salt Lake City, Utah, at night. After their dedication, Mormon temples are closed to all but active members of the Church. © CHRIS ROGERS/CORBIS.

cially with respect to their personal salvation and church responsibilities.

MORAL CODE OF CONDUCT The Latter-day Saints subscribe to the classic ethical values associated with New Testament Christianity: love of God and love of neighbor (broadly defined). In addition to its emphasis on moral integrity, the church places a high value on sexual chastity, including abstinence prior to, and fidelity within, marriage.

SACRED BOOKS The LDS canon includes four books that are considered equally authoritative: the Bible, the Book of Mormon, the Pearl of Great Price, and the Doctrine and Covenants. The church prefers the King James Version of the Bible. The Book of Mormon, a 500-page narrative of an Israelite civilization in the Americas, includes an account of Christ's postresurrection ministry. The Pearl of Great Price comprises Smith's other revelations, many of which elaborate upon the biblical narrative. The Doctrine and Covenants contains Smith's revelations concerning the organization of the church and elucidation of its doctrines.

SACRED SYMBOLS On top of every LDS temple is a statue of an angel blowing a trumpet. A common motif in LDS imagery, this figure symbolizes both a specific event and a religious ideal. Historically it refers to the angel Moroni, who gave Joseph Smith the golden plates upon which the Book of Mormon was based. Moreover, since Moroni is equated with the angel prophesied in Revelation 14:6, the statue also symbolizes the church's sense of divine commission to evangelize the entire world.

EARLY AND MODERN LEADERS Besides Joseph Smith, Brigham Young, who played a significant role in colonizing the western United States, is probably the most famous Latter-day Saint. In 1995 Gordon B. Hinckley became the church's fifteenth president. His administration has been defined by an increasing internationalization of the church.

MAJOR THEOLOGIANS AND AUTHORS The Latter-day Saints do not engage in traditional theological reasoning, and scholastic theology does not carry any doctrinal authority for them. This, in large part, is a result of their view that philosophical disputes corrupted early Christianity, their inheritance from Joseph Smith of a large body of canonical writing, and their belief in the revelatory power of their contemporary prophet. Those within the church who write about doctrinal matters tend to do so as commentaries on LDS scripture or in the form of homilies published by the church's press.

ORGANIZATIONAL STRUCTURE LDS congregations are organized geographically and are called "wards." Several wards form a "stake," and several stakes make up an "area," the aggregation of which covers the world. Each unit is presided over by a lay presidency serving a limited tenure; all are under the direction of the church's lifetime appointed president and its quorum of twelve apostles.

HOUSES OF WORSHIP AND HOLY PLACES Formal LDS worship occurs in both chapels and temples. Chapels are the site of regular Sunday worship services and are architecturally distinctive by the absence of the cross, which reflects the LDS emphasis on the resurrection. More distinctive are the more than one hundred temples built throughout the world. After their dedication, temples are closed to all but active members of the church. Highly symbolic in design, temples portray LDS cos-

Five men herald the opening of a performance of the Mormon Pageant on Hill Cumorah in Palmyra, New York. To the left is a statue of the angel Moroni, who, according to Mormon belief, led Joseph Smith to the hiding place of the golden plates of the Book of Mormon in 1823. © BETTMANN/CORBIS.

mology and its theology of the immediacy of the divine. Certain locations, such as Temple Square in Salt Lake City and places associated with Joseph Smith's ministry, are deeply meaningful to the Latter-day Saints as sites of religious sacrifice or revelatory experience.

WHAT IS SACRED? The Latter-day Saints do not ascribe particular sanctity to objects. Rather, they take literally the Hebrew Bible's notion of a priestly people who, in virtue of their covenantal relationship to God, are able to mediate the divine for the sake of the world. In this manner, Latter-day Saints believe that God acts to sanctify the world through humans who can consecrate, bless, and heal through prayer, anointing, and laying on of hands.

HOLIDAYS AND FESTIVALS The Latter-day Saints observe the primary events of the Christian calendar: Easter and Christmas. They also commemorate the Mormon exodus from Illinois and heroic crossing of the American continent. Each year celebrations are held in

Utah's cities (in addition to smaller observances held worldwide in Latter-day Saint congregations) to commemorate, with parades and reenactments, the entry of the first pioneers into the Salt Lake Valley in 1847.

MODE OF DRESS Latter-day Saints dress in the fashion of their respective cultures, adapting it only to observe certain standards related to modesty. Temple-going church members wear at all times an undergarment that symbolizes, not unlike a clerical collar, their formal dedication to serving God.

DIETARY PRACTICES Latter-day Saints continue to observe a dietary code, divinely revealed to Smith in 1833, that forbids the consumption of alcohol, tea, coffee, and tobacco and advocates wise eating habits as foundational to both spiritual and physical strength.

RITUALS The LDS Church's prophetic and lay priestly tradition, coupled with a belief in the necessity of sacraments, has created a rich set of ritual practices that order both communal and personal life. Infants are introduced into the congregation through rituals of naming and blessing, usually by the father. Sunday services, while in the Protestant model of sermons and classes, are focused on the administration of Communion. On Monday nights the home is the site of family worship designed to teach gospel principles and strengthen family relationships through wholesome activities. On any day but Sunday, a member who receives the necessary authorization (based on worthiness) may attend the temple to perform ordinances, such as baptism, for a deceased person who did not receive such ordinances while alive.

RITES OF PASSAGES Membership in the church is signified by baptism and confirmation at the age of eight. Full-time missionary work and marriage in a temple mark important transitions to adult status within the church, as well as increased responsibility for it. The temple is the preferred site of LDS marriages, since only in the temple may a couple be joined for time and eternity. Those who choose to be married in LDS chapels are considered joined until death. The dead are buried in simple ceremonies that emphasize the certainty of resurrection and include prayers over the grave.

MEMBERSHIP In 2003 the LDS Church had 60,000 missionaries, organized by the church's central administration into 330 missions in over 120 countries. Serving voluntarily and at their own expense, LDS missionaries devote up to three years introducing people to the church. In addition, the church invites public interest in its beliefs through television and radio programming, as well as websites.

RELIGIOUS TOLERANCE Its doctrine of the necessity of free choice, and its experience of religious violence, make the LDS Church supportive of religious tolerance. The church welcomes opportunities to cooperate with other religions for the benefit of society at large, but believing itself to be uniquely authorized by God, the church does not participate in doctrinally motivated ecumenical movements.

SOCIAL JUSTICE The church requires a biblically based 10-percent tithe on its member's income that is reallocated to ensure economic equality among its congregations. Additional donations support educational programs. Members are also expected to make generous offerings for the benefit of the poor by fasting two

The Latter-day Saint Movement

Based in Salt Lake City, Utah, the Church of Jesus Christ of Latter-day Saints, with an international membership of 12 million, is the largest and best-known group that traces its origins to Joseph Smith. But it is not the only one. The next largest is the Community of Christ, which is headquartered in Independence, Missouri, and has fewer than 200,000 members. The Community of Christ evolved doctrinally and ecclesiastically in ways that allowed rapprochement with mainstream American Protestantism but that caused schism with a third of its membership, who wished to retain a "restorationist" orientation (seeking a restoration of the early practices of the Christian church).

The remaining religious groups who look to Smith for their origins are typically small, almost tribal organizations located primarily in the western United States. The best known among them are called "Fundamentalist Mormons" and are identifiable by their continuing practice of "plural marriage," or polygamy. This is in contrast to the Community of Christ, which never practiced polygamy, and the Church of Jesus Christ of Latter-day Saints, which abandoned the practice in the nineteenth century. The various churches that make up the Latter-day Saint movement share the conviction that Smith was a modern prophet, though the definition of this role may range from a mild acknowledgment of his religious genius to a strong conviction that he was a Moses-like lawgiver and mediator of heavenly power.

meals one day a month and donating at least their cash equivalent for distribution to the poor.

SOCIAL ASPECTS One of the distinctive and central beliefs of the LDS Church is that the family is ordained by God to function for the salvation of its members and is empowered to do so through temple ordinances. Thus, the well-being of the family is the paramount duty of each of its members, especially the parents. "No success," states a common church teaching, "can compensate for failure within the home." The religious authority of home and family, as well as the ministerial functions of the church, are ensured through a program of ordaining all worthy male members over the age of twelve years. Depending on the particular priesthood office, lay male members are authorized to perform the sacraments of the church, preside over the membership at large, and make church policy. Male dominance, however, is mitigated by women's authority to teach and preach to the general congregation, as well as to administer church programs that do not require them to direct priesthood-holding males.

CONTROVERSIAL ISSUES The church's sacramental view of marriage and the family places it on the conservative side of many controversial questions, especially those related to sex and gender. The church discourages delay of childbearing, mothers working outside the home, and divorce. It proscribes abortion except in certain extreme circumstances related to the health of the mother, rape, or incest. The church is a leader in the political resistance to legalizing same-sex unions. Homosexual practice is regarded as a sin, though the church is careful not to take a position on whether the origin of homosexuality is in nature or human choice.

CULTURAL IMPACT Through dramatic representations in literature and film, the Latter-day Saints have long symbolized certain elements in the American mythos, especially the paradoxical aspects of the West (pioneering individualism and communal settlement). In the twenty-first century the Latter-day Saints have come to represent the American middle class—as seen, for example, in Tony Kushner's famed Broadway play and subsequent film *Angels in America*. Cultural productions by the church itself include weekly broadcasts by the Mormon Tabernacle Choir and elaborate plays staged at various LDS historical sites, such as the Hill Cumorah pageant in New York. These sites have been meticulously restored by the church to encourage tourism and the propagation of its message.

Kathleen Flake

See Also Vol. 1: *Christianity*

Bibliography

Allen, James B., Ronald W. Walker, and David J. Whittaker, eds. *Studies in Mormon History, 1830–1997: An Indexed Bibliography.* Urbana: University of Illinois, 2000.

Bushman, Richard L. *Joseph Smith and the Beginnings of Mormonism.* Urbana: University of Illinois, 1984.

Daynes, Kathryn M. *More Wives than One: Transformation of the Mormon Marriage System, 1840–1910.* Urbana: University of Illinois, 2001.

Givens, Terryl L. *By the Hand of Mormon: The American Scripture That Launched a New World Religion.* Oxford: Oxford University Press, 2002.

New Mormon Studies: A Comprehensive Resource Library. CD-ROM. Smith Research Associates, 1998.

Selected Collections from the Archives of the Church of Jesus Christ of Latter-day Saints. Provo, Utah: Brigham Young University, 2002.

Shipps, Jan. *Mormonism: The Story of a New Religious Tradition.* Urbana: University of Illinois, 1985.

Whittaker, David J., ed. *Mormon Americana: A Guide to Sources and Collections in the United States.* Provo, Utah: Brigham Young University, 1994.

Coptic Christianity

FOUNDED: 48 C.E.

RELIGION AS A PERCENTAGE OF WORLD POPULATION: 0.12

OVERVIEW The Coptic Orthodox Church adheres to the original apostolic traditions. It follows the decisions of the Councils of Nicea (325), Constantinople (381), and Ephesus (431) and uses the original liturgies written by Saints Mark, Basil of Alexandria, and Gregory of Nazianzus.

During the first Christian centuries, when Egypt was part of the Roman Empire, Copts contributed to the development of the monastic life and Christian theology as formulated by the ecumenical councils. After Arab rule replaced the Byzantine Empire in Egypt in 641–42, Christianity was slowly overshadowed by Islam through intermarriage and conversion. The majority of the contemporary Egyptian Muslim population is of Coptic origin. In spite of its minority position, the Coptic Church was able to survive, and beginning in the 1950s Coptic Christianity experienced a religious revival. Concurrent with this revival a movement of Coptic immigration to Western countries started during the 1960s. The majority of the immigrants settled in the United States, Canada, Australia, and New Zealand. By the twenty-first century more than 180 Coptic churches existed outside Egypt.

The name Copt is derived from Qibt, the Arabic translation of the Greek Aigyptios, itself a derivation of Hikuptah, a reference to Memphis, the capital of ancient Egypt.

HISTORY According to tradition, Christianity was introduced to Egypt by Saint Mark the Evangelist in 48 C.E., and it is to this event that the Coptic Orthodox Church traces its origins. From the first century C.E. Christianity spread rapidly, unleashing violent persecutions by the Roman emperors. So many Christians were murdered during the rule of Diocletian (reigned 284–305) that the Coptic Church started its calendar at the year of his enthronement in order to commemorate the martyrs on whose blood the church was built. After the Edict of Milan (313), Christians were free to worship, and many Egyptians embraced the Christian faith. By the fourth century Egyptian Christians started to withdraw into the desert, eventually creating the monastic movement.

The fourth and fifth centuries were marred by doctrinal controversies, especially concerning the nature of Christ. One of the main issues centered on the teaching of Arius (c. 250–336), who maintained that Christ was created by God and not equally eternal. Arius was declared heretical, and, according to the Nicene Creed (325) that Athanasius (reigned 328–73) helped formulate, Christ was affirmed fully one with God. As different parties refined their ideas about Christ's divinity and humanity, they also came to represent opinions in the eastern and western part of the Byzantine Empire. Various emperors tried to promote a single accepted doctrine but failed. By the seventh century a schism had occurred between the churches of the East, including the Coptic Church, and the churches of Rome and Constantinople. It ran along religious, geographical, and political lines and has endured through modern times.

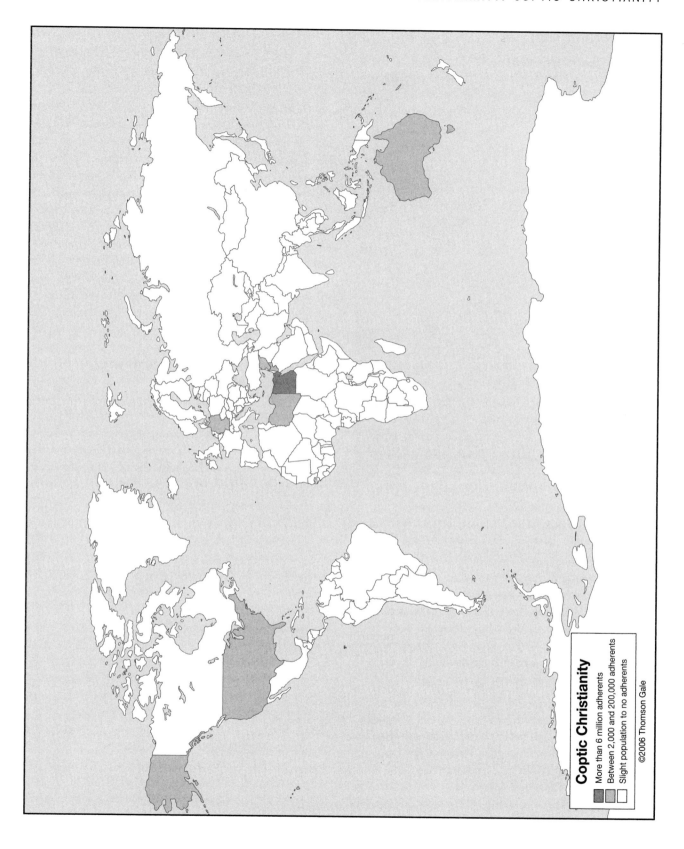

Coptic Christians gather to celebrate St. Mary's Day. The deaths of Coptic saints are commemorated by moulids, *festivals of church-related activities and entertainment.* © ED KASHI/CORBIS.

In 629 Byzantium tried to suppress Coptic Christianity, replacing the Coptic patriarch with a Byzantine church ruler. After the Arabs invaded Egypt in 641–42, the Copts were initially allowed to practice their religion freely. Coptic Christians were Egypt's religious majority until the Middle Ages, although they suffered sporadic persecutions by Muslims. Copts remained in the secondary status of *dhimmi*s (protected citizens) until 1856.

The ruler Mohammed Ali (1805–13) modernized Egypt, providing economic and educational opportunities for the Copts. This represented the beginning of the revival of the Coptic Church that has continued into the twenty-first century. The impetus for this revival came from the Sunday School Movement (1918), which inspired many young, well-educated men and women to serve the church.

Copts fought with the Muslims against the British occupation (1882–1922), and for a few decades rela-

tions between Muslims and Christians were relatively good. Twice a Copt briefly served as prime minister. This changed when, in the 1940s, the Islamic Brotherhood started to propagate an Islamic agenda.

The 1952 revolution led by Gamal Abdal Nasser introduced land reforms and deprived Copts of 75 percent of their wealth, which led to school closures and deterioration of Coptic possessions. Nasser, however, suppressed the Islamic Brotherhood, and Copts enjoyed relative safety. When Anwar as-Sadat became president in 1970, he allowed the Islamic Brotherhood more freedom, and incidents of religious strife increased again. During Hosni Mubarak's regime, which began in 1981, extremist Islamic groups aggravated this strife.

CENTRAL DOCTRINES Cyril I (412–44) formulated the Coptic Christology now known as Miaphysitism, which holds that Christ is truly God and man as his nature is "divine and human—mystically united in one, without confusion, corruption, or change." At the Council of Chalcedon (451), the Western churches accepted the formula that Christ had unity of person but duality of natures.

The center of Coptic Church life is the seven sacraments: Eucharist, baptism, confirmation (with holy chrism), confession and absolution, unction of the sick, matrimony, and consecration into one of the holy orders of priesthood. The Eucharist is at the core of Coptic religious life, and in order to participate in the Eucharist, a person must be a full member of the Coptic Church through baptism and confirmation. A person may receive Communion only after confession and absolution.

MORAL CODE OF CONDUCT Copts developed a moral code of conduct that, to a large extent, conforms with that of its Middle Eastern and Islamic environment. Believers rarely drink alcohol or eat pork, and forms of indulgence, such as overeating or sleeping long hours, are deemed incompatible with the ascetic character of the Coptic Church. Coptic society is patriarchal. Although many contemporary Coptic women are successful professionals, men are considered the head of the family.

SACRED BOOKS Copts use three liturgies: the Liturgy of Saint Basil, the Liturgy of Saint Gregory of Nazianzus, and the ancient liturgy of Saint Mark, also known as the Liturgy of Saint Cyril.

The lectionary (*Katamaros*), a study of the various stages of Christ's life, is used throughout the liturgical year. The *Agbiya*, the book of the hours, contains the Psalms, prayers, and Gospels for the seven daily prayers. In addition, Copts use a psalmody, a book of doxologies (praise), and the *Synaxarium*, a book that commemorates Coptic saints.

Parts of the sacred literature appear in the ancient Coptic language that was derived from the pharaonic times and was spoken and written in a form of the Greek alphabet until about 1300 C.E. Coptic, considered a sacred language, is part of the Coptic culture and identity.

SACRED SYMBOLS Apart from the Eucharist and liturgies in Coptic, the most sacred symbol in the Coptic Church is the cross, including a tattooed cross on the right wrist. Originally the tattoo was an identification mark so that Coptic children would not be mistaken for Muslims in times of upheaval. In modern times the cross has become a powerful mark of Christian identity in Egypt.

EARLY AND MODERN LEADERS Copts, who have never had access to political power, have rallied around their patriarchs and bishops for guidance in both religious and secular affairs. They have had numerous prominent leaders, including Athanasius, the church father who was exiled five times as a result of political and theological controversies. Patriarch Cyril I (reigned 412–44) violently persecuted non-Christians and fought Nestorius for his refusal to call Mary the Mother of God, since he considered her to be only the mother of the human Jesus. Cyril IV (reigned 1854–61) called the Father of Reform, changed education, including what was offered to girls. Cyril V (reigned 1875–1927) fought against foreign intrusion by Catholic and Protestant missionaries, and Cyril VI began the modern revival of the Coptic Church.

Important lay leaders have included Habib Girgis, the founder of the Sunday School Movement (1918), and the Ghali family, which counts among its members former Egyptian prime minister Boutros Ghali and former general secretary of the United Nations Boutros Boutros-Ghali.

MAJOR THEOLOGIANS AND AUTHORS The catechetical school in Alexandria produced illustrious theologians, such as Clement of Alexandria (born c. 150) and

A young girl displays a tattoo of a cross on her right wrist. Apart from the Coptic Eucharist and liturgies, the most sacred symbol in the Coptic Church is the cross. © REZA; WEBISTAN/CORBIS.

Origen (c. 185–c. 251). They framed their arguments within Greek philosophy, defending Christianity against gnosticism and paganism. Athanasius and Cyril I were both prolific theologians. Saint Anthony (c. 250–356) led the Copts in the development of solitary monasticism, while Saint Pachomius (born c. 290) originated the communal monastic life. Shenute (348–451?) was the first theologian to write in the Coptic language.

In the thirteenth century several writers, known as the Awlad al-Assal, translated Coptic theological texts into Arabic. Father Matta el-Meskeen, the abbot of the Saint Macarius Monastery, is one of the most influential contemporary theologians.

ORGANIZATIONAL STRUCTURE The Coptic Orthodox Church hierarchy is headed by the patriarch of Alexandria and includes approximately 60 bishops, who must be monks and members of the Coptic Holy Synod. The Coptic lay council facilitates relations between church and state, and the lay-clerical committee mediates between clergy and laity.

HOUSES OF WORSHIP AND HOLY PLACES Coptic churches have the sanctuary oriented to the east. The altar is located behind a screen, or iconostasis. Churches are decorated with icons, wall paintings, carved wood, stuccos, and fabrics. Women sit separately from men.

Coptic Monastic Life and Church Renewal

The renewal of the Coptic Orthodox Church began through the activities of well-educated lay Copts who became impatient with the lethargic attitudes of patriarchs after the reformer Cyril IV of the mid-1800s. They adopted the model of Protestant Sunday schools to teach Coptic children about their faith, history, and culture. By the 1950s former Sunday school students, after obtaining graduate degrees from universities, were joining the church as priests, monks, or nuns. Under Patriarch Cyril VI (reigned 1959–71) these developments were consolidated into a reform movement, which has continued under Shenouda III, who took office in 1971.

The central developments in this movement include daily celebration of the Eucharist, a strengthened monastic movement, new options for women to serve the church as active nuns and deaconesses, intense Sunday school programs, and new seminaries to educate priests. In addition, church renewal has reclaimed the Coptic archeological and cultural heritage.

Many churches, monasteries, and convents stand on sites where the Holy Family stayed or that are connected to a saint or martyr.

WHAT IS SACRED? Coptics hold the Eucharist most sacred. Furthermore, relics and icons of the saints are held sacred. Locally there are hundreds of places dedicated to martyrs, saints, and the Holy Family. Copts carry objects connected to these places or persons, such as holy oil, pictures, and crosses, as sources of *baraka* (blessing).

HOLIDAYS AND FESTIVALS The deaths of Coptic saints are commemorated by *moulids*. These festivals consist of church-related activities and entertainment, and they are sometimes attended by Muslims. *Moulids* also provide opportunities to make pilgrimages to shrines of saints and martyrs.

MODE OF DRESS Copts typically wear Western clothing. In villages Coptic women wear veils similar to those of Muslim women. Monks and nuns wear a skullcap called a *qalansuwa* that is divided into two halves, with crosses embroidered on each half. The split symbolizes the struggle Saint Anthony experienced in the desert with the devil, who tore his cap in two.

DIETARY PRACTICES Copts fast from all animal products, including meat, eggs, milk, and butter, every Wednesday and Friday, as well as during the days of Lent, Advent, and several other feasts, for a total of more than 200 days a year. The aged, children, and pregnant women are not excused from the fasts. Copts also fast for a minimum of nine hours before officiating at, or partaking in, the Eucharist. Fasting is a physical and a spiritual exercise and includes sexual abstinence.

RITUALS Daily Coptic prayer rituals are directed toward preparation for the Eucharist. Following the book of the hours, the day starts at sunset, in keeping with the time of Christ's death. Throughout the day Copts pray seven times, commemorating Christ's suffering.

The marriage ceremony is ruled by Coptic canon law and includes prayers and readings that lead to the *al-iklil* (the crowning ceremony), wherein the couple is crowned with two diadems that symbolize the high spiritual status of marriage.

Funeral liturgies vary according to the status (clergy or lay), age, and gender of the deceased. Burial occurs on the same day as death. Copts believe that the soul lingers for three days, and thus they perform a ritual for the spirit on the third day. On the 40th day after death, there is a church ceremony in front of a portrait of the deceased.

RITES OF PASSAGE The most important rites of passage initiate children into the community and church. One week after birth a cluster of celebrations is held called *subu'*, or seventh-day feast, which is celebrated by Muslims and Christians alike for good luck and protection. The child is given a name, and the child's status changes from newborn to family member. These ceremonies for Copts often include the *salawat al-tisht* (washbasin prayers), at which time a priest gives the child its first bath while chanting prayers and verses from the Bible. Circumcision for boys and for many girls is performed sometime during early childhood. Having received the sacraments of baptism, confirmation, and

Communion, a boy becomes a full member of the church on his 40th day and a girl on her 80th. The new mother, whom the church considers unclean after having given birth, undergoes a cleansing ritual.

MEMBERSHIP Copts are forbidden by Islamic law to proselytize. Church growth within Egypt is purely demographic, while outside Egypt intermarriage adds new members. In the late twentieth century the Coptic Church started missionary activities in sub-Saharan Africa and established several churches there. The Coptic Church participates in ecumenical dialogues and was among the founding members of the World Council of Churches.

RELIGIOUS TOLERANCE The Egyptian state is not based on Islamic laws and, in principle, allows Copts full rights as citizens. Copts, however, are not allowed to practice their religion openly. Special governmental permits are needed to build a new church or repair an existing one. Churches cannot be established in the vicinity of a mosque. Copts suffer numerous forms of hidden discrimination when seeking employment or scholarships.

SOCIAL JUSTICE The Coptic Church has designed vocational training and special Bible studies for the poorest of the poor. It also has worked on interfaith and peacemaking activities through youth workshops and integrated schools for Muslim and Coptic children. Coptic leaders have been active in protesting the practice of female circumcision.

SOCIAL ASPECTS The sacrament of marriage sanctifies a physical and spiritual union that cannot be broken. The family unit is considered the core of the Coptic faith. It is considered indivisible and functions like a small church that experiences the work of God and holds specific spiritual responsibilities. The family transmits the extensive Coptic tradition and teaches children the faith.

CONTROVERSIAL ISSUES The Coptic Church allows the practice of birth control but forbids abortion. It condemns homosexuality. Women are considered caregivers who raise the future generation. The Coptic Church still follows some Old Testament laws that deem a woman impure during menstruation and after childbirth. These rules, in combination with specific interpretations of the New Testament, bar women from holding official, ordained offices in the church hierarchy. Women can be Sunday school teachers, pastoral workers, and nuns.

CULTURAL IMPACT Christianized themes on shrouds and textiles of antiquity represent the beginning of Coptic art. The most important monuments of early Coptic art are monasteries and the frescoes preserved within them, such as those in the Wadi Natroun Oasis and in the Monastery of Saint Anthony. In the eighteenth century a fertile period of icon painting began, and in the 1970s Isaak Fanous established a school for neo-Coptic iconography. Early Coptic sculpture depicts people with wide-set eyes, a characteristic that has returned in contemporary iconography to reflect the idea that the saint has grasped a divine truth.

Nelly van Doorn-Harder

See Also Vol. I: *Christianity*

Bibliography

Atiya, Aziz S., ed. *The Coptic Encyclopedia.* 8 vols. New York: Macmillan, 1991.

Cannuyer, Christian. *Coptic Egypt: The Christians of the Nile.* New York: Harry N. Abrams, 2001.

Doorn-Harder, Pieternella van. *Contemporary Coptic Nuns.* Columbia: University of South Carolina Press, 1995.

Doorn-Harder, Pieternella van, and Kari Vogt, eds. *Between Desert and City: The Coptic Orthodox Church Today.* Eugene, Ore.: Wipf and Stock Publishers, 2004.

Hassan, Sana. *Christians versus Muslims in Modern Egypt: The Century-Long Struggle for Coptic Equality.* New York: Oxford University Press, 2003.

Kamil, Jill. *Christianity in the Land of the Pharaohs: The Coptic Orthodox Church.* London: Routledge, 2002.

Watson, John H. *Among the Copts.* Sussex, England: Sussex Academic Press, 2000.

Eastern Catholicism

FOUNDED: Twelfth century C.E.

RELIGION AS A PERCENTAGE OF WORLD POPULATION: 0.2 percent

OVERVIEW The Eastern Catholic Churches are Eastern Churches that obey the authority of the Roman Catholic Church. They are also called the Catholic Churches of Eastern Rites and the Uniate Churches (because of their union with Rome). These churches maintain their own ecclesiastical traditions and rites—sometimes with minor changes influenced by the Latin tradition—and preserve certain levels of autonomy and self-organization but have otherwise accepted the dogmatic teaching of the Roman Catholic Church.

There are more than 20 Eastern Catholic Churches, with followers all over the world. The different churches officially united with Rome at various times between 1182 and 1961. Most new adherents are in eastern Europe, the Middle East, India, Egypt, western Europe, and North America.

HISTORY The Eastern Catholic Churches trace their origin to the twelfth century, when the Roman Catholic Church began to absorb Eastern Orthodox Christian Churches of different theological traditions. Rome's efforts were not successful until it established a strong presence in the Near East and Anatolia during the Crusades. Two influential Christian communities declared their unity with Rome at that time: the Maronite Church in 1182 and the Armenian Church in 1198 (a

union destroyed by the Tatar invasion of 1375 and reestablished in 1742).

The Catholic Church of Byzantine Rite in southern Italy and Sicily absorbed a mass migration of Orthodox Albanians in the fifteenth and sixteenth centuries and became the Italo-Albanian Church in 1595. The first Eastern Catholic community in India was the Syro-Malabar Church, which officially united with Rome in 1599. Some of the hierarchy and followers of the Malankara Orthodox Syrian Church established the Syro-Malankara Catholic Church in India in 1930.

Several Eastern Catholic Churches were formed after internal conflicts within Orthodox Churches led groups of clergy and their followers to look for support from Rome. The Chaldean Church of the East-Syrian, or Nestorian tradition (formed in 1552, with adherents mainly in Iraq and Iran); the Syrian Church of the West-Syrian, or Jacobite tradition (formed in 1662); and the Melkite Church of the Byzantine tradition (formed in 1724) were proclaimed in this way.

In the sixteenth and seventeenth centuries bishops' synods and uniting councils brought in several churches of the Byzantine rite in Eastern Europe. The Ukrainian and Belarusian ecclesiastical traditions and churches formed after the Brest Union Council in 1596. The Uzhorog Union with Rome in 1646 brought the Ruthenian Church in the United States (a separate metropoly since 1969) and the Greek-Catholic diocese of Mukachiv in the Ukraine into the Eastern Catholic movement. The Romanian Church joined in 1700 after the bishops of the Transylvania region agreed to unite with Rome.

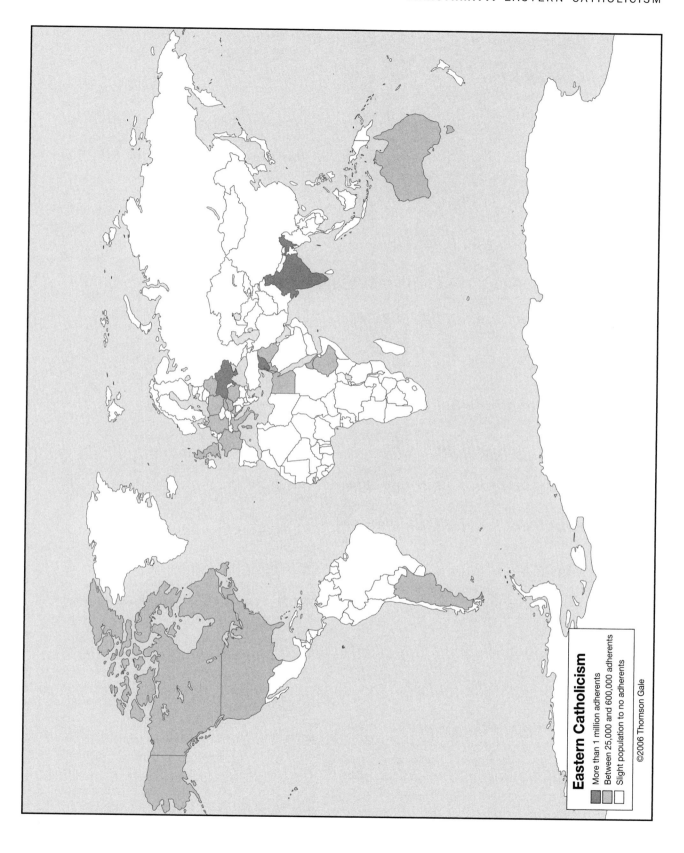

Eastern Catholicism

More than 1 million adherents

Between 25,000 and 600,000 adherents

Slight population to no adherents

©2006 Thomson Gale

Cardinal Liubomyr Huzar, the major archbishop of the Ukrainian church, conducts a service in 2001. © REUTERS NEWMEDIA INC./CORBIS.

The eighteenth century brought in the Coptic Catholic Church of Egypt (1741) and the Byzantine Church in the former Yugoslavia (1777). Other Eastern Catholic Churches were established in the twentieth century: the Greek (1911); the Hungarian (1912); the Russian, with two separate exarchates (1917 and 1928); the Bulgarian (1926); the Slovak (1937); the Albanian (1939); and the Ethiopian (1961).

CENTRAL DOCTRINES Though not obligated to do so, all Eastern Catholic Churches accept the central doctrines of the Roman Catholic Church, including those that have caused controversy between Western and Eastern churches—for example, the doctrines of Filioque, papal infallibility, and the Immaculate Conception. The most latinized churches are those that have the longest history of organizational unity with Rome, those directly supervised by the Latin hierarchy, and those too

small to maintain their distinctive traditions in the face of regional Eastern Orthodox influences without direct support of the Latin hierarchy.

A movement to preserve and restore the unique doctrines of Eastern Christianity began in the nineteenth century. The Melkite Church has been one of the most active proponents of this trend along with the Syro-Malankaran, Ethiopian, Syrian, and, increasingly, Ukrainian churches.

MORAL CODE OF CONDUCT As a general rule Eastern Catholic Churches observe the same moral principles as the Eastern Churches, especially in regions where Eastern Catholics and Orthodox Christians coexist: the state of Kerala in India, Syria, Lebanon, big cities in Iraq, Cairo and upper Egypt, the western Ukraine, and Romanian Transylvania. Eastern Catholics take a more liberal approach to moral principles than Orthodox Christians, however, and have more conservative patterns of conduct than Latin Catholics. In the traditional societies, as well as in diasporian communities, Eastern Catholics mostly develop interpersonal relations—marriage in particular—within the church community.

SACRED BOOKS Eastern Catholic Churches use the liturgical books and texts of traditional Eastern Christianity, including the Euchologions, the Books of Needs, the Anthologions, the Festal Anthologies, the Floral and the Lenten Triodions, Oktoechos, Horologions, Typikons, Menologions, Menaions, the Books of Akathistos, and the Books of Commemoration. Some churches accept Latin editions of these works.

SACRED SYMBOLS Eastern Catholics consider holy crosses of various forms (including Greek, Saint Andrew the First Called, Coptic, and Slavic) as important sacred symbols in liturgical as well as private contexts. The Heart of Jesus Christ and the Virgin Mary (a red heart in conjunction with such symbols as drops of blood, wreaths, crowns, or red rays) has become an important symbol in some churches since the end of the nineteenth century, notably the Coptic, the Syro-Malabar, and to some extent the Ukrainian and other churches of the Byzantine tradition.

EARLY AND MODERN LEADERS The founders of specific Eastern Catholic Churches are especially important: Jeremias II al-Amshitti, the first patriarch (1199–1230) of the Maronite Church; Simon III, the first patriarch (1552–1555) of the Chaldean Church; Bishop Jacob, head of the Christians of Saint Thomas, who established informal unity with Rome at the beginning of the sixteenth century; Abraham Pierre I, the first patriarch of the Armenian Church in the eighteenth century; and Michel Jarweh, the first patriarch of the Syrian Church, who helped restore church traditions in 1782. Saint Josaphat Kuntsevych, murdered by his opponents in Polotsk (now Belarusia) in 1623, is especially well known among Eastern European Catholics as a symbol of faithfulness to Rome.

Especially distinguished members of the Eastern Catholic Churches' contemporary hierarchy include Cardinal Ignatius Mous Daud I, the patriarch of the Syrian Church since 1998; Cardinal Nasrallah Sfeir, the patriarch of the Maronite Church since 1986; and Cardinal Liubomyr Huzar, the major archbishop of the Ukrainian Church since 2000.

MAJOR THEOLOGIANS AND AUTHORS The modern-day theology of the Eastern Catholic Churches is based on the works and activities of several theologians from the late nineteenth century (including Josef Audo, the patriarch of the Chaldean Church, and George II, the patriarch of the Melkite Church). In the early twentieth century Andrij Sheptytsky, the metropolitan of the Ukrainian Church, had a significant impact on the development of the Eastern European churches.

While Eastern Catholic theology formerly focused on the Byzantine tradition, several late-twentieth-century authors from the Arabic and Indian Eastern Catholic traditions, including Reverend Mathew Vellanikal from India, Reverend Samir Khallil from Lebanon, and Chaldean Reverend Peter Jusif, introduced other types of Eastern spirituality into consideration.

ORGANIZATIONAL STRUCTURE The Eastern Catholic Churches fall into four groups: patriarchates, major archepiscopacies, metropolies, and others. The six patriarchal Eastern Catholic Churches—the Maronite, Armenian, Chaldean, Syrian, Melkite, and Coptic churches—have the highest level of autonomy and consist of numerous (sometimes two or three dozen) dioceses, which in some cases are joined in regional metropolies or exarchates (one step above a metropoly). The Ukrainian Church and the Syro-Malabar Church in India are major archepiscopacies (archbishoprics), which also consist of numerous dioceses and metropolies or exarchates.

Women pray at an Eastern Catholic church in Lviv, Ukraine. Eastern Catholic church buildings come in a variety of styles, each with its own priest and clergy. © PETER TURNLEY/CORBIS.

Each of the four metropolitan (metropolitinate) Eastern Catholic Churches—the Ethiopian, the Syro-Malankara, the Romanian, and Ruthenian—consist of dioceses only. The 10 other Eastern Catholic Churches have internal autonomy but receive direct guidance from the Vatican. The Italo-Albanian and the Slovak Churches each have two dioceses; the Hungarian Church and the Byzantine Church in the former Yugoslavia have one diocese each; the Bulgarian and Greek Churches exist as exarchates; the Belarusian and the Russian Churches, with an extremely limited number of parishes and adherents, have only organizations at the parochial level; and the Albanian Church exists only in name, having never recovered from Communist repression. The Greek-Catholic diocese of Mukachiv in the Transcarpathian region of Ukraine, denied the possibility of becoming part of the Ukrainian Greek-Catholic Church, identifies with the Ruthenian Metropoly in the United States and depends organizationally directly on Rome.

HOUSE OF WORSHIP AND HOLY PLACES Eastern Catholic church buildings come in a variety of styles,

each with its own priest and other clergy. In large cities the Eastern Catholic traditions led by archbishops or metropolitans offer services in cathedrals. Chapels intended for private prayer (particularly for travelers) in various places (sometimes far from cities or villages, occasionally at memorial sites or crossroads) do not have permanent clergy. Other popular holy places for prayer and veneration are missionary crosses and statues of Christ, the Virgin Mary, or popular saints found near churches, in the center of villages or cities, in hospitals, in the countryside, and in private houses.

WHAT IS SACRED? In the Eastern Catholic Churches the bread and wine used in the sacrament of Communion are the most sacred things. Icons painted on wood or canvas are objects of special veneration, as are crosses, church buildings, the liturgical clothing of the clergy, and ecclesiastical texts.

HOLIDAYS AND FESTIVALS As in Eastern Christianity, Easter is the most significant holiday for Eastern Catholics because of its symbolism of victory over the death. The other main Eastern Catholic holidays are a combination of the 12 traditional holidays in Eastern Christianity (including Christmas, Theophany, Holy Trinity, Transfiguration, Dormition of the Most Pure Mother of God, Exaltation of the Holy Cross, Christmas of the God's Mother, and Entering of the God's Mother into the Temple), several holidays from Western Christianity (including Holy Eucharist and the Christ's Heart), and certain holidays celebrating specific events and saints from regional Eastern Catholic traditions—for example, the Day of Saint Josafat Kuntsevych, observed by Eastern European Catholics, and the Day of Mykola Charnetsky, a newly proclaimed saint in the Ukrainian Church.

MODE OF DRESS The clergy of the most latinized Eastern Catholic Churches (the Syro-Malabar, Maronite, Armenian, and Romanian Churches and the church in the former Yugoslavia, as well as the Basilian monastic order in the Eastern European churches) dress according to Western Christian tradition in black robes with white collars. Some ideological movements that originated in the early 1900s have called for a mode of dress based exclusively on the Eastern tradition: long black (sometimes grey, rarely green or dark red) robes with wide sleeves.

DIETARY PRACTICES According to the common Orthodox tradition, Eastern Catholic Churches observe no specific dietary limitations or prohibitions. Fasts have a more significant role in the church than they do in Western Christianity, however. When adherents fast, they may not eat any product of animal origin or drink alcohol; they must limit public appearances and sexual activity; they may not organize or conduct celebrations or intensive spiritual exercises; and they more frequently attend worship services and pray. Eastern Catholics fast on Wednesdays and Fridays throughout the year and participate in four longer fasts: Lent, the Fast of the Holy Apostles, the Fast of the Dormition of the Most Pure Mother of God, and Advent. Several contemporary churches have eliminated fasting obligations on certain dates (New Year's Day in the Ukrainian Church, for example); relaxed general fasting requirements (permitting the use of eggs and milk and shortening the length of fasting periods); and exempted several groups of people from fasting, including children, the elderly, pregnant women, travelers, and those who are ill. These churches still support strict rules during Lent (the Great Fast).

RITUALS The liturgy (the main service, which includes confession and Communion) is the focal point of ritual practice in the Eastern Catholic Churches. Each of the five main ecclesiastical and liturgical traditions (Byzantine, Coptic, Armenian, Chaldean, and Syrian, or Jacobite) uses its own unique texts, but all have three main parts (the Latin liturgy has only two): Proskomide (introduction and preparation of the saint's gifts for Communion); the Liturgy of Oglashenny, or Catechumens (those preparing to be baptized); and the Liturgy of Adherents. Influenced by the Latin tradition and a general tendency to simplify and shorten rituals, some Eastern Catholic Churches make a point of rejecting certain forms of worship—for example, all-night vigils and "little vespers"—that are traditional components of Eastern Christianity.

Eastern Catholic Churches recognize the seven sacraments (the most holy mysteries) and emphasize baptism, marriage, confession, and Communion. Other rituals important to Eastern Catholics include Chrismation (which involves the application of myrrh after baptism), the consecration of priests, and consecration by oil for bodily and spiritual recovery.

RITES OF PASSAGE Although their level of religious activity and their involvement in religious life are high compared with Western (Latin) Catholics, the majority of Eastern Catholics do not attend weekly services. Eastern Catholics do generally adhere to those rituals connected with birth, adulthood, marriage, and death. Children are baptized within several days after their birth, when the parents choose godparents to support the spiritual growth of the child. Unlike in the Orthodox tradition, some Eastern Catholic Churches accept the Latin practice of confirmation for older children. In marriages between Eastern and Western Catholic spouses, the children accept the rite of the parent of their gender: boys inherit their father's rite and girls take their mother's. Funeral services are attended by special commemorations, which are repeated on the ninth and fortieth days after the death and again one year after the death.

MEMBERSHIP Eastern Catholic Churches that exist in predominantly non-Christian environments, particularly the Coptic, Chaldean, and Syrian traditions, are limited in their ability to evangelize openly, so their communities have remained relatively closed and without growth for several decades. Eastern European Catholic Churches were prohibited and persecuted after World War II by Communist regimes. The Soviet Ukrainian, Romanian, and Czechoslovakian churches were liquidated in a uniform way: with the support of Communist regimes, former clergy declaring their desire to join the Orthodox Church gathered special councils—in Lviv (Ukraine) in 1946, in Cluj-Napoca (Romania) in 1948, in Uzhorod (Ukraine) in 1949, and in Presov (Czechoslovakia) in 1950—that agreed to terminate ecclesiastical relations with Rome. Bishops and priests who refused to recognize the decisions of these councils were arrested or banned from ecclesiastical activity. After the late 1940s adherents of Eastern Catholic Churches in these Communist countries met illegally. Poland and Yugoslavia were allowed to retain their Eastern Catholic dioceses (along with their relations to Rome).

In 1968 the Slovakian Church gained the freedom to expand, but the strong opposition of the local Orthodox Churches prevented it from regaining its prewar status. Other Eastern European churches have evangelized openly only since the fall of Communism in the late 1980s; the Romanian Church has witnessed some growth, while the Ukrainian Church has actually exceeded its previous influence. The Belarussian and Russian churches, however, have grown very slowly, while the Albanian Church never resumed activities, despite regaining the liberty to do so.

RELIGIOUS TOLERANCE Eastern Catholic Churches are fairly open to external ecumenical contacts, although they observe the Vatican's lead and do not generally participate independently in interdenominational communications. Eastern Catholic ecumenical activities usually encounter strong opposition from the Orthodox Churches, however, which do not recognize the union of the Eastern Catholic Churches with Rome as an appropriate way to restore Christian unity. The Orthodox Churches regard Eastern Catholicism as a form of contemporary Catholic proselytism and an attempt to obtain new adherents in the traditional Orthodox territories, curtailing Orthodox influence on the Christian world. They see the Eastern Catholic Churches as a major obstacle in their efforts to establish their own lasting relations with the Vatican on the basis of principles of church organization from the first Christian millennium, which designated five main centers—Rome, Constantinople, Alexandria, Antiochia, and Jerusalem. In this schema Rome would have only spiritual leadership. The bishops of the Melkite Church have been leading advocates of making the reintegration of Eastern Catholic Churches into their corresponding Eastern Orthodox Churches a precondition to reconciliation between Western and Eastern Christianity.

SOCIAL JUSTICE The position of specific Eastern Catholic Churches on poverty and other social problems is generally determined by that church's position in society. Adherents of the Maronite and Armenian Churches in Lebanon represent the wealthier sector of society and have founded prestigious educational institutions (including universities) and many supportive organizations for the poor. Followers of the Chaldean (in Iraq and Iran), Coptic (in Egypt), and Syrian (in Syria and Turkey) Churches belong to the poorer classes. Eastern European Catholics, who represent the middle class, have used the help of Western Catholic institutions to organize support of the poor within their societies. All the churches try to provide theological and general education for their followers, with support from Rome and other Catholic organizations throughout the world.

SOCIAL ASPECTS Traditional family values form the basis of the social doctrine of the Eastern Catholic Churches. Preparation and special education before marriage have become an obligatory practice for the majority of the churches. Marriage between Eastern Catholics and non-Catholics is not widespread or supported in church communities.

Unlike their counterparts in the Western Catholic Church, the majority of Eastern Catholic clergy (except bishops, monks, and hieromonks, who can serve as parochial priests) are married. The Latin observance of celibacy is accepted by the Syro-Malabar, Italo-Albanian, and Armenian Churches and by several small churches of the Byzantine tradition in Europe. The private family life of married Eastern Catholic priests must serve as a model for the interpersonal relations of the society in general. The presence of these priests in dioceses in the West has at times put the Eastern Catholic Churches at odds with local Roman Catholic groups.

CONTROVERSIAL ISSUES The Eastern Catholic custom of maintaining distinctive local traditions within their connection to the Vatican has frequently led to disagreements about proper practice. The Syro-Malabar Church just recently normalized relations with the Catholic Church of the Latin Rite in India after a dispute over jurisdiction; the Vatican had not allowed the Malabar Church to establish new dioceses in the state of Kerala, which is the historical motherland of that church. As the most numerous in members and dynamic in its contemporary development, the Ukrainian Greek-Catholic Church was to have received patriarchal status from the Vatican, but the Vatican has backed down in the face of opposition from Orthodox churches, particularly the Moscow Patriarchate. Since the early 1990s the post-Soviet-era legalization and restoration of the Ukrainian and Romanian Greek-Catholic Churches' organizational structures have caused many ideological and other conflicts (especially concerning the possession of church buildings) with Orthodox Churches that strongly opposed the process. The desire in the second half of the 1990s of the majority of the region's Greek-Catholics to find or rediscover the Eastern roots of their ecclesiastical identity has lessened the opposition between the two communities, which now work to reach mutual understanding.

CULTURAL IMPACT The Eastern Catholic Churches have had a powerful impact on the cultural development of nations and societies, especially those where Eastern Catholics have been or are the majority or an essential part of the local society, such as Iraq, India, the western Ukraine, and Romanian Transylvania. In the visual and decorative arts, Eastern Catholicism has contributed iconography and other elements of temple decoration, including many famous local images of Christ, the Virgin Mary, and different saints, as well as clerical clothing and liturgical objects. Eastern Catholic architecture in churches, bell towers, and chapels sometimes includes Latin or Western additions that distinguish them from Orthodox buildings. Eastern Catholicism has included polyphonic singing (an obligatory part of the Eastern Orthodox liturgy) in its liturgy, and it has produced a great variety of liturgical, ecclesiastical, historical, and educational works.

Andrij Yurash

See Also Vol. I: *Christianity*

Bibliography

Attwater, Donald. *The Christian Churches of the East.* 2 vols. Milwaukee: Bruce, 1961.

Code of Canons of the Eastern Churches. Washington, D.C.: Canon Law Society of America, 1992.

Fortescue, A. *The Lesser Eastern Churches.* London: Catholic Truth Society, 1913.

Liesel, N. *The Eastern Catholic Liturgies: A Study in Works and Pictures.* Westminster, Md.: Newman Press, 1960.

Oriente Cattolico: Cenni storici e statistiche. Vatican City: Congregation for Oriental Churches, 1974.

Pallath, Paul. *Catholic Eastern Churches: Heritage and Identity.* Rome: Mar Thoma Yogam, 1994.

Parry, Ken, Dmitri Brady, Sidney H. Griffith, David J. Melling, and John Healy, eds. *The Blackwell Dictionary of Eastern Christianity.* Oxford: Blackwell Publishers, 1999.

Religions of the World: A Comprehensive Encyclopedia of Beliefs and Practices. 4 vols. Santa Barbara, Calif.: ABC-CLIO, 2002.

Roberson, Ronald G. *The Eastern Christian Churches.* Rome: Orientalia Christiana, 1995.

Sayagh, Maximos, IV, ed. *The Eastern Churches and Catholic Unity.* New York: Herder and Herder, 1963.

Eastern Orthodoxy

FOUNDED: 325 C.E.

RELIGION AS A PERCENTAGE OF WORLD POPULATION: 3.5 percent

OVERVIEW Along with Roman Catholicism and Protestantism, Eastern Orthodoxy is one of the three major branches of Christianity. It exists as a fellowship of 18 independent or semi-independent church bodies, each headed by a bishop (sometimes called a patriarch). The largest are the Russian Orthodox Church and the Romanian Orthodox Church. The honorary head of Eastern Orthodoxy is the patriarch of Constantinople (Istanbul, Turkey), who holds no jurisdiction over the church as a whole. Today most Eastern Orthodox Christians live in Russia, the Balkans, and the Middle East.

In Greek the word "orthodoxy" (*orth* and *doxa*) means "correct praise" or "correct teaching." The first use of the word "orthodox" by Greek theologians occurred in the fourth century C.E., when what came to be known as "Orthodox Catholic" Christianity confronted "erroneous" teaching. The essential tenets of Orthodox theology were confirmed over the course of seven ecumenical councils, held between 325 and 787 C.E. Constantinople, the historical center of Eastern Christianity, separated from Rome in a schism that began in 1054. This breach widened to include all of Eastern Orthodoxy and was made permanent by the destruction of Constantinople in 1204 during the Fourth Crusade.

Orthodox Christianity emphasizes the mystical activity of God in his creation. God's presence is located primarily, but not exclusively, in the sacraments (or mysteries). Central among the sacraments is the Eucharist, or Holy Communion. Orthodox Christians refer to icons—representations of Christ, his mother, and the saints—as the "painted Word." They do not regard icons primarily as "art" but as another way in which the Scriptures teach.

HISTORY Christianity was officially prohibited in the Roman Empire until 313 C.E., when Emperor Constantine I issued the Edict of Milan, extending religious toleration to Christians throughout the realm. Thereafter Orthodox Catholic Christianity emerged in the eastern, Greek-speaking half of the empire, which included present-day Turkey, Greece, Bulgaria, Romania, and Serbia. In 330 C.E. Constantine founded Constantinople (formerly the Greek city of Byzantium), establishing it as the new capital city of the Christian empire of Byzantium.

Seeking to define its "correct teaching," Orthodoxy emphasized the primacy of tradition and the necessity of conciliar consensus (as opposed to papal decree) concerning Scripture. Further, according to "correct teaching," it was imperative that Orthodox doctrine articulate both that Christ is God (equal to God and in perfect communion with God and the Holy Spirit) and that Christ was truly human (the Incarnation). Beginning with the First Ecumenical Council at Nicea (now Iznik, Turkey) in 325 C.E., seven ecumenical councils were held to establish universal standards of doctrine and practice for the Orthodox faith.

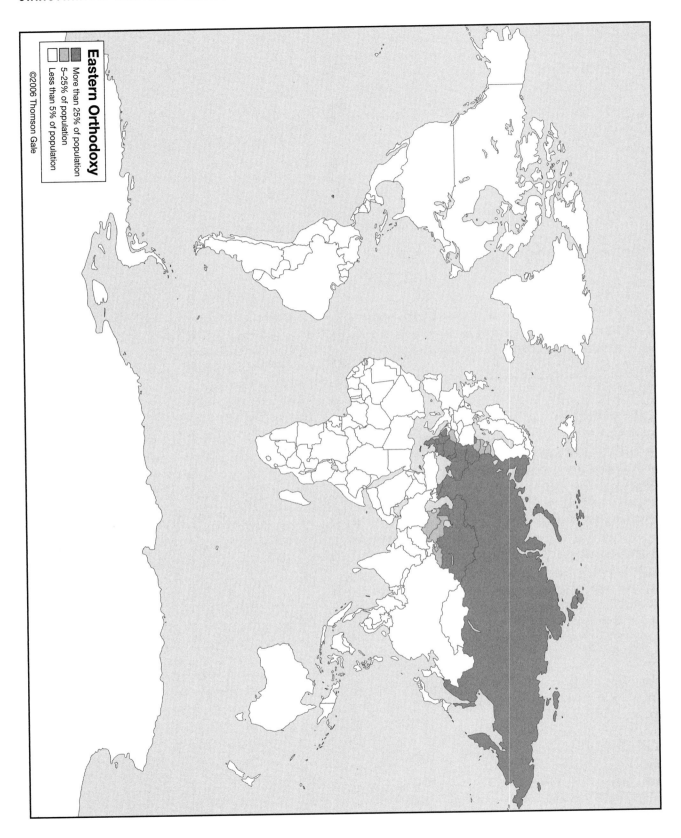

Eastern Orthodoxy

More than 25% of population
5–25% of population
Less than 5% of population

©2006 Thomson Gale

By the Fourth Ecumenical Council at Chalcedon (now Kadiköy, Turkey) in 451 C.E., church leadership was structured as a "pentarchy," based on the Roman imperial model. At the top level of the hierarchy were five bishops, specially designated as "patriarchs" according to the historical and political significance of their cities. Originally Rome, Alexandria, and Antioch were named because of the many Christians martyred in those cities. Constantinople (recognized as the "New Rome") and Jerusalem (revered as the place of Christ's death and resurrection) were later added. At the second tier of the hierarchy were archbishops, or metropolitans, who governed large church territories within the empire.

Although tensions between the pope (patriarch) of Rome and the other patriarchs surfaced as early as the 400s, Orthodoxy in the eastern half of the empire was able to maintain communion with Rome for another 800 years. During this time the East was troubled by Persian invasions into its territories, the rise of Islam in the 700s, and the loss of Christian areas in Syria, Persia, Armenia, and India to bishops who rejected the teachings of the Fourth Ecumenical Council. Relations between East and West were also strained by the attack on icons led by a series of Christian emperors, but Rome stood with Eastern defenders of the icons in condemning these attacks, and a vindication of icons was formally issued at the Seventh Ecumenical Council of in 787 C.E.

Just 13 years later, however, when Pope Leo III crowned Charlemagne as "Emperor of the Romans" at Rome on Christmas Day, the dominions of pope and Roman emperor became strategically linked, thus further marginalizing the Byzantine emperor and the eastern patriarchs. Thereafter Orthodoxy began increasingly to recognize the East as the sole province of "right worship" and "right teaching".

The eastern patriarchs' distrust of the Roman papacy was longstanding. They were wary of the papacy's claim to primacy and infallibility and to Rome as the "mother of all churches." They took further exception to the western church's addition of the words "and from the Son" to the Christian Creed (Nicene Creed), which was written at the first two ecumenical councils (in 325 and 381). The decision by Rome to amend the creed unilaterally, without the consent of an ecumenical council, proved a significant blow to the overall unity of the Church.

Acrimony between East and West continued to grow. In 988 the eastern church began a vigorous expan-

Orthodox priests line up to pay their last respects to Greek Orthodox Patriarch Diodoros during funeral ceremonies in the Old City of Jerusalem. © REUTERS NEWMEDIA INC./CORBIS.

sion, Christianizing Bulgaria, Moravia, Serbia, Romania, and Kieven Russia. In 1054 Cardinal Humbert of Rome excommunicated the patriarch of Constantinople, Michael Cerularius, precipitating what became known as the Great Schism between East and West. Although Cerularius in turn excommunicated the Roman pope, some patriarchs—notably Peter of Antioch—continued to commemorate the pope in his liturgy.

The decisive break came in 1204, when western Crusaders invaded and sacked Constantinople. With the violent establishment of a Latin kingdom in the heart of the Greek-speaking Orthodox East, the rift between East and West became irreparable. The Byzantines retook Constantinople in 1261 and went on to close the Latin monastery of Saint Mary on Mount Athos (a critical holy sight for eastern monasticism) in 1287. Weakened by decades of plunder, however, the city was vulnerable to invasion by the Ottoman Turks. Indeed, Constantinople fell to the Turks in 1453, further embittering the "eastern" Orthodox against western Christians.

Under the Ottoman Turks all Orthodox Christians were organized as the *Rum millet* (Roman nation). Greek, Arabic, Egyptian, Romanian, Serbian, and Bulgarian Orthodox peoples became subject to the political jurisdiction of the patriarch of Constantinople and his appointees, known as the "Phanariot Greeks" (named for

An Orthodox Christian retrieves a wooden crucifix thrown into the waters of the Bosphorus strait in Istanbul, Turkey, during a ceremony celebrating the baptism of Jesus Christ in Jordan River. © REUTERS NEWMEDIA INC./CORBIS.

the Phanar, the Christian area in Istanbul). Russia was the only Orthodox country that remained free from Muslim domination throughout the Ottoman centuries. With the Mongol destruction of Kievan Orthodoxy in 1237, Moscow (formerly an insignificant outpost Christianized by Kievan missionaries) emerged as the new center of Orthodoxy. The capitol city declared its autocephaly (complete independence) from the patriarchate of Constantinople in 1589 and came to regard itself as the "Third Rome."

In the centuries that followed, the autonomy of the Moscow patriarchate was repeatedly restricted. In 1721 the patriarchate was abolished altogether by Peter the Great, and the Orthodox Church was consigned to function as an arm of the Tsarist government under the authority of the Holy Synod. The Synod, or council, continued to curtail the independence of the church's activities until it, too, was abolished on the precipice of the Russian Revolution in 1917. The Moscow patriarchate thus enjoyed a short-lived return to independence, only to be crushed by the strenuous repression of the new Communist regime, which culminated in the widespread massacre of Orthodox clergy, monastics, and laity. The Orthodox Church was further fragmented by the 1927 declaration of support for the Soviet re-

gime by Patriarch Sergius, a statement that divided Orthodox opinion at home and abroad and devastated Russian missionary efforts from Asia to North America.

The composition of the Orthodox Church has undergone various other shifts during the nineteenth and twentieth centuries. Following a protracted decline in the influence of the patriarch of Constantinople, an independent Greek Church reemerged in 1833. Constantinople regained a position of prominence, however, in the aftermath of World War I and the devastation of the Russian Orthodox patriarchate under Soviet Communism. Orthodoxy has continued to decline in all parts of the Middle East and Egypt, with the exception of modern Syria, where it maintains a stable presence. Since 1945 missionary efforts and indigenous interest have led to the spread of Orthodoxy in Africa, Latin America, Australia, and Asia. In North America ethnic Orthodox groups have been united under the autocephalous (independent) Orthodox Church in America (1970) and the self-governing Antiochian Orthodox Christian Archdiocese (2004). Significantly, too, Orthodoxy has experienced a resurgence in Russia and eastern Europe since the fall of Communism and the collapse of the Soviet Union in 1989.

CENTRAL DOCTRINES The concept of *theosis* (English: "deification') is central to Orthodox doctrine. Somewhat analogous to the Western Christian concept of sanctification, it teaches that the mission, or journey, of humanity is to become as holy, free of sin, and united with God as possible. *Theosis* does not suggest that man may transcend his own created being to become equal with God (a blasphemy) but rather that he should seek communion with God and other beings, receiving the omnipresent energies of God in order to restore his own human nature to its original purpose. The doctrine of *theosis* also influences Orthodox interpretations of sin and redemption.

Theosis involves the participation in several sacraments, known as mysteries: the initiation (baptism); Chrismation (anointing with holy oil), reception of Holy Communion; anointment of the sick for restoration of bodily and spiritual health (unction); confession of sins committed after baptism (penance); and holy matrimony, the mystery in which men and women find salvation through mutual sacrifice on behalf of each other. Indeed, Orthodoxy considers marriage as an ordination and even an entrance into martyrdom because of the extreme commitment it entails. Ordination to the

CHRISTIANITY: EASTERN ORTHODOXY

ranks of deacon, priest, and bishop (the taking of holy orders) is also regarded as one of the mysteries, although ordination is not necessarily permanent, as clerics can be deposed, or reduced, from their office for grave offenses. Monastic life offers another path on the journey of *theosis*. Monks and nuns, whether as solitaries or in communities (the latter is more common), are bound by rules first taught by Antony of Egypt and Pachomius, who emphasized cycles of communal and private prayer, rigorous fasting, and the conquest of human passion through the virtue of humility. Unlike ordained clergy, such as deacons and priests, who may marry under Orthodoxy, monks and nuns devote themselves to a life of celibacy.

The Orthodox deny that physical death is a barrier to communion and pray that a person's journey of *theosis* may continue after death, despite his or her earthly sins and offenses. Mary, the "God bearer" (Theotokos), represents an ideal in this regard, as one whose faith and obedience resulted in a *theosis* that included bodily translation from the grave. Thus, Mary holds a special place of honor as a unique model and foretaste of the destiny of the saved.

MORAL CODE OF CONDUCT Bound by a general awareness that humans possess the capacity for both good and evil, Orthodox Christians accept the moral code of the Ten Commandments. Still, Orthodox place the highest importance on the aspiration to selfless love, as personified by Christ and reflected in the faith and obedience of his own mother, the Apostles, the martyrs, and saintly men and women throughout history. Prayer, fasting, almsgiving, and the regular participation in the mysteries are considered essential components of a spiritual life.

SACRED BOOKS By the early fourth century Eastern Orthodox Christians had named and accepted as sacred 27 books of the New Testament. Today their scriptural canon also includes 50 books of the Old Testament. Orthodoxy uses the Septuagint Greek version of the Old Testament, including several books often referred to as the Apocrypha (or "hidden" writings) but more commonly called a "second canon" (deuterocanonical) by the Orthodox. Originally translated from Hebrew in Alexandria, Egypt, in about 300 B.C., this was the first vernacular version of the Bible. Orthodoxy also accepts the Greek New Testament because this is the oldest surviving version of Christian scripture written by the Holy Apostles Matthew, Mark, Luke, John, Paul, James,

Peter, and Jude. These books include the Gospels, the apostolic letters, the Acts of the Apostles, and the Book of Revelation.

Subordinate but also critical to the Orthodox "right interpretation" of Scripture are the writings of the church Fathers, including both clerical and lay reflections and teachings on Scripture and Christian life. These works also encompass hymns and sayings recorded by desert monastics, both male and female. Lastly, in certain parts of the Orthodox world, local and regional synods or meetings of bishops can issue decrees or rulings that eventually find acceptance among all the Orthodox.

SACRED SYMBOLS The central sacred symbol of Eastern Orthodoxy is the cross. In church services the processional cross signifies to worshipers the entrance of Christ to the Sanctuary. The priest carries a hand cross as a symbol of his role as a teacher and sanctifier of worshipers. Orthodox Christians also normally wear crosses around their necks as a way of publicly confessing their faith. When making the sign of the cross, the fingers of the right hand are held in a particular way to convey "right teaching and right praise." The thumb and first two fingers are joined to represent the One God in Three Persons, while the last two fingers are joined together and held against the palm of the hand to represent the Divine and human natures of Christ.

EARLY AND MODERN LEADERS Flavia Iulia Helena (248–329 C.E.)—mother of Constantine, also known as Saint Helena and Helena of Constantinople—was responsible for building many of the shrines at significant Christian sites in Palestine. The Emperor Justinian I (527–565 C.E.) briefly reunited the eastern and western parts of the empire; his codification of Roman law (Corpus Juris Civilis) profoundly influenced church law. Theodore Abu Qurrah (750–824 C.E.) was notable among Arabic Orthodox Christians as the author of a detailed response to Islam defending the Orthodox veneration of icons. Significant emperors include John Tzimiskes (969–76) and Basil II (976–1025), both credited with restoring the Byzantine Empire; and Theophilus (829–42), who revived the University of Constantinople. Mark, archbishop of Ephesus, single-handedly defended Orthodoxy against a proposed union with Roman Catholicism at the Council of Florence (1438–39).

Defining leaders in the Russian Orthodox Church include Patriarch Nikon (1605–81), who initiated reforms in Russian liturgical customs designed to align the Russian church more closely with Greek Orthodox churches; and Avvakum Petrovich (1620–82), a Russian archpriest who led a faction called the Old Believers in opposing the reforms and who was ultimately burned at the stake. The missionary vision of Orthodox Russia is best represented by John Veniaminov (1797–1879), later known as Saint Innocent of Alaska.

Twentieth-century figures include Mother Maria Skobtsova (1891–1945), a Russian Orthodox nun who gave safe haven to Jews in Paris during the Nazi occupation and who was killed in a concentration camp; and metropolitans Stefan of Sofia, Kiril of Plovdiv, and Neofit of Vidin, all of whom conspired to protect Bulgaria's Jews from the Nazis. Athenagoras, patriarch of Constantinople (1948–72), was responsible for strengthening ties among Orthodox churches and opening dialogues with Roman Catholics. Archbishop Makarios III (1950–77) devoted his civil and church career to resolving tensions between Greeks and Turks on the island of Cyprus. The reemergence of Orthodoxy in the post-Communist Balkans has benefited from the remarkable leadership of Archbishop Annastasios Yannoulatos of Tirana and Albania. Elisabeth Behr-Sigel, an Alsatian-born convert to Orthodoxy, has been influential in raising questions about the status of women in Orthodoxy. The late Ugandan bishop Rauben Sebanja Mukasa Spartas (1890–1982) was largely responsible for the spread of Orthodoxy in modern Africa. Patriarch Ignatius of Antioch IV (1979–) has initiated ecumenical dialogues with Roman Catholic and non-Chalcedonian Orthodox (also known as Oriental Orthodox, who reject the provisions of the Fourth Ecumenical Council of Chalcedon) and encouraged consideration of a universal date for the celebration of Pascha (Easter) among Christians.

Finally, the Russian Saint Silouan (1866–1938), a monk of Mt. Athos, and Father Amphilochios (1888–1970), abbot of the Monastery of St. John on the Island of Patmos, are revered among the most important Orthodox spiritual leaders of the twentieth century.

MAJOR THEOLOGIANS AND AUTHORS Saint Basil the Great (329–379 C.E.) was a brilliant thinker and defender of the Orthodox faith, as well as a principal founder of the monastic life in the East. Born in 329 in Caesarea, the capital of Cappadocia, he studied at universities in Constantinople and Greece and went on to become bishop of Caesarea. A prolific writer on theology and canonical law, he devoted considerable attention to issues relating to the Holy Spirit and its relationship in the Holy Trinity. Basil also composed a set of rules for monasticism still practiced today by most Eastern Orthodox monks. Along with his contemporaries, Saint Gregory Nazianzus and Saint Gregory of Nyssa, he belonged to a trio known as the Cappadocian doctors of the church. Saint John Chrysostom (347–407 C.E.) is also regarded as a "doctor" of Orthodoxy, whose extensive writings were seminal to the foundation of official church doctrine. Born John of Antioch, he became Archbishop of Constantinople. After his death he was given the title "Chrysostom" ("golden-mouthed") because of his exceptional oratory skills. Other founding Orthodox theologians include Saint Maximus the Confessor (sixth–seventh century), Saint John of Damascus (seventh–eighth century), Saint Photius the Great (ninth century), Saint Symeon the New Theologian (tenth century), and Saint Gregory Palamas (fourteenth century).

Compilers and editors of *The Philokalia,* (monastic reflections on asceticism and mysticism) include eighteenth- to twentieth-century saints Macarius and Nicodemus of the Holy Mountain (among the Greeks) and Paissy Velichkovsky and Father Dumitru Staniloae (among Russians and Romanians). Nineteenth-century Russian theology was transformed by Alexis Khomiakov (1804–60), who sought to establish a revitalized Orthodox tradition unfettered by western scholastic theological terms and categories. Important twentieth-century theologians include Saint John of Kronstadt, author of the classic *My Life in Christ;* Panagiotis Nellas and John Zizioulas, the Greek revitalizers of mystical theology; and Vladimir Lossky, Georges Florovsky, Paul Evdokimov, and Alexander Schmemann, all of whom were Russian exiles. Interpreters of Orthodoxy in English who converted to the faith include British-born Bishop Kallistos Ware and Americans Father Peter Gillquist and Francis Schaeffer.

ORGANIZATIONAL STRUCTURE The Orthodox Church is structured as a fellowship of independent or semi-independent churches. The Patriarch of Constantinople is honored above all officials, but his primacy is merely symbolic, as his actual authority does not extend beyond his own patriarchate. Patriarchs of Alexandria (Egypt), Antioch (now in Syria), and Jerusalem retain ultimate independence in the governance of their own patriarchates. In addition, the Monastery of Mount Sinai and nine other nationally-based autocephalous churches (including Russia, Romania, Serbia, and Greece) are completely self-governing. At a lesser level of independence are autonomous national churches (e.g. Finland, China, and Japan) that exercise the right to elect their own metropolitans (archbishops), subject to the approval of the synod, or council, of the patriarchate. Each national church is governed by its own Holy Synod, or council of bishops, which is the deciding body in matters of doctrine and administration. Finally, there are provinces scattered throughout traditionally non-Orthodox areas of the world that are still subject to one of the autocephalous churches—for example, the Greek Orthodox Archdiocese of North America. The clergy of each church also includes priests and deacons, who are subject to the authority of the bishops.

HOUSES OF WORSHIP AND HOLY PLACES The foundation of an Orthodox temple requires the blessing of a bishop, adherence to specific requirements in construction, and a ritual of formal consecration when the building is complete. Within each parish church a chair is reserved for the bishop, even in his absence, to signify that the church and its worshipers are his responsibility. The Orthodox altar always faces east toward the sunrise, symbolic of Christ as the light of the world. Traditionally, Orthodox temples do not have pews, since standing is the normal posture for Orthodox prayer. In Western countries and some Mediterranean nations, however, pews and occasionally organs may be incorporated into the temple.

The most prominent and distinctive feature of an Orthodox church is the iconostasis ("wall of icons"), a screen that separates the central prayer area ("nave") from the altar area ("sanctuary"), representing a gateway into the latter Holy Place. The iconostasis bears three entrances (usually doors) to the altar: the Royal Doors stand at center, with Deacon's doors on either side. Only bishops, priests, and deacons may pass through the Royal Doors in performing their duties. An icon of Christ always occupies the place of honor to the right of the Royal Doors, while an icon of the Theotokos (Mary, the "God bearer") always occupies the place to the left. The rest of the screen is filled with icons of the angels, apostles, or saints that reflect the regional traditions of that church.

Monasteries are also regarded by the Orthodox as holy places. Dedicated to God for prayer and penitence, they are not open to visitors except as permitted by the ruling abbot or abbess. The Orthodox make pilgrimages to these and other sites where saints lived or were martyred.

WHAT IS SACRED Because of his love and mercy, the holiness of God extends to his entire creation. Humans can choose to be sinful, but the victory of Christ over death has transformed the entire cosmos. Orthodox Christians believe that no part of the world is evil or lacking in holiness. Because of their emphasis on *theosis*, Orthodox believe that God's holiness is always present, is especially intense in the mysteries of the church, and is at work in the lives of believers as well.

Humans who achieve a high degree of deification in this world are venerated as saints. No formal process exists to recognize saints. Rather, such extraordinary holiness may be manifested by an individual's reputation before death, his or her association with miraculous cures or answers to prayers, or the inexplicable incorruption of his or her body after death. Among the most widely venerated of Orthodox saints is Nicholas, the archbishop of Myra in Lycia (present-day Turkey) during the fourth century, who was severely persecuted for his faith under the Emperor Diocletian and renowned for his compassionate humility. Nicholas is popularly known as the "wonder-worker" for the miracles he is believed to have performed during his lifetime and afterward.

HOLIDAYS/FESTIVALS The cycle of time in Orthodoxy revolves around Pascha, or Easter, the day of the resurrection of Christ. While Easter is the most important holiday in the Orthodox calendar, every Sunday is also regarded as a "little Pascha." In all there are 12 major festivals or feasts in Orthodoxy, marking special days in honor of Christ, the Theotokos (Mary), the apostles and saints, and significant events in the history of the church. Christmas, Epiphany, and Pentecost also hold special importance, as they celebrate the incarnation and baptism of Christ and the descent of the Holy Spirit upon the apostles.

Periods of fast precede the celebration of major holidays: the Great Fast (Lent) before Pascha; the Nativity Fast before Christmas and Epiphany; the Fast of the Apostles before the Feast of Saints Peter and Paul (29 June); and the Dormition Fast before the Dormition of the Theotokos (15 August). The custom of these fasts derives from the tradition of church members fasting and praying with candidates preparing to be baptized on Pascha, Christmas, Epiphany, and Pentecost.

MODE OF DRESS Orthodoxy does not impose particular requirements on everyday dress. Laymen and laywomen are expected to dress modestly. In some places women wear a veil or head covering in church, but this is no longer a universal custom.

The vestments worn by the clergy during public worship are evolved from the dress of Roman imperial officials. Outside of worship, bishops, priests, and deacons wear black cassocks or, in Western countries, black suits with clerical collars. Monks and nuns wear a black habit including a veiled hat (for monks) or a veil (for nuns).

DIETARY PRACTICES Orthodoxy influences the daily diet of its believers through its demand for regular fasting, although a completely vegan diet is not permitted lest one be tempted to spiritual pride and lack of gratitude to God for the goodness of creation (which includes the primacy of humans over other created life).

Orthodox Christians observe four major periods of fasting (mentioned above in HOLIDAYS/FESTIVALS), during which they limit themselves to one meal per day and refrain from meat, dairy, wine, and oil. In addition, they fast on Wednesdays and Fridays throughout the year (except Bright Week, the week following Pascha, the week following Pentecost, and the 12 days from Christmas to Epiphany). Some churches now refrain from fasting during the entire Paschal season (between Easter and Pentecost).

RITUALS Orthodox Christian worship invokes all the senses. Rituals include the burning of incense and candles or oil lamps. Common gestures include making the sign of the cross, bowing, and prostrating. Nearly all parts of worship services include a capella singing.

The ecclesiastical day begins at sunset, as indicated by Moses, whose description of God's creation of the world began with evening. Evening prayer service is called vespers. Private evening prayer, called compline, is often recited before the family altar (located in an east corner of the home), which normally holds icons, a lamp or candle, and a copy of the Holy Scripture. Morning prayer, called Orthros, precedes the Divine Liturgy (Eucharist). Throughout the rest of the day monastics and some laity pray at the third, the sixth, and the ninth hour. Specific rituals accompany each of the mysteries. The Great Blessing of Waters occurs on the Feast of Epiphany in honor of the baptism of Christ; another common ritual involves the commemoration of a deceased on the anniversary of his or her death.

RITES OF PASSAGE Forty days after birth Orthodox infants are baptized and chrismated. Baptism is enacted by full, triple immersion (for both infants and adults), once for each person of the Trinity. Chrismation (analogous to the Roman Catholic rite of confirmation, although confirmation in the West since about the year 1000 is normally conferred upon adolescents) is the sacrament of anointing the recipient with holy oil, or *chrism*, which has been consecrated by the bishop. Immediately after the recipient has been baptized and chrismated, he or she receives the Eucharist.

Betrothal and holy matrimony mark the entrance into the married estate. As Orthodoxy emphasizes the spiritual rather than the legal bond of marriage, participation in the sacrament does not include the taking of vows. The rite does include the exchange of rings and is completed by placing "crowns of glory and honor" upon the heads of the couple to signify roles as "king" and "queen" of their own family under God. The crowns also signify the martyrdom of marriage, as an act of sacrifice and unwavering devotion.

Ritual prayers are said for children beginning a school year. Priests anoint the sick upon request and all worshipers on the Wednesday of Holy Week (preceding Pascha). Ritual prayers are said for the dying, as well as at the time of death. Specific rites also exist for the conversion of new adherents to Orthodoxy and for the restoration to communion of those who have been excommunicated.

MEMBERSHIP Anyone baptized, chrismated, and communed is a full member of the Orthodox Church. Non-Christian converts are received by baptism and Chrismation, while Christians converts (who have already received a valid Trinitarian baptism) may be received by Chrismation alone. Excommunication is incurred by those who, in spite of admonition from their priest, willingly and knowingly violate the teachings of the Church as laid down by the councils or regularly ignore the canons or "measures" of the church that seek to guide the implementation of council teachings in everyday life.

RELIGIOUS TOLERANCE Orthodoxy extends tolerance to Christians thought to be "in error," as well as non-Christians, even while it claims itself to be the one true church. Such tolerance is based on Orthodoxy's basic principle of freedom of conscience, as well as the understanding that it cannot know the exact boundaries of God's mercy and must reserve judgment on the spiritual condition of those not in communion with the church. Still, in Russia and other historically Orthodox nations, restrictive measures toward non-Orthodox citizens or preferential treatment for the Orthodox have led to tensions and calls for freedom of religion.

SOCIAL JUSTICE Orthodoxy has always called for the giving of alms and relief of human suffering as essential components of Christian life. In the Byzantine and the Russian empires, imperial support was extended for church relief efforts. Today Orthodox churches in developed nations support international relief efforts and issue declarations that condemn ethnic or racial warfare and economic injustice and advocate an equitable share of the world's resources for all humans.

SOCIAL ASPECTS Orthodox ethics reflect the aspiration to *theosis*—God's "image and likeness"—in each human, which is the Holy Trinity's gift. Murder, abortion, infanticide, and euthanasia are impermissible as violations of Orthodox theological and social vision.

Marriage is normally to be entered into once and is considered an eternal sacrament. The Orthodox church, however, takes a compassionate view of divorce when all avenues of reconciliation have failed. Remarriage is permitted (up to three times), although the ceremony for a second marriage includes prayers of repentance for the previous divorce and is not celebrated to the same degree as the first marriage. The church considers procreation to be one of the fundamental purposes and duties of marriage and therefore regards it as sinful to use contraception to avoid completely the birth of any children. On the other hand, for married couples seeking to limit family size, some church authorities sanction the use of contraception, arguing that regular sexual relations (as opposed to abstinence) are fundamental to preserving the health and sanctity of the marriage, as well as being one of its privileges and obligations for mutual *theosis*.

CONTROVERSIAL ISSUES Orthodoxy remains divided between the most traditional monastics and countries that remain on the Julian, or "old," calendar and those who have adopted a limited use of the Western, or Gregorian, calendar. The dispute between Orthodoxy and the Christian West over a common date for Pascha (Easter) remains volatile and ongoing. Similarly charged are Orthodoxy's attempts at reconciliation with non-Chalcedonian Christians (e.g., the Coptic and Ethiopian churches and the Syrian Orthodox) and Roman Catholics. Also, the continued decline of Christianity in the Middle East has provoked tension among Orthodox Christians who feel concerned by a resurgent and sometimes violent Islam in Egypt and Palestine, a lack of sympathy in Israel, and the perceived indifference of Western nations.

After the Russian patriarchate was attacked in Soviet Russia, a major Pan-Orthodox Congress was held in Constantinople from 10 May to 8 June 1923, and plans were begun for an ecumenical council. Despite subsequent preparatory committee reports and repeated urgings from various patriarchs and bishops over the next decades, such a council, or even the creation of a pan-Orthodox Synod to resolve urgent contemporary issues in dispute, remained an unfulfilled dream. Some Orthodox leaders have called for an international forum, perhaps held through the Internet, as a more realistic way of moving forward a discussion of issues.

CULTURAL IMPACT The cultural impact of Orthodoxy, beginning in the Byzantine Empire, has been immense. The history of Greece, Russia, the Balkans, and eastern Europe cannot be understood without appreciating the role Orthodox Christianity has played in shaping the cultures of these regions. Even in Syria, Palestine, Israel, and Egypt, the presence of Orthodoxy has contributed to literary, scientific, artistic, and musical expression.

In the realm of music, many scholars believe that all forms of Christian chant, east or west, may have derived from the Syrian chant tones that can be documented from the fourth century C.E. Equally influential, artists such as the Cretan Domenikos Theotocopoulos (1541–1614)—commonly called "El Greco" (the Greek)—developed his painting style in Spain on the basis of his earlier work in Byzantine iconography. Romanesque architecture, including the stunning church of San Vitale in Ravenna, Italy, reflects the Orthodox understanding of sacred space, as do two German struc-

Icons

One of the most distinctive aspects of Orthodox Christianity is the significance it gives to icons. Icons are representations of Christ, his mother, the Apostles, and scenes from Scripture and the life of the church. They may also depict stories from Holy Scripture as taught in the tradition of the Orthodox Church. Icons have existed throughout the entire known history of Orthodoxy, as revealed by wall paintings in Roman catacombs, as well as a few examples that survive in Syria and Asia Minor. In the contemporary church the most common icons are those of Christ and his mother displayed to the right and left, respectively, of the central entrance to the altar.

In the 720s C.E. the Roman emperor Leo III launched an attack on icons, charging that their veneration was tantamount to idolatry. Those who sought to condemn and destroy icons were called iconoclasts. The defenders of icons—members of both the western and eastern churches—were called iconophiles (or iconodules). The iconophiles argued that icons were not idols but symbols, which were not intended to be divine in themselves but dynamic human expressions of the divine.

tures—the chapel at Aachen and the Benedictine monastery in Fulda—both of which attempted to replicate the church of the Holy Sepulchre in Jerusalem. One can hardly imagine Russian literature apart from the massive influence Russian Orthodoxy worked on the imagination of its major authors, including Fodor Dostoyevsky (1821–81) and Leo Tolstoy (1828–1910). Similarly, the criticisms of Western society leveled by Alexandr Solzhenitsyn (b. 1919) cannot be understood apart from the writer's Russian Orthodox perspective. Not even those who were bitterly critical of the Church—such as the Lebanese-born Khalil Gibran (1833–1931)—could avoid Orthodoxy as a subject and cultural context for their work. The same must be said for the Greek writer Níkos Kazantzákis (1885–1957).

A. Gregg Roeber

See Also Vol. I: *Christianity*

Bibliography

Clendenin, Daniel B., ed. *Eastern Orthodox Theology: A Contemporary Reader.* 2nd ed. Grand Rapids, Mich., Baker Academic: 2003.

Coniaris, Anthony M. *Introducing the Orthodox Church: Its Faith and Life.* Minneapolis, Minn: Light and Life Publishing, 1982.

Fairbairn, Donald. *Eastern Orthodoxy through Western Eyes.* Louisville and London: Westminster John Knox Press, 2002.

Gillquist, Peter E. *Becoming Orthodox: A Journey to the Ancient Christian Faith.* Ben Lomond, Calif.: Conciliar Press, 2002.

Nellas, Panayiotis. *Deification in Christ: The Nature of the Human Person.* Crestwood, N.Y.: St. Vladimir's Seminary Press, 1997.

Stokoe, Mark, and Leonid Kishkovsky. *Orthodox Christians in North America 1794–1994.* Wayne, New Jersey: Orthodox Christian Publishing Center, 1995.

Terzopoulos, Constantine, trans. *What Do You Know About Icons? An Aesthetic, Historical and Theological Approach to the Icons of the Orthodox Church in the Form of Questions and Answers.* Kareas, Attiki, Greece: Sacred Monastery of St John the Baptist, 2001.

Ware, Timothy (Bishop Kallistos). *The Orthodox Church.* Rev. ed. London and New York: Penguin Books, 1997.

Christianity

Evangelicalism

FOUNDED: Seventeenth century C.E.

RELIGION AS A PERCENTAGE OF WORLD POPULATION: 12 percent

OVERVIEW Evangelicalism is a movement within Christianity that emphasizes reliance on Scripture over tradition and that holds conversion to be the foundation of the life of the believer. The doctrine that Jesus Christ died to atone for the sins of mankind is central to evangelical beliefs. Pentecostalism, a charismatic movement, is usually considered to be a part of evangelicalism.

Evangelicalism originated in the 1600s in the Pietism of Philipp Jakob Spener, a Lutheran pastor in Germany. By the eighteenth century it had spread to England and by the nineteenth century to the United States. Today evangelicalism is a worldwide movement of some 750 million believers.

HISTORY Evangelicalism, which began in the seventeenth century in the Pietism of the Lutheran pastor Philipp Jakob Spener and others, was a response to the formality and perceived rigidity of the Reformation. Evangelicals called for a religion of the "open air and the human heart." On 24 May 1738 the Anglican priest Charles Wesley felt "his heart strangely warmed," and from that time until his death in 1791, Wesley preached in churches and open fields throughout England and the United States, calling people to conversion and organizing small Bible groups for prayer. His strategies were enormously successful and resulted in the founding of

world Methodism. With equal passion figures like the English Baptist John Bunyan, author of *The Pilgrim's Progress*, stressed a believer's baptism, rejecting both Protestant and Roman Catholic forms of infant baptism and demanding that each Christian make up his or her own mind about belief in Jesus Christ. In the nineteenth century this message spread to ever widening circles in Europe and the United States through American revivalists like Charles Grandison Finney and Dwight L. Moody. Moreover, out of the movement came a worldwide evangelical mission to South America, Africa, and Asia. By the end of the nineteenth century Christian leaders confidently spoke of the "evangelization" of the entire world.

This hope was deflected in the twentieth century by controversies over the interpretation of Scripture that fragmented the evangelical movement. In the post–World War II years a new movement called "neoevangelicalism," led by the former fundamentalist Billy Graham, created a loose coalition of evangelicals. This movement developed into several streams of evangelical religion in the United States: in the popular media in televangelism and the so-called prosperity gospel; in the cultural advocacy of the Moral Majority led by the Baptist Jerry Falwell; and in political circles in the Christian Coalition of the Pentecostal pastor Pat Robertson. At the same time the spread of evangelicalism to other countries, including Brazil, South Africa, South Korea, and the Philippines, brought further growth.

CENTRAL DOCTRINES Evangelicalism is not a particular denomination. Evangelicals are found in the Roman

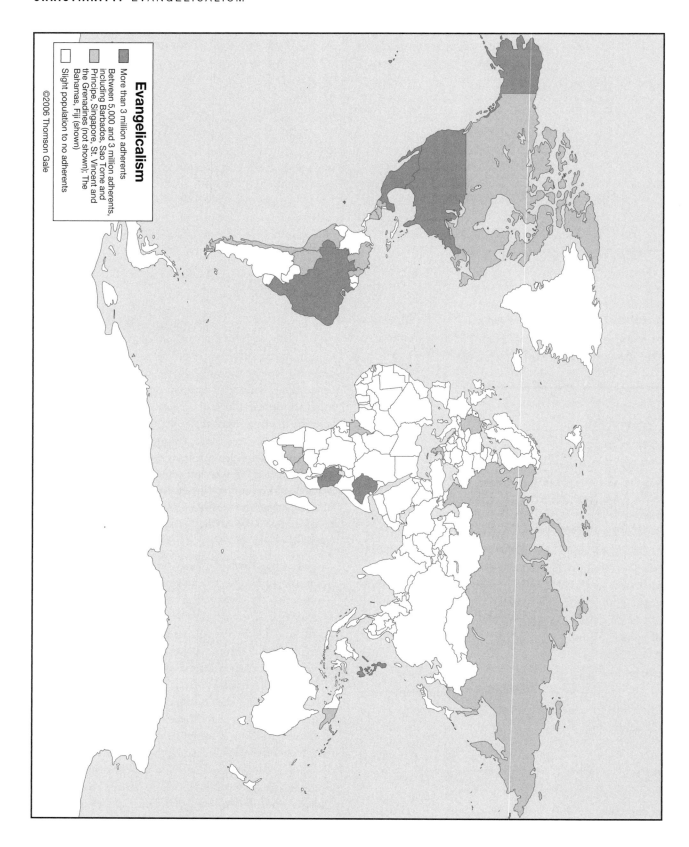

Evangelicalism

More than 3 million adherents

Between 5,000 and 3 million adherents, including Barbados, Sao Tome and Principe, Singapore, St. Vincent and the Grenadines (not shown); The Bahamas, Fiji (shown)

Slight population to no adherents

©2006 Thomson Gale

Catholic communion and across the Protestant spectrum. Evangelicalism is best defined by its beliefs and practices: (1) the authority of Scripture as a core principle for faith and practice (biblicism); (2) the importance of a heartfelt conversion to the faith (conversionism); (3) the centrality of Christ's death on the cross to atone for each person's sin (crucicentrism); and (4) the call and obligation to share the "good news" of Jesus Christ with all people (activism). With subtle variations these beliefs are held by the groups that are called evangelical, whether mainstream Protestant churches, such traditional evangelical denominations as Baptist, Seventh-day Adventist, and Christian and Missionary Alliance, or the Pentecostal network of churches that includes Assemblies of God, Four Square, and the predominately African-American Church of God in Christ. Pentecostals often include a focus on the "gifts and fruits of the spirit"—healing, exorcism, and speaking in tongues—and the fastest growing evangelicals in the Southern Hemisphere feature Pentecostal forms of evangelicalism.

Evangelicalism differs from mainstream Protestant denominations in emphasizing the exclusive truth of the gospel message and the obligation to evangelize others and to lead them to conversion. Evangelicalism is distinct from Roman Catholicism in four principal ways: (1) an emphasis on Scripture over historical traditions; (2) a focus on religious experience in conversion and healing; (3) the independence of churches from one another; and (4) pronounced lay participation in leadership, often including women as missionaries and occasionally as pastors.

MORAL CODE OF CONDUCT Because evangelicalism had its origins in the Pietism and Holiness movements of the seventeenth through nineteenth centuries, purity of personal conduct has been a central mode of its expression. While this strictness has decreased over time, in general a person is expected to abstain from tobacco, alcohol, and sex outside marriage. At one time dancing was forbidden, and in the early twentieth century movies as well. The latter two restrictions have dropped away, but faithfulness in marriage has remained critical. After the 1960s, however, divorce was no longer an automatic reason for dismissal from the church or indeed from leadership as a pastor.

SACRED BOOKS The sacred book for evangelicals is the Christian Scriptures, the Old and New Testaments. In this sense evangelicalism has adopted the Reformation

In much of the world the image of a person with Bible in hand has come to be a classic symbol of evangelicalism. For evangelicals, however, this is not so much a symbol as witness of their faith in the power of Scripture. © BOJAN BRECELJ/CORBIS.

theme of *solo scriptura*, the belief that it is by Scripture alone that a person can know God. Correct biblical interpretation is a critical issue. Some evangelicals say that the Scriptures are "infallible" (without error regarding salvation), while other say that they are "inerrant" (without error in matters of both science and salvation).

SACRED SYMBOLS From its inception Protestantism has been iconoclastic, rejecting any object or person that might take the place of God in the hearts of believers. Thus, symbols—whether in stained glass, rosaries, or icons—have been rejected by many churches. Nonetheless, in much of the world the image of a man or woman with a Bible in hand has come to be a classic image of evangelicalism. For evangelicals, however, this is not so much a symbol as a witness of their faith in the power of Scripture.

EARLY AND MODERN LEADERS The founders of evangelicalism include Philipp Jakob Spener (Pietism), Charles Wesley (Holiness movement), Charles Grandison Finney (revivalism), and, in the early twentieth century, Aimee Semple McPherson, an American who was one of the leaders of the Pentecostal movement. In the second half of the twentieth century, the American Billy

Evangelicals gather for the German Evangelical Congress in Frankfurt, Germany. For evangelicals membership is a matter of conversion to the faith, which is the primary rite of passage. © AFP/CORBIS.

Graham became a pivotal figure in carrying the evangelical message across the globe. Since evangelicalism has become a worldwide phenomenon, most leaders have been indigenous to their own countries. An example is Edir Macedo, who rose from the lower middle class of Brazil to found one of the largest churches in Latin America, the 4-million-member Universal Church of the Kingdom of God, in 1977.

MAJOR THEOLOGIANS AND AUTHORS One of the most important evangelical theologians was one of its first, the Congregationalist minister Jonathan Edwards. From his parish in Northampton, Massachusetts, Edwards led a revival and wrote numerous theological works, including the classic *A Treatise concerning Religious Affections* (1746), a nuanced reflection on evangelical religious experience. In the nineteenth century Charles Hodge, a biblical theologian at Princeton Theological Seminary, created a scientific biblicism to counter the Darwinian movement and the German historical critical method of understanding the Bible. In the twentieth century British evangelicals like C.S. Lewis and John R.W. Stott wrote apologetic works that, along with the

theology of James I. Packer, attracted a worldwide readership. In the contemporary period there has been a movement among American evangelicals promoting the idea of an intelligent designer, supported by the legal scholar Philip Johnson, the biochemist Michael Behe, and the philosopher William Dembski. The American theologian Stanley J. Grenz has become an interpreter of evangelical faith in the postmodern period.

ORGANIZATIONAL STRUCTURE The organizational structures of evangelicals are enormously diverse, with no central authority. This elasticity and the ability to adapt to the needs of particular cultural systems have allowed evangelical leaders to plant new churches quickly, with little or no bureaucratic approval. The authority of local evangelical leaders frequently depends on their personal charisma.

HOUSES OF WORSHIP AND HOLY PLACES The houses of worship of evangelicals vary dramatically. They include Edir Macedo's mother church in São Paulo, which has an arched-girder roof with a 230-foot clear span and holds 25,000 worshipers, as well as Robert Schuller's Crystal Cathedral in Orange Grove, California. Evangelical worship centers are diverse, ranging from stadiums to churches that are no more than thatched huts.

For evangelicals there are few holy places, but for some believers the doctrine of biblical prophecy called premillennial dispensationalism foretells that during the "last days" Jews will return to their homeland, Christians will be taken to heaven, and in 7 years Christ will return with his followers and rule for 1,000 years from the restored Temple in Jerusalem. In part this is the reason political support for Israel is strong in U.S. evangelical politics.

WHAT IS SACRED? For evangelicals the Scriptures are the sacred witness to Jesus Christ as the only salvation for a person's soul for eternity.

HOLIDAYS AND FESTIVALS In general evangelicals do not follow the traditional Christian liturgical year. This is not to say that evangelicals do not celebrate Christmas, which they do, or recognize Easter, which they see as the focus of their faith. Evangelicals, however, tend to interpret liturgical patterns as overly ceremonial. A common phrase in American evangelical parlance is that "Christianity is not a religion but a relationship with Jesus." Thus, liturgical formality is downplayed, and conversion becomes a central focus of worship and of holidays, with festivals often serving as occasions for evangelical outreach.

MODE OF DRESS Although modes of dress for evangelicals vary by region, informality is the rule for both believers and clergy. In warm climates, for example, one may see a young pastor in shorts, while in colder climates he may wear pants and a shirt but without a coat or tie. There are, however, evangelical clergy in the Anglican and Catholic traditions who maintain the practice of wearing robes and collars.

DIETARY PRACTICES Dietary restrictions for evangelicals often include a prohibition on the consumption of alcohol, although this varies by region. Otherwise, there are no notable restrictions.

RITUALS The evangelical movement is marked both by its core beliefs and by dramatic cultural adaptations in worship and rituals. One may, for example, see spirit dancing in an African congregation, a staid worship service in a Korean Presbyterian evangelical congregation, spirit healing and exorcism in a Brazilian house church, and contemporary music and drama in American nondenominational churches. Holy Communion, which serves as congregational fellowship, is often followed by a period of prayer that invokes the "gifts" of the Holy Spirit in healing and prophecy. Weddings are most often seen by evangelicals as an occasion for witnessing to the family, with funerals a celebration of the moment at which believers receive their promise of eternal life.

RITES OF PASSAGE Because the rite of baptism signifies conversion, it is central to evangelicalism. This passage is the "new birth" that marks the believer as a disciple. Indeed, for evangelicals baptism is the only rite of passage that matters. It is often remembered as a birth date, and it is referred to as the major turning point in the course of a person's life, marking one's identity and sealing one's salvation.

MEMBERSHIP For evangelicals membership is a matter of conversion to the faith, which is the primary rite of passage. A person must repent, turn from sin, and give his or her heart to Jesus Christ. Membership is demanding in the sense that there is an expectation of personal change, a challenge of moral purity, an obligation to participate in worship, and an expectation that the person will reach out to others with the message of the "gospel of Jesus Christ." In this sense the passage is from the "old life of sin" to the "new life in Christ." There is often, though not always, an expectation that the person will tithe. Proselytization is central to evangelicalism, and the extensive use of mass media reflects this mission.

RELIGIOUS TOLERANCE Religious freedom is a key issue for evangelicals, particularly those in the Southern Hemisphere. There is political oppression in countries where Protestantism is the minority faith, and in many countries the lives of evangelicals and their families are in danger from secular as well as other religious groups. In Latin America, where Catholicism remains culturally and often politically dominant, Protestantism must struggle for both political and public acceptance. In some nations of Africa and Asia, Muslims have made it illegal for Christians to evangelize Muslims. In the United States evangelicals have supported religious freedom and tolerance, although as a context in which evangelization can take place rather than as a celebration of religious pluralism. Because evangelicals lack a broad ecumenical movement, international connections are rare, and institutional cooperation is not common.

SOCIAL JUSTICE In the nineteenth century evangelicalism featured a strong mission of social amelioration that included schools, children's homes, orphanages, prison reform, hospitals, and centers for the care of the sick, elderly, and handicapped. Moreover, the English evangelical William Wilberforce, a member of the House of Commons, advocated an end to the slave trade, which was finally abolished by Parliament in 1807. All British slaves were freed in 1833, a month after Wilberforce's death.

In the twentieth century evangelicalism has grown in places where there is significant poverty. Part of its appeal in Africa, for example, lies in its claim and in its ability to empower the poor in countries like Nigeria and South Africa. Although evangelicalism focuses on the importance of spiritual fruits, in some cases these fruits are held to manifest themselves in material blessings. Evangelicalism focuses less on programs for social justice, however, than it does on personal transformation, which often means a stronger work ethic and personal discipline, and on ameliorating social problems such as hunger and the effects of natural disasters. Nonetheless, some of the largest nongovernmental global social service agencies, such as World Vision, are evangelical. Human rights are important to, but not the focus of, evangelical advocacy.

SOCIAL ASPECTS Whereas American evangelicalism has focused on specific social issues, for example, by taking a pro-life position on abortion or by opposing rights for homosexuals, evangelicals in the Southern Hemisphere have been less single-minded and have tended to focus on religious freedom. Moreover, evangelicals generally are less loyal than American evangelicals to specific economic policies (Western capitalism) or political ideologies (liberal democracy). Nonetheless, in some countries evangelicals have entered politics by forming political parties (Latin America has more than 20 evangelical parties) and running candidates (Brazil elected its first evangelical legislator in 1933).

In the United States the politicization of what is often called the Christian right has had effects on both American evangelicalism and on politics, including a shift toward the Republican Party. This shift is often framed by an emphasis on strengthening marriage and the family. Focus on the Family, an organization headed by the American psychologist James Dobson, sponsors radio broadcasts and distributes printed material that promotes its views and challenges conservative Christians to push this agenda in the public sphere.

CONTROVERSIAL ISSUES The evangelical record is mixed on women's rights. From its beginning in the United States, Pentecostalism was a tradition in which women attained religious leadership. This tradition has continued, but women in evangelical churches are most often found as missionaries or as Christian educators. In families women are honored as mothers and caregivers but not usually as equals. Nonetheless, many women encourage the conversion of their husbands precisely because evangelicalism advocates that males exemplify moral discipline, monogamy in marriage, and hard work in providing for the family. Evangelicals tend to favor contraception and divorce as options, however, particularly in Catholic countries where these practices are outlawed. Abortion is universally condemned, and adoption is encouraged as the last, best option.

CULTURAL IMPACT It is not clear what the cultural impact of evangelicalism might eventually be on those countries in the Southern Hemisphere where it is growing so rapidly. At some point, for example, the expan-

Explosive Growth

Evangelicalism is the fastest growing religious movement in the world. By 2000, for example, there were 360 million Christians in Africa, many of whom were evangelical or Pentecostal. Whereas there were only a handful of evangelicals in Latin America in 1900, by 2000 there were more than 50 million. Growth in Asia has been substantial as well; South Korea and the Philippines are majority Christian nations with large evangelical populations. There are more than 10 million evangelicals in South Korea and about 4 million in the Philippines, which represents a doubling in 30 years. It has been estimated that in 2000 one-third of all Christian pastors worldwide were evangelical or Pentecostal. If these growth trends were to continue, by the middle of the twenty-first century Africa and Asia would have the largest populations of Christians in the world.

sion of evangelicalism in Latin American countries might allow Protestantism to displace the region's traditional Catholic culture. In Africa evangelicalism has not displayed clear cultural consequences, and in Asia it has remained a personal faith.

In the United States, however, evangelicals have been highly successful in adapting popular forms of culture to their uses. This can be seen, for example, in the best-selling series of Left Behind novels by Tim LaHaye and Jerry B. Jenkins, in the proliferation of Christian self-held books, and in the development of Christian rock.

James K. Wellman, Jr.

See Also Vol. I: *Christianity*

Bibliography

Barrett, David B., George T. Kurian, and Todd M. Johnson. *World Christian Encyclopedia.* 2nd ed. New York: Oxford University Press, 2001.

Boyer, Paul. *When Time Shall Be No More: Prophetic Belief in Modern American Culture.* Cambridge, Mass.: Belknap Press, 1992.

Brasher, Brenda E. *Godly Women: Fundamentalism and Female Power.* New Brunswick, N.J.: Rutgers University Press, 1998.

Edwards, David L. *Christianity: The First Two Thousand Years.* Maryknoll, N.Y.: Orbis Books, 1997.

Freston, Paul. *Evangelicals and Politics in Asia, Africa and Latin America.* Cambridge: Cambridge University Press, 2001.

Grenz, Stanley J. *A Primer on Postmodernism.* Grand Rapids, Mich.: William B. Eerdmans, 1996.

Jenkins, Philip. *The Next Christendom: The Coming of Global Christianity.* Oxford: Oxford University Press, 2002.

Lewis, C.S. *Mere Christianity.* 1952. Reprint, New York: HarperCollins, 2001.

Marsden, George. *Understanding Fundamentalism and Evangelicalism.* Grand Rapids, Mich.: William B. Eerdmans, 1991.

Martin, David. *Pentecostalism: The World Their Parish.* Oxford: Blackwell, 2002.

Noll, Mark A. *American Evangelical Christianity: An Introduction.* Oxford: Blackwell, 2001.

Ward, W.R. *The Protestant Evangelical Awakening.* New York: Cambridge University Press, 1992.

Jehovah's Witnesses

FOUNDED: 1879 C.E.

RELIGION AS A PERCENTAGE OF WORLD POPULATION: 0.24

OVERVIEW Jehovah's Witnesses were known as Bible Students until 1931. In 1870 their founder, Charles Taze Russell, an Allegheny, Pennsylvania, businessman, had started a study group that became a congregation. Russell was influenced by members of the Advent Christian Church and an independent Second Adventist, George Storrs (1796–1879). Later Russell drew most of his "end-times" teachings from Nelson Barbour (1824–1906), a former disciple of William Miller.

Jehovah's Witnesses deny the Trinity, believe that hell is the grave, teach that only 144,000 elect will receive heavenly immortality, and assert that the rest of saved humanity will live eternally on earth. The Witnesses have frequently been in conflict with other religions and secular governments. They suffered persecution under Nazism and Communism, have been banned in many countries, and were mobbed repeatedly in the United States from 1940 through 1943.

HISTORY In 1876 Charles Taze Russell, the founder of the Bible Students, met Nelson Barbour and accepted Barbour's end-times chronology, which asserted that Christ had been present invisibly since 1874, that their fellowship would be taken to heaven in 1878, and that Jesus' millennial kingdom would be established on earth in 1914. In 1879 Russell broke with Barbour. He then established the journal *Zion's Watch Tower and Herald of Christ's Presence,* and in 1884 he and several associates incorporated Zion's Watch Tower and Tract Society to promote a massive publicity campaign.

Beginning about 1895 the Bible Students came to regard Russell as the "faithful and wise servant" of Matthew 24:45–47 and the channel through whom "new light" was delivered. Although Christ's kingdom did not replace the nations of the world in 1914 as he had expected, Russell believed till his death two years later that World War I would lead to their destruction in the battle of Armageddon.

In January 1917 Joseph Franklin Rutherford was elected the second president of the Watch Tower Society. Shortly thereafter a struggle began at the Watch Tower headquarters in Brooklyn, New York, between Rutherford and a majority of the society's board of directors. In July Rutherford ousted four board members and increased his control over the society.

Rutherford and seven associates were imprisoned briefly in the Atlanta, Georgia, federal penitentiary in 1918, allegedly for opposing conscription. Following the release of Rutherford and the others on appeal in 1919, the Bible Students grew dramatically until 1926. The cause of this growth was the revised teaching that the millennium would begin in 1925. When that did not happen, and when Rutherford began revising Russell's teachings and assuming centralized control over Bible Student congregations, a majority of Bible Students broke with him. Yet, by his death in 1942, Rutherford had rebuilt the movement, by then known as Je-

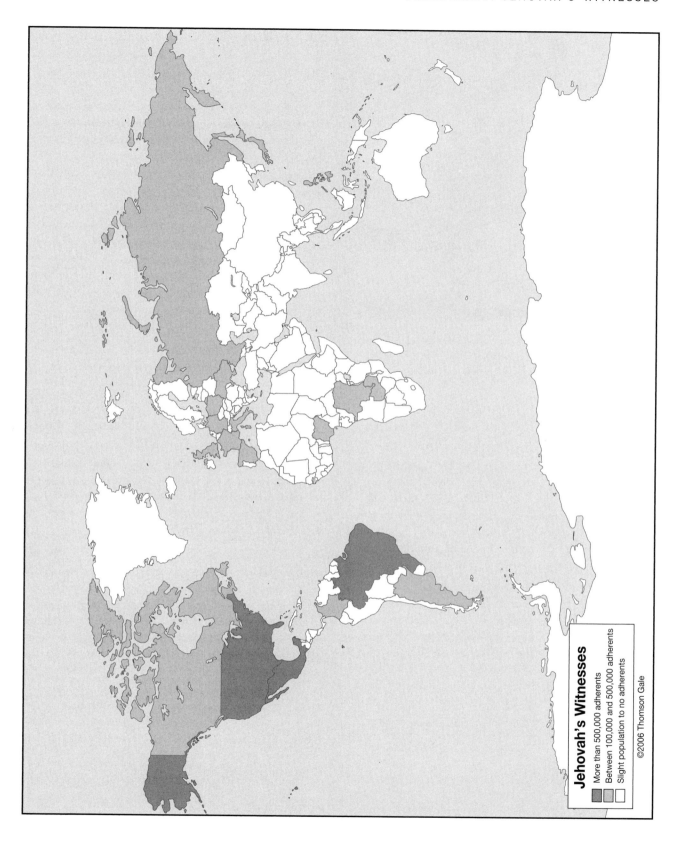

Jehovah's Witnesses

More than 500,000 adherents
Between 100,000 and 500,000 adherents
Slight population to no adherents

©2006 Thomson Gale

A Jehovah's Witness sells copies of the religion's magazine. Jehovah's Witnesses consider themselves to be the only true Christians, in part because they dismiss many Orthodox Christian doctrines as false, pagan teachings.
© ROBERT MAASS/CORBIS.

hovah's Witnesses, despite bitter international persecution.

Under Rutherford's successors the Witnesses have grown into a worldwide religion. Although they count only "publishers" (persons actively involved in public religious educational work), their number of adherents is far larger. In 2002, while there were only 6,304,645 publishers, nearly 15,600,000 persons attended the annual spring Memorial of Christ's death.

While Jehovah's Witnesses are found in most countries, there are more in the United States than in any other. They make up a larger percentage of the population, however, in some Latin American and African nations. For example, while there was one Witness publisher for every 280 persons in the United States in 2002, there was one for every 181 in Mexico. Their numbers are growing much faster in the Third World and the former Soviet Union than in major industrialized lands.

CENTRAL DOCTRINES Jehovah's Witnesses consider themselves to be the only true Christians, in part because they deny many orthodox Christian doctrines as false, pagan teachings. The Witnesses hold that Jehovah is God, the Father, and that he alone exists throughout eternity. The Logos, or Word, was his first creation and

only begotten son, through whom the rest of creation came into being. The Witnesses regard the Genesis accounts of creation as basically literal, although they interpret the creative days of the first chapter as six thousand-year periods.

Witnesses believe that, as a consequence of the Fall in Eden, Adam passed sin to all humankind, that the Mosaic Law was given to the Israelites as a tutor leading to Christ, and that Christ came to ransom Adam's descendants from sin and death. Concerning these teachings, they are in general agreement with most conservative Christians, particularly Evangelicals. But they deny that Jesus was divine; rather, he was simply a sinless man. By offering a perfect atoning sacrifice to Jehovah, he bought back what Adam had lost and laid the foundation for a New Creation as the "last Adam." This New Creation will be composed of the "church class," which is held to be the 144,000 of Revelation chapters 7 and 14, and a "great crowd," described in Revelation 7:9, 10. While the "church class" is literally made up of 144,000 individuals predestined as a class and saved by grace, the "great crowd" must work out their salvation and will receive eternal life on a restored paradise earth only if they remain faithful through a final testing, which is to follow a literal millennium.

Central to contemporary Witness teachings is the belief that humankind has been living in the "last days" since 1914 and that all Witnesses must bring testimony to as many as possible through house-to-house preaching work prior to an imminent Great Tribulation. At the end thereof, all—except Jehovah's Witnesses—will be annihilated. Then Satan will be bound for a thousand years, and Christ will begin his millennial reign over the earth.

All Jehovah's Witnesses are baptized by water immersion, but only a small group of roughly 8,000 take Communion once a year to indicate that they have a heavenly hope. This group is called the "anointed remnant" of the 144,000 and the "faithful and discreet slave" class. The Witnesses teach that all "new light" and spiritual direction must come through this class. While all members of the Governing Body must be "anointed," other members of the class play little part in the oversight of the movement.

MORAL CODE OF CONDUCT Jehovah's Witnesses are stern moralists. Although they have no prohibitions against any food (except blood products) or drinks, including alcoholic beverages, their Governing Body prohibits many other activities. These include the use of tobacco or any hallucinogen, saluting flags, standing for national anthems, participating in politics, serving in armed forces, working in factories producing weapons of war, and taking blood transfusions. They hold abortion and euthanasia to be murder. They permit birth control and sanction divorce for marital unfaithfulness. Otherwise, they insist on traditional, monogamous, heterosexual sexual values.

The Governing Body also asserts that questioning official Witness doctrine as promulgated through the Watch Tower Society is a serious violation of spiritual authority that may be regarded as apostasy. Any Witness who violates any of these proscriptions may face expulsion from the Witness community through "disfellowshipment" and shunning by other Witnesses, including family members.

Moral rules have often changed. For example, for some time Jehovah's Witnesses were told that they could not accept organ transplants or perform alternative civilian service in lieu of serving in the armed forces. Furthermore, they could not accept medically administered blood fractions, such as blood plasma or platelets. Over the years, however, the bans on organ transplants and alternative civilian service have been lifted, and Witnesses can now accept certain blood fractions.

SACRED BOOKS The Witnesses regard the Protestant canon of the Bible as originally written to be inspired and inerrant. They have produced their own version, The New World Translation of the Holy Scriptures, in many modern languages.

SACRED SYMBOLS Jehovah's Witnesses have no sacred symbols. Since they hold that Jesus was "impaled" on an upright stake rather than crucified, they regard the cross as an emblem of "false Christianity."

EARLY AND MODERN LEADERS Because of the nature of their community, which has emphasized withdrawal from the secular world and has generally been hostile to higher education, Jehovah's Witnesses have produced few outstanding historical figures besides the first four presidents of the Watch Tower Society: Charles Taze Russell, Joseph Franklin Rutherford, Nathan Homer Knorr (1905–77), and Fredrick William Franz (1893–1992). Two of their outstanding lawyers, Hayden Covington (1911–79) and W. Glen How (born in 1921), however, are recognized for their civil liberties victories

Jehovah's Witnesses study scriptures. Central to contemporary Witness teachings is the belief that humankind has been living in the "last days" since 1914 and that all Witnesses must bring testimony to as many as possible through house-to-house preaching. © ROBERT MAASS/CORBIS.

before the U.S. and Canadian Supreme Courts. The only other prominent Witnesses have been either entertainers or athletes. These have included George Benson, Eve Arden, and Venus and Serena Williams. Although entertainer Michael Jackson was raised a Witness, he left the movement some years ago under pressure.

MAJOR THEOLOGIANS AND AUTHORS Although Charles Russell, Joseph Rutherford, and Fredrick Franz produced a great number of religious writings, and Franz was the primary translator of The New World Translation of the Holy Scriptures, none of these Watch Tower presidents was a professional theologian in the usual sense of that term.

ORGANIZATIONAL STRUCTURE The organization of the Jehovah's Witnesses is hierarchical. At the top is the Governing Body, which selects all new members of that body as well as, indirectly, zone, branch, district, and circuit overseers, plus congregational elders and ministerial servants (deacons). All are males in these positions. The Jehovah's Witnesses have no clergy.

HOUSES OF WORSHIP AND HOLY PLACES Jehovah's Witness congregations meet in Kingdom Halls. The homes for officials and workers at their American headquarters and branch offices are called Bethels.

WHAT IS SACRED? Besides the Bible and their organization, Jehovah's Witnesses place a high value on both

The Slave Class

The doctrine of the "faithful and wise servant," or "faithful and discreet slave," is central to the Jehovah's Witnesse's authority structure. Originally, Bible Students (as Jehovah's Witnesses were called until 1931) taught that Charles Russell was the "faithful and wise servant." In 1927, however, Joseph Rutherford dropped this teaching and proclaimed that all Bible Students made up a "slave class" as the living remnant of the 144,000 members of Christ's church. Other Christians could go to heaven as a "great multitude" (the "great crowd"). But in 1935 Rutherford asserted that this great multitude would gain earthly salvation, not heavenly immortality. Since then the only Jehovah's Witnesses called to the slave class by the Holy Spirit have been replacements for those who had become unfaithful. Witnesses who feel they have a heavenly calling manifest this by partaking of Communion. Governing Body members must do so, and they speak and act in the name of the entire slave class.

human and animal life. They must not take human life except in self-defense, and they must not take animal life for sport. Obedience to God is, however, regarded as more important than life itself, and martyrdom for such obedience is esteemed.

HOLIDAYS AND FESTIVALS The celebration of all religious and national holidays is condemned as either pagan or "worldly." Witnesses do meet annually, however, on Nisan 14, according to the Jewish calendar, to celebrate Communion on the Memorial of Christ's death.

MODE OF DRESS Jehovah's Witnesses dress in the common apparel of the countries in which they live and have no unique garb. They do stress that their apparel must be "chaste and modest" since they are "God's ministers."

DIETARY PRACTICES Jehovah's Witnesses have no prohibitions against any foods or beverages except those that include blood or blood products.

RITUALS Jehovah's Witnesses gather five times a week for religious services in meetings that are practically the same in form and content throughout the world. Central to these meetings are sermons and study materials provided by the Governing Body through various legal societies. Kingdom Songs (hymns) are sung at the beginning and end of most meetings.

RITES OF PASSAGE All Jehovah's Witnesses at the age of understanding are encouraged to be baptized as acts of dedication to Jehovah through Christ and "Jehovah's spirit directed organization." Only members of the "anointed remnant"—those who hope to receive a heavenly resurrection—partake of Communion.

MEMBERSHIP All baptized Jehovah's Witnesses are considered members of the community and may be disciplined as such. Only those involved in preaching work are counted as "active." Witnesses regard growth in the number of converts as a sign of Jehovah's favor.

RELIGIOUS TOLERANCE Through their litigation in the courts of the United States, Canada, and a number of other countries, the Jehovah's Witnesses have made important contributions to such civil liberties as freedom of speech, freedom of the press, and freedom of religion. But they regard all other religions as satanic.

SOCIAL JUSTICE Because of their refusal to participate in most political activities, Jehovah's Witnesses do not support social justice movements. In Canada during the 1940s and 1950s, however, they campaigned for a constitutionally guaranteed Bill of Rights. In their congregations they emphasize social, ethnic, and interracial harmony, and they have attracted large members of ethnic and racial minorities in many countries.

SOCIAL ASPECTS Jehovah's Witnesses are extremely conservative in most personal aspects of life. They hold that monogamous marriage is sacred and can only be broken by sexual unfaithfulness. They condemn masturbation, premarital sex, adultery, and homosexuality.

CONTROVERSIAL ISSUES Jehovah's Witnesses have often come into conflict with other religions and secular governments, even in liberal societies. Their preaching and proselytizing work, their unwillingness to engage in politics, their refusal to participate in patriotic exercises, their conscientious objection, and their rejection of blood transfusions, even in the face of death, have brought them much criticism and persecution.

CULTURAL IMPACT Because Jehovah's Witnesses separate themselves from everything they consider "worldly," and because they place emphasis on their preaching work at the expense of all other activities, they have had little impact on either the fine or liberal arts.

M. James Penton

See Also Vol. 1: *Christianity*

Bibliography

Beckford, James A. *The Trumpet of Prophecy: A Sociological Study of Jehovah's Witnesses.* New York: John Wiley and Sons, 1975.

Bergman, Jerry, comp. *Jehovah's Witnesses: A Comprehensive and Selectively Annotated Bibliography.* Westport, Conn., and London: Greenwood Press, 1999.

Botting, Gary. *Fundamental Freedoms and Jehovah's Witnesses.* Calgary: University of Calgary Press, 1993.

Franz, Raymond. *Crisis of Conscience: The Struggle between Loyalty to God and Loyalty to One's Religion.* 3rd ed. Atlanta: Commentary Press, 2000.

Harrison, Barbara Grizzuti. *Visions of Glory: A History and a Memory of Jehovah's Witnesses.* New York: Simon and Schuster, 1978.

Jehovah's Witnesses: Proclaimers of God's Kingdom. Brooklyn, N.Y.: Watchtower Bible and Tract Society of New York, 1993.

King, Christine Elizabeth. *The Nazi State and the New Religions: Five Case Studies in Non-Conformity.* New York and Toronto: Edwin Mellen Press, 1982.

Penton, M. James. *Apocalypse Delayed: The Story of Jehovah's Witnesses.* 2nd ed. Toronto: University of Toronto Press, 1997.

Peters, Shawn Francis. *Judging Jehovah's Witnesses: Religious Persecution and the Dawn of the Rights Revolution.* Lawrence: University Press of Kansas, 2000.

Lutheranism

FOUNDED: 1517 C.E.

RELIGION AS A PERCENTAGE OF WORLD POPULATION: 1.0 percent

OVERVIEW Lutheranism, named after the German preacher and professor Martin Luther (1483–1546), began with the publication of his Ninety-five Theses (1517), an attack on abuses of the Catholic Church, which precipitated the Protestant Reformation. Shaping the agenda of early modern Western Christianity, Lutheran theology argued that salvation came from faith alone and that Scripture, not the church, was the only basis of religious authority. The movement quickly spread from Germany across northern Europe, becoming one of the main strands of Protestantism.

Luther and his followers initially opposed the term "Lutheran," used derisively by opponents of his reforms. Many early churches preferred the term "Evangelical" (meaning "Gospel centered"), which became part of the official name of the church in many countries. In the seventeenth century Lutheranism was challenged by the Catholic Church's Counter-Reformation, which reduced the strength of Lutheran churches, especially in Hungary, Slovakia, and Poland; Communist oppression in central Europe further weakened the Lutheran movement.

By 2001, however, Lutheranism remained one of the largest Protestant groups, with 65 million adherents gathered in more than 200 churches in some 100 countries. The majority of these churches were founded dur-

ing the Reformation in Germany, Scandinavia, and the Baltic countries. Newer churches in the European Lutheran tradition have been organized by immigrants in North and Latin America, Australia, and South Africa. Churches established by missionaries—especially in Indonesia, Ethiopia, Tanzania, Madagascar, Papua New Guinea, South Africa, India, and Namibia—have been growing rapidly.

HISTORY Luther's call for reform initially concerned the Catholic practice of indulgences. An indulgence is a papal dispensation from punishment in purgatory, which in Luther's time could be earned by the performance of good works (good deeds) or by giving money to the church. Luther, a Catholic priest and professor at the University of Wittenberg, attacked the practice in his Ninety-five Theses on Indulgences, which he nailed to the door of the Wittenberg Castle Church on 31 October 1517. The document spread rapidly through the new medium of print, and it launched a movement that became organized as Lutheran territorial churches in Germany, Scandinavia, and parts of central Europe. In 1521 the pope excommunicated Luther. Lutheranism was first defined in the Augsburg Confession (1530) of Luther's Wittenberg colleague Philipp Melanchthon (1497–1560). A second colleague, Johannes Bugenhagen (1485–1558), pioneered a new church order by authoring constitutional documents for many territories and cities.

After significant disagreements among Luther's and Melanchthon's students, theologians produced the Formula of Concord (1577) and then the Book of Concord

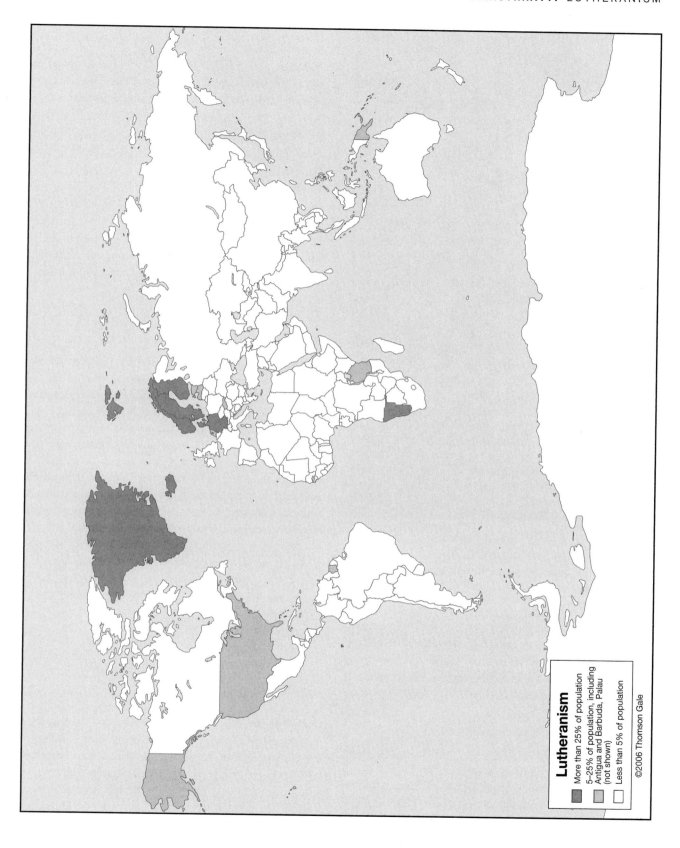

Lutheranism

More than 25% of population

5–25% of population, including Antigua and Barbuda, Palau (not shown)

Less than 5% of population

©2006 Thomson Gale

A stained-glass window depicts Martin Luther in the chapel of Coburg Castle in Coburg, Germany. A German preacher and professor, Luther precipitated the Protestant Reformation with his Ninety-five Theses (1517), an attack on various abuses of the Catholic Church. © DAVE BARTUFF/CORBIS.

(1580). The latter contained the Formula and other Lutheran confessions of faith, and it initiated an era of "Orthodoxy" (1580–1750). The leading theologians of Orthodox Lutheranism—including Johann Gerhard (1582–1637)—wrote massive works on Christian dogma that relied on the metaphysics of Aristotle.

Criticism that the Lutheran church had become sterile and failed to cultivate religious devotion within society led to the Pietist movement, spurred on in the later seventeenth century by Philipp Jakob Spener (1635–1705), a pastor in Frankfurt and Berlin. This movement was centered in the German towns of Württemberg and Halle, where August Hermann Francke

(1663–1727) started a foundation that promoted parish and individual renewal, Bible reading, and missionary activity. In 1748 Heinrich Melchior Mühlenberg (1711–87) organized the Pennsylvania Ministerium, the first Lutheran synod in the United States.

In the eighteenth century Lutheranism entered a period of Rationalism, which placed emphasis on reason, and leading theologians of the era modified or laid aside traditional biblical doctrines. Opposing this Rationalism of the church, Claus Harms (1778–1855) of Kiel began a "confessional revival" (returning to sixteenth-century doctrinal standards) in 1817. N.F.S. Grundtvig (1783–1872) in Denmark and Gisele Johnson and Carl P. Caspari in Norway also advocated traditional Lutheran teaching to oppose the rationalist criticism of biblical doctrines. This struggle continued until the end of the nineteenth century, when Lutheranism experienced a rise in liberal theology, an attempt to adapt the church's message to prevailing social trends of the time.

In the nineteenth century German, Nordic, and Slovak emigrants established Lutheran churches in the Americas, Australia, and South Africa. At the same time, European missionaries took their message and customs to Asia, Africa, and Latin America. In the United States a movement to "Americanize" Lutheranism under the leadership of Samuel Simon Schmucker (1799–1873) was countered in the 1860s by Charles Porterfield Krauth (1823–83), among others, while Carl Ferdinand Wilhelm Walther (1811–87) organized the synod of Missouri along strictly confessional lines.

Pietistic revivals in Scandinavia, led by Hans Nielsen Hauge (1771–1824) in Norway, Heinrich Schartau and Carl Olof Rosenius (1816–68) in Sweden, Frederik Gabriel Hedberg in Finland, and Vilhelm Beck (1829–1901) in Denmark, revitalized nineteenth- and twentieth-century parish life. Twentieth-century Lutheran churches experienced a variety of theological movements, including the existentialism of German scholar Rudolf Bultmann (1884–1976).

CENTRAL DOCTRINES Lutheranism, in its theology, has tended to follow Martin Luther's understanding of the Christian faith. Luther believed that human beings are righteous, or free from sin, in two different sets of relationships. As God's creations, they are righteous through his grace and favor; they enter this relationship through trust or faith in God. In relation to other creatures, especially other human beings, human beings practice righteousness in acts of love (corresponding to

God's commands) at home, at work, and in political and religious communities. Because human beings, according to Lutheranism, do not love and trust God above all he has made, they exist as sinners in a broken relationship with God; this is exhibited in their failure to love his other creatures. To restore human being's trust in him, God the Son (Luther maintained the traditional Christian doctrine of the Trinity) became human as Jesus Christ, suffered the condemnation that God had pronounced on sinners, died, and reclaimed life for them through his resurrection. God justifies (restores to righteousness) sinners by forgiving their sins; through Christ he creates within them trust in God; and through the Holy Spirit he calls and moves them to new obedience, which enables them to practice love toward their neighbors.

Luther taught that certain people are chosen by God to be saved (although no one is excluded from salvation). In this form of predestination, people are brought to trust in God by the Holy Spirit through the "means of grace"—oral, written, and sacramental forms of God's Word. The Word is given authoritatively, according to Luther, in the Holy Scriptures, which the Holy Spirit inspired. Bible reading and preaching form the foundation of Lutheran piety.

Luther had initially emphasized baptism as a primary way that God creates believers, but its importance for daily life receded as subsequent generations regarded it only as an entry point to the Christian life and not the basis for pious living. Lutherans continued to focus, however, on the Lord's Supper (the Eucharist, or Communion) as a means through which God expresses his will to forgive and provide life. Luther believed that Christ's body and blood were present in the bread and wine of the Lord's Supper—bestowing on recipients God's grace and forgiveness—but he did not try to define the nature of this mysterious presence (unlike the Catholic Church, which used the Aristotelean concept of substance in its doctrine of transubstantiation). Differing views over the true presence of Christ in the bread and wine led to conflict between the Lutheran and Reformed strands of Protestantism; the latter viewed Christ as spiritually, but not literally, present in the Lord's Supper. The two traditions attempted to resolve this conflict with the Leuenberg Agreement of 1973.

MORAL CODE OF CONDUCT Luther taught that faith in Christ, not moral living and the performance of good works, leads to salvation. Even so, flowing from their

Interior of the Cathedral of Oslo in Oslo, Norway. Because Lutheran liturgies emphasize music, the organ is an integral part of Lutheran churches. © LE SEGRETAIN PASCAL/CORBIS SYGMA.

faith in Christ, believers have an obligation, or a "new obedience," to perform good works. It is Christ's forgiveness, liberating believers from sin and evil, that frees them to serve their neighbors in love. Lutheran Pietists emphasize a strict adherence to moral codes, some forbidding pleasures such as dancing or card playing.

SACRED BOOKS Lutherans view the Bible as the only authority for their teachings and approach to life, and Luther insisted that doctrine come from Scripture alone (though he did not mean it was to be used apart from Christian tradition). Most Lutherans have also turned to the Augsburg Confession (composed in 1530 by Philip Melanchthon) and to a collection of confessions of faith compiled with it in the Book of Concord (1580), which have provided an interpretation and summary of Lutheran teachings.

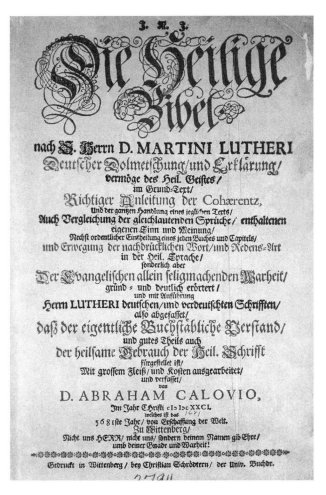

Title page of a German-language bible, with commentary by Martin Luther. Lutherans view the Bible as the only authority for their teachings, and Luther believed that doctrine came from Scripture alone. © ARCHIVO ICONOGRAFICO, S.A./CORBIS.

SACRED SYMBOLS Lutherans retained most of the central symbols of the medieval Catholic Church. Unlike some Protestants, they are not opposed to the use of images, although they discarded representations of saints that involved superstitious practices. The crucifix (a cross with the body of the suffering Christ) is often the preferred expression of the cross.

EARLY AND MODERN LEADERS Sixteenth- and seventeenth-century territorial princes encouraged the development of Lutheran theology, culture, and values and gave the church political support. Such princes included John (1468–1532), John Frederick (1503–54), and August (1526–86) of Saxony (now in Germany), electors of the Holy Roman Empire; Landgrave Philip (1504–67) of Hesse (now in Germany); King Gustavus Adolphus (1710–71) of Sweden; and Duke Ernst the Pious (1601–65) of Saxe-Coburg-Gotha (now in Germany).

In the nineteenth and early twentieth centuries, Lutherans took political leadership in various movements for national identity. For example, Lajos (Louis) Kossuth (1802–94) led the 1848 revolution in Hungary, and Milan Rastislav Stefanik (1880–1919) was a leader in the movement to create Czechoslovakia at the end of World War I.

The Swedish bishop Nathan Söderblom (1866–1931) led the ecumenical movement Life and Work; he won the Nobel Peace Prize in 1930. Although many church leaders, including Lutherans, compromised with or promoted National Socialism, some opposed its tyranny; for example, the Lutheran theologian Dietrich Bonhoeffer (1906–45) was executed for plotting to overthrow Hitler. That Ishmael Noko of Zimbabwe was appointed director of the Lutheran World Federation in 1994 indicates the growing significance of the mission churches for world Lutheranism.

MAJOR THEOLOGIANS AND AUTHORS Johannes Brenz (1499–1570) and Urbanus Rhegius (1489–1541), both contemporaries of Luther, helped shape Reformation teaching. Luther's student Matthias Flacius Illyricus (1520–75) composed the first Protestant hermeneutics (study of the principles of biblical interpretation) and pioneered Protestant church history. Martin Chemnitz (1522–86), Jakob Andreae (1528–90), and David Chytraeus (1530–1600) summarized the reformer's teaching in the Formula of Concord (1577). Johann Gerhard, Abraham Calov (1612–86), and Johann Andreas Quenstedt (1617–88) exemplify the thinkers of seventeenth-century Lutheran Orthodoxy.

The so-called Erlangen school of the nineteenth century (which included F.H.R. von Frank, Theodosius Harnack, and J.C.K. von Hofmann) attempted to use historical Lutheran thought to address modern problems. The work of Albrecht Ritschl (1822–89) and Adolf von Harnack (1851–1930) represents an attempt to depart from traditional Lutheran theology in order to discuss the modern world on its own terms. In the twentieth century reactions against their ideas came from professors in the Erlangen school, such as Werner Elert (1885–1954) and Paul Althaus (1888–1966).

ORGANIZATIONAL STRUCTURE Lutheran theology prescribes no organizational structure. During the Reformation the church in Sweden retained bishops; most other territorial churches were governed by consistories (government-appointed commissions for the administration of the church) until the twentieth century, when some Lutheran churches adopted an episcopal form of government. Churches organized by immigrants or missionaries in the Americas, Africa, Asia, or elsewhere embrace a variety of governing approaches, including the autonomy of local congregations.

HOUSES OF WORSHIP AND HOLY PLACES Lutheran reformers converted medieval Catholic churches with few, if any, changes in their structure or furnishings. The importance of proclaiming the Word of God makes the pulpit a central point of worship, and the altar and baptismal font are also significant because there God bestows life and forgiveness of sins through the Lord's Supper and baptism. Because Lutherans emphasize music, the organ is an integral part of the church.

WHAT IS SACRED? Lutherans reject the idea that divine power is mediated through objects. Thus, they do not hold any objects to be sacred.

HOLIDAYS AND FESTIVALS Lutherans continued to follow the liturgical calendar of the medieval Catholic Church and its system of pericopes (lessons read in Sunday worship), although the number of saint's days was drastically reduced to secondary celebrations of a few New Testament figures. Christmas, Easter, and Pentecost anchor the church year, and there is a focus on Christ's suffering during Passion Week, with special attention to Good Friday. In 1617 the Festival of the Reformation (31 October) was introduced.

MODE OF DRESS Lutherans have never prescribed modes of dress, and there are a variety of clerical vestments in Lutheran practice. In Sweden and in certain areas of Germany, the medieval vestments have continued to be used; in other territories pastors wear a robe similar to sixteenth-century academic garb, sometimes with clerical bands or the ruff collar. The liturgical revival, or return to ceremonial worship, in the twentieth century led to the widespread use of the cassock (a full-length robe, usually black) and the surplice (a white outer garment) and later the alb (a long white robe) as vestments, particularly in North America.

DIETARY PRACTICES There are no special dietary practices in Lutheranism. Compulsory fasting was abolished during the Reformation, though Luther urged its pious use. Moderation in eating and drinking is expected of believers.

RITUALS Luther adapted the liturgy of the medieval Catholic Church and translated it into German. Over the years Lutheran churches have used the core of this historical liturgy, translated into the vernacular, for their services, emphasizing two elements: the sermon and the Lord's Supper. Congregational hymn singing plays a significant role in worship.

RITES OF PASSAGE The Lutheran church practices infant baptism. Through baptism God establishes a relationship with a human being, leading him or her toward faith. Confirmation of adolescents affirms the baptismal gift of forgiveness of sins and serves as a person's entry into the Lutheran community.

MEMBERSHIP In the traditional Lutheran areas of Europe, all children were baptized. In churches organized elsewhere by immigrants or missionaries, membership has also been bestowed through baptism, but there is the expectation that the person will receive instruction in the faith, often on the basis of Luther's Small Catechism (1529). Since the twentieth century Lutheran mission societies and church-run missions have spread their message to non-Christians through radio, television, and printed materials, and they have attempted in many countries to train members for evangelism.

RELIGIOUS TOLERANCE Luther insisted that only God's Word should be used to persuade those outside the accepted faith, although Lutheran rulers in the early modern period sent dissidents into exile. Lutherans were active in forming the interdenominational movements Faith and Order and Life and Work, which merged to form the World Council of Churches in 1948. The Lutheran World Federation negotiated a "Joint Declaration on the Doctrine of Justification" with the Roman Catholic Church (1999), recognizing a broad consensus between the two churches, noting remaining differences, and lifting historic mutual condemnations.

SOCIAL JUSTICE Influenced by Luther's emphasis on God's Word and the fundamental place of the Bible in Christian practice, early Lutherans promoted literacy and education throughout central and northern Europe. In the nineteenth century, as industrialization brought poverty and other social and economic changes, the church leadership failed to meet the needs of urban workers in Europe. This led to a widespread "Inner Mission," focusing on charitable works, in Lutheran areas. Notable were German pastors Theodor Fliedner (1800–64) and Johann Heinrich Wichern (1808–81), who worked in prisons, education, and hospital care.

In the twentieth century Lutherans led independence movements in Africa, in particular the former European colonies of Namibia (South-West Africa) and Tanzania (Tanganyika). European and North American Lutherans have also provided leadership in movements for social justice. Lutherans have founded their own groups, such as the North American organization Lutherans for Life, but they have often joined existing groups or worked with others to found organizations.

SOCIAL ASPECTS Luther's teachings on marriage (that it was the most honorable calling from God and the foundation of God's order for the world), his criticism of monasticism (rejecting a higher calling for monks), and his own marriage in 1525 (until 1521 he was a Catholic priest and unable to marry) provided a new model for sixteenth-century Christians. Parents continue to use Luther's Small Catechism in educating their children in the faith.

CONTROVERSIAL ISSUES There is significant disagreement about abortion and homosexuality within North American and European Lutheran churches. Elsewhere—in Africa and Asia, for example—Lutherans generally hold more conservative positions concerning these issues. Of particular concern has been the question of ordaining homosexual pastors and whether to bless same-sex relationships.

CULTURAL IMPACT Luther's gift for linguistic expression helped shape modern German, particularly through his translation of the Bible, and Lutherans have subsequently contributed to the national literature in various countries. In Slovakia, for example, Ludovit Stur (1815–56) and Josef Miloslav Hurban (1817–88) established a literary language and produced works that helped form the country's emerging national identity.

Although the great artists Albrecht Dürer (1471–1528) and Lucas Cranach the Elder (1472–1553) were among Luther's earliest followers, Lutheran contribu-

The Small Catechism

Since 1529 Lutheran children have learned the basics of their faith from Martin Luther's Small Catechism, a brief handbook for Christian living. Luther wrote the catechism to help the "common people, especially in the villages, [who] have no knowledge whatever of Christian doctrine." After a brief preface, it includes simple explanations of each line of the Ten Commandments, the Apostle's Creed (a statement of Christian belief dating from about 500 C.E.), and the Lord's Prayer (the prayer Jesus gave his disciples in Luke 11:1). It then answers basic questions about baptism, confession, and the Lord's Supper; provides instruction on daily prayers; and lists Bible verses summarizing the duties and responsibilities of Christians in everyday life.

tions to the visual arts have paled in comparison with the musical accomplishments of its composers—above all, Johann Sebastian Bach (1685–1750), who expressed his faith in his compositions. He built on a heritage of hymnody and composition that was begun in Luther's own circle by Johann Walther (1684–1748) and others and that was continued in the seventeenth century by Heinrich Schütz (1585–1672), Samuel Scheidt (1587–1654), and Johann Hermann Schein (1586–1630).

Robert Kolb

See Also Vol. I: *Christianity, Protestantism*

Bibliography

Bachmann, E. Theodore, and Mercia Brenne Bachmann, eds. *Lutheran Churches of the World.* Minneapolis: Fortress Press, 1989.

Benne, Robert. *Ordinary Saints.* Minneapolis: Fortress Press, 2003.

Bergendoff, Conrad. *The Church of the Lutheran Reformation.* St. Louis: Concordia Publishing House, 1967.

Bodensieck, Julius, ed. *The Encyclopedia of the Lutheran Church.* Minneapolis: Augsburg Publishing House, 1965.

Brecht, Martin. *Martin Luther.* Translated by James L. Schaaf. 3 vols. Minneapolis: Fortress Press, 1985–93.

Elert, Werner. *The Structure of Lutheranism.* Translated by Walter Hanson. St. Louis: Concordia Publishing House, 1962.

Gassmann, Günter. *Historical Dictionary of Lutheranism.* Lanham, Md.: Scarecrow Press, 2001.

Kolb, Robert, and Timothy J. Wengert, eds. *The Book of Concord: The Confessions of the Evangelical Lutheran Church.* Minneapolis: Fortress Press, 2000.

Luther's Works. 55 vols. St. Louis: Concordia Publishing House; Philadelphia: Muhlenberg/Fortress Press, 1958–86.

Nischan, Bodo. *Lutherans and Calvinists in the Age of Confessionalization.* Aldershot, England: Variorum, 1999.

Piepkorn, Arthur Carl. *The Survival of the Historic Vestments in the Lutheran Church after 1555.* St. Louis: Concordia Seminary, 1958.

Preus, Robert D. *The Theology of Post-Reformation Lutheranism.* 2 vols. St. Louis: Concordia Publishing House, 1970–72.

Repp, Arthur. *Confirmation in the Lutheran Church.* St. Louis: Concordia Publishing House, 1964.

Sasse, Hermann. *Here We Stand: The Nature and Character of the Lutheran Faith.* Translated by Theodore G. Tappert. New York: Harper and Row, 1938.

Schlink, Edmund. *A Theology of the Lutheran Confessions.* Translated by Paul F. Koehneke and Herbert J.A. Bouman. St. Louis: Concordia Publishing House, 1961.

Wenz, Gunther. *Die Theologie der Bekenntnisschriften der evangelisch-lutherischen Kirche.* 2 vols. Berlin: de Gruyter, 1996–98.

Wingren, Gustav. *Luther on Vocation.* Translated by Carl C. Rasmussen. Philadelphia: Muhlenberg Press, 1957.

Christianity

Methodism

FOUNDED: 1729 C.E.

RELIGION AS A PERCENTAGE OF WORLD POPULATION: 1.17 percent

OVERVIEW Methodism, a form of Protestant Christianity, was founded by John Wesley (1703–91) as a means of promoting disciplined Christian living within the Church of England. Ordained an Anglican priest in 1728, Wesley formed a small religious society in about 1729 while a fellow and tutor of Lincoln College, Oxford, England. As the movement grew and spread, it was characterized by open-air preaching focused on God's forgiving love toward all people (justification), the possibility of holy living (sanctification), disciplined living "by method and rule," Christian nurturing in close-knit societies, and an organizational structure closely monitored by Wesley himself. Opposing itself to the Calvinist doctrine of predestination, the Wesleyan revival stressed God's "free grace" to all and attracted many poor people who felt excluded by the elitist teachings and practices of the Church of England.

As the eighteenth century progressed, Methodism eventually spread to Ireland, Scotland, and colonies across the Atlantic. As a consequence of the American Revolution, the movement became a separate denomination in the United States in 1784. Only in 1795, after Wesley's death, did Methodism in Great Britain become a separate body from the Church of England. In the nineteenth century Methodism grew rapidly in the United States and became a major participant in the worldwide missions movement. Denominations with roots in the Wesleyan movement have about 40 million members in the U.S. and worldwide.

HISTORY John Wesley's father, an Anglican priest who implemented a religious society in his parish at Epworth, and his wife, Susanna, instilled an interest in disciplined Christian living in their sons. As an Oxford fellow and tutor, John, along with his brother Charles (1707–88) and some other students, formed a study group in 1729. Within three years critics were characterizing their Arminian theology (opposing predestination and maintaining the possibility of salvation for all) and religious activities as "Methodist." Within the university they were disparaged for their zealous study and devotion, conscientious attendance at worship, and beneficent assistance to the poor of the community. Nevertheless, they soon attracted a following of some four dozen people in the university and town, including such later church notables as James Hervey, Benjamin Ingham, and George Whitefield.

In 1738 the Wesley brothers met Peter Boehler, a Moravian pastor who stressed the Reformation doctrine of salvation by faith alone. His mentorship led them to a spiritual awakening. Although John never promoted his experience of "assurance of faith" as explicit paradigm for his followers, the idea of a sudden spiritual "conversion" became typical in the Wesleyan movement.

The revival began in earnest in 1739 when Wesley followed George Whitefield's example in Bristol and

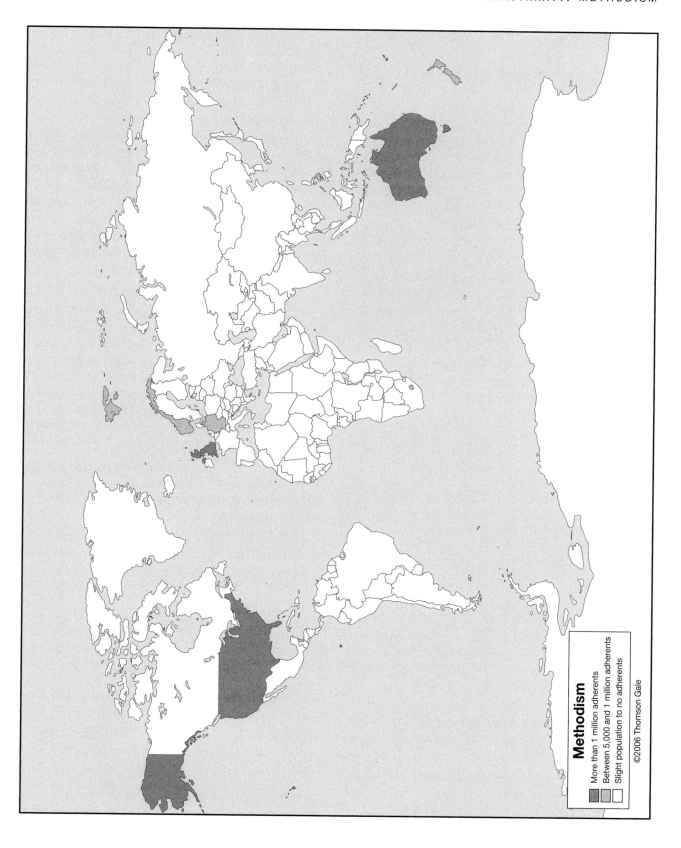

Methodism

More than 1 million adherents
Between 5,000 and 1 million adherents
Slight population to no adherents

©2006 Thomson Gale

Members of a Methodist church hold up Thanksgiving turkeys. Methodism emphasizes programs that assist the poor. © KEVIN FLEMING/CORBIS.

began preaching in outdoor venues, such as market places and brickyards. Such "field preaching" was irregular but attracted large numbers of people, including many who did not normally attend church. As groups began to grow in London, Newcastle, and other parts of England, Wesley adopted the name United Societies of People Called Methodists. Wesley soon began setting apart lay preachers (his "sons in the gospel") to lead the societies. He invited clergy and lay preachers to an annual conference to maintain uniformity of doctrine and practice. Wesley published the "Minutes," spelling out the doctrinal and disciplinary guidelines for the movement; several volumes of his sermons, to furnish the lay preachers with theological guidelines; and pamphlets with hymns and sacred poems for use during services. Although Wesley did not officially select any women as preachers, they provided much of the leadership within the small group structure of the Methodist societies, and a few women were encouraged by Wesley to "expound" and "exhort" within their societies.

Wesley felt God had raised up the Methodist preachers "to reform the nation, especially the Church, and spread scriptural holiness across the land." Although he explicitly denied any inclination to separate from the Anglican Church, his reforms gave the movement its own identity and eventuated in a separation after Wesley's death.

Methodist immigrants to America formed into societies in the 1760s, and before the decade was over, Wesley sent preachers, including Francis Asbury in 1771 and Thomas Rankin in 1773. Harry Hosier, a black lay preacher, increased black membership in the societies. Partly because Wesley opposed the colonies' rebellion against English rule, most British lay preachers (except Asbury) joined the flow of Anglican priests back to England beginning in 1775. In 1784, after the United States had established political and religious independence, Wesley sent Thomas Coke to the new country, made him and Asbury general superintendents (they soon adopted the term "bishops"), and provided a plan for the formation of a separate denomination, the Methodist Episcopal Church.

During the nineteenth century Methodists provided leadership within the growing world missions movement, spreading their beliefs around the globe. Methodism expanded significantly in Great Britain during this time. Methodists also participated in revival services and camp meetings, which were especially strong in the United States, and Methodist Episcopal Church membership grew by 20 times, making Methodism the largest Protestant denomination in the country before mid-century (more than 5 percent of the total population).

The prevalence of Methodists in the general population, but specifically in positions of authority, has led many to view the nineteenth century as the "Methodist Age" in the United States. Nineteenth-century Methodists combined a tendency to view morality in negative terms (promoting various prohibitions) with a tendency to see moral value in positive programs (those that support family values); thus, Methodism joined many other denominations in backing such political movements as women's rights, temperance, labor unions, racial tolerance, and peace. Many of the organizations that promoted these causes were led by Methodists, including Harriet Tubman, Frederick Douglass, Frances Willard, Frank Mason North, and Harry Ward. By 1900 social issues, political tensions, and doctrinal disputes fragmented Methodism into a number of separate denominations in both the United States and Britain, but the growth of the segments continued unhampered for 60 further years.

The twentieth century witnessed efforts at unification among Wesleyan groups. After the political failure of the Prohibition movement, the negative approach to morality was generally replaced with a more positive emphasis on ways Methodists could responsibly exhibit love in their personal, social, civic, and political relationships. Methodists are still active in political leadership. For instance, in the United States three of the four presidential and vice-presidential candidates of the Republican and Democratic parties in 2004 were United Methodists.

As with many mainline Protestant denominations, overall Methodist membership decreased in the last half of the twentieth century, though it continues to grow in areas of the southern United States and all across Oceania, Africa, and Asia. A single Methodist congregation in Korea has just under 100,000 members, and the Methodist Pentecostal Church in Chile has about 800,000 members. Among the denominations with the largest membership are the United Methodist Church (uniting three American bodies in 1968), with nearly 10 million members; the African Methodist Episcopal Church, with over 3 million members, and the African Methodist Episcopal Zion Church, with nearly 1.5 million members, both in the United States; the Church of the Nazarene (Wesleyan in theology), with 1.4 million members; and the Methodist Church of Great Britain (uniting the five main British groups in 1932), with over 300,000 members. The World Methodist Council, whose history goes back to 1881, includes members from Methodist and Wesleyan denominations in 132 countries, which together attract some 75 million members and adherents.

CENTRAL DOCTRINES Methodism shares the main doctrines of classical Protestantism. The doctrinal standards of Methodism (official measures of "orthodoxy") are, within each denomination, contained in a document often called the Articles of Religion of Confession of Faith, following the pattern John Wesley set in 1784 when he abridged the articles of the Church of England for the Methodist Episcopal Church in America. Within such groups as the United Methodist Church, the disciplinary rules do not allow anyone, clergy or laity, to disseminate doctrines contrary to those standards. Further statements of doctrine include Wesley's *Sermons on Several Occasions*; his biblical commentary, *Explanatory Notes upon the New Testament*; and the liturgy found in each denominational hymnbook or book of worship. The practical implications of these doctrines for the disciplines of Christian living are spelled out in the "General Rules," written by Wesley in 1743 and still contained in most Methodist by-laws.

A Methodist preacher leads a service in San Francisco, California. Contemporary Methodists generally hold Sunday morning and evening worship services in churches and chapels. © KEVIN FLEMING/CORBIS.

The defining doctrinal emphases of the Methodist movement from the beginning have been what Wesley called the "three grand doctrines": repentance, faith, and holiness (or, in more theological language, original sin, justification, and sanctification). The most distinctive doctrine of Methodism is Christian Perfection (entire sanctification), the idea that believers can, with God's assistance (grace), love God and neighbor fully in this life—that is, they can live without any conscious, voluntary, willful sin, defined as a breaking of the known will of God. Another characteristic of Wesleyan doctrine is that of Assurance, which maintains that one can have a conscious knowledge that at any given time he or she is a child of God, forgiven of sins and empowered for holy living (loving God and neighbor). Assurance is never a guarantee of final blessedness, however. Backsliding ("falling from grace") is a real possibility at any point in life.

Methodism emphasizes Scripture as the primary source and criterion of truth, "the only rule, and the sufficient rule, both of our faith and practice." Within this framework Wesley also bequeathed to Methodism a healthy regard for the traditions of the Church during the first four or five centuries of Christianity as primal interpretations of the Gospel, a trust in reason as a means of perceiving God's truth, and the more radical view that one can experience God's truth directly through the divine presence acting in the life of the believer.

These doctrines are the basis for both the devotional piety (personal and communal) and the social action typical of Methodism over the last 250 years. Wesley believed that both works of piety (loving God) and works of mercy (loving neighbor) were "means of grace," or ways of appropriating the transforming power of God in human life. Although Wesley was careful to maintain a synergism of these energies, some segments of the contemporary movement have emphasized one side more than the other, so that revivalist and activist wings often disagree about the true nature of the church.

MORAL CODE OF CONDUCT Methodists have never been slow to translate doctrine into discipline—personal, organizational, and programmatic. Wesley's work on translating biblical theology into personal morality resulted in the document "Nature, Design, and General Rules of the United Societies." Still contained in most Methodist handbooks, these rules are in themselves simple and short: Members should "evidence their desire of salvation" (1) "by avoiding evil of every kind," (2) "by doing good of every possible sort," and (3) "by attending upon all the ordinances of God" (all the means through which God's power can affect a person's life). Each rule is accompanied by a list of examples that have remained unchanged since the eighteenth century. Many people now view the examples as antiquated, so the rules have been largely neglected for the last hundred years.

SACRED BOOKS According to the preface of the 1788 edition of the Articles of Religion, the Bible is the sole standard of Christian truth for Methodists. It is the only book considered truly sacred, though not the only source of knowledge or inspiration.

SACRED SYMBOLS Methodists use many Christian symbols to represent sacred realities. These range from traditional visual symbols grounded in the life of Christ (such as the cross and others related to the crucifixion and resurrection) to the many representations of ideas and events from the long history of God's action in human history (such as the rainbow, the flame, and the alpha and omega).

EARLY AND MODERN LEADERS John Wesley was assisted by a number of notable eighteenth-century contemporaries, such as his brother (Charles Wesley), George Whitefield, Selina Countess of Huntingdon, Mary Bosanquet, Francis Asbury, and Thomas Coke. In America groups that would later join with the Method-ists were led by Philip Otterbein (United Bretheren) and Jacob Albright (Evangelical Association). In the nineteenth century American Methodism fragmented into several separate denominations, such as African Methodist Episcopal, African Methodist Episcopal Zion, Methodist Protestant, Wesleyan Methodist, Free Methodist, and Colored Methodist Episcopal, under leaders such as Richard Allen, James Varick, Nicholas Snethen, Orange Scott, Benjamin Roberts, and William H. Miles. Many bishops have provided strong leadership, including Joshua Soule and Matthew Simpson in nineteenth-century America. In the United Methodist Church the Council of Bishops has begun to provide theological and pastoral leadership through the development of such programs as the Bishops' Initiative on Children in Poverty.

MAJOR THEOLOGIANS AND AUTHORS John Wesley set the course for Methodist theology with an approach grounded in the thought of the Church of England but influenced by patristic (following the Church fathers), puritan (using biblical guidelines for morality and organization), and pietist (stressing bible study and personal religious experience) thought, producing a synthesis that was catholic, reformed, and evangelical.

Early theological leaders included Wesley's friends John Fletcher and Adam Clarke, followed in the nineteenth century by Richard Watson in Great Britain and Asa Shinn, Wilbur Fisk, and Thomas Summers in the United States. Georgia Harkness, Borden Parker Bowne, and Edwin Lewis were among the important theologians of twentieth-century Methodism. Albert C. Outler was the major ecumenical leader among Methodists of that century, as well as being one of the leading Wesleyan theologians.

ORGANIZATIONAL STRUCTURE Most Methodist bodies maintain an episcopal polity—a structure led by bishops. The legislative authority for most Methodist denominations rests in a representative quadrennial general conference that, since the late nineteenth century, has included laity as well as clergy. From the beginning Methodism has stressed local organization and small group meetings. Local congregations are connected in a structure that includes district, regional ("annual"), and jurisdictional conferences in increasingly larger geographical areas. Clergy are ordained and appointed to their ministerial positions by the bishops and their assistants—the district superintendents—and they maintain membership in an "annual conference."

HOUSES OF WORSHIP AND HOLY PLACES Early Methodists held nonsacramental meetings in "preaching houses" (later often called "chapels") as a supplement to Anglican parish church services. Contemporary Methodists generally hold Sunday morning and evening worship services in churches and chapels. Revival services often take place in tents, "brush arbors," amphitheaters, or other outdoor venues that echo the early Methodist "field preaching." Prayer meetings, church school classes, and other meetings of subgroups of a given congregation often meet in educational buildings, the homes of members, or at campgrounds.

Some Methodist denominations designate historic shrines and landmarks, but when Methodists talk of a "pilgrimage" to Wesley's birthplace at Epworth, England, or to Francis Asbury's home near Gloucester, Massachusetts, or to John Fletcher's home in Madeley, Shropshire, they are not speaking of a spiritual exercise similar to a Roman Catholic's at Compostella or a Muslim's at Mecca.

WHAT IS SACRED? Methodists believe in a doctrine of God's creation, but nothing in that creation has the same sacred status as the divine being of the Trinity. Churches are often called "sacred space," and persons are seen as having "sacred worth," but these are metaphorical uses of the term.

HOLIDAYS AND FESTIVALS Most Methodist bodies follow the liturgy and holidays of the Christian Year, in which holy days represent events in the life of Jesus. The Church of England celebrates a festival of John and Charles Wesley on 3 March (the day after John's date of death in 1791), but the Methodists more often celebrate 24 May, the day John Wesley experienced "assurance of faith" at a society meeting in Aldersgate Street, London, in 1738. Many Methodist congregations emphasize other historical events, educational themes, and social concerns on specially designated Sundays.

MODE OF DRESS Some Methodist clergy wear clerical garb, including a clerical collar and such liturgical vestments as a stole, robe, alb, cross, or other paraphernalia, especially during worship services, other services (such as funerals and weddings), and pastoral occasions (such as hospital visits). Many British Methodist clergy follow Wesley's habit of wearing Geneva tabs (a form of clerical collar) as a sign of their ministerial status. Other clergy typically dress like the members of their congrega-

tions. Laity in most Methodist denominations are usually undifferentiated from the general population, although some with closer ties to the nineteenth-century Holiness movement (which stressed personal piety) still encourage simplicity of dress and denigrate the wearing of jewelry or fine clothing.

DIETARY PRACTICES Many Methodist groups officially observe temperance in eating and drinking, with a historical focus on abstinence from alcoholic beverages; this has extended to a stance against drug abuse.

RITUALS Since the nineteenth century Methodist churches have usually followed the Protestant move toward a "free church," impromptu approach to ritual, straying from Wesley's interest in the more formal ritual of the Church of England. Most Methodist books of worship, however, still include versions of the historical rituals for worship and the Eucharist (Communion), as well as for baptisms, marriages, funerals, and other significant religious rites of passage. Distinctive Methodist rituals include a Covenant Service (based on Wesley's idea of renewing one's covenant with God) at the beginning of each new year and the Love Feast, closely patterned after the Moravian service (also from Wesley's day).

RITES OF PASSAGE Methodists celebrate two Christian sacraments, baptism and the Lord's Supper. Entrance into the body of Christ is celebrated in baptism, usually in infancy, and membership in the community of faith is marked by confirmation, as a child approaches teen years. Marriage is usually solemnized in church but is not considered a sacrament.

MEMBERSHIP Historically people become members of Methodist churches by professing faith in Christ or transferring from other recognized Christian denominations. Continued membership requires active participation in and support of the ministries of the church. The early tradition of closed membership ceased in the last half of the nineteenth century. Methodists have traditionally evangelized through preaching services, mission outreach, and small group encounters.

RELIGIOUS TOLERANCE Like many groups that started out as minorities, Methodists have historically promoted religious tolerance, and for over a century they have joined in ecumenical dialogue on both the national and international level.

SOCIAL JUSTICE In the late nineteenth and early twentieth centuries, Methodism provided leadership in various movements for social justice. The American Methodist "Social Creed" (1908) was one of the first major statements that summarized the church's concern for societal problems. Methodists have historically included persons of all economic and social groups and are still markedly diverse in membership. The early interest in reaching out to those who suffer in poverty and incorporating them into the fellowship of believers, however, has often shifted, especially in North America, to an emphasis on mission programs that simply send help to the poor. Methodist promotion of education and health issues has resulted in the prevalence of Methodist-related hospitals, retirement homes, educational institutions, and summer institutes and camps. The present social action programs are promoted by several boards and agencies of the churches, such as the Methodist Federation for Social Action.

SOCIAL ASPECTS Methodists have a long history of supporting the traditional importance of healthy marriages and strong families; because of a desire to uphold the family, the nineteenth-century Methodist Frances Willard (among others) fought for women's rights and temperance. The more recent concern for children in poverty is another reflection of this emphasis.

CONTROVERSIAL ISSUES The Methodist family of denominations exhibits a great variety of positions on many controversial social issues. Most follow the consensus represented by other mainline Protestant groups, such as the allowance of divorce, the limited approval of abortion, the promotion of birth control, the support of unionization, the prohibition of ordaining homosexuals, the declaration that "the practice of homosexuality is incompatible with Christian teaching," and the equal role of women at all levels of the church. Methodist debate is not closed on issues that cause a division of opinion in society. The stance of most Methodist denominations can be defined or changed only by their governing body, such as the General Conference of the United Methodist Church.

CULTURAL IMPACT One of the primary influences of Methodism on religious culture has been the wide use of Charles Wesley's hymns in most Christian denominations. Methodist churches are some of the best architectural examples from particular periods and regions,

The Name "Methodist"

The name "Methodist" derives from several possible sources. John Bingham of Christ Church, Oxford, used the term in derision in about 1732. He may have been describing the group's Arminian theology (opposing predestination), thus likening them to the "New Methodists" of the previous century, who, according to the Calvinists, used a "new," or bad, method in theology. John Wesley, the founder of Methodism, thought Bingham was referring to an ancient sect of Greek physicians called "Methodists," who promoted good health by prescribing a strict regimen of diet and exercise.

Although the name was thrust upon the group, Wesley adopted it for his movement, often using the phrase "the people called Methodists." In his compact English dictionary Wesley defined "Methodist" as "one who lives by the method described in the Bible." The regular and disciplined patterns of living that typified early Methodism are now most often cited as the source of the name, even though the term also applies to their theology.

forming an ecclesiastical architectural history of the last three centuries. In the last two generations Methodist churches have introduced special services that reflect the music, art, poetry, and various other multimedia expressions of contemporary cultures. The Chautauqua Institution, founded in 1874 by Methodist Episcopal bishop J.H. Vincent to reflect the denomination's interest in combining religion, education, and the arts, has been widely imitated.

Richard P. Heitzenrater

See Also Vol. 1: *Christianity, Protestantism*

Bibliography

Davies, Rupert, A. Raymond George, and Gordon Rupp, eds. *A History of the Methodist Church in Great Britain.* 4 vol. London: Epworth Press, 1988.

Field, Clive D., Frank Baker, Sheila Himsworth, John A Vickers, and Alison Peacock. *The People Called Methodists: A Documentary History of the Methodist Church in Great Britain and Ireland* Microfiche. Leiden: IDC, 1999.

Heitzenrater, Richard P. *Wesley and the People Called Methodists.* Nashville: Abingdon Press, 1995.

Norwood, Frederick. *The Story of American Methodism.* Nashville: Abingdon Press, 1974.

Rack, Henry. *Reasonable Enthusiast.* London: Epworth Press, 1988.

Richey, Russell E., and Kenneth E. Rowe, eds. *The Methodist Experience in America.* Nashville: Abingdon Press, 2000.

Rowe, Kenneth E. *Methodist Union Catalog.* Metuchen, N.J.: Scarecrow Press, 1975.

Streiff, Patrick. *Methodism in Europe.* Tallinn: Baltic Methodist Theological Seminary, 2003.

Wesley, John. *The Works of John Wesley.* Bicentennial Edition. Projected 35 vols. Nashville: Abingdon Press, 1978.

Pentecostalism

FOUNDED: 1901 C.E.

**RELIGION AS A PERCENTAGE OF
WORLD POPULATION:** 8.5 percent

OVERVIEW Pentecostals are Christians who believe in an experience called "baptism with the Holy Spirit." This form of baptism refers to the descent of the Holy Spirit upon a person, allowing the person to speak in tongues and to manifest other spiritual gifts. It is mentioned several times in the New Testament, including the following passage from Matthew 3:11: "I indeed baptize you in water unto repentance: but he that cometh after me is mightier than I, whose shoes I am not worthy to bear: he shall baptize you in the Holy Spirit and in fire." The name Pentecostalism comes from the Pentecost, which is the day, discussed in the Acts of the Apostles, when the Holy Spirit descended upon Jesus' apostles.

Pentecostalism began in the United States in January 1901, when Charles Fox Parham, an independent Holiness evangelist in eastern Kansas, preached that speaking in tongues was the biblical evidence of baptism with the Holy Spirit. His teaching was taken to Los Angeles in 1906 and sparked the Azusa Street Revival, whose publications attracted radical evangelical groups across the United States.

Today much of Pentecostalism's numerical strength lies outside the United States. In the *World Christian Encyclopedia*, David B. Barrett estimates there were 65.8 million Pentecostals worldwide in 2000. If the count in-

cluded those outside Pentecostal denominations but who had been influenced by waves of twentieth-century charismatic renewal, the total, he suggests, would exceed 520 million.

HISTORY Many late-nineteenth-century Protestants on the margins of the church establishment taught that baptism was with the Holy Spirit rather than with all three persons of the Trinity (Father, Son, and Holy Spirit). Among them were those who embraced the idea that the evidence of such baptism was speaking in tongues.

This was the view of evangelist Charles Fox Parham. A native of Iowa, Parham spent his formative years in Kansas, where he began preaching among Methodists. His strong independent inclinations led him to launch out on his own, however. During the mid-1890s he preached throughout eastern Kansas, imbibing homespun religious opinions. In 1898 he opened a healing home and mission in Topeka and began publishing the newspaper *Apostolic Faith.* Working "by faith," he received no salary and passed no collection plates at the mission. With his wife, Sarah Thistlethwaite Parham, he developed enough of a following to open a Bible school in the fall of 1900. Aware of growing interest in topics related to the Holy Spirit, Parham read and traveled to keep abreast of the latest popular views.

In January 1901 Parham began teaching that speaking in tongues was always evidence of baptism with the Holy Spirit. He also thought that speaking in tongues, by circumventing the need for language study, would allow the gospel to be proclaimed rapidly around the

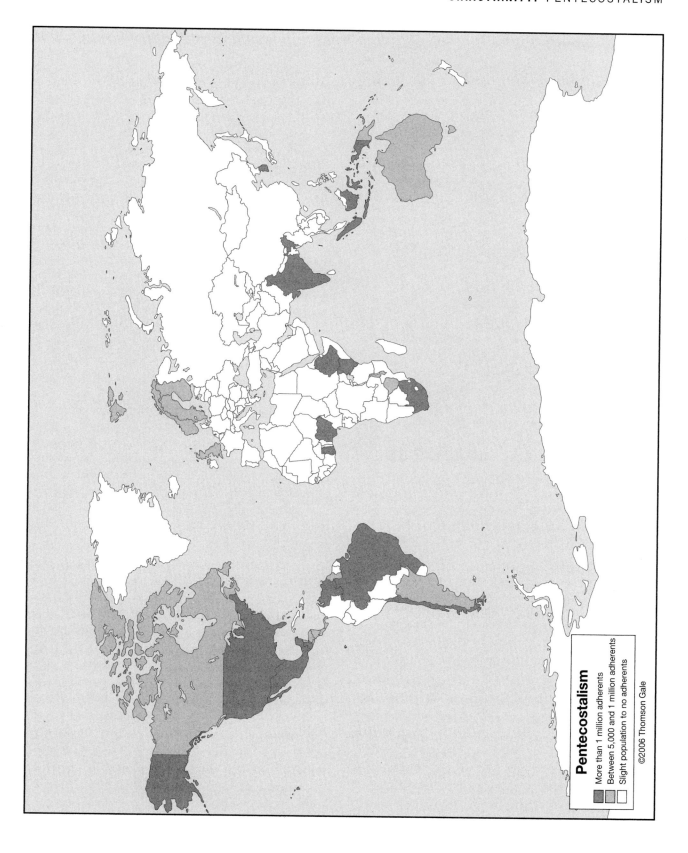

Pentecostalism

More than 1 million adherents
Between 5,000 and 1 million adherents
Slight population to no adherents

©2006 Thomson Gale

A Brazilian Pentecostal woman, with face in Bible, prays in the street, while others pray behind her. Though it began in the United States, Pentecostalism has spread all over the globe, owing largely to the evangelization efforts of its members. © RICARDO AZOURY/CORBIS.

world. Parham understood baptism with the Holy Spirit to be the third in a series of "crisis experiences" he urged everyone to embrace. Conversion and sanctification, the latter freeing the penitent from the power of sin, were the first two. The third, baptism with the Holy Spirit, provided the fully sanctified believer with the power for service, which was widely understood as preaching.

Parham's message started to spread in 1903, when he began a series of meetings in Joplin, Missouri. His efforts then spread to Texas, where he converted William J. Seymour, a local African-American Holiness pastor, who carried the views to Los Angeles in 1906. Between 1906 and 1908 there were revivals at Seymour's Azusa Street Mission. Reports of "Pentecosts" around the globe filled the pages of the mission's four-page monthly, *Apostolic Faith.* Leaders of various grassroots networks embraced the mission's message of restoring

early Christian practices, and by 1907 regional clusters, most of them small associations, began to identify with Pentecostalism. Among them were the Church of God, established by Ambrose J. Tomlinson near Cleveland, Tennessee; the Pentecostal Holiness Church around Dunn, North Carolina; and the largely African-American Church of God in Christ, with congregations in northern Mississippi and southwestern Tennessee. Camp meetings, periodic conventions, and a flurry of inexpensively produced periodicals sustained fervor and slowly built an enduring religious movement out of an emotion-packed revival.

After World War II a renewal movement that included Pentecostal practices erupted in both mainstream Protestantism and Roman Catholicism. This charismatic, or neo-Pentecostal, movement also contributed to the growth of independent ministries. Oral Roberts became a key figure when he moved from the Pentecostal Holiness Church to the Methodist Church and then to an independent fellowship that bridged charismatic and older Pentecostal influences. Pentecostal evangelists traveled the globe to testify to experiences described in the movement's press, and the Pentecostal focus on possession by the Holy Spirit, physical healing, and the immediacy of the divine presence found a ready response in some non-Western cultures. Such media-savvy Pentecostals as Americans Jimmy Swaggart and Benny Hinn promoted their message throughout the world, and German Reinhard Bonnke and American T.L. Osborne conducted crusades featuring "signs and wonders evangelism."

CENTRAL DOCTRINES Charles Fox Parham's belief that speaking in tongues, or tongues speech, was always evidence of baptism with the Holy Spirit lay at the core of early Pentecostal identity. The views of the handful of Pentecostals who objected that this gave undue prominence to one spiritual gift or disagreed about the meaning of speaking in tongues were soon overwhelmed by the force of the majority. The idea that speaking in tongues was useful in missionary work was taught briefly at Azusa Street, but increasing numbers of Pentecostals embraced the view that speakers in tongues generally employed heavenly languages.

The interweaving of two other convictions also influenced the movement's core identity. First, Pentecostals thought they lived at the end of history. As premillennialists, they anticipated the imminent "rapture" of the church to heaven, and they wanted to be ready. This translated into an interest in personal holiness and public witness of their faith. Second, Pentecostals believed that the Bible promised an end-times revival, a "latter rain" that would rival the power of New Testament Christianity. They saw the restoration of the gift of tongues as the sign that the end-times revival had arrived.

Pentecostals believed that all New Testament spiritual gifts belonged to the contemporary church, and they embraced with particular enthusiasm the doctrine of divine healing. They thought that healing was part of the Atonement, and they anointed and laid hands on the sick and prayed for their recovery, eschewing the use of medicine. They thought of themselves as people of faith and believed that faith supplied their physical and temporal, as well as spiritual, needs.

For Pentecostals sanctification was not an abstract doctrine. Becoming holy had everything to do with how they lived. In the movement's formative years most Pentecostals thought of sanctification as a "second definite work of grace," in which the tendency to sin had been uprooted. Like their cousins in the Holiness movement, Pentecostals received this "second blessing" in a crisis moment, often by coming forward for prayer and generally after much agonized self-searching and repentance. In 1910 Chicago Pentecostal evangelist William Durham offered an alternate view he called "the finished work of Calvary." Durham deemphasized the crisis aspect of sanctification and stressed the moment-by-moment subduing of sin effected by Christ "reigning" within the soul. Durham's supporters thought of sanctification as a process rather than an instantaneous event. This caused an enduring rift in the Pentecostal movement between those who insisted that three crisis experiences (conversion, sanctification, and Spirit baptism) marked the Christian life and those who were satisfied with two (conversion and Spirit baptism).

By 1912 the baptismal formula had led to yet another controversy. Observant Pentecostals noticed that, according to the Acts of the Apostles, early Christians were baptized "in the name of Jesus" rather than "in the name of the Father, the Son, and the Holy Spirit." Some members promptly introduced this pattern, and by 1913 prominent preachers called for rebaptism of the faithful in the name of Jesus. In some areas Pentecostals largely heeded the summons. By the end of the decade, proponents of rebaptism had begun rejecting traditional views of the Trinity in favor of an emphasis on Jesus as the New Testament manifestation of the Old Testa-

A man raises his arms during a Pentecostal baptism ceremony. Pentecostals believe in an experience called "baptism with the Holy Spirit." This form of baptism allows a person to speak in tongues and to manifest other spiritual gifts. © KEVIN FLEMING/CORBIS.

ment Jehovah. They came to be known as Oneness, or sometimes Apostolic, Pentecostals.

MORAL CODE OF CONDUCT Pentecostals draw their moral code of conduct from Scripture. Early Pentecostals dreaded worldliness and separated themselves from the world in decisive ways. Movies, theaters, spectator sports, dance halls, bars, and the like were off-limits. Adherents dressed modestly and shunned jewelry, and women wore their hair long, avoided makeup, and wore skirts rather than slacks. One Southern U.S. denomination, the Fire-Baptized Holiness Church, divided over the worldliness of men's ties. Others argued about the propriety of wedding rings. In tobacco-growing regions Pentecostals wrestled with the conflict presented by making their livelihood from a product they denounced. Pentecostals also abstained from alcohol.

After World War II many of these proscriptions began to change, especially those related to dress and entertainment. Objections to movies and theaters gave way to sponsored dramatic competitions, as early notions of worldliness yielded to the press of popular culture. Like other evangelicals, Pentecostals have moved away from the lists that once governed conduct to general guidelines that leave many such decisions to individual choice. Oneness Pentecostals have tended to be the most conservative on these issues.

SACRED BOOKS The Bible is the only book Pentecostals regard as sacred. They value the devotional writings common among evangelicals, however, and they regularly publish new resources and materials. Pentecostal how-to and therapeutic manuals are as popular as the classics.

SACRED SYMBOLS Pentecostals have no sacred symbols in any traditional sense, and the movement sustains no concept of sacred space. While some churches display a cross or a scripture text, others display no Christian symbols.

EARLY AND MODERN LEADERS Leading Pentecostal figures include Charles Fox Parham, the self-proclaimed "founder and progenitor" of the movement; William J. Seymour, an African-American preacher and constant presence in the ever-changing scene at the Azusa Street Mission in Los Angeles; Ambrose J. Tomlinson, founder of the Church of God movements that identify with Pentecostalism; William Durham, articulator of the process of grace as an alternative to crisis sanctification; J. H. King, founder of the Pentecostal Holiness Church; Charles H. Mason, founder of the Church of God in Christ; Aimee Semple McPherson, founder of the Los Angeles–based International Church of the Foursquare Gospel and nationally known evangelist; Oral Roberts, evangelist and broadcaster; and Jack Hayford, pastor of the Church on the Way in Van Nuys, California, as well as educator, broadcaster, author, and popular speaker, who has bridged the Pentecostal and charismatic movements.

MAJOR THEOLOGIANS AND AUTHORS Pentecostals have not historically valued formal theology, and the movement in the West has produced few theologians recognized beyond Pentecostalism. Some leading Pentecostal theologians include Donald Gee, George Taylor, Ernest Williams, Stanley Horton, Gordon Fee, and the charismatic Presbyterian J. Rodman Williams. Each denomination values its own theologians, few of whom cross over to other constituencies. Pentecostals with an academic interest in theology tend to value the work of evangelical theologians.

ORGANIZATIONAL STRUCTURE The Pentecostal movement involves members in numerous Christian denominations and in a vibrant independent sector. Larger groups include the Church of God in Christ; Assemblies of God; International Church of the Foursquare Gospel; United Pentecostal Church; Church of God, Cleveland, Tennessee; Pentecostal Holiness Church; and Pentecostal Assemblies of the World.

HOUSES OF WORSHIP AND HOLY PLACES Pentecostal congregations meet in all kinds of buildings, from mega-churches filled with the latest technology to small frame buildings. The movement has no holy places, though the memory of the Azusa Street Revival has a hallowed place in rhetoric and collective identity.

WHAT IS SACRED? While Pentecostals do not generally denote objects or spaces as sacred, in practice they regard both the teaching of Scripture and the "moving of the Spirit" as sacred. They understand the Holy Spirit to move among gathered believers when spiritual gifts are exercised and emotions are touched. Ecstasy, individual audible praise, prostration, uplifted hands, dance, or tears may mark such moments.

HOLIDAYS AND FESTIVALS Pentecostals have no holidays or festivals of their own. Some, however, take special note of the day of Pentecost, the seventh Sunday after Easter, to celebrate the movement's particular emphasis on speaking in tongues and baptism with the Holy Spirit, experiences recorded in the second chapter of the Acts of the Apostles as having marked the first Christian Pentecost.

MODE OF DRESS Pentecostals vary in their customs of dress. Some emphasize modesty, but they interpret this in a variety of ways. Pastors often wear business suits, although some adopt clerical collars and others wear robes. African-American congregations may feature deaconesses, or congregational mothers, who dress in white and take a prominent part in the life and worship of the community. A few denominations object to the wearing of jewelry.

DIETARY PRACTICES In general Pentecostals view the body as God's temple and urge believers to exercise good stewardship of their health. Many Pentecostals participate enthusiastically in the popular evangelical culture of religiously based diet books—with titles like *What Would Jesus Eat?*—and some churches host diet-support groups. Pentecostals oppose smoking and the consumption of alcoholic beverages.

RITUALS Pentecostal congregations have worship services on Sunday mornings as well as midweek prayer and Bible studies with a family emphasis. In the United States, Sunday evening services are increasingly less common. Rituals include prayers for healing, often accompanied by anointing with oil; exorcisms; and altar calls (invitations to the penitent or those seeking healing or Spirit baptism to come forward for prayer). Annual or biennial denominational business meetings attract huge numbers of members. The fall convention of the Church of God in Christ, for example, draws tens of thousands of people to Memphis, Tennessee. At these mammoth gatherings of the faithful, both lay and clerical, rituals for cleansing, healing, and reconciliation are reenacted around business sessions.

RITES OF PASSAGE Most Pentecostal congregations offer a service of infant dedication, in which parents promise to provide their child with a Christian home and church education. Once they reach an age of accountability, children may choose to be baptized. Both new converts and anyone who received baptism as an infant are encouraged to be baptized on a profession of faith. Pentecostals regard baptism as obedience to a command, as a sign of something from the past rather than as a moment of grace. In some Pentecostal denominations it is not necessary to be baptized to receive Communion.

MEMBERSHIP Pentecostals evangelize eagerly. They are extremely conscious of numbers, and they tend to equate success with growth. Pentecostal denominations support thousands of career and short-term missionaries around the globe. Pentecostals employ many modes of outreach, both in the United States and elsewhere. They readily embrace new media to assist their evangelistic efforts. Pioneers in radio and televangelism, Pentecostals also use the Internet and nontraditional missionaries to reach countries closed to missionary work.

RELIGIOUS TOLERANCE Pentecostals support freedom of worship. In the United States they have historically been wary of the ecumenical movement. This distrust has been nurtured by the liberal theology and political views of ecumenical agencies and by the Pentecostal belief in the prophecy of a coming world church. Pentecostals cooperate, however, in the efforts of evangelical agencies to support relief work and evangelism.

Numbers of Pentecostal Groups

Classic Pentecostals are those who were influenced by the Azusa Street Revival of 1906–08 in Los Angeles. Most often they belong to Pentecostal denominations, and they emphasize speaking in tongues as evidence of Spirit baptism. In the *World Christian Encyclopedia*, David B. Barrett estimated there were 65,832,970 such Pentecostals worldwide in 2000. Charismatics are those in historic denominations, both Protestant and Roman Catholic, who in the 1950s and 1960s turned their attention to experiencing the Holy Spirit and recovering New Testament spiritual gifts. Barrett estimated their numbers at 175,856,690. Neocharismatics include a wide variety of nondenominational and indigenous movements that focus less on speaking in tongues but that maintain openness to spiritual gifts and embrace a Pentecostal worship style (raised hands, praise, and worship music). Barrett estimated that in 2000 there were 294,405,240 neocharismatics.

Barrett distributed participants in these twentieth-century renewal movements worldwide as follows: Latin America, 141,432,880; Asia, 134,889,530; Africa, 126,010,200; North America, 79,600,160; Europe, 37,568,700; and Oceania, 4,265,520. In the United States the principal Pentecostal groups are the Church of God in Christ, which claims 5.5 million members; the Assemblies of God, with 2.5 million members and adherents; the Pentecostal Assemblies of the World, with 1.5 million members; the United Pentecostal Church, with 1 million members; the Church of God, Cleveland, Tennessee, with 896,000 members; and the Pentecostal Holiness Church, with more than 200,000 members.

SOCIAL JUSTICE White Pentecostals in the United States have not taken strong public stands on issues related to social justice, except to support human rights elsewhere, especially religious freedom, with petitions, prayers, and public statements. African-American Pentecostals have been much more involved than white Pentecostals in the civil rights and poverty issues that affect their constituencies.

SOCIAL ASPECTS Pentecostals work hard at building strong families. They promote Marriage Encounter, James Dobson's Focus on the Family, and a wide variety of other programs that are infused with conservative views on marriage, relationships in the family, and male headship in the home. The realities of modern life have forced them to respond as well to the needs of the divorced and of single parents and blended families. Pentecostals regard homosexuality and abortion as sinful practices.

CONTROVERSIAL ISSUES Pentecostals discourage divorce and remarriage. For most of their history, Pentecostal ministers refused to remarry a person whose earlier spouse was living, and most Pentecostal denominations routinely refused ordination to divorced persons. In the 1990s some denominations altered this stance in favor of a case-by-case approach. Pentecostals have no proscriptions on birth control, but they absolutely reject abortion. Some Pentecostal denominations ordain women, and to sustain their outreaches, all of them depend heavily on the volunteer efforts of women, who constitute a majority of the membership.

CULTURAL IMPACT Music is the area in which Pentecostals have had the most cultural influence. The Pentecostal emphasis on religious experience has assured a prominent role for music, and their styles of music have affected both Christian sacred and secular popular music. Instead of traditional hymns, it was gospel hymns, with roots in late-nineteenth-century revivals

emphasizing testimony and experience, that found favor at the movement's outset. Since the mid-1960s the musical revolution associated with the charismatic renewal has brought into many Pentecostal congregations simple scriptural choruses (Bible verses or phrases set to music), along with music focused on praise and worship. While these changes in religious music did not necessarily originate in Pentecostal circles, Pentecostals have embraced them in their yearning for renewal of their worship practices. Thus, the emphasis on personal worship has made Pentecostals major contributors to the praise-and-worship music used widely in contemporary Christian services.

Edith Blumhofer

See Also Vol. I: *Christianity*

Bibliography

Anderson, Robert M. *Vision of the Disinherited: The Making of American Pentecostalism.* New York: Oxford University Press, 1979.

Blumhofer, Edith. *Restoring the Faith.* Champaign: University of Illinois Press, 1993.

Burgess, Stanley M., ed. *The New International Dictionary of Pentecostal and Charismatic Movements.* Rev. and enl. ed. Grand Rapids, Mich.: Zondervan, 2002.

Sanders, Cheryl. *Saints in Exile: The Holiness-Pentecostal Experience in African American Religion and Culture.* New York: Oxford University Press, 1996.

Synan, Vinson. *The Holiness-Pentecostal Tradition: Charismatic Movements in the Twentieth Century.* 2nd ed. Grand Rapids, Mich.: William B. Eerdmans, 1997.

Wacker, Grant. *Heaven Below: Early Pentecostals and American Culture.* Cambridge, Mass.: Harvard University Press, 2001.

Protestantism

FOUNDED: 1517 C.E.

RELIGION AS A PERCENTAGE OF WORLD POPULATION: 5.8 percent

OVERVIEW Along with Roman Catholicism and Eastern Orthodoxy, Protestantism is one of the three major branches of Christianity. It is divided into numerous groups, often called "denominations," that are marked by their own institutional characteristics. Each denomination has its own history, and each possesses unique beliefs, emphases, organizations, and practices that set it apart from other groups in the Protestant family. These extensive differences make Protestantism appear fragmented compared with the highly centralized structures of authority that mark Catholicism and Eastern Orthodoxy. A common conviction of Protestantism is that humans are saved not by good deeds or other actions but by faith in Jesus Christ alone. Humans receive this salvation though the work of the Holy Spirit, who illuminates the readers of Holy Scripture with the gift of faith.

The early Protestant groups emerged in sixteenth-century Europe in what came to be called the Reformation. The term "Protestant" was first used in 1529, when five German princes seeking church reform issued a statement (Latin, *protestatio*) at the Diet of Speyer. This statement of belief declared solidarity against the powerful Roman Catholic majority. Later in the sixteenth century the term came to describe two reforming movements that separated from the Catholic Church: Luther-

anism, based on the teachings of Martin Luther (1483–1546), and Reformed, based on the work of Huldrych Zwingli (1484–1531) and John Calvin (1509–64). An additional stream of protest against the Catholic Church, which featured a rejection of infant baptism, was called "Anabaptist." In England a "middle way" between Catholicism and Protestantism was developed, resulting in the Church of England, or Anglicanism. Protestantism has subsequently spread throughout the world, although some contemporary groups have moved away from and beyond their Protestant roots.

HISTORY The beginnings of Protestantism are traditionally associated with an event that took place on 31 October 1517; Martin Luther, then a Catholic priest, nailed his "Ninety-five Theses" to a church door in Wittenberg, Germany. Criticizing elements within the Roman Catholic Church that Luther viewed as not rightly based on Scripture, these were intended as items for debate. Luther's emerging critique of the Catholic Church and his developing theology led to his excommunication by Pope Leo X in 1520. His writings and reforming activities gave rise to the formation of "evangelical" churches that opposed Catholic theology and sought to focus authority for Christian faith and practice on the Old and New Testaments instead of the teachings of the church.

The joint "protestation" of princes at the second Diet of Speyer in 1529 led to the use of "Protestant" to describe those who opposed the halting of the reform movement, something Roman Catholics at the diet proposed to do. But the term also had a positive meaning.

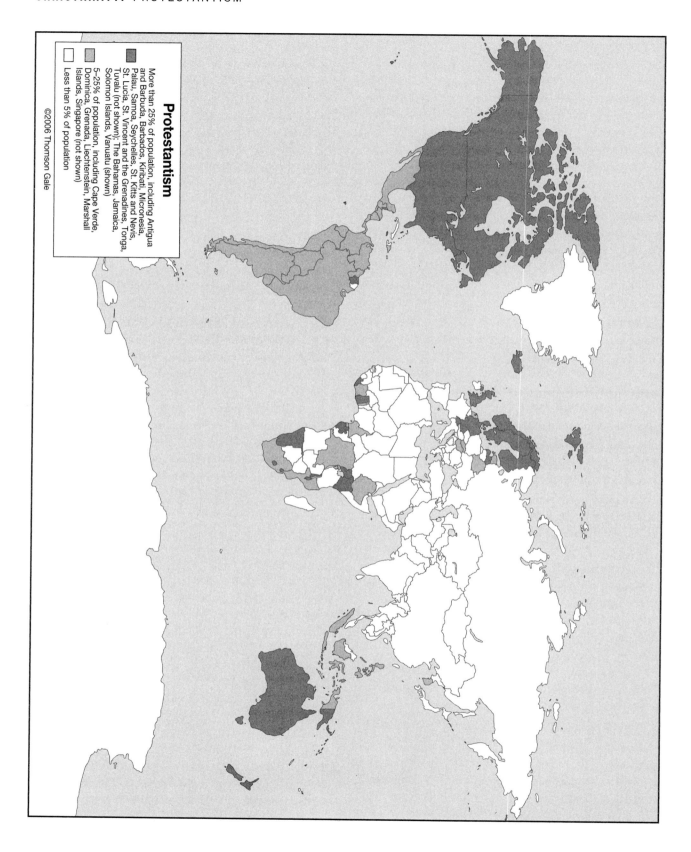

Protestantism

More than 25% of population, including Antigua and Barbuda, Barbados, Kiribati, Micronesia, Palau, Samoa, Seychelles, St. Kitts and Nevis, St. Lucia, St. Vincent and the Grenadines, Tonga, Tuvalu (not shown); The Bahamas, Jamaica, Solomon Islands, Vanuatu (shown)

5–25% of population, including Cape Verde, Dominica, Grenada, Liechtenstein, Marshall Islands, Singapore (not shown)

Less than 5% of population

©2006 Thomson Gale

The Latin *protestari* means "to witness," "to profess," or "to declare formally," which was consistent with the desire of those at the Diet of Speyer to "testify openly before God . . . and likewise before all persons and creatures" according to their consciences. Thus, Protestants are those who witness, or testify, to their Christian faith.

Although the term did not appear until 1529, during the 1520s new churches had begun to emerge that could be called "Protestant." These bodies opposed the doctrines, organization, and juridical functions of the Catholic Church. The new churches and movements represented the theological beliefs of Luther and, later, those of Huldrych Zwingli, John Calvin, and the Anabaptist Menno Simons (1496–1561).

The followers of Luther established Lutheran churches, whereas those who followed Zwingli and Calvin were called "Reformed" or "Calvinist." The name "Reformed" recognized the impulse of these two men to reform the church "according to Scripture." Zwingli and Calvin had theological disagreements with Luther about such issues as the Lord's Supper, or Communion (opposing Luther's view that during the Lord's Supper the bread and wine were transformed into the physical body and blood of Christ). The Anabaptist stream of Protestantism was made up of groups that emphasized baptism not for infants but for mature believers who professed their faith in Jesus Christ. This view made Anabaptists suspicious in the eyes of Catholics as well as Lutherans and the Reformed. Typically Anabaptism was also marked by a strong sense of social radicalism, the desire to order the church according to New Testament patterns and practices, and an expectation of the imminent end of the world.

Since the sixteenth century there has been a proliferation of Protestant bodies worldwide. These groups are termed "denominations" (Latin, *denominare;* "to name") in the United States. Among the most prominent denominational families are Adventist, Anglican (Episcopal in the United States), Baptist, Brethren, Campbellite/Restorationist, Christian Church, Church of God, Congregational, Friends (Quaker), Holiness, Lutheran, Mennonite, Methodist, Moravian, Pentecostal, Presbyterian, and Reformed. Today so-called mainline denominations have their own identities, while Protestants across denominational lines sometimes primarily identify themselves as "evangelicals," stressing the need for a personal relationship with Jesus Christ, or as "fundamentalists," interpreting Scripture in a literal sense. As these groups function through church bo-

dies in different countries, they incorporate various cultural practices that accompany their theological beliefs. There is no single head or leader of Protestantism, each church family instituting its own form of church government.

CENTRAL DOCTRINES Protestantism emerged out of Martin Luther's protest against the doctrines and practices of the Roman Catholic Church as he understood them in the context of sixteenth-century Germany. Protestants today continue to be marked by a rejection of Catholic dogma, church structure, and views on authority. They also differ from Eastern Orthodoxy in theological views and in matters of church government and authority.

The critique of Catholic teachings can be summarized through Reformation slogans that became watchwords among Protestant adherents. The first of these is "Scripture alone" (*sola scriptura*). Luther's initial criticism of Catholic teachings involved the practice of indulgences, the paying of money to reduce the number of years spent in purgatory. Luther believed that the practice was not scriptural. His developing theology was centered on the conviction that it is Scripture alone, not Catholic teaching (magisterium) or tradition, that provides authority for the church and the Christian. Scripture is God's Word and is the source from which theological understandings are developed. This contrasts with the Catholic view that it is the church through its traditions that interprets Scripture and thus that tradition plus Scripture are the sources of authority. Because of the conviction that it is in Scripture that God's Word and presence are found, Protestantism focuses on the interpretation of the Bible.

A second slogan is "Christ alone" (*solus Christus*). The Scriptures bear witness to Jesus Christ as God's incarnate Word, for it is in him that the full expression of God is found. As the second person of the Trinity, Jesus became a human being, and he is the only agent through whom salvation can be accomplished. Protestantism stresses that salvation—a restored relationship with God in which human sin is overcome—is possible only through the work of Christ in his life, death, and resurrection. For Protestants, Christ is the sole agent of salvation, and one can be saved apart from the church and its sacraments, which are emphasized in Catholicism.

A third slogan is "grace alone" (*sola gratia*). Protestant theology emphasizes that salvation is God's free gift. Salvation is not earned; it is not gained by human works or by righteousness of any kind. Humans are sinful and incapable of performing any actions that can remove their sin or make them right, or "just," in the eyes of God. Yet God showed his love by sending Jesus Christ to die for the sins of the world so that the relationship between God and humans that had been ruptured by sin could be restored. Salvation is provided solely through God's gracious love in Christ. This view contrasts with the traditional Roman Catholic belief that humans can cooperate with God's grace and thus provide an element of their salvation through the doing of works that are good in God's sight.

Finally, there is "faith alone" (*sola fide*). Humans receive the gift of salvation by faith. Luther's critical insight was that "the just shall live by faith" (Rom. 1:17). This means, Luther believed, that it is by faith, or trust, in God's gift in Jesus Christ, who died for the sin of the world (Rom. 5:8), that humans receive the gift of salvation. This contrasts with the traditional Roman Catholic position that it is faith plus human works that produce salvation. According to the Protestant view, the Christian does works that are pleasing to God but does them as an expression of faith, not as a cause for salvation.

These major characteristics of Protestantism are also the basis for other distinctive views on such matters as sin, the church, the sacraments of baptism and the Lord's Supper, and eschatology (future life). For example, on the basis of Scripture, Protestants reject the Catholic classification of sins as either "mortal" or "venial" and the doctrine of purgatory.

MORAL CODE OF CONDUCT As guides for living a Christian life, Protestantism looks to the centrality of love and justice as expressed in the person of Jesus Christ. Jesus himself embodied God's love and commanded his followers to express this love. He saw love as the fulfillment of the law and the prophets of the Old Testament (Matt. 22:40), and Protestants look to the life of Jesus as a model for living faithfully before God and in right relationships with other people.

Protestants also emphasize that those Christians who are related to God by faith and who follow Jesus Christ can live their lives in freedom as the children of God. The power of sin as the controlling force in life is broken by the forgiveness that comes through the death of Christ on the cross (Eph. 1:7; Col. 1:14). The power of the moral law to condemn sinners also is broken by the grace of God in Christ (Rom. 6:14). Christian life is life in the Spirit who dwells in believers (Rom. 6:9–11). This gives Christians the freedom to follow Christ as their guide for moral conduct and to be open to the leading of God's Spirit in determining how to live and how to act. Christian freedom involves the responsibility of seeking the will of God in all things. For Protestants the goal of Christian living is to "do everything for the glory of God" (I Cor. 10:31).

Freedom in Jesus Christ does not mean, however, that the moral law of God expressed in the Ten Commandments no longer has a role to play. The Reformed tradition of Protestantism has especially stressed the place of the law in Christian life. The law is seen as an expression of the will of God, which was fulfilled in Christ. The Ten Commandments are guides to the kind of conduct God desires humans to follow, and those who love God in Christ will keep the law and obey the commandments out of thankfulness for the forgiveness and salvation given in Christ. Christians live an ethic of gratitude for the love of God expressed in Christ.

Christian freedom, with an emphasis on thankfulness expressed through obedience to God's will, leads Protestant churches to emphasize the "fruit of the Spirit"—characteristics such as love, joy, peace, and kindness (Gal. 5:22–26)— both in individual lives and in the ministry and mission of the church. The will of God as expressed through the Old Testament prophets also provides ethical direction, for the power of sin requires that the cries of the prophets for justice, righteousness, and peace be repeated in every age. This involves the church and its members in struggles for justice and peace and in active involvement in the problems of society. These ethical concerns emerge from biblical perspectives and are motivated by the call of Jesus Christ to follow him (Mark 2:14).

SACRED BOOKS Protestants believe in the authority of the Bible. The canon of Scripture in Protestantism consists of the 39 books of the Old Testament and the 27 books of the New Testament. The Apocrypha, or deuterocanonical books, may be studied but do not possess theological status as part of the canon. Theological writings, pronouncements of church councils, confessions of faith, and creeds are subordinate standards for understanding the Bible, which for Protestants is authoritative as God's Word.

SACRED SYMBOLS Protestant churches vary in the amount of symbolism they display in their sanctuaries and during worship. As the central symbol of Christianity, the cross is nearly always displayed in church buildings. Protestants usually display an empty cross, recognizing that Jesus Christ has been raised from the dead, rather than a crucifix, displaying Christ on the cross, as in the Roman Catholic tradition. Most Protestants allow the cross to be worn in various forms of jewelry.

EARLY AND MODERN LEADERS One early Protestant leader of high standing was Martin Bucer (1491–1551), of Strasbourg, who had strong ecumenical impulses and tried to bring reconciliation between the emerging theological positions of Lutheran and Reformed Christians. In England, George Fox (1624–91), the founder of the Religious Society of Friends (Quakers), possessed tremendous organizing abilities to accompany his magnetic personality and spiritual vitality. The founder of the Methodist movement was John Wesley (1703–91), whose itinerant preaching in England and voluminous writings, along with his great capacity for leadership, gained many followers and established a significant body of those who rejected the tenets of Calvinism.

Throughout the years Protestants have been leading figures in many areas of endeavor. Well-known Protestants in modern times whose influence has been worldwide include Albert Schweitzer (1875–1965), best known for his medical work in Africa; Dietrich Bonhoeffer (1906–45), a German theologian who opposed Adolf Hitler; Toyohiko Kagawa (1888–1960), a Japanese Presbyterian minister, social worker, and evangelist; Martin Luther King, Jr. (1929–68), a U.S. civil rights leader; Archbishop Desmond Tutu (born in 1931), a leading South African foe of apartheid; and Billy Graham (born in 1918), an American evangelist who has preached throughout the world.

A number of Protestant women have made important contributions. One early leader was Katharina Schütz Zell (1497/98–1562), of Strasbourg, who was a tireless provider for the needs of the poor, a strong advocate of toleration of both Roman Catholics and Anabaptists, and a zealous preacher of the gospel in word and deed. Queen Elizabeth I (1533–1603) was instrumental in establishing a moderate Protestantism in England, and Selina Hastings, Countess of Huntingdon (1707–91), was a lay leader in the eighteenth-century British evangelical revival. Anne Hutchinson (1591–1643), a New England colonist, was an early ad-

vocate of religious liberty and women's rights. Other important Protestant women in the United States have included Harriet Beecher Stowe (1811–96), author of *Uncle Tom's Cabin* (1852); Susan B. Anthony (1820–1906), Quaker social reformer; Elizabeth Cady Stanton (1815–1902), women's rights leader; Lucretia Mott (1793–1880), Quaker minister and social reformer; and Jane Addams (1860–1935), settlement house founder and peace activist.

MAJOR THEOLOGIANS AND AUTHORS Martin Luther (1483–1546) provided Protestantism with its earliest theological expressions, while Philipp Melanchthon (1497–1560) was an important participant in theological disputations. Huldrych Zwingli (1484–1531) was a Swiss who began reforms in Basel and who, along with John Calvin (1509–64), was one of the leading theologians of the Reformed stream of Protestantism. Major early Anabaptist theologians included Thomas Müntzer (c. 1489–1525), Balthasar Hubmaier (c. 1485–1528), Hans Denck (1495?–1527), Pilgram Marpeck (died in 1556), and Menno Simons (1496–1561). So-called second-generation Protestant theologians included Theodore Beza (1519–1605), Martin Chemnitz (1522–86), and Francis Turretin (1623–87). Later important Protestant theologians included Friedrich D. E. Schleiermacher (1768–1834), known as the father of liberal theology; Philipp Jakob Spener (1635–1705), German Pietist; Albrecht Ritschl (1822–89); Jonathan Edwards (1703–58), perhaps the most brilliant of American theologians; Charles Hodge (1797–1878); Abraham Kuyper (1837–1920), Dutch theologian, politician, and statesman; P. T. Forsyth (1848–1921); Herman Bavinck (1854–1921); Adolf von Harnack (1851–1930), a brilliant German historian of dogma; Paul Tillich (1886–1965), the most prolific and influential twentieth-century Protestant theologian; Karl Barth (1886–1968); and H. Emil Brunner (1889–1966). Other theologians of note have included Helmut Thielicke (1908–86); Jürgen Moltmann (born in 1926), who has reestablished the importance of eschatology for theology; Wolfhart Pannenberg (born in 1928), who sees theology as a science with universal scope; and John Cobb (born in 1925), a leading proponent of process theology, the view that God "evolves" with the world and that humans share in the process of his emerging identity and actions. Prominent authors in evangelical theology have included Carl F. H. Henry (1913–2003) and Donald G. Bloesch (born in 1928). Important women theologians in the United States have included

Georgian Harkness (1891–1974), Letty Russell (born in 1929), and Sallie McFague (born in 1933).

ORGANIZATIONAL STRUCTURE Three forms of church government (polity) are found in Protestantism. Episcopal polity is hierarchical and features government by bishops, who have authority over local pastors and congregations. Presbyterian polity centers authority in presbyteries composed of elders and ministers from local churches within a region. Larger bodies, such as synods and a general assembly, also have governing roles. Congregational polity focuses on the local church body, which adopts its own standards for belief, organization, and practice.

HOUSES OF WORSHIP AND HOLY PLACES Protestant churches vary greatly in their architectural styles. This is true not only in terms of the country in which churches are located but also in regard to the particular denomination to which a church belongs. To emphasize the centrality of the Word of God, Protestant sanctuaries feature a pulpit, which is often located in the center front of the sanctuary. An altar, where the bread and wine for the Lord's Supper are placed, is featured prominently in the front of the sanctuary as well. Reformed churches speak of a "communion table" instead of an altar. Churches also have a baptismal font or a baptistery for baptism by immersion. Other particular features of the sanctuary are distinctive to each Protestant tradition. For example, although almost all sanctuaries feature an empty cross, the size, type, and placement vary.

WHAT IS SACRED? Protestants historically have focused on Jesus Christ as the Word of God, thus making subordinate all other persons, objects, or entities. Yet Protestants have also recognized various religious and even natural symbols as "pointers to the divine." Some Protestant denominations with highly developed worship liturgies, such as Anglican churches, use extensive religious symbolism. Other Protestant bodies, such as Baptist churches, do not, but because of their emphasis on the Bible, they are sometimes accused of turning the Bible itself into a sacred object.

HOLIDAYS AND FESTIVALS Festivals of the Christian year, as recognized by the universal Church, are observed by most Protestant denominations. Among others these include Advent, Christmas, Epiphany, Lent, Maundy Thursday, Good Friday, Palm Sunday, Easter, and Pentecost. Reformed churches initially rejected holiday and festival celebrations, but today most celebrate the major festivals. The ways in which these holidays and festivals are commemorated vary widely among Protestant churches. Local customs and practices may play a role in the way observances are carried out. Other days honoring saints and commemorating events in the traditions of specific churches are also observed. Individual congregations may recognize special days in their own locales. In a number of Protestant traditions, use of the Common Lectionary, or list of Bible readings for Sundays, provides a way by which celebration of the church's festivals are integrated into the worship practices of each congregation.

MODE OF DRESS For worship some Protestant clergy wear special vestments, which may include a clerical collar, a cassock or an alb, and a cross. In other Protestant traditions, however, the clergy dress in the same way as their parishioners. The variations in dress for clergy apply both to men and to women. Protestants have no prescribed modes of dress for laypersons, which vary according to time, place, and culture. Outside worship some clergy wear clerical garb, which clearly sets them apart from other persons and testifies to the clerical vocation. In other Protestant traditions clergy do not wear special garments outside worship, the emphasis being on their common unity with the laity.

DIETARY PRACTICES Most Protestants do not subscribe to or participate in special dietary practices. Protestants historically have not emphasized fasting in the same way Roman Catholics have. Although fasting is not a prescribed activity, Protestants may at times fast voluntarily. In Protestantism there are no specific bans against eating meat or, for a number of Protestants, against using alcohol. Some Protestants, particularly in the United States, however, regard alcohol as sinful, which has led many churches to substitute grape juice for wine in the Lord's Supper. Many Protestants see the Lord's Supper in a sacramental sense as an "eating and drinking with Jesus." For them the blessing of Jesus for fellowship around a table with food and drink gives Christians the freedom to enjoy these created, God-given elements as gifts that can and must be shared with others.

RITUALS In practice there is great diversity among the worship services of Protestant churches. The varieties exist between Protestant denominations and also within denominations themselves. Most Protestant traditions have clear liturgical practices that prescribe or suggest the elements of ritual for each worship service and the patterns by which worship is to be carried out. Church "bulletins" often list the order of worship and provide instructions for the congregation to follow. Protestant worship services typically consist of prayers, Scripture readings, hymns, an offering, and a sermon, as well as the sacraments of baptism and the Lord's Supper. Not all Protestant churches celebrate the Lord's Supper in each worship service. Baptism may be administered as appropriate, always to adults in the Protestant tradition and, for the Lutheran and Reformed streams, also for infants. Anabaptists insist that only adult baptism is valid. Some churches have a tradition of holding regular "revivals," while others emphasize glossolalia, or speaking in tongues, and some practice foot washing. Weddings and funerals are typically special services. Weddings are usually held in a church sanctuary, whereas a Protestant funeral may be conducted in a church, a home, or a funeral parlor.

RITES OF PASSAGE Most of Protestantism recognizes two sacraments, baptism and the Lord's Supper. In Anabaptist traditions these are regarded not as sacraments, in which God has promised to be present and which provide the benefits of salvation, but as "ordinances," that is, as memorials or acts of obedience. The Lutheran and Reformed traditions baptize infants, whereas Anabaptist traditions recognize only adult baptisms. Baptism in general is the incorporation of the person into the household of God. For Protestants the Lord's Supper nurtures the faith of believers, who are "nourished" by the bread and the wine. Unlike Roman Catholics, Protestants do not believe that the "substance" of the bread and wine is changed into the body and blood of Christ. Other rites of passage typically include confirmation, a rite whereby those baptized as infants are "confirmed" by making personal affirmations of Christian faith. Ordination in Protestantism marks a person for a ministry or function in the church. Clergy are ordained, and in some Protestant traditions laity are also ordained as church officers. Wedding ceremonies are performed by Protestant clergy and typically take place apart from the weekly worship services. Wedding services witness to the blessing of God upon marriage. Funerals serve as a witness to the Resurrection and, in many Protestant traditions, also as a celebration of the life of the deceased.

MEMBERSHIP Most Protestant denominations seek to expand their membership through evangelism or other means. In the history of Protestantism there has been a wide variety of evangelistic practices, ranging from special services featuring "altar calls," or the opportunity for people to confess their faith in Jesus Christ, to door-to-door efforts, in which believers witness to their Christian faith to strangers. Many Protestant bodies have also been vigorous practitioners of mass evangelism through radio, television, and the Internet. Western Protestant churches historically have been deeply involved in missionary efforts to take the Christian gospel to people in other countries. In contemporary times, with recognition of the negative ways in which Western mores and culture were part of the traditional missionary enterprise, many of these efforts have taken different forms, including efforts to develop indigenous leaders.

RELIGIOUS TOLERANCE Because a number of Protestant churches were persecuted in their origins, many—especially in the Anabaptist stream—have stressed religious toleration and sought freedom to worship. After the sixteenth century degrees of toleration were granted in various European lands, and in some nations Protestant bodies became the state churches. In the American colonies religious intolerance was common, but with the adoption of the U.S. Constitution in 1788, freedom of religion became a founding ideal, and today Protestants and other groups enjoy religious toleration. To varying degrees Protestants have been involved in the ecumenical movement, seeking points of contact and agreement with Roman Catholicism and Eastern Orthodoxy. There also are dialogues among Protestants, both at official and local levels. Churches of Christ Uniting (COCU), originally the Consultation on Church Union, is ongoing in the United States.

SOCIAL JUSTICE Protestants have made strong commitments to education, and many schools and universities owe their origins to Protestant church bodies. Education is seen as a gift of God and thus as a Christian responsibility. Protestant churches also have been concerned with the alleviation of poverty and have worked both legislatively and through local congregations to provide relief for the plight of the poor. In the United States the Social Gospel movement of the early twentieth century was a Protestant effort that made concern for the poor a central focus, believing that Christian responsibility for the less fortunate was both a personal and a collective mission. Some Protestant churches have been outspoken in their support for human rights. Through their official bodies Protestant denominations regularly issue pronouncements that address a wide range of issues in social justice.

SOCIAL ASPECTS Marriage and the family have been important concerns for Protestant churches. Protestants view marriage as ordained by God and intended to be permanent. Many Protestant denominations, however, have dropped prohibitions on divorce and no longer consider it a disqualification for leadership. While marriage is not regarded as a sacrament, it is considered to be a sacred obligation. Nonetheless, given human brokenness, marriage is sometimes better ended through divorce, and divorced people may legitimately remarry. Because Protestantism did not adopt the requirement that clerics be celibate, marriage and family experience have been features of the life of the clergy. Protestants have not generally been opposed to birth control, believing that stewardship of the family is a responsibility of parents. Protestant's views differ on the ethical legitimacy of abortion.

CONTROVERSIAL ISSUES A number of contemporary issues create divisions among Protestants. There are, for example, strong differences over the legitimacy of ordaining women to pastoral offices. Issues of war and peace are sometimes divisive, although political contexts and convictions play as great a role as formal theological views. The appropriateness of homosexuality and of homosexuals in church leadership is strongly debated. The great variety of political and cultural settings in which Protestant churches exist means that they are not unanimous in their perspectives on a number of other controversial issues. Among these are stem-cell research, cloning, and end-of-life issues.

CULTURAL IMPACT A primary Protestant affirmation, that Christians are called to serve God in the midst of the world, has been a strong impetus for believers to engage their cultures fully and, at times, decisively. For example, the musical works of Johann Sebastian Bach (1685–1750) were composed in the service of the German Lutheran Church but provide religious depth for all Christians. George Frideric Handel (1685–1759) is perhaps best remembered for his oratorio Messiah. The Protestant tradition in hymnody has produced thousands of songs. Among writers the Puritan poet John Milton (1608–74), author of *Paradise Lost*, and John

Priesthood of All Believers

Martin Luther emphasized that all Christians are "priests" and thus are able to approach God directly through Jesus Christ. Baptism incorporates believers into the household of God, where as part of the "people of God" they are a "royal priesthood" (1 Peter 2:9). In the sixteenth century, however, "priesthood" had predominantly come to mean the ordained hierarchy of the Roman Catholic Church. Luther's rediscovery of the biblical usage became an important part of his theological understanding and a key point of Protestant doctrine. Christians may pray to God directly without the need for an ordained priest as a "mediator." This view also implied that Christian believers can directly interpret the Scriptures without the need of priestly intermediaries.

Bunyan (1628–88), author of *The Pilgrim's Progress,* stand out. Protestant literary traditions continue through the poet William Blake (1757–1827) to the present day with the contemporary Left Behind series, based on a reading of Scripture. The astronomer Johannes Kepler (1571–1630) and the mathematician Isaac Newton (1642–1727) were both Protestants.

Donald K. McKim

See Also Vol. I: *Christianity*

Bibliography

Balmer, Randall, and Lauren F. Winner. *Protestantism in America.* New York: Columbia University Press, 2002.

Benedetto, Robert, Darrell L. Guder, and Donald K. McKim. *Historical Dictionary of Reformed Churches.* Lanham, Md.: Scarecrow Press, 1999.

Cameron, Euan. *The European Reformation.* New York: Oxford University Press, 1991.

Chadwick, Owen. *The Reformation.* Pelican History of the Church, vol. 3. Baltimore: Penguin Books, 1968.

Dillenberger, John, and Claude Welch. *Protestant Christianity: Interpreted through Its Development.* New York: Macmillan, 1988.

George, Timothy. *Theology of the Reformers.* Nashville: Broadman, 1988.

Gritsch, Erich W., and Robert W. Jenson. *Lutheranism: The Theological Movement and Its Confessional Writings.* Philadelphia: Fortress Press, 1976.

Hillerbrand, Hans J., ed. *Encyclopedia of Protestantism.* New York: Routledge, 2004.

————, ed. *Historical Dictionary of the Reformation and Counter-Reformation.* Lanham, Md.: Scarecrow Press, 1999.

————, ed. *The Oxford Encyclopedia of the Reformation.* 4 vols. New York: Oxford University Press, 1996.

Latourette, Kenneth S. *History of Christianity.* Vol. 2 of *Reformation to 1975.* New York: Harper and Row, 1975.

Lindberg, Carter. *The European Reformations.* Cambridge, Mass.: Blackwell, 1996.

MacCullough, Dairmaid. *The Reformation: A History.* New York: Viking, 2003.

McGrath, Alister E., and Darren C. Marks. *Blackwell Companion to Protestantism.* London: Blackwell, 2004.

Marty, Martin E. *Varieties of Protestantism.* New York: K.G. Saur, 1992.

Pelikan, Jaroslav. *The Reformation of Church and Dogma 1300–1700.* Vol. 4 of *The Christian Tradition.* Chicago: University of Chicago Press, 1984.

Troeltsch, Ernst. *Protestantism and Progress: The Significance of Protestantism for the Rise of the Modern World.* Philadelphia: Fortress Press, 1986.

Weber, Max. *The Protestant Ethic and the Spirit of Capitalism.* Translated by Talcott Parsons. 1904–05. Reprint, New York: Routlege, 1992.

Welch, Claude. *Protestant Thought in the Nineteenth Century.* 2 vols. New Haven: Yale University Press, 1972–85.

Williams, George H. *The Radical Reformation.* Kirksville, Mo.: Sixteenth Century Publishers, 1992.

Reformed Christianity

FOUNDED: Sixteenth century C.E.

RELIGION AS A PERCENTAGE OF WORLD POPULATION: 1.19 percent

OVERVIEW Reformed Christianity emerged in the sixteenth century out of the Lutheran and Anabaptist traditions of the Protestant Reformation. "Reformed" refers to a number of church bodies worldwide. The World Alliance of Reformed Churches, a voluntary organization, represents approximately 70 percent of the world's Reformed Christians. In 2003 it had 218 churches in 107 countries with more than 75 million members (who subscribed to more than 60 different confessions of faith). Most churches are called Congregational, Presbyterian, Reformed, and United, and most are minorities in their countries.

Reformed churches are diverse, but they share a common heritage going back to John Calvin (1509–64) and other important figures. These theologians stressed God's freedom as well as his desire to enter into covenantal relationships with humanity. They believed that God worked through the Old Testament nation of Israel and ultimately sent Jesus Christ into the world to live and die and be raised again to provide salvation for those who believe. God freely bestows the gift of faith in Christ to those whom God chooses. These believers constitute the church and become the people God uses to share the message of Jesus Christ and to serve God's purposes in the world. These emphases on God's free-dom and his covenant are key beliefs in Reformed Christianity.

HISTORY Reformed Christianity is rooted in the sixteenth-century reforms begun by Martin Luther (1483–1546), yet developed on a separate path. Such major reformers as Ulrich Zwingli (1484–1531) and John Calvin (1509–64), as well as Martin Bucer (1491–1551), John Knox (c. 1513–72), and Heinrich Bullinger (1504–75), gave impetus to the movement. The Reformed agreed with Luther's criticisms of Roman Catholicism but disagreed on certain theological issues. Calvin's writings, especially his *Institutes of the Christian Religion,* articulated Reformed theology.

After Calvin's death, Reformed Christianity advanced throughout Europe. It took root in Switzerland and Germany, expanded into France, and spread to Scotland, the Netherlands, and England with particular effectiveness. The Synod of Dort (1618–19), in the Netherlands, rejected Jacobus Arminiu's views on predestination and promulgated the five points of Calvinism: total depravity, unconditional election, limited atonement, irresistible grace, and perseverance of the saints (TULIP). Later the Westminster Assembly (1643–48), in England, produced the Westminster Confession of Faith (1647), which articulated doctrinal understandings and a presbyterian form of church government by elders through presbyteries. Church bodies that held theological beliefs similar to those of Presbyterians but who advocated a local, independent form of church government became known as Congregationalists.

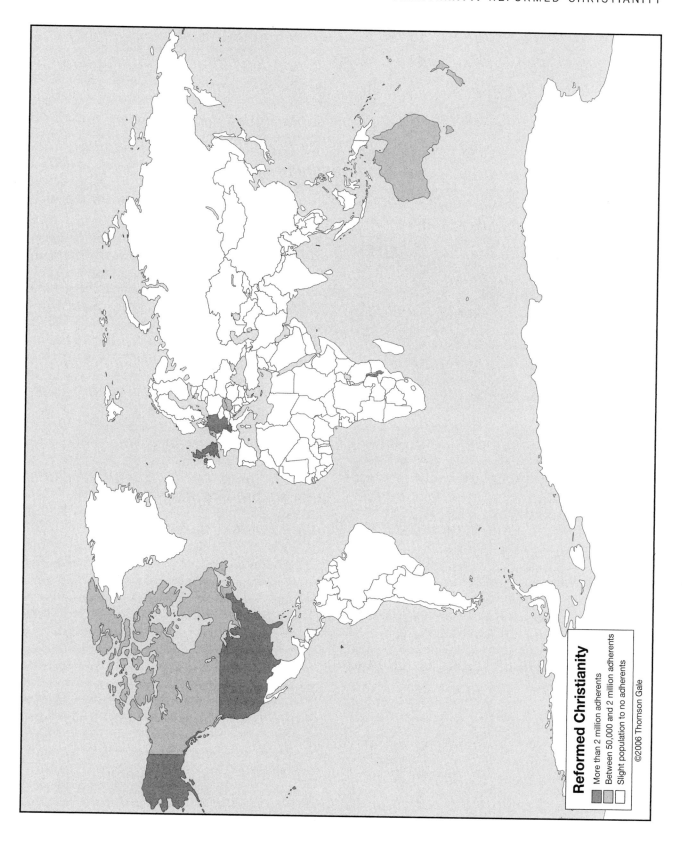

Reformed Christianity

More than 2 million adherents
Between 50,000 and 2 million adherents
Slight population to no adherents

©2006 Thomson Gale

A model of a church sits above directions to a Reformed church in North Dakota. Reformed churches are diverse, but they share a common heritage dating back to John Calvin and other important figures. © ANNIE GRIFFITHS BELT/CORBIS.

Large numbers of Reformed Christians emigrated from the British Isles and Europe to the American colonies, and the early history of the United States demonstrates the strong influence of Calvinists, who were involved in the nation's political, cultural, and religious life. Eighteenth- and nineteenth-century missionary movements spread the Reformed faith throughout the world. Dedicated missionaries established churches and ministered through education and health care in South America, Africa, and Asia. The effects of their efforts are still found today.

Throughout the twentieth century many Reformed churches participated in worldwide ecumenical and missionary endeavors. During this period Reformed Christianity grew strongly in the Southern Hemisphere, where a majority of the world's Reformed Christians now live. A large number of Reformed Christians are also found in Asia, with Presbyterians the largest Protestant group in South Korea. In western Europe and North America, Reformed Christians are a declining percentage of the population.

CENTRAL DOCTRINES Reformed Christians share common beliefs with other Christian traditions, particularly the doctrines of the Trinity and the person of Jesus Christ. They recognize God as triune (the unity of Father, Son, and Holy Spirit) and sovereign over all. The centrality of Jesus Christ is crucial, with the Reformed confessing him as "God with us" (the Incarnation) and "truly God and truly human"—the eternal Son of God who lived and died and was raised again to provide salvation, which is the restoration of the loving relationship between God and humans that has been broken by sin.

Reformed Christians affirm the doctrines of Protestantism, emphasizing that salvation is the freely given gift of God, offered by God's grace, and received by sinners through faith. Faith is focused on belief and trust in Jesus Christ as the savior who has taken upon himself human sin. Through Christ's death on the cross and resurrection from the dead, sinners are adopted into the family of God and are saved. Salvation comes by God's grace, through faith, and not by human efforts or actions. The Reformed affirm the Bible (Holy Scripture) as the Word of God and as the medium through which the knowledge of God and God's actions through Jesus Christ are known.

Reformed Christianity may often emphasize the doctrine of election, or predestination, as associated with the followers of Calvin. Election is a biblical theme indicating that it is God's grace alone that gives people the gift of salvation. God has chosen, or elected, a people to enter into relationship with him and to glorify and serve him in the world. The elect serve him through the covenant community, the church. The church is the people of God, who order their life in accord with his Word in Scripture. The people of God seek to be faithful stewards of the creation entrusted to human care and to worship the one, true God—known in Jesus Christ by the work of the Holy Spirit in human hearts—rather than any other person, power, or ideology, which would be the sin of idolatry. God's people work for justice and peace in society, as these are God's purposes for all people. These beliefs lead Reformed Christians to take active roles in society and culture, seeking their transformation through God's power.

Reformed Christians stress God's initiatives. God "made the first move" in creating the world, in coming to sinful humanity in Jesus Christ, in extending salvation through grace, and in giving the gift of faith to the people of God by the work of the Holy Spirit. The Christian's response is to live a life of gratitude and to praise God for this wondrous love. The Christian turns from sin and lives in obedience to God's will and law as a grateful response to the gift of salvation in Jesus Christ.

MORAL CODE OF CONDUCT Reformed Christians believe salvation is a gift of God's grace, received through faith (trust) in Christ, and made possible by the work of the Holy Spirit, whose regenerative power causes the believer to be born again, or made into a new person. Thus, Christians are oriented toward serving and loving God rather than sinfully turning inward toward their own needs.

The Reformed acknowledge that Christians continue to sin and do not always act in accord with God's will. God's forgiveness is extended to them, in Jesus Christ, when they confess their sin in repentance and then resolve to follow God's will.

Reformed Christians look to the Bible as the source of their knowledge of God's will. A Christian code of conduct is basically to seek to follow the example of Jesus Christ. More broadly, Reformed Christians stress that Christians follow God's law as revealed in Scripture and that this is the way to know the conduct God wants of Christian people. The moral law, revealed especially in the Ten Commandments, is God's declaration of the way human society and human lives should be ordered.

Reformed Christians emphasize that Christians must willingly follow God's law. They do so not to gain their own salvation—that is, in the belief that by obeying God's law they will earn salvation. Instead, obedience to God's will as expressed in his law arises as a Christian's grateful response for the free salvation given in Jesus Christ. Following the law of God is the result of salvation, not its cause. The Christian willingly obeys God's law as a grateful expression of love and gratitude for the gift of salvation in Jesus Christ.

SACRED BOOKS Reformed Christians honor the Bible as the Word of God. Here God is uniquely and authoritatively revealed. No other book or source can convey the true knowledge of God in the way the Bible does. Reformed Christians look to the Scriptures as the supreme source of the knowledge of God, the means of communication God has used to convey to humanity who he is and what he has done.

SACRED SYMBOLS The cross stands at the center of Christianity. Reformed Christians, like other Protes-

Portrait of John Calvin, whose works became the most important Reformed theological writings. GETTY IMAGES.

tants, honor the empty cross of the resurrected Christ as a sacred symbol of their faith. An empty cross topped by a crown is often a symbol in Reformed churches, while historically a rooster adorning their steeples is a reminder of Christ's coming return in judgment.

Most often the Reformed are wary of investing symbols with much prominence. They fear that the symbols themselves will detract from the realities they represent. Any absolutizing of a symbol would be a form of idolatry—one of the central sins to be avoided.

EARLY AND MODERN LEADERS Reformed Christians have been active in many contexts. Well-known historical figures who were adherents of Reformed Christianity include Isaac Watts (1674–1748), an English nonconformist minister and prolific hymn writer; George Whitefield (1714–70), a Church of England evangelist whose tour of the American colonies was pivotal in New England's Great Awakening; David Livingstone (1813–73), a Scottish physician, missionary, and explorer in Africa; and Robert E. Speer (1867–1947), an American

Presbyterian lay leader and a central figure in the American missionary movement.

MAJOR THEOLOGIANS AND AUTHORS Among the most important historical and contemporary figures for Reformed Christians are those theologians who have provided biblical and systematic expositions of the Reformed faith. These include Ulrich Zwingli, who began the Swiss Protestant Reformation, and John Calvin, whose works became the most important Reformed theological writings. Later important theologians include Theodore Beza (1519–1605) and Francis Turretin (1623–87). Leading Reformed theologians in the Netherlands include Abraham Kuyper (1837–1920) and Herman Bavinck (1854–1921), who each wrote important works in systematic theology. An important Reformed theologian in the United States was Jonathan Edwards (1703–58), who wrote penetrating theological treatises. Charles Hodge (1797–1878), of Princeton Seminary, produced the significant, three-volume work *Systematic Theology*. The Swiss theologian Karl Barth (1886–1968), through his massive *Church Dogmatics,* was a dominant Reformed voice in the twentieth century.

ORGANIZATIONAL STRUCTURE Reformed churches are either presbyterian or congregational in church government. Presbyterianism features a series of graduated governing bodies, with the presbytery as the central governing unit. This central governing unit is composed of ministers and elders (elected leaders of local congregations) from a specific geographical area. In a congregational polity each local church has complete jurisdiction over its own church life.

HOUSES OF WORSHIP AND HOLY PLACES In the Reformed view there are no holy places. Worship can take place anywhere. Reformed Christians build houses of worship to promote and enhance the worship of God.

The architecture of Reformed churches has been significantly influenced by the conviction that the proclamation of the Word of God and the sacraments are central to worship. This has resulted in a central pulpit in the worship space, often raised to emphasize the importance of preaching. The Lord's Supper is administered from a Communion table set on the level of the congregation, as opposed to a high altar, to emphasize the equality and fellowship of all congregants.

WHAT IS SACRED? Reformed Christians do not recognize any human elements as sacred. That which is sacred is God—known in the Trinity as Father, Son, and Holy Spirit. As Jesus Christ has ascended into heaven, there are no sacred objects, persons, or places on earth to be worshiped. To worship thus, in the Reformed view, is to practice idolatry, which gives undue honor to that which is not God. In general, this is the theological view of other Protestant churches. The use of symbols in worship and in other liturgical practices, however, is more prominent in some other Protestant bodies than among the Reformed.

HOLIDAYS AND FESTIVALS The festivals celebrated in the lives and churches of Reformed Christians are the historic festivals of the universal Christian church, particularly Advent, Christmas, the baptism of the Lord, Lent, Palm Sunday, Good Friday, Easter, Ascension Day, Pentecost, and Christ the King Sunday. Individual congregations may have their own traditions and practices around some of these holiday festivals. In general, worship during these days is oriented toward the religious meaning of the particular festival. Historically some Reformed churches have eliminated the traditional Christian round of holy days.

MODE OF DRESS Reformed Christians' mode of dress varies according to the particular societies and cultures in which they live. While normal Christian prescriptions for modesty and avoidance of ostentation are present, Reformed Christians are free to adopt modern-day dress in their own cultural settings.

DIETARY PRACTICES There are no dietary practices prescribed or suggested for Reformed Christians. The Reformed regard food as a good gift of God, necessary for the sustenance and enjoyment of life.

RITUALS Weekly worship services are a central part of the Christian experience. The Reformed emphasize that worship is for the people of God, who gather to honor and worship him, to pray, to listen to his Word, to celebrate the sacraments, and to be nurtured in their lives of faith to serve God in the world in all they do. Worship services feature hymns, prayers, a sermon, the sacraments, an offering, and, often, announcements related to the local congregation.

Sacraments are an outward ritual or sign of an inward reality. In contrast to some other traditions, the Reformed usually do not celebrate the sacrament of the Lord's Supper at every worship service. The frequency

The Word of God

Reformed Christians have oriented much of their theological lives around an understanding of the Word of God. Karl Barth, a Swiss theologian, spoke of the "threefold form of the Word of God." Primarily the Word of God refers to Jesus Christ, who, as the full expression of God, is the incarnate Word. The Word of God is also Holy Scripture, as the Scriptures witness to Jesus Christ and convey the full expression of God's will for humanity. Finally, the Word of God refers to preaching, in which the will of God is expressed in the here and now by humans.

The three forms of the one Word of God are interrelated. The incarnate Word is revealed through the written Word and the preached Word. All share as ways God is known and his will is expressed.

of celebration in Reformed churches varies. The Lord's Supper, instituted by Christ, is given to strengthen the faith of believers and is a means by which the benefits of salvation achieved by Jesus Christ are sealed in the lives of those who have faith. Jesus Christ is spiritually present in the sacrament but not in a physical or substantial form.

The sacrament of baptism is occasionally celebrated during worship. The Reformed tradition typically stresses infant baptism, while also acknowledging adult baptism as the means by which, through a profession of faith in Christ, a person is received as a member of the Christian community. In the case of infants who are baptized, both the parents and the local congregation make promises to raise the child with a knowledge of God's love in Jesus Christ. When the child comes to an age of accountability (the exact age varies, though many churches set age 12 as standard), a personal confession of faith can be made as the young person becomes a church member. This process is called confirmation.

RITES OF PASSAGE While Reformed churches acknowledge only two sacraments, baptism and the Lord's Supper, other dimensions of Christian experience, or rites of passage, are also part of church life. Weddings

are performed in Reformed churches to acknowledge marriage. Funerals are often held in Reformed churches as a service of witness to the Resurrection as well as to acknowledge death and the life to come. The focus of funerals in Reformed churches is on the eternal life that Jesus Christ gives as a result of his resurrection rather than on the life of the deceased alone.

MEMBERSHIP Membership in Reformed churches is open to all. Reformed churches seek to bring others into their communities of faith through sharing the gospel of Jesus Christ. Reformed churches use traditional as well as innovative forms of missionary activities, such as contemporary media, including the Internet. Reformed Christians hold that the gospel of Jesus Christ is to be shared with all people and that vigorous efforts must always be made to spread Christ's message through words and deeds. They also recognize that the Holy Spirit causes a person to make a profession of Christian faith.

RELIGIOUS TOLERANCE Many Reformed Christians support the freedom to worship, religious tolerance, and ecumenical participation. Not all Reformed churches are as committed to ecumenical endeavors as others. Reformed Christianity sees itself as one stream of Christian belief, or one part of the Christian family. Despite theological differences with other churches, Reformed Christians can celebrate the great commonalities of Christian faith and recognize that the ties that bind them together with other Christians are more and greater than the doctrines that divide them. Reformed Christians have often fought against political oppression, while working for peace and justice for all persons.

SOCIAL JUSTICE Reformed Christianity is sometimes said to adopt the paradigm of "Christ the transformer of culture." This means the emphasis of the Reformed church is to bring the gospel to bear on all societal and cultural institutions and practices, so that the power of God can work within the structures of a community or country. The quest for social justice is part of this paradigm. Reformed churches have consistently made social pronouncements that focus on contemporary issues, and they have been active in efforts to fight poverty, support education, and champion human rights.

SOCIAL ASPECTS Social dimensions of life are important for Reformed Christians. Support for healthy marriages and stable families is shared by the Reformed with other Christians. While the Reformed view marriage as ordained by God and intended to be permanent, Reformed Christians can also recognize that error and sin are part of Christian existence, and so they may recognize the validity of divorce on occasions. The Reformed may also view the human family as a witness, or pointer, to the family of God, the church, into which believers in Jesus Christ are adopted through faith.

CONTROVERSIAL ISSUES There is no unanimity among Reformed Christians on contemporary controversial issues such as birth control, divorce, abortion, and the role of women in religion. Societal and cultural differences may affect the way these issues are understood in different settings. Theological arguments on different sides of these issues can be, and are, made and debated. This means Reformed thinking and practice vary among the global Reformed churches.

CULTURAL IMPACT Reformed theologians have spoken of God's "common grace," which is God's restraint of human sin. This view enables Reformed Christians to participate fully in cultural life, including the liberal arts and those other aspects of human society that promote positive values and communal life. Thus, Reformed Christians are free to participate widely and vigorously in all dimensions of culture—political, economic, social, and religious. They may join in common cause with non-Christians to promote shared values and collective goals.

Reformed contributions to the arts and sciences include the work of Rembrandt van Rijn, the seventeenth-century Dutch painter, who gave visual artistic expression to Reformed ideas. In the political sphere, Oliver Cromwell (1599–1658), English soldier and political leader, embraced a Calvinist faith in his attempt to reform English government. Woodrow Wilson (1856–1924), president of the United States from 1913 to 1921, was a devout Reformed believer whose faith greatly influenced his approach to politics and his zeal for a League of Nations.

In the Netherlands Abraham Kuyper (1837–1920), a leading Reformed theologian, was also a prom-

inent journalist—as well as a member of parliament, founder of the Calvinist Free University of Amsterdam, and prime minister. Yoshitaka Kuman (1899–1981) was a Japanese minister and theologian who, through many writings, was significant for contextualizing Christian theology within Japanese life and culture. Samuel Habib (1928–98), an Egyptian church leader and president of the Protestant Council of Egypt, wrote more than 70 books. American cultural icon Fred M. Rogers ("Mister Rogers"; 1928–2003)—an educator and popular host of children's television programs—was a Presbyterian minister.

Donald K. McKim

See Also Vol. 1: *Christianity*

Bibliography

Barth, Karl. *Church Dogmatics.* 13 vols. Edinburgh: T. and T. Clark, 1936–77.

Benedetto, Robert, Darrell L. Guder, and Donald K. McKim. *Historical Dictionary of Reformed Churches.* Lanham, Md.: Scarecrow Press, 1999.

Benedict, Philip. *Christ's Churches Purely Reformed: A Social History of Calvinism.* New Haven: Yale University Press, 2002.

Calvin, John. *Institutes of the Christian Religion.* Edited by John T. McNeill and translated by Ford Lewis Battles. 2 vols. Philadelphia: Westminster Press, 1960.

Leith, John H. *Introduction to the Reformed Tradition.* Atlanta: John Knox Press, 1980.

McKim, Donald K. *Introducing the Reformed Faith.* Louisville: Westminster John Knox Press, 2001.

———, ed. *Encyclopedia of the Reformed Faith.* Louisville: Westminster John Knox Press, 1992.

———, ed. *Major Themes in the Reformed Tradition.* Eugene, Ore.: Wipf and Stock Publishers, 1998.

McNeill, John T. *The History and Character of Calvinism.* New York: Oxford University Press, 1967.

Rogers, Jack. *Presbyterian Creeds: A Guide to the Book of Confessions.* Louisville: Westminster John Knox Press, 1991.

Rohls, Jan. *Reformed Confessions: Theology from Zurich to Barmen.* Translated by John Hoffmeyer. Louisville: Westminster John Knox Press, 1997.

Religious Society of Friends (Quakers)

FOUNDED: 1652 C.E.

RELIGION AS A PERCENTAGE OF WORLD POPULATION: 0.006 percent

OVERVIEW The Religious Society of Friends, also known as Quakers, emerged in the 1650s in England and soon expanded to the American colonies and elsewhere. The term "Friend" derives from John 15:14, where Jesus says, "Ye are my friends, if ye do whatsoever I command you." According to one account, the name "Quaker" was given to Friends by a judge who observed their tendency to tremble under divine conviction.

The immediacy of religious experience is held by Friends to be the core of the spiritual quest. In their commitment to integrity and authenticity, Friends have provided several "testimonies" about the unmediated character of worship, the spiritual nature of the sacraments, peace and nonviolence, plainness in speech and lifestyle, and a method of decision making in which believers are led by God in unity.

There are now some 400,000 Friends throughout the world: 95,000 in North America; 25,000 in Britain and Europe; 180,000 in East and Central Africa; 90,000 in Latin America; and 10,000 in Australia and Asia.

HISTORY George Fox, the founder of the Quakers, was born at Drayton-in-the-Clay, Leicestershire, England, in 1624. A preacher, he received a vision in 1652 of "a

great people to be gathered," and when he later gave a three-hour sermon at Firbank Fell, the vision was fulfilled. The crowd was so moved by the experience that several dozen, called the "Valiant Sixty," set off to preach the good news. Within a decade the movement had grown to more than 10,000 people, and despite restrictive laws, by the turn of the century the number had reached 50,000. After William Penn, a Quaker, founded Pennsylvania in the 1680s, Friends continued to migrate from England to the colonies, where they had a great impact upon the development of American democracy and social ethos.

British and American Friends contributed significantly to the abolitionist movement and other social reforms. In the United States Friends living in slaveholding regions migrated north and west, later to became the backbone of the pastoral and evangelical developments among Quakers. In 1827 a major split developed among American Friends, as the followers of Elias Hicks split off from orthodox Friends in an attempt to preserve the inwardness of religious experience and authority. Followers of John Wilbur also split off, seeking to preserve the plain testimonies of Friends in speech and dress and reacting against more expressive and ordered approaches to worship and teaching. The pastoral Friends, or those employing pastors, emerged in the 1870s and 1880s as Quaker preachers joined with other revivalist ministers in the healing of the nation after the Civil War. This accounts for four major groupings of Friends in the United States and beyond: Friends General Conference (Hicksite, nonpastoral, and theologically liberal), Friends United Meeting (orthodox and largely pastoral), Evangelical Friends Interna-

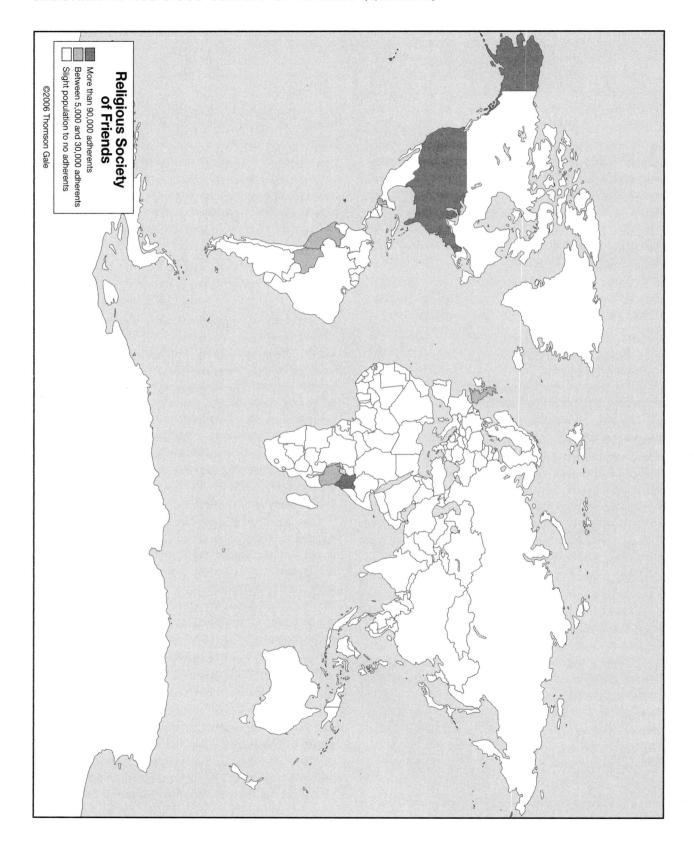

Religious Society
of Friends

More than 90,000 adherents
Between 5,000 and 30,000 adherents
Slight population to no adherents

©2006 Thomson Gale

tional (pastoral and theologically conservative), and Conservative Friends (Wilburite, nonpastoral, and theologically conservative). The most significant demographic development among Friends during the twentieth century was the missionary expansion into Latin America, Africa, and Asia.

CENTRAL DOCTRINES Despite the fact that Friends consider themselves noncredal, they have doctrines and expectations of moral conduct. Among the yearly meetings of Friends around the world, each has its own *Constitution and Discipline* or *Faith and Practice,* in which central doctrines are spelled out. The leading theological treatises of Friends include Robert Barclay's *Apology for the True Christian Divinity* (1678) and Joseph John Gurney's *Peculiarities of Friends* (1824). The closest thing to a common confession is the "Richmond Declaration of Faith," a statement approved in 1887 by orthodox Friends gathered from most sectors of American Quakerism but excepting Hicksites and Wilburites. The statement was drafted by Joseph Bevan Braithwaite of the London Yearly Meeting, and following the conference, most Friends affirmed it.

According to the declaration, Friends affirm one holy, all-wise, and everlasting God. They affirm the redemptive and revelatory mission of Jesus Christ, through whose saving death believers receive remission of sins and through whose presence they are granted life and direction. Friends believe in the sanctifying power of the Holy Spirit and in its ability to deliver humanity from the grip of sin. The Holy Scriptures are seen as having been given by inspiration and are held to be authoritative for faith and practice. On these matters most Friends are quite close to orthodox Christian groups, although liberal Friends have placed greater emphasis on the universal and continuing work of revelation.

Being somewhat at odds with such faith statements, Hicksite (Friends General Conference) and British Friends especially have upheld the doctrine of the Inward, or Inner, Light, existing within every person. Rooted in the biblical teaching that Christ was the "Light" that illuminated all humanity (John 1:9), Friends have believed that all persons have access to the saving and revealing work of God regardless of their era, where they live, or their religion. The Light is apprehended inwardly, although its origin comes from beyond the individual. George Fox described Christian witness as "speaking to that of God in everyone," and Friends are happy to affirm authentic spirituality with-

The Quaker Third Haven Meetinghouse in Easton, Maryland. Because a church is not considered a building but rather the gathered people of God, Friends refer to the local congregation as a "meeting" and the place at which they gather as the "meetinghouse." © LEE SNIDER/PHOTO IMAGES/CORBIS.

out restricting it to credal definitions—Christian or otherwise.

Friends hold several other distinctive positions on doctrinal issues. These include baptism, in which the spiritual experience is held to be more important than the ceremony. The true evidence of spiritual baptism is not the water of the rite but the changed life of the believer. On the Lord's Supper, Friends affirm that the presence of Christ is encountered within the meeting for worship and that authentic communion happens as believers abide in Christ and he in them. Authentic worship is held to be mediated solely by the workings of God within and among the hearts of persons and not by human agents, such as priests or pastors. Friends hold that liberty of conscience may require a person to defy civil authorities. Peace and nonviolence are required of believers, and oaths are seen as going against the command of Jesus.

Because the Light of Christ is accessible to all, Friends believe that effective witnessing involves listening as well as sharing. The conversion process is described not as proselytization but as "convincement." Friends hold that the ministry is a calling for all believers. Ministry has its roots in a transforming experience and a sense of calling, and it depends on the operation of the Holy Spirit in a person's life rather than on organizational structure or formal education.

MORAL CODE OF CONDUCT For Friends moral conduct is central to the life of the spirit and calls for adher-

A group of Quakers marches for peace in Britain. Quakers advocate nonviolence and hold that liberty of conscience may require a person to defy civil authorities. © TOUHIG SION/CORBIS SYGMA.

ence to a number of commitments based on the teachings of Jesus. Among them are nonviolence and peacemaking. Friends have historically opposed capital punishment, and they take great care to be fair and honest. Friends are known for practicing plain speech and simple living. Friends have suffered at the hands of judges for refusing to swear oaths in court, although they will "affirm" that they are speaking the truth.

The causes embraced by Friends have included prison reform, care for the mentally ill, advances in medicine and technology, the abolition of slavery and racism, woman suffrage, ecological concerns, and Third World development. Friends have sought to be good stewards, returning their bounty to the service of humanity and the glory of God. It is believed that a person's calling should not be contrary to his means of employment but complementary to it. Friends have often given their lives

to the service and educational professions, with 11 colleges and universities in North America alone having been founded by Friends.

SACRED BOOKS In addition to the Bible, Friends use such modern anthologies as *Christian Faith and Practice* and *Quaker Faith and Practice.* Thomas Kelley's *A Testament of Devotion* (1941) and Hannah Whitehall Smith's *The Christian's Secret of a Happy Life* (1875), in addition to the journals of George Fox and John Woolman, have become devotional classics.

SACRED SYMBOLS Because Friends focus on spiritual reality, they have resisted the use of sacred symbols. The transformed human life and the fruit of the spirit are considered to be the true outward evidence of God's presence and work. Nonetheless, the meeting for worship is sometimes closed with a handshake.

EARLY AND MODERN LEADERS George Fox (1624–91) is credited with founding the Religious Society of Friends. In the 1680s William Penn founded the Quaker colony of Pennsylvania (Penn's woods). Elizabeth Fry was known for her championing of prison reform in nineteenth-century England. In the twentieth century two U.S. presidents, Herbert Hoover and Richard Nixon, had Quaker backgrounds, though of the two, only Hoover was a practicing Quaker while in office. Henry J. Cadbury, a leading twentieth-century New Testament scholar at Harvard University, was a founder of the American Friends Service Committee, a pioneering organization in peace and justice work. In 1947 he received the Nobel Peace Prize on behalf of the committee, while Margaret Backhouse accepted the award on behalf of the British Friends Service Council, later renamed Quaker Peace & Social Witness.

MAJOR THEOLOGIANS AND AUTHORS Robert Barclay (1648–90) is credited with being the first genuine Quaker theologian. During the mid-nineteenth century Joseph John Gurney outlined a systematic theology of Friends and furthered progressive orthodoxy among American Friends. The nineteenth-century American poet John Greenleaf Whittier and the twentieth-century novelist James Michener were both Quakers. In the twentieth century Everett Cattell contributed to the founding of the National Association of Evangelicals and the Evangelical Fellowship of India, and Douglas Steere broadened an appreciation for the spirituality of world religions. Among modern writers Rufus Jones, D. Elton Trueblood, Parker Palmer, and Richard Foster are among the most noted.

ORGANIZATIONAL STRUCTURE The organizational structure among Friends is informal. The presiding officer at "meetings for worship" at which business is conducted is called a "clerk," and councils of elders, overseers, and stewards care for the needs of the local meeting. "Unprogrammed" Friends do not employ pastors or preachers, but "programmed" Friends "release" pastors and others for the ministry.

HOUSES OF WORSHIP AND HOLY PLACES Because a church is not considered to be a building but rather the gathered people of God, Friends refer to the local congregation as a "meeting" and the place at which they gather as the "meetinghouse." Meetinghouses tend to be plain, and they characteristically have a large room for worship along with rooms for other purposes. The worship room is often arranged with the chairs or pews facing one other or in a semicircle and with the "facing bench," at the front, occupied by elders, or "weighty Friends," who have been recognized for their spiritual maturity and effectiveness in spoken ministry. Pastoral Friends use buildings similar to those of other Protestant churches, and they sometimes refer to their congregation as a church rather than a meeting.

WHAT IS SACRED? Friends honor the sanctity of human life and seek to be effective stewards of the created order. They hold relationships to be of first importance. Because obedience to God is the first step of discipleship, waiting in silence is often considered a sacred endeavor for discerning the divine will.

HOLIDAYS AND FESTIVALS Friends hold all days to be sacred and of equal importance before God, and they have traditionally refused to honor national and religious holidays. In the past Friends also rejected the ordinary names for days and months, such as Sunday and January, because of their pagan roots, choosing instead to use numbers—"first day" (Sunday), "second day" (Monday), and "first month" (January)—as is done in Scripture.

MODE OF DRESS Friends oppose a person's setting off his or her status by means of dress or ornaments and therefore have testified against distinctive clothing. In

previous centuries Friends advocated plain dress, often gray or black.

DIETARY PRACTICES Quakers advocate healthy diets. Some Friends have supported animal rights and been advocates for cooperative systems of food production. In providing alternatives to more addictive substances, Friends were forerunners in the chocolate industry, and root beer was first introduced in 1876 as a marketable product by Charles Hires, an American Quaker.

RITUALS There are considerable differences in worship between "unprogrammed" and "programmed" Friends. Within the four main organizations of Quakers, Friends General Conference and Conservative Friends are largely unprogrammed, not using pastors or orders of worship, while Friends United Meeting and Evangelical Friends International use pastors and an informal order of worship.

Worship among unprogrammed Friends is unstructured, with periods of silence providing an opportunity for those who feel led to speak to do so. Silence is not the goal but rather involves creating the opportunity to attend and respond to the presence of God. The meeting for worship tends to run an hour in length. As people enter the room, they do so in silence, and the first half hour or so is a time of "centering" thoughts and sentiments upon God. Several people may feel led to speak, but rarely is a person expected to speak more than once in a meeting. A person's contribution is released to the rest of the meeting, and if it resonates with others, the message is built upon. Sometimes a passage of Scripture or another text is read, and in more expressive meetings singing is not uncommon.

The weddings and funerals of unprogrammed Friends follow the same format. A minister does not officiate at a Quaker wedding. Instead, God joins the couple in matrimony as vows are exchanged in the presence of family and friends. It is customary for all present to sign the certificate of marriage as witnesses. At a Quaker funeral spontaneous sharing is expected, especially as those present share thoughts about what the life of the deceased has meant to them.

Meetings of programmed Friends are often similar to other Low Church (less formal), Protestant orders of service. Programmed friends employ pastors and other leaders of worship, and the service might include hymns, public prayers, and a message by the pastor. There is also time set aside for open (unprogrammed)

Quotes from George Fox, Founder of the Quakers

A 1647 passage from George Fox's *Journal* illustrates how the idea for the Religious Society of Friends began in his own life experience: "And when all my hopes in them [religious leaders] and in all men were gone, so that I had nothing outwardly to help me, nor could I tell what to do, then, Oh then, I heard a voice which said, 'There is one, even Christ Jesus, that can speak to thy condition', and when I heard it my heart did leap for joy."

Another (1656) shows his conception of how Friends should live: "And this is the word of the Lord God to you all, and a charge to you all in the presence of the living God: be patterns, be examples in all countries, places, islands, nations, wherever you come, that your carriage and life may preach among all sorts of people, and to them; then you will come to walk cheerfully over the world, answering that of God in every one."

worship, sometimes called "communion after the manner of Friends." Although it is customary for the pastor to speak, primary emphasis is placed upon responding to the leadings of Christ with spontaneity.

Friends, both unprogrammed and programmed, advocate regular times of personal prayer and devotional reading.

RITES OF PASSAGE With a few exceptions Friends are understated in the celebration of rites of passage. When attenders become members, they are introduced to the meeting, and if they have not already done so, they give testimony to their spiritual experience and commitments. Especially in programmed traditions babies are dedicated to God and prayed for, as parents and members alike pledge themselves to their careful upbringing. Upon entering adulthood, those born into the meeting, or "birthright" Friends, are invited to declare their own interest in becoming full members.

MEMBERSHIP Criteria for membership are determined within each yearly meeting. While Friends do not prose-

lytize, most believe in evangelism, or the sharing of good news. Pastoral Friends have followed enthusiastically in the tradition of the early Quakers, who sought to reach the world for Christ, and missions of evangelical Friends are the primary reason the movement doubled in size and expanded to Latin American and Africa during the twentieth century. More liberal Friends have been prolific as writers and pamphleteers.

RELIGIOUS TOLERANCE Friends have been among the most tolerant of religious groups. Many in the twentieth century extended their inquiry into global spirituality by sharing fellowship with those from other religious traditions. Friends have been active in the ecumenical movement and have strongly opposed religious oppression and discrimination.

SOCIAL JUSTICE Friends have been forerunners in areas of social justice, including education, alleviation of poverty, and human rights. The Retreat (in England), opened in 1796, was the first facility designed for the care of the mentally ill, and in the nineteenth century Joseph Lancaster developed a program for offering free education to street children in London. In the United States, John Woolman and Anthony Benezet were leaders in the eighteenth-century abolitionist movement, and in the nineteenth and twentieth centuries, Lucretia Mott and Susan B. Anthony were leaders in woman suffrage.

SOCIAL ASPECTS Quaker egalitarianism extends to family life. Husbands and wives share roles equally and seek to work in a complementary partnership. Parents seek to explain to their children why a decision is worthy and try to help them understand the larger principles behind it. Because corporal punishment is at odds with Quaker commitments to nonviolence, parents resort to other means in exercising their authority.

CONTROVERSIAL ISSUES On abortion evangelical and pastoral Friends tend to be pro-life, while liberal Friends tend to be pro-choice. Liberal Friends oppose capital punishment, although some more conservative Friends favor it for violent crimes. On homosexuality evangelical and more conservative Friends believe that repentance and providing the necessary support to overcome the practice is the loving approach, while liberal Friends tend to be affirming of same-sex relationships.

A minority of Friends, mostly within unprogrammed meetings, have argued that although the Quaker movement had Christian beginnings, its universal ethos transcends Christianity to include other religions (especially the Baha'i faith and Buddhism) and even atheism. Most Friends, however, while appreciating the interest of inclusivity, view this tendency as a departure from the historical and spiritual basis of Quaker faith and practice, which is Christ-centered in both religious experience and commitment.

CULTURAL IMPACT While Quakers oppose self-aggrandizing aspects of the arts, they have nonetheless made distinctive artistic contributions. Quaker musicians have composed works with a social or spiritual message, and revivalist Friends have excelled in musical ministries. Edward Hicks (1780–1849), who is known as one of the foremost American folk painters, produced more than 100 renditions of Isaiah's "Peaceable Kingdom" motif, characteristically featuring William Penn's treaty with the Indians. Likewise known for their social commentary are the wood-block prints of Fritz Eichenberg (1901–90), more than 100 of which were featured in *Catholic Worker* magazine.

Paul N. Anderson

See Also Vol. 1: *Christianity, Protestantism*

Bibliography

Anderson, Paul. *Meet the Friends*. Rev. ed. Newberg, Ore.: Barclay Press, 2003.

Barbour, Hugh, and J. William Frost. *The Quakers*. New York: Greenwood Press, 1988.

Barbour, Hugh, and Arthur O. Roberts, eds. *Early Quaker Writings*. Grand Rapids, Mich.: William B. Eerdmans, 1973.

Barclay, Robert. *Barclay's Apology in Modern English*. Edited by Dean Freiday. Newberg, Ore.: Barclay Press, 1991.

———. *Barclay's Catechism and Confession of Faith*. Edited by Dean Freiday and Arthur O. Roberts. Newberg, Ore.: Barclay Press, 2001.

Fox, George. *George Fox's "Book of Miracles."* Edited by Henry J. Cadbury. Philadelphia: Friends Uniting in Publication, 2000.

———. *The Journal of George Fox*. Edited by John L. Nickalls. London: Religious Society of Friends, 1975.

Garman, Mary, Margaret Benefiel, Judith Applegate, and Dortha Meredith, eds. *Hidden in Plain Sight: Quaker Women's Writings, 1650–1700*. Wallingford, Eng.: Pendle Hill Press, 1995.

Hamm, Thomas. *The Transformation of American Quakerism*. Bloomington: Indiana University Press, 1988.

Houlden, David. *Friends Divided: Conflict and Division in the Society of Friends*. Richmond, Ind.: Friends United Press, 1988.

Punshon, John. *Encounter with Silence*. Richmond, Ind.: Friends United Press, 1987.

———. *Portrait in Grey: A Short History of the Quakers*. London: Quaker Home Service, 1984.

———. *Reasons for Hope: The Faith and Future of the Friends Church*. Richmond, Ind.: Friends United Press, 2001.

Trueblood, D. Elton. *The People Called Quakers*. Richmond, Ind.: Friends United Press, 1971.

Woolman, John. *The Journal and Major Essays of John Woolman*. Edited by Philips Moulton. New York: Oxford University Press, 1971.

Roman Catholicism

FOUNDED: First century C.E.

RELIGION AS A PERCENTAGE OF WORLD POPULATION: 17 percent

OVERVIEW The term "catholic" is derived from a Greek word meaning "universal" or "worldwide," and it was first applied to the church in the early second century C.E. It originally distinguished the "worldwide" church from various sectarian or splinter groups. The adjective "Roman" is not part of the name of the Catholic Church but identifies its distinguishing feature: acceptance of the supreme authority of the bishop of Rome (the pope). The matter is complicated by the fact that the Catholic Church comprises a variety of rites. The term "rite" here designates a distinct tradition in worship and church discipline. Most Catholics belong to the Latin (or Roman) Rite, but many, especially in Eastern Europe and the Middle East, belong to Eastern Rites, chiefly the Byzantine, Alexandrian, Antiochene, Armenian, and Chaldaean Rites. These "Eastern Catholics" do not usually call themselves Roman Catholics but do accept the authority of the pope.

The Catholic Church does not regard itself as one denomination of Christians among others. According to the Second Vatican Council (1962–65), the Church, in the sense of the entire community of those united and saved in Jesus Christ, "subsists in" the Catholic Church, and all baptized Christians not officially joined to the Catholic Church "have some real, though imperfect, communion with it."

There are somewhat more than one billion Roman Catholics in the world. Of these, around 13 percent are in Africa, 21 percent in North and Central America, 29 percent in South America, 10 percent in Asia, 26 percent in Europe, and 1 percent in Oceania. The heaviest concentration of Catholics is in Central and South America, where they form approximately 85 percent of the population.

HISTORY The Catholic Church claims it was founded by Jesus Christ (died in 30 or 33 C.E.) in his call for disciples, who were led by 12 apostles. It traces the pope's authority to Jesus' appointing Saint Peter as leader of the apostles (Matt. 16:18–19) and to the traditional link between Saint Peter and the church of Rome, where he is said to have been martyred. Saint Peter is considered to be the first pope of the Catholic Church.

After the death, resurrection, and ascension of Jesus, the apostles assumed leadership of the new Christian community. Though the apostles had the primary authority in the churches they founded, they had to provide for local leadership; hence, leadership by bishops developed. By the second century the structure whereby each local church had a single bishop prevailed throughout the Christian world.

The authority of the bishop of Rome, or pope, developed slowly. In 95 C.E. the First Letter of Clement shows the church of Rome exercising supervision over the church of Corinth. Furthermore, the eminence of the church of Rome—as the church of Peter and Paul as well as the empire's capital city—was recognized by early Christian writers. In 190 C.E., however, when the

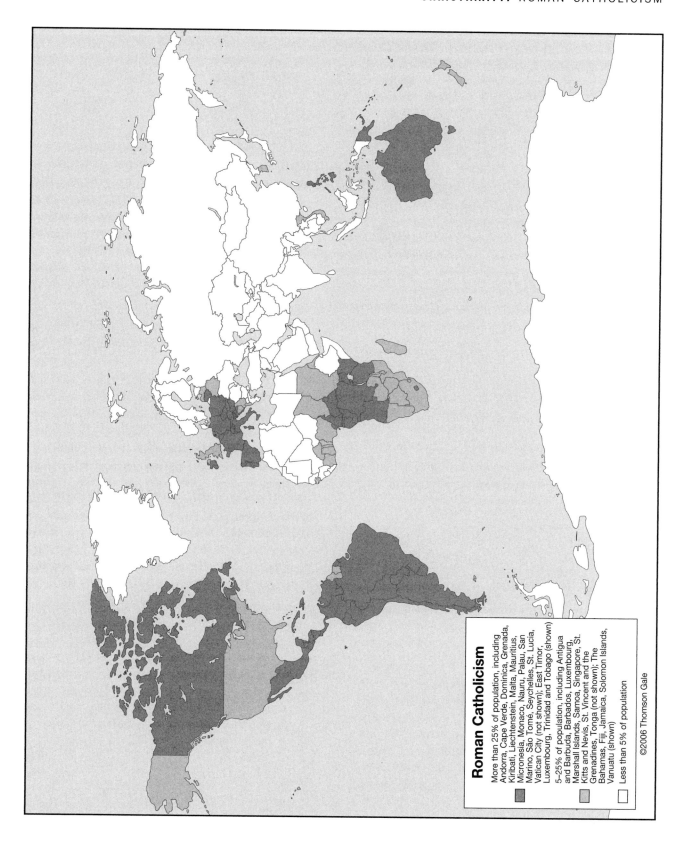

Roman Catholicism

More than 25% of population, including Andorra, Cape Verde, Dominica, Grenada, Kiribati, Liechtenstein, Malta, Mauritius, Micronesia, Monaco, Nauru, Palau, San Marino, São Tomé, Seychelles, St. Lucia, Vatican City (not shown); East Timor, Luxembourg, Trinidad and Tobago (shown)

5–25% of population, including Antigua and Barbuda, Barbados, Luxembourg, Marshall Islands, Samoa, Singapore, St. Kitts and Nevis, St. Vincent and the Grenadines, Tonga (not shown); The Bahamas, Fiji, Jamaica, Solomon Islands, Vanuatu (shown)

Less than 5% of population

©2006 Thomson Gale

A woman takes Communion outside of Notre Dame Cathedral in Paris, France. The central act of the Catholic liturgy, commonly known as the Mass, is the celebration of the Eucharist. © OWEN FRANKEN/CORBIS.

bishop of Rome sought to impose the Roman date for Easter on the churches of Asia Minor, he met with strenuous resistance. In the late fourth century the bishops of Rome began to speak as though they were the voice of Peter and to exercise formally judicial power over other churches. Papal authority was enhanced when the Council of Chalcedon (451 C.E.) accepted Pope Leo I's solution to the problem of Jesus' divinity and humanity. In western Europe papal power grew from the fifth century onward, when there was often no other effective civil authority.

For the first millennium of Christianity, the history of Catholicism almost coincides with that of Christianity generally, except for the churches that did not accept the Councils of Ephesus (431 C.E.) and Chalcedon. Those churches were the ancestors of today's Assyrian Church of the East, as well as of the Armenian, Coptic, Ethiopian, Eritrean, Syrian Orthodox, and Malankara Orthodox churches.

Among the churches that did accept the early councils, there was a gradual separation between the Eastern, primarily Greek-speaking churches (ancestors of today's Eastern Orthodox churches) and the Western Catholic Church. The division was formalized by mutual anathemas (condemnations) in 1054 and was sealed by the Fourth Crusade in 1204, when Western armies sacked Constantinople.

A further division occurred in the West with the Protestant Reformation, usually dated from 1517. Catholics and Protestants disagreed on the role of church authority and sacraments in mediating a Christian's relation to God. Other issues involved the financial and political dealings of church leaders in western Europe. The Council of Trent (1545–63) restated church doctrines without much accommodation to Protestant concerns, but it also reformed church practices, ending many of the worst abuses. Seminaries were instituted to train the clergy, whose ignorance, even illiteracy, had been an embarrassment. Most of northern Europe became Protestant, while southern Europe (including France, Spain, Portugal, and Italy) remained Catholic. During the baroque period (seventeenth and eighteenth centuries) a revival of Catholic spirituality and art took place in these countries.

The age of western European exploration and colonization—lasting from the late fifteenth century to the nineteenth century—spread Catholicism to the Americas, central and southern Africa, and Asia. Catholicism grew mainly in areas that were colonized by Spain, Portugal, and France.

After the French Revolution of 1789 overthrew Catholic power in France, the popes and much of the European church took a defensive stance against Protestantism, Enlightenment secular thought, and modern secular states. In the late nineteenth century new developments—notably, modern papal teaching on social issues—began to occur, culminating in the teachings of the Second Vatican Council of 1962–65. Since that time the Catholic Church has actively taken part in Christian ecumenism and interreligious dialogue. It has also been preoccupied by how to adapt and become indigenous to non-Western cultures, thus becoming genuinely a world church. The anathemas of 1054 were lifted in 1965, but Catholicism and Eastern Orthodoxy remain divided; the pope's authority is a principal divisive issue.

CENTRAL DOCTRINES Like many Christians, the Catholic Church affirms the Apostle's Creed and the Nicene Creed. The Catholic Church teaches many other doctrines, a summary of which can be found in the Catechism of the Catholic Church. The doctrines taught most authoritatively are called dogmas. Dogmas must be accepted by all church members; to knowingly deny a dogma is heresy. A pope may proclaim a dogma of Catholic faith by proclaiming it ex cathedra—that is, with the explicit intention of invoking his supreme authority to define a doctrine to be believed by the whole church. When he does so, he is understood to teach in-

A crucifix stands in the Igreja da Ordem Terceira de Sao Francisco in Salvador, Brazil. Catholics are more likely than many other Christians to employ the crucifix, a cross that bears the figure of the crucified Christ. © JEREMY HORNER/CORBIS.

fallibly (without error). An ecumenical council (a gathering of bishops and other leaders representing the worldwide Church) may, with the pope's approval, define a dogma. Such definitions are also considered infallible.

The most distinctively Catholic doctrine is that of the supreme authority (primacy) of the pope, including his infallibility and his jurisdiction over the whole church (some other Christians would accept a primacy of the pope but not exactly as Catholics understand it). Doctrines about the Blessed Virgin Mary are also among those that distinguish the Catholic Church from many other Christian groups. These include the Assumption (Mary's bodily ascent into heaven at the end of her life), Mary's lifelong virginity, and her Immaculate Conception (her conception free from original sin). Mary is the first among the saints, holy people now enjoying eternal life with God. Catholics regard saints as intercessors who pray for the church on earth. Because the saints are saved by Jesus Christ, and their prayer is joined to his, the Catholic Church does not regard

prayers addressed to saints as diminishing Jesus' role as sole savior. Other Catholic doctrines are that there are seven sacraments (baptism, penance or reconciliation, the Eucharist, confirmation, matrimony, order, and anointing the sick) and that, after death, there is a temporary state of purification, called purgatory, through which many people must pass before entering heaven.

MORAL CODE OF CONDUCT The Catholic Church prescribes a traditional Christian code of conduct, often specified in terms of the biblical Ten Commandments. While some of the commandments are understood as God's direct orders otherwise unknowable by humans, most are considered to be knowable by human reason without special divine revelation. Catholic teaching commonly follows medieval tradition, especially the teaching of Saint Thomas Aquinas, in referring to moral principles knowable by reason as the natural law. Accordingly, the Catholic Church—in specifying conduct required of, permitted of, or forbidden to humans—makes greater use of philosophy than do many Christian

representing the crucifixion of Jesus. Catholics are more likely than many other Christians to employ the crucifix, a cross that bears the figure of the crucified Christ.

Pope John Paul II baptizes an infant girl. The late pontiff is one of the dominant Catholic figures of the twentieth century. © REUTERS NEWMEDIA INC./CORBIS.

churches. A body of Canon Law governs the internal life of the church.

SACRED BOOKS Catholics believe in the authority of the Bible. They accept 46 books of the Old Testament—the 39 from the Hebrew canon and the 7 deuterocanonical books (which most Protestants call Apocrypha). Like most Christians, Catholics accept 27 books in the New Testament. The Catholic Church regards the entire Bible as the inspired word of God, free from error. It locates that freedom from error, however, not necessarily in the literal text but in the "truth that God, for the sake of our salvation, wished the . . . text to contain" (according to the Second Vatican Council). Because God is understood to have worked through humans who were genuine authors, the biblical books may well contain what would be error when judged by the standards of modern history or science.

SACRED SYMBOLS Catholicism uses a wide range of symbols to signify the sacred. Most central is the cross,

EARLY AND MODERN LEADERS Until the division between Eastern and Western Christianity, the leading figures in Catholicism were the same as the leading figures in Christianity, and up to the Protestant Reformation, the leading figures in Catholicism were the same as those in Western Christianity.

After the Reformation new religious orders, such as the Jesuits, founded by the Spaniard Saint Ignatius of Loyola (1491–1556), and reformed orders, such as the Carmelites of the Spanish saints Teresa of Avila (1515–82) and John of the Cross (1542–91), helped to revitalize the life of the church. Saint Francis de Sales (1567–1622), Saint Jane Frances de Chantal (1572–1642), and Saint Vincent de Paul (1581–1660) similarly revived spiritual life in France.

In the nineteenth century Pope Pius IX (reigned 1846–78) consolidated papal authority, culminating in the definition of papal infallibility at the First Vatican Council (1870), while Pope Leo XIII (reigned 1878–1903) inaugurated modern Catholic social teaching. The two dominant figures of the twentieth century were Pope John XXIII (1958–63) and Pope John Paul II (1978–2005). John XXIII called the Second Vatican Council (1962–65) to reform and modernize the church. John Paul II had to strengthen internal church discipline while exercising leadership in world affairs. Mother Teresa of Calcutta (1910–97) won global admiration and a Nobel Peace Prize for her service to India's poor, while Dorothy Day (1897–1980) combined service to the poor in the United States with an influential witness against war.

MAJOR THEOLOGIANS AND AUTHORS The writings of Saint Thomas Aquinas (1225/6–1274) shaped later Catholicism more than those of any other theologian; in 1878 his writings were granted official status. In the period after the Reformation, the writings of Saint Teresa of Avila, Saint John of the Cross, and Saint Francis de Sales, as well as those of Blaise Pascal (1623–62), the greatest French Catholic thinker of the time, helped develop a distinctively Catholic spirituality.

In the twentieth century there was a major revival of Catholic theology, culminating in the Second Vatican Council (1962–65). Among its principal figures were Henri de Lubac (French, 1896–1991), Yves Congar

(French, 1904–95), Bernard Lonergan (Canadian, 1904–84), Karl Rahner (German, 1904–84), Hans Urs von Balthasar (Swiss, 1905–88), Edward Schillebeeckx (Dutch, born in 1914), and John Courtney Murray (American, 1904–67).

ORGANIZATIONAL STRUCTURE The pope exercises supreme power in the Catholic Church. The bishops share in this power. The Catholic Church is divided into mostly geographic districts, called dioceses (often called eparchies in the Eastern churches); a diocese is governed by a bishop. Bishops are usually organized into national or regional episcopal (or bishop's) conferences. In some of the Eastern churches, a bishop called a patriarch is second in authority to the pope. The sacrament of order (ordination, holy orders) has three degrees: a bishop has the fullness of the sacrament, a priest holds the second rank, and a deacon the third. All ordinations must be performed by bishops, who are considered successors of the apostles. A diocese is divided into parishes, governed ordinarily by a priest called the pastor. Cardinals, who include all the patriarchs, are bishops who have authority to elect the pope. Men and women who make special commitments to poverty, chastity, and obedience are called religious. Some of the men are priests; the women (who are not ordained) are called sisters or nuns. People who are not ordained are laypersons or laity; often these terms are further restricted to those who are not "religious" in the above sense.

The pope governs the worldwide church through the Roman Curia, the central administrative offices in Vatican City (a sovereign state governed by the pope and located within the city of Rome).

HOUSES OF WORSHIP AND HOLY PLACES Catholic houses of worship are called churches. There is an altar at the front or center, along with a pulpit or lectern for reading and speaking. The most common structure is based on a type of Roman public building called a basilica; the term "basilica" is now used to indicate special honor for a church, regardless of structure. A diocese's principal church is called the cathedral. Smaller churches or churches designated for particular communities (other than parishes) may be called chapels. A shrine is a place of prayer, especially a site for pilgrimages; it may be a church, a building, or another location, indoors or outdoors.

WHAT IS SACRED? For Catholics most sacred objects are linked to the rituals called sacraments (explained below under RITUALS). After bread and wine have been consecrated in the Mass, they are held sacred as the body and blood of Christ (although still appearing as bread and wine). Also sacred are baptismal water, the oil (chrism) used in confirmation and ordination, and the oil of the sick, used for anointing. Some objects that are less centrally connected to a sacrament, such as wedding rings, are called sacramentals.

The church also venerates the relics (bodily remains or personal objects, such as clothing) of saints, who will share in the final bodily resurrection of the dead.

HOLIDAYS AND FESTIVALS The Catholic Church divides the week and the year according to the liturgical calendar. The week centers on Sunday, the day of Jesus' resurrection. Catholics are obligated to attend Mass on Sunday and, to the extent possible, to observe it as a day of rest. The year centers on Easter, the annual feast of Jesus' resurrection; it falls on the Sunday following the first full moon after the spring equinox. A secondary focus is Christmas, 25 December. The Sacred Triduum celebrates the death and resurrection of Jesus; it begins on Holy Thursday (the Thursday before Easter) and continues through Good Friday (commemorating Jesus' death), Holy Saturday, and the Easter Vigil (held on the Saturday evening before Easter Sunday) to Easter Sunday.

Pentecost, which commemorates the coming of the Holy Spirit to the apostles after Jesus' resurrection, is celebrated on the seventh Sunday after Easter. Holy Days of Obligation—feasts on which Catholics are obligated to attend Mass—are Christmas and the feasts of Mary, Mother of God (1 January), Epiphany (6 January, unless moved to Sunday), Saint Joseph (19 March), Ascension (the fifth Thursday after Easter, unless moved to Sunday), the Body and Blood of Christ (Corpus Christi; the second Thursday after Pentecost, unless moved to Sunday), Saints Peter and Paul (29 June), the Assumption of Mary (15 August), All Saints (1 November), and the Immaculate Conception of Mary (8 December). Bishop's conferences usually transfer some of these to Sunday and waive the obligation to attend Mass on some others.

MODE OF DRESS The following vestments are worn by ministers in the church's liturgy: alb, a full-length white robe; cincture, a cord that serves as a belt for the alb; stole, a scarflike garment worn by a priest or deacon; chasuble, a sleeveless outer garment worn by a priest;

and dalmatic, a sleeved outer garment worn by a deacon. The colors of the stole, chasuble, and dalmatic vary with the liturgical season or with the nature of the feast. Liturgical vestments are based on the ordinary clothing of civil officials in the late Roman Empire. On public occasions outside of liturgy, a priest is expected to wear clerical dress, which in many countries means a black suit with a stiff white collar known as a Roman collar. Men and women religious (discussed above under ORGANIZATIONAL STRUCTURE) sometimes wear habits, which are based on ordinary medieval clothing but which vary from one religious community to another. There is no distinctive dress for Catholic laity.

DIETARY PRACTICES Latin Rite Catholics are required to fast (reduce food consumption) on Ash Wednesday (the first day of Lent, a six-week period before Easter) and Good Friday. Canon Law also calls for Catholics to abstain from meat on Ash Wednesday and on all Fridays (although, since 1966, bishop's conferences have been allowed to mitigate the last requirement, and in some areas, such as the United States, Friday abstinence has been confined to Lent). It is also required that Catholics abstain from all food and drink except water for one hour before receiving Communion (the Eucharist; explained below in RITUALS).

RITUALS The official public prayer of the Catholic Church is called the liturgy. The central act of the liturgy, commonly known as the Mass, is the celebration of the Eucharist. The Mass consists of the Liturgy of the Word, which includes readings from the Bible and preaching, and the Liturgy of the Eucharist, in which bread and wine are understood to become the body and blood of Christ and are eaten in Communion. The Mass is celebrated every day except Good Friday.

The Eucharist is one of the seven sacraments of the church. The others are baptism, confirmation (a ritual ratification of baptism understood to bring about a special presence of the Holy Spirit in the person confirmed), penance or reconciliation (a ritual forgiveness of sins), marriage, order (holy orders or ordination), and anointing of the sick. There are also liturgies for funerals, church dedications, and other occasions. The Liturgy of the Hours consists of prayers (chiefly psalms) and readings at certain times of day, particularly morning and evening. Priests and religious must pray it, publicly or privately; laity may do so.

Nonliturgical prayers and rituals include the rosary, a prayer commemorating events in the lives of Jesus and Mary and consisting of repetitions of the Lord's Prayer, the Hail Mary, and doxology; Stations of the Cross, which commemorate events from Jesus' trial to his burial; pilgrimages to Rome, the Holy Land, and shrines or other holy places; and processions on certain feasts of importance in particular localities. In a retreat an individual or group withdraws from ordinary activities to engage in an intensive period of prayer, often at a location set apart for such activities. Catholic private prayer takes a wide variety of forms; the most common prayers are the Lord's Prayer ("Our Father"), the Hail Mary (based on the angel's greeting to Mary in Luke 1), and the doxology ("Glory [be] to the Father . . .").

RITES OF PASSAGE Certain sacraments function as rites of passage for Catholics. Baptism is a ritual of entry into the church. It may be administered to infants or to adults; for adults it is preceded by a process of preparation called the catechumenate. Confirmation functions as a ritual of adolescence for many Catholics baptized as infants, though this is not the essential nature of the sacrament; for adults it is administered immediately after baptism, and in the Eastern churches infants receive confirmation immediately after baptism. Marriage and ordination are official recognitions of commitments typical of adulthood. The anointing of the sick is for those who are seriously ill, especially when in danger of death. Dying Catholics are to receive viaticum (Holy Communion), and there are special prayers for the "Commendation of the Dying" to the mercy of God. In funeral and burial rituals the community publicly entrusts the dead person to God's mercy.

MEMBERSHIP The Catholic Church welcomes new adult members, who are, ideally, to be received at the Easter Vigil, through baptism, confirmation, or a rite of reception, followed by the Eucharist. From the earliest days of the church, missionaries have used all available media to spread Jesus' message. Especially after the Second Vatican Council, missionaries have accepted the plurality of human cultures and are careful to distinguish evangelization (the proclamation of Christian faith) from the spread of Western culture. Recognizing God's presence outside the formal boundaries of the Catholic Church, they generally reject aggressive proselytizing and seek instead to embody Catholic faith and to practice in a way that is welcoming to those outside the church.

RELIGIOUS TOLERANCE The Catholic Church officially embraced religious freedom at the Second Vatican Council. The dignity of the human person, who possesses reason and free will, the council argued, requires that humans be free from coercion in matters of conscience. The church also endorsed the ecumenical movement (the pursuit of unity among Christians), and since that time it has participated actively in two-party and many-party dialogues. With the goal of mutual understanding, the Catholic Church has been actively engaged in dialogue with representatives of non-Christian religions.

SOCIAL JUSTICE Drawing upon earlier Catholic teaching, Pope Leo XIII in 1891 inaugurated modern Catholic social teaching with an encyclical (an authoritative statement), *Rerum Novarum*, addressing the oppression of working persons in modern industrial society. Since then popes and bishops have elaborated a substantial body of teaching. Principal themes are (1) the unique dignity of the human person, (2) the social nature of the person, (3) the dignity and rights of labor, (4) the right of all persons to participate in political and economic decisions, (5) justice in the distribution of the world's goods, (6) peace and cooperation among nations (though at times war may be justified, as explained below under CONTROVERSIAL ISSUES), and (7) the need to protect the "integrity of creation" against environmental degradation.

Social ministry and action is carried out by the church on all official levels, from the Vatican to local parishes (for instance, Catholic Relief Services, sponsored by the U.S. bishops, is one of the largest nongovernmental relief and development agencies in the world). It is also carried out by Catholic groups that do not have official status, though they may have official approval.

Liberation theology originated in the Catholic Church in Latin America in the 1960s. Defined by Gustavo Gutiérrez (born in 1928) of Peru as "critical reflection on Christian praxis in the light of the Word (of God)"—where "praxis" primarily means action to transform oppressive structures—liberation theology gained great prominence in Latin America and spread from there to other continents and social contexts. It has been criticized by the church for its reliance on Marxist social analysis and for excessive politicization of faith, but some of its emphases have found their way into official church social teaching. Two examples are "social

sin" (sin that is embedded in unjust social structures and that thus leads to individual sin) and the "option for the poor" (the notion that the church should give priority to the viewpoint of the poor and powerless in its socioeconomic teaching and action).

SOCIAL ASPECTS The Catholic Church regards the family as the fundamental unit of society, and hence it opposes both public policies and social conditions (such as poverty and excessive hours of labor) that it perceives to threaten the family. Without prejudice against "extended families," the church sees the core of the family as a marriage between a man and a woman. For centuries the primary good of marriage was understood to be procreation; today Catholic teaching gives equal emphasis to the love and support between the partners.

Since the twelfth century marriage has been considered a sacrament; this applies even to many non-Catholic marriages, since the ministers of the sacrament are understood to be the couple themselves. Marriage is permanent and indissoluble; hence, the church forbids remarriage after divorce. Many marriages, however, lack some condition necessary to be "sacramentally valid"—that is, truly to be a sacrament—and in such cases an annulment, a declaration that the marriage is sacramentally (not civilly) invalid, may be issued by the church. People whose marriages have been annulled are free to marry again.

CONTROVERSIAL ISSUES Issues of human life and sexuality are controversial both within the Catholic Church and between the church and the larger society. The Catholic Church teaches that the dignity and sanctity of human life begins at (or probably at) conception and continues to the end of life. Hence, it forbids abortion, infanticide, suicide, and euthanasia. Killing in self-defense is permitted, and, because they are somewhat analogous to self-defense, war and capital punishment have been allowed under some circumstances. Catholic teaching since the late twentieth century, however, has limited those circumstances (in the case of capital punishment, to near zero), and it has been increasingly negative toward modern war.

The church holds that sexual activity is reserved for marriage and must be of such a sort that the possibility of procreation is not deliberately foreclosed. On the basis of these principles, premarital and extramarital sex are forbidden, as are nonprocreative sexual acts such as homosexual relations and masturbation, as well as the use of most forms of birth control within marriage. Natural family planning, which regulates family size by timing sexual intercourse for periods when the woman is probably infertile, is allowed.

Two other highly controversial issues are clerical celibacy and the ordination of women. Priests in the Latin Rite must be celibate; that is, they are forbidden to be married (or to engage in other sexual relationships). Married men may be ordained deacons, and some married men, previously ministers in other Christian churches, have been ordained as Catholic priests. Many Eastern Rite priests are married. Women may not be ordained as deacons, priests, or bishops. Official church teaching recognizes the requirement of celibacy to be a changeable matter of church discipline but regards the restriction of priesthood to men as a matter of the essence of priesthood. The status of the rule against women deacons is less clear, as there were women deacons (possibly not equivalent to male deacons) in the early centuries of the church.

CULTURAL IMPACT The Catholic Church has long promoted the arts, "so that," as Vatican II says, "the things that form part of liturgical worship"—such as church architecture, decoration, and music—"can be . . . signs and symbols of the things above." The church has also been a patron of religious art outside the immediate context of worship. Though it has sometimes been accused of idolatry, it has sought to distinguish the derivative veneration owed to images from the veneration owed to that which they represent.

The history of the visual and performing arts in Catholicism from the late Roman Empire up to the Protestant Reformation almost coincides with the history of the arts in the West. The great cathedrals of Europe, Gregorian chant in music, the *Divine Comedy* of Dante, and the paintings and sculptures of the Italian Renaissance, for instance, are all treasures of the Catholic Church and of Western culture generally. Since the Reformation the church has sponsored art, architecture, and music in the baroque and modern styles. It has made use of newer art forms, such as film, and it has been increasingly making use of non-Western art forms and traditions.

William J. Collinge

See Also Vol. 1: *Christianity*

The Second Vatican Council

An ecumenical, or general, council is a gathering of the bishops (and other leaders) of the worldwide church. The Catholic Church usually counts 21 ecumenical councils in its history, of which the Second Vatican Council (1962–65) is the most recent. It was the largest council in the history of the church and produced the largest body of official documents. The Second Vatican Council was summoned by Pope John XXIII (reigned 1958–63) to renew the church and to update it in light of contemporary conditions. Its 16 documents provided an authoritative statement of Catholic teaching on the nature and mission of the church. Most important were four "constitutions": on the church, on liturgy, on divine revelation (scripture and tradition), and on the church in the modern world. Other important documents addressed ecumenism (the movement to reunite the Christian churches), non-Christian religions, and religious freedom.

Bibliography

Carlen, Claudia, ed. *The Papal Encyclicals (1740–1981).* 5 vols. Wilmington, N.C.: McGrath, 1981.

Catechism of the Catholic Church. 2nd ed., revised in accordance with the official Latin text promulgated by Pope John Paul II. Washington, D.C.: U.S. Catholic Conference, 2000.

The Catholic Almanac. Huntington, Ind.: Our Sunday Visitor, annual.

Collinge, William J. *The A to Z of Catholicism.* Lanham, Md.: Scarecrow Press, 2001.

Downey, Michael, ed. *The New Dictionary of Catholic Spirituality.* Collegeville, Minn.: Liturgical, 1993.

Dwyer, Judith, ed. *The New Dictionary of Catholic Social Thought.* Collegeville, Minn.: Liturgical, 1994.

Fink, Peter E., ed. *The New Dictionary of Sacramental Worship.* Collegeville, Minn.: Liturgical, 1990.

Kelly, J.N.D. *The Oxford Dictionary of Popes.* New York: Oxford University Press, 1986.

Komonchak, Joseph A., Mary Collins, and Dermot A. Lane, eds. *The New Dictionary of Theology.* Collegeville, Minn.: Liturgical, 1987.

Levillain, Philippe, ed. *The Papacy: An Encyclopedia.* 3 vols. London and New York: Routledge, 2002.

Marthaler, Berard L., ed. *The New Catholic Encyclopedia.* 2nd ed. 15 vols. Detroit: Gale, 2003.

McBrien, Richard P., ed. *The HarperCollins Encyclopedia of Catholicism.* San Francisco: HarperSanFrancisco, 1995.

Tanner, Norman P., ed. *Decrees of the Ecumenical Councils.* 2 vols. Washington, D.C.: Georgetown University Press, 1990.

Seventh-day Adventists

FOUNDED: 1863 C.E.

RELIGION AS A PERCENTAGE OF WORLD POPULATION: 0.2 percent

OVERVIEW The Seventh-day Adventist Church originated in the United States in the mid-nineteenth century. With more than 13 million members in over 200 countries, it is among the world's ten largest international religious organizations.

Although in many countries Adventists constitute only a small part of the population, they have made significant contributions in the areas of health and medical care, education, humanitarian relief, religious liberty, and other fields. While working for the betterment of humanity in the present, Adventists believe that it is God alone who will ultimately solve the world's ills through the Second Coming, or Advent, of Jesus Christ. For this reason preaching the gospel of Jesus Christ is their highest priority.

HISTORY The Seventh-day Adventist Church originated in the United States from the widespread Advent Awakening of the mid-nineteenth century. The Great Disappointment of the Millerite movement in October 1844, so called because Jesus Christ did not return as expected, led many Advent believers to a deeper study of the Scriptures, especially the books of Daniel and Revelation. A renewed hope in Christ's Second Coming and a growing conviction that God had called them to proclaim the everlasting gospel to the world resulted in the formation of the General Conference of Seventh-day Adventists in 1863.

The next 50 years witnessed the growth of Seventh-day Adventism into a worldwide movement with a range of diversified ministries. Not only did the membership of the young denomination grow from a few thousand to more than a hundred thousand but Adventist missions were started on every inhabited continent on the globe and on the islands of the Pacific Ocean. During this same period publishing houses, sanitariums, schools, and colleges were established in a Christ-centered approach to bring healing and to restore the image of God in human beings.

Significant organizational changes in the early twentieth century laid the groundwork for the growth of the Adventist Church into the world church of today. While in the first 60 years the mission outreach of the church was predominantly from the so-called developed countries to other parts of the world, in the latter part of the twentieth century Seventh-day Adventism became embedded and self-reliant in many countries around the globe.

At the end of 2001 the educational system of the Adventist Church operated about 5,000 elementary schools and 1,350 secondary schools, colleges, seminaries, and universities worldwide. More than 550 hospitals, sanitariums, clinics, and dispensaries provided medical care for millions of patients. Loma Linda University in California is known for progressive medical research and advanced surgical technology. In Africa the church has established an international center to combat the AIDS epidemic. The Adventist Development and

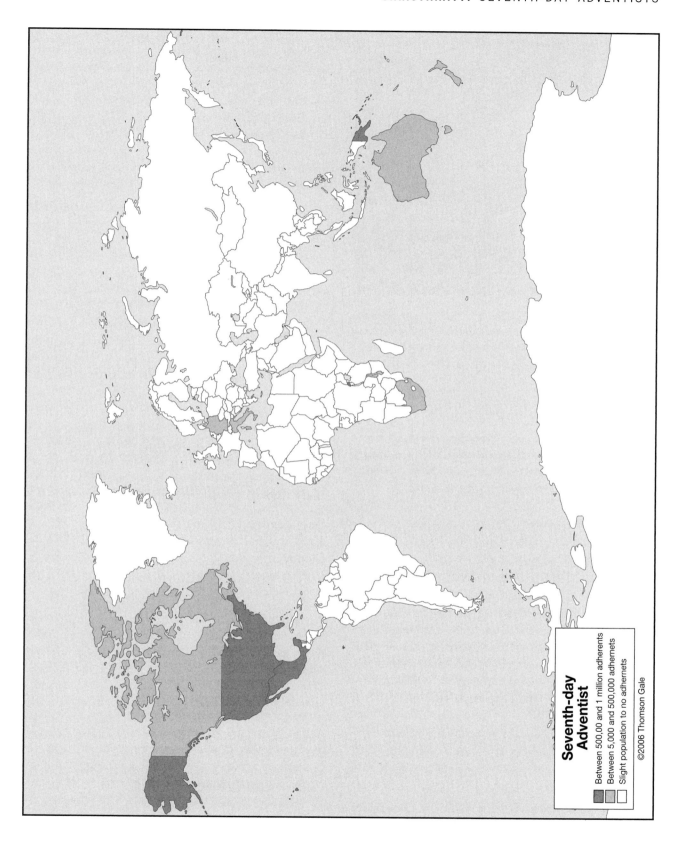

Seventh-day
Adventist
Between 500,00 and 1 million adherents
Between 5,000 and 500,000 adherents
Slight population to no adherents

©2006 Thomson Gale

A Seventh-day Adventist church in Chicago, Illinois. Adventists believe that it is God alone who will ultimately solve the world's ills through the Second Coming, or Advent, of Jesus Christ. © SANDY FELSENTHAL/CORBIS.

Relief Agency maintains development projects in many countries and provides humanitarian relief in scores of areas stricken by disasters. Adventists believe, however, that no institutional ministry can substitute for a Christlike life and witness, so that ultimately Adventist history is the history of Christ living in believers and working through them for the salvation of the world.

CENTRAL DOCTRINES Seventh-day Adventists hold many doctrines in common with other Christians. They believe in the triune God—Father, Son, and Holy Spirit—and in Jesus Christ, truly God and truly man, as the unique Savior of the world. Christ crucified, risen, interceding, and returning forms the center of their faith and doctrine. They believe that salvation is through grace alone, by faith alone, as revealed in Scripture alone. This is the everlasting gospel, which, according to the three angel's messages in Revelation 14, must be made known to all nations, tribes, and peoples. Adventists accept the entire Bible as the Word of the living God, and they hold the Scriptures to be the authentic record of the creation of the world, of the first human beings, of their fall and its terrible results, and of God's dealings with humanity in history.

Among biblical doctrines held by Adventists, though not exclusively, is the doctrine of the great controversy. Behind the struggle between good and evil in the world, the Bible reveals a conflict of cosmic dimensions between rebellious angels, led by Satan, and the Godhead. The central issue in the controversy is the character and law of God. Satan, once an exalted angel in heaven, impeached God's character and government as selfish and tyrannical. He incited other angels to join him in his rebellion and also successfully tempted the first human beings to sin. Christ's incarnation, life of selfless service, and sacrificial death on the cross proved Satan's accusations to be false. They also constitute the divine provision for the salvation of the human race.

In common with the mainstream Christian tradition, Adventists believe the law of God, the Ten Commandments, to be binding upon all humanity. Consequently, they also believe that the fourth commandment—to keep holy the seventh day of the week, which is Saturday, not Sunday—remains the God-ordained day of rest for the whole human family. In this their religious practice differs from many other Christians. Basic Adventist beliefs are summed up in the statement "Fundamental Beliefs of Seventh-day Adventists," which is published in each *Yearbook of Seventh-day Adventists.*

MORAL CODE OF CONDUCT While Adventists accept the Ten Commandments as God's moral code for all humanity, they firmly believe that salvation is not earned through keeping the law, which is legalism, but only received through grace. They also believe, however, that faith in Christ results in the desire and will to obey God's law. Grace does not abrogate the law, which is the doctrine of antinomianism. Jesus in his life on earth fulfilled the law perfectly and taught that whoever loves him will obey God's commandments. In fact, only genuine love for God and neighbor fulfills the law.

Adventists recognize that there are distinctions in Scripture between eternal principles and temporary laws, but they hold that God's moral principles are binding upon human beings in all ages and cultures. They see the moral law as an expression of God's character, fully exemplified in the life of Christ and unchangeable, because God's character and will do not change. Any human laws or traditions that are in conflict with God's law or are substituted for God's commandments are condemned by Christ and should be rejected by his followers.

SACRED BOOKS The Scriptures are held by Adventists to be the sacred oracles of God. While aware that some changes may have occurred in the transmission of the original text, they believe that the whole Bible is the God-given standard by which all other writings and teachings should be judged. Adventists also accept the writings of Ellen White as having been given through the spirit of prophecy, but as she herself insisted, they are to be held subject to the Scriptures.

SACRED SYMBOLS For Adventists, as for many Christians, the cross is the major symbol of their faith in Christ. It symbolizes Christ's death on the cross for the sins of humans and also the life of self-denial to which he calls his followers. Another symbol, unique to Adventists, is that of three flying angels, derived from the angel's messages in Revelation 14. Adventists apply this symbol to their church in the humble conviction that they have been called to proclaim these messages as God's final call to faith and repentance before Christ's Second Coming.

EARLY AND MODERN LEADERS Adventists refer to the early leaders of the church as pioneers. Prominent among them were James Springer White (1821–81), his wife Ellen Gould (Harmon) White (1827–1915), and Joseph Bates (1792–1872). Of the three Ellen White is best known among Adventists because of her multifaceted ministry and influence during the first 70 years of the church's history. Her writings have been, and still are, a major factor in the growth of the church and its diverse ministries, in leading thousands of people to Christ, in encouraging a thorough study of the Scriptures, and in fostering a deeper relationship with God.

Many capable leaders have served the Adventist Church during the 140 years of its organized existence. Brief biographies of these men and women are given in the *Seventh-day Adventist Encyclopedia.*

MAJOR THEOLOGIANS AND AUTHORS Since the establishment of the first theological seminary in 1934, Adventists have increasingly stressed the importance of theological study. Today qualified theologians staff Adventist seminaries and college departments of religion around the world. Few of them have world renown, but many have made significant contributions to theological scholarship.

ORGANIZATIONAL STRUCTURE There are five levels of organization in the world Adventist Church. First are local churches, of which there are more than 51,000. Next are conferences or missions, made up of local

A poster advertises a visit to London by an American Seventh-day Adventist preacher. Evangelism and missions have played a prominent role in Adventist history. © HULTON-DEUTSCH COLLECTION/CORBIS.

churches in a defined geographical area, of which there are more than 500. There are 94 union conferences or union missions, made up of conferences and missions. Fourth are the 12 world divisions that coordinate the work in a number of unions. Finally, there is the General Conference, which is the main governing body of the world church. Leaders at every level of organization are elected for specified periods of time by representatives at regular sessions of the respective organizations. General Conference sessions are held every five years.

HOUSES OF WORSHIP AND HOLY PLACES Adventist church buildings range from large modern structures to small jungle chapels. With a rapidly growing membership, especially in parts of Latin America, Africa, and Asia, there is a great need for houses of worship. Many are built by volunteers. Simplicity characterizes most Adventist churches.

WHAT IS SACRED? Adventists believe that only God can make or declare something sacred or holy. Although human beings cannot make anything holy, they are

Seventh-day Adventist: What's in a Name?

When the early Advent believers decided to organize as a church, they had to choose a name. Different names were suggested, but the choice became clear. It would be Seventh-day Adventist. The name succinctly expressed, and still expresses, the faith. They are called "Adventist" because they live in the expectation that Christ, the crucified and risen Savior, will soon return to give eternal life to all who believe in him. They are called "Seventh-day" because they accept the seventh day of the week, the Sabbath, as the day of the Lord, the memorial of creation, and the sign of salvation. Thus, the name sums up God's intention for Christ's followers as "those who keep the commandments of God and the faith of Jesus" (Revelation 14:12).

called upon to keep holy what God has made sacred. For this reason Adventists keep the Sabbath holy and receive the Bible as God's sacred book.

HOLIDAYS AND FESTIVALS For Adventists worldwide the Sabbath is the weekly recurring festival of joyful worship and fellowship. There are no other prescribed religious festivals.

MODE OF DRESS Simplicity, modesty, true beauty, and cultural appropriateness are considered to be the guiding principles by Adventists not only for the way they dress but also for their total manner of life. Their aim is to follow the example of the Lord.

DIETARY PRACTICES Adventists believe that God is greatly interested in the well-being of his human children, and they accept the biblical laws on health as still valid. Consequently, Adventists abstain from all harmful substances, including addictive drugs, alcohol, and tobacco. They promote a vegetarian diet as God's ideal for humanity.

RITUALS Like most Protestants, Adventists practice the Christ-ordained rites of baptism and Communion. Baptism is by immersion on a profession of faith in Christ. Infants are dedicated to God but are not baptized. The Communion service is preceded by the mutual washing of feet, following Christ's example and command.

RITES OF PASSAGE There are no rites of passage that are distinctive to the Adventist Church.

MEMBERSHIP Adventists fully accept the command of Jesus to preach the everlasting gospel and to make disciples of all nations. Consequently, evangelism and missions have played a prominent role in Adventist history. Through public and personal evangelism, through the printed page, via radio and television, and in contemporary times via satellite and the Internet, the gospel and the message of Christ's Second Coming are broadcast around the world. Since the 1960s mission institutes have prepared thousands for cross-cultural ministries. Supportive lay ministries, such as Maranatha Volunteers International and Adventist Frontier Missions, complement the worldwide missionary outreach of the church. Global Mission, a contemporary initiative, focuses on taking the Adventist message to formerly unreached groups.

RELIGIOUS TOLERANCE For more than a century Adventists have been in the forefront of upholding and defending religious liberty for all human beings. Since 1906 the Church has promoted principles of religious liberty through the publication of *Liberty: A Magazine of Religious Freedom*. In cooperation with other religious organizations and several governments, Seventh-day Adventists have also sponsored international conferences on religious liberty. Adventists understand religious liberty to be more comprehensive than religious tolerance.

SOCIAL JUSTICE Adventists believe that the most powerful liberating force in the world is the gospel of Jesus Christ. At the same time, however, through development projects, literacy programs, medical care, and education, Adventists endeavor to break the shackles of poverty, ignorance, sickness, and social degradation.

SOCIAL ASPECTS Adventists believe in marriage between one man and one woman, as ordained by God at creation. On the basis of the Bible, they hold all sexual relationships outside a monogamous marriage to be in conflict with God's express command. They consider solid Christian homes as essential for the prosperity of both the church and society.

CONTROVERSIAL ISSUES The Adventist Church believes that, as a result of sin and its consequences, the world is imperfect. There are, therefore, no easy answers to such issues as abortion, birth control, and divorce. A number of controversial issues are addressed from an Adventist perspective in the book *Statements, Guidelines, and Other Documents: A Compilation.*

CULTURAL IMPACT Adventists foster a variety of arts in their homes and educational institutions, music probably taking pride of place. Adventist choirs and soloists have performed on many prominent occasions. In addition, the works of Adventist writers, painters, and sculptors have met with wide appreciation and professional recognition.

Peter M. van Bemmelen

See Also Vol. I: *Christianity*

Bibliography

Adventist Television Network. 16 Jan. 2004. www.adventist.tv.

Dabrowski, Ray, ed. *Statements, Guidelines and Other Documents: A Compilation.* 2nd ed. Silver Spring, Md.: General Conference of Seventh-day Adventists, 2000.

Dederen, Raoul, ed. *Handbook of Seventh-day Adventist Theology.* Hagerstown, Md.: Review and Herald Publishing Association, 2000.

Neufeld, Don F., ed. *Seventh-day Adventist Encyclopedia.* 2nd rev. ed. 2 vols. Hagerstown, Md.: Review and Herald Publishing Association, 1996.

Seventh-day Adventist Church. 16 Jan. 2004. www.adventist.org.

Seventh-day Adventist Yearbook. Silver Spring, Md.: General Conference of Seventh-day Adventists.

Unitarianism and Universalism

FOUNDED: 1565 C.E. (Unitarianism) and 1723 C.E. (Universalism)

RELIGION AS A PERCENTAGE OF WORLD POPULATION: 0.005 percent

OVERVIEW Unitarianism and Universalism began as independent traditions emerging from the liberal Protestant Reformation period of the Christian faith. Unitarianism was founded on the belief that God is one and that Jesus was not of the same substance as God (as opposed to the orthodox Trinitarian view). Universalism's defining belief was universal salvation: A loving God would not condemn his children to eternal suffering. Distinct Unitarian and Universalist communities around the world share a common commitment to the belief that individuals must find answers to the great questions of human existence for themselves through the use of reason rather than blindly accepting dogma or unexamined tradition. Over time the two traditions became more similar theologically, and in 1961 they merged in North America to form the Unitarian Universalist Association. Outside the United States, older organizations in this tradition are identified as Unitarian, while more recently established ones are typically Unitarian Universalist. As a global organization, the International Council of Unitarians and Universalists connects the various national and regional bodies but has no ecclesiological authority over them.

HISTORY Unitarian and Universalist beliefs existed within the early Christian Church but were declared heretical (often by narrow votes) at church councils in the 300s–500s C.E. Since that time Unitarian and Universalist beliefs have reemerged repeatedly as Christianity has spread throughout the world. For the most part these movements have been independent and indigenous and not the result of missionary activity.

The oldest continuous thread of these traditions emerged early in the Reformation. Spaniard Miguel Servetus published *On the Error of the Trinity* in 1531, was convicted of heresy by both the Catholic and Reformed churches, and was burned at the stake in Geneva in 1553. The Minor Reformed Church of Poland was the first organized body founded (1565) on Unitarian theology. The first body to use the name Unitarian emerged in Transylvania through the preaching of Ferenc Dávid (1510–79). The Italian Faustus Socinus (1539–1604), from whom the Polish Socinians took their name, had a profound influence on the emerging Unitarianism in both Poland and Transylvania.

Unitarianism in Great Britain began with the writings of John Biddle in the mid-1600s but did not organize until Theophilus Lindsay began the first Unitarian church in England in 1774 (though the Dissenting Presbyterians, who were Unitarian in theology, began in the early 1700s).

The English minister Joseph Priestley influenced the early development of Unitarianism in North America, but it is a primarily indigenous movement. Although some churches calling themselves Unitarian predate it, organized American Unitarianism began as a schism

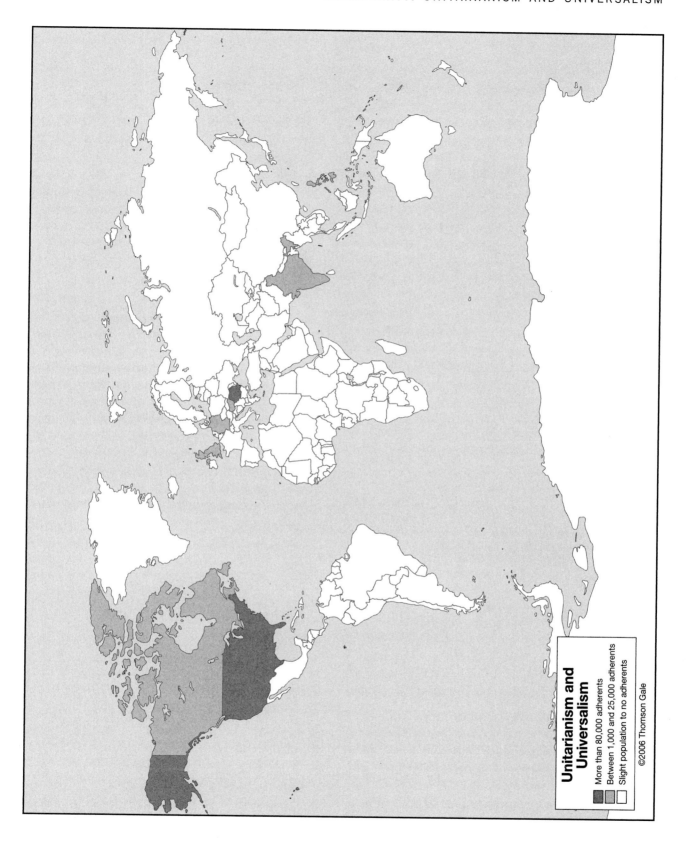

Unitarianism and
Universalism

More than 80,000 adherents

Between 1,000 and 25,000 adherents

Slight population to no adherents

©2006 Thomson Gale

The interior of a Unitarian meetinghouse designed by Victor Lundy in Hartford, Connecticut. Unitarian Universalist houses of worship vary tremendously, from the stark white clapboards of a New England meetinghouse, to the churches designed by Unitarian Frank Lloyd Wright, to ultramodern structures of glass and steel. © G.E. KIDDER SMITH/CORBIS.

within the New England Congregational tradition. The corporate birth of Unitarianism in the United States occurred in 1819, when minister William Ellery Channing delivered a sermon that changed the label of "Unitarian" from a theological slur to the name of a distinct religious movement. The American Unitarian Association began in 1825.

Unitarianism in Canada, Australia, and New Zealand is primarily the result of immigration. It was introduced to northern Europe by natives who were exposed to it in the United States.

Universalism began in England in the early 1700s but was carried to North America by such ministers as John Murray and George de Benneville. Circuit-riding preachers carried its teachings out of New England and into the Midwest. The forerunner of the American Universalist Church was organized in 1833.

Unitarianism and Universalism in North America had a long history of contact and cooperation and discussed a merger in 1899 and 1931. In 1961 the Unitarian Universalist Association was formed. While UU churches are found in every U.S. state, they are much more prevalent in New England. There are more Unitarian Universalists (160,000) in the United States than in any other country in the world.

The presence of Unitarian Universalism in other parts of the world is small but continuing. Only in Japan is it the result of missionary outreach. The UU communities of South Africa, the Philippines, India, and Pakistan, as well as a few small communities in South America, developed their own indigenous UU theologies and then later discovered and affiliated with the larger UU world. In India, Unitarians are concentrated in two pockets: in the southwest around Madras and in the Khasi Hills area of the northeastern state of Meghalaya. All of the UU churches in the Philippines are located on the island of Negros. The country with the largest percentage of its population belonging to a Unitarian or Universalist church is Romania, at 0.4 percent.

CENTRAL DOCTRINES It is difficult to generalize the central doctrines of Unitarian Universalists (UUs) worldwide. Some national UU groups have formal creeds and catechisms to which all members must subscribe. Others, especially in North America, pride themselves on being a noncreedal church. Historian Earl Morse Wilbur wrote that the three primary principles of Unitarianism are freedom, reason, and tolerance. Other than a common historical root, what UUs primarily share is a commitment to the notion that the individual conscience is the ultimate arbiter of religious truth. Theologian James Luther Adams used the phrase "prophethood of all believers" to describe the notion that revelation is never sealed and that each individual is capable of unique religious insight.

Of the various strands of Unitarianism, that of Transylvania has maintained the strongest connection to its Christian roots. In the theology of this tradition the purpose of religion is this-worldly, to improve humanity's lot here and now rather than focusing on the afterlife. The Bible is a guidebook for living. Jesus is not God; it is his humanity that is celebrated. Jesus is seen as a leader, an ethical role model, and a teacher rather than as a savior. The Lord's Supper is not a sacrament but is a symbolic expression of the congregation's commitment to imitating his life.

Modern Unitarian Universalism in Western countries has been described as post-Christian. A shift toward a more naturalist and humanist theology began with the transcendentalists, such as Ralph Waldo Emerson and Henry David Thoreau, in the mid-1800s and continued through the rise of religious humanism in the 1920s and 1930s. While in recent years an interest in greater spirituality and a growing identification with neopagan and Buddhist traditions have occurred, surveys have shown that humanism is still a dominant view among U.S. and Canadian UUs.

During its history American UUism has undergone a shifting theological landscape, which has caused it to

A Unitarian demonstrates against World War II in 1944. Like other traditions of liberal Christian origin, many Unitarian Universalists have been involved in antiwar efforts regarding every modern American armed conflict. © BETTMANN/CORBIS.

experience repeated crises of identity. The question of what UUs hold in common that binds them together arises periodically.

MORAL CODE OF CONDUCT The application of theological ideals to issues of daily life has always been an important part of the Unitarian and Universalist traditions. The early Unitarians in Eastern Europe stressed that individuals should attempt to live the ethics of Jesus. The English and American Unitarians of the Enlightenment had a similar emphasis.

The so-called Jefferson Bible provides a good example of this emphasis on morality. While Thomas Jefferson was never a Unitarian by affiliation, he referred to himself as Unitarian in his writings several times, and he "took scissors and paste to the Gospels" only because his friend Joseph Priestley (a Unitarian minister) died before producing a revision of the story of Jesus. Jefferson was interested primarily in the morals of Jesus and how they should be put into practice in one's life. The activism of many UU individuals and communities, as seen in their involvement in issues of social justice and welfare, is an outcome of this view—that religious faith is lived through deeds, not creeds.

Over the centuries Unitarians and Universalists have produced many catechisms, statements of agreement, and other corporate theological documents. The morality of behavior has been a core issue in each of these. The current "Principles and Purposes" of the Unitarian Universalist Association in the United States, for example, includes foundational principles that are relevant to interpersonal relationships; acceptance of and compassion toward others; the primacy of the individual conscience; the value of a democratic society; war, peace, and justice in a global context; and ecological and environmental issues.

The last issue is of particular importance to many UUs around the world: the vision of humanity as only one part of an interdependent web of environmental connections has grown in importance. The burgeoning interest in nature-based, neopagan religious traditions in part reflects this perception of human being's place in the world.

SACRED BOOKS Because Unitarian Universalism is a faith with Christian roots, many Unitarian Universalists consider the Bible to be a sacred, albeit not inerrant, text. Reasoned interpretation of the Scriptures was one of the defining characteristics of the early European Unitarians. In many UU congregations the sacred writings of all religions are respected and included in worship services, as are modern prose and poetry.

SACRED SYMBOLS Unitarian Universalists throughout the world attach varying significance to the Christian cross. A variety of world religious symbols can be found in many UU congregations. The nearest thing to a uniquely, universal UU symbol would be the flaming chalice symbol adopted by the Unitarian Service Committee during its World War II relief efforts in Europe. The use of this symbol has spread informally, and it is now common in several countries.

EARLY AND MODERN LEADERS Important international Unitarian figures include Brock Chisholm, first executive secretary of the World Health Organization; Irish poet and nationalist William Drennan; and Cana-

dian inventor Alexander Graham Bell. In the United States important historical Unitarians and Universalists include several Revolutionary War figures (Thomas Paine, Ethan Allen, Paul Revere, and Benjamin Franklin); Presidents John Adams, John Quincy Adams, Millard Fillmore, and William Howard Taft; diplomat Adlai Stevenson; Nobel Peace Prize winners Emily Greene Balch and Linus Pauling; inventor Lewis Lattimer; engineer and architect Buckminster Fuller; Urban League founder Whitney Young; and the Reverend James Reeb, who was killed while participating in Martin Luther King's march on Selma. Contemporary American UUs include two former secretaries of defense (William Perry and William Cohen), *Columbia* astronaut Laurel Clark, and actor Christopher Reeve.

MAJOR THEOLOGIANS AND AUTHORS In addition to the early founders, notably Ferenc Dávid and Faustus Socinus, other early influences on Unitarian theology include William Ellery Channing, Ralph Waldo Emerson, and Theodore Parker. Important Unitarian theologians of the twentieth century include James Luther Adams, Charles Hartshorne, and Henry Nelson Wieman. On the Universalist side Theophilus Lindsay, Hosea Ballou, and Clarence Skinner were influential theologians. Important contemporary theological work is being produced by Thandeka, Forrest Church, Sharon Welch, and Paul Rasor.

ORGANIZATIONAL STRUCTURE National and regional Unitarian Universalist bodies vary tremendously in their structure. Eastern European Unitarian groups, such as the Transylvanian church in Romania with its elected bishop, tend toward a more ecclesiastical structure. UUs in the United States, on the other hand, trace their lineage in part to the Pilgrim churches of early New England and so have a strong tradition of congregational polity, rooted in the Cambridge Platform of 1648. In 1994 the International Council of Unitarians and Universalists was formed to help connect the various strands of the faith.

HOUSES OF WORSHIP AND HOLY PLACES Unitarian Universalist houses of worship vary tremendously, from the stark white clapboards of a New England meetinghouse, to the churches designed by Unitarian Frank Lloyd Wright, to ultramodern structures of glass and steel. Some smaller groups may meet in a rented space or a private home. While "holy" may not be an appropriate word, important places typically are associated with significant historical events and people, such as the prison in Romania where Ferenc Dávid was held and died.

WHAT IS SACRED? For most Unitarian Universalists all of existence is sacred. The natural world is holy, and the preservation of it is considered by many to be a religious duty. Specific objects are not sacred in the sense that they are especially sanctified or possessing of special or magical qualities. Even the bread and wine of the Communion, where it is still celebrated, are valued for their symbolic nature.

HOLIDAYS AND FESTIVALS Most UU congregations, even ones that are humanistic in approach, tend to commemorate the Christian holidays of Christmas and Easter. Some also commemorate holidays and festivals of other religious traditions. There are no universally held, uniquely Unitarian or Universalist holidays. The closest would be the Flower Ceremony, originally created by Czech Unitarian minister Norbert Capek for his Prague congregation during the 1930s. Each attendee is asked to bring a flower to the ceremony, which is usually held in the spring but not on any specific date. These flowers are combined into large bouquets and blessed, after which each individual leaves the ceremony with a different flower than the one he or she contributed. The flowers celebrate the community of the congregation and the contribution made by each person.

MODE OF DRESS Unitarian Universalists generally are embedded in their local culture. There are no special modes of dress that set UUs apart. Congregational expectations concerning formality of dress vary greatly. In some churches ministers wear robes, at least on special occasions, and in others they never do.

DIETARY PRACTICES Unitarian Universalists tend to follow the dietary customs of their culture. Among North American and European UUs there is a greater proportion of vegetarians than in the general population, but this is for individual reasons and is not a tenet of the organized faith.

RITUALS Regular worship services are most commonly held on Sunday mornings and typically follow the Protestant format of readings, hymns, and prayers surrounding a sermon. The content of the readings and hymns varies greatly, especially in terms of the degree of Christian content. In some congregations the Bible may be the referent for the entire service. In others biblical references may only be heard around Christian holidays.

In North America and western Europe, where humanism and theological diversity mix, prayer is highly individualistic, depending on personal theology, and congregational prayer typically is couched in sufficiently general terms as to cover a range of forms. Some congregations have more specific prayer practices, but this is not typical. Among eastern European churches, where a liberal Christian theology prevails, prayer is more theistically centered, and the Lord's Prayer is always part of congregational worship.

Wedding and funeral rituals follow a similar dichotomy: In countries where liberal Christianity has been maintained, the wedding and funeral ceremonies are more traditional, in the Protestant mold. In other regions, such as North America, weddings are highly individualized and based on the wishes and preferences of the couple. Among UUs in Western countries weddings of same-sex couples are common, and in fact UU ministers often are called upon to perform services of union for non-UU same-sex couples. Among American UUs religious rituals immediately following a death are often limited to family and close friends. Cremation is common, and a memorial service for the community is often held at a later time.

RITES OF PASSAGE The rites of passage celebrated by Unitarian Universalists are similar to those of other traditions emerging from Protestantism. Naming ceremonies are held for infants. A confirmation or coming-of-age ceremony is commonly held for young teens. In North America the term "bridging" refers to a ceremony in recognition of the passage from youth to adulthood and is often associated with graduation from high school.

MEMBERSHIP Unitarian Universalism is generally a faith of converts. In North America several surveys in the 1980s and 1990s found that only about 10 percent of members are raised in the faith. Evangelism and outreach activities are focused on attracting people who already hold UU views as opposed to changing people's beliefs. Corporate social justice work provides a means by which others can see the faith lived. Media like TV and radio are sometimes used for advertising or local broadcast of services, and North American UUs use the

Evolution of a Unitarian Martyr

Ferenc Dávid was born in Transylvania in 1510. After becoming a Catholic priest, Dávid became the minister of a Lutheran church in 1553, and by 1557 he was bishop of the Transylvanian Lutherans. He later decided that John Calvin's views were more consistent with Scripture than Martin Luther's, and by 1564 he was serving as Transylvanian bishop of the Reformed Church. In 1564 Dávid began to question the truth of the Trinity. His notoriety as a preacher brought him to the attention of King John Sigismund.

By 1566 Dávid was preaching openly against the Trinity, and his views began to spread to other churches. In 1568 he became the first Unitarian bishop. In 1571 the king granted the Unitarians the same legal rights as Catholics, Lutherans, and Calvinists and named Dávid the official court preacher.

Following John Sigismund's death later in 1571, a more conservative king was crowned at the same time that Dávid's theology was becoming more liberal. Dávid was found guilty of religious innovation and imprisoned, dying on 15 November 1579. By the time of Dávid's death there were 300 Hungarian-speaking Unitarian churches.

Internet extensively for both outreach and internal communication. In other parts of the world, especially eastern Europe, Unitarianism is more of a cultural church, and conversion is less of a factor in its growth.

RELIGIOUS TOLERANCE The tradition's support for religious tolerance dates from 1563, when John Sigismund, Unitarian king of Transylvania, signed the Edict of Torda, giving equal religious freedom to the Catholic, Reformed, Lutheran, and Unitarian faiths in his kingdom. Unitarians were among the organizers of the World's Parliaments of Religions and the International Association for Religious Freedom. In North America, UU congregations and ministers commonly are in-

volved in interfaith efforts and organizations to the extent to which they are welcomed by the dominant Christian faiths. Groups for UUs who identify with Christianity, Buddhism, Judaism, humanism, and pagan traditions have been organized and have chapters in many local congregations.

SOCIAL JUSTICE In Great Britain and North America, Unitarian Universalists have been leaders in every major social justice movement. Many vocal and active proponents of the abolition of slavery, mental health and prison reform, poverty relief, child labor reform, and reproductive rights have been UUs. Like other traditions of liberal Christian origin, many UUs have been involved in peace movements and antiwar efforts regarding every modern American armed conflict. On the issue of women's rights and suffrage, Unitarians were in the forefront in North America, Great Britain, Australia, and the Scandinavian countries. In recent years the rights of gay, lesbian, bisexual, and transgender persons have been a major focus for North American UUs.

SOCIAL ASPECTS The social attitudes of Unitarian Universalists depend in part on their cultural context. As a movement, North American UUism has embraced a broad and liberal definition of "family," and UU congregations generally are welcoming of multicultural, single-parent, and same-sex families. Globally, UUs tend to hold attitudes toward family issues that are progressive relative to the surrounding culture.

CONTROVERSIAL ISSUES Religious liberalism is commonly (but not universally) associated with political liberalism. Especially in the United States, Unitarian Universalists are involved in liberal movements, such as support for reproductive rights, drug policy and prison reform, death with dignity, elimination of the death penalty, and civil rights for sexual minorities. Universalist Olympia Brown was the first woman ordained by an American religious organization (1864), and Unitarian Martha Turner was the first woman minister in Australia (1874). Women now outnumber men in the UU ministry in North America.

CULTURAL IMPACT Unitarians and Universalists have had a disproportionate impact on culture and society, especially in the fields of science and literature. In England the scientists Isaac Newton and Charles Darwin and authors Charles Dickens and Mary Shelley, among others, altered humanity's view of itself and its place in the universe. In the United States the intellectual climate of the 1800s was influenced by Unitarian writers and lecturers, such as Walt Whitman, Louisa May Alcott, and especially the transcendentalists, including Ralph Waldo Emerson, Henry David Thoreau, and Margaret Fuller. More recently Unitarian Universalists—for example, cognitive scientist Herbert Simon; Tim Berners-Lee, inventor of the World Wide Web; essayist and retired UU minister Robert Fulghum; writers Beatrix Potter, Edwin Markham, James Michener, Ray Bradbury, Carl Sandburg, E.E. Cummings, and Kurt Vonnegut; musicians Pete Seeger and Malvina Reynolds; TV producer Rod Serling; and actor-producer Paul Newman—have continued this tradition. Internationally, culturally influential UUs include Hungarian composer Béla Bartók, Bengali poet Rabindranath Tagore, and Canadian painter Arthur Lismer.

James Casebolt

See Also Vol. 1: *Christianity*

Bibliography

Buehrens, John A., and Forrest Church. *A Chosen Faith.* Boston: Beacon Press, 1998.

Bumbaugh, David E. *Unitarian Universalism: A Narrative History.* Chicago: Meadville Lombard, 2000.

Hill, Andrew M., Jill K. McAllister, and Clifford M. Reed. *A Global Conversation: Unitarian/Universalism at the Dawn of the 21st Century.* Prague: International Council of Unitarians and Universalists, 2002.

McEvoy, Don. *Credo: Unitarians and Universalists of Yesteryear Talk about Their Lives and Motivations.* Rancho Santa Fe, Calif.: Lowell Publishing, 2001.

———. *Credo International: Voices of Religious Liberalism from around the World.* Del Mar, Calif.: Humanunity Press, 2002.

Parke, David B., ed. *The Epic of Unitarianism.* Boston: Skinner House, 1985.

Robinson, David. *Unitarians and Universalists.* Westport, Conn.: Greenwood, 1985.

Wilbur, Earl M. *A History of Unitarianism in Transylvania, England, and America.* Boston: Beacon Press, 1952.

Williams, George H. *American Universalism.* 4th ed. Boston: Skinner House, 2002.

Christianity

United Church of Christ

FOUNDED: 1957 C.E.

RELIGION AS A PERCENTAGE OF WORLD POPULATION: .02 percent

OVERVIEW The United Church of Christ (UCC), founded in the United States in 1957, was the product of four preexisting religious groups: the Congregational Church, the Christian Churches (or Christian Connexion), the German Reformed Church, and the German Evangelical Church. With common commitments to Christian unity and theological openness, these groups went through several mergers prior to the 1957 creation of the United Church of Christ. The UCC is recognized as one of the most theologically and socially progressive of the mainline American Protestant denominations.

With membership only in the United States (with the exception of four congregations in Canada that are part of the church's North Dakota Conference), the UCC is not a global church. It is, however, one of several merged Christian communions internationally that share the name "United Church."

HISTORY Congregationalism, the largest and oldest of the UCC's member traditions, arose in the late 1500s as a protest against the Church of England (Anglican Church). The Pilgrims, who advocated total separation from the Church of England, and the Puritans, a larger and more influential group who hoped to change and purify the church, migrated to New England in the early seventeenth century. They established independent local congregations of believers (from which the name "Congregationalist" derives), which, rather than a national or regional body, defined the "true church." Both Congregational groups adapted Genevan reformer John Calvin's ideas to the American environment and considered religious homogeneity in church and community essential.

The Christian Churches, the UCC's smallest and only indigenous strain, emerged in the early 1800s as a diverse, bible-based fellowship. Arriving at similar conclusions about the nature of church and faith, defectors from three groups—Baptists in New England, Methodists in Virginia, and Presbyterians in Kentucky—gathered in small churches in the early 1800s in rural and frontier America. Eschewing creeds, confessions, and the formalities of both church life and traditional theology, they accepted the Bible as their sole authority, rejected sectarianism, and insisted that right action, rather than right belief, was the most important factor in a Christian's life. Members embraced theological positions ranging from unitarian to evangelical. In 1931, drawn together by common commitments to church unity and theological openness, the General Convention of Christian Churches merged with the National Council of Congregational Churches, becoming the Congregational Christian Churches.

The German Reformed came to the American East and Midwest in two separate migrations in the eighteenth and nineteenth centuries to escape war, poverty, and social unrest in their homeland. Theologically similar to Congregationalists, the Reformed differed in their understanding of "church" as an aggregate, unified by

266

Worldmark Encyclopedia of Religious Practices

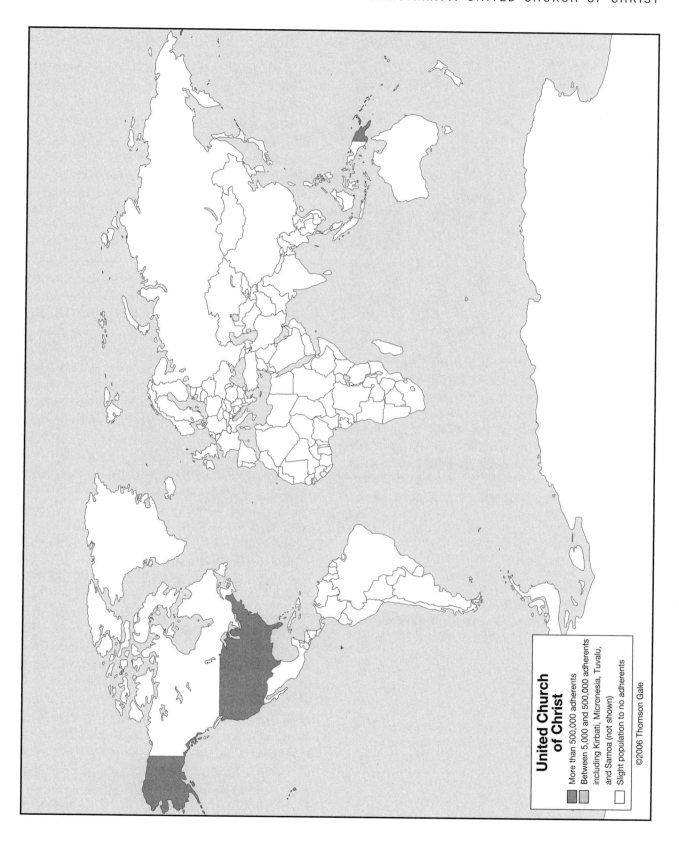

United Church
of Christ

More than 500,000 adherents

Between 5,000 and 500,000 adherents
including Kirbati, Micronesia, Tuvalu,
and Samoa (not shown)

Slight population to no adherents

©2006 Thomson Gale

The United Church of Christ (UCC) in Coral Gables, Florida. The UCC, founded in 1957, is one of the most theologically and socially progressive of the mainline American Protestant churches. © MORTON BEEBE/CORBIS.

common worship and polity, rather than as a group of individual congregations. The UCC's second largest tradition, the German Reformed also had an ecumenical bent.

The German Evangelicals, forming the youngest UCC tradition, began migrating to Illinois and Missouri in the 1830s. Independent, open-minded, and often indifferent to doctrinal particularities, they stood for the tradition of "unionistic" Protestantism that had flourished in their homeland. In the United States they were influenced not only by their isolation on the frontier but also by Swiss missionaries who emphasized the importance of religious experience over theology. Strong ecumenical commitments and ties of history and ethnicity led the German Reformed Church to unite with the General Convention of the Evangelical Synod in 1934, becoming the Evangelical and Reformed Church.

Recognizing similarities in their history, theology, and social commitments, leaders of these two larger bodies—the Congregational Christian Churches and the Evangelical and Reformed Church—began informal conversations in 1937. Questions over independence, authority, and legality postponed the union until 1957, when they became the United Church of Christ.

CENTRAL DOCTRINES The heritage of the United Church of Christ is essentially orthodox: Most adherents believe in the Trinity (the unity of Father, Son, and Holy Spirit), claim as their own the ancient creeds and reformulations of the Protestant Reformation, rely on the Bible as the religious authority, and recognize the two sacraments of baptism and Communion. Within that orthodoxy, theological perspectives vary from evangelical to liberal, though the latter dominates. The original and continuing need to mediate differences among the four constituent traditions necessitates theological openness. The UCC is known for its diversity, and most members agree with a saying common among Protestant humanists in the sixteenth century: "In essentials, unity; in non-essentials, liberty; in all things, charity."

Perspectives about the nature of the church also vary, but members generally agree that the UCC is founded on the Bible, the writings of the Protestant reformers, and the inspired understandings of each new generation. In believing that Jesus Christ is the sole head of the church, they affirm that all human leadership is radically equal and that all members share a common Christian experience and a responsibility for the church's mission in the world. The church has four basic purposes: to proclaim the gospel through Scripture, sacrament, and witness; to gather and support communities of the faithful for celebration and mission; to manifest more fully the unity of church, humankind, and creation; and to work to further God's realm of justice, peace, and love.

MORAL CODE OF CONDUCT Though the Ten Commandments are part of its foundation, the UCC insists on no "black and white" moral or ethical codes. UCC members are expected—but never directed—to behave out of obedience to God, love for neighbor, and respect for self, as specific situations demand. The church respects the right of private judgment in these situations and the need to allow for changing historical and cultural circumstances.

SACRED BOOKS Like other mainline Protestant denominations, the UCC sees the Bible as the foremost and final revelation of God's word. Members do not understand it literally, however, as a rulebook for Christian conduct or an accurate historical record but as the dramatic story of God's grace, God's people, and God's mercy and admonishment through the ages. Members believe that the Bible, though divinely inspired, was written by human beings for a variety of purposes and audiences and that its primary purpose is to reveal God's plan for the world and bring people to God's redeeming love. Faithful interpretation requires an awareness of the particular contexts that influenced and limited the Bible's writers, as well as a knowledge of contemporary realities.

SACRED SYMBOLS The UCC inherited from the Swiss Reformation a general opposition to venerating religious images, and in its early history the UCC insisted on a simplicity of pulpit, font, and communion table. The nineteenth and twentieth centuries, however, saw an increasing use of visual symbolism. Some UCC members wear crosses as symbols of their faith and their fidelity to Christ, and most church sanctuaries include an altar cross, but these are not venerated or treated with ritual care.

EARLY AND MODERN LEADERS The UCC's Congregational tradition has provided the greatest number of famous historical figures, including John Winthrop (1588–1649), lay leader and first governor of Massachusetts Bay Colony; Richard Mather (1596–1669), Increase Mather (1639–1723), and Cotton Mather (1663–1728), architects and historians of the "New England way," emphasizing the independence of local churches and the church community as a way of life; and Washington Gladden (1836–1918), pastor and pioneer of the Social Gospel movement. In 1853 Antoinette Brown Blackwell (1825–1921) became the first Congregationalist woman to be ordained.

Revivalist Charles Grandison Finney (1792–1875), associated with both the Presbyterian and Congregational churches, helped introduce Arminian theology into the solidly Calvinist Congregational tradition. (Arminius's doctrines opposed the absolute predestination of strict Calvinism and maintained the possibility of salvation for all.) Finney later became president of Oberlin College. Among other UCC leaders were Elias Smith (1764–1846) and Abner Jones, the publishers of

A caretaker stands inside the First United Church of Providence in Providence, Rhode Island. UCC houses of worship range from the simple to the ornate, but the trend in new churches is toward multipurpose buildings with flexible space for worship and other activities. © BOB ROWAN; PROGRESSIVE IMAGE/CORBIS.

the first religious newspaper in the Christian tradition, the *Herald of Gospel Liberty,* and such civil rights activists as Andrew Young (b. 1932) and Benjamin Chavis (b. 1948).

MAJOR THEOLOGIANS AND AUTHORS The denomination's most famous theologian is Jonathan Edwards (1703–58), a Congregationalist and major figure in the "Great Awakening" revivalist movement of the 1740s. From the Reformed tradition, John Williamson Nevin (1803–86) and Philip Schaff (1819–93) helped shape the path of ecumenical progress in the mid-nineteenth century. German evangelicals and brothers Reinhold Niebuhr (1892–1971) and H. Richard Niebuhr (1894–1962) were internationally prominent twentieth-century theologians who helped articulate a scripture-based movement that became known as neo-orthodoxy.

Prominent figures in today's church include systematic theologian and ecumenist Gabriel Fackre; former seminary president and church history professor Barbara Brown Zikmund, an expert on theological education and women's issues; ethicist Max Stackhouse; and John Thomas, general minister and president of the denomination and a noted promoter of Christian unity.

ORGANIZATIONAL STRUCTURE The UCC's government contains both autonomous and cooperative elements. Local churches are independent but are grouped in associations, which have responsibilities for ordaining, installing, and disciplining pastors; for receiving (and dismissing) churches; and for caring generally for the welfare of local congregations in the area. Associations are subunits of larger conferences, which provide services, counsel, venues for common mission, and administrative support to churches and associations. The general synod, the national representative body, issues pronouncements and sets priorities for the denomination but speaks "to, not for" the churches.

HOUSES OF WORSHIP AND HOLY PLACES UCC houses of worship range from simple white clapboard buildings—the familiar "New England meeting-house"—to the substantial stone and stained-glass churches of Pennsylvania and other regions. The trend for new churches is to create multipurpose buildings with flexible space for both worship and other activities.

WHAT IS SACRED? UCC members typically do not recognize either places or particular objects as inherently holy or sacred. Rather, God is sacred, and the holiness inherent in religious gatherings (where members worship or do the work of God) derives from the sacredness of God.

HOLIDAYS AND FESTIVALS Like other Protestant groups, the UCC emphasizes Christmas and Easter. Because of contacts with other churches and new members from more liturgical (such as German heritage) traditions, local churches are increasingly observing Lent (culminating in Maundy Thursday and Good Friday services), Advent, and Pentecost. Some United Churches also mark Passion Sunday, Ascension Day, and Reformation Day with special preaching or prayers.

MODE OF DRESS During services UCC pastors generally wear a white alb (full-length, long-sleeved vestment), black Geneva gown, or academic-style robe and a stole, the color of which is determined by the season of the church year. Casual or street dress is the rule outside of church. Some of the clergy, particularly those of Evangelical and Reformed background, wear a clerical collar when conducting worship, and a few wear it when in street dress. A minority prefer to wear no clerical garb at all, arguing that since ministry is the responsibility of all the people of God, clergy should not dress distinctively.

DIETARY PRACTICES Members of the United Church of Christ observe no notable dietary restrictions.

RITUALS The UCC prescribes no particular ritual forms. Although the Congregational-Christian tradition had a common format for service, they had no set prayers and were historically devoid of other ritual. Many UCC churches still closely follow services in the *Pilgrim Hymnal* or *Free Church Worship Book.* The influence of the Evangelical and Reformed Church and ties with other churches have moved the UCC toward greater formality, especially in the eucharistic liturgy and in settings and events beyond the local church. Public celebrations are often innovative within the boundaries of tradition and sometimes involve the arts. Individual members often develop private rituals, such as prayer, meditation, journal writing, and other devotional practices.

RITES OF PASSAGE The denomination's *Book of Worship* offers alternatives from both contemporary and traditional sources for sacraments, marriages, funerals, dedications, installations of pastors and church officers, leave-takings, and confirmation. Children acknowledge their baptisms and are formally accepted as church members during confirmation, which typically takes place at 12 or older. Children used to receive their first Communion at confirmation, but parents are increasingly allowing younger children to take Communion, believing that children need do nothing to merit grace.

MEMBERSHIP Evangelization has become more important to the UCC as the American population becomes ever more diverse. Slow to use new technologies for this work, the denomination since 2000 has sought new members through a website, identity videos, and internally produced television programs. The UCC is formally committed to becoming a multicultural, multiracial communion, accessible to all, and has focused its evangelizing efforts on various ethnic groups (including African American, Hispanic, Native American, and Asian) and religious traditions (such as Armenian Evangelical, German Congregational, Hungarian Reformed). These religious and ethnic groups, outside the UCC's four founding communions, have significantly informed and influenced the contemporary church. Though not in great numbers, members of these groups play a highly visible role in UCC leadership.

RELIGIOUS TOLERANCE Born out of the passionate desire for church unity among its founders and formed in an era of social upheaval, the UCC is open, inclusive,

From the Preamble, UCC Constitution

The United Church of Christ acknowledges as its Head, Jesus Christ, Son of God and Savior. It acknowledges as kindred in Christ all who share in this confession. It looks to the Word of God in the Scriptures, and to the presence and power of the Holy Spirit, to prosper its creative and redemptive work in the world. It claims as its own the faith of the historic Church expressed in the ancient creeds and reclaimed in the basic insights of the Protestant Reformers. It affirms the responsibility of the Church in each generation to make the faith its own in reality of worship, in honesty of thought and expression, and in purity of heart before God. In keeping with the teaching of our Lord and the practice prevailing among evangelical Christians, it recognizes two sacraments: Baptism and the Lord's Supper or Holy Communion.

and tolerant of diversity, both theologically and structurally. The founders chose an inclusive name, without historical antecedent. The UCC participates in national and international ecumenical discussions (including the National and World Councils of Churches, Churches Uniting in Christ, and the World Alliance of Reformed Churches) and has relationships with other churches around the globe.

SOCIAL JUSTICE One of the most socially active American Protestant churches, the UCC has taken strong and often controversial stands against numerous injustices, in particular racism, war (UCC is a "just peace church"), and economic oppression. The Puritans placed a high value on an educated electorate, and the UCC has supported public schools. The general synod, individual conferences, and local churches regularly take action and issue formal pronouncements about social issues, including the death penalty, sexual harassment, sexism, the right of women to choose abortion, and gay rights. The UCC routinely accepts openly gay and lesbian applicants into the ordained ministry and other leadership positions.

SOCIAL ASPECTS Like other Protestant denominations, the UCC supports marriage and strong family ties, yet recognizes that, given human imperfection, marriages must sometimes be dissolved. Many members also recognize nontraditional families. An increasing number of United Church ministers conduct services of union for same-sex couples, arguing that committed partnership should be blessed, not rejected, by the church.

CONTROVERSIAL ISSUES In the mid-seventeenth century disagreements over the "Half-Way Covenant" led to a major controversy in Puritan Congregational communities. Puritans granted church membership only to people with a personal experience of conversion or revelation, and though the children of the original Puritan colony had been baptized, few had conversion experiences. Thus, when they wanted their own children baptized, they were denied this privilege because they were not church members themselves. This created a crisis in Congregational churches. Some compromised their strict ideals by allowing these children to be baptized; these churches subscribed to what they called the Half-Way Covenant. Other Puritan Congregationalists wanted to keep the stricter rule.

In the nineteenth century Charles Grandison Finney's introduction of Arminian theology, the basic position of the Methodists, into the Calvinist Congregationalist tradition caused some controversy. Finney opposed Calvin's idea of predestination (in which only those selected by God could be saved) with the idea that every person has the choice to accept God's offer of salvation.

Since the founding of the United Church of Christ in 1957, UCC members have debated various issues, including labor organizing, abortion, war, and sexual orientation.

CULTURAL IMPACT The Puritan tradition of the UCC—particularly the strong work ethic, the insistence on an educated electorate, and the idea that the local community should be free to govern its own affairs—has had a profound influence on American culture in the areas of commerce, education, and politics. Although art, especially of a representational sort, has not been an emphasis of the denomination or its antecedent traditions, many men and women of letters were among early New England Congregationalists, including Puritan poet Anne Bradstreet (the first female author published in the American colonies), William Cullen Bryant, Henry Wadsworth Longfellow, Emily Dickinson, and James Russell Lowell.

Elizabeth C. Nordbeck

See Also Vol. 1: *Christianity*

Bibliography

Book of Worship. New York: United Church of Christ Office for Church Life and Leadership, 1986.

Gunnemann, Louis. *The Shaping of the United Church of Christ: An Essay in the History of American Christianity.* Cleveland: United Church Press, 1999.

———.*United and Uniting: The Meaning of an Ecclesial Journey.* New York: United Church Press, 1987.

Johnson, Daniel L., and Charles Hambrick-Stowe, eds. *Theology and Identity: Traditions, Movements, and Polity in the United Church of Christ.* New York: Pilgrim Press, 1990.

The Living Theological Heritage of the United Church of Christ. 7 vols. Cleveland: Pilgrim Press, 1995–2003.

The New Century Hymnal. Cleveland: Pilgrim Press, 1995.

Shinn, Roger. *Confessing Our Faith: An Interpretation of the Statement of Faith of the United Church of Christ.* New York: Pilgrim Press, 1990.

Zikmund, Barbara Brown, ed. *Hidden Histories in the United Church of Christ.* 2 vols. New York: United Church Press, 1984–1987.

Confucianism

FOUNDED: c. 1050–256 B.C.E.

RELIGION AS A PERCENTAGE OF WORLD POPULATION: 0.1 percent

OVERVIEW The term Confucianism is derived from Confucius, the conventional name for Master Kong, the most revered sage of this religious tradition. Although Master Kong (551–479 B.C.E.) is the putative founder of the tradition, its practitioners, including the master himself, venerated sages who predated Kong by hundreds of years, and most modern scholars view the tradition as having evolved only after Kong's death. Historically, Confucianism was not an organized religion that spread across continents in the manner of, say, Buddhism or Christianity. To borrow the terminology of scholar C.K. Yang, Confucianism, rather than being an "institutionalized" religion, was a "diffused" one that permeated existing social entities, such as the family and the state. This diffusion happened first in China and later in Vietnam, Korea, and Japan, as Chinese familial and governmental practices spread to those countries, along with Chinese philosophy, language, and art.

Because Confucianism permeated so many areas of East Asian life, there have been controversies over how to define it. Is it religion or philosophy, ritual or ethics, family custom or bureaucratic protocol? In different contexts it has been all of these and more. Above all, it has been a value system that has penetrated almost all aspects of East Asian societies. For this reason its modern critics—as well as its modern supporters—have considered it synonymous with East Asian culture, sometimes overlooking the contributions of Buddhism, Taoism, and other traditions. Ironically, in the first half of the twentieth century, many blamed Confucianism for the failure of national efforts to modernize, while more recently others have praised it for facilitating the rapid economic development of East Asian nations.

Without exaggerating its impact, it is best to approach Confucianism primarily as the source of moral values and ritual practices that have influenced personal development, family life, social relations, and political behavior in East Asia. Its main moral values have included filiality (obedience and respect toward elders, especially parents), loyalty, humaneness, just action, mutual trust, reciprocity, and moral courage. Its ritual practices, derived from Chinese texts more than 2,000 years old, have influenced East Asian weddings, banquets, funerals, coming-of-age ceremonies, and official protocols into the twenty-first century. Moreover, as indicated by this list of activities, Confucian rituals have often concerned human interrelations rather than relations between humans and divine beings.

Of course, Confucianism has been more than a system of social values and public rituals. In particular it has served as a path of spiritual cultivation for individuals. It has also been a philosophical tradition within which different schools of thought have pursued competing interpretations of the Confucian heritage. The latter remains especially vibrant today, with various new interpretations of the Confucian heritage having been inspired by the challenge of Western thought.

HISTORY The history of a religious tradition begins when it becomes conscious of itself as a tradition and

RU. The Chinese character ru, meaning "scholar" or "literatus," is a common symbol of Confucianism. It is from this character that Confucianism gets its Chinese name, *ru-jiao* ("tradition of scholars"). (THOMSON GALE)

when it seeks to preserve and develop the teachings of its founder(s). In the case of the Confucian tradition, historians see this happening in the century after the death of Master Kong. It should nonetheless be noted that followers of the tradition have often stressed a sacred history that traces its origins to ancient sage rulers, such as the legendary emperors Yao and Shun (supposedly prior to 2000 B.C.E.), and to early rulers of the Zhou Dynasty (c. 1050–256 B.C.E.): King Wu, King Wen, and the Duke of Zhou.

In the centuries following his death, during the late Zhou and early Han (206 B.C.E.–220 C.E.) dynasties, the followers of Master Kong produced collections of sayings attributed to him and progressively enhanced his reputation from teacher to sage and, at least for some, from sage to deity. During the same period, the Confucians established themselves as custodians of ancient China's ritual, political, and historical traditions. In addition to Master Kong's sayings (known as the *Analects*), they preserved records of teachings attributed to other early sages, such as Master Meng (also Mencius; c. 391–308 B.C.E.) and Master Xun (also Hsün Tzu; c. 298–235 B.C.E.), as well as various ritual, political, and historical records that would later become authoritative Confucian sacred books. This process of formulating sacred books neared culmination during the Han period, just as the tradition was becoming a major social and political force in China.

At the start of the Han period the Confucian tradition's imminent success was not self-evident to its pro-

ponents. Rulers of the preceding Qin Dynasty (221–206 B.C.E.) had burned Confucian texts because of their support for the Zhou Dynasty. Han literati debated which texts to accept as well as what the texts meant. Nevertheless, they agreed that Master Kong was a great sage. They considered him not only the source of the famous *Analects* but also the author or editor of the texts that would come to be known as the *Five Scriptures* (also *Five Classics*). These books grew in importance to the point that, in 175 C.E., the emperor Han Xiaoling issued an edict to have stone stelae (pillars) inscribed with the sacred texts erected outside the national university. The Confucians also benefited from becoming the custodians of ancient rituals. Chinese rulers knew that magnificent ceremonies held an air of majesty, and in their way of thinking, the ritual dimension of statecraft was as important as its practical aspects. In the case of sacrificial offerings, it kept a ruler in good standing with his royal ancestors and the forces of nature (such as Heaven, Earth, Sun, and Moon). In the case of audience rites (ceremonial meetings a ruler grants to persons who wish to encounter him), it also brought order to a ruler's relations with his government officials and foreign neighbors.

Among the earliest Confucians to gain imperial favor was Dong Zhongshu (c. 176–104 B.C.E.), who served under the Han emperor Wudi. On Dong's advice the emperor established positions for the study of Confucian scriptures as well as the national university in front of which Han Xiaoling would later erect his famous stelae. In developing an examination for aspiring imperial scholars, Dong established the basis for the state examinations that later East Asian governments used to recruit government officials. Dong was himself an expert on the sacred book *Chunqiu* (Spring and Autumn Annals), and his famous commentary on it, *Chunqiu fanlu* (Luxuriant Dew of the Spring and Autumn Annals), indicates key trends in Han Confucian thought. In his view Master Kong—the *Annal's* reputed author—was a great sage and uncrowned king. This portrayal matched ongoing efforts to deify Kong and develop the practice of performing sacrificial rites at his tomb and in Master Kong temples and government schools. Synthesizing yin-yang thought of the late Zhou era with Confucian ideas, Dong also established numerological and cosmological correspondences between Heaven (Tian) and humanity within a microcosm-macrocosm theory (a microcosm is a miniature model of the larger universe, or macrocosm). Yin-yang thought was based

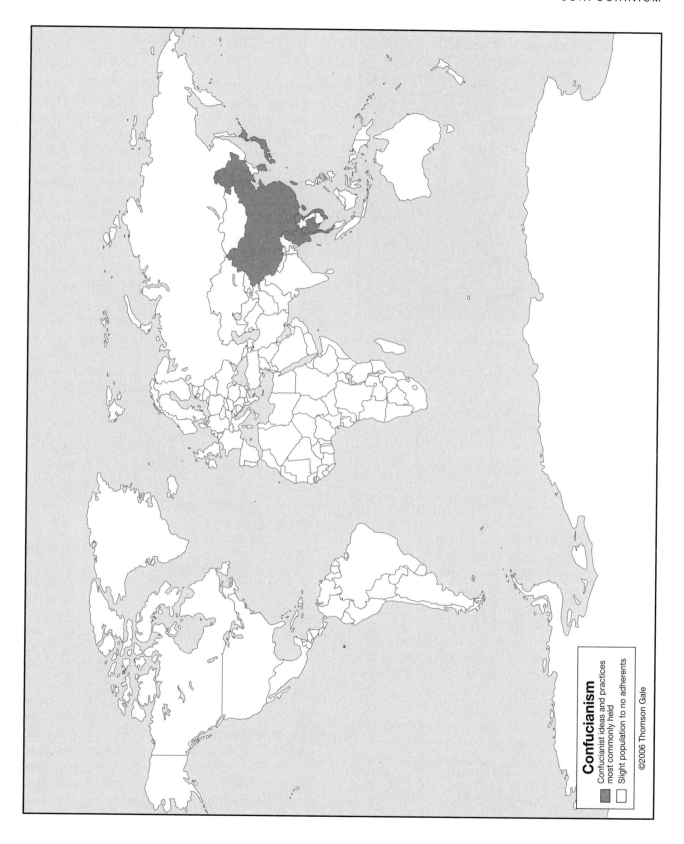

Confucianism

■ Confucianist ideas and practices most commonly held

□ Slight population to no adherents

©2006 Thomson Gale

Dancers in traditional costumes celebrate Master Kong's birthday. The holiday is celebrated in many ways, with various kinds of East Asian cultural performances. © NATHAN BENN/CORBIS.

on the idea of pairs of complementary opposites in the world, including (in yin-yang order) dark and light, cold and hot, wet and dry, female and male, winter and summer, night and day, and the sun and the moon. Exemplifying the microcosm-macrocosm theory, a balance of yin and yang made for a healthy person (a microcosm) as well as for a harmonious universe (the macrocosm).

Dong also further developed the old idea of a Mandate of Heaven (*tianming*), according to which Heaven granted the right to rule to a line of rulers and expressed its evaluation of them through natural phenomena or other omens. This corresponded to a fundamental Confucian belief that social order must follow cosmic order in the harmonious relations between its parts and in the hierarchical structuring of its high and low parts (for example, Heaven and Earth, yang and yin). To maintain harmony with Heaven, people must observe the doctrine of the Three Bonds: subject to ruler, son to father, and wife to husband. Many Han Confucians followed Dong's cosmological ideas, which implicitly supported autocratic rule. (Some Han emperors supported Confucian thought but ruled in the autocratic fashion of the first emperor of the Qin Dynasty, who had burned Confucian texts.) Later, Confucian scholars would play a dual role, supporting the emperor as a "Son of Heaven" yet reminding him that Heaven wanted its "Son" to practice benevolence and justice (*ren* and *yi*).

In later history political and social trends favored the spread of authoritarian tendencies in the Confucian tradition rather than the flowering of its moral ideals. In the name of Master Kong leaders stressed views of harmony and filiality that held that people should subordinate themselves to social units (family, clan, and state) and remain subservient to those who ranked higher in generation, age, or gender. Han scholars defined women's roles in various ways: Stories of self-sacrificing women were collected in the *Lienü zhuan* (Biographies of Exemplary Women) by Liu Xiang (79–8 B.C.E.), and the virtues of ideal womanhood were presented in the Lessons for Women (*Nüjie*) by Ban Zhao (died in 116 C.E.), a female scholar from an elite family. *Biographies of Exemplary Women* presented women in their role as upholders of social morality but also included negative examples of women whose selfish, sensual demands destroyed social morality, their husbands, and even dynasties. Ideal figures were mothers who reared their sons well and gave their husbands moral guidance. On the one hand, *Lessons for Women* contained strong statements against spousal abuse and stressed male respect for women. On the other hand, it painted a picture of the ideal (marriageable) girl as a model of obedience who possesses the "four virtues": "womanly virtue" itself, which involves being chaste and demure; "womanly words," which are always polite and never quarrelsome; "womanly bearing," which is ever erect and clean, never slovenly or dirty; and "womanly work," which is domestic and industrious.

Available evidence indicates that, by the time of the Han Dynasty texts just mentioned, families already preferred newborn boys to girls, clans expected wives to be completely obedient to their husbands and in-laws, and social leaders excluded women from positions of power. In the centuries that followed, Confucian scholars did little to challenge these social values. Some later wrote to condemn the most egregious abuses against women, such as wife beating and foot binding. In late imperial history there were rare individuals, such as Li Zhi (1527–1602) and Tang Zhen (1630–1704), who advocated that women have educational and life opportunities similar to those afforded men. Mainstream Confucian scholars, however, mainly reinforced the patriarchal values of traditional society in China (and, later, in Vietnam, Korea, and Japan).

Typically, the Confucian Way for a man meant a life of public service, informed by the study of Confucian scriptures and the practice of inner cultivation. For

Mourners participate in a Confucian funeral. Like other Confucian rituals, the event is a family affair, with the sons of the deceased, rather than religious professionals, performing key roles. © SETBOUN/CORBIS.

a woman the Confucian Way involved a search for personal fulfillment through a life of service to the men in her life. Excluded from the path of formal study that led to government service, most women took this prescribed path. If a woman wanted a less domestic spiritual life, she had to seek it on another path, such as that of a Buddhist nun or Taoist priestess. For families, ritual traditions based on Confucian scriptures spread among social elites before ultimately reaching society's lower levels. Having a Confucian-style marriage for one's daughter, coming-of-age ceremony for one's son, or funeral for one's deceased parent marked upward social movement.

Over time the Confucian tradition came under the influence of Taoism and Buddhism, the latter having gained strength in post-Han China. By the time of the Tang Dynasty (618–906 C.E.), most literati were content to share the stage with Buddhism and Taoism, the other two of China's "three teachings" (*san jiao*). Some felt the true Confucian Way had been lost, however. By the time of the Song Dynasty (960–1279), this view became more widely held, and a major Confucian renaissance movement began. The movement had so many new elements that modern scholars came to call it Neo-Confucianism. Despite the Neo-Confucian's avowed opposition to Buddhism and Taoism, the new elements can be traced mainly to those religions. Of special importance was the fact that Neo-Confucians adopted the originally Indian idea that ascetic self-denial should play

a necessary role in spiritual development. This development tended to undermine certain salutary elements of early Confucian thought, with its positive evaluation of human emotions, the human body, and the natural world. It affected the behavioral ideals promoted by Confucians for women as well as men. While Song literati did not themselves advocate foot binding or seclusion for women, the ascetic turn in their thinking had subtle links to the development and spread of such practices.

Looking beyond China, these later developments played a key role in determining which Confucian beliefs and practices would be adopted in Vietnam, Korea, and Japan and thus had a momentous effect on the lives of men and women throughout East Asia. For example, Zhu Xi (1130–1200), the leading Song Confucian thinker, presented the tension between the ideal of heavenly principle (*tianli*) and the actuality of human desires (*renyu*) as the basic problem of philosophical understanding and moral cultivation. Moreover, when Confucian teachings were transmitted to Vietnam, Korea, and Japan from China's Song, Yuan (1279–1368), and Ming (1368–1644) dynasties, Zhu Xi's new orthodoxy held a central place in both its social and philosophical aspects. Indeed, Zhu Xi was known throughout East Asia as much for the book *Zhuzi jiali* (Master Zhu's Family Rituals) as for his philosophical writings.

The Confucian tradition first arrived in Vietnam long before China's Song era, for the area was frequently

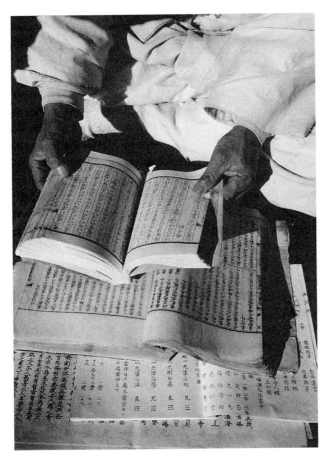

A South Korean villager pages through a stack of books. Confucianist texts have been used for hundreds of years to educate children throughout East Asia. © SETBOUN/CORBIS.

ments of the Confucian tradition, Korean leaders would ultimately adopt Neo-Confucian ideals in attempting a full-fledged transformation of their state and society. They introduced examinations for the recruitment of officials, rules to establish honesty in government, ceremonies to add civility to public life, and the ideal of benevolent rule. At the same time Korean Confucian loyalists sought conformity to social norms that deprived women of established social privileges in the areas of inheritance, freedom of movement outside the home, relations with their natal families, and status within their marriages. This effort began during the Koryo Dynasty (918–1392) and continued during the Yi (Chosôn) Dynasty (1392–1910), which became aligned with the Confucian tradition to the extent that it even suppressed Korean Buddhism.

Chinese Confucian influence in Japan also predated the Song period. During the seventh and eighth centuries Japan adopted various social norms, administrative practices, and intellectual trends of China's Tang Dynasty. Confucian governmental traditions borrowed directly from the Tang Dynasty state codes were particularly important in Japan's first attempts at centralized rule. Nonetheless, it was later Confucian influence (in the post-Song era) that led to the creation of lasting philosophical schools and that had widespread social effects in Japan.

During the Kamakura (1185–1333) and Muromachi (1392–1568) periods in Japan, Zen Buddhists helped spread new Confucian ideas and practices. The meditative practices of Buddhist *zazen* and Confucian *seiza* (quiet sitting; from the Chinese *jingzuo*) became popular, along with the synthesis of other Buddhist and Confucian personal development practices. Against this background, Bushido (Way of the Warrior) later developed as the way of the feudal knights known as Samurai.

The Samurai ascended to power under Tokugawa rule (1600–1868), and their rise was accompanied by Tokugawa support for Confucian scholars who followed Zhu Xi's Neo-Confucian orthodoxy. Yamaga Sokō (1622–85), admired for formulating the Bushido code, was once banished from the capital (Edo) for ten years (1666–75) for advocating that Confucians overlook Zhu Xi in favor of the "ancient learning" (*kogaku*) of early Confucian sages. Japanese political conservatives usually preferred Zhu Xi's orthodoxy, while progressives adopted the activist and intuitionist alternative associated with the scholar Wang Yangming (1472–1529) of China's Ming Dynasty. Progressive Confu-

under Chinese control. Chinese writing was introduced to Vietnam as early as the Han period. Later, Vietnamese scholars competed in state examinations and became officials of the Chinese government. Nonetheless, as in Korea and Japan, the extensive Confucian penetration of Vietnam occurred later, during the Ly (1010–1225), Tran (1226–1400), the second Le (1428–1789), and Nguyen (1802–1945) dynasties. Despite the fact that the country's society was originally less patriarchal than that of China, Vietnamese leaders encouraged adoption of the rituals and values in Confucian scriptures as interpreted by Zhu Xi and other Chinese Neo-Confucians. State ceremonies, like state administrative practice, followed Chinese models. Vietnamese leaders idealized the hierarchical pairings in father-son, husband-wife, ruler-subject, and, in addition, teacher-student relationships.

Korea's history reveals a situation similar to that in Vietnam. Following earlier exposure to isolated ele-

Glossary

de virtue; potential goodness conferred on a person by *Tian* (Heaven)

Five Scriptures *Wujing;* Confucianism's most sacred texts

Four Books *Sishu;* central texts of Confucian philosophy and education

haoxue love of (moral) learning

jingzuo "quiet sitting"; meditation

li cosmic ordering principle

li norms for the interaction of humans with each other and with higher forces (a different Chinese character from the other *li*, meaning "principle," above)

liangzhi innate moral knowledge

Lixue "study of principle"; Neo-Confucian philosophical movement

neisheng waiwang "sage within and king without"; phrase used to describe one who is both a spiritual seeker and a social leader

qi matter-energy; life force pervading the cosmos

ren humaneness; benevolence

renzheng humane government

renyu human desires

tao (also dao) "the way"; the Confucian life path

Three Bonds obedience of subject to ruler, child to parent, and wife to husband

Tian "Heaven"; entity believed to represent cosmic and moral order

tianli ultimate, Heaven-rooted cosmic ordering principle permeating all phenomena

tianming Mandate of Heaven

xin heart-mind; human organ of moral evaluation

xing inner human nature

Xinxue "study of mind"; Neo-Confucian philosophical movement

yi rightness; to act justly

---

cians were among those who brought about the Meiji Restoration of 1868, which marked the beginning of Japan's era of modernization.

Confucian teachings thus affected Japan's male world of warriors and statecraft. At the same time, they also had an impact on women in Tokugawa Japan that mirrored their effects under pro-Confucian regimes in Korea and Vietnam. It seems, however, that the Japanese emphasis on the emotional and sensual dimensions of life kept the puritanical features of the Neo-Confucian value system from penetrating Japanese society as deeply as it had other East Asian societies. Nonetheless, since Japanese society was the most explicitly feudal of premodern societies in East Asia, Confucian views on loyalty, filiality, and female subservience also reinforced the Tokugawa social structure.

Lacking distinct institutional forms of its own, Confucianism relied on existing social institutions, such as the family and the state, to preserve and transmit its teachings. As these institutions changed in each of the East Asian societies where it traditionally held sway, Confucianism also changed. Moreover, in each of these

societies intellectuals promoting modernization attacked the tradition as a conservative obstacle to change. As a result, the Confucian tradition eventually entered a crisis comparable to an identity crisis in an individual.

This is best seen in the case of China, where Confucianism was born. Indeed, after the fall of the Qing Dynasty (1644–1911), telltale trends against Confucianism emerged in the first decade of the new Chinese republic. In 1915 a group of intellectuals led by Chen Duxiu (1879–1942) of Beijing University founded the journal *New Youth* and initiated a movement that produced mass student demonstrations on 4 May 1919. Known as the May Fourth Movement, it made Confucianism a key target of its attack on traditional culture. As indicated by the articles and short stories published in *New Youth,* the movement saw Confucianism as the main obstacle to achieving what it defined as China's key goals: male-female equality, scientific thinking, economic development, and democracy. The journal came to epitomize the spirit of the era and was followed by similar journals, including some dedicated specifically to women's rights, such as *The New Woman* and *The Woman's*

Bell. Chen, who later founded the Chinese Communist Party, was joined by literary figures—such as Lu Xun (1881–1936), the period's greatest short-story writer—and political essayists, including Hu Shi (1891–1962). Hu and other proponents of the Western liberal tradition disagreed with Chen and other Communists about many things, but both groups of social reformers agreed on the need to criticize Confucianism.

One needed a great deal of courage to defend Confucianism in this milieu. There were those, however, who not only defended the tradition but also insisted that a Confucian revival was just what would lead China out of its national crisis and into a bright future. Building on the work of such turn-of-the-century thinkers as Kang Youwei (1858–1927) and Liang Qichao (1873–1929), Liang Shuming (1893–1988) was the first of Confucianism's post–May Fourth defenders. In 1922 he published *Dongxi wenhua ji qi zhexue* (Eastern and Western Cultures and Their Philosophies), a work in comparative thought and culture that argued Chinese culture was supreme and that true Confucianism was China's salvation. For Liang, as for other modern Confucians, true Confucianism transcended the imperial system with which it had once been identified and was, in fact, compatible with science and democracy. Xiong Shili (1885–1968), another scholar of Liang's generation, trained many students who continued to revive and redefine the Confucian tradition. These students included a famous group of four self-styled New Confucians: Mou Zongsan (1909–95), Tang Junyi (1909–78), Xu Fuguan (1903–82), and Zhang Junmai (1886–1969).

Due to its apologetic tone, the foursome's attempt at Confucian revival has been termed Fundamentalism. Yet, these scholars and their living students, notably Shu-hsien Liu (born in 1934) and Wei-ming Tu (born in 1940), have seen themselves as modernizers of their tradition, seeking to find a place for it in contemporary theology and philosophy. Until recently these Confucian apologists were alone in their defense of the tradition. Since the economic success of Japan and the "Four Little Dragons" (Hong Kong, Singapore, South Korea, and Taiwan), however, a new breed of Confucian apologists has emerged. These defenders are social scientists armed with data on rapid economic development as well as surveys demonstrating the perseverance of such so-called Confucian values as diligence, thrift, loyalty to authority, and conformity to social norms. They claim Confucianism facilitates, rather than obstructs, economic modernization.

Despite this new assessment of Confucianism's economic role, many remain less sanguine about its role in social and political modernization. The tradition's key representatives, all of whom are men, have not dealt extensively with its patriarchal norms and sexist historical record. Socially, while other religious traditions—Buddhism, Christianity, and Islam, for example—have striven to take into account feminist movements, Confucianism has yet to see such a movement emerge within its ranks. While other traditions have given rise to progressive movements that are socially and politically active, like Engaged Buddhism and "Social Gospel" Christianity, the Confucian tradition has not produced any social activists. Its modern political champions, such as Chiang Kai-shek (1887–1975) and Lee Kuan Yew (born in 1923), have been authoritarian rulers rather than social activists. This has hurt its chances for developing what William Theodore de Bary, for example, has called the "liberal tradition" in Confucianism.

CENTRAL DOCTRINES Through its doctrines every religious tradition seeks to answer three questions. In their simplest form these are: (1) What's wrong with people (as individuals or as a group); (2) what ideal state should people seek (salvation, enlightenment, moral perfection, or the perfect society); and (3) what means should people use to transform themselves from their present (flawed) state to the ideal state? Frederick J. Streng, a scholar of comparative religious studies, has explained that each religion is "a means of ultimate transformation" because, in answering the third question, it tells people they can change—or be changed by divine will or grace—to become ultimately different from the sinful, selfish, ignorant, or morally lax persons they are now.

While Master Kong and other early Confucian thinkers never presented people as evil or ignorant by nature, they were completely dissatisfied with people's behavior and with the state of human society. They argued that people behaved in a selfish and morally lax manner because the world lacked true moral leadership of the kind once provided by ancient sage rulers. Master Kong is quoted as saying that "the world is without the Way (of moral behavior)." For Kong the Way (*dao*; also, tao) came from a cosmic and moral entity called Tian (Heaven). It was a spiritual path inherent in existence and accessible to human understanding. Confucians believed the Way could be found in the behavior of exemplary sages, including Master Kong, as well as in themselves.

People can find the Way in themselves in the sense that they possess a moral potential that has been conferred on them. Depending on the context, Confucians have called this potential *de* (virtue) as well as *xing* (inner nature). When this potential is developed, a person exists in an ideal moral-spiritual state that enables him or her to have a powerful positive influence over others. This realized moral potential has been called *ming de* (brightly shining virtue). Another way of saying humans are born with a powerful moral potential is to argue, as have most Confucians since Master Meng, that "a person's inner nature is originally good" ("renxing ben shan"). In other scriptures the two concepts were merged in such phrases as *zun dexing* (honoring virtuous nature), which comes from the text *Zhongyong* 27:6 (Centrality and Commonality).

This account would be incomplete without mention of the "heart-mind" (*xin*), a special human capacity for moral feeling and thinking. Using this reflective capacity, a person is able to distinguish between good and bad behavior as well as to discern the part of the self that tends toward goodness and that should be developed in order to restore the Way in the world.

Over the centuries Master Kong and his followers, in declaring "the world is without the Way," blamed social leaders for setting poor examples for the masses. By indulging their selfish desires, they had grown out of touch with the suffering of the masses, as well as with their own potential for goodness. If leaders would practice moral-spiritual cultivation, they could not only transform themselves but also have a transforming effect on the common people, according to the Confucians. In Master Kong's words: "As grasses bend with the wind, so will the masses bend [toward goodness] under the sway of a true moral gentleman" (*Analects* 12:19). Because such gentlemen were not in power, every kind of moral outrage existed. Leaders ignored the welfare of the common people and used them as cannon fodder in their wars; ministers set bad examples in their own behavior yet punished others for minor infractions of strict laws; sons attacked their own fathers; and ministers rebelled against their rulers. Master Kong exclaimed, "Fathers should be true fathers, sons should be true sons, rulers should be true rulers, ministers should be true ministers" (*Analects* 12:11). This suggests that, in an ideal society, each person fulfills his or her role, setting an example for those over whom he or she has influence. While this would seem to favor the development of a rigid social structure, in Confucian doctrine

the harmonious society was considered one in which each person would have a chance to flourish individually while making a contribution to social harmony. Thus, the goal of the Confucian individual is to become the kind of sage who can be a social leader, not the kind who leaves society or seeks to transcend the material world. Confucians have used the phrase "sage within and king without" (*neisheng waiwang*) to describe an ideal person who has the characteristics of both a spiritual seeker and a social leader. It is easy to see how this individual ideal is linked to the collective goal of a peaceful, harmonious, and just society. Like Master Kong and Master Meng, later Confucians argued that personal development should be pursued for the sake of improving society. The standard passage describing personal development as the basis for social service is chapter one of *Daxue* (Great Learning), which states: "The ancients who wished to manifest brightly shining virtue throughout the empire, first brought order to their own states. Wishing to order their own states, they first regulated their families. Wishing to regulate their families, they first cultivated their own persons. Wishing to cultivate their persons, they first rectified their heart-minds. Wishing to rectify their heart-minds, they first sought to be sincere in their thoughts. Wishing to be sincere in their thoughts, they first extended their knowledge. The extension of knowledge lay in the investigation of things . . . From the Son of Heaven down to the mass of the people; all must consider cultivation of the person as the root."

This passage is essential not only for understanding the nature of the Confucian goal but even more so for understanding the characteristic Confucian path. Confucians have identified eight principles, or eight stages, of personal cultivation in chapter one of the Great Learning. The first four are interpreted as aspects of inner cultivation, concluding with "rectifying the heart-mind" by making it fully present but not under the influence of negative feelings. The explanation of this in chapter seven of *Daxue* reads: "If one is under the influence of passion, one will be incorrect in one's conduct. One will be the same if one is under the influence of fear, or under the influence of fond regard, or under that of sorrow. When the mind is inattentive, we look and do not see, we hear and do not understand, we eat and do not know the taste of our food." With the heart-mind rectified, a person can perfect outward behavior; and, with the "brightly shining virtue" stressed in *Daxue*, he or she can assume a role of leadership in the family, the local state, and, then, the world.

In practice the Confucian path not only involved efforts to develop one's inner moral potential, it also involved adherence to the complex rules of propriety (*li*) that governed the gentleman's life in ancient China. Indeed, over time these ritual norms came to govern the behavior of almost all Chinese. Although an ancient saying proclaimed that "the *li* do not reach down to the common people" ("li bu xia shu"), Confucians ultimately encouraged their observance on all of the important occasions in people's lives—birth, puberty, marriage, and ancestor worship, for example.

The doctrine of *li*, however, has involved more than prescribing correct ritual behavior for social occasions. It is a doctrine that has encapsulated the Confucian perspective on life at all levels: the individual, the family, society, and the cosmos. Believing the *li* were grounded in nature, Confucians saw adherence to these ritual norms as a way to maintain harmony between people in society as well as between human society and the natural world. As in the case of the need for inner moral cultivation, this was true "from the Son of Heaven down to the common people." Whether it was the imperial sacrifices to Heaven, Earth, Sun, and Moon or a common person's observation of ancestral rites, the ultimate motivation for the observance of *li* lay in the search for harmony.

As has already been discussed, the transformation of individuals was linked with the transformation of society, which was seen as leading to an era of great peace and harmony for all. Of course, while each individual could be transformed, it was particularly important for society's leaders to become sages. Indeed, the entire process of social transformation began with the ruler who held the Mandate of Heaven. According to this central Confucian religio-political doctrine, the man who held the mandate not only gained political legitimacy, he also inherited a deep moral obligation; and, if he did not fulfill this obligation, he would lose the mandate. The doctrine of the Mandate of Heaven specified that Heaven was a model for the king (who was sometimes called the Son of Heaven), and the king a model for all his subjects. In ritual behavior he had to act in accordance with Heaven's seasonal cycle, and in political behavior he had to lead his subjects, above all, by exemplifying the development of human moral potential. As a moral sage, he could rule with benevolence and justice (*ren* and *yi*) as well as engage in the transformative instruction (*jiaohua*) of his subjects. These two activities went hand-in-hand, for a just and benevolent ruler provided the material conditions within which people could morally educate themselves and, at the same time, gave them a model to emulate.

An ideal Confucian king who fulfilled this dual role was himself emulating Heaven, which was not only the source of all natural and social goods but also a just and compassionate guide for the ruler. Whenever the ruler strayed from the true Kingly Way (*wangdao*), Heaven sent forth signs of displeasure—strange natural phenomena, for example, or even natural disasters. A ruler who failed to heed such warnings would not last long. In theory, at least, the doctrine of Heaven's Mandate thus assumed that a ruler would take seriously his obligations to perform the rituals required to maintain harmony within society as well as between human society and the cosmos; to establish laws that would deter his subjects from following their selfish instincts into misbehavior; and to provide moral guidance that would help his subjects develop the better part of themselves (the good nature endowed by Heaven). Success in all these areas would be enough to usher in an era of great peace and harmony, the ultimate goal of Confucian personal and social development.

MORAL CODE OF CONDUCT Identifying a basic code of conduct, such as the Ten Commandments of Judaism and Christianity or the five precepts of Buddhism, is not possible in Confucianism because of its nature as a diffused, rather than institutional, religion. Confucian-based moral codes that affected people's behavior were found, for example, within Chinese law, imperial edicts issued to improve social morality, and clan rules that governed family behavior. The *Liji* (Book of Rites) and other ancient texts about *li* are the most important sources for these Confucian moral codes. Other texts with an emphasis on practical morality, such as the *Scripture of Filiality, Instructions for Women*, and *Master Zhu's Family Rituals*, were also influential.

Ethics concerning social relations is at the heart of Confucian morality, from the basic moral principles established by the masters Kong and Meng to the specific codes of conduct found in clan rules and imperial edicts. The most consistently important example of this was a list of five principles governing social relations found in *Mengzi* (Master Meng) 4A:12. The principal of loyalty governs the relationship between a ruler and his officials; filiality, that between a father and his son; proper order, that between an elder and a younger brother; separation of duties, that between a husband and his wife; and mutual trust, that between friends.

How these principles and other aspects of Confucian ethics affected moral codes can be seen in Chinese law, clan rules, and imperial edicts. It must be noted that the basis of Chinese imperial law was not originally Confucianism but rather Legalism, to use the name frequently given to an early rival of the Confucian school. The School of Law (*Fa Jia*) saw its legal traditions adopted by the Qin Dynasty (221–206 B.C.E.), the first dynasty to unite China under a central bureaucracy, and, with revisions, all later dynasties in China. According to Legalist thought, laws should be created so as to apply universally to all subjects of the empire, and laws should be enforced with equal strictness in all situations. In contrast, in Confucian thought, the *li* were created to reinforce social distinctions and to prescribe different behavior in different situations. What scholars have called the "Confucianization of law" was the process whereby the spirit and many of the details of the Confucian teachings penetrated the Chinese legal system.

For example, penalties prescribed for crimes against others were adjusted according to the social status of the perpetrator and the victim. A heavy penalty was prescribed for a commoner harming an official (or a child offending a parent), but a light penalty was prescribed in reverse circumstances. Confucian relational principles, such as filiality and loyalty, also affected the legal system, reinforcing the idea that persons in subordinate social roles—such as children, commoners, or wives—committed an especially grave offense when they harmed one of their superiors. Even more indicative of the influence of Confucian on Legalist ideology was the priority of filiality over loyalty when the two principles came into conflict, pitching one's need to serve parents against the needs of the state. For example, throughout imperial history people were allowed to conceal the crimes of close relatives in accordance with Master Kong's strong disapproval of a son who had reported his father's theft of a sheep to the authorities (*Analects* 13:18). Another example is the law that allowed judges to repeal the sentences of criminals who were the sole supporters of aged relatives or even the sole male descendants of deceased parents in need of the customary ancestral offerings. By lessening the punishment meted out to a sole surviving son, the judge allowed the son to fulfill the requirements of the principle of filiality.

Such cases raised the related issue of efforts to enshrine into law the Confucian principle of "humane government" (*renzheng*). Providing for the support of elderly parents by commuting the sentences of their son was an example of this, but only one among many. When judges meted out death sentences, higher courts and the emperor reviewed these sentences, often prescribing lesser punishments in order to make a show of their support for the Confucian principle of humane government. Imperial amnesties were frequently announced for the same reason, allowing those imprisoned to return to their families. In some cases the young, the elderly, the handicapped, and women were judged less harshly than other subjects of the state. All such cases were largely the result of efforts to have a code of behavior that accorded with the principle of humaneness (*ren*) and the various ritual norms (*li*) found in Confucian scriptures.

Clan codes represented even more explicit efforts to "Confucianize" the rules by which people were supposed to live. Indeed, among all Chinese social institutions, the family clan, or *zu* (lineage), came closest to being a Confucian moral church. A clan was established to honor its founding patriarch and other clan ancestors, which often involved the construction of an ancestral temple in which to worship their spirits. The clan's raison d'être was the pursuit of achievements that would glorify those ancestors. Toward this end, clan rules prescribed filial behavior for all situations in which children related to parents and older siblings, wives related to husbands and parents-in-law, and living clan members related to dead ancestors. The rules also emphasized honesty and hard work as the means to succeed in life and to glorify one's ancestors. Finally, the rules prescribed charitable behavior toward less fortunate clan members and the building of schools for clan youths in order to honor the Confucian principles of humanity (*ren*) and the love of learning (*haoxue*), respectively.

Many of the principles of the clan codes are also evident in "sacred edicts" (*sheng yu*), which represented the emperor's efforts to provide guidelines for moral behavior. In fact, clan rules often quoted passages from these edicts. The best known among them was the sacred edict of the Kangxi emperor, issued in 1670, with its famous Sixteen Instructions. The first six demonstrate how the instructions enshrined the principles of filiality, harmony, diligence, and love of learning: (1) In order to honor proper human relations, maintain filial and brotherly duties. (2) In order to manifest cordial behavior, be sincere in familial relationships. (3) In order to prevent discord and lawsuits, promote harmony in your village and neighborhood. (4) In order to provide adequate food and clothing, honor farming and silk production. (5) In order to be efficient in expenditures, esteem thrift and frugality. (6) In order to establish scholarly practices, support building schools. Next to the family clan, the traditional Chinese state was the most important surrogate Confucian church, with the emperor and his officials committed, at least in word, to the moral principles set forth by Master Kong and his followers. It was, therefore, appropriate that the state enshrined Confucian morality not only in its legal system but also in its efforts at moral suasion. After all, according to Confucian teachings, rulership that employs moral suasion and personal example is better than rulership that depends on legal statutes and punishments.

SACRED BOOKS For the past 1,000 years, Confucians have considered 13 books to be their *jing* (scriptures). These books include the earlier and more basic *Wujing* (Five Scriptures) as well as the later, but more frequently used, *Sishu* (Four Books). The 13 are the *Yijing* (Book of Changes), *Shujing* (Book of Documents), *Shijing* (Book of Odes), *Liji* (Book of Rites), *Zhouli* (Rites of Zhou), *Yili* (Book of Etiquette and Ritual), *Lun yu* (Analects), *Xiaojing* (Scripture of Filiality), the Chinese dictionary *Erya*, *Mengzi* (Master Meng), and *Chunqiu* (Spring and Autumn Annals), which is included three times, in each instance accompanied by a different commentary. The *Four Books* were drawn from the Thirteen Scriptures and include the *Analects, Master Meng, Daxue* (Great Learning), and *Zhongyong* (Centrality and Commonality), the last two being chapters of the *Book of Rites.* The *Four Books* became popular as a basic catechism for young boys being introduced to classical Chinese thought as well as the standard set of texts whose meanings were explored in essays by candidates taking state examinations. For 800 years they have been part of the curriculum recommended by educators throughout East Asia, with rare exceptions, such as the educators who were followers of the Communist leader Mao Zedong.

SACRED SYMBOLS Today, the most recognizable symbol of the Confucian tradition is an image of Master Kong. Historically such images, whether paintings or sculptures, were also common symbols. For hundreds of years, however, the correct representation of the master in Master Kong temples was his ancestral tablet engraved with the words "supreme sage and ancient teacher."

Master Kong temples, found in major cities throughout East Asia, are themselves powerful symbols of the tradition. Traditionally the officials who performed ceremonies in Master Kong temples dressed in mandarin robes that also symbolized the tradition, especially for the common folk, who saw them as emblems of sacred authority.

Within Master Kong temples, placards were found upon which were written famous Confucian phrases in the hand of a leading scholar, state official, or even an emperor. Because of the importance of calligraphy in East Asia, as well as the importance of sacred words, these placards have also been regarded as sacred symbols of the tradition. Finally, sacred texts have been important symbols of the tradition, revered by the literate and illiterate alike because they contain the words of holy sages.

EARLY AND MODERN LEADERS The ancestral cult of Master Kong has always been led by a Kong clan patriarch who is a descendent of the master. The current clan patriarch, Kong Decheng (born in 1920), has lived in exile in Taiwan in recent decades. Historically there have been several instances when descendants of the master became more than just patriarchs of the clan, such as when Kong Anguo (died in 74 B.C.E.) and Kong Yingda (574–648 C.E.) became leading Confucian intellectuals in the Han and Tang eras, respectively.

But neither the Kong clan patriarch nor any other figure could have been considered the religious leader of all Chinese Confucians, let alone of those in Japan, Korea, and Vietnam. In fact, the problem is not only that it is hard to identify a leader but also that it is hard to locate his flock, given that Confucianism is a diffused rather than an institutional religion.

Since Confucianism was diffused throughout the state system, the reigning monarch of an East Asian state that promoted Confucian ritual and ideology was by default a Confucian leader. He performed the state ceremonies prescribed by Confucian ritual tradition, was ultimately responsible for recruiting Confucian-educated officials, and, as in the case of China's Kangxi emperor, led efforts to cause the populace to embrace Confucian morality. High-ranking Confucian officials were also leaders responsible for providing moral and political guidance for the literati in general. These leaders could galvanize others to engage in collective action, sometimes in opposition to their reigning monarch.

In serving as the political ideology for the premodern states of East Asia, Confucianism played a dual role. It supported monarchies, yet, at the same time, preserved conventions of protest according to which a loyal official could remonstrate against a corrupt monarch. Even the *Scripture of Filiality* quotes Master Kong as saying that, when confronted with what is unrighteous, a son must remonstrate against his father, and the minister against his ruler. In China this ideal manifested itself in an institution, the Censorate, as well as in the actions of courageous individuals. The Censorate was a product of the merger of Confucian and Legalistic ideology, for it combined the function of surveillance on behalf of the monarch with that of remonstrance against a monarch's misdeeds. One famous case of the latter was the protest of officials against the Tianqi emperor (reigned 1620–27) and his powerful palace eunuch, Wei Zhongxian (1568–1627). According to the imperial censor Zuo Guangdou and his colleagues, palace eunuchs preferred taxing the people to lessening expenditures on palace luxuries and coddling the emperor to telling him the truth about the poor condition of national defense and popular welfare. Most important of all, Confucian officials accused Wei Zhongxian, perhaps the most powerful eunuch in all of Chinese history, of usurping the emperor's unique right to rule.

In 1624 Wei convinced the Tianqi emperor to have hundreds of Wei's opponents rounded up and punished. Some lost only their jobs, but others, including Zuo Guangdou, lost their lives (Zuo died under torture in 1625). In a world where power politics could trump Confucian ideals, Zuo could not be saved, despite decades of service under two imperial ancestors, the father and grandfather of the reigning emperor. This fact exposes a key irony of Confucian political life: Adherence to Confucian ideals in the service of the ruler could easily engender imperial wrath rather than imperial gratitude.

While some Confucians thus became famous for their political activities, the best-known Confucian leaders in history earned their reputations as intellectuals and teachers. They became famous for their individual philosophical contributions and for establishing Confucian academies (*xueyuan*). In some cases these academies were the training ground for Confucian scholars who would lead future philosophical, social, or political movements. Thus, serving as a teacher could make one a Confucian leader, since a Confucian scholar's reputa-

tion was furthered above all through teaching a body of dedicated disciples.

In fact, one way of enhancing Master Kong's reputation was through building legends about the large number of disciples he taught. By the first half of the Han Dynasty, when Sima Qian wrote the *Shiji* (Records of the Grand Historian), China's first comprehensive history, the author reported that Kong had 3,000 disciples, of whom 72 could be named. As in other lists of major disciples, usually numbering about 70, the author includes the names of 25 disciples who appear in the *Analects*. Although the evidence from the *Analects* and pre-Han sources gives little credence to later legends, it verifies that a group of Master Kong's immediate disciples began an intellectual lineage that still survives. By the time Master Meng taught, a century-and-a-half later than Master Kong, the idea of an intellectual lineage was so strong that Meng considered Kong the sage and uncrowned king (*suwang*) whose teachings had to be spread to save the empire. Meng's effort to spread these teachings was recorded in turn by Meng's disciples in the book *Mengzi* (Master Meng).

At every major stage in the later history of the Confucian intellectual lineage, there were moral-spiritual leaders who are remembered for their contributions to education as well as to philosophical and political life. The great Han Dynasty Confucian Dong Zhongshu convinced the emperor Wudi to establish a state college for the study of Confucian scriptures, which initiated trends that would ultimately give China a Confucian-based civil service examination system. During the Song era Zhu Xi developed the renowned White Deer Grotto Academy and other schools. Wang Yangming, the famous Ming era adversary of Zhu Xi, took up the life of a teacher at Kuiyang Academy after being banished to outlying Guizhou Province for writing a defense of a Confucian official who had been arrested by the powerful eunuch Lin Jin. As explained below in MAJOR THEOLOGIANS AND AUTHORS, these same men were also philosophical luminaries in Confucian intellectual history.

As in China, leading Confucians in other East Asian countries often had political as well as intellectual influence. Nevertheless, some scholars in, for example, Vietnam and Japan showed surprising resistance to Neo-Confucianism centuries after its rise to prominence in their countries. This occurred in part because resistance to Chinese influence as such was expressed through resistance to current Chinese ideologies and in part be-

Is Confucianism a Religion?

Many have asked, is Confucianism a religion, a philosophy of life, or a system of ethics? This is a misleading question, as all three are correct. Confucianism has a religious aspect along with its philosophical, moral, and other dimensions. In some cases its religious dimension is obvious, such as when China's emperors made sacrificial offerings to Heaven, Earth, Sun, or Moon in accordance with instructions from Confucian scriptures, such as the *Book of Rites.* In other contexts, such as the behavior of a person on the path toward sagehood, the religious dimension is manifested in more subtle ways—for example, in a person's efforts to understand the transcendent aspect of inner human nature (*xing*), which other traditions may refer to more explicitly as a quest for "the God within." In various ways, obvious and subtle, a religious dimension is apparent in Confucianism that is parallel to that of other major Asian traditions, including Buddhism, Taoism, and Hinduism. While lacking the personal God of various Western monotheistic faiths, these traditions construct temples and other sacred structures, have collections of holy scriptures, advocate spiritual paths toward perfection, and perform rituals that involve human as well as trans-human forces. Confucianism is no exception.

cause the Vietnamese and Japanese scholars in question were reformers who drew their ideas from Confucianism's earliest sources, bypassing more recent interpretations that were, in their minds, of lesser value.

When the Tâyson rebellion in late-eighteenth-century Vietnam overthrew the Le Dynasty, the country was ripe for intellectual as well as institutional change. Ngo Thi Nham (1746–1803), already a leading Confucian, took the opportunity to provide for the new Tâyson emperor a suitable ideology, the influence of which extended well into the succeeding Nguyen Dynasty. Nham shunned the scholasticism that characterized the Neo-Confucianism of his day, criticizing the method of rote memorization favored by many of his Vietnamese contemporaries. He stressed direct parallels

between the political situation in Vietnam and the travails of the ancient Zhou Dynasty during its Spring and Autumn era (722–481 B.C.E.), as recorded in the scriptural *Spring and Autumn Annals.* Although the *Annals* described a world that predated by more than two millennia Nham's Vietnam, it captured the latter country's need of leadership to "save the age" (*tê thê*). By challenging his contemporaries to abandon the relative security of the scholastic method for the direct experience of a world in crisis, with the chronicle of the ancient Zhou experience as a guide, Nham reinvigorated the Confucian tradition in Vietnam.

Confucianism's traditional influence in Japan regained strength during the Meiji period (1868–1912). Although the Meiji period is best known for its connection with Japanese modernization, it is also known for efforts to revive certain Confucian teachings. Motoda Nagazane (1818–91), the Meiji emperor's tutor and advisor, was the Confucian leader most responsible for these efforts. While the government promoted the Westernization of Japan's economy, society, and culture, Motoda argued for the revival of Confucianism as a countervailing force. As a Confucian lecturer in the Imperial Household Ministry and the primary author of the famous 1890 Imperial Rescript on Education, which gave renewed emphasis to Confucian and Shinto values, he was able to achieve a certain success.

In particular, Motoda advocated an enhanced role for Confucian ethics in modern Japanese education. Modern knowledge, he argued, must be ethically based, built on Confucianism's Four Virtues of benevolence, righteousness, loyalty, and filiality. Like other traditionalists in late-nineteenth-century Japan, he supported movements to establish private schools and societies for Confucian learning and himself authored an ethics textbook, which was widely distributed in 1882 under the auspices of the emperor. By the time of the Imperial Rescript on Education, which assured the role of Confucian ethics in the standard curriculum for Japanese schools, Confucianism had been merged with Imperial Shinto as the basis for Japanese nationalism. Thus, as perhaps unintended consequences of Motoda's leadership, the Japanese government promoted Confucianism for two main reasons: (1) to reinforce people's feelings of loyalty and filiality toward the emperor and (2) to establish Confucianism as the common cultural heritage in the areas of East Asia that Japan was beginning to conquer.

MAJOR THEOLOGIANS AND AUTHORS Prior to today, the most innovative Confucian thinkers emerged during the time of classical Confucianism (fifth through third centuries B.C.E.) and during the era of so-called Neo-Confucianism, more than a thousand years later. The leading figures of the classical era were the masters Kong, Meng, and Xun. In the development of Neo-Confucianism, two figures stood out: Zhu Xi and Wang Yangming. In the twentieth century a group of thinkers called New Confucians initiated efforts to revive Confucian thought.

Much has already been said about the role of Kong and Meng in Confucian history. Master Xun was a brilliant thinker who influenced Legalists as well as early Confucians. He was not fully appreciated by later Confucians, however, perhaps because he disagreed with Master Meng's view on the goodness of human nature, which became a mainstay of Confucian orthodoxy. Nonetheless, Master Xun's views on li (ritual norms) did influence later Confucianism. These views were actually linked to his position on human nature, which held that the latter tended toward selfish behavior and, therefore, was needful of the social training provided by li. In an argument suggestive of the theories of modern sociology, he asserted that ritual behavior functions to create social harmony as well as to have a civilizing effect on the acts and feelings of individuals.

Early Confucians focused on the outward behavior—both political and ritual—that was needed for a person's moral development. The Neo-Confucians, responding to Buddhism and Taoism, took up a stronger interest in the inner life. They produced two main schools of moral and mental cultivation, one known as Lixue (learning to understand li [meaning, in this case, fundamental principle, not ritual norms]) and the other as Xinxue (learning of the heart-mind). Lixue was championed by Zhu Xi, while Wang Yangming promoted Xinxue. Master Zhu held that the mental practice of being attentive to principle as it was manifested in each thing could lead to the realization of the fundamental principle permeating all phenomena, which he called heavenly principle (tianli).

The other two linchpins of the Neo-Confucian perspective on humanity and nature were heart-mind (xin) and matter-energy (qi). While the principle manifested in things was held to be ultimately unified, the dynamic nature of matter-energy was thought to account for the unceasing change in the cosmos as well as for the differences among its myriad phenomena. Like all other cos-

mic entities, humans embody the dynamic interaction of li and qi, principle and matter-energy. Indeed, Zhu conceived each person as having a heart-mind that, ideally, could unify li and qi as manifested in the inner nature endowed by Heaven, on the one hand, and human feelings rooted in physicality, on the other. This perspective on humanity and nature was the basis for Zhu's follower's seeking to attain the goal in which "Heaven and human become one" (tian ren heyi). They began their quest with an effort to understand li (principle) as it is manifested in the myriad phenomena of the cosmos. From this starting point, Zhu asserted, a person could ultimately awaken to the unifying tianli permeating all phenomena, human and nonhuman.

Three centuries later Wang Yangming would disagree with Zhu, asserting that the quest for Confucian awakening should begin with the heart-mind itself. While this version of Neo-Confucian self-cultivation seemed close to Buddhism—to the Chan (Zen) school in particular—Wang's followers distinguished themselves from the so-called mind-emptying, society-fleeing monks and nuns of Buddhism. One sees justification for their position when one looks at the political as well as philosophical career of Master Wang. Banished to a remote area following a youthful confrontation with the powerful eunuch Liu Jin, Wang was restored to favor following Liu's execution in 1510, at which point he began a remarkable career as a civil administrator and military commander. His reputation was so great that, in 1527, he was asked to come out of retirement to govern two southern provinces of China that were plagued by insurgents. He succeeded in his final assignment and died on his way back home in 1529.

How could this socially involved official be identified, especially by critics, as someone responsible for a Buddhist turn in Neo-Confucian thought? Biographers trace his philosophical shift to a spiritual experience he had during his banishment in Guizhou. As a result of this experience he realized that his inner nature was itself sufficient for attaining sagehood and that he could find li (principle) within his own heart-mind. In fact, in Wang's view, Zhu Xi had made a crucial error in separating li from heart-mind, thus leading followers to believe they could find li in things outside the self. Because Wang believed heavenly principle is inherent in the human heart-mind, he said it should be sought there through inner contemplation. Quiet sitting (jingzuo), the Confucian equivalent of Buddhist meditation, was thus even more central for Wang's followers than for those of Zhu Xi. Moreover, the former also embraced the idea that moral practice could gain greater guidance from a person's inner knowledge of the good (*liangzhi*) than through more outward moral learning. Wang's approach toward moral and spiritual matters would become the inspiration for the New Confucians of the late twentieth century.

After Neo-Confucian thought spread to Korea and Japan, Zhu Xi orthodoxy achieved prominence in those countries. In both countries, however, there were efforts to revise, and even to oppose, Zhu Xi's thought. Yi T'oegye (1501–70) played a central role in reinforcing the status of Zhu Xi's thought in Korea, yet his revision of Master Zhu's ideas also gave him a reputation as one of Korea's most original thinkers. Ogyu Sorai (1666–1728), a major figure in the so-called Ancient Learning (*kogaku*) movement in Japan, took the even more radical step of committing himself to the study of early Confucian scriptures, ignoring the commentary of Zhu Xi and deriving fresh ideas of his own.

Yi T'oegye earned his place in Korean intellectual history by advancing the Confucian conceptualization of how principle (*li*) relates to matter-energy (*qi*). Zhu Xi had made this relationship central to Confucian thought but had left it somewhat unclear. For Zhu, although principle had a certain priority—by virtue of its relation to tao (and coequally heaven) and inner human nature (*xing*)—over physical things and human emotions, the precise character of this priority remained ambiguous. In his work on ethics and psychology, T'oegye, uncomfortable with this ambiguity, clearly described the way in which principle had priority. For him, in the ideal order, principle manifests itself first, and matter-energy second. This order results in goodness. By contrast, if matter-energy becomes manifest first and veils principle, evil can result. On this basis he explained the origin of evil tendencies in human behavior and provided guidance for people on how to prevent evil from arising in their behavior.

In T'oegye's view, since principle is always good, the moral status of something depends on the quality of its matter-energy. For humans a return to the inner nature, which is aligned with principle, establishes the basis for developing good tendencies at the level of matter-energy. This return can be accomplished by cultivating the moral aspect of one's mind, or the mind of tao, as opposed to the merely human mind. More concretely, this means that the "seeds," as Master Meng had called them, of the Four Virtues issue from principle and are

grasped by the mind of tao, whereas the emotions issue from the human mind. In this way T'oegye established the priority of the mind of tao over the ordinary human mind in parallel with the priority of principle over matter-energy. During his life and for centuries afterward, debate continued over his solution to perceived problems in orthodox Zhu Xi thought. Nonetheless, he had done more than any other Korean thinker to frame the context of the debate.

In Japan debate focused not on a correct interpretation of Chinese Neo-Confucianism but, rather, on the possible need for a radical alternative to it. For thinkers in the Ancient Learning movement, this alternative was found by returning directly to early Confucian texts. They believed the metaphysical and psychological theories that fascinated T'oegye and other Neo-Confucians were distractions from the correct Confucian path. Ogyu Sorai, the best known among these thinkers, founded the Kobunjigaku (School of Ancient Words and Phrases) and made good use of his skills as a scholar of ancient Chinese texts to identify concrete Confucian moral, ritual, and governmental practices. In his attack on the thought of Zhu Xi and other Neo-Confucians, he argued for the importance of actual rites and institutions created by the ancient kings, as recorded in ancient texts. According to Ogyu, reverence for heaven expressed through prescribed ceremonies and the adoption of correct ritual norms in daily life would transform individuals and society, whereas acting upon the belief that the inner nature linked persons to heavenly principle would only lead to arrogance. Just as an earlier proponent of Ancient Learning, Yamaga Sokō, had advocated the adoption of early Confucian models for personal behavior in developing Bushido, or the Way of the Warrior, Sorai furthered an abiding interest in ancient Chinese *li* (ritual norms) within Japanese civilization. Although he did not deter other Japanese thinkers from continuing with Neo-Confucian philosophical speculation, his contribution to the richness of Japanese ritual thought and practice lasted into modern times.

In the twentieth century many East Asian intellectuals opposed Confucianism. Their opposition was grounded in the view that Confucian traditions were responsible for their society's difficulties with modernization. Nonetheless, some intellectuals remained loyal to Confucian thought and, moreover, strove to show its relevance to the modern world. One clear example of this has been the work of the New Confucians.

On 4 May 1919 demonstrations occurred throughout China that became symbolic of the antitraditionalist efforts of Chinese intellectuals. The first well-known traditionalist response was the book *Dongxi wenhua ji qi zhexue* (Eastern and Western Cultures and Their Philosophies), by Liang Shuming (1893–1988). Two of his like-minded contemporaries, Zhang Junmai (Carson Chang; 1886–1969) and Xiong Shili (1885–1968), inspired and taught a second generation of modern Confucians who were labeled New Confucians. Three of them—Tang Junyi (1909–78), Xu Fuguan (1903–82), and Mou Zongsan (1909–95)—left China proper and were instrumental in educating a third generation of New Confucians in Hong Kong and Taiwan. These three scholars, along with Zhang Junmai, produced and signed a manifesto introducing their teachings in 1958. Zhang was living in the United States at the time and was the first to suggest the idea of a manifesto that would provide other scholars with a more positive assessment of Chinese thought and a more optimistic view of its contribution to world thought.

Although the manifesto of 1958 was addressed, in key respects, to Western scholars, the English translation appeared four years later in an abbreviated version that had little impact at the time. Published in Chia-sên Chang's *The Development of Neo-Confucian Thought* (1962), the translation was titled "A Manifesto for a Reappraisal of Sinology and a Reconstruction of Chinese Culture." The four authors were disappointed with prevailing studies of traditional Chinese culture because such studies treated it as a dead object and failed to understand its spiritual essence. They believed that a correct understanding of Chinese culture would improve the prospects for healthy future developments in China and throughout the world. Correctly understood, they argued, the essence of Chinese culture lies in moral and metaphysical teachings that have universal value rather than a value limited to their being aspects of Chinese history or modern Chinese nationalism. These teachings originated in Confucianism and are far more spiritual in nature than others are willing to admit. While others consider Confucianism important and identify *xin* (heart-mind) and *xing* (inner nature) among its key concepts, they fail to see its spiritual value. Too influenced by modern, Western views of mind and human nature, they misunderstand *xin* and *xing*. *Xin* designates a person's transcendental moral mind, and *xing* designates the sense of moral reason that is conferred on a person by Heaven. By following the learning of moral mind and moral reason (*xinxing zhi xue*), one can attain a state of conformity in virtue (*de*) with Heaven (Tian).

According to the 1958 manifesto, Confucian moral metaphysics, unlike Western moral metaphysics, does not need to posit God's existence. Instead, it grounds itself in the experience of the limitless nature of the transcendental moral mind possessed by every person. While moral practice can emerge from consciousness of moral mind and moral reason, such consciousness grows only through regular moral practice. Thus, Confucian philosophy is never merely theoretical, as is so often true in the West. It is always practical and close to everyday living. Therefore, although Western philosophy produced the kind of abstract theory and rigorous logic that helped modern science to develop, it can still learn much from Asian thought. In particular, there are five areas in which the West can learn from the East. In its relentless pursuit of progress the West betrays an underlying insecurity that makes its societies keep driving ahead. With experience of the transcendental moral mind as the basis of all temporal value, people can appreciate resting in contentment as a counterbalance to the will to drive ahead. Proceeding from abstract truths to their application in concrete situations, the modern West is not only exceedingly oriented toward progress, it is also quite inflexible in its manner of observing and handling specific situations. All must conform to supposedly universal legal, scientific, or religious principles. By appreciating that the human mind must stay in contact with immediate reality, an Asian perspective can lead us to a more dynamic and flexible approach to world problems. The West can also learn from the East in regards to the practice of compassion. The love and enthusiasm for helping others that is grounded in Western religions carry the danger of distortion and allow selfish tendencies to play a role. To prevent these tendencies from emerging, a person must remove them at their roots by experiencing what Buddhists call "great compassion." A person can then love and respect every other person as one in whom God (Heaven, great compassion) also dwells. Westerners should also learn from the East how to perpetuate their culture. In its pursuit of progress and world mastery, the West not only lacks a sense of contentment but also a sense of historical consciousness that incorporates human as well as cosmic roots. Westerners need to have a sense of filial gratitude toward their roots as the basis for prolonging the culture and history of their ancestors. Finally, with their traditional beliefs in original sin and a salvation that is limited to members of a particular religion, Westerners need to develop a greater sense of "one world, one family." Holding that each person is originally good and having no requirement of church membership, Confucianism can lead the way toward people's acceptance of all others as brothers.

Students of the New Confucian thinkers who wrote the 1958 manifesto continue to be active, developing their ideas and seeking new ways to respond to Western religions and philosophies. Perhaps the best known among them is Wei-ming Tu, a Chinese-American scholar at Harvard University. In his optimistic assessment, contemporary Confucians are beginning a Third Epoch in the history of Confucian thought as they respond to Western ideas. During the First Epoch (Han period), according to Tu, Confucians successfully faced the challenge of competing Chinese schools of thought. In the Second Epoch (Song period) they reformulated their tradition in response to Indian Buddhism. In the Third Epoch they will match their earlier intellectual accomplishments in facing the challenge of the West.

ORGANIZATIONAL STRUCTURE Confucianism's organizational structure was typically the same as that of existing social institutions, such as the family and the state. Those who led and preserved the tradition over the centuries were clan patriarchs and state officials. Other organizations that served as Confucianism's "carriers," to use the concept of the sociologist Max Weber, included the Confucian academies aligned with certain philosophical schools and the syncretic religious groups that promoted Confucian teachings along with Buddhist, Taoist, and other teachings.

With the demise of East Asian monarchies and with clan organizations existing only as shadows of their former selves, the successors of the Confucian academies and syncretic religions remain as the primary carriers of Confucian teachings and practices. Such groups as the New Confucian school of philosophers continue to serve the function of Confucian academies, and some religious organizations, such as Yiguan Dao (Way of Unity) and Falun Gong, preserve Confucian teachings as part of a syncretic mixture.

HOUSES OF WORSHIP AND HOLY PLACES The most sacred place for Confucians is Qufu, Shandong Province, China. The town contains the gravesite of Master Kong (in a Kong family graveyard) and the homes of many living descendants of the Kong family. In addition, Qufu is the site of the oldest and largest Master Kong temple. Throughout East Asia are similar temples, where official rites for Master Kong were traditionally performed. Only a few such temples continue to have these rites and do so partly to keep the tradition alive and partly to serve the tourist industry.

One can also include the ancestral halls and gravesites of East Asian families other than the Kong family as places of Confucian worship. Traditionally, at these two sites, family members performed Confucian-style ceremonies in commemoration of their ancestors. This practice has continued but on a reduced scale, though there has been a revival of these ceremonies in China since the death of Mao Zedong.

WHAT IS SACRED? In his book *Confucius: The Secular as Sacred* (1972), the scholar Herbert Fingarette presented the view that people should find sacredness in the ordinary activities of human interaction. According to this view, what Confucians consider sacred is fully within the natural and social worlds in which people live. In the natural world Tian (Heaven) and key representations of the yin and yang forces, such as Moon and Sun, are sacred. In the social world each human being is sacred and potentially a sage, yet a person's own elders and ancestors are to be most revered. Even the tradition's main deity—to the extent that Master Kong is treated as one—has only rarely been associated with anything miraculous or supernatural. Like other revered sages of Confucianism, he is sacred because he was able to maximize human virtue and wisdom.

HOLIDAYS AND FESTIVALS The most specifically Confucian holiday is 28 September, the celebration of Master Kong's birthday, which for some East Asians is also Teacher's Day. It is celebrated in many ways, with various kinds of East Asian cultural performances, including traditional sacrificial rites at Master Kong temples. During premodern times these were biannual rites performed on spring and fall festival days.

In a strict sense there are no other Confucian festival days. Most people, however, acknowledge the strongly Confucian nature of ancestral festivals, when family members ritually express their filial gratitude toward ancestors. These festivals include days for visiting gravesites, such as the Chinese Qing Ming festival (5 April), as well as days when family members present offerings to ancestors on the family altar at home, such as New Year's Day.

MODE OF DRESS Contemporary Confucians, even leaders, have no specific mode of dress. The only exception occurs on Master Kong's birthday, when dignitaries wear robes similar to those worn by traditional Confucian officials. In premodern times the mandarin robes that were the daily attire of officials enhanced the reverence in which they were held by the common people. The robes worn on ritual occasions were quite ornate, featuring images of birds and other animals that indicated the type (civil or military) and rank (grades one through nine) of an official's position. When a large number of officials wearing these robes stood in ceremonial formations, both color and cosmic significance were added to the rites being performed.

DIETARY PRACTICES The Confucian scriptures and related traditions had much to say about eating in general but not about dietary restrictions or prohibited foods. These sources, especially the ones about *li* (ritual), covered good table manners, seasonal observances, and proper awareness of the social hierarchy in the serving of food. For example, the *Book of Rites* prescribes the following: Do not make noise in eating; do not snatch food; do not use chopsticks for millet porridge; do not gulp soup; do not keep picking the teeth; and, if a guest asks for condiments, the (insulted) host will apologize for not making a better soup. While modern East Asians may not know the source, most will certainly recognize the table manners it recommends.

Seasonal and hierarchical aspects of eating also had religious and social significance. The discussion of seasonal observances in Confucian ritual texts included information about what to eat so as to be in harmony with a given time of year. For example, the "Monthly Ordinances" chapter of the *Book of Rites* prescribes wheat and mutton for a ruler's spring meals; beans and fowl for his summer meals; hemp seeds and dog's flesh for his autumn meals; and millet and pork for his winter meals. As with other aspects of the ruler's behavior—such as the color of his robe and the type of carriage or shape of vessel used—the food he ate had to harmonize with the elemental agent of each season: wood for spring, fire for summer, metal for autumn, and water for winter.

Reflecting a broader enforcement of social hierarchy through symbolic acts, ritual procedures for serving food revealed the same penchant for careful differentiation by age, gender, and social status that are found in Confucian ritual procedures for other areas of life, from court protocol to funeral ceremonies. An especially in-teresting passage from the part of the *Book of Rites* covering table manners tells about the five ways to serve a melon based on the social status of the person who will eat it. For the Son of Heaven (the emperor), the melon must be in eight parts and covered with fine linen; for the ruler of a state, it should be in four parts and covered with a course napkin; for a great officer, it should be in four parts but left uncovered; for a lesser officer, it should simply be served with the stalk cut off; and, for the common man, no preparation is needed, since he "will deal with it with his teeth."

RITUALS As discussed above, *li* (ritual norms, propriety) have played a central role in Confucianism, and throughout East Asia, ritual norms for important ceremonies, such as marriages and funerals, originated in ancient Confucian scriptures. In addition, a whole range of state rituals were performed in accordance with the requirements of the Confucian scriptures, such as the *Book of Rites,* from each ruler's worship of his own ancestors to the imperial sacrifices to Heaven that Chinese emperors performed at the Altar to Heaven on the day of the winter solstice. In a general sense, all of these events were Confucian rituals. The rites performed for Master Kong at Confucian temples, however, were historically the ones most closely identified with Confucianism, and today this is even truer because they are virtually the only (formerly state) rituals that continue to be performed.

Temple rites for Master Kong began as a Kong family affair. Over time, however, they became a national tradition in China and other East Asian countries. Centuries after Master Kong's death, during the Han Dynasty, the Chinese emperor first made offerings at Master Kong's ancestral temple in the hometown of the Kong family. Later the system of official rites for Master Kong expanded greatly. A major temple for Master Kong was constructed in the national capital, and lesser temples were built at all local administrative centers. At the main altar in each temple the master was worshiped under his official title, "supreme sage and ancient teacher," and, at various secondary altars, lesser Confucian sages were revered. Similarly, ordinary families built clan ancestral temples for the worship of male ancestors, who were represented by tablets showing their names and official titles.

Since the fall of the premodern states in China, Korea, and Vietnam, only a shadow of the former system of Confucian temple rites has been maintained.

Cultural conservatives and foreign tourists in contemporary East Asia are periodically able to enjoy ceremonies performed for Master Kong. But these ceremonies no longer serve a central role in a state religion. Like other aspects of the modern Confucian tradition, they have an uncertain future.

RITES OF PASSAGE Three major rites of passage in East Asia developed under Confucian influence: coming-of-age, marriage, and funeral ceremonies. Confucian mourning and ancestral rites can be viewed as extensions of the practices of Confucian funeral ceremonies. The *Book of Rites* was the original source for most information on how to perform these rites of passage. Since the twelfth century, however, *Zhu Xi's Family Rituals* has been the immediate source of information for most families. In addition to carrying the commentary and imprimatur of Master Zhu, it briefly covers each of the key rites of passage: capping and pinning, weddings, funerals, and sacrificial rites for ancestral and seasonal events.

While the existence of the capping and pinning ceremonies for boys and girls suggests ritual parity between males and females, in actuality only the capping ceremony for boys was a major event. Girls were "pinned" (given a cap, a jacket, and an adult name) as part of the betrothal process, sometimes just prior to their marriage. The capping ceremony, by contrast, was a major event in the lives of boys from upper-class families who had reached the age of 14 (15 in Chinese reckoning). The process began three days before the actual capping with an announcement at the family offering hall by an elder (usually the boy's father or grandfather). The capping ceremony itself occupied a day of ritual activities that culminated in a meal for the sponsor (an important friend or associate of the elder) and the introduction of the boy to his father's friends and other local elders.

Confucian influences on marriages extend from the details of the rituals as such to the patriarchal values underlying them. Even today many traditional marriages conform to the pattern of "six rites" that is described in Confucian ritual texts. First, the groom's family hires a go-between to inquire about the prospective bride. Second, the go-between makes another visit to request the prospective bride's astrological information. Third, if the bride's family provides this information, then an astrologer will be asked to compare the astrological information of the young woman and the man to assure that their marriage will be a match made in heaven. Fourth, there is a formal engagement involving the ex-

change of gifts between the families. The most important gifts go from the groom's to the bride's family in the form of a "bride's price," which compensates the girl's family for giving away their daughter to become another family's helpmate as well as its hope for continuing the family line. The fifth rite sets an auspicious date on which the wedding ceremony will take place. The sixth rite, the wedding ceremony itself, has several parts: The bride departs her home amid acts marking her impending separation from her natal family; she arrives at the groom's home to witness rituals that celebrate her arrival but also express the subordinate position she will have in her new home; and the bride joins the groom as a guest of honor at the wedding banquet, with its various acts and foods symbolizing key values, including prosperity and posterity, above all.

The only other family rituals that match marriage ceremonies in importance are those that follow death: funerals, mourning, and the veneration of ancestors. A Confucian funeral is, above all, a final opportunity for sons and daughters to express the depth of their filial gratitude. Although Master Kong advised against lavish funerals, most people express filial gratitude to their cherished ancestors by spending heavily on funerals, often hiring Taoist priests or Buddhist clerics to perform additional rites for the sake of the deceased person's soul. As a Confucian ritual, the event is a family affair, with sons of the deceased, rather than religious professionals, performing key ritual roles. As death becomes imminent, the elder is moved to the main hall of the home, where the altar to the ancestors is located. After death family members wash the corpse and place it in a coffin, which is then ritually sealed. Following filial rites in the main hall of the home, participants in the funeral procession carry the coffin to its burial site. After the burial the ancestral tablet carried by a son at the head of the procession is returned to the home and ritually installed on the ancestral altar.

Mourning rites offer opportunities to continue to express filial gratitude to one's deceased ancestors. Mourning responsibilities are divided into five grades (*wu fu*) defined by the *Book of Rites*. These range from first-grade mourning, which is observed by the wife and children of a deceased man, to fifth-grade mourning, which is observed by his distant relatives. The higher, or stricter, kinds of mourning last longer (up to 27 months), involve severe restrictions on behavior, and require the wearing of coarse attire as an expression of respect and sadness. In addition to mourning activities, ancestral rites were the final obligations required of family members. These will be covered below in connection with Confucian state rituals.

The main official rituals in Confucian states consisted of sacrifices to three kinds of entities: cosmic forces, royal ancestors, and Confucian sages. State sacrifices to cosmic forces were considered an important part of government because they maintained harmony between human society and the universe. The timing, location, and content of these sacrificial offerings were key aspects of maintaining this harmony. For example, the Chinese emperor, as the Son of Heaven, worshiped Heaven on the day of the winter solstice (when the heavenly yang principle begins to grow) at the Altar to Heaven, south of the capital city (that is, the yang direction). Because the sacrifice to Heaven was a "Great Sacrifice," it involved offering all three main sacrificial animals: an ox, a sheep, and a pig. The emperor offered a sacrifice to Earth at the time of the summer solstice at an altar to the north of the capital, while he revered the Sun and Moon in the east and west, respectively, at times that were also fixed in accordance with the yin-yang cosmology. As the representative of human society, the emperor acted according to the principles of the yin-yang cosmology specifically in order to maintain harmony between humanity and the natural world.

In the world of Chinese state ritual, the Son of Heaven's royal ancestors were second in importance only to Heaven. In fact, throughout East Asia, monarchs worshiped their ancestors in accordance with the Confucian principle of filial gratitude. In China ritual offerings were made at the imperial ancestral temple near the imperial palace and also at the imperial tombs outside the capital. Families throughout the empire conducted these practices on a smaller scale. They made offerings to their own ancestors at altars in the main halls of their homes as well as at their ancestor's gravesites. These rituals celebrated the accomplishments of the ancestors, the continuity of the family line, and the anticipated achievements of future generations. While contemporary East Asian leaders honor their forebears in private ancestral rites, just as ordinary citizens do, public commemorative rites for deceased national leaders and heroes are also common.

MEMBERSHIP Has Confucianism been a universal religion—that is, one that spreads a message for all humanity from one area to others in the manner of Buddhism, Christianity, and Islam? Or has it been a cultural religion, one that maintains itself primarily among one ethnic or national group, as has been the case with Judaism and Hinduism? Confucianism seems to fall between these two types of religion. On the one hand, it evolved and long remained within Chinese society. On the other hand, Confucianism ultimately spread from China to Korea, Japan, and Vietnam along with various features of Chinese culture. Because Confucian doctrines had a strong appeal to certain leaders in those countries, they promoted these doctrines with missionary zeal. But this does not mean that Confucianism is an evangelistic tradition. Rather, it has moved with societal, governmental, and intellectual traditions as they spread throughout East Asia and beyond. Even outside East Asia, immigrants—not missionaries—brought Confucian teachings and practices into new areas. Nonetheless, modern followers of Master Kong, such as the New Confucians, argue that people everywhere can embrace Confucian teachings on being filial, humane, trustworthy, and morally courageous. More than ever, Confucianism is a universal tradition but not an evangelizing one.

RELIGIOUS TOLERANCE There is no question that contemporary Confucians are content to accept their tradition as one among several world religions that should respect one another. In fact, several leading Confucian scholars are simultaneously interested in Confucianism and Buddhism or Taoism, while yet others are practicing Christians. In addition, they have been willing to participate in interreligious conferences, which are the modern world's best examples of mutual tolerance among religions. In particular, in the late twentieth century there were four major Confucian-Christian conferences—in Hong Kong (1988), Berkeley (1991), Boston (1994), and Vancouver (1997).

In premodern times the Confucian record with regard to religious tolerance was more mixed. Confucian states in China, Korea, and Vietnam were generally more tolerant of different religion's beliefs than their Christian counterparts in Europe. Periodically, however, there were persecutions of Buddhists by Confucian states as well as the infamous long-term suppression of Buddhism under Korea's Yi dynasty. Moreover, Confucian states often betrayed a suspicion of popular syncretic religious groups, which had roots in Buddhism, claiming that they had subversive tendencies. If deemed necessary, they used military force to control, or even eliminate, these sects.

SOCIAL JUSTICE During most of its history Confucianism has been aligned with established powers in society rather than with social justice movements that challenged these powers. As modern Confucians have argued, however, the tradition has a "prophetic" (social justice) dimension that they can develop, since Confucianism is now separated from the premodern monarchies that once supported and defined it. This dimension emerged during China's Warring States period (480–221 B.C.E.), when Master Meng, in particular, was one of few voices calling for peace, social welfare, and popular protest against inhumane monarchs. At that time Confucians, who considered themselves an ignored minority preaching humaneness and justice, lacked social and political influence.

Some modern scholars have found populist, and even democratic, tendencies in Master Meng's thought. They have pointed to occasions on which he approvingly quoted proto-democratic sayings, such as "Heaven sees as the people see; Heaven hears as the people hear" (*Mengzi* 5A:5). They also have argued that he believed in popular rebellion when it was justified. For example, in conversation with the king of the state of Qi, he told the king that the people will treat a ruler who abuses them as a robber and an enemy. A bit incredulous, the king asked, "May a subject assassinate his sovereign?" Master Meng explained, "He who mutilates humaneness is just a mutilator; he who cripples justice is a mere crippler." He added that this kind of behavior turns a king into an "outcast," so that his murder would not count as the assassination of a sovereign (*Mengzi* 1B:8). As for conducting wars, Master Meng considered this to be one of the great crimes monarchs committed against their peoples. Although those skilled at war were highly valued in his time, he said "death is too light a punishment for such men." He stated his justification for this view as follows: "In wars to capture territory, the dead fill the plains; in wars to capture cities, dead bodies litter the urban landscape" (*Mengzi* 4A:14). Thus, the Confucian tradition has the intellectual resources to support social justice movements, although historically it has a weak record in using them.

Education is one area in which Confucianism has a strong historical record. With its positive assessment of human potential, Confucianism has made education central to its views on social as well as individual development. This trend began in the time of the masters Kong and Meng with the idea that social leaders should be those who have themselves learned about govern-

ment, ritual, and virtue, not simply those born the sons of aristocrats. It later developed into East Asia's most important social program to counteract aristocratic privilege: the state examination system. With roots going back as far as the Han period, the system of state examinations evolved first in China and was later adopted in other areas of East Asia and, ultimately, the world. Confucian leaders sought to develop state-run examinations that would become the path by which the sons of any family could enter key government positions.

While the examination system excluded women and was not completely successful in replacing aristocracies with meritocracies, it established education as a path to success and stressed selection by merit as a cure for the widespread social ills of nepotism and favoritism. In contemporary East Asia, the battle between these social ills and the meritocratic ideal has continued, with young women as well as young men placing their fate in the hands of examination systems that determine access to educational as well as career opportunities.

SOCIAL ASPECTS The family has always been the central social institution in Confucian thought. In fact, the second institution stressed by Confucians, the government, was in key ways modeled on the family, with the monarch filling the role of patriarch. Traditionally, the family and the state in Confucian societies were both hierarchically ordered. More recently, there have been efforts to change this by promoting equality between husbands and wives and by promoting democracy as the best system for forming governments.

Representatives of Confucianism hold conservative views on the value of the family, viewing it as preferable to other social arrangements, from communes to unmarried couples. Many, however, would like to see democratization in family relationships as well as in political ones. One recommendation has been to rearrange the famous Five Relationships, described above in MORAL CONDUCT, so that the central one would be a balanced husband-wife relationship instead of the hierarchical father-son relationship, the latter relationship also becoming more equable. Such an arrangement represents two fundamental shifts in social values. First, women are valued as much as men and are believed to have the same right to pursue careers. Second, no one in the family is stuck perpetually in a powerless, subordinate role. The wife is freed from a life of subordination to her mate. Children are given the space to develop as independent individuals, although they still must learn to express filial gratitude to the mother and father who have sacrificed to help them develop.

CONTROVERSIAL ISSUES Many issues on which modern Confucians have taken a stand concern the nature of the Confucian tradition itself. Focused on saving Confucianism and, in many cases, traditional culture as such, they have rarely commented on the issues that dominate much religious debate—abortion, birth control, divorce, and homosexuality, for example. In fact, they have expended most of their intellectual capital defending the tradition against the attacks of its critics. In the process they have had to respond to the following key questions: (1) Is Confucianism so attached to the past that it is unable to contribute to a brighter future in East Asia; (2) do Confucian values run counter to the economic needs of modernizing societies; (3) is Confucianism relevant to East Asia's quest for democracy; and (4) can Confucianism find roles for and enhance the status of women within the tradition as well as in society as a whole?

Contemporary Confucians are admittedly conservative in the sense that they find much of value in traditional culture. Most claim, however, that they are willing to abandon useless elements of traditional culture while preserving useful elements and combining them with the best contributions from the West. The need to preserve the past while moving forward to keep pace with the West has dominated the thinking of East Asian intellectuals since at least the mid-nineteenth century, when the Confucian scholar Zhang Zhidong (1837–1909) coined the slogan "Chinese learning as foundation, Western learning as application." The polarity between *ti* (foundation, substance) and *yong* (application, function) had been important in Confucian thought prior to the nineteenth century, but Zhang placed it at the center of a controversy that has lasted for well over a century.

Confucians have generally believed that Western learning provides useful tools for developing East Asian nations but that Asian thought (Confucianism, in particular) continues to provide the basic values by which these nations should be developed. They have admired certain Western contributions, such as science for technological development and democracy for political development, but they have rejected "wholesale Westernization." They do not want Western materialistic and utilitarian values to replace Confucianism's spiritual humanism and its commitment to forms of social harmony that mitigate competition between individuals.

In the mid-twentieth century Western social scientists all seemed to agree that elements of the Confucian social harmony model—familism, deference to authority, suppression of assertive individualism—would stand in the way of economic development. By the 1980s, however, social scientists in East Asia as well as the West found themselves having to explain the economic success of Japan and the four "mini-dragons": Hong Kong, Singapore, South Korea, and Taiwan. Contemporary explanations attribute economic success in these areas to the presence of the East Asian social harmony model as well as to such other "Confucian" elements as frugality, diligence, and delayed gratification. This has emboldened Confucians to claim that, indeed, there is a way to remain culturally Confucian while using Western tools to modernize, at least economically. The jury is still out on the issue of democratization in East Asia, however. Despite the region's economic modernization, it is still possible to argue that, as long as the political culture of East Asian countries remains subtly but essentially Confucian, they will continue to have trouble with political modernization.

Some modern Confucians have claimed that ancient Confucian political thought was not authoritarian—that, in fact, it contained democratic tendencies. Nonetheless, controversy has continued to rage over whether or not Confucianism can contribute positively to the process of democratization in East Asia. Even the New Confucian thinker Mou Zongsan has acknowledged that the Confucian political tradition lacked the means for practicing democracy, even though it supported philosophically the idea of government by and for the people. Others have been even less sanguine, wondering whether Confucianism can do anything at all to help democratization except stay out of the way as the process occurs. Moreover, Confucians have had trouble convincing people that their tradition is friendly to democracy, because a number of modern authoritarian regimes have promoted Confucian values, such as loyalty and filiality, to cultivate people's obedience. The governments of Chiang Kai-shek in Taiwan (1949–75), Lee Kuan Yew in Singapore (1959–90), and, more recently, Jiang Zemin in China (1993–2003) have made use of the Confucian tradition to secure people's compliance. Philosophically oriented Confucians have tried to distance themselves from this trend, but it clearly has led people to view claims about the compatibility of Confucianism and democracy with skepticism.

Confucians confront an equally difficult situation in making the case that their tradition is in a good position to champion women's rights. They face an uphill battle in reinterpreting their tradition in a way that establishes gender-neutral respect for human dignity. Scriptural discussions of the human potential for virtue and wisdom seem always to assume a gendered male subject, and the historical record on the treatment of women in Confucian societies is abysmal. It is therefore not surprising that no prominent feminist intellectuals in East Asia have identified themselves with Confucianism. All prominent representatives of Confucianism are men. For the most part these men have been willing to repudiate the attitudes toward women found in Confucian scriptures and in premodern Confucian societies. Nonetheless, they have not been affected as much by the global women's movement as have men in other world religions, primarily because women have been mostly unable or unwilling to join their ranks. Whether deserved or not, their tradition has an extremely poor reputation with feminists.

CULTURAL IMPACT As the teachings of Master Kong and his successors spread over East Asia, something called "Confucianization" occurred in the affected parts of China, Japan, Korea, and Vietnam. This process extended from the previously discussed areas of moral, spiritual, and political life to the arts, including architecture, literature, and painting.

In the case of architecture, public buildings, especially the residences and audience halls of rulers, were built to conform to sacred principles laid down in Confucian scriptures. These included the principle of north-south axiality, according to which building entrances faced south—the beneficent yang direction—with their backs to the north. The related principle of directionality determined what ritual structures could be built to the east, west, north, or south of the main hall or residence. Finally, the principle of concentricity assured that the most sacred building, such as the primary audience hall or royal residence, was at the center of the whole complex of walls and buildings. Lesser structures were built on the periphery in locations determined by the principles of directionality and north-south axiality. Even the structures of other traditions, such as Buddhist monastery complexes in East Asia, were built according to these principles.

While Confucianism's influence on music and dance was less pervasive than its influence on architecture, it had a special impact on the performance of public rituals that featured music and dance. Intoned ritual commands mixed with the sounds of drums and bronze bells came to characterize public rituals throughout East Asia. Moreover, the positions of participants in the ritual reflected originally Confucian conceptions of social hierarchy, with the highest-ranking participant (perhaps the ruler himself) marking the center of power, and those of lesser and lesser ranks standing in locations farther and farther away from this central figure.

Turning to the realm of literature, it is clear that Confucian officials wrote more than ritual commands and the texts of memorials to their kings. Indeed, the *Book of Odes* was not only one of Confucianism's original *Five Scriptures* but also the primary source of examples and inspiration for East Asian poets. Moreover, Confucian officials were always found among the ranks of poets, and learning to write poetry was always part of a good Confucian education. For better or worse, poetry writing required skills possessed only by members of the educated elite. Poet's verses had to conform to strict rules about rhyming, line length, and so forth. Poets also needed the erudition that would allow them to create, as well as to recognize, literary allusions to the contents of earlier poetic works, including the *Book of Odes*.

In fact, the topics and themes of poetry, going back to the *Book of Odes,* often reflected Confucian values and a Confucian lifestyle. Such topics and themes included descriptions of being in harmony with the seasonal changes of the cosmos, praise for good rulers and their loyal ministers, subtle condemnation of corrupt rulers through portrayals of social abuses, and expressions of the nostalgia for one's native place that was felt by officials who were stationed far from home. Finally, the events celebrated in occasional verse were often connected with the public and private lives of Confucian officials, including such occasions as a parting from home to take up a new official position, a private gathering of the literati, or even a visit to a friend.

Confucianism also exerted an influence on painting. In fact, a movement called "literati painting" emerged in China that, ultimately, had an impact in other areas of East Asia as well. Literati painters were self-professed "amateurs" in their lives away from court. They self-consciously avoided the professionalism of those who painted court portraits or realistic scenes from upper-class life. One of the results of their effort to avoid pro-

Confucian Civil Religion

Scholars most often use the concept "civil religion" when discussing beliefs and rituals that are connected to a nation rather than to any particular organized religion. The term is also useful, however, for understanding the role of Confucianism in premodern China, Korea, and Vietnam, especially since Confucianism usually lacked the organizational forms (churches or religious groups, for example) found in other world religions. Like modern civil religion in the United States and elsewhere, Confucianism provided the religious dimension of the state through the beliefs that its representatives promoted and the rituals that they performed.

This situation is well exemplified by Korea's Yi Dynasty (1392–1910), which aligned itself with Confucianism to perhaps the greatest extent of any East Asian state in history. Following the Koryo Dynasty (918–1392), in which Buddhism expanded its influence in Korean life, the Yi Dynasty promoted Confucianism over both foreign Buddhism and indigenous Korean shamanism. The dynasty's first king, T'aejo (reigned 1392–98), began construction of a Confucian school and temple complex called Sŏng gyun' gwan (Hall of Perfection and Equalization), which still exists in modern Seoul at its original location. He and many of his royal successors identified closely with Master Kong, whose descendants lived in the neighboring Shandong Province of China and migrated to Korea in significant numbers. Ultimately,

the national Master Kong Temple at Sŏng gyun' gwan housed the spirit tablets of Korean Confucian sages as well as those of Master Kong and his famous Chinese disciples.

Korean royalty performed rites of commemoration for Master Kong twice each year at this temple, thereby exhibiting their commitment to Confucian virtues. The master was revered as a human sage, not as a divine being, although elaborate sacrificial offerings were prepared to honor his spirit. This civil religious rite thus reinforced preferred social beliefs and served as a ritual model of a harmonious social hierarchy. In parallel with this and related Confucian civil rituals, the Korean state promoted Confucian civil beliefs regarding, for example, the loyalty of subject to ruler, the subservience of wife to husband, and the filial obedience of younger to older family members. These beliefs mainly concerned human relations, not the relationships between humans and divine beings. They were promoted, however, with the enthusiasm characteristic of religious missionaries. Within several generations of the Yi royal family's adoption of various Confucian beliefs and rituals, most of the Korean populace had embraced this "civil religion." Without actual missionaries, faith in the will of God, or even a church, a population was converted to a sacred tradition of foreign origin. The Confucian civil religion was celebrated by the Yi Dynasty until its end in 1910, and it continues to exert an influence in the lives of all Koreans, including those who swear allegiance to Protestant denominations or Buddhist revival movements.

fessional realism was the somewhat expressionist look for which literati landscape paintings are now so well known and adored. They offer personal expressions of the beauty and mystery of nature rather than photographic reproductions of it.

This discussion of Confucianism's impact on cultural developments in East Asia would be incomplete without mentioning calligraphy and the carving of seals. These two art forms had a special connection with East Asia's Confucian elite, who viewed their handwriting and signature seals as expressions of human character on paper. All educated people studied the art of using a

brush to write traditional Chinese characters. In premodern times a calligraphic scroll written by a great brush master or a famous historical figure had more value than most paintings. Perhaps even more surprising to students of East Asia, the carving of seals was often considered a major art form there, of no less importance than painting or calligraphy. After all, stamping one's seal on a document in East Asia continues to serve the same function as signing a document elsewhere in the world. Who else but Confucians would create an art form out of an important tool of the bureaucracy: the seal used to guarantee the authenticity of a state document?

This discussion demonstrates that, as the Confucian tradition spread over East Asia, it brought with it various cultural forms rooted in the private and public lives of Confucian scholars. The impact of these cultural forms has been as deep and abiding as the influence of the philosophical ideas and governmental practices for which Confucianism is better known.

Christian Jochim

Bibliography

Anh, Dao Duy. "Influence of Confucianism in Vietnam." *Vietnamese Studies* 111 (1994): 23–35.

Bellah, Robert. *Tokugawa Religion: The Cultural Roots of Modern Japan.* New York: The Free Press, 1985.

Carlitz, Katherine. "The Social Uses of Female Virtue in Late Ming Editions of Lienu Zhuan." *Late Imperial China* 12, no. 2 (1991): 117 ff.

Chang, Chia-sên. *The Development of Neo-Confucian Thought.* Vol. 2. New York: Bookman Associates, 1962.

Chow, Tse-tsung. *The May Fourth Movement: Intellectual Revolution in Modern China.* Cambridge, Mass.: Harvard University Press, 1960.

Confucius. *The Analects.* Translated by D.C. Lau. Harmondsworth, England: Penguin Books, 1979.

Dardess, John. *Confucianism and Autocracy: Professional Elites in the Founding of the Ming Dynasty.* Berkeley: University of California Press, 1983.

De Bary, William Theodore, and the Conference on Seventeenth-Century Chinese Thought. *The Unfolding of Neo-Confucianism.* New York: Columbia University Press, 1975.

De Bary, William Theodore, and JaHyun Kim Haboush, eds. *The Rise of Neo-Confucianism in Korea.* New York: Columbia University Press, 1985.

Deuchler, Martina. *The Confucian Transformation of Korea: A Study of Society and Ideology.* Cambridge, Mass.: Council on East Asian Studies, Harvard University, 1992.

Ebrey, Patricia Buckley. *Confucianism and Family Rituals in Imperial China: A Social History of Writing about Rites.* Princeton, N.J.: Princeton University Press, 1991.

Elman, Benjamin A., John B. Duncan, and Herman Ooms, eds. *Rethinking Confucianism: Past and Present in China, Japan, Korea, and Vietnam.* Los Angeles: UCLA Asian Pacific Monograph Series, 2002.

Fingarette, Herbert. *Confucius—The Secular as Sacred.* New York: Harper and Row, 1972.

Jensen, Lionel M. *Manufacturing Confucianism: Chinese Traditions and Universal Civilization.* Durham, N.C.: Duke University Press, 1997.

Kelleher, Theresa. "Confucianism." In *Women in World Religions.* Edited by Arvind Sharma, 135–60. Albany: State University of New York Press, 1987.

Legge, James, trans. *Li Chi: Book of Rites.* New Hyde Park, N.Y.: University Books, 1967.

Levenson, Joseph Richmond. *Confucian China and Its Modern Fate: A Trilogy.* Berkeley and Los Angeles: University of California Press, 1968.

Li, Chenyang, ed. *The Sage and the Second Sex: Confucianism, Ethics, and Gender.* Chicago: Open Court, 2000.

Liu, Shu-hsien. *Understanding Confucian Philosophy: Classical and Sung-Ming.* Westport, Conn.: Greenwood Press, 1998.

Makeham, John. *New Confucianism: A Critical Examination.* New York: Palgrave, 2003.

Mencius. *Mencius.* Translated by D.C. Lau. Harmondsworth, England: Penguin Books, 1970.

Meyer, Jeffrey F. *The Dragons of Tiananmen: Beijing as a Sacred City.* Columbia: University of South Carolina Press, 1991.

Nivison, David S., and Arthur F. Wright, eds. *Confucianism in Action.* Stanford, Calif.: Stanford University Press, 1959.

Nosco, Peter, ed. *Confucianism and Tokugawa Culture.* Princeton, N.J.: Princeton University Press, 1984.

Palmer, Spencer J. *Confucian Rituals in Korea.* Berkeley, Calif.: Asian Humanities Press, 1984.

Shryock, John. *The Origin and Development of the State Cult of Confucius.* New York: Paragon Reprint Corp., 1966.

Smith, R.B. "The Cycle of Confucianism in Vietnam." In *Aspects of Vietnamese History.* Edited by Walter F. Vella, 1–29. Honolulu: University of Hawai'i Press, 1973.

Swann, Nancy Lee. *Pan Chao: Foremost Woman Scholar of China, First Century A.D.* New York: The Century Co., 1932.

Taylor, Rodney L. *The Religious Dimensions of Confucianism.* Albany: State University of New York Press, 1990.

Tu, Wei-ming. "Confucianism." In *Our Religions.* Edited by Arvind Sharma, 139–227. San Francisco: HarperSanFrancisco, 1993.

Tu, Wei-ming, ed. *Confucian Traditions in East Asian Modernity: Moral Education and Economic Culture in Japan and the Four Mini-Dragons.* Cambridge, Mass.: Harvard University Press, 1996.

Tu, Wei-ming, and Mary Evelyn Tucker, eds. *Confucian Spirituality.* 2 vols. New York: Crossroad Publishing, 2003–04.

Wilson, Thomas A., ed. *On Sacred Grounds: Culture, Society, Politics, and the Formation of the Cult of Confucius.* Cambridge, Mass.: Harvard University Asia Center, 2002.

Woodside, Alexander. *Vietnam and the Chinese Model: A Comparative Study of Nguyen and Ch'ing Civil Government in the First Half of the Nineteenth Century.* Cambridge, Mass.: Harvard University Press, 1971.

Yang, C.K. *Religion in Chinese Society: A Study of Contemporary Social Functions of Religion and Some of Their Historical Factors.* Berkeley and Los Angeles: University of California Press, 1961.

Yao, Xinzhong. *An Introduction to Confucianism.* New York: Cambridge University Press, 2000.

Yao, Xinzhong, ed. *RoutledgeCurzon Encyclopedias of Confucianism.* London; New York: Routledge, 2003.

Zhu, Xi. *Chu Hsi's Family Rituals: A Twelfth-Century Manual for the Performance of Cappings, Weddings, Funerals, and Ancestral Rites.* Translated by Patricia Buckley Ebrey. Princeton, N.J.: Princeton University Press, 1991.

Zhu, Xi, and Lü Zuqian, comps. *Reflections on Things at Hand: The Neo-Confucian Anthology.* Translated by Wing-tsit Chan. New York: Columbia University Press, 1967.

Hinduism

FOUNDED: before 3000 B.C.E.

RELIGION AS A PERCENTAGE OF WORLD POPULATION: 14 percent

OVERVIEW Hinduism is the religion of almost a billion people. While most of them are in India, there are almost two million in the United States and substantial numbers in Great Britain, Canada, the Caribbean, Australia, and East Africa. Marked by diverse beliefs, practices, and organizational structures as well as multiple chains of authority, Hinduism is one of the largest and oldest religious traditions in the world. The tradition has been transmitted through performing arts, texts, visual art, and architecture. Hindus may think of the supreme being as beyond thought and word; as a supreme power that is immanent in the universe and that also transcends it; as male, female, or simultaneously male and female; as beyond gender; as one, as many; as a local colorful deity; and as abiding in the human soul or even as identical with it. Hinduism can be spoken of both as one umbrella category or as several traditions, and the larger Hindu culture encompasses not just beliefs and texts but also practices that include healing, performing arts, astrology, geomancy, and architecture.

The Hindu tradition does not have a particular year or even century of birth. It is generally believed that the Hindu tradition originated in the civilization that existed in India about five thousand years ago and possibly in the culture of the Indo-European people. Whether these two cultures were the same or distinct is a matter of scholarly debate. While Hinduism has been largely associated with India over the last two millennia, it has spread to many parts of the world through maritime contacts, traders, businessmen, educators, bonded workers, and learned priests.

The names "Hindu" and "India" are derived from "Sindhu," the original name of the river Indus. It was a word that most Hindus did not use for themselves in the past, and in India it had more geographical than religious overtones, at least until the thirteenth or fourteenth centuries C.E. The word "Hinduism" came to be used increasingly by the British in the eighteenth century, when they began to extend their colonial rule over India. There were numerous concepts and practices that connected the many "Hindu" groups and communities, but Western scholarship has questioned whether the concept of "Hinduism" as a unified tradition existed in the precolonial era. Despite their regional, sectarian, and linguistic differences, many Hindus point to concepts of caste, texts, and theologies—as well as practices such as pilgrimage and the celebration of festivals—to support the idea that there were diverse but connected precolonial traditions.

HISTORY In the traditional recording of events in India (called *iti-hasa,* or "thus it has been"), the deeds of gods and goddesses are combined with those of heroic kings, thoughtful and resourceful women, celestial beings (*devas*), and the wicked demon-like characters known as *danavas* or *asuras.* The sense of "history" in many of the Hindu texts called *Puranas* ("Ancient Lore") is a sense of valorous and gracious actions; it involves learning to act with a sense of what is righteous (dharma), compas-

OM. The "Om" (Aum) symbol is the written form of the sacred "Om" sound. It is the most holy of all the Hindu mantras. The symbol also represents the trinity of God in Brahma (the creator), Vishnu (the preserver), and Shiva (the destroyer). (THOMSON GALE)

sion, and gratitude. This sense of "thus it has been" is different from narrating a linear sequence of events, which constitutes a customary understanding of "history" in other parts of the world. Recording linear history has also been, however, practiced by many Hindu rulers. It is important to recognize that the well-known markers in the last few millennia are those people, events, and movements that have been privileged by contemporary minds as worthy of being preserved and therefore tell us only some aspects of the history of the Hindu traditions.

Most scholars believe that the earliest civilization in India of which we have records existed from about 3000 to 1750 B.C.E. near the river Indus. While some city centers were in Harappa and Mohenjo-Daro (both of which are in modern-day Pakistan, the country that borders India to the northwest), the civilization seems to have existed in many parts of the subcontinent. The people of the Harappa civilization were impressive builders and lived in what appears to have been planned urban centers. At Mohenjo-Daro there is a huge structure, resembling a swimming pool, that archaeologists call "the Great Bath." Scholars believe that it was meant for religious rituals. Archaeological evidence also suggests that the people of this culture worshiped a goddess and a god with the characteristics of the later Hindu deity Shiva.

The original homeland of the Indo-European people (who called themselves Arya, or "noble ones") is one of the most debated issues in Indian history. Although

many Western scholars maintain that the Indo-Europeans migrated from Central Asia in about 2000 B.C.E., some scholars think that the migration began in about 6000 B.C.E.—and from other regions (possibly the areas near Turkey). The work of these scholars suggests that it was a peaceful migration, possibly undertaken because of the farming interests of the population. Others say that the original homeland of these people was the Indian peninsula and that the civilization was continuous with the Harappan civilization. The dates for the Indo-European occupation of this area could thus be several centuries—if not millennia—earlier than 1500 B.C.E.

The Indo-Europeans spoke a language that developed into the ancient language of Sanskrit. They composed many poems, and eventually manuals, on rituals and philosophy. For a long time none of these were written down. The traditions were committed to memory and passed from generation to generation by word of mouth. Mnemonic devices were used to ensure accurate pronunciation, rhythm, and utterance. Many Hindus think of their earliest history as being recorded in these Indo-European compositions, called Veda, or "knowledge."

In the hymns that were composed by about 1000 B.C.E. there is speculation on the origins of the universe and a description of the sacrifice of a primeval man through which creation began. One of the hymns explicitly mentions the beginnings of the social divisions that are today called "caste."

The sacrificial worldview of the early Vedic age gave way to philosophical inquiry and discussion in the *Aranyaka*s and the Upanishads, composed during the seventh and sixth centuries B.C.E. The sophisticated philosophy of the Upanishads was coeval with the spirit of critical enquiry in many parts of northern India. Religious leaders—notably, Gautama Siddhartha (eventually called the Buddha, or the Enlightened One) and Mahavira the Jina (the Victorious One)—challenged the notion that the Vedas were revealed and authoritative. They relied on their own spiritual experiences to proclaim a path to liberation that was open to all sections of society. The followers of Mahavira are today called Jains. Early religious texts such as the Upanishads focus on the goal of liberation from the cycle of life and death, but most later Hindu literature in Sanskrit (after about 400 B.C.E.) deals directly or indirectly with dharma or righteous behavior.

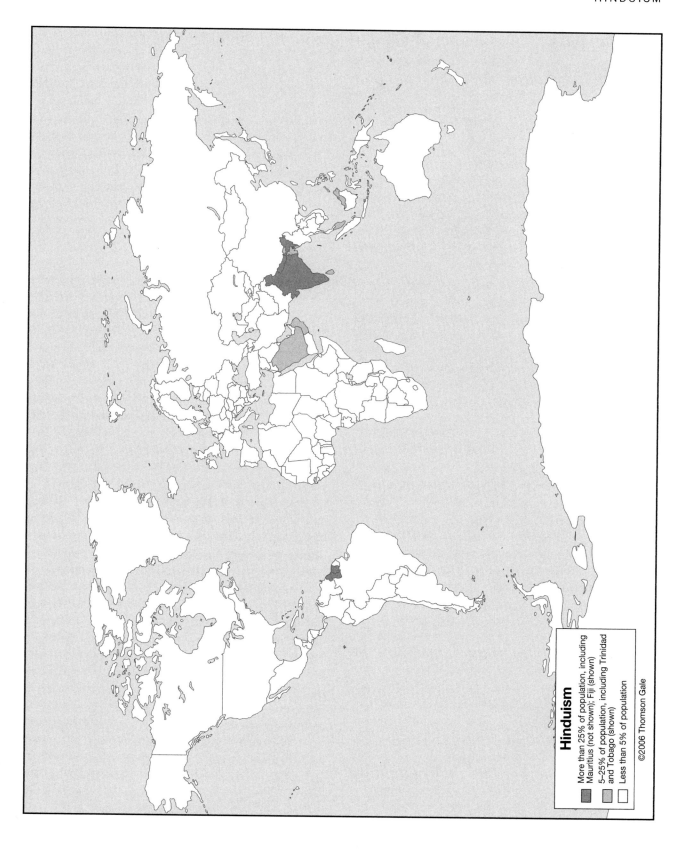

Hinduism

More than 25% of population, including
Mauritius (not shown); Fiji (shown)

5–25% of population, including Trinidad
and Tobago (shown)

Less than 5% of population

©2006 Thomson Gale

Women worship a young girl who symbolizes the goddess Durga during a Durga Puja observance in Calcutta, India. © AFP/CORBIS.

Although Buddhism and Jainism were patronized by many monarchs, by the fourth century C.E. the Gupta dynasty in northern India had facilitated the growth of Hinduism by encouraging the building of Hindu temples and the composition of literary works. Temple construction was taken up enthusiastically by kings and queens as well as citizens in many parts of India after the sixth century.

Bhakti, the expression of devotional fervor, is perhaps most evident after the seventh century C.E. Men and women from different castes poured out their devotion to the gods and goddesses in vernacular languages. Several features contributed to the spread of *bhakti.* One was the use of vernacular languages; the composition after the sixth century C.E. of devotional hymns in the classical (but spoken) language Tamil was an important development in Hinduism. The songs became popular, appealing both to intellectual commentators and philosophers and to the larger population. Another factor was *bhakti'*s appeal across all social classes. A canon was anthologized, with poems drawn from various castes and classes. Many of the most renowned devotional poet-

saints were perceived as being from low castes. The building of temples also promoted devotion; from at least the fourth or fifth centuries Hindu temples have been built in both India and Southeast Asia. Temples in India became centers for devotion, rituals, poetry, music, dance, scholarship, and economic distribution as well as emblems of power and prestige for patrons. Many temples were centers for art and, according to many scholars, also for astronomy. Kings and queens in the Gupta dynasty (fourth–sixth centuries C.E.) in northern India and the Western Chalukya dynasty in central India (c. sixth century C.E.) subsidized temples for the Hindu deities Shiva and Vishnu and the various goddesses.

Treatises on healing, surgery, astrology, and architecture that were composed (by authors such as the physician Caraka) in the early centuries of the Common Era are all framed in religious discourses. These subjects are presented as conversations between Hindu gods and goddesses and holy men. In some cases the texts say that the practice of these arts and sciences will lead to liberation. There were several forms of healing, including systems such as Ayurveda ("knowledge of a long life") and Siddha. Ritual prayers, pilgrimage, and exorcism were also used for healing. Descriptions of various hospitals and civic healing centers in India date back to the fifth century.

Hinduism spread to Southeast Asia during the first millennium of the Common Era. It was probably taken there by traders and merchants. By the fourth century there were kings with Indian names in the kingdom of Funan in Cambodia. The "Indianization" of Southeast Asia is a significant event in world history. It is a matter of scholarly debate whether Hindus migrated to Southeast Asia or whether scholars and ritual specialists from Southeast Asia had their training in India and selectively adapted practices to their regions. The cultural and religious worldviews of the Hindu and Buddhist traditions were selectively adapted by local populations, leading to the construction of some of the greatest temples and monuments in the world. By the early ninth century Jayavarman II was crowned in Cambodia in accordance with rituals specified by Hindu texts. Men and women in Southeast Asia donated manuscripts, endowed temples, and patronized religious rituals. In Cambodia, Indonesia, and other places large temple complexes were built following precise ritual regulations. Hindu temples flourished in Java and Bali. Buddhism became the prevalent religion after the thirteenth century in Cambodia

Hindu priests perform a ritual during Durga Puja, the biggest five-day festival of Bengali Hindus, on the banks of the River Hooghly in Calcutta, India. In Hindu mythology, Durga Puja is the celebration of the triumph of good over evil. © JAYANTA SHAW/REUTERS NEWMEDIA INC./CORBIS.

and after the fourteenth and fifteenth centuries in Java and Bali. Hinduism continued to exist in Bali, but with the eventual dominance of Buddhism and Islam, it died out in many other Southeast Asian countries.

A number of renowned Hindu theologians lived between the seventh and fifteenth centuries C.E. Many of them, including Shankara (c. eighth century), Ramanuja (c. 1017–1137), and Madhva (c. thirteenth century), interpreted Sanskrit texts that were considered to be canonical.

Sailors and merchants from the Middle East took Islam to southern India probably in the seventh century C.E. The encounter between Hindus and Muslims in this region seems to have been relatively peaceful. Almost two centuries later Muslim conquerors went to northern India, and by the twelfth century the first Muslim dynasty had been established in Delhi. In the following centuries another Muslim dynasty, the Mughal empire,

came to power. The relationships between the traditions differed in various parts of India.

After the fifteenth century the Portuguese, Dutch, English, and French made their way to India and established settlements there. In time the foreign powers became involved in local politics, and possession of territory became part of their agendas. The disintegration of the Mughal empire in the eighteenth century led to the formation of many small kingdoms that invited the military help of European traders. By the late eighteenth century the domination of the East India Company and the British had led to a loose unification of large parts of the Indian subcontinent under British control. While most Hindu and Muslim forms of rule had generally accepted local autonomy, the British, who were Christians, felt a moral and political obligation to govern the entire country. Many foreign missionaries scrutinized the Hindus' social and religious practices. Their criticisms were

PL.I.   PL.LIV.

Vichnou.

A drawing of Vishnu, one of the most important Hindu gods. © HISTORICAL PICTURE ARCHIVE/CORBIS.

particularly severe regarding "idolatry," the caste system, and some of the practices applied to women.

In the early nineteenth century the Hindu theologian Ram Mohan Roy, discussed below under EARLY AND MODERN LEADERS, founded a reform movement that came to be called the Brahmo Samaj (society of Brahma). Later in the century Dayananda Sarasvati, also discussed below under EARLY AND MODERN LEADERS, started the Arya Samaj reform movement. Other significant religious leaders in the nineteenth century included Ramakrishna (1836–86) and his disciple Vivekananda (1863–1902). During the nineteenth century *sanatana dharma* (eternal dharma)—a term that had been used in the texts on dharma and in the epics to denote virtues that are normative for all human beings— became popular for denoting Hinduism in general. Some nineteenth-century Hindus, who saw the religion as one rather than many disparate traditions, began to use this term for their faith tradition.

The spread of Hinduism throughout the world has been one of the most significant developments of the nineteenth and twentieth centuries. After the abolition

of slavery, colonial powers from the Western world (principally England) took Indians as workers— sometimes as indentured servants—to many parts of the world, including eastern and southern Africa, Fiji, and the Caribbean. Hindu practices in these lands depended on the origin, caste, and class of the Hindu workers who went there. As soon as they were financially and physically able to do so, these Hindus built temples.

Other forms of Hinduism or practices derived from Hindu teachings are also seen in the diaspora. Some practices, such as ISKCON (the International Society for Krishna Consciousness, a group that is more popularly known as the Hare Krishnas), require a fair amount of "Indianization"—such as adopting Indian names and clothing. Other practices, such as Transcendental Meditation and certain forms of yoga, have been separated from their cultural and religious contexts in India and are presented as physical and mental exercises that anyone, regardless of religious affiliation, can practice.

The many traditions that make the tapestry of Hinduism continue to flourish in the diaspora. Just as the Hindus who migrated to Southeast Asia in the first millennium C.E. sought to transmit their culture through the building of the great temples of Cambodia and Java, Hindu immigrants to England and the United States seek to perpetuate their culture into the next millennium through establishing temples, which serve as the religious and cultural nucleus of a Hindu community.

CENTRAL DOCTRINES There are many Hindu schools of thought and practice and many Hindu communities. Only a few ideas and concepts are common to most Hindus. There is no creed or pillar of faith and no doctrine that all Hindus must believe in to be considered Hindus. Nevertheless, many schools of philosophy have held that acceptance of the sacred compositions called the Vedas as a source of divine authority is a litmus test of orthodoxy. Hindu doctrines are expressed and transmitted by epic narratives, which are frequently performed as music, dance, recitation, and drama. The sophisticated and extensive written traditions in Sanskrit and other languages have been the province of a small percentage of educated scholars.

In the Hindu tradition there are numerous gods and goddesses and many books and stories about them. According to one account, a conversation in the Upanishads (Hindu sacred texts composed in about the seventh century B.C.E.), there are three hundred million gods and goddesses. In the course of this conversation

Glossary

acharya a formal head of a monastery, sect, or sub-community

ashrama one of the four stages of life

atman the human soul

Ayurveda "knowledge of a long life"; a Hindu healing system

Bhagavad Gita one of the most sacred texts of the Hindus; a book of 18 chapters from the epic the *Mahabharata*

bhakti devotion; the practice of devotion to God

Brahma a minor deity; the creator god

Brahman the term used in the Upanishads to refer to the supreme being

Brahman the upper, or priestly, caste

caste a social group (frequently one that a person is born into) in Hindu society

deva a divine being

Devi in the Sanskrit literary tradition, the name for the Goddess

dharma duty, or acting with a sense of what is righteous; sometimes used to mean "religion" and "ethics"

Dharma Sastra any of a set of treatises on the nature of righteousness, moral duty, and law

Durga a manifestation of the Goddess (represented as a warrior)

Ganesha a popular Hindu god; a son of the goddess Parvati, he is depicted with an elephant head

Goddess a powerful, usually gracious, deity in female form sometimes seen as a manifestation of Parvati, the wife of Shiva; she is called any number of names, including Shakti, Durga, Kali, or Devi

gotra a clan group

guru a charismatic teacher

jati birth group

karma literally "action"; the system of rewards and punishments attached to various actions

Krishna a manifestation of the supreme being; one of the most popular Hindu deities, he is considered by many Hindus to be an incarnation of the god Vishnu

kundalini the power that is said to lie dormant at the base of a person's spine and that can be awakened in the search for enlightenment

Lakshmi a goddess; wife of the god Vishnu

Mahabharata "Great Epic of India" or the "Great Sons of Bharata"; one of the two Hindu epics

mandala a geometric design that represents sacredness, divine beings, or sacred knowledge or experience in an abstract form

mantra a phrase or string of words, with or without meaning, recited repeatedly during meditation

moksha liberation from the cycle of birth and death

Parvati a goddess; the wife of the god Shiva

puja religious rituals performed in the home

Purana "Ancient Lore"; any of a set of sacred texts known as the old narratives

---

the question "How many are there?" is reiterated several times until the final answer is given: just one. Thus, it is correct to say that Hindus worship many gods and one god. Ultimately, the supreme being is infinite and beyond words—the same being can therefore be said to be both one and many. To deny the manifoldness or the unity of the supreme being would be to deny its infinity.

Hindus may say that they worship one God, even as they recite prayers and sing in devotion to the many deities of the Hindu pantheon. Some Hindus claim that, although there are many deities, only one is supreme. Others say that all gods and goddesses are equal but that one is their favorite or that their family worships a particular deity. Some believe that there is only one god, and all other deities are manifestations of that being. Many Hindus contend that numbers are like gender—they are human ideas foisted upon the divine.

The Upanishads call the supreme being Brahman. Brahman is considered to be ineffable and beyond all human comprehension. Other texts, such as the *Puranas*,

Ramayana "Story of Rama"; one of the two Hindu epics

samadhi the final state of absorption into, and union with, the divine

samsara continuing rebirths; the cycle of life and death

sanatana dharma "eternal dharma"; in the *Dharma Sastra*s, virtues common to all human beings; also, a word used to denote Hinduism in general after the nineteenth century

shakti energy or power, frequently used for the power of the Goddess; also a name for a manifestation of the Goddess

Sanskrit a classical language and part of the Indo-European language family; the language of ancient India

Shiva "the auspicious one"; a term for the supreme being; one of the most important deities in the Hindu tradition

smriti "remembered"; a set of sacred compositions that includes the two epics, the *Purana*s, and the *Dharma Sastra*s

sruti "that which is heard"; a set of sacred compositions more popularly known as the Vedas

swami "master"; a charismatic teacher

Tamil a classical language of southern India that is still spoken

Tantra literally "loom" or "to stretch"; generic name given to varied philosophies and rituals that fre-

quently involve mantras, meditation on mandalas, or forms of yoga, leading to a liberating knowledge and experience

upadesa the sacred teaching

Upanishad any of the Hindu sacred texts composed in about the sixth century B.C.E; generally considered to be the "last" and philosophically the most important part of the Vedas

Vaishnava a member of a group of people devoted to Vishnu; also used to describe an object or an institution devoted to Vishnu

varna literally "color"; the social class into which a person is born

varna-ashrama dharma the behavior recommended for each class and each stage of life

Veda literally "knowledge"; any of a set of compositions dating from the second millennium B.C.E. that is the highest scriptural authority for many educated Hindus

Vedanta a philosophical school within Hinduism

Vishnu literally "all-pervasive"; a term for the supreme being; one of the most important deities in the Hindu tradition; his incarnations include Rama and Krishna

yoga physical and mental discipline by which one "yokes" one's spirit to a god; more generally, any path that leads to final emancipation

yuga in Hindu cosmology, any of four ages into which each cycle of time is divided

say that this supreme being assumes a form and a name to make itself accessible to human beings. Viewed from these perspectives, Hindus speak of the supreme being as being both *nirguna* ("without attributes," specifically "without inauspicious attributes") and *saguna* ("with attributes" such as grace and mercy). Some texts identify this supreme being as the god Vishnu ("all-pervasive"); others call it Shiva ("the auspicious one"). Still others

believe that the supreme being assumes the form of the Goddess and is called Shakti (Sanskrit for "energy"), Durga, Kali, or any one of a thousand names. Although Vishnu, Shiva, and the Goddess are the most important gods in the texts, others—such as Ganesha (a son of Parvati); Kartikkeya, or Murugan (a son of Shiva); and Hanuman (a devotee of Rama, an incarnation of Vishnu)—are popular among Hindus. Ganesha is depicted as riding a mouse. Hindus worship him before beginning any new task or before embarking on any journey or project.

Devotees of any deity may perceive him or her to be the supreme being. In some early accounts there was an idea of a trinity sharing various functions; Brahma was the creator, Vishnu the preserver, and Shiva the destroyer. This idea, however, was never really popular except in art and sculpture, and in time Brahma (a minor creator god who worked under the orders of a powerful being) became marginal. The functions of creation, preservation, and destruction were combined.

Shiva is one of the most important deities within the Hindu tradition. The manifold aspects of Shiva's power are expressed by his simultaneous and often paradoxical roles: threatening but benevolent, creator but destroyer, exuberant dancer but austere yogi (practitioner of yoga). He is depicted as an ascetic and as the husband of the goddess Parvati. Stories of his saving powers describe him granting wisdom and grace to his devotees.

Many Hindus also deify natural phenomena such as rivers. Hindus revere planets and propitiate the *navagraha* (nine planets) with rituals. The "nine planets" include the Sun, the Moon, Venus, Mercury, Mars, Jupiter, Saturn, and two mythical entities called Rahu and Ketu, identified with the ascending and descending nodes of the Moon. In addition to the pan-Hindu deities there are many local gods and goddesses who may have distinctive histories and functions. Because some of the deities have specific functions, a person may worship a particular deity for career success, a particular goddess for a cure from illness, and so on.

Hindus pride themselves on being part of a tradition that has continuously venerated the divine in female form for more than two thousand years. The Goddess, sometimes called Devi in Sanskrit literary tradition, has usually been seen as a manifestation of Parvati, the wife of Shiva. In her beneficent aspect she is frequently called Amba or Ambika (little mother). As a warrior goddess she is Durga, represented in iconography with a smiling countenance but a handful of weapons (which shows that she is ready to help her devotees). Durga is one of the most popular goddesses in India. As Kali, the Goddess is a dark, disheveled figure with a garland of skulls. Even in this manifestation she is called "mother" by her devotees. There are local goddesses in every part of India. In some regions a goddess may be known only by the provincial name and celebrated with local stories.

Many texts speak of the relationship between the human soul (*atman*) and the supreme being (Brahman), but invariably they suggest rather than declare the connection between the two. For instance, in a conversation in the Chandogya Upanishad, a father asks his son to dissolve salt in water and says that Brahman and *atman* are united in a similar manner. The father ends his teaching with the well-known dictum "tat tvam asi" (you are that). In this statement, the "that" refers to Brahman and the "you" to *atman*. Philosophers who later interpreted this passage understood it in different ways. The philosopher Shankara (c. eighth century C.E.) wrote that "you are that" means that Brahman and *atman* are the same identity. On the other hand, Ramanuja (eleventh century) interpreted it to mean that, while Brahman and *atman* are inseparably united, they are not identical. Shankara's philosophy came to be called nondualist—that is, there is no ultimate distinction between Brahman and *atman*. Ramanuja's philosophy, which nuances this identity, is called "qualified nondualism" by later devotees. Other philosophers declared that the human soul and the supreme being are different. The philosophy of Madhva (thirteenth century) is known as "dualism" because he speaks about the real and eternal difference between the human soul and the supreme being.

According to Hindu thought, there is a quest for a higher, experiential knowledge, the knowledge of Brahman. The Upanishads distinguish "lower" knowledge, or that which can be conceptualized and articulated, from the "higher" knowledge of true wisdom. This higher wisdom comes from experientially knowing the relationship between the human soul (*atman*) and the supreme being (Brahman). Brahman pervades and yet transcends the universe as well as human thought. Ultimately, Brahman cannot be described. According to many Upanishads, to know Brahman completely is to reach the ultimate goal of human beings: to enter a new state of consciousness. This state is said to be ineffable; with our lower conceptual knowledge, we cannot put into words what is ultimately beyond words.

The notions of karma and reincarnation are common to the Hindu, Buddhist, and Jain traditions. Karma literally means "action," especially ritual action, but it has come to mean the system of rewards and punishments attached to various actions. Thus, it refers to a system of cause and effect that may span several lifetimes. The law of karma dictates that human beings are rewarded or punished according to their behavior. Actions produce merit or demerit, and this will affect the quality of one's future life, either in this lifetime or several lifetimes later. Good deeds and bad deeds do not balance each other out; one has to experience the results of good actions and bad actions.

The idea of karma is closely connected with the concept of the immortality of the soul. Although in the early Vedas there was only a nebulous notion of the afterlife, by the time of the Upanishads the human soul was said to live beyond death. Thus, the theory of karma also implies continuing rebirths (*samsara*). Liberation from them (*moksha*), according to the Upanishads, comes from a supreme, experiential, transforming wisdom. When one gets this transforming knowledge, one is never reborn and never dies; one is immortal. Ultimately, therefore, even good karma is to be avoided, for it ties one to the cycle of reincarnation.

In general, the texts do not discuss the details of what happens immediately after death or what happens to a soul between lifetimes. Only the truly evolved souls are said to remember all their past lives. Some theistic texts speak about the soul's journey after death. If the soul is emancipated, it is said to cross a river called Viraja ("without passion") and enter a heaven-like place called Vaikuntha or Kailasa. Vaikuntha is Vishnu's abode, and Shiva lives in Kailasa. Philosophical texts of the Hindu tradition give various accounts of what happens to the soul when it is liberated from the cycle of life and death. The many Hindu texts describe different relationships between the human soul and the supreme being. Theistic philosophies (which assert the ultimate reality of a personal deity) speak about a devotional relationship being joyously experienced in the afterlife. Some theistic schools think of the ultimate liberation as a state of passionate separation between the human soul and God. God is thought of as Krishna in this tradition, and the soul is cast in the role of one of Krishna's cowherd girlfriends, who felt the intensity of their love for him only when separated from him.

While many texts speak about the miserable nature of this life and urge people to seek the everlasting "real" life of liberation, others say that glorifying God on Earth is like experiencing heaven in this lifetime. Sacred pilgrimage centers are considered to be a break in the earthly rhythm and to reflect divine revelation. In this devotional context, some Hindus consider life on Earth to be a joyful experience comparable to the status of liberation.

Although reincarnation and liberation are the most frequently discussed aspects of the afterlife, some of the

Puranas talk of many kinds of heavens and hells. In some texts, seven states of netherworlds and seven heavens are described in detail. Different kinds of karma may entail rebirth in these states of heavens or hells. The difference between the hells in Hindu texts and the Judeo-Christian notion of hell is that, within the Hindu tradition, a soul's stay in hells are temporary. Hindu texts recognize a heaven that could be permanent (Vaikuntha) as well as those that are like a temporary paradise (*svarga*). Descriptions of temporary paradises include dancing girls and wish-fulfilling trees—standard, generic imagery of an androcentric (male-centered) place of delight. A soul is reborn in these paradises if it has certain kinds of karma; once this karma is exhausted, the soul moves on into a different kind of life form.

For more than 2,500 years the religious traditions of India have portrayed the human being as caught in a cycle of life and death. The way out of this misery is to seek and obtain liberation from the cycle. There are several paths to liberation. These can be divided into two general perspectives. The first perspective is characteristic of the Hindu traditions that believe that the human soul (*atman*) is identical to the supreme being (Brahman) and that liberation is the final, experiential knowledge that one is, in fact, divine. The teacher Shankara (c. eighth century C.E.) described this worldview best. His followers (and those who belong to some other schools) ultimately emphasize human effort and striving, which will result in the transforming wisdom. The second perspective on paths to liberation comes from the theistic schools that speak of an ultimate distinction between the human being and God. Proponents of this worldview advocate devotion to the supreme being and reliance on God's grace.

The *Bhagavad Gita* ("Sacred Song") discusses the ways to liberation. Some Hindus say that the text portrays multiple paths to the divine, and others say that all paths are aspects of one discipline. In the course of the *Bhagavad Gita* Krishna, talking to the warrior Arjuna, describes three ways to liberation: the way of action (*karma yoga*), the way of knowledge (*jñana yoga*), and the way of devotion (*bhakti yoga*).

The way of action (*karma yoga*) entails the path of unselfish action; a person must do his or her duty (dharma), but it should not be done either for fear of punishment or for hope of reward. By discarding the fruits of one's action, one attains abiding peace. The second is the way of knowledge (*jñana yoga*). Through attaining scriptural knowledge, a person may achieve a transforming wisdom that destroys his or her past karma. True knowledge is an insight into the real nature of the universe, divine power, and the human soul. This wisdom may be acquired through learning texts from a suitable and learned teacher (guru), meditation, and physical and mental control in the form of the discipline called yoga. Later philosophers say that when a person hears scripture, asks questions, clarifies doubts, and eventually meditates on this knowledge, he or she achieves liberation. The third way, the way of devotion (*bhakti yoga*), is the most emphasized throughout the *Bhagavad Gita.* Ultimately, Krishna makes his promise to Arjuna: If a person surrenders to the Lord, he will forgive the human being all sins.

Bhakti yoga is perhaps the most popular path among Hindus. Many consider the only way to get salvation to be devotion to a god or goddess, surrendering oneself to that deity, and leaving oneself open to divine grace. Others believe that *karma yoga*, the way of "detached action," is the best way to get rid of karma and acquire liberation from the cycle of life and death. This is acting for the good of humanity and not with selfish motives. It is believed that by doing all action in a compassionate manner, one can get supreme liberation. *Jñana yoga*, the path of striving with wisdom and yoga, is considered laudable but are not practiced much by the average Hindu.

Yoga entails physical and mental discipline by which a person "yokes" his or her spirit to a god. It has been held in high regard in many Hindu texts and has had many meanings in the history of the Hindu tradition. Its origins are obscure, but it is generally thought to have come from non-Aryan sources. Many Hindus associate yoga with Patañjali (c. third century B.C.E.) and consider his text, the *Yoga Sutras* (composed of short, fragmentary, and aphoristic sentences), significant. Yoga was probably an important feature of religious life in India several centuries before the text was written. Patañjali's yoga requires moral, mental, and physical discipline; it involves meditation on a physical or mental object as the single point of focus. Proper bodily posture is one of the unique characteristics in the discipline of yoga. Detaching the mind from the domination of external sensory stimuli is also important.

Perfection in concentration (*dharana*) and meditation (*dhyana*) lead one to *samadhi*, the final state of absorption into, and union with, the divine. *Samadhi* has many stages, the ultimate of which is a complete emancipation from the cycle of life and death. The state is spo-

ken of variously as a coming together, uniting, and transcending of polarities; the state is empty and full, it is neither life nor death, and it is both. In short, this final liberation cannot be adequately described in human language.

While many scholars consider Patañjali's yoga to be the classical form of yoga, there are dozens of other varieties. At the broadest level the word has been used to designate any form of meditation or practice with ascetic tendencies. More generally, it is used to refer to any path that leads to final emancipation. Since the nineteenth and twentieth centuries a distinction between two avenues of discipline—Raja Yoga and Hatha Yoga—has been drawn. Raja Yoga deals with mental discipline; occasionally, this term is used interchangeably with Patañjali's yoga. Hatha Yoga largely focuses on bodily posture and control over the body. This form of yoga is what has become popular in Western countries.

A philosophical and ritual practice called Tantra (which etymologically means "loom") began to gain importance in the Hindu and Buddhist traditions in about the fifth century. The Tantric tradition influenced many sectarian Hindu movements; Shaiva, Vaishnava, and Shakta (pertaining to Shakti, or the Goddess) temple liturgies, still practiced, are in large measure derived from tantric usage. Much of Tantra has fused with devotional practices and is no longer known officially as "tantra."

In some forms of the Tantric tradition we find an emphasis on a form of yoga known as *kundalini* yoga. The term *kundalini* refers to the *shakti* (power of the Goddess) that is said to lie coiled at the base of one's spine. When awakened, this power rises through a passage and six chakras, or "wheels," to reach the final wheel, or center, located under the skull. This final chakra is known as a thousand-petaled lotus. The ultimate aim of this form of yoga is to awaken the power of the *kundalini* and make it unite with Purusa, the male supreme being, who is in the thousand-petaled lotus. With this union the practitioner is granted several visions and given psychic powers. The union leads eventually to final emancipation.

Whereas concepts of the deity, reincarnation, and the immortality of the soul are central to the texts, in practice many Hindus focus on notions of purity and pollution, auspiciousness and inauspiciousness. Ritual purity is not directly linked to moral purity. Certain actions, events, substances, and even classes of people can be ritually defiling. Thus, urinating, menstruating, the shedding of blood (even during childbirth), death, and some castes traditionally perceived to be "low" can be polluting. Physical cleansing or the lapse of certain time periods restores the ritual purity to a person or a family. While many of these practices are no longer followed, many held sway until the mid-twentieth century. A few practices, such as menstruation taboos, continue to be followed in some sectors of society, including by some people in urban situations and in the diaspora.

Concepts of what is auspicious and what is not are significant in understanding Hindu life. Certain times of the day, week, month, and year are propitious. In general, what is life-affirming and what increases the quality of life is considered to be auspicious. The right hand is associated with auspicious activities, such as gift-giving, eating, and wedding rituals. The left hand is associated with the inauspicious: insults, bodily hygiene, and funeral (including ancestral) rituals.

Doctrinally and theistically, the Hindu tradition is pluralistic. Each one of the many traditions (*sampradayas*) of Hinduism has specific doctrines and a precise theology. These theologies have been articulated with faith and in great detail, and the several commentaries hammer out the nuances of every word. Thus, if we look at individual traditions, we find that they are doctrine-specific; if we take Hinduism as a whole, we find a spectrum of ideas and concepts.

MORAL CODE OF CONDUCT Hindus today use the word "dharma" to refer to religion, ethics, and moral behavior in general and to their religion in particular. Since the nineteenth century the term *sanatana dharma* (the eternal or perennial dharma) has been used to designate the Hindu tradition. Buddhists, Jains, and Hindus use the term "dharma" to indicate a fairly wide variety of concepts and issues. In the last two centuries the texts on dharma (composed in the beginning of the Common Era) also formed the basis for formulating the administration of law in India. The "moral code" for most Hindus is a combination of traditional customs and practices that are ordinarily even more important than the code of behavior advocated in the texts on dharma. Hindus have been concerned with ritual purity and impurity and auspiciousness and inauspiciousness as areas of importance in correct behavior. In philosophy and in ordering their lives the two categories that have had overriding importance are dharma and *moksha* (liberation).

The meaning of dharma depends upon the context; further, there have been changes in the emphases over the centuries. Dharma may mean religion, the customary observances of a caste or sect, law usage, practice, religious or moral merit, virtue, righteousness, duty, justice, piety, morality, or sacrifice, among other things. The word "dharma" appears several times in the early Vedic texts. In many later contexts it means "religious ordinances and rites," and in others it refers to "fixed principles or rules of conduct." In conjunction with other words, "dharma" also means "merit acquired by the performance of religious rites" and "the whole body of religious duties." The prominent meaning of dharma eventually came to refer to the duties and obligations of a human being (primarily a male) in connection with his caste and particular stage of life. Texts on dharma both described and prescribed these duties and responsibilities and divided the subject matter into various categories.

For many educated Hindus dharma deals with behavior, justice, repentance, and atonement rites. Dharma also includes the duties of each class or caste of society; sacraments from conception to death; the duties of the different stages of life; the days when one should not study the Vedas; marriage; the duties of women; the relationship between husband and wife; ritual purity and impurity; rites of death and rituals for ancestors; gifts and donations; crime and punishment; contracts; inheritance; activities done only at times of crises; and rules concerning mixed castes. It is obvious that the areas and concerns of what is deemed to be righteous behavior in the Hindu tradition differ from the Western notions of ethics.

The earliest texts on dharma are the *Dharma Sutras*. These are part of the *Kalpa Sutras*, which are considered to be ancillaries to the Vedas. By the first centuries of the Common Era many treatises on the nature of righteousness, moral duty, and law were written. These are called the *Dharma Sastras* and form the basis for later Hindu laws. The best known of these is the *Manava Dharmasastra*, or the "Laws of Manu." These were probably codified in about the first century and reflect the social norms of the time.

Far better known than these treatises on dharma are the narrative literature of the epics (the *Ramayana* and the *Mahabharata*) and the *Puranas* ("Ancient Lore"). Hindus in India and the diaspora understand stories from these texts as exemplifying values of dharma and situations of dharmic dilemmas. The people in these epics are paradigms to be imitated or avoided.

Dharma is not homogenous, and there are many varieties that are discussed and practiced. There are some virtues and behavior patterns that are recommended for all human beings; others are incumbent on the person's caste, stage of life, and gender. Many Hindus in the nineteenth and twentieth centuries emphasized what has been called the common (samanya or sadharana) dharma for all human beings; some speak of this as the "universal" dharma. The epics also call this the sanatana dharma (eternal dharma).

Gautama Siddhartha's Dharma Sutra, one of the earliest texts on dharma, extols the ultimate importance of eight virtues: compassion toward all creatures; patience; lack of envy; purification; tranquility; having an auspicious disposition; generosity; and lack of greed. A person with these qualities may not have performed all sacraments but will still achieve the ultimate goal of being with Brahman, the supreme being. While these virtues and recommendations for behavior are considered to be common to all human beings, the texts on dharma really emphasize the specific behavior enjoined for people of the four major castes and for male members who are in various stages of life. There are also considerable discussions on women's duties (stri dharma). The longest discussions focus on marriages, death rituals, food laws, and caste regulations.

While there are common virtues that all human beings should have, the texts on dharma speak of context-specific dharma that is incumbent on the different classes (varna) of society. The texts say that male members of the upper three classes—the "priestly" Brahmans, the rulers, and the merchants—should ideally go through four stages (ashrama) of life. The behavior recommended for each class and each stage of life is called varna-ashrama dharma. The responsibility to behave thus is called sva (self) dharma. Whenever books describe the decline of the social order in the world, they refer to the abandoning of the duties that are incumbent upon a person by virtue of his or her station in life.

The "Laws of Manu" and the Bhagavad Gita say that it is better for a person to do his or her own dharma imperfectly than to do another's well. The law books, however, acknowledge that in times of adversity a person may do other tasks. In many parts of India custom and tradition override the dharma texts. While the moral codes of Manu were much exalted by colonial rulers, scholars have shown that they had limited import—

that in fact the law was mitigated by learned people, and each case was decided with reference to the immediate circumstances.

The texts of law recognized four stages of life, called the ashramas, for males of the upper three classes of society. First, a young boy was initiated into the stage of a student; his dharma was to not work for a living and to remain celibate. After being a student, a young man was to marry, repay his debt to society and his forefathers, and repay his spiritual debt to the gods. A householder's dharma was to be employed and to lead a conjugal life with his partner in dharma (saha-dharmachaarini).

The "Laws of Manu" give details of two more stages: those of a forest dweller and an ascetic. Manu says that when a man sees his skin wrinkled and his hair gray or when he sees his grandchildren, he may retire to the forest with his wife and spend the time in quietude and in reciting the Vedas. The final stage, sannyasa, was entered by few: A man apparently staged his own social death and became an ascetic. The ascetic owned nothing, living off the food given as alms and eating but once a day. He was to spend his time cultivating detachment from life and pursuing knowledge about salvation. With the increasing popularity of the Bhagavad Gita, which stresses detached action, the need to enter formally into this stage of life diminished considerably within the Hindu tradition.

Sanskrit and vernacular texts on dharma extol the importance of becoming an ascetic (sannyasi). Indeed, in India (and wherever Hindus have traveled) there are such ascetics in ochre or saffron clothes. While the texts on dharma specify that only male members of the upper three classes of society have the right to become ascetics, women have also embraced this stage of life. When a person enters this stage, he or she usually conducts his or her own death rituals. The ascetic is now socially dead and is formally disassociated from all relationships. An ascetic is religiously (and in India legally) a new person without connections.

SACRED BOOKS There are multiple lines of religious authority in the Hindu traditions. While sacred texts are significant—and there have been hundreds of them—many were known only by a small minority of literate people. On the other hand, the popular epics and the stories from the books known as the Puranas have been passed on through oral and ritual traditions and through the performing arts.

The highest scriptural authority in philosophical Hinduism is a set of compositions known as *sruti* (that which is heard), more popularly known as the Vedas ("knowledge"). They date from about the second millennium B.C.E. Many Hindu traditions consider the Vedas to be of nonhuman origin. The Vedic seers (*rishi*) are said to have visually perceived and transmitted the mantras, poetry, and chants; according to traditional belief, they did not compose them. The *rishi* transmitted the words to their disciples, starting an oral tradition that has come down to the present. The words are said to have a fixed order that has to be maintained by a tradition of recitation.

There are four Vedic collections, known as Rig, Sama, Yajur, and Atharva. Each one is divided into four parts. The first two parts—the *samhita* and the *brahmana*—deal with sacrificial rituals and the hymns to be recited during them, and the last two parts are more philosophical in nature. The last section, known as the Upanishads (literally "coming near" [a teacher for instruction]), focuses on existential concerns and the relationship between the human soul and the supreme being. The Upanishads were composed between the seventh and sixth centuries B.C.E. The Vedas also have appendices on the observance of ritual.

There are other fields of knowledge, called Vedangas, that are considered to be ancillary to the Vedic corpus. They include subjects such as phonetics and astronomy, which were considered to be extremely important. In addition, such areas of study as archery, music and dance (*gandharva veda*), and the science of health and long life (*Ayurveda*) were considered to be vital to the well-being of men and women.

The Vedic corpus was followed by a set of books called *smriti* (remembered) literature. Though acknowledged to be of human authorship, the *smriti* is nonetheless considered inspired. This literature is theoretically of lesser authority than the Vedas, but it has played a far more important role in the lives of Hindus for the last 2,500 years. Sometimes this category is divided into three subfields: the two epics, the old narratives (*Puranas*), and the codes of law and ethics (*Dharma Sastras*).

For most Hindus the two epics, the *Ramayana* ("Story of Rama") and the *Mahabharata* ("Great Epic of India," or the "Great Sons of Bharata"), are the most significant texts. They deal, above all, with situations of dharma. The epics are widely known among the many communities and sectarian divisions within the Hindu

tradition, and they provide threads of unity through the centuries and across social divides.

The *Ramayana* has been memorized, recited, sung, danced, and enjoyed for 2,500 years. It has been a source of inspiration for generations of devotees in India and in other parts of the world. The story of the *Ramayana* centers on the young prince Rama. On the eve of Rama's coronation his father exiles him. In the forest Ravana, the demon-king of Lanka, captures Rama's beautiful wife, Sita; the epic focuses on Rama's struggle to get her back. After a protracted battle Rama kills Ravana and is reunited with Sita. They eventually return to the kingdom and are crowned. Rama is held to be a just king; the term "Ramrajya" (kingdom or rule of Rama) has become the Hindu political ideal.

There have been many local versions of the *Ramayana*, including vernacular renderings, and the story has been theologically interpreted in many ways. The epic is regularly danced and acted in places of Hindu (and Buddhist) cultural influence in Southeast Asia (Indonesia, Cambodia, and Thailand). The capital of Thailand for several centuries was named after Rama's capital, and the kings there bore the name "Rama" as part of their title.

The other epic, the *Mahabharata*, with approximately 100,000 verses, is considered to be the longest poem in the world. It is the story of the great struggle among the descendants of a king called Bharata; Indians call their country Bharat after this king. The main part of the story deals with a war between the Pandavas and the Kauravas. They are cousins, but the Kauravas try to cheat the Pandavas out of their share of the kingdom and will not accept peace. A battle ensues in which all the major kingdoms are forced to take sides. The Pandavas emerge victorious but at a great emotional cost. All their sons and close relatives are killed in the battle.

The *Bhagavad Gita* ("Sacred Song") is a book of 18 chapters from the *Mahabharata*. It is esteemed as one of the holiest books in the Hindu tradition. People learned it by heart for centuries. The complete *Mahabharata* is not a book one would find in a typical home, but the *Bhagavad Gita* is widely copied. It is a conversation that takes place on a battlefield between Krishna and the warrior Arjuna. Just as the war of the *Mahabharata* is about to begin, Arjuna (one of the Pandava brothers) becomes distressed at the thought of having to fight against his cousins, uncles, and other relatives. Putting down his bow, he asks his cousin Krishna (who is portrayed as an incarnation of Vishnu) whether it is correct to fight a war in which many lives, especially those of one's own kin, are to be lost. Krishna replies in the affirmative; it is correct if we fight for what is right. One must fight for righteousness (dharma) after trying peaceful means. The *Bhagavad Gita* speaks of loving devotion to the Lord and the importance of selfless action. Krishna instructs Arjuna (who is generally understood to be any human soul who seeks spiritual guidance) on God, the nature of the human soul, and how one can reach liberation. A person may reach Vishnu/Krishna through devotion, knowledge, or selfless action. Some later interpreters think of these as three paths, and others consider them to be three aspects of the path of loving surrender to the supreme being.

The *Puranas* ("Ancient Lore") contain narratives about the Hindu deities and their manifestations on Earth to save human beings as well as accounts of the cycles of creation and destruction of the cosmos. In recounting the deeds of the various gods and goddesses, most of the Sanskrit *Puranas* focus on the supremacy of either Shiva, Vishnu, or the goddess Durga (more popularly known as Devi). There are also *Puranas* dedicated to Ganesha and other deities; Tamil *Puranas* speak about the valorous and saving acts of Murugan, the son of Shiva and Parvati. The *Bhagavata Purana*, one of the most popular of the Sanskrit *Puranas*, speaks at length about the various incarnations of Vishnu.

The Hindu understanding of time, which is explained in the *Puranas*, is that it has no beginning and no end. Time is an endless series of intervals, each one of which is the lifetime of a minor creator god called Brahma, which lasts for 311,040,000 million human years. Throughout each cycle the cosmos is periodically created and destroyed. At the end of each Brahma's life, the universe is absorbed into Vishnu, a new Brahma emerges, and a new cycle begins.

According to the *Puranas*, the cosmos is continually created and destroyed in cycles that are understood as the days and nights of the creator god Brahma. Within each of these days there is a basic cycle of time, a *mahayuga*, composed of four smaller units known as yugas, or aeons. Each yuga is shorter and worse than the one before it. The golden age (*Krita Yuga*) lasts 4,800 divine years. The years of the divine beings called *devas* are much longer than earthly years; a divine year is 360 human years. Therefore, the golden age lasts 1,728,000 earthly years. During this time dharma (righteousness) is on firm footing. The *Treta* age is shorter, lasting 3,600 divine years; dharma is then on three legs. The *Dvapara*

age lasts 2,400 divine years, and dharma is then hopping on two legs. During the *Kali Yuga,* the worst of all possible ages, dharma is on one leg, and things get progressively worse. This age lasts for 1,200 divine years. We live in the degenerate *Kali Yuga,* which, according to traditional Hindu reckoning, began in about 3102 B.C.E. There is a steady decline throughout the yugas in morality, righteousness, life span, and human satisfaction. At the and of the *Kali Yuga*—obviously still a long time off—there will be no righteousness, no virtue, no trace of justice.

One thousand *mahayugas* make up a day of Brahma, which is approximately 4,320 million earthly years. The nights of Brahma are of equal length; it is generally understood that during Brahma's night creation is withdrawn. A total of 360 such days and an equal number of nights makes a year of Brahma, and Brahma lives for 100 divine years (311,040,000 million earthly years). After this the entire cosmos is absorbed into the body of Vishnu (or Shiva) and remains there until another Brahma is evolved.

The many texts of righteousness and duty, known as *Dharma Sastras,* were composed in the first millennium C.E. These focus on the issues of right behavior, including those that pertain to caste. Texts relating to astrology, medicine, sexual love, and power—all framed in religious discourses—were also composed in the first few centuries of the Common Era. The importance of many texts has been highlighted by calling them the fifth Veda.

While many of the Sanskrit texts are known in the vernacular all over India, there is also an extensive array of classical and folk literature that was composed in the vernacular languages. Tamil, a classical language that is still spoken, is one of the old languages and has a hallowed tradition of sophisticated literature going back well into the beginning of the Common Era. The earliest literature in Tamil, known as the Sangam texts, dealt primarily with love and war. Many local deities, including Ganesha and Murugan, sons of Shiva and Parvati, were greatly beloved in Tamil-speaking regions. Even from the earliest times there was extensive interaction and mutual influence between Sanskrit and vernacular texts. Tamil devotional literature was heavily influenced by the Sanskrit stories and texts. The Tamil "Sacred Utterance" (composed by the poet Nammalvar in the ninth century) was also known as the Tamil Veda and was introduced alongside the Sanskrit Vedas in temple and domestic liturgies.

The vernacular texts from the south moved north in the second millennium. By the second millennium there was extensive literature in many Indian languages. Particularly noteworthy are the poems written by the great devotional poets of South India as well as of the regions of Orissa, Bengal, Maharashtra, and Gujarat. These texts are well known and continue to be performed in many parts of India; they are more closely a part of Hindu life than the Vedas and other Sanskrit texts.

SACRED SYMBOLS Hinduism is known for its numerous icons and images. Deities are represented in many postures and in various materials. The question of whether these are "symbols" or reality itself has been much contested within the Hindu traditions. Some philosophical schools think of them as symbols leading a person through meditation and concentration to reality; others think of the icons in the temples as actual incarnations of the deity itself. Some Hindus think that, just as the incarnations of the supreme being as Rama and Krishna are real manifestations and not illusory or symbolic, the infusion of the supreme in the material body of a sculpture or icon is real.

Gods and goddesses are identified with specific iconography and every position of the hands or feet. Many deities have several hands, each carrying a weapon or a flower to protect the devotees from harm. Some Hindus interpret the many arms of a deity as representing omnipotence. The numerous attributes of the deities, as well as their weapons, are seen as symbolic of values, concepts, or qualities, and there is no general agreement on their interpretation. For instance, the conch shell and wheel of Vishnu are sometimes understood to be the weapons he uses to destroy evil, but others think of them as representing space and time.

Many Hindu deities are associated with animals or birds. Although the sacred texts give traditional reasons for this, some believers understand the iconography in an allegorical way. Vishnu reclines on a serpent and flies on a bird called Garuda. Lakshmi is flanked by elephants; Murugan rides a peacock; and Ganesha has an elephant head and rides a small mouse. There is no uniform understanding of what these represent or symbolize, but there are many viewpoints. Vishnu's serpent, called Sesha, is seen as a paradigmatic servant of Vishnu, transforming his form to serve the deity's many manifestations. The serpent is also known as Ananta (literally "infinite"), and according to some people, it represents

the coils of time. For some devotees the bird Garuda represents the celestial forces in contrast to the terrestrial powers of the serpent. Garuda also symbolizes the Vedas in traditional literature. Elephants are said to represent royalty, auspiciousness, and rain-laden monsoon clouds. Ganesha's elephant head, on the other hand, is thought to symbolize his ability to overcome obstacles.

Shiva and Parvati are frequently represented as abstract forms known as *linga* and *yoni. Linga* means distinguishing mark or gender, and *yoni* is translated as a womb; thus, many textbooks on Hinduism tend to depict the *linga* and *yoni* as sexual symbols. Most Hindus, however, do not see them as phallic or as having sexual connotations but rather as representing the masculine and feminine creative energies of the universe.

Many Hindus also venerate mandalas—large, geometric patterns that represent the supreme being in aniconic (abstract) form. These square or circular designs are symbols of the entire universe or of various realms of beings. The diagrams are a visual analog to the strings of words known as mantras. The most important mantra in the Hindu tradition is "Om," which is recited either by itself or as a prefix to the many mantras dedicated to various deities. "Om" is considered to be made up of three letters: *a, u,* and *m.* The various Hindu traditions give different meanings to these letters, which may be understood as aural symbols.

Perhaps the most ubiquitous symbol in Hindu art is the lotus flower. Red and gold lotuses dominate literature, art, and theologies, and they have a wide variety of interpretations. The lotus is said to be a symbol of auspiciousness; for others, it may symbolize the grace of the Goddess (she is often depicted sitting on a lotus). Still other traditions think of the thousand-petaled lotus flower as being near the crown of the head and believe that the spiritual power that rises up a person's spine reaches the lotus on enlightenment.

EARLY AND MODERN LEADERS Scholars, priests, teachers, and ritual specialists have all been considered inspired and inspiring teachers of the Hindu traditions. Ram Mohan Roy (1772–1833) was a theologian who is frequently called a reformer. Born into an orthodox Brahman family, he became familiar with Western social life and the Christian scriptures. He also read the Upanishads and the books of dharma and came to the conclusion that what he objected to in Hindu practice was not part of classical Hinduism. Roy discarded most of the epic and Puranic materials as myths that stood in the way of reason and social reform. In 1828 he set up a society to discuss the nature of the supreme reality (Brahman) as portrayed in the Upanishads. This organization came to be called the Brahmo Samaj (congregation of Brahman). Roy translated some of the Upanishads and other selected texts and distributed them for free. A pioneer for education, he started new periodicals, established educational institutions, and worked to improve the status of Hindu women.

Dayananda Sarasvati (1824–83) started the Arya Samaj, another reform movement. Dayananda considered only the early hymns of the Rig Veda to be the true scripture. Because these hymns were action-oriented, Dayananda advocated a life of education and vigorous work. He taught that a good society is one in which people work to uplift humanity and that this in itself leads to the welfare of a human soul and body. The Arya Samaj is popular in parts of northern India and is almost unknown in the south.

A well-known figure in the twentieth century was Vivekananda, founder of the Ramakrishna mission (in India). He spoke about the Hindu traditions at the Parliament of World Religions in Chicago in 1893 and became the face of Hindu thought in the West. He had been inspired by Ramakrishna (1836–86; a Bengali teacher considered by many to be a saint), and he articulated a form of Vedanta philosophy based loosely on the interpretation of the eighth-century philosopher Shankara, discussed below under MAJOR THEOLOGIANS AND AUTHORS. Vivekananda's influence on later Hinduism was tremendous. His vision of Hinduism as a "universal" and "tolerant" religion, a form of open tradition that incorporates many viewpoints, has been popular among Hindus in the diaspora in the twentieth and twenty-first centuries.

Other twentieth-century teachers considered to be saints (a word that is used in the Hindu tradition to mean an enlightened teacher) include female gurus such as Anandamayi Ma (1893–1972), Amritanandamayi Ma (born in 1953), and Karunamayi Ma (born in 1956) and male gurus Shirdi Sai Baba (died in 1918) and Satya Sai Baba (born in 1926). The latter is a charismatic teacher from Andhra Pradesh in southern India. His followers believe he is an avatar (incarnation) of the deities Shiva and Shakti (the Goddess).

One of the best-known teachers in the West is Maharishi Mahesh Yogi (born c. 1911), whose articulation of Transcendental Meditation has explicit Hindu origins and overtones. Nevertheless, Transcendental Medi-

tation is not ordinarily identified as Hindu or even as "religion" but more as a stress-reduction technique. The teachings, however, of Bhaktivedanta Prabhupada, who arrived in New York in 1965 and started a devotional school of Hinduism called the International Society of Krishna Consciousness (ISKCON), and Swami Chinmayananda (1916–93), who taught a nondualistic form of Vedanta, are identified with specific traditions within Hinduism.

While Mahatma Gandhi (1869–1948) is not considered to be a religious leader, his actions were strongly influenced by religious texts and practices. His ideas of nonviolence and actions based on truth-principles have all been part of the larger Hindu tradition in the last few millennia.

MAJOR THEOLOGIANS AND AUTHORS Most of the important Hindu theologians in the last 1,500 years can broadly be classified as teachers of a philosophical school called Vedanta. This field of philosophical enquiry remains important in Hinduism. The term Vedanta was traditionally used to denote the Upanishads, the final part of the Vedas, but the term has more popularly been used to denote systems of thought based on a coherent interpretation of three works, the Upanishads, the *Bhagavad Gita*, and the *Brahma Sutra* (a text composed possibly after the first century). The *Brahma Sutra*, which has short aphorisms, was meant to be a mnemonic aid, summarizing the teachings of the other two texts. Because many phrases did not have an obvious meaning, Vedantic philosophers wrote extensive commentaries on this text.

Shankara, who lived in about 800 C.E., was a prominent interpreter of Vedanta. He spoke of this Earth and life cycle as having limited reality; once the soul realizes that it is and always has been Brahman (the supreme being), "this life passes away like a dream." For Shankara, reality is nondual (*advaita*). There is only one reality, Brahman, and this Brahman is indescribable and without any attributes. Liberation is removal of ignorance and a dispelling of illusion through the power of transforming knowledge. Shankara is said to have established monasteries in different parts of India. There is reportedly an unbroken succession of teachers in these monasteries, and all of them have the title of "Shankara, the teacher" (Shankaracharya).

Shankara's philosophy was criticized by later Vedanta philosophers such as Ramanuja (traditionally 1017–1137) and Madhva (c. 1199–1278). Ramanuja was the most significant interpreter of theistic Vedanta for the Sri Vaishnava, a community in South India that worships Vishnu and his consorts Sri (Lakshmi) and Bhu (the goddess Earth). Ramanuja proclaimed the supremacy of Vishnu-Narayana and emphasized that devotion to Vishnu would lead to ultimate liberation. According to Ramanuja, Vishnu (whose name literally means "all-pervasive") is immanent in the entire universe, pervading all souls and material substances but also transcending them. The philosopher Madhva, in classifying some souls as eternally bound, is unique in the Hindu tradition. For him, even in liberation there are different grades of enjoyment and bliss. He was also one of the explicitly dualistic Vedanta philosophers, holding that the human soul and Brahman are ultimately separate and not identical in any way. The devotional philosophy of Chaitanya (sixteenth century) has been popular in the eastern state of Bengal and, in the twentieth century, in the United States (through the ISKCON community).

Reactions to colonial rule can be seen in the teachings and activism of Ram Mohun Roy (1772–1833), Dayananda Saraswati (1825–83), and the poet-philosopher Aurobindo (1872–1950). Ram Mohun Roy, discussed above under EARLY AND MODERN LEADERS, advocated educational and social reforms. Dayanand Saraswati opened educational institutions for women and raised people's consciousness about Vedic teachings. Aurobindo was initially a radical who protested against British rule. He eventually taught a new interpretation of Vedanta that portrayed the ascent of the human spirit combining with the descent of the divine into the human being.

Other leaders, such as the novelist Bankim Chandra Chatterjee (1838–94), also challenged the presence of the British in India; the philosopher, writer, and religious activist Bal Gangadhar Tilak (1856–1920) advocated a more activist approach to achieve independence from the colonial powers. Political and cultural philosophies came together in the writings of Veer Savarkar (1883–1966), who championed the concept of "Hinduness" (*Hindutva*). He distinguished this from the religion itself and argued—on the basis of shared culture, geography, and race—for the unification of the inhabitants of India.

ORGANIZATIONAL STRUCTURE The social organization of the Hindu tradition can be discussed in many ways. The word "Hindu" was not commonly used to describe people's identity in India until the nineteenth century. A person's social class (*varna*, literally "color"), subgroup or caste, sectarian community, philosophical group, and linguistic community contribute to creating the sense of "self" within the Hindu tradition. There are many communities within Hinduism, and many of them have their own chains of leaders. In addition to these communities, there are charismatic teachers (gurus) who command large followings around the world. Sometimes clan groups (*gotra*, literally "cow-pen") and the region of origin also figure in the organization of Hindus. In diaspora communities Hindus tend to congregate along linguistic lines.

The word "caste" (derived from a Portuguese word meaning "a division in society") is used as a shorthand term to refer to thousands of stratified and circumscribed social communities that have multiplied through the centuries. "Caste" has sometimes been used to mean *varna* (class) and other times to mean *jati* (birth group). The beginnings of the caste system are seen in the "Hymn to the Supreme Person" in the Rig Veda, with its enumeration of four classes, or *varna*: priestly (Brahman), ruling (Kshatriya), mercantile (Vaishya), and servant (Sudra) classes. From the simple fourfold structure eventually arose a plethora of social and occupational divisions. The texts on dharma specify the names of various subcastes that come from marriages between the various classes. Ritual practices, dietary rules, and sometimes dialects differ between the castes.

Although the Vedas spoke of four major social divisions (*varna*s), most Hindus historically have identified themselves as belonging to a specific birth group, or *jati*. In many parts of India the word *jati* may be translated as caste or community, but the numerous *jati*s do not neatly fit into the fourfold caste system. There are several hundred *jati*s in India. It has been a matter of controversy whether a person is born into a caste or whether caste could be decided by a person's qualities and propensities. Although there have been many arguments in favor of the latter concept, the idea of birth group gained hold in India, and now a person's caste in India is determined at birth. Caste is only one of the many factors in social hierarchies; age, gender, economic class, and even a person's piety figure in the equation. At various times the hierarchies were reversed by exalting "lower"-caste devotees, but they were seldom discarded.

Contrary to popular perceptions, there was, historically, a great deal of caste mobility in India. This was particularly true in the case of warriors. Kings and war-

The *Tilaka* and Religious Affiliation

The *tilaka,* the forehead mark worn by many Hindus, is often cosmetic, but in many cases the color, shape, and material with which it is made indicates whether someone is a follower of a particular god. These sectarian marks may be created with materials such as white clay, sandalwood paste, *kajal* (made from the soot of an oil-lamp), or specific kinds of ash.

In general, vertical forehead marks (which are often *U*-shaped) denote that a person is a follower of the god Vishnu and the goddess Lakshmi or a devotee of the lord Krishna (whom some Hindus hold to be an incarnation of Vishnu). Such marks are usually made of white clay; sometimes the materials are taken from places where Krishna is supposed to have lived. The *U*-shaped mark represents the foot of Vishnu and signifies his grace. There may be a red line in the middle; this symbolizes Lakshmi, who is considered to be inseparable from Vishnu. Horizontal or slightly curved crescent marks made of ash or other substances, with a red dot in the middle, denote that the person worships Shiva and the goddess Parvati. The three horizontal lines are sometimes interpreted as representing the three syllables of the mantra "Om" or the three gods Brahma, Vishnu, and Shiva. The ash is also symbolic of the destruction of one's ego. Combinations of various dots and crescents usually show a preference for the Goddess (Devi) in one of her many manifestations.

Some sectarian forehead marks are two vertical lines with an empty space in between; others include a round dot (*bindu*). The empty space or the dot is considered to indicate the ineffable nature of the supreme being. Both theistic and nontheistic believers in the Hindu traditions understand the supreme being as beyond description, and the void expresses this sentiment. In an extension of this belief, some Hindus wear two dots, one white and one black. The white dot is said to portray the supreme being (Brahman); the black dot symbolizes the belief that the supreme deity has glorious qualities such as mercy, compassion, and generosity.

---

riors (*kshatriyas*) generally traced their ancestry to either the lineage of the sun (*surya vamsa*) or the lineage of the Moon (*chandra vamsa*), both of which go back to the primeval progenitors of humanity. This harking back to the right genealogies was even done in places such as Cambodia and Java, where there were Hindu rulers. These are classic instances of the ruling class seeking legitimacy by invoking divine antecedents; even usurpers of thrones eventually began to trace their ancestries thus. In the Hindu tradition, both then and now, lines of claimed biological descent are all important. The *Kshatriya* ("royal" or "warrior") families held the power of rulership and governance, and rituals of later Hinduism explicitly emphasized their connection with divine beings.

Outside the circuit of the castes, there are many other groups collectively called "out-caste" in English. These resulted either from mixed marriages or, more often, from association with professions deemed inferior. Such occupations included working with animal hides and dealing with corpses, because dead animal or human flesh is considered polluting.

While texts and practices clearly imply hierarchy within the castes, some Hindus have interpreted the castes as a division of labor, with each caste being responsible for a particular function in society. This concept may have been predominant historically in the practice of social divisions in Hindu communities of Cambodia. From inscriptional evidence it seems probable that Cambodian kings awarded castes and caste names to groups of people or even to an entire village. These names suggest ritual functions in the palace or connections with work, and in Southeast Asia the caste system seems not to be based on birth groups.

Sectarian divisions cut across caste lines and form a different template for social divisions. Some Hindu groups are divided along lines of which god they worship; the followers of Vishnu are called Vaishnavas, Shiva's devotees are called Shaivas, and so on. Members of sectarian communities and castes tend to be endogamous. In addition to caste and sectarian affiliation, philosophical communities have formed social divisions in many parts of India.

There is no single teacher or religious leader who speaks for all Hindus, nor are there neatly arranged denominations or groups. There are thousands of communities and groups, each with multiple leaders. There are several kinds of teachers in the Hindu tradition. A religious teacher within the many sectarian Hindu communities may be called *acharya* or guru. Usually, the term *acharya* designates any formal head of a monastery, sect, or subcommunity—a teacher who comes in a long line of successive leaders. Some of the more enduring lines of *acharya* succession can be seen in the communities that follow a noted theologian. The followers of teachers such as Shankara (eighth century), Ramanuja (eleventh century), Madhva (thirteenth century), Chaitanya (fifteenth century), and Swaminarayan (nineteenth century) have long, unbroken chains of teachers. The philosophical traditions founded by Ramanuja and Chaitanya, among others, venerate the religious teacher almost as much as the deity they worship. In their pious writings the living, human teacher is seen to be more important than God. Absolute surrender to the teacher is said to be a path to liberation. In addition to these, there have been thousands of ascetics—women and men possessed by a god or spirit—who have been revered. There have been mediums, storytellers, and *sadhus* (holy men) who have participated in the religious leadership of the Hindu traditions. These leaders have commanded anything from veneration to absolute obedience. Any charismatic leader may be known by his followers as guru (teacher) or swami (master).

Some followers consider their teachers to be an avatar (incarnation) of the supreme being on Earth. Others consider these teachers to be spiritual masters who are highly evolved souls—that is, beings who have ascended above the cares of human life to a state of self-realization or perfection.

In the late twentieth century the Internet became an important tool of communication for Hindus. Devotees of various traditional teachers or gurus or followers of a particular community organize cyber-communities for discussions on their teachings. These Hindu communities have been enormously successful, mobilizing and connecting people from around the globe. Teachers from India regularly address these devotees by what are called *tele-upanyasam*, or tele-sermons.

HOUSES OF WORSHIP AND HOLY PLACES Hundreds of thousands of villages, towns, forests, groves, rivers, and mountains in India are considered sacred. In a larger religio-political context, India is personified as a mother in literature and practice, and almost every part of this motherland is said to be sacred. In recent centuries it has been hailed in many songs as "Mother India" (Bharata Mata) and as a compassionate mother goddess. While many early texts advocated living in India as part of one's religious duties, Hindus have also migrated to other countries—starting with Southeast Asia in the centuries before the Common Era—and recreated the sacred lands in their new homes.

Although there are many standard Hindu pilgrimage itineraries, some places are considered especially sacred. Pilgrimage routes are often organized thematically. For instance, in India devotees may visit the 108 places where *shakti*, or the power of the Goddess, is said to be present; the 68 places where emblems of Shiva are said to have emerged "self-born"; the 12 places where Shiva appears as the "flame of creative energies" (*jyotir linga*); the 8 places where Vishnu spontaneously manifested himself (a form called *svayam vyakta*); and so on. Hindu holy texts extol the sanctity of many individual sites. For pious Hindus, to live in such places or to undertake a pilgrimage to one of them is enough to destroy a person's sins and to assist in the attainment of liberation from the cycle of life, death, and rebirth.

Texts that discuss the sanctity of the holy places tend to have narratives about how a particular deity manifested himself or herself there and promised rewards in this life and in the afterlife for all the worshipers. Most holy places also have temples to mark this hierophany (divine revelation). The temple itself is like a "port of transit," a place from which a human being may "cross over" (*tirtha*) the ocean of life and death. Because water is also considered to be purifying, many temples and holy places are located near an ocean, lake, river, or spring. When such a body of water is not close by, there is usually an artificial ritual well or pool, a feature that may date back to the time of the Harappan civilization (c. 3000 to 1750 B.C.E.). Pilgrims sometimes cleanse themselves in these pools before praying in the temple.

Mountains, lakes, groves, and rivers are also sacred. The Ganges, Yamuna, Cauvery, and Narmada rivers are believed to be so holy that bathing in them destroys a person's sins. Confluences of two rivers or of a river and the sea are particularly sacred. Pilgrims journey regularly to bathe at Triveni Sangama ("Confluence of Three Rivers") at Prayag (an ancient city now the site of Allahabad), where the Ganges, the Yamuna, and a mythical underground river, the Sarasvati, all meet. Small sealed jars of holy water from the Ganges are kept in homes and are used in domestic rituals to purify the dead and dying.

Many temples are located on hills and mountains because they are considered to be sacred. In Southeast Asia, where there were no hills, artificial mountain-temples were erected. It is not clear exactly when temples became popular in India, because the earlier houses of worship were probably made of perishable materials. Inscriptions in Champa (now Vietnam) mention Hindu houses of worship that existed in Southeast Asia during the early centuries of the Common Era.

Some of the early places of worship were in the Chalukya capital of Vatapi (modern Badami), where in the late sixth century C.E. exquisite carvings of Vishnu and Shiva were carved into rock caves. That an adjacent cave is a Jain holy site is evidence of the amicable coexistence of religious traditions in India. Experimental modes of temple architecture can be seen in nearby Aihole and Pattadakal (c. seventh–ninth centuries).

Temple architecture was different in northern and southern India, with many variations within both areas. Temples, palaces, and all buildings were part of the guided practices of the Hindu tradition. Texts on architecture, dwelling places, and choice of building sites gave instructions on how to build these structures and on the ratio of the measurements. Large complexes have many shrines, each oriented in a specific direction. Temples were major religious, cultural, and economic centers. They were (and to a large extent continue to be) built to represent the whole cosmos, and there are elaborate rules that determine their design. Many temples, such as Angkor Wat in Cambodia, also include proportions connected with Hindu systems of time measurement. For instance, the various measurements of a temple could correspond to the number of years in the various yugas (ages). Many temples were also built in accordance with the observed movements of the Sun, Moon, and stars. The sun would shine on icons, sculptures, or specific areas of the temple at certain times, such as the summer and winter solstices and the equinoxes.

The main part of a temple is an inner shrine where a deity is consecrated. Hindu worship is not generally congregational, so the entrances to the inner shrine allow only small groups of people to enter. For many sectarian movements, the deity in this shrine is not a symbol; it is the actual presence of the god or goddess in the midst of human beings, a veritable incarnation. The deity resides in the temple as long as the devotees worship there. Devotees believe that the presence of God in the temple does not detract from his or her presence in heaven, immanence in the world, or presence in a human soul. The deity is always complete and whole no matter how many manifestations take place.

In most parts of southern India the pan-Hindu deities are known and worshiped only with local names; in the Tirumala-Tirupati temple (the wealthiest religious institution in India), for instance, Vishnu is known as Venkateswara, or the Lord of the Venkata Hills. Many of the temple complexes in India are associated with the major sects—that is, they enshrine Vishnu, Shiva, or the Goddess and their entourages. In many of them the deities are known by their local or regional names. A typical temple may have separate shrines for the deity, his or her spouse, other divine attendants, and saints. Temples in the diaspora generally cater to a broader community of worshipers and have images of Shiva, Vishnu, the Goddess, and other deities enshrined under one roof.

WHAT IS SACRED? A holy space in the Hindu tradition is one in which devotees come to see the enshrined deity and hear sacred words from holy texts. In the past religious teachers were careful about whom they imparted their teachings to, and they screened their devotees carefully. Today, however, the Internet allows anyone to see images of deities, teachers, and gurus and even to hear the recitation and music sacred texts and songs. Some websites call their home pages "electronic ashrams." An ashram is a traditional hermitage or place of learning.

Some Hindus believe that there is no aspect of life that is not sacred to them, but not all Hindus interpret sacredness this way. In Hinduism the lines between the sacred and the secular are blurred and depend on context. Every paper and every book is sacred because they represent knowledge; if a person's feet come into contact with a sheet of paper, a Hindu may spontaneously do a small act of veneration to compensate for the disrespect.

While many aspects of nature are sacred, a few important emblems are notably holy. Special ash that the devotees of Shiva put on their forehead is holy. Hindus venerate particular plants that are said to be sacred to Vishnu (tulsi leaves and flowers of the parijata tree) or

Shiva (leaves of the *bilva* tree). Cows are not worshiped, but they are held as sacred and venerated. In ritual contexts snakes are considered emblematic of good fortune or fertility and are deemed worthy of respect.

HOLIDAYS AND FESTIVALS Hindus celebrate festivals throughout the year. There are domestic, temple, and public celebrations. The birthdays of the many deities, especially Ganesha, Krishna, and Rama, are popular. Hindus have a lunar calendar that is periodically adjusted to the solar year; thus, while the dates of the festivals change, they come within the span of a month. Most festivals are marked in the lunar calendar, and many Hindus know whether the divine birthdays occur on the waxing or waning moon cycles.

Festivals can be local or pan-Indian. Holi and Onam are examples of regional festivals. Holi, a spring festival celebrated in some parts of northern India with bonfires and an exuberant throwing of colored powder on friends and crowds, commemorates various events narrated in the *Purana*s. In the state of Kerala, Onam is celebrated in August and September; the fifth incarnation of Vishnu as a dwarf-Brahman is remembered in that festival.

Other festivals, such as Navaratri and Dipavali (known as Divali in some areas), are more or less pan-Hindu festivals. The festival of Navaratri (a word meaning "nine nights") lasts for nine nights and ten days. It is celebrated by Hindus all over India, but in different ways and for different reasons. The festival begins on the new moon that occurs between 15 September and 14 October. In southern India Navaratri is dedicated to the goddesses Sarasvati, Lakshmi, and Parvati, and in northern India it commemorates the battle between the prince Rama and the demon-king Ravana.

In the region of Tamil Nadu, Navaratri is largely a festival for women. A room is set apart and filled with exquisite dolls for the play of the goddesses. Elaborate tableaux are set up depicting epic and Puranic scenes. Every evening women and children dressed in bright silks visit one another, admire the *kolu* (display of dolls), play musical instruments, and sing songs, usually in praise of one of the goddesses. Some Hindus believe that the goddess Durga killed the buffalo-demon Mahisa during these nine or ten days. Hindus in the state of West Bengal call this festival Durga Puja. They make sumptuous statues of Durga and worship her. In the state of Gujarat the Navaratri celebration includes performing two traditional dances at night: *garbha,* a circular dance in which a sacred lamp is kept in the center as a manifestation of the goddess, and *dandiya,* a dance with sticks, reminiscent of the dance that Krishna is said to have done with the cowherd girls.

The last two days of Navaratri are called Ayudha Puja (veneration of weapons and machines). Hindus acknowledge the importance of all vehicles and many other instruments that day. On the ninth day of the festival the goddess Sarasvati, the patron of learning and music, is worshiped. People place musical instruments, writing implements, and textbooks in front of her and the display of dolls, to be blessed by her for the rest of the year. The next day is the victorious tenth day (Vijaya Dasami), dedicated to Lakshmi. People start new ventures, account books, and learning on that day.

Dipavali (literally "necklace of lamps"), one of the most popular Hindu festivals, occurs on the new moon between 15 October and 14 November. Seen as the beginning of a New Year in some parts of India, it is celebrated by decorating houses with lights, setting off firecrackers, and wearing new clothes. As with Navaratri, Hindus celebrate Dipavali for many reasons. In southern India it is believed that on that day at dawn, Krishna killed the demon Narakasura, thus insuring a victory of light over darkness. Fireworks are used in celebrations all over India. In North India Rama's return to the city of Ayodhya and his coronation are celebrated on Dipavali.

MODE OF DRESS Every region and every community in India has its own code of dress. Historically, most Hindu communities celebrated the body and wore clothes to enhance and adorn it. After the arrival of Islam in northern India in the twelfth century C.E., the covering of the body initially became fashionable and then a way of depicting one's modesty, especially in northern India. In the south there was less covering, and even now on ritual occasions men in the Brahmanic communities may not wear much on the upper part of their bodies. In the north, however, women cover their heads, a custom that is completely avoided in the south.

Most women wear the sari; they wrap a piece of cloth (varying between six and nine yards) around the waist, and a piece of it is then draped over the breasts and over one shoulder. While the six-yard sari has become standard in post-independence India, there are many variations in the way it is tied. Many urban Hindu women have adopted Western clothes.

In the Hindu tradition the human body is a carrier of a person's cosmology and worldviews. The way Hindus care for it, adorn it, carry and move it, and dispose of it all reflect something about their engagement with the world, the universe, and the divine.

The most common, yet ambiguous, manifestation of Hindu religion and culture is the forehead mark worn by many adherents. Traditionally women most often wear the mark, but in many parts of India male ascetics, temple priests, and devotees also put on the marks in a prominent manner. While women wear it every day, many men wear it only for religious rituals. These marks have several meanings. How the mark is interpreted depends upon factors such as the gender and marital status of the person wearing it, the occasion for which the mark is worn, the shape and materials with which it is made, the particular sectarian community from which the person comes, and occasionally a person's caste.

At the simplest level the mark, known as a *tilaka* (meaning "small, like a *tila*" [sesame seed]), is a form of adornment with decorative value, part of a large repertoire of ornamentation used to enhance appearance. Over the centuries men and women in India have painted different parts of their bodies and faces; the drawing of the *tilaka* was one central piece in this decorative exercise. In this spirit most of the marks worn by women today are stickers in different colors and shapes with little theological value. As such, many people dismiss it as not being a "religious" mark because it seems more distinctive of a geographic region than of a religious tradition. *Kumkum*, a red powder made from turmeric, is frequently dabbed onto the image of the Goddess in a temple and then distributed among the devotees. Hindus regularly use this *kumkum*, which is blessed by the deity, to make their forehead marks. Even women who wear plastic stickers often pause to put a hint of this sacred powder on their foreheads to proclaim that their husbands are alive.

The marks are not always merely decorative. Many also denote sectarian or religious affiliation. When worn correctly in ritual situations, the shape and color not only indicate which god or goddess the person worships but also to which socioreligious community he or she belongs. It also specifies which theologian or philosopher is important in the religious community from which the person hails.

Some texts and images portray the god Shiva as having a third eye in the center of his forehead. While most Hindus believe that this eye is unique to Shiva, oc-casionally, in folklore and meditative practice, it is held that all human beings have a nascent "eye" of wisdom in their foreheads. This eye is said to generate spiritual heat and will be opened at a time of intense religious experience. Thus, the forehead mark is said to represent this third eye of wisdom. Some interpreters say that the use of herbal powders on the skin of the forehead regulates this spiritual energy for the devotee.

A round, decorative, forehead mark is seen as a symbol of *saubhagya* (good fortune) in many texts and in popular practice in India. Androcentric (male-centered) texts interpret good fortune for a woman as the state of being married and having her husband alive. Thus, married women often wear the mark as a symbol of their married status and as a sign of the role that they play in society. In many communities of Hinduism, it is mandatory for the woman to remove this symbol of good fortune if she is widowed. Such practices display a long tradition of customs that belittle and objectify some women. In certain traditions, such as the Vaishnava (followers of Vishnu), however, marital status does not affect the wearing of the sectarian mark. A woman who belongs to any of these communities would consider herself to be in a state of "good fortune" in being a devotee of Lakshmi and Vishnu and would always wear it.

DIETARY PRACTICES Perhaps one of the most important areas of Hindu life is food. The treatises on dharma spend the most amount of time discussing the issue of marriage, and the second area of interest is food. What is consumed, who consumes it, who prepares the food, when it is done, how much is eaten, with whom one eats, what direction one faces when one eats, and more details are all addressed with great detail—but are often negated in the contexts of faith and devotion.

Food regulations may differ not only between the various castes and communities of the Hindu traditions but also by region, gender, the stages of a person's life, the times of the year, the phases of the Moon, the ritual calendar, and an individual's obligations. Contrary to the perception of many Westerners, most Hindus are not vegetarians. Whether a Hindu practices vegetarianism is determined by his or her membership in a specific community or caste. The cow is seen as a nurturing mother. Sometimes cows are considered the "residence" of the goddess Lakshmi. Hence, most Hindus in the last two millennia have tended not to consume beef.

Women's Contributions to the Hindu Tradition

Although the literature on dharma does not give many rights to a woman, there have been a number of strong women who have contributed to Hindu society. Women gave religious advice and wrote scholarly works. These women were respected, honored, and in some cases even venerated. In the Rig Veda there are hymns to various deities composed by women such as Ghosha, Apala, and Lopamudra. In the Upanishads, Maitreyi, the wife of the philosopher Yajñavalkya, questions him in depth about the nature of reality. Gargi Vachaknavi, a woman philosopher, challenges Yajñavalkya with questions in a public debate. There were probably more women composers and philosophers, but they are not noted in the texts. In time, many parts of the text, including verses composed by women, were lost. It is also possible that when literature became more androcentric (male-centered), the women's compositions that came after the Vedas were suppressed. Nevertheless, women continued to be involved in poetry and philosophy. Starting in the eighth century women poets such as Andal, Karaikkal Ammaiyar, and Akka Mahadevi rejected married life and dedicated passionate poetry to Vishnu and Shiva. They have been honored and venerated as saints in the Sri Vaishsnava, Shaiva, and Vira Shaiva traditions.

Women, especially those from royal families, were also benefactors of temples and other institutions. For example, in 966 C.E. in Tiru Venkatam (the city of Tirupati, in southern India), a woman called Samavai endowed money to celebrate major festivals and to consecrate a processional image of the lord. The temple at Tirupati has the largest endowments and sources of revenue in India today. Studies have shown that Samavai was not an isolated example. We know, for instance, that queens of the Chola dynasty (c. 846–1279) were enthusiastic patrons of temples and religious causes for the Shaiva community of South India in about the tenth century.

There are regular periods of fasting and feasting in the Hindu calendar, and these periods differ for each community. Many Vaishnavas (followers of Vishnu) have typically fasted or avoided grain on *ekadashi* day (the 11th day of the waxing or waning Moon). Others fast during specific festival seasons such as Navaratri. Some fasts are specific—refraining from grains, rice, salt, and so on for a period of time. Men and women sometimes fast for half a day or for several hours on days when they have performed rituals to the ancestors.

For many Hindus it is not enough just to be a vegetarian; food, like many other material substances, is said to have three qualities. These are *sattva* (purity); *rajas* (passion, energy, movement); and *tamas* (sloth, stupor, rest). Thus, some Hindu communities refrain from having onions and garlic because they are said to have a preponderance of *rajas* and *tamas*. Several vegetables are also prohibited for similar reasons; for example, food that has been tasted by others and leftover food are considered to be ritually polluted and are also prohibited. While there are hundreds of restrictions on food, there are certain devotional contexts where food that can be considered ritually polluting is made acceptable because of a devotee's faith. There are several Hindu narratives about how prohibited food was offered to the deity and it was accepted because the devotee offered it with love.

In many temples ritual food is offered to the deity and then distributed to the worshipers as divine favor (*prasada*). For more than a thousand years devotees have endowed land and monies to temples so that the revenue from them could be used for the preparation of food and then distributed to the pilgrims. Many families even now sponsor feasts or donate food in temples to celebrate birthdays or in memory of family members.

Right eating is not just what a person can eat or avoid; in the texts on dharma as well as in orthoprax (orthodox in practices) houses, it involves issues such as the caste and gender of the cook (preferably a high-caste male or any woman, except at times when she is menstruating); the times a person may eat (for example, twice a day and not during twilight); and not eating food cooked the day before.

The greatest amount of discussion in the *Dharma Sastra* texts is spent on forbidden foods, which varied in different time periods and between authors. It is generally agreed that most people ate meat, even beef, possibly up to the beginning of the Common Era. It is a matter of some controversy whether Indians ate beef during the time of the Vedas and whether the cow was a protected animal; however, it is fairly well accepted that most Indians ate other kinds of meat and fowl then.

RITUALS Hindu temple rituals are complex, and in many temples there may be a celebration almost every other day. Ritual worship is divided into daily, fortnightly, monthly, and annual cycles. On ritual occasions in southern India the deity is taken in a procession through the streets near the temple in special floats or enormous chariots. Most of the larger temples take notions of ritual purity seriously, and therefore women are not allowed to worship during the time of menstruation. In many South Indian temples there is not much gender segregation during the rituals. Worship is individual rather than congregational, and the modes of prayer are dictated by many texts. Frequently the priest—a male member of the Brahman caste—offers the prayers on behalf of the devotee. Usually only the priests are allowed to enter the inner shrines of a temple. After the ritual prayer a lamp or camphor light is waved in a circle in front of the deity in a ritual called *arati*, and in northern India a special song is sung at this time.

Rituals performed in the home are generally called *puja* (literally "worship"). Worship of the deity or of a spiritual teacher at a home shrine is one of the most significant ways in which Hindus express their devotion. Many Hindu households set aside some space (a cabinet shelf or an entire room) at home where pictures or small images of the deities are enshrined. *Puja* may involve simple acts of daily devotion, such as the lighting of oil lamps and incense sticks, recitation of prayers, or offering of food to the deity. In home worship simpler versions of some temple rituals take place. In daily worship family members lead the rites, but more elaborate or specialized rituals of worship, such as the ones to Satyanarayana (a manifestation of Vishnu) on full-moon days, may involve the participation of a priest or special personnel. The concept of appropriate hospitality guides home worship. The image of the deity receives the hospitality accorded to an honored guest in the home, including ritual bathing, anointing with ghee (clarified butter), offerings of food and drink, lighted lamps, and garlands of flowers.

Domestic rituals by women may be performed on a daily, recurring, or occasional schedule. While many of the well-known rituals are performed for the welfare of the family and for earthly happiness, a few are performed for personal salvation or liberation. Many rituals, such as pilgrimages, worshiping at home shrines or temples, and singing devotional songs, are similar to patterns of worship practiced by men, but some are unique to married women whose husbands are alive. Underlying many of the rites is the notion that women are powerful and that rites performed by them have potency. While many rituals conducted by Hindu women share certain features, there are significant differences among the many communities, castes, and regions.

Perhaps in no rite within the Hindu tradition is there more regional variation than in a wedding ceremony. Choosing the right spouse for a daughter or son is usually accomplished with the help of an extensive family network and sometimes by advertising in newspapers or on the Internet. In many communities, after the prospective couple's caste, community, economic, and educational compatibility is addressed, the detailed horoscopes of the bride and bridegroom are matched. Apart from the several regional and community rites that accompany it, the sacrament of marriage involves several basic features for it even to be considered legal. These include the *kanya dana* (the gift of the virgin by the father), *pani grahana* (the clasping of hands), *sapta padi* (taking seven steps together around fire, which is the eternal witness), and *mangalya dharana* (the giving of auspiciousness to the bride). In addition to these, the bride and bridegroom exchange garlands.

The ceremony itself lasts several hours and may involve several changes of elaborate clothing for the bride, who is adorned with expensive jewelry. Often the couple sits on a platform with a fire nearby, to which offerings are made. The bride's parents have an active role to play, as do specific relatives (the groom's sister and the bride's brother and maternal uncle) at particular moments in the ritual, but the hundreds of guests are free to come and go as they please. In one of the central rituals the bridegroom's family presents the bride with "the gift of auspiciousness." The gift is a necklace or string, called the *mangala sutra* (string of auspiciousness or happiness). It may be a gold necklace, a string of black beads, a yellow thread, or anything else that the woman may wear around her neck. The necklace is adorned with the insignia of the god the family worships. The South Indian bridegroom ties this string or places the necklace around the bride's neck as her symbol of marriage. It corresponds to a wedding ring in Western society. There is no equivalent symbol for the bridegroom, but in the castes in which a man wears the sacred thread, married men wear a double thread. The central rituals are to take place only near a sacred fire.

Death causes a state of pollution for the family. This pollution is observed for a period that may last from 12 days to almost a year. The body is usually removed from the home within a few hours. In most communities cremation is the final sacrament, and the eldest son usually performs these rites. In a few communities, and for people in certain stages of life (such as an infant or an ascetic), the body may be interred. Until the body is removed and the cremation fire is lit, no fire is to be lit or tended in the house where death occurred. Each religious community has its own list of scriptures from which to recite. These include portions of the Vedas and the *Bhagavad Gita.*

RITES OF PASSAGE Two factors are important to note in discussing life-cycle rites. First, not all are pan-Hindu, and even those that are may have little importance in some communities. Second, many of the important rites, especially those that are celebrated for girls or women, may not be discussed in any classical text on dharma. This is possibly because many of the texts were written by men. Women were treated as the partners of males, who were the main focus of the books. It may also be that some of these rites emerged after these texts were written.

Many life-cycle rituals are called auspicious. The English word "auspiciousness" has been used as a shorthand term for a rather wide category of features in Hindu life. Auspicious times are chosen for the conduct of all sacraments; these times are in agreement with the person's horoscope.

A person's sacraments (*samskaras*; literally "perfecting") begin prenatally. Two of these, called *pumsavana* (seeking a male offspring) and *simanta* (hair parting), are followed by many communities in India. Although formerly performed in the fifth month of pregnancy, they are done much later now for the safe birth of a child, preferably a male. After childbirth a ceremony called *jatakarma* (birth ceremony) is performed. In earlier days this was supposed to be done before the umbilical cord was cut, but it is now done much later. The moment of birth is also noted, so that the exact horoscope of the child can be charted. Childhood sacraments include naming, the first feeding of solid food, tonsure or cutting of the child's hair, and piercing of the ears (which was historically done for both boys and girls but now

only applies to girls). The beginning of education for a child is called *vidya arambha* (literally "the beginning of learning").

The ritual that initiates a young Brahman boy into the study of the Vedas is called *upanayana* or *brahma upadesa.* The word *upanayana* has two meanings; it may mean "acquiring the extra eye of knowledge" or "coming close to a teacher" to get knowledge. *Brahma upadesa* means receiving the sacred teaching (*upadesa*) concerning the supreme being (Brahman). The ritual of *upanayana* traditionally initiates a young boy at about age eight into the first stage of life, called *brahmacarya.* This word literally means "traveling on the path that will disclose the supreme being," that is, studenthood. The central part of the ritual is the imparting of the sacred teaching. As the boy sits with his father and the priest under a silk cloth (symbolizing the spiritual womb, according to some), a sacred mantra (sentence for chanting) is given to him. He is to repeat this mantra 108 times, 3 times a day. The mantra, known as the *gayatri*, is short: "I meditate on the brilliance of the sun; may it illumine my mind." In Vedic times, and possibly even well into the first millennium of this era, the young boy began his Vedic studies at this stage and went to live with his new teacher for several years. The ceremony is now conducted with considerable social overtones in many communities. Traditionally, male members of the upper three classes went through this ritual, but it is now performed mainly by the Brahmanic sections of the Hindu community.

The auspicious marriage is a way to fulfill obligations to society. According to the *Dharma Sastra* texts, a wife is a man's partner in fulfilling dharma, and without her a man cannot fully perform his religious obligations.

MEMBERSHIP Hindu traditions have not sought to convert, nor have they actively proselytized. It has been widely debated whether a person has to be born a Hindu or whether it is possible to convert to the tradition. A widely held opinion is that a person may be initiated to specific traditions (*sampradaya*) such as ISKCON or the Sri Vaishnava faith within Hinduism, but the word "convert" is largely seen as an irrelevant concept. Because Hinduism is used as an umbrella category for hundreds of castes, communities, and traditions, a person cannot be a generic Hindu; a Hindu always has to be part of a group, whether he or she is born into it or not. Because there is no formal organization or institution for all Hindus (or even for most of them), the question of membership is problematic. Legally, however, it is important to know who a Hindu is because family law in India is different for Hindus, Muslims, Christians, and Zoroastrians. A Hindu, according to legal texts, is held to be anyone who is not a Christian, Muslim, or Zoroastrian and who is domiciled in the territories of India. Thus, at least for the purposes of the law, Buddhists, Jains, and Sikhs in India are considered to be Hindus, even though theologically, and sometimes socially, they are distinct groups.

There are also thousands of people around the world who adopt facets and selected practices of Hindu life, such as meditation, yoga, diet, and recitation of mantras. While those who are initiated into specific traditions such as ISKCON consider themselves part of the larger Hindu tradition, others may accept some features of Hindu life without necessarily having any formal affiliation with the tradition.

RELIGIOUS TOLERANCE In the nineteenth and twentieth centuries religious leaders such as Vivekananda and Mahatma Gandhi emphasized the importance of tolerance in the Hindu tradition. For centuries, if not millennia, Hindus have lived with Buddhists, Jains, Parsis (also called Zoroastrians), Sikhs, Jews, Christians, and Muslims in relatively long periods of peace. Hindu rulers have funded and encouraged the building of monasteries and houses of worship for Buddhists in India and Southeast Asia; in India they endowed lands to Muslim saints as well as to Jain and Buddhist institutions. Because Hindus are the majority in post-independence India (after 1947), many of the minority traditions are given special privileges.

While religions in India have for the most part peacefully coexisted, historically there have been a few instances of tension between the Shaiva and Vaishnava traditions as well as between these groups and Jainism. There have also been both harmonious as well as extraordinarily acrimonious relationships between Hindus and Muslims in South Asia. Hundreds of Hindu temples in South Asia were destroyed for political, economic, and religious reasons. The real and perceived persecutions under Muslim rulers culminated in violence in 1947, when the subcontinent was partitioned into the separate countries of India (with a Hindu majority) and Pakistan (with a Muslim majority). In the last few years of the twentieth century political parties with Hindu nationalist interests were perceived to be encouraging hostility toward minority religions. Unlike in colonial days,

when the missionary activity of Christian churches in India was accepted, some Hindu groups now try to stem the strong evangelizing exercises.

SOCIAL JUSTICE Issues of social justice in Hinduism revolve around the caste system and the status of women. The caste system has been complex and different in the many regions of India. Power has been distributed in different ways across the community groups; in many areas there has been discrimination against those who do not fall within the traditional caste system. There are many communities that are collectively called "outcaste" in the Western world and that, in India, are now given the administrative labels of "scheduled caste" or "scheduled tribe." The names of these groups are part of a larger governmental program in India of granting not just equal opportunity but preference to those perceived as not having had the advantage of formal education in the last few centuries. Thus, many federal and state jobs as well as admissions to professional colleges and institutions of higher learning depend to a large extent on one's caste, and there are quotas and reservations exceeding 70 percent in some places for the "scheduled caste" applicants. The quota system has been controversial, especially for those who believe that they have been passed over in favor of those who are less qualified.

The status of women has largely depended on caste, economic class, age, and even piety. It is extremely difficult to make generalizations about the role of women in Hindu society. Androcentric (male-centered) texts have tended to disparage them, yet they had specific religious roles, and without them men could not perform their own duties. It has been a general rule that women in the so-called higher castes had less freedom than those in the so-called lower castes. Widows, especially, were discriminated against in the past, particularly in Brahmanic societies. Unlike many other religions, however, Hinduism has had varied resources that it has drawn upon for the advancement of women in society. Historically there have been powerful women—devotees, poets, patrons of arts, and philosophers—many of whom were known only regionally. These women have served as role models in the late twentieth century and into the twenty-first century.

Several groups in India are dedicated to various forms of social justice. One of the best-known movements was initiated by Vinoba Bhave (1895–1982). His movement focused on *bhu daan* (literally "gift of land") to the poor as a way of redistributing resources.

Swami Agnivesh (born in 1939) has mobilized mass campaigns to fight bonded labor, child labor, and the ecological destruction of Third World countries. He attacks these problems primarily through the legal system as well as with direct activism and social work.

SOCIAL ASPECTS Hinduism is not just a religion focusing on the individual's relationship to the divine but a network of social relationships and power. Elaborate kinship arrangements and connections are laid out in text and practice, and every family member has specific ritual functions to perform. The family is the center of most social, cultural, and religious events. Social divisions are part of a complex system of castes, communities, subcommunities, and linguistic groups. Among some higher castes, families may have a name called a *gotra* (literally a "cow-pen"), a word referring loosely to a clan. While a person is expected to marry within a subcommunity and caste, he or she must marry outside his or her *gotra.*

Throughout the history of the Hindu tradition some men have practiced polygamy, but since the passing of the Hindu Marriage Act of 1955–56 monogamy has been the only legal option. Inheritance, succession, divorce, adoption, and other issues are all dealt with under codified Hindu family acts. There have been occasional instances of polyandry in Hindu narratives, and it was not uncommon in matrilineal states. Except for the matrilineal culture in the state of Kerala and a few other castes and tribes, Hindu traditions have largely been patriarchal and patrilineal.

Large extended families were common in India until the late twentieth century. Marriages were and still are arranged between men and women of the same caste, and marriage is seen not so much as a union of individuals but of families. While divorce has become increasingly accepted in many levels of society, it remains relatively rare.

In many Hindu communities a woman who is "auspicious" is honored and respected. Auspiciousness refers to prosperity in this life. It is seen in terms of wealth and progeny, along with the symbols and rituals connected with these. In the classical literature dealing with dharma, and in practice, it is auspicious to be married and to fulfill one's dharmic obligations. A *sumangali*—a married woman whose husband is alive—is the ideal woman with the ideal amount of auspiciousness, who can be a full partner in dharma (duty), *artha* (prosperity), and *kama* (sensual pleasure); through whom children are born; and through whom wealth and religious merit are accumulated. Only a married woman bears the title Srimati (meaning "the one with *sri* [auspiciousness]"). She is called *griha-laksmi* (the goddess Lakshmi of the house) and is the most honored woman in Hindu society, especially if she bears children.

The ethical issues surrounding reproductive technology are debated. Some of their basic logic may at first seem to run contrary to the *smriti* literature dealing with dharma. Books on dharma written about 2,000 years ago by Manu and others emphasized the importance of married couples having children. Many Hindus today accept advances in reproductive technology, such as artificial insemination, as a means of achieving this goal. Members of higher castes sometimes reject sperm banks as a source because they value the purity of their lineage. For similar reasons, adoption of an unknown child is not always acceptable for caste-conscious Hindus. The Hindu epics and the *Puranas* offer stories about supernatural means of conception and giving birth. Even though these tales, which legitimate the new reproductive technologies, are generally not invoked, the technologies seem to have been accepted easily.

CONTROVERSIAL ISSUES Abortion, homosexuality, and other issues that are controversial in the West are not often publicly spoken about in India. While the texts of dharma condemn abortion and encourage the birth of many children, laws permitting abortion passed in India without prolonged debate or any strong dissent from religious leaders. Many Hindus are not even aware of the pronouncements of the texts of dharma; the dharma texts simply have not had the compelling authority that religious law has had in some other religious traditions. Preference for male children in some parts of India has led to cases of female feticide (sex-selective abortion), which was made illegal in 1996.

Homosexuality is explicitly acknowledged only in some groups. Many middle-class families would not approve of it, but to a considerable extent it is not seen as a political embarrassment or liability for elected officials. Extramarital sex, on the other hand, is frowned upon if a married woman is involved; premarital sex with someone who does not become one's spouse may be extremely damaging to a woman and her family. As in many cases, the rules and mores of the Brahmanic and the so-called higher castes are more stringent than others.

Many traditional teachers argue against the authority of women and some so-called "lower castes" to recite the Vedas or conduct religious rituals. Despite these opinions, there are several movements that periodically bypass such Brahmanic values and simply initiate practices that may have been forbidden earlier. Thus, some groups train women to recite the Vedas, and in some families women may perform funeral rites that were forbidden to them; all these activities become woven into the social fabric without any chastisement or repercussions because there is no centralized authority to condemn such acts.

CULTURAL IMPACT India's contribution to religion, culture, art, and science has been tremendous. Many of these fields have been framed in religious discourses; thus, healing, astronomy, and architecture are all presented as part of religion. Many of these concepts and practices, however, have spread to other cultures without the religious framework and have been adapted for local consumption.

Hindu philosophies had a major impact in many parts of the world from about the third century B.C.E. Many philosophies and practices traveled to East and Southeast Asia with Buddhism; others were spread to the western hemisphere by trade routes and through traffic with West Asia and Greece. Beginning in the eighteenth century, through colonial scholarship, many of the important Sanskrit texts were transmitted through translation to Europe and then to the United States. Thus, in the nineteenth century American Transcendentalists such as Ralph Waldo Emerson and Henry David Thoreau selectively took what they considered to be the best offerings of India and integrated texts such as the *Bhagavad Gita* and the *Vishnu Purana* into their writings. Entire passages from these texts, for instance, can be seen in Emerson's poems "Brahma" and "Hematreya."

With the arrival of Vivekananda (1863–1902) and other teachers in the United States in the late nineteenth and early twentieth centuries, yoga and some Hindu forms of meditation became well known in the West. These were presented without connection to Indian cultures and were initially adapted as spiritual exercises. With the spread of counterculture movements in the 1960s, yoga became popular as a physical exercise, and today it is taught in practically every gym and physical education class in the United States and Canada. Its popularity is so overwhelming that most practitioners do not perceive it as being connected with Hindu culture.

Perhaps the greatest impact within India itself has come from the cumulative dance traditions; dance itself has been considered to be sacred. Although there are parts of dance traditions that have been continuous for several centuries, many of the formal classical dances that had fallen out of practice were reconstituted in the twentieth century by studying sculptures in temples. The revival of musical and dance forms along with the religious culture in which they are embedded has been a significant development in the late twentieth century. The performing arts, especially music and dance, have thrived in the diaspora, and they help transmit the stories of the epics, the *Puranas*, and the *Iti-hasa* (the stories of "thus it has been") to a new generation of Hindus.

Much of the cultural impact in the twentieth and twenty-first centuries has occurred through learning from oral traditions and through selecting and adapting traditional thought and practices rather than from textual materials. In this regard Hinduism in the twenty-first century has been congruent with the traditions of two millennia ago.

In Java and Bali the many inscriptions in Hindu temples are evidence of the popularity of the epics, the *Puranas*, and the books on dharma. Parallels can be seen in origin stories, art, and architecture from particular parts of India (such as Kanchipuram and Kalinga) and Cambodia. While one can certainly speak of the "Indianization" of Southeast Asia, it is important to realize that stories and practices significant in India were not all transferred in the same hierarchical order to other places. For example, stories relatively minor in the Hindu tradition in India became extremely significant in Cambodia.

Vasudha Narayanan

See Also Vol. I: *Shaivism, Vaishnavism*

Bibliography

Babb, Lawrence. *Redemptive Encounters: Three Modern Styles in the Hindu Tradition.* Berkeley: University of California Press, 1986.

Baird, Robert. *Religion and Law in Independent India.* New Delhi: Manohar, 1993.

Bhagavata Purana. Translated by Ganesh Vasudeo Tagare. Delhi: Motilal Banarsidass, 1978.

Bose, Mandakranta, ed. *Faces of the Feminine in Ancient, Medieval, and Modern India*. New York: Oxford University Press, 2000.

Bryant, Edwin. *The Quest for the Origins of Vedic Culture: The Indo-Aryan Migration Debate*. NewYork: Oxford University Press, 2003.

Bryant, Edwin, and Maria Eckstrand. *The Hare Krishna Movement: The Postcharismatic Fate of a Religious Transplant*. New York: Columbia University Press, 2004.

Caraka Samhita. Translated by A. Chandra Kaviratna and P. Sharma. Delhi: Sri Satguru Publications, 1996.

Carman, John, and Frederique Marglin. *Purity and Auspiciousness in Indian Society*. Leiden: E.J. Brill, 1985.

Chapple, Christopher Key, and Mary E. Tucker. *Hinduism and Ecology: The Intersection of Earth, Sky, and Water*. Cambridge, Mass.: Harvard University Press, 2000.

Dehejia, Vidya. *Royal Patrons and Great Temple Art*. Bombay: Marg, 1988.

Eck, Diana. *Darsan*. New York: Columbia University Press, 1998.

Hawley, John Stratton. *Devi: Goddesses of India*. University of California Press, 1996.

Hawley, John Stratton, and Mark Juergensmeyer. *Songs of the Saints of India*. New York: Oxford University Press, 1988.

Hess, Linda, and Shukdev Singh. *The Bijak of Kabir*. New Delhi: Motilal Banarsidass, 1986.

Jackson, William J. *Tyagaraja, Life and Lyrics*. New York: Oxford University Press, 1991.

Jacques, Claude. *Angkor: Cities and Temples*. London: Thames and Hudson, 1997.

Kane, Panduranga Vamana. *History of Dharmasastra*. Poona, India: Bhandarkar Oriental Research Institute, 1968–74.

Lutgendorf, Philip. *The Life of a Text*. Berkeley: University of California Press, 1991.

Miller, Barbara Stoler, trans. *The Bhagavad Gita: Krishna's Counsel in Time of War*. New York: Columbia University Press, 1986.

Narayan, R.K. *The Mahabharata*. Chicago: The University of Chicago Press, 2000.

———. *The Ramayana: A Shortened Modern Prose Version of the Indian Epic*. New York: Penguin Books, 1993.

Narayanan, Vasudha. *The Vernacular Veda: Revelation, Recitation, and Ritual*. Columbia: The University of South Carolina Press, 1994.

Nelson, Lance. *Purifying the Earthly Body of God: Religion and Ecology in Hindu India*. Albany: State University of New York Press, 1998.

Olivelle, Patrick, trans. *The Law Code of Manu*. New York: Oxford University Press, 2004.

———, trans. and ed. *Dharmasutras: The Law Codes of Ancient India*. New York: Oxford University Press, 1999.

Orr, Leslie C. *Donors, Devotees, and the Daughters of God: Temple Women in Medieval Tamilnadu*. New York: Oxford University Press, 2000.

Patton, Laurie, ed. *Jewels of Authority: Women and Textual Tradition in Hindu India*. New York: Oxford University Press, 2002.

Ramanujan, A.K. *Hymns for the Drowning*. Princeton, N.J.: Princeton University Press, 1981.

———. *Speaking of Siva*. Harmondsworth, England: Penguin Books, 1979.

Richman, Paula. *Many Ramayanas: The Diversity of a Narrative Tradition in South Asia*. Berkeley: University of California Press, 1991.

Sivaramamurti, C. *Nataraja in Art, Thought and Literature*. New Delhi: National Museum, 1974.

Williams, Raymond Brady, ed. *A Sacred Thread: Modern Transmission of Hindu Traditions in India and Abroad*. Chambersburg, Penn.: Anima, 1992.

Wilson, H.H. *The Vishnu Purana: A System of Hindu Mythology and Tradition*. 3rd ed. Calcutta: Punthi Pustak, 1961.

Hinduism

Shaivism

FOUNDED: Second century C.E.

RELIGION AS A PERCENTAGE OF WORLD POPULATION: 3.2 percent

OVERVIEW Shaivism is a complex body of South Asian traditions centered on the worship of the Hindu male deity Shiva, or Śiva (Sanskrit: "Auspicious One"). Together with Vaishnavism (those sects devoted to the god Vishnu) and Shaktism (those devoted to the goddess Shakti ["Creative Power"], who is also known as Devi), Shaivism forms one of the most important currents of classical and modern Hinduism.

The origins of Shaivism can be traced to at least the second century B.C.E. and to such semihistorical figures as the sage Lakulisha, though its roots probably lie much earlier in the history of Indian religions. In classical Hindu mythology Shiva is portrayed both as the destroyer, who annihilates the universe at the end of each cosmic cycle, and as the lord of yoga and asceticism. As such, he is a deeply paradoxical deity—called by some the erotic ascetic—associated with the forces of both creation and destruction.

Shiva lives high in the Himalayas. His body is smeared with ashes, and his hair is in long, matted locks. He carries a trident and wears a cobra as a garland and a crescent moon as his hair ornament. He is often accompanied by his wife Parvati and his two sons, Skanda and the elephant-headed Ganesha.

The worship of Shiva assumes a wide range of forms and sectarian expressions, ranging from popular devotional worship (bhakti) to the more extreme and esoteric groups, such as the Kapalikas (Skull Bearers) and Tantrics, who use deliberately transgressive elements such as wine, meat, and sexual intercourse in their rituals. By the eleventh or twelfth century, Shaivism had spread throughout most of South Asia in a wide array of different sects, philosophical systems, and devotional forms. In modern times it has spread throughout the globe in a variety of new popular media, attracting not only an Indian audience but also a powerful European and American following through the work of international gurus such as Swami Muktananda and Sathya Sai Baba.

HISTORY The historical origins of Shaivism are not entirely clear and have been the subject of debate among modern scholars. Many have identified a kind of proto-Shiva as early as the Indus Valley civilization, which flourished from roughly 2500 to 2000 B.C.E. in what became modern Pakistan and northwestern India. A small seal found in the Indus Valley area depicts what appears to be a figure seated in a yogic posture with an erect penis surrounded by animals, which many have taken to be an early form of Shiva in his role as Pashupati, Lord of Creatures. A more likely predecessor is found in the earliest Sanskrit texts, the Vedas (1500–400 B.C.E.), which describe a frightening and violent figure called Rudra ("The Howler"). A minor deity in the Vedas, Rudra is a fierce and terrible figure associated with disease and uncontrolled aspects of nature, such as storms. In the last portion of the Vedas, called the Upanishads (700–400 B.C.E.), Rudra-Shiva is described as the Lord (Ishvara), who is at once the cause of the uni-

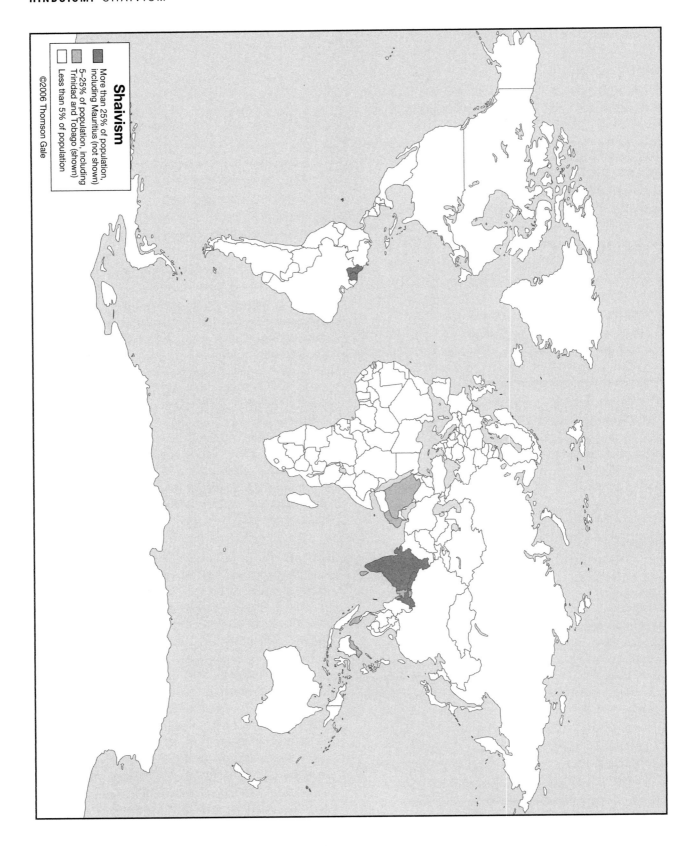

Shaivism

More than 25% of population, including Mauritius (not shown)

5–25% of population, including Trinidad and Tobago (shown)

Less than 5% of population

verse, the magician who sustains all things through his power, and the divinity who transcends the cosmos and yet dwells within the heart of all beings.

By the time of the early classical period of Hindu literature (c. 500 B.C.E.–1000 C.E.), Rudra-Shiva had emerged as a powerful deity with a rich mythology, as seen in the Sanskrit epic poem the *Mahabharata* (500 B.C.E.–500 C.E.) and the body of mythological compendia known as the *Puranas* (300–1200 C.E.). Together with Brahma and Vishnu, Shiva is typically imagined as part of the classical Trimurti, or three forms of god. In later texts Shiva is usually identified as the "Destroyer," Brahma as the "Creator," and Vishnu as the "Preserver," even though all three activities can be attributed to each deity, especially in the sectarian texts. Next to his popular image as the long-haired, ash-covered Lord of Yoga, Shiva also appears as Nataraja, the Lord of the Dance, whose multiarmed whirling dance creates, sustains, and finally engulfs the entire universe.

The earliest known Shaivite sect, the Pashupata tradition, which emerged around the second century C.E., is dedicated to Shiva as the Lord of Creatures. From at least the sixth or seventh century, a new movement, known as Tantra, emerged within both the Hindu and Buddhist traditions. The Shaivite Tantric texts claim both to incorporate and to transcend the authority of the Vedas. As such, these texts provided the inspiration for a proliferation of Shaivite Tantric groups, such as the highly developed Trika and Krama schools of Kashmir. By the thirteenth century a wide variety of Shaivite groups appeared, ranging from highly ascetic groups like the Lakulishas and Kalamukhas, to yogi sects like the Natha Siddhas, to devotional movements like the Lingayats of South India. In the modern era Shaivism has proliferated into a wide array of sect schools and popular forms, not only throughout South Asia but throughout the world, in new transnational Shaivite movements like Siddha Yoga and in the following of global gurus like Sathya Sai Baba.

CENTRAL DOCTRINES The basic doctrines of most Shaivite sects do not differ tremendously from those of other Hindu traditions; like other Hindus, Shaivites assume the laws of karma and reincarnation, and they have as their ultimate goal liberation from this material world, which is seen as illusory and filled with suffering. The primary difference in Shaivism lies in making Shiva the central deity as the origin, cause, and end of existence. According to one of the more developed and in-

A Shaivite prays near the Ganges River in India. Prayer to Lord Shiva follows the model of other Hindu traditions, centering on the repetition of mantras, sacred sounds holy to Shiva, such as "Om Nama Shivay." © CHRIS HELLIER/CORBIS.

fluential Shaivite schools, the Shaiva Siddhanta, reality consists of three basic tenets: the *pati* (the Lord), the *pashu* (the beast, or created beings), and the *pasha* (the bond). In this context the Lord is Shiva, the cause and master of all things; the beast is the soul or self; and the bond is the illusory phenomenal universe in which the living soul is enmeshed. The goal of Shaiva Siddhanta practice is, therefore, to free the living soul from its entanglement in the universe and to realize its own inherent divinity.

Various Shaivite traditions do differ somewhat in their core doctrines. The Shaiva Siddhantas, for example, are generally dualist—that is, they maintain a clear distinction between the Lord and the soul. Other schools, such as the Kashmir Shaivites, tend to be strongly monistic, asserting the ultimate unity of God and the soul.

A statue of Shiva. In classical Hindu mythology Shiva is portrayed both as the destroyer, who annihilates the universe at the end of each cosmic cycle, and as the lord of yoga and asceticism. © JANEZ SKOK/CORBIS.

MORAL CODE OF CONDUCT Like the paradoxical ascetic-erotic deity Shiva himself, the moral code of the various Shaivite sects differs widely and may appear contradictory. While some sects are highly ascetic and austere, others are explicitly antinomian and involve deliberate violations of conventional moral boundaries. Thus, the earliest Shaivites, the Pashupatas, were strict renunciants—traditionally Brahman (priestly class) males who maintained celibacy and abandoned householder life and family. The Pashupata initiate was required to take a vow and engage in spiritual practice that involved three main stages. First, the disciple, smeared in ashes, would live in a Shiva temple, worshiping the deity through meditation, mantras, singing, and dancing. During the second stage he would then leave the temple, go out in public, and behave in various bizarre antisocial ways—such as acting insane and making lewd gestures toward women—deliberately inviting the abuse and re-

proach of passersby. In the third stage he would withdraw to some remote place, such as a cave or empty house, in order to immerse himself in meditation; ultimately, he would retreat to a cremation ground where he would await his final union with Lord Rudra at death.

More extreme Shaivites, like the Kapalikas and Tantrics, however, sought a more radical means to union with Shiva. The Kapalikas took as their role model Shiva in his most terrible form—Bhairava, the fearsome Lord who wanders the earth carrying the skull of the god Brahma, whom he had beheaded. Like Bhairava, the Kapalika is in a sense beyond good and evil, beyond the moral limitations that confine ordinary human beings. Indeed, a Kapalika sought to transcend the very distinction between pure and impure, clean and unclean by deliberately violating normal social and ethical boundaries; by consuming impure substances such as meat, alcohol, and sexual fluids; or by engaging in sexual intercourse in violation of class restrictions. By systematically overstepping conventional social taboos, the Kapalika hoped to achieve *siddhi,* a divine power beyond conventional human social limits, like that of the awesome Shiva himself.

SACRED BOOKS In addition to early Upanishads, such as the Shvetashvatara, other classical Shaivite texts include the Shaivite *Puranas,* or cosmological and mythological works, such as the Shiva Purana and Linga Purana. Individual Shaivite groups also generated their own texts; for example, the *Pashupata Sutra* is sacred to the Pashupatas, Lakulishas, and other sects. Finally, with the rise of Hindu Tantra beginning in the fourth or fifth century C.E., a wide range of Shaivite Tantric material was composed, including the various Tantras, Agamas, and Nigamas, said to be revealed by Shiva or Parvati themselves, as well as the sophisticated philosophical works of the Kashmir Shaivite schools. Among the more important of the vast body of Kashmir Shaivite texts are the works of Abhinavagupta (950–1025 C.E.), who composed a monumental synthesis of Shaivite traditions in his Tantraloka and Tantrasara.

SACRED SYMBOLS The primary symbol of Shiva is the linga, a stylized representation of the male sexual organ. This image is typically an abstract, upright phallus that may vary in size from a few inches to several feet in height and is seated on top of the yoni, or female sexual organ. In addition, a variety of other sacred objects are associated with Shiva, including the *mala* (rosary) made of dried Rudraksha seeds, used for recitation of mantras; the trident, signifying Shiva's power to destroy ignorance and evil; the begging bowl, symbolizing the renunciation of worldly society; the *vibhuti* (ashes), with which Shaivite ascetics smear their bodies in imitation of Shiva as the Lord of Destruction, who also creates new life from the ashes of destruction; the cobra worn around Shiva's neck, representing Shiva's power to subdue danger and transform venom into nectar; and Nandi, the bull who symbolizes the perfect devotee.

EARLY AND MODERN LEADERS Other than Lord Shiva himself, Shaivism has no known founder, though there have been a wide range of historical figures associated with the spread of Shiva's worship. One of the earliest recorded Shaivite teachers is Lakulisha, said to have been the incarnate form of Rudra-Shiva, who appeared by entering and reanimating the corpse of a Brahman in the cremation ground. Over the last 1,800 years India has seen the rise of numerous Shaivite leaders, ranging from ecstatic devotees to erudite philosophers. The semimythical yogi Gorakhnath, who is believed to have lived sometime between the ninth and twelfth centuries, was considered by many to be an incarnation of Shiva and to have helped spread devotion to Shiva as Lord of Yoga. In South India one of the most inspiring Shaivite leaders was Basava (died in 1167), a social and religious reformer in the Lingayat movement who was known both for his deeply moving devotional poetry and his radically egalitarian social doctrines.

During the latter half of the twentieth century, several new movements emerged that brought ancient Shaivite teachings to a new international audience. One of the most influential of these movements is the Siddha Yoga Dham of America (SYDA), which was founded in 1974 by Swami Muktananda (died in 1982). Claiming to be rooted in the traditional teachings of Kashmir Shaivism, the SYDA movement has had a tremendous appeal to a new generation of students in the United States. It has spread to Europe and other parts of the world, as well.

Perhaps the best-known and most influential figure in modern times is Sathya Sai Baba. Born in 1926 in Andhra Pradesh, Sathya Sai Baba claims to be the avatar (human incarnation) of Shiva and that he has manifested himself for this most violent and chaotic age. Sathya Sai has been both tremendously popular and increasingly controversial because of his alleged ability to

materialize various small objects, coins, trinkets, and sacred ash from his hands. Significantly, Sathya Sai has also emerged as a powerful international guru who has attracted a variety of high-profile Western devotees.

MAJOR THEOLOGIANS AND AUTHORS Shaivism has had a tremendous and lasting impact on Indian philosophy from at least the time of the Upanishads to the modern era. Shankara (700?–750? C.E.), the greatest figure in the development of Advaita Vedanta, or absolute nondualism, was himself a devotee of Shiva. Historically, however, the most influential Shaivite theologians came from the Shaiva Siddhanta and Kashmir Shaivite schools. Such Shaiva Siddhanta philosophers as Sadyogoti (eighth century C.E.) and Bhojadeva (eleventh century C.E.) argued for a dualist system in which the self is ultimately equal to, but fundamentally distinct from, God. Conversely, the Pratyabhijna, or "recognition," school, which adhered to a more radically monist view of God and the self, emerged among the Kashmir Tantric Shaivites. For Kashmiris like Abhinavagupta and Utpala (925–975), the self is characterized by pure consciousness. Once it recognizes its own inherent nature, the self is one with Lord Shiva, who is himself supreme being, consciousness, and bliss. In the twentieth century, the Kashmir Shaivite philosophy was revived and newly propagated by several influential figures, such as the Bengali-born scholar and philosopher Kopinath Kaviraj (1887–1976), who developed a new system of Akhanda-Mahayoda (Great Integral Yoga), and the Kashmiri teacher Swami Laksman Joo (1907–91), who claimed to have tapped into and newly transmitted the traditional oral teachings of the Kashmir schools.

ORGANIZATIONAL STRUCTURE The basic organizational structure common to virtually all Shaivite sects is the master-disciple (*guru-sishya*) relationship, which typically involves initiation at the hands of the guru, who then imparts the teachings orally to his disciples. Most Shaivites can trace a lineage of masters and disciples extending back hundreds of years to an original founder, such as Lakulisha, Gorakhnath, or to Shiva himself. Beyond this the organization of the various Shaivite groups differs widely, from withdrawn solitary ascetics like the Pashupatas to more coherent intellectual and philosophical circles like the Trika school that emerged in Kashmir.

HOUSES OF WORSHIP AND HOLY PLACES Shaivite temples and holy places range dramatically, from tiny household altars or village shrines to vast temple complexes. Shaivite temples and shrines can be found in every corner of India and Nepal; they may be as small as roadside lingas or as large as great temple complexes, such as the vast Lingaraj Temple in Bhubaneswar or the Cidambaram Temple in Tamil Nadu, which is dedicated to Shiva as Nataraja, the Lord of Dance. Traditionally there are said to be 12 sacred places in India where Shiva's linga shone forth in a fiery column of light, as well as 68 sites where lingas are said to have emerged self-born from the earth itself.

The most sacred holy place of the Shaivite tradition—and, indeed, for all of India—is the city of Varanasi, which is itself called the city of Shiva. According to Hindu mythology, Varanasi is Kapalamocana, the site where the skull was released. According to classical mythology, Brahma had desired to commit incest with his daughter and was beheaded by Shiva (in his wrathful Bhairava form). Because he had killed a Brahman, Bhairava was condemned to wander the earth with Brahma's skull in his hand until it was released at this holy site. Hundreds of linga shrines of varying sizes are found in Varanasi, and the city also contains some of the most important Shiva temples, such the Vishvanatha. Outside of India one of the largest Shaivite centers is the Pashupatinath Temple near Kathmandu, Nepal.

WHAT IS SACRED? For the Shaivite the sacred can manifest itself in anything from the lowliest stone carved into a linga to a vast temple complex consecrated as the body of Lord Shiva himself. Specific geographic regions, such as the Himalaya Mountains, and specific individuals, such as sadhus and gurus, can also be physical embodiments of the sacred. Ultimately for most Shaivite traditions, the goal is to see all things as sacred, for all things are in effect created by, and reflections of, Lord Shiva.

HOLIDAYS AND FESTIVALS The central holy day in the Shaivite calendar is Maha Shivaratri, the "Great Night of Shiva," held on the 14th night of the new moon during the dark half of Phalgun, the month in the Hindu calendar that overlaps February and March. The festival is said to mark the manifestation of Shiva's vast *jyotirlinga*, or linga of light. According to Hindu mythology, Vishnu and Brahma had been quarreling over who was the more powerful deity. Shiva then manifested himself as a great shining linga so vast that Brahma could not find its top, and Vishnu could not find its

bottom, thus asserting Shiva's preeminence among the gods. During Maha Shivratri, the linga is bathed with the five sacred offerings of a cow—milk, sour milk, urine, butter, and dung. Then the five foods of immortality—milk, clarified butter, curd, honey, and sugar—are placed before the linga. Devotees fast during the day and then pray and make offerings to the Lord throughout the night.

In addition to Maha Shivaratri, individual regions and temples have specific festivals that are celebrated with special fanfare. For example, at the Kapalishvara Temple in Madras there is a unique festival held in March or April known as Brahmotsavam, the Festival of Brahma, believed to have been founded by Brahma himself. During the 10-day celebration, a bronze image of Shiva is seated on a gigantic image of the bull Nandi and then pulled in procession throughout the city until he is returned to his home in the temple.

MODE OF DRESS Most modern Shaivite priests and devotees would not stand out from other Hindus in their particular mode of dress. Shaivite sadhus (holy men) and sannyasis (renunciants), however, are typically known for their imitation of Lord Shiva in their dress, markings, and hairstyle. Shaivite sadhus and sannyasis will typically smear their bodies in ash, wear their hair in long, snakelike locks, carry the trident and begging bowl, and mark their foreheads with ash in three horizontal lines, symbolic of Shiva's trident.

DIETARY PRACTICES Most Shaivite sects do not differ significantly from other Hindus in their dietary practices. As in other Hindu traditions, diet varies somewhat according to one's class status, so that Brahmans tend to be more strictly vegetarian, while lower classes may consume poultry, fish, and mutton, with various regional differences. Exceptions to this general rule include the more extreme Shaivite sects, such as the Kapalikas, Aghoris, and left-hand Tantrics, who often deliberately ingest substances that are considered impure by orthodox standards—such as beef, wine, and sexual fluids—in order to prove their transcendence of all conventional dualities. Some Aghoris, literally "those without fear," are known to consume human flesh as a sign that they have fully overcome the distinction between purity and impurity that confines ordinary human beings.

RITUALS Shaivite worship follows the general model of *puja* (honor) that is common in most other Hindu traditions. Lord Shiva is believed to be literally, not just symbolically, present in his various physical representations, whether it be an abstract linga or an anthropomorphic sculpture of the deity. He is to be revered with offerings that involve all the senses—taste, touch, sight, smell, and hearing. Thus, at most Shaivite shrines the linga is bathed, dressed, and adorned with flowers and incense; various substances (such as sandalwood paste, milk, honey, and mashed fruit) may be poured over it as offerings. Prayer to Lord Shiva also follows the model of other Hindu traditions, centering on the repetition of mantras (sacred sounds holy to Shiva) such as "Om Nama Shivay."

Devotees make long journeys to various Shaivite temples throughout India. In addition to the holy city of Varanasi, major pilgrimage sites include the Mahakaleshwar Temple, said to be the place where Shiva manifested his *jyotirlinga* in Ujjain, Madhya Pradesh, as well as several sacred sites in Shiva's mountain realm in the Himalaya foothills of Uttar Pradesh, such as Kedarnath, Badrinath, Nilkanth, and Gangotri, the source of the Ganges River.

In a few areas, particularly in Nepal, Shiva is also worshiped with animal sacrifice. The Kala (black) Bhairava and Seto (white) Bhairava images in Kathmandu, for example, are still regularly honored with the severed heads and blood of goats and buffaloes.

RITES OF PASSAGE As in other Hindu traditions, most Shaivite householders accept the basic life cycle rites, or *samskaras*, that mark major stages of life, such as baptism, first haircutting, marriage, and first impregnation. Most of the Shaivite sects also require some form of initiation (*diksha*) at the hands of a qualified guru. According to the Shaiva Siddhanta tradition, the practitioner (*sadhaka*) undergoes two initiations to remove impurities from the soul. The first of these is the lesser initiation (*samaya-diksha*), which ushers the practitioner into the rituals and scriptures of the cult, and the second is the liberating initiation (*nirvana-diksha*), which ensures the soul's final liberation.

MEMBERSHIP Early Shaivite sects tended to be quite exclusive in their membership. The Pashupatas required that initiates be of a certain social caste; Kapalikas and Tantrics required initiates to engage in highly esoteric rituals. Later devotional movements, such as the Lingayats, however, made an explicit attempt to break down class barriers and to appeal to men and women of all

social strata, from Brahmans to untouchables. Since the late twentieth century neo-Shaivite gurus like Sathya Sai Baba have made free use of a wide variety of modern media and technologies.

RELIGIOUS TOLERANCE Prior to the twentieth century most Shaivite sects showed little interest in ecumenical activity; indeed, they were long considered by other sects as non-Vedic, heterodox, or outside the fold of Brahminical ritual. Some later Shaivite theologians, such as Abhinavagupta, attempted to synthesize and categorize all the known religious systems, creating an elaborate hierarchy of teachings with his own Trika system at the pinnacle. In modern times many neo-Hindu leaders have tended to promote a kind of universal spirituality in which all the world's religions are regarded as so many paths leading to the same divine summit. Sathya Sai Baba, the self-proclaimed avatar of Lord Shiva, represents this globalized Hindu spirit, which at once declares the unity of all religions and also asserts the superiority of Hinduism as the most inclusive and universal of all faiths.

SOCIAL JUSTICE Most Shaivite sects tend to accept the social order established by the Vedas and the system of class and the four stages of life (*varnashramadharma*). There are, however, some influential Shaivite traditions, such as those practiced by the Lingayats of South India. The Lingayat twelfth-century poet and spiritual leader Basava was himself a Shaivite Brahman at the court of King Bijjala of Kalyana (reigned 1156–67). Basava preached vehemently against the class system and advocated an egalitarian, classless vision of society in which Brahmans and untouchables might live together equally. Most modern Shaivite teachers have also taught either a serious reform or complete abolition of the class system and new rights for women; an important exception, however, is Sathya Sai Baba, who has argued for the importance of traditional class and gender roles as a crucial foundation for a strong culture and social order.

SOCIAL ASPECTS Shaivite attitudes toward marriage and family generally do not depart significantly from other Hindu traditions. There are both married householder Shaivites and renunciants, like the Pashupatas, who abandon women and family. While a few more radical groups, such as the Lingayats, oppose the class system and traditional marital laws, most of the more orthodox schools accept the *varna* (class) system, the authority of Brahmans, and the sacrament of marriage.

Shaivite Tantra

One of the most controversial forms of Shaivism—and one of the most popular forms in the United States—is Tantra. A complex body of religious practices common to Hindu and Buddhist traditions since at least the fifth century, Tantra has long held a deeply ambivalent place in both the Indian and Western imaginations. Tantric theology and practice centers in large part on the polarity of male and female energies, the masculine and feminine forces that create and sustain the universe. In Hindu Tantra these complementary forces are Lord Shiva, the passive male pole identified with pure consciousness, and Shakti, the active power or energy of the goddess, who creates and pervades the cosmos.

Tantra has been particularly controversial because of its deliberate use of substances and practices that are normally considered impure by orthodox moral standards. The most infamous of these are the five Ms (panchamakara), or five things beginning with the syllable ma in Sanskrit—namely, meat (mamsa), fish (matysa), wine (madya), parched grain (mudra), and sexual intercourse (maithuna), often in violation of class laws. In the rite of sexual intercourse, the male and female are said to be the embodiments of Shiva and Shakti, whose union leads to the realization of the supreme unity and bliss of the absolute reality beyond all duality. Typically Tantric sects are divided into "right-handed" (dakshinachara) and "left-handed" (vamacharara) traditions; whereas the former tradition takes the five Ms purely symbolically, as things to be meditated upon but not practiced physically, the latter takes them literally and performs them, typically in esoteric ritual circles (chakras) of initiated male and female partners.

While Tantra in India has traditionally been a highly esoteric movement demanding strict secrecy and guarded initiation, it has become increasingly popularized in the United States, where it is mass-marketed as a kind of "spiritual sex" or "nookie nirvana." Indeed, one need only browse the shelves of bookstores or surf the Internet to find a wide array of popular books, magazines, websites, and mass-marketed "ceremonial-sensual" merchandise.

CONTROVERSIAL ISSUES Since at least the nineteenth century and the encounter with British colonialism and European scholarship, one of the more controversial aspects of Shaivism is the worship of the linga, or phallus. Indeed, after two centuries of attack and criticism by Western authors for their alleged "primitive phallicism" and even "erotomania," some Hindus deny that the linga has anything to do with the male genitalia.

A more recent political controversy, however, surrounds some of the extreme fundamentalist Pan-Hindu movements that have emerged since the latter half of the twentieth century—particularly the Shiva Sena, or "Army of Shiva." The Shiva Sena movement has become increasingly controversial because of its often xenophobic and anti-Muslim stance. Members of Shiva Sena were a major force in the destruction of the Babri Masjid (Mosque) in Ayodhya, Uttar Pradesh, in 1992, which in turn ignited horrific violence and bloodshed between Hindus and Muslims throughout South Asia.

CULTURAL IMPACT Shaivism has had a deep and lasting impact on virtually every aspect of Indian and, increasingly, Western culture, from dance and music to literature and painting. As Nataraja, the Lord of Dance, Shiva is often identified as the spiritual inspiration for classical Indian dance, and his image has given birth to a 2000-year-old tradition of sculpture, temple architecture, and painting. There is, moreover, a vast body of literature dedicated to Shiva, ranging from the classical Sanskrit of the epics and *Puranas* to the vernacular poetry of authors like Basava and the South Indian Lingayat tradition. Finally, arguably the greatest aesthetic theorist in Indian history was Abhinavagupta, the same Kashmiri theologian who synthesized the major Shaivite and Tantric schools of his day. Abhinavagupta developed a sophisticated aesthetic system based on the various *rasas,* or "flavors," of aesthetic experience, which has had a lasting impact on Indian poetry, drama, and religious literature through modern times. Indeed, for Abhinavagupta the ultimate aesthetic experience was *santa-rasa* (peace), which is the same experience of tranquillity that is experienced in the nondual union of the self and absolute reality.

Hugh B. Urban

See Also Vol. I: *Hinduism*

Bibliography

Bhandarkar, R.G. *Vaisnavism, Saivism, and Minor Religious Systems.* New York: Garland, 1980.

Davis, Richard. *Ritual in an Oscillating Universe: Worshipping Siva in Medieval India.* Princeton, N.J.: Princeton University Press, 1991.

Dhavamony, Mariasusai. *Love of God according to "Saiva Siddhanta."* Oxford: Oxford University Press, 1971.

Dyczkowski, Mark S.G. *The Aphorisms of Siva: The Siva Sutra with Bhaskara's Commentary, the Varttika.* Albany: State University of New York Press, 1992.

Eck, Diana L. *Banaras: City of Light.* Princeton, N.J.: Princeton University Press, 1982.

Eliade, Mircea. *Yoga: Immortality and Freedom.* Princeton, N.J.: Princeton University Press, 1969.

Gonda, Jan. *Visnuism and Sivaism: A Comparison.* London: Athlone, 1970.

Kramrisch, Stella. *The Presence of Siva.* Princeton, N.J.: Princeton University Press, 1981.

Lorenzen, David. *The Kapalikas and Kalamukhas: Two Lost Saivite Sects.* Berkeley: University of California Press, 1972.

Meister, Michael. *Discourses on Siva.* Philadelphia: University of Pennsylvania Press, 1984.

Muller-Ortega, Paul Eduardo. *The Triadic Heart of Siva: Kaula Tantricism of Abhinavagupta in the Non-Dual Saivism of Kashmir.* Albany: State University of New York Press, 1989.

O'Flaherty, Wendy Doniger. *Siva: The Erotic Ascetic.* New York: Oxford University Press, 1981.

Padoux, Andre. *Vac: The Concept of the Word in Selected Hindu Tantras.* Albany: State University of New York Press, 1990.

Pandey, Kanti Chandra. *Abhinavagupta: An Historical and Philosophical Study.* Varanasi, India: Chowkhamba Sanskrit Series, 1963.

Ramanujan, A.K., trans. *Speaking of Siva.* Harmondsworth, England: Penguin, 1973.

Sanderson, Alexis. "Purity and Power among the Brahmans of Kashmir." In *The Category of the Person.* Edited by Michael Carrithers, Steven Collins, and Steven Lukes. Cambridge: Cambridge University Press, 1986.

———. "Saivism and the Tantric Traditions." In *The World's Religions.* Edited by S.L. Sutherland. London and New York: Routledge, 1988.

Shulman, David Dean. *Tamil Temple Myths: Sacrifice and Divine Marriage in the South Indian Saiva Tradition.* Princeton, N.J.: Princeton University Press, 1980.

Urban, Hugh B. *Tantra: Sex, Secrecy, Politics, and Power in the Study of Religion.* Berkeley: University of California Press, 2003.

White, David Gordon. *The Alchemical Body: Siddha Traditions in Medieval India.* Chicago: University of Chicago Press, 1996.

———, ed. *Tantra in Practice.* Princeton, N.J.: Princeton University Press, 2000.

Vaishnavism

FOUNDED: c. 500 B.C.E.

RELIGION AS A PERCENTAGE OF WORLD POPULATION: 9.5 percent

OVERVIEW Vaishnavism is the name given to the faith and practices of those Hindus who hold Vishnu ("the all pervasive one") and the goddess Lakshmi as supreme deities. The Sanskrit term Vaishnava means "follower of Vishnu."

Devotion to Vishnu seen in the Vedas and later Sanskrit literature, amalgamated with the worship of many local deities and texts, eventually gave rise to the Vaishnava faith. Vaishnavas also worship Vishnu's many incarnations, especially his appearances as Rama and as Krishna, as well as his manifestations in iconic form in several temples. These manifestations in temples are considered to be actual incarnations of Vishnu in a worshipable form. In addition, many Vaishnavas also revere various poet-saints and theologians whom they consider to be paradigmatic devotees. There are several traditions of Vaishnava theologies, but a Vaishnava does not have to be affiliated with any one of them. It is thus difficult to determine the exact number of Hindus who practice Vaishnavism.

HISTORY While the deity Vishnu appears in the Vedas, the earliest Sanskrit sacred compositions in India (c. 1500 B.C.E.), it is believed he became a mighty and supreme deity a millennium later. The distinctive characteristics of Vaishnava faith, which upholds Vishnu as

the supreme being who alone can grant salvation, seem to have gathered force with the compositions of the epics *Ramayana* and the *Mahabharata* around 500 B.C.E. and particularly with the Bhagavad Gita, a section of the *Mahabharata* that may have been composed around the second century B.C.E.

Vishnu also became identified with the deities Narayana and Vasudeva sometime in the first millennium B.C.E. Narayana is a supreme deity eulogized in several texts, including the *Mahabharata*, as well as in books associated with goddess traditions that are called *agamas*. Archaeological evidence from the second century B.C.E. suggests that Vasudeva was worshiped in both northwestern as well as central India.

The deity Mal in the Tamil-speaking lands of South India was also first venerated in the early centuries of the Common Era. He is identified with Vishnu, and some of the stories connected with Mal, such as the churning of the mythical ocean of milk, are attributed to him. In this story divine beings (*devas*) and demonic beings (*asuras*) churn the ocean of milk for the elixir of immortality. When the enterprise seems to fail, Mal-Vishnu incarnates himself in several forms, including that of a tortoise, to help them.

During the reign of the Gupta dynasty (c. fourth–fifth centuries C.E.) in the north and the Chalukyas dynasty in the Deccan Plateau of south central India (after the sixth century C.E.), royal patronage and increased temple building gave rise to the devotional fervor of Vaishnava devotees. It was about this time, the first half of the first millennium C.E., that the major *Pu-*

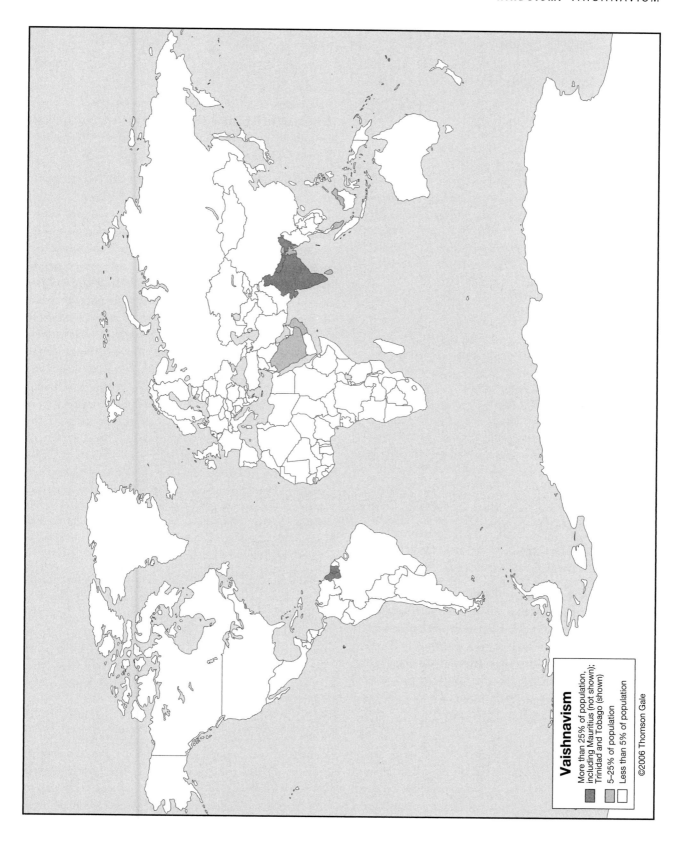

Vaishnavism

More than 25% of population, including Mauritius (not shown); Trinidad and Tobago (shown)

5–25% of population

Less than 5% of population

©2006 Thomson Gale

An Indian woman covers her head with a garment called a sari, as is the custom in northern India. © LINDSAY HEBBERD/CORBIS.

ranas, texts that praise the deities in the Hindu tradition, were compiled in their present forms.

Perhaps the greatest stimulus to the Vaishnava tradition came through the composition of vernacular hymns, which first appeared in the seventh century C.E. Tamil-speaking devotees from the south of India composed these songs in praise of Vishnu-Narayana, especially in the form in which he was enshrined in the many temples of southern India. It is believed that these devotees made pilgrimages, visiting sacred sites in various parts of India. Twelve poet-saints (men and women distinguished by their devotion to Vishnu) came to be called Alvars, or those immersed deeply in the love of God. It was the first time that devotional poetry was composed in a local, but classical, language, and by the tenth and eleventh centuries the Vaishnava community that revered these poems, known as Sri Vaishnavas, came to regard them as equivalent to the Sanskrit Vedas.

Devotion to Vishnu and Vaishnava traditions can be found in almost every part of India. Vaishnava texts and practices, however, have not been confined to India. By the fifth century C.E. devotees worshiped Vishnu in Cambodia, and Vishnu temples flourished in that country. Icons of Vishnu are found all the way from Thailand to Japan, where some of his manifestations are subsumed in Buddhist lore.

The popularity of Vaishnavism can be attributed to many factors. Sanskrit texts were known all over India, from possibly as early as several centuries before the Common Era, and formed a common substratum for the Vaishnavas; however, it was the local vernacular texts of passionate devotion that led to the rapid spread and sustenance of the many Vaishnava traditions. Philosophical texts by the major theologians gave it orthodoxy; hagiographical texts entertained and educated the masses. Many of the texts were told and retold in local languages, and some were expressed through performing arts. The songs of the Alvars, for instance, were sung and acted out in temples. In later centuries religious leader Chaitanya (1485–1533) took his emotional worship of Lord Krishna and devotional singing to the streets, a practice that was adopted by the members of International Society of Krishna Consciousness (ISKCON), or the Hare Krishna movement, in the twentieth century. The emphasis on devotion also led to the softening of gender roles and the roles incumbent upon one by way of caste; people from all castes of society could be considered to be Vaishnava.

CENTRAL DOCTRINES Like almost all other practitioners of schools of Hindu thought and practice, Vaishnavas believe in the immortality of the soul and a supreme being. They also take for granted that the soul is caught in a cycle of life and death. Unlike other forms of Hinduism, however, Vaishnavas believe that it is devotion to Vishnu that will save them from endless rebirth. In practice this monotheism is rather elastic. Worship also includes devotion to the Goddess Sri, or Lakshmi, the many incarnations of Vishnu, his manifestations in local temples in southern India, his emanations in a theological framework called *vyuha*, the paradigmatic celestial devotees Hanuman and Garuda, and the Alvars, the exalted human devotees. Many of these celestial and mortal beings are seen in icons that have been consecrated in temples and are part of the ritual universe of the Vaishnavas.

The theology of the various schools of Vaishnavism is significantly different from each other. While all the schools have distinctive features that describe the relationship between the human being, the created universe, and the supreme being, all believe that it is devotion to Vishnu and Lakshmi as well as Vishnu's salvific grace that will grant liberation from the cycle of life and death for the human devotee.

In all Vaishnava contexts the object of devotion is Vishnu, who is also known as Narayana. In the Rigveda, Vishnu-Narayana is seen as having paced the universe in giant strides. The two epics *Ramayana* and the *Mahabharata* portray Rama and Krishna, who ultimately are considered the most important incarnations of Vishnu. Eventually various stories about Vishnu, Narayana, and Vasudeva come together into a cohesive theory of the descent (*avatarana*) of the supreme being to earth in one of many incarnations. While the early Puranas composed in the beginning of the Common Era speak of as many as 24 incarnations, a later version includes 10 incarnations.

The Bhagavad Gita, a section of the epic *Mahabharata,* and one of the most important texts in Hindu literature, gives a clear reason for Vishnu's multiple incarnations. Krishna, an incarnation of Vishnu, says in this text that whenever dharma (righteousness) falters on earth, Vishnu comes down to destroy evil and protect the good people.

While Vishnu's many incarnations, especially those of Rama and Krishna, serve as the focal point of devotion, some Vaishnava texts known as the *Pancharatra* agama, which is held as authoritative by the Sri Vaishnava community, describe various emanations of Vishnu. In the *Pancharatra* agama, as well as other *Puranas*, Vishnu is portrayed lying down in an ocean, and a fourfold manifestation called *vyuha* appears from him to take care of various cosmogonic functions, such as the creation and destruction of the universe. The Sri Vaishnava community believes that Vishnu has five forms, all of which exist simultaneously and completely. Vishnu abides in heaven, or Vaikuntha; he appears on the ocean of milk, the locus from which the emanations as the *vyuha* originate to perform the cosmogonic functions; he descends to earth periodically as the avatara, or incarnation, assuming a form appropriate for the purpose and for the time; he resides in a ritually consecrated icon in a temple; and, finally, he is all pervasive and abides in every soul. Some Vaishnava communities also believe that Vishnu incarnates himself in temples in a form that can be worshiped so as to be accessible to human beings. This iconic form in a temple is held, therefore, to be an actual manifestation of Vishnu, not just a symbol or a focal point of concentration as some other Hindus may believe.

Vaishnavas also venerate Lakshmi, who is considered to be inseparable from Vishnu. She has her own shrine in many South Indian temples. In icons she is portrayed as abiding on a lotus, a symbol of auspiciousness, and also as residing on Vishnu's chest, as an articulation of divine grace.

Devotion (bhakti) to Krishna and Vishnu is the distinguishing characteristic of Vaishnavism. In some discussions several kinds of devotion are highlighted: One may pray to Vishnu with the attitude of a servant, a parent, a lover, or a friend. While all forms of devotion are considered valid in the Sri Vaishnava tradition, Chaitanya's school privileges devotion that is colored with the passion of romantic or sometimes erotic love. The love of Radha—the consort, or in some Vaishnava traditions the girlfriend, of Krishna—becomes paradigmatic of the love that should be obtained between the devotee and the supreme being. In these theologies the role of the cowherd girl Radha is ambiguous; some devotees think of her as the ideal devotee, and others as a goddess-consort of Krishna.

MORAL CODE OF CONDUCT Most Vaishnava schools accept the epics and the dharmasastras (texts of dharma or righteousness) as important sources of moral conduct, but like most Hindus, Vaishnavas would not be familiar with the content of these texts. The main teachings of the Bhagavad Gita would be known in some form to most devotees. For example, adherents hold devotion to Krishna paramount, and all action should be done in the name of Krishna/Vishnu-Narayana. The Bhagavad Gita enjoins devotees to act in a detached manner without being focused on the results of one's actions. The moral code incumbent upon men and women, which varies from region to region, is also applicable to Vaishnavas. As in other devotional movements, however, devotion trumps all textual and practiced notions of dharma. Devotion to Vishnu and the quest for liberation wins over the codes for conduct in everyday life.

Virtues associated with the Vaishnava faith, and spoken of in the texts of dharma known as *samanya dharma,* or the code of conduct applicable to all human beings, include compassion, purity, humility, and the notion of ahimsa, or nonviolence.

Attitudes toward caste issues have evolved and those issues continue to be reinvented within the devotional Vaishnava contexts. By the eleventh century C.E., when the poetry of the Alvars was anthologized, it was clear that some of the paradigmatic devotees were, in fact, of the so-called lower castes and in some cases even an outcaste. While some Hindu texts have spoken of caste as a matter of individual potential and behavior, the practice over the millennia has overwhelmingly been to think of it as fixed by birth into a particular family and community. In the late twentieth century C.E. Bhaktivedanta (also known as Swami) Prabhupada (1886–1977), the founder of ISKCON, addressed the issue of caste. Prabhupada spoke about a simpler version of caste to the new Euro-American Vaishnava devotees he had converted. Instead of the complex caste system, Prabhupada described a fourfold division originally mentioned in the Vedas, but the idea was not followed in its entirety. A few male members of the ISKCON movement wear a sacred thread, an emblem of the upper castes in India. No specific caste name is given to most devotees.

SACRED BOOKS Almost every Vaishnava school has its own set of books that it considers canonical; however, almost all Vaishnava traditions hold sacred the Vedas (as in many other Hindu communities), the two epics of *Ramayana* and the *Mahabharata,* and the Vaishnava *Puranas.* Among the *Puranas,* the Vishnu *Purana* and in later traditions the Bhagavata *Purana* are considered to be significant. In addition to these texts, every Vaishnava tradition has several genres of works both in Sanskrit and in the local vernacular. The vernacular languages, in many cases, are also classical languages. There are philosophical treatises written by the major theologians; there are devotional panegyrics; there is hagiographical literature; and there are texts and narratives transmitted through song and dance.

SACRED SYMBOLS Vishnu is said to hold several weapons in his hands to destroy evil, and among these the conch and the discus are considered to be most important. The conch is blown before a battle; the discus is hurled to slice and destroy anything evil. Many Vaishnavas etch these sacred symbols on wedding necklaces. These marks are also used during initiation into some communities. In the Sri Vaishnava community, for instance, the spiritual teacher brands these marks on the

shoulders or upper arms of the devotee who seeks initiation.

Perhaps the most ubiquitous body marking in India is that worn by men and women on their foreheads, a mark that is both secular and sectarian. Many of the marks, especially those worn for ritual occasions, indicate the sectarian community to which a Hindu may belong. Many Vaishnavas are known by U- or Y-shaped forehead marks. These marks, made with white clay from a sacred place, usually symbolize the foot of Vishnu. The red line or red dot in the middle indicates the inseparability of the Goddess Sri from Vishnu. In some Vaishnava communities the forehead marks may indicate Rama, his wife Sita, and his brother Lakshmana; in others the marks represent the reality of a supreme being who is without qualities and simultaneously has all good attributes.

EARLY AND MODERN LEADERS There have been many important Vaishnava leaders and teachers, as well as leaders who happen to be Vaishnavas. Many musical composers are particularly well known and admired in India. The compositions of the late fifteenth-century composers Annamacharya and Purandara dasa are still sung by exponents of Carnatic music in South India. Perhaps the best-known Vaishnava musician is Tyagaraja (1767–1847), whose compositions to Rama are honored every year in India and in the diaspora with the annual Tyagaraja Festival. Mohandas Karamchand (Mahatma) Gandhi (1869–1948) was born into a Vaishnava family. Vaishnava texts, such as the Bhagavad Gita, and Vaishnava codes of conduct, such as the emphasis on nonviolence, were significant in his life.

MAJOR THEOLOGIANS AND AUTHORS Ramanuja (c. 1017–1137) is probably one of the best-known exponents of the Vaishnava tradition. He expressed his philosophy of qualified nondualism in his commentaries and texts, especially the Sri Bhashya and the Gitabhashya. Madhvacarya (1296–1386), a major theologian in the Kannada-speaking area of southern India, preached a philosophy called dualism, or *dvaita,* in which the soul is seen as distinct from the supreme deity Vishnu.

Madhva's followers have a philosophically and socially distinct form of Vaishnava tradition. While the Sri Vaishnava and Madhva schools of philosophical Vaishnavism flourished in southern India, the followers of Vallabhacharya (b. 1479) and Chaitanya (1485–

1533) were primarily from the northern and northeastern parts of India. These theologians significantly increased the number of Vaishnava devotees through the devotional schools of philosophy and practice that they espoused. Chaitanya and his followers, who eventually came to be called Gaudiya Vaishnavas or Vaishnavas from the land of Bengal, conceptualized the supreme reality as Krishna, which is distinct from the belief of many other Hindus who think of Krishna as one of the many incarnations of Vishnu. Several traditions also came to think of Rama as the supreme being, and over the centuries those who think of Rama or Krishna as the primordial deity have come to be called Vaishnava. Ghanshyam (better known as Swaminarayan; b. 1781) established one of the most influential schools of Vaishnavism in the western state of Gujarat. The Swaminarayan movement is a socially engaged form of Vaishnavism with several forms of outreach activities. No list of Vaishnava theologians would be complete without the profound influence of Bhaktivedanta Prabhupada, the founder of ISKCON, better known as the Hare Krishna movement. It was largely through his teaching and practices that Vaishnavism came to be adopted by a number of Euro-Americans.

ORGANIZATIONAL STRUCTURE The many Vaishnava traditions have distinctive organizational structures. It is important, however, to recognize that one can be a Vaishnava without ever belonging to an institution or to a philosophical tradition. Many of the Vaishnava singers and poets were not affiliated with specific schools of thought.

Although most Vaishnavas are lay people, leadership is frequently held by a small number of sannyasins, or renunciants. In the Swaminarayan, Sri Vaishnava, and Pushti marg (Vallabha) communities, some of the initiating teachers (*acharyas*) are householders who have descended from those men appointed by the original founding teacher of each sect.

HOUSES OF WORSHIP AND HOLY PLACES India abounds with sacred places connected with the Vaishnava faith. Pilgrimage traditions have been religiously, socially, culturally, and economically significant in the last two millennia. Of the thousands of such places, a few cities and towns are strikingly important. While many of the northern Indian traditions consider places connected with Krishna—such as Govardhana, Gokula, and Mathura—as the most significant, southern Indian Sri

Vaishnava Theology

Although there are great differences between various schools of Vaishnavism, all reject the philosophy of pure nondualism taught by Shankara (700?–750), the Indian theologian and exponent of the Advaita Vedanta school. Shankara had taught that the ultimate reality is Brahman, the ineffable supreme being, and in the highest stage of realization there is no difference between the individual soul and the supreme being. While many Vaishnava schools subscribe to forms of nondualism (with the exception of Madhva), they do not think of the soul as Isvara, or the supreme being. The philosophy of Ramanuja (c.1017–1137), known as Visistadvaita (qualified nondualism), is considered by many as an "anchor" Vaishnava movement. According to Ramanuja, the supreme being, Brahman or Vishnu, is understood to be the soul of the entire universe. The entire universe, including all sentient and insentient matter, form the body of Vishnu. In theory, if not in actual practice, most Vaishnava schools accept the significance of this school; the Swaminarayan school of Vaishnavism, for instance, calls itself Navya Visistadvaita, or "Neoqualified nondualism."

Vaishnavas may deem the many temple towns such as Srirangam and Tirumala-Tirupati as the most important sites. People from the state of Kerala consider the Krishna Temple at Guruvayur to be the most significant pilgrimage site. Vaishnava devotees from Maharashtra make annual pilgrimages to see Vithoba in Pandaripur. Puri, on the east coast of India, in the state of Orissa, has been one of the most important pilgrimage centers for at least the last millennium. The tenth-century Prasat Kravan Temple and the twelfth-century Angkor Wat Temple, both near Siem Reap in northwestern Cambodia, were built through the patronage of noble and royal Cambodian families. Angkor Wat is one of the biggest Vishnu temples in the world, and it has the largest bas-relief ever completed on any work of architecture.

The iconic manifestation of Vishnu in all these temples is considered by most Vaishnavas to be a revelation in action. Devotees think of the enshrined icon as a continuous revelation of the supreme being, not as an idol made of material substance. Vaishnavas consider this icon to be God—on earth as He is in heaven.

While the temple is extremely holy and significant in Vaishnava faith, the home and the human body are also considered to be sacred. Icons and pictures of Vishnu are kept in home altars, and daily worship at such household altars signifies that the deity is treated as an honored guest. He is woken up, bathed, offered food, and made to sleep at night. One can be a good Vaishnava without ever having to set foot outside the home.

The human body is also a container of the divine. In daily exercises, when Vaishnava symbols are anointed on different parts of one's body, the various names of Vishnu are recited. One is therefore enjoined to keep one's body physically and mentally pure. This deity in one's heart is not different from or lesser than the deity in the temple or the one in heaven.

WHAT IS SACRED? Vishnu is also seen as abiding in a fossil called a salagrama, which is found in lakes in the Himalayan region. The salagrama fossil is believed to have a complete presence of Vishnu, and when the salagrama is present at home, it is treated like a temple deity. Ordinarily only men handle a salagrama.

HOLIDAYS AND FESTIVALS The Vaishnava traditions share many holidays and festivals with other Hindus, and these vary by region and by community. Like most other Hindus, the Vaishnavas celebrate Deepavali, the Festival of Lights, on the new moon or the day before that comes between 15 October and 15 November. The festival is celebrated for various reasons. Vaishnavas in northern India celebrate this as the day Rama returned from Lanka after defeating the demon Ravana, whereas devotees in the south believe that on dawn that day Krishna and his wife, Satyabhama, together defeated Narakasura, the demon of Hell.

Southern Indian Vaishnavas, along with other Tamil-speaking people from Tamil-Nadu, celebrate Pongal, a festival of harvest and thanksgiving. Although celebrated in mid-January, this three-day festival marks the winter solstice in the Hindu calendar. It is called the beginning of the *uttarayana punya kala,* the blessed time when the sun travels north. The Sri Vaishnava community also celebrates the songs of the Alvars in a festival

of recitation in the month of Margasirsa (mid-December to mid-January). The songs are recited and sung, and in some holy temples like Srirangam and Srivilliputtur, men from families who have the hereditary right to do so act out some of the poems.

Vaishnavas tend to celebrate the birthdays of their spiritual teachers as well as the birthdays of Rama and Krishna. The birthdays of the deities—the astrological date on which they are said to have incarnated themselves—are days of considerable celebration with the preparation and consumption of many sweets and dishes.

MODE OF DRESS Vaishnava garb for men and women varies depending on the region. On ritual occasions in southern India, men wear a *veshti,* a piece of white cotton cloth that is twirled around the legs. Also on ritual occasions both priests and Brahman men in southern India do not ordinarily wear a shirt. The sacred thread that they wear over their shoulders announces their caste. At one time many men in all parts of India, especially the Brahmans, tended to shave their heads except for a tuft of hair that resembles a ponytail on the top of their heads, but this custom is seldom followed now. Orthoprax ("correct practice") Brahman women belonging to the Sri Vaishnava community wear a special, nine-yard sari on ritual occasions, especially weddings. Men and women in the north tend to cover themselves more fully. In general, women from the north tend to veil their heads or drape their saris lightly over their heads in modesty; whereas women from the south do not follow this custom. In the past only widows covered their heads in southern India.

DIETARY PRACTICES The Vaishnava calendar is marked with days of feasting and fasting. Ekadashi, or the eleventh day after the new moon or full moon, is ordinarily a day of fasting when grain is not consumed, and a diet of fruits and dairy products is recommended. There are other days of complete fasting, such as the hours just before the birthday of Krishna or during eclipses.

Vaishnavas are said to prescribe to the Sanskrit dictum "ahimsa paramo dharmah" (nonviolence is the highest virtue) and tend to be vegetarians. Several Vaishnava theologians have written extensively on dietary regulations; this is, in fact, one of the most important aspects of premodern Vaishnavism. While many if not most of these regulations are not followed now,

Vaishnavas had strict rules on what, when, and with whom they ate, as well as who cooked the food. Generally the food had to be cooked by a Vaishnava of the same caste; orthoprax pilgrims still take a cook with them on their tours to be sure their diet is not compromised.

RITUALS Daily, weekly, fortnightly, monthly, and annual rituals are celebrated at Vaishnava homes and temples. In temples the deities are "woken" up from their sleep with special prayers and bathed and adorned before formal worship. Every temple has its own schedule. In Nathdwara, Rajasthan, for instance, Krishna is worshiped in the form of a baby. The understanding is that a baby needs to sleep, and, therefore, the times opened for devotee worship (*darshan,* literally "viewing") are very limited. As in most Hindu temples, worship in Vaishnava temples is ordinarily not congregational, though that can be found in a few communities. Devotees take fruits and flowers, and the Brahman priest performs a *puja* (worship) on behalf of the worshiper to the enshrined deity. While most Vaishnava priests in India are male and belong to the Brahman caste, women in the ISKCON tradition have an active role in the bathing and adorning of the deities.

Domestic rituals vary by caste and gender. There is daily worship at the home altar that may be done by any member of the family and may range from simply lighting a lamp to more elaborate rituals. Singing classical and popular songs to the various manifestations of Vishnu, and reciting the 108 or 1,008 names of Vishnu, Lakshmi, or any one of their many manifestations is also considered to be meritorious.

RITES OF PASSAGE Vaishnavas, like other Hindus, follow sacraments that are common all over India, as well as those that may be specific to their community or their local areas. Thus, all children go through rites of passage in which they are named and given the first solid food. In addition, one's first birthday and sometimes the formal starting of education are marked with rituals. Boys of the upper castes also go through the *upanayana* ceremony in which they are invested with a sacred thread that marks a young man's spiritual birth.

The wedding is frequently the most important sacrament in a Vaishnava's life. Sixtieth and eightieth birthdays are marked with religious rituals that include propitiatory rites to various deities for peace in one's life. In death the body is cremated, and the ashes immersed in a holy river. Local or community Vaishnava rites of passage may include celebrations to mark menarche and prenatal rituals for pregnant mothers.

MEMBERSHIP One may be born into a Vaishnava family or become a Vaishnava by choice. Most frequently the person who becomes a Vaishnava does so by simply accepting Vishnu as the supreme being and perhaps by following some of the dietary and ritual practices. On the other hand, those who formally want to become Vaishnavas may get initiated into a particular Vaishnava tradition by one of the many spiritual teachers. The initiation ceremony may involve the giving of a mantra, a name that now articulates the devotee's new status, and perhaps the marking of the upper arms with the signs of Vishnu—the conch and the discus.

Hundreds of websites cater to the Vaishnava subgroups, creating transnational communities. While some communities have had periods of active proselytizing, in general, Vaishnava traditions do not focus on new recruitment; rather, the websites as well as the individual teachers try to get the existing Vaishnavas to be better devotees.

RELIGIOUS TOLERANCE While there is no persecution against Vaishnavas today, there have been occasional historical cases of struggle between Vaishnavas, Shaivites, and Jains in southern India. In general, a sense of religious pluralism among Hindus has prevailed in most communities in India and elsewhere at most times.

SOCIAL JUSTICE Many of the Vaishnava traditions highlight the importance of faith and devotion and place these traditions as more important than social class or caste. Thus, there are many narratives that speak about how religious leaders befriended those of the "lower" castes. There have also been several Vaishnava movements to include members of the outcaste groups into the social fabric. In this logic of devotion (which may be different from the rules of ethics that apply in a day-to-day situation), women, too, are considered to be qualified for salvation. In practice, however, women and those who belong to the "lower" castes have not had priestly roles in temples.

SOCIAL ASPECTS Vaishnava traditions celebrate the importance of community. Devotees frequently sing or compose poems longing to live with other devotees. Such a life with other devotees is considered to be the "real" society (*sat sangh*)—that is, the ideal society in which one should aspire to live. There is much reverence given to devotees of Vishnu, and frequently more respect is given to such devotion than to age, caste, or gender. In spite of these concepts, the caste system that exists in Hinduism is present in the Vaishnava traditions as well.

CONTROVERSIAL ISSUES Many Vaishnava groups have internal tensions over succession issues, and after the death of a charismatic leader, these groups frequently splinter over issues of philosophical interpretation and social practices. Controversies over the authority of certain castes to have sacerdotal functions or the authority of women to do certain rituals and recite certain mantras or prayers also exist. In general, the Vaishnava leaders, like most Hindu leaders of other traditions, do not speak out publicly on such issues as birth control, abortion, and gay marriages.

CULTURAL IMPACT Vaishnava traditions are perhaps best appreciated in the arts, and for centuries Vaishnavism tenets have been transmitted through the performing arts rather than through books or sermons. Whether it is a simple *bhajan* (devotional song) or a complex dance performance, the power of the narratives is brought out through articulating the emotion with performing arts. The glory of the various incarnations of Vishnu as well as the soul's longing for union with the divine is frequently portrayed in classical dances. The dancer takes on the role of a young woman pining for her lover in an allegory for the soul's search for God. Folk songs and dances, such as the *ras* in Gujarat, also reenact incidents from the life of Krishna.

The various hand gestures adopted by dancers are also seen in iconography. Vishnu icons abound in South and Southeast Asia, with some spectacular ones seen in southern India and in Cambodia. Vishnu can be portrayed as standing, sitting, reclining, or striding; and there are hundreds of ways in which Rama, Krishna, or the other incarnations can be portrayed.

Vaishnava themes, especially stories relating to the life of Krishna, have been the focus of miniature painting for the last four centuries in northern India. Some incidents depicted in the paintings are seen as expressive of particular modes of music (ragas) and are projected as the visual dimension of aural aesthetics.

Vasudha Narayanan

See Also Vol. I: *Hinduism*

Bibliography

Bryant, Edwin. *The Hare Krishna Movement: The Postcharismatic Fate of a Religious Transplant.* New York: Columbia University Press, 2004.

Carman, John. *The Theology of Ramanuja.* New Haven: Yale University Press, 1974.

Haberman, David. *Journey through the Twelve Forests: An Encounter with Krishna.* New York: Oxford University Press, 1994.

Hawley, John Stratton. *Krishna: The Butter Thief.* Princeton, N.J.: Princeton University Press, 1983.

———. *Songs of the Saints of India.* New York: Oxford University Press, 1988.

Narayanan, Vasudha. *The Way and the Goal.* Cambridge: Center for the Study of World Religions, Harvard University, 1988.

Williams, Raymond Brady. *An Introduction to Swaminarayan Hinduism.* Cambridge: Cambridge University Press, 2001.

Islam

FOUNDED: 622 C.E.

RELIGION AS A PERCENTAGE OF WORLD POPULATION: 20 percent

OVERVIEW The religion of Islam was revealed to Muhammad ibn Abdullah, who became known as the Prophet Muhammad, in central Arabia between 610 and 632 C.E. Muhammad did not think that he was founding a new religion with a new scripture but, rather, bringing belief in the one God, a belief already held by Christians and Jews, to the Arabs. The Koran's revelations were seen as a return in the midst of a polytheistic society to the forgotten past, to the faith of the first monotheist, Abraham. Muslims believe that God sent revelations first to Moses, as found in the Hebrew scriptures (the Torah), then to Jesus (the Gospels), and finally to Muhammad (the Koran).

The revelations Muhammad received led him to believe that, over time, Jews and Christians had distorted God's original messages to Moses and, later, to Jesus. Thus, Muslims see the Torah and the Gospels as a combination of the original revelations and later human additions, or interpolations. For example, Christian doctrines such as the Trinity and the divinity of Jesus (his elevation from prophet to Son of God) are seen as changes to the divine revelation from outside or foreign influences.

The Koran contains many references to stories and figures in the Old and New Testaments, including Adam and Eve, Abraham and Moses, David and Solomon, and Mary and Jesus. Indeed, Mary, the mother of Jesus, is mentioned more times in the Koran than in the Gospels. Muslims view Jews and Christians as People of the Book, who received revelations through prophets in the form of revealed books from God.

In addition to belief in a single, all-powerful God, Islam shares with Judaism and Christianity belief in the importance of community-building, social justice, and individual moral decision-making, as well as in revelation, angels, Satan, a final judgment, and eternal reward and punishment. Therefore, Islam was not a totally new monotheistic religion and community that sprang up in isolation. Muslims believe that Islam was, in fact, the original religion of Abraham. The revelations Muhammad received were calls to religious and social reform. They emphasized social justice (concern for the rights of women, widows, and orphans) and warned that many had strayed from the message of God and his prophets. They called upon all to return to what the Koran refers to as the straight path of Islam or the path of God, revealed one final time to Muhammad, the last, or "seal," of the prophets.

The diversity of Islam, the world's second largest religion, is reflected by the geographic expanse of the 56 countries that have Muslim majorities. The world's approximately 1.2 billion Muslims are found not only from Africa to Southeast Asia but also in Europe and North America. Only 20 percent of the world's Muslims are Arab, with the majority of Muslims living in Asian and African countries. The largest Muslim populations are found in Indonesia, Bangladesh, Pakistan, India, and Nigeria. Islam is also a significant presence in the West, as the second largest religion in Europe and

CRESCENT MOON AND STAR. The Crescent Moon and Star is a symbol frequently associated with the Islamic faith. The crescent moon in particular is of considerable significance. The sighting of the crescent moon, for example, signals the beginning and end of Ramadan, the holy month of fasting. The symbol is often found on the flag of Muslim nations. (THOMSON GALE)

projected to become the second largest in the United States. While Muslims share certain core beliefs, there are many interpretations and cultural practices of Islam. Beyond the two major branches of Islam—Sunni (approximately 85 percent of the Muslim community) and Shiite (15 percent)—there are many theological and legal schools, as well as the diversity of thought and practice illustrated by Sufism (Islamic mysticism).

Islam's many faces across the world are seen in diverse cultures. They are seen in Muslim women's dress and in their varied educational and professional opportunities, as well as in their participation in mosques and societies that differ widely from country to country. They are also seen in politics and society when Islamic activists peacefully press for the implementation of religion in the state, when members of Islamic organizations are elected to parliaments (as in Turkey, Algeria, Jordan, Egypt, Kuwait, Yemen, Pakistan, Thailand, and Malaysia), and when Islamic associations provide inexpensive and efficient educational, legal, and medical services in the slums and lower middle-class neighborhoods of Cairo and Algiers, Beirut and Mindanao, the West Bank and Gaza. At the same time, on 11 September 2001 violent extremists and terrorists headed by Osama bin Laden and al-Qaeda, acting in the name of Islam, hijacked commercial airliners and flew them into the towers of the World Trade Center in New York

City and into the Pentagon in Washington, D.C., resulting in the loss of almost 3,000 lives. The hijackers who committed this act reflect a religious radicalism that, for several decades, has threatened governments and societies in the Muslim world and in the West. The challenge, however, is not only to be aware of the threat from Muslim extremist groups but also to know and understand the faith of the vast majority of mainstream Muslims across the globe.

HISTORY Like Judaism and Christianity, Islam originated in the Middle East, in Mecca and Medina in Arabia. The origins of Islam, like those of Judaism and Christianity, would have seemed improbable as forecasters of a great world religion. Just as few would have anticipated the extent to which Moses and Jesus, a slave and a carpenter's son, would become major religious figures, so one would not have predicted that the followers of an orphaned, illiterate caravan manager, Muhammad ibn Abdullah, would become the world's second largest religion, a global religious, political, and cultural presence and power.

Muslims see themselves, as well as Jews and Christians, as children of Abraham, belonging to different branches of the same religious family. The Koran and the Old Testament, or Hebrew Bible, both tell the story of Abraham, Sarah, and Hagar, Sarah's Egyptian servant. While Jews and Christians are held to be descended from Abraham and his wife, Sarah, through their son, Isaac, Muslims trace their religious roots to Abraham through Ismail (Ishmael), his firstborn son by Hagar. This connection to Abraham, Hagar, and Ismail is commemorated each year in the rituals of the pilgrimage to Mecca.

According to both Hebrew and Muslim scripture, when, after many years, Sarah did not conceive a child, she urged Abraham to sleep with her maidservant Hagar so that he might have an heir. As a result of the union between Abraham and Hagar, a son, Ismail, was born. After Ismail's birth Sarah also became pregnant and gave birth to Isaac. Sarah then became jealous of Ismail, who as firstborn would be the prime inheritor and overshadow her own son, and she pressured Abraham to send Hagar and Ismail away. Abraham reluctantly let Hagar and his son go, because God promised that he would make Ismail the father of a great nation. Islamic sources say that Hagar and Ismail ended up in the vicinity of Mecca in Arabia, and both the Bible and the Koran say

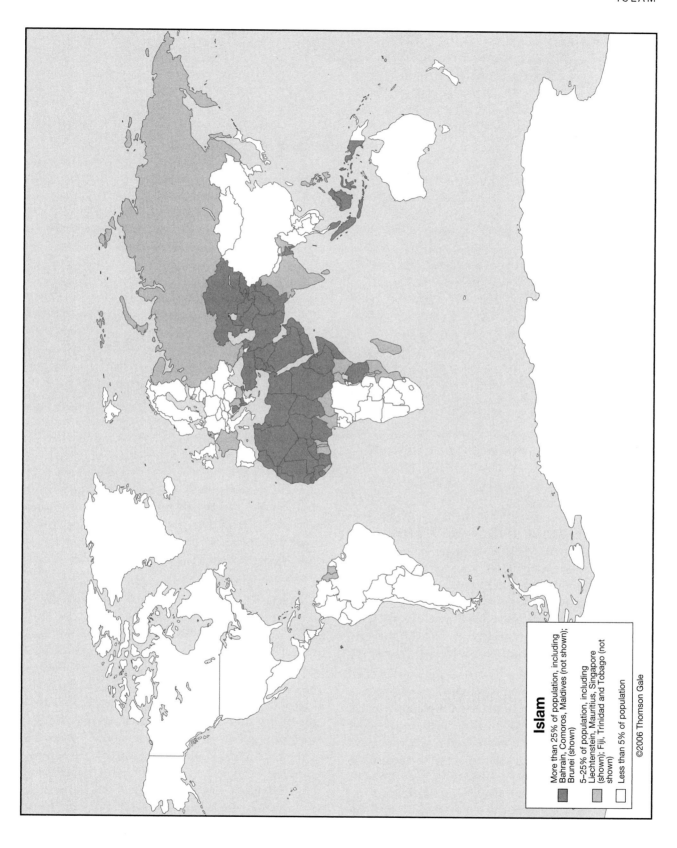

Islam

More than 25% of population, including Bahrain, Comoros, Maldives (not shown); Brunei (shown)

5–25% of population, including Liechtenstein, Mauritius, Singapore (shown); Fiji, Trinidad and Tobago (not shown)

Less than 5% of population

A young woman reads from the Koran. The Koran raised the status of women by, among other things, prohibiting female infanticide, abolishing women's status as property, and establishing their legal capacity. © J A GIORDANO/CORBIS SABA.

that they nearly died but were saved by a spring that miraculously gushed from the desert.

In seventh-century Arabia, where Muhammad ibn Abdullah was born, war was the natural state. Arabia was located in the broader Near East, which was divided between two warring superpowers, the Byzantine (Eastern Roman) and the Sasanian (Persian) empires, that were competing for world dominion. Located along the profitable trade routes of the Orient, Arabia was affected by the rivalry and interventions of its powerful imperial neighbors.

Pre-Islamic Arabia was tribal in its religious, social, and political ideas, practices, and institutions. Tribal and family honor were central virtues. Manliness (chivalry, upholding tribal and family honor, and courage in battle) was a major virtue celebrated by the poets of the time. There was no belief in an afterlife or a cosmic moral purpose or in individual or communal moral responsibility. Thus, justice was obtained and carried out through group vengeance or retaliation. Arabia and the city of Mecca, in which Muhammad was born and lived and received God's revelation, were beset by tribal raids

and cycles of vendettas. Raiding was an integral part of tribal life and society and had established regulations and customs. Raids were undertaken to increase property and such goods as slaves, jewelry, camels, and livestock. Bloodshed was avoided, if at all possible, because it could lead to retaliation.

Religion in Arabia at the time was predominantly polytheistic. Various gods and goddesses who were feared, not loved, served as protectors of the many tribes. These gods were the objects of cultic rituals and supplication at local shrines, reflecting the tribal nature and social structure of society. Mecca was a rising commercial and religious center that housed the Kaaba, a cube-shaped structure that contained representations of approximately 360 different tribal gods and goddesses. At the head of the shrine's pantheon was the supreme god, Allah, who was seen as the creator and sustainer of life and the universe but who was remote from everyday concerns. Mecca was also the site of a great annual fair and pilgrimage to the Kaaba, a highly profitable event. It brought worshipers of the different gods from far and wide, along with their money and their business interests. In addition to the prevailing tribal polytheism, Arabia was also home to a variety of monotheistic communities, in particular Jews, Christians, and Zoroastrians, which Muhammad encountered in his travels as a businessman.

The traditional sources for information about Muhammad's life are the Koran, as well as biographies of the Prophet and hadith (tradition) literature. Muhammad ibn Abdullah (Muhammad, the son of Abdullah) was born in 570 C.E. in Mecca. Although born into the ruling tribe, the Quraysh, Muhammad was among the "poorer cousins." Orphaned at an early age (his father died before he was born, and his mother died when he was six years old), Muhammad was raised by his uncle, Abu Talib, a well-respected and powerful member of the Quraysh, who provided Muhammad and, later, his community with protection. As a young man Muhammad earned his living as a business manager for the caravans of a wealthy widow named Khadijah. At the age of 25, Muhammad married Khadijah, who was 15 years older. Tradition records that they were married for 24 years and had two sons who died in infancy and four surviving daughters, the most famous of whom was Fatimah, who married Ali, the fourth caliph. Khadijah was the first person to believe in the revelation Muhammad had received, making her the first Muslim convert. She was Muhammad's strongest supporter and adviser, particularly during the early, difficult years after his call as a prophet.

By the age of 30, Muhammad had become a respected member of Meccan society, known for his business skills and trustworthiness (he was nicknamed al-Amin, "the trustworthy"). Reflective by temperament, Muhammad often retreated to the quiet and solitude of Mount Hira to contemplate life and society. It was there, during the month of Ramadan in 610, on a night remembered in Muslim tradition as the Night of Power, that Muhammad, the Meccan businessman, was called to be a prophet of God. Muhammad heard a voice commanding him to "recite." He was frightened and replied that he had nothing to recite. After the angel, identified as Gabriel, repeated the command, the words finally came: "Recite in the name of your Lord who has created, created man out of a germ cell. Recite for your Lord is the Most Generous One, who has taught by the pen, Taught man what he did not know."

This was the first of what would be many revelations from Allah, "the God" in Arabic, communicated through the angel Gabriel. Muhammad continued to re-

Muslim women gather in front of the Dome of the Rock Mosque in Jerusalem. The Dome of the Rock is among the most prominent religious symbols in Islam. © RICHARD T. NOWITZ/CORBIS.

ceive revelations over the next 22 years, until his death in 632. The revelations were preserved verbatim orally and written down by scribes, and they were later collected and compiled into the Koran, the Muslim scripture. The reformist message Muhammad received, like that of Amos and other prophets before him, represented a powerful but unwelcome challenge to religious and tribal leaders and to businessmen, who comprised the religious and political establishment. Muhammad denounced corrupt business practices and called for social justice for the poor and women, and for children and orphans, the most vulnerable in society. He emphasized the religious equality of men and women and expanded the marriage and inheritance rights of women. Muhammad's prophetic message summoned the people to strive and struggle (jihad) to live a good life based on religious belief rather than loyalty to their tribe and to reform their communities. Most importantly, Muhammad's revelation in the Koran rejected the common practice of worshiping many gods, insisting that there was only one true God. He therefore threatened the livelihood of those who profited enormously from the annual pil-

Muslim men wash their hands and feet before prayer. The ablution consists of washing the face, both arms up to the elbows, the head, and the feet. The ablution should be performed before praying and circumambulating the Kaaba shrine. © ANDERS RYMAN/CORBIS.

grimage honoring many different gods, the equivalent of a giant tribal convention.

During the first 10 years of Muhammad's preaching, his community of believers remained small and under constant pressure and persecution. In an increasingly hostile environment they were compelled to struggle to stay alive. The life and livelihood of the community were eventually threatened by sanctions that prevented them from doing business and that were literally starving them out. This hardship may have contributed to the death of Khadijah, and after his fortunes were destroyed, Abu Talib, Muhammad's protector, also died. Muhammad was now a likely and proximate target for assassination.

It was at this low point in his life that Muhammad had a mystical experience: the Night Journey, or Ascension. One night, sleeping near the Kaaba, Muhammad was awakened by the angel Gabriel. Muhammad was mounted on a mystical steed called Buruq, who flew him from Mecca to Jerusalem, which is referred to in the

Koran as *al-masjid al-aqsa* (Further Mosque) and which is the site of the Temple Mount, where the ancient Temple of Solomon once stood. There, according to tradition, Muhammad climbed a ladder leading to the throne of God. Along the way to the throne, Muhammad met Abraham, Moses, Joseph, John the Baptist, and Jesus, as well as other prophets. During his meeting with God, Muhammad received guidance for the final number of daily prayers that Muslims should perform, set at five. The Night Journey, which is understood by many Muslims as a mystical experience, made Jerusalem the third holiest city in Islam and affirmed the continuity of Islam with Judaism and Christianity.

Faced with increasing hardships, Muhammad was invited in 622 by a delegation from Yathrib, a city in the north that was caught in a bitter feud between its Arab tribes, to be their binding arbitrator. That his decisions were to be accepted by all the tribes was testimony to Muhammad's wide reputation as a trustworthy and just man. Muhammad began sending his followers to

Glossary

al-hajj / al-hajji pilgrim; prefix added to a name to indicate that the person has made the hajj

Allah God

caliph successor; deputy to the Prophet Muhammad

dawa call to Islam; propagation of the faith

dhimmi protected person, specifically a Jew or Christian

dua personal prayer

fast of Ramadan fast during ninth month; fourth pillar

fatwa legal opinion or judgment of a mufti, a specialist in Islamic law

Five Pillars of Islam fundamental observances

ghusl ritual cleansing before worship

hadith tradition; reports of Muhammad's sayings and deeds

hajj pilgrimage to Mecca; fifth pillar

halal meat slaughtered in a religious manner

hijab Muslim dress for women, today often referring to a headscarf

hijra (hegira) migration of early Muslims from Mecca to Medina

imam Shiite prayer leader; also used as the title for Muhammad's successors as leader of the Muslim community, consisting of male descendants through his cousin and son-in-law Ali

Islam submission to the will of God; peace

jihad strive, struggle

jizya poll, or head, tax paid by Jews and Christians

juma Friday congregational prayer

Kaaba sacred structure in Mecca; according to tradition, built by Abraham and Ismail

Koran (Quran) revelation; Muslim scripture

madrasah Islamic religious school

masjid place for ritual prostration; mosque

mihrab niche in mosque indicating the direction of Mecca

millet protected religious community

minbar raised platform in mosque; pulpit

People of the Book Jews and Christians, who Muslims believe received divine revelations in the Torah and Gospels, respectively

riba usury

sadaqah almsgiving for the poor, for thanksgiving, or to ward off danger

salat prayer or worship; second pillar

shahadah declaration of faith; first pillar

Shariah Islamic law

Shiite member of second largest Muslim sect, believing in the hereditary succession of Ali, the cousin and son-in-law of Muhammad, to lead the community

Sufi mystic

sunnah example of Muhammad

Sunni member of largest Muslim sect, holding that the successor (caliph) to Muhammad as leader of the community should be elected

surah chapter of the Koran

tawhid oneness, or unity, of God; monotheism

ulama religious leader or scholar

ummah the transnational community of followers of Islam

wali friend of God; Sufi saint

wudu ablution before worship

zakat purification; tithe or almsgiving; third pillar

Yathrib, and he followed a short time afterward, thus escaping those plotting to kill him. Yathrib would later be renamed Medina, or Medinat al-Nabi (City of the Prophet). This migration (*hijra*, or hegira) of the Muslim community from the traditional safety of tribe and kinsmen in warring Arabia to form alliances with alien tribes based upon a broader Islamic ideal was a concept introduced by Muhammad, one that would have remarkable success.

The migration to Medina and the creation of the first Islamic community (*ummah*) underscores the primary importance of community in Islam. It is so significant that when Muslims devised their own calendar they dated it, not from the year in which Muhammad was born or from the first revelation of the Koran, but from the creation of the Islamic community at Medina. Thus, 622 C.E. became I A.H. (year [*anno*] of the *hijra*). This act reinforced the meaning of Islam as the realization of God's will on earth and the centrality of the Islamic community. It became the basis for Muslim belief in Islam as a world religion, a global community of believers with a universal message and mission.

The experience and example of Muhammad's new community would provide the model for later generations. In times of danger the twin ideals of *hijra* (to emigrate from a hostile anti-Islamic environment) and jihad (to resist and fight against oppression and injustice) were established. These concepts became guiding principles for responding to persecution and rejection, to threats to the faith, and to the security and survival of the community. Today both mainstream and extremist movements and self-proclaimed "holy warriors," such as Osama bin Laden, who emigrated from Saudi Arabia to establish his movement and training bases in Afghanistan, have selectively used the pattern of migration and struggle, armed resistance, and warfare for their own purposes.

In Medina the Muslim community thrived, resulting in the establishment of the first Islamic community-state. Muhammad was not only a prophet but also a head of state, political ruler, military commander, chief judge, and lawgiver of a multireligious community consisting of Muslims, Arab polytheists, Jews, and Christians. The Constitution, or Charter, of Medina, as established by Muhammad, set out the rights and duties of the citizens and the relationship of the Muslim community to other communities, thus reflecting the diversity of this society. The charter recognized the People of the Book (Jews and Christians who had received God's revelation through the prophets Moses and Jesus) as an allied community. These People of the Book were entitled to live in coexistence with Muslims and to retain and practice their religion in return for loyalty and the payment of a poll tax, or *jizya.*

With establishment of the community at Medina, the bitter conflict between Mecca and Muhammad and his followers continued. Muhammad threatened the economic power and political authority of the Meccan leaders with a series of raids against their caravans. In addition, several key battles occurred that are remembered in Muslim tradition as sources of inspiration and guidance. In 624 Muslim forces, although greatly outnumbered, defeated the Meccan army in the Battle of Badr, in which they believed they were aided by divine guidance. The Koran (3:120) declares that thousands of angels assisted the Muslims in battle. This battle has special significance for Muslims because it represents the victory of monotheism over polytheism, of good over evil, of the army of God over the army of ignorance and unbelief. Badr remains an important sacred symbol for contemporary Muslims. For example, Egypt's President Anwar as-Sadat launched the 1973 Arab-Israeli war as a jihad with the code name Operation Badr.

The Battle of Uhud, in 625, represented a major setback for the Muslims when the Meccans bounced back and soundly defeated them, wounding Muhammad. The Battle of the Ditch, or Battle of the Trench, took place in 627, when the Meccans mounted a siege against the Muslims, seeking to crush them permanently. The Battle of the Ditch proved to be a major turning point, however. The Muslims dug a trench to protect themselves from the Meccan cavalry and doggedly resisted the Meccan siege. In the end the Meccans were forced to withdraw, and a truce was struck at Hudaybiyah, a pact of nonaggression that proved a face-saving device for both parties. The truce granted the Muslims the right to make the pilgrimage to Mecca the following year but required that Muhammad end his raids and the attempt at an economic blockade. At the same time, the truce signaled recognition of the political legitimacy of Muhammad.

In 629 Muhammad extended Muslim governance over the Hejaz, in central Arabia, and led the pilgrimage to Mecca. In 630 the feud between Mecca and Medina came to an end. After client tribes of Mecca and Medina clashed, Muhammad declared the truce broken and moved against Mecca with an army of 10,000, and the Quraysh surrendered without a fight. After 20 years Muhammad had successfully returned to Mecca and brought it within the Pax Islamica. In victory Muhammad proved magnanimous and strategic, preferring diplomacy to force. Rather than engaging in vengeance and plunder, he offered amnesty to his former enemies, rewarding a number of its leaders with prominent positions and gifts. Regarding the Kaaba shrine in Mecca as the original house of God built by Abraham and Ismail, Muhammad destroyed its pagan idols and rededicated it to the one true God. The majority of Meccans converted to Islam, accepted Muhammad's leadership, and became part of the Islamic community.

The conquest of Mecca established Muhammad's paramount political leadership. He continued to employ his religious message, diplomatic skills, and, when necessary, force to establish Muslim rule in Arabia. In 632 the 62-year-old Muhammad led a pilgrimage to Mecca and delivered his farewell sermon, a moment remembered and commemorated each year during the annual pilgrimage: "Know ye that every Muslim is a brother unto every other Muslim, and that ye are now one brotherhood. It is not legitimate for any one of you, therefore, to appropriate unto himself anything that belongs to his brother unless it is willingly given him by that brother." When Muhammad died in June 632, all of Arabia was united under the banner of Islam.

Few observers of seventh-century Arabia would have predicted that, within a hundred years of Muhammad's death, a religious community established by a local businessman, orphaned and illiterate, would unite Arabia's warring tribes, overwhelm the eastern Byzantine and Sasanid empires, and create its own vast empire stretching from North Africa to India. Within a brief period of time, Muhammad had initiated a major historical transformation that began in Arabia but that would become a global religious and political movement. In subsequent years Muslim armies, traders, and mystics spread the faith and power of Islam globally. The religion of Islam became intertwined with empires and sultanates from North Africa to Southeast Asia.

After the death of Muhammad, his four immediate successors, remembered in Sunni Islam as the Rightly Guided Caliphs (reigned 632–61), oversaw the consolidation of Muslim rule in Arabia and the broader Middle East (Egypt, Palestine, Iraq, and Syria), overrunning the Byzantine and Sasanid empires. A period of great central empires was followed with the establishment of the Umayyad (661–750) and then the Abbasid (750–1258) empires. Within a hundred years of the death of Muhammad, Muslim rule extended from North Africa to South Asia, an empire greater than Rome at its zenith.

Under the Abbasids trade and industry, a strong central bureaucracy, law, theology, literature, science,

and culture developed. The Abbasid conquest of the central Umayyad empire did not affect the existence of the Spanish Umayyad empire in Andalusia (modern-day Spain and Portugal). There, where Muslims were called Moors, Muslim rule ushered in a period of coexistence and culture developed by Muslims, Christians, and Jews in major urban centers. The Spanish Umayyad empire was less a threat to the Abbasids than was the Fatimid (Shiite) empire in the tenth century, carved out in North Africa and with its capital in Cairo. From the tenth to the twelfth centuries, the Fatimids challenged a weakened and fragmented Abbasid empire, spreading their influence and rule across North Africa, Egypt, Syria, Persia, and Sicily. The Fatimids were not brought under Abbasid rule until 1171, when the great general Salah ad-Din (Saladin) conquered Cairo. Despite this success, however, by the thirteenth century the Abbasid empire had become a sprawling, fragmented group of semiautonomous states governed by military commanders. In 1258 the Mongols captured Baghdad, burned and pillaged the city, slaughtered its Muslim inhabitants, and executed the caliph and his family.

Although the fall of Baghdad seemed to be a fatal blow to Muslim power, by the fifteenth century Muslim fortunes had been reversed. The central caliphate was replaced by a chain of dynamic states, each ruled by a sultan, stretching from Africa to Southeast Asia, from Timbuktu to Mindanao. They included three imperial sultanates: the Turkish Ottoman Empire (1322–1924), which encompassed major portions of North Africa, the Arab world, and eastern Europe; the Persian Safavid Empire (1501–1722); and the Mughal Empire (1520–1857), which included much of the Indian subcontinent (modern-day Pakistan, India, and Bangladesh).

Like many parts of the world, Muslim societies fell victim to European imperialism. When Christian Europe overpowered North Africa, the Middle East, and South and Southeast Asia in the nineteenth century, reducing most Muslim societies to colonies, many Muslims experienced these defeats as a religious, as well as a political and cultural, crisis. It was a symbol not only of the decline of Muslim power but also of the apparent loss of divine favor and guidance. Colonialism brought European armies and Christian missionaries, who accompanied the bureaucrats, traders, and teachers, to spread the message of Western (Christian) religious and cultural superiority and dominance. Europe legitimated its colonization of large areas of the underdeveloped Muslim world in cultural terms. The French spoke of a "mission to civilize" and the British of "the white man's burden."

Muslim responses to Europe's political and religious penetration and dominance varied significantly, ranging from resistance or warfare (jihad) in "defense of Islam" to accommodation with, if not outright assimilation of, Western values. The result of Western imperialism for Muslims was a period of self-criticism and reflection on the causes of their decline. Responses spanned the spectrum from liberal secularism to Islamic modernism. Islamic modernists sought to respond to, rather than react against, the challenge of Western imperialism. They proclaimed the need for Islamic reform through a process of reinterpretation and selective adaptation (Islamization) of Western ideas and technology. Islamic modernism sought to reinterpret Islam to demonstrate its compatibility with Western science and thought and to resist European colonialism and meet the changing circumstances of Muslim life through religious, legal, political, educational, and social reforms.

Some Muslims, however, rejected both conservative and modernist positions in favor of religious activism. The Muslim Brotherhood (Ikhwan al-Muslimin) of Egypt and the Jamaat-i Islami (Islamic Society) of the Indian subcontinent are prominent examples of modern neorevivalist Islamic organizations that linked religion to activism. Their leaders, the Muslim Brotherhood's Hasan al-Banna and Jamaat's Mawlana Abul Ala Mawdudi, were pious Muslims whose upbringing and education exposed them to modernist Islamic thought and Western learning. In contrast to Islamic modernists, who justified adopting Western ideas and institutions because they were compatible with Islam, al-Banna and Mawdudi sought to produce a new interpretation, or synthesis. Rather than leaving their societies, they organized their followers into an Islamically oriented community with a dynamic nucleus of leaders capable of transforming society from within. Joining thought to action, these leaders provided Islamic responses, both ideological and organizational, and inspired political as well as social activism.

Though anti-Western, the Muslim Brotherhood and Jamaat were not against modernization. They engaged in building modern organizations and institutions, provided modern educational and social welfare services, and used modern technology and mass communications to spread their message and to mobilize popular support. They addressed the problems of modernity, analyzing the relationship of Islam to nationalism, democracy, capitalism, Marxism, work, modern banking, education, law, women, Zionism, and international relations. The organizations established by al-Banna and Mawdudi remain vibrant today and have served as an example to others throughout much of the Muslim world.

CENTRAL DOCTRINES Like Jews and Christians, Muslims are monotheists. They believe in one God, Allah, who is the creator, sustainer, ruler, and judge of the universe. The word "Allah" appears in the Koran more than 2,500 times.

The word "Islam" means "submission" to the will of God and "peace," the interior peace that results from following God's will and creating a just society. Muslims must strive or struggle (jihad) in the path (*Shariah*) of God in order to implement his will on earth by working to establish a just society or to expand or defend the Muslim community.

Muslims believe that the Koran is the final, complete, literal, eternal, uncreated word of God, sent from heaven to the Prophet Muhammad as a guide for humankind (Koran 2:185). Thus, the Koran does not reveal God per se but, rather, God's will, or law, for all of creation. Although God is transcendent and thus unknowable, his nature is revealed in creation and his will in revelation, and his acts in history. God in the Koran is all-powerful and is the ultimate judge of humankind, but he is also merciful and compassionate.

The proclamation of God's mercy and compassion is made in the opening verse of the Koran, which begins, "In the Name of God, the Merciful, the Compassionate." In the Muslim world this phrase is used by pious believers at the beginning of letters, speeches, books, and articles. Many people recite the phrase as they begin to drive a car, eat a meal, or begin any task. God's mercy exists in dialectical tension with his role as the ultimate judge. Although it can be tempered by mercy for the repentant, justice requires punishment for those who disobey God's will. On Judgment Day all human beings are to be judged according to their deeds and either punished or rewarded on the basis of their obedience or disobedience.

Muslims believe that sacred scriptures exist because throughout history God has sent his guidance to prophets so that his will might be known and followed by humankind. Thus, Muslims believe not only in the Prophet Muhammad but also in the prophets of the Hebrew

Bible, including Abraham and Moses, and of the New Testament, John the Baptist and Jesus. Those prophets who have also brought God's revelation in the form of a sacred scripture or book—for example, Moses and the Torah and Jesus and the Gospels—are also called "messengers" of God. Thus, not all prophets are messengers, but messengers are also prophets. Jews and Christians are regarded as the People of the Book, a community of believers who received revelations, through prophets, in the form of scriptures, or revealed books, from God.

The Koran confirms the Torah and the Gospels as revelations from God, but Muslims believe that, after the deaths of the prophets, extraneous, nonbiblical beliefs infiltrated the Torah and the Gospels, altering the original, pure revelation. For example, the Koran declares an absolute monotheism, which means that associating anyone or anything with God is the one unforgivable sin of idolatry, or associationism. Muslims therefore do not believe in the Christian doctrine of the Trinity (one God in three persons), and although Muslims recognize Jesus as a prophet, they do not recognize him as God's son. Thus, Muslims believe that the Koran was sent as a correction, not as a nullification, or abrogation, of the Torah and the Gospels, and they see Islam as the oldest of the monotheistic faiths, since it represents both the original and the final revelation of God.

The Koranic universe consists of three realms—heaven, earth, and hell—in which there are two types of beings: humans and spirits. All beings are called to obedience to God. Spirits include angels, jinn, and devils. Angels are created from light, are immortal and sexless, and serve as the link between God and human beings. They serve as guardians, recorders, and messengers from God who transmit his message to human beings by communicating with prophets. Thus, the angel Gabriel is believed to have communicated the revelation of the Koran to Muhammad. Jinn, beings created by fire, are between angels and humans and can be either good or bad. Although invisible by nature, jinn can assume visible form. Like human beings, they are to be rewarded or punished in the afterlife. Jinn are often portrayed as magical beings, such as genies, as in the story of Aladdin and his lamp. Devils are fallen angels or jinn that tempt human beings torn between the forces of good and evil. Satan (*shaytan*, or Iblis), leader of the devils, represents evil, which is defined as disobedience to God. Satan's fall was caused by his refusal to prostrate himself before Adam upon God's command.

Because God breathed his spirit into Adam, the first human being, humans enjoy a special status as God's representatives on earth. The Koran teaches that God gave the earth to human beings as a trust so that they can implement his will. Although Muslims believe in the Fall of Adam and Eve in the Garden of Eden, in contrast to Christianity there is no doctrine of an inherited original sin and no belief in a vicarious suffering or atonement for humankind. The punishment of Adam and Eve is believed to result from their own personal act of disobedience to God. Each person is held responsible for his or her own actions. Human beings are mortal because of the human condition, not because of sin or the Fall of Adam and Eve. Sin is the result of an act of disobedience rather than a state of being. In Islam the Fall demonstrates human sin, God's mercy, and human repentance. Islam emphasizes the need to repent by returning to the straight path of God. The Koran does not emphasize shame, disgrace, or guilt but, rather, the ongoing human struggle—jihad—to do what is right and just.

A Muslim's obligation to be God's servant and to spread his message is both an individual and a community obligation. The community is bound not by family or tribal ties but by a common faith, which must be acted out and implemented. The primary emphasis is upon obeying God as prescribed by Islamic law, which contains guidelines for both the individual and the community. In contrast to Christianity, in which theology is the queen of the sciences, for Islam, as for Judaism, the primary religious science is law. Christianity therefore emphasizes orthodoxy (correct doctrine or belief), while Islam, as witnessed by the Five Pillars (fundamental observances), emphasizes orthopraxy (correct action).

Many Muslims describe Islam as "a total way of life." They believe that religion cannot be separated from social and political life, since religion informs every action a person takes. The Koran provides many passages that emphasize the relationship of religion to the state and society. Muslims see themselves as God's representatives, with a divine mandate to establish his rule on earth in order to create a moral and just society. The Muslim community is thus seen as a political entity, as proclaimed in the Koran 49:13, which teaches that God "made you into nations and tribes." Like Jews and Christians before them, Muslims believe that they have been called into a covenant with God, making them a community of believers who must serve as an example

Islamic Law

Islamic law, which includes requirements for worship as well as for social transactions, has been seen as providing the ideal blueprint for the believer who asks, "What should I do?" The law covers regulations for religious rituals and for such social transactions as marriage, divorce, and inheritance and sets standards for penal and international law. Traditionally religious scholars (ulama) and judges, courts, or governments have been responsible for elaborating and applying the law.

Sunni Muslims recognize four official sources of law: (1) the Koran, which contains moral directives; (2) the *sunnah* (example) of Muhammad as recorded in stories or traditions describing his activities, illustrating Islamic faith in practice and explaining Koranic principles; (3) *qiyas,* reasoning by analogy, used by scholars facing a new situation or problem when no clear text can be found in the Koran or *sunnah*; and (4) consensus (*ijma*), which originated with a reported saying of Muhammad, "My community will never agree on an error," which came to mean that consensus among religious scholars could determine the permissibility of an action.

Concern for justice led to the development of subsidiary legal principles: equity (*istihsan*), which permits exceptions to strict, or literal, legal reasoning, and public interest (*maslaha*) or human welfare, which give judges flexibility in arriving at just and equitable decisions. Shiites also include collections of the traditions of Ali, who they believe was the first caliph to succeed Muhammad, and of other imams, the ruling descendants of Muhammad through Ali, whom they regard as supreme authorities and legal interpreters.

The diverse geographic, social, historical, and cultural contexts in which jurists have written also account for differences in Islamic law. Many ulama, representing conservative strains in Islam, continue to equate God's divinely revealed law (Shariah) with legal manuals developed by early law schools. Reformers, however, call for changes in laws that are the products of social custom and human reasoning, saying that duties and obligations to God (worship) are unchanging but that social obligations to one's fellow man reflect changing circumstances. They reclaim the right of *ijtihad* (independent reasoning) to reinterpret Islam to meet modern social needs.

to other nations (2:143): "You are the best community evolved for mankind, enjoining what is right and forbidding what is wrong" (3:110).

Social justice is a central teaching of the Koran, with all believers equal before God. The equality of believers forms the basis of a just society that is to counterbalance the oppression of the weak and economic exploitation. Muhammad, who was orphaned at an early age and who witnessed the exploitation of orphans, the poor, and women in Meccan society, was especially sensitive to their plight. Some of the strongest passages in the Koran condemn exploitation and champion social justice. Throughout history the mission to create a moral and just social order has provided a rationale for Islamic activist and revivalist movements, both mainstream and extremist.

In response to European colonialism and industrialization, issues of social justice came to the forefront of

Muslim societies in the early twentieth century. The influx of large numbers of peasants from the countryside into urban areas in many developing countries created social and demographic tensions. In Egypt, for example, the Muslim Brotherhood, founded in 1928, emerged as a major social movement whose Islamic mission included a religious solution to poverty and assistance to the dispossessed and downtrodden. Its founder, Hasan al-Banna, taught a message of social and economic justice, preaching particularly to the poor and uneducated. In al-Banna's vision Islam was not just a philosophy, religion, or cultural trend but also a social movement seeking to improve all areas of life, not only those that were inherently religious. That is, rather than being simply a belief system, Islam was a call to social action.

In the contemporary era emphasis on Islam's message of social justice by Islamic movements, both moderate and militant, has been particularly powerful in gaining adherents from poorer and less advantaged groups in such countries as Algeria and Indonesia. In Israel and Palestine, and in Lebanon, groups like Hamas and Hezbollah devote substantial resources to social welfare activities and call for the empowerment of the poor and weak. They teach that social justice can be achieved only if the poor rise up against their oppressive conditions.

MORAL CODE OF CONDUCT The Shariah (Islamic law) provides a blueprint of principles and values for an ideal society. At its core are the Five Pillars of Islam, which unite all Muslims in their common belief. Following the pillars involves a Muslim's mind, body, time, energy, and wealth. Meeting the obligations required by the pillars translates beliefs into actions, reinforces an everyday awareness of God's existence and presence, and reminds Muslims of their membership in a worldwide community of believers.

The first pillar is the declaration of faith. A Muslim is one who bears witness, who testifies that "There is no god but God [Allah] and Muhammad is the messenger of God." This statement, known as the *shahadah,* is pronounced and heard 14 times a day by those who meet the requirement of praying five times daily, and it is repeated at many other occasions in a Muslim's life. To become a Muslim, one must make only this brief and simple declaration, or profession, of faith.

The first part of the declaration reflects absolute monotheism, Islam's uncompromising belief in the oneness, or unity, of God (*tawhid*). Associating anything else with God is idolatry, considered the one unforgivable sin. To avoid any possible idolatry resulting from the depiction of figures, for example, Islamic religious art tends to use calligraphy, geometric forms, and arabesque designs and is thus abstract rather than representational.

The second part of the declaration emphasizes that Muhammad is not only a prophet but also a messenger of God, the one who received a book of revelation from him. For Muslims, Muhammad is the last and final prophet, who serves as a model for the community through his life. Unlike Jesus, however, Muhammad is held to have been only human, although he is believed to have been a perfect man, a follower of God. Muslim's efforts to follow Muhammad's example in their private and public conduct reflect the emphasis of Islam on religious observance, or practice, that is expressed in the remaining pillars.

The second pillar of Islam is prayer, or worship (*salat*). Throughout the world Muslims worship five times a day (daybreak, noon, mid-afternoon, sunset, and evening), sanctifying their entire day as they remember to find guidance in God. In many Muslim countries reminders to pray, or "calls to prayer," echo across the rooftops. Aided by a megaphone from high atop a mosque's minaret, a muezzin calls all Muslims to prayer. Modern technology has also provided novel audio and visual reminders to pray, including special wristwatches, mosque-shaped clocks, and a variety of computer programs.

Prayer is preceded by a series of ablutions, which symbolize the purity of mind and body required for worshiping God. Facing the holy city of Mecca, Islam's spiritual homeland where the Prophet was born and received God's revelation, Muslims recite passages from the Koran and glorify God as they stand, bow, kneel, touch the ground with their foreheads, and sit. Muslims can pray in any clean environment, in a mosque or at home or at work, alone or in a group, indoors or outside. Although not required, it is considered preferable and more meritorious to pray with others, thus demonstrating and reinforcing Muslim brotherhood, equality, and solidarity. Regardless of race or language, all Muslims pray in Arabic. After a formal ritual prayer, individuals may offer personal prayers (*dua*) of petition or thanksgiving. Each week on Friday, the Muslim Sabbath, the noon prayer is a congregational prayer (*juma*) at a mosque or Islamic center.

The third pillar of Islam is called the *zakat,* a tithe or almsgiving. *Zakat,* which means "purification," and *salat,* or worship, are often mentioned in the same Koranic verse, reinforcing their significance. As an early Muslim observed, "Prayer carries us half-way to God; fasting brings us to the door of His praises; almsgiving procures for us admission."

By caring for the poor, Muslims as individuals, and the Muslim community collectively, demonstrate their concern and care for their own. It is in this spirit that *zakat* can be viewed as a social responsibility, combating poverty and preventing the excessive accumulation of wealth. The redistribution of wealth also underscores the Muslim belief that everything ultimately belongs to God. Human beings are simply caretakers, or vice-regents, for God's property, which must be fairly allocated within the broader community.

Thus, *zakat* is not viewed as voluntary giving, as charity, but, rather, as an act of individual self-purification and as a social obligation, reflecting Islam's emphasis upon social justice for the poor and vulnerable in society. Payment of the tithe purifies both the soul of the person and what is given. It reminds Muslims that their wealth is a trust from God. *Zakat* expresses worship of, and thanksgiving to, God by meeting the needs of the less fortunate members of the community. It functions as an informal type of social security in a Muslim society and resembles forms of tithing found in Judaism and Christianity.

Paid during Ramadan, the ninth month of the Islamic lunar calendar and the month of fasting, *zakat* requires an annual contribution of 2.5 percent of a person's total wealth and assets, not merely a percentage of annual income. Original Islamic law stipulated clearly and specifically those areas subject to *zakat*—silver and gold, animals, and agricultural products. Today modern forms of wealth, such as bank accounts, stocks, and bonds, are included.

There are other religious taxes in Islam. In Shiite Islam the *khums,* meaning "one-fifth," is an obligatory tax paid to religious leaders. Among the many forms of almsgiving common to all Muslims is the *sadaqah,* voluntary alms given to the poor, in thanksgiving to God, or to ward off danger. It is the *zakat,* however, that is the obligatory form of almsgiving for all Muslims.

The fourth pillar of Islam is the fast of Ramadan, which occurs during the month in which the first revelation of the Koran came to Muhammad. The primary emphasis of fasting is not simply on abstinence and self-mortification but, rather, on spiritual self-discipline, reflection on human frailty and dependence on God, and performance of good works in response to the less fortunate. During this month-long fast Muslims whose health permit abstain from dawn to sunset from food, drink, and sexual activity. Those who are sick, pregnant, or weakened by old age are exempted. Muslims on a journey may postpone fasting and make it up at another time. Ramadan is also a special time to recite or listen to the recitation of the Koran. This is popularly done by dividing the Koran into 30 portions to be recited throughout the days of the month. Near the end of Ramadan, on the 27th day, Muslims commemorate the Night of Power, on which Muhammad received the first of God's revelations.

The fifth pillar, and probably the best known among non-Muslims, is the pilgrimage, or hajj, to Mecca in Saudi Arabia, which occurs about 60 days after the end of Ramadan. Every adult Muslim who is physically and financially able is required to make the pilgrimage, becoming a person totally at God's service at least once in his or her lifetime. Many who are able to do so make the pilgrimage more often. Muslim tradition teaches that God forgives the sins of those who perform the hajj with devotion and sincerity. Thus, many elderly make the pilgrimage with the hope that they will die cleansed of their sins.

Every year more than 2 million believers, representing a tremendous diversity of cultures and languages, travel from all over the world to the Al-Haram Mosque in Mecca to form one community living their faith. Just as Muslims are united five times each day as they face Mecca in worship, so the pilgrimage to the spiritual center of Islam enables them to experience the unity, breadth, and diversity of the Islamic community. Muslims who have made the hajj are entitled to add the prefix "pilgrim," *al-hajj* or *hajji,* to their names, which many proudly do. Like *salat,* the pilgrimage requires ritual purification, symbolized by the wearing of white garments, which represent purity as well as the unity and equality of all believers, an equality that transcends class, wealth, privilege, power, nationality, race, or color.

Jihad is sometimes referred to as the sixth pillar of Islam, although it has no such official status. In its most general meaning jihad pertains to the difficulty and complexity of living a good life by struggling against the evil in oneself, by being virtuous and moral, by making a serious effort as individuals and as a community to do good works and help reform society, and by fulfilling the universal mission of Islam to spread its community through the preaching of Islam or the writing of religious tracts, these latter referred to as "jihad of the tongue" and "jihad of the pen." Today jihad may also be used to describe the personal struggle to keep the fast of Ramadan, to fulfill family responsibilities, or to clean up a neighborhood, fight drugs, or work for social justice. In addition, jihad includes the sacred struggle for, or the defense of, Islam or the Muslim community, popularly referred to as "holy war." The two broad meanings of jihad, nonviolent and violent, are contrasted in a well-known Prophetic tradition that reports Muhammad returning from battle to tell his followers, "We return from the lesser jihad [warfare] to the greater jihad." The greater jihad is the more difficult and more important struggle against ego, selfishness, greed, and evil.

Despite the fact that jihad is not supposed to include aggressive (offensive as opposed to defensive) warfare, this has occurred throughout history. Muslim rulers have used jihad to legitimate their wars of imperial expansion, often with the approval of religious leaders or scholars (ulama). Religious extremist groups assassinated Egypt's President Anwar as-Sadat in 1981, and they have slaughtered innocent civilians in suicide bombings in Israel and Palestine and murdered thousands in acts of global terrorism in the United States, Saudi Arabia, Morocco, Indonesia, and other countries. At the same time, wars of resistance or liberation have been fought as jihads in Afghanistan against Soviet occupation, in Bosnia and Herzegovina, in Kosovo, and, in the eyes of many Muslims, in Palestine and Israel, Jammu and Kashmir, and Chechnya.

In addition to the Five Pillars of Islam, the Koran provides Muslims with other rules of conduct. Consuming pork and alcohol is forbidden, and there are strict prohibitions against gambling, prostitution, adultery, murder, and other criminal offenses. A host of regulations about the just treatment of debtors, widows, the poor, and orphans emphasizes the key importance of social justice. Those who practice usury are strongly rebuked. In addition, both men and women are required to dress and to act modestly, and they are encouraged to marry and procreate. Thus, Islam provides a set of common beliefs, values, and practices that are to guide Muslim life.

SACRED BOOKS The Koran—"recitation" in Arabic— is the Muslim scripture. It contains the revelations received by the Prophet Muhammad from God through the angel Gabriel over a period of 23 years, beginning when Muhammad was 40 years old and continuing until his death in 632. For Muslims, Muhammad, who was illiterate, was neither the author nor the editor of the Koran. Rather, he functioned as God's intermediary, reciting the revelations he received. The Koran, therefore, is the eternal, literal word of God, preserved in the Arabic language and in the order in which it was revealed.

Muslims believe that the Koran's 114 chapters (surahs) were initially preserved in oral and written form during the lifetime of Muhammad. The entire text was collected in an official standardized version some 15 or 20 years after his death. The Koran is approximately four-fifths the size of the New Testament. Its chapters were assembled and ordered from the longest to the shortest, not thematically. This format proves frustrating to some non-Muslims, who find the text disjointed. The organization of the Koran, however, enables a believer simply to open the text at random and to start re-

citing at the beginning of any paragraph, since each represents a lesson to be learned and reflected upon.

The recitation of the Koran is central to a Muslim's life, and many Muslims memorize the Koran in its entirety. Recitation reinforces what Muslims see as the miracle of hearing the actual word of God expressed by the human voice. There are many examples throughout history of those who were drawn to, and converted to, Islam upon hearing the Koran recited.

SACRED SYMBOLS Because of the sensitivity in Islam to representational sacred art, lest any human being or physical object become the subject of worship or idolatry, major symbols are more limited in scope than in many other religions, including Christianity and Hinduism. The Kaaba, Dome of the Rock, and calligraphy are among the more prominent religious symbols in Islam.

The Kaaba is considered the most sacred space in the Muslim world and the spiritual center of the earth, the point Muslims turn toward when they pray and the direction toward which their heads point in burial. It is thought to mark the location where the earth was created. The Kaaba symbolizes an earthly image of the divine throne in heaven, and it is therefore believed that actions that take place at the Kaaba, such as circumambulation, are duplicated in heaven at the throne of God.

Another major symbol is the Dome of the Rock in Jerusalem, popularly referred to as the Mosque of Umar. Jerusalem first came under Muslim rule in 638, during Umar's reign. The shrine itself, however, was built later, in around 692, by the caliph Abd al-Malik ibn Marwan. It was constructed over the rock on the Temple Mount, where Muslim tradition holds that the Prophet Muhammad departed on his Night Journey to heaven. (The Temple Mount itself is also the site of the Temple of Solomon and of the Christian Dome of the Holy Sepulcher, and is thus sacred to all three great monotheistic traditions.) The octagonal shaped shrine, with its golden dome, dominates the skyline. It is majestically decorated inside and out with some 240 yards of calligraphic designs consisting of Koranic inscriptions. Among Muslims today pictures and representations of the Dome of the Rock are probably second in popularity only to those of the Kaaba, both because it symbolizes the Prophet's Night Journey and is located in the third holiest city of Islam and because it has become a popular symbol for the liberation of Jerusalem and Palestine.

Arabic calligraphy originated from the desire for a script worthy of divine revelation in copying the Koran.

Because of its association with the Koran, calligraphy assumed a sacred character and became the highest form of art. Since Islamic art does not represent human forms, calligraphy is used to capture and symbolize meaning and message. Thus, for example, Allah written in calligraphic form became a powerful symbol representing the divine. It is also common to see the names of Allah and Muhammad, or of Allah, Muhammad, and Ali, written in calligraphy as religious symbols, whether on paper, in plaster on walls, or on such ornamental objects as plates or medals. Other popular phrases, such as the *shahadah* (There is no god but God and Muhammad is the messenger of God), Allahu Akbar (God is great), or Ya Rabb (the Lord), are also depicted in calligraphic art that adorns walls and buildings throughout the Islamic world.

EARLY AND MODERN LEADERS Throughout history Islam has been integral to politics and civilization. Intellectuals and writers, religious rulers and activists have often exercised leadership and had a significant impact on government and society. The relationships of faith to power, reason, science, and society have been enduring and interconnected concerns and issues.

The period of Muhammad and his first four successors, the Rightly Guided Caliphs (reigned 632–61), has remained an ideal to which most Muslims look for inspiration and renewal. During the reign of the Rightly Guided Caliphs, Arab Muslim rule over the heartlands of the Middle East was established. Each of these caliphs had been a close companion to Muhammad, and all belonged to the Quraysh tribe. The period of their rule is considered the golden age of Islam, when rulers were closely guided by Muhammad's practices. Abu Bakr, the first caliph (reigned 632–34), had been an early convert who was also Muhammad's close advisor and father-in-law. A man respected for his piety and sagacity, Abu Bakr had been the one appointed to lead the Friday communal prayer in Muhammad's absence. After Muhammad's death Abu Bakr was selected as Muhammad's successor by the majority of Muslims, called Sunnis, or followers of the *sunnah* (example) of the Prophet, based on their belief that leadership should pass to the most qualified person.

The second caliph, Umar (reigned 634–44), seen as the dominant personality among the four, was responsible for establishing many of the fundamental institutions of the classical Islamic state. During the reign of the personally pious third caliph, Uthman (reigned 644–56), the Koran was collected and put into its final form. Uthman's lack of strength in handling unscrupulous relatives, however, led to his murder by malcontents and to a period of disorder and civil war. The fourth caliph, Ali (reigned 656–61), was the cousin and son-in-law of Muhammad and the first male to convert to Islam. Ali, who was also a distinguished judge and brave warrior, was the first caliph recognized by Shiite Muslims, who believed that succession should be based on heredity and who thus considered the first three caliphs to be usurpers. Ali's political discourse, sermons, letters, and sayings have served as the Shiite framework for Islamic government. His rule was marked by political strife, however, and he was assassinated while praying in a mosque. Shiite Muslims recognize only Ali, as well as the brief reign of Ali's son Hussein (reigned 661). Following the Rightly Guided Caliphs, the dynasty of the Umayyads, who reigned from 661 to 750, was established to became a powerful Arab military aristocracy.

Throughout the following centuries, from the rise of Islam to the modern period, Islamic empires, sultanates, and movements flourished. They were led or influenced by rulers and military men like Saladin and Suleiman the Magnificent; theologians, historians, and legal scholars like Muhammad al-Ghazali and Ibn Taymiyya; and leaders of revivalist movements like Muhammad ibn Abd al-Wahhab in the Arabian Peninsula, the Mahdi of the Sudan, and Uthman dan Fodio of Nigeria.

From the late nineteenth century Islamic movements, both mainstream and extremist, have sought to revitalize and reform Islam. They have been influenced by a core group of Islamic intellectual-activists. Two in particular, Islamic modernism and Islamic revivalism, or "fundamentalism," have been particularly influential. Both have sought a modern reformation but with somewhat differing visions and styles.

Among the more important modern reformers were Muhammad Abduh (1849–1905) in the Middle East and Sayyid Ahmad Khan (1817–98) and Muhammad Iqbal (1876–1938) in South Asia. The Egyptian Abduh received a traditional religious education. He taught at Cairo's Al-Azhar University, renowned throughout the Islamic world as the principal center for Islamic education and orthodoxy. Abduh also taught at the newly created Dar al-Ulum College, which provided a modern education for Al-Azhar students who wanted to qualify for government positions. In the 1870s Abduh became an enthusiastic follower of Jamal al-Din al-Afghani (1838–97), born in Iran and educated in Iran and then India. Al-Afghani, an activist who is known as the father of Muslim nationalism, traveled from India to Egypt to promote Islamic intellectual reform as a prerequisite to overcoming European colonial influence and rule and achieving independence. In the 1880s Abduh and Al-Afghani were exiled to Paris for their participation in a nationalist uprising against British and French influence in Egypt. When he returned to Cairo in 1888, Abduh accepted the existing political situation and devoted his energies to religious, educational, and social reform.

A religious scholar, Abduh reinterpreted scripture and tradition to provide an Islamic rationale for modern reforms. When Abduh became mufti, head of Egypt's religious court system, in 1899, he introduced changes in the Shariah courts. As a judge, he interpreted and applied Islam to modern conditions, using a methodology that combined a return to the fundamental sources of Islam with an acceptance of modern rational thought. Critical of many religious leaders' inability to address modern problems, Abduh also modernized the curriculum at Al-Azhar University, whose graduates became religious leaders throughout the Muslim world, to change their training and intellectual outlook. Abduh called for educational and social reforms to improve and protect the status of women, supporting their access to education and arguing that the Koranic marriage ideal was monogamy, not polygamy.

On the Indian subcontinent, in what is today Pakistan, India, and Bangladesh, Sayyid Ahmad Khan and, later, Muhammad Iqbal were prominent voices for Islamic reform. Khan responded to the fall of the Mughal Empire. The Sepoy Mutiny against British colonial influence and de facto rule became the pretext for the British to officially take charge, and it left the Muslim community, largely blamed by the British, in disarray. Initially overwhelmed by the chaos and devastation, Khan had considered leaving India. Instead, he chose to stay and rebuild the Muslim community. In contrast to Al-Afghani and others, he argued that Indian Muslims should accept British rule as a political reality and reform their community within these limits. He wished to respond both to Muslim reform and to the criticisms and attacks leveled at Islam by Christian missionaries.

In the tradition of past Islamic revivalists, Khan claimed the right to reinterpret Islam. He rejected the classical formulations of Islam fashioned by the ulama and sought to return to the original Islam of the Koran

and Muhammad. Arguing that Islam and science were compatible, he advocated a new theological formulation, or reformulation, of Islam. To implement his ideas and produce a new generation of Muslim leaders, he established the Muhammadan Anglo-Oriental College at Aligarh, India, in 1874. Renamed Aligarh University in 1920, it was modeled on Cambridge University, with a course of studies that combined the best of a European curriculum with a modernist interpretation of Islam. He and his disciples published journals that dealt with religious reform and women's rights in Islam.

In the 1930s three trailblazers—Hasan al-Banna (1906–49) and Sayyid Qutb (1906–66) of the Muslim Brotherhood in Egypt and Mawlana Abul Ala Mawdudi (1903–79) of the Jamaat-i-Islami (Islamic Society) in South Asia—had an incalculable impact on the development of Islamic movements throughout the Muslim world. Both organizations constructed a worldview based on an interpretation of Islam that informed social and political activism. These men were the architects of contemporary Islamic revivalism, their ideas and methods studied and emulated by scholars and activists from the Sudan to Indonesia. The two movements emerged at a time when the Muslim world remained weak and in decline, much of it occupied and ruled by foreign powers. Egypt was occupied by Britain from 1882 to 1952, and the Indian subcontinent was ruled by Britain from 1857 to 1947, when modern India and Pakistan achieved independence.

Although the Muslim Brotherhood and the Jamaat have been called fundamentalist, they were quite modern, though not necessarily Western, in their ideological agenda, organization, and activities. Rather than fleeing the modern world, they sought to engage and control it, but on their own terms.

Hasan al-Banna, a schoolteacher, was born in a small town outside Cairo. His early traditional religious education was supplemented by his father, who had studied at Al-Azhar University during the time of Muhammad Abduh. After studying at a local teacher-training college, al-Banna went to Cairo to study at Dar al-Ulum College, with its modern curriculum. There he came into contact with disciples of Abduh and with the reformist thought of Abduh and Al-Afghani. After completing his studies, al-Banna took a teaching position at a primary school in Ismailia. Convinced that only through a return to Islam could the Muslim community revitalize itself and its fortunes and throw off European colonial domination, he ran discussion groups and, in

1928, established the Muslim Brotherhood (Ikhwan al-Muslimin).

Mawlana Abul Ala Mawdudi was born in Aurangabad in central India. His father supervised his early education in religious disciplines. It was only later that Mawdudi learned English and studied modern subjects. He turned to a career in journalism and quickly became editor of the newspaper of India's Association of Ulama. Mawdudi also became active in the Khilafat movement, which called for a restoration of the caliphate, and the All-India National Congress. He soon became convinced, however, that the identity, unity, and future of Indian Muslims were threatened not only by European imperialism but also by Hindu and Muslim nationalism. Mawdudi believed that a gradual social, rather than a violent political, Islamization of society from below was needed to create an Islamic state and society. He became editor of the journal *Exegesis of the Quran,* in which he published articles on his Islamic alternative. In 1938 he moved to Lahore (today in Pakistan) at the invitation of Muhammad Iqbal and, in 1941, organized the Jamaat-i-Islami (Islamic Society).

Both al-Banna and Mawdudi believed that their societies were dominated by, and dependent on, the West, both politically and culturally. Both men advocated an "Islamic alternative" to conservative religious leaders and modern Western secular-oriented elites. The ulama were generally regarded as passé, a religious class whose fossilized Islam and co-option by governments were major causes for the backwardness of the Islamic community. Modernists were seen as having traded away the very soul of Muslim society out of their blind admiration for the West.

For decades the symbol of revolutionary Islam was Ayatollah Ruhollah Khomeini (1902–89), leader of Iran's Islamic revolution of 1978–79. Born in the village of Khomein, he studied in Qum, a major center of Islamic learning, and then taught Islamic law and theology. In the mid-1960s Khomeini spoke out against the policies of the shah, Mohammad Reza Pahlavi, delivering fiery sermons that denounced laws or imperial decrees that directly affected religious endowments, extended the vote to women, and granted diplomatic immunity to the American military. He condemned Iran's increasingly authoritarian and repressive government, the growing secularization and Westernization of Iranian society, and the country's relationship with the United States and Israel. He was forced to live in exile from 1964 to 1979, first in Turkey, then in Iraq, and finally in France. Increasingly during the 1970s, Khomeini moved from calling for reform to advocating the overthrow of the Pahlavi dynasty, which he denounced as un-Islamic and illegitimate, and its replacement with an Islamic republic. His calls from exile, distributed secretly through audiocassettes and pamphlets, might have remained marginal had it not been for the increasing broad-based opposition to the shah and his repressive response. Khomeini, who had early on been a voice of protest and opposition and was relatively free to speak out in exile, attracted a broad and diverse following: men and women, religious and secular intellectuals and students, journalists, politicians, liberal nationalists, socialists, and Marxists. However different, all were united in their opposition to the shah and by the desire for a new government.

After the revolution Khomeini surprised many when, in setting up an Islamic republic, he moved away from a constitutional government in which the clergy would advise on religious matters to advance the notion of clerical rule, a clergy-dominated government with himself at the apex as the supreme jurist. For a decade Khomeini, as supreme guardian of the republic, oversaw the implementation of his Islamically legitimated vision domestically and the export of Iran's revolution internationally.

MAJOR THEOLOGIANS AND AUTHORS Islamic religion and civilization have produced many great intellectuals and writers, including philosophers, theologians, legal scholars, and scientists, who have sought to understand their faith and its relationship to the world. From earliest times a key issue has been the relationship of reason to revelation.

Yaqub ibn Ishaq as-Sabah al-Kindi (795–866), known in Europe as "the philosopher of the Arabs," was among the early great Islamic philosophers. A prolific, encyclopedic author, he made significant contributions to philosophy, medicine, astronomy, mathematics, chemistry, and the theory of music. Al-Kindi drew heavily on the Greek philosophers Plato and Aristotle and was especially influenced by Neoplatonism. He championed inquiry into the source of all being and unity, which, he believed, reinforced the Muslim belief in the existence of God, the world's creation, and the truth of prophetic revelation. In the more than 300 volumes attributed to him, al-Kindi addressed a wide range of classical learning that encompassed logic, metaphysics, ethics, and astronomy and developed a scientific and philosophical vocabulary that influenced his successors. Like many who followed him, he resolved apparent contradictions between reason and revelation by resorting to an allegorical, rather than a literal, interpretation of the Koran.

The Persian Abu Bakr ar-Razi (865–923) was also a great admirer of Greek philosophy but was diametrically opposed to al-Kindi on the relationship between philosophy and revelation. For ar-Razi revelation was superfluous, since only reason was needed to lead to truth and the development of morals. His concept of the five eternal principles (the creator, soul, matter, space, and time), some of which had a basis in Plato, led to his designation as Islam's greatest Platonist. Ar-Razi incorporated Plato's concepts of the soul, creation in time, and the transmigration of the soul into his own philosophical system.

Even more influential in shaping the direction of Islamic thought was Abu Nasr al-Farabi (878–950), from northern Persia, who was known as the founder of Islamic Neoplatonism and political philosophy. Drawing upon the Koran, al-Farabi also developed the terminology of Arab scholasticism, which was adapted into Latin and later used by the great Christian theologian Thomas Aquinas. Al-Farabi rejected the Sufi concept of a solitary life, believing, like Aristotle, that, because man was a political animal, happiness could be achieved only within society, within a "virtuous city" somewhat like Plato's ideal state. But as a Muslim, al-Farabi saw such a state as embodied in the ideal of Muhammad and the early Muslim community.

Al-Farabi's thought was further developed by the most famous Neoplatonist of Islam, Ibn Sina (Avicenna in Latin; 980–1037), the renowned physician and philosopher of the Middle Ages whose works became widely known in both the East and the West. Born in Bukhara, he worked as a physician, serving as court physician for a number of princes, and he traveled widely. Ibn Sina's Canon on Medicine was translated into Latin and remained a major text in Europe until the seventeenth century. His influence and reputation earned him the title "prince of the physicians." He wrote with authority on medicine, physics, logic, metaphysics, psychology, and astronomy.

Ibn Sina, who drew on the writings of both Plato and Aristotle, credited al-Farabi with giving him the first keys that led to his understanding Aristotle. He completed Aristotle's idea of the prime mover, developed the philosophy of monotheism, and taught that

creation was a timeless process of divine emanation. His rationalist thought was condemned by the religious establishment.

Abu Hamid Muhammad al-Ghazali (1058–1111), a philosopher, theologian, jurist, and mystic, was an extraordinary figure, remembered as the "renewer of Islam," who deeply affected the religion's later development. Born and raised in Iran, al-Ghazali received a first-class Islamic education. In Baghdad he became a renowned lawyer and wrote a series of books. Among the most influential was The Incoherence of the Philosophers, in which he refuted Avicenna, maintaining that, while reason was effective in mathematics and logic, applying it to theological and metaphysical truths led to confusion and threatened the fabric of faith. Al-Ghazali's teachings brought him fame and fortune. After several years, however, he experienced a crisis of faith and conscience, both spiritual and psychological, which rendered him unable to speak or function professionally. He withdrew from life and spent many years traveling, practicing Sufism, and reflecting. During this time he wrote what many consider his greatest work, The Revivication of the Religious Sciences, his great synthesis of law, theology, and mysticism.

Al-Ghazali lived in a turbulent time, when conflicting schools of thought emphasizing faith or reason or mysticism contended with one another, each claiming to be the only authentic view of Islam. "To refute," he said, "one must understand." His comprehensive knowledge of all of the schools and arguments, as well as of philosophy, theology, law, and mysticism, enabled him to establish a credible synthesis of the intellectual and spiritual currents of the time. He presented law and theology in terms that religious scholars could accept, while grounding the disciplines in direct religious experience and the interior devotion seen in Sufism, which he helped to place within the life of the Muslim community. He tempered rationalism by an emphasis on religious experience and love of God.

Because he criticized the blind acceptance of authority, and emphasized a thorough study of a discipline and objectivity of approach, al-Ghazali today receives considerable attention from both Muslim and Western scholars. His "modern" approach is seen in his focus on the essentials of religion, his willingness to entertain doubt and put it in perspective, and his concern for the ordinary believer.

Ibn Rushd (Averroës in Latin; 1126–98) was the greatest Aristotelian philosopher of the Muslim world.

His prominence and commentaries, which provided many Europeans in the medieval world with their only source of knowledge about Aristotle, led to his title "the commentator." His writings and ideas influenced Jewish and Christian thinkers such as Maimonides, Albertus Magnus, and Thomas Aquinas.

Born in Córdoba, Spain, Ibn Rushd sought to harmonize the Koran and revelation with philosophy and logic. Like Ibn Sina, he believed that there was no contradiction between religion and philosophy, although, while religion was the way of the masses, philosophy was the province of an intellectual elite. Some have called this a "two-truths" theory and labeled Ibn Rushd a "freethinker." But when he spoke of religion, Ibn Rushd, who recognized that the higher truth resided in revelation, was referring more specifically to the formulations of theology, the product of fallible human beings and theologians and thus subject to the limitations of language, and not to divine revelation itself.

Ibn Rushd's contributions in philosophy, theology, medicine, and Islamic jurisprudence were voluminous, comparable in comprehensiveness to the works of al-Farabi and Ibn Sina. His extensive influence in the West led to his condemnation by Muslim religious scholars opposed to the view that religious law and philosophy have the same goal and that creation is an eternal process. His intellectual stature, influence, and significance are demonstrated by the fact that European philosophers and theologians during the thirteenth century participated in major pro- and anti-Averroist battles.

Ibn Taymiyya (1268–1328) lived during one of the most disruptive periods of Islamic history, which saw the fall of Baghdad and the conquest of the Abbasid empire in 1258 by the Mongols. He was forced to flee with his family to Damascus, an experience that affected his attitude toward the Mongols throughout his life and made an otherwise conservative religious scholar a militant political activist. As with many who followed him, his writing and preaching earned him persecution and imprisonment. He combined ideas and action to express belief in the interconnectedness of religion, state, and society, thus exerting an influence on modern revivalist movements.

A professor of Hanbali law (Hanbali is the most conservative of the four Sunni schools), Ibn Taymiyya relied on a rigorous, literal interpretation of the sacred sources (the Koran and the examples of the Prophet and of the early Muslim community) for Islamic renewal and the reform of society. Like many who came after

him, he regarded the community at Medina as the model for an Islamic state. Ibn Taymiyya distinguished sharply between Islam and non-Islam (*dar al-Islam* and *dar al-harb*, respectively), the lands of belief and unbelief. In contrast to his vision of a close relationship between religion and the state, he made a sharp distinction between religion and culture. Although a pious Sufi, a practitioner of Islamic mysticism, he denounced as superstition such popular practices of his day as the worship of saints and the veneration of shrines and tombs.

Ibn Taymiyya's revolutionary ire was especially directed at the Mongols, who were locked in a jihad with the Muslim Mamluk rulers of Egypt. Despite their conversion to Islam, the Mongols continued to follow the code of laws of Genghis Khan instead of the Islamic law, the Shariah, and Ibn Taymiyya regarded them as no better than the polytheists of pre-Islamic Arabia. He issued a *fatwa* (legal opinion or judgment) that denounced them as unbelievers (*kafirs*) who were thus excommunicated (*takfir*). His *fatwa* established a precedent that has been used by contemporary religious extremists. Despite their claim to be Muslims, the Mongol's failure to implement Shariah rendered them, and by extension all Muslims who acted accordingly, apostates and hence the lawful object of jihad. Thus, "true" Muslims had the right, indeed duty, to revolt or wage jihad against such governments or individuals. Later generations—from the Wahhabi movement in Arabia to Sayyid Qutb in modern Egypt, from Islamic Jihad, the group that assassinated Egypt's President Anwar as-Sadat, to Osama bin Laden—would use the logic of Ibn Taymiyya's *fatwa* against the Mongols to call for a jihad against their "un-Islamic" Muslim rulers and elites and against the West.

The writings of Muhammad Iqbal (1873–1938) embodied the conflicting agendas of modernists. Educated at Government College in Lahore (now in Pakistan), he then studied in England and Germany, where he earned a law degree and a doctorate in philosophy. Iqbal's modern synthesis and reinterpretation of Islam combined the best of his Islamic heritage with the Western philosophy of Fichte, Hegel, Nietzsche, and Bergson. He was both an admirer and a critic of the West. Acknowledgment of the West's dynamic spirit, intellectual tradition, and technology was balanced by his sharp critique of European colonialism, the materialism and exploitation of capitalism, the atheism of Marxism, and the moral bankruptcy of secularism. Iqbal's reformist impulse and vision, embodied in his extensive writings and poetry, were succinctly summarized in *The Reconstruction of Religious Thought in Islam.*

Like other Islamic modernists, Iqbal rejected much of medieval Islam as static and stagnant, part of the problem and not the solution for a debilitated community. He saw Islam as emerging from 500 years of "dogmatic slumber" and compared the need for Islamic reform to the Reformation. Iqbal emphasized the need to reclaim the vitality and dynamism of early Islamic thought and practice, calling for a bold reinterpretation of Islam. Drawing on tradition, he sought to "rediscover" principles and values that would provide the basis for Islamic versions of such Western concepts and institutions as democracy and parliamentary government. He looked to the past to rediscover principles and values that could be reinterpreted to reconstruct an alternative Islamic model for modern Muslim society. Because of the centrality of such beliefs as the equality and brotherhood of believers, Iqbal concluded, democracy was the most important political ideal in Islam. He maintained that, although the seizure of power from Ali by Muawiyah, the founder of the Umayyad dynasty, had ended the period of the Rightly Guided Caliphs, led to the creation of dynastic governments, and prevented the realization of an Islamic democratic ideal, it remained the duty of the Muslim community to realize this goal.

It would be difficult to overestimate the role played by Sayyid Qutb (1906–66) on both mainstream and militant Islam. His journey from educated intellectual, government official, and admirer of the West to militant activist who condemned both the Egyptian and the U.S. governments and who defended the legitimacy of militant jihad has influenced and inspired many militants, from the assassins of Anwar as-Sadat to the followers of Osama bin Laden and al-Qaeda.

Qutb's interpretation of Islam grew out of the militant confrontation in the late 1950s and the 1960s between the repressive Egyptian state and the Muslim Brotherhood. Like Hasan al-Banna, Qutb had a modern education at Dar al-Ulum College. After graduation he became an official in the Ministry of Public Instruction as well as a poet and literary critic. A devout Muslim who had memorized the Koran as a child, he began to write on Islam and the Egyptian state. In 1948 he published *Islam and Social Justice,* in which he argued that Islam possessed its own social teachings and that Islamic socialism avoided both the pitfalls of Christianity's separation of religion and society and those of communism's atheism.

An admirer of Western literature, Qutb visited the United States in the late 1940s. It proved to be a turning point in his life, transforming an admirer into a severe critic of the West. His experiences in the United States produced a culture shock that convinced him of the moral decadence of the West and made him more religious. He was appalled by U.S. materialism, sexual permissiveness and promiscuity, the free use and abuse of alcohol, and racism, which he experienced personally because of his dark skin. Qutb felt betrayed when he saw what he considered to be anti-Arab and pro-Jewish coverage in U.S. newspapers and movies that fostered contempt for Muslims. Shortly after his return to Egypt, Qutb joined the Muslim Brotherhood. He quickly emerged as a major voice in the organization and, amid a growing confrontation with Gamal Abdel Nasser's repressive regime, its most influential ideologue. Imprisoned and tortured for alleged involvement in a failed attempt to assassinate Nasser, he became increasingly militant and radicalized, convinced that the Egyptian government was un-Islamic and must be overthrown.

A prolific author, Qutb published more than 40 books, many translated into Persian and English and still widely distributed. During 10 years of imprisonment, Qutb developed a revolutionary vision captured in his most influential tract, *Milestones,* which was used as evidence against him and led to his being sentenced to death. His ideas would reverberate loudly in the radical rhetoric of revolutionaries.

Like Ibn Taymiyya before him, Qutb sharply divided Muslim societies into two diametrically opposed camps: the forces of good and the forces of evil, those committed to the rule of God and those opposed, the party of God and the party of Satan. His teachings recast the world in black and white; there were no shades of gray. Since the creation of an Islamic government was a divine commandment, he argued, it was not simply an alternative but, rather, an imperative that Muslims must strive to implement or impose immediately. Qutb used the classical designation for pre-Islamic Arabian society, *jahiliyyah* (a period of ignorance), to paint and condemn all modern societies as un-Islamic and anti-Islamic. Given the authoritarian and repressive nature of the Egyptian government and many other governments in the Muslim world, Qutb concluded that change from within the system was futile and that Islam was on the brink of disaster. Jihad was the only way to implement the new Islamic order.

For Qutb jihad, as armed struggle in the defense of Islam against the injustice and oppression of anti-Islamic governments and the neocolonialism of the West and the East (Soviet Union), was incumbent upon all Muslims. There could be no middle ground. Qutb denounced Muslim governments and their Western, secular-oriented elites as atheists, against whom all true believers must wage holy war.

ORGANIZATIONAL STRUCTURE In general, Islam does not have an official organizational structure or hierarchy. It technically lacks an ordained clergy, and major religious rituals, such as prayers or marriage ceremonies, do not require a religious official. Over time, however, the early scholars of Islam, the ulama (the learned), became a clerical class, asserting their prerogative as the guardians and official interpreters of Islam and adopting a clerical form of dress. They became the primary scholars of law and theology, teachers in schools and universities or seminaries (madrasahs), judges, muftis, and lawyers, as well as the guardians and distributors of funds from religious endowments that provided support for such institutions as schools, hospitals, and hostels and for the poor. In time, in some Muslim countries, senior religious officials were appointed by governments with titles such as grand mufti. Some forms of Shiism, in particular the Twelvers (Ithna Ashari) of Iran and Iraq, developed a hierarchical system of religious officials and titles. Their senior leaders are called ayatollahs, and at the apex of the system are grand ayatollahs.

The Sufi orders, or brotherhoods of Islamic mystics, also developed an institutional structure and organization of disciples, followers, and helpers led by the master (pir or shaykh), who functions as the spiritual leader and head of the community. Some of the more prominent brotherhoods developed international networks. At times the heads of Sufi brotherhoods also became military leaders. When these religious and social organizations turned militant, as with such eighteenth- and nineteenth-century jihad movements as the Mahdi in the Sudan, the Fulani in Nigeria, and the Sanusi in Libya, they fought colonial powers and created Islamic states.

HOUSES OF WORSHIP AND HOLY PLACES The word "mosque" comes from the Arabic masjid (place for ritual prostration). For many Muslims, Friday at a mosque is a day of congregational prayer, religious education ("Sunday school"), and socializing. The atmosphere is one of tranquility and reflection and also of relaxation.

A visitor to a mosque may see people chatting quietly or napping on the carpets, as well as praying and reading the Koran.

The mosque's main prayer area is a large open space adorned with Oriental carpets. When they pray, Muslims face the mihrab, an ornamental arched niche set into the wall, which indicates the direction of Mecca. Near the mihrab is the minbar, a raised wooden platform, like a pulpit, that is similar to the one the Prophet Muhammad used when giving sermons. Prayer leaders deliver sermons from the steps of the minbar. Most mosques also have a spot set aside, away from the main area, where Muslims can cleanse themselves before they pray.

Throughout history, wherever Muslims have settled in sufficient numbers, they have made erecting a mosque an important priority. In the United States, for example, the construction of mosques, which serve as community centers as well as places of worship, has increased greatly. More than 2,100 mosques and Islamic centers serve a diverse Muslim community in the United States, whose membership is often drawn along such ethnic or racial identities as Arab, South Asian, Turkish, and African-American. Mosques of various sizes are located in small towns and villages as well as major American cities.

In addition to individual worship and the Friday congregational prayer, mosques are often the sites for Koranic recitations and retreats, especially during the fast of Ramadan, and as centers for the collection and distribution of charitable contributions (zakat). Muslim pilgrims visit their mosques before they leave for, and when they return from, a pilgrimage to Mecca (hajj), and the bodies of those who have died are placed before the mihrab for funerary prayers. Mosques are also sites where marriages and business agreements are contracted and where educational classes are often held. In contemporary times mosques have become centers for political mobilization in those countries that control or ban public meetings or opposition politics. Preachers deliver sermons that incorporate political messages, criticizing government leaders, corruption, and injustice.

In Shiism the family of Ali and the imams became objects of imitation and veneration. Sites associated with their lives or deaths became mosques and shrines, the objects of veneration and pilgrimage. Shrines and holy cities such as Najaf (the burial place of Ali) and Karbala (the site of the martyrdom of Hussein), both in Iraq, or Mashhad and Qum, in Iran, became centers for learning and pilgrimage where rituals of commemoration, prayer, and celebration were performed. In Sunni Islam places associated with the Prophet Muhammad, his family, and companions, as well as with later martyrs and Sufi saints, became shrines and centers of pilgrimage and places for prayer, petitions, blessings, and miracles.

WHAT IS SACRED? Islam emphasizes the oneness, or unity, of God and rejects the substitution of anything for God that could be considered idolatrous. Thus, while animals and plants are regarded as part of creation, they are not sacred, a category reserved only for God.

Historically, however, in popular practice, especially in Sufism, some masters came to be viewed as *walis* (friends of God, or saints), and their tombs became the focus of pilgrimages, where they were appealed to for blessings and assistance. The master's spiritual power and intercession before God might be invoked to request a safe pregnancy, overcoming sickness, a prosperous business, or success in taking exams. Special rituals and celebrations were held to commemorate the dates of the master's birth and death.

For many Muslims, though certainly not all, objects reportedly associated with the Prophet Muhammad—a tooth or strand of hair, for example—have come to be regarded as relics. Similarly, a mosque in Cairo to which Hussein's head was transferred in the twelfth century has been a popular shrine for Sunni and Shiite alike.

HOLIDAYS AND FESTIVALS Muslims celebrate two great holidays. One is Id al-Fitr, the feast celebrating the breaking of the Ramadan fast. The second, which occurs two and a half months later, is Id al-Adha, or the Feast of Sacrifice. This latter holiday, the greater of the two, marks the end of the pilgrimage to Mecca and commemorates God's testing of Abraham by commanding him to sacrifice his son Ismail (Isaac in Jewish and Christian traditions). The feast is a worldwide celebration that lasts for three days.

The two holidays, which are a time for rejoicing, prayer, and social visits, represent a religious obligation as well as a social celebration. Both are occasions for visiting relatives and friends, for giving gifts, and for enjoying special desserts and foods that are served only at these times of the year. Many Muslim children stay home from school to celebrate the festivals, and in some areas school authorities recognize them as holidays for Muslim youngsters.

Muslims also celebrate other religious holidays, including the Prophet Muhammad's birthday. In Shiism the birthdays of Ali and the imams are also celebrated. Shiites annually commemorate the "passion" of Hussein during a 10-day period (*ashura*) of remembering, during which they ritually reenact and mourn the last stand of Imam Hussein and his followers against the army of the caliph.

MODE OF DRESS Islamic dress for men and women reflects a focus on modesty in public and private spaces as defined in the hadith (the reports of Muhammad's sayings and deeds) and in popular tradition. Historically dress in the Muslim world was also strongly influenced by hot and arid climates with wind- and sandstorms, where long and flowing garments ensured comfort and head coverings served as protection. In the Muslim world today dress varies greatly, depending on geographic location, diverse customs and Koranic interpretations, marital status, and differing ages, tastes, identities, occupations, or political orientations.

Nonetheless, there is a particular style of Islamic dress for men and women that was adopted in the twentieth century by Muslim communities throughout the world. Female dress consists of an ankle-length skirt and long-sleeved top or a long robe, unfitted at the waist, along with a head covering, low on the forehead and draped over the neck and sometimes the shoulders. Austere colors (black, white, dark blue, beige, or gray) and opaque materials are the most common. This outfit, called the *hijab* and voluntarily chosen by many Muslim women, is distinctly modern, bought ready-made in shops or sewn by hand.

Male dress, less popular than the female version, includes a traditional long-sleeved tunic and baggy pants or a robe, along with a prayer cap or other traditional head wrap. A beard, either untrimmed or trimmed but covering areas of the cheek, is also sometimes worn. Islamic dress is less popular among men because it often leads officials to identify them as activists subject to identification and arrest.

This Islamic dress represents a new public morality. It strengthens Islamic identity and is a sign of protest and liberation that distances the believer from Western values and its emphasis on materialism and commercialism. Some women believe that Islamic dress makes them better able to function as active, self-directed subjects, commanding respect and valued for who they are rather than what they look like. This dress code has also developed political overtones, becoming a source of national pride, desire for participatory politics, and resistance to authoritarianism and Western cultural and political dominance.

Special dress is worn on a pilgrimage. For women this includes an outer covering and a headscarf. Men on pilgrimage wear two seamless pieces of white cloth and a waistband, an outfit that symbolizes the equality of all believers.

DIETARY PRACTICES Muslims are required to eat meat that has been slaughtered in a religiously appropriate way (*halal*). A dietary prohibition against pork comes from the Koran (5:3). The widespread use of pork products and by-products by U.S. food manufacturers creates difficulties for American Muslims. Lard, commonly used in the United States as shortening, is sometimes an ingredient in cookies, for example, and potato chips may be fried in it.

The sale, purchase, and consumption of alcohol by Muslims is strictly prohibited by Islamic law, although in rare cases it is permitted for medicinal purposes. This prohibition is based upon the Koran (5:90–91), which specifically forbids the consumption of date wine. Most jurists, however, apply the injunction to all substances that produce an altered state of mind, including alcohol and narcotics.

Some mosques and Islamic centers circulate lists of specific products known to contain either pork or alcohol, so that they can be avoided. This includes mustard, some of which is made with white wine.

RITUALS In a well-known hadith Muhammad is reported to have said, "Purity is half of faith." This saying dramatically emphasizes the importance of purity and purification in the Islamic tradition, especially as a preparation for worship and an encounter with God. Thus, physical purification culminates in a spiritual purity that results from worship. The two major purification rituals are the bath (*ghusl*) and the ablution (*wudu*), the latter consisting of washing the face, both arms up to the elbows, the head, and the feet. A bath is a precondition for all forms of worship in Islam, but to overcome any impurities encountered during the day, an ablution should also be performed before praying (*salat*) and circumambulating the Kaaba.

The *salat* is a ritual performed five times daily. Individually or in groups, Muslims face the holy city of Mecca to pray in Arabic. Believers stand, bow, kneel, and touch the ground with their foreheads—an expression of ultimate submission to God—as they recite verses from the Koran, glorify God, declare their faith, and then privately and informally offer personal prayers of request or thanksgiving.

The most intricate of Islamic rituals is the pilgrimage (hajj) to Mecca, which every Muslim who is financially and physically able must make once in his or her lifetime. During the pilgrimage Muslims perform a series of symbolic and emotional rituals—reenactments of faith-testing events in the lives of Abraham, Hagar, and Ismail—as determined by Muhammad shortly before his death. Muslims pray at the spot where Abraham, the patriarch and father of monotheism, stood. But the focus of the pilgrimage is the Kaaba, the cube-shaped structure that Muslim tradition teaches was originally built by Abraham and his son Ismail to honor God. The black stone the Kaaba contains is believed to have been given to Abraham by the angel Gabriel. Thus, it is a symbol of God's covenant with Ismail and, by extension, with the Muslim community. Pilgrims circumambulate the Kaaba seven times, symbolizing the believer's entry into the divine presence. They try to touch or kiss the black stone as they pass by in their procession around the Kaaba.

Pilgrims also walk or run between the nearby hills of Safa and Marwa to commemorate Hagar's frantic search in the desert for water for her son Ismail. In the midst of her running back and forth, water sprang from the earth, from the well of Zamzam. According to Islamic tradition, both Hagar and Ismail are buried in an enclosed area next to the Kaaba. Pilgrims cast small pebbles, a symbolic stoning, toward the three pillars where Abraham was tempted by the devil to disobey God and refuse to sacrifice his son. Finally, they visit the Plain of Arafat, near the Mount of Mercy, the site where Muhammad delivered his last sermon, to seek God's forgiveness for themselves and for all Muslims throughout the world. At the culmination of the hajj, the important ritual of Id al-Adha (Feast of Sacrifice) celebrates the ram substituted by God when Abraham, in a test of his faith, offered to sacrifice his son Ismail.

Collectively the hajj celebrates renewal and reunion across cultures and the continuity over time of the worldwide Islamic community (*ummah*). Individually it often coincides with major events in the believer's life cycle—adulthood, marriage, retirement, illness, a personal crisis or loss—and thus is also viewed as a key rite of passage. The simple garments pilgrims wear, which symbolize the equality and humility of all Muslims regardless of their class, gender, nationality, or race, is often used years later as their burial shroud.

RITES OF PASSAGE Life cycle rituals in Islam serve to provide meaning and reinforce an individual and communal worldview. In addition to the Five Pillars of Islam, rites of passage for birth, puberty, marriage, and death symbolize the theme that a Muslim's purpose is to serve God by submission and thanksgiving.

At birth the call of prayer is recited in the infant's right ear. Names for babies are often derived from those of the prophets or their wives or companions, or a name is formed from the prefix *abd* (servant) and an attribute of God, such as "servant of the Almighty" (Abd al-Aziz). In addition, a goat or sheep is sacrificed to express gratitude to God and joy at the birth, as well as to form an association with Abraham's willingness to sacrifice his son for God. Although circumcision of males is sometimes practiced, it has no doctrinal basis in Islam and is viewed as an act of hygiene. Puberty, the entrance into adulthood, represents the beginning of religious and social responsibility, the obligation to perform purification rituals to ensure physical cleanliness and daily prayers, and participation in the fast during Ramadan.

In Islam marriage (*nikah*) is encouraged as an integral part of humanity, and celibacy is discouraged. Marriage is considered a contract, however, not a sacrament. As with other rites of passage, marriage customs in the Muslim world reflect local customs. Because Islam views sexuality as a part of life requiring rules that preserve social morality, the Koran and *sunnah* (example of the Prophet) provide guidelines for prayer before, as well as a ritual bath (*ghusl*) after, conjugal relations.

Death in Islam is seen as the transition from life in this world to life in the next. Burial normally occurs on the day of death, after funerary rituals, based on practices of Muhammad, that include bathing and wrapping the body. The *salat al-janazah,* a funeral prayer led by a relative or an imam, is said in the mosque after any of the daily prayers, and the *shahadah* (declaration of faith) is recited by the family and friends at the burial. The deceased is placed in the grave with his or her face turned toward Mecca. To reinforce humility and the mindfulness of death, each funeral participant contributes three handfuls of earth toward filling the grave.

MEMBERSHIP Islam is a world religion in geographic scope and mission. All followers have an obligation to be an example to others and to invite them to Islam. Muslims believe that Islam is the religion of God, possessing his final and complete word, the Koran, and his final prophet, Muhammad. Thus, while God's revelation had been revealed previously and covenants had been made with other communities, such as Jews and Christians, Muslims believe that Islam possesses the fullness of truth and that they have a divine mandate to be an example to others and to preach and spread their faith.

The "call" (*dawa*) to Islam, or propagation of the faith, has been central from the origins of the Muslim community. It has a twofold meaning: the call to non-Muslims to become Muslim, and the call to Muslims to return to Islam or to be more religiously observant. From earliest times commercial and military ventures were accompanied by the spread of Islam, with traders, merchants, and soldiers its missionaries. Caliphs also used the spread of Islam as a means to legitimate their authority over Muslims and to justify imperial expansion and conquest.

Modern interpretations of *dawa* have taken many forms—political, socioeconomic, and cultural—as governments, organizations, and individuals have sought to promote Islam's message and impact. Governments and modern Islamic movements and organizations have supported diverse activities, including the distribution of the Koran; the building of mosques, libraries, hospitals, and Islamic schools in poor Muslim countries; and greater Islamization of law and society in Muslim countries. As part of their foreign policies, some governments, including Saudi Arabia, Libya, and Iran, have created Dawa, or Call, organizations to promote Islam and their influence in the Muslim world and in the West. At the same time, nongovernmental Islamic organizations throughout the world have created strong networks of educational institutions and medical and social services. While the majority of these activities have been supported by mainstream groups, extremist organizations have also used social services to enhance their credibility, recruit supporters, and provide aid for the widows and families of their fighters.

RELIGIOUS TOLERANCE The Koran stresses religious tolerance, teaching that God deliberately created a world of diversity: "O humankind, We have created you male and female and made you nations and tribes, so that you might come to know one another" (49:13). In addition, the Koran stresses that "there is to be no compulsion in religion" (2:256).

Islam regards Jews and Christians as People of the Book, as people who have also received revelations and scriptures from God. It is recognized that followers of the three great Abrahamic religions, the children of Abraham, share a common belief in the one God, in such biblical prophets as Moses and Jesus, in human accountability, and in a final judgment followed by eternal reward or punishment. In later centuries Islam extended recognition to other faiths.

Historically, while the early expansion and conquests spread Islamic rule, Muslims in general did not try to impose their religion on others or force them to convert. As People of the Book, Jews and Christians were regarded as protected people (*dhimmi*), permitted to retain and practice their religions, be headed by their own religious leaders, and be guided by their own religious laws and customs. For this protection they paid a poll, or head, tax (*jizya*). While by modern standards this treatment amounted to second-class citizenship, in premodern times, compared with the practices of Christianity, for example, it was highly advanced.

The most frequently cited example of religious tolerance is that of Muslim rule in Spain (Andalusia, or Al-Andalus) from 756 to about 1000, which is usually idealized as a period of interfaith harmony, or *convivencia* (living together). Muslim rule offered the Christian and Jewish populations seeking refuge from the class system elsewhere in Europe the opportunity to become prosperous small landholders. Christians and Jews occupied prominent positions in the court of the caliph in the tenth century, serving as translators, engineers, physicians, and architects. The archbishop of Seville commissioned an annotated translation of the Bible for the Arabic-speaking Christian community.

In the contemporary era religious and political pluralism has been an issue in the Muslim world, threatened by political and socioeconomic tensions and conflicts. Discrimination and conflict between Muslims and Christians, for example, have occurred from Egypt, the Sudan, and Nigeria to Iran, Afghanistan, Pakistan, and Indonesia. The situation has been exacerbated in many of those countries, such as the Sudan, Iran, Pakistan, and Afghanistan, that have attempted to implement self-described Islamic states or Islamic law. A major factor has been extremist religious groups that have targeted non-Muslims. Religious conflict and violence have also occurred within Islam, between Sunnis and Shiites in countries like Pakistan and Afghanistan under the Taliban.

The Israeli-Palestinian conflict is a major example of religion and politics intimately intertwined. Both Jewish and Islamic activist organizations have brought a religious dimension to the conflict between Israeli and Palestinian nationalism. The use of suicide bombings, with their connection to martyrdom, by such Palestinian organizations as Hamas and Islamic Jihad has added a further religious element to the conflict. The struggle over the future of Jerusalem has come to symbolize the religious dimension of the conflict.

A key Islamic issue today regarding tolerance and pluralism is the relationship of past doctrine to current realities. Mainstream conservative Muslims call for a reinstatement of the gradations of citizenship that accompanied the *dhimmi* status, which, however progressive in the past, would deny equal rights to non-Muslims today. Others recognize that this approach is not compatible with the pluralistic realities of the contemporary world or with international standards of human rights. Muslim reformers, who do not approve of the application of the classical tradition in modern times, insist that non-Muslims be afforded full citizenship rights. Advocates of reform maintain that pluralism, rather than being a purely Western invention or ideology, is the essence of Islam as revealed in the Koran and practiced by Muhammad and the early caliphs. Thus, while militants and traditionalists advocate classical Islam's *dhimmi* or *millet* (protected religious community) system, reformers call for a reinterpretation of pluralism.

SOCIAL JUSTICE Muslims, like Christians and Jews before them, believe that they have been called to a special covenant with God, as stated in the Koran, constituting a community of believers intended to serve as an example to other nations (2:143) in establishing a just social order (3:110). The Koran envisions a society based upon the unity and equality of all believers, in which morality and social justice counterbalance economic exploitation and the oppression of the weak. The new moral and social order called for by the Koran reflects the fact that the purpose of all actions is obedience to God's law and fulfillment of his will, not individual, tribal, ethnic, or national self-interest. Men and women are equally responsible for promoting a moral order and adhering to the Five Pillars of Islam.

Sunnis and Shiites

Sunnis (approximately 85 percent) and Shiites (15 percent), the two largest groups within the Muslim community, formed as the result of disagreements about who should succeed Muhammad, whose death in 632 meant the end of direct, personal guidance from the Prophet and thus direct revelation from God. The majority, the Sunnis, or followers of the *sunnah* (example of the Prophet), believed that Muhammad had not established a system for selecting a successor, and they selected Abu Bakr, his close friend and trusted adviser, to be the caliph (successor, or deputy). An early convert who had also become Muhammad's father-in-law, Abu Bakr was respected for his sagacity and piety. Thus, Sunni Muslims adopted the belief that leadership should pass to the most qualified person through a process of selection or election.

A minority of the Muslim community, the Shiites, or party of Ali, believed that succession should be hereditary and that Ali, Muhammad's first cousin and closest living male relative as well as the husband of his daughter Fatimah, should be the leader, or imam, of the Islamic community. Despite their views Ali was passed over three times, not gaining his place as caliph for 35 years, only to be assassinated a few years later. To make matters worse, Ali's charismatic son Hussein, who led a rebellion against the Sunni caliph Yazid, was overwhelmed and massacred along with his followers.

Thus, the differences between Sunnis and Shiites are based on leadership, on who is qualified to be the Muslim community's leader. Although they share many fundamental beliefs and practices, their diverse experiences also have resulted in differences in belief and ritual, as well as different views about the meaning of history.

Historically Sunnis have almost always ruled Shiites, who have existed as an oppressed and disinherited minority. (Today Shiites are a majority only in Iran, Iraq, Bahrain, and Lebanon.) Thus, Shiites have come to understand history as a test of the righteous community's perseverance in the struggle to restore God's rule on earth. While Sunnis can claim a golden age in which they were a great world power and civilization, which they see as God's favor upon them and a historic validation of Muslim beliefs, Shiites see in this same history the Sunni ruler's illegitimate takeover at the expense of a just society. Shiites view history more as a paradigm of the suffering and oppression of their righteous minority community and of their need to struggle constantly to restore God's rule on earth under his divinely appointed imam.

In the twentieth century Shiite history was reinterpreted in a way that provided inspiration and mobilization to fight actively against injustice rather than passively accept it. This reinterpretation has had the most significant impact among Shiites in Lebanon, who struggled to achieve greater social, educational, and economic opportunities during the 1970s and 1980s, and in Iran, where, during the Islamic revolution of 1978–79, the shah was equated with Yazid and Ayatollah Khomeini and his followers with Hussein. Thus, the victory of the Islamic revolution was declared to be the victory of the righteous over illegitimate usurpers of power.

The socioeconomic reforms of the Koran are among its most striking features. Muslims are held responsible for the care and protection of members of the community, in particular the poor, the weak, women, widows, orphans, and slaves (4:2, 4:12, 90:13–16, 24:33). Bribery, false contracts, the hoarding of wealth, the abuse of women, and usury are condemned. The practice of *zakat,* giving 2.5 percent of one's total wealth annually to support the less fortunate, is a required social responsibility intended to break the cycle of poverty and to prevent the rich from holding on to their wealth while the poor remain poor: "The alms [*zakat*] are for the poor and needy, those who work to collect them, those whose hearts are to be reconciled, the ransoming of slaves and debtors, and for the causes of God, and for travelers" (9:60). The redistribution of wealth underscores the Muslim belief that human beings are care-takers, or vice-regents, for God's property, that everything ultimately belongs to God.

Opposition to interest, seen as exploitation of the poor, originates in Koranic verses that prohibit usury, or *riba,* an ancient Arabian practice that doubled the debt of borrowers who defaulted on their loans and doubled it again if they defaulted a second time. Today opposition to interest comes from the Koranic prohibition against *riba* and the belief that interest gives an unfair gain to the lender, who receives money without working for it, and imposes an unfair burden on the borrower, who must repay the loan and a finance charge regardless of whether his money grows or he suffers a loss. Opponents also believe that interest transfers wealth from the poor to the rich, promotes selfishness, and weakens community bonds. Reformers argue that the condemnation of *riba* does not refer to the practices of modern banking but to usury, for, as the Koran warns, usurers face "war from God and His Prophet" (2:279).

Koranic reforms in marriage, divorce, and inheritance sought to protect and enhance the status and rights of women. While the Koran and Islam did not do away with slavery, which was common in pre-Islamic Arabia and thus presumed to be part of society, Islamic law set out guidelines to limit its negative impact and assure the just treatment of slaves. It forbade the enslavement of free members of Islamic society and, in particular, orphans and foundlings. Slaves could not be abused, mutilated, or killed. The freeing of slaves was regarded as an especially meritorious action. Similarly, in war clear regulations were given to protect the rights of noncombatants and the clergy.

The Koran and *sunnah* teach that Muslims should make every effort, or struggle (jihad), to promote justice. This includes the right, if necessary, to engage in armed defense (jihad) of the rights of the downtrodden, in particular women and children (4:74–76) and victims of oppression and injustice, such as those Muslims who were driven out of their homes unjustly by the Meccans (22:39–40).

SOCIAL ASPECTS Marriage and family life are the norm in Islam. In contrast to Christianity, marriage in Islam is not a sacrament but, rather, a contract between a man and a woman, or perhaps more accurately between their families. In the traditional practice of arranged marriages, the families or guardians, not the bride and groom, are the two primary actors. The pre-

ferred marriage, because of concerns regarding the faith of the children, is between two Muslims and within the extended family. In Islam, as in Judaism, marriage between first cousins has been quite common.

As in most societies, the early form of the family in Islam was patriarchal and patrilineal. (The term "patriarch," referring to Jewish and Christian prophets, exemplifies this tendency.) Islam, however, brought significant changes to the seventh-century Arabian family, significantly enhancing the status of women and children. The Koran raised the status of women by prohibiting female infanticide, abolishing women's status as property, establishing their legal capacity, granting women the right to receive their own dowry, changing marriage from a proprietary to a contractual relationship, and allowing women to retain control over their property and use their maiden name after marriage. In addition, the Koran granted women financial maintenance from their husbands and controlled the husband's free ability to divorce. The hadith (Prophetic tradition) saying that "The best of you is he who is best to his wife" also reflects Muhammad's respect for, and protection of, women.

Islamic law views the relationship of husband and wife as complementary, reflecting their differing capacities, characteristics, and dispositions, as well as the different traditional roles of men and women in the patriarchal family. In the public sphere, the primary arena for the man, the husband is responsible for the support and protection of the family. The woman's primary role of wife and mother requires that she manage the household and supervise the upbringing and religious training of their children. Both men and women are seen as equal before God, having the same religious responsibilities and equally required to lead virtuous lives, but women are viewed as subordinate in family matters and society because of their more sheltered and protected lives and because of a man's greater economic responsibilities in the extended family.

In Muslim countries, to a greater extent than in the West, the extended family, which includes grandparents, uncles, aunts, and cousins, has traditionally provided its members with counseling, child care, financial assistance, insurance, and social security. Women in the family have always been seen as the bearers of culture, the center of the family unit that provides a force for moral and social order and the means of stability for the next generation. In the nineteenth century the family provided religious, cultural, and social protection from colonial and Western domination, as well as a site for political resistance. In a rapidly changing, unpredictable, and sometimes hostile twentieth century, the family in many Muslim countries came to face economic and political and personal pressures brought about by unemployment and economic need and by disruption from war and forced migration. Debates throughout the Muslim world center on better family support from the state, as well as the changing roles and rights of men, women, and children.

Islam has always recognized the right to divorce under certain circumstances. Both the Koran and Prophetic traditions, however, underscore its seriousness. Muhammad is reported to have said, "Of all the permitted things, divorce is the most abominable with God," and an authoritative legal manual describes divorce as "a dangerous and disapproved procedure as it dissolves marriage . . . [It is] admitted, but on the ground of urgency of relief from an unsuitable relationship."

CONTROVERSIAL ISSUES In Islam procreation is considered an important result of marriage, and for this reason many Muslims oppose abortion. According to Muslim religious scholars, abortion after the fetus obtains a soul (views differ on whether this occurs at fertilization or after 120 days) is considered homicide. The Koran emphasizes the preservation of life (17:31), with neither poverty nor hunger justifying the killing of offspring, and stresses that punishment for unlawfully killing a human being is to be imposed both in this life and in the afterlife (4:93). Therapeutic abortions, performed as a result of severe medical problems, are justified by a general principle of Islamic law that chooses the lesser of two evils. Instead of losing two lives, the life of the mother, who has important duties and responsibilities, is given preference.

Muslim voices differ regarding birth control. Islam has traditionally emphasized the importance of large families that will ensure a strong Muslim community. Although family planning is not mentioned in the Koran, some traditions of the Prophet mention coitus interruptus. Some conservative ulama (religious scholars) object to the use of birth control because they believe it opposes God's supreme will, can weaken the Muslim community by limiting its size, and contributes to premarital sex or adultery. Today, however, the majority of ulama permit contraception that is agreed to by both the husband and the wife, since this guarantees the rights of both parties. On the other hand, steriliza-

tion is opposed by most ulama on the grounds that it permanently alters what God has created.

The Koran declares men and women to be equal in God's eyes, to be equal parts of a pair (51:49) or like each other's garment (2:187). Their relationship should be of "love and mercy" (30:21). The Koran states, "The Believers, men and women, are protectors of one another; they enjoin what is just, and forbid what is evil; they observe regular prayers, pay *zakat* and obey God and His Messenger. On them will God pour His mercy: for God is exalted in Power, Wise. God has promised to Believers, men and women, gardens under which rivers flow, to dwell therein" (9:71–72). This verse was the last to be revealed, and as a result some scholars believe that it defines the ideal, a relationship of equality and complementarity.

Nonetheless, one of the most controversial issues in Islam today is the status of women and their lack of legal rights in family law. Many of the problems, however, can be traced not to Islam but, rather, to the customs of the patriarchal societies in which Islamic laws were originally interpreted. Until the twentieth century women were not actively engaged in interpreting the Koran, hadith, or Islamic law. For example, in order to control a husband's unbridled right to divorce, the Koran requires the man to pronounce his intention three times over a period of three months before the divorce becomes irrevocable (65:1). The delay allows time for a possible reconciliation and time to determine if the wife is pregnant and in need of child support. Despite these guidelines an abbreviated form of divorce, allowing the man to say "I divorce you" three times in succession, became a common phenomena. Although considered a sinful abuse, this kind of divorce was nevertheless declared to be legal, and it affected women's rights in many Muslim countries.

Using the Koran and the courts, many Muslim countries have instituted reforms to control divorce and to improve women's rights. In many countries today, Muslim women can obtain a divorce in court on a variety of grounds, although there are other patriarchal Muslim societies in which custom continues to allow extensive rights of divorce for men but only restricted rights for women. There also have been significant reforms in women's rights in other spheres. In the overwhelming majority of Muslim countries, women have the right to a public education, including education at the college level. In many countries they also have the right to work outside the home, to vote, and to hold public office. Among the most important reforms have been the abolition of polygamy in some countries and its severe limitation in others; expanded rights for women to participate in contracting marriage, including the stipulation of conditions favorable to them in the marriage contract; expanded rights for financial compensation for a woman seeking a divorce; and the requirement that a husband provide housing for his divorced wife and children as long as she holds custody over the children. There also have been reforms prohibiting child marriages and expanding the rights of women to have custody over their older children.

CULTURAL IMPACT Muslim views of music have been influenced by hadith (Prophetic traditions) that caution against music and musical instruments. Nothing in the Koran bans music, however, and historically music has been a popular and significant art form throughout the Muslim world. It has played an important role in religious festivals and in life cycle rituals, including those for birth, circumcision, and marriage. In addition, throughout Muslim cities the daily calls to prayer are traditionally sung or chanted by a muezzin and projected from on high from loudspeakers on minarets. The most important musical form in Islam, however, is recitation of the Koran, done as a chant, in which annual competitions are held throughout the Muslim world. Recordings of Koran recitation are widely sold, and some of Islam's best-known singers have been reciters of the Koran. The Egyptian singer Umm Kulthum and others have imitated Koran recitation in their music.

As part of their devotions, the Sufi orders typically use music, both vocal, through repetition of words or phrases and in chanting, and instrumental. For Sufis music is a vehicle for spiritual transcendence and a means of attaining the experience of divine ecstasy. Folk music has also been an important expression of culture throughout the Muslim world, used to express moral and devotional themes as well as heroism and love. The music produced by the Muslims of Andalusia, like their poetry, had an enormous impact on the development of classical music in Europe.

In Islamic visual art concerns about idolatry have led historically to bans on the representation of human beings. Thus, the Islamic art that is most cherished is based upon the use of Arabic script in calligraphy (the art of beautiful writing) or of arabesque (geometric and floral) designs. A hadith attributed to the Prophet Muhammad says that one who beautifully writes the phrase

"In the name of God the Merciful, the Compassionate," the first words in the opening chapter of the Koran, will enter paradise. The belief that God's direct words in the Koran should be written in a manner worthy of divine revelation has led to the development of calligraphy in many styles and forms. Calligraphy sometimes uses the stylized lettering of Koranic quotations or religious formulas to reflect animal, flower, or even mosque figures. Today interest in calligraphy remains high, as is evidenced in its varied use as decorations for holiday cards, announcements of important events, and book covers. Computer programs have been developed that can create decorations from Arabic script.

Because figures are not used in Islamic art, a form of decoration that came to be known in the West as arabesque—the use of natural forms such as stems, leaves, vines, flowers, or fruits to create designs of infinite geometric patterns—developed as a major artistic technique. Arabesque designs are used to decorate such objects as interior and exterior walls, mosque furniture like the *minbar* (pulpit), and fine Koran manuscripts. Some designs combine calligraphy with colorful geometric and floral or vegetal ornamentation.

Designs in Islamic art are often enhanced by exuberant colors, for example, in the glittering golden or azure domes and multicolored tiles of buildings or in the colors of pottery, textiles, and manuscripts. Colors are used symbolically in Islamic literature, although their meanings and associations are determined by context. For example, black can be associated with the black stone in the Kaaba in Mecca or with vengeance, violence, or hell. White is less ambiguous, usually representing faithfulness (as in the cloths worn by pilgrims on hajj), lightness, royalty, or death (as in its use as a burial shroud). Blue is the color of magical qualities, which can be used to protect a person from evil spirits or, in contrast, to dispense evil. Green was the color of the Prophet and of turbans worn by descendants of the Prophet, and it was also the color of the cloak of Ali, for Shiites the first imam. As the color of living plants, green is also symbolic of youth and fertility.

The ambiguities of color in Islamic art are matched by the Arabic language itself, which facilitates plays on words and the varied interpretations that result. These multiple meanings contribute to the enjoyment of both unchanging and variable insights and thus represent part of the appeal of Islamic literature. As the direct word of God, the Koran is viewed as religious literature as well as a perfect literary document.

Although in pre-Islamic Bedouin society poetry was the dominant literary form, the first centuries of Islam were dominated by a fear that poetry might conflict with the Koran's divinely inspired words. In the emotionally charged atmosphere generated by mysticism in the tenth and eleventh centuries, however, Sufi poems of longing for the divine beloved proliferated. By the twelfth century poetry emphasizing praise of the Prophet had developed in a number of forms, from short devotional verses to long, elaborate descriptions of Muhammad's greatness to pious songs. These forms are found in almost all literatures of the Muslim world today. The development of such modern technology as audio- and videotapes has fostered the growth of Islamic religious poetry in regional languages and in remote areas of the world.

Islamic prose forms include Koranic verses, the hadith, and biographies and autobiographies. Along with poetry and plays, novels, short stories, and autobiographies are used to advocate a religious way of life. Modern autobiographies place emphasis on the individual, in contrast to classical texts, which focused primarily on collective Islamic norms.

John L. Esposito

See Also Vol. 1: *Shiism, Sunnism*

Bibliography

Armstrong, Karen. *Islam: A Short History.* New York: Modern Library, 2000.

———. *Muhammad: A Biography of the Prophet.* San Francisco: Harper, 1993.

Asad, Muhammad, trans. *The Message of the Quran.* Chicago: Kazi Publications, 1980.

Barlas, Asma. *"Believing Women" in Islam: Unreading Patriarchal Interpretations of the Quran.* Austin: University of Texas Press, 2002.

Bloom, Jonathan, and Sheila Blair. *Islam: A Thousand Years of Faith and Power.* New York: TV Books, 2000.

Coulson, Noel J. *A History of Islamic Law.* Edinburgh: Edinburgh University Press, 1964.

Denny, Frederick. *An Introduction to Islam.* New York: Macmillan, 1994.

Esposito, John L. *Islam: The Straight Path.* 3rd ed. New York: Oxford University Press, 1998.

———. *Unholy War: Terror in the Name of Islam.* New York: Oxford University Press, 2002.

———. *What Everyone Needs to Know about Islam.* New York: Oxford University Press, 2002.

———, ed. *The Oxford Dictionary of Islam.* New York: Oxford University Press, 2003.

———, ed. *The Oxford History of Islam.* New York: Oxford University Press, 1999.

Fakhry, Majid, trans. *The Quran: A Modern English Version.* London: Garnet Publishing, 1997.

Haddad, Yvonne Y., and John L. Esposito. *Islam, Gender and Social Change.* New York: Oxford University Press, 1998.

———. *Muslims on the Americanization Path?* New York: Oxford University Press, 2000.

Haneef, Suzanne. *What Everyone Should Know about Islam and Muslims.* Chicago: Library of Islam, 1995.

Heim, Heinz. *Shiism.* Edinburgh: Edinburgh University Press, 1991.

Hunter, Shireen. *Islam, Europe's Second Religion.* Westport, Conn.: Praeger, 2002.

Lings, Martin. *What Is Sufism?* Cambridge: Islamic Texts Society, 1999.

Nasr, Seyyed Hossein. *The Heart of Islam.* San Francisco: Harper, 2002.

———. *Islamic Spirituality.* London: SCM Press, 1989.

Nielsen, Jorgen. *Muslims in Western Europe.* Edinburgh: Edinburgh University Press, 1995.

Peters, F.E. *Islam: A Guide for Jews and Christians.* Princeton, N.J.: Princeton University Press, 2003.

Rahman, Fazlur. *Major Themes of the Quran.* Minneapolis: Bibliotheca Islamica, 1980.

Ramadan, Tariq. *To Be a European Muslim.* Leicester, England: Islamic Foundation, 1999.

Schimmel, Annemarie. *Mystical Dimensions of Islam.* Chapel Hill: University of North Carolina Press, 1975.

Smith, Jane. *Islam in America.* New York: Columbia University Press, 1999.

Voll, John O. *Islam: Continuity and Change in the Muslim World.* Syracuse, N.Y.: Syracuse University Press, 1994.

Wadud, Amina. *Quran and Woman.* New York: Oxford University Press, 1999.

Waines, David. *An Introduction to Islam.* Cambridge: Cambridge University Press, 1995.

Watt, W.M. *The Formative Period of Islamic Thought.* Edinburgh: University of Edinburgh Press, 1973.

Wolfe, Michael. *Hadj: An American's Pilgrimage to Mecca.* New York: Atlantic Monthly Press, 1993.

Islam

Shiism

FOUNDED: 632 C.E.

RELIGION AS A PERCENTAGE OF WORLD POPULATION: 2.2 percent

OVERVIEW One of the two major branches of Islam, Shiism represents about 15 percent of the worldwide Muslim population. The initial split among Muslims occurred in Medina (western present-day Saudi Arabia) in 632 C.E. over the question of who would succeed the prophet Muhammad, but it took several decades before the division between the two branches, Shiism and Sunnism, became official. According to Shiites, the spiritual and temporal authority in the Muslim community rightfully belonged to Ali, the Prophet's cousin and son-in-law, and a succession of his descendants, known as the imams.

While Shiites live all over the world, they are most concentrated in Iran, where Shia Islam is the state religion. The majority of Iraq's population is also made up of Shiites. Other considerable Shiite communities live in Lebanon, Syria, the Gulf States, Saudi Arabia, East Africa, Afghanistan, Central Asia, India, and Pakistan.

Shiism consists of a number of major and minor subgroups. The most prevalent, representing about 80 percent of all Shiites, are the Twelvers (Shia Imamiyyah, or Ithna Ashariyyah), named after the number of imams the group recognizes; they are active mostly in Iran, Iraq, and Lebanon. Other important groups with substantial followers are the Seveners, or Ismailiyah (likewise, a description reflecting the number of recognized imams),

active mostly in the Indian subcontinent and East Africa; and the Fivers, or Zaydiyah, found primarily in Yemen.

The Seveners divided from the Twelvers on the death of the sixth imam in 765 C.E., when they decided to recognize his son Ismail as the seventh imam (instead of another son, Musa al-Kazim, whom the Twelvers accept). The Fivers had seceded from the majority earlier (c. 720) when they recognized Zayd bin Ali as the fifth imam instead of his half brother Muhammad al-Baqir. Although these schisms grew out of theological, legal, and political differences, all Shiites share the fundamental belief that Ali and his descendants (through Fatima, Ali's wife and Muhammad's daughter) are the true successors of the Prophet. This entry focuses on the history and practices of the Twelvers, the dominant Shiite group.

HISTORY The formation of Shiism was a gradual process. During the decades immediately following the Prophet's death in 632 C.E., there emerged a number of religiopolitical dissent movements whose members expressed allegiance to Ali (Muhammad's cousin and son-in-law) and his sons (Muhammad's grandchildren) as the Prophet's true successors. These Muslims came to be known as the Shia (Arabic: "party" or "partisans") of Ali. The Shiite's claim of Ali's right to this succession was based on a number of events in which Muhammad showed special consideration for Ali. Shiites have understood these events as an indication of the Prophet's will to designate Ali as his successor and as his recognition of Ali's superior qualification for the role.

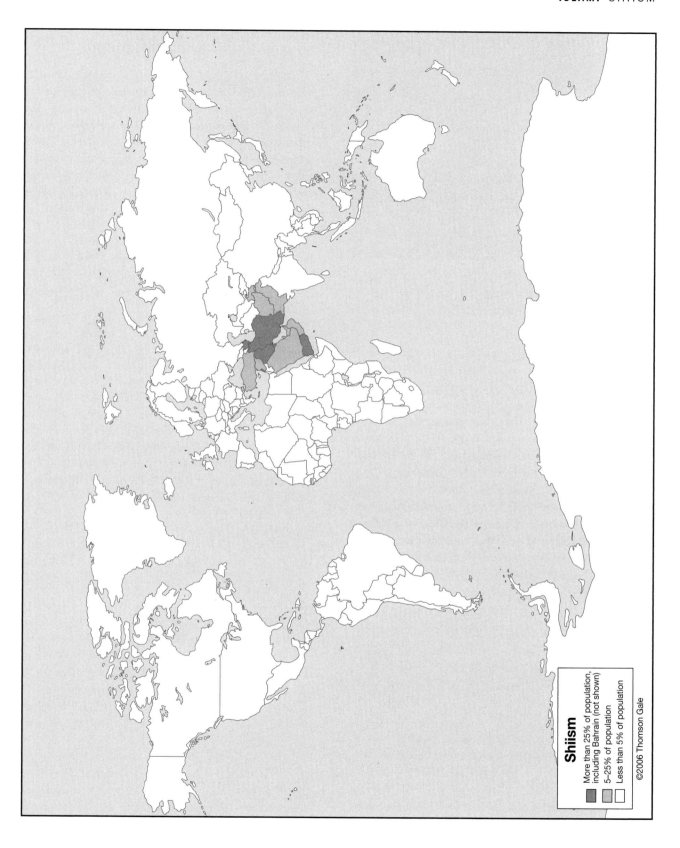

Shiism

More than 25% of population, including Bahrain (not shown)

5–25% of population

Less than 5% of population

©2006 Thomson Gale

Shiite Muslims touch the tiled walls of the shrine of Imam Husayn in Karbala, Iraq. The shrines of the imams are considered holy and play important roles in Shiite religious life. © MICHAEL APPLETON/CORBIS.

The most notable of these events occurred at the oasis of Ghadir-e Khum, where the Prophet, in a sermon during his last hajj (pilgrimage), stated, "He of whom I am the *mawla*, Ali, also, is his *mawla*. O God, be the friend to those who befriend him and be the enemy of him who is his enemy, support those who support him and abandon those who abandon him." There has been major disagreement between Shiites and Sunnis over how to interpret this passage. For Shiites the extraordinary manner in which the Prophet equated Ali in authority and affection with himself remains the strongest basis for their claim. They have taken the word *mawla* to mean leader, master, and guardian and thus see it as an explicit designation of Ali as his successor, whereas the Sunnis have interpreted *mawla* as friend and confidant.

After the Prophet's death Ali did not immediately become caliph (successor of Muhammad and head of Islam); three other senior companions of the Prophet preceded him. Indeed, although Ali's partisans held the view that he was the true successor of the Prophet, Ali did not contest the leadership of his predecessors, and he pledged allegiance to them in order to avoid dissension in the *ummah* (Islamic community). Ali finally became caliph in 656, but his reign lasted only until 661, when he was assassinated. None of Ali's descendants ever formally assumed the office of caliph, for they were either imprisoned or killed by the Sunni authorities. In 681 C.E. the Umayyads (a Sunni dynasty) brutally suppressed an uprising in Karbala (central Iraq) of Ali's son

Husayn; this inaugurated a long period of denying the rights of Ali's descendants to the caliphate.

For most of their early history the Shiites lived as a persecuted Muslim minority scattered throughout the Islamic lands. In the tenth century C.E., however, the Shiites briefly gained political control of almost all the Muslim world, with each part ruled by one Shiite group or another. Notable among them were the Buyid dynasty (945–1055) in Iran, Iraq, and Syria and the Fatimid dynasty (909–1171), led by Sevener Shiites, in Egypt and North Africa. This Shiite domination was eventually brushed aside by Sunni Turks who established the Seljuq dynasty (eleventh–thirteenth centuries). In the sixteenth century the Safavids (1502–1736) adopted Twelver Shiism as the state religion of the Persian (Iranian) Empire. Since then Iran has remained the homeland of the majority of Shiite Muslims.

CENTRAL DOCTRINES There are three fundamental principles of belief that both Sunni and Shia Islam agree upon: *tawhid* (unity of God), *nubuwwah* (prophecy), and *maad* (resurrection). To these the Shia add two other principles: *imamah* (the imamate) and *adl* (justice of God). *Imamah* is the authority and leadership of the imams, who are regarded as the Prophet's legitimate successors, inheriting his authority in both its spiritual and temporal dimensions. It is these inherited qualifications, particularly the spiritual one, that make the Shiite concept of imamate distinct from the Sunni concept of caliphate, which is essentially a temporal office. An imam may not assume the temporal leadership of the community—indeed, none except Ali did so—yet he remains exclusively the highest spiritual authority in the *ummah*, or Islamic community.

Imamah is the prerogative bequeathed by God to the Prophet's family, who are known as *ahl al-bayt*, consisting of the Prophet, his daughter Fatima, his cousin Ali, Hasan and Husayn (children of Ali and Fatima), and certain of their descendants. Through divine inspiration each imam designates his successor during his lifetime. Embodied in this doctrine is the idea that an imam is a divinely inspired individual who possesses a special knowledge of religion (*ilm*), which includes both the explicit (*zahir*) and the esoteric (*batin*) meanings of the Koran. By virtue of possessing this special knowledge of religion, an imam continues one of the Prophet's functions—*velayat* (guardianship). Shiism is clear, however, in its insistence that prophetic revelation ended with the prophet Muhammad.

The principle of *adl* was adopted by Shiites during the twelfth and thirteenth centuries C.E. Of the two contesting schools of theology, Ashari and Mutazilah, during that time, Shiism adopted the latter, which stressed free will and reason rather than predestination. As such, individuals are responsible for their own actions, which, on the Day of Judgment, will be evaluated by God according to his justice. *Maad* and the Last Judgment would be irrelevant if a person's actions were predetermined by God.

MORAL CODE OF CONDUCT Shiites strive to live a moral life, the guidelines of which are defined in the Shariah (Islamic law) and exemplified in the lives of the Prophet and the imams. An imam is understood to be the embodiment of spiritual transcendence, wisdom, rationality, and justice. Stories of the imam's commitment to social justice and moral uprightness are widespread among Shiites. Because free will exists, personal accountability and responsibility for one's actions are emphasized. It is everyone's duty to "command good and forbid wrong" in his or her community.

SACRED BOOKS The only sacred book accepted by both Sunnis and Shiites is the Koran. Yet each branch has its own collections of prophetic hadith (exemplary traditions). The four canonical Shiite collections, which also include the words of the imams, are *Kitab al-Kafi* by al-Kulayni (died in 939), *Man la Yahduruhu al-Faqih* by Ibn Babuyah (died in 991), and *Tahdhib al-Ahkam* and *al-Istibsar*, both by Shaykh al-Tusi (died in 1067). The *Nahj al-Balaqhah*, a collection of Imam Ali's sermons, is another distinctively Shiite text. The *Sahifah Sajjadiyyah*, a book of hymns and prayers attributed to the fourth imam, Imam Sajjad (659–712/13), is widely used by Shiites in their devotional prayers and rituals.

SACRED SYMBOLS Shiism has no sacred symbols. At some point during the period of the Abbasids—a pro-Shiite dynasty (750–1258) centered in Baghdad—the color green came to be recognized as representative of the Shiites. At the top of all major Shiite shrines is a green flag. The only exception is the shrine of Imam Husayn in Karbala, which flies a red flag to designate him as the chief martyr.

EARLY AND MODERN LEADERS Although all the imams are considered important to Shia Islam, there are three outstanding figures among them: Ali (c. 600–61),

Photographs of Shiite imams are sold in the streets of Baghdad, Iraq. The imam is the highest spiritual authority in the Islamic community. © ANTOINE GYORI/AGP/CORBIS.

the first imam and founder of Shiism; Husayn (626–80), the third imam and martyr of Karbala; and Jafar al-Sadiq (702–65), the sixth imam and founder of the Shiite school of law and theology. There are also two outstanding female figures, Fatima and Zeynab, who were, respectively, daughter and granddaughter of the Prophet, wife and daughter of Ali, and mother and sister of Husayn. They are venerated not only for having been members of the Prophet's family, or *ahl al-bayt*, but also because of their own personal merits and for being models of socially and politically conscious Muslim women.

Among notable twentieth-century figures in Twelver Shiism are Ayatollah Ruhollah Khomeini (died in 1989), the leader of the Iranian Revolution in 1979; Ayatollah Muhammad Baqir al-Sadr, a political leader of Shiites in Iraq who was executed by Saddam Hussein's regime in the 1980s; and Imam Musa al-Sadr, a political leader of Shiites in Lebanon (he disappeared in 1979 and was allegedly kidnapped by Libyan secret police).

MAJOR THEOLOGIANS AND AUTHORS Because the imams are considered the true authorities after the Prophet, their sayings and interpretations of religion were significant in the development of Shiite religious thought. As such, early scholarly efforts were directed toward collecting their sayings, called the hadith, and their formulations of Shiite law. The compilers of the four canonical collection of Shiite hadith (*al-Kutub al-arbaah*, or "The Four Books") are al-Kulayni (died in 939), Ibn Babuyah (died in 991), and Shaykh al-Tusi (died in 1067). Shaykh al-Tusi (also known as Shaykh al-Taifah) and two other jurists, Shaykh al-Mufid (died in 1022) and Sayyid Murtada (died in 1044), are known for their fundamental contributions to Shiite theology, which was strongly influenced by the Mutazilah school of theology. They attempted to elaborate and systematize the principles of imamite theology and jurisprudence as set down by the fifth and sixth imams. Among later figures of philosophical theology are Khwajah Nasir al-Din al-Tusi (died in 1274), known for his contributions in astronomy, mathematics, philosophy, and theology; and his commentator, Allamah Hilli (died in 1325). Nasir al-Din's book *Tajrid al-itiqad* ("Plain Doctrines") is considered the beginning of systematic Shiite theology. A convergence between the mystical teachings of Ibn Arabi (1165–1240) and Shiite theology led to a new trend of theosophy (theoretical mysticism) best manifested in *Jami al-Asrar* ("The Compilation of Secrets"), the monumental work of its leading figure, Sayyid Haydar al-Amuli (died after 1383 C.E.).

During later periods, and particularly under the Safavid dynasty (1502–1736) in Iran, Shiism experienced a remarkable revival of intellectual activity. While Islamic philosophy had ceased to flourish in other parts of the Islamic world, it reached its peak in Iran because of the philosophical "School of Esfahan." It was a creative synthesis of the Aristotelian-based philosophy of Ibn Sina (spelled Avicenna in English; 980–1037), the illuminationist theosophy of Suhravardi (died in 1191), the mysticism of Ibn Arabi, and Shiite theology. The masters of this new metaphysics were Mir Damad (died in 1631), Mulla Sadra (died in 1640), Baha al-Din al-Amili (died in 1622), Mulla Muhsin Fayd al-Kashani (died in 1680), and Abd al-Razzaq Lahiji (died in 1661). Also emerging during the Safavid period was Allamah Majlisi (died in 1699), known for his voluminous hadith collection, *Bihar al-Anwar* ("Oceans of Lights"). Shiite jurisprudence received further elaboration by Wahid Bihbahani (died in 1790) and Murtada Ansari (died in 1864).

Notable Shiite interpreters of the Koran include al-Tabrisi (died in 1153), author of *Majma al-Bayan* ("Collection of Elucidations"); Mulla Muhsin Fayd al-Kashani, author of *Tafsir Safi* ("The Pure"); and the twentieth-century philosopher, mystic, and exegete Allamah Muhammad Hossein Tabatabai (died in 1980), author of *Tafsir al-Mizan* ("The Balance").

ORGANIZATIONAL STRUCTURE During their lifetimes the imams were the central authority in Shiite Islam. Twelver Shiites believe the twelfth and last imam has been in occultation (concealment) since 878 and will not return until the end of time. After the occultation Shiite jurists and traditionists (hadith specialists) came to be considered the imam's general deputies.

In the late eighteenth century, with the dominance of the Usuli school of jurisprudence over the Akhbari school, a leadership position called the *marja al-taqlid* (source of emulation) was established. In each generation there have been only a few senior jurists recognized by public consensus—on the basis of their knowledge and impeccable piety—as *marja*, the highest religious authority. The opinions and verdicts of a *marja* are binding upon his followers, who send religious taxes and donations to him.

At the lowest rank of the clerical hierarchy are the seminary students, *tullab*, who receive study stipends from the *marja* of their choice. In between are *mujtahids*, graduates of seminaries whose main function is to lead prayers in mosques and to resolve day-to-day religious problems.

HOUSES OF WORSHIP AND HOLY PLACES Shiites, like Sunnis, perform daily prayers in a mosque, which, in addition to being a holy place, usually serves as the local center of religious activities in each community. Besides Mecca and Medina—the two most sacred places for all Muslims—the shrines of the imams are also considered holy and play important roles in Shiite religious life as both sites of pilgrimage and centers of religious learning. The most important of these sites are located in Iraq (the shrines of Imam Ali in Najaf, of Imam Husayn in Karbala, of the fifth and ninth imams in Kazemayn, and of the tenth and eleventh imams in Samarra), Iran (the shrines of the eighth imam [Ali al-Rida] in Mashhad and of his sister [Masumah] in Qum), and Syria (the shrine of Sayyidah Zeynab, the sister of Imam Husayn, outside of Damascus).

WHAT IS SACRED? The Koran is regarded as the only sacred object by Shiite Muslims. Highly respected among Shiites as a kind of relic is *turbat-e Imam Husayn*, or *turbat-e Karbala* (dust or baked mud from the earth of Karbala, where Imam Husayn and other martyrs fell). This dust, which has a pleasant and soothing scent, is believed to carry the blessings of the imam and is used in some popular and devotional religious practices, particularly in birth and death rituals.

HOLIDAYS AND FESTIVALS Shiite holidays and festivals may be divided into two categories: celebrations and occasions of mourning. In the first category, Shiites share with Sunni Muslims the celebration of the two major feasts of Id al-Fitr and Id al-Adha. In addition, they also celebrate an exclusively Shiite feast called Id al-Ghadir, which falls eight days after Id al-Adha and celebrates the Prophet's designation of Ali as his successor at Ghadir-i Khum.

Moreover, the birth of the Prophet (also recognized by Sunnis) and those of the imams are celebrated. Although not all these birthdays are recognized as major holidays, and few of them are publicly celebrated, the births of the Prophet and Ali, Husayn, and Mahdi (the first, second, and twelfth imams, respectively) are widely observed. During these holidays there are festive gatherings of families and friends, public distribution of sweets and special meals, and visits to elderly relatives. Because blessings are attributed to these days, people may perform special prayers or even fast. In public gatherings speakers usually recite poetry praising the imam being honored, after which the crowd may chant one or two phrases.

Commemoration of the deaths of the Prophet and the imams constitutes the second set of Shiite holidays. Mourning ceremonies for the Prophet, Ali, Fatima, and Husayn are the main public events observed by all Shiites. On these occasions devout Shiites wear black clothing and participate in public ceremonies, which are held in almost every neighborhood by devout families or local religious organizations and mosques.

The suppression of Shiites in Karbala and the martyrdom of Husayn are commemorated every year during the month of Muharram. Shiite mourning ceremonies culminate on the tenth day, Ashura, which corresponds to the day in 681 C.E. when Imam Husayn and his 72 companions and family members were massacred by the army of Yazid, the Umayyad caliph. Muharram ceremonies include the *Rawda Khani*, a recitation by a cleric of the martyr's sufferings. At the high point of these meetings the audience weeps and publicly laments the losses of Karbala. Another distinctive feature of the Muharram commemorations is the street processions, which often attract large crowds (mostly men) marching in rows through the streets from one place of ceremony to another, chanting eulogies to the martyred imam while beating their chests rhythmically. Some strike their shoulders with chains, while in various parts of the Shiite world there are devotees who even strike their heads

The Love for *ahl al-bayt*

At the heart of Shiite teachings is love for the *ahl al-bayt,* or holy family, consisting of the prophet Muhammad, his daughter Fatima, his cousin Ali (who married Fatima), and Hasan and Husayn (children of Fatima and Ali). For Twelvers, the dominant Shiite group, *ahl al-bayt* comprises "the Fourteen Infallibles"—namely, the Prophet, Fatima, and the twelve imams (or successors of the Prophet, including Ali, the first imam). Below is a chronological list of the imams, who were born between the seventh and ninth century C.E.

Ali ibn Abi Talib

Hasan ibn Ali

Husayn ibn Ali

Ali ibn al-Husayn

Muhammad al-Baqir

Jafar al-Sadiq

Musa al-Kazim

Ali al-Rida

Muhammad al-Taqi

Ali al-Naqi

Hassan al-Askari

Muhammad al-Mahdi (the Awaited Imam)

The twelfth imam, Mahdi (the Rightly Guided One), disappeared in 878 C.E. According to the Twelver Shiites, Mahdi is still alive and in occultation (concealment). While hidden from ordinary eyes, he takes a hand in world affairs by guiding current spiritual leaders and his qualified followers. It is believed that his return at the end of the time will usher in an era of ultimate peace and justice on earth.

with swords (a popular act usually not authorized by religious authorities). This self-flagellation is a symbolic act indicating regret that they could not be present in Karbala to help the imam and his innocent family; it is also a means of sharing their suffering.

Muharram commemoration ceremonies, known by various names in different countries (*Rawda* in Iran, *Majlis* in India, and *Quarry* in Iraq), are often followed by public distribution of meals and sweet drinks in remembrance of the hunger and thirst that Husayn and his family suffered in Karbala. This is customary among Shiite families and is often done in fulfillment of a vow. Also part of the ceremonies is the *Taziyah,* a theatrical reenactment of the Karbala tragedy (referred to by some as the Shiite passion play), which began in Iran under the Safavids and continues to be performed in some parts of Iran, Iraq, and Lebanon.

MODE OF DRESS No specific mode of dress is adopted by ordinary Shiites. Shiite clergy are distinguished from laypersons by their professional dress, which consists of a long gown (*aba*) and a turban (*ammamah*). The color of the turban, black or white, indicates whether the person is a sayyid. The sayyids (who wear black turbans) claim genealogical ties to one of the descendants of the Prophet.

DIETARY PRACTICES The Shiite school of law confirms the dietary regulations prescribed in the Koran and elaborated in the Shariah. As such, it does not differ from the four Sunni schools of law on what types of food are *halal* (permissible) or *haram* (forbidden). Drinking water, however, has special meaning for a devout Shiite: It reminds him or her of the suffering of Imam Husayn and his companions, who were denied access to water for some days prior to their massacre in Karbala. Shiites teach their children from an early age that before drinking water they should say, "May I drink in remembrance of Husayn."

RITUALS Twelver Shiism shares with Sunni Islam the fundamental rituals of daily prayer, fasting in the month of Ramadan, hajj (pilgrimage), and payment of *zakat.* There are, however, minor differences in the performance of prayers. Although the times of day, number of prayer units (*rakah*), prayer content, and postures are the same, Shiites usually, but not necessarily, shorten the waiting time (one to two hours among Sunnis) between the noon and afternoon prayers by saying them a few minutes apart. The waiting time is similarly shortened between the evening and night prayers. The Shiite call to prayer (*adhan*), moreover, states Ali's name following that of the Prophet. Shiites refrain from crossing their hands over their chests or abdomens during prayer, and

they insist that during the prostration phase the forehead should be placed on nonanimal, natural objects, mostly dust, stone, or the earth. Out of practicality small blocks of baked mud, called *muhr,* are used, preferably made from *turbat-e Karbala* (dust from the earth of Karbala).

Shiites are also required to pay *khums,* a tax that amounts to one-fifth of their total annual savings and of any net increase in their property. This practice is mentioned in the Koran and was performed during the Prophet's time. *Khums, zakat,* and other religious donations are paid to a *marja al-taqlid* (who functions as a representative of the hidden twelfth imam) and are used for helping the needy and for establishing and maintaining mosques and religious education centers.

There are no fundamental differences in burial rites between Shiites and Sunnis. Shiites observe a longer period of mourning and hold special ceremonies on the third, seventh, and fortieth days following a death, as well as on the anniversary. They also often visit the tombs of their deceased relatives, whose burial markers, engraved with biographical information, are kept in good condition for many generations.

RITES OF PASSAGE There are no distinctive Shiite rites of passage.

MEMBERSHIP In its early phase the Shiite population grew naturally, as some members of the *ummah,* or Islamic community, chose to join the followers of Ali or other imams. Even in its later phase, when Twelver Shiism developed its own organizational structure, there was no office with the specific task of missionary activities. Nevertheless, Shiism has always been open to accepting new members, and there have been some Shiite clergy and mosques involved in proselytizing.

RELIGIOUS TOLERANCE Generally speaking, the Shariah (Islamic law), which is based on the Koran, is tolerant of People of the Book—Jews, Christians, and other religious minorities that possess divine scriptures and have received revelations from God. Excluded is any religious tradition that proclaims a prophecy after Muhammad. For this reason the Bahai tradition, which developed from an offshoot of nineteenth-century Shiite thought (Babism) and claims to offer a new prophecy, has not been tolerated in Iran, where Shiism is the state religion. As a minority, Shiites themselves have been

Seveners and Fivers

A minority of Shiites, about 20 percent, are members of the Sevener (Ismailiyah) or Fiver (Zaydiyah) subgroups. Their political histories, theologies, and religious practices are radically different from those of the Twelvers (Ithna Ashariyyah), who represent the remaining 80 percent of Shiites. These groups formed over disagreements about the selection of an imam, or successor to the prophet Muhammad.

The Fivers, or Zaydiyah, were founded in 720 C.E. when Zayd, a grandson of Husayn (the third imam), rebelled against the Sunni leader of the Umayyad empire. Zayd's followers recognized him as the fifth imam (thus the name Fivers), unlike other Shiites, who believed the imam was Zayd's half brother Muhammad al-Baqir. According to the Fivers, now mostly in Yemen, the rightful imam may be any descendent of Husayn (son of the Shiite founder, Ali) who establishes himself through an armed rebellion. This view is reflected in their tendency to be more politically active—and, during their formative years, militant—compared with other Shiites.

When the sixth imam died in 765 C.E., most of his followers accepted his son Musa al-Kazim as the seventh imam, but a minority recognized his eldest son, Ismail, instead. Since then the latter have followed a succession of imans who descend from Ismail. Ismaili Shiites are referred to as Seveners because they disagree with Twelver Shiism over the selection of the seventh imam.

At the end of the eleventh century another dispute over succession caused the Seveners to subdivide into the Nizari and the Mustali factions. The Nizaris are now known as the Khojas and live primarily in Pakistan, India, Iran, Yemen, and East Africa; their spiritual leader is called the Aga Khan. The Mustalis are now known as Bohras, and the majority live in the state of Gujarat in India.

Seveners follow few traditional Muslim practices. For instance, instead of mosques, they have *jama/at khanah*s ("gathering houses"). They follow the Five Pillars of Islam, but the interpretation of these, and of the Koran, may be changed by the reigning imam. This is because they emphasize a highly esoteric and symbolic meaning of both the scripture and the acts of worship. For Ismailis, hajj (pilgrimage) is fulfilled not by a trip to Mecca but rather by seeing the imam.

subject to persecutions and prejudices to varying degrees throughout their history.

SOCIAL JUSTICE Shia Islam has from its inception been concerned with social justice and has upheld the egalitarian spirit of the Koran and the Prophet. Indeed, it was over the issue of social justice that many of the Prophet's prominent companions and other members of the *ummah* turned to Ali. Ali's concern for social equality and his reign as caliph set the example for *adl wa qist* (justice and fairness) for both Sunni and Shiite Muslims. In Islamic, and particularly Shiite, literature, Ali's name is invariably associated with justice. *Khums,* the obligatory religious tax for Shiites, indicates an institutionalized concern for maintaining social and economic justice. In addition to discussing the Prophet's exemplary treatment of the poor and downtrodden, Shiite ethical texts include numerous examples from Ali's life, which was devoted to the cause of the poor, orphans, widows, and

other disadvantaged groups. Ali symbolizes contentment, rejection of material attachment, and standing for the cause of justice.

In addition to *khums, zakat,* and general charities, Shiites also donate money to the shrines of different imams, which have large endowments and charity organizations.

SOCIAL ASPECTS Family constitutes the core unit of Shiite society and the foundation of its religious life. The laws on marriage and divorce are fundamentally the same among Twelver Shiites and Sunnis, as both ground their rules on the Koran and the Shariah. There is, however, one major exception: The Shiite school of law allows, yet strictly regulates, temporary marriage (*mutah*), in which a duration, such as a day, a month, or three years, is chosen for the marriage. This practice was permitted at the time of the Prophet and his first successor, Abu Bakr. It was prohibited by the second caliph, Umar, and then it was restored by Ali, the fourth caliph.

Divorce in Shiite law is generally more difficult. Distinct from the Sunni schools, the statement of the divorce formula should be made explicitly and in the presence of two witnesses. It is not acceptable if made in a state of intoxication or anger. Also, Shiite law does not allow innovated divorce (*talaq al-bidah*), in which three pronouncements of divorce (rendering it irrevocable) are made on a single occasion.

CONTROVERSIAL ISSUES Like Sunni Islam, Shiism is opposed to abortion and homosexuality. Abortion is permitted only if the mother's life is at risk, though some jurists allow it before the "ensoulment" period (before the soul enters the fetus, occurring 120 days after conception). The majority of Shiite jurists permit the use of contraceptives, and family planning and population control programs (which promote contraceptives and other methods) are not considered religiously unlawful. Such programs are permitted even in Iran under the Islamic regime, which is in the hands of Shiite jurists.

CULTURAL IMPACT The twelve imams provide models for both the temporal and spiritual domains of life. Shiite literature is replete with stories about the imam's patience, wisdom, piety, self-sacrifice, and resistance to injustice. In Twelver Shiism there is a messianic expectation that the twelfth imam, Mahdi, will come out of his concealment and bring ultimate peace and justice to the world. A special genre of Shiite poetry in celebration of Mahdi's virtues reflects the depth of yearning for his return.

Although Shiites, like Sunnis, insist that there is no intermediary between God and humankind, it is a common Shiite practice to appeal to the imams, as *walis* (divine guardians), for spiritual or even temporal aid. The Shiite perception of Ali as a supreme *wali* is reflected in popular Shiite paintings that portray him sitting in a powerful posture yet with a majestic simplicity. Although Muslims are not supposed to portray any religious figure, it is possible to find such pictures of Ali in the houses of devotees who want to visualize the subject of their love. Such pictures, however, are not used as objects of worship.

The suppression of Shiites in Karbala has had a notable impact on all aspects of Shiite life and culture. The artistic expressions and imagination of Shiites are inextricably inspired by the themes of this event. *Musibat*, a genre of religious epic that narrates the events of Karbala, occupies a prominent place in Shiite literature. Themes of martyrdom, heroism, the suffering of the oppressed, and messianism are commonly used in paintings and the performing arts. The *Taziyah*, a reenactment of the Karbala tragedy, has served as the precursor of modern theater among Shiite Muslims.

Forough Jahanbakhsh

See Also Vol. 1: *Islam*

Bibliography

Daftary, Farhad. *The Isma'ilis: Their History and Doctrines*. New York: Cambridge University Press, 1990.

Jafri, S. Husain M. *Origins and Early Development of Shi'a Islam*. London: Longman, 1981.

Momen, Moojan. *An Introduction to Shi'i Islam: The History and Doctrines of Twelver Shi'ism*. New Haven: Yale University Press, 1985.

Nasr, S. Husayn, Hamid Dabashi, and S. Vali Reza Nasr, eds. *Expectation of the Millennium: Shi'ism in History*. New York: State University of New York Press, 1989.

Richard, Yann. *Shi'ite Islam*. Translated by Antonia Nevill. Oxford: Blackwell, 1995.

Sachedina, Abdulaziz. *Islamic Messianism: The Idea of Mahdi in Twelver Shi'ism*. Albany: State University of New York Press, 1981.

Sobhani, Jafar, and Reza Shah Kazemi. *Doctrines of Shi'i Islam: A Compendium of Imami Beliefs and Practices*. London: I.B. Tauris, 2001.

Tabataba'i, S. Muhammad Husayn. *Shi'a*. Translated by Sayyid Husayn Nasr. Qum, Iran: Ansariyan Publication, 1981.

Sunnism

FOUNDED: 632 C.E.

RELIGION AS A PERCENTAGE OF WORLD POPULATION: 15 percent

OVERVIEW Sunnism is the largest branch of Islam, representing more than 80 percent of all Muslims. The word itself derives from the Arabic *sunnah,* which means "accepted or established practice."

Sunnis claim that they represent the traditional, common understanding of Islam proclaimed by the prophet Muhammad ibn Abdullah (c. 570–632 C.E.), who founded Islam. As such, they differentiate themselves from the Shiites, the other major branch of Islam. Sunnism focuses on the collective will of the group, emphasizing consensus on religious, social, political, legal, and doctrinal issues.

After its founding in the seventh century C.E. Sunnism became entrenched as the religion of the expanding Islamic empire in the Middle East. It initially spread through state conquest, but eventually immigrants, merchants, and Sufi adherents carried its distinctive message eastward to Southeast Asia and China and westward to Africa and the Mediterranean basin. It has remained the favored perspective espoused by most governments and state institutions throughout the Islamic world. Today its adherents are found in almost every country in the world.

HISTORY The Koran, the sacred text of Islam, does not recognize a distinctive group called Sunnis. Rather, Sunnism is one of two broad movements that evolved in the Muslim community after the Prophet's death in 632 C.E. Disagreement over who was Muhammad's legitimate successor led to a schism between two groups, Sunnis and Shiites, resulting in two interpretations of Islam and two different sacred histories.

According to Sunnism, Muhammad left no written will at his death, and thus no one could claim to be his designated successor. On the day before he died, however, he had ordered a longtime associate, Abu Bakr, to lead the community in prayer. After Muhammad's funeral, members of the Islamic community chose Abu Bakr to be his successor without much apparent contention. They were convinced by the lofty position that Abu Bakr held in the community, as well as by his selection as prayer leader, which they saw as a signal from the Prophet. From that moment on, most Muslims believed that the majority view should decide crucial issues, including who should be its leader. Followers of this belief became known as *ahl al-sunnah wa'l-jama'ah* (people of established practice and of the community), or Sunnis.

A minority of Muslims opposed the Sunni position, claiming that during his last pilgrimage the Prophet had named Ali, his cousin and son-in-law, as his successor. They came to be known as the Shia (partisans) of Ali, later shortened to Shia or Shiites. The disagreement over succession spawned a series of four internal battles called *fitnah*s (seditions), which were interspersed between the years 632 to 819 C.E. The Sunnis argued that the Muslim community should be understood as the collectivity of all believers, which was responsible for

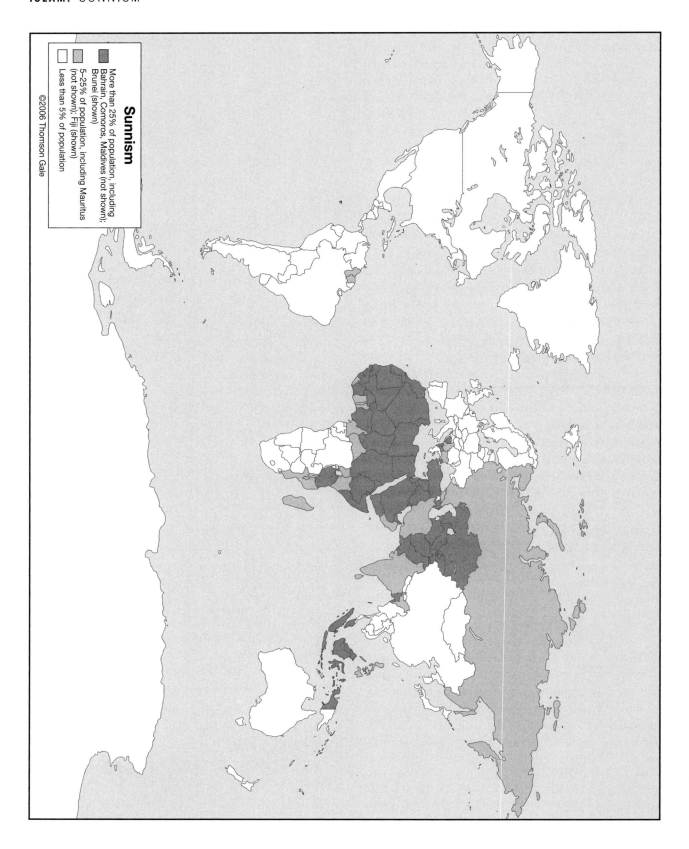

deciding what should be done about any controversial issue, including succession. They eventually argued that God guided the collective will of his believers. Although Ali was selected as the fourth caliph (successor of Muhammad) in 656, by the time Ali was assassinated five years later, the two groups were sufficiently differentiated that Muslims could identify to which faction a person belonged. Eventually Sunnis embraced their name as a way to affirm their loyalty to accepted traditions associated with the Prophet, which, they held, formed the basis of a growing Islamic consensus.

Over the years Sunnis often ruled Muslim empires, but they had to deal with explaining just what their defining value, consensus, entailed. Many problems required going beyond the simple statements that had been passed down to the rulers from the Prophet. Hence, Sunnis supported a wide range of intellectuals (physicians, Koranic interpreters, historians, scientists, and educators). A class of scholars known as the ulama developed, providing the basis for an international Sunnism to thrive. Scholars organized Islamic sources into legal texts (which were accepted as authoritative), and ordinary Sunnis gradually deferred to these scholars (or legists) on most matters of faith and law. These believers increasingly espoused the Shari'ah (the system of Muslim law) not just as a means to solve their legal problems but also as a way to understand and follow God's will.

Sunnis were not the only Muslims who embraced the Shari'ah as a spiritual guide, but because Sunnism provided the foundation for its development, the Shari'ah became inextricably connected to how people understood Sunnism. When scholars speak of the classical period of Islam (c. 900–1200 C.E.), they are usually referring to a time when consciousness of the Shari'ah combined with other great achievements throughout the Muslim world, forming the pinnacle of Islamic, and Sunni, civilization. For the ordinary believer the triumph of the Sunni perspective indicated that divine providence accompanied its system of values, and its success coalesced in the popular mind with that of worldwide Islam. By the end of the classical period, however, Sunnis faced an important question: whether new perspectives could be incorporated without seriously modifying the assumptions of its system. Some ulama argued that the door to new insights should be closed, and the result was a social order that found it difficult to confront changes associated with modernity.

Sunni girls pray during afternoon prayer at a mosque in Iraq. Sunnis embrace all the central rites of Islam, the most fundamental of which include daily prayer, fasting during Ramadan, almsgiving, and hajj (pilgrimage).
© LYNSEY ADDARIO/CORBIS.

Beginning in the thirteenth century a unified sense of Sunnism was also challenged by the emergence of independent states and emirates, who relied less on an international Sunni value system. That, along with the loss of any real power behind a unifying figure like the caliph, led to political fragmentation in the Islamic world, which signaled a weakening of Muslim cohesion. By the time of the Renaissance in Europe in the 1500s, when the West challenged Muslim civilization, the word Sunni had taken on a meaning close to "doctrinaire." Thus, Sunnism often appeared to Western commentators as Islam's "orthodoxy."

In the eighteenth and nineteenth centuries political issues increasingly dominated Sunnism. As a result of Western colonialism, the Muslim world was severed into small nation-states, each vying for legitimacy, further weakening Muslim cohesion. By the end of the twentieth century most Muslim countries were dealing with militant fundamentalist groups bent on reform. These anti-Western and anti-regime movements were characterized by a commitment to the international triumph of Islam and a rigid opposition to all things not of Islamic origin. Although such groups considered themselves Sunni, their views were not shared by the majority of Sunnis; instead, they represented a new Islamic identity that could not be understood in terms of classical Sunnism.

Sunni youth sit during a lesson in an Islamic school in Egypt. The scholarly class has exercised more control over the Sunni point of view than any other group, until, perhaps, the rise of Islamism, or fundamentalism, in the contemporary period. © AFP/CORBIS.

CENTRAL DOCTRINES Sunni doctrine affirms that God of Islam, or Allah, is the only God, a concept underlined in the Koran by the word *tawhid* (unity, or oneness of God). Shiite belief differs little on this issue.

Often the Koran calls for believers to heed what the Prophet says and does. Yet Sunnis insist that the Prophet was but a man, and they have forbidden not only the worship of the Prophet but also the creation of any images of him. Moreover, Sunnis affirm that Muhammad is the seal of the prophets (33:40), meaning that he brought the final and complete message from God. Sunnis are convinced that God will not speak again through any other spokesperson, so they have opposed newer claims to apostleship by other Muslims, such as the Ahmadiyya reformers in India and Pakistan.

Nevertheless, the Prophet was considered an ideal model, and memories of what he said and did were written down. Eventually these were collected in books known as the hadith (usually translated as "traditions"). Sunnis treasure six of these collections, beginning with

the ninth-century collections of Muhammad ibn Isma'il al-Bukhari and Muslim ibnu'l-Hajjaj.

Early in the classical age of Islam another view of the religion, known as Mu'tazilism, developed within Sunnism. The scholars who shaped this perspective tried to apply a rational and allegorical interpretation to the Koran. Ultimately Sunnis rejected their approach, insisting that the Koran was not a matter for philosophical speculation but rather a set of codes by which one should live. This is why some commentators do not speak about orthodoxy in Islam but "orthopraxy," meaning a standard way of living.

Sunnis have debated the issue of free will versus predestination. Most Sunnis hold that a person's life is intersected by God's will in many crucial but nonassertive ways, but the Koran states that God guides whom he will, implying that a person's destiny is in the hands of God. The Koran seems to offer a balance between the notion of free will and predestination. As a result, Sunnis believe that humans should live in submission to God, even while acknowledging that their end is in God's hands.

Islamic law does not function as law in the West does. The emphasis in Sunni courts is to guide Muslims toward living the true Islamic life and thus to turn society into a normative Muslim community. Sunnis generally practice according to one of four schools of law, which vary on some issues and are distributed regionally: Hanafi (Iraq, Turkey, India, Pakistan, Afghanistan), Maliki (North and West Africa), Shafi'i (Yemen, Egypt, Malaysia, Indonesia, Philippines), and Hanbali (Saudi Arabia). Because of historical factors such as population movements and changes in the ruling dynasties, Muslims in areas such as Syria or the West may find multiple schools in the same location.

MORAL CODE OF CONDUCT The Sunni moral code is a product of the Koran, which often expresses the importance of action over belief. In the same vein, the Prophet is said to have voiced the Muslim Golden Rule: "No man is a true believer unless he desires for his brother that which he desires for himself." Moreover, the Koran commands an ethics of retaliation (42:42)— that is, turning the other cheek is not acceptable when faced with an evil person.

Everyday activities are normally evaluated according to two concepts, *halal* (permissible) and *haram* (forbidden). *Halal* encompasses all things that the Koran, the hadith, and Sunni culture have decided are permitted. Thus, only animals killed according to proper procedures are permitted to be eaten. *Haram* applies to all those acts that the sources define as being forbidden, such as suicide or eating pork.

Sunni law developed more nuanced approaches to moral issues by classifying acts according to three further categories—neutral, recommended, and reprehensible—which, along with *halal* and *haram,* provided five possible *ahkam,* or rulings. There has been debate about how these principles should be applied to an individual's actions, and Sunni courts require that the context for such actions be established.

SACRED BOOKS The Koran is the sacred scripture for both Sunnis and Shiites. The prophet Muhammad received the holy text in 610 C.E. when the archangel Gabriel told him to "recite"; this revelatory process continued until Muhammad's death in 632. Immediately afterward Abu Bakr, the first caliph (successor to the Prophet), began collecting these revelations in what became the Koran, an activity that was completed by Uthman about 20 years later. This text was accepted as canonical, and all other versions were destroyed. Sunnis have stood by the veracity of this text, despite questions raised about it.

Sunnis regard the Koran as God's last instruction; it is the ultimate authority on all matters of doctrine, religious behavior, and faith. All Sunnis maintain that even though the version we know was compiled after the time of the Prophet, it reflects an eternal message; it is said that the original book ("the mother of the book") has always resided with God in heaven. Sunnis also hold that the Koran's message was sent to all prophets but that the other resulting sacred scriptures were either lost or reflect a modification of the pure original message. Thus, the Koran stands above all scriptures because of its claim to be God's word alone.

Sunni scholars consider Ibn Ishaq's *Sirat Rasul Allah* (late seventh century; "The Biography of the Prophet") to be of historical importance for depicting the setting of the Koran. This book has taken on almost canonical significance for its explanation of how the message came to be given through the prophet Muhammad. Among Sunnis, too, collections of the hadith (traditions) of the Prophet, as collected by the scholars Muhammad ibn Isma'il al-Bukhari (810–70) and Muslim ibnu'l-Hajjaj (819–75), are accorded a paramount place in its theological literature.

SACRED SYMBOLS Because in Islam only God's creations are to receive the greatest praise, and because turning an object into a totem or fetish is condemned, Sunnis venerate few human-made symbols. There are, however, some symbols of Muslim identity. The Kaaba, or cube, is the small, almost square building in the center of the courtyard of the Grand Mosque in Mecca. Muslims worldwide pray toward the Kaaba. While the Kaaba serves as the prime symbol for all Muslims, it has always been in the hands of Sunnis.

EARLY AND MODERN LEADERS All Sunni Muslims regard the "rightly-guided" caliphs—the first four leaders of the Muslim community (Abu Bakr, Umar, Uthman, and Ali)—to be the crucial early leaders. Over the years factionalism has determined which of these leaders Sunnis have honored most.

An important leader at the pinnacle of Islam's classical period was Harun al-Rashid (786–809), whose caliphate in Baghdad was seen as taking Sunnism to unsurpassed excellence and splendor. Sunnism was also invigorated by Akbar (1556–1605), a Mughal emperor who firmly established Islam in northern India.

Mustafa Kemal, known as Ataturk (1881–1938), was responsible for a major rethinking of traditional Islamic statehood. His reforms in Turkey shifted the state's goals away from embodying religious ideology and toward adapting Sunnism to a modern society. Muhammad Ali Jinnah (1876–1948) founded the Islamic republic of Pakistan in 1947, attempting to maintain a Sunni identity within a Western political structure. Gamal Abdel Nasser (1918–70) applied a socialist ideology to the Islamic state when he established a republic in Egypt in 1956.

Backlashes against non-Islamic trends have resulted in Sunni reform movements. One of the most important was Wahhabism, a conservative reform movement founded by Muhammad ibn 'Abd al-Wahhab (1703–92). A second movement emerged around Hasan al-Banna' (1906–49), whose Sunni Egyptian organization, the Muslim Brotherhood, spread throughout the Arab world, providing institutional growth for Islamism, or fundamentalism.

Sunni radical leadership has continued to express a wide variety of perspectives. Osama bin Laden (born in Saudi Arabia in 1957) encouraged the use of terror and indiscriminate violence to overthrow Western culture and political structures. Of perhaps equal relevance,

The Ideal Leader of an Islamic State

Traditional Sunnism holds that in a true Islamic state, religion and politics are united. What constitutes the true Islamic state, however, has been a matter of debate within the tradition, as have been the ideal qualities of the person who should lead the state. Some Sunnis believe that the true Islamic community is led by a religious person whose piety indicates that he or she is God's choice as political leader. For instance, Abu Bakr, the first caliph (or successor to the prophet Muhammad, 632–32), has long been seen as a pious man who had little skill in governance but whose closeness to the Prophet justified his position. Other Sunnis maintain that Muslims should be led by someone with political acumen but no special piety. An example is Gamal Abdel Nasser (1918–70), who in 1956 established Egypt as a republic compatible with Islamic principles; he possessed considerable political savvy but was not a particularly religious man.

though representing a different outlook, is Wallace Warith Din Muhammad (born in 1933), head of an Islamic movement in the United States—first called the Nation of Islam and then the American Muslim Society—begun by his father, Elijah Muhammad (1897–1975). Warith has dramatically changed an American sectarian movement into one of the most respected Sunni organizations in the Western world. In the United States the Muslim feminist perspective has been expressed effectively in the writings of Egyptian-born Leila Ahmed (born in 1940).

MAJOR THEOLOGIANS AND AUTHORS Rabi'ah al-Adawiyya (eighth century) of Basra, Iraq, was a devoted Sunni woman of Sufi (mystic) convictions; her asceticism inspired generations of *muridin* (devotees) to spend their lives in meditation. Abu Hamid al-Ghazali (1058–1111), head of a school in Baghdad, underwent such a spiritual revolution that he abandoned his career and wrote books reconciling the mystical tradition with Sunni legal thinking. Sunni civilization was also influ-

enced by writers such as Jalal al-Din al-Rumi (1207–73), a Sufi poet and savant; Ibn al-Arabi (1165–1240), a theosophist and metaphysical thinker; and Ibn Khaldun (1332–1406), who founded the study of societies (and by extension, sociology) with his concept of 'asabiyya (group cohesion).

Modern religious reformists include Jamal al-Din al-Afghani (1839–97), a political revolutionary who resisted British imperialism in Islamic territories; Sayyid Ahmad Khan (1817–98), a Muslim modernist and advocate of Westernizing reform in India; Muhammad Abduh (1849–1905), an advocate of Islamic modernism in Egypt; Sayyid Abdul Ala Mawdudi (1904–79), a neoconservative reformer and fundamentalist ideologue in Pakistan; and Sayyid Qutb (1906–66), the principal theorist of the contemporary radical Islamist movement.

ORGANIZATIONAL STRUCTURE Because Sunnism has no priesthood and no explicit religious hierarchy, there is no one spokesperson for the tradition. Over the course of history the ulama have come to be considered official authorities of Islamic learning, and they have often represented Sunnism. The scholarly class has exercised more control over the Sunni point of view than any other group, except, perhaps, until the rise of Islamism, or fundamentalism, in the contemporary period. Under the influence of Islamism another aspect of contemporary Sunni life has come to the fore: a small number of people, using media and technology, have been able to have a disproportionate power over public opinion.

HOUSES OF WORSHIP AND HOLY PLACES There are no essential differences between Sunnis and Shiites concerning places of worship. Indeed, though the mosque is the common house of worship, a Muslim needs no building to carry out his or her religious responsibilities. No representation of the human form appears in mosques, because Islam forbids any image to be worshiped. By far the best-known Muslim building is the Kaaba in the center of the Grand Mosque in Mecca. Sunnis who belong to a Sufi order may also pray in a meeting place called a *zawiya, takiyah,* or *khaniqah.* One corner of these buildings usually features the tomb of the order's saint or founder.

Some places are sacred, such as Mecca, Medina, Jerusalem. While they are not exclusively honored by Sunnis, they hold a special place in Sunni consciousness because they have been under Sunni control.

WHAT IS SACRED? All Muslims treat the Koran with special care. It is regarded by some as so powerful that it is deemed to have curative powers (a folk belief often found among ordinary Sunnis).

Lives of saintly figures such as Muhammad were early on thought to contain a powerful spiritual element called *baraka*. Moreover, founders and leaders of Sufi orders are often considered to have *baraka*, and seeking their help with some problem is recognized as a way of appropriating the saint's power to one's life. According to some Moroccan Sunnis, tombs of the saints can contain *baraka*, and consequently the countryside is dotted with sacred places for visitation.

HOLIDAYS AND FESTIVALS Sunnism observes all major Muslim holidays (including Id al-Fitr, celebrating the end of the Ramadan fast, and Id al-Adha, the Feast of Sacrifice). Most Sunni countries also celebrate the birthday of the Prophet. This is in contrast to Shiite communities, where Ali or other Shiite figures receive prominent attention.

MODE OF DRESS Sunnism has not developed a distinctive dress code. Diversity is the norm within Muslim communities, and ethnicity and culture have often had greater influence than religion on clothing. Nevertheless, at times throughout history some distinctive styles have been supported by Sunni culture.

Wearing the *hijab*, or veil, almost always identifies a woman as a conservative Muslim; some Sunni women go so far as to wear the *burqa*, a loose garment that covers the whole body, including the head and face, with only a slit for the eyes. A significant challenge to the Sunni use of the *hijab* was made by an Egyptian woman, Huda Sharawi (1879–1947), early in the twentieth century. She led like-minded feminists in discarding the veil. Supporters of the *hijab* point to the purported styles adopted by Muhammad's wives, while detractors argue that it arose in classical society as a way for the highest-class women to distinguish themselves from the working class and that it was thus not meant as a requirement for all women.

DIETARY PRACTICES Sunnis observe all the dietary laws of Islam. There are minor differences between the various Sunni law schools; for example, depending on the school, eating shellfish is classified as forbidden, reprehensible, or neutral.

RITUALS Sunnis embrace all the central rites of Islam, the most fundamental of which include daily prayer, fasting during Ramadan, almsgiving, and hajj (pilgrimage). There are only minor differences between Sunnis and Shiites in these areas.

RITES OF PASSAGE Sunnis practice four major rites of passage: birth, circumcision, marriage, and death. They celebrate the birth of child with the *'aqiqa*, a sacrifice of an animal on the seventh day after birth.

Circumcision of boys is a marker of Muslim, and Sunni, identity; for example, in Egypt it occurs when a boy has completed the recitation of the Koran, usually at about age 12. For many Middle Eastern Muslims, completing the Koran's memorization is a sign that the adolescent is ready to move into the realm of adult responsibility.

A small number of Sunni cultures also perform female circumcision, depending upon ethnic custom and the interpretation of a particular statement of the Prophet. In the societies that practice this rite, it takes place at the onset of puberty. Girls are then deemed capable of being married, so the rite is associated with passage to adulthood. Most Sunni cultures oppose female circumcision.

Sunnism regards marriage as a blessing from God and views sexuality within marriage to be healthy and beneficial, so the wedding is an occasion for great community festivity. Thereafter, both parties take their places as members of the adult community. A major difference between Sunnism and Shiism is the practice of *mut'ah* (temporary) marriage, in which a duration, such as a day, a month, or three years, is chosen for the marriage. Sunni law rejects it, and Shiite law accepts it (although it is rarely practiced).

MEMBERSHIP Because the Koran explicitly recognizes the legitimacy of other People of the Book (Jews and Christians), there is no attempt within Islam to launch a widespread program for conversion from other faiths. Generally speaking, Muslims, including Sunnis, are content to present information about Islam if asked.

Islamic law states that Muslim women may not marry non-Muslim men. In the West and in places where Muslims are a minority, however, male conversion through marriage is one means of community growth. In the United States the Nation of Islam has been particularly effective in organizing prison missions, with the result that many young African-American men are converted to Islam while incarcerated. Conservative Muslims are also energetic in presenting Islam's message to inquirers. One group that has sent "missionaries" throughout the world is the Tablighi Jamaat, a Sunni reformist group based in the Indian subcontinent; it argues that Muslim society must return to its spiritual roots and properly extol the virtues of true Islam. This group, however, focuses its attention on Muslims.

RELIGIOUS TOLERANCE Because Sunnism expanded through military conquest in the early days, Sunni's commitment to tolerance is often questioned. For example, members of the Ahmadiyya sect, who mainly live in Pakistan, claim widespread intolerance of their views by the majority Sunni population. Most observers, however, note that there is little evidence of systemic intolerance in Sunnism. For centuries Sunnis have lived in close proximity to all major religions without making any concerted attempt to undermine them, and in most cases they have constructed good working relationships with other religions. Most Sunnis regard attacks against adherents of other religions to be forbidden, and they strongly criticize ultra-conservative and reactionary factions who do this in the name of Islam. Almost all Sunnis condemned the terrorist attacks in the United States on 11 September 2001, and they have insisted that intolerance is a characteristic of radical Islamist groups, not of Sunnism as a whole.

SOCIAL JUSTICE Sunnism stresses egalitarian principles. The integration of religion and politics in Sunni community life means that politics cannot override what religion guarantees. Even a person of the lowest status can claim that God has provided him or her with certain rights. Thus, in dispensing justice within the community, a Sunni ruler or official is charged to uphold rights above all else. Most Sunnis believe that an individual's rights include freedom of religion, the right to existence, and the right to own property. In Pakistan groups such as the All-Pakistan Women's Association and Women's Action Forum, while not overtly Sunni in their approach, have affiliates that argue for women's rights as a value consistent with Sunni teachings on equality. Progressive Muslims have used Sunni notions of equality to advocate a "gender jihad," arguing for a vigorous rethinking of the traditional relationship between the sexes in Muslim societies.

SOCIAL ASPECTS Sunnis typically live in a close-knit environment emphasizing personal piety, private family festivities, public prayer in the mosque, and community celebration. A key to this environment is marriage. Embracing the notion that the normative Muslim life is married life, Muslim families spend a great deal of time and effort in securing a good marriage for their children.

CONTROVERSIAL ISSUES The most controversial aspect of Sunnism is the relationship between its tradition and the various fundamentalist or radical movements. Reflecting the Islamic revival that has been underway since the nineteenth century, some citizens of Muslim countries are reluctant to support secular governments on the grounds that Islam will be removed from the center of the state's values and that religious minorities will be granted the same political power as Muslims.

An important issue debated by Sunnis is whether Islam is compatible with Western-style democracy. At its extreme Sunni conservatism has given birth to anti-Western, antimodern religiopolitical governments (such as the Taliban of Afghanistan), as well as militant reactionary groups (such as al-Qaeda). Many Sunni theologians have been shocked by militant's promotion of politically motivated suicide, because all Sunni scholars have condemned suicide.

In Sunnism human existence is sacred; a human is regarded as the unique creation of God, and the entire person belongs to God. Therefore, euthanasia and abortion are not allowed. Because the body is required for resurrection and judgment, Sunnis traditionally resisted any alteration of the cadaver, including the use of the corpse for teaching and research purposes or even, at one time, for autopsy. Today autopsies are allowed.

CULTURAL IMPACT The Koran, as the primary element of Muslim life, has had an impact on most Sunni artistic expressions. The holy text itself has been glorified with elaborately developed scripts, which are used for decorative purposes in mosques and public buildings. Because Sunnis insist on consensus, what can or cannot be a subject of art has been a matter of public debate. The broad cultural synthesis that was characteristic of Sunnism in its golden age has been shattered in the modern era by influences that have largely arisen from the West and from modern technology. Mosque architectural style, for example, may now reflect worldwide tastes, but often the decor remains traditional, with arabesque, calligraphy, and domes. Popular Sunni musicians in the United States, Europe, and the Middle East have wedded religious words to rap and rock music to appeal to a new generation of Muslim youth.

Earle H. Waugh

See Also Vol. I: *Islam*

Bibliography

'Abduh, Muhammad. *The Theology of Unity.* Translated by Ishaq Musa'ad and Kenneth Cragg. London: Allen and Unwin, 1966.

Ahmed, Leila. *Women and Gender in Islam: Historical Roots of a Modern Debate.* New Haven, Conn., and London: Yale University Press, 1992.

Arberry, A.J., trans. *The Koran Interpreted.* 2 vols. London: Allen and Unwin; New York: Macmillan, 1955.

Boullata, Issa J. *Trends and Issues in Contemporary Arab Thought.* Albany: State University of New York Press, 1990.

Ibn Ishaq, Muhammad. *The Life of Muhammad: A Translation of Ibn Ishaq's Sirat Rasul Allah.* Translated by Alfred Guillaume. London and Karachi: Oxford University Press, 1955.

Madelung, Wilferd. *The Succession to Muhammad: A Study of the Early Caliphate.* Cambridge: Cambridge University Press, 1996.

Marsh, Clifton. *From Black Muslims to Muslims.* Metuchen, N.J., and London: Scarecrow Press, 1984.

Rahman, Fazlur. *Islam.* London: Weidenfeld and Nicolson, 1966.

————. *Islam and Modernity: Transformation of an Intellectual Tradition.* Chicago: University of Chicago Press, 1982.

Watt, W. Montgomery. *The Formative Period of Islamic Thought.* Edinburgh: Edinburgh University Press, 1973.

Yusuf Ali, Abdullah, trans. *The Holy Qur'an: Text, Translation, and Commentary.* Elmhurst, N.Y.: Tahrike Tarsile Qur'an, Inc., 1987.

Jainism

FOUNDED: c. 550 B.C.E.

RELIGION AS A PERCENTAGE OF WORLD POPULATION: 0.1 percent

OVERVIEW Jain doctrine states that the religion has been periodically renewed by enlightened people, or Jinas, since a beginningless time, but scholars date Jainism as it is practiced today to Lord Mahavira, a Jina who lived in India in the sixth century B.C.E. The religion spread from Bihar in the east to the south and west of India and later to other parts of the world. Today there are 3.35 million Jains in India, with several thousand elsewhere in Asia and in Europe, Africa, and North America. Although they are a minority, Jains are an influential force in India because of their affluence. Most Jains marry and thus are laypeople, although some renounce the life of householders to become monks and nuns.

Jainism is the most nonviolent and austere religion in the world, and it is perhaps the most difficult to practice. Not only do Jains attempt never to harm humans and animals, but the strict nonviolence followed by monks and nuns proscribes harm to any being, even microscopic organisms. Austerities include long and difficult fasts, and monks and nuns pull their hair out by the roots from two to five times a year and travel throughout India barefoot. Some monks do not wear any clothing. The purpose of practicing nonviolence and austerities is to purify karma, particles that cling to the soul and prevent it from reaching an enlightened state and avoiding reincarnation. Although Jain asceticism is severe, laymen are highly successful and are among the richest people in India. Their wealth is balanced, however, by their philanthropy and by the asceticism of Jain laywomen.

As with Buddhism and Hindu renunciation, Jainism is part of India's ascetic heritage. Like Buddhism, Jainism refused to recognize the authority of the Hindu Vedas, of Vedic sacrifices, or of Brahman priests. The Jain practice of renunciation also differed from that of Hindus, most pronouncedly by establishing a strong tradition of female renouncers.

HISTORY Jain doctrines and practices today are traced to Lord Mahavira in the sixth century B.C.E., but after his death Jainism divided into sects, subsects, and smaller groups called *gaccha*s. The two main Jain sects are Shvetambara and Digambara. The Sthanakwasi, Murtipujak, and Terapanthi subsects are divisions of the Shvetambara sect, and the Kharatara and Tapa Gacchas are subgroups of the Murtipujak subsect.

According to doctrine, in the current age there have been 24 enlightened Jinas (victors), also called Tirthankaras (fords or bridge builders). They include, in order from first to last, Rishabha (also known as Adinatha), Ajita, Sambhava, Abhinandana, Sumati, Padmaprabha, Suparshva, Chandraprabha, Suvidhi (Pushpadanta), Shitala, Shreyamsa, Vasupujya, Vimala, Ananta, Dharma, Shanti, Kunthu, Ara, Malli, Munisuvrata, Nami, Nemi, Parshva, and Mahavira (Vardhamana). Each Jina established the four-fold community of monks, nuns, laymen, and laywomen. Lord Mahavira, the 24th and last Jina, is believed to have lived from 599 B.C.E. to either

UNIVERSAL JAIN SYMBOL. The Jain symbol consists of various components. The outline of the symbol represents the universe. The arms of the swastika represent the four possible states of rebirth: human, heaven, hell, and animal. The three dots above the swastika represent the path of liberation. The crescent at top represents the place for liberated souls, with the dot above it representing such a soul. The raised hand means ìstopî and to act with wisdom and peace. The word in the middle of the wheel, ahimsa, means ìnon-violence.î The wheel represents the cycle of birth and death that one will follow repeatedly if ahimsa is not observed. (THOMSON GALE)

527 B.C.E. (according to the Shvetambara sect) or 510 B.C.E. (according to the Digambara sect).

The circumstances of Mahavira's conception are said to have been unusual. According to some scriptures, instead of remaining in one womb throughout his gestation, he was transferred from the womb of Devananda, a woman of the priestly caste, to the womb of Trishala, a woman of the warrior caste. Trishala's child was likewise transferred to Devananda's womb. Mahavira was born into luxury, but he renounced wealth, along with household life, in order to focus on his quest to eliminate karma, to win inner control and spiritual freedom, to reach enlightenment (*moksha,* or nirvana) and never be reborn, and to teach the Jain religion. Scriptures describe his tolerance of and lack of concern with the hardships he encountered from other people, demons, and animals, as well as with the hardships of the ascetic life in general, which included wandering, fasting, nakedness, and the lack of shelter and sleep.

After his enlightenment, at the age of 42, Mahavira preached to people regardless of their status in society or their gender, and he won many followers. Accounts of this part of his life describe not only the people whom Mahavira influenced but also the gods and animals that gathered to listen wherever he preached. After a long life of teaching Jainism, he died, never to be reborn. Today Jain ascetics strive for their own spiritual progress and that of others by following Lord Mahavira's example of austerity, nonviolence, and instruction.

Originating in eastern India, Jainism spread southward beginning around the second century B.C.E. and westward beginning in the fourth century C.E. Most Jains now live in the northwest and southwest of India. After Mahavira's death many sects of Jainism developed, and eventually there emerged the two main branches of Shvetambara, located mostly in the northwest, and Digambara, mostly in the southwest. Although the final split probably happened before the first century C.E., the schism evidently became fully established around the fifth century at the Council of Valabhi, during which Shvetambaras, without Digambaras present, decided on canonical scriptures. The schism was long in the making, however, and took place after a period of disagreement about scripture, doctrine, and clothing that dated to the fourth century B.C.E.

Digambaras rejected the Shvetambara canon. In fact, the only scripture accepted by both sects today is the Tattvartha Sutra. Other differences are doctrinal. One involves the state of an enlightened Jina. While Digambaras assert that an enlightened Jina did not eat, drink, or take part in common bodily processes and activities, Shvetambaras argue that an enlightened Jina continued to function like other humans until his death.

The disagreement over clothing is, however, probably the most important difference, and it also produced a disagreement about whether women, since they cannot renounce clothing, can reach enlightenment. While Shvetambaras (wearing white) believe that clothing is necessary for the spiritual path, Digambaras (wearing the sky) assert that to reach enlightenment a person must renounce all clothing. There is a large body of literature dating from 800–1700 C.E. concerning the debate, including the question of whether or not women can achieve enlightenment. Digambaras argue that women cannot attain *moksha* until they are first reborn as men, but Shvetambaras argue that women can do so in female bodies. Shvetambaras also believe that the 19th Jina,

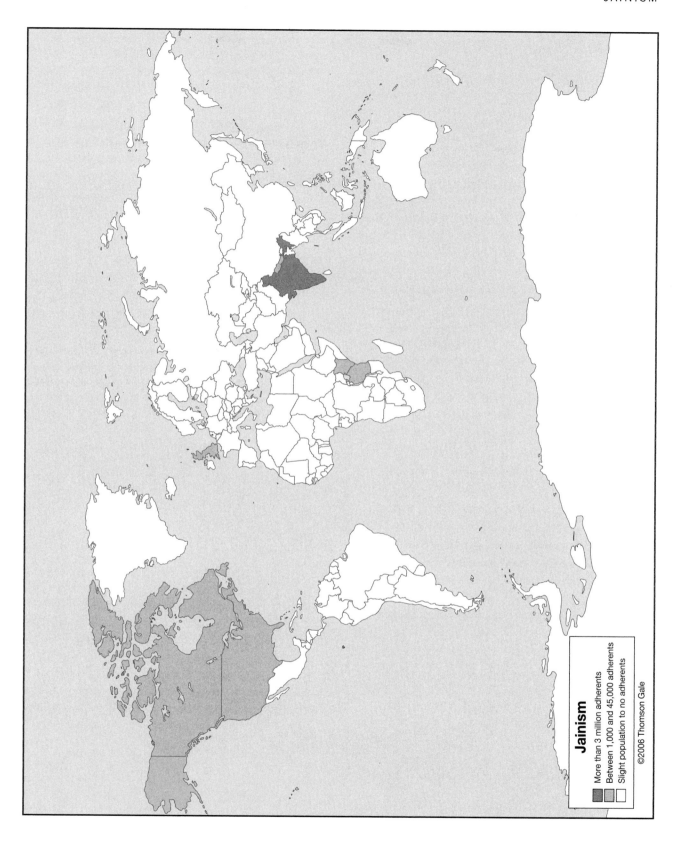

Jainism

More than 3 million adherents

Between 1,000 and 45,000 adherents

Slight population to no adherents

©2006 Thomson Gale

A *Shvetambara renouncer wears a white robe and mouth covering. They may wear only prescribed white clothing, and their possessions are limited to what is necessary to help them practice nonviolence.* © ROBERT HOLMES/CORBIS.

Mallinatha, was female, while Digambaras believe that this Jina was male. It is important to note, however, that Jains believe that it is impossible for anyone to achieve *moksha* in the current period, which is considered to be a degenerate age, so that all monks and nuns will have to wait in an heavenly realm for a more pure age before they can be reincarnated in human form again and achieve *moksha*.

The Shvetambara and Digambara sects further divided into subsects. The Shvetambara branch divided into the Sthanakwasi, Murtipujak, and Terapanthi subsects, and the Digambara into the Bisapanthi, Terapanthi, and Taranpanthi. Murtipujak Jains further divided into groups called *gacchas,* the most important of which are the Tapa and Kharatara Gacchas. The Shvetambara divisions are more clear-cut than those of the Digambara, although there are important differences among the Digambara divisions. Bisapanthi and Terapanthi Digambaras, for example, worship statues in temples, while Taranpanthis worship scriptures. Among the Bisapanthi, women may anoint Jain images in tem-

ples, and there are no restrictions concerning green vegetables. Among the Terapanthi, women are restricted from touching images of the Jinas, and the eating of green vegetables is restricted during certain times of the month.

Among Shvetambaras, those belonging to the Sthanakwasi and Terapanthi subsects do not engage in image worship, which helps set them apart from the Murtipujak subsect. The Sthanakwasi subsect traces its origins to aniconic advocates (that is, those opposed to images) who lived around the seventeenth century C.E. and who broke from Murtipujaks. Among them was Lavaji, who established the practice of living in abandoned structures instead of in buildings constructed for traveling monks and nuns. He also emphasized the renouncer practice of wearing a cloth, or *muhapatti,* over the mouth so as not to injure insects or other life forms in the air. On ritual occasions many Murtipujaks also wear such a cloth, but the Sthanakwasis, as well as the Terapanthis, wear a *muhapatti* most of the time.

Acharya Bikshu, who was born in Marwar Rajasthan in 1726, founded the highly organized Terapanthi subsect of the Shvetambaras. It is because of the organization of this subsect that scholars know more about Bikshu than about most other important Jains. Originally a Sthanakwasi renouncer, Bikshu eventually became disillusioned with the lax behavior of many of this fellow renouncers. He criticized them for living permanently in buildings constructed for them, for repeatedly going to the same households for food, for establishing connections with powerful lay Jains, for handling money, and for forbidding their lay followers from accepting initiations from other renouncers.

The early history of Bikshu and his followers resembles the legend of Lord Mahavira. Few laypeople were willing to give them food and shelter, and they faced extreme hardships. By the end of his life, however, Bikshu had initiated more than 100 monks and nuns, and his practice of allowing only one *acharya* (religious leader) and his doctrine of complete obedience to this *acharya* allowed the order to grow without division. Since Bikshu there have been nine other *acharyas,* the most important being the 9th, Acharya Tulsi, who lived from 1914 to 1997.

Most Murtipujaks belong to the group Tapa Gaccha, which was created by Jagachandrasuri in the early 1200s because of the lax practices he saw in his community. Jagachandrasuri emphasized *tap* (austere practices) in his life, and so his group became known as the Tapa

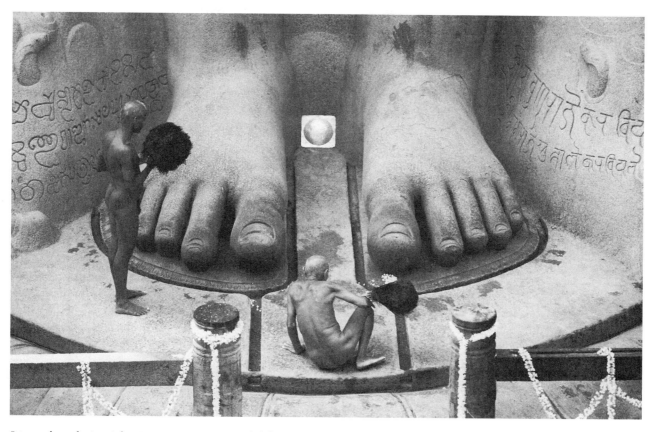

Jain monks at the feet of the fifty-seven-foot statue of Bahubali. Every ten to fifteen years, hundreds of thousands of pilgrims attend a spectacular head-anointing ritual. © CHRIS LISLE/CORBIS.

Gaccha. Prevalent in Gujarat, it has become the largest group of Jains in India. The Kharatara Gaccha is so named because of the exceptional power of its founder, Jinashvarasuri, in debating. He received the title *kharatar* (formidable) in 1024 from a king who hosted a debate between Jinashvarasuri and ascetics who argued that they should be able to own property and reside in temples. Needless to say, Jinashvarasuri won the argument. Today most members of the Kharatara Gaccha live in Rajasthan.

A later reformation that is very important for Tapa Gacchas today took place in the mid-1800s. At that time the majority of Tappa Gaccha renouncers were *yatis*, settled monks who owned property and sired heirs. Corrupt and even rich, they were associated with tantras, techniques linked to spells and magical powers, and therefore were associated with danger and sorcery. The *yatis* were eventually deemed lax by the Tapa Gaccha lay community and were largely expelled. There are now very few *yatis*.

These conflicts and divisions in Jainism are examples of the longstanding friction between sedentary and itinerant and between lax and strict renouncers. Some of the conflicts also indicate how lay and renouncer communities interact. Lay Jains need renouncers, who inspire them to follow the difficult rules of Jainism. In addition, giving to renouncers is one of the main sources of good karma (merit). If renouncers are not sincere or are lax, laypeople do not collect as much good karma from giving food and other necessities. In turn, because the laity provide food, clothing, and shelter, renouncers need them for survival.

CENTRAL DOCTRINES According to Jainism, there is an infinite number of intrinsically divine souls reincarnating in many forms, depending on their karma. These souls can achieve *moksha*, or nirvana, through detachment from karma only at relatively short times and in small places in the vast but finite universe. Souls progress to *moksha* through many stages, during which their innate divine qualities are gradually uncovered so that they

Jain nuns pray at a temple in India. One explanation for why there are more nuns than monks is that Jain women are used to hardship and so are more able to tolerate the austerities of Jainism. © CHRIS LISLE/CORBIS.

move from limited and contextualized knowledge to omniscience. After achieving *moksha,* enlightened souls are free from rebirth and constitute the divine, which is worshiped by the Jain community.

There is no creator God in Jainism. The finite universe and the infinite souls within it have always existed and will always exist. When, however, a human attains complete experiential knowledge of reality, he or she is understood to have attained a state of godhood and is worshiped accordingly. The nine *tattva*s (realities) that characterize the universe include souls (*jivas*), matter (*ajiva*), matter coming in contact with souls (*ashrava*), the binding of karma and the soul (*bandha*), beneficial karma (*punya*), harmful karma (*papa*), inhibiting the influx of karma (*samvara*), purifying the soul of karma (*nirjara*), and liberation (*moksha,* or nirvana). All souls are identical and equal, but they expand or contract to fit the body they inhabit at any given time. Their bondage to karma hides their inherently divine characteristics of perfect energy, perfect bliss, perfect perception, and perfect knowledge. Matter comes in five categories: space, change, stability, atoms, and time. Shvetambaras do not include time as a form of matter, and this categorization was probably not systematized in early Jainism.

Jain's motivations and practices reflect the worldview that all beings are part of a cycle of reincarnation (samsara) that extends from the heavens to the hells and that also includes a realm of beings who have attained enlightenment, or liberation from further rebirth (*moksha*). Jain cosmology divides the world into five parts: the hells, the middle world of humans and animals, the heavens, the abode of enlightened souls, and the abode of those beings with only one sense. Until they reach *moksha,* souls are reincarnated repeatedly in all of these parts. It was relatively late in Jain history when this world, or universe, came to be described as the "cosmic person," as it is known today. Needless to say, the cosmic person is enormously large.

From top to bottom, the cosmic person is measured by fourteen "ropes" that are said to be incalculably long. There is a narrow axis that runs vertically through the middle of the structure, outside of which no multisensed being may exist. It is only within a small section of this waist region that humans and animals may live, Jinas may be born, and enlightenment may be achieved. The other regions are dominated by sensual desire or are void of moral understanding. Below and above the waist there are, respectively, several infernal realms where souls suffer the fruits of bad karma and several celestial realms in which souls enjoy the fruits of good karma. Above the heavens is the realm of enlightened souls, who are free of all karma and who are worshiped collectively and individually as God. The largest section of the axis is constituted by the hells, the second largest by the heavens, and the smallest by the realms in which human birth and enlightenment take place. The largest population of souls, however, is constituted by animals and plants.

Souls may have one or more of the five senses: touch, taste, smell, sight, and hearing. Beings with only one sense, that of touch, are not self-propelling. They include microscopic *nigoda*s, earth-bodies, water-bodies, fire-bodies, air-bodies, and plant-bodies. Beings with two to five senses are self-propelling and are categorized as either sentient or insentient. Animals, heavenly and infernal beings, and most humans are considered sentient. The distinction is also made between those higher animals that are able to reason and those that are completely instinctive. Heavenly (gods and goddesses) and hell beings are born spontaneously, without parents, and have certain paranormal senses, such as clairvoyance.

Although these are the main classes of beings, there is further variety, especially among gods and goddesses.

Preponderance of Nuns over Monks

It is widely known among Jains and Jain scholars that there are more nuns than monks, but the reasons behind this fact have been little studied. Jain stories about heroic women, called Satis, and women's more consistent religiosity are important factors, but the situation is more complicated than this. It is an important issue for understanding Jainism, since the tradition survives mostly because of mothers and nuns. When asked about the matter, Jains give the following answers.

A common answer of Shvetambara nuns is that, because of an absence of desire, women can practice celibacy easily but that men are unable to control themselves sexually. Fewer men, therefore, renounce householder life to become monks. A common answer of nuns generally is that men can remarry if their wives die or leave them, while women cannot. Thus, men remarry, but women become nuns. When child marriages were prevalent among Jains, girls were encouraged to renounce if their husbands died.

Renunciation both protected young girls and helped them cope with their sexual feelings.

One of the most common answers is that women are more tolerant than men. They are used to hardships, and so they are able to tolerate the austerities of Jainism. Monks, nuns, and laywomen commonly say that women are softer and more sympathetic, compassionate, and sensitive, while men are more harsh and unfeeling. Because Jainism emphasizes nonviolence, renouncers must be compassionate.

Nuns of all sects and subsects say that, for women who do not become renouncers, there are limited opportunities for spiritual, educational, and personal growth. Those who do not renounce must marry, and care of their families leaves them no time for themselves.

Nuns and some laymen commonly say that it has always been the case, even in the times of the Jinas, that there were more nuns than monks. Laymen say that, because men are responsible for supporting their families and ensuring succession, parents do not let their sons renounce. It is also commonly said that Jain women are more religious in general.

Some gods and goddesses live in caves or in the woods and can help or harm others, and some—planetary gods and goddesses—live just below the heavenly realms. While some gods and goddesses have sexual relationships, others do not.

The most important physical matter in Jainism, however, is karma, microscopic physical particles that float in the universe. Beings control their own suffering and happiness through their physical, mental, and verbal actions. Their actions attract tiny karmic particles that stick to the soul and trap it in samsara. Karma determines the soul's situation and position within the cycle of reincarnation and hinders the soul's experience of its own true nature. Hinduism, Buddhism, and Jainism all agree that actions produce their own rewards and punishments, but Jainism is the only religion of the three in which karma is held to be physical particles.

Of these religions Jainism also has the most extensive categorization of karma, which is a function of its

pivotal importance in the Jain worldview. In Jainism karma determines where souls are reborn, and no soul may achieve enlightenment while still bound by karma. There are eight divisions of karmic particles that fall under two subheadings: destructive, or harmful, karmas and nondestructive, or secondary, karmas. Destructive karmas includes those that delude insight, conceal knowledge, cloud perception, and restrict energy. In short, the destructive karmas obscure the inherent qualities of the soul and therefore the soul's experience of itself.

Nondestructive karmas include those that determine feelings of pleasure or pain; control birth, sex, the body, the senses, color, and spiritual potential; govern longevity; and decide status and environmental factors. Karmic particles attach to individual souls by means of the passions, emotional states such as hatred, greed, lust, and anger. The passions act as both magnets that attract and the glue that holds karmic particles to the soul. The passions also determine the severity and the length of karmic results. Once karmic particles have manifested their results, they leave the soul.

Because only humans can achieve enlightenment and escape rebirth, being born as a human is considered to be a result of good karma. It is even better karma, however, to be reborn as a human at a time when and in a place where enlightenment is possible. To understand why this is so, it is necessary to understand certain details about Jain cosmology. Humans may exist only on a relatively small, horizontal terrestrial plain, which is a flat disk located at the waist of the cosmic person. Mount Meru, which is located in the middle of Jambudvip, the central continent of this disk, rises 800,000 miles. This continent, as well as surrounding ones, has seven sections that are completely separated from one another by mountain ranges. The inner continent of Jambudvip is surrounded by innumerable oceans and islands. Humans, however, may inhabit only the center-most of the surrounding islands, along with the inner part of the next island.

There are also areas designated as enjoyment-lands and karma-lands. The former are like heavenly realms, in that sustenance is readily available and there is no need to work. Asceticism is not appealing to those who inhabit the lands of enjoyment, and so enlightenment is not possible there. Those in karma-lands, however, must work, and so their lives are not always happy, which is conducive to spiritual reflection. It is only in karma-lands, which include half of Mahavideh and all of Bharat and Airavat, that enlightenment is possible and that Jinas can be incarnated. Mahavideh is particularly significant. Jinas are always present there, and because successive ages of increasing and decreasing happiness and suffering do not affect the area, liberation is always possible. Bharat, the human realm, is not as fortunate as Mahavideh, but it is a karma-land, which makes enlightenment possible.

Time is not the same everywhere in cosmic person, and this is something that affects Bharat and Airavat. Although in such realms as Mahavideh time does not change the quality of life, in Bharat and Airavat time consists of 12 sections that complete a cycle divided into ascending and descending modes. According to some sources, each mode lasts for two *kalpa*s (aeons, an enormous amount of time, such as 2 billion years) and, according to others, for "innumerable" lengths of time. The first six sections of time, in the ascending mode, are characterized by decreasing suffering and increasing happiness. They are called suffering-suffering, suffering,

suffering-happiness, happiness-suffering, happiness, and happiness-happiness. The second six sections, in the descending mode, are marked by a symmetrical increase in suffering and decrease in happiness. Each happier time lasts for a longer period, during which humans are characterized by greater morality, longer life spans, and larger bodies. Each more agonizing time lasts a shorter period, during which humans are characterized by greater immorality, shorter life spans, and smaller bodies.

In the happiest times there is so much abundance that no one need do anything, and culture need not exist for law and order to be maintained. Only in less happy times, when scarcity develops, do the common aspects of human existence become necessary. It is only during the times of suffering-happiness and happiness-suffering that Jinas are born and teach and that enlightenment is possible. In sections of time that are primarily characterized by suffering, humans are too overwhelmed by pain to realize that happiness or enlightenment is possible. In sections of time primarily characterized by happiness, humans have no understanding of suffering and therefore no incentive to strive for enlightenment. In each ascending and descending mode 24 Jinas are born, and thus 48 are born in each complete cycle. In the descending mode, at the end of the happiness-suffering age, Rishabha was the first Jina, and he lived a superhuman life span of 600,000 years. Lord Mahavira, at the end of the suffering-happiness age, was the last Jina, and his life span was less than 90 years.

There is only an extremely small number of beings with good karma who are born during the small intervals of time characterized by both happiness and suffering and who can therefore strive to attain enlightenment. Thus, Jain doctrine provides motivation for those who find themselves lucky enough to be born human during a time when enlightenment is possible. Now, according to Jain doctrine, humans are in the descending mode, in an age of suffering and nearing the age of suffering-suffering. For this reason it is not possible for anyone to become enlightened. Nevertheless, Jains are motivated not to waste their human lives, since it is believed that the pious are reborn in a heavenly realm. There they wait for the age of the next Jina, when they will be reincarnated as humans, according to Shvetambaras, or as males, according to Digambaras, to achieve enlightenment.

To embark on the path of liberation, beings need to accumulate good karma, but ultimately the path consists of purifying the soul of all karma. Not only are individuals responsible, through their karmic actions, for their fates in the round of rebirth, but each person is also responsible for his or her own liberation. Although fate is governed by karma, a person determines the amount and quality of karma through the actions he or she chooses. Furthermore, enlightenment is possible through a person's efforts by means of the three jewels: right faith, right understanding, and right conduct. Right faith refers to the aspirant's acceptance of the nine realities. Right understanding refers to the detailed knowledge of these nine realities that is found in many Jain scriptures and through meditative effort. Right conduct is behavior that will lead the aspirant to enlightenment. All of the three jewels are deemed necessary on the renouncer's path.

There are 14 stages through which a soul travels while making spiritual progress, or regression, the end point of which is enlightenment at death. They are known as the 14 "stages of qualities" and are likened to the rungs of a ladder. Each higher stage moves the practitioner from various states of ignorance, passion, bad conduct, and more karma to states of omniscience, less passion, perfect conduct, and no karma. This path to perfection is sometimes called the "path of purification."

Until omniscience is gained at the top of the ladder, a person cannot claim to know the whole truth of reality, so that every assertion must be qualified as a partial truth. The multiplicity, or many-sidedness, of truth is known as *anekant*. According to this doctrine, every statement about something must be accompanied by qualifying statements that limit its claim from being the whole truth to being a contextualized truth. A popular metaphor for this is to acknowledge that seeing something means seeing it from various points of view, from the top, bottom, left side, and so on. In other words, *anekant* refers to interpreting something from one's own point of view, environment, and spiritual state.

A popular story that illustrates the doctrine of *anekant* is that of the elephant and five blind men. According to the story, a king took five blind men to a large elephant. One man touched the trunk and claimed that it was a large snake. The second touched the tail and claimed that it was a rope. The third man felt a long, sturdy leg and claimed that it was a tree trunk. The fourth man touched an ear and stated that it was a winnowing fan. The fifth touched the elephant's side and stated that it was a wall. In disagreement with one another, they began to argue, each claiming that the others

were wrong. Unenlightened beings are like the blind men, while enlightened beings are like those who can see that all the blind men stated partial truths but that the object really is an elephant.

Jain's ideas about God are related to their ideas about enlightened beings. Like Hindus, Jains believe that all people have God within them as their soul (*jiva*) and that the spiritual path consists in becoming aware of this. Unlike Hindus, however, Jains believe that all enlightened souls travel to the apex of the universe, where they are worshiped as gods or together as God. Enlightened Jinas also reside there. Some Jains believe that these Jinas are completely detached from all worldly affairs and so do not bless or directly help their followers (the scriptural view) or that they help those who worship them (the devotional view).

MORAL CODE OF CONDUCT Ideas about karma are at the heart of the Jain code of right conduct, one of the three jewels. To be born human at a time when enlightenment is possible, a person must have lived highly moral past lives. When a person decides to attain enlightenment, moral actions help to eliminate karma from the soul. All karma, both good and bad, ultimately hinders the practitioner from achieving enlightenment. But moral actions are not enough to achieve the blissful state called *moksha*, or nirvana. Two further things are necessary. The practitioner must stop accumulating karmic particles (*samvara*) and must eliminate the karmic particles he or she has already collected (*nirjara*).

In order to stop the inflow of karmic particles, it is usually necessary to renounce the married life of a householder and to eliminate passions and violence through continual restraint and the denial of the pleasures of the senses. This is done through adherence to moral actions that are based on nonviolence. In order eliminate karmic particles that have already accumulated, the lifestyle of renunciation must be combined with internal and external austerities (*tap, tapas,* or *tapasya*). Internal austerities include such practices as meditation, study, and service, while external austerities include such bodily mortifications as fasting. Once the practitioner has halted the inflow of karmic particles and annihilated all accumulated particles, he or she attains *moksha* and will not be reborn again. The emancipated soul travels upward to the top of the universe and, with all of the liberated souls dwelling there, is worshiped as God.

The Jain code of moral conduct, through which practitioners endeavor to stop the collection of new karma, centers around the value of nonviolence (ahimsa) and is explicated in the five great or lesser vows. The great and lesser vows include nonviolence, truth, nonstealing, sexual restraint (*brahmacharya*), and nonpossession. They differ only in the strictness with which they are observed. All Shvetambara renouncers accept some version of the great vows. In the Digambara sect only the highest renouncers take the great vows, while other renouncers take the lesser vows. In both sects laypeople may choose to adopt the lesser vows, but if they do not, they still endeavor to live lives in accordance with the values expressed by them. While renouncers are extremely strict, laypeople are given more latitude. Renouncers also follow three types of restraints, or ways of being careful in their practice of the five great vows: being careful with their body, speech, and mind. This requires constant vigilance in all that is done, said, and thought. Such vigilance is not easy and may be described as a type of meditation, or awareness, in every moment.

The Jain vow of nonviolence prohibits harmful thoughts, words, and deeds and prescribes an attitude of compassion and friendship toward other beings. All Jains are vegetarians. Laypeople may act in self-defense, while renouncers may not. In addition, laypeople must choose nonviolent professions, such as business. Examples of renouncer's more extensive practice of nonviolence include checking their clothing for insects and brushing insects away with a soft broom before sitting down or while walking at night. The vow of truth prohibits lying, but if the truth would hurt someone, both renouncers and laypeople are told to remain silent. The vow of nonstealing means both that people should not acquire anything not given to them and that they should not think or talk about acquiring it. For many laypeople this includes honest business transactions as well as honesty in general.

For Jains the vow of sexual restraint is extremely important, with many renouncers claiming that it is the most important of their vows. For renouncers sexual restraint means complete celibacy in actions, words, and thoughts, something that may be more difficult than the other vows. If other vows are broken, renouncers may do penance to reestablish themselves, but if a renouncer has sexual relations, he or she is expelled from the Jain community. Furthermore, celibacy is seen as helping to retain the inner energy needed as fuel for the difficult path to enlightenment. Even one act of sexual misconduct dissipates this power. While the sexual restraint of monks and nuns requires complete celibacy, laypeople

observe the vow by remaining faithful to their spouses in thought, word, and deed. This is more important for laywomen than laymen, being the most important index of laywomen's general piety and honor and of the honor of their families.

Observing the vow of nonpossession also differs between renouncers and laypeople. For renouncers the vow not only signifies the absence of all possessions not needed for ascetic practice but also implies a sense of equanimity or detachment concerning possessions. In addition, there is a crucial difference between Shvetambara and Digambara interpretations of the vow. Shvetambaras believe that clothing is a necessary possession, but Digambaras believe that clothing should be renounced. Thus, while Shvetambara monks and nuns wear white clothing, full Digambara monks wear no clothing, and Digambara nuns wear white clothing. Laypeople who are in business are generally prosperous, and they demonstrate the value of nonpossession by donating large amounts of money to build temples, to provide shelters for wandering monks and nuns, and to support the many Jain charitable organizations in India.

Renouncers perform six rituals throughout the day. These are meditative awareness and equanimity at every moment; veneration of the 24 Jinas; veneration of the personal guru; repentance and karmic purification for any wrong thought, word, or deed; standing meditation, during which attention is directed away from the body and toward the immaterial soul; and the abandonment of transgressions, refraining from certain foods, and the performance of austerities through fasting. The rituals vary from sect to sect, and some are practiced by Jain laypeople as well, especially by women. These rituals help to stop karma from attaching itself to the soul and help to purify the soul of karma already attached.

By conforming to the five great and lesser vows, all religious Jains endeavor to stop bad karma from attaching to the soul. Renouncers, however, attempt to eliminate all karma, while laypeople try to accumulate as much good karma as possible. This distinction between the aims of laypeople and renouncers is less important in the current age of suffering, in which enlightenment is not possible.

Although few laypeople actually accept the five lesser vows, they may still attempt to follow them. Meritorious conduct such as charity, worship (*puja*), the singing of hymns, and celebration of another person's religious acts all collect good karma, and avoiding violence and fasting protect laypeople from, and purify, bad karma.

Such religiosity enables laypeople to maintain prosperous rebirths and also eventually to produce circumstances favorable for renunciation and the achievement of enlightenment.

Jain women are usually more religious than men. Women tend to follow food regulations more strictly and consistently, they educate their children about Jainism, they frequently visit renouncers and listen to their sermons, and most complete at least one significant fast. The principal karma-related practice for laywomen is fasting. The fasts, which are public undertakings, are celebrated with pride in Jain communities. They are performed for various reasons related to the purification of bad karma and the accumulation of good karma. Fasts are also performed in order to benefit the family, to acquire good husbands for themselves or their daughters, to demonstrate piety and faithfulness to their husbands and families, and to obtain notice within Jain communities for their religiosity. Although the most difficult of the fasts lasts for a month, there are a great variety of other fasts. These include fasting every other day, for a week, or for three days, as well as limiting the types of foods ingested. It is believed that only highly virtuous women can complete the more difficult fasts, and so these fasts demonstrate such women's honor and piety. Furthermore, because women are responsible for maintaining Jainism in the home, the fasts also indicate the honor and piety of their families.

For Jain men charity rather than fasting is the principal karma-related practice. Laymen give money for education, libraries, hospitals, animal shelters, temples, temporary shelters for renouncers, Jain images, and pilgrimages. As with fasting, charity is a highly public undertaking. There are public auctions to raise money for Jain causes, with the donor's names frequently displayed on what they have helped to create and maintain. Giving is important not just for accumulating good karma but also for establishing a good reputation and good business and marriage contacts within the Jain community.

Another common way of achieving merit is through celebration of the religious actions of others. Fasts and donations are celebrated by processions and feasts, through which religious actions are displayed and lauded. Initiation into an order of renouncers is also celebrated with great pomp. Members of the entire Jain community can thereby encourage piety and accumulate good karma that will continue their well-being and help them to renounce in a future life.

SACRED BOOKS Jain sacred literature is expressed in forms that are both classical and vernacular and includes narratives, treatises, and poetry. It is both written and oral and may be polemic and sectarian. The literature is studied, memorized, narrated, and worshiped. To say that there is a Jain canon in the Western sense of the term is somewhat misleading, but there are scriptures that are considered authoritative and sacred and that are commonly known. Through oral tradition, memorization, and worship, Jain sacred texts are part of a living and changing tradition.

Certain Jain texts are believed to have originated from the divine sound of the enlightened Lord Mahavira. While Shvetambaras believe that the sound emanated in languages suitable for different peoples and beings, Digambaras believe that it was one great, uniform sound. In either case, Lord Mahavira's immediate disciples compiled the sound, which became systematized Jain scripture.

Both Shvetambaras and Digambaras assert that the earliest Jain compositions consisted of 14 oral texts, called the Purvas. Both sects also assert that the Purvas have been lost, although some of the information contained in them is believed to have been incorporated in the Digambara texts Shatakanda Agama and Kashayaprabhrita and in the Shvetambara text Prajnapana Upanga, also called the Bhagavati Sutra. Evidence from other texts describing this literature suggests that they contained information about karma theory, cosmology, astronomy, astrology, and the acquiring of supernatural powers, as well as philosophical polemics.

The core scriptures of the Shvetambara tradition are numerous, consisting of 45 texts organized into five groups. The first 12 texts, called Angas ("Limbs"), include information about monastic rules, dangers on the ascetic path, limited heretical views, knowledge theory and logic, the nature of karma, and cosmology, along with narratives about devout Jains of the past. (Unlike Shvetambaras, Digambaras believe that all true Angas have been lost.) The second group, called Upanga ("Supplementary Limbs"), contains mostly narratives but also includes information about the soul, gods, and hell beings; how to attain liberation; and ontology, time cycles, doctrines, and cosmology. The third group of texts is the Chedasutras ("Delineating Scriptures"), which contain information about monastic hierarchy, monastic rules, and penance for breaking monastic rules. The fourth group is the Mulasutras ("Root Scriptures"), which monks and nuns first study after initiation. These texts include information about doctrine, conduct, rituals, caste, and caring for monastic possessions, as well as narratives. The fifth group of scriptures, Prakirnaka ("Miscellaneous"), contains a variety of subjects, from ritual death and astrology to lauding the Jinas.

Both Digambaras and Shvetambaras also produced the Anuyogas. The Digambaras especially hold the Anuyogas in high regard. They contain information about cosmology, doctrine, conduct, karma, and logic and philosophy, as well as praise for the Jinas and popular narrative literature. Among the most important Anuyogas, for Digambaras, are the Puranas (narratives) and the authoritative works of Kundakunda and, for Shvetambaras, the Trishashtishalakapurushacharitra (narratives).

The worship, or honoring, of sacred texts is common in Jainism. For example, when a renouncer finishes copying a text by hand, this is celebrated within the Jain community. If a renouncer successfully memorizes scriptures, he or she receives additional respect and veneration. During the Paryushan festival of the Shvetambaras, renouncers recite the Kalpa Sutra, while during the Dashalakshanaparvan festival of the Digambaras, members of the community recite the Tattvartha Sutra.

Jains generally do not know what is contained in all of the scriptures. Instead, many renouncers and most laypeople receive their knowledge of Jain history, doctrine, and practice from their mothers and from renouncers. Indeed, without the efforts of mothers and renouncers, the Jain tradition would soon die out. To inspire them to practice Jainism, mothers tell the narratives to their children, and renouncers tell them to large audiences and individuals. Young Jains also perform popular narratives in plays. It is this narrative tradition, not the erudite and complicated works themselves, that is significant in the daily life of Jains. Narratives often illustrate issues within the context of Jain history, and it is in this way that followers learn how to understand the workings of Jainism in their own lives. The majority of the narratives can be considered canonical, and they are included in the sacred texts. Most Jains, however, are not concerned about the texts from which the narratives come but rather in the oral retelling, which frequently includes details absent from the written versions.

Thus, narratives based on sacred texts are the preferred mode of explanation in Jainism, and for this reason the oral, not the written, word may be said to be more important. This means that much of Jain sacred literature cannot be separated from the people and their practices and also means that its content grows. As stories that recount exceptional contemporary Jains are composed, told, and retold, new narratives continue to be added to the Jain repertoire.

SACRED SYMBOLS The *svastika* is an ancient and sacred symbol for both Jains and Hindus. Most Westerners associate the symbol with the Nazis, but this is an abhorrent association for Jains, who are committed to nonviolence.

The *svastika* is a powerful symbol of auspiciousness in India, and the word itself means "well-being." In Jainism the symbol represents existence in samsara, the cycle of reincarnation, and the way to *moksha* (enlightenment), and it is incorporated into worship, appears on homes and temples, and is used in meditation. The four arms represent the four realms—human, animal and plant, heavenly, and hellish—into which souls may reincarnate. Three horizontal dots above represent the three jewels of right faith, right understanding, and right conduct that lead an aspirant to enlightenment. Above these are a crescent that represents the abode of enlightened souls at the top of the universe and another dot that represents the enlightened souls themselves.

EARLY AND MODERN LEADERS The most important historical leader in Jainism was Lord Mahavira, who lived in the sixth century B.C.E. and who determined the shape and practice of Jainism as it is known today. Other important historical leaders included those who established major divisions within Jainism. Among these was Lonka (Lonka Shah), who lived in Gujarat in the fifteenth century C.E. and to whom both the Sthanakwasi and Terapanthi subsects within Shvetambara Jainism are traced. Scholars have never determined exactly who Lonka was or what he advocated, but there is evidence to indicate some of his ideas and his place in Shvetambara society. According to Sthanakwasi legends, Lonka was a magnate and calligrapher who had political connections with the Muslim government and who eventually became a renouncer. Both legends and scholarship agree that he and his followers were aniconic—that is, that they viewed image worship as a corruption of Jainism. Some scholars, however, believe that Lonka probably was not rich and not a full renouncer. Others trace his aniconic ideas to his connections with the similarly minded Muslims, while some point out that this connection is not necessary to explain the origins of his stance, since such ideas can be seen in several early Jain texts. His followers in the Lonka Gaccha eventually returned to image worship, possibly influenced by a need to maintain business connections with image-worshiping Jains, and although the group still exists, it has only a small number of adherents. Nonetheless, Lonka was important in the development of the aniconic Sthanakwasi and Terapanthi subsects.

Acharya Tulsi, a twentieth-century Terapanthi, was pivotal for many reasons. He initiated more monks and nuns than any other *acharya* and in 1949, two years after the violence that accompanied the partition of India and Pakistan, founded the *anuvrat* movement. This movement encourages laypeople, both Jains and those in other religions, to adopt a version of the lesser vows (*anuvratas*) in order to create a more just, unified, and peaceful society. Acharya Tulsi also created the institution of lesser renouncers—*samanis* (female) and *samans* (male)—who are allowed to travel by vehicles in order to minister to Jains living abroad, including those in Europe and North America. In addition, the first Jain university was created through his efforts. Acharya Tulsi's work to improve the position of women in society was especially important in Rajasthan, where they are still routinely beaten and mistreated by their husbands and in-laws and where they must adhere to *parda* restrictions that limit them to the home and keep them veiled much of the time. He also supported widows, who are particularly vulnerable, and the few women who did not renounce but did not want to marry, a radical step for Jains, who are expected to do one or the other.

MAJOR THEOLOGIANS AND AUTHORS Jainism has a rich scholastic and literary tradition. It is so important that Jain libraries, which collect and preserve these works, are among the best in India. One of the most important writers was Umasvati (c. 300 C.E.), the author of the Tattvartha Sutra, which is the only scripture accepted by both Shvetambaras and Digambaras. The Tattvartha Sutra is a philosophical explanation of such key Jain principles as karma, cosmology, spiritual progress, and ethics.

Haribhadra (either sixth or eighth century C.E.) and Hemachandra (1089–1172) were two influential Shvetambara monk-scholars. While Shvetambaras claim that Haribhadra wrote 1,400 texts, scholars attribute only about one hundred 100 to him, although they remain some of the best Indian literature. In fact, scholars have identified two Haribhadras. One, who lived in the eighth century, was converted by the nun Yakini to Jain-

ism, and the other, who lived earlier, perhaps in the sixth century, had nephews who reportedly were killed by Buddhists when they were discovered spying. In any event, Haribhadra marked the beginning of an independent Shvetambara literary culture, with works concerning practice, ritual, scriptures, narrative, and logic. Another monk-scholar, Hemachandra, who is more concretely identifiable, also was important in Shvetambara Jainism. Born in Gujarat, he was still young when he was given to a group of monks headed by Devachandra. Hemachandra eventually proved to be intellectually superior in religious learning and so became Devachandra's successor, helped to organize Shvetambara Jainism, especially in western India, and composed such comprehensive literature as *The Lives of the Jain Elders, Universal History,* and *Treatise on Behavior.*

Jinasena and Virasena, who both lived in the ninth century C.E., are important to Digambaras. Both developed epic and narrative literature that included versions of stories also present in Hinduism, such as the *Mahabharata* and *Ramayana,* as well as purely Jain stories. Kundakunda is another important figure for Digambaras. He was a monk who probably lived around the eighth century or earlier, although little else is known about his life. His writings, on the other hand, are highly accessible and influential. Digambaras credit him with 16 treatises, although scholars believe that some of these were written by others. Kundakunda is known for the mystical orientation of his works toward the personal experience of the soul. In his view the soul is the only entity that is ultimately real, and all practice should be oriented toward it. Everything else is worldly and thus only partially real. These are the two levels of truth, ultimate and worldly. Duality, as between notions of good and bad or right and wrong, is significant only from the worldly point of view, so that any "good" acts that produce auspicious karma and influence the circumstances for rebirth have nothing to do with the soul. The soul is already enlightened and ultimately free of karma, but it is karma that obscures the person's realization or experience of this. Ascetic practices are valuable only in that they purify karma and lead to the experience of the soul. Kundakunda's most significant works include those that claim to describe the internal essence of religion: *The Essence of Scripture, The Essence of Doctrine,* and *The Essence of Restraint.*

ORGANIZATIONAL STRUCTURE The Jain community, which each Jina is held to have established or renewed, is divided into four groups: monks, nuns, laymen, and laywomen. Within the community Jains tend to be highly conscious of hierarchy and status, which are based mostly on gender, age, level of asceticism, piety, and prosperity.

In Jainism men are considered higher than women, but these hierarchies exist separately in lay and renouncer communities and in certain ascetic divisions of the Digambara sect. All renouncers, regardless of their gender, are above all laypeople. Thus, while laywomen are lower than laymen, laymen are lower than nuns, and nuns are lower than monks. Although nuns are theoretically lower than monks, this means little in many communities, however, since there are so few monks. Both Shvetambaras and Digambaras call the heads of their renouncer communities *acharya*s, and all but one in Jain history have been male. The only exception is Acharya Chandana (born in 1937), who became the head of an innovative and controversial group in the Sthanakwasi subsect in Bihar. This group makes service to the poor a part of renouncer practice and allows renouncers to travel in vehicles, neither of which is standard practice for monks and nuns. In the Terapanthi subsect there is only one *acharya* at a time, but in other sects and subsects there are multiple *acharya*s in charge of separate groups.

Jain hierarchies are also based on seniority, but while lay communities base seniority on age, renouncers base it on the number of years since initiation. Among laypeople, therefore, it is virtually impossible for a younger person to have seniority over an older relative of the same gender, but it is possible for a younger renouncer to have seniority over an older renouncer of the same gender. An *acharya* is typically the most senior male member of a group of renouncers, but this does not mean that he is the oldest.

Because of differing levels of austerities, the Digambara hierarchy of ascetics is even more complicated. Digambara ascetics consist of the following types, listed in order from the lowest in the hierarchy (based on gender and the difficulty of their austerities) to the highest: *brahmacarinis* (female), *brahmacarins* (male), *kshullikas* (female), *kshullaks* (male), *ailaks* (male), *aryikas* (female), and *munis* (male). Although all Shvetambara monks and nuns take the five great vows and so are considered full-fledged monks and nuns, in the Digambara sect only *munis* take the great vows. All of the other Digambara ascetics take the five lesser vows. The versions of the lesser vows taken by these Digambara ascetics are still extremely strict, but because they are lesser vows, these ascetics are officially only advanced laypeople. Thus, officially there are no Digambara nuns. In practice, however, all *kshullaks*, *kshullikas*, *ailaks*, and *aryikas* are considered to be relatively close to *munis*, and so these ascetics are considered higher than other laypeople, and the female *aryika*s are usually counted among the Digambara renouncer community.

Laypeople are ordered according to their piety (women) and monetary success (men). Women who are very religious and have completed more difficult fasts are higher than those who are not as religious and have not fasted. For poor and middle-class Jains, women largely determine familie's places in Jain society. Those lay Jains who have been successful in business or are members of a successful family, however, have higher status than do poor or middle-class Jains, even though the latter may be more religious. The female relatives of the successful therefore have less pressure to show their piety, although many may still be highly pious. Both piety and wealth are displayed publicly, and so both are a matter of public knowledge.

Because Jains belong to fewer castes and because they maintain high standards of purity, caste means less among Jains than among Hindus. Although some Jains come from farming backgrounds, most are of the merchant caste. While Hindus who are higher in the caste system maintain their purity and status by being vegetarians, all Jains are vegetarians. Thus, while Jains may be envied or resented for their business success, they are respected in the larger Hindu society for their high standards of nonviolence and purity. These standards tend to keep Jains from mixing with Hindus who do not hold the same standards. Jains therefore most often marry within the community, but they also sometimes marry Vaishnavas (Vishnu worshipers), who are generally vegetarians.

HOUSES OF WORSHIP AND HOLY PLACES Broadly speaking, a Jain holy place is wherever a Jain renouncer temporarily resides or where a religious act is taking place, but image-worshiping Jains, such as Digambaras and the Murtipujak subsect of Shvetambaras, also have important temples. Prominent image worship probably began in the third century B.C.E., and ancient Jain temples remain some of the most beautiful in India. For laymen especially, one primary merit-making activity continues to be the donation of money to construct temples and to fund the images within them.

Most places of pilgrimage are considered holy because of their connection with an enlightened being's life or because of miracles that took place there. For Shvetambaras, Kshitriyakund is held to have been the birthplace of Lord Mahavira, while Digambaras believe that he was born at Vaishali. Rijubaluka is associated with the 12 years of austerities before he reached enlightenment, Pavapuri with his enlightenment, and Pava with his physical death and passing from this world. All of these pilgrimage sites are in Bihar. Also important to Jinas are the hills of Parasnath (also called Shikarji) in Bihar, where 20 Jinas attained *moksha* (enlightenment), and Girnar in Gujarat, where the Jina Nemi achieved *moksha.*

One of the most impressive Digambara images and pilgrimage sites was constructed around the tenth century C.E. at Shravana Begola in Karnataka. It is a 57-foot image of Bahubali, a son of the first Jina, Rishabhadev. Although he fought his brother over who would be the universal ruler of their time, during the combat Bahubali realized his folly and withdrew to practice austerities. The enormous stature depicts him performing the austerity of standing for a long period of time, so long that vines grew up his body. Every 10 to 15 years hundreds of thousands of pilgrims attend a spectacular head-anointing ritual. Even before the image was constructed, the area was associated with the auspicious passings of Digambara monks who fasted to death there, and Jains also assert that it was connected with the original migration of Jains to the south and with their leader Bhadrabahu.

Some of the most beautiful Shvetambara temples were constructed from white marble, with intricate carvings of pious images. For this reason the temples on Mount Abu in Rajasthan are popular with both Jains and tourists. There also are important pilgrimage sites at Ranakpur in Rajasthan. The construction of the temples on Mount Abu and in Ranakpur dates from the eleventh to the fourteenth centuries C.E.. In Gujarat the impressive temples at Palitana are a place of pilgrimage for Shvetambaras. It is said that the Jina Rishabhadev visited the site 22 times.

WHAT IS SACRED? The Jain conception of God centers around inherently perfect and divine souls, all of which have perfect energy, bliss, perception, and knowledge. Every soul is sacred, and so all life is sacred, from liberated beings to microscopic *nigoda*s. Those who have attained enlightenment, or who are on the path to doing

so, are considered more sacred in that they are part of, or will be part of, the Jain concept of God. The sacredness of enlightened beings and of those making progress toward enlightenment is expressed in the Namaskar Mantra, which is sacred in and of itself and which is chanted by Jains of every sect and subsect.

All Jinas, the great men and women in Jain history, and renouncers are considered sacred. The great men and women in Jain history, both lay and renouncer, are described in the extensive narrative tradition. Their names are frequently recited in rituals in order to invoke auspiciousness and also so that those reciting may develop their qualities, such as religiosity, nonviolence, and chastity. The names of the Jinas and of the Satis, or virtuous women, are especially used in this way. The names of the Satis are Sita, Kunti, Damayanti, and Draupadi, who are known in Hinduism as well, and Chandanabala, Rajimati, Brahmi, Sundari, Subhadra, Pushpachula, Prabhavati, Shiva, Shalavati, Sulasa, Chellna, Anjana, Madanarekha, Mrigavati, Mainasundari, and Padmavati, who are unique to Jainism. The Jina's mothers (*jinamata*s) are sometimes also categorized with the Satis, but usually they are considered separately. (The names of the 24 Jinas are given above under HISTORY.)

While non-image-worshiping Jains focus much of their veneration on renouncers, there are many sacred sites that are of particular importance to image-worshiping Jains. Women especially worship daily in local temples in front of sacred images of the Jinas and of various lesser gods and goddesses. Strictly speaking, the gods and goddesses are not liberated and are therefore inferior to liberated souls and renouncers, but they may help with worldly affairs.

HOLIDAYS AND FESTIVALS Perhaps the most important "holiday" for Jains is *chaturmas,* a retreat that last for four months. It takes place during the rainy season, at a time when insects are thriving. During this period all Jain renouncers must remain in one location, lest in traveling they trample the insects. Laypeople provide food and shelter for renouncers during *chaturmas* and attend lectures and storytellings or receive teachings from them. In addition, there are a variety of celebrations, and even those who do not participate in Jain activities during the rest of the year often take part in *chaturmas.* Otherwise, unless they are in ill health or are undertaking a scholarly endeavor, renouncers are not allowed to stay in one place.

Both Shvetambaras and Digambaras celebrate Mahavira Jayanti, the birth of Lord Mahavira, at the same time during March–April. Otherwise Shvetambaras and Digambaras follow largely separate calendars of festivals. At the end of the rainy season retreat, Shvetambaras celebrate Paryushan, during which renouncers recite the Kalpa Sutra, while Digambaras celebrate Dashalakshanaparvan and recite part of the Tattvartha Sutra. Both Paryushan and Dashalakshanaparvan last for several days and are marked by fasting. On the final day Jains repent for any violence done to other beings, and laypeople send letters to friends and associates asking for pardons for any transgressions.

Like Hindus, Jains celebrate the Festival of Lights (Diwali) in October, during which Lakshmi is worshiped as the goddess of well-being. Other festivals include the Shvetambara Jnanapanchami (knowledge fifth) in October–November and the Digambara Shrutapanchami (scripture fifth) in May–June. Both festivals involve learning and scriptures. Akshayatriya (undying third) is a Shvetambara and Digambara celebration of the initiation of the first Jina, Rishabhadev, and his first acceptance of alms.

MODE OF DRESS While Jain laypeople follow local customs concerning dress, renouncer's clothing is more restricted. They may wear only prescribed white clothing, and their possessions are limited to what is necessary to help them practice nonviolence. The dress of full Shvetambara and Digambara renouncers differs. Shvetambara renouncers wear white. While most Digambara ascetics wear white, Digambara *muni*s do not wear any clothing. Other accoutrements associated with a renouncer include a soft broom and a mouth guard (*muhapatti*). The former is used to brush insects out of the way before sitting down, turning over during sleep, and sometimes when walking. The *muhapatti*, used in the Sthanakwasi and Terapanthi subsects, protects insects and one-sensed air-bodies from being injured or killed through inhalation and exhalation.

DIETARY PRACTICES All religious Jains are vegetarians, and renouncers must acquire their food from vegetarian households. The ritual collection of food by renouncers is one of the most significant religious practices in Jainism. "Begging," however, is not an appropriate word for this activity, for laypeople consider it an honor and a merit-making activity to provide for renouncers.

To eat meat of any kind means to violate the preeminent vow of nonviolence. Jains are also prohibited from eating foods, including honey, alcohol, eggplant, root vegetables, and some fruits, in which life forms may exist. Water must be boiled and strained so that no microscopic or tiny organisms are inadvertently ingested. Evening meals are eaten before sunset so that flying insects are not attracted to and die in the cooking fires.

There are minor dietary variations between sects and subsects. Among Digambaras, for example, Bisapanthis may eat green vegetables, while Terapanthis restrict the eating of green vegetables at certain times.

RITUALS All Jains who grow up in religious homes know the Namaskar Mantra, a simple mantra or prayer: "I bow to the Arihants [enlightened beings who still have bodies]. / I bow to the Siddhas [enlightened beings who have left their bodies]. / I bow to the Acharyas [heads of Jain orders]. / I bow to the religious teachers. / I bow to all renouncers."

Another common form of auspicious prayer involves recitation of the names of the Jinas and Satis, which encourages the growth of these people's religious qualities within those who chant their names. Not only are their names recited, but also hymns about their lives are sung. Although hymns are sung by laymen and renouncers, they are more important in the lives of laywomen, who continue to compose, record, and pass them on.

A Jain must either marry or renounce. This is an extremely important decision, for there is no socially sanctioned way to end a marriage, except through one or both partner's renunciation, and no socially sanctioned way to become a householder once a person has been initiated as a renouncer. Although the vast majority of Jains marry, many also choose to be initiated as monks and nuns. As in Lord Mahavira's renunciation, during *diksha* (initiation) the postulant leaves behind attachments to the world in order to engage in practices conducive to *moksha*, or nirvana. In the Shvetambara sect a postulant as young as six may be initiated, but in the Digambara sect an initiate must be an adult. Initiations are expensive celebrations and also opportunities for merit making.

For every Jain sect there are two initiation ceremonies, one that is publicly celebrated by laypeople and another that is more private, performed in the presence of renouncers. Between these two ceremonies there is usually a probation period of about a month, although it is as long as two years in the Terapanthi sect. During this period postulants fast and study the basic scriptures in order to test their resolve and to learn about Jain philosophy and the ascetic life. In Jainism, unlike Hinduism, renunciation is a suitable alternative to marriage for women. And unlike Hinduism, Jainism always celebrates renunciation, as well as marriage, as an auspicious event.

Although marriage and renunciation initiate different ways of life, there are a number of characteristics shared by the two rituals. Both are public and extravagant celebrations. Before they take place, there are numerous parties at which sweets are offered to large numbers of relatives. Both celebrations include processions accompanied by musical bands, and most of the community attends. The night before the ceremonies women sit up singing. In the morning the bride or initiate bathes and is then dressed in a wedding sari and gold jewelry. Wedding henna is applied to her hands and feet, and a saffron mark known as the *tikka* is placed on her forehead. Photos are taken, for collection in an album, and sometimes the event is also captured on videotape. There is usually much weeping during the ceremonies, in which the girl either leaves her family home to join her husband and in-laws or leaves her home to stay with nuns.

The conclusion of initiation ceremonies underscores the divergent nature of the two life choices. Before the private ceremony takes place, the postulant's clothes are changed to the simple white garb of a renouncer. The initiate then gives a speech in which she explains why she wants to renounce, pays her respects to the renouncer who is initiating her, is given a new name, and accepts the five great vows.

Jains treat initiations as pilgrimage events and travel to witness and celebrate them. The most important pilgrimages for many lay Jains, however, are those undertaken to meet with respected and well-known renouncers. Indeed, for non-image-worshiping Jains, such as the Terapanthi and Sthanakwasi, this is even more important. Terapanthis, for example, frequently travel to the place where the current leader or head nun is staying in order to take food and other donations and to receive blessings. In addition, many Jains view accompanying monks and nuns on their travels as a type of pilgrimage.

Jains also make pilgrimages to famous temples, shrines, and statues. One of the most significant Sh-

vetambara pilgrimage sites is Mount Shatrunjaya, in the village of Palitana in Gujarat. There pilgrims climb 3,600 steps up the mountainside to reach the zenith, which is covered with religious images. This pilgrimage is popular with Jain laypeople, and Murtipujak monks and nuns can be seen combining austerity and devotion by repeatedly ascending and descending the steps while limiting their food and drink. The town of Shravana Belgola in Karnataka is the site of an important Digambara pilgrimage site. A special pilgrimage to the town takes place every few years when the 57-foot statue of Bahubali is anointed.

Monks and nuns must, and laypeople may, choose to undertake the six Jain obligatory actions: establishing equanimity, praising the Jinas, honoring one's teachers, repenting, standing motionless, and abandoning certain foods and drink. The ritual of Pratikramana is particularly indicative of the Jain emphasis on nonviolence. During this ritual of repentance and purification, Jains confess and ask forgiveness for any harm they have caused others and purify the karma they have accrued through such harmful acts. The rite is performed twice a day by renouncers, often by laywomen, and perhaps once a year by laymen.

Singing is a common part of lay rituals and worship. It is largely a female activity, although renouncers, and to a lesser extent laymen, also participate in singing as a devotional and inspirational activity. Singing circles are an important religious and social activity for laywomen, who sometimes infrequently leave their homes otherwise. Women collect religious songs from their natal homes and communities in order to pass them on to their in-laws after they marry. Women create, memorize, change, and exchange such songs. They are included in women's own ever changing collections and repertoires and are also available in published books and on cassette tapes.

RITES OF PASSAGE The most distinctive Jain rite of passage is initiation, as explained above under RITUALS. In other rites of passage, such as birth, marriage, and death, Jains usually follow local Hindu customs.

Fasting to death (*sallekhana*), however, is a practice that is distinctly Jain, although it is undertaken by few today. When Jain renouncers find themselves too old or incapacitated to follow their vows, they may choose to fast until they die. This is not considered suicide, which is an act of violence, but instead a controlled

Glossary

acharya head of a subsect or smaller group of renouncers

ahimsa nonviolence

anekant doctrine of the multiplicity of truth

aryika a Digambara nun who wears white clothing

brahmacharya chastity in marriage or celibacy

Dashalakshanaparvan yearly Digambara festival during which the Tattvartha Sutra is read and that ends in atonement

Digambara wearing the sky; sect of Jainism, largely based in southern India, in which full monks do not wear any clothing

diksha rite of initiation for a monk or a nun

Jina victor or conqueror; periodic founder or reviver of the Jain religion; also called a Tirthankara (ford or bridge builder)

jiva soul; every soul is endowed with perfect energy, perfect bliss, perfect perception, and perfect knowledge

karma microscopic particles that float in the universe, stick to souls according the quality of their actions, and manifest a like result before becoming detached from them

Mahavira Jayanti celebration of the birth of Lord Mahavira, the 24th and last Jina of the current period, by Shvetambaras and Digambaras in March–April

moksha nirvana; enlightenment achieved when practitioners purify themselves of all karma so that they will not be reborn

muhapatti mouth guard worn by some renouncers to avoid harming insects and air beings

muni a Digambara monk who wears no clothing

Murtipujak a Shvetambara subsect that worships by means of images

Namaskar Mantra the preeminent mantra that all Jains know and recite

nigoda microscopic being

Paryushan yearly Shvetambara festival during which the Kalpa Sutra is read and that ends in atonement

puja rite of worship

Purvas oldest scriptures of Jainism, now lost

sallekhana ritual fasting until death

samsara the cycle of reincarnation

sati virtuous woman; a chaste wife or a nun

Shvetambara wearing white; sect of Jainism, largely based in northwestern India, in which monks and nuns wear white clothing

Sthanakwasi Shvetambara aniconic subsect

svastika well-being; symbol representing the four realms into which souls are reincarnated, the three jewels, the abode of enlightened beings, and the enlightened beings themselves

tap (tapas, tapasya) austerities performed to purify the soul of karma

tattva any of the nine realities that characterize the universe and that include souls (*jivas*), matter (*ajiva*), matter coming in contact with souls (*ashrava*), the binding of karma and the soul (*bandha*), beneficial karma (*punya*), harmful karma (*papa*), inhibiting the influx of karma (*samvara*), purifying the soul of karma (*nirjara*), and liberation (*moksha,* or nirvana)

Tattvartha Sutra the only Jain scripture shared by both Shvetambaras and Digambaras, composed by Umasvati in c. 300 C.E.

Terapanthi Shvetambara aniconic subsect that has only one *acharya*

three jewels right faith, right understanding, and right conduct

death. The practitioner renounces food and meditates, attempting to withdrawal his or her senses from the outside world in order to die in a meditative and completely nonviolent state.

MEMBERSHIP Jain scriptures are full of stories of scholars and renouncers who debated, preached, and converted people—and also gods, demons, and animals—in India. Unlike Buddhism, however, the growth of Jainism to other countries has been inhibited by ascetic's rules against traveling in vehicles. The only group that actively promotes Jain practices in India and elsewhere today is the Terapanthi subsect. They are able to do so because they have created a new form of renunciation, the institution of lesser renouncers (samanis and samans), to fit modern times. Although these renouncers follow most ascetic rules, they are allowed to travel in vehicles. Lesser Terapanthi nuns, and some monks, actively promote Jainism by traveling, lecturing, and ministering to Jains and others outside India, including those in the United States as well as European countries.

RELIGIOUS TOLERANCE Although there have been religious persecutions on the continent, many Asians today follow practices and beliefs of more than one religion. Hindus, for example, revere Mother Teresa, a Roman Catholic, as a saint and go to Dharmashala to receive blessings from the Dalai Lama, a Buddhist. Jains also have respect for such religious leaders and today live cordially with members of other religions in India. This was not always the case, however, especially in southern India, where Jains were persecuted by Hindus in the latter part of the first millennium C.E.

In contemporary times, with the reinterpretation of the doctrine of anekant (multiplicity of truth) to accommodate ecumenical movements, Jainism has headed in an even more tolerant direction. In the past this doctrine was used by scholars and debaters to establish the superiority of Jain teachings to the more partial truths of other religions. Now, however, especially among those living in the West, the more tolerant and relativistic side of Jainism is emphasized. Perhaps today's attitude is closer to that of Haribhadra's. Although he argued for the superiority of Jainism, he also advocated respect for the people of all religions.

In the same way Jains today argue that their religion already encompassed many concepts, such as microscopic organisms and environmentalism, before they were discovered by science. By demonstrating how broad their ideas are, Jains glorify their religion, a principal means of accumulating good karma, and they also assert that Jainism encompasses many points of view and perspectives, making it closest to the enlightened state of omniscient knowledge that was attained by Lord Mahavira. At the same time, Jains emphasize a more tolerant side of anekant, as did Haribhadra, and hold that, with the qualification that they should be nonviolent, the beliefs and practices of any religion may be respected.

SOCIAL JUSTICE Unlike monks, Jain laymen must earn money to support their families. Their professions are limited by the adherence to nonviolence, however, and it is for this reason that men tend to go into business. The Jain community is, therefore, affluent, and laypeople frequently give money to support their religion and other beneficial causes. Laypeople not only gain good karma from this, but they also purify bad karma.

Lay Jain activities involve supporting and running institutions dedicated to helping humans and animals. These include creating educational opportunities, providing for the poor, and working for peaceful solutions to political problems. Jain libraries contain not only Jain works but works from other religions as well. Jain hospitals provide medical care, and shelters provide care for animals. All such causes are time-honored recipients of charity, and as Jainism has expanded to the West, environmental causes have come to be included.

Most Jains are active in the promotion of learning, religious or otherwise. With the decrease in child marriages in India, Jain children, particularly girls, have time to pursue education. As in India generally, in the past education was less available to Jain girls and women than to men, but Jains have made more progress in this area than Hindus have. Even the Tapa Gaccha, a division of Murtipujak Shvetambaras and the most populous Jain group, in which nuns formerly did not have educational opportunities, has opened religious education to its nuns. Today there are many educated Jain laypeople and renouncers, including some who have earned doctorates and published books.

Historically there have been mixed attitudes in Jainism toward nature. On the one hand, the ultimate goal of asceticism is to escape rebirth in the world in order to reside with other liberated souls at the top of the universe. On the other hand, Jainism has institutionalized nonviolence toward all forms of life, which include embodied souls that are intrinsically divine even though their divinity may be hidden by karma. For Jains souls are embodied in what the West terms "nature," including earth, water, air, and plants. Thus, many Jains try to live nonviolently toward these life forms, and Jain ascetics are required to do so. Although the ascetic ideology tends to emphasize escape from this world, lay ideology does not. Further, because most ascetics cannot travel by vehicles, virtually all Jains in the West are laypeople. For this reason the ascetic ideal of escaping the world is less strong among Western Jains. Instead of looking toward escape, they have begun to create an ecological Jainism that, as an extension of nonviolence, aims to preserve the environment.

Jains believe in purification through suffering and are concerned with all souls, not just those presently inhabiting human bodies. For these reasons activity in promoting social justice has been limited, particularly in the past. Jains have traditionally focused on noninterfering types of nonviolence. Not only should Jains not interfere with another soul's happiness, but they also should not interfere with another soul's purification of karma through suffering. Alleviating the suffering of others, in the Jain view, does not eliminate suffering but only postpones it. For example, food and some medical care are provided to animals in shelters, but no matter how much they suffer, the animals are not euthanatized. Instead, they are made as comfortable as possible until they recover or die. At the same time, Jains are concerned with animal products used in consumer goods and with animal testing done for consumer products and in medical laboratories.

SOCIAL ASPECTS When they reach their teens and early 20s, Jains in India must decide between two different lives: marriage or renunciation. If a person does not marry, he or she must renounce, and vice versa. For most Indians marriage is the only option, and this is what the majority of Jains choose. Now that fewer child marriages take place, however, increasing numbers of Jain women are choosing to renounce. In addition, a man may remarry if his wife leaves him or dies, but a wife under the same circumstances should not remarry. Further, the only legitimate means of divorce for traditional Jains is to leave a spouse through renunciation.

Families in India tend to be extended, in which young women and girls leave their own families to live with their in-laws. Thus, children often grow up with grandparents, parents, aunts, uncles, brothers, sisters, and cousins around them. Jain family structure in India differs from region to region, however. Hierarchy in the family is based on seniority and gender, with the oldest and male members having the most authority, respect, and power. It is not surprising then that male children are valued more highly than female children. As in other Indian traditions, a Jain wife does not gain significant respect from her in-laws until she has given birth to her first son.

CONTROVERSIAL ISSUES Abortion, which is considered violence to a soul in the form of the unborn child, is forbidden in Jainism. In addition, human rebirth is an extremely rare occurrence, let alone in a time when Jain teachings are available. Human rebirth is therefore precious, and Jains are exhorted not to waste human life but to live with the ultimate goal of liberation in mind. If a pregnancy threatens the mother, however, abortion may be considered.

As in many other Indian traditions, divorce in Jainism is forbidden for women, although it does occasionally takes place, and it is frowned upon for men. If, however, a married person decides that he or she wants to become a renouncer, the marriage is dissolved. Although the practice has begun to change, traditionally a woman could marry only once and was to be faithful to her husband in body, speech, and mind. She was never to touch, speak to, or think of another man. Even if her husband was abusive, she was to submit to him, serve him, and not complain. If her husband died, left her, or decided to renounce, she was not allowed to remarry but had to tolerate the harsh life of a woman without a husband. In the past, however, men, especially kings, could marry more than one woman at a time. Today men may remarry if a wife dies or decides to renounce.

Women have greater rights among the Jains of southern India, where widows may remarry, and in Gujarat, where women have more authority. In Rajasthan, however, wives are frequently abused by their husbands and in-laws, despite the Jain proscription against violence. It is also more difficult to be a widow in Rajasthan. The situation there was alleviated in the twentieth century by Acharya Tulsi, who improved women's rights in the Terapanthi subsect.

Regardless of her situation, a Jain women is, or strives to be, a *sati* (virtuous women). Whereas in Hinduism the term describes both faithful wives and wives who die with their husbands on the funeral pyre, in Jainism the term describes faithful wives and female renouncers. Although there is some evidence to indicate that a few Jains participated in wife immolation in the past, this is no longer the case. Both types of *satis*, wives and nuns, accumulate power through their chastity and tolerance of hardship. For wives this means fidelity and

A Narrative of Jain Values

Nonviolence is the most important guiding principle of Jainism, but close behind is chastity. The ancient story of Jina Nemi, Sati Rajimati, and Rathanemi illustrates both principles.

As a prince, Nemi was on his way to be married to the princess Rajimati until he saw the animals that were about to be killed for his wedding feast. Because he could not be a part of such slaughter, he renounced householder life and became an ascetic. This left the princess overcome by grief. While she was contemplating her situation, Nemi's brother Rathanemi decided to ask the beautiful Rajimati to marry him instead. She had already determined to marry Nemi, however, and as a *sati* (virtuous woman) she could not feel the same way about another man. She convinced Rathanemi that she would not marry him, and she decided that it would be better for her to renounce and become a nun. Rathanemi decided to renounce as well and was initiated as a monk.

Sometime later Rajimati was caught in a downpour and took refuge in a cave. Thinking she was alone, she took off her soaked clothing in order to dry them but was seen naked by the monk Rathanemi, who was meditating in the cave. She was frightened and tried to hide her body, but he propositioned her. When she realized that he had succumbed to sensual desire, she warned him to control himself and to maintain his practice of celibacy. Rathanemi did so, and both eventually became enlightened.

obedience to husbands, and for nuns its means complete celibacy and the endurance of austerities.

The power that is accumulated through celibacy and austerities and that fuels spiritual progress is so important that it is preferable to end one's life rather than to lose this power. Although suicide is forbidden in Jainism, there are two circumstances in which deliberate death is allowed and appropriate, which separates Jain-

ism from most religious traditions. The first is fasting until death (*sallekhana*), which Jains may undertake in order to control the circumstances of their dying. The second applies mostly to nuns. By dissipating the internal energy stored within, one instance of sexual activity, voluntary or involuntary, ruins a monk's or nun's spiritual progress. Because celibacy is so important in the lives of monks and nuns, it is considered suitable for a nun threatened with rape to prevent the act by killing herself.

Although in many ways Jainism is highly egalitarian, most Jains look to monks as the highest authority and do not respect the traditions of laywomen. Jain laywomen, however, are more religious than laymen and are extraordinarily important in the religion. It is women who mostly frequent temples, perform rituals and fasts, sing hymns, and consult with renouncers, while men normally go to temples less often, attend or participate only in important rituals, and give religious donations. Women are in charge of their children's religious education and are therefore crucial for the continued existence of the Jain religion. In addition, today there are four times more Jain nuns than monks. Considering the larger Indian and Hindu culture, in which Hindu female renouncers are rare, this is highly unusual.

CULTURAL IMPACT There are no Jain images dating from before the common era. Although images of the Jinas are perhaps the most significant form of Jain visual art, scholars have tended to neglect them because of their uniformity across time and the sects. This uniformity, however, points to the sameness of all souls in Jainism, which is realized upon liberation and is therefore important to show in art. Even Shvetambara images of the Jina Mallinatha, who was female, adhere to the same male form, with a smooth and tubular, rather than muscular, limbs and torso to indicate dispassion in physical form and with wide open eyes to symbolize omniscience. Images of different Jinas are usually distinguishable from one another only by various emblems at the bases. Exceptions to this are images of Lord Parshva, who usually appears with cobra hoods emerging from behind, sheltering his head and body.

The once subtle Jain arts of drama and dance are now extinct, although local plays continue to be performed during devotions and celebrations. The more developed and subtler forms may have disappeared as a result of Jainism's emphasis on austerity, which shunned such sensual enjoyments as beauty and entertainment for detachment and equanimity. Some arts may also have been lost with Jainism's loss of support from and persecution by rulers. Furthermore, drama and dance have strong ties to devotional worship. Although worship is present in Jainism, it is not as prevalent as in Hinduism, in which theater and dance have continued to thrive. When Jain drama and dance existed, they were similar to the Hindu performing arts, while ingeniously incorporating aspects more suitable to the ascetic Jain tradition, such as an emphasis on spiritual heroism and calm equanimity.

Although the visual and performing arts are limited in Jainism, Jain literature is particularly significant. Jains have long commissioned the copying of their texts and have established libraries to protect collections of literature. Some collections were once so protected that Europeans found themselves barred from entering. Jainism has some of the most voluminous story literature of any tradition, including short didactic narratives and long epics. There are even Jain versions of such popular Hindu epics as the *Ramayana* and *Mahabharata*. The epic *Chivakachintomani*, composed by Tiruttakkatevar, has been particularly influential in Tamil Nadu, so much so that some Hindu compositions, such as Kampar's famous *Ramayanam*, were created to compete with it and imitated its style.

The beautiful poetics and subtle literary devices used in the *Chivakachintomani* make it a masterpiece, even in English translation. The main characters are the king Chachchantan, his queen Vichayai, his minister Kattiyankaran, and his son Chivakan. Chachchantan was a good king, but he was so in love with his queen that he decided to give his minister power to rule while he retired to enjoy sensual pleasures with her. Kattiyankaran was not satisfied ruling another man's kingdom, however, and plotted to kill Chachchantan so that he could claim the kingdom for himself. The king heard of the plan and devised a way for his pregnant wife to escape. When Kattiyankaran attacked, King Chachchantan was killed, but Queen Vichayai was able to escape to give birth to a son. Because of her dire circumstances she was forced give up the son, and she renounced to become a nun. The merchant Kantukatan found and raised her son, Chivakan, as his own. When the boy matured, his teacher told him of his true heritage and urged him to wait a year before taking back his father's kingdom. Before it was time to attack, Chivakan married eight women, and when he attacked Kattiyankaran, he was successful. Chivakan eventually followed his biological

and foster mothers to renounce the world, and he did so at the glorious feet of Lord Mahavira.

Sherry Fohr

Bibliography

Babb, Lawrence. *Absent Lord.* Berkeley: University of California Press, 1996.

Balbir, Nalini. "Women in Jainism." In *Women and Religion.* Edited by Arvind Sharma. Albany: State University of New York Press, 1994.

Carrithers, Michael. "Jainism and Buddhism as Enduring Historical Streams." *Journal of the Anthropological Society of Oxford* 21 (1990): 141–63.

———. "Naked Ascetics in Southern Digambara Jainism." *Man* 24 (June 1989): 219–35.

Carrithers, Michael, and Caroline Humphrey, eds. *The Assembly of Listeners.* Cambridge: Cambridge University Press, 1991.

Chapple, Christopher, ed. *Jainism and Ecology.* Cambridge, Mass.: Harvard University Press, 2002.

Cort, John E. *Jains in the World: Religious Values and Ideology in India.* New York: Oxford University Press, 2001.

———. "The Rite of Veneration of Jina Images." In *Religions of India in Practice.* Edited by Donald S. Lopez, Jr. Princeton, N.J.: Princeton University Press, 1994.

———. "The Śvetāmbar Mūrtipūjak Jain Mendicant." *Man* 26 (1991): 651–71.

———. "Two Ideals of the Shvetambara Murtipujak Jain Layman." *Journal of Indian Philosophy* 19 (December 1991): 1–30.

———. "Who Is God and How Is He Worshipped." In *Religions of India in Practice.* Edited by Donald S. Lopez, Jr. Princeton, N.J.: Princeton University Press, 1994.

———, ed. *Open Boundaries.* Albany: State University of New York Press, 1998.

Deo, S.B. *History of Jaina Monachism from Inscriptions and Literature.* Deccan College Dissertation Series, 17. Poona, 1956.

Dixit, K.K., trans. *Pt. Suklalji's Commentary on the Tattvārtha Sūtra of Vācaka Umāsvāti.* Ahmadabad: Institute of Indology, 1974.

Doniger, Wendy, ed. *Purāṇa Perennis: Reciprocity and Transformation in Hindu and Jaina Texts.* Albany: State University of New York Press, 1993.

Dundas, Paul. *The Jains.* London: Routledge, 2002.

Flügel, Peter. "The Codes of Conduct of the Terāpanth Samaṇ Order." *South Asian Research* 23, no. 1 (2003): 7–53.

Fohr, Sherry. "External Rules and Protection." In *Studies in Jain History and Culture: Disputes and Dialogues.* Edited by Peter Flügel. London: Routledge, 2005.

————. "Jain Nuns: Chastity and Power." Ph.D. diss., University of Virginia, 2001.

Folkert, Kendall W. "Jainism." In *A New Handbook of Living Religions.* Edited by John R. Hinnells. Cambridge: Blackwell, 1997.

Goonasekara, R.S.A. "Renunciation and Monasticism among the Jains of India." Ph.D. diss., University of California, San Diego, 1986.

Granoff, Phyllis. *The Forest Thieves and the Magic Garden.* New Delhi: Penguin Books, 1998.

Granoff, Phyllis, and Koichi Shinohara, eds. *Monks and Magicians.* Delhi: Motilal Banarsidass, 1994.

Jacobi, Hermann, ed. "Jaina Sutras." In *Sacred Books of the East.* Edited by Max Muller. Delhi: Motilal Banarsidass, 1964.

Jaini, Padmanabh S. *Gender and Salvation: Jaina Debates on the Spiritual Liberation of Women.* New Delhi: Munishiram Manoharlal Publishers, 1991.

————. *The Jaina Path of Purification.* Delhi: Motilal Banarsidass, 1979.

————. "The Pure and the Auspicious in the Jaina Tradition." In *Journal of Developing Societies.* Edited by John B. Carman and Frédérique Apffel Marglin. Leiden: E.J. Brill, 1985.

Kelting, Whitney. *Singing to the Jinas.* New York: Oxford, 2001.

————. "Who Is Running the Pūjā? A Jain Women's Maṇḍal and the Rituals of Performance." In *Approaches to Jaina Studies.* Edited by Olle Qvarnström and N.K. Wagle. Toronto: Centre for South Asian Studies, University of Toronto, 1997.

Pal, Pratapaditya. *The Peaceful Liberators: Jain Art from India.* London: Thames and Hudson; Los Angeles: Los Angeles County Museum of Art, 1994.

Reynell, Josephine. "Prestige, Honour, and the Family: Laywomen's Religiosity Amongst Śvetāmbar Mūrtipūjāk Jains in Jaipur." In *Bulletin d'etudes Indienne* 5 (1987): 313–59.

————. "Women and the Reproduction of the Jain Community." In *The Assembly of Listeners.* Edited by Michael Carrithers and Caroline Humphrey. Cambridge: Cambridge University Press, 1991.

Sangave, Vilas A. *Jaina Community.* Bombay: Popular Prakashan, 1980.

Shāntā, N. *La Voie Jaina.* Paris: O.E.I.L., 1985.

Vallely, Anne. *Guardians of the Transcendent.* Toronto: Toronto University Press, 2002.

Wagle, N.K., and Olle Qvarnström. *Approaches to Jaina Studies: Philosophy, Logic, Ritual and Symbols.* Toronto: University of Toronto Press, 1999.

Judaism

FOUNDED: c. eighteenth century
B.C.E.

**RELIGION AS A PERCENTAGE OF
WORLD POPULATION:** 0.25
percent

OVERVIEW Judaism had its beginnings some 3,800 years ago in Mesopotamia, today part of Iraq, with Abraham, the founding patriarch of the tribes of Israel. Judaism is a monotheistic faith affirming that God is one, the creator of the world and everything in it. God is also a transcendent being above and beyond the world and is thus without material form, and yet he is present in the world. His will and presence are especially, but not exclusively, manifest in his relationship with Israel (the Jewish people), to whom he has given the Torah (teaching), stipulating the laws that are to govern their religious and moral life, by virtue of which they are to be "a light unto the nations" (Isa. 49:6). Accordingly, Jews understand themselves as a chosen people, bound by a covenant with God.

In Judaism faith is less a matter of affirming a set of beliefs than of trust in God and fidelity to his law. Faith is thus primarily expressed "by walking in all the ways of God" (Deut. 11:22). These ways are specified in God's revealed law, which the rabbis, or teachers, appropriately called the Halakhah (walking). The commandments of the Halakhah embrace virtually every aspect of life, from worship to the most mundane aspects of daily existence. The precise details of the Halakhah are but adumbrated in the Torah, and they require elab-

oration to determine their contemporary applicability. This process is ongoing, for the Torah must be continually reinterpreted to meet new conditions, and the rabbis developed principles to allow this without violating its sanctity. The modern world has thus witnessed the emergence alongside traditional, or Orthodox, Judaism various movements—Reform, Conservative, and Reconstructionist—that have introduced new criteria for the interpretation of the Torah and for Jewish religious responsibility.

As early as 597 B.C.E.hasis>, with conquest by Babylonia, the Israelites were exiled from their homeland. Over the centuries the Jewish Diaspora came to include communities throughout the world but particularly in the Middle East, around the Mediterranean, and in Europe. In modern times Europe was the center of Jewish religious and cultural life until more than two-thirds of European Jews were murdered during the Holocaust. The center of Judaism then shifted to the United States and to the State of Israel, founded in 1948. Today there are smaller Jewish communities in Canada, Central and South America, and Australia, as well as several European countries.

HISTORY Judaism traces its origins to Abraham, who in the judgment of most scholars lived in the eighteenth century B.C.E. Jewish tradition regards Abraham as the first person to have believed that God is one. At the age of 75 Abraham was commanded by God to leave Mesopotamia and settle in the land of Canaan: "Go forth from your native land and from your father's house to the land that I will show you. I will make you a great

THE MENORAH. The Menorah, a seven-branched candelabrum, is the most enduring symbol of Judaism. First constructed by Moses at God's instruction (Exodus 25:31–38), it was placed in the portable sanctuary carried by the Israelites in the wilderness and then to the Temple of Jerusalem. When the temple was destroyed, the Menorah became the emblem of Jewish survival and continuity. The Star of David is a modern symbol of Jewish identity, although it has no religious content or scriptural basis. (THOMSON GALE)

nation" (Gen. 12:1–2). His descendants were to be called the Children of Israel, and the country they were promised the Land of Israel. Only much later, in the Hellenistic period (333–63 B.C.E.), were the Israelites called Jews.

According to the Bible, the history of the Israelites was determined by their relationship to God, which was sealed by two events. The first was the Exodus of the enslaved Israelites from Egypt, where they had settled after a famine had blighted the Promised Land. The deliverance of the Children of Israel from servitude marked their birth as a nation. Previously they had been a loosely knit group of 12 tribes, descendants of Abraham. God's intervention on their behalf was understood to be an act of love and undeserved grace, solely the fulfillment of a promise he had made. Acknowledging that its existence was owed to God, Israel was henceforth beholden to him. The Exodus story, which the Israelites were enjoined to remember through constant retelling, thus constituted Israel's understanding of itself as a people destined to serve God in love and gratitude.

The second event shaping the spiritual history of Israel occurred some three months after the Exodus. Wandering in the wilderness, the Israelites stopped at the foot of Mount Sinai when their divinely appointed leader, Moses, ascended the mountain. He returned with a decree from God calling upon them to enter into a covenant (*brit*). The people agreed, after which they experienced God's presence in "thunder, and lightning, and a dense cloud upon the mountain, and a very loud blast of the horn" (Exod. 19:16). Through Moses, God bestowed the Ten Commandments, proclaiming the people's duties to him and to their fellow humans. Overwhelmed by the experience, the people beseeched Moses to serve as their mediator with God. He obliged them and ascended the mountain once again. What followed was an extensive body of divine decrees, which Moses recorded in the books called the Torah and submitted to the people. With this act a covenant between Israel and God was established. The Mosaic Covenant is generally understood to be a renewal and elaboration of the original covenant between God and Abraham, confirmed by his son Isaac and grandson Jacob, but this time with the entire House of Israel.

Some 230 years after the Israelites returned from Egypt, they built the Temple in Jerusalem. This was the central site of Jewish prayer and pilgrimage and for the bringing of sacrifices as an expression of submission to God, as thanksgiving, and as atonement for sins. The Temple rites were conducted by a hereditary priesthood. In 587 B.C.E. the Temple was destroyed by the conquering armies of Babylonia, which resulted in the exile of most of the Israelite nobility and leadership. It was apparently during the Babylonian Exile that the institution of the synagogue as a house of prayer began to emerge. In 586 the Persian king Cyrus, who had defeated the armies of Babylonia, gave the exiles permission to return. Many, however, remained in Babylonia, which, together with Egypt, where Jews had also voluntarily settled, became the first community of the Diaspora. Those who did return found not only the Temple in ruins but also a dispirited people, bereft of spiritual leadership, who had neglected the Torah and had mixed with the heathen population and adopted their culture and religious practices.

The reconstruction of the Temple, which was rededicated in 516 B.C.E., failed to reassert the authority of the Torah. It was not until the return of two leaders that the process of assimilation was decisively reversed. The scribe and priest Ezra arrived in Jerusalem in 458,

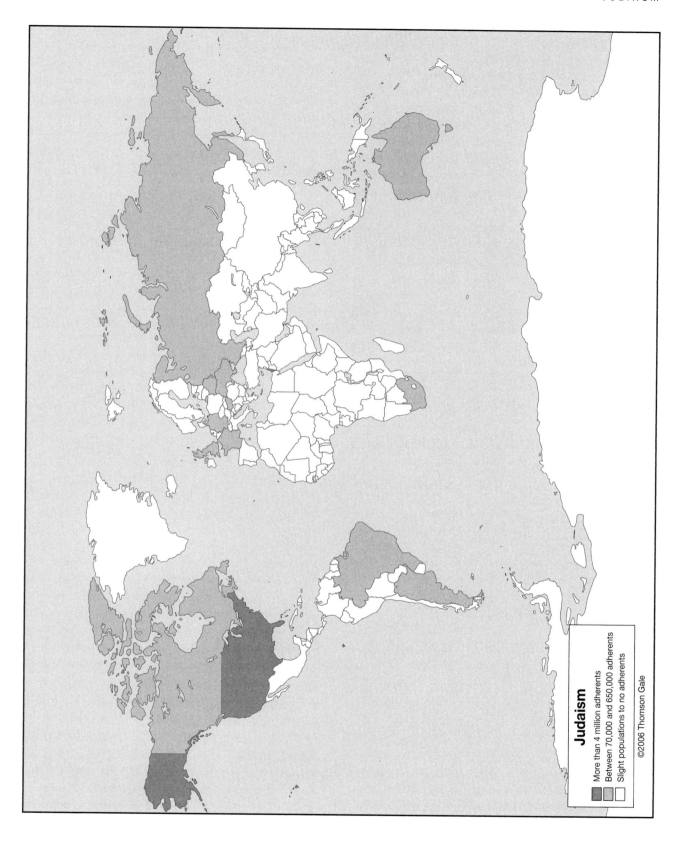

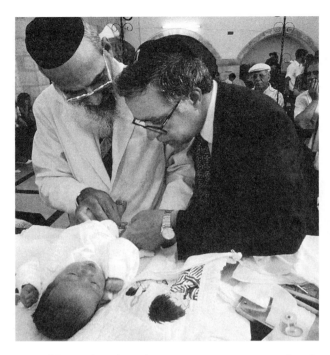

Brit Milah, a traditional Jewish circumcision ceremony, is carried out by a rabbi in a synagogue. Brit Milah is an important rite of passage among Conservative Jews. © BOJAN BRECELJ/CORBIS.

and three years later the Persian overlords appointed Nehemiah governor of the province of Judea. Together Ezra and Nehemiah set out to uproot pagan influences and to reform the life of the Jewish community. Nehemiah instituted civil regulations ensuring social justice and the rule of law. Ezra, who, according to the traditional account, was authorized by the Persian king to impose the laws of the Torah on the community, annulled the marriages with heathen wives and introduced strict observance of the Sabbath, including a ban on business transactions. Perhaps most important was his codification of the Torah as the five books of Moses, which were read and expounded before the people at the Sabbath afternoon prayer and during the morning prayers on Mondays and Thursdays. Overseeing the people's solemn rededication to the Torah and its study, Ezra was said to be a second Moses, and his comprehensive program of reform laid the foundation for what was to become known as rabbinical Judaism.

The destruction of the Second Temple by the Romans in 70 C.E. found the Jews prepared to face the tragedy. A body of teachers and expositors of the Torah—the rabbis—was solidly in place. The synagogue, established in virtually every community, replaced the Temple as the focus of ritual and prayer. Led by Joha-

nan ben Zakkai, the rabbis transferred many of the rites and ceremonies that had belonged to the Temple to the synagogue, where they were often recast as symbolic gestures. Sacrifices were replaced by acts of charity and repentance. The rabbis also recognized that, with the decentralization of religious authority, it was urgent to fix the biblical canon. Hitherto, aside from the Torah, the corpus of sacred writings had been fluid, with several competing versions. By the end of the first century the biblical text was sealed, with 31 books organized according to three parts—Torah (Pentateuch), Nevi'im (Prophets), and Ketuvim (Hagiographa), collectively known by the acronym Tanakh.

Sixty years after the destruction of the Temple, Simeon Bar Kokhba led the Jews in a revolt against their Roman overlords. After three years the tenacious and valiant forces of the revolt were put down, and Bar Kokhba himself was killed in the last decisive battle, in the summer of 135. (According to one account, he was taken captive and enslaved.) In the aftermath the Jews were banished from Jerusalem, and Jewish ritual practices, including circumcision, study of the Torah, and observance of the Sabbath, were prohibited. The spiritual leadership was summarily executed, and most of the remaining Jewish population fled. The Romans quickly repopulated Judea with non-Jews, and the Land of Israel, aside from Galilee, ceased to be Jewish.

The fugitives from Judea scattered throughout the Mediterranean. Joined by scholars, these Jews spread to Asia Minor and westward to Spain, Gaul (France), and the Rhine valley, where they organized self-governing communities. Those Jews remaining in the Land of Israel also slowly reorganized themselves. The Sanhedrin (Greek for Council of the Elders), which formerly had its seat in Jerusalem, was reconstituted in Jabneh (Yavneh) as the supreme representative body in religious and communal affairs. The institution continued until the early fifth century, when the Roman authorities abolished the office of the presidency of the Sanhedrin.

With the vast majority of the Jews living outside the Land of Israel, many in distant lands, the rabbis referred to the emerging Diaspora as the Exile, as a tragic national and religious state of homelessness. While many answers were given to explain the indignity and spiritual dislocation wrought by the Exile, the rabbis were united in their faith that God would redeem the exiles and regather them. This redemption was associated with the advent of God's appointed deliverer, the Messiah, who would be chosen from among the descendants of King David. A redeemed Jerusalem became the symbol of the hope for the coming of the Messiah, who would herald not only the liberation of the Jews from Exile but also the establishment of the universal kingdom of God upon earth. The messianic age would witness the perfection of creation and of the human order. The rabbis also taught, however, that in Exile the Jews were not utterly bereft of God's providential presence. Earlier God had told the Israelites, "Fear not to go down to Egypt, for I will go down with you into Egypt and surely bring you again" (Gen. 46:3–4), and he accompanied the Jews in Exile. This teaching allowed the Jews to develop a creative spiritual and religious life while they mourned the desolation of Zion, or Israel, and new centers of Jewish life emerged throughout the Diaspora.

The Babylonian Diaspora, whose origins date to the destruction of the First Temple and the decision of most of the exiles not to return, was the oldest and largest settlement of Jews for at least the first thousand years of the Exile. By the second century C.E. the Jewish community of Babylonia had reached between 800,000 and 1.2 million, constituting from 10 to 12 percent of the total population. Under the leadership of an exilarch (head of the Exile), a hereditary office occupied by descendants of King David, the Jews enjoyed religious freedom and communal autonomy. The exilarchs ruled according to the Torah and Halakhah and encouraged the establishment of rabbinical academies (yeshivas), which initially acknowledged the authority of the academy in Jabneh and elsewhere in the Land of Israel. But with the decline of Israel, the Babylonian academies became the center of Jewish learning and culture. They produced the commentary on the Mishnah (collection of oral teachings on the Torah) known as the Babylonian Talmud, a labor of seven generations and hundreds of scholars, who completed their task in approximately 500, and communities throughout the Diaspora turned to Babylonian rabbis for guidance. The preeminence of the Babylonian Jewish community lasted until the tenth century, when it was superseded by centers of Jewish learning in the West.

The establishment of Christianity as the official religion of the Roman Empire by Constantine (ruled 306–37) marked a turning point in the life of Western Jewry. Christians had an ambivalent attitude toward Jews. On the one hand, Jews were the people from whose midst Jesus and the first apostles of the church came, and they were the living custodians of the Old

A Jewish man worships at the first functioning synagogue since World War II, in Lviv, Ukraine. Europe was the center of Jewish religious and cultural life until more than two-thirds of European Jews were murdered during the Holocaust. © PETER TURNLEY/CORBIS.

Testament, which contained the prophecies of the advent of Jesus as the Messiah. On the other hand, Jews were despised for rejecting Jesus. Despite the resulting history of antagonism, which often occasioned discrimination and persecution, there was also a rich cultural exchange. Early Christians adopted many Jewish beliefs and practices. The Gregorian chants of the Orthodox Church, for instance, are said to bear traces of the music of the Temple, and the structure of the Christian liturgy and many of its prayers are derived from Judaism, as is the practice of baptism. Medieval Jewish scholars took Greek philosophy, a knowledge of which they had acquired under the tutelage of Islamic sages, to Christian Europe. In turn, Christianity exercised an influence on popular Jewish religious practices, music, folklore, and thought, especially mysticism.

Within Christian Europe, Jews developed an intellectually and spiritually vibrant culture. Communities in southern Italy, where Jews had lived since the second century B.C.E., were particularly creative in composing liturgical poetry in Hebrew, and they thereby laid the foundations of what was to be called the Ashkenazi rite,

Jews in Brooklyn, New York, observe the festival of Sukkoth by spending time in succahs, or temporary dwellings. Conservative Jews follow the traditional Jewish calendar in celebrating Sukkoth, one of three pilgrimage festivals. © DAVID H. WELLS/CORBIS.

a term designating the Jews who lived in medieval Germany and neighboring countries. In northern France and on the eastern banks of the Rhine, important centers of rabbinical scholarship crystallized in the tenth and eleventh centuries. The comprehensive commentary on the Bible and the Talmud by the French rabbi Rashi (1040–1105) continues to serve as the basic text of a traditional Jewish education. In the second half of the twelfth and in the thirteen centuries, these communities produced highly original mystical theologies, collectively known as Hasidei Ashkenaz. The Jewish communities of Provence, in southern France, and of Christian Spain witnessed not only a flowering of philosophy, biblical exegesis, and Talmudic learning but also the unfolding of a mystical literature that culminated in the composition of the *Zohar* ("Book of Splendor") in the thirteenth century.

In the wake of the Crusades of 1096, 1146–47, and 1189–90 and of the Black Death in 1348–49, however, the situation of the Jews in Europe steadily deteriorated. Whole communities were massacred, and others were expelled. By 1500, except for isolated communities in France and Italy, western Europe was virtually empty of Jews. By then Jewish life was largely centered in the Kingdom of Poland-Lithuania, where a unique brand of Ashkenazi piety and learning developed, and in the Islamic world.

Under Muslim rule, which spread rapidly from the far corners of Persia to Spain, Jews on the whole enjoyed a less precarious lot than in Christian Europe. The very fact that some of the most important works of Jewish philosophy and even of Halakhah were written in Arabic, whereas in medieval Europe Jews wrote exclusively in Hebrew, illustrates the degree to which they were integrated into Muslim culture. Islamic philosophers, who revived the dormant thought of the Greeks, recruited disciples among Jews, the best known being Maimonides (1135–1204). The efflorescence of Jewish culture reached its height in Muslim Spain in the tenth and eleventh centuries, which was a golden age of Talmudic scholars, poets, philosophers, and mystics.

Glossary

Aggadah nonlegal, narrative portions of the Talmud and Mishna, which includes history, folklore, and other subjects

Ashkenazim Jews whose ancestors in the Middle Ages lived in Germany (Ashkenaz in Hebrew) and the surrounding countries

bar mitzvah (son of commandment) initiation ceremony for boys at age 13, when they are held to be responsible for their actions and hence are obliged to observe all of the commandments of the Torah; bat mitzah, a similar ceremony for girls at age 12, is observed by some Jews

Brit Milah circumcision of a male infant or adult convert as a sign of acceptance of the covenant

Conservative Judaism largest denomination of American Judaism, with affiliated congregations in South America and Israel; advocating moderate modifications of Halakhah, it occupies a middle ground between Reform and Orthodox Judaism

Diaspora communities of Jews dispersed outside the Land of Israel, traditionally referred to as the Exile

Haggadah book used at the Passover seder, containing the liturgical recitation of the Passover story and instructions on conducting the ceremonial meal

Halakhah legal portions of the Talmud as later elaborated in rabbinic literature; in an extended sense it denotes the ritual and legal prescriptions governing the traditional Jewish way of life

Hasidism revivalist mystical movement that originated in Poland in the eighteenth century

Kabbalah mystical reading of the Scriptures that arose in France and Spain during the twelfth century, culminating with the composition in the late thirteenth century of the *Zohar* ("Book of Splendor"), which, especially as interpreted by Isaac Luria (1534–72), exercised a decisive influence on late medieval and early modern Jewish spiritual life

kasruth rules and regulations for food and its preparation, often known by the Yiddish "kosher"

Midrash commentary on the Scriptures, both Halakhic (legal) and Aggadic (narrative), originally in the form of sermons or lectures

Mishnah collection of the Oral Torah, or commentary on the Torah, first compiled in the second and third centuries C.E.

Orthodox Judaism traditional Judaism, characterized by strict observance of laws and rituals (the Halakhah)

The Christian Reconquista (Reconquest) of Spain in the twelfth century led to the expulsion of the Jews at the end of the fifteenth century. Jews were allowed to remain in Spain only on the condition that they convert to Catholicism. Among the converts, however, were those who secretly maintained allegiance to their ancestral faith and who, as a consequence, later became subject to the Inquisition. Most of those who refused to convert sought refuge in Muslim countries, their descendants becoming known as Sephardic Jews, from the Hebrew name for Spain. Beginning in the late sixteenth century there was a steady stream of Jews from Spain and Portugal, popularly known as Marranos, who settled in the Netherlands, where they returned to Judaism. Members of this community founded the first Jewish settlements in the New World.

Hence, on the threshold of the modern era the Diaspora was in the midst of a radical reconfiguration. Sephardic Jewry was establishing itself throughout the Ottoman Empire and North Africa, where it became the dominant constituency in Jewish cultural life. A much smaller but dynamic Sephardic community was established in the Netherlands and its colonies in the Americas. Ashkenazic Jewry was overwhelmingly concentrated in eastern Europe, particularly in Poland and Lithuania. The remaining Jews of Germany slowly began to recover. This process was encouraged by the Protestant Reformation, which in alliance with nascent capitalism adopted a more pragmatic and thus tolerant attitude toward Jews. In time democratic forces led to the political emancipation of the Jews and their integration into the social and cultural life of Europe.

Passover (Pesach) festival marking the deliverance of the Israelites from Egyptian bondage

Prophets (Nevi'im) second of the three part of the Tanakh, made up of the books of 7 major and 12 minor prophets

Reconstructionist Judaism movement founded in the United States in the early twentieth century by Mordecai M. Kaplan (1881–1983) that holds Judaism to be not only a religion but also a dynamic "civilization" embracing art, music, literature, culture, and folkways

Reform Judaism movement originating in early nineteenth-century Germany that adapted the rituals and liturgy of Judaism to accommodate modern social, political, and cultural developments; sometimes called Liberal Judaism

Rosh Hashanah Jewish New Year; also known as the Day of Judgment, it is a time of penitence

Sanhedrin supreme religious body of ancient Judaism, disbanded by the Romans early in the fifth century C.E.

Sephardim Jews of Spain and Portugal and their descendants, most of whom, in the wake of expulsion in 1492, settled in the Ottoman Empire and in North Africa; in the early seventeenth century small groups of descendants of Jews who had remained on the Iberian Peninsula and accepted Christianity settled in the Netherlands, where they reaffirmed their ancestral religion

Shabuoth (Feast of Weeks) originally a harvest festival, now observed in commemoration of the giving of the Torah to the Israelites

Talmud also known as the Gemara, a running commentary on the Mishnah written by rabbis (called *amoraim,* or "explainers") from the third to the fifth centuries C.E. in Palestine and Babylonia; the work of the former is called the Jerusalem Talmud and the latter the Babylonian Talmud, which is generally regarded as the more authoritative of the two

Tanakh anagram for Jewish Scriptures, comprising the Torah, Prophets, and Writings

Torah (Pentatuch or Law) first division of the Tanakh, constituting the five books of Moses

Writings (Ketuvim or Hagiographa) third division of the Tanakh, including the Psalms and other works said to have be written under holy guidance

Yom Kippur (Day of Atonement) end of 10 days of penitence that begin with Rosh Hashana; the most holy of Jewish days

The effect on Judaism was far-reaching. The Jews' embrace of the Enlightenment and of liberal culture gave birth to new expressions of self-understanding and of religious belief and practice. One of the tragic ironies of the integration of Jews into modern European culture and society, however, was the intensification of anti-Semitism. Virulent opposition to the civic and political parity of the Jews, which for the most part was based on secular and not religious grounds, culminated in the fanatic hatred of Adolf Hitler and the National Socialist German Workers' Party (Nazis) and in their efforts in the Holocaust (Shoah) to exterminate all Jews. More than two-thirds of the Jewish people of Europe, a third of Jews worldwide, were murdered in Auschwitz and other death camps. The survivors sought to rehabilitate themselves in the State of Israel, established in 1948, or in Jewish communities unscathed by the Holocaust, particularly in North and South America.

CENTRAL DOCTRINES Principally a way of life, Judaism emphasizes religious practices rather than articles of faith. Upon his descent from Mount Sinai, Moses explained to the Children of Israel, "And now, O Israel, what does God demand of you? Only this: to revere the Lord your God, to walk only in His paths, to love Him, and to serve the Lord your God with all your heart and soul, keeping the Lord's commandments and laws, which I enjoin upon you today . . ." (Deut. 10:12–13). Judaism thus began not with an affirmation of faith but with an acceptance of what the rabbis came to call "the yoke of the Torah." Even the Ten Commandments stress basic duties rather than principles of faith. Implicit in the Torah and its teachings are, of course, fundamental beliefs, for example, the belief in God as recorded in the declaration "Hear, O Israel, the Lord is our God, the Lord is One" (Deut. 6:4), which is incorporated into the morning and evening prayers.

In Judaism heresy is thus defined as denial of the existence of God and of his oneness. Nonetheless, the rabbis did not formulate a binding statement of Judaism's principles of faith. The philosopher Philo (c. 20 B.C.E.–50 C.E.) was the first to attempt the outline of such a statement. Focusing on the creation narrative in Genesis, he enumerated five essential articles of Jewish belief: the eternal existence and rule of God, the unity of God, the divine creation of the world, the unity of creation, and divine providence that extends over the whole world. Philo's summary of the Jewish creed had virtually no resonance in subsequent theological discourse, however.

From time to time other Jewish philosophers, like Philo prompted by the need to explain and defend Judaism in the face of rival faiths, sought to formulate a succinct statement of essential beliefs. But it was only the philosopher and rabbinical scholar Maimonides who, in the twelfth century, succeeded in formulating a statement of Jewish doctrine that obtained an authoritative status. In his commentary on the Mishnah, he delineated the "Thirteen Principles of Faith":

1. Belief in the existence of God

2. Belief in God's unity

3. Belief in God's incorporeality

4. Belief in God's eternity

5. Belief that God alone is to be worshiped

6. Belief in prophecy

7. Belief that Moses was the greatest of the prophets

8. Belief that the Torah was given by God to Moses

9. Belief that the Torah is unchangeable

10. Belief that God knows the thoughts and deeds of each human being

11. Belief that God rewards and punishes

12. Belief in the coming of the Messiah

13. Belief in the resurrection of the dead

These principles were soon incorporated into the prayer book as the hymn "Yigdal" ("May He be magnified . . . "), which in 1517 was supplemented by a more elaborate prose explication in the form of a personal attestation of belief ("I believe in perfect faith . . .").

With their inclusion in the traditional liturgy, the "Thirteen Principles" thus gained the status of an official catechism. Maimonides even went so far as to claim that anyone not subscribing to all of the principles of faith, even if the person observes the laws of Moses, will not have a share in the world to come. To underscore the overarching significance he attached to the principles, Maimonides held that an utter sinner, although he or she will be appropriately punished, will share in the world to come if the principles are affirmed. For Maimonides, then, a Jew is defined by what he believes and not by what he does, which amounted to a radical revision of Judaism. It is, therefore, not surprising that many rabbis and philosophers disputed the authority of the "Thirteen Principles," contending that they were not as basic and essential as Maimonides contended. For instance, the Spanish philosopher Yosef Albo (c. 1380–1444) argued that there are only three basic doctrines constitutive of Jewish belief: the existence of God, divine revelation, and divine reward and punishment. Another Spanish philosopher and biblical scholar, Isaac Abravanel (1437–1508), questioned whether it was necessary at all to formulate articles of belief. To his mind the faith implicit in the observance of the Torah was sufficient. He concluded nonetheless that Maimonides' "Thirteen Principles," although not to be construed as dogma, might be helpful for those unable to comprehend on their own the theological presuppositions of the Torah and its commandments.

Although Maimonides' "Thirteen Principles" as formulated in the liturgy are still affirmed by Orthodox and Conservative Jews, they are subject to interpretation. Reform Jews have periodically formulated alternative statements of the essential Jewish beliefs, but by and large they continue to endorse the first five, namely, the existence of God, that he is one, that he has no bodily form, that he is eternal, and that he alone is to be worshiped.

MORAL CODE OF CONDUCT Judaism does not distinguish between duties toward fellow human being and duties toward God. The Hebrew Bible and the rabbis regard moral and religious duties as inseparable. The emphasis is on attaining holiness, on "walking in God's ways" (Deut. 10:12–13), thus allowing his presence to dwell in one's midst. Through Moses, God told the Children of Israel, "You shall be holy, for I, the Lord your God, am holy" (Lev. 19:2), which is recited today by observant Jews in their morning and evening prayers.

This commandment is followed immediately by the injunction to honor one's parents and to observe the Sabbath. The weave of moral and ritual duties is maintained in a long list of commandments, from measures to aid the poor and secure their dignity to proper worship at the Temple, from fairness in commerce to the avoidance of pagan rites, from respect for the stranger to the sanctity of the firstfruits (Lev. 19:3–37), the earliest products of the harvest that are offered to God. A person attains holiness by observing the commandments and laws of God. As God is manifest only through his deeds, so a person is beckoned to imitate those deeds (Deut. 10:17–19).

The prophets, and the rabbis after them, typically warned that ritual piety unaccompanied by moral deeds is unacceptable to God. As the prophet Micah taught, "With what shall I approach the Lord, Do homage to God on high? Shall I approach Him with burnt offerings? . . . He has told you, O man, what is good / And what the Lord requires of you: Only to do justice / And to love goodness / And to walk humbly with your God . . ." (Mic. 6:6–8). But while upholding the primacy of morality over ritual, it was not the intention of Micah, or of any other prophet, to distinguish moral from religious virtue. The biblical conception of social responsibility as the axis of the ethical life was incorporated by the rabbis into the Halakhah. The rabbis elaborated biblical injunctions, codifying in great detail alongside the Jew's ritual duties the ethical principles of justice, equity, charity, and respect for the feelings and needs of others.

When asked to identify the overarching principle of the Torah, the rabbis pointed to its moral dimension. Hence, according to a Midrash on Leviticus 19:18, "Rabbi Akiva [c. 50–c. 136] said of the command, 'You shall love your neighbor as yourself,' that is 'a great principle of Torah.'" Rabbi Hillel (c. 70 B.C.E.–c. 10 C.E.) formulated the same principle with psychological insight: "What is hateful unto yourself do not to your fellow human being. This is the entire Torah, the rest is commentary. Go and study." Implicit in these encapsulations of biblical morality is that the ethical life requires sensibilities that often must go, as the rabbis would put it, "beyond the letter of the law." To love one's neighbor or to avoid treating one's neighbor in a manner that one would find repugnant—offensive, hurtful, humiliating—when done to oneself, requires a sensitivity that cannot be legislated.

The religious significance of the moral teachings of the Torah was summarized by a sixteenth-century rabbinical scholar from Prague, Judah Loew, popularly known as the Maharal. Through adhering to the moral teachings of the Torah, the Maharal taught, a person imitates God's ways and thus realizes his or her destiny as a being created in the image of God. Moral behavior, therefore, draws a person to God. Conversely, immoral conduct distances a person from God. The nineteenth-century German rabbi Samson Raphael Hirsch observed that "the Torah teaches us justice towards our fellow human beings, justice towards the plants and animals and the earth, justice towards our own body and soul, and justice towards God who created us for love so that we may become a blessing for the world."

SACRED BOOKS Judaism is a text-centered religion, the writings it regards as sacred constituting a vast library of thousands of volumes. Its foundational text is the Hebrew Bible, which is divided into three parts: the Torah, forming the five books of Moses (also called the Pentateuch); the Prophets (Nevi'im); and the Writings (Ketuvim or Hagiographa). Jewish tradition holds the Torah to be the direct, unmediated Word of God, whereas in the Prophets men said to be divinely inspired speak in their own voices, while the Writings are considered to be formulations in the words of men guided by the Holy Spirit.

Alongside the Torah and the other books of the Bible there developed an elaborate commentary explicating their teachings. This commentary was initially not written, but since it was regarded as divinely inspired, it was called the Oral Torah. Over the centuries the Oral Torah expanded to such a degree that it could no longer be contained by sheer memory. Hence, around the end of the second and the beginning of the third century C.E., Rabbi Judah the Prince (that is, the head of the supreme rabbinical council) compiled a comprehensive digest of the Oral Torah. This work, known as the Mishnah, assumed a canonical status. Written in Hebrew, the Mishnah is a multivolume work covering such subjects as the laws governing agriculture, Temple service, festivals and fast days, marriage and divorce, business transactions, ritual purity and purification, adjudication of torts, and general issues of jurisprudence. The Mishnah does not confine itself to Halakhic, or legal, matters. Under the rubric of Aggadah (narration), it contains reflections on Jewish history, ethics, etiquette, philosophy, folklore, medicine, astronomy, and piety. Typical of rabbinical discourse, the Aggadah and Halakhah are interwoven in the text of the Mishnah, complementing and amplifying each other.

Post-Mishnaic teachers and scholars in the Land of Israel and in Babylonia wrote running commentaries on the Mishnah. These commentaries, together with those on other, smaller works, were collected in two massive collections, one known as the Palestinian, or Jerusalem, Talmud and the other as the Babylonian Talmud. (Another term for the Talmud is Gemara, from an Aramaic word for "teaching.") These were completed around 400 and 500 C.E., respectively. The two Talmuds were written in Aramaic, a language related to Hebrew. Similar to the Mishnah, the Talmuds contain Aggadah and Halakhah woven into a single skein. In the centuries that followed numerous commentaries were written on the Talmuds, particularly on the Babylonian, which became the preeminent text of Jewish sacred learning. In the age of printing the Talmuds were published with the principal commentaries on them adorning the margins of each page.

From time to time collections of scriptural commentaries, originally in the form of sermons or lectures at rabbinical academies from the period of the Mishnah and Talmud, were made. They appear under the general name Midrash (inquiry, or investigation). The collections are classified as Halakhic and Aggadic Midrashhim. The Halakhic Midrashim focus on explicating the laws of the Pentateuch, whereas the Aggadic Midrashim have a much larger range, employing the Bible to explore extralegal issues of religious and ethical meaning. The most widely studied Aggadic Midrashim are the *Midrash Rabbah* ("The Great Midrash"), compiled in the tenth century by Rabbi David ben Aaron of Yemen, and the Midrash of Rabbi Tanhuma in the fourth century. Aggadic Midrashim were written until the thirteenth century, when they yielded to two new genres of sacred writings, philosophy and mysticism (Kabbalah).

The most widely studied Jewish philosophical work is *The Guide of the Perplexed*, written by Maimonides at the end of the twelfth century, and the seminal work of the Kabbalah is the *Zohar* ("Book of Splendor"), from the late thirteenth century. Written in form of a mystical Midrash, the *Zohar* purports to present the revelations of the mysteries of the upper worlds granted to the second-century sage Rabbi Simeon ben Yohai and his circle. It is a work of unbridled imagination and symbolism that exercised a profound impact on the spiritual landscape of Judaism. The *Zohar*'s far-reaching influence was registered in prayers and in such popular movements as Hasidism (the pious ones), which arose in eighteenth-century Poland and which produced hundreds of mystical teachings and tales, all of which are considered to illuminate divine truths and hence are regarded as sacred.

SACRED SYMBOLS Judaism has a culture rich in religious symbols, objects, and rituals that represent abstract concepts, particularly of God and his teachings and of his providential presence in Israel's history. Thus, God commanded Moses to instruct the Israelites to wear fringes, or tassels, on the corners of their garments as a reminder "to observe all My commandments and to be holy to your God" (Num. 15:38–40). On the basis of this commandment there arose the practice of wearing a shawl (tallith) with tassels (zizith). This is either a *tallith katan*, a small four-cornered shawl generally worn under garments, or a larger tallith worn over clothes during prayer.

As a reminder of their deliverance from Egyptian bondage, the Israelites were commanded to place a sign upon their heads and a symbol on their foreheads (Exod. 13:9, 16). Jewish tradition interpreted this commandment as an injunction to wear tefillin, or phylacteries, small leather boxes fastened to the forehead and the upper left arm by straps; each cube-shaped box contains the Scriptural passages in which the commandment appears (Exod. 13:1–10; Exod. 13:11–16; Deut. 6:4–7; Deut. 11:12–21). The tefillin are worn during the morning service except on the Sabbath and on holidays, which are themselves symbols of God's presence.

The Bible also enjoins Jews to fix a mezuzah to the doorposts of their dwellings (Deut. 6:9; 11:20). The mezuzah, from the Hebrew word for "doorpost," consists of a small scroll of parchment, usually placed in a case or box and often ornately decorated, on which are inscribed two biblical passages (Deut. 6:4–9; 11:13–21). The first includes the commandments to love God, study the Torah, read the Shema prayer (attesting to the unity of God), wear the tefillin, and affix the mezuzah. The second passage associates good fortune and well-being with the observance of God's commandments.

The preeminent symbol of Judaism is Brit Milah, the covenant of circumcision performed on a male child when he is eight days old or on an adult male convert as a sign of his acceptance of the covenant. The removal of the foreskin is a "sign in the flesh" of the covenant

God made with Abraham and his descendants (Gen. 17:9–13).

The *kippah*, known in Yiddish as the yarmulke, is the name of the skullcap, which may be any head covering, worn by males in prayer and by Orthodox Jews throughout the day. Covering the head is regarded as a sign of awe before the divine presence, especially during prayer and while studying sacred texts. The *kippah* was apparently introduced by the Talmudic rabbis, for there is no commandment in the Bible giving this instruction.

The menorah, a seven-branched candelabrum, is the most enduring symbol of Judaism. First constructed by Moses at God's instruction (Exod. 25:31–38), it was placed in the portable sanctuary carried by the Israelites in the wilderness and then in the Temple of Jerusalem. When the Second Temple was destroyed, the menorah became the emblem of Jewish survival and continuity. In modern times the six-pointed Star of David was adopted as a symbol of Jewish identity, although it has no religious content or scriptural basis.

EARLY AND MODERN LEADERS Abraham was the founding patriarch of the Jewish people and the paradigm of the moral and spiritual virtues—humility, magnanimity, and steadfast faith in God—incumbent upon Jews to attain. He was born into a heathen family in Mesopotamia in the eighteenth century B.C.E., and his path from idolatry to an affirmation of the one God is related in Genesis (11:27–25:18). The Bible does not tell why he was singled out by God, who promised to make of him a great nation, with abundant blessings, numerous offspring, and a land of its own. Abraham's selection is presented as an act of pure grace. The covenant God established with Abraham was symbolized by the rite of circumcision, which is reenacted by the circumcision of all Jewish male children. But Abraham was not only the father of his physical descendants; he is also the spiritual father of all who convert to Judaism. The prototypical Jew, Abraham is emblematic of a faith that resists all temptation, as when, to test his trust in God, he was commanded to sacrifice his son Isaac.

The leadership of the Israelite nation passed to Abraham's son Isaac and then to his grandson Jacob, the progenitor of the 12 tribes of Israel. (Jacob was renamed Israel by an angel with whom he wrestled [Gen. 32:25–33].) Jacob's favorite son, Joseph, persecuted by his envious brothers, found his way to Egypt, first as a slave to a high-ranking official and eventually as vice-regent of the country. When Joseph encountered his brothers,

he urged them to bring Jacob and their families to Egypt to avoid the famine blighting the Land of Israel. After Joseph's death the Children of Israel were enslaved by the Egyptians.

Among the Hebrew slaves was the child Moses. He was raised by the pharaoh's daughter, who found him as an infant among the reeds of the Nile, where his mother had hid him from the Egyptian soldiers ordered to kill every Israelite male infant. Brought up as an Egyptian prince, Moses nonetheless commiserated with his people. On one occasion, when he witnessed an Egyptian taskmaster about to kill a Hebrew slave, Moses intervened and slew the Egyptian. Obliged to flee, he found refuge in the desert. God appeared to Moses in a burning bush and ordered him to return to the pharaoh to demand that the Children of Israel be set free. After God had unleashed 10 plagues upon the Egyptians, the pharaoh freed the Children of Israel under Moses' leadership. As they were crossing the desert, however, the pharaoh had second thoughts, and he sent an army to recapture them. At the Red Sea, whose waters had miraculously parted to allow the Israelites to cross, the pursuing army drowned as the waters closed over them. When the Israelites arrived at Mount Sinai, God gave them the Ten Commandments. Moses then ascended the mountain, where he stayed for 40 days and received further laws and instructions, called the Torah. For 40 years he led the people through the wilderness, until they came to the Promised Land. Before being able to enter the land with his people, Moses died at the age of 120.

The successor of Moses was Joshua (twelfth century B.C.E.), leader of the Israelite tribes in their conquest of the Promised Land. As depicted in the Bible, he was a composite of a prophet, judge, and military leader. Upon Joshua's death the people were ruled by judges. Except for Deborah, they were not judges in the technical sense but rather inspired leaders who, guided by the spirit of God, arose on the occasion of a crisis. As temporary leaders, they generally had limited influence, and thus the period was one of political and social instability.

Samuel (eleventh century B.C.E.) was the last of the judges and a prophet who led Israel during a transitional period. In the face of a growing threat from the neighboring Philistines, conflict among the tribes of Israel, and the weak and corrupt leadership of the judges, the people called upon Samuel to anoint a king over them. In accordance with God's will, Samuel anointed Saul, but only after warning the people of the disadvantages of a monarchy. Indeed, Samuel was profoundly disappointed with the king, and he secretly appointed David to replace Saul. Jewish tradition judges Samuel to be of equal importance with Moses.

Saul (c.1029–1005 B.C.E.) was a successful military leader, but his differences with Samuel and his melancholic disposition led to fits of depression, which were eased by music. A young harpist named David was often summoned to play for him. David's increasing popularity, culminating in his slaying of the Philistine giant Goliath, along with his marriage to Saul's daughter Michal and his friendship with Saul's son Jonathan, served only to deepen the king's jealousy. His suspicion that David was bent on wresting the throne from him drove Saul mad with rage, and he tried to kill David, forcing him to flee. Saul met an inglorious end when a force of Philistines defeated the armies of Israel and the wounded Saul took his own life. The victorious Philistines displayed his decapitated body on the wall of the Israelite city of Beth-Shan.

David was anointed king and reigned from c.1010 to 970 B.C.E. He led the remaining troops of Israel to swift victories over the Philistines and other enemies. He then captured Jerusalem, declared it the capital of his kingdom, and had the Ark of the Covenant, containing the tablets of laws given by God to Moses, taken there. His plan to build a Temple was thwarted by the prophet Nathan, who claimed that God found David, a man of war, unsuitable for the sacred project. A warrior and statesman, David united the tribes of Israel and greatly expanded the borders of the kingdom. Although his reign was not free of intrigue and ill fortune, Jewish tradition regarded him as the ideal ruler. Indeed, it was held that the redeemer of Israel, the Messiah, would be a scion of the House of David (Isa. 9:5–6; 11:10).

It was given to David's son Solomon to build the Temple in Jerusalem. His 40-year reign was marked by peace, prosperity, and amiable ties with the surrounding countries. But Solomon taxed the people heavily to finance the construction of the Temple and an opulent palace and to strengthen his army. His many political marriages with foreign wives were also suspect in the eyes of the people. The festering resentment surfaced after his death and led to the division of the kingdom.

Upon the death of Solomon in 928 B.C.E., the 10 northern tribes of Israel seceded to establish the Kingdom of Israel. Solomon's son Rehoboam thus ruled over the southern Kingdom of Judah, which included only the tribes Judah and Benjamin and which was greatly diminished in territory. For the next 350 years the Kingdom of Israel was constantly beset by internal instability and external enemies. Although at times the rulers of the northern kingdom proved their mettle in battle, they failed to provide effective moral and religious leadership, and pagan practices spread. In response prophets arose in judgment of Israel's sins. In the ninth century the prophet Elijah inveighed against the idolatrous practices and decadent lives of the privileged classes. (Elijah was said not to have died but to have been taken to heaven in a chariot of fire, and later Jewish legend claimed that he would return to earth as the herald of the Messiah.)

In the eighth century B.C.E. the prophet Amos, who came from the Kingdom of Judah, fulminated against the oppression of the poor and disinherited members of society. Because of divine election, Amos taught, the Children of Israel, in both the north and the south, had a responsibility to pursue social justice. In contrast to Amos, who stressed justice, the contemporary prophet Hosea spoke of loving kindness. God loved his people, but they did not requite his love and "whored" with Baal, the pagan god of the Phoenicians. In a dream God commanded Hosea to marry a harlot to symbolize Israel's immoral behavior, while at the same time highlighting God's forgiveness and abiding love. The Kingdom of Israel came to an end in 722 when it was conquered by the Assyrians, who exiled the inhabitants. These 10 tribes of Israel were henceforth "lost" from history.

The kings of the Kingdom of Judah proved to be more resolute in fending off pagan influences, and they sought to strengthen knowledge of the Torah and its observance. Nonetheless, they were also subject to the wrath of the prophets. Active during the reign of four kings of Judah, the prophet Isaiah (eighth century B.C.E.) castigated the monarchs for forging alliances with foreign powers, arguing that the Jews should place their trust in God alone. Isaiah lent support to King Hezekiah (727–698), who instituted comprehensive religious reforms by uprooting all traces of pagan worship. The prophet Jeremiah (seventh–sixth centuries) denounced what he regarded as the rampant hypocrisy and conceit of the leadership of Judah. When the Babylonians reached the gates of Jerusalem, Jeremiah claimed that it would be futile to resist, and, accordingly, he urged the king to surrender and thus spare the city and its inhabitants from further suffering. His prophecy of doom earned for him the scorn of the leadership and masses alike. When the city fell in 597, he was not exiled to Babylonia with the rest of the political and spiritual elite. He eventually fled to Egypt, where he was last heard of fulminating against the idolatry of the Jews there.

In 538 B.C.E. the Persian emperor Cyrus, who had conquered Babylonia, allowed the exiled Jews to return to Judea (formerly Judah). At first only small groups were repatriated to their ancestral home, by then a province of the Persian Empire. The pace of the return gained momentum when Zerubbabel, a scion of King David, was appointed governor of Judea in about 521. Encouraged by the prophets Haggai and Zechariah, the governor led 44,000 exiles back to Judea. With the support of the prophets, Zerubbabel was able to overcome many political and economic obstacles, as well as the public's apathy toward the rebuilding of the Temple that had been destroyed by the Babylonians. The Temple, henceforth known as the Second Temple, was re-dedicated in 516. Under the leadership of the priest Ezra, another group of exiles returned to Judea in 458. Ezra was soon joined by Nehemiah, whom the Persians appointed governor, and the two worked together to rebuild Jerusalem and to reorganize and reform Jewish communal life. They pledged the people to renew the covenant and to rid themselves of foreign and pagan influences.

For the next 300 years Judea was a vassal state ruled by a Jewish governor appointed by the Persian overlords and a religious leader in the person of a high priest. In the last third of the fourth century B.C.E., Judea fell under the power of the Hellenistic world. The Greeks concentrated temporal as well as religious power in the hands of the high priest. To ensure their control, the Greeks also established colonies throughout the land, and their culture gradually penetrated the upper classes of the Jewish population. Hellenization intensified when Antiochus IV Epiphanes (175–164), the Seleucid ruler of Syria, laid claim to Judea and appointed Jason, a Hellenized Jew, to the office of high priest. Jason transformed Jerusalem into a Greek polis (city-state) named Antiochia, in honor of the Seleucid king, and had a sports arena built to replace the Temple as the focus of the city's social and cultural life. Dissatisfied with Jason, Antiochus replaced him with Menelaus, another Hellenized Jew, with whose conniving he plundered the Temple's treasures. In the wake of a revolt by Jason, Antiochus took further measures to obliterate the Jewish character of Jerusalem. He forbade Jews to practice their religion and forced them to eat foods forbidden by the Torah and to participate in pagan rites. The Temple was desecrated and rendered a site for the worship of Zeus. These harsh actions led to an uprising led by the Hasmoneans, a priestly family headed by Mattathias.

Mattathias and his five sons proved able warriors and leaders. Through guerilla warfare they liberated the countryside from Seleucid control. After Mattathias's death in 167 B.C.E., his son Judah Maccabees assumed leadership of the revolt. A brilliant strategist and tactician, he further routed the Seleucid armies and eventually dislodged them from Jerusalem. In 164 the Temple was ritually purified and rededicated, and to celebrate the event, the festival of Hanukkah was instituted. When Judas Maccabees fell in battle in 160, his brothers Jonathan and Simeon resumed guerilla warfare against the Seleucids. Through diplomatic and military efforts they prevailed and gained de facto independence of Judea. In 140 Simeon convened an assembly of priests and learned men who confirmed him, and his sons after him, as the high priest and commander in chief of the Jewish nation.

The Hasmonean Kingdom of Judea lasted for 80 years. During this period the territory was expanded to include virtually all of the Land of Israel. For the most part the Hasmoneans aligned themselves with the Pharisees, who regarded themselves as disciples of Ezra and Nehemiah and who sought to develop Judaism as a dynamic, evolving religion based on both the Written and the Oral Torah. The Hasmoneans also recognized the Sanhedrin as the supreme judicial institution of the Pharisees. For more than five centuries this body, composed of the 71 leading rabbis of the generation, and its president served as the central religious, and at times even temporal, authority of the Jewish people. The leadership of the Pharisees was solidified under the rule (76–67 B.C.E.) of Queen Salome Alexandra, the widow of King Alexander Yanai (103–76), whose father, Aristobulus I, had assumed the title of king (104–103).

Upon Queen Alexandra's death her sons waged a struggle for the throne and the high priesthood, and the resulting civil war rendered Judea vulnerable to invasion. In 63 B.C.E. Roman armies conquered the country, bringing an end to the independence of Judea. The Jewish state once again became a province of an empire. In 37 the Romans appointed Herod, an official in the Hasmonean administration and a descendent of converts to Judaism, king of Judea. With the help of a Roman army, he defeated Antigonus, a grandson of Alexandra who had led a successful revolt against the Romans and reclaimed the Hasmonean throne. Herod loyally served his Roman overlords, ruthlessly suppressing all opposition and reducing the power of the high priests and the Sanhedrin. On the other hand, he allowed the Pharisees to continue to teach and interpret the Torah. Ruling during a period of prosperity, Herod pursued a construction program that included renovation of the Temple. Further, he did not hesitate to intercede with Roman authorities on behalf of Jewish communities throughout the empire.

Herod's kingdom did not endure beyond his death in 4 B.C.E. With the consent of the emperor, he had divided his realm among his three sons, which proved ungainly and ineffective and which led to unrest. Once again the emperor reorganized Judea as a Roman province governed by a non-Jewish administrator. Although the Sanhedrin was allowed to reassemble as the supreme religious and judicial body of the Jews, heavy taxes and the presence of Roman troops in Jerusalem continued to cause discontent. The appointment of Pontius Pilate as governor in 26 C.E. ushered in a particularly oppressive regime. The land was rife with revolutionary and messianic ferment, although with the accession of Emperor Claudius in 41, the situation seemed to ease. The emperor appointed Herod's grandson, Agrippa I, as king, and he proved to be a shrewd political leader and a Jewish patriot. With his death in 44, however, the Roman authorities reimposed direct rule. Once again Judea was in the grips of discontent and messianic agitation, and groups of freedom fighters surfaced. The mounting resistance to Roman rule led to a revolt in 66, which was not put down until four years later when Titus led an army to conquer Jerusalem and destroy the Temple. With the fall of the desert fortress of Masada in 73, Jewish hopes for the restoration of political sovereignty were crushed.

There was a growing realization that an alternative to political and military leadership had to be found. This was offered by Rabbi Johanan ben Zakkai, a leader of the Pharisees during the first century. He had slipped out of Jerusalem during the city's siege and reconstituted the Sanhedrin in the coastal town of Jabneh, already a center of learning. Through his inspiration the Sanhedrin took measures to strengthen Judaism in the wake of the destruction of the Temple. When asked by one of his disciples how the Jews were to atone for their sins now that the Temple was destroyed and expiatory animal sacrifices were no longer possible, Johanan replied

by citing the prophet Hosea: "Do not fear, we now have charity as a substitute" (6:6). Johanan was joined by many of the leading sages of the time, and together they laid the ground for Judaism to continue as a faith independent of the Temple. Without relinquishing hope for the restoration of the Temple, they implicitly established a new scale of values, at whose pinnacle was the study of the Torah. At Jabneh the Jews truly became a People of the Book.

Upon Johanan's death in c. 80, Rabbi Simeon ben Gamaliel II was appointed president of the Sanhedrin, and he continued the work of reorganizing the national and religious life of the Jewish people. Gamaliel frequently traveled to Rome, where he was greeted as the head of the Jewish nation, and he negotiated with Roman authorities with determination and skill. Under him the community of sages gathered at Jabneh established guidelines for Judaism as a religious faith and practice. Toward this end they elaborated a body of theological, legal, ritual, and ethical teachings that Gamaliel's grandson, Judah ha-Nasi (c. 138–c. 217) brought together in the Mishnah.

Despite the efforts of the Sanhendrin to channel Jewish loyalties into a life of prayer and study, national feelings continued to erupt in revolts against Roman rule, both in the Diaspora and in the Land of Israel. In the early second century Jewish revolts broke out in Mesopotamia, Egypt, Cyprus, and the Land of Israel. When the emperor Hadrian disclosed plans to establish a Roman colony on the ruins of Jerusalem—to be called Aelia Capitolina in honor of himself, Aelius Hadrianus, and the god Jupiter Capitolinus—he provoked a war. Led by Simeon Bar Kokhba, the well-planned revolt, which broke out in 132, took the Romans by surprise. The Jewish rebels first liberated Jerusalem and then seized control of Judea and large parts of Galilee. Enthralled by Bar Kokhba's spectacular victories, many Jews, including Rabbi Akiva, widely regarded as the preeminent scholar of his generation, hailed him as the Messiah, and he was named the *nasi* (prince or president) of Judea. After three years, however, the revolt was suppressed, leaving 600,000 Jews dead in battle or from hunger and disease. Tens of thousands of others were sold into slavery, and many more, including scholars, fled the country. Judea was now empty of Jews.

The Sanhedrin was relocated to a small town in Galilee and through resolute leadership extended its authority throughout the Diaspora, where the majority of the Jews now lived. It retained the sole right to ordain rabbis, and emissaries were periodically dispatched to regulate the religious observances of the scattered communities and to collect a voluntary tax for the support of the Sanhedrin and its president. The Roman administration allowed the Sanhedrin to function as part of an implicit agreement that it act to restrain Jewish militants and national sentiments. During this period the Sanhedrin became not only a judicial but also a deliberative and legislative body, and its president, referred to by the Romans as the patriarch, served in effect as the chief executive of the Jewish people. In 420, however, the Romans withdrew their recognition of the patriarch and dissolved the Sanhedrin.

Alternative leadership was provided by the exilarch (in Aramaic, Resh Galuta, or "leader of the Exile") of the Jewish community of Babylonia, which in Jewish nomenclature corresponded to the Persian Empire. Since the days of the First Temple, the Babylonian Diaspora had grown in strength, and it emerged as a dynamic center of Jewish spiritual life and learning. Allowed to develop autonomous institutions, the community was headed by the exilarch, a hereditary office reserved for descendants of King David, who represented the community before the non-Jewish rulers of Babylonia. For 12 centuries after the abolition of the Sanhedrin and the office of the patriarch, the exilarch headed not only the Jewish community of Babylonia but also most other communities of the Diaspora. The exilarch was responsible for collecting taxes from the Jewish community, and he had the authority to impose fines and even to imprison delinquents. His office was strengthened by his administrative and financial control of the great rabbinical academies that had evolved in Babylonia. The spiritual significance of this relationship was underscored by the academies' practice of naming as the heir to the office the member of the deceased exilarch's family deemed the most erudite in the Torah. Under the tutelage of the exilarch, the academies of Babylonia produced the commentary on the Mishnah known as the Babylonian Talmud. By virtue of the esteem accorded this elaboration of Jewish law, it eclipsed the Talmud produced by the academies in Palestine and served to set the contours of Jewish religious life.

The academies of Babylonia drew students and scholars from throughout the Jewish world. The heads of the academies, known as *geonim* (singular, *gaon;* "pride" or "excellency"), thus exercised influence far beyond Babylonia, and they were a major factor in maintaining Jewish unity. From Egypt, North Africa, and Christian and Muslim Spain, questions on all aspects of Judaism were sent to the *geonim.* From the end of the sixth to the middle of the eleventh century, the *geonim* were considered the intellectual leaders of the Diaspora, and their decisions were regarded as binding by most Jewish communities.

The decline in the influence of the Babylonian academies and the *geonim* was to a great measure caused by their success. Through their power the Babylonian Talmud became the bedrock of Judaism, and eventually new centers of learning, along with great rabbinical scholars, emerged throughout the Diaspora. As a result, the dependence on the Babylonia academies and the *geonim* declined. Political divisions within Islam, which since the seventh century had come to reign over most of the lands of the Diaspora, were also a factor. The caliphs of Spain, for instance, did not appreciate the relationship of their Jews to Babylonia, which was governed by a rival caliph. Moreover, under the caliph of Baghdad, Babylonia entered a period of economic stagnation and impoverishment, which naturally affected the Jewish community and its ability to support the rabbinical academies. By the eleventh century the last of the great academies of Babylonia had closed, and the office of the exilarch, long diminished in stature, came to an end in the fifteenth century.

Centralized Jewish leadership thus also came to an end. The various Jewish communities established their own institutions to govern themselves and to represent their interests in non-Jewish societies. Fragmentation of the Jewish people was prevented by the firm foundation that rabbinical Judaism, as amplified especially by the Babylonian Talmud, had throughout the Diaspora. Despite the loss of a central religious and political authority, a worldwide network of correspondence among rabbis and the circulation of their writings served to reinforce the spiritual unity of the Jewish people.

MAJOR THEOLOGIANS AND AUTHORS Virtually all of the foundational texts of Judaism, starting with the Hebrew Bible, are of collective authorship. According to Jewish tradition, the first five books of the Bible, known as the Torah, are the Word of God as recorded by Moses. (The exception is the last section, describing his death and burial.) Tradition holds that the other two sections, the Prophets and Writings, were inspired by God, although not directly written by him. Modern critical scholarship, however, regards the Torah as the composite work of several human authors writing in different periods. Similarly, scholarly opinion judges the other books of the Bible to be the work of editors and not necessarily of the authors to whom individual books are ascribed within the texts.

Whether one follows the traditional view or that of modern scholars, the Bible is clearly a chorus of many different theological voices. Moreover, not all voices were included in the text as it was finally canonized. Some of these works have been preserved, although not always in the original Hebrew, in what is called the Apocrypha and Pseudepigrapha. This literature, which also embraces works written by Jewish authors in Aramaic and Greek, was sanctified in the canons of various Christian churches, often in translation in the sacred language of these churches—for example, Ethiopian, Armenian, Syriac, and Old Slavonic. Indeed, it is only by virtue of the sanctity these books have for Christianity that the voices have been remembered. This body of extracanonical Jewish writings was augmented in 1947 when the manuscripts now known as the Dead Sea Scrolls were discovered in caves near the Judean desert.

The voices that came to be a part of the Jewish Scriptures were ultimately determined by the Pharisees, who considered themselves disciples of the scholar and prophet Ezra and who emerged during the time of the Hasmoneans. During this period the dominant voice of the Pharisees was Hillel, known as Hillel the Elder (c. 70 B.C.E.–c. 10 C.E.). Born and educated in Babylonia, he developed interpretative principles that encouraged a flexible reading of the Torah. Above all, Hillel taught the virtue of Torah study, to be pursued for its own sake and without ulterior motives. He believed that learning, and learning alone, could refine a person's character and religious personality and endow him with the fear of God. It is told that Hillel was once approached by a would-be convert who asked to be taught the whole Torah while Hillel stood on one foot. He replied, "What is hateful to you, do not do unto your fellow human being; this is the whole Torah, all the rest is commentary. Now go and learn!" This, the "golden rule," Hillel suggested, is not only the best introduction to Judaism but also its sum total. Thus, Hillel played a decisive role in the history of Judaism. His hermeneutical rules expanded and revolutionized the Jewish tradition, while his stress on the primacy of ethical conduct and his tolerance and humanity deeply influenced the character and image of Judaism. Hillel was the patron of what has been termed "classical Judaism." To the worship of power and the state, he opposed the ideal

Contemporary Midrash

The affirmation of Judaism as a living faith has led a number of thinkers, particularly in the United States, to place sacred texts once again at the center of Jewish spirituality. Inspired by postmodernism and its critique of the Enlightenment's quest for objective truth, such thinkers as Arthur A. Green (born in 1941), Michael A. Fishbane (born in 1944), and Peter Ochs (born in 1950) have initiated what has become an ever increasing trend of reestablishing Judaism as a community of study in which the foundational texts are continuously reinterpreted without any claim for the absolute validity of a single reading. The study of these texts and their inexhaustible interpretation are said to renew the traditional understanding of Torah study, broadly called Midrash, as the principal medium of Israel's covenantal relation with God and his revealed Word.

of the community of those learned in Torah and of those who love God and their fellow human beings.

Hillel's teachings are woven into the Mishnah, an anthology of Pharisaic interpretations of the Written and Oral Torah that was edited by one of his descendants, Judah ha-Nasi (c. 138–c. 217), head of the Sanhedrin. Noting that over the centuries the Oral Torah had continued to grow exponentially, Judah ha-Nasi deemed it necessary, especially since a majority of Jews by then lived in the Diaspora, to have a written protocol of the most significant teachings. He prevailed upon each of the Pharisees, who bore the honorific title of rabbi (master or teacher of the Torah), to prepare a synopsis of the Oral Torah they taught in the various academies of the Land of Israel. He then edited and collated the material into the compendium titled the Mishnah, a name derived from the Hebrew verb *shanah*, meaning "to repeat," that is, to recapitulate what one has learned. In his work Judah ha-Nasi had been aided by other scholars who preceded him, in particular Rabbi Akiva (c. 50–c. 136).

Judah ha-Nasi intended the Mishnah to serve as a curriculum for the study of Jewish law. He thus did not seek to establish an authoritative text but rather provided variant opinions and rulings on the subjects discussed. The corpus of teachings gathered in the Mishnah did not exhaust the oral traditions of the rabbis, who in the collection are also called *tannaim* (singular, *tanna*; Aramaic for "teacher"), for there were teachings Judah ha-Nasi chose to exclude and others unknown to him. Further, the Oral Torah continued to develop. Later teachings were collected in a variety of anthologies, such as the Tosefta, literally the "addition" to the Mishnah. An important body of rabbinical teachings representing hundreds of different voices, it was apparently edited at the end of the fourth century, perhaps even later.

The crowning achievement of rabbinic Judaism was the two Talmuds. In the Land of Israel and in Babylonia scholars known as *amoraim* (Aramaic for "explainers") organized themselves into academies (yeshivas) to study the Mishnah and other collections of rabbinical teachings. The record of the reflections and debates of the *amoraim* was published as a commentary on the Mishnah in two multivolume works, the Jerusalem and the Babylonian Talmuds. Both encompass the work of many generations of scholars. The Jerusalem Talmud, actually composed in academies in Galilee, was concluded in about 400, and the Babylonian Talmud a century later. Because of the intensification of the anti-Jewish policy of the Roman authorities, which led to the flight of many scholars, the Jerusalem Talmud was hastily compiled. It thus lacks the editorial polish of the Babylonian Talmud, which was prepared under far calmer circumstances.

The *amoraim* also edited collections of the commentaries known as Midrashim. Whereas previous collections had been based on Halakhic (legal) discussions of the rabbis of the Land of Israel, the later Midrashim, edited in the fifth and sixth centuries, largely originated in the homilies of synagogues, which had become the central institution of Jewish religious life. These Midrashim were also devoted to an exegesis of Scripture, often in a sustained line-by-line commentary. There are, for example, such collections for the books of Genesis, Lamentations, Esther, the Song of Songs, and Ruth.

Another seminal work of collective authorship that emerged during this period was the Hebrew prayer book, which with local variations became authoritative for Jews everywhere. Although the Bible gives witness to personal prayers, it is not clear that Temple rituals were accompanied by communal prayers. Sacrificial rites were accompanied by a chorus of psalms chanted by Levites (descendants of Levi, the third son of Jacob, who were by hereditary privilege assigned a special role in the Temple service) but without the participation of the congregation. There is evidence, however, that in the Second Temple a form of communal prayer had begun to take shape. But it was only after the destruction of the Temple and the end of its rites that the rabbis at Jabneh began to standardize Jewish liturgical practice. Alongside the obligatory prayers instituted by the rabbis, there also developed the tradition of composing *piyyutim* (liturgical poems), many of which were incorporated into the prayer book.

Other than certain books of the Bible, the first work by a Jewish author to appear under the name of an individual was that of the philosopher Philo (c. 20 B.C.E.–50 C.E.), who lived in Alexandria. Writing in Greek, he composed an exegesis of the Bible in which many passages were interpreted as allegorical elucidations of metaphysical truths. His concept that God created the world through Logos had a profound impact on the Christian dogma that identified Jesus with the Logos. The Christian church therefore preserved many of Philo's writings, which, other than a few brief passages cited in the Talmud, were forgotten by his fellow Jews after his death.

Sustained Jewish interest in philosophy was to be manifest only under the impact of Islamic thought, which was nurtured by Greek philosophy, and by and large Jewish philosophy was philosophy of religion. Writing for the most part in Arabic, Jewish philosophers used the philosopher's tools to address religious or theological questions. It is significant that medieval Jewish philosophy was inaugurated by a *gaon* (head) of one the leading rabbinical academies in Babylonia, the Egyptian-born Saadiah Gaon (882–942). His *Book of Beliefs and Opinions*, written in Arabic and later translated into Hebrew, presented a rational analysis and proof of the basic theological concepts of Judaism.

Among the most important Jewish philosophers was Solomon ibn Gabriol (c. 1026–50), of Muslim Spain, who wrote a Neoplatonic defense of the biblical concept of creation that, translated from the Arabic into Latin as *Fons vitae* ("Fountain of Life"), deeply influenced Christian theology. Drawing on Islamic mysticism, Neoplatonic philosophy, and perhaps even esoteric Christian literature, Bahya ibn Pakuda (second half of the eleventh century), who also lived in Spain, wrote on ethical and spiritual life in *Duties of the Heart*, which first appeared in 1080 in Arabic. Through translations into Hebrew, the first of which had already appeared in the late twelfth century, and other languages, this guide is still widely studied within the Jewish community.

One of the most popular Jewish philosophical works of the Middle Ages was written by the poet Judah Halevi of Toledo (c. 1075–1141). Known for his Hebrew poems, some 800 of which are extant, Halevi was the author of the treatise *The Book of the Kuzars.* Written in Arabic in the form of a dialogue between a Jewish scholar and the king of the Khazars, who was subsequently to convert to Judaism, Halevi's book explores the conflict between philosophy and revealed faith. Exposing what he believes to be the limitations of Aristotelan philosophy, he argues that only religious faith that affirms God's transcendence and the gift of revelation, namely, the Torah and its commandments, can bring a person close to God. Another prominent Spanish philosopher writing in Arabic was Abraham ibn Daud (c. 1110–c. 1180). In *The Exalted Faith* Ibn Daud systematically sought to harmonize the principles of Judaism with Aristotelian rationalist philosophy.

The Jewish philosophical tradition in Spain had its most esteemed expression in the work of Rabbi Moseh ben Maimon, known as Maimonides (1135–1204). Writing like most of his colleagues in Arabic, he addressed *The Guide of the Perplexed* to those who had difficulty reconciling Greek philosophy, particularly Aristotelianism, with biblical faith. Like Philo, Maimonides read the Bible as allegorical expositions of philosophical truths and thus demonstrated that the conflict between faith and reason is but apparent. Accordingly, the authentically wise person realizes that intellectual and religious perfection, the latter to be achieved through the observance of God's laws, are identical. Maimonides also wrote, in Hebrew, a comprehensive codification of Jewish law called the *Mishnah Torah.*

All subsequent medieval Jewish philosophy may be viewed as either affirmative or dissenting footnotes to Maimonides. The Italian Jewish philosopher Hillel ben Samuel (c. 1220–c. 1295) devoted a Hebrew work to defending Maimonides' doctrine of the soul—survival of physical death as pure intellect—arguing that he did not mean to deny individual immortality. The Catalonian Jewish philosopher Isaac Albalag (thirteenth century), while seeming to affirm the survival of the individual soul after death, in fact subtlety rejected the notion,

suggesting that reason allows a person to speak only of the eternity of the universe.

The philosopher and rabbinical scholar Hasdai Crescas (1340–1410) refuted the Aristotelian premises of Maimonides. Indeed, he opposed all attempts to identify the principles of Judaism with those of Greek philosophy. For him man is a spiritual being, and hence his soul departs the body after death and survives. In contrast to Maimonides and followers of Aristotle, Crescas taught that love and rational knowledge are the highest good and, as such, that it is the love between man and God that determines the immortality of the soul. Joseph Albo (c. 1380–1445), who was regarded as the last of the great Jewish philosophers of the Middle Ages, was at home in the Latin Scholasticism of Christianity as well as in Islamic philosophy. This Spanish philosopher sought to forge a synthesis of Maimonides and Crescas. With regard to the question of the immortality of the soul, to which a large portion of his *Book of Principles,* written in Hebrew, was devoted, he endorsed Crescas's view that the soul is spiritual and not intellectual in nature but that it is, nonetheless, capable of attaining rational knowledge.

Although the Italian Renaissance witnessed a rebirth of Jewish philosophy, such writers as Judah Abrabanel (better known as Leone Ebreo; c. 1460–c. 154) and Joseph Delmedigo (1591–1655) essentially confined themselves to expositions of the teachings of their medieval predecessors. The Dutch philosopher Baruch Spinoza (1632–77), however, marked the end of the Jewish tradition in medieval philosophy. Gaining his initial instruction from the works of such philosophers as Maimonides and Crescas, Spinoza developed a philosophical system that abandoned all attempts to reconcile faith and reason, revelation and philosophy. He regarded faith in revelation or in a divine source of knowledge, held to be superior to or at least compatible with reason, as undermining the integrity of philosophy as a self-sufficient rational discourse. Spinoza thus boldly challenged the overarching concern of medieval philosophy, Jewish, Christian, and Islamic alike. His radical, implicitly secular views led to his excommunication from the Jewish community, whereupon he took the name Benedictus, the Latin equivalent of his Hebrew name.

Philosophy was not the only expression of medieval Jewish thought. Jews also developed a robust mystical tradition that gave birth to a rich and varied literature. Most of this literature is characterized by collective authorship or is pseudepigraphic—that is, ascribed to ancient or mythical authors. The first written evidence of Jewish mysticism was a collection of some 20 brief treatises originating from the Talmudic period (third century C.E.) and collectively known as Hekhalot ("Supernal Palaces") and Merkavah ("Divine Chariot") literature. The writings record a journey through the celestial palaces to the vision of God's chariot, or throne. In the second half of the twelfth century there emerged groups of scholars in the Germanic lands, known in Hebrew as Ashkenaz, who developed an acute mystical consciousness. Writing under the trauma of the massacres of Jews during the Crusades, they reflected on the mystery of the inner life of God as a key to understanding what seemed to be his ambiguous relationship to history and Jewish fate. Most of the literature produced by this mystical school, known as Hasidei Ashkenaz (pious men of Ashkenaz), was either anonymous or pseudepigraphic. In addition to speculative theosophical literature, these scholars produced ethical tracts that sought to inculcate a severe pietistic discipline touching virtually every aspect of life.

In neighboring France and Spain the seeds of a parallel school of Jewish mysticism, known as Kabbalah, were sown. Abraham ben David of Posquieres (c. 1125–98), in Provence, one of the most renowned rabbinical scholars of his age, was a fierce critic of Maimonides' attempt to reduce the Talmud to a code of law and to render Judaism a species of rational philosophy. Although a prolific writer, he limited his mystical teachings to oral instructions to his sons. They became the literary guides of the emerging Kabbalah movement, which purported to be based on an ancient tradition of esoteric readings of the Torah's deepest meanings.

These teachings were elaborated by Rabbi Moses ben Nahman (known as Nahmanides or the Ramban; 1194–1270) of Gerona. Deeply impressed by French rabbinical scholarship, he worked to raise the prestige and significance of Talmud study in Spain. He, too, objected to Maimonides' attempt to render philosophy the touchstone of religious truth. In his voluminous writings, some 50 of which are preserved, Nahmanides wove, particularly in his commentary on the Torah, his teachings in encoded form. Kabbalists of the late thirteenth and early fourteenth centuries devoted considerable effort to decode Nahmanides' teachings. As elaborated by his and Abraham ben David's disciples, Kabbalah spread throughout the Jewish world.

The various mystical impulses of Kabbalah culminated in the appearance in the late thirteenth century of the Zohar ("Book of Splendor"), which became its main text. The principal author of this multivolume pseudepigraphic work was identified by twentieth-century scholars as Moses de Lion (c. 1240–1305) of Castile. Written as a commentary on the Torah, the Zohar is presented as the esoteric Oral Torah taught by Rabbi Simeon ben Yohai, a tanna (teacher) of the fourth generation and one of the most prominent disciples of Rabbi Akiva and the teacher of Judah ha-Nasi, the editor of the Mishnah. Written in a symbolically rich Aramaic, the Zohar inspired numerous works that sought to develop further insights into the hidden layers of the Torah's meaning as the ground of the ultimate and most intimate knowledge of God.

The expulsion of the Jews from Spain and Portugal at the end of the fifteenth century engendered a profound sense of crisis and messianic longing. This was expressed through the speculations spawned by new schools of Kabbalah established in Greece, Italy, Turkey, and the Land of Israel. Presented as commentaries on the Zohar, these writings had the questions of evil and redemption as their central themes. In the sixteenth century the small town of Safed in Galilee became the center of this new, indeed revolutionary, trend in Kabbalah, which gained its fullest expression with Rabbi Isaac Luria (1534–72) and his disciples, especially Rabbi Hayyim Vital (1542–1620). Expounding a messianic theology based on motifs and images from the Zohar, Lurianic Kabbalah taught that the Exile and Israel's tragic history were but symbolic reflections of a higher reality in which part of God suffered exile, trapped in the material realm through a flaw in the process of creation. In fulfilling the precepts of the Torah with the proper mystical intent, the Jewish people redeemed both God and themselves. By virtue of this teaching, Kabbalah was transformed into a messianic myth that allowed the Jews to believe they could actively change the course of their history and at the same time cleanse the world of evil, which was a result of God's exile.

This teaching, especially as amplified through popular writings, captured the imagination of the Jewish people. The heightened hope that redemption was approaching led to the advent of a mystical Messiah in the person of Shabbetai Tzevi (1626–76). Through the writings of his disciples, especially Nathan of Gaza (1644–80), the Jewish world was electrified with excitement. All seemed to collapse, however, when Shabbetai, confronted by Turkish authorities who saw in the messianic movement that galvanized about him a political threat to their rule over the Land of Israel, was given the choice of death or conversion to Islam and chose the latter. Shabbetai's ignominious end left the Jewish people deeply perplexed.

Among the many responses to the energy induced by Lurianic Kabbalah and by Shabbetai Tzevi was a movement of popular mysticism called Hasidism that arose in eastern Europe in the eighteenth century. Founded by Israel ben Eliezer (known as Baal Shem Tov or by the acronym Besht; c. 1700–60), the movement reinterpreted Kabbalistic teachings so that they neutralized the sting of messianic disappointment that lingered after Shabbetai's death. Israel ben Eliezer and his disciples redirected the longing for redemption to the experience of God in the here and now through the everyday acts of prayer, ritual, and good deeds. Rejoicing in the all-pervasive presence of God through song and dance was also deemed to be a valid form of divine service. In addition to writing numerous works on Kabbalah, Hasidic teachers developed a unique genre of mystical parables and stories that were eventually collected in widely circulated collections. Many of these parables and stories are ascribed to Baal Shem Tov, who himself did not write any books. Rabbi Nahman of Bratzlav (1772–1811), his great-grandson, was a particularly gifted storyteller whose mystical tales and subtle theology, rich with psychological insight, continue to exercise a unique fascination on Jews beyond the Hasidic movement.

With the dawn of the modern world, Jewish religious thinkers were faced with the challenge of accommodating not only new conceptions of truth, which questioned divine revelation as a source of knowledge, but also with the task of articulating strategies that would allow Jews to participate in a culture that was essentially secular and universal while they preserved their commitment to Judaism as a distinctive way of life. The first philosopher to acknowledge this task was the German-born Moses Mendelssohn (1729–86). One of the leading proponents of the Enlightenment, he contributed highly acclaimed essays and books on such general subjects as metaphysics, aesthetics, and psychology. Hailed in his day as the German Socrates, he was obliged to explain publicly his abiding devotion to the Torah and its precepts. Many of his contemporaries wondered how he could be a Jew, beholden to biblical revelation, and at the same time a philosopher who acknowledged reason as the sole arbiter of truth. Mendelssohn published a defense of his allegiance to both Juda-

ism and philosophy in the book *Jerusalem* (1783). His answer was that Judaism understands revelation, not as a divine disclosure of propositions, but rather as divine instruction on how to conduct religious life. Intellectually, he held, Jews are totally free to pursue the rule of reason.

But as the social and cultural reality changed for an ever increasing number of Jews, Mendelssohn's reconciliation of traditional Judaism and philosophy no longer proved tenable. By sheer dint of their participation in modern culture, Jews found themselves occupying a new social and political space that led them, in varying degrees, to abandon the duties of traditional Judaism. In response to the new cultural reality, scholars and religious philosophers in the early nineteenth century, primarily in Germany, sought to develop a theology that would authenticate new conceptions of traditional obligations. Gathering under the banner of what came to be called Reform, or Liberal, Judaism, they wrote learned essays and monographs arguing that the essence of Judaism was to be found in its universal ethical teachings as opposed to time-bound ceremonial laws. Among the leading representatives of this school were Solomon Ludwig Steinheim (1790–1866), Samuel Holdheim (1806–60), and Abraham Geiger (1810–74).

A centrist position between Reform and Orthodoxy—as traditional Judaism has often been called since the early nineteenth century—was forged by Zacharias Frankel (1801–75). His blend of intellectual modernism and modified traditional practice sowed the seeds of what in twentieth-century North America came to be known as Conservative Judaism. Initially affiliated with Conservative Judaism, Mordecai M. Kaplan (1881–1983) developed a religious philosophy he called Reconstructionism. Believing that traditional conceptions of God as a supernatural, personal being were hopelessly out-of-date, he argued that fundamental presuppositions of Jewish religious thought must be revised and purged of anachronistic supernaturalism. Reconstructed as a "naturalistic" faith, Judaism would be more attuned both to the modern world and to the evolving spiritual and cultural aspirations of Jews. Judaism was best understood as a civilization, of which religion was but one, albeit central, component. In this respect Kaplan drew inspiration from Zionism, which in advancing its political program understood Jews as principally a nation and culture, to which a person might be affiliated on purely secular terms.

Traditional Jews did not remain indifferent to these developments. Moses Sofer (1762–1839), a German-born rabbi who was widely recognized as the leading Halakhah authority of his day, viewed all theological and organizational attempts to accommodate the modern world and its secular values as a mortal threat to Judaism. He is said to have coined the slogan "All innovation is forbidden by the Torah," about which Ultra-Orthodox Jews have since organized their uncompromising opposition to any deviation from Jewish tradition. Sofer's younger colleague, Samson Raphael Hirsch (1808–88), also a German-born traditional rabbi, regarded Sofer's principled resistance to all things modern as profoundly mistaken. Preferring to call himself a "Torah-true" rather than an Orthodox rabbi, Hirsch held that traditional Judaism not only could but also should affirm certain aspects of modern enlightened culture. Indeed, Jews should regard themselves as obligated to learn the physical and social sciences, for God is manifest in nature and history. Further, the humanistic ethic of the Enlightenment is compatible with the deepest ethical values of Judaism. In the twentieth century other Orthodox theologians, such as Joseph Dov Soloveitchik (1903–93) and Abraham Joshua Heschel (1907–72), have given their own twists to Hirsch's modern, or Neo-Orthodox, views.

Modern Jewish religious thought has also been characterized by theologies developed outside the denominational framework. Hermann Cohen (1842–1918), who held a chair in philosophy at the University of Marburg in Germany, employed philosophical categories derived from his studies of Immanuel Kant to present Judaism as a "religion of reason." According to his conception, human reason is assigned the "ethical task" of striving to perfect institutions promoting social justice and universal peace. As a religious community, Jews, whose spiritual and moral sensibilities are nurtured by their ancient liturgy and ritual, should exemplify a commitment to this task. He associated devotion to the task with the traditional Jewish concept of imitating God's holiness and serving as his partner in perfecting the work of creation.

For Franz Rosenzweig (1886–1929) the tendency to regard religion as but a handmaiden of ethics eliminated the core experience of divine revelation. Removing revelation as the ground of an existential relationship to God, Rosenzweig protested, amounted to "atheistic theology." He also directed his criticism against Martin Buber (1878–1965), who represented a tendency shared by both Jewish and Protestant thinkers to ascribe the "spirit" animating a community of faith with the national or ethnic "genius" of that community. In time Buber recognized the mistake of this essentially romantic, indeed nationalistic, conception of religion, and he sought in *Ich und Du* (1923; *I and Thou*) and other works to redefine the biblical concept of revelation as a dialogue between a human being and a transcendent, personal God. Rosenzweig also developed a dialogic view of revelation, although his took into account more traditional conceptions of Jewish religious practice. He set forth his views in a monumental volume titled *Der Stern der Erlösung* (1921; *The Star of Redemption*).

The legacy of European Jewish thought has continued to inspire American-born thinkers, including Will Herberg (1902–77), Milton Steinberg (1903–50), Arthur A. Cohen (1928–86), Eugene B. Borowitz (born in 1928), Richard Rubenstein (born in 1924), and David Hartman (born in 1931). Their writings have largely been characterized by interpretative commentaries on the thought of their European predecessors. This dependence may be indicative not only of a pervasive sense of being indebted heirs of their predecessors but also an awesome sense that they are their survivors. The tragic, catastrophic end of European Jewry created, in the words of Cohen, a profound "caesura," or rupture, in Jewish collective and personal existence, engendering a feeling of inconsolable mourning and obligation. In reflecting on the tragedy of the Nazi era and on its theological implications for the "surviving remnant" of Jewry, American Jews have been at their most original and probing. The resulting "theology of the Holocaust" may in many respects be viewed as a theology of survival, seeking to affirm the obligations of the remnant of Jewry to survive somehow as Jews. Auschwitz, in the words of Emil L. Fackenheim (1916–2003), issued "a commandment" to Jews to endure and to ensure the survival of Judaism.

Several Hasidic rabbis developed theological responses to the Holocaust, most significantly Menachem Mendel Schneerson (1902–94), head of the Lubavitcher, or Habad, branch of Hasidism. He viewed the Holocaust as the "birth pangs of the Messiah," the tribulations preceding Redemption, whose imminent advent was indicated by the "miraculous" birth of the State of Israel. The rabbi's messianic enthusiasm was expressed by his dedication to the spiritual "ingathering" of the exiled of Israel, which he pursued by establishing a worldwide program to instill in secularized and assimilated Jews a love of the Torah. Many of Rabbi Schneerson's followers believe that he himself was the longed-for Messiah, who, despite his death, will soon return as the manifest Redeemer of Israel and the world.

The commandment to endure also inspired the slow but impressive reconstruction of European Jewry, which has likewise witnessed the renewal of Jewish religious thought, most notably represented by Emmanuel Lévinas (1906–95) in France and Louis Jacobs (born in 1920) in England. Lévinas, one of the most esteemed philosophers of post-World War II France, represented a continuation of the existentialist thought pioneered by Rosenzweig and Buber. Employing the metaphysical phenomenology he developed as a critique of Edmund Husserl's and Martin Heidegger's concept of "the other," Lévinas sought to illuminate the religious meaning of Judaism. The moral experience of the other, borne by a compelling sense of responsibility toward him, is the only genuine knowledge of a person. Lévinas contrasted the antihumanistic tendency of Western culture—which, he held, masquerades as liberty but which is, in fact, bereft of responsibility for the other—with the biblical concept, especially as elaborated by the rabbis, of "a difficult liberty." (The title of his most important collection of essays on Judaism is *Difficile liberté* [1963; *Difficult Freedom,* 1990].) Paradoxically, the Jew obtains transcendence, and thus liberty, by living under God's law, which requires ethical and social responsibility for the other. Biblical man, Lévinas observed, with an oblique reference to Heidegger, "discovers" his fellow man before "he discovers landscapes." As the custodian of biblical humanism, Lévinas declared, Judaism stands before the contemporary world and defiantly proclaims that liberty entails ethical responsibility and obligation.

ORGANIZATIONAL STRUCTURE Since the abolishing of the Sanhedrin at the beginning of the fifth century C.E. and the decline of the office of the *geonim,* the heads of the Babylonian rabbinical academies, in the eleventh century, Judaism has not had a central religious authority acknowledged by all communities. In response some communities have organized themselves around a regional or countrywide leadership, such as a central rabbinical judicial court or even a chief rabbi. In fifteenth-century Turkey, for instance, the position of *hakham bashi* (chief sage) was established. In the nineteenth century the position was elevated by the Turkish authorities and assigned the function of chief rabbi of the Ottoman Empire.

In 1807 Napoleon Bonaparte convened what he ceremoniously called a Sanhedrin in order to gain rabbinical sanction for the changes in Jewish laws and theological orientation that he deemed would facilitate Jewish integration into the French state. Napoleon hoped that this body of representatives, two-thirds rabbis and one-third lay leaders from the French empire and the Kingdom of Italy, would gain the recognition of all Jewry. The world Jewish community greeted the French Sanhedrin with indifference or profound suspicion, however, and after doing the emperor's bidding, it ceased to exist. Thereafter, Napoleon instituted the office of a chief rabbi, which eventually was transferred from government auspices to the autonomous communal organization of French Jewry.

A chief rabbinate in England arose at the beginning of the nineteenth century and was officially recognized by the government in 1845, which assured that its authority would extend over the entire British Empire. In 1840, during the period of Ottoman rule, Jerusalem became a regional administrative center, and the *hakham bashi or rishon le-Zion* (First of Zion, or the chief rabbi of the Sephardic community) was recognized as the chief rabbi of the Land of Israel. In 1920 the British mandatory government of Palestine established two offices of the chief rabbinate, one for the Ashkenazim and the other for the Sephardim. The authority of these offices, which the State of Israel continues to support, is not universally acknowledged by all Jewish communities, however. Recurrent attempts to establish a chief rabbinate in the United States have failed. Instead, each denomination—Orthodox, Reform, Conservative, and Reconstructionist—has established its own organization.

HOUSES OF WORSHIP AND HOLY PLACES In Judaism, as in all biblical religions, the notion of specific holy places is ambiguous. If God is the universal God of creation, it is not clear how his glory or presence can be manifest in any one place rather than another. Some rabbis regard certain places as intrinsically holy because the divine presence objectively dwells in those spaces, namely, the Land of Israel and the Temple in Jerusalem. Others view holy places as sanctified by historical association, as sites evoking certain religious memories and, therefore, emotions. Among such holy places in Judaism are Mount Moriah, where Abraham bound Isaac (Gen. 22:14) and upon which, according to Jewish tradition, the Temple was built. The holiness of Mount Sinai, where God gave the Children of Israel the Torah, was limited to the time of divine revelation and subsequently has had no special status. Although the Land of Israel is regarded as the Holy Land and the Temple Mount as the most holy part of this land, some rabbis have debated what constitutes the holiness of this land and of the Temple Mount. It is significant that King Solomon, in his prayer at the dedication of the Temple, raised this very question: "For will God indeed dwell on the earth? Behold, the heaven and the heaven of the heavens cannot contain thee; how much less this house that I have built!" (1 Kings 8:27). As the twentieth-century theologian Abraham Joshua Heschel observed, "God has no geographical address nor a permanent residence." Nonetheless, after the destruction of the Second Temple, the remaining parts of its Western Wall, popularly known as the Wailing Wall, became a site of collective mourning and of the expression of messianic longing for its restoration.

Judaism also regards as holy the site in the city of Hebron where the patriarchs are said to be buried. Similarly, the tomb of Rachel, near Bethlehem, is revered as holy. Some Jewish communities regard as holy the grave sites of famed rabbis—for example, the grave at Meron in Galilee of Simeon ben Yohai, the second-century sage who figures prominently in the Mishnah and in the *Zohar.* Members of the Hasidic community following the teachings of Rabbi Nachman of Bratzlav make annual pilgrimages to his grave in the Ukrainian village of Uman.

After the destruction of the Jerusalem Temple in 70 C.E., the synagogue, from the Greek meaning "assembly," has served as the site of Jewish worship. (The Hebrew equivalent is *bet ha-keneset,* or "house of assembly.") In the Talmudic period there arose a parallel institution called *bet ha-Midrash,* or "house of study," designating a place where Jews went to study the Torah. The two institutions eventually were joined, and in Yiddish, the vernacular of eastern European Jewry, the synagogue is simply called a *Schul,* or "school." In order to signal that they no longer pray for the restoration of the Jerusalem Temple, Reform congregations often call their house of worship a temple.

WHAT IS SACRED? The Hebrew term for "holiness" is kedushah, meaning the act of "setting apart," or dedication to God, who as the holy one and the creator of the universe is the source of all holiness. The act of dedicating oneself and one's actions to God constitutes the sa-

cred in Judaism. Hence, it is said that Jews' relationship to God is preeminently through time and not space. It may, therefore, seem to be a paradox that one of the most frequent names for God in the Talmud is Makom, Hebrew for "space." The paradox is explained by a midrash ascribed to Rabbi Eliezer ben Hyrcanus (first–second centuries C.E.) on Psalm 90:1—". . . Lord, Thou has been our dwelling place in all generations"—pointing to the fact that wherever there are righteous and pious people "God is with them."

Through pious deeds Jews sanctify the objects (food, drink, a residence, an object of beauty) and natural activities (sex, work, beholding beauty as well as tragedy) of the created order and thereby render them receptive to God's holy presence. These deeds include those specified by the Torah, as elaborated by the Halakhah, and those acts of reverence and morality that one must legislate to oneself. The rabbis, however, have held that it is life itself that is most sacred, and in order to preserve a life the precepts of the Torah may be suspended. Accordingly, they interpreted Leviticus 19:16 to mean ". . . neither shalt thou stand aside when mischief befalls thy neighbor," and hence if someone is, say, assaulted, it is incumbent upon all who are in a position to help to do so, even if this entails abrogating the ritual commandments of the Torah.

In Judaism reverence is accorded to ritual objects, and in this sense they are regarded as sacred. Religious books written in Hebrew, "the sacred tongue," starting with the Bible, are regarded as sacred. Hence, when these books become worn and no longer fit for use, they are not simply discarded but rather are reverentially buried in a cemetery, often in the grave of a great scholar or particularly pious person. In some communities it is the custom to store Hebrew texts, including correspondence dealing with religious matters, that are no longer in use in a special vault, or *genizah* (hiding place), usually in the synagogue.

HOLIDAYS AND FESTIVALS The Sabbath, the seventh day of the week, is the paradigm for all holidays in Judaism. Associated with God's creation of the world and with the enduring source of life's ultimate meaning, the Sabbath is marked by a cessation of work and mundane activity and by dedication to worship, thanksgiving, study of the Torah, and reaffirmation of Israel's covenant with God. With important modifications, this pattern applies to all major Jewish festivals.

Two Israeli Holidays

Two holidays of the State of Israel are also marked throughout the Diaspora. One is Yom Ha-Shoah (Holocaust Memorial Day), on the 27th of Nisan, which commemorates the systematic killing of 6 million Jews by the Nazis during World War II. It was on this date in 1943 that the Nazis suppressed the Warsaw Ghetto Uprising, and the heroic resistance of Jewish partisans is thus also remembered on this day. Many Jewish congregations and communities throughout the Diaspora have incorporated Yom Ha-Shoah into their liturgical and communal calendars.

The second holiday is Yom Ha-Atzamaut (Israeli Independence Day), on the 5th of Iyyar, the eighth month of the Jewish calendar, which marks the proclamation of the State of Israel on 14 May 1948. Although it is an Israeli civil holiday, Yom Ha-Atzamaut is celebrated in most Jewish congregations with special prayers of thanksgiving.

The Jewish liturgical calendar essentially has five major festivals and two principal minor festivals, the former biblically ordained and the latter instituted by the Talmudic sages. While on the Sabbath all work is forbidden, on the major holidays the preparation of food is permitted. The major holidays are Rosh Hashanah; Yom Kippur, which is regarded as the Sabbath, with all work whatsoever forbidden; Sukkoth; Passover; and Shabuoth. In biblical times the latter three were celebrated by pilgrimages to the Temple in Jerusalem. The two principal minor festivals introduced by the rabbis are Hanukkah and Purim, which do not carry the prohibition against working or engaging in mundane activities. Similar rules apply to other minor festivals and fast days.

The holidays and festivals are ordered according to the ancient Jewish calendar, which is based on the monthly cycle of the moon, with adjustments to the seasonal pattern of the solar year. The Jewish New Year, or Rosh Hashanah, falls on the 1st of the month of Tishri, which generally corresponds to a day in September. Literally "head of the year," the holiday is also known as the Day of Judgment (Yom Ha-Din), on which a person stands before God, who judges his or her personal repentance. God's judgment is dispensed 10 days later, on Yom Kippur, the Day of Atonement. Rosh Hashanah is a festive celebration of divine creation and, at the same time, a solemn reckoning of one's sins. The period between Rosh Hashanah and Yom Kippur is known as the Days of Awe and is devoted to penitential prayer, which culminates with the fasting and intense expression of contrition and atonement that mark Yom Kippur. On this, the holiest day of the Jewish year, on which God's judgement is cast, Jews pray to be pardoned for their sins and for reconciliation with God.

Five days after Yom Kippur, on the 15th of Tishri, the autumn festival of Sukkoth (Tabernacles) takes place. Lasting a week, the festival is marked by the construction of provisional booths, or sukkahs (from the Hebrew *sukkoth*), as a reminder of the structures in which the Israelites dwelt during their 40 years' journey in the wilderness (Lev. 23:42). The roof of the sukkah, in which a person is to eat and, if possible, sleep for the duration of the festival, is to be made from things that grow from the ground, a symbol of God's care for the earth and its inhabitants. On the last day of the festival, called Hoshanah Rabbah (Great Hosannah), hymns are sung appealing to God for deliverance from hunger. Sukkoth is followed immediately by Shemini Atzeret, the "eighth day of assembly," on which God is entreated to bestow rain to ensure a good harvest, and the next day is Simhat Torah (Rejoicing of the Torah). On this day the annual cycle of the reading of the Torah is completed, hence the rejoicing. In the Land of Israel, Shemini Atzeret and Simhat Torah are observed on the same day.

Hanukkah (Dedication) is a winter festival that begins on the 25th of Kislev, the second month after Tishri. It celebrates the victory of the Maccabees over the Seleucids, although greater import is attached to the rededication of the Temple. According to the Talmud, the Maccabees could find ceremonial oil for only one night, but by a miracle its flames lasted for eight days until a fresh supply could be obtained. In commemoration of the miracle, lights are kindled in Jewish homes during the eight nights of Hanukkah, customarily in a special candelabrum.

Purim, or the Feast of Esther, falls on the 14th of Adar, the fifth month after Tishri. This festival commemorates the deliverance of the Jews from Haman, the chief minister of the king of Persia, who cast lots (Hebrew, *purim*) to determine the date on which the Jews in the kingdom would be killed. The Book of Esther is read in the synagogue on the night of Purim and on the next morning. During the reading it is customary for the congregation to "blot out" the name of Haman, held to be a descendent of Amalek (Exod. 17:8–16) and the forefather of those bent on destroying the Jewish people, by shouting raucously, pounding their feet, and rattling noisemakers. In general a carnival mood prevails, and many people, including children, dress in costumes.

Passover takes place from the 15th to the 22nd (in the Diaspora from the 15th to the 23rd) of Nisan, the seventh month after Tishri. The Hebrew name for the holiday, Pesach, denotes the lamb offered on the even of the festival during the time of the Temple. With a change in one vowel, the name becomes the past tense of the verb *pasach* (to pass over), alluding to God's having passed over the houses of the Children of Israel when he slew the firstborn of the Egyptians (Exod. 12:13). After the destruction of the Second Temple, the principal ritual focus of the holiday was transferred to the prohibition against eating leavened bread, with matzo becoming a symbol of affliction and poverty. A seder, or festive meal and religious service, is held in the home on the first night of Passover in Israel and for the first two nights in the Diaspora. At the meal the Haggadah relating the story of the Exodus, along with legends and homiletic commentaries on the Passover ritual, is recited.

Shabuoth falls on the 6th (in the Diaspora on the 6th and 7th) of Sivan, the ninth month after Tishri. It takes place 50 days after the Omer (sheaf of barley) was taken to the Temple on the second day of Passover. (Hence, it is called Pentecost [Greek for "50"] in Christian sources.) In biblical times Shabuoth was a harvest holiday, and it is celebrated as such by many secular Israelis today. The rabbis, however, understood its principal significance to be a commemoration of the giving of the Torah on Mount Sinai. The portion of the Torah read on the first day of Shabuoth is from Exodus (19:1–20:26). On the second day, in the Diaspora, a parallel passage from Deuteronomy 16:1–17 is read. It is also customary to read the Book of Ruth on Shabuoth, for of her own volition Ruth the Moabite entered into the covenant of Abraham. She is, therefore, the paradigm both of pure faith and of a genuine convert to Judaism. According to Jewish tradition, Ruth's grandson, King David, died on Shabuoth. Although there are no special rituals to mark Shabuoth, many customs have evolved over the centuries. The eating of dairy dishes, some especially prepared for the day, is a particularly popular custom. The Kabbalist custom of devoting the entire night of Shabuoth to Torah study was later adopted by other Jewish communities.

MODE OF DRESS Aside from the biblical commandment to attach fringes (zizith) to the four corners of garments (Num. 15:38–40; Deut. 22:12), which are also attached to a special shawl (tallith) worn by men during prayer, Jewish law does not prescribe any specific dress. Nonetheless, a dress code has indirectly been created by the prohibition against wearing garments containing a mixture of wool and flax (Deut. 22:11) and the injunction against men wearing women's clothing and women dressing like men (Deut. 22:5). A verse in Leviticus (19:27)—"You shall not round off the side-growth of your head, or destroy the side-growth of your beard"— was interpreted by the Talmudic sages as a prohibition against shaving with a razor, which was regarded as an act of disfigurement. The removal of facial hair with a scissors, or in modern times with an electric razor, is permitted, but the practice of wearing a beard and side locks (*peot*) has been widely adopted by traditional Jews.

Rules of modesty influence the manner of traditional Jewish dress. Since ancient times married women have covered their hair, considered one of the sources of a woman's allure. As an expression of piety, the custom has evolved for men to wear a skullcap, especially during prayer and while studying sacred texts, and many Orthodox men wear a head covering at all times. In Conservative and Reform circles the practice of women wearing a skullcap has increased. In the modern period Ultra-Orthodox Jews, especially Hasidim, have adopted special dress as a way of securing their religious identity, especially in the face of secularization and acculturation.

DIETARY PRACTICES Based primarily on passages in the books of Leviticus and Deuteronomy, traditional Judaism has developed an elaborate code governing foods that are permitted and forbidden. For instance, only animals that have cloven hooves and that chew the cud are permitted; hence, a person is not to consume pork, for the pig does not chew the cud. Similarly, only fish with scales and fins may be eaten; accordingly, shrimp and lobster are deemed unfit for consumption. There are also rules regulating the separation of meat and dairy products, while other laws determine how certain meats are to be slaughtered, prepared, and cooked. These regulations are known collectively as "kasruth" (often in English as "kosher" after the Ashkenazi pronunciation) from the Hebrew *kasher*, for "fit." As an expression of God's will, the dietary code is said to promote a life of holiness (Exod. 22:30; Lev. 11:44–45; Deut.14:21).

RITUALS As symbolic acts meant to endow life with holiness, Jewish rituals are generally derived from biblical commandments determining a person's relationship to the divine. This relationship is most often expressed ritually and ranges from the donning of tefillin to the manner of washing one's hands before eating, from the symbolic gestures and prayers with which one greets the Sabbath to the Habdalah (separation) ceremony at the end that marks the division between the day of rest and the remainder of the week.

Jewish ritual life embraces both the home and the synagogue, where the rituals are woven into the liturgy, and virtually all festivals are celebrated in both through prescribed rituals and prayers. This is especially true of the three "pilgrimages" specified in the book of Deuteronomy (16:16): "Three times a year—on the Feast of Unleavened Bread [Passover], on the Feast of Weeks [Shabuoth], and on the Feast of Booths [Sukkoth]—all your males shall appear before the Lord your God in the place that He will choose." The place of God's choice was the Jerusalem Temple, but with its destruction the pilgrimages came to be enacted symbolically through rituals. Some Jewish communities make pilgrimages to the graves of saintly rabbis.

In Judaism births, marriages, and deaths are noted with prescribed liturgies and rituals. All of these are rich in symbols.

RITES OF PASSAGE Eight days after birth a Jewish boy is received into the covenant of Abraham through the rite of circumcision (Brit Milah). Conservative and Reform Jews have introduced a parallel ceremony for girls, without circumcision, called Brit ha-Bat (covenant for a daughter). A male convert to Judaism undergoes circumcision, followed by immersion in a ritual bath (*mikveh*), while the conversion of a woman is marked by a ritual bath only.

When a Jewish boy reaches the age of 13, marking the beginning of puberty, he is held be intellectually and spiritually ready to assume full responsibility for his actions and hence obliged to observe all of the commandments of the Torah. He is thus said to be "bar mitzvah,"

that is, a "son of the commandment." Although this status is automatic by virtue of age, it is customarily marked by a ceremony held in the synagogue. The boy is called upon to read or chant a passage from the Torah and then a portion of the book of Prophets, determined by the liturgical calendar for that particular day. Often the boy is honored by being invited to deliver a discourse on the passages he has read, thus displaying his intellectual responsibility to be a learned and spiritually conscious Jew. The ceremony is followed by a festive party.

Girls reach the status of full religious responsibility at the age of 12. Until contemporary times no special ceremony was held to celebrate this. Increasingly, however, many congregations, especially those associated with Reform and Conservative movements, have introduced a ceremony for girls, called bat mitzvah, that replicates bar mitzvah. Most Orthodox congregations, which adhere to the ancient practice of separating the sexes in prayer, object to women reading from the Torah in the synagogue, although they may allow special worship services for women, at which time a bat mitzvah may read from the Torah.

Reform Judaism has introduced the rite of confirmation as supplementary to the bar and bat mitzvah ceremonies. Whereas the latter mark a technical change in status, confirmation, which is preceded by an extended and systematic study of Judaism, is held to reflect knowledge and thus a deepened sense of personal commitment. The rite, generally a group ceremony for boys and girls who have reached the age of 15, is usually part of the Shabuoth service.

MEMBERSHIP According to traditional law, a person is a Jew by virtue of being born to a Jewish mother or by conversion. The child of a Jewish mother and non-Jewish father is regarded as a Jew, whereas the child of a Jewish father and non-Jewish mother is not. By and large, however, Reform Judaism recognizes patrilineal descent, holding that it is sufficient for a child to have a Jewish father—that is, a father who is Jewish by birth or through conversion—to be considered a member of the Jewish people.

As a monotheistic religion affirming the oneness of God and thus of humanity, Judaism welcomes conversion. The classic example of the convert is Ruth the Moabite, who in accepting the God of Abraham declared, "For wherever you go, I will go; wherever you lodge, I will lodge; your people shall be my people, and your God my God" (Ruth 1:16). The fact that Ruth was the grandmother of King David, from whose descendants the Messiah is to emerge, underscores the esteemed status of the convert.

Until the destruction of the Second Temple, Judaism actively sought to proselytize. Thereafter, as a dispersed minority, missionary activity became difficult. Moreover, as they increasingly became subject to often aggressive Christian missionaries, Jews developed an aversion to active proselytizing. This attitude was reinforced by the Talmudic doctrine that "the righteous of all peoples have a share in the World to Come." Hence, a person need not be a Jew in order to be graced with God's love. All that is required of non-Jews is the observance of the seven Noahide Laws, the laws given to Noah and his "descendants," that is, all of humanity, after the Flood (Gen. 9:1–17): prohibitions against idolatry, blasphemy, murder, adultery and incest, robbery, and the eating of flesh torn from living animals (and by extension cruelty to animals), as well as the establishment of courts of justice. The rabbis considered these laws to be understood instinctively by all peoples. Nonetheless, sincere converts are welcome, their sincerity judged by a preparedness to accept the fate of the Jewish people and a commitment to observe the precepts and teachings of the Torah. The prevailing practice is to require the prospective convert to undertake an intensive course of study before submitting an application to a court of at least three rabbis.

RELIGIOUS TOLERANCE As implied by the Noahide Laws and the Talmudic doctrine that all righteous peoples will share in the world to come, members of other faith communities are to be accorded respect. The philosopher Maimonides argued that the Noahide Laws were based on belief in the God of Abraham, in effect limiting the principle of tolerance to followers of biblical religions. Most other rabbinical scholars, however, have not accepted this interpretation. Attitudes toward Gentiles—the term "goyim" is from the Hebrew for "nations," that is, other nations—are also determined by whether or not religious and cultural practices are understood as idolatrous. It has thus been suggested that, although Judaism is not a universal religion, a religion that seeks to embrace all of humanity, it is a universalistic religion.

SOCIAL JUSTICE The unyielding pursuit of justice is one of the overarching themes of the Bible: "Justice, jus-

tice shall you pursue . . ." (Deut. 16:20). Initially addressed to judges, beseeching them to administer the law with integrity, this injunction was interpreted both in the Bible itself and in later Jewish teachings as a commandment to be alert to the needs of disinherited members of society: the poor, the widowed and orphaned, the stranger, and the physically and mentally infirm. Indeed it is held that, unaccompanied by the pursuit of justice, the worship of God is vacuous: "Spare Me the sound of your hymns, And let Me not hear the music of your lutes. But let justice well up like water, Righteousness like an unfailing stream" (Amos 5:23–24). The rabbis recognized that justice must be grounded in the law and in a society's institutions.

Hence, rabbinical law (Halakhah) is an ongoing process—until this day in Orthodox communities—of review and refinement, representing a quest to understand how God's will, as embodied in the Torah and its principles, apply to the ever unfolding complex realities of life. The Bible sets forth certain criteria for social justice. Among these is that charity, the Hebrew term for which is derived from the word for "justice," should avoid humiliating the recipient. The needy are not to expose themselves to the humiliation of begging. The philosopher Maimonides therefore taught that the highest and purest form of charity is constituted by actions that prevent a person from becoming poor or that assist a person emerging from poverty by providing a decent job or other help. Implicit in this dictum, as many modern interpreters underscore, is the premise that the alleviation of suffering by individual acts of charity alone is insufficient. Equally if not more important is the establishment of just social institutions and laws.

The rabbis also recognized, however, the danger of relegating the pursuit of justice to social and legal institutions. Thus, they introduced the concept of benevolence (*gimilut hasadim*, or "bestowing kindness"). Whereas charity is invariably of a material nature, benevolence requires that a person give of the self, if merely a kind word or gesture, to another. Even those who enjoy material well-being are in need of benevolent attention. And whereas charity may be prompted by a sense of duty, benevolence is a spontaneous deed of the caring heart.

SOCIAL ASPECTS To marry and to bear children are supreme religious and social values in Judaism. As the rabbis observe, the first commandment issued by God was addressed to Adam and Eve: "Be fruitful and multiply . . ." (Gen. 1:28). But God created Eve as Adam's companion, not only as a partner for procreation. Male and female are bonded in companionship in order to create a family, to become husband and wife as well as father and mother to their common offspring. Marriage is thus regarded as a covenant. Indeed, the union of man and wife often serves as a metaphor for the relationship between God and Israel.

Although the Bible sanctions polygamy, the ideal marriage, as projected by the story of Adam and Eve, is monogamous. The practice of having more than one wife persisted, however, until the German Rabbenu (Our Rabbi) Gershom ben Judah (960–1028 C.E.) proclaimed a ban on such marriages, which has been universally honored since by Ashkenazi Jews. Today Sephardic Jews also reject polygamy. Divorce is permitted by Jewish law, although a rabbinical court sanctions divorce only if it is convinced that the breakdown in the marriage is beyond repair.

CONTROVERSIAL ISSUES Since the demise of the Sanhedrin in the fifth century C.E. and the parallel eclipse of the Babylonian academies, Judaism has had no central authority. In general, however, the various communities have recognized the rulings of esteemed rabbis. All rabbis are beholden to biblical and Talmudic teachings, as well as to the precedents of the ever unfolding development of Jewish law (Halakhah). Differences between rabbis are understood as a matter of interpretation of these teachings and precedents. The emergence in the modern era of denominations and of their subdivisions has further fragmented theological opinion.

Nonetheless, on various contemporary issues there is a rough consensus among Orthodox Jews. Abortion, for instance, is regarded as a grievous act akin to homicide. Yet as the rabbis of the Mishnah ruled, if a woman's life is endangered by a pregnancy, it is permitted to abort the fetus in order to save her life. If the child she is bearing already has begun to emerge from the womb, and is thus deemed a full-fledged being, it is not permitted to kill one life for the sake of another. There are cases, however, when the rabbis would allow even this principle to be overridden. Some rabbis have ruled that if, in the judgment of a physician, a child will be born with a severe physical or mental infirmity, abortion is permitted. Others have sanctioned abortion when the pregnancy resulted from rape by a man other than the woman's husband. All Orthodox rabbis object to abortion as a means of birth control. Conservative and especially Reform opinion tends to be far more liberal

on abortion, affirming a woman's inalienable right to choose to give birth or not to a child she bears.

The issue of using artificial means to prevent fertilization and conception is complex. The overarching reason for marriage is to bear children and establish a family. The rabbis also acknowledge, however, that sexual intercourse often is pleasurable. Hence, the question is whether or not it is permissible for a married couple to employ contraceptives and thus separate the pursuit of sexual pleasure from the divine commandment to procreate. (Extramarital sex is frowned upon as utterly sinful.) The rabbis generally approach the question in view of the biblical injunction against "spilling," or "wasting," one's seed (Gen. 38:9). The majority of contemporary Orthodox rabbis reason that, since this injunction applies only to a man, a woman may use a contraceptive device or take birth control pills. Such measures are particularly countenanced when pregnancy would be detrimental to the woman's health.

In consonance with biblical and rabbinical views, Orthodox Judaism is unambiguously patriarchal. Women not only are strictly separated from men in the synagogue and houses of study but also occupy a lower position in the religious life of the community. They are not counted in the minyan, or quorum, required for communal prayer, nor do they take an active part in the worship service, such as reading from the Torah or serving as a cantor and leading the congregation in prayer. Reform and Reconstructionist, and to a lesser extent Conservative, Judaism have adopted gender-inclusive positions, removing barriers to the full participation of women in religious life.

Advances in medical science have engendered an array of ethical and religious issues, such as organ transplants, artificial insemination, and genetic engineering. All branches of Judaism view these developments positively when they are understood as serving to enhance the sanctity of life. This attitude is guided by the rabbinical teaching that the preservation of life overrides all other considerations and religious prohibitions.

CULTURAL IMPACT Since its biblical beginnings Judaism has developed a rich history of religious expression through music, dance, and song. Miriam, Moses' sister, led the women of Israel in song and dance to celebrate the crossing of the Red Sea (Exod. 15:20). The Temple service was accompanied by singing and instrumental music (Ps. 150:3–5). The rabbis of the Talmud, however, deemed instrumental music to be a form of work and thus banned it on the Sabbath and during festivities. But prayers at home and in the synagogue were often chanted and sung. Indeed, song has remained a prominent feature of Jewish worship. Throughout the ages poets have written religious hymns (*piyyutim*), for which melodies were often composed. Songs and wordless melodies play a particularly significant role in Hasidism. In addition, Hasidim often punctuate their prayers with dance, which they regard as a form of worship. Dance and instrumental music are common features of weddings and other celebrations in all Jewish traditions.

Visual art is yet another important form of religious expression in Judaism. The Tabernacle (temporary sanctuary used by the Israelites in the wilderness) and later the Jerusalem Temples were richly adorned with ornamental art, apparently even pictorial paintings. The biblical prohibition against the fashioning of graven images pertains only to the creation of idols for the purpose of worship (Exod. 20:4; Deut. 4:15–19). Hence, there is a tendency in Jewish tradition to frown upon sculpture, especially if placed in the synagogue, although sculpture is not in itself prohibited. The synagogue is often richly adorned with paintings, although they tend to avoid the depiction of human images. The Torah scroll is usually bedecked in a finely embroidered mantle or decorated encasing and is adorned with specially crafted silver ornaments of bells and a breastplate, or shield, and topped with a crown. Other ceremonial objects, such as goblets and the cases for mezuzah (doorpost) parchments, are also especially crafted by artisans, and there is a long tradition of illuminated Aggadah manuscripts.

In contrast to the Temple in Jerusalem, which was built according to precise architectural blueprints, there are no guidelines regarding the construction of synagogues. Hence, the design of synagogues frequently reflects the influence of local architectural styles. The ark containing the Torah scroll, however, should face Jerusalem.

In traditional Judaism verbal imagination found expression in the Aggadah, the nonlegal portions of the Talmud and Mishna. A species of Midrash, the scriptural commentaries of the Aggadah provided the framework for developing ideas and perspectives on a variety of ethical and religious issues. The Aggadah also served to convey folklore and folktales. In the modern period Jews have adopted new genres, preeminently fiction,

theater, and film, to give expression to their verbal imagination.

Paul Mendes-Flohr

See Also Vol. 1: *Conservative Judaism, Orthodox Judaism, Reform Judaism*

Bibliography

Ben-Sasson, Hayim Hillel, ed. *A History of the Jewish People.* London: Weidenfeld and Nicolson, 1976.

Bergman, Samuel Hugo. *Faith and Reason: An Introduction to Modern Jewish Thought.* Translated by Alfred Jospe. New York: Schocken Books, 1972.

Berlin, Adele, and Marc Brettler. *The Jewish Study Bible.* Oxford: Oxford University Press, 2004.

Bland, Kalman. *The Artless Jew: Medieval and Modern Affirmations of the Visual.* Princeton, N.J.: Princeton University Press, 2000.

Bleich, J. David. *Bioethical Dilemmas: A Jewish Perspective.* Hoboken, N.J.: Ktav Publishing House, 1998.

Cohen, Arthur A., and Paul Mendes-Flohr, eds. *Contemporary Jewish Religious Thought: Original Essays on Critical Concepts, Movements, and Beliefs.* 2nd ed. New York: Free Press, 1989.

Elazar, Daniel J., and Rela Mintz Geffen. *The Conservative Movement in Judaism: Dilemmas and Opportunities.* Albany: State University of New York Press, 2000.

Frank, Daniel H., and Oliver Leaman, eds. *History of Jewish Philosophy.* London: Routledge, 1997.

Frankel, Ellen, and Betsy Platkin Teutsch, eds. *The Encyclopedia of Jewish Symbols.* Northvale, N.J.: Jason Aronson, 1992.

Holtz, Barry W., ed. *Back to the Sources: Reading the Classic Jewish Texts.* New York: Summit Books, 1984.

———, ed. *The Schocken Guide to Jewish History: Where to Start Reading about Jewish History, Literature, Culture, and Religion.* New York: Schocken Books, 1992.

Jacobs, Louis. *The Jewish Religion: A Companion.* Oxford: Oxford University Press, 1995.

Gillman, Neil. *Conservative Judaism: The New Century.* West Orange, N.J.: Behrman House, 1993.

Kaplan, Mordecai M. *Judaism as a Civilization: Toward a Reconstruction of American-Jewish Life.* Philadelphia: Jewish Publication Society of America, 1981.

Lamm, Norman. *The Religious Thought of Hasidism: Texts and Commentary.* New York: Yeshivah University Press, 1999.

Meyer, Michael A. *Response to Modernity: A History of the Reform Movement in Judaism.* New York: Oxford University Press, 1988.

Neusner, Jacob. *The Pharisees: Rabbinic Perspectives.* Hoboken, N.J.: Ktav Publishing House, 1973.

Safrai, Shmuel, ed. *The Literature of the Sages.* 2 vols. Philadelphia: Fortress Press, 1987.

Schiffman, Lawrence H. *From Text to Tradition: A History of Second Temple Rabbinic Judaism.* Hoboken, N.J.: Ktav Publishing House, 1991.

Scholem, Gershom G. *Kabbalah.* New York: Quadrangle, 1974.

———. *Major Trends in Jewish Mysticism.* New York: Schocken Books, 1961.

Seltzer, Robert M. *Jewish People, Jewish Thought: The Jewish Experience in History.* New York: Macmillan, 1980.

———, ed. *Judaism: A People and Its History—Religion, History, and Culture: Selections from "The Encyclopedia of Religion."* New York: Macmillan, 1989.

Sklare, Marshall. *Conservative Judaism: An American Religious Movement.* 2nd enl. ed. New York: Schocken Books, 1972.

Steinsaltz, Adin. *The Essential Talmud.* Translated by Chaya Galai. London: Weidenfeld and Nicolson, 1976.

Stone, Michael E., ed. *Dead Sea Scrolls: Selections.* New York: Oxford University Press, 2000.

———, ed. *Jewish Writings of the Second Temple Period.* Philadelphia: Fortress Press, 1984.

Urbach, Ephraim Elimelch. *The Sages: Their Concepts and Beliefs.* Translated by Israel Abrahams. Jerusalem: Magnes Press, 1979.

Washofsky, Mark. *Jewish Living: A Guide to Contemporary Reform Practice.* New York: UAHC Press, 2000.

Zohar, Noam J. *Alternatives in Jewish Bioethics.* Albany: State University of New York Press, 1997.

Conservative Judaism

FOUNDED: 1886 C.E.

RELIGION AS A PERCENTAGE OF WORLD POPULATION: 0.024 percent

OVERVIEW Conservative Judaism, developed in the United States, was a reaction to Reform Judaism's rejection of Jewish law and practice. In 1883 a group of traditional rabbis, vowing to "conserve" Judaism, came up with a moderate platform for a new movement under the motto "Tradition and Change," requiring fidelity to Jewish law and practice while acknowledging that Judaism had always been influenced by the societies in which Jews lived. The Conservative movement was officially launched in 1886 with the opening of the Jewish Theological Seminary of America (JTS) in New York City. By 1975 more American Jews were affiliated with Conservative synagogues than with those of any other Jewish movement. With the dawn of the twenty-first century, however, the number of Conservative adherents had declined, and the population in Conservative synagogues had begun to age.

Branches of the Conservative movement exist in Canada, Israel, Argentina, Brazil, and western and eastern Europe under the name Masorti, the Hebrew word for "traditional." Israel has a Conservative Zionist movement called Mercaz; a growing number of Masorti synagogues; Masorti youth groups, summer camps, and elementary and high schools; and a branch of the JTS.

HISTORY Although begun in the United States, the Conservative movement was influenced by developments in Europe, especially the teachings of Zecharias Frankel (1801–75), a German rabbi. Frankel, who promoted historical scholarship of Judaism, viewed Jewish law and custom not as static elements but as evolving from historical circumstances.

Until 1880 there was little traditional Judaism in the United States; of the 200 synagogues, 188 were Reform. In 1883 a group of traditional rabbis walked out of their graduation banquet at Hebrew Union College in Cincinnati because the menu was not kosher. Two years later, in 1885, the Reform movement published its radical Pittsburgh Platform, which further encouraged traditional rabbis to start a new movement in American Judaism. The coalition that launched the Conservative movement included German Reform and Sephardic Jews, as well as some of the first of several million Jews who emigrated from eastern Europe to the United States between 1880 and 1920. In 1886 the Jewish Theological Seminary of America (JTS) was established to train English-speaking, Americanized, but traditional rabbis to serve the new immigrants. The school combined the scientific study of Jewish texts with traditional practice. Graduates founded congregations where the language of prayer was Hebrew and the liturgy was traditional, but the sermon was delivered in English and often included events of the day alongside traditional explications of the text. The tenets of the movement were complex, and for decades most Conservative Jews saw themselves simply as Jews in the middle between Reform and Orthodox adherents.

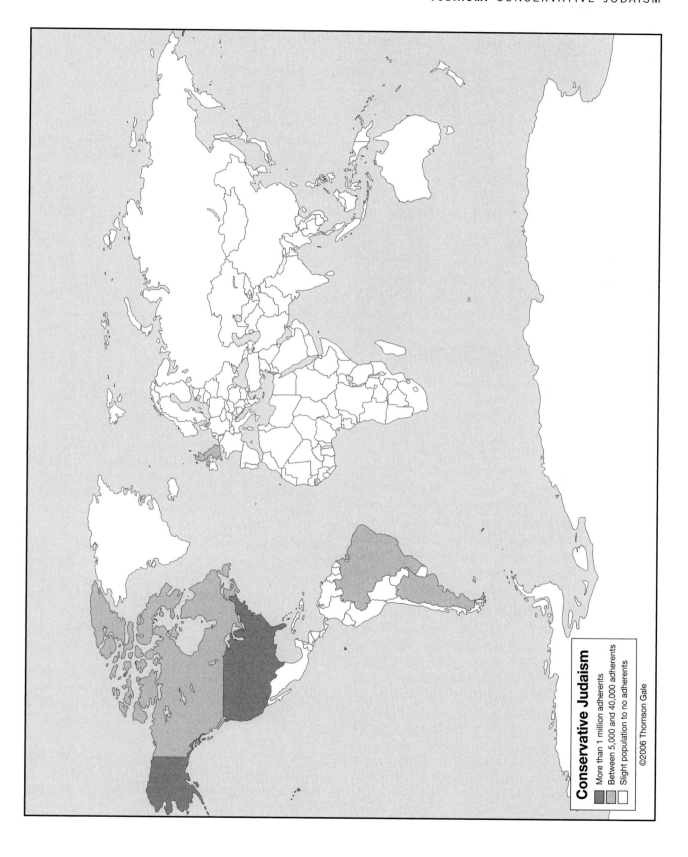

Conservative Judaism

More than 1 million adherents

Between 5,000 and 40,000 adherents

Slight population to no adherents

©2006 Thomson Gale

A Jewish girl reads from the Torah at her Bat Mitzvah, representing her transformation into Jewish adulthood. The Bat Mitzvah was created by Mordecai Kaplan in 1924 as a coming-of-age ceremony for his eldest daughter. © ROSE EICHENBAUM/CORBIS.

By the middle of the twentieth century, Conservative Judaism had taken hold in the United States among the second and third generations of eastern European Jewish immigrants, especially in suburbs of big cities. Today the movement has a worldwide membership but is still overwhelmingly American in numbers and character.

CENTRAL DOCTRINES Fundamental to Conservative Judaism is a fidelity to the rabbinic interpretation of halacha (Jewish law and practice), which is assumed to have developed over time. Because halacha has always been influenced by the cultures in which Jews lived, Conservative Jews believe that Jewish law and practice continue to develop but that they can be interpreted only by those who believe in the sanctity of tradition, adhere to its precepts, and are learned in Jewish law.

Conservative Jews accept the notion of revelation (without outlining a specific version that must be accepted) and acknowledge the existence of a covenant between God and the Jewish people that binds them to the 613 mitzvoth, or commandments, listed in the Torah (the first five books of the Hebrew Bible). Along

with ethical precepts, the mitzvoth include such ritual practices as kashruth (dietary laws). Conservative Judaism has also emphasized the unity of the Jewish people and a commitment to rebuilding a Jewish state in the land of Israel.

The Committee on Jewish Law and Practice—which includes faculty members from the JTS, members of the Rabbinical Assembly (the organization of Conservative rabbis), and some lay observers—rules on new questions of Jewish law. Only rabbis may submit these questions. If the law committee has permitted a range of practices in a given area, the rabbi of the individual congregation may choose any of the approved practices for his synagogue. The only recourse of a dissatisfied congregation is not to renew the rabbi's contract. If the law committee has unanimously ruled on a matter (such as the prohibition against officiating at an interfaith marriage), a Conservative rabbi who deviates from this practice may be asked to resign from the Rabbinical Assembly.

MORAL CODE OF CONDUCT Conservative Judaism's moral code of conduct is based on Jewish law and practice and is identical to that of traditional Judaism. In Judaism, monotheism requires brotherhood; the fact that everyone has descended from one person who was created by one God means that people must behave toward others with fairness. The role of human beings is to help create a good society on earth.

SACRED BOOKS Conservative Jews have the same sacred books as all other Jews: the Tanach (Hebrew Bible), which includes the Torah (the five books of Moses), and the Talmud (the body of Jewish law and lore).

SACRED SYMBOLS Like all traditional Jews, Conservative Jews revere as sacred symbols the Torah scrolls and other holy books, such as prayer books and the Talmud. Other symbols include the menorah (a candelabra with nine lights used in Jewish worship), the mezuzah (a parchment scroll containing sections from the Torah that is affixed to the doorpost of one's home as a sign of faith), and tefillin (phylacteries, or leather boxes containing scriptural passages that are worn on the head and left arm).

EARLY AND MODERN LEADERS Two distinguished rabbis, Sabato Morais and H. Pereira Mendes, along with a group of prominent lay leaders from Sephardic congregations in Philadelphia and New York, founded the JTS in 1886. Its mission was to preserve the knowledge and practice of historical Judaism. In 1887 the JTS held its first class of 10 students in the vestry of the Spanish-Portuguese Synagogue, New York City's oldest congregation.

The men considered the founders of the Conservative movement were Solomon Schechter, Louis Ginzberg, Cyrus Adler, and Mordecai Kaplan. Schechter (1847–1915) came from a teaching post at Cambridge University in 1902 to serve as the first president of the JTS. In 1913 he founded the United Synagogue of Conservative Judaism, representing Conservative synagogues in North America. Ginzberg (1873–1953) was the leading scholar of rabbinical literature at JTS from 1903 until his death. Adler (1863–1940) was president of the JTS from 1915 until 1940. Kaplan (1881–1983) founded the Teachers Institute at JTS in 1910 and taught there for more than fifty years, influencing generations of students. He also founded the Jewish Reconstructionist movement, which seceded from the Conservative movement after his retirement from the JTS. Kaplan was a strong supporter of the "synagogue center," an institutional trend encouraging the use of synagogues for community events, study, and social activities in addition to prayer. In 1924 he created the bat mitzvah—with synagogue rituals similar to those of the bar mitzvah, the traditional boy's coming-of-age ceremony—for his eldest daughter.

MAJOR THEOLOGIANS AND AUTHORS Theologian Abraham Joshua Heschel (1907–72) wrote important works on the relationship of human beings to God, the significance of the Sabbath, and the meaning of revelation. He served as a living model of ethical behavior for his students at the JTS during the civil rights movement of the 1960s and during the anti–Vietnam War protests.

Isaac Klein (1905–79) chaired the Committee on Jewish Law and Standards at JTS and authored *A Guide to Jewish Religious Practice*, the legal handbook of the Conservative movement.

ORGANIZATIONAL STRUCTURE The Conservative movement has three formal organizational structures in North America: the JTS, the Rabbinical Assembly (RA), and the United Synagogue of Conservative Judaism (USCJ). The RA, the organization of Conservative

A Jewish family sits at a dinner table reading from the Haggadah as they celebrate Seder. Seder, a service including a ceremonial dinner, is held on the first and second nights of Passover in commemoration of the Jewish exodus from Egypt. © ROGER RESSMEYER/CORBIS.

rabbis, began as an alumni association of JTS but currently has many members who were trained elsewhere. The USCJ, which represents 760 North American synagogues, is a layperson's organization, though its executive director has always been a rabbi. The umbrella organization for Conservative groups in other parts of the world is the World Council of Conservative Synagogues.

The individual synagogues form the grassroots core of the Conservative movement and contribute members to the Women's League of Conservative Judaism, the International Federation of Jewish Men's Clubs, and the United Synagogue Youth, which has 25,000 members.

HOUSES OF WORSHIP In Judaism, as in all biblical religions, the notion of specific holy places is ambiguous. If God is the universal God of creation, it is not clear how his glory or presence can be manifest in any one place rather than another. Some rabbis regard certain places as intrinsically holy because the divine presence objectively dwells in those spaces, namely, the Land of Israel and the Temple in Jerusalem. Others view holy places as sanctified by historical association, as sites evoking certain religious memories and, therefore, emotions. Among such holy places in Judaism are Mount Moriah, where Abraham bound Isaac (Gen. 22:14) and upon which, according to Jewish tradition, the Temple was built. The holiness of Mount Sinai, where God gave the Children of Israel the Torah, was limited to the time of divine revelation and subsequently has had no special status. Although the Land of Israel is regarded as the Holy Land and the Temple Mount as the most holy part of this land, some rabbis have debated what constitutes the holiness of this land and of the Temple Mount. It is significant that King Solomon, in his prayer at the dedication of the Temple, raised this very question: "For will God indeed dwell on the earth? Behold, the heaven and the heaven of the heavens cannot contain thee; how much less this house that I have built!" (I Kings 8:27). As the twentieth-century theologian Abraham Joshua Heschel observed, "God has no geographical address nor a permanent residence." Nonetheless, after the destruction of the Second Temple, the remaining parts of its Western Wall, popularly known as the Wailing Wall, became a site of collective mourning and of the expression of messianic longing for its restoration.

Judaism also regards as holy the site in the city of Hebron where the patriarchs are said to be buried. Similarly, the tomb of Rachel, near Bethlehem, is revered as holy. Some Jewish communities regard as holy the grave sites of famed rabbis—for example, the grave at Meron in Galilee of Simeon ben Yohai, the second-century sage who figures prominently in the Mishnah and in the *Zohar.* Members of the Hasidic community following the teachings of Rabbi Nachman of Bratzlav make annual pilgrimages to his grave in the Ukrainian village of Uman.

After the destruction of the Jerusalem Temple in 70 C.E., the synagogue, from the Greek meaning "assembly," has served as the site of Jewish worship. (The Hebrew equivalent is *bet ha-keneset,* or "house of assembly.") In the Talmudic period there arose a parallel institution called *bet ha-Midrash,* or "house of study," designating a place where Jews went to study the Torah. The two institutions eventually were joined, and in Yiddish, the vernacular of eastern European Jewry, the synagogue is simply called a *Schul,* or "school." In order to signal that they no longer pray for the restoration of the Jerusalem Temple, Reform congregations often call their house of worship a temple.

WHAT IS SACRED? The Hebrew term for "holiness" is kedushah, meaning the act of "setting apart," or dedication to God, who as the holy one and the creator of the universe is the source of all holiness. The act of dedicating oneself and one's actions to God constitutes the sacred in Judaism. Hence, it is said that Jews' relationship to God is preeminently through time and not space. It

may, therefore, seem to be a paradox that one of the most frequent names for God in the Talmud is Makom, Hebrew for "space." The paradox is explained by a midrash ascribed to Rabbi Eliezer ben Hyrcanus (first–second centuries C.E.) on Psalm 90:1—". . . Lord, Thou has been our dwelling place in all generations"— pointing to the fact that wherever there are righteous and pious people "God is with them."

Through pious deeds Jews sanctify the objects (food, drink, a residence, an object of beauty) and natural activities (sex, work, beholding beauty as well as tragedy) of the created order and thereby render them receptive to God's holy presence. These deeds include those specified by the Torah, as elaborated by the Halakhah, and those acts of reverence and morality that one must legislate to oneself. The rabbis, however, have held that it is life itself that is most sacred, and in order to preserve a life the precepts of the Torah may be suspended. Accordingly, they interpreted Leviticus 19:16 to mean ". . . neither shalt thou stand aside when mischief befalls thy neighbor," and hence if someone is, say, assaulted, it is incumbent upon all who are in a position to help to do so, even if this entails abrogating the ritual commandments of the Torah.

In Judaism reverence is accorded to ritual objects, and in this sense they are regarded as sacred. Religious books written in Hebrew, "the sacred tongue," starting with the Bible, are regarded as sacred. Hence, when these books become worn and no longer fit for use, they are not simply discarded but rather are reverentially buried in a cemetery, often in the grave of a great scholar or particularly pious person. In some communities it is the custom to store Hebrew texts, including correspondence dealing with religious matters, that are no longer in use in a special vault, or *genizah* (hiding place), usually in the synagogue.

HOLIDAYS AND FESTIVALS For Conservative Jews the 25-hour Shabbat (Sabbath), from sundown each Friday until an hour after sunset on Saturday, is the most sacred day besides Yom Kippur (the day of atonement). The Conservative movement follows the traditional Jewish calendar in celebrating the biblical high holidays of Rosh Hashanah (the new year) and Yom Kippur; the three pilgrimage festivals of Pesach (Passover), Shavuot (the Feast of Weeks), and Sukkoth (Tabernacles); and the minor festivals of Hanukkah and Purim. Contemporary innovations in the Jewish calendar include the celebration of Israeli Independence Day and the commemoration of Yom Hashoah (Holocaust Memorial Day).

MODE OF DRESS Conservative Jews do not have a distinctive dress. For daily prayer men, boys over the age of 13, and some women wear tefillin; for daily, Shabbat, and festival prayer men and some women wear *talitot* (prayer shawls). Men and many women cover their heads for prayer, and some Conservative Jews wear head coverings at all times. In the vast majority of Conservative synagogues, the rabbis and cantors wear the same ritual garb as the congregants, except on the high holidays, when the clergy wear white robes.

DIETARY PRACTICES Ideally Conservative Jews adhere to the laws of kashruth, which require that only biblically acceptable meats and fish be eaten, that meat be slaughtered according to rabbinic law, and that meat and dairy foods not be eaten together at the same meal. On the festival of Passover, stricter rules apply. Many Conservative Jews do not follow kashruth stringently.

RITUALS Conservative synagogues hold prayer services three times a day, with a fourth prayer service added on Shabbat and festival days. While decorum was important in early congregations, contemporary services emphasize informality, lay participation, and singing, and on Shabbat and festival days the rabbi often conducts a study session rather than a formal sermon. The basic liturgy, spoken in Hebrew, is the same in all congregations, but some large synagogues run "parallel services" with different styles of worship that may include study, music, or increased family participation.

RITES OF PASSAGE Conservative Jewish rites of passage include *brit milah* (circumcision) for boys and a special baby-naming ceremony, often called *simhat bat* (the joy of a daughter), for girls. *Simhat bat*, an outgrowth of the Jewish feminist movement, was created in the early 1970s and became widely observed in the late 1980s. When boys and girls turn 13, they celebrate their bar mitzvahs and bat mitzvahs, respectively, officially assuming religious duty and responsibility.

Traditional but personalized wedding ceremonies include a chuppah (canopy), a *ketubah* (the Aramaic wedding document), and the traditional seven benedictions. After the death of a close relative (a parent, spouse, child, or sibling), Conservative Jews "sit shiva," or stay home, for seven days, which is followed by 30 days of

The Masorti Movement in Israel

Because the official chief rabbi of Israel is Orthodox, the Masorti (Conservative) movement has suffered more limitations in Israel than in any other country. Conservative rabbis in Israel may not officiate at marriages or Jewish divorce proceedings. Mixed-gender Conservative groups are banned from praying at the main plaza in front of the Western Wall (the only remaining outer wall of the ancient Temple Mount). Non-Orthodox movements within Judaism are systematically excluded from government aid. The thorniest issue has been conversion to Judaism. Tens of thousands of immigrants to Israel from the former Soviet Union have wanted to convert to Judaism but have not wanted to become Orthodox, and the state recognizes only Orthodox conversion. Despite these obstacles, and particularly since the mid-1980s, the Masorti movement has created and maintained institutions in Israel, trained native-born rabbis and teachers, nurtured synagogues and a youth movement, and begun to support candidates for local political office.

intense mourning, or a year of mourning when each parent dies. As part of the mourning process, the kaddish prayer is recited in the synagogue three times a day.

MEMBERSHIP Any Jew can join and pay dues to a Conservative synagogue, but non-Jews and non-Jewish spouses of Jews may not be members or participate in traditional rituals. Children must have Jewish mothers or be converted to be accepted as Jews. After the Reform and Reconstructionist movements accepted patrilineal descent as a marker of Jewish identity in the 1980s, the Conservative movement's law committee unanimously reaffirmed the necessity of matrilineal descent.

The Conservative movement does not evangelize. It does, however, sponsor conversion classes for those interested in studying Judaism and encourages non-Jewish fiancés and spouses to take these classes along with their Jewish partners.

RELIGIOUS TOLERANCE One of the hallmarks of Conservative Judaism is its open-mindedness. Adherents are tolerant of Jews who differ in their interpretation of Judaism, of members of other religious groups, and of secular humanists.

SOCIAL JUSTICE Conservative Judaism highlights prophetic and rabbinic writings that urge adherents to create the "good commonwealth on earth," where social justice will prevail. Most congregations have social action programs and encourage members to give money to charity, to participate actively in making the world a better place, and to lobby state and federal governments to achieve social goals.

SOCIAL ASPECTS The central institutions of Conservative Judaism are the synagogue and the family. The movement is egalitarian and stresses the importance of parenting by both men and women. Divorce is permitted, but a Conservative rabbi will officiate at a second marriage only if the divorced person has obtained a Jewish divorce document in addition to a civil divorce.

CONTROVERSIAL ISSUES The most controversial issues in the last half century have related to Jewish law. In the middle of the twentieth century, controversy erupted over permission to ride in a car to the synagogue on the Sabbath and over the use of an organ or other live music in the synagogue. Today the vast majority of Conservative synagogues do not have organs, but they all have parking lots, and most Conservative Jews drive to services.

In the 1980s the movement's Committee on Jewish Law and Practice approved a woman's right to count in a minyan (the quorum of 10 people required for communal prayer), to read publicly from the sacred scrolls, and to enter rabbinical and cantorial schools. As a result, a small group called the Union for Traditional Judaism seceded, starting its own seminary, law committee, and synagogue organization.

As the incidence of marriage between Jews and non-Jews rose in the United States (the 2001 National Jewish Population Survey put the figure at 47 percent of all new marriages that included Jews), Conservative synagogue members put great pressure on the law committee to allow patrilineal (not just matrilineal) Jewish descent as the basis of Jewish identity. The law committee resisted this change.

By the 1990s Conservative Judaism was clearly differentiated from Orthodox Judaism (which opposed both the ordination of women and counting them in the quorum for prayer) and from Reform and Reconstructionist Judaism (which accepted rabbinic officiation at interfaith marriages, patrilineal descent as a basis for Jewish identity and the ordination of gay men and women).

Another controversy has been the status of openly practicing gay and lesbian Jews, who currently may not enter rabbinical or cantorial schools of the JTS and may not be placed as rabbis in Conservative congregations. Conservative rabbis are not permitted to officiate at same-sex commitment ceremonies.

CULTURAL IMPACT The Jewish Museum in New York City, which operates under the auspices of the JTS, contains a magnificent collection of traditional Jewish art and sponsors exhibits that have received national acclaim. The JTS cantorial school promotes Jewish music, and its professors have composed many melodies that have entered the liturgy. The Eternal Light, a pioneering Conservative Jewish radio program, was started in the 1950s by JTS, which now has a media department producing videos, television shows, and web-based programs.

Rela Mintz Geffen

See Also Vol. I: *Judaism*

Bibliography

Davis, Moshe. *The Emergence of Conservative Judaism.* Philadelphia: Jewish Publication Society, 1963.

Elazer, Daniel J., and Rela Mintz Geffen. *The Conservative Movement in Judaism: Challenges and Opportunities.* Albany: State University of New York Press, 2000.

Emet veEmunah. *Statement of Principles of Conservative Judaism.* New York: The Rabbinical Assembly, the Jewish Theological Seminary of America, and the United Synagogue of America, 1988.

Gillman, Neil. *Conservative Judaism: The New Century.* West Orange, N.J.: Behrman House, 1993.

Ruskay, John, and David Szioni, eds. *Deepening the Commitment: Zionism and the Masorti Movement.* New York: Jewish Theological Seminary of America, 1990.

Sklare, Marshall. *Conservative Judaism: An American Religious Movement.* Glencoe, Ill.: Free Press, 1955.

Waxman, Mordecai, ed. *Tradition and Change: The Development of Conservative Judaism.* New York: Burning Bush Press, 1958.

Wertheimer, Jack, ed. *Tradition Renewed: A History of the Jewish Theological Seminary of America.* 2 vols. New York: Jewish Theological Seminary of America, 1997.

Orthodox Judaism

FOUNDED: Nineteenth century C.E.

RELIGION AS A PERCENTAGE OF WORLD POPULATION: 0.04 percent

OVERVIEW Since the nineteenth century the term "Orthodoxy" (Greek *orth*, "correct," and *doxa*, "belief") has been applied to the most traditional movement within Judaism. This movement sees itself, compared with other Jewish groups, as the authentic carrier of Jewish tradition since ancient times. Orthodox Jews believe that the Torah (the first five books of the Hebrew Bible, also called the written law) is the word of God and, along with interpretations of the Torah known as the oral law, was divinely revealed to Moses on Mount Sinai. Because of its strict adherence to written and oral law (the latter compiled in the Talmud and codified in the Sholchan Aroch), the Orthodox community often calls itself "Torah-true Judaism."

Scholars generally partition Orthodox Judaism into two major groups: the "ultra-orthodox," or Haredi (awestruck), community and the Modern, or Neo-Orthodox, community. The Haredi community, in turn, can be divided into three general subgroups: the Hasidim (pious ones), the Mitnaggdim (opponents of Hasidim), and a relatively new phenomenon, Haredim of Sephardic and Oriental descent. The Hasidim and Mitnaggdim both originated in eastern Europe, and the ancestry of Sephardic and Oriental Haredim may be traced to the Iberian Peninsula and various Arab countries.

Some scholars divide the Orthodox world into three major groups, distinguishing a "centrist" Orthodox camp that falls somewhere between the Haredi and Modern Orthodox communities.

HISTORY Throughout the Middle Ages European, or Ashkenazi, Jews lived in autonomous, separate communities (often required to do so by law) that reinforced a cultural and religious aloofness from surrounding non-Jewish populations. In the mid-eighteenth century Hasidism, a revival movement with deep mystical tendencies, commenced among eastern European Jews. Opponents of the Hasidim, known as Mitnaggdim, attempted to thwart Hasidic innovations with orders of excommunication. Despite this opposition Hasidism soon dominated most of eastern European Judaism outside of Lithuania, leading to an ever-widening rift within the traditional Jewish world.

Because of the emancipation of Jews in central and western European societies, as well as the relaxing (if not abolishment) of discriminatory laws in the early nineteenth century, Jews were exposed to, and began to participate more equally in, the non-Jewish world. As a result, the traditional Jewish community was forced to grapple with the influence of surrounding cultures and the role of the emerging nation-state. Community cohesion gave way as Jews struggled to react to these societal shifts. Various reforms of Judaism were proposed to accommodate the changing times and to help Jews integrate with the societies around them. In 1795 the term "orthodoxy"(borrowed from Christianity) first appeared in a Jewish context—in an article published by

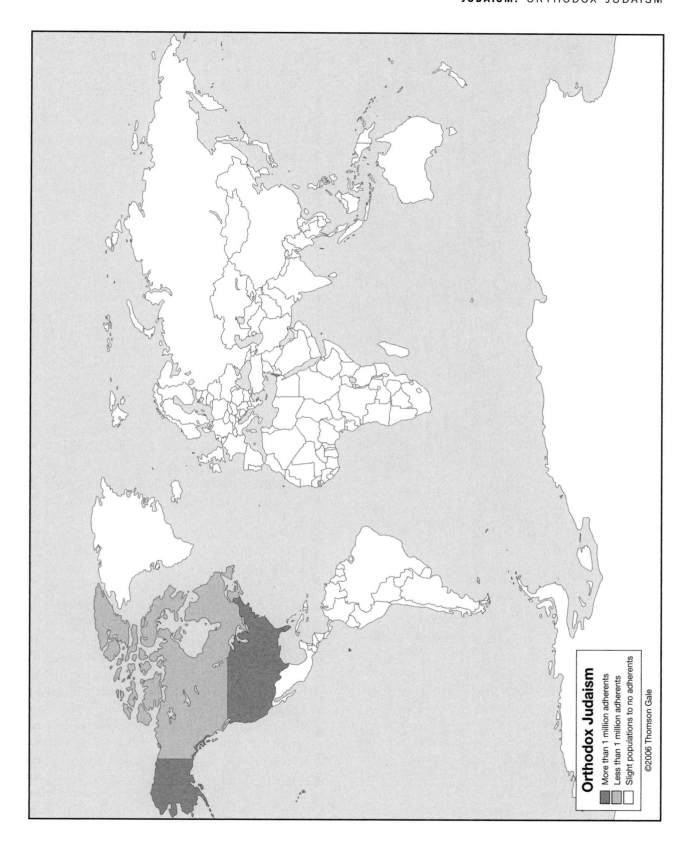

A rabbi studies the Torah. Orthodox Jews believe that the Torah is the word of God and that, along with interpretations of the Torah known as the Oral Law, it was divinely revealed to Moses on Mount Sinai. © RICHARD T. NOWITZ/CORBIS.

reformers intent on disparaging those who refused to modify Jewish practice or belief. Jewish traditionalism had previously required no specific designation.

In the early 1800s another bloc within traditional Judaism developed (this time in western Europe) that would come to be called Neo-Orthodoxy, or Modern Orthodoxy; its motto became "Torah Im Derekh Eretz" ("Torah in harmony with secular culture"). Modern Orthodoxy was characterized by a willingness to embrace some contemporary cultural forms but also by a rejection of reformist modifications in such areas as traditional liturgy, the authoritative nature of divine revelation, and the binding character of halakhah (Jewish law). As the challenge of modernity intensified in the nineteenth and twentieth centuries, divisions within Haredi Orthodoxy became less relevant as factions joined forces to fight modernizing trends.

From the mid-nineteenth century through the mid-twentieth century, Sephardic and Oriental Jews were exposed to modernization and European colonial culture. In more rural areas traditional Orthodox forms prevailed, whereas in urban centers Modern Orthodoxy emerged. In contrast to western Europe, however, the establishment of non-Orthodox Jewish denominations never developed within Sephardic and Oriental societies. In the latter part of the twentieth century, the majority of Sephardic and Oriental Jews immigrated to Israel.

CENTRAL DOCTRINES Judaism has never developed a universally accepted set of dogmas, thus making the appellation "Orthodoxy" something of a misnomer. What generally characterizes Orthodox Jews is a belief in three things: 1) "Torah Min HaShamayim," the divine revelation of the Five Books of Moses, representing direct supernatural communication of content from God to man; 2) the obligation to live according to traditional interpretations of halakhah (Jewish law); and 3) the authority of Orthodox rabbis to assist the believer in applying halakhah to his or her life. These attitudes usually inspire the believer to live and worship in an Orthodox community, where these values will be reinforced.

MORAL CODE OF CONDUCT The Orthodox code of conduct in both the ritual and moral realms is based upon a strict adherence to Jewish law, which determines what constitutes morality in every aspect of life. Issues concerning family relationships, sexuality, and conduct in business, among many others, are discussed and adjudicated in exquisite detail within Jewish sources, beginning with the Bible and extending to the responsa (answers to follower's questions) of modern rabbis.

SACRED BOOKS In Orthodox Judaism both the written law (Torah) and the oral law (finally written down c. 500 C.E. in the Talmud) are considered sacred; the latter in particular is an essential source of study throughout a Jewish man's life. Because of the complexity of the oral law, various attempts were made from the eleventh to the sixteenth centuries to summarize its rulings in comprehensive legal codes. The most recent and authoritative of these is Rabbi Joseph Caro's sixteenth-century work the *Shulkhan Arukh* ("Set Table"). It remains the foundation of the Orthodox Jewish lifestyle. These and other authoritative texts are considered fixed and binding for all time, reflecting God's will.

SACRED SYMBOLS Orthodox Jews do not have any sacred symbols that differ from those of other Jewish movements.

EARLY AND MODERN LEADERS The charismatic Rabbi Israel ben Eliezer, also called the Baal Shem Tov ("master of the good name"), founded the Hasidic movement in the eighteenth century. In the twentieth century Rabbi Menachem Mendel Schneerson served as rebbe (spiritual leader) of the Habad (Lubavitch) branch of Hasidism. He founded an educational network emphasizing worldwide outreach to all Jews and became a controversial figure when many of his followers claimed he was the Jewish messiah.

Within the non-Hasidic Haredi community, Rabbi Elijah ben Shlomo Zalman of Vilna, known as the Vilna Gaon, was in the late eighteenth century one of the intellectual giants of post-medieval Judaism and an implacable foe of the Hasidic movement. In the early nineteenth century Rabbi Moses Sofer, or the Hatam Sofer, gave voice to the anti-modernist, separatist faction within Orthodoxy. His legacy was continued in the United States by Rabbi Moses Feinstein, the leading non-Hasidic Haredi figure in the second half of the twentieth century.

Within the Modern Orthodox community, Rabbi Samson Raphael Hirsch (1808–88) is considered its founder. In the early twentieth century Rabbi Abraham Isaac Ha-Kohen Kook was the first Ashkenazi chief rabbi of Palestine and an early proponent of Religious Zionism. In the second half of the twentieth century Rabbi Joseph Dov Soloveichik influenced generations of Modern Orthodox rabbis in the United States.

Rabbi Ovadia Yosef, the former Sephardi chief rabbi of Israel (known as the Rishon Le-Zion), founded the Sephardic Haredi party Shas in the 1980s and has served as the de facto leader of Haredi as well as of more modern Orthodox Sephardi Jews.

MAJOR THEOLOGIANS AND AUTHORS Rabbi Shneur Zalman (1745–1812) of Lyady, Russia, founded Habad Hasidism; he developed a mystical theology detailed in *The Tanya* (1796), which became a fundamental text of Hasidic spirituality within the Habad (Lubavitch) movement. Rabbi Samson Raphael Hirsch elucidated the Modern Orthodox perspective in his work *Nineteen Letters* (1836).

Several Modern Orthodox thinkers emerged in the second half of the twentieth century. Rabbi Joseph Dov

An ultra-Orthodox Jew performs a ceremony known as Kaparot, which involves swinging a live chicken over his head. The ceremony is supposed to transfer the sins of the year to the chicken before Yom Kippur. © AFP/CORBIS.

Soloveichik in the United States wrote *Halakhic Man* (1944; originally published in Hebrew); Rabbi David Hartman in Israel wrote *A Living Covenant: The Innovative Spirit in Traditional Judaism* (1985); and Rabbi Irving (Yitz) Greenberg helped bridge the divide between Orthodoxy and other Jewish groups by founding the Center for Learning and Leadership in New York City in the 1970s. His wife, Blu Greenberg, wrote *On Women and Judaism: A View from Tradition* (1981), which led to new roles and learning opportunities for Orthodox women. In general non-Hasidic Haredi leaders promote their theology and outlook through their responsa, which are gathered into collections and published for the faithful.

ORGANIZATIONAL STRUCTURE Leadership in Orthodox communities is usually based upon a person's piety of practice and depth of Jewish knowledge. The synagogue rabbi or the rabbi of the community is ostensibly the most powerful figure, able to impose his interpretation of halakhah on the synagogue or community. Nevertheless, Orthodox communities are democratic in many ways; for instance, owing to the numerous subgroupings and synagogues in the Orthodox world, a person may always move to a more compatible environment.

HOUSES OF WORSHIP AND HOLY PLACES Orthodox Jews usually gather for prayer in a synagogue. Synagogues are situated in the center of an Orthodox community to enable worshipers easy access by foot on Sabbaths and festivals, when traveling by automobile is forbidden as a violation of the Sabbath rest. Men and women sit in separate sections, and no human images are allowed in the sanctuary. Sometimes prayer takes place in the *beit midrash* (house of study) or in a yeshiva (institution of higher Jewish learning), where students live and study on a daily basis over many years.

For many Orthodox Jews, living in Israel, the Holy Land, is encouraged, and visiting there on a regular basis is common. Within Hasidic and Oriental communities the graves of especially notable rabbis or biblical figures are considered holy places, worthy of pilgrimage.

WHAT IS SACRED? As the language of the Bible, Hebrew is known as the Holy Tongue (*lashon hakodesh*) and is endowed with special sanctity. As a result, over time its use was restricted to specific sacred objectives, such as study, prayer, or religious correspondence. The Orthodox insistence on using Hebrew as the exclusive language of prayer was a key issue in the emergence of Reform Judaism, whose advocates favored using the vernacular. During the late nineteenth and early twentieth centuries many in the Orthodox community fiercely opposed the transformation of Hebrew from a sacred language to the vernacular of Jews living in Israel. Many Ashkenazi Haredi Jews purposefully use Yiddish as their primary language.

HOLIDAYS AND FESTIVALS Holidays and festivals are the same for Orthodox Jews as for members of other Jewish movements. Orthodox Jews might differ from others in the manner and duration of their holiday observance. Out of respect for tradition Orthodox Jews living in the Diaspora, and many Conservative Jews as well, observe each holiday for two days (rather than one, as specified in the Torah). Some Haredi Jews refuse to mark modern holidays, such as Israel's Independence Day, because they were ordained by the government of the secular State of Israel rather than by God.

MODE OF DRESS Dress in the Orthodox world is quite varied. In keeping with a more separatist philosophy, those in the Haredi community dress in a quasi-uniform intentionally designed to make them stand out from the surrounding culture, as well as to preserve traditions specific to particular subgroups within the Haredi world. For men, this means always covering one's head with a hat or skullcap, wearing a beard and often earlocks, and displaying the biblically ordained fringes (*tzitzit*) outside of their upper garments. Orthodox men wear the *tallith katan*, a small prayer shawl, under their shirts. In the Hasidic world black caftans, black hats (fur hats on the Sabbath), and often some form of knee pants and black shoes are worn in a style traceable to Polish nobility. For women, pants are not permitted; all clothing must cover the chest to the neck and the arms to at least the elbows and fall below the knees. As a sign of modesty, married women hide their hair with a covering that may be a wig over a shorn head (in the most extreme cases), a wig over hair, a scarf, or a hat.

Modern Orthodox men and women might dress entirely in the fashion of the country in which they reside, albeit with a more modest cut of clothing. In general, men will put on a skullcap while eating and praying, if not all the time, and women will cover their hair during prayer or all the time.

DIETARY PRACTICES Orthodox Jews are generally meticulous in their observance of kashruth (Jewish dietary laws), seeing it as an essential expression of holiness commanded in sacred text as well as a means of cultural separation. The range of observances varies widely. Those in the Modern Orthodox world would try to eat only in kosher homes and establishments, but given no alternative, might eat uncooked, vegetarian, or dairy foods in a non-kosher environment. The majority of Orthodox Jews, however, confine themselves to homes or restaurants where the dietary laws are observed. Because there are different levels of scrupulousness regarding kashruth, those in the Haredi communities are even more stringent about where and what they will eat. In addition, blessings of gratitude are supposed to be recited before and after every meal as well as upon ingesting any food or drink.

RITUALS Orthodox Judaism is characterized by adherence to traditional practices, such as strict observance

Thirteen Principles of Belief

In his commentary on the Mishnah (Jewish oral law), Rabbi Moses ben Maimon (known as Maimonides; 1135–1204) articulated the basic tenets of Judaism. These principles are now a part of the Orthodox liturgy.

One must believe …

First principle: In the existence of God.

Second principle: That God is one.

Third principle: That God is incorporeal.

Fourth principle: That God is eternal; nothing existed before Him.

Fifth principle: That nothing beneath Him, such as angels, stars, planets, and the like, is worthy of worship or praise.

Sixth principle: That prophecy is possible.

Seventh principle: That Moses was superior to all other prophets before and after.

Eighth principle: That the entire written and oral Torah came from God through Moses.

Ninth principle: In the authenticity and divinity of the Torah.

Tenth principle: That God is omniscient.

Eleventh principle: That God rewards and punishes each according to their deeds.

Twelfth principle: That the Messiah will come.

Thirteenth principle: In the bodily resurrection of the dead.

If a man gives up any one of these fundamental principles, he has removed himself from the Jewish community and is considered a heretic and an unbeliever.

role for women within the synagogue as well as separation of the sexes during worship services and often in school classrooms after a certain age. Many rituals incumbent upon men, such as reading from the Torah or putting on the prayer shawl (tallith) or the phylacteries (*tefillin*), are largely frowned upon or forbidden for Orthodox girls and women.

Orthodox Jews firmly reject burial practices such as cremation, embalming, and even autopsies (except under certain exceptional conditions) as violations of Jewish law and expressions of disrespect to the deceased.

RITES OF PASSAGE Orthodox Jews observe the same basic ceremonies (circumcision, bar/bat mitzvah, wedding, burial) as other Jews, differing in the degree to which they adhere to traditional custom and what role women and girls may play. The influence of feminism on liberal Jews has led to greater emphasis in the Orthodox world on ceremonies marking rites of passage for girls, such as naming and bat mitzvah, though more so in the Modern Orthodox than in the Haredi community.

MEMBERSHIP The Holocaust in Europe decimated many Sephardic communities (in Amsterdam, Greece, and Italy, for example) and almost all of the eastern European Orthodox world by destroying entire families, towns, Hasidic dynasties, and major Orthodox educational institutions, disproportionate to the more liberal Jewish communities who lived abroad or managed to escape. As a result of high birthrates and, in some communities, extensive campaigns of outreach or proselytizing to less observant Jews, the Orthodox community worldwide has since rebounded.

RELIGIOUS TOLERANCE Within traditional Judaism there is a greater ideological tolerance shown toward gentiles than toward non-Orthodox Jews, because according to traditional Jewish thinking, non-Jews may achieve salvation by following a few basic universal practices, whereas Jews are considered sinners if they do not observe halakhah in full. Because of cultural and religious ties, however, Orthodox Jews, especially the Haredi, are generally more socially comfortable with non-Orthodox Jews than with non-Jews.

Few Orthodox leaders are willing to grant legitimacy to non-Orthodox expressions of Judaism, which cast doubt upon (or outright reject) the principle of "Torah Min HaShamayim" (the divine revelation for the Five

of the Sabbath and holidays, kashruth (dietary laws), and *taharat hamishpakhah* (commandments relating to family purity). Many engage in daily worship, regular and intensive study of sacred texts, and acts of charity. Modesty (*tsniut*) is an essential value, leading to a less public

Books of Moses) and the obligation to live based on halakhah as interpreted by Orthodox rabbis. While some among the Orthodox left might promote intra-Jewish dialogue, even on theological issues, and many more among the "modern/centrist" community would promote cooperation on a variety of intra-Jewish issues (such as charity work), the Haredi Orthodox embrace a calculated policy of separatism and withdrawal in nearly all matters not directly related to Jewish survival.

SOCIAL JUSTICE Performing kind deeds (*gemilut hesed*) and acts of charity (*tzedekah*) are considered commandments of the highest order in Judaism, though in general Orthodox Jews tend to devote themselves to causes within the Jewish world. Orthodox communities are often distinguished by their generosity to Jewish causes (giving at least 10 percent of one's income to charity is the norm) and the time given to care for those in need.

SOCIAL ASPECTS Because of strict prohibitions against premarital sex, marriage in the Orthodox community usually takes place at an earlier age than in the Jewish and general population. In some Haredi circles (particularly the children of prominent rabbis), marriages may be arranged by parents or by a matchmaker.

Family life is extremely important within the Orthodox community, and because of the biblical commandment to be "fruitful and multiply," families tend to be large. Men and women share in the childrearing tasks. An element that distinguishes Modern from Haredi Orthodoxy is that men in the latter community, particularly those in Israel, often engage in full-time study of sacred texts, leaving their wives to manage the home and to serve as breadwinners.

CONTROVERSIAL ISSUES Various controversies plaguing Orthodoxy include the role of women in communal and ritual life, the legitimacy of non-Orthodox ideologies, preserving the unity of the Jewish people, the proper amount of isolation from (versus assimilation into) non-Jewish culture, the sanctity of the State of Israel, the role of religion in Israeli political life, and the increasing concentration upon fastidiousness in ritual.

CULTURAL IMPACT It is difficult to identify cultural elements within Judaism and secular culture as a whole that are directly attributable to Orthodox Judaism. An exception is the collection and production of Jewish ceremonial and ritual objects, which are often handmade and of expensive materials, such as gold. This area of Jewish art has been growing, in part because *hiddur mitzvah* (beautifying a commandment), a value traditionally held by Orthodox Jews, has been increasingly adopted by Jews of all movements.

Zion Zohar

See Also Vol. I: *Judaism*

Bibliography

Ellenson, David Harry. *Tradition in Transition: Orthodoxy, Halakhah, and the Boundaries of Modern Jewish Identity.* Lanham, Md.: University Press of America, 1989.

Goldberg, Harvey E., ed. *Judaism Viewed from Within and Without: Anthropological Studies.* Albany: State University of New York Press, 1987.

Heilman, Samuel C. *Defenders of the Faith: Inside Ultra-Orthodox Jewry.* New York: Knopf Publishing, 1993.

Heilman, Samuel C., and Steven Martin Cohen. *Cosmopolitans and Parochials: Modern Orthodox Jews in America.* Chicago: University of Chicago Press, 1989.

Hundert, Gershon, ed. *Essential Papers on Hasidism: Origins to Present.* New York: New York University Press, 1991.

Sacks, Jonathan. *Arguments for the Sake of Heaven: Emerging Trends in Traditional Judaism.* Northvale, New Jersey: Jason Aronson, 1991.

Safran, Bezalel, ed. *Hasidism: Continuity or Innovation.* Cambridge, Mass.: Harvard University Press, 1988.

Verthaim, Aharon. *Law and Custom in Hasidism.* Hoboken, N.J.: Ktav, 1992.

Zohar, Zion. "Hasidic Jews of New York State." In *Encyclopedia of New York State.* Syracuse, N.Y.: Syracuse University Press, 2004.

————. "Oriental Jewry Confronts Modernity: The Case of Ovadia Yosef." *Modern Judaism,* May 2004.

————. "Sephardic Jews of New York State." In *Encyclopedia of New York State.* Syracuse, N.Y.: Syracuse University Press, 2004.

————. "Spirituality, Kavvanah, and Ethics: Ancient Wisdom for a Modern World." In *Studies in Jewish Civilization,* vol. 13. Edited by Leonard J. Greenspoon and Ronald A. Simkins. Lincoln, Nebr.: Creighton University Press, 2003.

Judaism

Reform Judaism

FOUNDED: Early nineteenth century C.E.

RELIGION AS A PERCENTAGE OF WORLD POPULATION: .06 percent

OVERVIEW Reform Judaism is a movement that believes in modifying traditional Jewish law and practice to make it consistent with contemporary social and cultural conditions. The movement began in the early nineteenth century, when Jewish reformers, responding to political and other changes in western and central Europe, began altering the Jewish worship service. Over time rabbis and laypeople sympathetic to these changes coalesced as a distinct group, and by the middle of the century, they had developed a set of ideological principles distinct from traditional Jewish doctrine. This Reform movement spread throughout most of western Europe, and by the end of the nineteenth century it had become a prominent feature of American Judaism.

Reform Jews are a minority of the Jewish population in most countries around the world, but they are a growing presence in Israel and the former Soviet Union, and they form the largest Jewish denomination in the United States. About a third of American Jews affiliated with a synagogue belong to a Reform synagogue.

HISTORY Influenced by the ideals of the Enlightenment and by promises of political and social freedom, the first reformers were German Jews seeking to live as both Jews and members of the larger society. They aimed to introduce modern aesthetics and strict decorum into the traditionally informal and jumbled Jewish worship service.

By the early 1840s a trained Reform rabbinic leadership emerged in central Europe. Reform conferences in Brunswick in 1844, Frankfurt in 1845, and Breslau in 1846 gave rabbis an opportunity to clarify their beliefs and discuss ways to derive innovative practices from those beliefs. Despite the shadow of anti-Semitism and the threat of forced conversion to Christianity, the movement continued to grow in Germany and much of central Europe throughout the nineteenth and early twentieth centuries.

The Reform movement in the United States developed in a much freer and more pluralistic atmosphere. From its beginnings in Charleston, South Carolina, in 1824, American Reform Judaism grew rapidly, especially after the large migration of German Jews to the United States in the late 1840s. During the 1870s and 1880s German immigrant Rabbi Isaac Mayer Wise founded the central institutions that formed the organizational basis of American Reform Judaism.

CENTRAL DOCTRINES Distinguishing Reform from other branches of Judaism is the belief that Jewish practices have evolved over time and should continue to do so. Most Reform Jews agree that God did not reveal the Torah (the written Jewish law) to Moses at one definitive moment. Rather the Torah and the vast corpus of Jewish literature developed gradually, reflecting changes in the social and cultural life of the Jewish people.

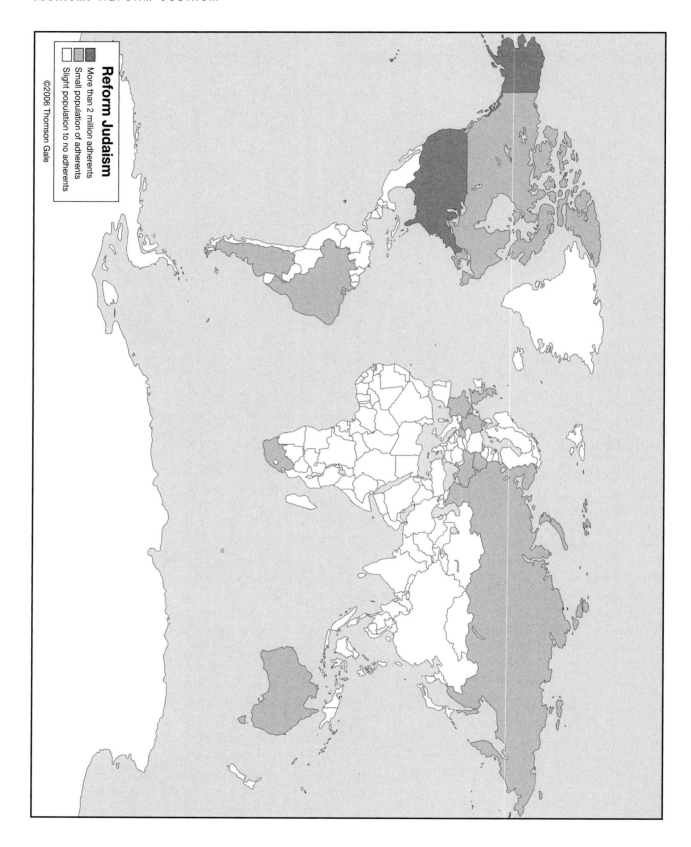

Reform Judaism and Conservative Judaism have common roots—the reaction of Jews to social and political forces in nineteenth-century Europe. The Reform branch, however, does not believe that Jewish law (including, for example, its dietary restrictions) is binding. Reform Jews have also emphasized the ethical component of Judaism over ritual practices, and Reform institutions have given lay Jews more authority in determining the legitimacy of various religious practices and principles.

MORAL CODE OF CONDUCT Reform Jews have emphasized the central role that ethics should play in a religious system. The prophets of the Bible, such as Micah, Isaiah, and Hosea, placed emphasis on social responsibility, and Reform Jews see the prophets as a model for their religious duty to teach the world an ethical vision for society.

By the late twentieth century the Reform movement had embraced many liberal notions of what is moral and ethical. In the United States the Reform branch differs most prominently from Conservative Judaism in its acceptance of intermarriage (between Jews and non-Jews), gay and lesbian marriage, and the ordination of gay rabbis. The Reform movement has also developed an ethical code on other issues, such as sexuality, proper business practices, and civic responsibility.

SACRED BOOKS The Reform movement has emphasized the importance of the Hebrew Bible (including the Torah) over the Talmud (comprising rabbinic discussions of Jewish law and practice). Early reformers felt the Talmud was overemphasized in traditional Jewish education, and Reform Jews have seen the Bible as having a more universal significance than the Talmud. The Reform movement has produced numerous prayer books for use in the home and the synagogue.

SACRED SYMBOLS Reform Jews have maintained traditional Jewish symbols, such as the menorah, but have sometimes interpreted them in a dramatically different way. They may see the Torah, the most sacred Jewish symbol, as an emblem of human freedom, whereas an Orthodox Jew may see it as representing the eternal commitment to Jewish law. Because the Reform movement stresses the autonomy of the individual, Reform Jews may interpret religious symbols in their own way.

EARLY AND MODERN LEADERS Israel Jacobson, one of the earliest figures of the Reform movement, estab-

A man is shown blowing the Shofar on the Jewish holiday of Yom Kippur.
© TED SPIEGEL/CORBIS.

lished the first Reform prayer chapel in 1801 in the German state of Westphalia. He made changes in Jewish worship and education, setting the pattern for lay-led innovations. Rabbi Isaac Mayer Wise emigrated from Bohemia to the United States in 1846 and built the American Reform movement. A populist who wholeheartedly embraced the use of English (rather than the more usual German) in Reform congregations, Wise founded the central institutions of American Reform Judaism, wrote a popular prayer book, and established a Jewish newspaper.

Rabbi Alexander M. Schindler, president of the Union of American Hebrew Congregations (UAHC) from 1973 to 1996, is known for his assertive support of civil rights, world peace, nuclear disarmament, a "Marshall Plan" for the poor, a ban on the death penalty, feminism, gay rights, and outreach to intermarried couples. Rabbi Eric Yoffie, who became president of the UAHC in 1996, is known for his advocacy of a

Rabbi Isaac Mayer Wise (1819-1900) was the greatest organizer of American Reform Jewish institutions. © BETTMANN/CORBIS.

"Reform revolution" that would involve more intensive Jewish education, greater liturgical innovation, and a reinvigoration of worship.

MAJOR THEOLOGIANS AND AUTHORS Among early Reform theologians, Rabbi Abraham Geiger and Rabbi David Einhorn stand out. Geiger was a leading pulpit rabbi and scholar in mid-nineteenth-century Germany. He believed that a critical understanding of Jewish history and an appreciation of the moral genius in Judaism should serve as the basis of a new Judaism shorn of archaic practices. Einhorn, who emigrated from Germany to the United States in 1854, was considered the leader of the radical wing of American Reform Judaism. His writings, which argued for a universal moral sensibility and a theologically unswerving attitude, conflicted with the more pragmatic program of his contemporary, Rabbi Isaac Wise, who emphasized responding effectively to changing social trends. Over time Wise's views have proved the more popular.

Rabbi Eugene Borowitz, a leading Reform Jewish theologian in the United States, has emphasized the responsibility of the individual Jew to engage with Jewish tradition in an open, critical manner.

ORGANIZATIONAL STRUCTURE The World Union for Progressive Judaism is an organizational body serving Reform and other congregations in more than 40 countries. The three central institutions of American Reform Judaism are the Union for Reform Judaism (representing more than 900 Reform congregations), the Central Conference of American Rabbis, and the Hebrew Union College–Jewish Institute of Religion (the largest Reform rabbinical school in the world, with campuses in Cincinnati, New York City, Los Angeles, and Jerusalem). The Leo Baeck College in London also trains Reform rabbis.

HOUSES OF WORSHIP AND HOLY PLACES Originally Jews named their houses of worship synagogues to distinguish them from the original Temple in Jerusalem, destroyed by the Romans in the year 70 C.E. Reform Jews, however, traditionally called their houses of worship temples, indicating that these structures replaced the original Temple as their center for prayer and that they did not aspire to rebuild the Jerusalem Temple or to return to live in Israel even in a future messianic time. The contemporary Reform movement sees the local temple as a place for worship, study, and fellowship and uses "temple" and "synagogue" synonymously.

WHAT IS SACRED? While the Torah and other religious articles have a degree of holiness, Reform Judaism discourages overly emphasizing symbols or places. The most sacred act is the study of the Torah, but all actions that do not violate human dignity are considered sacred and significant.

HOLIDAYS AND FESTIVALS Reform Jews observe all the major Jewish holidays, but shorten the length of Rosh Hashanah and Passover by a day. They also omit the festive seder meal on the second night of Passover. Reform Jews are not required to follow many of the traditional restrictions on behavior during Jewish holidays, such as not driving in cars and not writing.

MODE OF DRESS Reform Jews dress like non-Jews as part of the movement's commitment to integrating into the host society (maintaining a distinctive religion, but not at the expense of social segregation).

THE PLATFORMS OF REFORM JUDAISM

The Central Conference of American Rabbis has issued four platforms that define the principles of American Reform Judaism and reflect its ongoing mediation between tradition and modernity. The following are excerpts from these four platforms:

The Pittsburgh Platform (1885): "We consider ourselves no longer a nation, but a religious community, and therefore expect neither a return to Palestine, nor … the restoration of any of the laws concerning the Jewish state."

The Columbus Platform (1937): "Judaism as a way of life requires … the retention and development of such customs, symbols and ceremonies as possess inspirational value."

Centenary Platform (1976): "The widespread threats to freedom, the … explosion of new knowledge and of ever more powerful technologies, and the spiritual emptiness of much of Western culture have taught us to … reassert what remains perennially valid in Judaism's teaching."

The Pittsburgh Statement of Principles (1999): "We believe that we must … actively encourage those who are seeking a spiritual home to find it in Judaism."

DIETARY PRACTICES Reform Jews do not generally observe kashruth, the strict Jewish dietary laws. Some abstain from certain types of foods that are regarded as particularly nonkosher, such as pork and sometimes shellfish. Most Reform synagogues prohibit the serving of such foods at temple-sponsored events and may also require the traditional separation of milk and meat so that everyone can eat freely regardless of their level of observance.

RITUALS The Reform synagogue has services on Friday nights, and sometimes on Saturday mornings, in celebration of the Sabbath. The largest services are on Rosh Hashanah and Yom Kippur. The style of ritual in Reform congregations has changed over the past 50 years from formal to participatory. Many contemporary Reform Jews have reembraced ritual practice, but because they are looking for spiritual meaning rather than a faithfulness to God's command, they do so selectively.

RITES OF PASSAGE Reform Jews commemorate all the traditional Jewish rites of passage, but the Reform movement's flexibility allows members to individually design their rites to meet their spiritual needs. Reformers have also developed new rituals, believing that if a new ceremony is meaningful, there is no reason not to introduce it into practice. One nontraditional ritual is the passing of the Torah at many Reform bar mitzvahs (Jewish coming-of-age ceremonies). The grandparents hold the Torah and then hand it to the parents, who pass it to the 13-year-old, symbolizing the desire to pass Jewish family traditions from generation to generation.

MEMBERSHIP The Reform movement has adopted an active outreach program to families in which at least one of the parents is Jewish. Reform Jews also welcome non-Jewish religious seekers. Reform congregations in the United States have become increasingly multicultural, with significant numbers of African-American, Hispanic, and Asian members. Although historically membership in a synagogue required conversion to Judaism, people have increasingly become active in Reform congregations without formally converting. Still, most Reform rabbis encourage conversion for the sake of strengthening Jewish life and families.

RELIGIOUS TOLERANCE Reform Judaism is a very tolerant denomination and has been a leader in interfaith dialogue. As in other branches of Judaism, Reform Jews believe righteous individuals of all faiths can go to heaven. Therefore, it is not necessary to convert to Judaism in order to obtain salvation.

SOCIAL JUSTICE For Reform Jews practice is more important than belief, and ethics are more important than ritual. The early reformers believed deeply in working with their Christian neighbors to make the world more livable, peaceful, and just; this belief was central to their religious worldview. Reform Judaism has often been called "Prophetic Judaism" because of the movement's strong identification with the ethical and moral vision of the biblical prophets, who emphasized social responsibility. The Reform movement maintains a political-action office in Washington, D.C., and provides a variety of resources to synagogues that want to engage in social-action projects.

SOCIAL ASPECTS Most Reform Jews would agree that an ideal family consists of two loving partners—in a monogamous, religiously sanctified union—and their children. While sanctioning the traditional Jewish view that having and raising children is a sacred obligation, the Reform movement has opposed the "family-centered" agenda of the religious right.

CONTROVERSIAL ISSUES Women were regarded as equal to men from the beginning of the Reform movement. Religious roles remained traditionally gender based for much of the twentieth century, but since the 1970s women have read prayers, served on synagogue boards, and become rabbis and cantors.

The American Reform movement is unequivocally committed to supporting full social and legal equality for gays and lesbians, and it has appointed a considerable number as rabbis and cantors. Many Reform rabbis officiate at same-sex commitment ceremonies.

Reform Judaism has consistently upheld the right of women to choose to have an abortion and the duty of parents and schools to teach children about safe sex and birth control. The movement opposes the death penalty, favors protecting the environment, and supports gun-control legislation.

CULTURAL IMPACT The Reform movement has had a significant impact on the cultural life of many countries, especially the United States. This influence is reflected by its representation in literature, which commonly includes Reform Jews, synagogues, and rabbis, and in films and television shows, often featuring Reform synagogues or weddings ceremonies involving Reform rabbis.

Dana Evan Kaplan and Evan Moffic

See Also Vol. 1: *Judaism*

Bibliography

Borowitz, Eugene B. *Reform Judaism Today.* New York: Behrman House, 1983.

Hirt-Manheimer, Aron, ed. *The Jewish Condition: Essays on Contemporary Judaism Honoring Alexander M. Schindler.* New York: Union of American Hebrew Congregations Press, 1995.

Hoffman, Lawrence A. *The Journey Home: Discovering the Deep Spiritual Wisdom of the Jewish Tradition.* Boston: Beacon Press, 2002.

Kaplan, Dana Evan. *American Reform Judaism: An Introduction.* New Brunswick, N.J.: Rutgers University Press, 2003.

———. *Contemporary Debates in American Reform Judaism.* London and New York: Routledge, 2001.

———. *Platforms and Prayer Books.* Lanham, Md.: Rowman and Littlefield, 2002.

Kertzer, Morris N. *What Is a Jew?* New York: Macmillan, 1993.

Meyer, Michael A. *Response to Modernity: A History of the Reform Movement in Judaism.* New York: Oxford University Press, 1988.

Silverstein, Alan. *Alternatives to Assimilation.* Waltham, Mass.: Brandeis University Press, 1994.

Vorspan, Albert, and David Saperstein. *Tough Choices: Jewish Perspectives on Social Justice.* New York: Union of American Hebrew Congregations Press, 1992.

Washofsky, Mark. *Jewish Living: A Guide to Contemporary Reform Practice.* New York: Union of American Hebrew Congregations Press, 2001.

Shinto

FOUNDED: c. 500 C.E.

RELIGION AS A PERCENTAGE OF WORLD POPULATION: 1.8 percent

OVERVIEW The term Shinto refers to the worship of local divinities, called *kami*, in the Japanese archipelago. "Shinto" literally means "the way of the *kami*." It is difficult to pinpoint the historical origins of this Japanese religion. It has no founder, so its beginnings cannot be connected with an individual. Indeed, the location of the origins of Shinto in history depends upon how the term Shinto itself is defined. For centuries nativist scholars in Japan (*kokugakusha*) and apologists for the imperial family have claimed that Shinto is the expression of the natural and innate spirituality of the Japanese people. They have argued that this spirituality—styled Yamato-damashii, or "the spirit/soul of Yamato," Yamato being the name for ancient Japan—is unique to the Japanese as a people and has not changed over the centuries. They have projected the origins of Shinto back into the misty past and connected it with a divinely ordained political order. From a modern perspective, claims such as these are ideological and xenophobic in nature; they are not historically grounded. Yet, while it is impossible to accept this picture of Shinto as historically accurate, the very fact that so many Japanese scholars and Shinto apologists have proffered it is itself useful for the historian of religions. It tells us that defining and dating Shinto has always been a political act, one related to the rhetorical construction of a collective identity and to the goal of legitimating imperial rule.

The noun *kami*, which is both singular and plural in usage, is usually translated as "deities," "divinities," or "gods." In contrast to the mainstream traditions of the three Western monotheisms (Judaism, Christianity, and Islam), which hold that the divine and the human are categorically different forms of being, in Japan the line between the human and the divine is blurred. The emperor and empress, for example, were long held to be living *kami* in human form. The founders of some so-called new religions of the nineteenth and twentieth centuries were also considered to be living *kami* (*hitogami* or *ikigami*). More important, *kami* are not necessarily beings at all. Islands, mountains, rocks, trees, springs, rivers, waterfalls, whirlpools, and any number of other phenomena are referred to as *kami*. This has led some scholars to suggest that Shinto is a form of animism. Yet not all natural phenomena are sacred; only those that evoke a specific sort of response (for example, wonder, awe, a sense of the uncanny, or fear) in people are said to possess *kami* nature.

HISTORY In an important sense the terms Japan, the Japanese, and Shinto are anachronisms when they are used in reference to the Jōmon period (c. 8000–200 B.C.E.) or even the early centuries of the Common Era. No nation as such, no racially or ethnically distinct and unified people, and no unified religion were found in the Japanese archipelago during this time.

The earliest written records that may refer to the islands today known as Japan are Chinese texts. The third-century C.E. *Wei Chih* (History of the Kingdom of Wei), for instance, speaks of the land of the Wa, an is-

TORII. An important symbol of Shinto is the torii. It is an open gateway that consists of two upright bars and two crossbars. Torii are found in front of almost every Shinto shrine, functioning as a boundary between the physical and spiritual worlds. (THOMSON GALE)

land chain with many different principalities. The largest, Yamatai, was ruled by a woman who exercised shamanic powers, going into trances and communicating with the gods. The people practiced divination using tortoise shells and tattooed their bodies. It would be a stretch to call this Shinto, however, since so little is known about the religious beliefs and practices of the time. In the period just before writing was introduced, the people organized themselves into many extended clans (*uji*). Each clan was united by the shared worship of the clan *kami.* The political leader of each clan (*uji-gami*) also served as the chief ritualist—a pattern that was to be followed by the emperors and empresses later, after the establishment of a centralized kingdom. The people lived in an oral society in which all knowledge (e.g., religious, technological, and genealogical) was preserved and handed down from generation to generation by word of mouth. Immigrants from the present-day Korean peninsula brought writing to the islands, as well as other new technologies (iron forging, bronze casting, and pottery, for example), in the early centuries of the Common Era. They also introduced various aspects of the Chinese and Korean peninsular cultures, including religious values, concepts, and practices; cosmological constructions; and social and political structures.

Rice paddy culture was introduced to the region in the Yayoi period (c. 200 B.C.E.–250 C.E.). The subsequent agricultural revolution allowed the people to shift from a hunting-and-gathering stage of culture to one of

surplus food stores, expanded permanent settlements, differentiated social classes, and occupational specialization. Gradually, some clans gained hegemony over others and began to exercise broader control over more people. Numerous large burial mounds (*kofun*), often in the shape of a keyhole, date from this time. The largest of these, said to be the burial site of Emperor Nintoku (reigned 313–99 B.C.E.), covers 80 acres. Although it is anachronistic to refer to the rulers at this time as "emperors," the presence of such impressive *kofun* indicates that some clans had the power to marshal the labor of thousands of persons for extended periods of time.

The large-scale changes wrought by the introduction of agriculture were not limited to the socioeconomic realm, however. Equally important, agriculture produced a revolution in religious imagery, symbolism, and practice. It is no accident that the architectural form of Shinto shrines resembles that of ancient granaries in Southeast Asia and Polynesia. The ritual calendar of the people came to be punctuated with rites and festivals related to the agricultural cycle, from the rituals for the planting of rice seedlings to the harvest festival in the fall. Moreover, when a centralized sacred kingship developed in the sixth and seventh centuries, the rulers styled themselves as the guarantors of fertility and bountiful harvests throughout the land, just as the Chinese emperor did. This intimate relationship between the ruler and agriculture is clearly in evidence in the myths preserved in the eighth-century *Kojiki* (Record of Ancient Matters) and *Nihonshoki* (Chronicle of Japan), especially those concerning Amaterasu, the sun goddess.

In an important sense it is the dual presence of agricultural rites and a centralized sacral kingship that permits us to speak of the emergence of Shinto. The term Shinto or the phrase "the way of the *kami*" does not refer to a timeless indigenous religion. Rather, it was coined in response to the presence of other sacred ways, most especially Taoism and Buddhism, brought from the Asian mainland. In terms of East Asian civilizations, Japan is fairly young—much younger than the Korean or Chinese civilizations, for instance. The earliest narrative texts from Japan date only from the eighth century C.E. The *Kojiki* (712), *Nihonshoki* (720; also known as *Nihongi*), and the *Man'yōshū* (late eighth century), among the earliest texts from Japan, provide valuable information about the religion of this time (at least among the elite) and preserve many myths. It is difficult to say, though, how far back into the past the religious beliefs, values, and practices found therein can be projected. Only a few

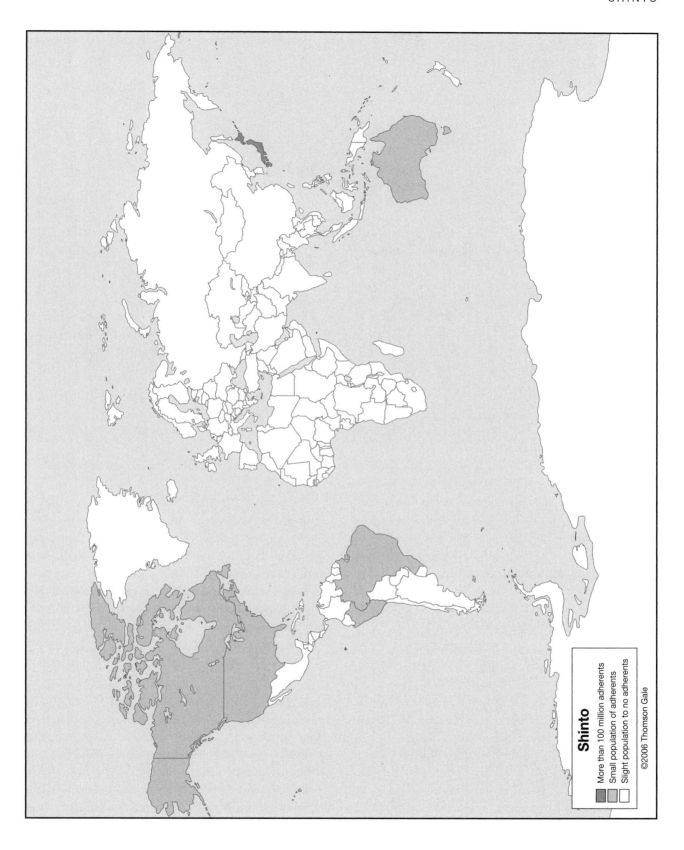

Shinto

More than 100 million adherents
Small population of adherents
Slight population to no adherents

©2006 Thomson Gale

Female shrine assistants perform kagura, *Shinto ritual dances at the end of a festival on Ikema Island, Japan. Shinto and Shinto-Buddhist festivals are known as* matsuri. © LINDSAY HEBBERD/CORBIS.

contemporary Shinto apologists accept the chronology of the *Nihonshoki,* which dates the founding of Japan to 660 B.C.E., during the reign of the legendary emperor Jimmu. No serious historian does so. This chronology includes legendary figures with Methuselah-like life spans, as well as historical figures who lived closer to the time of the chronicle's composition.

The so-called Japanese historical chronicles actually present a "mythistory," not unlike that found in the Hebrew Bible. A "mythistory" blends myths—narratives with divine actors—into historical narratives of human action in order to create an ontological distinction and a pedigree for the ruling elite or for a people. In this case, it also seeks to legitimate a social hierarchy with an uneven distribution of wealth, power, privilege, and prestige. The *Kojiki, Nihonshoki,* and *Man'yōshū* all came out of the elite sectors of society. The *Kojiki,* for instance, was first ordered to be committed to writing by the emperor Temmu (reigned 673–86). The "mythistory" these works recount claims that the imperial family is descended directly from Amaterasu, the sun goddess. Like the pharaohs of Egypt, the rulers of ancient Japan claimed to be suprahuman or, more precisely, *kami* in human form (*arahitogami*). It is unknown how many people believed this to be true, but the assertion became the official position and was at the center of the imperial cult.

In 645 and 646 court leaders promulgated the Great Reform (Taika) in an attempt to restructure the political realm, to formalize a social hierarchy with the emperor at the top, and to create a hierarchy of religious institutions. Land grants were made to numerous Shinto shrines (such as Ise, Izumo, and Kashima), which gained prestige by becoming identified with the imperial family. This reform was followed in 701 by the Taihō Code (Taihō Ritsuryo), which established a Bureau of State (Dajōkan) and a Bureau of Kami Affairs (Jingikan) at the top of the government hierarchy. The Taihō Code solidified the government's investment in the state-sponsored *kami* cults, both in economic terms and in terms of symbolic legitimation. It also sought to strengthen government control over Buddhist institutions. These reforms may be seen as efforts to weaken clan-based religio-political institutions and to replace these with imperially sponsored and controlled ones. While the Taihō Code was never fully implemented, the ideal of a divine emperor as the sacred center of the land and the cosmos was to continue to attract supporters down to the modern period.

As time went on, the imperial court began to grant additional titles, special hereditary rights, and prerogatives to specific families and to members of occupational guilds (be). From the second half of the ninth century until the mid-twelfth century, the Nakatomi family (later known as the Fujiwara) parlayed the hereditary status of its members as priests into real political power for several centuries. Nakatomi men became powerful ministers in the government, while daughters were strategically married into the imperial family in order to assure that Fujiwara grandchildren would accede to the throne. Numerous shrines and temples, controlled by aristocrats, were granted tax-free landholdings and estates and thus became sources of great wealth. As a result the religion of the wealthy elite, like their lifestyle, came to differ in some important ways from that of the peasants and laboring masses. Nevertheless, the religion of the elite and that of the commoners continued to share many beliefs and practices. Historians of Shinto have yet to investigate fully the ways in which the religious worlds of commoner and elite were both alike and different.

In the Nara period (710–94) Buddhism gained significant government support and patronage, most especially from the emperor Shōmu (reigned 701–56), who himself took the tonsure (i.e., shaved his head and donned Buddhist robes). From the start, however, Buddhism was assimilated with the kami cults in various ways. In 742 Shōmu issued an edict in which he declared that people should worship the kami but know that the original forms (honji) of these kami were actually various Buddhas. This is an expression of the Buddhist concept of assimilation, known in Japanese as honji-suijaku. An important example of the identification of a kami with a Buddha is the god Hachiman. The emperor sought to cast a great bronze Buddha (daibutsu) for Tōdai-ji, the Great Eastern Temple, as a protector of the country. Things did not go well, however. The casting failed, the imperial treasury ran short of funds, and many of the people in the countryside began to grumble

Shinto priests arrive for the beginning of a New Year's festival. This event is an example of a Shinto seasonal festival that is designed to renew time or to continue the cosmic and agricultural cycles of time. © REUTERS NEWMEDIA INC./CORBIS.

about being forced to contribute labor and funds. With the success of the project in jeopardy, two developments turned the tide.

First, according to the Shoku Nihongi, the kami Usa Hachiman in Kyushu delivered an oracle that he would "lead the kami of heaven and earth" to support the project. In gratitude the emperor had this kami enshrined in Tōdai-ji as its protective deity. There Buddhist priests recited sutras before this kami, who came to be known as a bodhisattva—that is, a fully enlightened being who forgoes entrance into paradise in order to bring all living things to enlightenment and salvation—and as the divinized spirit of the legendary emperor Ō. In time the syncretic cult of Hachiman would become one of the largest and most widespread in the country. It is important to recognize the extent to which the kami cults and the worship of Buddhist deities were intertwined. In the city of Nara the Buddhist temples Tōdai-ji and Kōfuku-ji and the Shinto Kasuga Shrine were, to use the term of the scholar Allan Grapard, an integrated "multiplex."

A visitor approaches the Tsurugaoka Hachiman Shrine in Kamakura, Japan. Most Shinto shrines should be thought of as consisting of both the buildings and the sacred sites on which they stand. © MICHAEL S. YAMASHITA/CORBIS.

That is, these institutions were not independent, just as the worship of Shinto and Buddhist deities was not distinct.

Second, Emperor Shōmu turned to Gyōgi (670–749), a charismatic Buddhist leader who had won widespread acclaim among the commoners. Gyōgi was not a fully ordained priest; rather, he practiced a shamanic form of Buddhism that blended mountain asceticism, divination, and faith healing with the boddhisattva ideal. Religious figures like Gyōgi were known as *ubasoku* or *hijiri*. They represent a type of religious leader, the holy man, who combines social activism with an implicit (if not explicit) critique of the religious and political establishment. As might be expected, some of the ecclesiastical heads of Buddhist institutions did not appreciate such unauthorized figures encroaching on what they considered to be their religious "turf." Reportedly,

Gyōgi traveled to the Ise Shrines in order to present a relic of the Buddha to Amaterasu. There he received a favorable communication from the *kami* authorizing him to solicit funds for the completion of the giant statue. (At a more mundane level, the discovery of new deposits of gold also enabled the court to complete the giant Buddha statue.) As was the case with Usa Hachiman, reports of oracles from *kami* served to suggest that Buddhist forms of devotion were not antithetical to the worship of the *kami*. Significantly, the commoners called Gyōgi "Gyōgi bosatsu"—the bodhisattva Gyōgi. In doing so, they extended the concept of *hitogami* (a *kami* in human form) to a Buddhist figure, though one outside the power elite associated with the court. The common people would continue to exercise their own power and prerogatives to acknowledge individuals as holy or divine over the following centuries, right down to the present.

The amalgamation of Buddhism and Shinto accelerated in the Heian period (710–1185), after the capital was moved to Kyoto. The two most influential schools of Japanese Buddhism—Tendai (in Chinese, T'ien-tai) and Shingon—were both esoteric schools. That is, they taught that, besides an exoteric truth and teaching that could be publicly communicated, there was also a deeper esoteric, or secret, religious truth. The concept of *honji-suijaku* (true essence and trace manifestation), found in the Lotus Sutra, was used to argue that Japanese *kami* were the temporally and spatially local manifestations of eternal Buddhas and bodhisattvas. The success of such identifications led to the building of Buddhist temples on Shinto shrine grounds, and vice versa, a pattern that was to be the norm through the 1870s. For their part, Shinto priests associated with Tendai and Shingon institutions formulated their own version of the identity of *kami* and Buddhist divinities. The origins of Sannō Itchijitsu Shinto (Mountain King-One Truth) can be traced to Saichō (767–822), the founder of the Tendai school. He worshiped the *kami* of Mount Hiei, where he established his headquarters and monastery, as the Buddhist avatar Sannō Gongen, the Mountain King, who was identified with Yakushi, the healing Buddha. Similarly, he worshiped the *kami* of Ōmiwa as the historical Buddha.

Shinto priests affiliated with the Shingon school of Buddhism promulgated Ryōbu Shinto, which identified the *kami* of the Inner Shrine of Ise with the Great Sun Buddha and the *kami* of the Outer Shrine with the Buddha of the Diamond Realm. This form of Shinto also

Glossary

Amaterasu the sun goddess

arahitogami a *kami* in human form

Fukko Shintō the "pure Shinto" of the scholar Motoori Norinaga

gon-gūji Shinto assistant head priest

goryō haunting spirit of a wronged individual

gūji Shinto head priest

Hachiman a Shinto-Buddhist deity popular with samurai

harae purification rites

himorogi sacred space demarcated by a rope (*shimenawa*) or other marker

hitogami a living *kami* in human form

honji-suijaku Buddhist philosophy of the assimilation of Buddhas and *kami*

iwasaka sacred stone circles

kagura Shinto ritual dances

kami Shinto deity or deities

kannushi lower-ranking Shinto priest

kegare bodily or spiritual pollution

ki vital spirit or energy

kokugaku Japanese nativist school of scholarship

Kojiki eighth-century Japanese mythological text

kokoro heart-mind

Man'yōshū eighth-century Japanese poetry anthology

marebito wandering spirits of the dead

matsuri Shinto festivals

miko female medium or shaman

Nihon shoki eighth-century chronicle of Japanese history

negi senior Shinto priest

norito Shinto liturgical prayers

oni demon

ubasoku, or hijiri mountain ascetics and holy men

yuitsu genpon sōgen shintō "unique original essence Shinto"

shinjin goitsu the essential identity of *kami* and humans

shintai the "body" of a *kami*, the object into which it descends following a ritual summons

torii gate marking the entrance to the grounds of a Shinto shrine

---

incorporated the use of such other elements of Buddhist practice as esoteric mantras (*dharani*); *mudra,* or magical hand signs; and mandalas (elaborate paintings used in meditative practice, as objects of worship, and as teaching devices) that represent key Buddhist concepts and beings. In 859 the Yoshida Shrine, a branch of the Kasuga Shrine in Nara, was established on a hill in the northeast sector of Kyoto. The *kami* enshrined there was Kasuga Daimyōjin, or Ame-no-koyane-no-mikoto, the ancestral deity of the Fujiwara. The Yoshida, or Urabe, family remained close to the imperial family and to the Fujiwara, which after all were also becoming one and the same through marriages of convenience. The Yoshida priests offered lectures on the *Kojiki* and the *Nihonshoki,* extolling the divine origins of the imperial family and the prestige of their own sacerdotal line.

Two other developments in the Heian period bear mention. First, the belief in goryō, the haunting spirits of persons who had died violently or who had been wronged, spread rapidly. Goryō were attributed with the power to cause illness, madness, death, fires, lightning strikes, and other calamities. One of the most famous goryō was that of Sugawara no Michizane (845–903), a scholar, poet, and government minister who was falsely accused of treason and sent into exile in Kyushu, where he died. After an oracle announced that a series of "natural" disasters had, in fact, been caused by Michizane's angry spirit, the emperor pardoned him posthumously and had his spirit enshrined and worshiped. This marked the formal beginning of the practice of deifying such individuals and of the pacification rites known as goryō-e. Tens of thousands of young people throughout contemporary Japan visit Shinto shrines dedicated to Temman Daijizai Tenjin, Michizane's divinized form. Popularly known as Tenjin-sama, this *kami* is prayed to for success in school entrance exams. Only the shrines dedicated to Inari, the rice harvest deity, or to Hachiman are more numerous.

The rise of the Kumano cults must also be noted. During the Heian period three shrines and sacred sites in the mountainous Kumano region—Hongu, Shingu, and Nachi—emerged as important pilgrimage sites, which were to become mass pilgrimage sites in the following centuries. The Kumano pilgrimage was popular with aristocrats and even emperors. Kumano is famous for its Shugendō priests, known as *shugenja* or *hijiri,* who practiced various forms of severe asceticism in the mountains. The cult was deeply influenced by the Shinto-Buddhist amalgamation described previously. The Kumano Mandala, which portrays the surrounding areas as a natural mandala, is a famous national treasure. Before the development of modern forms of transportation, simply getting to these pilgrimage sites was an arduous task that tested the faith and commitment of the pilgrims. Kumano remains an important religious area, though today visitors can travel there in comfort by rail, car, or ferry.

The Kamakura period (1185–1333) was marked by the rise of military rulers and the relative decline of the imperial family and old aristocracy. Minamoto Yoritomo (1147–99) moved the administrative capital north to Kamakura in 1192, leaving the court in Kyoto isolated and its trappings of prestige tattered. To be sure, the series of military dictators made more or less perfunctory nods to the imperial family, but real power had slipped from imperial into military hands. The military rulers at times supported Buddhist cults, but not surprisingly the amalgamated cult of Hachiman, the god of war, grew significantly at this time. Many samurai (members of the warrior caste) also practiced forms of Zen Buddhism, as well as worshiping at Shinto shrines. Again, many portrayals of Japanese history fail to convey the extent to which Buddhism (here Zen) and the *kami* cults were intertwined in the lives of the people.

The historical vicissitudes of the imperial family, as well as various powerful clans and military figures, all of whom rose to great heights of power and prestige only to fall to a ruinous state, seemed to many persons to be powerful and poignant evidence of the Buddhist teaching that this was the Age of Declining Dharma (*mappō*). This teaching held that the world and its inhab-

itants were in decline, with humans no longer able to practice and master earlier forms of religious practice. Millennial expectations of various sorts became widespread. Nichiren (1222–82), for example, was a Tendai Buddhist priest who came to believe that the teachings and practices of all the Buddhist sects, as well as of other religious traditions, were false and dangerous distortions of the Truth. Believing that he lived in the age of *mappō*, he placed his exclusive faith in the Lotus Sutra. Unlike most Japanese religious leaders, Nichiren attacked any position supporting religious pluralism or suggesting the identity or functional equivalence of different religions. Moreover, he offered a nationalistic, even xenophobic, vision of Japan's special role in salvational history. On the one hand, Nichiren promoted a message of religious exclusivity, but on the other, he saw Japan, "the land of the *kami*," as destined to play a critical role in sacred history. In other words, he viewed human history as a part of a universal plan of salvation. A strong supporter of the imperial cause, he was deeply troubled by the defeat of the imperial forces in 1221. He predicted absolute chaos and catastrophe for the country, including invasions by foreign forces, if the people did not return to an exclusive reliance upon the Lotus Sutra. When an invading Mongol fleet was destroyed in a typhoon, Nichiren credited this miraculous escape to *kami-kaze* ("divine winds"), a term he coined. He believed that Japan was destined to become a theocratic state ruled under a reformed Buddhism. Tellingly, his own priestly name combined the characters for "sun" and "lotus," suggesting a critical identification of the land and the Lotus Sutra in his own person. Indeed, he came to believe that he was an incarnation of Jōgyō (Viśistacāritra), the bodhisattva to whom the historical Buddha had entrusted the Lotus Sutra centuries earlier.

A Shinto response to a Buddhist claim of preeminence was forthcoming, although not immediately. Urabe (also Yoshida) Kanetomo (1435–1511) sought to revive the Ise Shinto cult and to restore its unique prestige and status. A noted scholar, he proffered his own form of exclusive and nationalistic religion, although in Shinto form. He argued against the concept and practices of *honji-suijaku* and for the restoration of a pure Shinto, which he called *yuitsu genpon sōgen shintō*—the unique original essence Shinto. In significant ways this form of Shinto remained influential over the following centuries.

The intertwined relationship of Buddhist and Shinto institutions and practices was radically altered in the

1870s when the Meiji government authorized the forced separation of Buddhist and Shinto deities in cultic sites, while establishing State Shinto as the national cult. The separate status of Buddhist temples and Shinto Shrines in present-day Japan is, thus, a modern development. It does not reflect the situation that had existed in the land for many centuries. The nineteenth and twentieth centuries also saw the development of many so-called new religions. These religions generally have a founder who underwent some form of divine possession or revelatory experience in which a *kami* or Buddha expressed its divine will. Often lay-based, these new religions come in Buddhist forms (for example, Reiyū-kai, Sōka Gakkai) and Shinto forms (for example, Tenri-kyō, Konkō-kyō), mixing aspects of faith healing with folk religious practices.

CENTRAL DOCTRINES Shinto is not a doctrinal religion. There is no formal, standardized, or orthodox system of belief per se. Rather, most shrines or sects are free to develop their own expressions of religious style and practice. Shrines affiliated with specific larger shrines, however, often follow the lead and ritual calendar of the head shrine. Since World War II the Association of Shinto Shrines (Jinja Honchō) has issued a series of publications through the Institute for Japanese Culture and Classics of Kokugakuin University, which serve as a general statement of Shinto beliefs and concepts. While Shinto priests are versed in topics such as morality, sincerity, purity, and so forth, they rarely preach on these subjects.

MORAL CODE OF CONDUCT Shinto does not have a moral code distinct from that of Japanese culture more generally, which has been deeply influenced by Confucian, Neo-Confucian, Taoist, and Buddhist values and ideals. Western authors have often noted, however, that Shinto does not possess a concept of sin akin to that found in the Western monotheisms, nor does it have a concept of humankind as fallen or inherently sinful. Rather, according to the religious anthropology of Shinto, human beings have an innate moral sense of right and wrong or—perhaps more precisely—of propriety and impropriety. This is because humankind is descended from the *kami* and, thus, there is no radical ontological distinction between *kami* and human beings. Indeed, Shinto authors speak of *shinjin goitsu*, the essential identity of *kami* and humans. For both *kami* and human beings, improper actions and improper interpersonal relation-

ships can lead to moral blemishes (*kegare*) or a state of pollution. These blemishes can be washed away, as it were, by performing rites of purification (*harae*) and by correcting personal attitudes and actions.

The mythic paradigm for understanding *kegare* and *harae* is found in the story of the *kami* Izanagi's descent into the underworld (told in the creation accounts of the *Kojiki* and *Nihonshoki*). There the female creator, Izanami, suffers severe burns in giving birth to the fire *kami*, passes away, and enters Yomi no kuni, the Land of Darkness. Her spouse, Izanagi, desires to see her again and descends into the realm of the dead. In the course of events, he violates a taboo on viewing her. This provokes her anger, and he is forced to flee the underworld, pursued by its denizens and cursed by Izanami. After his escape from this "most unpleasant land, a horrible, unclean land," Izanagi performs a rite of purification. In doing so he brings into existence a number of *kami*, including Amaterasu and her sibling, Susano-o.

In some respects Shinto proffers a form of situational ethics rather than absolute rights and wrongs. Suicide, for instance, may occasion either public censure or acclaim, depending on the circumstances. An individual who kills himself merely to escape personal problems may be judged to have been weak or selfish, while a person who commits suicide in order to take responsibility for a perceived failure that affected a collective unit (family, company, or the nation) is not. The figure of the loyal retainer, who faithfully serves his master or avenges his death but then commits ritual suicide (*junshi*) to take responsibility for his own failures and transgressions, has held sway in the Japanese popular imagination since the medieval period. From the many retellings of the eighteenth-century story of the 47 *rōnin* (masterless samurai or swordsmen) to the ritual suicides of General Nogi Maresuke and the writer Mishima Yukio in the twentieth century, each generation has grappled with the issues of what constitutes moral conduct and what to do in the face of conflicting moral duties.

It must be recognized that Shinto codes of moral conduct have changed over time, just as Christian ones have. The famous twentieth-century author Natsume Sōseki captured this in his novel *Kokoro* (1914). The novel's main protagonist, Sensei (Teacher), tries to explain in a letter to a young friend why he has decided to commit suicide after hearing that General Nogi had taken his own life following the death of Emperor Meiji: "Perhaps you will not understand clearly why I am about to die, no more than I can fully understand why General Nogi killed himself. You and I belong to different eras, and so we think differently. There is nothing we can do to bridge the gap between us." In other words, a moral imperative of one period may not prevail in another. Nor, for that matter, may the moral duty of one person or class of persons necessarily be the same for others. Thus, the moral code of the samurai class was not the same as that of farmers, merchants, or priests.

In general, the Shinto-based new religions of Japan place a heavy emphasis on each individual's responsibility for maintaining proper relationships with others, including one's ancestral spirits. They also teach that an individual must assume responsibility not only for his or her actions but also for the reactions of others to them. For instance, if a wife is ignored by her husband or finds him irritable, she should not blame him; rather, she is instructed to examine herself in order to discover what she may have done to provoke this reaction and, then, to rectify it. Shinto ethics, then, are informed by Confucian and Taoist elements and cannot be neatly separated from Japanese social ethics more generally. The Neo-Confucian emphasis on loyalty to one's superiors, the submerging of one's personal desires to the collective good, and moral obligation all were used in the modern period to mobilize the Japanese people in support of nationalist and expansionist policies.

SACRED BOOKS No Shinto texts have the status that the Bible has for Christians or that the Koran has for Muslims. That is, there are no divinely revealed works that all persons accept as the full and final word of God. Members of one of the Shinto-informed new religions have their own sacred texts, but the members of other religious communities do not recognize their status as scripture. To take but one example, the sacred texts of Tenri-kyō play no part in the communal life of the followers of Ōmoto-kyō; the converse is also true.

Largely because of the influential works of nativist scholars—such as Motoori Norinaga—in the early modern and modern periods, the *Kojiki* has come to hold a certain privileged status, but this has not affected the cultic status of hundreds of *kami* who were not mentioned in the *Kojiki*. Over the centuries, however, numerous shrines and priestly families have used inclusion in the *Kojiki* of a *kami* that they enshrine and ritually serve in order to gain status and prestige within the religious world of Japan. Similarly, the ancient *norito*, or sacred prayers that are recited at imperial shrines, have gained

a wider currency, although again they are hardly universal or required.

SACRED SYMBOLS Like the members of most religious communities, Shinto participants employ many symbols in their lives. White, for instance, is a ubiquitous symbol of purity. In the Great Purification Rituals at the end of the year and in late June, *hitogata* (literally "person-form"), or paper cutouts, are rubbed over a person's body in order to take on the aches and pains and to absorb the *tsumi* (*imi* or *kegare*—spiritual defilements) that have accumulated. Symbolizing long life and vitality, *kadomatsu* are New Year's wreaths made of pine boughs enclosing diagonally cut bamboo stalks. Amulets (*ofuda*) containing the name of a kami—and thus symbolizing the kami's presence and protection—may be carried in a purse or billfold or hung in a car.

At most shrines there are small wooden tablets tied to large wooden display boards. Visitors purchase these tablets and write simple petitions on the backs of them, such as "I want to find a husband" or "I want to pass the university entrance exam." These tablets, known as *ema* (literally "horse pictures"), are offered to the *kami*. The horse pictures symbolize the actual horses that were once offered to the deities, as well as a wish for the delivery of the petition. *Ema* may also have zodiac signs, shrine insignia, or natural scenes on them rather than horses.

EARLY AND MODERN LEADERS Shinto is a diffuse religion that was without an overarching ecclesiastical structure for most of its history. A number of historical leaders or innovators, however—proponents of Neo-Confucianism and members of the nativist, or National Learning, school (*kokugaku*)—bear mention.

Yamazaki Ansai (1618–82), a Neo-Confucian scholar, founded a form of Confucian Shinto known as Suika, or Suiga, Shinto—the Shinto of Divine Revelation and Blessings. He maintained that the one true teaching was that of Sarutahiko-no-mikoto, the earthly *kami* who had guided Amaterasu from the High Heavens to the earth and Japan. Ansai also promoted reverence for the emperor. He held that, as a direct descendent of Amaterasu, the Japanese emperor was united with the heavenly sun.

Yamaga Sokō (1622–85) was a member of the *kogaku*, or Ancient Learning school, which stressed the importance of returning to the original texts of both Confucianism and Shinto and using philological methods in the search for truth. He identified Shinto with the way of the Confucian sages, arguing that they were one and the same, not distinct traditions. He is representative of numerous thinkers and activists who sought to combine Neo-Confucian thought and ethics with Japanese emperor-worship and nationalism.

The nativist, or National Learning (*kokugaku*), movement maintained that the worship of the *kami*, especially the sun goddess, was the essence of "pure" Shinto (that is, Shinto before it became associated with Buddhism and Confucianism). Scholars locate the beginning of this movement in the work of a Shingon Buddhist priest, Keichū (1640–1701). Keichū came to believe that the poems of the *Man'yōshū* preserved the pure ancient Japanese language. Almost single-handedly he revived widespread interest in this poetry anthology, and he made it accessible to readers once again through his careful annotations. Keichū extended his critical methodology to other works of classical literature, including *The Tale of Genji* and *The Tales of Ise,* in an attempt to recover their original meaning and intent. This understanding of the significance of poetic language and its relationship to an earlier, pure spirituality recalls the ideas of the philosopher Giambattista Vico (1668–1744) and certain Romantic thinkers in Europe. The connection drawn between the *Man'yōshū* and other works of classical Japanese literature and a pure Japanese or Shinto spirituality by Keichū and other nativist scholars has remained influential in present-day Japan. For example, *The Manyōshū,* the English translation of 1,000 verses by the Nippon Gakujutsu Shinkokai, was first published in 1940, the year Japan formed an alliance with Nazi Germany and Italy under Benito Mussolini. The introduction to this anthology remains an important example of the modern ideological use of literary artifacts to construct a pure, unique, and innate Japanese spirituality and a "timeless" divine sociopolitical order.

Kada Azumamaro (1669–1736) and Kamo no Mabuchi (1697–1769) also contributed to the *kokugaku* movement. Kada, the son of a Shinto priest, continued Keichū's study of the *Man'yōshū* and classical Japanese literature. His immediate goal was to get the government to establish a school of National Learning, which would identify and eliminate Buddhist and Confucian obfuscations of the original meaning of Japanese texts. His proposed curriculum covered the way of the *kami*, history, law, and literature.

Kamo no Mabuchi became a disciple of Kada shortly before the latter died. Mabuchi continued and ex-

tended the work and teachings of his master. His school in Edo became widely influential, and his many works reached a large audience. In addition to studies of the *Man'yōshū,* he studied and wrote on the Shinto *norito* (liturgical prayers) of the *Engishiki* and other works of Japanese literature. He borrowed the Confucian concept of poetry as a guide and corrective to power politics, even as he substituted Japanese for Chinese verse and denigrated the Confucian tradition. Like other nativist scholars, Mabuchi romanticized the Man'yō period as a golden age in which the people spontaneously expressed themselves in poetry. Moreover, he argued that, because of the divine rule of the Japanese emperors, the land was blessed and the relations between the sovereign and the people were harmonious and free of all discord. Like many others before and after him, Mabuchi sought to identify Shinto with the Japanese national body (*kokutai*) and the imperial system.

Motoori Norinaga (1730–1801) was perhaps the most influential spokesman for the National Learning movement. Rather than emphasize the central importance of the *Man'yōshū*, however, he pointed to the *Kojiki.* For Norinaga the *Kojiki* was the repository of pure Japanese spirituality, or Yamato-damashii. He derided the thought of Yamazaki Ansai for attempting to promote Confucianism under the guise of Shinto. His goal was once again to restore Shinto to its original state of purity—thus, the name *Fukko Shintō* (Restoration Shinto) is sometimes used to refer to his school. Although Shinto is sometimes criticized for not having a well-developed system of ethics, Motoori Norinaga included national morality among his four subjects to be studied and taught, in addition to national history, national literature, and Shinto and the body politic. His work has also influenced the discourse on Shinto in numerous important ways, not least in his suggestion that human emotional responses to things and events in the world are the essence of a pure religion and spirituality, not reason or a set of beliefs. In his pioneering works on classical Japanese literature, he linked aesthetic responses to religious ones in ways that many Japanese scholars of religion and literature have continued to follow.

Hirata Atsutane (1776–1843) also promoted the restoration of imperial rule. His teachings were later to have great influence on samurai leaders of the Meiji Restoration, who overthrew the Tokugawa regime, reinstalled the emperor as the head of state, and sought to establish a national Shinto cult centered on the emperor. Hirata also posited the existence of a hidden or concealed world after death, where the spirits of the deceased continued to exist. This was a significant innovation in Shinto thought and one that introduced a dualism that some scholars have argued was influenced by Christianity.

Other important leaders have included the founders of new religious groups—the so-called new religions—in the Tokugawa, Meiji, and modern periods. Tenri-kyō, Konkō-kyō, Kurozumi-kyō, Ōmoto-kyō, Sukyō Mahikari, PL Kyōdan, Seicho-no-Ie, and Sekai Kyūsei-kyō are a few examples of Shinto-based "new religions." None of these founders ever became a spokesperson for the Shinto world as a whole; rather, their spheres of influence were more circumscribed. Nevertheless, their careers and religious roles collectively represent an important characteristic of Shinto history: Innovation and new revelations are always possible at the grassroots level through forms of divine possession and divine communication. Moreover, immediate contact with the *kami* is available not only to the clergy but also to laypersons—to women as well as men and to the uneducated as well as the highly educated.

Nakyama Miki (1798–1887) founded Tenri-kyō after experiencing repeated instances of divine possession by the *kami* Tenri-o-no-mikoto, or Oyagami (Parent Deity). Many of her visions and revealed teachings were recorded and are now the central sacred teachings and scripture of this populous, wealthy, and influential religion. Miki also performed faith healings and shamanic rites, including ecstatic dancing.

Kawate Bunjiro (1814–83), the founder of Konkō-kyō, was believed to be a *kami* in human form (*ikigami*). He taught a form of positive thinking while emphasizing that a person should live according to the will of the *kami* in this life and not search for an afterlife. If a person lived his or her life properly, according to Bunjiro, then the goodness, happiness, and prosperity that can be enjoyed in this life themselves become sacralized. The focus of Konkō-kyō and other new religions on this life, as well as the prevalence of prayers for practical benefits (*genze riyaku*), has recently attracted the attention of scholars studying religions in contemporary Japan.

Deguchi Nao (1836–1918) was a peasant woman who had been widowed and reduced to abject poverty. She sought to provide for her children by gathering and reselling rags and discarded clothing. Familiar with Konkō-kyō and Tenri-kyō from her youth, this illiterate woman began to experience attacks of divine possession,

which continued for more than twenty years. Nao's divine messages had millennial overtones, promising a rectification of the world order and the fall of the rich and powerful for having distorted the divine will. A son-in-law who took the name Deguchi Onisaburo (1871–1948) later assumed the leadership of the community that formed around Nao. He himself participated in the tradition of severe asceticism in the mountains, undertaking regimens that produced religious visions that he recorded in hefty volumes. Onisaburo was also a talented organizer and administrator and systematized the teachings and practices of Ōmoto-kyō. The rapid growth of the religion apparently threatened some members of the government, which led to his arrest in 1921 and the destruction of the Ōmoto-kyō headquarters. By the 1930s, however, Ōmoto-kyō had become a strongly nationalistic movement, though the independence of its leaders again led it afoul of the government. Over the years Ōmoto-kyō has spawned a large number of other new religious groups.

MAJOR THEOLOGIANS AND AUTHORS Several major theologians of Shinto were also important leaders in the development of the religion, as discussed above in EARLY AND MODERN LEADERS. One of the most important theologians was Urabe, or Yoshida, Kanetomo (1435–1511), the founder of Urabe Shinto, also known as Yuiitsu or Yoshida Shinto. In the wake of the devastation of the capital, Kyoto, in the Ōnin War, he promulgated teachings of the uniqueness of Japan, while rejecting *honji suijaku*, the Buddhist teaching that assimilated *kami* to various Buddhas and bodhisattvas. Perhaps in an effort to avoid the subsumption of the Yoshida Shrine by the Kamo Shrine, he strenuously promoted specific aspects of the Ise Shinto traditions. Among other things, he claimed that the *kami* Ame-no-koyane-no-mikoto was the original source of the uniqueness of Shinto and of Japan as a country. Buddhism and Confucianism were held to be the flowers and fruit of this root. Not surprisingly, this *kami* was the ancestral deity of the Nakatomi/Fujiwara family and the deity enshrined in the Urabe-dominated Kasuga Shrine in Nara and the Yoshida Shrine in Kyoto. In the *Kojiki* creation myth, Ame-no-koyane accompanies Ninigi-no-mikoto, the grandson of the Sun Goddess, in his descent from the High Heavens in order to pacify this world and to establish divine rule. Ame-no-koyane—and by extension the Urabe/Yoshida sacerdotal lineage—is closely associated with the imperial regalia. This is due in part to the claim of officials of the

Yoshida Shrine that in 1487 the *shintai* (objects into which the *kami* descend after a ritual summons) of the Inner and Outer Shrines of Ise had escaped a destructive fire by miraculously flying to the Yoshida Shrine. The teachings of Kanetomo were only the latest in a long line of theological "innovations" by members of the Urabe/Yoshida line of ritualists. These are more properly seen as permutations within the long-standing strategy of adapting to changing sociopolitical situations while protecting the prestige of the sacerdotal lineage. For example, in 1330 Urabe Jihen left the Yoshida Shrine in order to study the syncretic Tendai sannō cult and teachings at the monastic complex on Mount Hiei. Apparently he found the priority given to Buddhist figures in this cult unacceptable, however. He then traveled on to Ise, where he studied the esoteric tradition of the Watari priestly line of the Outer Shrine. Subsequently Jihen developed a theology in which even the Buddhas and bodhisattvas were declared to have *kami* nature. This essentially inverted the Buddhist *honji suijaku* teaching. Yui-itsu Shinto, which incorporated Buddhist and Confucian elements, was highly influential from the fifteenth century to the Meiji Restoration in the nineteenth century.

Mention also should be made of some of the major scholarly Japanese interpreters of Shinto to the West. Masaharu Anesaki's historical survey *History of Japanese Religion* (1930) remained the standard work until Joseph M. Kitagawa published his *Religion in Japanese History* (1966). In the early twentieth century Genchi Kato published several influential articles on Shinto in the *Transactions of the Japan Society of London,* as well as a translation of the ninth-century chronicle *Kogoshui.* Sokyo Ono's *Shinto: The Way of the Kami* (1962) is an insider's view, as are the publications of the Institute for Japanese Culture and Classics of Kokugakuin University. Tsunetsugu Muraoka's *Studies in Shinto Thought* (1964) and Naofusa Hirai's *Japanese Shinto* (1966) also bear mention. Hori Ichirō's *Folk Religion in Japan* (1968) was an important introduction to the significance of popular religious beliefs and practices for an appreciation of Japanese religions. Sōkichi Tsuda (1873–1961) is perhaps the best-known critical historian of Shinto and early Japanese history to have run afoul of governmental authorities for demonstrating that the historical chronology of the ancient imperial chronicles was unreliable. Kuroda Toshio (1926–93), for his part, argued persuasively that Shinto and Buddhism were institutionally intertwined through most of Japanese history.

ORGANIZATIONAL STRUCTURE The organizational structure of Shinto has varied greatly over time and from place to place. The early *kami* cults were local and independent in nature. Over time some shrines or shrine-temple multiplexes began to establish networks of branch shrines. This led to different "schools" of Shinto (for example, Yoshida Shinto) having their own organizational structures. At various points in history Japan's central government also sought to organize, and exercise control over, religious institutions. The Heian-period *Engishiki* listed 22 shrines in rank order, with Ise at the top. The later establishment of a system relating specific shrines to the imperial shrines of Ise is another example of how these institutions were organized. This section will discuss the general internal organization of Shinto shrines today and the current national organizational structure.

Individual shrines of sufficient size and resources generally have the following hierarchical leadership structure: the *gūji,* or head priest, who has day-to-day overall authority over the shrine, though he ultimately answers to a board of trustees; the *gon-gūji,* or assistant head priest; the *negi,* or senior priest(s); the *kannushi,* or priest(s); and the *miko,* or female shrine assistants (single young women who assist in rituals and perform *kagura,* or Shinto ritual dances).

The Association of Shinto Shrines (Jinja honchō), an organization created after World War II, regulates the Shinto shrines affiliated at a national level. This group represents the collective interests of the shrines in the political and legal spheres; it also takes the lead in handling public relations, both domestically and internationally. The association publishes a newspaper or newsletter, distributed to all members and to subscribers, which serves as the main vehicle for representing Shinto as a whole to the shrines themselves and to the world. The association also ranks shrines, as well as priests, in a hierarchy with the imperial shrines at Ise ranked at the top, as might be expected. The Jinja honchō is intimately involved in priestly appointments and licenses priests through examinations. Shrines dedicated to the *kami* Inari have their own organization and are not members of the Jinja honchō. Locally, priestly ranks are color coded, with the color of a priest's *hakama* (silk pantaloons) indicating his status. For example, in some shrines the head priest wears purple *hakama* with insignia; an assistant head priest wears purple with no insignia; and others wear light blue. Nationally, priests may be awarded one of four ranks, usually based on

What Is a Kami?

Translating the term *kami*, which is used to refer to Shinto divinities, has been a persistent problem, especially because Shinto concepts of divinity are different from Western ones. Etymologically the term means "high" or "superior," but in usage it refers more generally to all beings, places, and things that provoke a sense of awe or reverence in human beings. The eighteenth-century nativist scholar Motoori Norinaga offered one of the most famous definitions: "Generally speaking, 'kami' denotes, in the first place, the deities of heaven and earth that appear in the ancient texts and also the spirits enshrined in the [Shinto] shrines; furthermore, among all kinds of beings—including not only human beings but also such objects as birds, beasts, trees, grass, seas, mountains, and so forth— any being whatsoever which possesses some eminent quality out of the ordinary, and is awe-inspiring, is called kami."

length of service, which are distinct from an individual's local rank and status. All shrine priests are ordained after requisite studies at either Kogakkan University in Ise or Kokugakuin University in Tokyo. The latter was originally established as an institution dedicated to *kokugaku*, or nativist studies.

HOUSES OF WORSHIP AND HOLY PLACES Most Shinto shrines should be thought of as both buildings and the sacred sites on which these stand. This is because Shinto worship does not require physical structures to house the *kami*. Indeed, most of the earliest religious sites in the Japanese archipelago were holy sites where contact with the deities was possible. In prehistoric Japan circular arrangements of stones around a vertical pillar sometimes marked such spots. At other times trees or rocks demarcated such holy places. In present-day Japan *himorogi* (sacred sites) are demarcated by straw-plaited ropes (*shimenawa*), which are decorated with branches from evergreen *sakaki* trees and paper strips (*shide*). *Kami* are also regularly worshiped in open spaces known as *iwasaka*. Priests are not in residence at all shrines; rather, there are innumerable small and minia-

ture shrines throughout Japan where a Shinto priest might occasionally be called to perform a ritual but where more often laypersons offer their own prayers. Small, unattended shrines are also sometimes found in the midst of rice paddies, where the farmers offer their own prayers to the *ta no kami* (rice paddy *kami*) for a successful harvest. Visitors to the roofs of Japanese department stores, where carnival rides and (in the summer) beer gardens are located, will also often find miniature Shinto shrines, where rites of blessing and purification are occasionally performed by priests engaged for these services. Shrines may also be found in the wedding halls of hotels and department stores. All of these different forms represent places where the *kami* were (and are) ritually invited to descend in order to receive worship and prayers for practical, this-worldly concerns.

Shinto shrine buildings differ in architectural style. Some styles are named after the most famous shrines where they were used, such as the Gion, Hie, Hachiman, Kasuga, and Sumiyoshi styles. More readily recognizable as a distinctly Shinto architectural feature are the torii, or gate markers, at the entrances to shrine grounds. Torii generally consist of two upright pillars with two cross beams, which may be straight or curved. There is usually at least one torii at each entrance to the shrine grounds, although there can be more. Some shrines have a corridor of torii—sometimes consisting of hundreds of these gates—through which visitors walk. Individuals, families, businesses, or confraternities donate funds to purchase the torii, as well as the stone lanterns that dot the pathways. In addition, they may create endowments for the upkeep of the torii.

Shrine and temple grounds are often islands of green in the concrete jungle of modern industrial and urban centers in contemporary Japan. Visitors to Shinto shrines in urban centers are often struck by the atmosphere created by the mature trees, mosses, and ferns and the play of light and shadow surrounding the shrine buildings. It is important, however, to recognize the extent to which the contemporary religio-aesthetic experience of Shinto shrine grounds is shaped by the contrasting experience of the surrounding space. The sense of sacredness is not necessarily the same over time. Prior to the industrial age, the green space around Shinto shrines would not have been anything of special note or distinction, for most of the countryside was forested. It was only after the processes of industrialization and urbanization had covered over much of the green space in the cities of Japan that Shinto shrines (and Buddhist temples) became places where one could commune with nature.

It is a mistake—indeed, a form of anachronism—to project the modern concept of "nature" and a modern spiritual feeling for nature into the past. To be sure, many modern Japanese and Western scholars have made much of Shinto's being a nature religion or a "green" religion, with a built-in ecological sensitivity, but this characterization has been overdone. When this view is offered by Shinto priests and Japanese nationalists, it represents, at best, an overly romantic self-image and, at worst, a crass attempt to deflect attention from the extensive environmental destruction that Japanese industrialization and capitalist economic growth policies, which were not opposed by the Shinto establishment, have caused domestically and internationally. When Western scholars offer this representation of Shinto, they are participating either in an unexamined parroting of Japanese claims or in the continuing Western romanticization of an enchanted "traditional Japan" that, it is implied, is somehow still accessible. The assumption that nature is the same over time and in all places may be true in a pedantic sense (the sun and the moon are the same celestial objects everywhere, for example), but it is misleading in more important ways. The religious significance of, say, the rising and setting of the sun or the waxing and waning of the moon varies considerably not only among different cultures but over time within a given culture as well.

WHAT IS SACRED? Shinto *kami* are associated with phenomena of various sorts. Specific natural sites are considered to be sacred, including mountains, volcanoes, rivers and streams, rocks, waterfalls, caves, natural springs, ponds, and groves or individual trees. Some *kami* are identified with certain types of locations, such as roads, crossroads, paddy fields (*ta no kami*), and even toilets. Natural phenomena—including the wind, lightning, the sun, the moon, and the stars—also have *kami* associated with them. It is misleading, however, to suggest that Shinto is a nature religion, for many *kami* are not natural phenomena, nor is everything in the natural world sacred.

In order to define *kami*, some Western scholars have had recourse to Rudolf Otto's famous phenomenological definition of "the numinous" in his book *Das Heilige* (1917; *The Idea of the Holy* [1923]), but again the parallel is far from exact. For Otto "the holy," or the numinous, involves a sense of the wholly other (*ganz ander*); many

kami, however, are immanent in this world or, indeed, a part of it. Mount Miwa, near Nara, for example, is worshiped as a *kami*. It was not until the early Heian period (794–1185) that, in response to Buddhist art forms, the Japanese began to represent *kami* in human form in paintings and sculptures. Even today few Shinto shrines house an image of the *kami* worshiped there. Rather, shrines usually have an object—a sword or a brass mirror, for example—known as the *shintai* (body of the *kami*), into which the *kami* descends after being ritually summoned. The anthropomorphic statues of *kami* that do exist are also considered to be *shintai*.

In addition to the *kami* associated or identified with natural phenomena, there are two types of human *kami*. First, there are *hitogami* (living *kami* in human form). For example, some of the founders of new religions in the modern period are considered to be (or to have been) living *kami*, as is the emperor. Similarly, individuals may be recognized locally as *hitogami* because of their deep spiritual nature, their ascetic practices, their experiences of divine possession, and so on. The second type of human *kami* is the *goryō*. *Goryō* are the haunting spirits of deceased persons who suffered some great wrong while alive. They can cause mental illness, widespread disease, lightning strikes, and other troubles. Once a *goryō* has been identified through divination, the spirit is given a *kami* name and enshrined, and rites of pacification are performed for it. Prayers and petitions are subsequently offered to *goryō*.

In addition, in numerous festivals children are taken to embody the *kami* as they ride in the *mikoshi* (portable shrines in the form of a festival cart or palanquin) or as they perform *kagura* (sacred dances)—that is, they "house" the deity in their bodies for the duration of the ritual. Any thing or person that becomes the temporary "seat" of a deity is thereby made sacred for the duration of the deity's presence. Popular Japanese performance arts, such as *kagura*, No drama, Kabuki, and some traditional forms of puppetry also involve ritual acts of sacralization. For example, preceding the performance of the *okina* (Old Man) No plays, the actor performs a rite to call down a *kami* into the mask he will wear onstage. The actor "becomes" the deity during the performance. After taking off the mask, the actor performs a rite to send off the *kami*. Such practices are believed to be the traces of shamanic possession rites.

Another type of human *kami* is the *marebito*, a visiting or wandering god or demon. In earlier centuries the Shinto-Buddhist mountain ascetics known as *yamabushi*

SHINTO

were believed to be *marebito*. These mysterious figures lived on the periphery of towns and villages and were regarded with a mixture of fear and reverence because of the occult powers they reputedly gained in the mountains. When they visited villages, they functioned in certain regards as ritual scapegoats, performing exorcisms and purification rites before carrying evil and accumulated spiritual pollution out of the villages. In contemporary Japan local young men portray *marebito* or demons (*oni*) in many Shinto festivals of blessing, exorcism, and purification. The *namehage* of Akita, ferocious figures in masks and straw costumes, are instances of this type of deity.

Kami may also be animals, either species indigenous to Japan or mythological or fantastic beasts from China or India. Animal *kami* include deer, bears, monkeys, lions, tigers, dogs, foxes, badgers, serpents, eagles, catfish, and dragons.

HOLIDAYS AND FESTIVALS Shinto and Shinto-Buddhist festivals are known as *matsuri*. All *matsuri* have a tripartite structure involving calling down the *kami*, entertaining the kami (*kami asobi*), and sending off the *kami*. The primary function of a festival, then, is to ritually invite the temporary presence of a deity, provide entertainment, petition the deity for various reasons, and, finally, to effect a controlled return to the ordinary state of things, though with both the deity and the cosmos (or town) ritually renewed or purified. Renewal and purification are central to Japanese festivals, the purpose of which is to rejuvenate or "recharge" the world or to remove the pollution (*kegare*) that naturally accumulates.

Some *matsuri* are seasonal—that is, they are especially designed to renew time or to continue the cosmic and agricultural cycles of time. In the past the harvest festival (*niiname-sai*), which dates from the early historical period, not only celebrated the harvest but also served as the preferred time to ritually install a new emperor or empress. In this way it explicitly linked the renewal and continuity of the sociopolitical order to the agricultural cycle. The harvest festival is celebrated throughout Japan on 23 and 24 November. The emperor offers rice harvested from special paddy fields and other foods to the sun goddess and to other *kami*. He himself partakes of these offerings as he communes with the *kami*. Other seasonal festivals include New Year's; the Change of Seasons (*setsubun*) in February, which involves exorcism; the vernal equinox; rice planting time; and the autumnal equinox.

Yet other festivals are related to the stages or cycles of human life. In January there is the Coming of Age festival for those who have reached their majority (age 20 in contemporary Japan). In March the Doll Festival (*hina matsuri*) is celebrated by families with daughters, as well as at shrines around the country. A boy's festival is celebrated later in the year, at which time families with male children fly colorful windsocks in the shape of carp (*koi-nobori*) outside their homes. In November the Shichi-go-san festival is a rite of passage for five-year-old boys and girls aged three and seven. The nationwide festival of Ōbon sees many Japanese returning to their native towns for the festivities. The spirits of ancestors are invited back during this festival and led by lanterns or candles to special sites where ritual dances, known as *bon odori*, are performed to entertain them. Ancestors are considered to be continuing presences in the life of the community. Thus, death and the ritual transformation of the deceased into an ancestor are seen as stages in the natural order of things.

Towns and villages throughout Japan have their own annual festivals. It is impossible to list all of them or even the most famous ones. It will be useful, however, to note some of the different types of *matsuri* in terms of the character of their performance. In many festivals, the deity is transported through the streets in a *mikoshi* (a miniature shrine or palanquin). The *kami* may be present in the form of straw sandals, a seat cushion, pounded rice cakes, a sake barrel, a puppet or paper cutout, drums, or other object. In some *matsuri* young men, naked except for a loincloth, carry the *mikoshi*. These young men represent the strength and vitality of the community and undergo rites of purification prior to the festival's start. Numerous *matsuri* involve competitions, ranging from a tug-of-war or mock battle to searches for an object symbolizing divine power. Some festivals continue to feature sumo wrestling matches between adults or children, with the results believed to be a form of divination. Sumo wrestlers often take place names, recalling that in the past in ritual bouts they became the temporary hosts of the local earth *kami*. Related to these forms of competition are the various *kenka matsuri* (fighting *matsuri*) in which teams violently engage one other. In some rites competing teams attempt to knock the other team's *mikoshi* off the shoulders of the carriers or off the road. In some coastal festivals boats carrying *mikoshi* bump each other in races or ritual combat. The teams usually are sponsored by and represent specific neighborhoods, which are identified on the par-

Is Shinto a Religion?

When the term or category "religion" was introduced into Japan in the nineteenth century, a neologism—*shūkyō*—was created to translate it. An ongoing discussion then ensued over the question of whether Shinto was a religion. At first hearing, this sounds odd to Western ears, but the question is a serious one, and any answer to it has serious political and legal consequences. In the early Meiji period (1868–1912), Shinto priests—because of their long-standing performance of state rites devoted to the *kami*, or divinities—sought special recognition and status for the *kami* cults. Eventually only national and imperial shrines were granted this status, along with direct government support; most shrines did not receive such recognition.

After Japan's defeat in World War II, the issue of whether Shinto was a religion surfaced again. The new Japanese constitution included provisions for freedom of religion and the separation of religion and the state. In response, an influential group of conservative nationalists revived the argument that Shinto was not a religion per se; rather, they contended, it was an expression of the spiritual nature of the Japanese people. Since the late 1960s the consecutive conservative governments have repeatedly sought to pass legislation that would define the Yasukuni Shrine, the national shrine that offers rites and ceremonies for the spirits of Japan's war dead, as a nonreligious institution. The opposition to these efforts has been strong and vocal. In many ways this struggle resembles the ongoing contestation of issues concerning the separation of church and state in the United States. In both cases competing notions of national identity are also deeply involved.

od (794–1185) but ultimately were borrowed from Chinese ritual usage. When performing important rituals, priests wear hats known as *kanmuri*, which are distinguished by a taillike feature on the back. For more ordinary occasions they wear *eboshi*, pointed or thimble-shaped hats. Priests wear silk robes and pantaloons (*hakama*), with the color reflecting the season or the age and rank of the priest. Contemporary priests wear lacquered wooden shoes and carry a *shaku*, a flat elongated piece of wood that functions as a scepter.

Female shrine attendants wear vermilion *hakama* over white robes, and they wear special head ornaments on ritual occasions. These headdresses are usually in the form of flowers and blossoms, which traditionally were used to attract the *kami*. They recall the traditional role of women as ritual mediums (*miko*), as well as a number of popular beliefs. For instance, the long black hair of maidens was believed to be especially attractive to *kami*, including those that caused disease. During times of plague, women were warned to wear their hair up and never to comb their long hair in public for fear of attracting the *kami* of the plague.

DIETARY PRACTICES Shinto does not have strict dietary laws for participants. Most Japanese are not vegetarians and consume fish, fowl, and meat. On some occasions, however, an individual may abstain from consuming specific foods that are believed to offend a given *kami*. More commonly, special dietary practices involve the serving of certain foods during festivals. For example, pounded rice cakes (*mochi*), which symbolize the full moon, are commonly made and consumed during the New Year's holiday, though they are also frequently used in ritual offerings throughout the year. Rice wine (sake) is an integral part of all offerings made at shrines. After being ritually offered to the *kami*, it is served to the participants in the ritual and referred to as *o-miki*. Sake is also consumed at weddings and festivals and on other ritual occasions, while bottles or barrels of sake are often offered at shrines.

ticipant's *happi* coats (short, belted coats with wide sleeves) or headbands.

MODE OF DRESS Shinto worshipers are not required to wear any special form of dress during shrine visits. Shinto priests and female shrine attendants, however, wear distinctive forms of dress that date from the Heian peri-

RITUALS Shrine visits usually do not entail any formal worship service presided over by a Shinto priest. Rather, most visitors simply perform a simple purification rite by rinsing their mouth and washing their hands at the ever-present water basin; some may proceed to offer a prayer before the inner shrine. The petitioner will clap his or her hands three times, fold them together in prayer, bow his or her head, and silently offer a prayer or petition. A visitor may have a special rite or prayer offered on his or her behalf by a priest, however. Most shrines make available lists of the most popular rites and their respective prices. Such rituals can also be arranged by telephone or fax beforehand.

All Shinto shrines also have public rites that are performed at specific times. The Great Purification Rites of winter and summer are the most common such rites. These rituals are presided over by priests and shrine assistants, though laypersons may perform specific roles in the full festival performances.

All Shinto shrines seek to promote visits by the faithful, though depending on the shrine, they might attract people locally, regionally, or from throughout Japan. Some shrines have become major pilgrimage sites. Mount Fuji has long been a popular pilgrimage site, as have the Grand Shrines of Ise. Pilgrimage routes frequently include both Shinto shrines and Buddhist temples, a testimony to the fact that for most of Japanese history the typical religious structures were shrine-temple and temple-shrine complexes rather than discrete religious institutions. In addition, some new religions, such as Tenri-kyō, sponsor pilgrimages to the group's headquarters. Pilgrims often wear white *happi* coats and headbands inscribed with the group's name or with words of encouragement.

In contemporary Japan few Shinto shrines perform funeral rituals in part because death is considered to be polluting and dangerous. The ancient myth of Izanagi and Izanami tells how death came into the world and how humans became mortal. It also clearly implies that the pollution associated with death can be purified through ritual actions. With the introduction of the practice of cremation in the early eighth century, Buddhist priests assumed primary responsibility for funerary rites. Much later, in the wake of the government-sponsored separation of Shinto and Buddhism in the late nineteenth century, this division of labor became even more marked, as Buddhist temples were physically separated from Shinto shrines.

Whereas Buddhist priests perform funerary rituals, Shinto priests perform most weddings in Japan. In the twentieth century, however, many weddings moved from shrines proper to freestanding commercial wedding parlors or wedding halls in hotels or department stores. Weddings have become a big business in modern Japan, and Shinto priests have adapted to the shifts in consumer taste. They officiate in their traditional robes, hat, and so on, though the groom will wear a tuxedo and the bride a traditional kimono, to be quickly exchanged afterward for a Western-style bridal gown for a photo session. The newlyweds share a cup of sake to seal their vows.

RITES OF PASSAGE In addition to weddings, several other rites of passage are celebrated in Japan. Families often celebrate a newborn's first visit to a shrine. The annual Shichi-go-san festival held on 15 November honors girls who have reached the ages of three and seven and boys who have turned five. The *saiten-sai*, usually celebrated on 15 January, is a fairly recent innovation that marks the coming of age of twenty-year-olds. While these are the formal rites of passage, the liturgical calendar of every Shinto shrine includes "natural" rites of passage—that is, ceremonial markings of the passage of the solar year, the lunar cycle, and agricultural cycles of planting, growth, harvest, and dormancy. One of the central themes informing the Shinto worldview is the interrelatedness of human and natural cycles.

MEMBERSHIP Almost all Japanese participate in Shinto rites and activities, though there is no formal rite of initiation into the religious community akin to, say, baptism in Christianity. Shinto is not in general an evangelistic religion, so historically there has been little effort to convert other persons, especially non-Japanese, to Shinto. This being said, two important exceptions must be noted. First, during the modern period of Japanese imperialism in the twentieth century, the government established Shinto shrines in Korea, Manchuria, and other areas under Japanese control as part of its effort to legitimate its occupation under the ideological aegis of State Shinto. Members of the local population in these areas were sometimes required to participate in shrine activities. Second, some Shinto new religions, such as Tenri-kyō and Kurozumi-kyō, have sought to convert individuals both within Japan and abroad, though with mixed success.

RELIGIOUS TOLERANCE Throughout much of Japanese history, Shinto shrines were conjoined with Buddhist temples. Thus, religious intolerance has not characterized Shinto. The most notable exceptions to this are the violent repression of Christianity by the shoguns (military governors) Toyotomi Hideyoshi (1537–98) and Tokugawa Ieyasu (1543–1616) and the Meiji government's forcible separation of Shinto and Buddhist establishments in the late nineteenth century. The shogun's violent repression of Christian communities, known as *kirishitan,* seems to have been based on political considerations, including fear of the power of some *kirishitan daimyō* (provincial military rulers who had converted to Christianity) and the influence of foreign missionaries. While Shinto leaders did not instigate the persecution of Christians, neither did they oppose the government's policies. Their conduct was quite different in the nineteenth century, when some nationalists actively sought to restore Shinto as the state religion and to purify Shinto by excising all Buddhist elements from shrine grounds.

SOCIAL JUSTICE For much of its history Shinto has been a locally based religion. Most shrines served local villagers or the inhabitants of urban neighborhoods. Without an umbrella ecclesiastical organization, no explicit orthodoxy developed within Shinto, including any clear-cut statements on social justice. In some ways most Shinto leaders, like their Buddhist counterparts, were products of their ages and thus shared many of the widespread social and cultural prejudices. For instance, until the twentieth century few persons spoke out against the broad-based discrimination against *burakumin* (outcaste) communities in Japan or against persons of Korean descent. Those Shinto leaders who have spoken out against social injustice in Japan and around the world have done so as individuals rather than as spokespersons for Shinto as a whole. Since World War II many Shinto nationalists have resisted pressure from Asian nations to apologize for atrocities committed by Japanese forces. Similarly, they have been slow or unwilling to take responsibility for any complicity the Shinto establishment had in Japanese imperialism. More recently, a number of Shinto leaders have embraced ecological causes as an area in which Shinto has much to offer the world. Some have suggested that Japan's rice paddy culture is an ideal form of living responsibly in the natural world.

SOCIAL ASPECTS Shinto leaders support the values of the traditional East Asian patriarchal family. Based on Neo-Confucian ideals, the ideal Japanese family includes the husband as breadwinner, the wife as homemaker, their child or children, and perhaps the grandparents—all living under one roof. Caring for one's elderly parents is viewed as an act of filial piety. It is expected that the eldest son (or daughter, in the event there is no son) will bear this responsibility. In contem-

porary Japan, however, shifting social values and economic realities have led to a decline in the number of extended families living together, a fact that is lamented by more conservative religious leaders. Socioeconomic factors have also led to a negative birthrate in Japan precisely at the time when the elderly population is growing rapidly. The resultant situation has placed tremendous pressure on the social welfare system and revealed fissures in the family support system. The Shinto establishment, however, has not presented any clear-cut policy solutions to these problems. Shinto leaders often stress that a person's extended family also includes his or her ancestors. In important ways, the ancestral cult remains a central part of Shinto practice and the Shinto worldview in the twenty-first century. The Shinto-oriented "new religions," especially, have placed renewed emphasis on the moral importance of ancestral rites.

CONTROVERSIAL ISSUES Contemporary Shinto leaders are enmeshed in controversial issues facing the Japanese people as a whole. Frequently, these are political issues rather than social issues, such as abortion or divorce. The more conservative and nationalist faction has strenuously resisted pressure from former colonized nations for Japan to acknowledge its moral and legal responsibility for its imperialistic policies. Similarly, in the so-called textbook wars, Shinto nationalists have lobbied for history texts that downplay Japanese imperialism, mass killings of foreigners, the government's support of forced prostitution or the use of "comfort women" for the troops, and so on during the Pacific wars.

The Yasukuni Shrine in Tokyo, too, remains at the center of a long-standing dispute over the propriety of enshrining and memorializing the war dead, including convicted war criminals. Created in the early twentieth century as a part of the State Shinto apparatus, the Yasukuni Shrine and affiliated sub-shrines throughout the country have continued to provoke controversy concerning the proper relationship between religion and the state. Visits to Yasukuni by the prime minister and cabinet members regularly cause storms of protest domestically and elsewhere in East Asia, as does continued state support for the shrine. While no direct financial support is provided, more subtle forms of symbolic support for this cultic complex contribute to the blurring of the constitutional separation of church and state. Finally, in the wake of the Aum Shinrikyō affair—in which a controversial New Age religious group manufactured sarin nerve gas, released it in the Tokyo subway in 1995, and was involved in kidnapping and murder and in the "brainwashing" of members—official surveillance and regulation of religious groups has reemerged as a national issue. In general, Shinto organizations have not opposed the strengthening of government controls or the expansion of police powers in monitoring religious groups.

CULTURAL IMPACT The deep and lasting impact of Shinto throughout Japanese cultural history is undeniable. Conversely, the impact of history on Shinto has been equally great. Shinto shrine architecture has provided the inspiration for the clean and sparse lines of many other Japanese buildings, including houses. The modern architectural concept of negative space is indebted in part to the nonintrusive nature of Shinto architecture. Negative space focuses attention on the space between pillars and other physical structures rather than on the structures themselves.

Shinto ritual performances have influenced Japanese aesthetics and art forms, from dance and drama to puppetry. The concepts of purity and pollution have also impacted Japanese understandings of propriety and beauty. For many centuries Shinto and Buddhism were closely interrelated, as has been discussed; thus, it is difficult to clearly separate the cultural impact of Shinto and Buddhism in Japan.

Gary Ebersole

Bibliography

Anesaki, Masaharu. *History of Japanese Religion.* London: Kegan Paul, Trench, Trubner and Co., 1930.

Basic Terms of Shinto. Tokyo: Institute for Japanese Culture and Classics, Kokugakuin University, 1985.

Bock, Felicia Gressit, trans. *Engi-shiki: Procedures from the Engi Era.* Books VI–X. Tokyo: Sophia University, 1972.

Bocking, Brian. *The Oracles of the Three Shrines: Windows on Japanese Religion.* Richmond, England: RoutledgeCurzon, 2001.

Borgen, Robert. *Sugawara no Michizane and the Early Heian Court.* Cambridge, Mass.: Council on East Asian Studies, Harvard University, 1986. Reprint, Honolulu: University of Hawai'i Press, 1994.

Breen, John, and Mark Teeuwen, eds. *Shinto in History: Ways of the Kami.* Honolulu: University of Hawai'i Press; Richmond, England: RoutledgeCurzon, 2000.

Creemers, Wilhelmus H.M. *Shrine Shinto after World War II.* Leiden: E.J. Brill, 1968.

Fridell, Wilbur M. *Japanese Shrine Mergers, 1906–1912: State Shinto Moves to the Grassroots.* Tokyo: Sophia University, 1973.

Grapard, Allan G. *The Protocol of the Gods: A Study of the Kasuga Cult in Japanese History.* Berkeley and Los Angeles: University of California Press, 1992.

Hardacre, Helen. *Kurozumikyō and the New Religions of Japan.* Princeton, N.J.: Princeton University Press, 1986.

———. *Shinto and the State, 1868–1988.* Princeton, N.J.: Princeton University Press, 1989.

Harootunian, H.D. *Things Seen and Unseen: Discourse and Ideology in Tokugawa Nativism.* Chicago: University of Chicago Press, 1988.

Hirai, Naofusa. *Japanese Shinto.* Bulletin 18. Tokyo: International Society for Educational Information, 1966.

Hoff, Frank, trans. *The Genial Seed: A Japanese Song Cycle.* Tokyo and New York: Mushina/Grossman Publishers, 1971.

Holtom, Daniel Clarence. *The National Faith of Japan: A Study in Modern Shinto.* New York: Dutton, 1938. Reprint, New York: Paragon Book Reprint Corp., 1963.

Inoue, Nobutaka, ed. *Kami.* Translated by Norman Havens. Tokyo: Institute for Japanese Culture and Classics, Kokugakuin University, 1998.

Kageyama, Haruki. *The Arts of Shinto.* Translated by Christine Guth. New York: Weatherhill, 1973.

Kanda, Christina Guth. *Shinzō: Hachiman Imagery and Its Development.* Cambridge, Mass.: Council on East Asian Studies, Harvard University, 1985.

Kato, Genchi, and Hikoshiro Hoshino, trans. *Kogoshui: Gleanings from Ancient Stories.* 2nd ed. Tokyo: Meiji Japan Society, 1925.

Kitagawa, Joseph M. *Religion in Japanese History.* New York: Columbia University Press, 1966.

Kuroda, Toshio. "Shinto in the History of Japanese Religion." *Journal of Japanese Studies* 7, no. 1 (1981): 1–21.

Littleton, C. Scott. *Shinto: Origins, Rituals, Festivals, Spirits, Sacred Places.* New York: Oxford University Press, 2002.

Muraoka, Tsunetsugu. *Studies in Shinto Thought.* Translated by Delmer M. Brown and James T. Araki. Tokyo: Ministry of Education, 1964.

Nelson, John K. *A Year in the Life of a Shinto Shrine.* Seattle: University of Washington Press, 1996.

———. *Enduring Identities: The Guise of Shinto in Contemporary Japan.* Honolulu: University of Hawai'i Press, 2000.

Ono, Sokyo. *Shinto: The Kami Way.* Tokyo: Charles E. Tuttle, 1962.

Philippi, Donald L. *Kojiki.* Tokyo: University of Tokyo Press, 1968.

Philippi, Donald L., trans. *Norito: A New Translation of the Ancient Japanese Ritual Prayers.* Tokyo: Institute for Japanese Culture and Classics, Kokugakuin University, 1959.

Picken, Stuart D.B. *Essentials of Shinto: An Analytical Guide to Principal Teachings*. Westport, Conn.: Greenwood Press, 1994.

Ponsonby-Fane, R.A.B. *Studies in Shinto and Shrines: Papers Selected from the Works of the Late R.A.B. Ponsonby Fane, LL.D.* Rev. ed. Kakikamo, Kyoto: Ponsonby Memorial Society, 1953.

Reader, Ian, and George J. Tanabe, Jr. *Practically Religious: Worldly Benefits and the Common Religion of Japan.* Honolulu: University of Hawai'i Press, 1998.

Schattschneider, Ellen. *Immortal Wishes: Labor and Transcendence on a Japanese Sacred Mountain.* Durham, N.C.: Duke University Press, 2003.

Smyers, Karen A. *The Fox and the Jewel: Shared and Private Meanings in Contemporary Japanese Inari Worship.* Honolulu: University of Hawai'i Press, 1999.

Sonoda, Minoru, ed. "Studies on Shinto." Special edition of *Acta Asiatica* 51 (1987).

Tange, Kenzo, and Noboru Kawazoe. *Ise: Prototype of Japanese Architecture.* Cambridge, Mass.: M.I.T. Press, 1965.

Teeuwen, Mark. *Watarai Shinto: An Intellectual History of the Outer Shrine in Ise.* Leiden: Research School CNWS, 1996.

Teeuwen, Mark, trans. *Motoori Norinaga's "The Two Shrines of Ise": An Essay of Split Bamboo.* Wiesbaden: Harrassowitz, 1995.

Tyler, Susan C. *The Cult of Kasuga Seen through Its Art.* Ann Arbor, Mich.: Center for Japanese Studies, University of Michigan, 1992.

Watanabe, Yasutada. *Shinto Art: Ise and Izumo Shrines.* Translated by Robert Ricketts. Heibonsha Survey of Japanese Art, vol. 3. Tokyo: Heibonsha; New York: Weatherhill, 1974.

Sikhism

FOUNDED: c. 1499 C.E.

RELIGION AS A PERCENTAGE OF WORLD POPULATION: 0.3 percent

OVERVIEW Sikhism originated in the Punjab region of northwestern India five centuries ago. The founder, Guru Nanak, lived from 1469 to 1539. Sikhism is a monotheistic faith that stresses the ideal of achieving spiritual liberation within a person's lifetime through meditation on the divine name. It is also oriented toward action, encouraging the dignity of regular labor as a part of spiritual discipline. Family life and socially responsible living are other important aspects of Sikh teachings.

Sikhism is the youngest of the independent religions of India, where its members make up about 2 percent of the country's 1 billion people. Most live in the Indian state of Punjab. What makes Sikhs significant in India is not their numbers but their contribution in the political and economic spheres.

The global population of Sikhs is between 23 and 24 million. Substantial communities of Sikhs have been established in Southeast Asia, East Africa, the United Kingdom, and North America through successive waves of emigration. Beginning in the first decade of the twentieth century, a quarter million Sikhs settled in the United States. Observant male Sikhs everywhere are recognized by their beards and turbans, which are the very symbols of their faith.

HISTORY Sikhism is rooted in a particular religious experience, piety, and culture and is informed by the unique inner revelation of its founder, Guru Nanak, who declared his independence from other thought forms of his day. Those who claimed to be his disciples were known as *sikhs*, or "learners." Notwithstanding the influences he absorbed from the contemporary religious environment—particularly the devotional tradition of the medieval *sant*s, or "poet-saints," of North India, with whom he shared certain similarities—Guru Nanak established a foundation of teaching, practice, and community from the standpoint of his own religious ideals. Among the religious figures of North India, he had an especially strong sense of mission, compelling him to proclaim his message for the benefit of his audience and for the promotion of socially responsible living.

Nanak was born to an upper-caste professional Hindu family of the village of Talwandi, present-day Nankana Sahib in Pakistan. Much of the material concerning his life comes from hagiographical *janam-sakhi*s (birth narratives). His life may be divided into three distinct phases: his early contemplative years, the enlightenment experience accompanied by extensive travels, and a foundational climax that resulted in the establishment of the first Sikh community in the western Punjab. A local Muslim nobleman employed the young Nanak as a steward at Sultanpur Lodhi. Being a professional accountant of the Khatri (warrior) caste, he worked diligently at his job, but his mind was deeply absorbed in spiritual concerns. Thus, it is not surprising that he spent long hours of each morning and evening in meditation and devotional singing. Early one morning, when he was bathing in the Vein River, he disappeared with-

KHANDA. The Khanda is the universal symbol of the Sikh religion. The double-edged sword in the middle (also called a Khanda) symbolizes the divine power of the One, Infinite, Omnipresent, Formless, Fearless, Angerless, Omnipotent God. The circle is called the Chakar and symbolizes the perfection of God. The two swords that surround the Chakar represent those worn by the sixth Sikh Guru, Hargobind (1595–1644), symbolizing his spiritual (*piri*) and temporal (*miri*) authorities. Sikhs place an equal emphasis on spiritual aspirations and obligations to society. (THOMSON GALE)

out leaving a trace. Family members gave him up for dead, but three days later he stepped out of the water with cryptic words: "There is no Hindu, there is no Muslim."

This statement, made during the declining years of the Lodhi sultanate, must be understood in the context of the religious culture of the medieval Punjab. The two dominant religions of the region were the Hindu tradition and Islam, both making conflicting truth claims. To a society torn with conflict, Nanak brought a vision of a common humanity and pointed the way to look beyond external labels for a deeper reality. After his three-day immersion in the waters—a metaphor of dissolution, transformation, and spiritual perfection—Nanak was ready to proclaim a new vision for his audience. In one of his own hymns in the Adi Granth, the Sikh scripture, he proclaimed, "I was a minstrel out of work, the Lord assigned me the task of singing the divine Word. He summoned me to his court and bestowed on me [the] robe of honoring him and singing his praise. On me he bestowed the divine nectar [*amrit*] in a cup, the nectar of his true and holy Name" (Adi Granth, p. 150).

The hymn is intensely autobiographical, explicitly pointing out Guru Nanak's own understanding of his divine mission, and it marked the beginning of his ministry. He was then 30 years of age, had been married to Sulakhani for more than a decade, and was the father of two young sons, Sri Chand and Lakhmi Das. He set out on a series of journeys to both Hindu and Muslim places of pilgrimage in India and elsewhere. During his travels he came into contact with the leaders of different religious persuasions and tested the veracity of his own ideas in religious dialogues.

At the end of his travels, in the 1520s, Guru Nanak purchased a piece of land on the right bank of the Ravi River in West Punjab and founded the village of Kartarpur (Creator's Abode). There he lived for the rest of his life as the "spiritual guide" of a newly emerging religious community. His attractive personality and teaching won him many disciples, who received his message of liberation through religious hymns of unique genius and notable beauty. They began to use the hymns in devotional singing (*kirtan*) as a part of congregational worship. Indeed, the first Sikh families who gathered around Guru Nanak in the early decades of the sixteenth century formed the nucleus of a rudimentary organization of Nanak-panth. (The word *panth* literally means "path," but here it refers to those Sikhs who followed Guru Nanak's path of liberation.)

Guru Nanak prescribed the daily routine, along with agricultural activity for sustenance, for the Kartarpur community. He defined the ideal person as a Gurmukh (one oriented toward the Guru), who practiced the threefold discipline of "the divine Name, charity, and purity" (*nam-dan-ishnan*). Indeed, these three features—*nam* (relation with the divine), *dan* (relation with the society), and *ishnan* (relation with the self)— provided a balanced approach for the development of the individual and the society. They corresponded to the cognitive, the communal, and the personal aspects of the evolving Sikh identity. For Guru Nanak the true spiritual life required that "one should live on what one has earned through hard work and that one should share with others the fruit of one's exertion" (Adi Granth, p. 1,245). In addition, service (*seva*), self-respect (*pati*), truthful living (*sach achar*), humility, sweetness of the tongue, and taking only one's rightful share (*haq halal*) were regarded as highly prized ethical virtues in pursuit of liberation. At Kartarpur, Guru Nanak gave practical expression to the ideals that had matured during the period of his travels, and he combined a life of disciplined

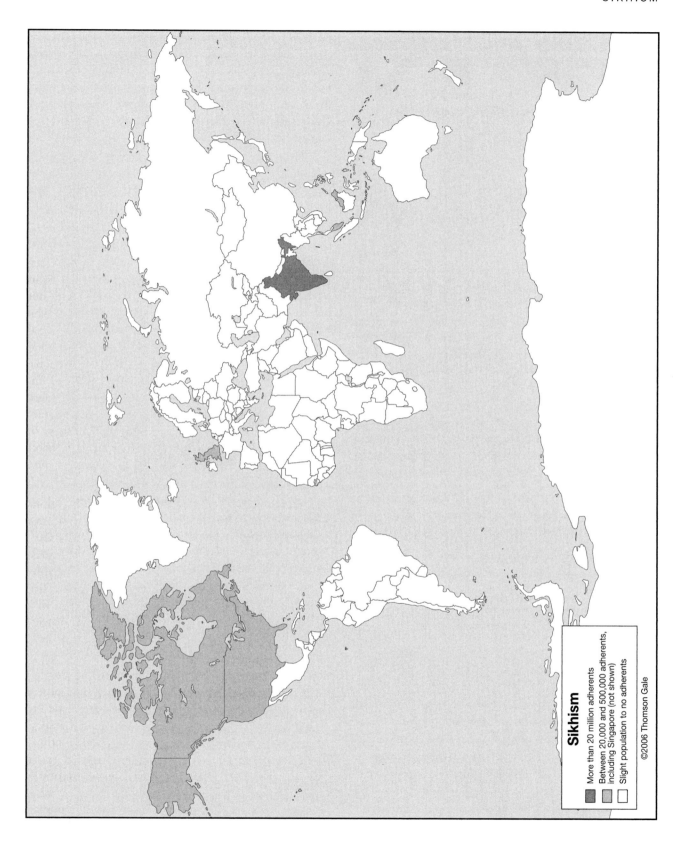

Sikhism

More than 20 million adherents

Between 20,000 and 500,000 adherents, including Singapore (not shown)

Slight population to no adherents

©2006 Thomson Gale

Three young girls of the Sikh faith. In India Sikh women continue to live in a patriarchal society. © SHELLEY GAZIN/CORBIS.

devotion with worldly activities set in the context of normal family life. As part of the Sikh liturgy, Guru Nanak's Japji (Meditation) was recited in the early hours of the morning, and So Dar (That Door) and Arti (Adoration) were sung in the evening.

Guru Nanak's spiritual message found expression at Kartarpur through key institutions: the *sangat* (holy fellowship), in which all felt that they belonged to one spiritual fraternity; the *dharamsala,* the original form of the Sikh place of worship; and the establishment of the *langar,* the dining convention that required people of all castes to sit in status-free lines (*pangat*) in order to share a common meal. The institution of *langar* promoted a spirit of unity and mutual belonging and struck at a major aspect of caste, thereby advancing the process of defining a distinctive Sikh identity. Finally, Guru Nanak created the institution of the Guru, or preceptor, who became the central authority in community life. Before

he died in 1539, Guru Nanak designated one of his disciples, Lehna, as his successor by renaming him Angad, meaning "my own limb." Thus, a lineage was established, and a legitimate succession was maintained intact from the appointment of Guru Angad to the death of Guru Gobind Singh (1666–1708), the 10th and last human Guru of the Sikhs.

The second Guru, Angad (1504–52), consolidated the nascent Sikh Panth in the face of the challenge offered by Guru Nanak's eldest son, Baba Sri Chand, the founder of the ascetic Udasi sect. Guru Angad further refined the Gurmukhi script for recording the compilation of the Guru's hymns (*bani*). The original Gurmukhi script was a systematization of two types of business shorthand Guru Nanak doubtless used professionally as a young man. This was an emphatic rejection of the superiority of the Devanagri and Arabic scripts (along with Sanskrit and the Arabic and Persian languages) and of the hegemonic authority they represented in the scholarly and religious circles of the time. The use of the Gurmukhi script added an element of demarcation and self-identity to the Sikh tradition. In fact, language became the single most important factor in the preservation of Sikh culture and identity and became the cornerstone of the religious distinctiveness that is part and parcel of the Sikh cultural heritage.

A major institutional development took place during the time of the third Guru, Amar Das (1479–1574), who introduced a variety of innovations to provide greater cohesion and unity to the ever-growing Sikh Panth. These included the establishment of the city of Goindval; the biannual festivals of Divali and Baisakhi, which provided an opportunity for the growing community to get together and meet the Guru; a missionary system (*manji*) for attracting new converts; and the preparation of the Goindval *pothi*s, collections of the compositions of the Gurus and some of the medieval poet-saints.

The fourth Guru, Ram Das (1534–81), founded the city of Ramdaspur, where he constructed a large pool for the purpose of bathing. It was named Amritsar, meaning "the nectar of immortality." To build an independent economic base, the Guru appointed deputies (*masand*s) to collect tithes and other contributions from loyal Sikhs. In addition to a large body of sacred verse, he composed the wedding hymn (*lavan*) for the solemnization of a Sikh marriage. Indeed, it was Guru Ram Das who explicitly responded to the question "Who is a Sikh?" with the following definition: "He who calls

People cross the bridge leading to the Golden Temple in Amritsar, India. The fifth Guru, Arjan, built the Harimandir, or Darbar Sahib (later known as the Golden Temple), which acquired prominence as the central place of Sikh worship. © BLAINE HARRINGTON III/CORBIS.

himself Sikh, a follower of the true Guru, should meditate on the divine Name after rising and bathing and recite Japji from memory, thus driving away all evil deeds and vices. As day unfolds he sings *gurbani* [utterances of the Gurus]; sitting or rising he meditates on the divine Name. He who repeats the divine Name with every breath and bite is indeed a true Sikh [*gursikh*] who gives pleasure to the Guru" (Adi Granth, pp. 305–6). Thus, the liturgical requirements of the reciting and singing of the sacred word became part of the very definition of being a Sikh. The most significant development was related to the self-image of Sikhs, who perceived themselves as unique and distinct from the other religious communities of North India.

The period of the fifth Guru, Arjan (1563–1606), was marked by a number of far-reaching institutional developments. First, at Amritsar, he built the Harimandir, or Darbar Sahib (later known as the Golden Temple), which acquired prominence as the central place of Sikh worship. Second, he compiled the first canonical scripture, the Adi Granth (Original Book), in 1604. Third, Guru Arjan established the rule of justice

and humility (*halemi raj*) in the town of Ramdaspur, where everyone lived in comfort (Adi Granth, p. 74). He proclaimed, "The divine rule prevails in Ramdaspur due to the grace of the Guru. No tax [*jizya*] is levied, nor any fine; there is no collector of taxes" (Adi Granth, pp. 430, 817). The administration of the town was evidently in the hands of Guru Arjan, although in a certain sense Ramdaspur was an autonomous town within the context and the framework of the Mughal rule of Emperor Akbar. Fourth, by the end of the sixteenth century the Sikh Panth had developed a strong sense of independent identity, which is evident from Guru Arjan's assertion "We are neither Hindu nor Musalaman" (Adi Granth, p. 1,136).

Fifth, dissensions within the ranks of the Sikh Panth became the source of serious conflict. A great number of the Guru's compositions focus on the issue of dealing with the problems created by "slanderers" (*nindak*), who were rival claimants to the office of the Guruship. The Udasis and the Bhallas, the latter formed by Guru Amar Da's eldest son, Baba Mohan, and his followers, had already established parallel seats of au-

Sikh men participate in the amrit sanskar *initiation ceremony. During the ceremony the novice drinks the* amrit *and has it sprinkled in his eyes and hair. The initiate takes the oath throughout each procedure.* © TIM PAGE/CORBIS.

thority and had paved the way for competing views of Sikh identity. The rivalry of these dissenters had been heightened when Guru Arjan was designated for the throne of Ram Das in preference to his eldest brother, Prithi Chand, who even approached the local Mughal administrators to claim the position of his father. At some point Prithi Chand and his followers were branded Minas (dissembling rogues).

Finally, the author of *Dabistan-i-Mazahib* ("The School of Religions"), a mid-seventeenth-century work in Persian, testifies that the number of Sikhs had rapidly increased during Guru Arjan's period and that "there were not many cities in the inhabited countries where some Sikhs were not to be found." In fact, the growing strength of the Sikh movement attracted the unfavorable attention of the ruling authorities because of the reaction of Muslim revivalists of the Naqshbandi order in Mughal India. There is clear evidence in the compositions of Guru Arjan that a series of complaints were made against him to the functionaries of the Mughal state, giving them an excuse to watch the activities of the Sikhs. The liberal policy of Emperor Akbar may have sheltered the Guru and his followers for a time, but in May 1606, within eight months of Akbar's death,

Guru Arjan, under torture by the orders of the new emperor, Jahangir, was executed. The Sikh community perceived his death as the so-called first martyrdom, which became a turning point in the history of the Sikh tradition.

Indeed, a radical reshaping of the Sikh Panth took place after Guru Arjan's martyrdom. The sixth Guru, Hargobind (1595–1644), signaled the formal process when he traditionally donned two swords, symbolizing the spiritual (*piri*) as well as the temporal (*miri*) investiture. He also built the Akal Takhat (Throne of the Timeless One) facing the Darbar Sahib, which represented the newly assumed role of temporal authority. Under his direct leadership the Sikh Panth took up arms in order to protect itself from Mughal hostility. From the Sikh perspective this new development was not taken at the cost of abandoning the original spiritual base. Rather, it was meant to achieve a balance between temporal and spiritual concerns. A Sikh theologian of the period, Bhai Gurdas, defended this martial response as "hedging the orchard of the Sikh faith with [the] hardy and thorny *kikar* tree." After four skirmishes with Mughal troops, Guru Hargobind withdrew to the Shivalik hills, and Kiratpur became the new center of the mainline Sikh tradition. Amritsar fell into the hands of the Minas, who established a parallel line of Guruship with the support of the Mughal authorities.

During the time of the seventh and eighth Gurus, Har Rai (1630–61) and Har Krishan (1656–64), the emphasis on armed conflict with the Mughal authorities receded, but the Gurus held court and kept a regular force of Sikh horsemen. During the period of the ninth Guru, Tegh Bahadur (1621–75), however, the increasing strength of the Sikh movement in rural areas again attracted Mughal attention. Guru Tegh Bahadur's ideas of a just society inspired a spirit of fearlessness among his followers: "He who holds none in fear, nor is afraid of anyone, Nanak, acknowledge him alone as a man of true wisdom" (Adi Granth, p. 1,427). Such ideas posed a direct challenge to the increasingly restrictive policies of the Mughal emperor, Aurangzeb, who reigned from 1658 to 1707. Not surprisingly, Guru Tegh Bahadur was summoned to Delhi by the orders of the emperor, and on his refusal to embrace Islam he was publicly executed in Chandni Chowk on 11 November 1675. The Sikhs perceived his death as the second martyrdom, which involved larger issues of human rights and freedom of conscience.

Glossary

Adi Granth Original Book; the primary Sikh scripture

Akal Purakh Timeless One; God

amrit divine nectar; sweetened water used in the initiation ceremony of the Khalsa

dan charity; a person's relation with society

granthi reader of scripture and leader of rituals in the gurdwara

gurdwara door of the Guru; house of worship

Gurmukh a person oriented toward the Guru

Guru spiritual preceptor, either a person or the mystical "voice" of Akal Purakh

Guru Granth, or Guru Granth Sahib the Adi Granth, or scripture, functioning as Guru

Guru Panth the Sikh Panth, or community, functioning as Guru

hukam divine order

ishnan purity

janam-sakhi birth narrative; a hagiographical biography

karah prashad sanctified food, prepared in a large iron dish, or karahi

karma influence of a person's past actions on his future lives

katha a discourse on scripture in a gurdwara; homily

Kaur female surname meaning Princess

Khalsa order of "pure" Sikhs, established by Guru Gobind Singh in 1699

kirpan sword

kirtan devotional singing

langar community dining

nam the divine name

panth path

pati the core of a person, including self-respect

rahit code

sangat holy fellowship; a congregation

sansar rebirth; transmigration

shabad the divine word

sikh learner

Sikh Panth the Sikh community

Sikh Rahit Maryada Sikh Code of Conduct

Singh male surname meaning Lion

vak divine command

Tradition holds that the Sikhs who were present at the scene of Guru Tegh Bahadur's execution shrank from recognition, concealing their identity for fear they might suffer a similar fate. In order to respond to this new situation, the 10th Guru, Gobind Singh, resolved to impose on his followers an outward form that would make them instantly recognizable. He restructured the Sikh Panth and instituted the Khalsa (pure), an order of loyal Sikhs bound by a common identity and discipline. On Baisakhi Day 1699 at Anandpur, Guru Gobind Singh initiated the first so-called Cherished Five (*panj piare*), who formed the nucleus of the new order of the Khalsa. The five volunteers who responded to the Guru's call for loyalty, and who came from different castes and regions of India, received the initiation through a ceremony that involved sweetened water (*amrit*) stirred with a two-edged sword and sanctified by the recitation of five liturgical prayers.

From the perspective of ritual studies, three significant issues were linked with the first *amrit* ceremony. First, all who chose to join the order of the Khalsa through the ceremony were understood to have been "reborn" in the house of the Guru and thus to have assumed a new identity. The male members were given the surname *Singh* (Lion), and female members were given the surname *Kaur* (Princess), with the intention of creating a parallel system of aristocratic titles in relation to the Rajput hill chiefs of the surrounding areas of Anandpur. Second, the Guru symbolically transferred his spiritual authority to the Cherished Five when he himself received the nectar of the double-edged sword from their hands and thus became a part of the Khalsa Panth and subject to its collective will. In this way he not only paved the way for the termination of a personal Guruship but also abolished the institution of the *masands*, which was becoming increasingly disruptive. Several of the *masands* had refused to forward collections to the Guru, creating factionalism in the Sikh Panth. In addition, Guru Gobind Singh removed the threat posed by the competing seats of authority when he declared that the Khalsa should have no dealings with the followers of Prithi Chand (Minas), Dhir Mal (Guru Har Rai's elder brother, who established his seat at Kartarpur, Jalandhar), and Ram Rai (Guru Har Krishan's elder brother, who established his seat at Dehra Dun). Finally, Guru Gobind Singh delivered the nucleus of the Sikh Rahit Maryada (Code of Conduct) at the inauguration of the Khalsa. By sanctifying the hair with *amrit*, he made it "the official seal of the Guru," and the cutting of bodily hair was thus strictly prohibited. The Guru further imposed a rigorous ban on smoking. He made the most visible symbols of external identity, the so-called five Ks, mandatory for the Khalsa, as explained below under SACRED SYMBOLS.

The inauguration of the Khalsa was the culmination of the canonical period in the development of Sikhism. Guru Gobind Singh also closed the Sikh canon by adding a collection of the works of his father, Guru Tegh Bahadur, to the original compilation of the Adi Granth. Before he died in 1708, he terminated the line of personal Gurus, and he installed the Adi Granth as the eternal Guru for Sikhs. Thereafter, the authority of the Guru was invested together in the scripture (Guru Granth) and in the corporate community (Guru Panth). Sikhism thus evolved in response to four main elements. The first of these was the ideology based on the religious and cultural innovations of Guru Nanak and his nine successors. The second was the rural base of Punjabi society. During the period of Guru Arjan the founding of the villages of Taran Taran, Sri Hargobindpur, and Kartarpur in rural areas saw large numbers of converts from the local Jat peasantry. It may have been the militant traditions of the Jats that brought the Sikh Panth into increasing conflict with Mughal authorities, a conflict that shaped the future direction of the movement. The third factor was the conflict created within the Sikh community by dissidents, which originally worked to counter and then, paradoxically, to enhance the process of the crystallization of the Sikh tradition. The fourth element was the period of Punjabi history from the sixteenth to the eighteenth centuries, in which the Sikh Panth evolved in tension with the Mughal authorities. All four elements combined to produce the mutual interaction between ideology and environment that came to characterize the historical development of Sikhism.

CENTRAL DOCTRINES The nature of ultimate reality in Sikh doctrine is succinctly expressed in the Mul Mantar (seed formula), the preamble to the Sikh scripture. The basic theological statement reads as follows: "There is one Supreme Being ['1' *Oankar*], the Eternal Reality, the Creator, without fear and devoid of enmity, immortal, never incarnated, self-existent, known by grace through the Guru. The Eternal One, from the beginning, through all time, present now, the Everlasting Reality" (Adi Granth, p. 1). The numeral "1" at the beginning of the original Punjabi text represents the unity of Akal Purakh (the Timeless One, or God), a concept that Guru Nanak interpreted in monotheistic terms. It affirms that Akal Purakh is one without a second, the source as well as the goal of all that exists. As the creator and sustainer of the universe, he lovingly watches over it. He is the source of love and grace and responds to the devotion of his humblest followers. Paradoxically, he is both transcendent (*nirguna*, "without attributes") and immanent (*saguna*, "with attributes"). Only in personal experience can he be truly known. Despite the stress laid on *nirguna* discourse within the Sikh tradition, which directs the devotee to worship a nonincarnate, universal God, in Sikh doctrine God is partially embodied in the divine name (*nam*) and in the collective words (*bani*) and in the person of the Guru and the saints.

With regard to the creation of the world, there is Guru Nanak's cosmology hymn in Maru Raga (Adi Granth, pp. 1035–36). He maintained that the universe "comes into being by the divine order" (Adi Granth, p. 1). Guru Nanak said further, "From the True One came air and from air came water; from water he created the three worlds and infused in every heart his own light" (Adi Granth, p. 19). He employed the well-known Indic ideas of creation through the five basic elements of air, water, ether, fire, and earth: "The Eternal One created nights, the days of the week, and the seasons of the year. With them came wind and water, fire and the regions established below. Amidst them all was set the earth, wherein the Maker meditates. Wondrous the creatures there created, boundless variety, countless their names. All must be judged for the deeds they perform, by a

The Adi Granth

The Adi Granth, the principal scripture of the Sikhs, has played a unique role as Guru, or preceptor, in the personal piety, liturgy, and corporate life of the Sikh Panth, or community. It has provided a framework for the shaping of the Sikh Panth and has been a decisive factor in giving Sikhs a distinctive identity. The Adi Granth occupies a central position in all Sikh ceremonies, and the experience of hearing it read has provided the Sikh tradition with a sense of the living presence of the divine Guru. The daily process of "seeking the divine command" by opening the scripture at random inspires Sikhs throughout the world and confirms the function of the scripture as Guru, known as Guru Granth Sahib. Indeed, the Guru Granth Sahib has given Sikhs a sacred focus for reflection and for discovering the meaning of life. It has functioned as a supratextual source of authority within the Sikh tradition. Thus, the ultimate authority within the Sikh Panth for a wide range of personal and public conduct lies in the Guru Granth Sahib. In a certain sense Sikhs have taken their conception of sacred scripture further than the People of the Book such as Jews and Muslims.

faultless judge in a perfect court" (Adi Granth, p. 7). As the creation of Akal Purakh, the physical universe is real but subject to constant change. For Guru Nanak the world was divinely inspired. It is a place that provides human beings with an opportunity to perform their duty and to achieve union with Akal Purakh. Thus, actions performed in earthly existence are important, for "all of us carry the fruits of our deeds" (Adi Granth, p. 4).

The notions of karma (actions) and sansar (rebirth, or transmigration) are fundamental to all religious traditions originating in India. Karma is popularly understood in Indian thought as the principle of cause and effect. The principle is logical and inexorable, but karma is also understood as a predisposition that safeguards the notion of free choice. In Sikh doctrine, however, the notion of karma underwent a radical change. For the

Gurus the law of karma was not inexorable. In the context of the Guru Nanak's theology, karma is subject to the higher principle of the "divine order" (hukam). The divine order is an "all-embracing principle" that is the sum total of all divinely instituted laws in the cosmos. It is a revelation of the divine nature. Indeed, the law of karma is replaced by Akal Purakh's hukam, which is no longer an impersonal causal phenomenon but falls within the sphere of Akal Purakh's omnipotence and justice: "The divine name can wash away millions of sins in a moment" (Adi Granth, p. 1,283). In fact, the primacy of divine grace over the law of karma is always maintained in Sikh teachings, and divine grace even breaks the chain of adverse karma.

Guru Nanak employed the following key terms to describe the nature of divine revelation in its totality: nam (the divine name), shabad (divine word), and guru (divine preceptor). The nam reflects the manifestation of the divine presence everywhere, yet because of their haumai, or self-centeredness, humans fail to perceive it. The Punjabi term haumai (I, I) signifies the powerful impulse to succumb to personal gratification, so that a person is separated from Akal Purakh and thus continues to suffer within the cycle of rebirth (sansar). Akal Purakh, however, looks graciously upon the suffering of people. He reveals himself through the Guru by uttering the shabad (divine word) that communicates a sufficient understanding of the nam (divine name) to those who are able to hear it. The shabad is the actual "utterance," and in "hearing" it one awakens to the reality of the divine name, immanent in all that lies around and within.

The institution of the Guru carries spiritual authority in the Sikh tradition. In most Indian religious traditions the term guru stands for a human teacher who communicates divine knowledge and provides his disciples with a cognitive map for liberation. In Sikhism, however, its meaning has evolved into a cluster of doctrines over a period of time. There are four focal points of spiritual authority, each acknowledged within the Sikh tradition as Guru: (1) doctrine of eternal Guru, (2) doctrine of personal Guru, (3) doctrine of Guru Granth, and (4) doctrine of Guru Panth. First, Guru Nanak used the term in three basic senses: the Guru is Akal Purakh; the Guru is the voice of Akal Purakh; and the Guru is the word, the truth, of Akal Purakh. To experience the eternal Guru is to experience divine guidance. Guru Nanak himself acknowledged Akal Purakh as his Guru: "He who is the infinite, supreme God is the Guru whom Nanak has met" (Adi Granth, p. 599). In Sikh usage, therefore, the Guru is the voice of Akal Purakh, mystically uttered within the human heart, mind, and soul (*man*).

Second, the personal Guru functions as the channel through whom the voice of Akal Purakh becomes audible. Nanak became the embodiment of the eternal Guru only when he received the divine word and conveyed it to his disciples. The same spirit manifested itself successively in those who followed. In fact, Guru Nanak bypassed the claims of his own son Sri Chand, disqualified by his ascetic ideals, in favor of a more worthy disciple. Guru Angad followed the example of his master when he chose the elderly disciple Amar Das in preference to his own sons. By the time of the third Guru, however, the hereditary pattern asserted itself when Amar Das designated as his successor his son-in-law, Ram Das, who, in turn, was followed by his youngest son, Arjan, the direct ancestor of all later Gurus. Nevertheless, the succession in each case went to the most suitable candidate, not automatically from father to eldest son. In Sikh doctrine a theory of spiritual succession was advanced in the form of "the unity of Guruship," in which there was no difference between the founder and the successors. Thus, all represented one and the same light (*jot*), just as a single flame can ignite a series of torches. The same principle is illustrated in the Adi Granth by the fact that the six Gurus contributing to the Sikh scripture signed their compositions "Nanak," each being identified by the code word *Mahala* (King) and the appropriate number. Thus, the compositions labeled Mahala I (M I) are by Guru Nanak, and those labeled M 2, M 3, M 4, M 5, and M 9 are by Guru Angad, Guru Amar Das, Guru Ram Das, Guru Arjan, and Guru Tegh Bahadur, respectively.

Third, in Sikh usage the Adi Granth is normally referred to as the Guru Granth Sahib, which implies a confession of faith in the scripture as Guru. As such, the Guru Granth Sahib carries the same status and authority as did the 10 personal Gurus, from Guru Nanak through Guru Gobind Singh, and it must, therefore, be viewed as the source of ultimate authority within the Sikh Panth. In actual practice Guru Granth Sahib performs the role of Guru in the personal piety and corporate identity of the Sikh community. It has become the symbol of ultimate sanctity for the Sikh Panth, and it is treated with the most profound respect when it is installed ceremonially in a *gurdwara* (Guru's house), the Sikh place of worship.

Finally, the key phrase Guru Panth is normally employed in two senses: first, as the Panth of the Guru, referring to the Sikh community in general; and second, as the Panth as the Guru, pointing specifically to the Sikh community's role as a Guru. This doctrine fully developed from the earlier idea that "the Guru is mystically present in the congregation." At the inauguration of the Khalsa in 1699, Guru Gobind Singh symbolically transferred his authority to the Cherished Five when he received initiation from their hands. Sainapati, the near contemporary author of *Gur Sobha* (1711), recorded that Guru Gobind Singh designated the Khalsa as the collective embodiment of his divine mandate: "Upon the Khalsa which I have created I shall bestow the succession. The Khalsa is my physical form and I am one with the Khalsa. To all eternity I am manifest in the Khalsa. Those whose hearts are purged of falsehood will be known as the true Khalsa; and the Khalsa, freed from error and illusion, will be my true Guru." Thus, the elite corps of the Khalsa has always claimed to speak authoritatively on behalf of the whole Sikh Panth, although at times non-Khalsa Sikhs interpret the doctrine of Guru Panth as conferring authority on a community more broadly defined. As a practical matter, consensus within the community of Sikhs is achieved by following democratic traditions.

In order to achieve a state of spiritual liberation (*jivan mukati*) within one's lifetime, one must transcend the unregenerate condition created by the influence of *haumai*. In fact, *haumai* is the source of the five evil impulses traditionally known as lust (*kam*), anger (*krodh*), covetousness (*lobh*), attachment to worldly things (*moh*), and pride (*hankar*). Under the influence of *haumai* a person becomes self-willed (*manmukh*), one who is so attached to his passions for worldly pleasures that he forgets the divine name and wastes his entire life in evil and suffering. This unregenerate condition can be transcended by means of the strictly interior discipline of *nam-simaran*, or "remembering the divine Name." This three-fold process ranges from the repetition of a sacred word, usually *Vahiguru* (praise to the eternal Guru), through the devotional singing of hymns with the congregation, to sophisticated meditation on the nature of Akal Purakh. The first and the third levels of this practice involve private devotions, while the second refers to a corporate activity. On the whole the discipline of *nam-simaran* is designed to bring a person into harmony with the divine order (*hukam*). The person thus gains the experience of ever growing wonder (*vismad*) in spiritual life, and he achieves the ultimate condition of blissful equanimity (*sahaj*) when the spirit ascends to the "realm of Truth" (*sach khand*), the fifth and the last of the spiritual stages, in which the soul finds mystical union with Akal Purakh, or God.

The primacy of divine grace over personal effort is fundamental to Guru Nanak's theology. There is, however, neither fatalism nor any kind of passive acceptance of a predestined future in his view of life. He proclaimed, "With your own hands carve out your own destiny" (Adi Granth, p. 474). Indeed, personal effort in the form of good actions has a place in Guru Nanak's view of life. His idea of "divine free choice," on the one hand, and his emphasis on a "life of activism" based on human freedom, on the other, reflect his ability to hold in tension seemingly opposed elements. Guru Nanak explicitly saw this balancing of opposed tendencies, which avoids rigid predestination theories and yet enables people to see their own free will as a part of Akal Purakh, as allowing Sikhs the opportunity to create their own destinies, a feature stereotypically associated with Sikh enterprise throughout the world.

MORAL CODE OF CONDUCT In his role as what the sociologist Max Weber called an "ethical prophet," Guru Nanak called for a decisive break with existing formulations and laid the foundations of a new, rational model of normative behavior based on divine authority. Throughout his writings he conceived of his work as divinely commissioned, and he demanded the obedience of his audience as an ethical duty. In fact, Guru Nanak repeatedly proclaimed that the realization of the divine truth depended upon the conduct of the seeker. At the beginning of his Japji (Meditation), he raised the fundamental question "How is Truth to be attained, how the veil of falsehood torn aside?" He then responded, "Nanak, thus it is written: submit to the divine order [*hukam*], walk in its ways" (Adi Granth, p. 1). Truth obviously is not obtained by intellectual effort or cunning but only by personal commitment. To know truth one must live in it.

The salient features of Sikh ethics are as follows. First, the Sikh ethical structure stands on the firm rock of a "living faith" in Akal Purakh. Accordingly, an action is right or an ideal is good if it contributes toward the love of Akal Purakh. Second, the seeker of the divine truth must live an ethical life. An immoral person is neither worthy of being called a true seeker nor capable of attaining the spiritual goal of life. Any dichotomy be-

tween spiritual development and moral conduct is not approved in Sikh ethics. In this context Guru Nanak explicitly said, "Truth is the highest virtue, but higher still is truthful living" (Adi Granth, p. 62). Indeed, truthful conduct (*sach achar*) is at the heart of Sikh ethics.

Third, the central focus in the Sikh moral scheme involves the cultivation of virtues such as wisdom, contentment, justice, humility, truthfulness, temperance, love, forgiveness, charity, purity, and fear of Akal Purakh. Guru Nanak remarked, "Sweetness and humility are the essence of all virtues" (Adi Granth, p. 470). These virtues not only enrich the personal lives of individuals, but they also promote socially responsible living. The Gurus laid great stress on the need to earn one's living through honest means. In particular, living by alms or begging is strongly rejected. Emphasizing hard work and sharing, Sikh ethics forbids withdrawal from social participation. Fourth, the Gurus offered their own vision of the cultivation of egalitarian ideals in social relations. Such ideals are based on the principle of social equality, gender equality, and human brotherhood. Thus, it is not surprising that any kind of discrimination based on caste or gender is expressly rejected in Sikh ethics.

Fifth, the key element of religious living is to render service (*seva*) to others in the form of mutual help and voluntary work. The real importance of seva lies in sharing one's resources of "body, mind, and wealth" (*tan-man-dhan*) with others. This is an expression toward fellow beings of what one feels toward Akal Purakh. The service must be rendered without the desire for self-glorification, and, in addition, self-giving service must be done without setting oneself up as a judge of other people. The Ardas (Petition, or Sikh Prayer) holds in high esteem the quality of "seeing but not judging" (*anadith karana*). Social bonds are often damaged beyond redemption when people, irrespective of their own limitations, unconscionably judge others. The Sikh Gurus emphasized the need to destroy this root of social strife and enmity through self-giving service.

Finally, in Guru Nanak's view all human actions presuppose the functioning of divine grace. Thus, one must continue to perform good actions at all stages of spiritual development to prevent a "fall from grace" and to set an example for others. Sikhism stresses the dignity of regular labor as a part of spiritual discipline. This is summed up in the following triple commandment: engage in honest labor (*kirat karani*) for a living, adore the divine name (*nam japana*), and share the fruit of labor with others (*vand chhakana*). The formula stresses both the centrality of meditative worship and the necessity of righteous living in the world. The Sikh Gurus placed great emphasis on a spirit of optimism (*charhdi kala*) in the face of adverse circumstances. They stressed the ideals of moderate living and disciplined worldliness in contrast to the ideals of asceticism and self-mortification. In this context Guru Nanak proclaimed, "As the lotus in the pool and the water fowl in the stream remain dry; so a person should live, untouched by the world. One should meditate on the Name of the Supreme Lord" (Adi Granth, p. 938).

SACRED BOOKS The Adi Granth (Original Book) is the primary scripture of the Sikhs. It contains the works of the first 5 and 9th Sikh Gurus, 4 bards (Satta, Balvand, Sundar, and Mardana), 11 Bhatts (panegyrists associated with the Sikh court), and 15 Bhagats (devotees such as Kabir, Namdev, Ravidas, Shaikh Farid, and other medieval poets of Sant, Sufi, and Bhakti origin). The standard version contains a total of 1,430 pages, and each page is identical. The text of the Adi Granth is divided into three major sections. The introductory section includes three liturgical prayers. The middle section, which contains the bulk of the material, is divided into 31 major ragas, or Indian musical patterns. The final section includes an epilogue consisting of miscellaneous works that could not be accommodated in the middle section.

The second sacred collection, the Dasam Granth (Book of the 10th Guru), is attributed to the 10th Guru, Gobind Singh, but it must have extended beyond his time to include the writings of others as well. Mani Singh, who died in 1734, compiled the collection early in the eighteenth century. Its modern standard version of 1,428 pages consists of four major types of compositions: devotional texts, autobiographical works, miscellaneous writings, and a collection of mythical narratives and popular anecdotes.

The works of two early Sikhs, Bhai Gurdas (1551–1636) and Bhai Nand Lal Goya (c. 1633–1713), make up the third category of sacred literature. Along with the sacred compositions of the Gurus, their works are approved in the official manual of the Sikh Rahit Maryada (Sikh Code of Conduct) for singing in the *gurdwara*s.

The last category of Sikh literature includes three distinct genres: the *janam-sakhi*s (birth narratives), the *rahit-nama*s (manuals of code of conduct), and the *gur-bilas* (pleasure of the Guru) literature. The *janam-sakhi*s

are hagiographical accounts of Guru Nanak's life produced by the Sikh community in the seventeenth century. The *rahit-nama*s provide rare insight into the evolving nature of the Khalsa code in the eighteenth and nineteenth centuries. The *gur-bilas* mainly focuses on the mighty deeds of two warrior Gurus, Guru Hargobind and, particularly, Guru Gobind Singh.

SACRED SYMBOLS All Sikhs initiated into the order of the Khalsa must observe the Sikh Rahit Maryada (Sikh Code of Conduct) as enunciated by Guru Gobind Singh and subsequently elaborated. The most significant part of the code is the enjoinder to wear five visible symbols of identity, known from their Punjabi names as the five Ks (*panj kakke*). These are unshorn hair (*kes*), symbolizing spirituality and saintliness; a wooden comb (*kangha*), signifying order and discipline in life; a sword (*kirpan*), symbolizing divine grace, dignity, and courage; a steel "wrist-ring" (*kara*), signifying responsibility and allegiance to the Guru; and a pair of short breeches (*kachh*), symbolizing moral restraint. Among Sikhs the five Ks are outer symbols of the divine word, implying a direct correlation between *bani* (divine utterance) and *bana* (Khalsa dress). The five Ks, along with a turban for male Sikhs, symbolize that the Khalsa Sikhs, while reciting prayers, are dressed in the word of God. Their minds are thus purified and inspired, and their bodies are girded to do battle with the day's temptations. In addition, Khalsa Sikhs are prohibited from the four cardinal sins (*char kurahit*): "cutting the hair, using tobacco, committing adultery, and eating meat that has not come from an animal killed with a single blow."

EARLY AND MODERN LEADERS During the eighteenth century the Khalsa Sikhs were largely occupied in fighting the armies of Mughals and Afghan invaders, until Sikhs emerged victorious with the establishment of rule in the Punjab under Maharaja Ranjit Singh, who reigned from 1799 to 1839. This brought settled conditions for the Sikh community, and territorial expansion attracted people of different cultural and religious backgrounds into the fold of Sikhism. The contemporary appearance of the Darbar Sahib at Amritsar owes much to the munificent patronage of the maharaja. He patronized scribes, who made beautiful copies of the standard version of the Sikh scripture that were sent as gifts to the Sikh *takhat*s (thrones) and other major historical *gurdwara*s. Maharaja Ranjit Singh's rule was marked by religious diversity within the Sikh Panth.

The loss of the Sikh kingdom to British India in 1849 created a new situation for the Sikh Panth. In fact, the modern religious and cultural transformation within the Sikh tradition took place during the colonial period at the initiatives of the Singh Sabha (Society of the Singhs). This reform movement began in 1873 at Amritsar under the leadership of four prominent Sikhs: Sardar Thakur Singh Sandhanvalia (1837–87), Baba Khem Singh Bedi (1832–1905), Kanvar Bikrama Singh (1835–87) of Kapurthala, and Giani Gian Singh (1824–84) of Amritsar. The principal objective of the Singh Sabha reformers was to reaffirm the distinctiveness of Sikh identity in the face of the twin threats posed by the casual reversion to Hindu practices during Sikh rule and the explicit challenges from actively proselytizing religious movements such as Christian missionaries and the Arya Samaj (Society of the Aryas). The Tat Khalsa (Pure Khalsa), the dominant wing of the Singh Sabha movement, succeeded in eradicating all forms of religious diversity by the end of the nineteenth century and established norms of religious orthodoxy and orthopraxy. The reformers were largely successful in making the Khalsa ideal the orthodox form of Sikhism, and they systematized and clarified the Khalsa tradition to make Sikhism consistent and effective for propagation. Indeed, the Tat Khalsa ideal of Sikh identity, which was forged in the colonial crucible, was both old and new.

Further, in the Anand Marriage Act of 1909 the Tat Khalsa reformers secured legal recognition of a distinctive ritual for Sikh weddings, and they reestablished direct Khalsa control of the major historical gurdwaras, many of which had fallen over the years into the hands of corrupt Mahants (Custodians) supported by the British. Inspired by the Tat Khalsa ideal, the Akali movement of the 1920s eventually secured British assent to the Sikh Gurdwaras Act of 1925. The immediate effect of the act was to make available to the Shiromani Gurdwara Prabandhak Committee (SGPC; Chief Management Committee of Sikh Shrines) the enormous political and economic benefits that came from control of the gurdwaras. In 1950, after a consensus was reached within the Sikh community, the standard manual, entitled Sikh Rahit Maryada, was published under the auspices of the SGPC. The manual has ever since been regarded as an authoritative statement of Sikh doctrine and behavior.

Master Tara Singh (1885–1967), a president of the SGPC, was the dominant figure on the Sikh political scene for the middle third of the twentieth century.

Later Gurcharan Singh Tohra (born in 1924) held the office of the president of the SGPC for more than two decades. The first woman ever to become president of the SGPC was Bibi Jagir Kaur, who held the office in1999–2000. Parallel to the SGPC, the Akali Dal (Army of the Followers of the Timeless One) has functioned as a Sikh political party. Two saintly figures, Sant Fateh Singh (1911–72) and Sant Harchand Singh Longowal (1932–85), were among the prominent leaders of the Akali Dal. After the 1984 assault by Indian government troops on the Darbar Sahib at Amritsar, however, the Akali Dal was divided into several factions, with Parkash Singh Badal becoming the leader of the dominant group.

MAJOR THEOLOGIANS AND AUTHORS The first acknowledged Sikh theologian was Bhai Gurdas (1551–1636), whom Guru Arjan chose to act as his assistant during the final recording of the Adi Granth. He was a poet of rare insight whose works are generally regarded as the "key to the Guru Granth Sahib." The most influential among his writings are 39 lengthy vars (ballads) that provide extensive commentaries on the teachings of the Gurus. Throughout his works Bhai Gurdas deals with essential doctrines taught by the Gurus (gurmat): the unity of Guruship, the Sikh way of life, Sikh morality, holy fellowship, the ideal Sikh who has turned toward the Guru (gurmukh), and so on.

Santokh Singh (1788–1843) was the most prominent of all Sikh hagiographers. He earned considerable popularity owing to the fact that he covered the complete range of the Guru's lives in Braj Bhasha, which consists of 51,820 verses. His magnum opus, Suraj Prakash, is frequently used in Sikh discourses (katha) in the gurdwaras. Kahn Singh Nabha (1861–1938) was a renowned scholar of Tat Khalsa ideals. His Mahan Kosh (1930), an encyclopedia of Sikh literature, is a permanent monument to his unmatched industry and erudition. The name of Max Arthur Macauliffe (1837–1913) is deeply revered in the Sikh Panth. A British civil servant assigned to Punjab, he rose to be a deputy commissioner in 1882 and a divisional judge in 1884. Meanwhile, he studied the literature of the Sikhs, and in 1893 he resigned his position to devote his time exclusively to the writing of the six-volume The Sikh Religion (1909), containing the lives of the 10 Gurus and of the poet-saints (bhagats) of the Adi Granth, together with extensive translations of their works. Bhai Vir Singh (1872–1957), a celebrated poet, scholar, and exegete, was the leading intellectual of the Singh Sabha movement and has continued to command considerable respect for his many literary works. Bhai Jodh Singh (1882–1981) was a patriarchal figure for many years in the field of Sikh theology, and his *Gurmat Niranay* (1932) offers a systematic statement of Sikh doctrines.

Ganda Singh (1900–87) was a doyen of Sikh history whose critical works became influential in northern India. Harbans Singh (1921–98), a distinguished interpreter of Sikh history and tradition, edited the four-volume *The Encyclopaedia of Sikhism* (1992–98), thus offering a valuable contribution in the area of Sikh studies. Khushwant Singh (born in 1915) has made his mark as a Sikh journalist, and his classic two-volume *A History of the Sikhs*, originally published in 1963 and published in India in 1977, is widely acclaimed. J.S. Grewal (born in 1927) is considered to be the father of the field of modern Sikh and Punjab studies. As a leading Western scholar of Sikh religion and history, W.H. McLeod (born in 1932) has single-handedly introduced, nourished, and advanced the field of Sikh studies. His works have been received with much enthusiasm and global critical acclaim, and on a number of occasions he has represented the Sikhs and Sikhism to both academic and popular audiences in the English-speaking world. The credit for exporting Sikhism to the West, however, goes to Harbhajan Singh Khalsa (born in 1929), popularly known as Yogi Bhajan, who founded the Sikh Dharma movement in the United States in 1971. The movement, which is best known as 3HO (Healthy Happy Holy Organization), claims several thousand Western adherents scattered over some 17 countries.

ORGANIZATIONAL STRUCTURE Sikhism is strictly a lay organization, which makes the issue of religious authority within the Panth a complex one. The Sikh Panth recognizes no priesthood, and there is no centralized "church" or attendant religious hierarchy. At the inauguration of the Khalsa on Baisakhi Day 1699, Guru Gobind Singh chose five Sikhs (*panj piare*, the "Cherished Five") of proven loyalty to receive the first initiation of the double-edged sword and then to administer it to the Guru himself and to others. He thus symbolically transferred his authority to the Cherished Five, who became responsible for conducting initiation ceremonies. According to well-established tradition, Guru Gobind Singh conferred his spiritual authority upon the scripture (Guru Granth) and the community (Guru Panth) together when he died in 1708. Since then the twin doc-

trines of Guru Granth and Guru Panth have successfully provided cohesive ideals for the evolution of the Sikh community.

In 1925 the Shiromani Gurdwara Prabandhak Committee (SGPC; Chief Management Committee of Sikh Shrines) came into being as an elected body to manage shrines in the Punjab. As a democratic institution, it eventually became the authoritative voice of the Sikh community in religious and political affairs. In order to maintain its control over the large Sikh community, it invokes the authority of the Akal Takhat in Amritsar, which is the seat of religious and temporal authority among Sikhs. The Akal Takhat may issue edicts (*hukam-nama*s) that provide guidance or clarification on any aspect of Sikh doctrine or practice. It may punish any person charged with a violation of religious discipline or with activity "prejudicial" to Sikh interests and unity, and it may place on record individuals who have performed outstanding service or made sacrifices for the sake of the Sikh cause.

The *gurdwara*s in the Sikh diaspora have their own managing committees. Each congregation (*sangat*) is a democratic community. Because there are no priests or ordained ministers, lay people actively participate in the various functions of a *gurdwara* on a voluntary basis. Each *gurdwara*, however, has an official *granthi*, or "reader" of the Sikh scriptures, who is responsible for conducting its routine rituals. As with other Sikh institutions, *gurdwara*s play a central role in community life by making it more religiously and culturally homogenous. They offer a wide variety of educational and cultural programs, such as the teaching and perpetuation of the Punjabi language and of Sikh music and songs among new generations. Some *gurdwara*s operate a Sikh version of a Sunday school, where children are given formal instruction in the tenets of Sikhism, while others support Sikh charitable and political causes.

HOUSES OF WORSHIP AND HOLY PLACES The Sikh house of worship is the *gurdwara*, which literally means "the door of the Guru." In fact, a *gurdwara* is any place that houses the Guru Granth Sahib. The preeminent *gurdwara* of the Sikhs is the Darbar Sahib in Amritsar, which is constructed in the center of a pool of particular sanctity. A *gurdwara* generally has an impressive white dome constructed on the model of the architecture of the Darbar Sahib. The presence of a public *gurdwara* is signaled by a triangular saffron Khalsa flag (*nishan sahib*) flying above it.

There are five major historic *gurdwara*s in India, each of which fulfills a special role in the Sikh Panth. These are the *takhat*s (thrones) that play a temporal role in addition to the spiritual functions of all *gurdwara*s. Akal Takhat is the supreme seat of temporal authority of the Sikh faith, and from its balcony all matters of vital importance to the Panth as a whole are promulgated. The remaining four *takhat*s are associated with the life of Guru Gobind Singh. They are Sri Harmandir Ji in Patna, marking his birthplace; Kesgarh in Anandpur Sahib, birthplace of the Khalsa; Sri Damdama Sahib in the village of Talvandi Sabo, where Guru Gobind Singh rested following his withdrawal to southern Punjab in 1706; and Sri Hazur Sahib in Nander, where he died in 1708. These holy places attract Sikh pilgrims from throughout the world.

WHAT IS SACRED? As the creation of Akal Purakh, all life is sacred in Sikhism. First, human birth is sacred because it is the epitome of creation: "All other creation is subject to you, [O man/woman!], you reign supreme on this earth" (Adi Granth, p. 374). Indeed, human life provides an individual with the opportunity to remember the divine name and ultimately to join with the Supreme Being. Second, all of the five elements of creation are sacred because they sustain life: "Air is the Guru, water the Father and earth the mighty Mother of all. Day and night are the caring guardians, fondly nurturing all creation" (Adi Granth, p. 8). The protection of the environment is, therefore, an act of sacred duty in Sikhism. Third, all historical places associated with the lives of the 10 Gurus are sacred. Similarly, the Guru's writings, their weapons, and other articles associated with them are sacred relics preserved by the Sikh community. Finally, bathing in the pool of the "nectar of immortality" at the Darbar Sahib at Amritsar is regarded as a sacred activity, since it offers an opportunity to the individual to listen to the continuous singing of the Guru's hymns. Thus, through spiritual cleansing one washes away one's sins.

HOLIDAYS AND FESTIVALS The most important day in the Sikh calendar is Baisakhi (Vaisakhi) Day, which usually falls on 13 April. It is celebrated as the birthday of the community, since on this day in 1699 Guru Gobind Singh inaugurated the Khalsa. Following a solar calendar, it is celebrated as New Year's Day in India, and Punjabis celebrate it as a grain harvest festival. Sikhs also celebrate the festival of lights, Divali, to mark the

Major Subgroups of Sikhs

Among the 23–24 million Sikhs in the world, only approximately 15–20 percent are Amrit-dharis (Initiated), those who follow the orthodox form of Khalsa (pure) Sikhism. A large majority (about 70 percent) of Sikhs, however, are Kes-dharis—that is, those who "retain their hair" and thus maintain a visible identity. Although they have not gone through the Khalsa initiation ceremony, these Sikhs follow most of the Khalsa *rahit* (code).

The number of Sikhs who have shorn their hair, and are thus less conspicuous, is quite large in North America and in the United Kingdom. Popularly known as Mona (Clean-Shaven) Sikhs, they retain a Khalsa affiliation by using the surnames *Singh* and *Kaur*. These Sikhs are also called Ichha-dharis because, although they "desire" to keep their hair, they cut it under compulsion. They are sometimes confused with Sahaj-dhari (Gradualist) Sikhs, those who have never accepted the Khalsa discipline. Although Sahaj-dhari Sikhs practice *nam-simaran* (remembering the divine Name) and follow the teachings of the Adi Granth, the Sikh scripture, they do not observe the Khalsa *rahit* and, in particular, cut their hair. The number of Sahaj-dharis declined during the last few decades of the twentieth century, but they have not disappeared completely from the Sikh Panth.

Finally, there are those who violate the Khalsa *rahit* after initiation by cutting their hair. These lapsed Amrit-dharis, who are known as Patit, or Bikh-dhari (Apostate), Sikhs, are found largely in the diaspora.

release of Guru Hargobind, who was imprisoned under the Mughal emperor Jahangir. The Darbar Sahib in Amritsar is illuminated for the occasion. The date of Divali varies according to the Indian lunar calendar, but it generally falls during October. Hindus celebrate with the theme of material wealth. It was the third Guru, Amar Das, who originally introduced the celebration of these two seasonal festivals to the Sikh Panth. Guru Gobind Singh added the observance of Hola Mahalla, the day after the Hindu festival of Holi (March/April), for the purpose of military exercises and organized athletic and literary contests. In addition, the anniversaries associated with the births and deaths of the Gurus are marked by the "unbroken reading" (akhand path) of the Sikh scripture by a relay of readers in approximately 48 hours. Such occasions are called Gurpurbs (holidays associated with the Gurus). In particular, the birthdays of Guru Nanak (usually in November) and Guru Gobind Singh (December/January) and the martyrdom days of Guru Arjan (May/June) and Guru Tegh Bahadur (November/December) are celebrated throughout the world.

MODE OF DRESS Sikh women in India often wear *salwars*, pajama-like trousers, with a long tunic called a *kameez* over them. This is regarded as a regional dress of the Punjab. The trousers and tunics are comfortable and functional in the rural Punjabi villages, where more than 70 percent of the Sikh population is concentrated. In addition, the sari has become popular among urban Sikh women. It is worn with a full blouse that covers the midriff, so that the injunction warning against "wearing clothes which cause pain to the body or breed lustful thoughts" (Adi Granth, p. 16) is obeyed. To cover their heads, Sikh women wear a muslin scarf (*dupatta/chunni*).

In villages Sikh men normally wear tight-legged pajama-like trousers with long shirts that hang on the outside. In towns and cities, however, most men wear Western-style trousers and suits, with shirts buttoned at the collar and occasionally a tie. Indeed, Western dress has influenced Sikh men more than women. The Sikh *granthi*s, *giani*s (traditional scholars), and *sant*s (saints) normally wear white dress that consists of a turban, a long outer shirt (*cholara*), tight-fitting trousers (*reb pajama*), a sash (*kamar-kasa*), and an undergarment (*kachh*), as well as a sword (*kirpan*) with a belt running diagonally over the right shoulder. These five garments are part of Khalsa dress (*bana*).

The turban has a particular prominence in Sikh dress. Most Sikhs normally wear turbans of three colors—deep blue, white, and saffron—all of which have religious significance. For Khalsa Sikhs the significance of deep blue lies in the "highest ideals of character" (*nili siahi kada karani*) and in the "deepest urges in the life of spirituality" (Adi Granth, p. 16), since the blue sky stands for the highest horizon and the blue ocean stands for the depth. The color white stands for purity, while saffron represents the spirit of sacrifice in Sikh mores.

Sikhs may wear a turban of any color, however, to match their clothes. They commonly wear a peaked turban to cover their long hair, unshorn out of respect for its original, God-given form.

DIETARY PRACTICES The Adi Granth does not prescribe dietary rules, although it lays emphasis on "consuming only those foods which do not cause pain in the body or breed evil thoughts in the mind" (Adi Granth, p. 16). Most Punjabi Sikhs have a diet of simple vegetables and milk products. One favorite is a diet of corn bread and mustard greens (*makki di roti* and *sag*) with buttermilk (*lassi*). Punjabis also eat rice and chapati, a flat wheat bread, supplemented by a lentil curry (*dal*) and other vegetables. The *Sikh Rahit Maryada* (Sikh Code of Conduct) strictly forbids the consumption of *kuttha* meat (*halal* meat prepared according to the Muslim convention) but permits the eating of *jhataka* meat (meat killed with a single blow). Sikhs in Punjabi villages frequently consume the meat of goats and chickens. In order to maintain the egalitarian emphasis of the Gurus, the serving of eggs and meat is not permitted in the community kitchens (*langar*s) of *gurdwara*s, where the food is exclusively vegetarian. The use of tobacco and other drugs is strictly prohibited to Khalsa Sikhs. Similarly, the consumption of alcohol is forbidden, although a large majority of the Punjabi population, particularly those from villages, is renowned for its use of hard liquor.

RITUALS The daily routine of a devout Sikh begins with the practice of meditation upon the divine name. This occurs during the *amritvela*, the "ambrosial hours" (that is, the last watch of the night, between three and six in the morning), immediately after rising and bathing. Meditation is followed by the recitation of five liturgical prayers, which include the Japji of Guru Nanak. In most cases the early-morning devotion concludes in the presence of the Guru Granth Sahib—that is, the scripture serving as Guru—in which the whole family gathers to receive the divine command (*vak laina*, or "taking God's word") by reading a passage selected at random. Similarly, a collection of hymns, Sodar Rahiras (Supplication at That Door), is prescribed for the evening prayers, and the Kirtan Sohila (Song of Praise) is recited before retiring for the night.

Congregational worship takes place in the *gurdwara*, where the main focus is upon the Guru Granth Sahib, installed in a ceremony every morning. Worship consists mainly of the singing of scriptural passages set to music, with the accompaniment of instruments. The singing of hymns (*kirtan*) in a congregational setting is the heart of the Sikh devotional experience. Through such *kirtan* the devotees attune themselves to vibrate in harmony with the divine word, which has the power to transform and unify their consciousness. The exposition of the scriptures, known as *katha* (homily), may be delivered at an appropriate time during the service by the *granthi* of the *gurdwara* or by the traditional Sikh scholar (*giani*). At the conclusion of the service, all who are present join in reciting the Ardas (Petition, or Sikh Prayer), which invokes divine grace and recalls the rich common heritage of the community. Then follows the reading of the *vak* (divine command) and the distribution of *karah prashad* (sanctified food).

RITES OF PASSAGE The central feature of the key life-cycle rituals is always the Guru Granth Sahib, the scripture serving as Guru. When a child is to be named, the family takes the baby to the *gurdwara* and offers *karah prashad* (sanctified food). After giving thanks and offering prayers through Ardas, the scripture is opened at random, and a name is chosen beginning with the same letter as the first composition on the left-hand page. Thus, the process of *vak laina* (divine command) functions to provide the first letter of the name. The underlying principle is that the child derives his or her identity from the Guru's word and begins life as a Sikh. To a boy's chosen name the surname *Singh* (Lion) is added, and to a girl's chosen name *Kaur* (Princess) is added. In some cases, however, particularly in North America, people employ caste names (for example, Ahluwalia, Dhaliwal, Grewal, Kalsi, Sawhney, or Sethi) as the last element, and for them *Singh* and *Kaur* become middle names. In addition, the infant is administered sweetened water that is stirred with a sword, and the first five stanzas of Guru Nanak's Japji are recited.

A Sikh wedding, according to the Anand (Bliss) ceremony, also takes place in the presence of the Guru Granth Sahib, and the performance of the actual marriage requires the couple to circumambulate the sacred scripture four times to take four vows. Before the bridegroom and the bride make each round, they listen to a verse of the Lavan, or "wedding hymn" (Adi Granth, pp. 773–74), by the fourth Guru, Ram Das, as given by a scriptural reader. They bow before the scripture and then stand up to make their round while professional musicians sing the same verse with the congregation.

During the process of their clockwise movements around the scripture, they take the following four vows: (1) to lead an action-oriented life based upon righteousness and never to shun the obligations of family and society; (2) to maintain a bond of reverence and dignity between them; (3) to keep enthusiasm for life alive in the face of adverse circumstances and to remain removed from worldly attachments; and (4) to cultivate a "balanced approach" (*sahaj*) in life, avoiding all extremes. The pattern of circumambulation in the Anand marriage ceremony is the enactment of the primordial movement of life, in which there is no beginning and no end. Remembering the four marital vows is designed to make the life of the couple blissful.

The key initiation ceremony (*amrit sanskar*) for a Sikh must take place in the presence of the Guru Granth Sahib. There is no fixed age for initiation, which may be done at any time the person is willing to accept the Khalsa discipline. Five Khalsa Sikhs, representing the collectivity of the original Cherished Five (*panj piare*), conduct the ceremony. Each recites from memory one of the five liturgical prayers while stirring the sweetened water (*amrit*) with a double-edged sword. The novice then drinks the *amrit* five times so that his body is purified from the influence of five vices, and five times the *amrit* is sprinkled on his eyes to transform his outlook toward life. Finally, the *amrit* is poured on his head five times to sanctify his hair so that he will preserve his natural form and listen to the voice of conscience. Throughout each of the procedures the Sikh being initiated formally takes the oath by repeating the following declaration: Vahiguru Ji Ka Khalsa! Vahiguru Ji Ki Fateh! (Khalsa belongs to the Wonderful Lord! Victory belongs to the Wonderful Lord!). Thus, a person becomes a Khalsa Sikh through the transforming power of the sacred word. At the conclusion of the ceremony a *vak* (divine command) is given, and *karah prashad* is distributed.

Finally, at the time of death, both in the period preceding cremation and in the postcremation rites, hymns from the Guru Granth Sahib are sung. In addition, a reading of the entire scripture takes place at home or in a *gurdwara*. Within 10 days of the conclusion of the reading, a *bhog* (completion) ceremony is held, at which final prayers are offered in memory of the deceased.

MEMBERSHIP Although Sikhism is an organized religion, the issue of membership is complex. Punjabi society is kinship-based, with most of the people Sikhs by birth. To a certain extent it is a closed society, and Sikhs are not ordinarily known as aggressively expansionist in urging their beliefs upon others. Despite the absence of an active agenda to proselytize non-Sikhs into the tradition, people may join Sikhism of their own free will. In fact, conversion to Sikhism indicates the extent to which a person incorporates the ideals of the Guru (*gurbani, prashad, amrit, rahit,* and so on) into his life when he formally joins the Khalsa order through the initiation ceremony. It is interesting to note that in Sikh society the idea of conversion does not carry with it the same notions as in Christianity, out of which the term originally evolved. On the one hand, Sikhism does not actively seek converts by knocking on people's doors, but, on the other, it does not refuse admission to any person who makes a conscious effort to join the Sikh fold.

In the 1970s a group of American and Canadian Caucasians converted to the Sikh faith at the inspiration of their Yoga teacher, Harbhajan Singh Khalsa (Yogi Bhajan), who founded the Sikh Dharma movement. These so-called white, or *gora,* Sikhs, male and female alike, wear white turbans, tunics, and tight trousers. They live and raise families in communal houses, spending long hours in meditation and chanting while performing various postures of tantric yoga. They have thus introduced the Sikh tradition into a new cultural environment. Most Punjabi Sikhs have shown an ambivalent attitude toward these converts. On the one hand, they praise the strict Khalsa-style discipline of the white Sikhs; on the other hand, they express doubts about the mixing of the Sikh tradition with the ideals of tantric yoga.

RELIGIOUS TOLERANCE The ability to accept religious pluralism is a necessary condition of religious tolerance. Religious pluralism requires that people of different faiths be able to live together harmoniously, which provides an opportunity for spiritual self-judgment and growth. It is in this context that Sikhism expresses ideals of coexistence and mutual understanding. Sikhism emphasizes the principles of tolerance and the acceptance of the diversity of faith and practice. It is thus able to enter freely into fruitful interreligious dialogue with an open attitude. Such an attitude signifies a willingness to learn from other traditions and yet to retain the integrity of one's own tradition. It also involves the preservation of differences with dignity and mutual respect.

The Sikh Gurus were strongly opposed to the claim of any particular tradition to possess the sole religious truth. Indeed, a spirit of accommodation has always been an integral part of the Sikh attitude toward other traditions. The inclusion of the works of the 15 medieval non-Sikh saints (*bhagat bani,* the "utterances of the devotees" of Sant, Sufi, and Bhakti origins), along with the compositions of the Gurus, in the foundational text of the Sikhs provides an example of the kind of catholicity that promotes mutual respect and tolerance. For instance, the Muslim voice of the devotee Shaikh Farid is allowed to express itself on matters of doctrine and practice. This is the ideal Sikhs frequently stress in interfaith dialogues.

The presence of the *bhagat bani* in the Sikh scripture offers a four-point theory of religious pluralism. First, one must acknowledge at the outset that all religious traditions have gone through a process of self-definition in response to changing historical contexts. Thus, in any dialogue the dignity of the religious identities of the individual participants must be maintained. One must be able to honor a commitment as absolute for oneself while respecting different absolute commitments for others. For this reason the quest for a universal religion and the attempt to place one religious tradition above others must be abandoned. Second, the doctrinal standpoints of different religious traditions must be maintained with mutual respect and dignity. Third, all participants must enter into a dialogue with an open attitude, one that allows not only true understanding of other traditions but also disagreements on crucial doctrinal points. Finally, the experience of the person of another faith must be incorporated into the self.

SOCIAL JUSTICE Guru Nanak advocated the virtue of justice in its legal sense and made it the principal characteristic of the ruler and the administrator. Thus, he severely condemned the contemporary Muslim jurist (*qazi*), who had become morally corrupt by selling justice and who had no concern for truth: "The *qazi* tells lies and eats filth" (Adi Granth, p. 662). In those days the *qazi* took "bribes" in order to deprive people of justice (Adi Granth, p. 951), and in Punjabi culture the phrase "to eat filth" came to refer to "unlawfully earned food." Guru Nanak further proclaimed, "To deprive others of their rights must be avoided as scrupulously as Muslims avoid the pork and the Hindus consider beef as a taboo" (Adi Granth, p. 141). Here one can see how, on religious grounds, Guru Nanak regarded the violation of human rights as a serious moral offense. The Sikh view of justice is, in fact, based on two principles: first, respect for the rights of others; and, second, the nonexploitation of others. To treat everyone's right as sacred is a necessary constituent of justice. A just person will not exploit others, even if he has the means and opportunity for doing so.

Guru Gobind Singh advocated the doctrine that, in the pursuit of justice, a person must try all peaceful means of negotiations. Only when all such methods of redress have failed does it become legitimate to draw the sword in defense of righteousness. The following celebrated verse of the *Zafarnama* ("Letter of Victory"), written to Emperor Aurangzeb, makes this point explicitly: "When all other methods have been explored and all other means have been tried, then may the sword be drawn from the scabbard, then may the sword be used" (verse 22). In this context W.H. McLeod, in his book *The Sikhs*, has made an important observation: "None of this should suggest that the Panth exists only to breathe fire or wield naked swords." The use of force is allowed in Sikh doctrine, but it is authorized only in defense of justice and then only as a last resort. Moreover, in the face of tyranny, justice can be defended and maintained only through sacrifices. The *Zafarnama* stresses that no sacrifice is too great for the sake of truth and justice: "It does not matter if my four sons have been killed, the Khalsa is still there at my back" (verse 78). For the Sikhs of the Khalsa the dominant ethical duty is the quest for justice. As McLeod has said in his book *Sikhism,* "The Khalsa was created to fight injustice, and fighting injustice is still its calling."

Indeed, Sikhism is dedicated to human rights and resistance against injustice. It strives to eliminate poverty and to offer voluntary help to the less privileged. Its commitment is to the ideal of universal brotherhood, with an altruistic concern for humanity as a whole (*sarbat da bhala*). In a celebrated passage from the *Akal Ustat* ("Praise of Immortal One"), Guru Gobind Singh declared that "humankind is one, and that all people belong to a single humanity" (verse 85). Here it is important to underline the Guru's role as a conciliator who tried to persuade the Mughal emperor Bahadur Shah to walk the ways of peace. Even though Guru Gobind Singh had to spend the major part of his life fighting battles that were forced upon him by Hindu hill rajas and Mughal authorities, a longing for peace and fellowship with both Hindus and Muslims may be seen in the following passage from the *Akal Ustat*: "The temple and the mosque are the same, so are the Hindu worship [*puja*] and Muslim prayer [*namaz*]. All people are one, it is through error that they appear different . . . Allah and Abhekh are the same, the Purana and the Qur'an are the same. They are all alike, all the creation of the One" (verse 86). The above verses emphatically stress the irenic belief that the differences dividing people are in reality meaningless. In fact, all people are fundamentally the same because they all are the creations of the same Supreme Being. To pursue this ideal, Sikhs conclude their morning and evening prayers with the words "Says Nanak: may thy Name and glory be ever triumphant, and in thy will, O Lord, may peace and prosperity come to one and all."

SOCIAL ASPECTS Rejecting the ascetic alternative, Guru Nanak stressed the way of the householder as the ideal pattern of life for the person who seeks liberation. His successors upheld the ideal of family life, expressing it in their own lives as well as in their teachings. The third Guru, Amar Das, proclaimed, "Family life is superior to ascetic life in sectarian garb because it is from householders that ascetics meet their needs by begging" (Adi Granth, p. 586). To understand family relationships, one must address issues of caste and gender from the Sikh perspective.

In Punjabi society family life is based upon broad kinship relationships. Every individual is a member of a joint family, a *biradari* (brotherhood), a *got* (exogamous group), and a *zat* (endogamous group). Like most other Indians, Sikhs are endogamous by caste (*zat*) and exogamous by subcaste (*got*). That is, a Sikh may marry within the same caste but not within the same subcaste. Descent is always patrilineal, and marriages link two groups of kin rather than two individuals. Within the framework of the patriarchal structures of Punjabi society, the cultural norms of honor (*izzat*) and modesty play a significant role in family relationships. The Gurus employed the term *pati*, which essentially refers to the core of a person, encompassing honor, self-respect, and social standing.

Guru Nanak and the succeeding Gurus emphatically proclaimed that the divine name was the only sure means of liberation for all four castes: the Khatri, originally the Kshatriya (warrior); the Brahman (priest); the Shudra (servant/agriculturalist); and the Vaishya (tradesman). In the works of the Gurus, the Khatris were always placed above the Brahmans in the caste hierarchy, while the Shudras were raised above the Vaishyas.

This was an interesting way of breaking the rigidity of the centuries-old caste system. All of the Gurus were Khatris, which made them a top-ranking mercantile caste in Punjab's urban hierarchy, followed by Aroras (merchants) and Ahluwalias (brewers). In the rural caste hierarchy an absolute majority (almost two-thirds) of Sikhs are Jats (peasants), followed by Ramgarhias (artisans), Ramdasias (cobblers), and Mazhabis (sweepers). Although Brahmans are at the apex of the Hindu caste hierarchy, Sikhs place Brahmans distinctly lower on the caste scale. This is partly because of the strictures the Sikh Gurus laid upon Brahman pride and partly because the reorganization of Punjabi rural society conferred dominance on the Jat caste.

Doctrinally, caste has never been one of the defining criteria of Sikh identity. In the Sikh congregation there is no place for any kind of injustice or hurtful discrimination based upon caste identity. In the *gurdwara,* Sikhs eat together in the community kitchen, share the same sanctified food, and worship together. The Sikh Rahit Maryada (Sikh Code of Conduct) explicitly states, "No account should be taken of caste; a Sikh woman should be married only to a Sikh man; and Sikhs should not be married as children." This is the ideal, however, and in practice most Sikh marriages are arranged between members of the same endogamous caste group. Caste, therefore, still prevails within the Sikh community as a marriage convention. Nevertheless, intercaste marriages take place frequently among professional Sikhs in India and elsewhere.

The Sikh Gurus addressed the issues of gender within the parameters established by traditional patriarchal structures. In their view an ideal woman plays the role of a good daughter or sister and a good wife and mother within the context of family life. They condemned both women and men alike who did not observe the cultural norms of modesty and honor in their lives. It is in this context that images of the immoral woman and the unregenerate man are frequently encountered in the scriptural texts. There is no tolerance for any kind of premarital or extramarital sexual relationships, and rape in particular is regarded as a violation of women's honor in Punjabi culture. Rape amounts to the loss of family honor, which in turn becomes the loss of one's social standing in the community. The notion of family honor is thus intimately linked to the status of women.

The third Guru, Amar Das, proclaimed, "They are not said to be husband and wife, who merely sit together. Rather, they alone are called husband and wife who have one soul in two bodies" (Adi Granth, p. 788). This proclamation has become the basis of Sikh engagement and marriage, which traditionally emphasizes a spiritual commitment between two partners over any material or physical advantages of the union. At every step the traditions surrounding Sikh marriages aim to ensure the spiritual compatibility of the couple to be married. To this end Sikh marriages are arranged by the families of the prospective couple. While the involvement of the couple itself has increased over time, the involvement and input of the family has remained vital. This emphasis on family, reflected in every aspect of Sikh life, from the communal eating halls of the *gurdwara*s to the common practice of identifying oneself through one's parentage, is among the most important precepts of Sikhism. At every stage in the Sikh process of engagement and marriage, the opinion of each partner's family is respected, considered, and valued.

CONTROVERSIAL ISSUES The issue of gender has received a great a deal of attention within the Sikh Panth. It is notable that the Sikh Gurus offered a vision of gender equality within the Sikh community and took practical steps to foster respect for womanhood. They were ahead of their times when they championed the cause of equal access for women in spiritual and temporal matters. Guru Nanak raised a strong voice against the position of inferiority assigned to women in society at the time: "From women born, shaped in the womb, to woman betrothed and wed; we are bound to women by ties of affection, on women man's future depends. If one woman dies he seeks another; with a woman he orders his life. Why then should one speak evil of women, they who give birth to kings?" (Adi Granth, p. 473). He sought to bring home the realization that the survival of the human race depended upon women, who were unjustifiably ostracized within society. Guru Amar Das abolished the customs among women of the veil and of *sati* (self-immolation) and permitted the remarriage of widows. He further appointed women as Sikh missionaries. Indeed, Sikh women were given equal rights with men to conduct prayers and other ceremonies in *gurdwara*s.

In actual practice, however, males dominate most Sikh institutions, and Sikh women continue to live in a patriarchal society based on Punjabi cultural assumptions. In this respect they differ little from their counterparts in other religious communities in India. Although there is a large gap between the ideal and reality, there is clear doctrinal support for the equality of rights for men and women within the Sikh Panth. In contemporary times the feminine dimension of the Sikh tradition has received considerable attention. Under the influence of feminist movements, for example, Sikh women have begun to assert themselves in addressing the bioethical issues of birth control and abortion. Sikhism does not approve of abortion just because raising a child would be "inconvenient to one's lifestyle" or, in the case of female children, "uneconomical." When, however, the mother's life is in danger, or in cases of incest and rape, Sikhism allows abortion of the fetus by medical procedure. On the other hand, it regards the cloning of humans as unethical, since this is seen as "playing God rather than walking in His will."

After the independence of India in 1947, there was growing hostility between the government and the Akali Dal, the Sikh political group, over the issue of increased autonomy for the provinces. The Congress government evidently sought to provoke disruption within the Akali ranks by promoting the interests of a young militant leader, Jarnail Singh Bhindranvale (1947–84), who followed a fundamentalist approach. He proved more radical than the moderate Akali leadership, and to instigate religious violence, he occupied the building of the Akal Takhat in the Darbar Sahib complex. This led to an assault by the Indian army on the complex in June 1984, which resulted in the death of Bhindranvale along with many other Sikhs. Consequently, Prime Minister Indira Gandhi was assassinated on 31 October 1984 by her own Sikh bodyguards. For several days unchecked Hindu mobs in Delhi and elsewhere killed thousands of Sikhs. The militancy in Punjab created a worldwide identity crisis within the Panth, with Sikhs becoming divided into liberal and conservative camps.

In the diaspora Sikhs have faced new issues and challenges with respect to the wearing of the five Ks. From time to time fierce controversy has erupted in particular over the right to wear the kirpan (sword) and over the minimum size required. Normally a total length of six inches, with a blade of about two and a half inches, is regarded as satisfactory. The constitution of India specifically protects the right of Sikhs to wear and carry a kirpan as a symbol of their faith. Many Canadians and Americans, however, perceive the kirpan to be a weapon and object to it on the grounds of public safety. Again and again, whenever the question of the kirpan as a religious symbol or a weapon has arisen, Sikhs have had to

fight legal cases. For instance, in January 1994 three Sikh students wearing kirpans were excluded from school in Fresno, California. In June 1994 a federal court judge turned down a request by the children that they be allowed to attend school wearing their kirpans while the lawsuit was being resolved. The U.S. Court of Appeals in San Francisco, however, ruled in September 1994 in favor of the Sikh children, overruling a lower-court decision that had backed the school district. The appellant court ruled that the school district had not tried to compromise with the children, who said they were willing to wear shorter, blunt kirpans sewn securely into a sheath. Thus, the children returned to school with their kirpans, and through mediation it was agreed to limit the length of the blade of the kirpan to the legal limit of two and a half inches.

Another problem for Sikhs is a widespread misunderstanding of who they are. This was shown, for example, after the terrorist attacks in the United States on 11 September 2001. The first victim of the backlash was a Sikh, Balbir Singh Sodhi of Arizona, who was shot dead by an angry gunman calling himself a patriot. Sodhi was a victim of mistaken identity, a target because the gunman took him to be a Middle Easterner. Indeed, there remains a great deal of ignorance in North America about Sikhs and their religious traditions. People simply do not know who and what Sikhs are, and they look at the Sikh turban and kirpan with suspicion. They do not realize, for example, that the Sikh style of turban is distinctively different from any style worn by people from the Middle East or Afghanistan or even from the Indo-Pakistani subcontinent. In response to such threats, the Sikh community has mobilized to reach out to various ethnic groups, with prominent Sikh leaders participating in interreligious dialogues as a way of bridging the gulfs of mutual ignorance and misunderstanding among different cultures of the world.

CULTURAL IMPACT Sikhism is the only world religion in which the founder was a musician who preached his message primarily through song and music, and it is thus a forceful example of the combination of religion and music. Indeed, sacred music is at the heart of the Sikh devotional experience. Guru Nanak and the succeeding Gurus laid great emphasis on ragas that would produce a balancing effect on the minds of both listeners and performers. Further, Guru Arjan created a theological and musical coherence in the very structure of the Adi Granth when he placed both classical and folk traditions side by side in the final sequence. The key organizing principle of the Sikh scripture is based upon a well-defined system of 31 classical ragas, along with an equal number of regional varieties. The Adi Granth presents a combination of lyrical and rational elements and is far more complex than any simple explanation or description. It should be added that understanding the ragas of the Adi Granth and their organization solely in terms of the modern North Indian musical tradition is inadequate. Modern North Indian music is unlikely to go back to traditions before Tansen (died in 1586), the most famous musician in the court of the Mughal emperor Akbar, and it is probably traceable only to the eighteenth or nineteenth century. In fact, scholars of music have taken a keen interest in examining the influence of both the Adi Granth raga system and of treatises of the time on modern North Indian musical traditions, since the former seems to be crucial in understanding the latter.

Sikh artistic activities began with the illumination of the manuscripts of scriptural traditions in the late sixteenth and early seventeenth centuries. The opening folio of the first canonical text of the Adi Granth (1604) was profusely decorated. Sikh scribes followed the Koranic tradition of illuminating the margins and the opening folios of the text. The earliest existing paintings of Guru Nanak go back to a *janam-sakhi* (birth narrative) of the mid-seventeenth century. Although the *janam-sakhi* genre of illustrations continued to evolve, it changed dramatically with the coming of the printing press to the Punjab in the nineteenth century. Sikh arts such as painting, carving, armour, brassware, jewelry, textiles, and architecture flourished under the patronage of Maharaja Ranjit Singh, who reigned from 1799 to 1839, and under other Sikh rulers. The works of artists and of writers such as Emily Eden, who published the well-known *Portraits and People of India* in 1844, have provided evidence of fine court paintings, the romantic artwork of visiting European dignitaries, the dazzling treasures of the Sikh kingdom, evocative images of the court of Ranjit Singh, with its handsome Sikh warriors, and the distinctive elements of Sikh architecture. Murals and frescoes, in particular, became popular at the time of the reign of Ranjit Singh. There are wall paintings of major events from Sikh history at the Darbar Sahib and at other historical *gurdwaras*.

In the twentieth century, in addition to the popular art of bazaar posters, great works of art emerged from the talent of renowned Sikh artists such as Sobha Singh (1901–86) and Kirpal Singh (1923–90). Sobha Singh, who was particularly known for his portraits of the Gurus, was skilled in the Western classical technique of oil painting, but his themes came from the romantic lore of the Punjab, from Indian epics, and from the Sikh tradition. Kirpal Singh's specialization was capturing on canvas episodes from Sikh history, including awe-inspiring scenes of martyrs and the realistic portrayal of battle scenes. Some of his original works are displayed in the Central Sikh Museum in the Darbar Sahib complex at Amritsar. A number of Sikh women have also made a name for themselves as artists. For instance, Amrita Shergill (1911–41) was a talented artist who depicted scenes of Indian village life. The works of Amrit Kaur Singh and Rabindra Kaur Singh have shown the cohesion of modern Sikh family life in the multicultural north of England. Similarly, Arpana Caur's painting *1984*, depicting the massacre that occurred during the Indian army's assault on the Darbar Sahib complex, shows the dark side of India.

A rich literary tradition began in the early Sikh community with the writing of the Guru's hymns in the Gurmukhi script. The principal source of Sikh devotional literature is, of course, the Adi Granth, which may be seen as the main inspiration behind the poetic works of Bhai Gurdas and other Sikh writers. The *janam-sakhi*s, which represent the first Punjabi prose form, belong to a second category of devotional literature. As a literary genre they enjoyed complete dominance before the emergence of the twentieth-century novel. It is easy to see the impact of Sikh devotional literature on the writings of celebrated modern authors such as Bhai Vir Singh, Kahn Singh Nabha, and Mohan Singh Vaid. Their writings reflect a spirit of optimism, resolute determination, faith, and love toward fellow human beings. Max Arthur Macauliffe, who went to India as a civil servant of the British government, resigned from his post to devote his life to Sikh devotional literature. It was people such as these who played a leadership role in the Singh Sabha reform movement of the late nineteenth and early twentieth centuries. Although Western forms have become common in contemporary Punjabi literature, Sikh devotional literature is still a source of inspiration for the passionate lyricism of the new generation of writers, as it was for Bhai Vir Singh, whose cosmic vision can be traced to the works of the Gurus.

Pashaura Singh

Bibliography

Brown, Kerry, ed. *Sikh Art and Literature*. London and New York: Routledge, in collaboration with the Sikh Foundation, 1999.

Cole, W. Owen. *The Guru in Sikhism*. London: Darton, Longman, and Todd, 1982.

———. *Sikhism and Its Indian Context, 1469–1708*. London: Darton, Longman, and Todd, 1984.

Cole, W. Owen, and Piara Singh Sambhi. *The Sikhs: Their Religious Beliefs and Practices*. London: Routlege and Kegan Paul, 1978.

Fenech, Louis E. *Martyrdom in the Sikh Tradition: Playing the Game of Love*. New Delhi: Oxford University Press, 2000.

Grewal, J.S. *Contesting Interpretations of the Sikh Tradition*. New Delhi: Manohar, 1998.

———. *Guru Nanak in History*. Chandigrah: Panjab University, 1969.

———. *The Sikhs of the Punjab. The New Cambridge History of India*. Vol. 2, bk. 3. Cambridge: Cambridge University Press, 1991.

Khalsa, Gurudharam Singh. *Guru Ram Das in Sikh Tradition*. New Delhi: Harman Publishing House, 1997.

Macaulifee, Max Arthur. *The Sikh Religion: Its Gurus, Sacred Writings, and Authors*. Vol. 3. Oxford: Clarendon Press, 1909.

Mann, Gurinder Singh. *The Making of Sikh Scripture*. New York: Oxford University Press, 2001.

McLeod, W.H. *Popular Sikh Art*. Delhi: Oxford University Press, 1991.

———. *Sikhism*. London: Penguin Books, 1997.

———. *The Sikhs: History, Religion, and Society*. New York: Columbia University Press, 1989.

———. *Sikhs and Sikhism*. New Delhi: Oxford University Press, 1999.

———. *The Sikhs of the Khalsa*. New Delhi: Oxford University Press, 2003.

Oberoi, Harjot. *Construction of Religious Boundaries*. New Delhi: Oxford University Press, 1994.

Shiromani Gurdwara Prabandhak Committee. *Shabadarath Sri Guru Granth Sahib Ji*. 5th ed. 4 vols. Amritsar: Shiromani Gurdwara Prabandhak Committee, 1936–41.

Singh, Avtar. *Ethics of the Sikhs*. Patiala: Punjabi University, 1970.

Singh, Harbans. *Guru Nanak and the Origins of the Sikh Faith*. Bombay: Asia Publishing House, 1969.

———. *Heritage of the Sikhs*. 2nd ed., rev. New Delhi: Manohar, 1983.

———, ed. *Berkeley Lectures on Sikhism*. New Delhi: Guru Nanak Foundation, 1983.

———, ed. *The Encyclopaedia of Sikhism*. 4 vols. Patiala: Punjabi University, 1992–98.

Singh, Khushwant. *A History of the Sikhs*. 2 vols. New Delhi: Oxford University Press, Oxford India Paperbacks, 2001.

Singh, Mohinder, ed. *Sikh Forms and Symbols*. New Delhi: Manohar, 2000.

Singh, Nikky-Guninder Kaur. *The Feminine Principle in the Sikh Vision of the Transcendent*. Cambridge: Cambridge University Press, 1993.

———, trans. *The Name of My Beloved: Verses of the Sikh Gurus*. San Francisco: HarperCollins, 1995.

Singh, Nripinder. *The Sikh Moral Tradition*. New Delhi: Manohar, 1990.

Singh, Pashaura. *The Bhagats of the Guru Granth Sahib: Sikh Self-Definition and the Bhagat Bani*. New Delhi: Oxford University Press, 2003.

———. *The Guru Granth Sahib: Canon, Meaning and Authority*. New Delhi: Oxford University Press, 2000.

Singh, Patwant. *The Golden Temple*. New Delhi: Times Books International, 1988.

———. *The Sikhs*. New York: Alfred A. Knopf, 2000.

Singh, Teja, and Ganda Singh. *A Short History of the Sikhs*. Rev. ed. Patiala: Punjabi University, 1989.

Stronge, Susan, ed. *The Arts of the Sikh Kingdoms*. London: V&A Publications, 1999.

Uberoi, J.P.S. *Religion, Civil Society and the State: A Study in Sikhism*. New Delhi: Oxford University Press, 1996.

Taoism

FOUNDED: c. 450–500 c.e.

RELIGION AS A PERCENTAGE OF WORLD POPULATION: 1 percent

OVERVIEW Taoism is a Chinese religious tradition emphasizing personal transformation and integration with the unseen forces of the universe. The Taoist's name for their religion is *Tao-chiao* ("the teachings of the Tao"), a term that goes back to leaders such as Lu Hsiu-ching (406–77), highly educated aristocrats who wove together many diverse traditions and practices to form an inclusive new cultural and religious framework. That framework was designed to preserve all that was good and worthwhile within the indigenous religious heritage of China so that it could survive the challenge of Buddhism, which became prominent in China beginning in the fourth century c.e. The term "Tao," literally "the way" in Chinese, has been variously understood in Taoism, though it generally refers to the highest dimensions of reality.

Taoism evolved not among superstitious peasants (as modern Confucians taught Westerners to imagine) but rather among China's most powerful, most cultured, and most educated classes. Taoist writings of all periods—few of which have been translated into modern languages or even read—provide models of personal practice designed for the tastes of scholars, artists, rulers, and intellectuals. Centuries of Taoist leaders produced scholarly and scientific works of every description, developed sophisticated medical techniques, and won the admiration of Chinese scholars and officials, military and civilian functionaries, poets and painters, and respectful emperors.

After its beginnings in the fifth century, Taoism quickly gained acceptance among men and women of all social levels in every region of China, and it was well respected by China's rulers up through the mid-eighteenth century. The universal respect for Taoism among the Chinese people resulted from the immense range of practices and beliefs for men and women of every taste, every social stratum, and every level of education. Even today within China's rapidly modernizing society, men and women preserve the living heritage of traditional Taoism, maintaining its temples, traditions, and rich panoply of ancient practices for self-cultivation.

Even so, Taoism is probably the most poorly understood of the world's major religions, both inside China and around the world. Centuries of Confucian dominance and decades of Communist rule left the people of China and the rest of the modern world with distorted ideas about the tradition. For instance, many Taoist practices, such as *ch'i-kung* (*qigong*, the skill of attracting vital energy), are popular among people who are largely ignorant of their Taoist underpinnings, while the men and women who practice Taoism in temples throughout China often keep mum about the vitality of their religion, fearing persecution by Communist authorities. Moreover, decades of Westerners were mistakenly taught that the Chinese themselves distinguish "religious Taoism" from "philosophical Taoism." In reality, that belief arose not from any difference among various types of Taoists or even among varying types

YIN YANG. Taoism does not have a central symbol, but it does employ images that obliquely suggest the effectiveness of spiritual practice. One example is the crane, whose red crown is understood as representing cinnabar, a symbol of spiritual perfection. The ancient Chinese symbol Yin Yang, a circle with swirling dark (yin) and light (yang) hemispheres, is commonly associated with Taoism. Each hemisphere contains a dot of the opposite color. The swirl represents change—the only constant factor in the universe. (THOMSON GALE)

of Taoist thought or practice. Rather, it was the propaganda of a would-be elite in nineteenth and twentieth-century China, who labored to be perceived as "more enlightened" than practitioners of Taoism.

HISTORY Trying to pinpoint the beginning of Taoism is like trying to identify the beginning of Judaism: One could place it here or there, depending upon exactly how"Taoism" is defined. Writings that have survived from "classical China" (i.e., before 221 B.C.E.)—and archaeological finds of the 1990s—show that by the late fourth century B.C.E. there were people who saw the world in holistic terms. Eventually some of them wrote about practices of self-cultivation that could lead to a kind of spiritual harmony. The earliest such writing seems to have been the long-overlooked *Nei-yeh* ("Inner Cultivation"), likely a prototype for the well-known *Tao te ching*. The *Nei-yeh* teaches one to quiet one's *hsin* (heart/mind) by governing thought and emotion; one can thereby preserve one's *ching* (vital essence) and attract and retain the elusive forces of life—Tao, *ch'i* (life-energy), and *shen* (spirit, or spiritual consciousness). Related ideas found their way into the *Tao te ching* (also

known as the *Lao-tzu*), which was probably completed c. 285 B.C.E. by an editor at the Chi-hsia academy. It seems to preserve oral traditions of the southern land of Ch'u, repackaging them as a sociopolitical program that could vie with Confucianism and other competing groups.

Yet in "classical China" there were actually no "Taoists," in the sense of a group of people who knew each other and agreed that they all shared ideas and practices that set them apart from other groups. Such a self-conscious group did not emerge until centuries later (about 500 C.E.). Near the end of the third century B.C.E., Legalists helped Ch'in Shih-huang-ti become the first emperor of a unified China, but his regime was soon overthrown, and the early rulers of the subsequent Han dynasty (206 B.C.E.–221 C.E.) often looked to the *Tao te ching* for guiding principles. "Lao-tzu," its legendary "author," was divinized by the Han imperial government, and for centuries thereafter both emperors and religious leaders frequently claimed a spiritual legitimacy bestowed upon them by Lord Lao (Lao-chün).

One movement that made just such a claim sprang from writings that had emerged from the Han court at the end of the first century B.C.E. They culminated in a little-known text called the *T'ai-p'ing ching* ("Scripture of Grand Tranquillity"). It echoes the *Tao te ching* by saying that ancient rulers had actualized *t'ai-p'ing* (grand tranquillity) by practicing *wu-wei* (nonaction)—a behavioral ideal of trusting to the world's natural processes instead of to one's own activity. "Grand tranquillity" was, however, disrupted when later rulers meddled with the world, and as a result, people now need practical advice for reintegrating themselves with the natural order. The *T'ai-p'ing ching*'s recipes included moral rectitude, meditation practices, medicine, acupuncture, hygienic practices such as breath control, and even music therapy. Notably it portrays some of its teachings as instructions that a *t'ien-shih* (celestial master) gave to a group of disciples called *chen* (perfected or realized ones).

Sometime later an obscure healer named Chang Tao-ling claimed a revelation and *meng-wei* (covenant) from Lord Lao authorizing him to found a new social and religious order. Chang's followers hailed him as the "Celestial Master" and built a religious organization whose men and women officiants (libationers) offered people of all social backgrounds absolution from inherited sins by means of confession and good works. The result was healing, not physical or spiritual immortality. The title "Celestial Master" was handed down among

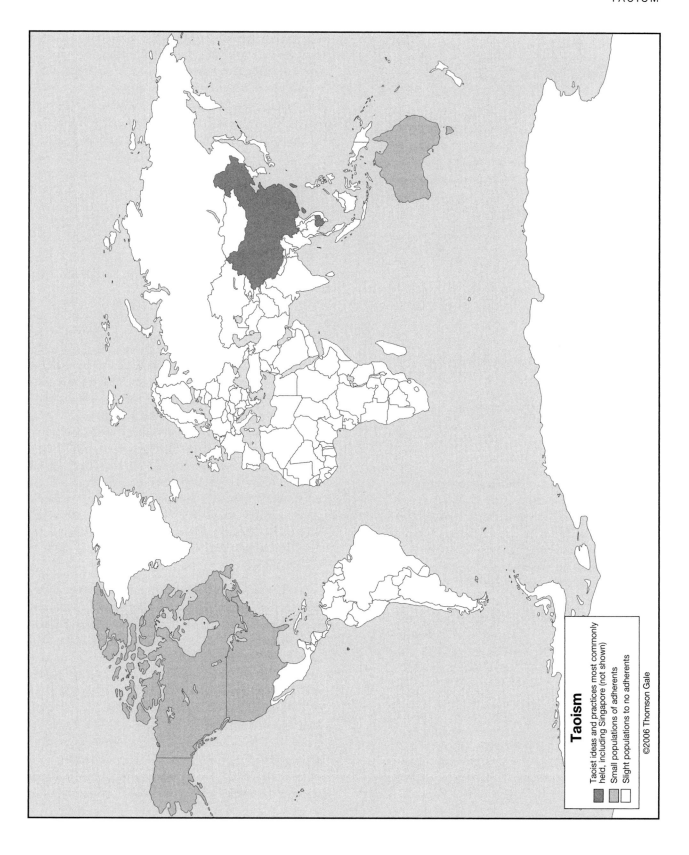

Taoism

■ Taoist ideas and practices most commonly held, including Singapore (not shown)

▨ Small populations of adherents

☐ Slight populations to no adherents

©2006 Thomson Gale

The crane, whose red crown is understood as representing cinnabar, a symbol of spiritual perfection, is present on this Taoist priest's robe. © PETER HARHOLDT/CORBIS.

Chang's descendants, one of whom presumably produced a text called the *Hsiang-erh* ("Just Thinking"). Couched as a commentary on the *Lao-tzu*, it integrated the self-cultivation teachings of the *Nei-yeh* with the *T'ai-p'ing ching*'s general worldview, even adding a set of moral precepts. The *Hsiang-erh* was thus the first text to offer something for everyone.

When northern China fell to non-Chinese invaders in the early fourth century, the "Celestial Master" leaders fled south. The rich indigenous culture of the south included ideas about *wai-tan* (alchemy)—a process of self-perfection involving the preparation of spiritualized substances called *tan* (elixirs). As explained in the scriptures of the *T'ai-ch'ing* ("Great Clarity") tradition—which apparently interested mostly aristocrats—the successful practitioner would be elevated to a heavenly sphere characterized by "great clarity." As these various beliefs and practices became known to elements of society that had theretofore been quite distinct from each other—socially, culturally, and geographically—they stimulated even more religious ferment. They would eventually come together to form "Taoism."

Two new developments were said to have begun as revelations from divine beings and held the interest of an indeterminable segment of the highly educated southern aristocracy. In the 360s, for instance, according to tradition, angelic beings called *chen-jen* (perfected ones) channeled an array of sacred texts through a human medium, revealing how a practitioner could ascend to their heavenly realm, called Shang-ch'ing

("Supreme Clarity"). A primary element of Shang-ch'ing practice was visualizational meditation, such as visualizing marriage between the human practitioner and one of the beneficent female "perfected ones." The Shang-ch'ing revelations also promised that mortals who perfected themselves by these practices would survive the world's imminent purgation: "the Sage of the Latter Days" (*hou-sheng*, sometimes translated "the Sage Who Is to Come") will soon appear, eliminate the negative forces that plague our world, and establish a new world order for the "seed people" who have perfected themselves under the guidance of the "perfected ones." The influence of these revelations on later centuries of Taoists was fairly limited, largely because the predicted date for the Sage's arrival passed without the promised felicities.

Consequently, at the end of the fourth century another set of southern aristocrats produced a different set of revelations, called Ling-pao ("Numinous Treasure"). The primary Ling-pao scripture was the *Tu-jen ching* ("Scripture for the Salvation of Humanity"). It teaches that at the beginning of the world the Tao became personified as a compassionate divine being who has now decided to save humanity by revealing the *Tu-jen ching*—itself an emanation of the Tao. The practitioner who recites the *Tu-jen ching* reactualizes the deity's primordial recitation of its words and thus assimilates himself into the Tao itself. No one knows how many people actually engaged in this practice, but the universalistic values underlying the Ling-pao message—borrowed in part from Mahayana Buddhist ideas—found a lasting place in Taoist tradition.

In the fifth century another southern aristocrat, a Ling-pao master named Lu Hsiu-ching, discussed below under EARLY AND MODERN LEADERS, initiated the effort to consolidate all the unrelated traditions outlined above into an ecumenical religious tradition that could compete with Buddhism, which had gained great acceptance in China. Lu reformulated earlier ritual practices—some from popular sources, some from imperial ceremonies—into standard liturgical forms. The resulting *chiao* and *chai* liturgies are practiced by Taoists today. Lu also shaped the entire later Taoist tradition by proposing a collection of texts that would define the contents and the boundaries of *Tao-chiao* ("the teachings of the Tao")—the term that Taoists ever since have used for their own religious traditions. Originally called *San-tung* ("The Three Caverns"), this massive "Library of the Tao" grew century after century, culminating in today's *Tao-tsang*, discussed below under SACRED BOOKS.

During the T'ang period (618–907), illustrious emperors took Taoist holy orders from great masters such as Ssu-ma Ch'eng-chen and Li Han-kuang, and imperial princesses entered the Taoist priesthood. The T'ang was also a time when new subtraditions began to emerge; an example is Ch'ing-wei ("Clarified Tenuity") Taoism, a system of therapeutic rituals founded by a young woman, Tsu Shu, in about 900.

During the Sung dynasty (960–1279) changes in Chinese society led to new challenges for Taoism. In the Northern Sung dynasty—from 960 to 1126—Taoism prospered and continued to enjoy respect throughout society, and the emperor Hui-tsung (reigned 1100–25) supported Taoism as earlier rulers had done. Soon, however, northern China was conquered by various non-Chinese peoples, and by the late thirteenth century Taoism had lost much of its social, political, and cultural prominence. The institutions that had evolved among medieval Taoists survived, but Taoism itself was modified by new "vernacular" traditions: Non-Taoist religious movements, with their own social and cultural constituencies, came to be accepted as part of the Taoist heritage.

Meanwhile, Taoist intellectuals repackaged age-old self-cultivation practices to appeal the new gentry class that had supplanted the ancient aristocracy. The prime example of "gentry Taoism" is Ch'üan-chen ("Integrating the Perfections"). It sprang from the teachings of Wang Che, otherwise known as Wang Ch'ung-yang (1113–70). Ch'üan-chen, which was especially popular among women, soon adopted a monastic setting. Its teachings featured a reinterpretation of the Taoist practices of spiritual refinement through meditation known as *chin-tan* ("Golden Elixir") or *nei-tan* ("Inner Alchemy"). This living tradition is now known as "Northern Taoism."

The history of Taoism over the last thousand years or so remains largely unknown, even to most specialists in Taoist studies. In general, late-imperial Taoism can be described as an amalgam of (1) elements of the common *Tao-chiao* of T'ang times; (2) new ritual traditions founded before the conquest period (approximately the twelfth through fourteenth centuries), such as Ch'ingwei; and (3) new models for self-cultivation, such as Ch'üan-chen. The ritual traditions of late-imperial times included "literati" participants, but they generally deemphasized self-cultivation (both "Inner Alchemy" and

Taoist priests are, at most, ritual intermediaries between humans and the higher powers—never evangelists who labor to shape practitioners' beliefs or clerics who confirm believers' conformance to established creeds. © REUTERS NEWMEDIA INC./CORBIS.

the earlier biospiritual practices) and seldom attempted to integrate Confucian or Neo-Confucian models of religious practice. Eventually, all those ritual traditions—both those that emphasized public liturgies and those more focused on individual ritual activity—blended together under a single rubric: "Southern Taoism." Its hereditary leaders purported to be descendants of Chang Tao-ling, founder of the ancient "Celestial Master" organization. Their Cheng-i ("Orthodox Unity") tradition had actually emerged during the conquest period, and their historical "lineage"—like those devised by Ch'an (Zen) Buddhists of the same period and by later "Dragon Gate" Taoists—was largely fabricated.

The turning point for Taoism was the period from 1279 to 1368, when China was ruled by the Mongols. The conqueror Chingghis (widely called Genghis Khan) continued to support the newly established Ch'üan-chen tradition, as his predecessors in northern China—a

Worshippers at the Dragon and Tiger Pagodas in Kaohsiung, Taiwan, enter through the mouths of the dragon and tiger. For 2,000 years Taoists have set up special places for their spiritual practices. © BOHEMIAN NOMAD PICTUREMAKERS/CORBIS.

Manchurian people called the Jurchen—had done. Chingghis even summoned its founder's most prominent disciple to explain Taoist principles at his court. Chingghi'ss successor, Qubilai (commonly called Khublai Khan), however, decided that his effort to consolidate Mongol control over the Chinese populace would be enhanced by establishing a "religious monopoly." Qubilai gave the Cheng-i leadership exclusive authority over Taoists throughout the south, and he denied the validity of any ordination given by other Taoist leaders.

The rulers of the ensuing Ming dynasty (1368–1644) were native Chinese, but they continued the Mongol's recognition of the Cheng-i priesthood and even intermarried with Cheng-i priests. In 1374 the Ming founder praised Cheng-i Taoists while denigrating Ch'üan-chen Taoists and Ch'an Buddhists for "devoting themselves to the cultivation of the person and the improvement of the individual endowment"—activities that did nothing to help the government control people's lives. Nonetheless, Ch'üan-chen models survived among literati of Ming times, mainly in a new

subtradition called Ching-ming ("Pure Illumination") Taoism, which remains little known even among scholars.

The Manchus—a people descended from the Jurchen—maintained the Ming ruler's domination of Taoism. Manchu rulers continued official recognition of Cheng-i Taoist leaders, sometimes even summoning them to perform rites at the imperial court. One emperor even named a Cheng-i priest "grand minister" of the nation, as T'ang emperors had earlier done. The harsh emperor known as Ch'ien-lung (reigned 1736–96) banished all Taoists from his court, however, and soon they lost virtually all their political influence. By the time the Western powers won the Opium Wars and took control of China in the mid-nineteenth century, the Manchus no longer bothered to recognize any Taoist.

Yet that is not to say that Taoism itself came to an end. Despite their loss of imperial sanctions, Cheng-i priests continued to perform their liturgies. The literati traditions of Taoist self-cultivation passed from Ching-ming hands into the Lung-men ("Dragon Gate") tradition. Like Ching-ming Taoism, "Dragon Gate" Taoism was carefully crafted to pass government muster while preserving the inherited social institutions of Taoism as well as traditional self-cultivation practices. Into the twenty-first century China's Taoists have preserved their living traditions and practices at temples across China, despite brutal attacks on religious centers of all faiths during the Cultural Revolution of 1966–76.

CENTRAL DOCTRINES There have never been any doctrines to which all Taoists were expected to subscribe. Unlike founded religions such as Buddhism, Christianity, or Islam, Taoism has never looked back to one great person and keyed its beliefs to his life or teachings. Unlike Christians or Muslims, Taoists never fought proponents of other faiths to gain or retain social or political supremacy. Hence, Taoists never felt pressed to reduce their faith to a set of core teachings that could determine whose side a person was truly supporting. Nor has Taoism ever had a priesthood that tried to enforce conformity to certain creedal formulations in order to maintain the faith's "purity" or to ensure its authority over practitioners. Taoist priests are, at most, ritual intermediaries between humans and the higher powers—never evangelists who labor to shape practitioner's beliefs or clerics who confirm believer's conformance to established creeds.

Taoism never based itself upon a premise that its followers consist of those who assent to certain propositions about life, as distinguished from people who do not. The idea that religious faith or practice must logically proceed from a proposition or belief—for instance, that religion begins inside a person's head and is then expressed in what one does with one's "external" life—is alien to the realities of Taoism, as indeed it is to the traditions of many indigenous peoples. For those reasons Taoists never engaged in disputation regarding the relative validity of different beliefs or worried that someone's faith might not be sound. Taoists never feared that their faith would be threatened by leaving matters of "belief" up to practitioners themselves.

Yet it would be a mistake to conclude that any and all beliefs could equally qualify as "Taoist." By analyzing the teachings and practices of Taoists throughout history, certain themes and principles can be identified that have been shared by most Taoists over the centuries and that have distinguished Taoists from those who embrace other traditions. What is found is that Taoism has

always emphasized practice rather than belief and that the kind of practice that it emphasizes has generally been spiritual self-cultivation. Self-cultivation is at the core of what it means to practice Taoism. Modern audiences must be careful to understand such matters on Taoist terms. For example, the very term "self-cultivation" misleads modern audiences to imagine Taoists as romantic individualists who treasure their sovereign "selves." The Taoist term *hsiu-lien* (literally, "cultivation and refinement") actually makes no reference to any "self." Modern people who narcissistically sanctify their own "self"—imagining it to be threatened by "outside forces" such as society or a Supreme Being—are not embracing Taoist premises. In fact, there is no word in Chinese that even remotely corresponds to a term like "the self." In Taoism there have never been any beliefs or practices premised upon dualistic assumptions of any description, for example, that the individual is at odds with society; good is in a struggle against evil; spirit is intrinsically alien to nature or matter; or that man is ontologically different from, and inferior to, the divine.

Even traditional Chinese ideas of yin and yang—often mistakenly imagined to be characteristic elements of Taoist belief—assumed those basic realities to be complementary, not antagonistic. Only in modern times did some Chinese writers, Taoist and non-Taoist, begin attributing a positive value to yang and a negative valuation to yin. Some late-imperial intellectuals conceived Taoist practice as leading to an integration of "the two," as seen in "Inner Alchemy" texts such as the *Hsing-ming kuei-chih* ("Balanced Instructions about Inner Nature and Life-Realities") of 1615. All such ideas, however, evolved in multiple (even, to non-Taoist eyes, discordant) ways, as different minds reformulated various inherited ideas.

If it is a mistake to project onto Taoism the dualistic assumptions that underlie some other culture's ideas, it would also be wrong to think that Taoism is monistic. The notion that "all things are one" is found nowhere in Taoism. Taoist practice is rarely explainable in such terms as "becoming one with Tao" (understood as some static transcendent absolute) or in such terms as transcending "time" or "the material world" to enter "eternity" or "heaven" (understood as a state ontologically different from our current life). Most certainly, no Taoist ever saw his or her practice in such terms as penetrating the "illusion" of the world of multiplicity and perceiving some underlying "unity."

Indeed, today's best scholars of Taoism frequently struggle with getting their inherited conceptual terminology to match up with what Taoists seem to be saying and doing. The interpretive categories derived from studying Christianity, Hinduism, Platonism, or Sufism simply do not fit Taoism. Looking back at the ways in which many centuries of Taoists, and their classical predecessors, have explained their understanding of how people should live, it is fair to say that Taoism rests upon a holistic worldview and a transformational ethos.

To understand the historical and theoretical parameters of the Taoist worldview and ethos more fully, it is helpful to examine the meanings of the term "Tao." Even if an exploration of Tao is confined to ideas found in the *Tao te ching* and other well-known classical texts such as the *Chuang-tzu*, a careful analysis yields no coherent results. In the *Tao te ching*, for instance, the usage of the term leads us to conclude that "Tao" is something simultaneously aware but not personal, neither transcendent nor immanent, unfeeling yet deeply maternal in its loving kindness, beyond human grasp yet easily graspable for anyone trying to wage a war or manage a government. In sum, the various contributors to the *Tao te ching* incorporated many unrelated concepts and left readers to take their pick.

In *Chuang-tzu* it is hard to see "Tao" as much more than a rhetorical element used to suggest the condition one experiences when one leaps beyond human valuation and cultural constructs. In the *Nei-yeh*, on the other hand, "Tao" suggests "realities that one ought to cultivate" and is used interchangeably with terms such as *ch'i* (life-energy) and *shen* (spirit)—transient spiritual forces that the successful practitioner learns to attract by proper management of body, mind, heart, and spirit. Those ideas endure among Taoists down to the present day and are found in many different Taoist models of practice. By contrast, the specific associations of "Tao" that one finds in the *Tao te ching* and *Chuang-tzu* were mostly ignored by later Taoists or preserved as rhetorical flourishes.

In most Taoist formulations, as in most other East Asian usages, the term "Tao" (literally "the way") was not a philosophical concept but rather a term for "personal practices that follow wise and ancient principles." In classical China, even in the teachings of Confucius himself, "Tao" was a term of common discourse meaning something like "our teachings about how we should live our lives" or "what we do in order to live most meaningfully." Such associations endure in certain Japa-

nese terms that contain the character "do" (the Japanese pronunciation of "tao"), such as *aikido* (the "way" of harmonious *ch'i*), a form of martial art, and *chado* (the "way" of tea), the traditions associated with the tea ceremony. That fact shows that by T'ang times (618–907)—when Japan adopted many elements of Chinese culture, though not Taoism itself—the term "Tao" suggested something like "an admirable complex of traditional practices." In all those contexts, as in Taoist tradition, the practices are not just activities related to certain ideas but rather means by which people embed themselves in, and manifest anew, cherished principles.

In Taoism those principles pertain to subtle realities that link the living practitioner to other practitioners of past and present, to other living things (human and nonhuman), and to the interconnected matrix of time, space, consciousness, life, spirit, and society within which all life's activities take place. From *Chuang-tzu* through the Shang-ch'ing revelations and T'ang Taoism into the present, Taoists frequently refer to religious practice as *hsiu chen* (cultivating reality) and to a person whose practice has reached its culmination as a *chen jen* (realized person). Nearly synonymous is the term *hsiu tao* (cultivating Tao), which became a standard summation of the practice of Ch'üan-chen Taoism and which endures in "Northern Taoism" today.

In sum, Taoists have always understood themselves as people who learn, and engage in, practices of spiritual transformation within a holistically interlinked universe. Taoists, however, have never devoted time or effort to pinning down the precise terms in which one should conceptualize such matters.

MORAL CODE OF CONDUCT Most twentieth-century writers mistakenly insisted that China's Taoists, unlike Confucians, ignored moral issues and formulated no moral teachings. In reality, Taoists always agreed with Confucians about the need for living a moral life and about the importance of moral conduct in society. While Confucians grounded their moral principles in the traditional Chinese social order, however, Taoists grounded theirs in holistic realities. That is, Taoists sought to integrate themselves not just with other humans but also with life's deeper realities.

In general, the principle of Taoist morality is that one should practice self-restraint while working to cultivate and refine oneself, for in that way one brings benefits to others as well as to oneself. The *Tao te ching* called this principle *shan* (goodness) and argued that it corre-

Glossary

"Celestial Masters" tradition (T'ien-shih) Taoist tradition of late Han times, with which several later traditions, especially Cheng-i, claimed affiliation

chen perfection or realization; ultimate spiritual integration

chen-jen perfected ones; a term used both for angelic beings and for the human ideal of fully perfected or realized persons

Cheng-i "Orthodox Unity"; Taoist tradition that emerged during the conquest period (approximately the twelfth through fourteenth centuries) and became a part of "Southern Taoism"

ch'i life-energy

chiao extended Taoist liturgy; a sequence of events over several days that renews the local community by reintegrating it with the heavenly order

chai type of Taoist liturgy that originated in the Ling-pao tradition in the fifth century

ch'i-kung (qigong) the skill of attracting vital energy

Chin dynasty dynasty that ruled China from 266 to 420 C.E.

chin-tan "Golden Elixir"; a set of ideas about spiritual refinement through meditation

Ch'ing dynasty dynasty that ruled China from 1644 to 1911; also called the Manchu dynasty

ching vital essence

Ching-ming "Pure Illumination"; a Taoism subtradition that emerged during the Ming dynasty; it was absorbed into the "Dragon Gate" tradition

Ch'ing-wei "Clarified Tenuity"; a Taoism subtradition the emerged in the tenth century; it involves a system of therapeutic rituals

ch'uan-ch'i type of traditional Chinese literary tale

Chuang-tzu classical text compiled c. 430 to 130 B.C.E.

Ch'üan-chen "Integrating the Perfections"; practice that originated in the eleventh century and continued in modern "Dragon Gate" Taoism; sometimes called "Northern Taoism"

classical China the period before 221 B.C.E.

"Dragon Gate" tradition (Lung-men) Taoist tradition that originated in the seventeenth century, incorporating Ch'üan-chen and Ching-ming; the dominant form of Taoism in mainland China today

Han dynasty dynasty that ruled China from 206 B.C.E. to 221 C.E.

Hsiang-erh "Just Thinking"; text that is couched as a commentary on the *Lao-tzu*

hsin heart/mind

hsing inner nature; internal spiritual realities

hsiu chen cultivating reality; term by which Taoists frequently refer to religious practice

hsiu-lien cultivation and refinement; an enduring Taoist term for self cultivation

hsiu tao cultivating Tao; nearly synonymous with *hsiu chen*

Inner Alchemy *nei-tan*; a generic term used for various related models of meditative self-cultivation

Jurchen Manchurian tribe; founders of the Chin dynasty (1115–1234)

kuan Taoist abbeys or temples

Lao-tzu the supposed author of the *Tao te ching*; also another name for the *Tao te ching*

Legalism Chinese school of philosophy that advocated a system of government based on a strict code of laws; prominent in the fifth through third centuries B.C.E.

libationers *chi-chiu*; men and women officiants in the early "Celestial Masters" organization

sponds to wholesome natural principles seen in the environment (for example, in water) and the characteristics of an imperceptible force called *Tao*.

In the *Tao te ching* that modern readers know, there is no suggestion that the practitioner should follow any specific code of behavior. In fact, many later Taoists

lien-shih refined master or mistress; an honorific term that was the highest Taoist title in T'ang times

Ling-pao "Numinous Treasure"; a set of Taoist revelations produced in the fourth century C.E.

meng-wei covenant

ming destiny; the realities of a person's external life

Ming dynasty dynasty that ruled China from 1368 to 1644

Mongols originally nomadic people who established the Yüan dynasty in China in the thirteenth century

nei-tan "Inner Alchemy"; the practice of spiritual refinement through meditation

Nei-yeh "Inner Cultivation"; an early Taoist text, likely a prototype for the well-known text *Tao te ching*

Neo-Confucianism Confucian teachings that were turned into a sociopolitical orthodoxy in China in the twelfth century

Northern Sung dynasty dynasty that ruled China until 1126; part of the Sung dynasty

"Northern Taoism" modern term for Taoist traditions (Ch'üan-chen and Lung-men) that stress self-cultivation

shan goodness

Shang-ch'ing "Supreme Clarity"; a tradition involving visualization meditation

shen spirit; spiritual consciousness

shen-hsien spiritual transcendence

"Southern Taoism" modern term for the Cheng-i Taoist tradition that survives mainly in Taiwan and along China's southeast coast; it stresses public liturgies such as *chiao* rather than self-cultivation

Sung dynasty dynasty that ruled China from 960 to 1279

T'ai-ch'ing "Great Clarity"; a tradition involving ritual alchemy

T'ai-p'ing ching "Scripture of Grand Tranquillity," an important early Taoist text

t'ai-p'ing grand tranquillity; a classical Chinese term for peace and harmony throughout the world; the most common Taoist political ideal

T'ang dynasty dynasty that ruled China from 618 to 907 C.E.

Tao classical Chinese term for any school's ideals and practices; among Taoists a term generally used to suggest the highest dimensions of reality, which can be attained by practitioners of traditional spiritual practices

Tao-chiao the teachings of the Tao; the Taoist's name for their religion

Taoism *Tao-chiao*; a Chinese religious tradition that emphasizes personal transformation and integration with the unseen forces of the universe

tao-shih Taoist priest or priestess; a person recognized by the Taoist community as having mastered a specific body of sacred knowledge and the proper skills and dedication necessary to put that knowledge into effect for the sake of the community

Tao te ching classical Taoist text; also known as the *Lao-tzu*

Tao-tsang today's library of Taoist literature

t'ien-shih celestial master; historical title for certain eminent Taoists, especially figures related to Chang Tao-ling

wai-tan alchemy; a process of self-perfection involving the preparation of spiritualized substances called *tan* (elixirs)

wu-wei nonaction; in the *Tao te ching*, a behavioral ideal of trusting to the world's natural processes instead of to one's own activity

continued to understand "goodness" as a general element of personal self-cultivation. By about the third century, however, Taoists had begun reading the *Tao te* *ching* as an expression of the wisdom of Lord Lao (Lao-chün), a divine being whom the emperors of the Han dynasty (206 B.C.E.–221 C.E.) had begun venerating.

Taoists thus began reading the *Tao te ching* as explaining Lord Lao's expectations regarding moral conduct. A fragmentary commentary from that period, the *Hsiang-erh* ("Just Thinking"), advocates biospiritual cultivation, yet it once also included 36 moral precepts. Nine of them promote virtues tagged to the *Tao te ching* (for example, stillness and clarity), while the others proscribed negative behaviors that had been obliquely criticized in the *Tao te ching* and the *T'ai-p'ing ching*.

By the fourth century Taoists had become familiar with the monastic precepts of Chinese Buddhists, which inspired them to particularize their own moral ordinances further in order to be more competitive with the Buddhist's model. The eventual result was *The 180 Precepts of Lord Lao*, which scholars wholly ignored until the closing years of the twentieth century. No one knows when the *180 Precepts* were first compiled. The scholar-aristocrat Ko Hung seems to have been familiar with some such precepts, and when later aristocrats such as Lu Hsiu-ching wove together Taoist traditions in the fourth and fifth centuries, they considered the *Precepts* essential for living the Taoist life. The *Tao-tsang* contains several versions of the *Precepts*, showing that they had remained important to centuries of Taoists.

Overall, the *Precepts* require that a person govern his behavior and restrain all thoughtless and self-indulgent impulses. By doing so, the person ensures that he does no harm to others or to the world in which we live. In format the *180 Precepts* follow the *Hsiang-erh*'s briefer list: They first explain what "you should not" do (140 precepts) and then outline what "you ought to" do (the remaining 40). The dicta gave specific standards concerning what is right and wrong regarding common aspects of everyday life. For instance, they require proper restraint in eating and drinking and respectful behavior toward women, servants, family members, teachers, disciples, and the general public. The *Precepts* also forbid abuse of animals, both wild and domestic; one ought not even frighten birds or beasts, much less cage them. Proper respect for nature is also required by prohibitions against improperly felling trees, draining rivers and marshes, or even picking flowers. Generally, a person should avoid activities that might harm anyone or anything and should assuredly take no part in the killing of anyone, even the unborn.

The audience of Lord Lao's *Precepts* apparently consisted of men. (Precepts intended specifically for women appeared in a now-lost text called the "Pure Precepts of Grand Yin.") Research has shown that the people expected to follow the *180 Precepts* were laymen, not clerics. Nevertheless, it is hard to say how fully Taoists of any era may have believed in such itemized codes of morality. By medieval times Taoist writers seldom mentioned Lord Lao's *Precepts*. In monastic institutions, however, detailed codes of behavior endured into the twentieth century.

One might be tempted to construe the *180 Precepts* as "the Taoist Ten Commandments," but their role was different from that of the Decalogue in Jewish or Christian tradition. Lord Lao was never viewed as "the One True God" by Taoists of any stripe, nor was "obeying the will of Lord Lao" ever part of any "Taoist catechism."

Some scholars believe that the "Celestial Master" community of late antiquity paralleled that of the Hebrews in the so-called wilderness period—a closed community that conceived its distinctive identity in terms of a covenant handed down by a deity who simply "chose" them. Surviving texts show that the early "Celestial Masters" expressly distinguished themselves from followers of other "cults" in the surrounding society. After the sixth century, however, most Taoist leaders were highly cultured aristocrats who had no worries about differentiating their religion from superstitious cults (as the earlier "Celestial Masters" had struggled to do). Thus, Lord Lao's *Precepts* faded into the background, and their underlying principles simply became taken for granted as general moral expectations. Without a theology of sin or a worldview assuming a fight between good and evil, Taoists were usually confident that any serious practitioner of their faith would seldom need more than occasional reminders that the spiritual life must rest upon a solid foundation of good character and moral conduct. Such reminders restated the common Taoist virtues—such as stillness, purity, and self-restraint—and trusted the practitioner to cultivate them as he or she worked toward spiritual perfection.

SACRED BOOKS Unlike Christians, Jews, and Muslims, Taoists have never understood their religion as the faithful practice of teachings found in a clearly defined set of writings. Certain "Taoist ideas" did originate in classical texts like the *Nei-yeh* and the *Tao te ching*, but research has not yet revealed any "religious community" devoted to following their teachings. In that sense, the first "Taoist scripture" may have been the *T'ai-p'ing ching* ("Scripture of Grand Tranquility")—a massive work of late antiquity. In another sense, the first "scripture" could be said to have been the *Tu-jen ching* (late fourth century; "Scripture for Human Salvation"), which presents itself as a verbalization of Tao itself.

History shows that some Taoist writings that had been influential in early periods eventually lost their impact. For instance, neither "Northern Taoists" nor "Southern Taoists" today make much use of ancient texts such as the *T'ai-p'ing ching* or *Tu-jen ching*. Likewise, the writings of subtraditions such as T'ai-ch'ing and Shang-ch'ing are read today only by scattered practitioners at Taoist temples and by a few dozen scholars around the world. On the other hand, the beliefs and practices presented in ancient texts on self-cultivation—particularly the *Nei-yeh*—were preserved over the centuries, because they were continually repackaged in new writings that appealed to ever-changing audiences. For instance, the *Nei-yeh*'s promotion of "biospiritual cultivation" reappeared in works as disparate as the "philosophical" *Huai-nan-tzu* (second century B.C.E.); the early "Celestial Master" *Tao te ching* commentary called the *Hsiang-erh* (second century C.E.); a still-used guide to Taoist practice called the *T'ien-yin-tzu* (c. 700 C.E.); and even a late-imperial novel, *Ch'i-chen chuan* ("Seven Taoist Masters"). So a true understanding of Taoist practice requires not just the study of one basic "scripture" but rather careful study of centuries of such largely-unknown texts, which were produced by men and women of different social classes and spiritual aspirations and which were honored and read but never "canonized" in quite the sense that the Bible was.

In the fifth century Lu Hsiu-ching hoped to create a sense of Taoist identity, so he compiled a list of writings that expressed ideas that would appeal to other like-minded aristocrats. The actual gathering of those writings (sixth century) resulted in a collection called "The Three Caverns" (*San-tung*), which stressed texts of the Ling-pao and Shang-ch'ing subtraditions. Soon *fu* (supplements) were added, including such writings as the *Tao te ching* and *T'ai-p'ing ching*, texts on ritual alchemy, and texts from the "Celestial Master" movement. "The Three Caverns" continued to grow, incorporating writings by and about Taoists of every description, partly because centuries of emperors wished to honor the Taoist community. For instance, the T'ang emperor Hsüan-tsung (reigned 713–56) commissioned the first systematic assemblage of Taoist writings. Such imperial sponsorship was vital before printing was invented (in the tenth century), for Taoist manuscripts—theretofore copied by hand—otherwise easily perished. In the

twelfth century the Sung emperor Hui-tsung ordered the engraving of a new and larger "Library of Tao," and the subsequent Jurchen rulers did likewise. The result was the most massive collection of Taoist writings in history, completed in 1244 under the auspices of the new Ch'üan-chen movement. Later Mongol rulers, however, were less tolerant, and in 1258 Qubilai (commonly called Khubilai Khan) ordered all Taoist writings except the *Tao te ching* to be burned. Many survived, but today's library of Taoist literature, called the *Tao-tsang*, is far smaller than that of Jurchen times, despite its inclusion of materials composed in the intervening years.

Today's *Tao-tsang* consists of 1120 separate works totaling 5,305 volumes. They include all of the Taoist writings that could be found in the year 1445, from the *Tao te ching* and *Chuang-tzu* to the texts of all later segments of Taoism. Late-imperial Confucians despised Taoism, however, so the "Library of Tao" was ignored both by centuries of Chinese scholars and by their Western disciples. Nonetheless, it was preserved by Taoists at such centers as the White Cloud Abbey in Beijing. A lithographic edition (1926) gradually found its way into some major libraries.

Yet few of its contents have been studied by scholars, and fewer still have been translated into any modern language—not even modern Chinese. Hence, most Taoist texts remain inaccessible to all but the most expertly trained scholars, and even they must travel to a major library to find it. Though many persist in calling the *Tao-tsang* the "Taoist canon," it should be thought of not as a sacred "canon" but rather as an ever-expanding library of materials in which Taoists have found value. There has never actually been a definitive collection of "canonical" scriptures that Taoists—of any period—have honored to the exclusion of "noncanonical" works, nor has there been any boundary between "sacred scripture" and other cherished texts.

SACRED SYMBOLS Given the nature of Taoist values, there has never been a central symbol, in the sense of a visual representation believed to convey a transcendent truth. The well-known yin-yang symbol is actually a common element of Chinese culture, not a symbol specific to Taoism, and it has held little importance for most Taoists throughout history. Instead, Taoist "symbolism" consists of an array of varied images that obliquely suggest the effectiveness of spiritual practice. An example is the crane, whose red crown is understood as representing cinnabar, a symbol of spiritual perfection.

EARLY AND MODERN LEADERS For two generations scholars associated the beginnings of the religious institutions of Taoism with a shadowy figure of Han times (206 B.C.E.–221 C.E.) named Chang Tao-ling. Hitherto unstudied texts, mostly from the *Tao-tsang*, led those scholars to believe that Chang was a major historical figure. Those writings suggested that he had founded the "Celestial Master" (*T'ien-shih*) organization, which the modern Cheng-i priests of Taiwan (the only region of China accessible to foreigners from the 1950s to the 1980s) claimed to have maintained. Scholars eager to redeem the reputation of living Taoist traditions—dismissed by earlier audiences as popular superstition—were excited by the apparent discovery that today's Cheng-i liturgists maintained practices that went back nearly two millennia to a figure who could even be likened to Moses. Texts of uncertain date report that in 142 C.E. Chang received a revelation from Lord Lao, who recognized Chang as the "Celestial Master" promised in the *T'ai-p'ing ching* and established a *meng-wei* (covenant) with Chang to take over from the failing Han emperors. Today scholars are unsure whether Chang was even a historical person, and they debate the historical impact of the traditions associated with his name.

Despite the early-fourth-century migration of the "Celestial Master" leadership to the south, Taoists in the north did not abandon their religion. One site where Taoism flourished was the Lou-kuan Abbey. It had been established near the spot where people of that era said that "Lao-tzu" had "departed to the west," so many Lou-kuan texts feature teachings of Lord Lao, a divine being who periodically descends to earth to impart his wisdom. A major Lou-kuan text was the *Hsi-sheng ching* ("Scripture of Western Ascension"), which features practices of self-cultivation from classical times, updated for contemporary tastes.

According to most scholars, the most influential figure of this era was an aristocrat named K'ou Ch'ien-chih (365–448). K'ou tried to restore the "Celestial Master" community in the north. He reported that he had received a revelation from Lord Lao in 415, primarily in the form of the "Precepts of the New Code" for the Taoist community. It is unclear whether anyone at the time accepted K'ou's claims, but by 424 he had befriended a Confucian official at the court of the Wei dynasty (386–534/35), founded by a people called the Toba who were influenced by Chinese culture. Together K'ou and his ally made themselves important by granting the Wei emperor the title of "Perfected Ruler of Grand Tranquillity," and later Wei emperors were ceremonially inducted into Taoist holy orders. The Toba rulers ordered that K'ou's "Precepts of the New Code" be put into effect throughout the countryside. Some have therefore said that the Toba adopted Taoism as a state religion, but it is unclear whether their decrees really affected many people's lives. After K'ou died, state patronage ceased, and other Taoist (and Buddhist) traditions gained more impetus. K'ou is thus a notable figure, though he was not really an heir to Chang Tao-ling's "Celestial Master" organization, and his historical effect may have been less important than was once thought.

For centuries Taoist leaders allied themselves with the rulers who were then in power. Such was true of the pivotal master Lu Hsiu-ching (406–77). Until the 1980s few had ever heard of Lu. At that time scholars began realizing that Lu Hsiu-ching had played a crucial role in stimulating a sense of common identity, and even common institutions, among people who had previously followed quite distinct traditions. Lu is best remembered for having conceptualized the first great Taoist "canon"—a forerunner of today's *Tao-tsang* ("Library of Tao"). Lu also helped codify and spread new models for Taoist liturgies, such as the *chiao*, and he instituted a religious establishment that once again legitimized the rulers of his day (the Liu-Sung dynasty, 420–79). Taoist leaders such as Lu and his eventual successor, T'ao Hung-ching (456–536), recognized those emperors (and their successors) both as fulfillers of earlier messianic prophesies and as the legitimate successors of the powerful rulers of Han times (206 B.C.E.–221 C.E.). Leaders such as Lu and T'ao established a model that would help centuries of later Taoist aristocrats secure government blessings and spread Taoist teachings and practices more fully throughout society.

The T'ang period (618–907) was when China was at its most powerful; its civilization overflowed into neighboring lands, from Tibet to Japan. It was also the time when Taoism was at its height. The many great leaders of T'ang Taoism belonged not to the tradition of the "Celestial Masters" (then all but extinct) but rather to the aristocratic traditions that such figures as Lu Hsiu-ching and T'ao Hung-ching had built up during the fifth and sixth centuries. A representative T'ang leader was Li Han-kuang (683–769), disciple and successor to the great Ssu-ma Ch'eng-chen. Like Ssu-ma, Li was a skilled calligrapher and accomplished scholar; he compiled a pharmacological guide as well as writings about *Lao-tzu* and *Chuang-tzu*. Li was also responsible for preserving the texts of the "Supreme Clarity" revelations and for rebuilding the religious center at Mount Mao, an active Taoist center today. Because of Li's aristocratic lineage, scholarly attainments, and position as Ssu-ma's spiritual heir, the great emperor Hsüan-tsung persistently summoned him to the court and even accepted formal religious orders in a ceremonial transmission from Li.

The living Ch'üan-chen tradition, commonly called "Northern Taoism," arose from the life of Wang Che (1113–70, also known as Wang Ch'ung-yang). Wang was a scholar and poet from a well-to-do family and the presumed author of a clear guide to living the Taoist life, known as "The Fifteen Articles." They teach that a person can achieve "spiritual immortality" within this life by cultivating one's internal spiritual realities (*hsing*) and harmonizing them with the realities of one's external life (*ming*). Wang's seven renowned disciples included a woman, Sun Pu-erh (1119–82), who couched some of her teachings in the form of poetry and presumably helped stir the great interest in Ch'üan-chen Taoism among Chinese women. Another disciple of Wang was Ch'iu Ch'u-chi (1148–1227, also known as Ch'iu Ch'ang-ch'un), who taught Taoism to several rulers, even the Mongol general Chingghis (widely called Genghis Khan).

By Ming times (1368–1644) the leading form of Taoism among scholars was called Ching-ming ("Pure Illumination"). Like most other Taoist traditions of that day, it traced its origins back to a legendary figure of early medieval times. By the twelfth century Ching-ming Taoism had combined self-cultivation with talismanic rituals and ethical teachings. Soon after the Mongol conquest a man named Liu Yü (1257–1308) reformulated the movement, teaching that ritual activity helped stimulate the virtues of loyalty and filial devotion, which in turn facilitated the stilling of the heart/mind. Over the next few centuries Confucian scholars were drawn into the practice of Ching-ming Taoism, which was finally absorbed into the "Dragon Gate" tradition of "Northern Taoism." Like Ching-ming Taoism, the Lung-men ("Dragon Gate") tradition was designed to preserve Taoist institutions within society so that Taoist self-cultivation practices could survive the oppressive social and political environment of late-imperial times.

"Dragon Gate" Taoism originated among disciples of Wu Shou-yang (1552–1641), who reputedly had received divine certification linking him and his teachings back to the early Ch'üan-chen leader Ch'iu Ch'u-chi. Eventually his "Dragon Gate" credentials were passed to a young man named Wang Ch'ang-yüeh, who established the "Dragon Gate" tradition at the White Cloud Abbey in Beijing in 1656. Wang thus established the form in which "Northern Taoism" would endure to the present day. "Dragon Gate" Taoism integrated ethical teachings that would suit all social classes with both the meditative tradition of "Inner Alchemy" and the priestly institutions that went back to Lu Hsiu-ching. By modern times its practitioners increasingly identified their tradition as a continuation of the Ch'üan-chen movement. Consequently, the achievements of "Dragon Gate" leaders such as Wang Ch'ang-yüeh are generally overlooked, though today's "Northern Taoism" owes much to them.

In China today it is difficult to identify any great Taoist leaders. That is not because of a shortage of conscientious men and women practicing Taoism at China's temples but rather because of the restrictive society in which they live. As a result, Taoist leaders—whether from the White Cloud Abbey, Mao-shan, or any of Taoism's other living centers—are not in a position to achieve acclaim among the populace of China or a conspicuous position in government, academia, or the media.

MAJOR THEOLOGIANS AND AUTHORS Taoism has had few "theologians"—people concerned with intellectual analysis or articulation of doctrinal principles. For more than 2,000 years it has had writers who explained their own views and values but who frequently did so anonymously. Moreover, many of their writings have long been lost, and of those that survive, few have yet to receive much attention from scholars or the public. A few of the Taoist writers whose works are known to today's scholars illustrate the range of Taoist ideas and activities.

The most renowned and well-studied Taoist thinker is Chuang Chou, the presumed author of the "inner chapters" of a classical text known as the *Chuang-tzu*. The *Chuang-tzu* is one of the most colorful and compelling works of world literature, and the writers who took part in compiling it—from perhaps 430 to 130 B.C.E.—were as witty as they were profound. The actual text that has been handed down to us, however, is really the work of a "commentator" of the third century C.E. named Kuo Hsiang. Kuo inherited 52 chapters of material bearing Chuang's name, threw away the parts that he confessed himself too dense to understand, and left 33 chapters that "made some sense" to him.

Virtually nothing is known of the historical life of Chuang himself, except that he lived in the second half of the fourth century B.C.E. At the end of the twentieth century many scholars believed that internal references to "Chuang Chou" within the text itself can be accepted as autobiographical confessions. In reality, the *Chuang-tzu* consists of tales and parables whose characters include not just Chuang himself but Confucius, unknown beings, and even birds and insects—all of whom simply appear to express and debate ideas from the minds of the *Chuang-tzu*'s contributors.

For the most part, those contributors urge readers to question the utility of rational thought as a reliable guide to life, to see "common-sense" ideas as cultural constructs bearing no clear relationship to truth, and to "leap into the boundless" instead of trying to figure out life and make it work as we wish it to. Yet as fascinating as those ideas may be, nothing in the text tells the reader how to do those things or what to do about real-life problems. Though Chinese and Western writers often tried to explain the *Chuang-tzu* and the *Tao te ching* together—as the "primary texts" of "classical Taoism"—the two works have little in common and were clearly not composed by people whose ideas about life were the same.

Until the 1970s it was widely, though inaccurately, believed that a primary "theoretical" work of "religious Taoism" was the *Pao-p'u-tzu* ["(The Writings of) the Master who Embraces Simplicity"]. The *Pao-p'u-tzu* was written by Ko Hung (283–343), an aristocrat of the early fourth century to whom are attributed various other Taoist writings, including the *Shen-hsien chuan* ("Accounts of Divine Transcendents"). In some senses Ko was indeed a key figure, though less for his thought, or for his effect on people of his day, as for the fact that he collected (or at least reported) all manner of data that were later accepted as "Taoist." For scholars today the writings attributed to Ko are thus a treasury of early-medieval "Taoism," particularly in regard to the tradition of ritual alchemy called T'ai-ch'ing. Yet in Ko's day Taoism had not yet coalesced, and if twentieth-century scholars were correct in thinking of the "Celestial Masters" as Taoism's main tradition, Ko clearly lived and worked on its fringes. Nor did Ko think that classical

texts such as *Chuang-tzu* or *Lao-tzu* held the answers to life.

Far from having been an "alchemist," as most once believed, Ko was a Confucian official who held minor military and clerical posts before retiring to Mount Luo-fu near the south coast. The so-called "Outer Chapters" of his *Pao-p'u-tzu* express the interests and values of the Confucians of his day so thoroughly that the only scholar ever to translate them calls Ko "a conservative defender of common sense." Ko was also proud to own various writings on alchemy and ritual, some of which had been bequeathed to him by his own ancestors. The "inner chapters" of his *Pao-p'u-tzu* maintain that the ritual methods described in those writings could elevate a person to a deathless state. Such an outspoken advocate of "immortality" struck later generations of Confucians—and the Western scholars whom they mentored—as so bizarrely "un-Chinese" (and contrary to modern beliefs) that caricatures of his ideas were long cited to show how stupid the Taoists of imperial times supposedly were. In reality, Ko was simply an eclectic aristocrat who might best be called a maverick Confucian. By maintaining that a pursuit of immortality—a goal to which both the *Lao-tzu* and *Chuang-tzu*, unlike "Celestial Master" texts, often allude—was a fitting goal for upstanding "gentlemen" like himself, Ko attempted to integrate the divergent beliefs and traditions that gave his own life meaning and value.

Arguably the single most influential Taoist of all time was Ssu-ma Ch'eng-chen (646–735). He was the greatest Taoist leader of an age when Taoism was a major force among the Chinese elite. Ssu-ma was descended from relatives of the rulers of the Chin dynasty (266–420), and his father and grandfather had both held government posts. An associate of renowned poets such as Li Po, Ssu-ma was not only an accomplished poet but also a musical composer and a distinguished painter and calligrapher. For centuries Chinese annals of history's greatest artists all celebrated Ssu-ma Ch'eng-chen. It is thus no surprise that when he died, Ssu-ma's life was commemorated in eulogies by government officials and even by the emperor Hsüan-tsung himself. Ssu-ma had been a frequent guest at the court of several emperors, and he was remembered as a sagely counselor who helped give their reign legitimacy. His disciples include Li Han-kuang, discussed above under EARLY AND MODERN LEADERS, and Chiao Ching-chen, a *lien-shih* (refined mistress) who was also acclaimed by the land's most eminent poets.

Of more lasting importance was Ssu-ma's work copying, collating, and composing Taoist texts. His expertise on the *Tao te ching*, for instance, was so great that the emperor commissioned him to write it out in three styles of script so that "the correct text" could be engraved in stone. He also edited T'ao Hung-ching's "Secret Directives for Ascent to Perfection" and himself wrote the now-lost "Esoteric Instructions for Cultivating Perfection." Some writings attributed to Ssu-ma are probably not in fact his work, but scholars today acknowledge him as the author of such important works as the *Fu-ch'i ching-i lun* ("On the Essential Meaning of the Absorption of Life-Energy [Ch'i]") and the *Tso-wang lun* ("On 'Sitting in Forgetfulness'")—a meditation text known in the West as "Seven Steps to the Tao." The teachings in that work were influenced by those of the Taoist physician Sun Ssu-miao in his *T'sun-shen lien-ch'i ming* ("Visualization of Spirit and Refinement of *Ch'i*"). Ssu-ma hails the unknown "Master of Heavenly Seclusion," T'ien-yin-tzu, whose brief introduction to the Taoist life Ssu-ma edited.

Ssu-ma taught that the path to spiritual transcendence (*shen-hsien*) requires a lifestyle of moderate self-discipline and practices designed to "cultivate and refine" both one's body and one's spiritual energies. Like other Taoist aristocrats of his day, Ssu-ma offered a model of Taoist practice intended to appeal to scholars and officials who had limited knowledge of earlier Taoism and who thus might appreciate clear, simple guidelines. Those models reappeared in the lives and teachings of centuries of "literati Taoists," including Wang Ch'ung-yang, Liu Yü, and Wang Ch'ang-yüeh, discussed above under EARLY AND MODERN LEADERS.

From today's perspective the most important Taoist of T'ang times may have been Tu Kuang-t'ing (850–933). Besides writing poetry and short stories that people continue to read, the court official Tu also composed numerous little-known religious works of great historical importance. He wrote commentaries on Taoist scriptures and classical texts, instructions for performing liturgies, and a number of historical and biographical collections that tell us much about the Taoists of medieval times. One, called the *Li-tai ch'ung-tao chi* ("Records of Reverence for Taoism over the Ages"), tells how centuries of rulers sponsored Taoists and their institutions. Another, the *Yung-ch'eng chi-hsien lu* ("Records of the Assembled Transcendents of the Walled City"), assembled biographies of great Taoist women and female "transcendents." Few of Tu's writings, however, have yet been studied or fully translated.

Around Tu Kuang-t'ing's time some Taoist writers began using the terminology of earlier alchemical traditions to express—and sometimes camouflage—their ideas about spiritual refinement through meditation. Those ideas—known among Taoists as *chin-tan* ("the Golden Elixir")—have become more generally known as *nei-tan* ("Inner Alchemy"). That ongoing tradition of meditative practices remains poorly understood in the West, though it has been the central tradition of Taoist self-cultivation practices for the last thousand years.

"Inner Alchemy" actually refers to "purifying the heart/mind" in order to achieve tranquillity and to harmonize oneself with the primordial Tao. In the *Wu-chen p'ien* ("Folios On Awakening to Reality") of Chang Po-tuan (eleventh century) and in *Chung-ho chi* ("On Centered Harmony") by Li Tao-ch'un (thirteenth century), "Inner Alchemy" practices are couched in such cryptic symbols as "uniting the dragon and the tiger." As literacy increased among the expanding "gentry" class, writers of Ming (1368–1644) and Ch'ing (1644–1911) times increasingly recast "Inner Alchemy" in clearer, more accessible terms. One good example is the anonymous *Hsing-ming kuei-chih* ("Balanced Instructions about Inner Nature and Life-Realities"), published in 1615.

Though these facts are still largely unknown to modern audiences, scholars of the Ch'ing (Manchu) period continued to write about "mind-cultivation," drawing upon those older traditions. Some, such as Min I-te (1758–1836), became regarded as leaders of the "Dragon Gate" tradition. Another was a scholar named Liu I-ming (1734–1821). One of Liu's writings was the *Wu-tao lu* ("Record of Awakening to Tao"), whose title recalls the *Wu-chen ko* ("Song of Awakening to Tao") by Wang Ch'ung-yang, the founder of "Northern Taoism." Liu's numerous writings on self-perfection have survived, but they have seldom been studied or properly translated. When future scholars bring such writings to the attention of readers around the world, the enduring Taoist tradition of self-cultivation will become better appreciated.

ORGANIZATIONAL STRUCTURE Most people who learned about Taoism from twentieth-century representations would assume that Taoism could, by its nature, have no organization at all. Of course, Taoism has never had a hierarchy like that which the emperor Constantine imposed upon Roman Christians in the early fourth century. For many centuries there have been Taoist priests, male and female alike, but they have never supervised the religious lives of all believers in a parish, nor have they reported to a bishop who reports to a pope. For that reason, today's scholars of Taoism are often reluctant to use any terminology drawn from Christian traditions when trying to explain Taoist institutions. The truth is that centuries of Taoists did attempt to organize their practitioners to some degree, sometimes following successful Buddhist models. Because Taoist's historical challenges, however, were different from those that Christians or Buddhists faced, Taoists could usually flourish with only a limited organizational structure, and they have never attempted any actual unification.

Before the second or third century C.E., there was no "Taoist community" to be organized. The followers of Chang Tao-ling's "Celestial Master" tradition assigned specific roles to its local leaders, the *chi-chiu* (libationers). Those forerunners of the later Taoist clergy could be male or female, Chinese or "barbarian," and they were ranked according to their level of religious attainment. The organization's headman claimed descent from Chang himself. The organization clearly died out in medieval times, but in the early modern era a band of Taoists surnamed Chang, based at Dragon-and-Tiger Mountain (Lung-hu shan), claimed to continue the old "Celestial Master" lineage. Until the mid-nineteenth century emperors nominally recognized the Cheng-i leaders, but Western reports that Cheng-i leaders were Taoist "popes" had no basis in fact. Even leading scholars of Taoism have inadvertently perpetuated some confusion about the role of Taoist leaders in relation to the religious community and its institutions. Some continue to believe that the Cheng-i liturgists of "Southern Taoism" truly continue institutions put in place by Chang Tao-ling. In other words, they see modern Cheng-i authorities as veritable papal successors to Chang himself. Since about the year 2000, other scholars have increased that confusion by labeling certain ill-defined traditions of early-medieval times the "Southern Celestial Masters" and the "Northern Celestial Masters." Most of those traditions seem to have little to do with either the earlier organization of Chang Tao-ling or the modern Cheng-i tradition.

Originally the term *t'ien-shih* (celestial master) simply meant an especially insightful teacher. Such "celestial masters" appear as characters in both the *Chuang-tzu* and the *T'ai-p'ing ching* but clearly not as historical figures related to Chang Tao-ling. In early medieval times the title "celestial master" was claimed by, or applied to, a wide variety of historical individuals—all apparently male—in various contexts. Few of them were named Chang, and none had any clear connection to the earlier followers of Chang Tao-ling. Chang's descendants appear in early-medieval sources, but there is no evidence that any of them claimed the title *t'ien-shih*, much less that anyone in that day regarded them as "apostolic" leaders.

Even less "papal" was the only person surnamed Chang to be mentioned as a *t'ien-shih* in regard to T'ang times (618–907), when Taoism was at its zenith. That man, Chang Kao, first appears in a text written in about 1300, which claims that the emperor Hsüan-tsung gave him the title of "Celestial Master in the Han Lineage." Taken at face value, that report would appear to bolster the idea of an "apostolic lineage" of leaders named Chang. Historical analysis has conclusively demonstrated, however, that no such event is mentioned in any historical or religious sources prior to the year 1300. The abundant sources of the period in question—including the detailed chronicles of the eminent Taoist historian Tu Kuang-t'ing—nowhere mention "Chang Kao" and nowhere mention any other person receiving such a title from a T'ang emperor.

T'ang sources do call quite a few historical Taoists "celestial masters" but in ways that show that in those days *t'ien-shih* was a general honorific term that could be casually applied to any memorable Taoist. The "celestial masters" of T'ang times thus included Ssu-ma Ch'eng-chen and his successor, Li Han-kuang; the aforementioned historian Tu Kuang-t'ing; a famous poet named Wu Yün; and even the wonder-worker Yeh Fa-shan (who was thought to have miraculous powers). Clearly none of those men were "popes." In T'ang times, in fact, the highest Taoist title may have been *lien-shih* (refined master/mistress), a title sometimes applied to venerable women as well as men. *Lien-shih* was apparently also an honorific term, not an ecclesiastical office that gave one person authority over other's religious lives.

By the twelfth century followers of Ch'an (Zen) Buddhism had concocted a story designed to legitimize one particular set of teachers as heirs to an apostolic lineage that was traceable back to the historical Buddha (15 centuries earlier). That lineage was entirely fabricated, as is clear from the fact that no such beliefs can be found among the earliest Ch'an Buddhists—not even in writings by or about their earliest Chinese "patriarchs." Yet the story proved effective in stimulating interest in

"Northern Taoism" and "Southern Taoism"

The people of modern China, including Taoists, generally distinguish two notably different living forms of Taoism. "Southern Taoism" survives mainly in Taiwan and along the southeastern coast of mainland China. It is an outgrowth of the Cheng-i liturgical tradition that has been based at Dragon-and-Tiger Mountain (Lung-hu shan) since the eleventh century. Its hereditary priests continue to perform liturgies such as the *chiao*, which harmonizes the local community with the cosmos. They also make a living by performing healing rituals and exorcisms for the public—activities shunned by "Northern Taoists." Before 1976 few outsiders were allowed to enter mainland China, so late-twentieth-century depictions of Taoism focused exclusively upon Taoist activity in Taiwan. A few Western scholars were even ordained as Cheng-i priests.

Until the 1980s outsiders were unsure that Taoism even remained alive in mainland China. It soon became apparent that, despite the persecution of members of all religions in China from 1966 to 1976, Taoism had indeed survived. Most Taoists in mainland China identify themselves as followers of "Northern Taoism," a continuation of the Ch'üan-chen tradition founded by Wang Ch'ung-yang in the twelfth century. "Northern Taoism," like Ch'an (Zen) Buddhism and even Neo-Confucianism (all of which deeply influenced each other), stresses individual moral and spiritual discipline; it also preserves self-cultivation practices that can be traced back to the classical text *Nei-yeh*. Its headquarters is the White Cloud Abbey (Pai-yün kuan) in Beijing, where Wang Ch'ang-yüeh established the "Dragon Gate" tradition in 1656. "Northern Taoism" remains largely unknown to Westerners.

ticed. That group wrote up "historical records" designed to show that the recipients of the Shang-ch'ing revelations in the fourth century had founded a lineage of *tsung-shih* ("Grand Masters"), which had run through such historical figures as Ssu-ma Ch'eng-chen before culminating in the leaders of Mao-shan in that day. The competing group was composed of the Taoists of Lung-hu shan, who purported to be descendants of Chang Tao-ling.

The reason that modern people, including most scholars of Taoism, have often talked about the "Celestial Masters" of Lung-hu shan but never about the "Grand Masters" of Mao-shan is simply that centuries of emperors gave political precedence to the Taoists of Lung-hu shan, thereby disempowering the Taoist leaders of Mao-shan and other centers. Imperial recognition of the Cheng-i lineage ended only in the mid-nineteenth century, at precisely the time that Western powers wrested real control of China away from the Manchus. Nevertheless, even that recognition never gave Cheng-i leaders any actual power; they could never do anything more than control the distribution of ordination certificates. So it would be a serious mistake to imagine them ever to have been "Taoist popes."

Likewise, the roles of Taoist "priests" must not be misconstrued. Scholarly explanations of the Taoist priesthood have often been confused and misleading. One problem is that few such scholars have ever had extensive personal contacts with living Taoist priests. Because of historical and political factors Taoist priests have been displaced for generations from China's government, academic institutions, and public media. Even in China today most Taoist priests have little contact with the educated public or the outside world. People trying to understand the roles and functions of Christian or Buddhist priests have generally been able to meet, observe, and learn from priests. Students of Taoism have had few such opportunities and were further misled by twentieth-century scholars who frequently confused literary images with historical data and who even anachronistically conflated social data from contemporary Taiwan with data from ancient and medieval texts. Moreover, some such scholars used terms such as "Taoist priest" or "Taoist master" as an indiscriminate translation for a range of unrelated Chinese terms, making it difficult for today's readers to get an accurate idea of Taoist priests through the ages.

In ancient times *tao-shih*, or "priest," was a vague literary term for idealized characters or a reference to peo-

Buddhism (even among modern Westerners), and two contemporary groups of Taoists fabricated analogous stories of an "apostolic succession." One group was based at a mountain called Mao-shan, where certain historical Taoists, such as Li Han-kuang, had earlier prac-

ple with unusual abilities. The actual institutions of the early "Celestial Master" organization remain poorly known, but they called their officiants *chi-chiu* (libationers), not *tao-shih.* Some scholars now argue that libationers were never really clergy, just leading lay participants.

The term *tao-shih* originated among the aristocratic *Tao-chiao* of early medieval times, when Taoist leaders such as K'ou Ch'ien-chih and Lu Hsiu-ching began trying to organize Taoist traditions to seem more competitive with Buddhist institutions. For a century or two, writers produced texts intended to particularize the ranks and duties of Taoist clerics. Those texts never agreed with each other, but they generally distinguished the *tao-shih* from lower-order functionaries such as *fa-shih* (ritual masters). Notably, however, such texts never designated separate orders for women priests.

From T'ang times on, Taoists used the word *tao-shih* as the standard designation for any person recognized by the Taoist community as having mastered a specific body of sacred knowledge and the ritual skills necessary to put that knowledge into effect for the sake of the community. The title also distinguished Taoist religious specialists from those of Buddhism as well as from those of nonrecognized traditions.

Throughout history the social status of *tao-shih* has generally remained high. In medieval times male *tao-shih* were often highly educated scholars, physicians, poets, and government officials. Leaders such as Ssu-ma Ch'eng-chen were members of China's high aristocracy, with social standing to match their ancient bloodline and scholarly attainments. Modern misconceptions (which remain common both in China and in the West) that Taoist practitioners in imperial times were mostly ignorant peasants—and thus not deserving respect—are an item of propaganda from a narrow circle of Confucian elitists who became Western scholars' "native guides" to Chinese civilization.

The medieval texts purporting to standardize the Taoist priesthood seem to have carried no weight in real life. Taoists remained so disinterested in formalizing their clerical institutions that T'ang emperors even tried to set clerical standards for them. Government supervision of the Taoist clergy has lingered to the present day, though no secular or religious authority ever had either the power or the will to impose a regulated ecclesiastical hierarchy upon Taoist practitioners. Consequently, later Taoists were free to reorganize as they saw fit, and occasional twentieth-century scholars likened early-modern

movements such as Ch'üan-chen to those of the Protestant reformers in Christianity. But such analogies are misleading, for those Taoists were not rebelling against any powerful hierarchy, and they were not united by common scriptures or creeds.

After losing imperial recognition in the nineteenth century, Cheng-i priests maintained their institutions and practices until the Communist revolution in the twentieth century, which drove their leaders to Taiwan. In mainland China today, virtually all Taoist abbeys or temples (*kuan*) are recognized as preserving Ch'üan-chen traditions, often called "Northern Taoism." Beijing's White Cloud Abbey (Po-yün kuan) has received official recognition as the country's principal Taoist center, and a loose coalition called the Chinese Taoist Association is headquartered there. With government blessings and modest funding, that association publishes Taoist books and magazines and holds classes for youths who aspire to the priesthood. Under the auspices of the Taoist Association, representatives from China's other temples sometimes gather to converse and provide each other with moral support. Yet the authority of each temple remains autonomous, and no attempt has been made—either by the government or by temple leaders—to standardize Taoist teachings and practices or to unify China's Taoists into a truly coherent organization.

Taoist traditions are also maintained among the various branches of the Chinese diaspora in other modern nations. In each such setting local autonomy remains the rule. National Taoist associations, paralleling the one based in Beijing, have been formed in such lands. For instance, the Hong Kong Taoist Association sponsors a Taoist college in addition to hosting scholarly conferences and publishing Taoist books and periodicals. By the 1990s national associations outside China began trying to establish greater communication and cooperation, though those efforts remained hampered by distance, a lack of financial resources, and lingering political tensions. An umbrella group called the International Taoist Association has been formed to combat those problems and to promote the ongoing vitality of Taoist traditions throughout the world.

HOUSES OF WORSHIP AND HOLY PLACES Taoism has never had houses of worship comparable to Christian churches or Muslim mosques. For 2,000 years, however, Taoists have set up special places for their spiritual practices. In medieval times Taoists began establishing *kuan* (temples, or abbeys), where male and female practitioners could go to immerse themselves in Taoist practice. Over time Taoists borrowed ideas from Buddhist institutions and added temple activities such as preserving old writings, housing traveling dignitaries, and providing a supplemental site for imperial ceremonies.

Today *kuan* across China are generally identified with the Ch'üan-chen tradition ("Northern Taoism"). During the 1960s reign of terror called the Cultural Revolution, most Chinese temples of all religions were forced to close, and their clerics and other practitioners were harshly persecuted. By the 1990s many *kuan* had been not only reopened but also partially restored, especially near tourist sites. Both at those well-known "temples" and at smaller sites further from the centers of modern life, Taoist men and women continue to practice self-cultivation and perform ceremonies to produce blessings for themselves and for all living things.

WHAT IS SACRED? Because of the diversity of Taoist traditions, understandings of what is sacred vary. Given the holistic perspective common to most of Taoism, a conceptual dichotomy of sacred and profane is hard to uphold. In fact, the classical text *Chuang-tzu*—identified by later Taoists as a "scripture"—includes an episode in which Chuang Chou intentionally shocks a philosopher-friend: Chuang answers the question "where is Tao?" by declaring that it is even in bodily waste. His intention was to ridicule the very question and to demonstrate the foolishness of imagining "Tao" as somehow apart from elements of our everyday world.

From other perspectives it is clear that all models of Taoist practice are based on an assumption that spiritual practice elevates a person's personal reality, lifting him or her out of a mundane state into a more fully *chen* (real) state. In that sense, one could say that Taoists believe in turning away from a "profane" life (understood as confusion and futility) and ascending to a "sacred" state (understood as reassimilation to the subtle realities of life).

In addition, Taoists have sometimes identified certain natural substances as somehow pointing to, or even leading to, such states of spiritual realization. For instance, ingesting a certain plant called *ling-chih* (efficacious fungus) has long been thought to help facilitate one's efforts at spiritual refinement. Individuals, however, are always free either to accept or to ignore such ideas, so in Taoism nothing is "sacred" in the sense of being normative for all Taoist's religious practice.

HOLIDAYS AND FESTIVALS The Taoist life has seldom been anchored to segments of the temporal year. Taoism has never had a "Sabbath," a common liturgical calendar, or holy seasons comparable to Easter and Christmas among Christians or Ramadan among Muslims. Generally, Taoists have observed the holidays and festivals common in the surrounding society, sometimes adding specifically Taoist ceremonies to the observance of such occasions. In early medieval times some Taoists suggested the observance of new holy days, but such observances never became standard. In general, laity continue to observe most of the holidays common to Chinese society and may also take part in additional activities at Taoist temples. Hence, specifically Taoist days of religious observance are generally limited to clerics who live and work full time at Taoist temples.

MODE OF DRESS Taoists have no distinctive items of apparel. The clerics of "Northern Taoism" favor simple cotton apparel in solid, muted colors, with formal robes for ceremonial occasions. The priests of "Southern Taoism" attract attention to their liturgical rites by wearing highly ornate silk robes, richly embroidered with images of heavenly bodies and animals such as fish and dragons, signifying the priest's role as unifier of all spheres of existence.

DIETARY PRACTICES No uniform dietary practices are expected of all Taoists. Historically, most Taoists accepted the general ideal that one should avoid foods that hinder self-refinement and should favor foods more conducive to spiritual practice. In medieval literature beneficial foods were so idealized that the perfect diet consisted solely of intangible life-essences, such as *ch'i* (vital energy) or even the emanations from stars. Few, however, have ever taken such idealizations literally. Under Buddhist influence some Taoists began avoiding meat and other "stimulating" foods such as onions; earlier, the prime food to avoid was any kind of grain. Generally, Taoists have tended to regard rice and vegetables as wholesome, but there have never been dietary requirements for laypeople.

RITUALS Evidence suggests that Taoists have never engaged in worship services comparable to those of Christians or Muslims. The idea that the believers in a local community should gather on a regular basis to pray, sing, hear a sermon, and forge or renew a relationship to a higher being is generally alien to Taoism. There has never been a Taoist "Sabbath" or a standard liturgical year.

Analogies for Taoist rites must be sought not in Christian or Muslim worship services but rather among the varied ritual traditions found in Hinduism, Shinto, and Native American cultures. In those settings we might profitably distinguish social ceremonies, such as weddings and funerals; liturgical rites, designed to integrate the community; and rites of passage, by which an individual moves from one stage of life to another.

There have never been Taoist weddings per se. Many Taoists have considered celibacy to be fundamental, as explained below under SOCIAL ASPECTS. Those who embraced marriage usually followed the wedding procedures common to Chinese social tradition, as they did in regard to funeral rites. Taoists developed various liturgies called *chai*, some of which sought to establish beatitude for deceased ancestors. Those rites were performed long after the demise of the ancestors in question, and they constituted a recommendation to the higher powers that the deceased should be accorded due recognition upon their arrival on the higher plane of existence.

Other *chai* liturgies had different purposes. One aimed to forestall natural disasters and to reintegrate the sociopolitical order with the cosmos, while another aimed to avert disease by expiating moral transgressions through communal confession. A more extended liturgy is the *chiao*, a sequence of events over several days that renews the local community by reintegrating it with the heavenly order. Under Lu Hsiu-ching these liturgies combined ritual frameworks from the imperial court with those of the local village and unified them through the actions of *tao-shih* (Taoist priests). Both "Northern Taoism" and "Southern Taoism" continue such liturgical traditions.

RITES OF PASSAGE Taoists have no standard rites of passage keyed to boy's or girl's natural growth and maturation. Rather, Taoists tend to integrate their own rites—generally intended to signify an individual's spiritual development—with the generic rites of passage common throughout Chinese society.

Taoism is not a religion into which a person is born, nor is it one into which a child's parents ritually induct him or her. There is thus no rite intended to confirm an infant as a member of the religion. Nor are there puberty rites that are specifically linked to Taoist reli-

gious identity. Rather, Chinese social traditions—disrupted by modernity—preserved ancient rites of ascendance (called "capping"), which have generally been regarded as Confucian, though they were never really tied to any doctrinal or scriptural authority. Boys and girls alike had the choice, from puberty onward, to move beyond such rites—which simply confirmed a person in standard social roles—and to enter a specifically Buddhist or Taoist community. In early medieval times it was not uncommon for boys or girls to take that step in early adolescence. There has never been any regulation in this area, and entry into the religious community remains elective for any person at any age.

MEMBERSHIP There has seldom been any formal membership in Taoism. The texts of "classical Taoism" were generally produced by isolated individuals or anonymous groups, and in neither case is there evidence of a community with a defined membership.

From the late second century the "Celestial Master" organization seems to have had a fluid membership, open to people of all origins, including non-Chinese peoples from neighboring regions, whom the Chinese commonly regarded as "barbarians." Its participants understood themselves to be followers of a *meng-wei*, a special covenant between Chang Tao-ling and Lord Lao, and they renounced participation in the "cults" practiced among the surrounding populace. Those who accepted the authority of the "Celestial Masters" could thus be called members of a distinct religious organization, though it did not survive beyond the seventh century.

The more aristocratic traditions of that period (including T'ai-ch'ing, Shang-ch'ing, and Ling-pao) had no comparable organization, though they did share a sense that their practices were superior to those of other traditions. It was only after the fifth century that a common Taoist tradition came into being; its follower's sense of identity rested mainly in being different from Buddhists. Other than among the "Celestial Master" leaders, there is little evidence that Taoists who had children raised them as Taoists. Instead, boys and girls would choose to become Taoists during adolescence or adulthood. Such remains the case today.

Taoism has never been evangelical. Taoists have always accepted any who wish to practice their tradition, but they have never attempted to convert followers of other traditions. Participation in Taoism has remained primarily a matter of personal interest within a society that has never assumed that individuals must have a single, exclusive religious affiliation.

Today the Taoists of China live in a highly regulated society. The government tolerates traditional religious institutions, but with no true freedom of religion, China's Taoists have little presence in the public media. Taoists have made no outreach to foreigners, and other than a few Western scholars who have been ordained as Cheng-i priests in Taiwan, only native Chinese practice Taoism at China's temples. Even Chinese emigrants to the West have generally not solicited the participation of non-Chinese, though in the late twentieth century a few emigrant Taoists began to accept Western participants into their small religious communities.

RELIGIOUS TOLERANCE In premodern China intolerance was rarely a feature of any religious tradition. In the twentieth century there was a common misconception that Taoism arose as a reaction against Confucianism. There is no validity whatsoever to such ideas. Confucians and Taoists generally lived in harmony, sharing many common beliefs and values and deeply respecting each other and each other's traditions and practices. Such was demonstrably the case up to the twelfth century, when rulers began turning the teachings of "Ch'eng/Chu" Confucians—widely called Neo-Confucianism—into a sociopolitical orthodoxy. Today's scholarship makes clear that Neo-Confucianism never really became the monolithic, all-powerful cultural force that twentieth-century audiences believed. Taoism flourished, even among so-called Confucian literati, well into modern times.

It is true that early-medieval Taoists first conceived their tradition in contradistinction to Buddhism, but they never understood the two traditions as standing in contradiction. Taoists were seldom hostile toward Buddhists or contemptuous of their teachings and practices. Rather, Taoists simply felt that Buddhism was not "who we are." During two brief periods emperors forced Buddhist and Taoist leaders to stage public debates. Though records show contempt for Taoism among some Buddhists, most show Taoists expressing respect and understanding for Buddhists and their beliefs. There were a few anomalous political acts by emperors who tried to curtail Buddhist's or Taoist's social, economic, and political power. But even those acts—often exaggerated in modern accounts—were seldom motivated by religious factors. Despite modern claims that there were persecutions here and there, there was nothing comparable to what occasionally happened during the dark days of European religious wars. There were never, for example, Chinese people—Buddhist, Taoist, or Confucian—burned at the stake, nor were there interred bodies exhumed and defiled. China has never had a religious war.

Modern accounts seldom acknowledge that centuries of Chinese rulers, intellectuals, and ordinary men and women happily endorsed the mutual validity of "the Three Teachings" (san-chiao): Buddhism, Taoism, and Confucianism. To them that term suggested a pleasant diversity, never conflict or contradiction. The modern misconception that Neo-Confucians ran late-imperial society conceals the reality that even Confucian intellectuals, and most emperors, usually agreed that "the Three Teachings are one" (san-chiao wei i).

There has also never been any discord within Taoism. During the mid-twentieth century some scholars called elements of post-Han Taoism "sects" and even tried to distinguish "sectarian Taoism" from a supposed "philosophical school." It is now known that those depictions have no validity. Taoism has been a kaleidoscope of ever-changing traditions and movements, and at no time did any of them denounce each other. Taoism is distinctive precisely for its persistently nonsectarian heritage.

SOCIAL JUSTICE Most people believe that Taoists have never cared about issues of social justice. Indeed, few Taoist traditions have ever been organized in ways that produce conspicuous examples of social advocacy, and it is hard to find any in "Southern Taoism" at all. Meanwhile, in mainland China Taoists remain guarded about taking social positions that might disturb political authorities.

Unlike religions that feel a sense of mission to convert their religious ideals into social action, Taoists have generally been skeptical of activism, preferring subtle—indeed, often secret—modes of benefiting others. Taoists believe that their liturgical rites, and even their self-cultivation, can and do indirectly transform the conditions under which all people live. That belief is grounded firmly upon the ancient Tao te ching: it cautions us to be like Tao itself, which "never presumes to act" (pu kan wei). Rather than presuming that we must go out and act to "make the world right," the Taoist faith—holistic, not humanistic—maintains that the world will naturally become and remain perfect but only if humans refrain from interventional activity.

A concept such as "rights" is hard to find in Taoism, for such concepts presume a world in which good must struggle lest evil prevail—presumptions no Taoist would accept. Nonetheless, some of the largely unexplored texts in the *Tao-tsang* show that, throughout history, Taoists were a leading voice against social abuses such as female infanticide. The ancient *T'ai-p'ing ching* makes clear that such injustices violate the integrity of life.

Because Chinese religions have usually been restricted by governments that fear social activism, modern Taoists have generally avoided taking positions that might provoke greater government oppression. Yet in Taoist terms, such restraint illustrates neither callousness nor cowardice but rather an abiding faith in the power of *Tao* to right life's wrongs by itself, with no need for premeditated human action.

SOCIAL ASPECTS According to twentieth-century misconceptions, it was China's Confucians—never Taoists—who valued the family. In reality, Taoists accepted the value of all existing social and political institutions, though many chose to live as exceptions to the prevailing rules.

Prior to the third century C.E., writers of "Taoist" texts seldom said anything about marriage or the family. From the third century to early modern times, Taoist movements fully recognized men and women of every station, regardless of marital status. The history of Taoism is replete with figures who married and had children—or who entered the religious life after having raised a family—and few Taoists felt pressed to develop any doctrinal guidelines regarding such matters.

Under Buddhist influence early modern Taoists evolved away from medieval Taoist's acceptance of marriage. "Northern Taoism" has historically intimated that spiritual practice is best undertaken by celibates. In "Southern Taoism," meanwhile, marriage has always been expected of clerics, and the Cheng-i "lineage" has traditionally been represented as an actual biological succession within the Chang clan. "Northern Taoists," however, like Ch'an (Zen) Buddhists, have always claimed a lineage that was spiritual, never biological.

For the laity, decisions about marriage and family matters have always been left up to individuals. Such decisions have seldom been mentioned in connection with Taoist doctrine or moral teachings. Though celibacy became a common ideal for most Taoists, other lifestyle decisions were not criticized or deprecated, and Taoists seldom posed as arbiters of family values for people outside of their tradition.

CONTROVERSIAL ISSUES The social, political, and historical influences on Taoism are such that there have seldom been religious authorities taking a public stance on issues that are today commonly considered controversial. Statements about divorce, abortion, or birth control are practically unknown among today's Taoists.

Such was not always the case. The early "Celestial Master" movement articulated principled positions on many social issues. The *T'ai-p'ing ching*, for instance, denounced the common practice of female infanticide—a position encountered virtually nowhere else in Chinese civilization until the twentieth century. *The 180 Precepts of Lord Lao* explicitly command respect for all life; they forbid not only slavery but also "the use of herbal medicine to perform abortions."

One issue that is often controversial in Western religions has never been controversial in Taoism: the role of women. In traditional Chinese society the roles and expectations for women were, in general, highly limiting. The religious life, however, was not governed by those expectations, for women's secular roles as wives and mothers did not carry over into religious settings. Moreover, whereas Confucians took pride in maintaining social tradition, Taoists took pride in rising above the ordinary. Consequently, Taoists of most traditions welcomed women and men on comparable terms.

The primary office in the early "Celestial Master" organization—the libationer—was reportedly open to women and men alike, and some women libationers, such as Wei Hua-t'sun (251–344), remained well known for centuries. Ritual functions could be performed by women as well as men, and ranks and titles were parallel. Beginners were *tao-nan* or *tao-nü* (Taoist men or Taoist women); intermediate-level practitioners were *nan-kuan* or *nü-kuan* (capped men or capped women); and advanced participants were *tao-fu* or *tao-mu* (Taoist father or Taoist mother).

After Lu Hsiu-ching began consolidating Taoism, women clerics held the same title as men, *tao-shih*, (priest or priestess), though female *tao-shih*, such as Huang Ling-wei (c. 640–721), were fewer in number. In 739 there were 550 abbeys for women compared with 1137 for men. Priests of each gender were frequently ordained during puberty, and the procedures for women's ordination differed only in that certain ritual actions proceeded from right to left instead of left to right. In the eighth and ninth centuries at least a dozen imperial princesses underwent such ordination. The performance of the great liturgies—*chiao* and *chai*—were sometimes reserved for male officiants, however.

Prominent women abounded in later Taoism. One early-modern movement, Ch'ing-wei ("Clarified Tenuity"), was reportedly founded by a young woman, Tsu Shu (flourished c. 900). Tradition says that her teachings were transmitted through a line of female leaders until the twelfth century, when men became included. By then lay practitioners of Taoism had become more common among the gentry, as illustrated by T'sao Wen-i (flourished 1119–25), a woman poet who wrote commentaries on earlier Taoist texts and who was honored at the Sung court. Meanwhile, the early Ch'üan-chen movement was so popular among women that 20 to 40 percent of its clergy were female.

After Mongol times Chinese society became increasingly oppressive, and women Taoists became less prominent. Women never had any meaningful role in the liturgical Cheng-i tradition, and in "Southern Taoism" women are effectively marginalized. In mainland China today, however, women priests participate in "Northern Taoist" temples alongside men, and some hold local leadership positions.

CULTURAL IMPACT Of all the aspects of Taoism, the ones that remain least appreciated are those in which Taoists have expressed themselves in media other than the written word. Twentieth-century Sinologists—like the Confucian scholars who mentored them—relied almost exclusively upon written texts when collecting and assessing data. Few scholars of Chinese religion have tried to integrate the study of concrete, visible artifacts—much less musical traditions—into their understanding of Taoism. At the end of the twentieth century art historians such as Stephen Little began finding unrecognized works of Taoist art buried away in the archives of great museums. In China, meanwhile, the delicate position of Taoism has inhibited active exploration of Taoist art, architecture, and music.

Taoist religious music—vocal and instrumental—goes back at least to K'ou Ch'ien-chih in the fifth century. On imperial order T'ang Taoists such as Ssu-ma Ch'eng-chen and Ho Chih-chang composed now-lost musical works, and the Ming emperor known as Yung-lo (reigned 1402–24) himself composed pieces of Tao-

ist music and had them assembled into an anthology. The influence of Taoist music on the broader musical heritage of China remains unstudied, however.

In "Northern Taoism" today most music is vocal and conforms to historical patterns linked to the *chai* rituals that go back to medieval times. In "Southern Taoism" music is mostly instrumental and is more flavored by local styles and folk elements.

Because scholars are generally obsessed with reading texts, it is surprising that the extensive Taoist influences on Chinese literature have been little studied. All surveys of Chinese literature hail the elegant prose of the *Chuang-tzu*. Taoism, however, also played an influential role in the development of later Chinese prose and verse alike. Renowned poets such as Li Po (701–62) were deeply steeped in medieval Taoist ideas and practices, and priests such as Ssu-ma Ch'eng-chen and Wu Yün were among the most accomplished poets of their times. Scholars have not studied the Taoist dimensions of later Chinese poetry.

Another T'ang Taoist, the chronicler Tu Kuang-t'ing, was a pioneer of the Chinese short story. Literary tales called *ch'uan-ch'i* often reflect themes from *Chuang-tzu*, such as the idea that our usual frames of reference are really just conventions and that the world in which we truly live is much more wondrous than we imagine. Imperial collections such as the *T'ai-p'ing kuang-chi* ("Expansive Records of the Reign of Grand Tranquillity"), completed in 978 by order of a founder of the Sung dynasty, preserve hundreds of stories. These, like *Chuang-tzu*, were intended to expand people's perceptions of reality by opening their eyes to wonders and marvels that show that the cosmos consists of multiple interlinked dimensions. Many collections of *ch'uan-ch'i*, the most well known of which is P'u Sung-ling's *Liao-chai chih-I* (1679; "Strange Stories from Make-Do Studio"), kept Taoist ideas and images in the minds of later Chinese readers.

The extensive Taoist influence on the traditional Chinese novel remains only partly appreciated. The sixteenth-century novel *Hsi-yu chi* ("The Journey to the West," also known as "Monkey") is partly an extended Taoist allegory. Other late-imperial novels, such as the *Feng-shen yen-i* ("The Creation of the Gods") and *Tung-yu chi* ("Journey to the East"), introduced self-cultivation traditions of "Inner Alchemy" to thousands of readers who would never have direct involvement with Taoist teachers or practitioners. Also well known is the late-Ming *Ch'i-chen chuan* ("Accounts of the Seven Perfected

Ones," otherwise called "Seven Taoist Masters"). It turns the historical lives of Wang Ch'ung-yang (founder of "Northern Taoism") and his primary disciples into a primer of Ch'üan-chen self-cultivation practices, and it is an illustration of the results of Taoist practice: Through dedication, sacrifice, and meditative discipline, the novel's characters overcome their personal failings and demonstrate the process of moral and spiritual maturation that constitutes the Taoist life.

Since the late twentieth century many such elements have also been transformed into components of Chinese movies, particularly in Taiwan. But by the turn of the millennium movies from mainland China also began to expand into these areas, and such popular fare as the film *Crouching Tiger, Hidden Dragon* tantalized Western audiences with stories influenced by Taoist values and practices.

J. Russell Kirkland

Bibliography

Bell, Catherine. "Lu Hsiu-ching." In *Encyclopedia of Religion.* New York: Macmillan, 1987.

Bokenkamp, Stephen. "Lu Xiujing, Buddhism, and the First Daoist Canon." In *Culture and Power in the Reconstitution of the Chinese Realm, 200–600.* Edited by Scott Pearce et al. Cambridge, Mass.: Harvard University Press, 2001.

Daoist Studies. 17 Aug. 2004. www.daoiststudies.org.

Despeux, Catherine, and Livia Kohn. *Women in Daoism.* Cambridge, Mass.: Three Pines Press, 2003.

Hendrischke, Barbara, and Benjamin Penny. "The 180 Precepts Spoken by Lord Lao." *Taoist Resources* 6.2 (1996): 17–29.

Kirkland, Russell. "Responsible Non-Action in a Natural World." In *Daoism and Ecology.* Edited by N.J. Girardot et al., 283–304. Cambridge, Mass.: Harvard University Press, 2001.

———. "The Roots of Altruism in the Taoist Tradition." *Journal of the American Academy of Religion* 54 (1986): 59–77.

———. "Self-Fulfillment through Selflessness." In *Varieties of Ethical Reflection.* Edited by Michael Barnhart, 43–81. New York: Lexington Books, 2002.

———. "Taoism." In *The Encyclopedia of Bioethics.* 2nd ed. Vol. 5, 2463–69. New York: Macmillan, 1995.

———. "Taoism." In *Encyclopedia of Women and World Religion.* Vol. 2, 959–64. New York: Macmillan, 1999.

———. *Taoism: The Enduring Tradition.* London and New York: Routledge, 2004.

———. "Varieties of 'Taoism' in Ancient China: A Preliminary Comparison of Themes in the *Nei yeh* and Other 'Taoist Classics.'" *Taoist Resources* 7.2 (1997): 73–86.

Kohn, Livia. *Daoism and Chinese Culture.* Cambridge, Mass.: Three Pines Press, 2001.

———, ed. *Daoism Handbook.* Leiden: E.J. Brill, 2000.

———. *God of the Dao: Laozi in History and Myth.* Ann Arbor: University of Michigan, Center for Chinese Studies, 1998.

———. *The Taoist Experience: An Anthology.* Albany: State University of New York Press, 1993.

Little, Stephen, and Shawn Eichmann. *Taoism and the Arts of China.* Berkeley: University of California Press, 2000.

Miller, James. *Daoism: A Short Introduction.* London and New York: OneWorld Publications, 2003.

Porter, Bill. *The Road to Heaven.* San Francisco: Mercury House, 1993.

Schipper, Kristofer. "Daoist Ecology: The Inner Transformation." In *Daoism and Ecology.* Edited by N.J. Girardot et al., 79–93. Cambridge, Mass.: Harvard University Press, 2001.

Sivin, Nathan. "On the Word 'Taoist' as a Source of Perplexity." *History of Religions* 17 (1978): 303–31.

Zoroastrianism

FOUNDED: Second millennium B.C.E.

RELIGION AS A PERCENTAGE OF WORLD POPULATION: 0.0023 percent

OVERVIEW Zoroastrianism, established at least 3,000 years ago, is the religion of pre-Islamic Iran. It survives in Iran (where followers are called the Zardushtis) and in India (where they are called the Parsis), as well as in diaspora communities around the world. The term "Zoroastrianism" is derived from the name of the founder, Zoroaster (as he is known in Greek; his Iranian name is Zarathustra). The *Fravarane,* a confessional text in the ancient Iranian language of Avestan, identifies the religion as the worship of the god Ahura Mazda (Lord Wisdom) according to the teachings of Zarathustra.

In Iran Zoroastrianism traditionally described itself as either the "Good Religion" or as Mazdeanism (from Ahura Mazda). It was the state religion of the two great pre-Islamic Iranian dynasties, the Achaemenids (550–330 B.C.E.) and the Sasanians (224–651 C.E.). After the fall of the Sasanians to the Arab Muslims who conquered Iran, the religion lost its patron but survived in the area. Members also migrated to India. In the modern period they have dispersed throughout the world, though the number of adherents has become infinitesimal; the worldwide population is only about 150,000. Even so, the impact of this tradition on the formation of Iranian culture and of other religions, including Judaism, Christianity, and Islam, has been enormous.

HISTORY The sources for reconstructing the history of Zoroastrianism before the fall of the Sasanians are textual and archaeological. The surviving literature in Avestan (an East Iranian language that is a part of the Indo-Iranian language family) is the starting point, but even with this material almost everything about the history of the tradition is obscure and contested.

Because tradition held that Zoroaster lived 258 years before Alexander the Great (356–323 B.C.E.), scholars once dated Zoroaster to the sixth century B.C.E. That figure has since been questioned, and scholars now believe he lived between 1800 and 1000 B.C.E. He is thus dated to the period of the Indo-Iranian migrations. There is no certainty about his homeland, though the fact that Avestan is an East Iranian language means it was somewhere in Central Asia or Eastern Iran. Zoroaster is connected by tradition to Balkh, in northern Afghanistan, and in a much later period he was identified with sites in western Iran. Western scholarship is divided between two sites as Zoroaster's original homeland—Khorezm, a historic region south of the Aral Sea (in present-day Uzbekistan and Turkmenistan), and the region of Seistan in southeastern Iran.

Zoroater has often been seen as a lone monotheist reformer and devotee of Ahura Mazda who attempted to suppress cultic practices and to proclaim in their place a new ethical vision; this view was based on the model of Old Testament prophets. This is also how the Zoroastrian tradition would come to understand him, especially after the ninth century C.E., when the pervasive influence of Islam on Iranian culture began. By the twelfth century C.E. the legend of Zoroaster had been

THE GUARDIAN SPIRIT. The Guardian Spirit, or Fravahar, is the most important symbol of Zoroastrianism. The figure, facing to the left and encircled in a ring that represents the soul, depicts Zoroaster, the founder of Zoroastrianism. The three wing sections represent the three pillars of the Zoroastrian faith: good thoughts, good words, and good deeds. (THOMSON GALE)

recast according to the model of Islamic prophecy. In the Greek world Zoroaster was known as an ancient wise man and sage. The only source of information about Zoroaster is the *Gāthās*, which are the 17 hymns, divided into five chapters, traditionally ascribed to him (his name appears in 9 of them). The small corpus and the abstractness of the *Gāthās* make it impossible to derive much historical information from them, though they do reflect a largely pastoral setting. The hymns were composed on behalf of a royal patron, Vishtasp, who was obviously a powerful figure who supported Zoroaster.

The followers of Zoroaster preserved his hymns for as long as a millennium, but we know next to nothing about this group. They kept material only from this one figure. They were active in the eastern Iranian territories, but at some point they took the tradition to the west, where it became triumphant as the cult of the entire Iranian plateau. Evidence suggests that a high priest—who bore the title *zarathustrema* (supreme Zoroaster)—headed them, and they might have functioned as a priesthood, perhaps on the model of the priestly group known as the Magi. The Magi were primarily active in western Iran under a tribe called the Medes, but some scholars have argued that they were the carriers of this Zoroastrian material.

The *Gāthās* are contained in the *Yasna*, the main liturgical text of Zoroastrianism (composed in younger Avestan, which differs from the Gathic dialect). The other main text is the *Yasht*s, a group of hymns to Iranian deities (also composed in younger Avestan). These two texts in different ways describe the situation of the Iranians in the middle of the first millennium B.C.E. The Iranians had settled on the Iranian plateau more than a millennium earlier and were closely related to the Aryan (Indo-Iranian) conquerors of India, whose earliest religious traditions are found in the Vedas (a collection of hymns).

The Vedas, in fact, show important similarities to the Iranian texts of Zoroastrianism, and the two traditions also share elements in their world outlooks: the vision of the cosmos as having an order (*asha*, providing a criterion for judging actions), the importance of the cow, and similar ritual practices. Central to both is the role of the religious specialist, the priest, in carrying the tradition. One difference is the position of the *daeva*s (demons). The word has the same root as "divinity" in the Indo-European languages. At some point (possibly before Zoroaster) the Iranians demoted that category of divinities into demons. This has been called the "Iranian reform," but it is impossible to understand exactly what the background or significance of this "reform" was. Several Vedic deities appear in the Iranian sources as demons. The reform may reflect the making of another group of divinities—the *ahura*s—into exclusive objects of worship. Another difference between the Vedas and the Iranian texts is the Iranian worship of a single god, Ahura Mazda. The Iranians retained elements of the Vedic polytheist system, but their focus on a single deity contrasts with the Vedas, which centers on a pantheon of divinities (the most important being the warrior god Indra, who became a demon in the Zoroastrian texts). There is no parallel to Ahura Mazda in the Vedas, but that may be because "Ahura Mazda" is not a proper name; rather, it is an epithet for an unnamed deity.

The Achaemenian empire (founded in 550 B.C.E.) brings the Iranian plateau more clearly into the light of history. The inscriptions left by the Achaemenid kings testify to the devotion of the royal house to the worship of Ahura Mazda. They suggest a struggle for truth and articulate a consciousness of Iranian identity. The empire was famed for its tolerance of other religious traditions. The founder of the empire, Cyrus the Great (c. 585–529 B.C.E.), is especially celebrated for allowing exiled Jews to return to Palestine to rebuild the Temple

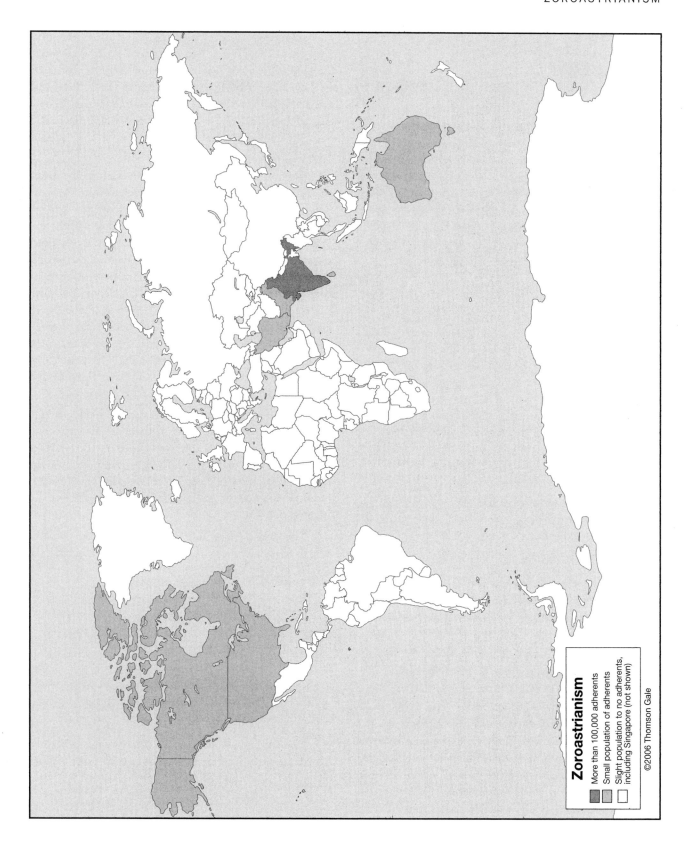

Zoroastrianism

More than 100,000 adherents

Small population of adherents

Slight population to no adherents,
including Singapore (not shown)

©2006 Thomson Gale

A Parsi priest leads a girl in the initiation navjote, *in which the child will learn the rudiments of the faith.* © LINDSAY HEBBERD/CORBIS.

this should not be overinterpreted, but it is a reminder that the Achaemenids did not proclaim their worship of Ahura Mazda in Zoroaster's name. Because Zoroaster became known to the Greeks during the Achaemenid period, it is clear that his followers had carried knowledge of him throughout the Achaemenid empire, including Asia Minor, where the empire met the classical Greek world.

The Achaemenids rose to prominence by uniting two western Iranian tribes, the Medes and the Persians. The Magi, a hereditary priestly tribe of the Medes, played an important political role in the court of the Achaemenids. The description of Persian religious practices by the fifth-century Greek historian Herodotus serves as an invaluable—but also puzzling—testimony to the religious scene in western Iran during his time. He reported that the Persians did not erect statues, altars, or temples to their gods but worshiped instead their chief god, Zeus (undoubtedly Ahura Mazda), on the tops of mountains. He wrote that they also worshiped the sun, the moon, the earth, fire, water, and winds as their other deities.

The Achaemenids left significant archeological remains, the most important being their ceremonial center in Persepolis, near their ancestral center in the province of Fars (in present-day southwestern Iran). That site was devoted to the celebration of kingship, in which different peoples of the empire offered gifts to the king on New Year's Day.

The Zoroastrian tradition is reflected in three additional features of the Achaemenian empire. First, the tombs of the Achaemenid kings were carved directly into cliffs. Zoroastrian rules forbid polluting the pure elements of fire and earth, so the dead were not cremated or buried. Second, archaeologists have found a large number of mortars and pestles, which might have been used to prepare *haoma* (a drink made from a sacred plant) in the main Zoroastrian ceremony, the *yasna*. Finally, the symbol of the fire altar exists in numerous reliefs at Persepolis and is also widely found on cylinder seals and other carvings throughout the region.

The subsequent history of Zoroastrianism may be broadly divided into two parts: from the fourth century B.C.E. to the coming of Islam (ninth century C.E.) and from that time to the present. After the fall of the Achaemenids (330 B.C.E.) the religion ceased to have imperial sponsorship but survived. Although Zoroastrianism may not have been the official state religion during the Seleucid empire (312 B.C.E.–64 B.C.E.) and the Parthian

at Jerusalem. That tolerance had its limits, but what it likely indicates is that local religions were left alone in the name of maintaining social order. Rulers also understood their objects of worship belonged to the royal house and were not gods for the empire as a whole.

Two features of the Achaemenid inscriptions are central to reconstructing the religion of the empire. The first is that Ahura Mazda was the sole divinity invoked by the earliest rulers, Darius I (ruled 522–486 B.C.E.) and Xerxes I (ruled 486–465 B.C.E.), but the later rulers of the empire invoked three gods: Ahura Mazda, Mithra, and Anahita. It is difficult to know what this development means. It need not be evidence of a return to polytheism by the royal house, because even the earliest rulers had acknowledged other, lesser gods in addition to Ahura Mazda. The second feature is that the Achaemenid inscriptions make no mention of Zoroaster. Because the inscriptions are brief and largely formulaic,

empire (247 B.C.E.–224 C.E.), it was widely practiced in Iran and as far west as Anatolia (Turkey), where it mixed with Greek religious beliefs. It is only with the establishment of the Sasanian empire (224–651 C.E.) that we can speak securely of a Zoroastrian church. With the rise of the Sasanian dynasty, the Zoroastrian church emerged as an ally of the royal house and embodiment of Iranian imperial ideology. The Sasanian court was interested in establishing orthodoxy as a source of its legitimacy.

The Sasanians arose in Fars province, the homeland of the Achaemenids. While historical memory of the earlier empire had dissolved into myth, the Sasanians seem to have seen themselves as the carriers of Achaemenid glory. They centralized their control of the Iranian plateau and were a threat to the Byzantine Empire. The Sasanian family was connected with a shrine to Anahita (an ancient Iranian goddess of fertility, war, and royalty) and organized a priestly hierarchy in the service of empire, which had two official titles for priests—*hērbad* (teaching priests) and *mōbed* (ritual priests), the latter apparently with higher ecclesiastical authority.

Evidence does not suggest much continuity between Achaemenid and Sasanian sponsorship of the Zoroastrian church, but the Sasanians believed the empire needed an official church given the potentially disruptive presence of other universalizing religions, such as Christianity, Buddhism, and Manichaeism. Sasanian ideology supported the idea that a symbiotic relationship should exist between kingship and religion (that is, both must support one another if the empire is to prosper). The alliance of Zoroaster and his royal patron Vishtasp was the model for this relationship.

Zoroastrianism was still primarily the religion of the Iranians and usually did not seek converts among its conquered people. The one exception was in Armenia. Armenia was a buffer state between the Roman and Sasanian empires. The Armenians seem to have been Zoroastrian before the Sasanians, but in 314 C.E. they converted to Christianity to maintain their independence. The Sasanians attempted to reverse that under Yazdegird II (reigned 438–57), leading to war in 451 C.E., but Armenian identity remained closely tied to Christianity. Although Zoroastrianism continued to be the official religion of the Sasanian empire, the other proselytizing religions, especially Nestorian Christianity, found significant numbers of converts among the Iranian population.

Parsi priests, following the seasonal calendar, engage in a ceremony to celebrate the naw ruz, *the first day of spring, which begins the new year.* © TIM PAGE/CORBIS.

Important in Zoroastrianism was the construction of fire temples, known as *atashkadeh*s (places of fire), found in Iran as well as in non-Iranian lands (presumably to serve Iranian populations). In their simplest form, fire temples were *chahar tāq*s (Persian: "four arches")—that is, single, square, domed buildings built on four arched walls. Individual sacred fires were maintained in these buildings. It is likely that state-supported priests conducted the religious life of the community, including the daily practice of the *yasna*. In addition, there were holy fires in shrines around the country dedicated to the different classes of society and to the royal house.

The establishment of an ecclesiastical hierarchy among the Zoroastrians, even if its reach into the laity was not deep, also meant the establishment of a Zoroastrian orthodoxy, which is reflected in the Pahlavi (middle Persian) texts. There is, in addition, some evidence of heterodox movements and heresies. The most important was Zurvanism, which placed the god Zurvan (time) above the combating deities Ahura Mazda and Angra Mainyu. This move toward monism demoted the position of Ahura Mazda and promoted a rather remote

The Dakhme-ye Zartoshti are funerary towers in Yazd, Iran. The towers were used by Zoroastrians to expose the dead to vultures. Zoroastrian rules forbid polluting the pure elements of fire and earth, so the dead were not cremated or buried. © BRIAN A. VIKANDER/CORBIS.

figure, Zurvan, as the actual creator of the world. Scholars, however, have expressed strong reservations about this doctrine being formally a heresy rather than an interpretation of orthodox belief. There is little evidence for this teaching in the Zoroastrian sources, which are strictly dualist. Much more significant and troubling was Manichaeism (established in the third century), which shared theological concepts with Zoroastrianism. Manichaeism taught that the world was the battleground between good, represented by a divine light, and evil, found in the material world; it thus completely rejected the material world, arguing that good could be released from its entanglement with matter through continual purification. The founders of the Sasanian dynasty had showed some initial interest in Manichaeism but ultimately rejected it. The Sasanian monarch, at the urging of the high priest Kirdīr, had Mani, the religion's founder, executed in 276. The church Mani founded remained active in Iranian lands, as well as in the Roman Empire, Central Asia, and China. Manichean teaching contributed to the heterodox movement of

Mazdak, a Zoroastrian priest who in 494 proclaimed a social revolutionary movement against the Sasanian state with the hope of establishing an egalitarian social order. The Sasanians eventually suppressed the movement, executing Mazdak in 524.

The defeat of the last Sasanian emperor in 651 C.E. brought the Iranian plateau under Muslim rule and initiated the conversion of the area to Islam. In the first century of Islam eastern Iran became a seedbed for opposition movements to the Umayyad rule based in Damascus. In 750 the overthrow of the Umayyad dynasty was achieved by Arab forces from eastern Iran that included recent Iranian converts to Islam. This led to the shift of the symbolic center of the Islamic empire to the east and to the increasing role of Persian culture in the formulation of Islamic culture and political life. Unrest continued in eastern Iran, and there were periodic local revolts, usually accompanied by Zoroastrian expectations for a messiah and Mazdak's heterodox message.

The status of Zoroastrians under Islam rule was initially clarified by the second caliph, Umar, who declared

Glossary

Achaemenian dynasty dynasty that ruled Iran from 550 to 330 B.C.E.

afrinagan Zoroastrian ceremony involving the distribution of blessings

Ahura Mazda supreme deity of Zoroastrianism; likely an honorific title meaning "Wise Lord" rather than a proper name

Amesha Spentas the six entities that aid Ahura Mazda, sometimes with an additional figure, Spenta Mainyu, to compose the divine heptad (group of seven)

Angra Mainyu primordial evil spirit, twin of Spenta Mainyu

asha truth; righteousness

atashkadeh "place of fire"; fire temple; more narrowly, the enclosed chamber in a fire temple that contains a fire continuously fed by the priests

Avestan ancient East Iranian language

barashnum Zoroastrian purification ceremony used primarily by priests to prepare for their ordination

daeva demon

dakhma "tower of silence"; a tower in which a corpse is traditionally exposed

dar-i Mihr "the court of Mithra"; the room in a fire temple where the *yasna* is performed

dastur "master"; honorific title for a Zoroastrian priest

fasli seasonal calendar that places New Year's Day in March; compare with *qadimi*

frashkard the renewal of the world at the end of history

Gathic older Avestan dialect

getig form; physical world

Gahambar one of six five-day Zoroastrian festivals

Gāthā one of the 17 hymns traditionally ascribed to Zoroaster

haoma sacred drink, now pressed from ephedra and pomegranate twigs

---

that Zoroastrians were "People of the Book" who would therefore be protected by Islam if they abided by the rules of their status and paid the *jizya* (the tax levied on non-Muslims). The social position of the Zoroastrian community became increasingly difficult, however, especially as the process of Muslim conversion began to take hold.

According to legend, in 917 C.E. a group of Zoroastrians from northeastern Iran, led by a priest who was frustrated by the declining fortunes of the community, left the country. They eventually settled in the Gujarat region on the western coast of India in 936. They won the patronage of the local ruler and founded the city of Sanjan. The necessary ritual implements later arrived, and the highest level of fire temple was established. The fire was moved to Udvada, where it continues as one of the most holy fires of the tradition. This was the basis for the Parsi community that is located primarily around Mumbai (formerly Bombay). Parsis also settled in northern India in areas that are now Pakistan.

Other Zoroastrians remained in Iran, and the tradition survived, especially in the desert cities of Yazd and Kerman. The Iranian community remained the authority of the tradition through the eighteenth century, and Parsis in India consulted Zoroastrians in Iran for guidance in their religion. This relationship changed in the nineteenth century, when Parsis were able to support educational institutions to maintain the tradition. As a minority cultivated by the British imperial rulers, Parsis also became financially and politically powerful in India, allowing them to exercise greater influence on their surrounding environment.

In the twentieth century opportunities for education and the development of trade encouraged some Zoroastrians to move to other parts of the British Empire. The Iranian revolution of 1978–79, which made Iran an Islamic republic, led to a significant exodus of Zardushtis (Iranian Zorastrians), especially to western European countries, the United States, and Canada.

jashan festival

kusti sacred cord worn around the torso by Zoroastrians and tied and untied during prayer

Magi priestly group that was initially active in western Iran under the Medes

Pahlavi middle Persian language of the Sasanian period; also the name of an Iranian dynasty (twentieth century)

parahom sacred drink prepared during the *yasna*; a mixture of *haoma* and milk

Parsi member of a Zoroastrian group living mainly in western India and centered around Mumbai (Bombay)

qadimi "old" Zoroastrian calendar, which has New Year's Day in late July; compare with *fasli*

raspi assistant priest, who feeds the fire during the *yasna*

sadre sacred shirt; a thin, white, cotton garment worn that is worn under clothes and should never be removed

Sasanian dynasty dynasty that ruled Iran from 224 to 651 C.E.

Spenta Mainyu primordial good spirit, twin of Angra Mainyu

Yasht one of a group of hymns to Iranian deities

yasna main Zoroastrian ritual; also the name of the main liturgical text, which is recited during the ritual

yazata any of a number of Zoroastrian divinities, the two most important of which are Mithra and the river goddess Anahita

zaotar priest

Zardushti name for the Zoroastrian tradition in Iran

Zoroaster founder of the Zoroastrian tradition; his Iranian name is Zarathustra

Zoroastrianism religion of pre-Islamic Iran; now represented by two communities, Parsi (Indian) and Zardushti (Iranian)

zot chief priest who performs the *yasna*

CENTRAL DOCTRINES The primary doctrine of Zoroastrianism is worship of Ahura Mazda, the creator and chief god of the world. As such, it is a monotheistic faith and shares the common problem of monotheism: how to account for the presence of evil. An ethical dualism (in which the spirit world is divided between the forces of good and evil) pervades the *Gāthā* hymns and the Achaemenid inscriptions requiring a deliberate choice of the good. This dualism constitutes the Iranian contribution to the religious history of humankind; it compromises God's omnipotence but has the benefit that the creator is blameless for the presence and power of evil in the world.

Ahura Mazda is above all connected with creation. The moment of creation established the dualistic world over which Ahura Mazda reigns. This event involved not him but two primordial spirits—the twins Spenta Mainyu (the good spirit) and Angra Mainyu (the evil spirit, who becomes Ahriman in Middle Persian)—who made diametrically opposed choices in the beginning. The language the *Gāthās* use to describe this event sug-

gests that, rather than being just a moment in the past, creation is an ongoing process of dividing the world along the lines of these choices.

In response to Muslim and Christian criticisms, some contemporary Zoroastrians have wanted to deny the dualist elements of the tradition and insist that the tradition teaches a pure monotheism. To judge by the major theological statements reflecting Sasanian theology, Zoroastrian orthodoxy was characterized by a strict dualism between Ahura Mazda and Angra Mainyu. They were locked in continual combat, and it was the duty of the followers of the religion to ally themselves firmly with Ahura Mazda. This dualism was an ethical one and did not in any way suggest a rejection of the physical world. It was in fact in the physical world (*getig*) that this combat was fought, and the forces of good had weapons at their disposal that guaranteed their eventual victory. Ahura Mazda dwells in the *menog* (spiritual world) but created the *getig* as the arena for conflict. Those who dwell in the *getig* are the primary combatants against Angra Mainyu. The efforts made in the material world are valued and are the chief means for the defeat of the forces of evil. In the end Ahura Mazda will enter into the material world to lead the final *yasna* ceremony that will transform the world, eliminating the power of Angra Mainyu once and for all.

Important to Zoroastrianism are the divine figures who aid Ahura Mazda. In the *Gāthās* Ahura Mazda interacts with and works through a number of abstract entities. These are not only available to Ahura Mazda but also related to human faculties, through which Ahura Mazda and human beings connect to one another. Numerous passages in the *Gāthās* refer to this idea of an intermediary between divine and human. In the *Gāthās* these entities are not systematized or given a group name, but in the *Yasna Haptanhāiti* (a later prose text in the ancient Gathic dialect) they are called the Amesha Spentas (bounteous immortals). Six figures comprise the Amesha Spentas: Vohu Manah, (good thought), Asha (truth), Khshathra Vairya (desirable dominion), Spenta Armaiti (beneficent devotion), Haurvatat (wholeness), and Ameretat (immortality). A seventh figure, Spenta Mainyu (the good spirit), was later added to the others, together forming the Divine Heptad.

In their abstraction the seven good agents are best thought of as the means by which Ahura Mazda interacts with the material world. This organization of good forces is arrayed against a counter-organization of seven evil forces headed by the evil spirit Angra Mainyu. To judge by the *Gāthās*, the male Vohu Manah and the female Spenta Armaiti (who was the daughter of Ahura Mazda and the goddess of earth) seem to have played the most important role in communicating divine speech to Zoroaster. Traditionally the Amesha Spentas came to be linked with various ritual and material elements: Vohu Manah to cattle, Asha to fire, Khshathra Vairya to metal, Spenta Armaiti to earth, Haurvatat to water, and Ameretat to plant life (including the sacred plant, *haoma*).

The divine world of Zoroastrianism is populated by a number of other divinities, some of whom receive worship in the other great Avestan text, the *Yashts*. The *Yashts* are 21 hymns that present a world that is consistently dualist but in which Ahura Mazda shares the divine stage with a number of other divinities (*yazatas*), the two most important of which are Mithra (also a Vedic god) and the river goddess Anahita (the pure one, corresponding to the Hindu goddess Saraswati). These and a number of other figures, as well as the sacred drink,

haoma (which is part of the *yasna* service), all have separate hymns dedicated to them.

The unsolved question about these hymns is what purpose they served. They are much closer to oral-formulaic poetry (poetry that is memorized and performed rather than written down) than are the *Gāthās*, and thus their wording was probably continually improvised. Some of them are presented as spoken to Zoroaster by Ahura Mazda. They were likely composed over an extensive period of time; some of the later *Yashts* were written as late as the Achaemenid period (550–330 B.C.E.). They appear to be connected with the development of the Zoroastrian liturgical calendar, a complicated daily and monthly cycle of times devoted to particular *yazatas*. This cycle specified the days on which particular hymns were to be recited to their associated divine beings. In contemporary Zoroastrianism, with the exception of the *Yasht* to the *haoma*, these hymns no longer have any liturgical purpose.

While each *Yasht* narrates incidents of an individual deity or discusses a more abstract notion—such as *sraosha* (obedience, the lord of prayer) or *xwarnah* (the kingly glory of Iran)—together they contain the outlines of a coherent epic history that features the coming of Zoroaster and predicts the unfolding of the future. This history is divided into three eras: creation, an epic history of the physical world (in which good and evil are mixed), and a period of renewal. In the first era six elements of the world (stone, water, earth, vegetation, animals, and humanity) are created. The earth is divided in seven "climes," or regions, with Iran at the center. At the moment of creation good and evil spirits appear, and the world subsequently exists as a site of the commingling of good and evil. The two earliest creations, the ox and the first man, are both killed by the evil spirit, Angra Mainyu, but from them arise animals and humanity.

Kingship comes to be a defining feature of human society. The epic history narrates the rise of heroes and kings who vie for power and who seek to defend the central clime of Iran against its natural enemies, the Turanians. Zoroaster comes at the midpoint of that history, with a revelation that guarantees the eventual triumph of good over evil. His legend begins with the miracles connected with his birth—including the light that glowed brightly and his escape from attempts to kill him—and continues with his reception of revelation, his early preaching, and his heroic defeat of enemies. He was famous for his virtue and his kindness to animals.

The conversion of the ruler Vishtasp and Zoroaster's alliance with him are the centerpiece of the story; it lays the groundwork for the spread of the "Good Religion" throughout the world. Zoroaster is eventually killed during a Turanian attack by a priest of a rival cult. Each of the next three millennia are initiated by a savior born of Zoroaster's semen, which is preserved in Hamun Lake in the region of Seistan (in southeastern Iran). The arrival of the last savior, Saoshyants, and the final defeat of the evil spirit achieve the promised *frashkard,* or renewal of the world.

Until the *frashkard* each soul at the end of its life arrives at Chinvat Bridge, "the bridge of the separation," where it is judged by the divinities Mithra, Sraosha, and Rashnu. The soul's deeds appear to him or her in the form of a beautiful maiden or an old hag, depending on the person's moral worth. Those who have been good cross the bridge, which has been made wide, and arrive in heaven, the realm of infinite lights. Those who have been evil fall off the bridge, which has become razor thin, making his or her demise inevitable. Those whose deeds are evenly balanced dwell in an intermediate region where there is no joy or torment. This fate exists only until the *frashkard,* when all evil is cleansed from the world, those suffering in hell complete their torments, and all receive the rewards of a transformed world. This structure of salvation history—with its apocalyptic expectation of a coming savior and the vision of individual judgment after death—likely influenced the development of neighboring religious traditions.

MORAL CODE OF CONDUCT The commandment "good thoughts, good words, good deeds" underlines the deeply ethical teachings of the tradition. Zoroastrians believe that the material world was created as the site of a struggle that will eventually result in the defeat of evil. The material world itself is not evil, but it requires protection from evil's pollution and needs to be marshaled for the weapons it provides for the struggle.

A Sasanian catechism called "The Selected Counsels of the Ancient Sages," or "The Book of Counsel of Zardusht," summarizes what every Zoroastrian should understand of his or her faith. They need to know that they are created beings who belong to Ahura Mazda, not Angra Mainyu. They must believe that Ahura Mazda's kingdom is infinite and pure, while the Evil Spirit will be destroyed. They must perform five duties: keeping the faith and keeping goodness and evil apart; marrying and procreating; cultivating the soil;

treating livestock justly; and spending one-third of one's time studying the religion and attending the fire temple, one-third tilling the earth, and one-third in eating, rest, and enjoyment. As this text shows, there is a special premium placed upon the cultivation of the land and the care of livestock. It could be said that peasants have the ideal Zoroastrian life, because the protection and cultivation of the pure elements water and earth lies with them.

More important is the cultivation of the individual and civic virtues that are expected of every Zoroastrian man and woman. The virtues of righteousness (*asha*) are central; they entail upholding the good order of the world and avoiding lying (the great opponent of order). Education and the quest for knowledge are also highly prized and expected of all. The virtues of charity and concern for the poor are important; the tradition envisioned an alliance of royalty and church to cultivate the virtues and create a good society. The values of education and charity continue to be hallmarks of contemporary Zoroastrian life.

SACRED BOOKS The holy language of the tradition is Avestan. Sacred texts exist in two dialects: older (Gathic) Avestan and younger Avestan.

The main surviving texts are collected in the *Yasna,* which is used in the daily liturgy. The *Yasna* contains the *Gāthās,* 17 hymns in older Avestan that are honored as the most sacred utterances of Zoroaster. The hymns were composed on behalf of a royal patron, Vishtasp; other figures, including priests of opposing cults, also appear in the hymns. The remainder of the *Yasna,* totaling 72 chapters, contains materials in younger Avestan. There are two other large texts in younger Avestan: the *Yasht*s, hymns to deities or divine entities, and the *Vidēvdād* (also known as the *Vendidad*), a collection of legends and purity rules that is recited during one occasionally performed ritual. There are also a number of smaller texts that function as liturgical guides for the priesthood and laity.

The tradition holds that the these sacred texts, known as the Avesta, originally contained 21 books. All but one, the *Vidēvdād,* were lost during the conquest of Iran by Alexander the Great in the fourth century B.C.E. Remnants were kept in oral circulation for as long as a millennium. They were finally written down in the Avestan alphabet (based on Aramaic), which was likely invented in the Sasanian period (224–651 C.E.), occurring after Avestan had ceased to be a living language.

The contents of the remaining 20 books, though lost, were generally known and summarized.

SACRED SYMBOLS In the nineteenth century an emblem of Persian royal glory, a winged disk with the torso of a bearded man, was found at the site of Persepolis. Called the Fravahar, it has since been adopted as a key Zoroastrian symbol. The emblem is often used to decorate fire temples, and along with the fire altar, it is used as a general symbol of the religion. Many interpret it as a symbol of Ahura Mazda, though originally it likely referred to the royal glory of the Achaemenids.

EARLY AND MODERN LEADERS The priesthood has been the primary source of leadership for the tradition. During the Sasanian period two priests seem to have played a crucial role in reorganizing the tradition. The first is Tansar (or Tosar), head of the priestly establishment under Ardashir (died in 240 C.E.), who was first ruler of the dynasty. Tansar is known for advising an interdependent relationship between royalty and religion; he believed both are necessary, and each must reinforce the other for prosperity and peace to reign. He is also said to have organized and edited the Avesta, helping the early Sasanians establish orthodoxy.

Tansar's putative successor was Kirdīr (or Kartir), who rose to prominence under Shapur I (240–72 C.E.) and continued to be prominent into the reign of Varahan II (276–93 C.E.). Kirdīr is known from a self-promoting rock inscription, which exists in four versions. In this inscription he tells of his rise to power, his governance of the state church, and his persecution of foreign religions in the Sasanian realm—including Jews, Buddhists, Hindus, Nasoreans (a baptismal sect), and Christians. It was under his influence that the Sasanian court turned against Mani (founder of Manichaeism) and executed him. The names of a number of priests from the Sasanian period survive in commentaries on the Avesta, suggesting the intellectual vitality of Zoroastrianism during that period. The authors of the Pahlavi texts written in the ninth century are evidence of the survival of the tradition under Muslim rule.

While priests have retained their status as leaders and interpreters of the tradition, modernity has seen a number of lay leaders who have played essential roles in their community. Four particularly prominent Parsis and Zardushtis illustrate the range of their activities. Manekji Limji Hataria (1813–90) was a Parsi and an early delegate of the Society for the Amelioration of the

The Impact of Zoroastrianism on Major Religions

As the ancient faith of Iran, Zoroastrianism extended its influence on neighboring religious traditions, including Judaism, Christianity, and Islam. This is reflected in the Old Testament by the Achaemenian king Cyrus the Great (as the "Lord's Anointed"; Isaiah 45:1); in the New Testament by the story of the Magi at Jesu's birth (Matthew 2:1–12); and in the Koran by the appearance of the Magi (22:17). Zoroastrianism gained prominence by being the state religion of two Iranian dynasties—the Achaemenid (550–330 B.C.E.), which controlled Israel, and the Sasanian (224–651 C.E.), under which rabbis dwelling in Babylonia produced the Babylonian Talmud. Zoroastrianism remained a vibrant and influential undercurrent after Islam became the dominant religion of the Iranian Plateau during the ninth century C.E.

Judaism, Christianity, and Islam all embrace Zoroastrianism ideas: a single god as the creator of the world, the development of an agent of evil, the judgment of the dead, and the promises of a coming savior, the renewal of the world, and bodily resurrection. They also share elements of Zoroastrian ecclesiastical organization and ritual practice. Historians cannot be certain whether surrounding religions borrowed Zoroastrian ideas or whether they merely came to recognize affinities between Zoroastrian ideas and their own internally generated beliefs. It is likely that both occurred.

Zarathustrians of Persia. He traveled twice to Iran investigating and documenting the state of the Zardushti community throughout Iran. He helped facilitate a number of charitable efforts for education and the rebuilding of fire temples and *dakhma*s (funerary towers), and he convinced the Shah to relieve the burdensome *jizya* tax on the Zarathustrian community. K.R. Cama (1831–1909) was a Parsi businessman from a distinguished family in Europe. He established contact with leading European scholars and was instrumental in bringing their research back to India, where he established the K.R. Cama Society, the leading center for the study of the Zoroastrian tradition. Bhikaji Rustom Cama (1861–1936), the daughter-in-law of K.R. Cama, was a leading Indian nationalist. She was a strong critic of the British colonization of India and a leader in the movement for Indian independence. She famously unfurled the first Indian flag at the International Socialist Conference in Stuttgart in 1907. Arbab Rustam Guiv (1888–1980) was a businessman from Yazd who eventually settled in Tehran. He was leader of the Tehran Zoroastrian Anjuman (association) from 1940 and a member of parliament representing the Zardushtis in 1942. He supervised the repair and construction of fire temples and led many charitable and educational initiatives for the community in Iran. He established a Zoroastrian center, the Arbab Rustam Guiv Darbe-Mehr, in New Rochelle, New York, in 1977, and he was involved in the construction of temples in Chicago, Toronto, Vancouver, and Anaheim, California.

MAJOR THEOLOGIANS AND AUTHORS The history of Zoroastrian thought since the fall of the Sasanians (seventh century C.E.) can be divided into three parts. Each developed in conversation with a powerful culture, to which Zoroastrians looked with a combination of uncertainty and respect.

The first period was the early centuries of Islam. The great works of that era, written in the ninth century, include the *Denkard* ("Acts of the Religion"), edited finally by Adurbad Emedan; the *Bundahishn* ("Creation"), edited by Farrobay i Ashawahishtan; and *Wizidagiha* ("Selections") of Zadspram. All are encyclopedic collections designed to regularize and preserve the tradition. Another ninth-century text, the *Shkand-gumānīg Wizār* ("Doubt-Dispelling Exposition") by Mardanfarrokh i Ohrmazddad, is a fascinating handbook justifying the Zoroastrian faith and answering attacks on the faith by Jews, Christians, Manichaeans, and Muslims. The various collections of Zoroastrian legal decisions mirror a community wrestling with the problems of conversion and the tradition's diminished status. These include the *Dadistan-i Denig* ("Religious Decisions," by the priest Manushchihr), the *Sad Dar* ("A Hundred Subjects"), and the *Shayast ne Shayast* ("Proper and Improper"), each reflecting the deteriorating condition of the Zoroastrian community under Muslim rule.

In the tenth century, after fleeing Iran for India, the Parsis began a second period of Zoroastrian thought, influenced by Indo-Muslim culture. The Parsis attempted to address both the doctrinal and the practical concerns of their Indian rulers. Under Mughal rule (1525–1748) Indian Muslim rulers took a wide interest in the religions of their territories. In 1573 the emperor Akbar called the learned priest Meherji Rana to his court to testify about Zoroastrian beliefs. Akbar's attempt to integrate all religions into a new faith, Dīn-e Ilāhī ("Divine Religion"), bore the mark of Zoroastrian influence.

Interaction with the West—above all with the British, who established rule over most of India in the nineteenth century—marked the third period. Intellectually the British presented three trends to which the Parsis responded. There was first the missionary effort begun in 1829 by the Anglican John Wilson, who criticized the tradition's dualism, ritualism, superstition, and focus on pollution. In response, there emerged a kind of "Protestant" defense of the tradition, represented by M.N. Dhalla (1875–1956), who viewed the tradition as an ethical monotheism and underplayed the role of ritual; he became known as the "Protestant Dastur" (*dastur* is the term for a high priest). The second trend was occultism, promoted by the Theosophical Society; the most important figure in this trend was Behramshah Naoroji Shroff (1858–1927). Claiming special initiation by Iranian masters, Shroff presented a highly spiritualized view of the tradition that focused on the occult significance and power of Avestan. He considered Zoroastrianism as the highest stage of religious evolution. He founded a movement known as Ilm-i Kshnoom (the science of spiritual satisfaction), invoking a word that appears once in the *Gāthās*. Deeply influenced by Hindu teachings, he also taught vegetarianism. The third trend was the rediscovery of the tradition's historical complexity through the philological study of Zoroastrian texts; Western scholars began this work, but a number of Zoroastrian scholars have also made significant contributions. This scholarship has tended to support a more traditional view of Zoroastrianism, emphasizing, for example, the importance of ritual. Many in this camp have been priests, including Darab Dastur Peshotan Sanjana (1857–1931), J. J. Modi (1854–1933), and, in the contemporary period, H. D. K. Mirza, F. M. Kotwal, and K. M. Jamasp Asa. Lay thinkers such as K. Mistree and R. R. Motafram have made this more traditional view widely available to the laity.

ORGANIZATIONAL STRUCTURE Urbanized Zoroastrians in Iran and India have governed themselves by councils of notables—partly hereditary and partly elected. The most significant in India is the Bombay Parsi Punchayet, established in 1728. These councils have managed all the affairs of the community, providing charity to those in need, encouraging education, and maintaining the priesthood. Zoroastrians elsewhere have organized local organizations throughout Europe, North America, Pakistan, Singapore, and Australia. The Federation of Zoroastrian Associations of North America coordinates the work of 24 such associations in the United States and Canada. The World Zoroastrian Organization, founded in the United Kingdom in 1980, serves the entire world community.

Priesthood is hereditary. Only men are priests, and they exist at two levels. The *navar* are able to perform the lesser ceremonies, and the *martab* can perform the *yasna* as well. Training for the priesthood, which begins at a young age with the mastery of the sacred texts, includes extensive language training in both Avestan and middle Persian.

HOUSES OF WORSHIP AND HOLY PLACES In Zoroastrianism the primary religious activity is the daily maintenance of a sacred fire. There are various levels of fires, some of which may even be in the possession of an individual. Most sacred fires are in a fire temple, where priests maintain them. To allow the fire to be extinguished would be a catastrophic sin. Some of the major fires have survived for centuries.

Every temple has an *atashkadeh* ("place of fire"), an enclosed chamber that contains a continuously burning fire on a metal grate or vase (*atashdan*). The fire receives continual tending. In addition to the *atashkadeh* there is also an area called the *dar-i Mihr* ("court of Mithra"; Mithra is the most important divinity, or *yazata*, in the tradition and is connected especially with the sun and the maintenance of covenants). This is a room that contains one or more *pawi*, rectangular consecrated spaces marked off by furrows. Each *pawi* contains a fire vase and two platforms; on one the priest sits, and on the other the priest prepares the offerings that are consecrated during the *yasna*.

These temples often contain schools for training priests. Both Iranian and Indian communities have sacred sites (connected either with legends or with historical memory) that are the object of popular pilgrimage. The main act of worship, prayer five times a day, is not performed at the temple but rather anywhere before a fire or the sun by all Zoroastrians.

WHAT IS SACRED? Because of the importance of fire in Zoroastrianism, the religion was erroneously characterized as "fire worship." Fire, however, is the highest kind of material; it is *getig* (physical world) connected to *asha* (truth). It is seen as animate, as a living creature that makes physically present the divine light of Ahura Mazda. Connected to one of the Amesha Spentas (entities that aid Ahura Mazda), fire is Ahura Mazda's most potent weapon in the material world. Other material elements connected to the Amesha Spentas—the cow, earth, and water—are also considered sacred. The fear of polluting these sacred elements dictates the special honor they receive.

HOLIDAYS AND FESTIVALS The Zoroastrian calendar is composed of 12 months of 30 days; each month and day bears the name of a divinity or concept. In addition, there are five Gatha days at the end of the year that are named after the five chapters of the *Gāthās*.

There are six Gahambars (five-day festivals) spread throughout the year: Maidhyōizarêmaya (mid-spring feast), Maidhyōishêma (mid-summer feast), Paitishaya (feast of "bringing in the harvest"), Ayathrima ("bringing home the herds"), Maidhyaiya (mid-year/winter feast), and Hamaspathmaêdaya (feast of All Souls). The last one is held during the Gatha days. Each Gahambar is a period to focus on worship and do only necessary work. Originally these festivals appear to have marked the change of seasons, and they came to be connected with the six elements of creation: stone, water, earth, vegetation, animals, and humanity.

The first day of spring, *naw ruz* (new day), is the pan-Iranian festival that begins the new year. It is the most important *jashan* (festival) of the year. There are 18 other *jashans* (a word derived from *yasna*); 12 of them occur when the name of the day and name of the month coincide. These are all periods for family gatherings and the sponsorship of ceremonies in the home. Another important *jashan* is Mehregan, a day in honor of the god Mithra.

The 365-day calendar has gradually lost its seasonal connection. As a result, it has become an object of major debate. Presently there are two calendars used in Iran. The *fasli*, or seasonal calendar, places *naw ruz*, or New Year's Day, in March. It was adopted in 1939 in Tehran, but it was rejected in more traditional Yazd, which follows the *qadimi* (old calendar) and has *naw ruz* in late July. Parsis observe three calendars: the two already mentioned, as well as the Shenshai calendar, which places *naw ruz* in August.

MODE OF DRESS There are two pieces of dress that every Zoroastrian is expected to wear after being initiated. The *sadre* is the sacred cotton shirt, a thin white garment that is worn under clothes and should never be removed. The *kusti* is a sacred cord, woven from wool, which traditionally was composed of 72 threads in recollection of the 72 chapters of the *Yasna*. It is wrapped around the body three times as a reminder of the commandment "good thoughts, good words, good deeds." It is tied and untied during the five daily prayers; the retying marks an intensification of commitment.

DIETARY PRACTICES Zoroastrians are permitted to eat anything edible in the good part of creation. It is meritorious to kill animals of the evil creation (such as snakes, insects, and frogs), but those are not to be eaten. Silence is maintained while eating so as not to confuse the two functions of the mouth, eating and speaking. Eating or drinking at night is discouraged, because that is when demons might be able to steal some of what is consumed. There are no formal rules for slaughtering an animal, though a portion of what is killed should be consecrated. As a result of Hindu influences, some Parsis practice vegetarianism.

RITUALS It is often argued that the *Gāthās* denounce ritual, especially extreme forms of ritual connected with the preparation and consumption of *haoma* (a hallucinogenic drink, which is now pressed from ephedra and pomegranate twigs) and with sacrifice. Because Zoroaster was engaged in the religious practices of his community, it is more likely that the ritual of opponents, rather than ritual itself, was being denounced.

Priests are responsible for the ritual life of the community. Rituals are of two kinds—those that take place in the sanctified space of a fire temple (the inner ceremonies in the *dar-i Mihr*, or court of Mithra) and those that occur outside. The key inner ceremony is the *yasna*, which is performed daily by two priests. In the ceremony, which lasts about two hours, the 72 chapters of the *Yasna* text are recited. The *yasna* takes place before a fire, with water at the right hand of the *zot*, the chief priest who performs the ceremony. The assistant priest, the *raspi*, feeds the fire during the ceremony.

The Diminishing Population of Zoroastrians

Population decline is the most pressing issue for the future of Zoroastrianism. In India, where most Zoroastrians, or Parsis, live, a demographic study predicted that the number of Parsis there would drop by more than half between 2003 and 2020. This decline is partially the result of low reproduction rates. Moreover, almost one in four Parsi women marry outside the community, and almost as many do not marry at all. Conversion to Zoroastrianism, even by spouses, is prohibited in most places, and children of intermarriages are not allowed to undergo a *navjote* (initiation) or to enter a fire temple.

Appeals have been made to increase the family size of Parsis, and cash incentives have been offered to Parsi families to have a third child. Neither has had much success, as having a larger family conflicts with the predominantly middle-class interests of most Parsis. Also unsuccessful have been calls to recognize the children of intermarriage as Zoroastrian.

The ceremony progresses with both ritual action and words. The heart of the ritual action consists of the sanctification of bread and butter (representing the vegetable and the animal worlds) and the preparation of *parahom*, a sacred drink made by adding milk to *haoma*. The bread and butter are distributed to the sponsors of the ceremony and other laity, so that they may be nourished by the sacred forces that have been concentrated in the food. Sponsors may also consume a portion of the drink, but the bulk of it is poured into a well to strengthen the water's power to remain pure and to sustain life.

The purpose of the ritual is to strengthen the material world and its inhabitants with concentrations of divine power. The six elements of creation, as part of the material world, are represented in the ceremony. Zoroastrians believe that the world was created in a primordial *yasna* conducted by a much larger number of officiants. At the end of the material era, Ahura Mazda will perform a final *yasna*, which will herald the *frashkard*, or renewal of the world, marking evil's defeat.

Priests also conduct the outer ceremonies, which may be performed outside the fire temple and may be witnessed by both Zoroastrians and non-Zoroastrians. The most important such ritual is the *afrinagan*, the distribution of blessings. In this ceremony fruit, wine, milk, eggs, flowers, and water are placed on a cloth on the floor before a fire vase, and the *zot* blesses them. The primary ritual in the ceremony is the exchange of flowers between the *zot* and the *raspi*, which is understood to be an exchange between the *getig* (physical world) and the *menog* (spiritual world). The ritual results in a concentration of sacred power, which is then funneled out through blessings to the assembled community.

The main act of worship required of all Zoroastrians is daily prayer. Five times a day the Ahunvar—the holiest prayer of the tradition, taught by Zoroaster—is recited anywhere before a fire or the sun. The meaning of the "Ahunvar" is obscure; it functions more like a mantra. It invokes two human agents who serve Asha (truth) and Vohu Manah (good thought), and it promises Ahura Mazda's special protection of the poor.

After initiation, discussed below, the two other life-cycle rituals are for marriage and death. There is a preference for performing the wedding in the bride's home in the evening, but that is not always possible. The ceremony is preceded by a ritual bath by both the bride and groom. The ceremony itself takes place before a fire, with a priest officiating.

The custom surrounding death are perhaps the best-known feature of Zoroastrianism. Death is the ultimate form of pollution and the most important sign of the continuing power of the evil spirit Angra Mainyu. Because it is forbidden to pollute fire or earth with a corpse, the body cannot be burned or buried. A special group of Zoroastrians is responsible for transporting a corpse, and they take on the inevitable pollution such work entails. The corpse is first taken to a special site and washed with bull's urine (thought to be a powerful antiseptic). Then it is laid out for three days, during which it is watched over by a dog, who was traditionally thought to be able to discern life and death and to be an especially effective slayer of demons. After three days the corpse is taken to the *dakhma*, (tower of silence), a large, round tower open to the elements. There the corpse is devoured by birds. The remaining bones are then gathered in a common container in the *dakhma*, where they will be reassembled into the individual resur-

rection bodies formed during the *frashkard*. Although an ancient custom, it has recently encountered opposition in urban areas. As a result, there has been a trend to replace exposure with cremation, done with the use of electricity rather than fire, or with above-ground burial. The practice of exposure, however, continues in some South Asian cities.

Another ritual practice to eliminate pollution is called the *barashnum*. This nine-day ceremony is composed of three ritual baths in a carefully laid out area, where the candidate will wash himself 18 times with bull's urine. A dog will also be presented to him 13 times. Traditionally all orthodox Zoroastrians sought to undergo this ceremony at least once, but now it is almost exclusively restricted to priests. A priest will likely undergo this ritual upon his initial consecration and at further points in his life as is needed.

RITES OF PASSAGE During the fifth month of a woman's pregnancy, a lamp is lit, representing the divine light that Zoroaster's mother displayed during her pregnancy. Shortly after birth a newborn is given a taste of *parahom* (a mixture of *haoma* and milk) if it is available. After delivery the mother traditionally was isolated for 40 days to allow the impurities of birth to diminish. The twentieth century has seen a decline of these practices.

The primary ritual for a child is initiation. The Parsis call the initiation *navjote* (new birth), while the Zardushtis call it *sudra-pushun* (the wearing of the *sadre*, or sacred shirt). The age of initiation varies, but the child cannot be younger than seven years old. The child must learn prayers and the rudiments of the faith. In the ceremony he or she is given the *sadre* and the *kusti* (sacred cord). The child then receives the blessings of a priest and is sprinkled with rice. A large party celebrating the boy or girl follows.

MEMBERSHIP Both Iranian and Parsi communities disapprove of conversion, as do most (but not all) diaspora communities. Because Zoroastrian identity is so strongly connected with Iranian descent, most feel that only those born to Zoroastrian parents can be Zoroastrian. Some more liberal diaspora communities have allowed conversion of non-Zoroastrian spouses.

The contemporary Zoroastrian community is defined by two important factors—their small numbers and the historical divisions maintained by the surviving remnant. The most important division is between the

Iranian and Parsi communities. These two traditions developed independently, despite periodic contact since the arrival of the Parsis in India. Since the mid-twentieth century thousands of Zoroastrians have immigrated to Europe, Australia, and North America. In the diaspora members of the Parsi and Iranian communities have come together and learned about what they share and where they differ. For both communities the most significant issues are the survival of the tradition and what should be passed on to the next generation.

RELIGIOUS TOLERANCE As a minority group in the last millennium, Zoroastrians have regularly experienced discrimination and persecution. This has encouraged Zoroastrians to work for religious tolerance, both for themselves within the wider community and between members of their own tradition.

The view that Zoroastrians are part of an exclusive, hereditary religion has also contributed to their tolerance of others. Most Zoroastrians believe that not only their tradition but all religions are founded on the highest insights and principles. They have no need to insist that Zoroastrianism is in exclusive possession of the truth, since their religion is not available to those born outside the tradition.

SOCIAL JUSTICE A commitment to education and charity has characterized the Zoroastrian community. In both Iran and India education has been the path to economic security, and both communities are highly educated.

The Parsi community in India has been dedicated to charitable work, both for poorer Parsis and for society in general; Parsis have established medical, educational, and social services. It has been argued that the generosity of the Parsi community has helped prevent resentment toward them within India. In poor Iranian communities charity also has played and important role, endowing festivals, temples, and other projects.

The strong ethical orientation of the tradition has inspired the Zoroastrian community to seek social justice for all. The Parsi community has provided leaders to a number of political and social reform movements in India, including the movement for independence from British rule (1917–47). Under the Pahlavi dynasty in Iran (1926–79), Zardushtis supported development efforts and played a special role in the formulation of Iranian nationalist ideology. That ideology—stressing modernization, social development, and the glories of

the pre-Islamic Iranian period—drew upon the country's Zoroastrian past.

SOCIAL ASPECTS In the modern era Zoroastrian women have risen to prominence in many fields, though they have confronted social obstacles common in their countries. Family is a central value, so it is incumbent upon all Zoroastrians to marry and produce offspring. Among more conservative Zoroastrians there is a strong movement to encourage marriage only within the community. Social sanctions have occasionally been taken toward those, especially women, who marry non-Zoroastrians. For example, Parsi women who have married outside the community have been denied Zoroastrian funerals. In the name of gender equality, this rule has been increasingly extended to men.

CONTROVERSIAL ISSUES The issue of conversion remains highly controversial. Orthodox Zoroastrians are convinced that Zoroastrianism has never accepted converts (history is largely on their side). The argument against conversion has been mixed with troubling claims to racial purity, which proponents of conversion find particularly offensive. Proponents also point out that prohibiting conversion implicitly denies freedom of choice.

The Parsi and Iranian communities tend to resist conversion for different reasons. Parsi self-identity has been influenced by the Indian caste system, supporting a strong sense of endogamy and exclusiveness. The Iranian community, on the other hand, is more concerned that it might violate the Islamic prohibition on proselytizing. Individual cases of conversion, either by a spouse or by anyone else, are generally not recognized, except by a few communities in the diaspora.

The controversy over conversion has tended to pit the clergy (who are more conservative) against the laity. This has led to a larger question concerning the identity of the religion. Some see Zoroastrianism as primarily characterized by the priests, who serve the community but who are cut off in many ways from modern life. Others view Zoroastrianism primarily as an ethical value system that provides direction to all its members and encourages them to apply those values in the modern world.

CULTURAL IMPACT Zoroastrianism is one of the world's oldest religions, with a proud history and cultural influence dating back more than 3,000 years. As the religion of an ancient empire in Iran, it had a notable influence on the culture of classical Greece, a competing power. The interaction between Greek and Iranian culture is seen in the relief sculpture at Persepolis, which appears to contain ancient Near Eastern themes interpreted by Greek craftsmen. This is significant because the Zoroastrian tradition otherwise seems not to have made pictorial representations or sculptures, though there are occasional references to statues, especially of the goddess Anahita.

The *chahar tāq,*—the square, domed fire temple with four arched walls developed during the Sasanian period—has survived as a fundamental form of Iranian architecture. The significance of the dome as symbol of the cosmos has had an impact on Christian and Muslim architecture, and it has been argued that it also played a role in the development of the Buddhist stupa (a shrine with a dome).

The opulent style and art of the Zoroastrian Sasanian court also had a legacy in the Islamic world, particularly in caliphal palaces and royal symbolism. The reemergence of the Persian language—beginning in the ninth century C.E. in northeastern Iran—helped preserve Zoroastrian epic history, with its interdependence of royalty and religion and its epic hero defending the Iranian realm. Persian poetic and musical forms later drew upon this history.

Contemporary Zoroastrians—such as Zubin Mehta (former conductor of the New York Philharmonic), the postmodern theorist Homi Bhabha, the Indian-born Canadian author Rohinton Mistry (whose fiction deals with themes of Parsi identity and Zoroastrian faith), and the Pakistani-born author Bapsi Sidhwa—have made major cultural contributions.

William Darrow

Bibliography

Boyce, Mary. *A History of Zoroastrianism.* 3 vols. to date. Leiden: E.J. Brill, 1975–.

———. *Zoroastrians: Their Religious Beliefs and Practices.* London and New York: Routledge, 1979.

———, ed. *Textual Sources for the Study of Zoroastrianism.* Manchester, England: Manchester University Press, 1984.

Choksy, Jamsheed K. *Conflict and Cooperation: Zoroastrian Subalterns and Muslim Elites in Medieval Iranian Society.* New York: Columbia University Press, 1997.

———. *Evil, Good, and Gender: Facets of the Feminine in Zoroastrian Religious History.* New York: Peter Lang Publishing, 2002.

———. *Purity and Pollution in Zoroastrianism: Triumph over Evil.* Austin: University of Texas Press, 1989.

Clark, Peter. *Zoroastrianism: An Introduction to an Ancient Faith.* Brighton: Sussex Academic Press, 1998.

Dhalla, M.N. *A History of Zoroastrianism.* New York: Oxford University Press, 1938.

Godrej, Pheroza, and Firoza P. Mistree, eds. *A Zoroastrian Tapestry: Art, Religion, and Culture.* Mumbai: Mapin Publishing, 2002.

Hinnells, John. *Zoroastrians in Britain.* Oxford: Clarendon Press, 1996.

Insler, Stanley. *The Gathas of Zarathustra.* Leiden: E.J. Brill, 1975.

Kellens, Jean. *Essays on Zarathustra and Zoroastrianism.* Translated by Prods Oktor Skjærvø. Costa Mesa, Calif.: Mazda Press, 2000.

Luhrmann, T.M. *The Good Parsi: The Fate of a Colonial Elite in a Postcolonial Society.* Cambridge, Mass.: Harvard University Press, 1996.

Mehr, Farhang. *The Zoroastrian Tradition: An Introduction to the Ancient Wisdom of Zarathustra.* Costa Mesa, Calif.: Mazda Press, 2003.

Mirza, H.D.K. *Outlines of Parsi History.* Bombay: The Industrial Press, 1974.

Mistree, K. *Zoroastrianism: An Ethnic Perspective.* Bombay: Zoroastrian Studies, 1982.

Modi, J.J. *The Religious Ceremonies and Customs of the Parsees.* 1922. Reprint, New York: Garland, 1979.

Motafram, R.R. *Mysticism, Mystic Sects among the Jews, Mohmedans and the Zoroastrians: A Comparative Study.* Mumbai: H.J.M. Desai and H.N. Modi, 1996.

Shaked, Shaul. *Dualism in Transformation: Varieties of Religion in Sasanian Iran.* London: School of Oriental and African Studies, 1994.

———. *From Zoroastrian Iran to Islam.* Aldershot, England: VARIORUM, Ashgate Publishing, 1995.

West, Edward William. *Pahlavi Texts.* 5 vols. The Sacred Books of the East. Oxford: Clarendon Press, 1879–1910.

Zaehner, Robert C. *The Dawn and Twilight of Zoroastrianism.* New York: Putnam, 1961.

———. *The Teachings of the Magi: A Compendium of Zoroastrian Beliefs.* New York: Oxford University Press, 1956.

———. *Zurvan: A Zoroastrian Dilemma.* New York: Biblo and Tannen, 1972.

Index

E

F

L

Laayeen order, Senegal, **3**:303, 304, 305
Labor. *See* Work
Labrang Tashikyil, **1**:80
Labuling. *See* Labrang Tashikyil
Laden, Osama bin, **1**:350
Laestadianism, **2**:368, 370
Laestadius, Lars Levi, **2**:368
Lafuente, Anselmo Llorente y, **2**:247
Laity
    China, **2**:226–227, 227
    Honduras, **2**:462
    Lithuania, **2**:630
    Mongolia, **3**:83, 85
    Myanmar, **3**:105
    Nepal, **3**:124
    Norway, **3**:168
    Peru, **3**:214
    San Marino, **3**:289–290
    South Korea, **3**:364
    Sri Lanka, **3**:378, 379
    Togo, **3**:451
    Tunisia, **3**:472
    United States, **3**:526
Lake Manasarovar (Tibet), **1**:97
Lakshmi, **1**:316, 319, 322, 323, 340,
    343
Lakulisha, **1**:335
Lakwena, Alice, **3**:491
Lama Temple, **1**:80
Lamaism. *See* Tibetan Buddhism
Lamas, **1**:95–96, 96, 98
    See also Dalai Lama
Lan Na. *See* Thailand
Land of Israel, as holy, **1**:445, 446, 458
Landmark controversy, **1**:150
Langar, **1**:500
Lao, Lord, **1**:522, 530–531, 533
Lao Evangelical Church, **2**:592
Lao-tzu. *See* Tao te ching
Laos, **2**:*586*, **586–591**
Lassy Zerpherinism, **3**:247
Last Testament Church (Russia), **3**:261
Last things, doctrine of. *See* Eschatology
Lateran Treaties (1929), **3**:552, 553
Latin America
    Bahai faith, **1**:28
    Christianity, **1**:101, 107–108
    Evangelicalism, **1**:187, 188
    Pentecostalism, **1**:217
    Religious Society of Friends, **1**:235
Latin crosses, **1**:116
Latin Rite. *See* Roman Catholicism
Latin rite churches. *See* Roman
    Catholicism
Latvia, **2**:*593*, **593–597**
Laval, Jacques Désiré, **3**:55

Law
    Confucianization of, **1**:283
    Hindu membership and, **1**:327
    Shiite, **1**:383–384
    See also Islamic law
Law, Islamic. *See* Shariah
Law Code (1184), **2**:63
Law of God. *See* Ten Commandments
Law of huququllah, **1**:42
Laws, Robert, **3**:18
Laws of Manu. See Manava Dharmasastra
Lay Buddhists, **1**:53
    dress mode, **1**:66
    holidays and festivals, **1**:65–66
    monks and, **1**:65
    moral code of conduct, **1**:60–61, 78,
        88
    rites of passage, **1**:68
    rituals, **1**:67
    temples and, **1**:80
    Theravada Buddhism and, **1**:83
Lay Jains, **1**:399
    lesser vows and, **1**:408–409
    organizational structure, **1**:412
    renouncers and, **1**:403
    social justice and, **1**:417
LDS Church. *See* Church of Jesus Christ
    of Latter-day Saints
Leaders. *See* Clergy and religious leaders;
    Politics and government
League of African Churches in
    Swaziland, **3**:398
Lebanon, **1**:361, **2**:*598*, **598–602**
Lebaran. *See* Id al-Fitr
Lebrun, Jean, **3**:57
Lectionary, **1**:163
Ledermann, Ilse, **1**:64
Ledi Sayadaw, **3**:104
Lee, Ann. *See* Ann, Mother
Lee Kuan Yew, **1**:280, 295
Leen, James, **3**:55
Lefebvre, Marcel, **2**:374
Left Behind novels, **1**:188, 226
Left-handed Tantric tradition, **1**:338
Legalism, **1**:254, 283
Legba, **1**:6–7
Legion of Mary (Africa), **1**:134
Legras, Louise de Marillac, **2**:375, 377
Leibovich, Yeshayahu, **2**:522
Leland, John, **1**:150
Lenca, **2**:325
Lent, **1**:122
    See also Abstinence and fasting
Leo III, Emperor, **1**:182
Leo III, Pope, **1**:105, 175
Leo XIII, Pope, **1**:109, 127, 128, 246,
    249, **3**:528
Leopold II, King of Belgium, **2**:281,
    283

Lesbianism, **1**:460, 474
    See also Burial rites and funerals
Lesotho, **2**:*603*, **603–609**
Lesser renouncers, **1**:411, 417
Lessons for Women, **1**:276
Letter to Artists, **1**:137
Leuenberg Agreement, **1**:199
Lévinas, Emmanuel, **1**:445
Lewis, C. S., **1**:133, 186
Lewis, Edwin, **1**:208
Leymang, Gérard, **3**:548, 549
Lhabap Duchen, **1**:97
Lhamo, Pasang, **1**:98
Lhamo Lhatso (Tibet), **1**:97
Li, doctrine of. *See* Property rights
Li Han-kuang, **1**:533–534, 535, 537
Li Zhi, **1**:276
Liang Fa, **2**:229
Liang Shuming, **1**:280, 289
Libationers, **1**:522, 537, 543
Liberal Judaism. *See* Reform Judaism
Liberation
    Buddhism, **1**:48
    Hinduism, **1**:310–311, 312
    Jainism, **1**:400, 402, 406–407
    Judaism, **1**:445
    Sikhism, **1**:498, 506, 515
    Upanishads, **1**:302
    Vaishnavism, **1**:343
Liberation theology, **1**:109, 115, 120,
    128–129, 249
    Belize, **2**:97
    Brazil, **2**:139–142
    Cameroon, **2**:175
    Colombia, **2**:237
    Costa Rica, **2**:249
    Cuba, **2**:268
    Ecuador, **2**:313
    El Salvador, **2**:328
    focus of, **3**:211–212
    Guatemala, **2**:427
    Haiti, **2**:458, 459
    Honduras, **2**:462
    Jamaica, **2**:538
    Mexico, **3**:61, 62, 64
    Panama, **3**:194–195
    Paraguay, **3**:207
    Peru, **3**:214, 215
    Uruguay, **3**:538
    Venezuela, **3**:559
Liberia, **2**:*611*, **611–616**
Liberty: A Magazine of Religious Freedom,
    1:256
Library of Tao. *See* Tao-tsang
Libya, **2**:*618*, **618–622**
Liechtenstein, **2**:*623*, **623–626**
Lien-shih, **1**:537
Lienü zhuan (Biographies of Exemplary
    Women), **1**:276

Vaishnavism and, I:342
Veronese, I:135
Vesak, I:66, *86*, 90
Vessantara, King, I:60
Vestments. *See* Dress mode
Vichayai, Queen (fictional character), I:420
Victory Chapel (Palau), 3:188, 191
Vietnam, I:277–278, 285–286, 3:*562*, **562–567**
Vietnam War, Buddhism and, I:70
Vietnamese Buddhist Church, 3:562, 563
Vijaya Dasami, I:322
Vikström, John, 2:368
Vinaya (Discipline), I:53, 88, 89
Vinaya Pitaka, I:61, 65
Vincent de Paul, Saint, 2:375, 377
Vincentians. *See* Congregation of Priests of the Mission
Violence, religious. *See* Religious tolerance
Virasena, I:411
Virgin Mary, I:121–122, 163, 245
  Andorra, 2:19
  Angola, 2:26
  Argentina, 2:36–37
  Belgium, 2:91
  Bolivia, 2:*116*, 117
  Brazil, 2:139
  Chile, 2:215
  China, 2:229
  Colombia, 2:*137*, 238
  Costa Rica, 2:248
  Croatia, 2:261
  Cuba, 2:264, 265, 266
  Cyprus, 2:271, 272
  Dominica, 2:301
  Dominican Republic, 2:305
  East Timor, 2:309–310
  Ecuador, 2:314
  Egypt, 2:318
  El Salvador, 2:328
  France, 2:375
  Greece, 2:415
  Guatemala, 2:426
  Honduras, 2:463
  Hungary, 2:467, 469
  Indonesia, 2:495–496
  Italy, 2:530
  Liechtenstein, 2:624, 625
  Lithuania, 2:629
  Luxembourg, 2:633, 634
  Malta, 3:41
  Mexico, 3:61, 62, 63
  Nicaragua, 3:140–141
  Panama, 3:194, 195
  Peru, 3:212, 213
  Poland, 3:*224*, 225–226
  Portugal, 3:233
  Slovakia, 3:333
  Spain, 3:371
  Trinidad and Tobago, 3:465
  Ukraine, 3:501
  Uruguay, 3:538
  Venezuela, 3:*557*, 558
Virtues. *See* Moral code of conduct
Vishnu, I:*306*, 308, 310, 315, 342, 343, 2:79
  Cambodia and, 2:169
  festivals for, I:322
  plants sacred to, I:321
  Ramanuja on, I:318
  Shiva and, I:333, 336
  symbolism and, I:316
  tilaka and, I:319
  Tirumala-Tirupati temple and, I:321
  See also Vaishnavism
Vishwanath, Atmaram, 3:53
Visigoths, Spain and, 3:368, 369
Visistadvaita. *See* Qualified nondualism
Vissarion, 3:261
Visual arts. *See* Art
Vivekananda, I:317, 327, 329
Vladimir Kantarian, 3:73–74
Vlk, M., 2:275–276
Vodou, Haiti, 2:454–458
Vodú. *See* Vodun
Vodun, I:2, *4*, 5
  Benin, 2:101, *102*, 102–105
  Dominican Republic, 2:303–307
  Togo, 3:449, 450, 452–455
Vohu Manah, I:555
Voodoo. *See* Vodun
Vows, greater and lesser, I:408

W

Waddel, Hope Masterton, 3:154
Wadii, Muqbil al-, 3:574
Wahhabi Islam, I:393
  Côte d'Ivoire, 2:253
  Ethiopia, 2:354, 355
  India, 2:486
  Iraq, 2:510
  Kazakhstan, 2:557
  Kuwait, 2:574–579
  Morocco, 3:87
  Pakistan, 3:181, 183, 185
  Qatar, 3:236, 237
  Russia, 3:260
  Saudi Arabia, 3:298, 300
  Tunisia, 3:473
  United Arab Emirates, 3:506
  Uzbekistan, 3:541
  Yemen, 3:571, 574
Wahid, Abdurrahman, 2:492
Wai-tan. *See* Alchemy
Wailing Wall (Israel), I:446
Waite, Terry, I:142
Waldensian Church, Italy, 2:527, 532
Waldenström, Paul Petter, 3:406–407
Wali Allah, 2:491
Waliggo, John, 3:494
Walleser, Salvador, 3:190
Wang Ch'ang-yüeh, I:534
Wang Che, I:525, 534
Wang Ch'ung-yang. *See* Wang Che
Wang ritual, I:97
Wang Yangming, I:278, 285, 287–288
Wani, Silvanus, 3:493
War
  Christianity and, I:131–132
  Jews *vs.* Romans, I:437
  Protestantism and, I:226
  Roman Catholicism and, I:249
  Unitarian Universalism and, I:*261*
  See also Civil war; Jihad
War of the Triple Alliance (1865-1870), 3:207
Ward, Louis J., 3:154
Warring States period (China), I:294
Warriors
  Hinduism, I:318–319
  Sikhism, I:515, 516
Warsaw Ghetto Uprising, I:447
Water
  Hinduism and, I:320–321
  in Shiism, I:386
  See also Baptism
Wats. *See* Temples
Wattasid dynasty, Morocco, 3:87, 88
Watts, Isaac, I:231
The Way
  Confucianism, I:280–281, 528
  Taoism, I:524, 528
Way of action, I:310–311
Way of devotion, I:310–311
Way of knowledge, I:310–311
Way of the Warrior. *See* Bushido
Way of Unity. *See* I-kuan Tao
Wazir, Ibrahim ibn Muhammad al-, 3:572
WCC. *See* World Council of Churches
Wealth
  Bahai faith on, I:42
  Buddhism and, I:60
  Islam and, I:361–362, 375–376
  redistribution in Tanzania, 3:441
Weapons
  Hindu symbolism, I:316
  Vaishnavism symbolism, I:344
Weber, Max, I:115, 132
Websites. *See* Internet
Weddings. *See* Marriage and weddings
Wei dynasty, Taoism and, I:533
Wei Hua-tsun, I:543